Human
Exceptionality

Human Exceptionality

Society, School, and Family

Seventh Edition

Michael L. Hardman
UNIVERSITY OF UTAH

Clifford J. Drew
UNIVERSITY OF UTAH

M. Winston Egan
BRIGHAM YOUNG UNIVERSITY

Allyn and Bacon

Boston London Toronto Sydney Tokyo Singapore

Executive Editor: Virginia Lanigan
Developmental Editor: Linda Bieze
Marketing Manager: Amy Cronin
Composition Buyer: Linda Cox
Manufacturing Buyer: Megan Cochran
Production Administrator: Deborah Brown
Editorial-Production Service: Barbara Gracia
Textbook Designer: Seventeenth Street Studios
Electronic Composition: Karen Mason
Photo Researchers: Julie Tesser, Deborah Brown
Cover Administrator: Linda Knowles

Copyright 2002, 1999, 1996, 1993, 1990, 1987, 1984 by Allyn and Bacon
A Pearson Education Company
75 Arlington Street
Boston, Massachusetts 02116

Internet: www.ablongman.com

Between the time Web site information is gathered and published, some sites may
have closed. Also, the transcription of URLs can result in typographical errors. The
publisher would appreciate notification where these occur so that they may be
corrected in subsequent editions.

Library of Congress Cataloging-in-Publication Data

Hardman, Michael L.
  Human exceptionality: society, school, and family/Michael L.
Hardman, Clifford J. Drew, M. Winston Egan.—7th ed.
  p. cm.
  Includes bibliographical references and indexes.
  ISBN 0-205-33750-3
  1. Handicapped. 2. Exceptional children. 3. Handicapped—
Services for. 4. Learning disabilities. I. Drew, Clifford J.,
1943– . II. Egan, M. Winston. III. Title.
  HV1568.H37 2001
  362–dc21

                                    20010033673

Printed in the United States of America

10 9 8 7 6 5 4 3 2 1 RRD 05 04 03 02 01

Photo credits appear on page 632, which constitutes an extension of the copyright page.

This book is dedicated to people with differences everywhere, who have risen to the challenge of living in a society that is sometimes nurturing, but all too often ambivalent.

To our families, a loving and appreciative thank you for being so patient and caring during the more than 20 years of writing, rewriting, and revising this text.

MLH
CJD
MWE

Brief Contents

Contents

![PART III icon]

PART III

High-Incidence Disabilities

PART IV

Low-Incidence Disabilities

CHAPTER 11

PEOPLE WITH SEVERE AND MULTIPLE DISABILITIES 347

CHAPTER 12

PEOPLE WITH AUTISM 375

Selected Features

■ TODAY'S TECHNOLOGY

■ DEBATE FORUM

*I have walked with people whose eyes are full of light but who see nothing in sea or sky,
nothing in city streets, nothing in books. It were far better to sail forever in the night of blindness
with sense, and feeling, and mind, than to be content with the mere act of seeing. The only
lightless dark is the night of darkness in ignorance and insensibility.*

—Helen Keller

ELCOME TO THE SEVENTH EDITION of *Human Exceptionality: Society, School, and Family.* We would like to help your exploration of lives who are exceptional by providing some perspective on features from the sixth edition as well as what is new and different in this edition. This text is about people—people with diverse needs, characteristics, and lifestyles—people who for one reason or another are called exceptional. What does the word *exceptional* mean to you? For that matter, what do *disordered, deviant, disabled, challenged, different,* or *handicapped* mean to you? Who or what has influenced your knowledge and attitudes about these terms and the people behind them? Up to this point in your life, you have probably been more influenced by life's experiences than by formal training. You may have a family member, friend, or casual acquaintance who is exceptional in some way. It may be that you are exceptional in some way. Then again, you may be approaching this subject with little or no background. You will find that the study of human exceptionality is the study of being human. Perhaps you will come to understand yourself better in the process. As suggested by novelist Louis Bromfield,

There is a rhythm in life, a certain beauty which operates by a variation of lights and shadows, happiness alternating with sorrow, content with discontent, distilling in this process of contrast a sense of satisfaction, of richness that can be captured and pinned down only by those who possess the gift of awareness.

Organizational Features

n addition to providing current and informative content, we are committed to making your first formal experience with exceptionality interesting, enjoyable, and productive. To this end, we have chosen features that should greatly enhance your desire to learn more about human exceptionality.

■ TO BEGIN WITH . . .

"To Begin With . . ." (excerpts on the first page of each chapter) introduce the chapter topic from several points of view. These quotes offer a variety of current facts and figures related to each particular subject area.

■ SNAPSHOT

The *Snapshot* series of personal insights focuses on the lives of people with differences; they are teachers, family members, friends, peers, and professionals, as well as persons who are exceptional. All chapters of this edition open with at least one snapshot of an individual who is exceptional. These snapshots are in no way representative of the range of characteristics associated with a given area of exceptionality. At best, they provide a frame of reference for reading and show that we are talking about real people who deal with life in many of the same ways that you do. We believe the snapshots will be one of the most enriching aspects of your introduction to exceptionality.

INTERACTING IN NATURAL SETTINGS

Another feature, *Interacting in Natural Settings,* provides brief tips on ways to communicate, teach, or socialize with people who are exceptional across a variety of settings (home, school, and community) and age spans (early childhood through the adult years). The tips are not exhaustive lists of the many possible ways to interact effectively with people who are exceptional, but we hope they provide some stimulus for further thinking on how to include these individuals as family members, school peers, friends, or neighbors.

REFLECT ON THIS

Every chapter includes *Reflect On This* boxes. Each one highlights a piece of interesting and relevant information that will add to your learning and enjoyment of the chapter. Offering a temporary diversion from the chapter narrative, these features provide engaging facts about topics such as dads who make a difference, giftedness that is encouraged in girls, facts about employment and the Americans with Disabilities Act (ADA), and characteristics of effective schools and classrooms.

TODAY'S TECHNOLOGY

The seventh edition features information on the expanding use of technology for people who are exceptional. *Today's Technology* highlights innovations in computers, biomedical engineering, assistive technology, and instructional systems. These boxes focus on topics such as learning language skills through devices that synthesize speech, electronic readers for people with vision loss, and word processing programs with specialized features that help students with learning disabilities to develop writing skills.

DEBATE FORUM

Every chapter concludes with a *Debate Forum.* The purpose of these forums is to broaden your view of the issues concerning people with differences. The debate forums focus on issues that have sparked some philosophical differences of opinion, such as whether the ADA levels the playing field or creates advantages, inclusive education for students with disabilities, the meaning of a high school diploma, or the appropriateness of an intervention strategy. For each issue discussed, a position taken *(point)* and an alternative to that position *(counterpoint)* are given. The purpose of the debate forum is not to establish right or wrong answers, but to call attention to the diversity and complexity of issues concerning individuals who are exceptional.

Improving Your Study Skills

Each chapter is organized in a systematic fashion to increase learning effectiveness:

■ PREVIEW THE CHAPTER   In the margins of each chapter there are *focus questions* that highlight important information. Survey these questions before reading the chapter to guide your reading. Then, examine key chapter headings to further familiarize yourself with chapter organization.

■ ASK QUESTIONS   Using the focus questions as a guide, ask yourself what you want to learn from the chapter. After reviewing chapter headings and the focus questions, write down any additional questions you may have and use them to guide your reading. Then, organize your thoughts and schedule time to read the chapter.

■ READ   Again using the focus questions as your guide, actively read the chapter.

■ RECITE   After reading the chapter, turn back to the focus questions and respond orally and in writing to each question. Develop a written outline of the key points to remember.

■ REVIEW   Each chapter concludes with a review section. Each focus question is repeated in this section along with key points from the chapter's text. Compare your memory of the material and your written outline to the points addressed in the review. If you forgot or misunderstood anything, return to the focus questions in the chapter and reread the material. Follow this process for each chapter. You may also consider developing your own short-answer essay tests to improve your understanding of the material in each chapter.

A *Study Guide* is available to help you master the information included in *Human Exceptionality.* Each chapter of the study guide is organized to promote effective methods for studying. It provides information on what to preview, questions to ask, keys to effective reading, and how to recite, review, and reflect on the most important concepts in each chapter of the book. Exercises for mastering key terms, multiple-choice practice tests, fill-in-the-blank study sections, and activities that encourage further exploration into various topics of interest are included.

Human exceptionality is a relatively young and unexplored field of study. Those of you seeking careers in fields concerned with exceptional people will be part of the exploration. If, after reading this book, you are excited and encouraged to study further in this area, then we have met our primary goal. It would be unrealistic and unfair if we said this book provides everything there is to know about people who are exceptional. What it does provide is an overview of exceptional people in their communities, at school, and living with families.

New Features of the Seventh Edition

- A new chapter, *Persons with Attention-Deficit/Hyperactivity Disorder* (Chapter 7), expands our coverage of this high-visibility topic that you will encounter often in schools and social service agencies.
- *Fuller coverage of the IDEA 1997 and the March 1999 implementation regulations* in Chapter 1 provides the most current information available on laws affecting the lives of people with disabilities.
- *An expanded discussion of Section 504/Americans with Disabilities Act,* also in Chapter 1, with major sections on reasonable accommodations, impact on schools and businesses, and eligibility, focuses on how these laws apply in daily life.
- *Sections on standards-based education reform* in Chapter 4 show how it impacts students with disabilities.
- Added coverage of *self-determination and choice for individuals with disabilities* in Chapter 5 will help you understand the lives of persons with exceptionalities.
- *Comprehensive coverage of inclusion issues* in each chapter will heighten your awareness of integrating persons with disabilities into educational and social settings.
- *Expanded coverage of reading disabilities* and *at-risk students,* two categories of growing concern in education, in Chapter 6, will help you understand these special needs.

Instructional Supplements and Course Enrichment Materials

- Instructor's Manual and Test Bank
- Computerized Test Bank (cross-platform)
- Video—*Professionals in Action: Teaching Students with Special Needs*

   (© 2000, 120 minutes in length) This *Professionals in Action* video consists of four modules (15–30 minutes in length) presenting viewpoints and approaches to teaching students with various disabilities, in general education classrooms, separate education settings, and various combinations of the two. Each module explores its topic via actual classroom footage, and interviews with general and special education teachers, parents, and students themselves. The four modules are entitled Working Together: The Individualized Education Program (IEP); Working Together: The Collaborative Process, Instruction, and Behavior Management; Technology for Inclusion; and Working with Parents and Families.

- The "Snapshots" Video Series for Special Education

   Snapshots: Inclusion Video (© 1995, 22 minutes in length) profiles three students of different ages and with various levels of disability in inclusive class settings. In each case, parents, classroom teachers, special education teachers, and school administrators talk about the steps they have taken to help Josh, Eric, and Tonya succeed in inclusive settings.

   Snapshots 2: Video for Special Education (categorical organization) (© 1995, 20–25 minutes in length) is a two-video set, comprised of six segments designed specifically for use in the college classroom. Each segment profiles three individuals, their families, teachers, and experiences. You'll find these programs to be of high interest to your students. Instructors who have used the tapes in their courses have found that they help in disabusing students of stereotypical viewpoints and put a "human face" on course material. The topics explored are behavior disorders,* learning disabilities,* mental retardation,* traumatic brain injury, hearing impairment, and visual impairment.

*Segments available with closed captioning for the hearing impaired.

- The Allyn & Bacon Special Education Transparency Package (© 2002). The transparency package has been revised and expanded to include approximately 100 acetates, over half of which are full color.
- NEW! Allyn & Bacon's Digital Media Archive (DMA) for Special Education. The digital media archive electronically provides charts, graphs, tables, and figures on one cross-platform CD-ROM, and then goes one step further by including weblinks and video clips.
- NEW! Companion Web Site with Online Practice Tests. The companion Web site for *Human Exceptionality: Society, School, and Family* [www.ablongman.com/hardman7e] features information about the authors—including their perspectives on human exceptionality—a snapshot video guide, chapter objectives, practice tests for the students, debate forums, community service learning activities, weblinks, case studies with essay functions, and more.
- Egan et al. *What's Best for Matthew?: Interactive CD-ROM Case Study for Learning to Develop Individualized Education Programs* and Gibb and Dyches's *Guide to Writing Quality Individualized Education Programs* are separate products for sale, which may also be shrinkwrapped with copies of the Hardman et al. 7/e text at a reduced price. Please ask your Allyn & Bacon/Longman representative for details.

Acknowledgments

We begin with a very big thank you to our colleagues from around the country who provided in-depth and constructive feedback on both the sixth and seventh editions of *Human Exceptionality*: Elizabeth W. Beale, Auburn University–Montgomery; Darlene Fewster, Towson University; Michael Jakupcak, University of Montana; David S. Katims, University of Texas at San Antonio; Kimberly Knesting, University of Wisconsin–Eau Claire; Kimber W. Malmgren, University of Maryland–College Park; Ann Monroe-Baillargeon, Nazareth College; William A Myers, University of Texas at Austin; Judith Reymond, Loyola University–Chicago; Robert S. Ristow, St. Ambrose University; and Keith Storey, Chapman University.

As authors, we are certainly grateful for the strong commitment of the Allyn and Bacon editorial and production team in bringing to fruition the highest-quality text possible. As is true with other editions, the team has sought to consistently improve the readability, utility, and appearance of the book. Thanks to Paul A. Smith, vice president and editor-in-chief, for his leadership in promoting an atmosphere of professionalism that supported cooperative efforts of the Allyn and Bacon team and yours truly—the authors. We are indebted to our senior editor, Virginia Lanigan, and her editorial assistant, Erin Liedel. Virginia's knowledge of the needs and interests of professors and students in the field of education helped us cast this edition into a comprehensive text for the 21st century. We genuinely appreciated the opportunity to work with Linda Bieze, senior development editor, and her attention to content quality. We sincerely thank Barbara Gracia, editorial production service, for her unwavering attention to the critical details related to text figures, tables, sentence and paragraph structure, typographical errors, and APA style that can make or break a text. To Karen Mason, we extend our appreciation for her efforts in laying out the electronic composition of the text. As always her work was first-rate. Last, but certainly not least, many thanks to Deborah Brown, production administrator, for her leadership in bringing this new edition home. We also thank Deborah and Julie Tesser for the outstanding job of locating photos that brought our narrative to life.

To Marti Hoge at the University of Utah, thank you for the painstaking proofing, copying, and mailing of the manuscript. Marti, we couldn't have completed this new edition without you.

Michael L. Hardman
Clifford J. Drew
M. Winston Egan

Human
Exceptionality

A Multidisciplinary View of Exceptionality

To begin with . . .

As we chart our personal and collective course for this new millennium, there are some sobering predictions that will cause us to think deeply about who we are as a people and what we value in ourselves. . . . How do we make sense of a world that is so very *diverse* in so many ways. . . . We will see a rapid growth of ethnic, linguistic, and cultural diversity. Terms such as "minority" and "majority" will lose their current relevance. More persons with exceptionalities will be in the workplace. . . . On October 12, 1999, the world population reached six billion with expectations of population growth reaching nine billion by 2030. And so, what relevance does this have . . . for educators, and particularly for special education as a profession? The relevance rests in . . . our appreciation of the gifts, talents, unique characteristics, and needs our students and families bring to our schools and communities. (Bogdan, 2000, p. 4)

For me, a multicultural, inclusive world is not really possible through the cognitive avenue only. That is, you cannot just "read and discuss" about others. You have to study, work, live, eat, talk, etc., with them. The more this happens, the more likely one can develop an appreciation, and hopefully, acceptance and understanding of the diversity of the human race. (Paul, 1998, p. 16)

Inclusive education is not a reform of special education. It is a convergence of the need to restructure the public education system, to meet the needs of a changing society, and the adaptation of the separate special education, which has been shown to be unsuccessful for the greater number of students who are served by it. It is the development of a unitary system that has educational benefits for both typical students and students with special needs. It is a system that provides quality education for all children. (Lipsky & Gartner, 1999, p. 15)

Nondisabled Americans do not understand disabled ones. That was clear at the memorial service for Timothy Cook, when longtime friends got up to pay tribute to him. "He never seemed disabled to me," said one. "He was the least disabled person I ever met," pronounced another. It was the highest praise these nondisabled friends could think to give a disabled attorney who, at 38 years old, had won landmark disability rights cases, including one to force public transit systems to equip buses with wheelchair lifts. But more than a few heads in the crowded chapel bowed with embarrassment at the supposed compliments. It was as if someone had tried to compliment a black man by saying, "You're the least black person I ever met," as false as telling a Jew, "I never think of you as Jewish," as clumsy as flattering a woman with "You don't act like a woman." (Shapiro, 1994, p. 3)

1

Franklin Delano Roosevelt

This snapshot was adapted from the remarks of Senator Robert Dole to his colleagues in the United States Senate on April 14, 1995. Senator Dole, disabled himself following a serious injury in World War II, remembers President Franklin Roosevelt as a master politician; an energetic and inspiring leader during the dark days of the Depression; a tough, single-minded commander-in-chief during World War II; a states-man; the first elected leader in history with a disability; and a dis-ability hero.

■ FDR'S SPLENDID DECEPTION

In 1921, at age 39, Franklin Roosevelt was a young man in a hurry. He was following the same political path that took his cousin Theodore Roosevelt to the White House. In 1910 he was elected to the New York State Senate, and later was appointed assistant secretary of the Navy. In 1920, he was the Democratic candidate for vice president. Then, on the evening of August 10, while on vacation, he felt ill and went to bed early. Within three days he was paralyzed from the chest down. Although the muscles of his upper body soon recovered, he remained paralyzed below the waist. His political career screeched to a halt. He spent the next seven years in reha-bilitation, determined to walk again. He never did. He mostly used a wheelchair. Sometimes he was carried by his sons or aides. Other times he crawled on the floor. But he did perfect the illusion of walking—believing that other-wise his political ambitions were dead. He could stand upright only with his lower body painfully wrapped in steel braces. He moved for-ward by swinging his hips, leaning on the arm of a fam-ily member or aide. It worked for only a few feet at a time. It was dangerous. But it was enough to convince people that FDR was not a "cripple." FDR biographer Hugh Gal-lagher has called this effort, and other tricks used to hide his disability, "FDR's splendid deception." This deception was aided and abetted by many others. The press were co-conspirators. No reporter wrote that FDR could not walk, and no photographer took a picture of him in his wheelchair. For that matter, thousands saw him struggle when he "walked." Maybe they didn't believe or under-stand what they saw. In 1928, FDR ended his political exile, and was elected gover-nor of New York. Four years later, he was president. On March 4th, 1933, standing at the East Front of this Capitol, he said, "The only thing we have to fear is fear itself." He was 35 feet from his wheel-chair. Few people knew from what deep personal experi-ences he spoke. Perhaps the only occasion where FDR fully acknowledged the extent of his disability in public was a visit to a military hospital in Hawaii. He toured the amputee wards in his wheel-chair. He went by each bed, letting the men see him exactly as he was. He didn't need to give any pep talks— his example said it all.

■ FDR: A DISABILITY HERO

Earlier I called FDR a "dis-ability hero." But it was not for the reasons some might think. It would be easy to cite his courage and grit. But FDR would not want that. "No sob stuff," he told the press in 1928 when he started his comeback. Even within his own family, he did not dis-cuss his disability. It was sim-ply a fact of life. In my view, FDR is a hero for his efforts on behalf of others with a disability. In 1926, he pur-chased a run-down resort in Warm Springs, Georgia, and over the next 20 years turned it into a unique, first-class rehabilitation center. It was based on a new philosophy of treatment—one where psy-chological recovery was as important as medical treat-ment. FDR believed in an independent life for people with disabilities—at a time when society thought they belonged at home or in insti-tutions. Warm Springs was run by people with polio, for people with polio. In that spirit, FDR is the father of the modern independent living movement, which puts peo-ple with disabilities in control of their own lives. He also founded the National Foun-dation for Infantile Paralysis— known as the "March of Dimes"—and raised millions of dollars to help others with polio and find a cure. In pub-lic policy, FDR understood that government help in reha-bilitating people with disabili-ties is "good business"—often returning more in taxes and savings than it costs. It is unfortunately a philosophy that we often pay more lip service than practice.

■ DISABILITY TODAY AND TOMORROW

Our nation has come a long way in its understanding of disability since the days of President Roosevelt. For example, we recognize that disability is a natural part of life. We have begun to build a world that is accessible. No longer do we accept that buildings—either through design or indifference—are not accessible, which is a "keep out" sign for the dis-abled. We have come a long way in another respect—in attitudes. Fifty years ago, we had a president who could not walk and believed it was necessary to disguise that fact from the American people. Today, I trust that Americans would have no problem in electing as president a man or woman with a disability (Dole, 1995).

Snapshot

fRANKLIN DELANO ROOSEVELT (FDR) has been hailed as one of the greatest U.S. presidents in history. *Time* magazine (December 31, 1999, *www.Time.com*) named FDR as one of the three finalists for the most important person of the 20th century, describing him as a statesman who helped define the political and social fabric of our time. What *Time* didn't talk about was FDR's life as a person with a disability and why he was forced to hide the fact he had polio and couldn't walk. In the opening snapshot, we learn of Roosevelt's deception and why he is considered by many to be a disability hero even though he publicly denied his physical differences. Throughout his life, FDR did everything possible to avoid being *labeled* as a person with a disability. In Roosevelt's time, disability connoted "weakness" and he believed that revealing a paralysis would jeopardize his standing as a national leader. Fortunately, we have a much better understanding of human diversity in today's society—that is, everyone is unique in some way. In fact, a 1995 Lou Harris survey found that more than 80% of Americans knew FDR was paralyzed. Of those who knew of his disability, 75% favored the depiction of him in a wheelchair at the new FDR national monument in Washington, D.C. (N.O.D./Harris & Associates, 1995).

Labeling People with Differences

To address differences, society creates descriptors to identify people who vary significantly from the norm. This process is called *labeling*. Sociologists use labels to describe people who are socially deviant; educators and psychologists use labels to identify students with learning, physical, and behavioral differences; and physicians use labels to distinguish the sick from the healthy.

Common labels used by professionals to describe physical and behavioral differences include *disorder, disability,* and *handicap*. These terms are not synonymous. **Disorder,** the broadest of the three terms, refers to a general malfunction of mental, physical, or psychological processes. It is defined as a disturbance in normal functioning. A **disability** is more specific than a disorder and results from a loss of physical functioning (e.g., loss of sight, hearing, or mobility) or from difficulty in learning and social adjustment that significantly interferes with normal growth and development. A **handicap** is a limitation imposed on the individual by environmental demands and is related to the individual's ability to adapt or adjust to those demands. For example, Franklin Roosevelt used a wheelchair because of a physical disability—the inability to walk. He was dependent on the wheelchair for mobility. When the physical environment didn't accommodate his wheelchair (e.g., a building without ramps, accessible only by stairs), his disability became a handicap.

When applied as an educational label, *handicapped* has a narrow focus and a negative connotation. The word *handicapped* literally means "cap in hand"; it originates from a time when people with disabilities were forced to beg in the streets merely to survive. This term may be used to describe only those individuals who are deficient in or lack ability.

Exceptional is a much more comprehensive term. It may be used to describe any individual whose physical, mental, or behavioral performance deviates substantially from the norm, either higher or lower. A person with exceptional characteristics is not necessarily an individual with a handicap. People with exceptional characteristics may need additional educational, social, or medical services to compensate for physical and

focus 1
Why do we label people according to their differences?

DISORDER. A disturbance in normal functioning (mental, physical, or psychological).

DISABILITY. A condition resulting from a loss of physical functioning; or, difficulties in learning and social adjustment that significantly interfere with normal growth and development. A person with a disability has a physical or mental impairment that substantially limits the person in some major life activity.

HANDICAP. A limitation imposed on an individual by the environment and the person's capacity to cope with that limitation.

EXCEPTIONAL. A term describing any individual whose physical, mental, or behavioral performance deviates so substantially from the average (higher or lower) that additional support is required to meet the individual's needs.

While labels have been the basis for developing and providing services to people, they can also promote stereotyping, discrimination, and exclusion.

behavioral characteristics that differ substantially from what is considered normal. These differences can be **learning disorders, behavior disorders, speech and language disorders, sensory disorders, physical disorders, health disorders,** or **gifts and talents.**

Labels are only rough approximations of characteristics. Some labels, such as **deaf,** might describe permanent qualities; others, such as *overweight,* might describe temporary qualities. Some labels are positive, and others are negative. Labels communicate whether a person meets the expectations of the culture. A society establishes criteria that are easily exceeded by some but are unreachable for others. For example, a society may value creativity, innovation, and imagination and will value and reward those with these attributes with positive labels, such as *bright, intelligent,* or *gifted.* A society, however, may brand anyone whose ideas drastically exceed the limits of conformity with negative labels, such as *radical, extremist,* or *rebel.* Moreover, the same label may have different connotations for different groups, depending on each group's viewpoint. For example, a high school student may be labeled a *conformist.* From the school administration's point of view, this is probably considered a positive characteristic, but to the student's peer group, it may have strong negative connotations.

What are the ramifications of using labels to describe people? Reynolds (1991) contended that the use of labels has produced mixed results at best: "At the extremes, human classification can be a demeaning process, causing stigma and leading to the isolation and neglect of those in unfavored classes; it, conversely, can be the basis on which extraordinary services and favors are rallied in support of selected groups" (p. 29). Labels are based on ideas, not facts. "When we create or construct them [labels], we do so within particular cultural contexts. That is, someone observes particular behaviors or ways of being and then describes these . . . with a label" (Kliewer & Biklen, 1996, pp. 83–84). Thus, even though labels have been the basis for developing and providing services to people, they can also promote stereotyping, discrimination, and exclusion. This view is shared by several professionals who indicate that the practice of labeling children in order to provide appropriate services has perpetuated and reinforced both the label and the behaviors it implies (Forts, 1998; Lipsky & Gartner, 1996; Minow, 1991; Reynolds, 1994; Stainback, Stainback, & Ayres, 1996).

If the use of labels can have negative consequences, why is labeling used so extensively? One reason is that many social services and educational programs for exceptional individuals require the use of labels to distinguish who is eligible for services and who is not. Kauffman (1998), discussing the need to label students with learning and behavior differences, argued that "either all students are treated the same or some are treated differently. Any student who is treated differently is inevitably labeled . . . Labeling a problem clearly is the first step in dealing productively with it" (p. 12). Funding may even be contingent on the numbers and types of individuals who are deemed eligible. To illustrate, Maria, a child with a hearing problem, by federal and state law must be assessed and labeled as having a hearing loss before specialized educational or social services can be made available to her. Another reason for the continued use of labels is that they assist professionals in

■ LEARNING DISORDERS. Problems resulting in learning performance that is significantly below average when compared to that of others of a comparable chronological age.

■ BEHAVIOR DISORDERS. Conditions in which the emotional or behavioral responses of individuals in various environments significantly differ from those of their peer, ethnic, and cultural groups. These responses seriously affect social relationships, personal adjustment, schooling, and employment.

■ SPEECH AND LANGUAGE DISORDERS. Difficulties in communicating effectively. Speech disorders are characterized by difficulties in voice quality, production of sounds, or speech rhythm. Language disorders are characterized by an inability to produce or understand messages.

communicating effectively with one another and provide a common ground for evaluating research findings. A third reason is that labeling helps identify the specific needs of a particular group of people. Labeling can help in determining degrees of needs or in setting priorities for service when societal resources are limited.

■ FORMAL VERSUS INFORMAL LABELING

Labels may be applied by both formal and informal labelers (Kammeyer, Ritzer, & Yetman, 1997). Formal labelers are sanctioned by society. For example, members of the criminal justice system—including the arresting officer, jury, and court judge—label the person who commits a crime a *criminal*. A criminal may be incarcerated in a penal institution and consequently be labeled a *convict*. Formal labelers speak for their society, as when a court judge pronounces sentence on a convicted felon on behalf of all who live in the community. Additional examples of formal labelers include doctors, educators, and psychologists. They use formal labels including *gifted and talented, mentally ill, mentally retarded, blind,* and so forth. Formal labels affect our perception of the individual and in turn may change the individual's self-concept.

An informal labeler is usually some significant other—such as a family member, friend, or peer—and the applied label is meaningful only to this person or to a restricted group. Informal labels may be expressed in a number of ways. They can be derogatory slang terms, such as *stupid, cripple, fat,* and *crazy.* Some informal labels, such as *witty, smart,* and *cool,* reflect more favorably on the individual. Other informal labels, such as *ambitious* and *conformist,* are open to individual interpretation.

■ APPROACHES TO LABELING

Significant physical and behavioral differences are found infrequently in every society. Most people in any given culture conform to its established standards. *Conformity*—people doing what they are supposed to do—is the rule for most of us, most of the time (Baron & Byrne, 1997). Usually, we look the way we are expected to look, behave the way we are expected to behave, and learn the way we are expected to learn. When someone does deviate substantially from the norm, a number of approaches can be used to describe the nature and extent of the differences (see Figure 1.1).

■ THE DEVELOPMENTAL APPROACH   The **developmental approach to labeling** is based on deviations from what is considered normal physical, social, or intellectual growth. To understand these human differences, which result from an interaction of biological and environmental factors, we must first establish what is normal development.

According to the developmental view, normal development can be described statistically, by observing in large numbers of individuals those characteristics that occur most frequently at a specific age. For example, when stating that the average 3-month-old infant is able to follow a moving object visually, *average* is a statistical term based on observations of the behavior of 3-month-old infants. When comparing an individual child's growth pattern to that group average, differences in development (either advanced or delayed) are labeled accordingly.

■ THE CULTURAL APPROACH   The **cultural approach to labeling** defines what is normal according to the standards established by a given culture. Whereas a developmental approach considers only the frequency of behaviors to define differences, a cultural approach suggests that differences can be explained partly by examining the values inherent within a culture. What constitutes a significant difference

■ SENSORY DISORDERS. Differences in vision and hearing that affect performance.

■ PHYSICAL DISORDERS. Bodily impairments that interfere with an individual's mobility, coordination, communication, learning, and/or personal adjustment.

■ HEALTH DISORDERS. Conditions or diseases that interfere with an individual's functioning but do not necessarily or initially affect the ability to move about independently in various settings.

■ GIFTS AND TALENTS. Extraordinary abilities in one or more areas.

■ DEAF. A term used to describe individuals who have hearing losses greater than 75 to 80 dB, have vision as their primary input, and cannot understand speech through the ear.

■ DEVELOPMENTAL APPROACH TO LABELING. Labeling based on deviations in the course of development from what is considered normal growth.

■ CULTURAL APPROACH TO LABELING. Approach by which *normalcy* is defined according to the standards established by a given culture.

FIGURE 1.1

Approaches to labeling: What is normal?

Developmental Approach

Cultural Approach

Individual Approach

focus 2

Identify three approaches that can be used to describe human differences.

changes over time, from culture to culture, and among the various social classes within a culture. As Kammeyer et al. (1997) suggested, deviance begins when a person does something that is disapproved of by other members within the dominant culture. For example, in some cultures, intelligence is described in terms of how well someone scores on a test measuring a broad range of abilities, and in other cultures, intelligence relates much more to how skillful someone is at hunting or fishing. The idea that human beings are the products of their cultures has received its greatest thrust from anthropology, which emphasizes the diversity and arbitrary nature of cultural rules regarding dress, eating habits, sexual habits, politics, and religion. The human infant is believed to be so flexible that the child can adjust to nearly any environment.

■ THE INDIVIDUAL APPROACH   The **individual approach to labeling** asserts that all people engage in a self-labeling process that others may not recognize. Thus self-imposed labels reflect how we perceive ourselves, not how others see us. Conversely, the culture uses a given label to identify a person, but that label may not be accepted by that person. Such was the case with Thomas Edison. Although the schools labeled Edison as an intellectually incapable child, he eventually recognized that he was an individualist. He proved himself by identifying his individual abilities and pursuing his own interests as an inventor. (See the Reflect on This feature on pages 8 and 9, and take a quiz on other famous people with disabilities.)

■ INDIVIDUAL APPROACH TO LABELING. The process of labeling oneself as a reflection of how one perceives oneself.

THE EFFECTS OF LABELING

Reactions to a label differ greatly from one person to another but can often be negative (Gustavsson, 1999; Hastings, 1994; Lapadat, 1998; Walker & Bullis, 1991; Walther-Thomas & Brownell, 1999). Smith, Osborne, Crim, and Rho (1986) surveyed special education teachers, school officials, and parents to determine their perceptions of the label *learning disabilities,* and they found that these individuals attached multiple and sometimes conflicting meanings to the term. In two studies of college students' reactions to various labels used to describe people with **mental retardation** and learning disabilities, researchers found that older terms, such as *mental subnormality* and *mental handicap,* generate a more negative reaction than newer terms, such as *learning difficulty* or *learning disability* (Hastings & Remington, 1993; Hastings, Songua-Barke, & Remington, 1993). However, only one term, *exceptional,* received a positive rating from the college students studied. The authors attributed this positive reaction to the students defining *exceptional* as meaning "much above average."

SEPARATING THE PERSON AND THE LABEL

Once a label has been affixed to an individual, the two may become inseparable. For example, Becky has been identified as having mental retardation. The tendency is to refer to Becky and her condition as one in the same—Becky *is* retarded. Becky is described by her label (retardation), which loses sight of the fact that she is first and foremost a human being, and that her exceptional characteristics (intellectual and social differences) are only a small part of who she is. To treat Becky as a label rather than as a person with special needs is an injustice, not only to Becky but to everyone else as well.

ENVIRONMENTAL BIAS

The environment in which we view someone can clearly influence our perceptions of that person. For example, it can be said that, if you are in a mental hospital, you must be insane. In a classic study, Rosenhan (1973) investigated this premise by having himself and seven other "sane" individuals admitted to a number of state mental hospitals across the United States. Once in the mental hospitals, these subjects behaved normally. The question was whether the staff would perceive them as people who were healthy instead of as patients who were mentally ill. Rosenhan reported that the seven pseudopatients were never detected by the hospital staff but were recognized as imposters by several of the real patients. Throughout their hospital stays, the pseudopatients were incorrectly labeled and treated as schizophrenics. Rosenhan's investigation demonstrated that the perception of what is normal can be biased by the environment in which the observations are made.

▪ MENTAL RETARDATION. Substantial limitations in functioning, characterized by significantly sub-average intellectual functioning concurrent with related limitations into two or more adaptive skills. Mental retardation manifests itself prior to age 18.

Bringing About Social Change

A HISTORY OF DISCRIMINATION AND ISOLATION

Throughout recorded history, people perceived as different have been vulnerable to practices such as infanticide, slavery, physical abuse, and abandonment. These practices reflect a common societal fear that the so-called mentally and morally defective would defile the human race. It has been widely believed that most deviance is caused by hereditary factors that, if left unchecked, would result in widespread social problems (Gelb, 1995).

focus 3
Identify four indicators of quality supports and services for persons with disabilities.

Reflect on This

Match the names to the descriptions:

_____ 1. He was diagnosed with amyotrophic lateral sclerosis (ALS–Lou Gehrig's disease) at the age of 21. He must use a wheelchair and have round-the-clock nursing care. His speech has been severely affected, and he communicates through a computer by selecting words from a screen that are expressed through a speech synthesizer. Acknowledged as one of the greatest physicists in history, he developed a theory on black holes that provided new insights into the origin of the universe. Currently, he is professor of mathematics at Cambridge University, a post once held by Sir Isaac Newton.

_____ 2. He did not learn to read at all until he was 12 years old and continued having difficulty reading all his life. He was able to get through school by memorizing his teachers' entire lectures. Acknowledged as one of the greatest strategists in military history, he gained fame as a four-star general in World War II.

_____ 3. She was disabled by an accident in 1914 and eventually had to have part of her leg amputated. Regarded as one of the greatest French actresses in history, she continued her career on stage until her death in 1923.

_____ 4. A well-known, tireless humanitarian advocate for children, the homeless, and human rights, also involved in

a. Albert Einstein

b. Sarah Bernhardt

c. Nelson Rockefeller

d. Stephen Hawking

e. Whoopi Goldberg

f. George S. Patton Jr.

g. Walt Disney

h. Tom Cruise

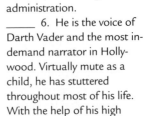

i. James Earl Jones

the battles against substance abuse and AIDS, this Oscar-winning actress and Grammy winner is a high school dropout with an acknowledged reading disability.

_____ 5. He was diagnosed with severe dyslexia, which made reading very difficult for him throughout life. He became a four-term governor

of New York and was appointed vice president of the United States during the Nixon administration.

_____ 6. He is the voice of Darth Vader and the most in-demand narrator in Hollywood. Virtually mute as a child, he has stuttered throughout most of his life. With the help of his high

school English teacher, he overcame stuttering by reading Shakespeare aloud to himself and then to audiences. He went on to debating and finally to stage and screen acting.

_____ 7. He was regarded as a slow learner during his school years and never had much success in public education. Later, he became the most well known cartoonist in history, producing the first full-length animated motion picture.

_____ 8. He did not speak until the age of 3. Even as an adult he found that searching for words was laborious. Schoolwork, especially math, was difficult for him, and he was unable to express himself in written language. He was thought to be "simple-minded" (retarded), until he discovered that he could achieve through visualizing rather than the use of oral language. His theory of relativity, which revolutionized modern physics, was developed in his spare time. *Time* magazine named him the most important person of the 20th century.

_____ 9. He has never learned to read due to severe dyslexia and was unable to finish high school. Today he is regarded as one of most accomplished actors of his time. Although unable to read, he can memorize his lines from an auditory source (cassette tape or someone reading to him).

Source: The source of this quiz is unknown. It was adapted from the *Family Village web site* (*http://www.familyvillage.wisc.edu/index.htmlx*) And from *Take a Walk in My Shoes—A Guide Book for Youth on Diversity Awareness Activities* by Yuri Morita, June 1996, Office of Affirmative Action, Division of Agriculture & National Resources, University of California, 300 Lakeside Drive, 6th Floor, Oakland, CA 94612-3560. Phone 510/987-0096.

Answers: 1(d), 2 (f), 3(b), 4(e), 5(c), 6(i), 7(g), 8(a), 9(h)

Humanitarian reform finally began in the last half of the 18th century, bringing with it optimism concerning the treatment and eventual cure of people described as deviant. However, when deviance wasn't cured and continued to be a major social problem well into the 19th century, many professionals became convinced that it was necessary to sterilize and segregate large numbers of these *mental and social degenerates.* Legal measures were undertaken to prohibit these people from marrying. Eventually, legislation was expanded to include compulsory **sterilization** of such individuals, and soon laws were passed in an effort to reduce the number of so-called deviates. Laws in some countries contained provisions for sterilizing people with mental retardation, individuals with epilepsy, the sexually promiscuous, and criminals. In addition to marriage and sterilization laws, measures were passed to move large numbers of individuals from their local communities to isolated special-care facilities. These facilities became widely known as **institutions.** Institutions have had many different labels: school, hospital, colony, prison, and asylum.

The institutions of the early 20th century became more and more concerned with social control as they grew in size and as financial resources diminished. To manage large numbers of individuals on a limited financial base, these facilities had to establish rigid rules and regulations, stripping away individuals' identities and forcing them into group regimentation. For example, individuals could not have personal possessions, were forced to wear institutional clothing, and were given identification tags and numbers. Institutions were characterized by locked living units, barred windows, and high walls enclosing the grounds. Organized treatment programs declined, and the number of "terminal," uncured patients grew, resulting in institutional expansion and the erection of new buildings. Given the public and professional pessimism concerning the value of treatment programs, this growth meant diminishing funds for mental health care. This alarming situation remained unchanged for nearly five decades and declined even further during the Depression years of the 1930s. By the early 1950s, more than 500,000 persons were committed to mental hospitals throughout the United States, and comparable numbers of persons with mental retardation lived in segregated institutions referred to as colonies, hospitals, or training schools. Several attempts to reform institutions were initiated. The American Psychiatric Association led efforts to inspect and rate the nation's 300 mental hospitals and called attention to the lack of therapeutic intervention and deplorable living conditions.

■ FROM ISOLATION TO INCLUSION: SUPPORTING PEOPLE WITH DISABILITIES IN FAMILY AND COMMUNITY SETTINGS In spite of the growth of segregated institutions in the 20th century, the vast majority of people

■ STERILIZATION. The process of making an individual unable to reproduce, usually accomplished surgically.

■ INSTITUTION. An establishment or facility governed by a collection of fundamental rules.

The inclusion of people with disabilities into schools and neighborhood settings recognizes and accepts the range of human diversity.

with disabilities remained at home within their families. For families, the choice to keep the child at home meant they were on their own, receiving little or no outside support. Government resources were very limited, and available funding was directed to support services outside of the family, often even beyond the community in which they resided (Bradley, Knoll, & Agosta, 1992). For the better part of this century, many families who had a child with a disability were unable to get help for basic needs, such as medical and dental care, social services, or education.

In response to the lack of government support and coinciding with the civil rights movement in the United States, parents of children with disabilities began to organize in about 1950. The United Cerebral Palsy Organization (UCP) was founded in 1949, and the National Association for Retarded children[1] (NARC) began in 1950. The UCP and NARC joined other professional organizations already in existence, such as the National Association for the Deaf, the American Association on Mental Deficiency,[2] the Council for Exceptional Children, and the American Federation for the Blind, to advocate for the rights of persons with disabilities. The purpose of these national organizations was to get accurate information to families with disabilities, professionals, policy makers, and the general public. Each organization focused on the rights of people with disabilities to be included in family and community life and have access to medical treatment, social services, and education (Berry & Hardman, 1998). Other parent groups followed, including those of the National Society for Autistic Children (1961) and the Association for Children with Learning Disabilities[3] (1964).

The inclusion of people with disabilities into community settings—such as schools, places of employment, and neighborhood homes—is based on a philosophy that recognizes and accepts the range of human differences. One way to evaluate the success of community services is to look at whether and how such supports make a difference in one's life. As such, the quality of community services for people with disabilities can be viewed in terms of four indicators:

1. Do services and supports promote personal autonomy?
2. Do opportunities for social interaction and **integration** exist?
3. Does the individual have a choice of lifestyle?
4. Do opportunities for economic self-sufficiency exist?

Each of these questions relates to different outcomes, depending on the age of the individual. For the preschool-age child, the world is defined primarily through the family and a small, same-age peer group. As the child grows older, the world expands to include the neighborhood, the school, and eventually a larger, more

■ INTEGRATION. The physical placement of individuals with disabilities in the natural settings of community, home, or general education class or school with their nondisabled peers.

---

[1] The National Association for Retarded Children became the Association for Retarded Citizens in 1974. It is now known as the ARC—A National Organization on Mental Retardation.

[2] It is now called the American Association on Mental Retardation.

[3] It is now called the Learning Disabilities Association (LDA).

diverse group called the community. The questions for professionals then change: How can services and supports be structured to foster full participation as the individual's world expands? What barriers obstruct full participation, and how do we break them down?

We will now examine some of the ways in which society supports as well as limits the participation of people with disabilities in community settings.

The Americans with Disabilities Act (ADA)

In 1973, the U.S. Congress passed an amendment to the Vocational Rehabilitation Act that included a provision prohibiting discrimination against persons with disabilities in federally assisted programs and activities. Section 504 of the Vocational Rehabilitation Act (herein referred to as Section 504) set the stage for passage of the most sweeping civil rights legislation in the United States since the **Civil Rights Act of 1964**: the **Americans with Disabilities Act (ADA)** signed into law in 1990. The purpose of ADA is to prevent discrimination on the basis of disability in employment, programs and services provided by state and local governments, goods and services provided by private companies, and commercial facilities. (See the nearby Reflect on This feature—This Wouldn't Have Happened Without the ADA.)

In the past, individuals with disabilities have had to contend with the reality that learning to live independently did not guarantee access to all that society had to offer in terms of services and jobs. Although several states have long had laws that promised otherwise, access to places such as public restrooms and restaurants and success in mainstream corporate America have often eluded those with disabilities, primarily because of architectural and attitudinal barriers. ADA is intended to change these circumstances, affirming the rights of more than 50 million Americans with disabilities to participate in the life of their community. Much as the Civil Rights Act of 1964 gave clout to the African American struggle for equality, the ADA has promised to do the same for those with disabilities. Its success in eliminating the fears and prejudices of the general community remains to be seen, but the reasons for such legislation were obvious. First, it was clear that people with disabilities faced discrimination in employment, access to public and private accommodations (e.g., hotels, theaters, restaurants, grocery stores), and services offered through state and local governments (N.O.D./Harris & Associates, 1994, 1995, 1999). Second, because the historic Civil Rights Act of 1964 did not even mention people with disabilities, they had no federal protection against discrimination except through the somewhat limited provisions in Section 504. As stated by the National Council on Disability,

ADA is the most comprehensive policy statement ever made in American law about how the nation should address individuals with disabilities. Built on principles of equal opportunity, full participation, independent living and economic self-sufficiency, the law reflects the disability community's convictions and determination to participate as first-class American citizens and to direct their own futures. (1996, p. 23)

In April 1999, The National Organization on Disability (N.O.D.) and Harris and Associates released the results of a survey on how Americans were perceiving ADA ten years after its passage. The survey found a strong and sustained public endorsement of this landmark civil rights legislation.

- Sixty-seven percent were aware of the ADA. Of those who had heard of the Act, 87% approved of what it is trying to accomplish.

focus 4

What is the purpose of the Americans with Disabilities Act?

▪ CIVIL RIGHTS ACT OF 1964. Legislation passed in the United States that prohibits discrimination against individuals on the basis of race, sex, religion, or national origin.

▪ AMERICANS WITH DISABILITIES ACT (ADA). Civil rights legislation in the United States that provides a mandate to end discrimination against people with disabilities in private sector employment, all public services, public accommodations, transportation, and telecommunications.

Reflect on This

THIS WOULDN'T HAVE HAPPENED WITHOUT THE ADA

At precisely 1:25 P.M. on Hayes Street near Franklin in San Francisco, Mary Lou Breslin's motorized wheelchair spat out a shower of sparks and died. Breslin, 50, disabled by polio since childhood, had been shopping with her friend, Kathy Martinez, 36, who is blind. "I haven't been dead in the water for years," Breslin muttered angrily. With that, she and Martinez began to "strategize," their term for improvising in the face of emergencies. As able-bodied pedestrians moved past in a hurried blur, Breslin pulled out her cellular phone and started making calls.

Despite Breslin's wheelchair breakdown, a day with them on the streets of the San Francisco area shows that commonplace life has improved dramatically for them since the advent of the Americans with Disabilities Act. Several years ago, for example, Breslin stopped at a drugstore near her home in Berkeley. The tight turnstiles at the entrance made access difficult, the checkout aisles were too narrow for her wheelchair, and Breslin had to wheel backward against the flow of other shoppers after she paid her bill. On a recent visit, she found that the store, now run by a different retailer, was much easier to deal with. There were no turnstiles to negotiate, and a wide checkout counter had been installed. "Without the ADA," Breslin said, "this wouldn't have happened."

Yet annoyances remain. An assistant manager seemed vaguely huffy when Martinez asked for help finding cough drops. The clerk assigned to the task was polite but, Martinez confided, "Sometimes they just take my [walking] stick and pull me along."

Later, at a Bay Area Rapid Transit station in Berkeley, Breslin had to wheel backward into a small, smelly elevator, while other people used escalators. Martinez, who also rides BART, feels safe there, thanks to bumps, or "edge detection strips," that warn the blind away from the edge of the platforms. Despite the tight elevator problem, BART is regarded as a disability-rights pioneer. "It was such a treat to take this train when I came to California years ago," says Breslin, who was raised in the Midwest. "I'd never lived anywhere where there was access."

But when the train pulled into the San Francisco Shopping Center, a mall on Market Street admired for its accessibility, the wheelchair lift refused to work. Breslin tinkered and finally made it move by asking a bystander to hold the bottom gate tightly shut while she pushed buttons inside. Later she spoke of the frustrations of "the Blanche DuBois life," a reference to the lonely, high-strung character in *A Streetcar Named Desire* who relies on "the kindness of strangers."

When Breslin's chair broke down an hour later, she was once again at the mercy of others. After telephoning a disabled-access taxi service, she had to wait nearly two hours. The driver charged $90 to transport her and Martinez to a wheelchair-repair shop across the bay. Strapped in her chair like furniture, Breslin rocked uncomfortably in the rear of the van with each high-speed freeway turn. A technician fixed her electric motor, and soon a friend arrived to help her get home. Such is the life of the disabled: determined, resourceful, and, all too often, reliant on the kindness of strangers.

Source: From "Under Their Own Power," by J. Willwerth, July 31, 1995, *Time*, p. 55. Reprinted by permission.

- Seventy-five percent believed that the benefits to people with disabilities are worth the additional costs to governments and businesses.
- Eighty-three percent felt that creating opportunities for those with disabilities will decrease welfare rolls and increase employment opportunities, whereas 12% felt it will be very expensive and not worth the cost for employers to hire more people with disabilities.
- Ninety-four percent believed employers should not discriminate against any qualified job candidate with a disability.
- Ninety-one percent wanted to see public transportation made accessible to disabled people.
- Ninety-five percent agreed that public places, such as hotels, restaurants, theaters, stores, and museums, must not discriminate against visitors with disabilities.

■ THE ADA DEFINITION OF DISABILITY

ADA uses a functional definition of disability that was originally established in federal law under Section 504. A person with a disability is defined as (1) having a physical or mental impairment that substantially limits him or her in some major life activity, and (2) having experienced discrimination resulting from this physical or mental impairment. The following is an illustrative list from the U.S. Congress of what constitutes a physical impairment:

any physiological disorder or condition, cosmetic disfigurements, or anatomical loss affecting one or more of the following body systems: neurological; musculoskeletal; special sense organs; respiratory, including speech organs; cardiovascular; reproductive; digestive; genito-urinary; hemic and lymphatic; skin; and endocrine.

An illustrative list of what constitutes a mental impairment includes "any mental or psychological disorder, such as mental retardation, organic brain syndrome, emotional or mental illness, and specific learning disabilities" (West, 1991).

■ MAJOR PROVISIONS OF ADA

ADA mandates protections for people with disabilities in public and private-sector employment, all public services, and public accommodations, transportation, and telecommunications. ADA charged the federal government with the responsibility of ensuring that these provisions be enforced on behalf of all people with disabilities (National Council on Disability, 1999). The intent of ADA is to create a "fair and level playing field" for eligible persons with disabilities. To do so, the law specifies that **reasonable accommodations** need to be made that take into account each person's needs resulting from his or her disabilities. As defined in law, the principal test for a reasonable accommodation is its effectiveness: does the accommodation provide an opportunity for a person with a disability to achieve the same level of performance and to enjoy benefits equal to those of an average, similarly situated person without a disability?

The major provisions of the ADA include the following:

- *Employment.* ADA mandates that employers may not discriminate in any employment practices, including job application procedures, hiring, firing, advancement, compensation, training, and other terms, conditions, and privileges of employment. It applies to recruitment, advertising, tenure, layoff, leave, fringe benefits, and all other employment-related activities. The law applies to any business with 15 or more employees. (See the nearby Reflect on This feature.)

- *Transportation.* ADA requires that all new public transit buses, bus and train stations, and rail systems must be accessible to people with disabilities. Transit authorities must provide transportation services to individuals with disabilities who cannot use fixed-route bus services. All Amtrak stations must be accessible to people with disabilities by the year 2010. Discrimination by air carriers in areas other than employment is not covered by the ADA but rather by the Air Carrier Access Act (49 U.S.C. 1374 [c]).

- *Public accommodations.* Restaurants, hotels, and retail stores may not discriminate against individuals with disabilities. Physical barriers in existing facilities must be removed, if removal is readily achievable. If not, alternative methods of providing the services must be offered. All new construction and alterations of facilities must be accessible.

- *Government.* State and local agencies may not discriminate against qualified individuals with disabilities. All government facilities, services, and communications must be accessible to people with disabilities.

- *Telecommunications.* ADA requires that all companies offering telephone service to the general public must offer telephone relay services to individuals with hearing loss who use telecommunication devices or similar equipment.

■ REASONABLE ACCOMMODA-TIONS. Requirements within ADA to ensure that a person with a disability has an equal chance of participation. The intent is to create a "fair and level playing field" for the person with a disability. A reasonable accommodation takes into account each person's needs resulting from their disability. Accommodations may be arranged in the areas of employment, transportation, or telecommunications.

Reflect on This

WHAT EVERYONE NEEDS TO KNOW ABOUT EMPLOYMENT AND THE AMERICANS WITH DISABILITIES ACT (ADA)

■ *What is the Americans with Disabilities Act?*

ADA is a federal law that protects people with a disability against many kinds of discrimination. Discrimination keeps people with a disability from getting a job just because someone says they have a disability. One part of ADA protects them against discrimination at work. ADA can "open doors." It can make it easier for people with a disability to apply for a job. The law can help each individual get a job, learn to do the job, and keep the job. The employer is responsible to help each person work faster and learn the job efficiently.

■ *Which jobs can people with a disability apply for?*

They can apply for any job for which they can do the important parts of the work, with or without help. ADA refers to the most important parts of a job as the "essential functions." They are the parts that must be done. Here are some examples. A mailroom clerk might have three essential functions: getting mail from a bag, sorting mail, and delivering it. A job that involves putting machine parts together might have four essential functions: getting supplies from a room, choosing the parts needed, putting the parts together, and packing the shipping boxes. These are only exam-

ples. Every job has its own essential functions. A person with a disability is qualified for a job if he or she can do the essential functions, with or without help.

■ *What are "reasonable accommodations"?*

A "reasonable accommodation" is any change or help that makes it easier for a person with a disability to find a job and do the work. Some of the help may come from coworkers. Some may come from job coaches. There are many several kinds of "reasonable accommodations" for employment.

If help is needed getting a job:
■ Bring a friend or family member along to apply for a job.
■ Ask the employer to read the application aloud.
■ Ask the employer to write information on the application.
■ Ask the employer to let the person with a disability show how he or she would do the job.

Remember—ADA protects people with disabilities against discrimination. Employers cannot ask whether a person has a disability. They cannot ask whether the person takes certain medicine or has been in an institution. They can ask the person to have a medical exam, but only after offering a job.

If the person with a disability can't do some "non-essential" parts of a job:

Ask the manager for "job restructuring." This means someone else will do the less important parts of the job. The person with a disability will still have to do the most important parts, or essential functions.

■ *How can a person with a disability get "reasonable accommodations"?*

A person with a disability (with assistance as necessary) can talk to the employer. Together they can decide what reasonable accommodations will help at work. There are many possible reasonable accommodations. They depend on the job and the individual's needs.

■ *What kind of assistance can people with disabilities ask for?*

They can ask for help applying for a job. They can ask for a reasonable accommodation for learning or doing the job. They can also ask for help with learning the rules at work. If they have trouble getting to work on time, they can ask to change the starting time.

■ *When can people with disabilities ask for assistance?*

They can ask for reasonable accommodations any time. They can ask when they apply for a job. They can ask when

they start a job. They can ask after beginning work. When they start a job, it's important to talk to the employer about the help they might need. They may find that they need more help once they are working. They can ask the employer about a new reasonable accommodation anytime.

■ *Does the employer have to provide a "reasonable accommodation"?*

Not always. Giving help may cause the employer "undue hardship." The employer doesn't have to give a reasonable accommodation if it costs too much. The employer doesn't have to give a reasonable accommodation if the work won't get done, even with help.

■ *Can someone come to work to assist people with disabilities?*

Yes. A job coach or counselor can help the individual learn a job. An agency may pay for a job coach or a counselor to help learn the job. Or the employer might let a friend or someone in the family help. The employer does not have to pay for this assistance.

Source: Adapted from *Opening Doors for You,* The Joseph P. Kennedy Jr. Foundation, n.d., Washington, D.C.: Author.

Living and Learning in Community Settings

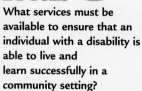

focus 5

What services must be available to ensure that an individual with a disability is able to live and learn successfully in a community setting?

egislating against discrimination is one thing; enforcing laws against it is another. The purpose of ADA was to ensure that comprehensive services (e.g., employment, housing, educational programs, public transportation, restaurant access, and religious activities) be available to all individuals within or as close as possible to their family and community lives. Individuals should also be able to purchase additional services at will: dental examinations, medical treatment, life insurance, and so forth. Access to these services allows people the opportunity to be included in community life. Successful inclusion is based on two factors: (1) the individual's ability, with appropriate education and training, to adapt to societal expectations, and (2) the willingness of society to adapt to and accommodate individuals with differences.

Access to adequate housing and **barrier-free facilities** is essential for people with physical disabilities. A barrier-free environment may be created by renovating existing facilities and requiring that new buildings and public transportation incorporate barrier-free designs. People in wheelchairs or on crutches need entrance ramps to and within public buildings; accessibility to public telephones, vending machines, and restrooms; and lifts for public transportation vehicles. Available community living environments could include private homes, specialized boarding homes, supervised apartments, group homes, and foster homes.

Recreation and leisure opportunities within the community vary substantially according to the individual's age and the severity of his or her disability, and the availability of such opportunities also varies from community to community. Thus many persons with disabilities may not have access to dance and music lessons, gymnastics training, swimming lessons, and scouting—activities that are generally available to others within the community. Similar problems exist for children, adolescents, and adults with exceptional characteristics, many of whom may do little with their leisure time beyond watching television.

Recreational programs must be developed to assist individuals in developing worthwhile leisure activities and more satisfying lifestyles. Therapeutic recreation is a profession concerned specifically with this goal: using recreation to help people adapt their physical, emotional, or social characteristics to take advantage of leisure activities more independently in a community setting.

Work is essential to the creation of successful lifestyles for all adults, including those with disabilities. Yet many individuals with disabilities are unable to gain employment during their adult years. A 1998 National Organization on Disability/Harris poll found significant gaps between the employment rates of people with disabilities in comparison to their nondisabled peers. Only 29% of people with disabilities (ages 18 to 64) work full- or part-time, compared to 79% of people who are not disabled, a gap of 50 percentage points. Of the people with disabilities who are not working, 72% say that they would prefer to work. A comparison of working and nonworking disabled individuals revealed that working individuals were more satisfied with life, had more money, and were less likely to blame their disability for preventing them from reaching their potential (N.O.D./Harris & Associates, 1998).

■ BARRIER-FREE FACILITY. A building or other structure that is designed and constructed so that people with mobility disabilities (such as those in wheelchairs) can move freely through all areas without encountering architectural obstructions.

FIGURE 1.2

Common terminology of
fields of study concerned
with individuals who are
exceptional

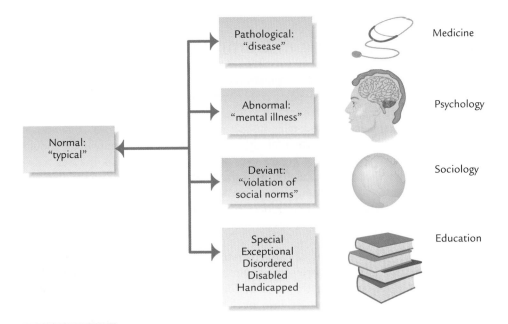

Medicine

Psychology

Sociology

Education

Medical, Psychological, and Sociological Understandings of People with Disabilities

To gain a broader understanding of the nature and extent of human differences, we will briefly examine several disciplines concerned with individuals who are exceptional. These disciplines include medicine, psychology, and sociology. Each is unique in its approach to exceptionality, as reflected in the labels it uses to describe a person with exceptional characteristics. Figure 1.2 provides the common terminology associated with each field.

■ MEDICINE

The **medical model** has two dimensions: normalcy and pathology. *Normalcy* is defined as the absence of a biological problem. **Pathology** is defined as alterations in an organism caused by disease, resulting in a state of ill health that interferes with or destroys the integrity of the organism. The medical model, often referred to as the *disease model,* focuses primarily on biological problems and on defining the nature of the disease and its pathological effects on the individual. The model is universal and does not have values that are culturally relative. It is based on the premise that being healthy is better than being sick, regardless of the culture in which one lives.

When diagnosing a problem, a physician carefully follows a definite pattern of procedures that includes questioning the patient to obtain a history of the problem, conducting a physical examination and laboratory studies, and in some cases, performing surgical exploration. The person who has a biological problem is labeled the *patient,* and the deficits are then described as the *patient's disease.*

We must go back more than 200 years to find the first documented attempts to personalize medical treatment programs to serve the needs of people with differences. During the 16th and 17th centuries, people with mental or emotional disturbance were viewed as mad persons, fools, and public threats to be removed from society. This view changed during the 18th and 19th centuries, when many physicians contributed to expanding our understanding of human differences. Jean-Marc

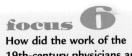

focus 6

How did the work of the
19th-century physicians and
philosophers contribute to
our understanding of people
with differences?

■ MEDICAL MODEL. Model by
which human development is
viewed according to two dimensions: normal and pathological.
Normal refers to the absence of
biological problems; *pathological*
refers to alterations in the organism caused by disease.

■ PATHOLOGY. Alterations in
an organism that are caused
by disease.

Itard (1775–1838) epitomized the orientation of professionals during this period, and his work is reflected in our modern medical, psychological, social, and educational intervention models.

In 1799, as a young physician and authority on diseases of the ear and education of those with hearing loss, Itard worked for the National Institute of Deaf-Mutes in Paris. He believed that the environment, in conjunction with physiological stimulation, could contribute to the learning potential of any human being. Itard was influenced by the earlier work of Philippe Pinel (1742–1826), a French physician concerned with mental illness, and John Locke (1632–1704), an English philosopher. Pinel advocated that people characterized as insane or idiots needed to be treated humanely, but his teachings emphasized that they were essentially incurable and that any treatment to remedy their disabilities would be fruitless. Locke, in contrast, described the mind as a "blank slate" that could be opened to all kinds of new stimuli. The positions of Pinel and Locke represent the classic controversy of **nature versus nurture:** what are the roles of heredity and environment in determining a person's capabilities?

Itard tested the theories of Pinel and Locke in his work with Victor, the so-called wild boy of Aveyron. Victor was 12 years old when found in the woods by hunters. He had not developed any language, and his behavior was virtually uncontrollable, described as savage or animal-like. Ignoring Pinel's diagnosis that the child was an incurable idiot, Itard took responsibility for Victor and put him through a program of sensory stimulation that was intended to cure his condition. After five years, Victor developed some verbal language and became more socialized as he grew accustomed to his new environment. Itard's work with Victor documented for the first time that learning is possible even for individuals described by most professionals as totally helpless.

Following Itard's ground-breaking work in the early 19th century, some European countries began establishing special schools and segregated living facilities for people with disabilities (such as mental illness, retardation, or hearing or sight loss). As explained by McCleary, Hardman, and Thomas (1990), expertise and knowledge about people with disabilities were extremely limited during this period. Most programs focused on care and management rather than treatment and education. Although many professionals had demonstrated that positive changes in individual development were possible, they had not been able to cure conditions such as insanity and idiocy.

Medical services for people with disabilities have evolved considerably. The typical course in the early part of the 20th century involved treatment primarily in a hospital or institutional setting. The focus today is directly on the individual in family and community settings. In many cases, the physician is the first professional with whom parents have contact concerning their child's disability, particularly when the child's problem is identifiable immediately after birth or during early childhood. The physician is the family adviser and communicates with parents regarding the medical prognosis and recommendations for treatment. However, too often physicians assume that they are the family's only counseling resource (Drew & Hardman, 2000). Physicians should be aware of additional resources within the community, including other parents, social workers, mental health professionals, and educators.

Medical services are often taken for granted simply because they are readily available to most people. This is not true, however, for many people with disabilities. It is not uncommon for a pediatrician to suggest that parents seek treatment elsewhere for their child with a disability, even when the problem is a common illness such as a cold or a sore throat.

▌NATURE VS. NURTURE. Controversy concerning how much of a person's ability is related to sociocultural influences (nurture) as opposed to genetic factors (nature).

It would be unfair to stereotype medical professionals as unresponsive to the needs of exceptional people. On the contrary, medical technology has prevented many disabilities from occurring and has enhanced the quality of life for many people. However, to ensure that people with disabilities receive comprehensive medical services in a community setting, several factors must be considered. The physician in community practice (e.g., the general practitioner, pediatrician) must receive more medical training in the medical, psychological, and educational aspects of disability conditions. This training could include instruction regarding developmental milestones; attitudes toward children with disabilities; disabling conditions; prevention; screening, diagnosis, and assessment; interdisciplinary collaboration; effective communication with parents; long-term medical and social treatment programs; and community resources.

Physicians must also be willing to treat patients with disabilities for common illnesses when the treatment is irrelevant to the patient's disability. Physicians need not become disability specialists, but they must have enough knowledge to refer patients to appropriate specialists when necessary. For instance, physicians must be aware of and willing to refer patients to other nonmedical community resources, such as social workers, educators, and psychologists. The medical profession must continue to support physician specialists and other allied health personnel who are well equipped to work with people with disabilities. These specialized health professionals include **geneticists** and **genetic counselors, physical therapists** and **occupational therapists,** public health nurses, and nutritional and dietary consultants.

■ PSYCHOLOGY

Psychology and sociology are similar in that both fields are concerned with the study of human behavior. Sociology is the science of social behavior, whereas psychology studies the person as a separate being.

Modern psychology is the science of human and animal behavior, the study of the overt acts and mental events of an organism that can be observed and evaluated. Broadly viewed, psychology is concerned with every detectable action of an individual. Behavior is the focus of psychology, and when the behavior of an individual does not meet the criteria of normalcy, it is labeled *abnormal.*

Psychology, as we know it today, is more than 100 years old. In 1879, Wilhelm Wundt (1832–1920) defined psychology as the science of conscious experience. His definition was based on the *principle of introspection*—looking into oneself to analyze experiences. William James (1842–1910) expanded Wundt's conception of conscious experience in his treatise *The Principles of Psychology* (1890) to include learning, motivation, and emotions. In 1913, John B. Watson (1878–1958) shifted the focus of psychology from conscious experience to observable behavior and mental events.

In 1920, Watson conducted an experiment with an 11-month-old child named Albert. Albert showed no fear of a white rat when initially exposed to the animal, seeing it as a toy and playing with it freely. Watson then introduced a loud, terrifying noise directly behind Albert each time the rat was presented. After a period of time, the boy became frightened by the sight of any furry white object, even though the loud noise was no longer present. Albert had learned to fear rats through **conditioning,** the process in which new objects or situations elicit responses that were previously elicited by other stimuli. Watson thus demonstrated that abnormal behavior could be learned through the interaction of the individual with environmental stimuli (Watson & Rayner, 1920).

In spite of Watson's work, most theorists during the first half of the 20th century considered the medical model to be the most logical and scientific approach to understanding abnormal behavior. The public was more accepting of the view that people with psychological disturbances were sick and not fully responsible for their problems.

focus

Distinguish between abnormal behavior and social deviance.

▪ GENETICIST. A professional who specializes in the study of heredity.

▪ GENETIC COUNSELOR. A specially trained professional who counsels people about their chances of producing a seriously ill infant, in reference to their genetic history.

▪ PHYSICAL THERAPIST. A person who performs physical therapy, a treatment of a physical problem by stretching, exercise, or massage.

▪ OCCUPATIONAL THERAPIST. A professional who specializes in designing and delivering instruction related to potential work-related activities.

▪ CONDITIONING. The process by which new objects or situations elicit responses that were previously elicited by other stimuli.

18

The **ecological approach,** emerging in the latter half of the 20th century, supported Watson's theories. This approach views abnormal behavior more as a result of an individual's interaction with the environment than as a disease. The approach theorizes that social and environmental stress, in combination with the individual's inability to cope, lead to psychological disturbances.

We cannot live in today's society without encountering the dynamics of abnormal behavior. The media are replete with stories of murder, suicide, sexual aberration, burglary, robbery, embezzlement, child abuse, and other incidents that display abnormal behavior. Each case represents a point on the continuum of personal maladjustment that exists in society. Levels of maladjustment range from behaviors that are slightly deviant or eccentric (but still within the confines of normal human experience) to **neurotic disorders** (partial disorganization characterized by combinations of anxieties, compulsions, obsessions, and phobias) to **psychotic disorders** (severe disorganization resulting in loss of contact with reality and characterized by delusions, hallucinations, and illusions).

The study of abnormal behavior historically has been based in philosophy and religion in Western culture. Until the Middle Ages, the disturbed or mad person was thought to have "made a pact with the devil," and the psychological affliction was believed to be a result of divine punishment or the work of devils, witches, or demons residing within the person. The earliest known treatment for mental disorders, called *trephining,* involved drilling holes in a person's skull to permit evil spirits to leave (Carlson & Buskist, 1999).

Today's psychologists use myriad approaches in the treatment of mental disorders, including behavior therapy, rational–emotive therapy, group psychotherapy, family therapy, or client-centered therapy. According to Carlson and Buskist (1999), the majority of psychologists describe their therapeutic philosophy as eclectic. They choose from many different approaches in determining the best way to work with an individual in need of psychological help.

■ SOCIOLOGY

Whereas psychology focuses primarily on the behavior of the individual, sociology is concerned with modern cultures, group behaviors, societal institutions, and intergroup relationships. Sociology examines individuals in relation to their physical and social environment. When individuals meet the social norms of the group, they are considered normal. When individuals are unable to adapt to social roles or to establish appropriate interpersonal relationships, their behaviors are labeled **deviant.** Unlike medical pathology, social deviance cannot be defined in universal terms. Instead, it is defined within the context of the culture, in any way the culture chooses to define it.

Even within the same society, different social groups often define deviance differently. Groups of people who share the same norms and values will develop their own rules about what is and what is not deviant behavior. Their views may not be shared by members of the larger society, but the definitions of deviance will apply to group members (Kammeyer et al., 1997).

Four principles serve as guidelines in determining who will be labeled socially deviant:

1. Normal behavior must meet societal, cultural, or group expectations. Deviance is defined as a violation of social norms.
2. Social deviance is not necessarily an illness. Failure to conform to societal norms does not imply that the individual has pathological or biological deficits.
3. Each culture determines the range of behaviors that are defined as normal or deviant and then enforces these norms. Those people with the greatest power

■ ECOLOGICAL APPROACH. An approach in psychology that ascribes abnormal behavior more to the interaction of an individual with the environment than to disease.

■ NEUROTIC DISORDERS. Behavior characterized by combinations of anxieties, compulsions, obsessions, and phobias.

■ PSYCHOTIC DISORDERS/PSYCHOSIS. A general term referring to a serious behavior disorder resulting in a loss of contact with reality and characterized by delusions, hallucinations, or illusions.

■ DEVIANT. A term used to describe the behavior of individuals who are unable to adapt to social roles or to establish appropriate interpersonal relationships.

within the culture can impose their criteria for normalcy on those who are less powerful.

4. Social deviance may be caused by the interaction of several factors, including genetic makeup and individual experiences within the social environment.

Today, many different kinds of sociologists specialize across more than 50 subfields and specialties. Within each specialty area, sociologists undertake a systematic study of the workings and influence of social groups, organizations, cultures, and societies on individual and group behavior. The sociologist accumulates and disseminates information about social behavior (including disability) in the context of the society as a whole (Kammeyer et al., 1997). The following are just a few examples of specialties within sociology that may include an emphasis on disability: deviant behavior and social disorganization, aging, criminology and criminal justice, family and marriage, medicine, and education.

Bringing About Educational Change

■ ACCESS TO EDUCATION

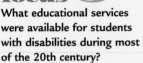

focus 8
What educational services were available for students with disabilities during most of the 20th century?

As children progress through formal schooling, their parents, teachers, peers, and others expect that they will learn and behave according to established patterns. Most students move through their educational programs in about the same way, requiring the same level of service and progressing within similar time frames. Students who do not meet educational expectations of normal growth and development may be labeled according to the type and extent of their deviation. They may also be provided with services and resources that differ from those provided for typical students.

Access to education is a basic American value, reflecting the expectation that each individual should have an opportunity to learn and develop to the best of his or her ability. From this value emerges some of the most fundamental goals of education. Schools exist to promote literacy, personal autonomy, economic self-sufficiency, personal fulfillment, and citizenship. McLaughlin, Shepard, and O'Day (1995) suggested that schools must prepare all students, not just the academically capable, to gain knowledge and apply what they learn in order to be productive workers and citizens. Full participation for everyone, regardless of race, cultural background, socioeconomic status, physical disability, or mental limitation, is the goal. Unfortunately, in the United States, it has taken more than two centuries to translate this value into actual practice in educating students with disabilities.

■ SPECIAL EDUCATION: 1900–1975

In the United States, education of children with exceptionalities began in the early 1900s with the efforts of many dedicated professionals. Those efforts consisted of programs that were usually separate from the public schools, established mainly for children who were slow learners or had hearing or sight loss. These students were usually placed in segregated classrooms in a public school building or in separate schools. Special education meant segregated education. Moreover, students with substantial differences were excluded from public education entirely.

Because the schools needed to have some way of determining who would receive a public education, an assessment device was developed to determine who was intellectually capable of attending school. The result was an individual test of intelligence developed by Alfred Binet and Theodore Simon (1905). It was first used in France to predict how well students would function in school, and in 1908, it was translated into English. The Binet-Simon Scales, revised and standardized by Lewis Terman at Stanford University, were published in 1916 as the **Stanford-Binet Intelligence Scale.** This test provided a means of identifying children who deviated significantly from the average in intellectual capability, at least in terms of what the test actually measured.

From 1920 to 1960, the availability of public school programs for exceptional children continued to be sporadic and selective. Most states merely allowed for special education; they did not mandate it. Services to children with mild emotional disorders (discipline problems) were initiated in the early 1930s, but mental hospitals continued to be the only alternative for most individuals with severe emotional problems. Special classes for children with physical disabilities were also started in the 1930s, primarily for those with crippling conditions, heart defects, and other health-related problems that interfered with participation in general education programs. Separate schools for these children, very popular during the late 1950s, were specially equipped with elevators, ramps, and modified doors, toilets, and desks.

During the 1940s, special school versus general school placement for students with disabilities emerged as an important policy issue. Educators became more aware of the need for these students to be educated in an environment that would promote "normal" social interaction.

By the 1950s, many countries began to expand educational opportunities for students with disabilities in special schools and classes funded through public education. Two separate events had a significant impact on the evolution of educational programs for students with disabilities. First, in many countries, parents of children with disabilities organized in order to lobby policy makers for more appropriate social and educational services for their children. Second, professionals from both the behavioral and medical sciences became more interested in services for individuals with disabilities, thus enriching knowledge through research, which could then be integrated into effective practice.

The number of public school classes for students with mild mental retardation and those with behavior disorders increased in the late 1950s. For the most part, these children continued to be educated in an environment that isolated them from nondisabled peers. The validity of segregation continued to be an important issue. Several studies in the 1950s and 1960s (e.g., Cassidy & Stanton, 1959; Johnson, 1961; Jordan & deCharms, 1959; Thurstone, 1959) examined the efficacy of special classes for children with mild mental retardation. Johnson (1962), summarizing this research, suggested that the academic achievement of learners with mental retardation was consistent regardless of whether they were placed in special or general education classes, although the child's social adjustment was not harmed by the special program. Although numerous criticisms regarding the design of efficacy studies have been made over the years, they did result in a movement toward expanding services beyond special classes in public schools. An example of this outcome was the development of a model whereby a child could remain in the general class program for the majority, if not all, of the school day, receiving special education when and where it was needed.

The 1960s brought other major changes in the field of special education as well. Under the leadership of President John F. Kennedy, the federal government took on an expanded role in the education of children with exceptional needs. University programs for teacher preparation received federal financial support and initiated programs to train special education teachers throughout the United States. The Bureau of Education for the Handicapped (BEH) in the Office of Education (presently the Office of Special Education and Rehabilitative Services in the U.S.

■STANFORD-BINET INTELLIGENCE SCALE. A standardized individual intelligence test, originally known as the Binet- Simon Scales, which was revised and standardized by Lewis Terman at Stanford University.

Department of Education) was created as a clearinghouse for information at the federal level. Demonstration projects were funded nationwide to establish a research base for the education of students with disabilities in the public schools.

focus 9

Identify the principal issues in the right-to-education cases that led to eventual passage of the national mandate to educate students with disabilities.

■ LEGAL REFORMS[4] AND SPECIAL EDUCATION

The 1970s have often been described as a decade of revolution in the field of special education. Many of the landmark cases addressing the right to education for students with disabilities were brought before the courts during this period. In addition, major pieces of state and federal legislation were enacted to reaffirm the right of students with disabilities to a free public education.

The rights of students with disabilities came to the public forum as a part of a larger social issue in the United States: the civil rights of people from differing ethnic and racial backgrounds. The civil rights movement of the 1950s and 1960s awakened the public to the issues of discrimination in employment, housing, access to public facilities (e.g., restaurants and transportation), and public education.

Education was reaffirmed as a right and not a privilege by the U.S. Supreme Court in the landmark case of *Brown v. Topeka, Kansas, Board of Education* (1954). In its decision, the court ruled that education must be made available to everyone on an equal basis. A unanimous Supreme Court stated, "In these days, it is doubtful that any child may reasonably be expected to succeed in life if he is denied the opportunity of an education. Such an opportunity, where the state has undertaken to provide it, is a right which must be made available to all on equal terms" (*Brown v. Topeka, Kansas, Board of Education,* 1954).

Although usually heralded for striking down racial segregation, this decision also set a major precedent for the education of students with disabilities. Unfortunately, it was nearly 20 years before federal courts were confronted with the issue of a free and appropriate education for these students.

In 1971, the Pennsylvania Association for Retarded Citizens filed a class-action suit on behalf of children with mental retardation who were excluded from public education on the basis of intellectual deficiency (*Pennsylvania Association for Retarded Citizens v. Commonwealth of Pennsylvania,* 1971). The suit charged that these children were being denied their right to a free public education. The plaintiffs claimed that children with mental retardation can learn if the educational program is adjusted to meet their individual needs. The issue was whether public school programs should be required to accommodate children who were intellectually different. The court ordered Pennsylvania schools to provide a free public education to all children with mental retardation of ages 6 to 21, commensurate with their individual learning needs. In addition, preschool education was to be provided for children with mental retardation if the local school district provided it for children who were not disabled.

The case of *Mills v. District of Columbia Board of Education* (1972) expanded the Pennsylvania decision to include all children with disabilities. District of Columbia schools were ordered to provide a free and appropriate education to every school-age child with a disability. The court further ordered that, when general public school assignment was not appropriate, alternative educational services had to be made available. Thus, the right of students with disabilities to an education was reaffirmed. The *Pennsylvania* and *Mills* cases served as catalysts for several court cases and pieces of legislation in the years that followed. Table 1.1 (on pages 24 and 25) summarizes precedents regarding the right to education for students with disabilities.

■ PUBLIC LAW 94-142 (THE EDUCATION FOR ALL HANDICAPPED CHILDREN ACT). Part B of the Education of the Handicapped Act, passed in 1975 and mandating that all eligible students regardless of the extent or type of handicap receive at public expense the special education services necessary to meet their individual needs.

■ INDIVIDUALS WITH DISABILITIES EDUCATION ACT (IDEA—PUBLIC LAW 101-476). The new name for Public Law 94-142 (The Education for All Handicapped Children Act) as per the 1990 amendments to the Education of the Handicapped Act. IDEA also added two new categories of disability: autism and traumatic brain injury.

---

[4] Because the legal reforms discussed in this section exclude students who are gifted and talented, the more narrowly defined term *disability* has been used.

The Individuals with Disabilities Education Act (IDEA)

focus 10

Identify five major provisions of the Individuals with Disabilities Education Act.

In 1975, the U.S. Congress saw the need to bring together the various pieces of state and federal legislation into one comprehensive national law. **Public Law 94-142** (PL 94-142) made available a free and appropriate public education to nearly 4 million school-age students with disabilities in the United States between the ages of 6 and 21. The law was renamed the **Individuals with Disabilities Education Act** in 1990 and is referred to throughout this text as **IDEA.**

In 1986, Congress amended IDEA to include provisions for preschool-age students. **Public Law 99-457** (PL 99-457) established a new mandate extending all the rights and protections of school-age children (ages 6 through 21) to preschoolers ages 3 through 5. This law required that states receiving federal funds ensure that all 3- through 5-year-old children with disabilities receive a free and appropriate public education. Another provision of PL 99-457 was the establishment of a state grant program for infants and toddlers up through 2 years old. Infants and toddlers who are developmentally delayed, as defined by each state, are eligible for services that include a multidisciplinary assessment and an **individualized family service plan (IFSP).** Although this provision did not mandate that states provide services to all infants and toddlers who were developmentally delayed, it did establish financial incentives for state participation. (The IFSP and other provisions of PL 99-457 are discussed in more depth in Chapter 4 of this text.)

■ WHAT IS SPECIAL EDUCATION?

Referred to as the **zero-exclusion principle,** IDEA requires that public schools provide special education and related services to meet the individual needs of all eligible students, regardless of the extent or type of their disability. *Special education means specially designed instruction provided at no cost to parents in all settings (such as the classroom, physical education facilities, the home, and hospitals or institutions).* IDEA also stipulates that students with disabilities are to receive any related services necessary to ensure that they benefit from their educational experience. **Related services** include the following:

transportation, and such developmental, corrective, and other supportive services (including speech–language pathology and audiology services, psychological services, physical and occupational therapy, recreation, including therapeutic recreation, social work services, counseling services, including rehabilitation counseling, orientation and mobility services, and medical services, except that such medical services shall be for diagnostic and evaluation purposes only) as may be required to assist a child with a disability to benefit from special education, and includes the early identification and assessment of disabling conditions in children. (1997 Amendments to IDEA, PL 105-17, Sec. 602[22])

■ WHO IS ELIGIBLE FOR SPECIAL EDUCATION?

In order for an individual to receive the specialized services available under IDEA, two criteria must be met. First, the individual must be identified as having 1 of the 12 disability conditions identified in federal law or their counterparts in a state's special education law. These conditions include mental retardation, specific learning disabilities, serious emotional disturbances (behavior disorders), speech or language impairments, vision loss (including blindness), hearing loss (including deafness), **orthopedic impairments,** other health impairments, deafness–blindness,

■ PUBLIC LAW 99-457. U.S. legislation that extended the rights and protections of IDEA (formerly Public Law 94-142) to preschool-age children (ages 3 through 5). The law also established a program for infants and toddlers with disabilities.

■ INDIVIDUALIZED FAMILY SERVICE PLAN (IFSP). A plan of intervention for infants and toddlers, similar in content to the IEP. It includes statements regarding the child's present development level, the family's strengths and needs, the major outcomes of the plan, specific interventions and delivery systems to accomplish outcomes, dates of initiation and duration of services, and a plan for transition into public schools.

■ ZERO-EXCLUSION PRINCIPLE. A principle which advocates that no person with a disability can be rejected for a service regardless of the nature, type, or extent of their disabling condition.

■ RELATED SERVICES. Those services necessary to ensure that students with disabilities benefit from their educational experience. Related services may include special transportation, speech pathology, psychological services, physical and occupational therapy, recreation, rehabilitation counseling, social work, and medical services.

■ ORTHOPEDIC IMPAIRMENTS. Bodily impairments that interfere with an individual's mobility, coordination, communication, learning, and/or personal adjustment.

Court Cases and Federal Legislation	Precedents Established
Brown v. Topeka, Kansas, Board of Education (1954)	Segregation of students by race is held unconstitutional.
	Education is a right that must be available to all on equal terms.
Hobsen v. Hansen (1969)	The doctrine of equal educational opportunity is a part of the law of due process, and denying an equal educational opportunity is a violation of the Constitution.
	Placement of children in educational tracks based on performance on standardized tests is unconstitutional and discriminates against poor and minority children.
Diana v. California State Board of Education (1970)	Children tested for potential placement in a special education program must be assessed in their native or primary language.
	Children cannot be placed in special classes on the basis of culturally biased tests.
Pennsylvania Association for Retarded Citizens v. Commonwealth of Pennsylvania (1971)	Pennsylvania schools must provide a free public education to all school-age children with mental retardation.
Mills v. Board of Education of the District of Columbia (1972)	Declared exclusion of individuals with disabilities from free, appropriate public education is a violation of the due-process and equal protection clauses of the 14th Amendment to the Constitution.
	Public schools in the District of Columbia must provide a free education to all children with disabilities regardless of their functional level or ability to adapt to the present educational system.
Public Law 93-112, Vocational Rehabilitation Act of 1973, Section 504 (1973)	Individuals with disabilities cannot be excluded from participation in, denied benefits of, or subjected to discrimination under any program or activity receiving federal financial assistance.
Public Law 93-380, Educational Amendments Act (1974)	Financial aid is provided to the states for implementation of programs for children who are exceptional, including the gifted and talented. Due-process requirements (procedural safeguards) are established to protect the rights of children with disabilities and their families in special education placement decisions.

multiple disabilities, **autism,** and **traumatic brain injury.** Each disability will be defined and described in depth in subsequent chapters of this text.

In 1997 the Congress amended IDEA[5] and gave states and local education agencies (LEA) the option of eliminating categories of disability (such as mental retardation or specific learning disabilities) for children ages 3 through 9. For this age group, a state or LEA may define a child with a disability as

(i) experiencing developmental delays, as defined by the State and as measured by appropriate diagnostic instruments and procedures, in one or more of the following areas: physical development, cognitive development, communication development, social or emotional development, or adaptive development; and (ii) who, by reason thereof, needs special education and related services. (PL 105-17, Sec. 602[3][B])

The second criterion for eligibility is the student's demonstrated need for specialized instruction and related services in order to receive an appropriate education.

■ AUTISM. A childhood disorder with onset prior to 36 months of age. It is characterized by extreme withdrawal, self-stimulation, intellectual deficits, and language disorders.

■ TRAUMATIC BRAIN INJURY. Direct injuries to the brain, such as tearing of nerve fibers, bruising of the brain tissue against the skull, brain stem trauma, and swelling.

[5]The 1997 Amendments to IDEA are herein referred to as IDEA 97.

TABLE 1.1   *(continued)*

Court Cases and Federal Legislation	Precedents Established
Public Law 94-142, Part B of the Education of the Handicapped Act (1975)	A free and appropriate public education must be provided for all children with disabilities in the United States. (Those up through 5 years old may be excluded in some states.)
Hendrick Hudson District Board of Education v. Rowley (1982)	The U.S. Supreme Court held that in order for special education and related services to be appropriate, they must be reasonably calculated to enable the student to receive educational benefits.
Public Law 99-457, Education of the Handicapped Act amendments (1986)	A new authority extends free and appropriate education to all children with disabilities ages 3 through 5 and provides a new early intervention program for infants and toddlers.
Public Law 99-372, Handicapped Children's Protection Act (1986)	Reimbursement of attorneys' fees and expenses is given to parents who prevail in administrative proceedings or court actions.
Public Law 101-336, Americans with Disabilities Act (1990)	Civil rights protections are provided for people with disabilities in private sector employment, all public services, and public accommodations, transportation, and telecommunications.
Public Law 101-476, Individuals with Disabilities Education Act (1990)	The Education of the Handicapped Act amendments are renamed the Individuals with Disabilities Education Act (IDEA). Two new categories of disability are added: autism and traumatic brain injury. IDEA requires that an individualized transition plan be developed no later than age 16 as a component of the IEP process. Rehabilitation and social work services are included as related services.
Public Law 105-17, Amendments to the Individuals with Disabilities Education Act (1997) (Commonly referred to as IDEA 97)	IDEA 97 expands the emphasis for students with disabilities from public school access to improving individual outcomes (results). The 1997 amendments modify eligibility requirements, IEP requirements, public and private placements, disciplining of students, and procedural safeguards.

This need is determined by a team of professionals and parents. Both criteria for eligibility must be met. If this is not the case, it is possible for a student to be identified as disabled but not eligible to receive special education services under federal law. These students may still be entitled to accommodations or modifications in their educational program under the Americans with Disabilities Act (see the later section on ADA and students with disabilities).

Five basic tenets of IDEA drive the determination of eligibility for services, design of an instructional program, and educational placement:

1. Nondiscriminatory and multidisciplinary assessment of educational needs
2. Parental safeguards and involvement in developing each child's educational program
3. A free and appropriate public education (FAPE)
4. An individualized education program (IEP)
5. Education in the least restrictive environment (LRE)

IDEA mandates a free and appropriate public education for children with disabilities ages 3 to 21.

■ NONDISCRIMINATORY AND MULTIDISCIPLINARY ASSESSMENT

IDEA incorporated several provisions related to the use of nondiscriminatory testing procedures in labeling and placement of students for special education services. Among those provisions are the following:

- The testing of students in their native or primary language, whenever possible
- The use of evaluation procedures selected and administered to prevent cultural or racial discrimination
- Validation of assessment tools for the purpose for which they are being used
- Assessment by a child-study team, utilizing several pieces of information to formulate a placement decision

Students with disabilities were too often placed in special education programs on the basis of inadequate or invalid assessment information. One result of such oversights was the placement of a disproportionate number of ethnic minority children and children from low socioeconomic backgrounds in special education programs.

■ PARENTAL SAFEGUARDS AND INVOLVEMENT

IDEA granted parents the following rights in the education of their children:

- To give consent in writing before the child is initially evaluated
- To give consent in writing before the child is initially placed in a special education program
- To request an independent education evaluation if they feel the school's evaluation is inappropriate
- To request an evaluation at public expense if the parent disagrees with the school's evaluation
- To participate on the committee that considers the evaluation of, placement of, and programming for the child
- To inspect and review educational records and challenge information believed to be inaccurate, misleading, or in violation of the privacy or other rights of the child
- To request a copy of information from the child's educational record
- To request a hearing concerning the school's proposal or refusal to initiate or change the identification, evaluation, or placement of the child or the provision of a free and appropriate public education

The intent of these safeguards is twofold: first, to create an opportunity for parents to be more involved in decisions regarding their child's education program; and second, to protect the student and family from decisions that could adversely affect their lives. Families thus can be secure in the knowledge that every reasonable attempt is being made to educate their child appropriately.

Some professionals and parents have argued that IDEA's provision for a parent and professional partnership has never been fully realized. Powell and Graham (1996) suggested that many barriers exist between the school and the home, such as "a lack of understanding, mistrust, a decrease in services as the child ages, and limited coordination of services" (p. 603). These authors further indicated a need to prevent the adversarial relationships that often result from due-process hearings. Such hearings may lead to mistrust and long-term problems.

IDEA 97 (PL 105-17) responded to the need for a mediation process to resolve any conflict between parents and school personnel and to prevent long-term adversarial relationships. This law requires states to establish a mediation system in which parents and schools voluntarily participate. In such a system, an impartial individual would listen to parents and school personnel and attempt to work out a mutually agreeable arrangement in the best interest of the student with a disability. But although mediation is intended to facilitate the parent and professional partnership, it must not be used to deny or delay the parents' right to a due-process hearing.

■ A FREE AND APPROPRIATE PUBLIC EDUCATION (FAPE)

IDEA is based on the value that every student can learn. As such, all students with disabilities are entitled to a **free and appropriate public education (FAPE)** based upon individual ability and need. The IDEA provisions related to FAPE are based on the 14th Amendment to the U.S. Constitution guaranteeing equal protection of the law. No student with a disability can be excluded from a public education based on a disability (the zero-exclusion principle). A major interpretation of FAPE was handed down by the U.S. Supreme Court in *Hendrick Hudson District Board of Education v. Rowley* (1982). The Supreme Court declared that an appropriate education consists of "specially designed instruction and related services" that are "individually designed" to provide "educational benefit." Often referred to as the "some educational benefit" standard, the ruling mandates that a state need not provide an ideal education but must provide a beneficial one for students with disabilities.

■ THE INDIVIDUALIZED EDUCATION PROGRAM (IEP)

The vehicle for delivering a free and appropriate public education to every eligible student with a disability is a written statement referred to as an **individualized education program (IEP).** The IEP provides an opportunity for parents and professionals to join together in developing and delivering specially designed instruction to meet student needs.

■ **THE IEP TEAM**   According to IDEA 97, the team responsible for developing the IEP should consist of the student's parents; at least one special education teacher; at least one regular (general) education teacher if the child is, or may be, participating in the regular (general) education environment; and a representative of the local education agency (LEA). The LEA representative must be qualified to provide, or supervise the provision of, specially designed instruction to meet the unique needs of children with disabilities. This individual must also be knowledgeable about the general curriculum and the availability of resources within the LEA.

■ FREE AND APPROPRIATE PUBLIC EDUCATION (FAPE). Provision within IDEA that requires every eligible student with a disability be included in public education. The Supreme Court declared that an appropriate education consists of "specially designed instruction and related services" that are "individually designed" to provide "educational benefit."

■ INDIVIDUALIZED EDUCATION PROGRAM (IEP). Provision in IDEA requiring that students with disabilities receive an educational program based on multidisciplinary assessment and designed to meet individual needs. The program must include consideration of the student's present level of performance, annual goals, short-term instructional objectives, related services, percent of time in general education, timeline for special education services, and an annual evaluation.

The development of an IEP is a collaborative process involving parents, professionals, and students.

The IEP team must also include an individual who can interpret the instructional implications of evaluation results. Other individuals who have knowledge or special expertise regarding the child (including related services personnel as appropriate, and whenever appropriate, the student with disability) may be included at the discretion of the parents or LEA.

■ **IEP REQUIREMENTS** The intended result of the IEP process is more continuity in the delivery of educational services for students on a daily as well as an annual basis. The IEP also promotes more effective communication between school personnel and the home. IDEA 97 requires that each child's IEP must include

- *a statement of the child's present levels of educational performance, including how the child's disability affects involvement and progress in the general curriculum. For preschool children the statement must describe how the disability affects the child's participation in appropriate activities.*

- *a statement of measurable annual goals, including benchmarks or short-term objectives related to meeting the child's needs that result from the disability. The annual goals should enable the child to be involved and make progress in the general curriculum and meet each of the child's other educational needs that result from the disability.*

- *a statement of the special education and related services and supplementary aids or services to be provided to, or on behalf of, the child. The statement must include (1) any program modifications or supports for school personnel that will be provided for the child to advance appropriately toward attaining the annual goals, (2) how the child will be involved and progress in the general curriculum and participate in extracurricular and other nonacademic activities, (3) how the child will be educated and participate with other children with disabilities and nondisabled children, and (4) an explanation of the extent, if any, to which the child will not participate with nondisabled children in the regular [general education] class and in the activities described above.*

- *a statement of any individual modifications in the administration of state or district-wide assessments of student achievement that are needed in order for the child to participate in such assessment. If the IEP team determines that the child will not participate in a particular state or district-wide assessment of student achievement (or part of such an assessment), there must be a statement of why that assessment is not appropriate for the child and how the child will be assessed.*

- *the projected date for the beginning of the services and modifications, and the anticipated frequency, location, and duration of those services and modifications.*

- *a statement of how the child's progress toward the annual goals will be measured and how the child's parents will be regularly informed (by means such as periodic report cards), at least as often as parents are informed of their nondisabled children's progress, of their child's progress toward the annual goals. The statement should include the extent to which that progress is sufficient to enable the child to achieve the goals by the end of the year. (IDEA 97, PL 105-17, Sec. 614[d])*

Further discussion of the IEP process and a sample IEP form can be found in Chapter 4.

■ EDUCATION IN THE LEAST RESTRICTIVE ENVIRONMENT

All students have the right to learn in an environment consistent with their academic, social, and physical needs. Such a setting constitutes the **least restrictive environment (LRE).** IDEA mandated that students with disabilities receive their education with nondisabled peers to the maximum extent appropriate. To meet this mandate, federal regulations required schools to develop a continuum of placements, ranging from general classrooms with support services to homebound and hospital programs. About 96% of students with disabilities between the ages of 6 and 21 receive their education in a general education school building, with the remaining 4% in a separate day school, residential facility, or hospital/homebound program (U.S. Department of Education, 2000a). An educational services model is presented in Figure 1.3.

At Level I in this continuum, a student remains in the general education classroom and receives no additional support services. Adaptations necessary for a given

■ LEAST RESTRICTIVE ENVIRONMENT (LRE). Students with disabilities are to be educated with their nondisabled peers to the maximum extent appropriate.

FIGURE 1.3

Educational service options for students with disabilities

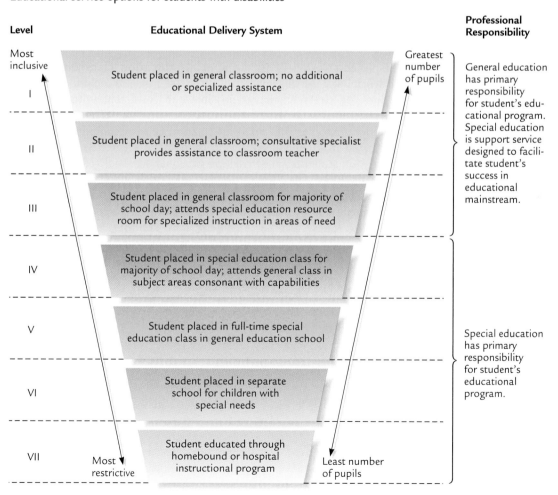

student are handled by the classroom teacher. Consequently, a student's success depends on whether his or her general education teacher has skills in developing and adapting programs to meet individual needs.

A student placed at Level II also remains in the general education classroom, but **consultative services** are available to both the teacher and the student. These services may be provided by a variety of professionals, including special educators, speech and language specialists, behavior specialists, physical education specialists, occupational therapists, physical therapists, school psychologists, and social workers. Services may range from assisting a teacher in the use of tests or modification of curriculum to direct instruction with students in the classroom setting.

The student placed at Level III continues in the general education classroom for the majority of the school day but also attends a **resource room** for specialized instruction in deficit areas. A resource room program is directed by a qualified special educator. The amount of time a student spends there varies according to his or her needs; it may range from as short as 30 minutes to as long as 3 hours a day. Instruction in a resource room is intended to reinforce or supplement the student's work in the general education classroom and includes the assistance necessary to help him or her keep pace with general education peers. The resource room is the most widely used public school setting for students with disabilities.

At Levels I, II, and III, the primary responsibility for the student's education lies with the general education classroom teacher. Consultative services, including special education, are intended to support the student's general education class placement. At Levels IV and beyond, the primary responsibility shifts to special education professionals.

The student placed at Level IV is in a **special education classroom** for the majority of the school day. At this level, provisions are made to include him or her with general education peers whenever possible and consistent with his or her learning capabilities.

Level V placement involves full-time participation in a special education class. Although still situated in a general education school, the student is not included with general education students for formal instructional activities. However, some level of social inclusion may take place during recess periods, lunch assemblies, field trips, and tutoring. Placement at Level VI involves transferring the student from the general education facility to a classroom in a separate facility specifically for students with disabilities. These facilities include **special schools,** where the education program is one aspect of a comprehensive treatment program.

Those students who, because of the severity of their disabilities, are unable to attend any school program must receive services through a homebound or hospital program. Placement at Level VII generally indicates a need for an **itinerant teacher** to visit an incapacitated student on a regular basis to provide tutorial assistance. Some students with chronic conditions, such as certain types of cancer, may be placed at this level indefinitely, whereas others are served while recuperating from short-term illnesses.

The issue of placement in the LRE continues to be a matter of public and private debate. Clearly, IDEA favors educating students in general education settings, mandating that students with disabilities be educated with their nondisabled peers to the maximum extent appropriate. An examination of the placement of students in segregated environments suggested that 4.0% of all students with disabilities between the ages of 6 and 21 receive their education in separate schools and residential facil-

▪ CONSULTATIVE SERVICES. Assistance provided by specialists in general education settings to improve the quality of education or other intervention for a student with a disability.

▪ RESOURCE ROOM. An educational placement option for students with disabilities, involving specialized instruction for a specified time period during the day to address the student's needs. Most of the student's day, however, is spent in the general education classroom. The specialized assistance provided in the resource room reinforces and supplements general education class instruction.

▪ SPECIAL EDUCATION CLASSROOM. A classroom setting under the supervision of a qualified special educator that provides specially designed instruction to meet the needs of a student with a disability.

▪ SPECIAL SCHOOLS. A general term applied to a separate educational placement for students with disabilities outside of a general education school. Students who are not disabled generally do not attend special schools.

▪ ITINERANT TEACHER. Teacher who moves from place to place to provide instruction and support to students, such as a teacher who regularly visits an incapacitated student in the home or a hospital to provide tutorial instruction. The term may also describe a teacher who moves from school to school to provide specialized instructional services.

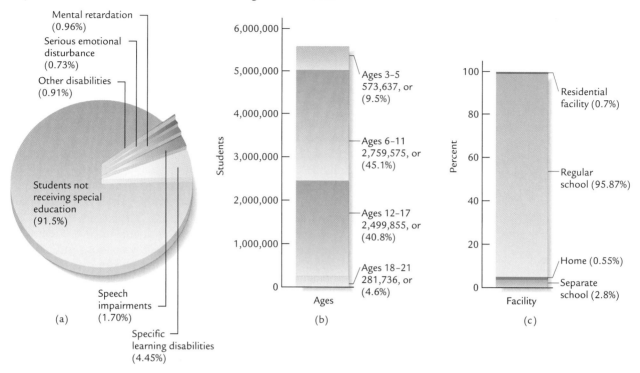

FIGURE 1.4 A profile of special education in the United States (school year 1998–1999): (a) Disabilities of students ages 6–21 receiving special education as a percentage of all students ages 6–21; (b) number of students with disabilities receiving special education services by age under IDEA (6,114,803 children served); (c) percentage of special education students in the school building and other sites.

[Source: The 22nd Annual Report to Congress on the Implementation of the Individuals with Disabilities Education Act, 2000a, Washington, DC: U.S. Government Printing Office.]

ities (U.S. Department of Education, 1999a). For a closer look at who is being served in special education programs, and where, see Figure 1.4.

Current Trends in the Education of Students with Disabilities

■ SAFE SCHOOLS, STUDENTS WITH DISABILITIES, AND IDEA 97

In the past several years, maintaining a safe school environment for America's children has become a critical priority for parents, school personnel, policy makers, and government officials. Today, 1 out of every 620 school-age children in America is killed by gunfire before the age of 20—about 13 children every day (Children's Defense Fund, 1998a). About 10% of America's schools experience one or more serious or violent crimes each year (National Center for Education Statistics, 1998b). In 1994, the U.S. Congress passed the Gun-Free Schools Act

focus 11

Under IDEA 97, describe the actions a school may take when a student brings a dangerous weapon to school or buys, sells, or possesses illicit drugs.

■ ZERO TOLERANCE. The consequences for a student's misbehavior are predetermined and any
individual reasons or circumstances are not to be considered.

as part of the Improving America's Schools Act. This federal legislation mandated that every state receiving federal funds under the Elementary and Secondary Education Act must enact a law requiring all local educational agencies (LEAs) to expel for at least one year any student who brings a firearm to school. The federal law and the corresponding state legislation employ the principle of **zero tolerance.** This principle states that the consequences for a student's misbehavior are predetermined (e.g., a one-year expulsion) and any individual reasons or circumstances are not to be considered. In the 1996–1997 school year, 6,093 students in the U.S. were expelled from schools for bringing a firearm or other dangerous weapon to school (Sinclair, Hamilton, Gutmann, Daft, & Bolcik, 1998). The National Center for Education Statistics (1997) reported that the proportion of public schools having zero tolerance policies ranged from 79% for violence and tobacco to 94% for firearms.

While the zero-tolerance principle has it supporters and detractors, it has posed a particularly serious problem for students with disabilities receiving services under the provisions of IDEA. IDEA employs a *zero rejection* principle requiring that an eligible student with a disability cannot be denied access to a free and appropriate public education (FAPE). As such, how can a student with a disability be expelled from school under any circumstances?

The issue of whether education services could be terminated and a student with a disability expelled because of dangerous or violent behavior arose in Congress during discussions on the 1997 amendments to IDEA. The concern was focused on incidents in which a student with a disability (1) brings a dangerous weapon to school or to a school function, (2) knowingly possesses or distributes illicit drugs or sells or solicits the sale of a controlled substance while at school or a school function, (3) is substantially likely to cause injury to self or others, and (4) exhibits any other behaviors that violate the school's written code of conduct.

Many professionals and parents of students with disabilities were concerned that if Congress allowed a cessation of services, it would undermine IDEA's zero-exclusion principle. Others argue that students with a disability should be treated no differently than nondisabled students when the individual is likely to cause injury to others and themselves. (See the Debate Forum for Chapter 7.)

In dealing with this controversial issue, IDEA 97 reiterated that a free and appropriate public education must be available to all students with disabilities and that there should be no cessation of services. Schools must seek to employ instructional alternatives to expulsion—that is helping children to learn decision-making and problem-solving skills that promote acceptable behavior. Hartwig and Ruesch (2000) suggested that it is important to have a balanced approach to discipline that includes " . . . both proactive strategies to prevent problem behavior and well-specified, procedurally sound responses to problem behavior" (p. 246).

Federal regulations prescribe the following actions when a student with a disability brings a dangerous weapon to school or buys, sells, or possesses illicit drugs:

■ *The ten-day rule.* To the extent removal would be applied to children without disabilities, school personnel may remove a child with a disability for not more than ten consecutive school days and for additional removals of not more than ten consecutive school days in that same school year for separate acts of misconduct, as long as the additional removals do not constitute a change in placement. Services need not be provided under IDEA to a child with a disability during the first ten school days in a school year that a child is removed for violations of school conduct rules, when necessary and appropriate to the circumstances and if services are not provided to a child without disabilities. After a child has been removed from his or her current placement for more than ten school days in the same school year, during any subsequent days of removal the public agency must provide services to the extent required under FAPE.

■ *Misconduct relating to weapons and drugs.* School personnel may order a change in placement of a child with a disability to an appropriate interim alternative educational setting for the same amount of time that a child without a disability would be subject to discipline but for not more than 45 days.

■ *Functional behavioral assessment and behavioral intervention plans.* After either first removing a child for more than ten school days in a school year or commencing a removal that constitutes a change in placement (including removals for weapons and drug misconduct), the public agency must convene an IEP meeting to develop a **functional behavioral assessment plan.** As soon as practical after developing the functional behavioral assessment plan, and completing the assessments required by the plan, the LEA must convene an IEP meeting to develop appropriate behavioral interventions to address the behavior and must implement those interventions. If the child already has a behavioral intervention plan, the IEP team must meet to review the plan and its implementation and modify the plan and its implementation as necessary, to address the behavior. If, subsequently, a child who has a behavioral intervention plan and who has been removed from his or her current educational placement for more than ten school days in a school year is subjected to removal that does not constitute a change of placement, the IEP members shall individually review the behavioral intervention plan and its implementation and if one or more of the team members believe that modifications are needed, the IEP team shall meet to modify the plan and its implementation.

■ *Determination of the interim alternative educational setting.* The interim alternative educational setting must be determined by the IEP team so as to enable the child to continue to participate in the general curriculum and continue to receive those services and modifications described in the child's current IEP. The setting must also include services and modifications to address the behavior relating to weapons and drugs, injury to child or others, that are designed to prevent the behavior from recurring.

■ *Manifestation determination (Is the student's misbehavior a manifestation of his or her disability?).* School officials must conduct a **manifestation determination** review whenever they contemplate (a) removing a child for behavior relating to weapons or the illegal use of drug, (b) seeking an order from a hearing officer to place a child in an interim alternative educational setting because of behavior that is substantially likely to result in injury to self or others, or (c) removing a child when such removal constitutes a change in placement for a child with a disability who has engaged in other behavior that violated any rule or code of conduct of the LEA that applies to all children. If the behavior is determined not to be a manifestation of the student's disability, the school may use disciplinary procedures applicable to nondisabled students.

■ *Parent notification.* When school officials decide to change a child's placement, the parents must be notified and procedural safeguards as described in IDEA must be followed. (Federal Register 34 C.F.R. Part 300.517, March 12, 1999; adapted from Silverstein, 1999)

■ FUNCTIONAL BEHAVIORAL ASSESSMENT PLAN. A plan that includes an explicit definition of problem behaviors, predicts when and under what conditions the behaviors occur, and specifies the function that a behavior serves in meeting the needs of the child or youth.

■ MANIFESTATION DETERMINATION. Process required in IDEA 1997 to determine if a student's misbehavior is caused by or directly related to his or her identified disability.

One out of every 620 school-age children in America is killed by gunfire before the age of 20. Here a teacher in California conducts a playground drill to prepare students for a random shooting.

focus 12

Distinguish between students with disabilities eligible for services under the Americans with Disabilities Act and those eligible under IDEA.

■ STUDENTS WITH DISABILITIES AND THE AMERICANS WITH DISABILITIES ACT

Today's schools must provide supports and services to two groups of students with disabilities. One group qualifies for special education services under IDEA, based upon educational need. Another group, while not eligible for special education, meets the definition of disability under Section 504 of the Vocational Rehabilitation Act that was incorporated into the Americans with Disabilities Act (ADA) of 1990.

Students eligible under ADA are entitled to reasonable accommodations or modifications as a means to "create a fair and level playing field" in their educational program. A plan for individually designed instruction must be developed for each student qualified under ADA. Numerous accommodations or modifications can be made for students, depending on identified need. Some examples include untimed tests, extra time to complete assignments, change in seating arrangement to accommodate vision or hearing loss or distractibility, opportunity to respond orally on assignments and tests, taped textbooks, access to peer tutoring, access to study carrel for independent work, use of supplementary materials such as visual or auditory aids, and so on. A comparison of the IDEA and ADA provision can be found in Table 1.2 on pages 36 and 37. The ADA definition of disability encompasses a broader group of students than those eligible under IDEA. This definition may include individuals with conditions such as HIV infection, heart disease, drug addiction, or alcoholism, in addition to the disability conditions identified in IDEA. The actual number of students covered under ADA is unknown.

■ STUDENTS WITH DISABILITIES AND SCHOOL REFORM

The current wave of school reform in the United States began with a report by the National Commission on Excellence in Education (1983), entitled *A Nation at Risk: The Imperative for Educational Reform. A Nation at Risk* is considered by many to be the basis for the current educational restructuring movement, which is centered on finding new and better ways to enhance student achievement. The rallying cry in today's schools is "higher expectations for all students." The call for high expectations has resulted in a standards-based approach to reforming schools—set high standards for what should be taught and how student performance should be measured. Four common elements characterize **standards-based reform** in America's schools:

■ STANDARDS-BASED REFORM. An educational reform movement focused on student achievement as the primary measure of school success. The movement emphasizes challenging academic standards of knowledge and skills and the levels at which students should demonstrate mastery of them.

1. A focus on student achievement as the primary measure of school success
2. An emphasis on challenging academic standards that specify the knowledge and skills students should acquire and the levels at which they should demonstrate mastery of that knowledge
3. A desire to extend the standards to *all* students, including those for whom expectations have been traditionally low
4. Heavy reliance on achievement testing to spur the reforms and to monitor their impact. (National Research Council, 1997)

Some advocates for standards-based reform have strongly emphasized the importance of acknowledging student diversity both in terms of ability and needs. O'Day and Smith (1993), for example, argue that the standards movement must respond to student differences.

Not to accommodate student differences . . . could effectively deny access to large numbers of students. . . . For the reform to be successful, the approaches taken by all schools must be based on common curriculum frameworks and all students must be expected and given the opportunity to perform at the same high standards on a common assessment. (p. 265)

Yet, in spite of the call to include *all* students in school reform initiatives, concerns have arisen that students with disabilities and other disadvantaged students are being left out. Research suggests that the participation of students with disabilities in the general education curriculum and statewide assessments of student performance vary considerably from state to state and district to district (Erickson, 1998; Erickson, Thurlow, & Thor, 1995; McLaughlin, 1998). The National Research Council (1997) indicates anecdotal evidence that states and local school districts are keeping students with disabilities out of their accountability systems because of fears that they pull down scores.

In response to these concerns, IDEA 97 required that a student's IEP must describe how the disability affects the child's involvement and progress in the general education curriculum. In addition, the IEP goals must enable the child to access the general education curriculum when appropriate. The law requires an explanation of any individual modifications in the administration of state- or district-wide assessment of student achievement that are needed in order for the child to participate.

As the movement to a standards-based system moves forward and students with disabilities gain more access to the general education curriculum, several questions are yet to be answered:

- How will the standards-based system deal with the diverse needs and functioning levels of students with disabilities?
- Will participation of students with disabilities in a standards-based general education curriculum result in higher academic achievement?
- Are the knowledge and skills learned in the standards-based general education curriculum the same ones that are necessary for the successful transition out of school and into adult life?
- Will a variety of student performance measures be used, or will criteria be based solely on standardized achievement tests? If the criteria are standardized tests, will schools continue to exclude students with disabilities in the testing program to avoid lowering the school's overall achievement scores? (McLaughlin & Tilstone, 2000)

	IDEA	ADA
General purpose	This federal funding statute provides financial aid to states in their efforts to ensure adequate and appropriate services for children and youth with disabilities.	This broad civil rights law prevents discrimination on the basis of disability in employment programs, and services provided by state and local governments, goods and services provided by private companies, and in commercial facilities.
Eligibility	IDEA identifies 12 categories of qualifying conditions. IDEA 97 allows states and school districts the option of eliminating categories for children age 3 through 9. The child may be defined as having developmental delays.	ADA identifies students as disabled if they meet the definition of qualified handicapped [disabled] person (i.e., student has or has had a physical or mental impairment that substantially limits a major life activity, or student is regarded as disabled by others).
Responsibility to provide a free and appropriate public education (FAPE)	Both require the provision of a free and appropriate education, including individually designed instruction, to students covered under specific eligibility criteria.	
	IDEA requires a written and specific IEP document.	ADA does not require a written IEP document, but does require a written plan.
	"Appropriate education" means a program designed to provide "educational benefit."	"Appropriate" means an education comparable to the education provided to students who are not disabled.
Special education or general education	A student is eligible to receive IDEA services only if the child-study team determines that the student is disabled under 1 of the 12 qualifying conditions and requires special education. Eligible students receive special education and related services.	An eligible student meets the definition of qualified person with a disability: one who currently has or has had a physical or mental impairment that substantially limits a major life activity or who is regarded as disabled by others. The student is not required to need special education in order to be protected.
Funding	IDEA provides additional funding, if a student is eligible.	ADA does not provide additional funds.

TABLE 1.2 A comparison of the purposes and provisions of IDEA and ADA

TABLE 1.2   *(continued)*

	IDEA	ADA
Accessibility	IDEA requires that modifications be made, if necessary, to provide access to a free and appropriate education.	ADA includes regulations regarding building and program accessibility.
Notice safeguards	Both require notice to the parent or guardian with respect to identification, evaluation, and/or placement.	
	IDEA requires written notice.	ADA does not require written notice, but a district would be wise to do so.
	It delineates required components of written notice.	Particular components are not delineated.
	It requires written notices prior to *any* change in placement.	It requires notice only before a "significant change" in placement.
Evaluations	IDEA requires consent before an initial evaluation is conducted.	ADA does not require consent, but does require notice.
	It requires reevaluations at least every 3 years.	It requires periodic reevaluations.
	It requires an update and/or review before any change in placement.	Reevaluation is required before a significant change in placement.
	It provides for independent educational evaluations.	Independent educational evaluations are not mentioned.
Due process	Both statutes require districts to provide impartial hearings for parents or guardians who disagree with the identification, evaluation, or placement of a student with disabilities.	
	Specific requirements are detailed in IDEA.	ADA requires that the parent have an opportunity to participate and be represented by counsel. Other details are left to the discretion of the local school district. These should be covered in school district policy.
Enforcement	IDEA is enforced by the Office of Special Education Programs in the Department of Education.	ADA is enforced by the Office for Civil Rights in the Department of Justice.

A discussion on current trends would not be complete without addressing the topic of **inclusive education.** Over the years, four terms have emerged as standards for describing the placement of students with disabilities in general education settings. In order of their evolutionary appearance and usage, these terms are **mainstreaming,** *the least restrictive environment,* integration, and inclusion. We have already discussed the least restrictive environment in the context of IDEA; we will now take a more in-depth look at this term as it relates to other terminology associated with the placement of students with disabilities in general education settings. We will then move into the terminology of the 21st century, whereby inclusive education has become the vernacular of choice to describe educating students with disabilities side by side with nondisabled peers and friends.

■ MAINSTREAMING   The expression "mainstreaming students with disabilities" dates back to the very beginnings of the field of special education. It didn't come into widespread use until the 1960s, however, with the growth of classes for children with disabilities in the public schools, most of which segregated students with disabilities from their nondisabled peers. The validity of segregated programs was called into question by some professionals. Dunn (1968) charged that classes for children with mild retardation could not be justified: "Let us stop being pressured into continuing and expanding a special education program that we know now to be undesirable for many of the children we are dedicated to serve" (p. 5). Dunn, among others, called for a placement model whereby students with disabilities could remain in the general education class program for at least some portion of the school day and receive special education when and where needed. This model became widely known as mainstreaming. Although mainstreaming implied that students with disabilities would receive individual planning and support from both general and special educators, this did not always happen in actual practice. In fact, the term *mainstreaming* fell from favor when it became associated with placing students with disabilities in general education classes without providing additional support, as a means to save money and limit the number of students who could receive additional specialized services. Such practices gave rise to the term *maindumping* as an alternative to *mainstreaming.* The term *mainstreaming* still remains in use today as one way to describe educating students with disabilities in general education settings. However, with the advent of Public Law 94-142 (now the Individuals with Disabilities Education Act) in 1975, a new term was incorporated into practice: *the least restrictive environment.*

■ THE LEAST RESTRICTIVE ENVIRONMENT   Over the past 20 years, *least restrictive environment (LRE)* has become the term most often used in the United States to describe a process by which students with disabilities are to be placed in educational settings consistent with their individual educational needs. As defined in IDEA, the intent of LRE is to educate students with disabilities with their nondisabled peers to the maximum extent appropriate. Federal regulations require that the removal of a child from the general education setting is to occur only when the nature and severity of the child's disability is such that education in general education classes with supplementary aids or services cannot be achieved satisfactorily (34 C.F.R. Sec. 300.550[b]). Although the concept of the LRE suggests a strong preference for students with disabilities to be educated alongside their nondisabled peers, it also states that this should occur only when appropriate. As such, *LRE and mainstreaming are not synonymous.* The LRE may be any one of a "continuum of place-

■ INCLUSIVE EDUCATION. The education of students with disabilities side by side with nondisabled peers and friends in general education settings.

■ MAINSTREAMING. The process in education whereby students with disabilities are integrated into general education classes with their nondisabled peers; refers to both instructional and social integration.

IDEA requires that students with disabilities are to be educated side by side with their nondisabled peers to the maximum extent appropriate.

ments," ranging from the general education classroom to separate educational environments exclusively for students with disabilities. School districts are required to provide such a continuum for students who cannot be satisfactorily educated in general education classes. Whenever possible, however, students should be educated in or close to the school they would attend if not disabled (see 34 C.F.R. Sec. 300.552[a][3] & 330.552[c]).

The concept of LRE implied within IDEA has been criticized in recent years. The concern is that, despite LRE's strong preference that students be educated with their nondisabled peers, it also has legitimized and supported the need for more restrictive, segregated settings. Additionally, LRE has created the perception that students with disabilities must "go to" services, rather than having services come to them. In other words, as students move farther from the general education class, the resources available to meet their needs increase concomitantly.

■ INTEGRATION   Whereas *LRE* is most often associated with the United States, *integration* is the term most often used to describe programs and services in several other countries throughout the world. For example, Italy mandates by law the integration of students with disabilities into general education classes. Australia may be described as moving toward full integration of these students, while to a lesser extent France, the United Kingdom, and Germany all have major initiatives promoting the integration of students with disabilities in general education settings.

In the United States, the term *integration* is most closely associated with social policy to end separate education for students of color. In the landmark *Brown v. Topeka, Kansas, Board of Education* in 1954, the U.S. Supreme Court ruled that education must be made available to everyone on an equal basis. Separate education for African American students was ruled as inherently unequal to that of white students. The increasing use of the term *integration* by many professionals and parents to describe the value of educating students with disabilities alongside their nondisabled peers coincided with the U.S. civil rights movement for people with disabilities of the

1980s, a movement that culminated in the passage of the Americans with Disabilities Act (ADA) in 1990. In fact, ADA moved away from the concept of the least restrictive environment as defined in IDEA, mandating that people with disabilities be placed in integrated settings appropriate to their individual needs.

■ INCLUSIVE EDUCATION   At its most fundamental level, inclusive education promotes the value of students with disabilities attending the same school they would attend were they not disabled. This value promotes acceptance and belonging, focusing on services and supports coming to the student within the natural setting of the general education school and classroom rather than students having to go to services in an isolated environment. Wade and Zone (2000) described the value as "building community and affirming diversity. . . . Struggling learners can be actively involved, socially accepted, and motivated to achieve the best of their individual and multiple abilities." Landers and Weaver (1997) indicated that "inclusion is an attitude of unqualified acceptance and the fostering of student growth, at any level, on the part of all adults involved in a student's education" (p. 7). These authors further suggested that the responsibility for ensuring a successful inclusive program lies with adults. "Adults must be able to design appropriate educational opportunities that foster the individual student's growth within the context of the student's talents and interests among age-appropriate peers" (p. 7).

Another approach to defining inclusion is a call for specific changes in the education system. For example, both the National Association of State Boards of Education (NASBE) and the National Center on Educational Restructuring and Inclusion (NCERI) define inclusive education as **home school placement,** with the supports necessary to ensure an appropriate educational experience for the student. NASBE (1992) indicates that

inclusion . . . means that students attend their home school with their age and grade peers. It requires that the proportion of students labeled for special services is relatively uniform for all of the schools within a particular school district, and that this ratio reflects the proportion of people with disabilities in society at large. Included students are not isolated into special classes or wings within the school. To the maximum extent possible, included students receive their in-school educational services in the general education classroom with appropriate in-class support. (p. 12)

NCERI (1994) describes inclusive education as

providing to all students, including those with severe handicaps, equitable opportunities to receive effective educational services, with the needed supplementary aids and support services, in age-appropriate classes in their neighborhood schools, in order to prepare students for productive lives as full members of society. (p. 4)

Putnam (1993) and Nisbet (1992) addressed inclusion as a *support network* or *circle of friends:* "An inclusive classroom setting is one in which the members recognize each other's individual differences and strive to support one another's efforts" (Putnam, p. xiii). "This supportive network can comprise family, friends, classmates, coworkers, neighbors, and others who care. This network has been described as the individual's circle of support, circle of friends, or personal board of directors" (Nisbet, p. 4).

Inclusion may also be defined by the level of participation and support the individual receives in the educational setting. Two terms are used to describe this level of participation: *full inclusion* and *partial inclusion.* **Full inclusion** is an approach whereby students with disabilities or at risk receive all instruction in a general education classroom setting; support services come to the student. **Partial inclusion**

■ HOME SCHOOL PLACEMENT. Education in the school that a student with disabilities would attend if not labeled as having a disability.

■ FULL INCLUSION. The delivery of appropriate, specialized services to students with disabilities in a general education classroom. These services are usually directed at improving students' social skills, developing satisfactory relationships with peers and teachers, building targeted academic skills, and improving the attitudes of nondisabled peers.

■ PARTIAL INCLUSION. Inclusion whereby students with disabilities receive most instruction in general education settings but are pulled out to a special education class or resource room when appropriate.

involves students with disabilities receiving most of their instruction in general education settings but being "pulled out" to another instructional setting when appropriate to their individual needs. The success of both full and partial inclusion programs depends on the availability of both formal and natural supports in the general education setting. **Formal supports** are those provided by, and funded through, the public school system. They include qualified teachers, paraprofessionals, appropriate curriculum materials, and technology aids. **Natural supports** in an educational setting most often consist of the individual's family and classmates. As described by Jorgensen (1992), "Natural supports bring children closer together as friends and learning partners rather than isolating them" (p. 183).

A more in-depth discussion of inclusive education and the characteristics of inclusive schools and classrooms can be found in Chapter 4.

■ STUDENTS AT RISK BUT NOT DISABLED

Although most of our discussion on education has focused on students who have been identified as having disabilities, a growing number of children in schools do not necessarily meet the definitions of disability but are at considerable risk for academic and social failure. Definitions of **students at risk** are very broad and vague. As suggested by Montgomery and Rossi (1994), there is a great deal of confusion and disagreement about "which children are at risk, why they are at risk, and what can be done to improve their chances for success in school and adult life" (p. v).

For the purposes of our discussion, we will address students at risk from the perspective that the individual is not identified as disabled but, due to myriad factors, *needs specialized instruction and/or support to succeed in a school setting.* As described by Manning and Baruth (1995), specific conditions associated with at-risk students include but are not limited to the following:

- *Lower achievement.* Students at risk for lower achievement develop a pattern of failure that is compounded through the school years. Once a lower achiever falls behind, the pattern of failure increases with each succeeding grade level. Lower achievers have poor self-concepts, are less ambitious about career aspirations, and are more likely to drop out of school.

- *Dropping out of school.* Approximately one out of every ten students between the ages of 16 and 24 drops out of school each year (National Center for Education Statistics, 1999). More males drop out than females, and Hispanic students have the highest dropout rates (over three times as high as that of Caucasian students). In the 1996–1997 school year, 366,479 students between the ages of 14 and 18 dropped out of school (National Center for Education Statistics, 1999). One out of every four of these school dropouts is unemployed, and two thirds of those employed are earning minimum wage.

- *Teenage pregnancy.* Teenage pregnancy is considered a serious problem by 70% of all high school teachers in the United States (Metropolitan Life/Harris & Associates, 1996). This condition is the major reason that students leave school. More than half of all high school students are sexually active but do not use contraceptives consistently. Nearly 20% of all sexually active teens have an unintended pregnancy. Pregnant teenagers are more likely to withdraw from school (40%) and become welfare recipients (73% within four years of becoming pregnant).

- *Use of tobacco, alcohol, and other drugs.* By the age of 17, about 16% of American teenagers report that they are using marijuana; 36% indicate they are consum-

focus 14

Identify the conditions that are most closely associated with students identified as at risk.

■ FORMAL SUPPORTS. Supports funded through government programs (such as the public schools) for people with disabilities.

■ NATURAL SUPPORTS. Supports for people with disabilities, which are provided by family, friends, and peers.

■ STUDENTS AT RISK. Students described as vulnerable to failure in the public schools. The designation may include students who drop out of school, live in poverty, are directly affected by substance abuse, are homeless, have no medical care, are latchkey kids, are abused and neglected, come from single-parent families, become pregnant as teenagers, and come from differing cultural backgrounds and may have limited English-speaking abilities.

Children have a better chance of becoming literate, self-assured, and productive adults in schools that are safe and conducive to both learning and promoting positive esteem.

ing alcohol, and 25% smoke cigarettes (U.S. Department of Health and Human Services, 1996). The use of tobacco, alcohol, and other drugs increases the probability of teenage pregnancy, health problems, and dropping out of school.

- *Involvement in delinquency, hate crimes, gangs, and criminal behavior.* Violence against teenagers in American schools is at a critical level. Approximately 1% of American high school students (255,000 total) are victims of serious violent crimes at school or while going to and from school. Over 21,000 American high school students are attacked in school each month. One out of every 12 secondary-age students misses school each month out of fear. In 1996, there were 79 thefts for every 1,000 students (ages 12 to 18) at school. Theft accounted for about 62% of all crimes against students at school that year. Eight out of 10 high school students report that they have engaged in some form of delinquent behavior, ranging from drinking, theft, and truancy to destruction of property, assault, and gang fighting (Seifert & Hoffnung, 1997; U.S. Department of Education, 1998). Today's gangs are well organized and prone to violence, extortion, and the illegal trafficking of drugs and weapons. Hate crimes, caused by a number of factors, are on the increase.

- *Poverty and lower socioeconomic conditions.* In the United States, more than 13 million children under the age of 18 live below the poverty line (Dalaker, 1999); as many as 500,000 children are homeless in any given year (National Law Center on Homelessness and Poverty, 1999); and nearly 10 million (1 in every 7) children have no access to regular and appropriate medical care (U.S. Bureau of the Census, 1997). Poverty and lower socioeconomic status (SES) are correlated with low ability, lack of motivation, and poor health. Poor children are more likely to go to school hungry, fall behind in school, have below-average basic academic skills, and drop out of school than teenagers above the poverty line. (Children's Defense Fund, 1998b)

- *Teenage suicide.* Every four hours a child or youth under the age of 20 commits suicide. Teen suicide has tripled in the past 30 years and now accounts for more than 20% of all deaths among teenagers. Of all the children killed by gunfire every year in the United States, nearly 33% died from suicide. Guns remain the most common method of suicide for children. (Children's Defense Fund, 1999)

- *Health problems.* Adolescents are more likely to have health problems than either younger children or adults. Students who exhibit delinquent behavior are at greater risk for automobile accidents, alcohol and drug abuse, unwanted pregnancy, inadequate health care, and eating disorders. Poor health contributes to higher school absences, falling behind in school, and the inability to concentrate when in school. (Seifert & Hoffnung, 1997)

Students at risk are often described as *educationally disadvantaged* because they enter school with "two strikes" against them. By the time they get to high school, many of these students have not mastered even the basic level of skills necessary to complete school or succeed in adult living. For a number of reasons (such as poverty, socioeconomic status, non-English-speaking families, etc.) these children tend to have low academic achievement and high dropout rates.

Although schools are often taken to task for their inability to meet the needs of students at risk, clearly these students are the products of conditions that go far beyond the educational system. It will take the cooperation of many agencies— including those involved in health, social services, and education—to even begin to understand the extent of the challenges, let alone find the solutions. Conservative estimates have suggested that as many as four of every ten children in America are at risk for educational failure (Natriello, McDill, & Pallas, 1990).

What can be done to meet the needs of students at risk? Given the complexity of factors associated with failure in the schools, short-term solutions obviously will not suffice. First and foremost, the full extent of the problem must be recognized, and then successful solutions must be identified and incorporated into public education. Sagor (1993) suggested that it is critical to clearly understand the basic psychological needs of at-risk students as suggested in the work of Abraham Maslow and William Glasser. These needs include feelings of competence, belonging, usefulness, potency, and optimism. We also know that "intensive instructional programs, conducted in school climates that are safe and conducive to both learning and promoting positive self-esteem, can remarkably enhance the chances of disadvantaged children to become literate, self-assured, and eventually productive adults" (Davis & McCaul, 1991, pp. 130–131).

Montgomery and Rossi (1994) emphasized the need to enhance the living conditions of low-income families, to strengthen the family and prevent abuse, to expand youth programs (before and after school), and to increase parent–teacher collaboration. These authors pointed out that the schools must be ready and willing to teach students from "diverse backgrounds," and they suggested some strategies for enhancing the school environment:

- *Improvement in school administrative and support services.* Examples include improved psychological and guidance counseling, flexible schedules for teen

Case Study

SARINA

Over the past several years, many changes have occurred in Sarina's life. After spending most of her life in a large institution, Sarina, now in her late 30s, move into an apartment with two other women, both of whom have a disability. She receives assistance from a local supported-living program in developing skills that will allow her to make her own decisions and become more independent in the community.

Over the years, Sarina has had many labels describing her disability, including mental retardation, epilepsy, autism, physical disability, chronic health problems, and serious emotional disturbance. She is very much challenged both mentally and physically. Medical problems associated with epilepsy necessitate the use of medications that affect Sarina's behavior (motivation, attitude, etc.) and her physical well-being. During her early 20s, while walking up a long flight of stairs, Sarina had a seizure that resulted in a fall and a broken neck. The long-term impact from the fall was a paralyzed right hand and limited use of her left leg.

Sarina's life goal has been to work in a real job, make money, and have choices about how she spends it. For most of her life, the goal has been out of reach. Her only jobs have been in sheltered workshops, where she worked for next to nothing, doing piecemeal work such as sorting envelopes, putting together cardboard boxes, or folding laundry. While most of the focus in the past has been on what Sarina "can't do" (can't read, can't get along with supervisors, can't handle the physical requirements of a job), her family and the professionals on her support team are looking more at her very strong desire to succeed in a community job.

A job has opened up for a stock clerk at a local video store about 3 miles from Sarina's apartment. The store manager is willing to pay minimum wage for someone to work 4 to 6 hours a day stocking the shelves with videos and handling some basic tasks (such as cleaning floors, washing windows, and dusting furniture). Sarina loves movies and is really interested in this job. With the support of family and her professional team, she has applied for the job.

■ APPLICATION

1. As Sarina's potential employer, what are some of the issues you would raise about her capability to meet the essential functions of the job?

2. What would you see as the "reasonable accommodations" necessary to help Sarina succeed at this job if she were to be hired?

---

mothers and working students, and support for highly mobile and homeless students.

- *Enhanced relevance and rigor of instruction.* Examples include use of the cultural knowledge that children bring to the classroom as "scaffolding" to build their skill acquisition, culturally relevant curriculum, high academic expectations, sensitivity to differences in learning styles, and heterogeneous instructional groupings.

- *Equitable and efficient use of resources.* Examples include increased funding for needy schools and targeting of resources to attract better school staff and teaching materials. (p. vii)

As we move into subsequent chapters on multicultural education, the family, education through the lifespan, categories of people with disabilities, and people who are gifted and talented, we will focus on effective practices for working with all students with exceptional characteristics, including those defined as at risk.

Debate Forum

Casey Martin was born on June 2, 1972, with a very rare congenital disorder (Klippel-Trenauny-Weber Syndrome), a condition that has no known cure. The disorder is degenerative and causes serious blood circulation problems in Casey's right leg and foot. His right leg is about one-half the size of his left one, and when forced to walk on it, Casey experiences excruciating pain and swelling. Casey can only expect the problems to worsen as he grows older, and there is a possibility of leg amputation at some time in the future.

While the condition would be difficult and very painful under any normal circumstances, Casey's occupation is professional golf—a career that was fostered early in life and one that he is very good at. During his college years, Casey went to Stanford and played with Tiger Woods on the team that won the 1994 NCAA championship. In 1995, Casey joined the Nike pro tour and was just one step away from the pinnacle of golf—the Professional Golf Association (PGA) tour. However, his condition continued to deteriorate, and the pain in his right leg and foot grew steadily worse. He finally reached the point where he could no longer walk a golf course but had to use a cart to get around. Although the

PGA had modified the rules of golf for disabled players in recreational settings, the organization did not permit the use of a golf cart during *competitions*. Given the progressive state of his disability, Casey requested an exemption that would allow him to ride and not walk. The PGA refused his request, and Casey took the ruling to court, claiming discrimination on the basis of the Americans with Disabilities Act. In February 1998, a U.S. magistrate found in Casey's favor. Casey played the events on the Nike tour throughout 1998 and 1999, qualifying for his first PGA tour event in January 2000. In March 2000, the U.S. Court of Appeals for the Ninth Circuit ruled that using a cart would not give Casey an unfair advantage. Meanwhile, the decision to allow Casey to ride a cart was appealed by the PGA, to the U.S. Supreme Court.*

The debate surrounding Casey Martin is whether he has been given an advantage over his fellow pro golfers by being able to ride a golf cart when others must walk. Is riding a cart an advantage for Casey, or does the golf cart simply allow the "playing field" to be leveled as intended in the Americans with Disabilities Act?

■ POINT

The PGA's attempt to disallow Casey Martin to use a

golf cart is an act of discrimination against a person with a disability. The PGA is a public entity, and golf courses are places of public accommodation under the Americans with Disabilities Act. Therefore, the association must provide *reasonable accommodations* for someone with a permanent disability. Casey meets all the ADA requirements. He has a permanent disability, and without a reasonable accommodation (riding in a golf cart) he could not participate in his chosen profession. The PGA argues that riding in a cart creates an advantage for Casey. Couldn't it be argued that riding is actually a disadvantage? From a sitting position, Casey can't get the same look and feel for the course that his competitors have. The PGA also argues that it should have the right to determine its own rules for competitions. Fine! Change the rules to allow Casey and any other seriously disabled golfer to use a cart. In the end, if letting Martin ride means that the PGA must allow every golfer to use a cart, so be it. Isn't the PGA's motto "anything is possible"?

■ COUNTERPOINT

One cannot help but express admiration for the grit and determination of Casey Martin. There is no doubt that he is a person with a

tragic medical disability. However, in passing the ADA, Congress never intended for the law to require an organization such as the PGA to change its basic rules of operation and thus create an advantage for one golfer over another. Physical requirements, including walking up to five miles on any given day in unfavorable weather, is an *essential element* of golf at its highest level. Any golfer that is allowed to ride in a cart, disabled or not, will have an unfair advantage over other competitors. If the PGA allows this for one player, it will create hardship for others, which is exactly what the ADA did not want to see happen. The real issue here is that a fundamental rule of golf has stood from its beginning hundreds of years ago—players in the highest levels of competition must walk the course as part of the test of their skills. One set of rules must apply to all players.

*In a 7-2 decision on May 29, 2001, the U.S. Supreme Court ruled that Casey Martin must be allowed to ride a cart during competition. Allowing Casey access to the cart would not "fundamentally alter" the game of golf or give him any advantage over other golfers on the course.

Review

focus 1

Why do we label people according to their differences?

- Labels are an attempt to describe, identify, and distinguish one person from another.
- Many medical, psychological, social, and educational services require that an individual be labeled in order to determine who is eligible to receive special services.
- Labels help professionals communicate more effectively with one another and provide a common ground for evaluating research findings.
- Labels enable professionals to differentiate more clearly the needs of one group of people from those of another.

focus 2

Identify three approaches that can be used to describe human differences.

- The developmental approach is based on differences that occur in the course of human development from what is considered normal physical, social, and intellectual growth. Human differences are the result of interaction between biological and environmental factors. Normal growth can be explained by observing large numbers of individuals and looking for characteristics that occur most frequently at any given age.
- The cultural approach to describing human differences defines *normal* according to established cultural standards. Human differences can be explained by examining the values of any given society. What is considered normal will change over time and from culture to culture.
- The individual approach to labeling suggests that labels may be self-imposed. Such labels reflect how we perceive ourselves, although those perceptions may not be consistent with how others see us.

focus 3

Identify four indicators of quality supports and services for persons with disabilities.

- They promote autonomy.
- They create opportunities for social interaction and inclusion.
- They give the individual a lifestyle choice.
- They create opportunities for economic self-sufficiency.

focus 4

What is the purpose of the Americans with Disabilities Act?

- ADA provides a national mandate to end discrimination against individuals with disabilities in private-sector employment, all public services, and public accommodations, transportation, and telecommunications.

focus 5

What services must be available to ensure that an individual with a disability is able to live and learn successfully in a community setting?

- Comprehensive community services must be available, including access to housing, employment, public transportation, recreation, and religious activities.
- The individual should be able to purchase services such as medical and dental care as well as adequate life insurance.

focus 6

How did the work of 19th-century physicians and philosophers contribute to our understanding of people with differences?

- Early 19th-century physicians emphasized that people with disabilities should be treated humanely.
- Jean-Marc Itard demonstrated that an individual with a severe disability could learn new skills through physiological stimulation.

focus 7

Distinguish between abnormal behavior and social deviance.

- Human behavior is the focus of psychology. When the behavior of an individual does not meet the criteria of *normal,* it is labeled *abnormal.*
- Sociology is concerned with modern cultures, group behaviors, societal institutions, and inter-group relationships. When people are unable to adapt to social roles or establish interpersonal relationships, their behaviors are labeled *deviant.*

focus 8

What educational services were available for students with disabilities during most of the 20th century?

- Educational programs at the beginning of the 20th century were provided primarily in separate, special schools.
- For the first 75 years of the 20th century, the availability of educational programs for special students was sporadic and selective. Special education was allowed in many states but required in only a few.
- Research on the efficacy of special classes for students with mild disabilities suggested that there was little or no benefit in removing students from general education classrooms.

focus 9

Identify the principal issues in the right-to-education cases that led to eventual passage of the national mandate to educate students with disabilities.

- Education was reaffirmed as a right and not a privilege by the U.S. Supreme Court.
- In Pennsylvania, the court ordered the schools to provide a free public education to all children with mental retardation of ages 6 to 21.
- The *Mills* case extended the right to a free public education to all school-age children with disabilities.

focus 10

Identify five major provisions of the Individuals with Disabilities Education Act.

- The labeling and placement of students with disabilities in educational programs required the use of nondiscriminatory and multidisciplinary assessment.
- Parental safeguards and involvement in the educational process included consent for testing and placement and participation as a team member in the development of an IEP. Procedural safeguards (e.g., due process) were included to protect the child and family from decisions that could adversely affect their lives.
- Every student with a disability is entitled to a free and appropriate public education.
- The delivery of an appropriate education occurs through an individualized education program (IEP).

- All children were given the right to learn in an environment consistent with their academic, social, and physical needs. The law mandated that children with disabilities receive their education with nondisabled peers to the maximum extent appropriate.

focus 11

Under IDEA 97, describe the actions a school may take when a student brings a dangerous weapon to school or buys, sells, or possesses illicit drugs.

- To the extent removal would be applied to children without disabilities, school personnel may remove a child with a disability for not more than ten consecutive school days.
- School personnel may order a change in placement of a child with a disability to an appropriate interim alternative educational setting for the same amount of time that a child without a disability would be subject to discipline but for not more than 45 days.
- The public agency must convene an IEP meeting to develop a functional behavioral assessment plan and appropriate behavioral interventions to address the behavior.
- An interim alternative educational setting must be determined by the IEP team so as to enable the

child to continue to participate in the general curriculum and continue to receive those services and modifications described in the child's current IEP.

- School officials must conduct a manifestation determination review whenever they contemplate (a) removing a child for behavior relating to weapons or the illegal use of drugs, (b) seeking an order from a hearing officer to place a child in an interim alternative educational setting because of behavior that is substantially likely to result in injury to self or others, or (c) removing a child when such removal constitutes a change in placement for a child with a disability who has engaged in other behavior that violated any rule or code of conduct of the LEA that applies to all children.
- When school officials decide to change a child's placement, parents must be notified and procedural safeguards as described in IDEA must be followed.

focus 12

Distinguish between students with disabilities eligible for services under the Americans with Disabilities Act and those eligible under IDEA.

- Students eligible under ADA are entitled to accommodations and/or modifications to their educational program that will ensure

that they receive an appropriate education comparable to that of their nondisabled peers.

- Students eligible under IDEA are entitled to special education and related services to ensure they receive a free and appropriate education.

 focus 13

Define inclusive education.

- Inclusive education may be defined as placing students with a disability in a general education setting while making available the necessary supports (or support networks) to ensure an appropriate educational experience.
- Inclusive education may be defined as both full (all instruction received in the general education classroom) or partial (students pulled out for part of their instructional program).

focus 14

Identify the conditions that are most closely associated with students identified as at risk.

- Low achievement
- Dropping out of school
- Teenage pregnancy
- Use of tobacco, alcohol, and other drugs
- Involvement in delinquency, hate crimes, gangs, and criminal behavior
- Poverty and lower socioeconomic conditions
- Teenage suicide
- Health problems

Multicultural and Diversity Issues

To begin with . . .

Taken as a group, minority children are comprising an ever larger percentage of public school students. . . . More minority children continue to be served in special education than would be expected from the percentage of minority students in the general school population. Poor African-American children are 2.3 times more likely to be identified by their teacher as having mental retardation than their white counterparts. (The 1997 Amendments to the Individuals with Disabilities Education Act [Sec. 687 (c) (7–8)])

In practice, many culturally and linguistically diverse (CLD) students still do not receive the type and quality of education to which they are legally guaranteed. (Baca & de Valenzuela, 1998, p. 4)

The average income deficit for poor families (the average dollar amount needed to raise a poor family out of poverty) was $6,620 in 1998; this was statistically unchanged from 1997. (U.S. Census Bureau, 1999)

An action research study aimed at enhancing teachers' thinking about their students' cultures showed positive practical applications in classroom settings. Pre- and post-treatment interviews suggested that the participating teachers exhibited behavior and thinking that was more sensitive to ethnic differences after the intervention. (Cadray, 1998)

Existing research on multicultural aspects of teacher education in both general and special education has been rather narrow and predominantly used pre/post research designs to measure student growth. (Webb-Johnson et al., 1998)

49

Raphael

Ten-year-old Raphael lives with his adoptive parents. He is proud of his deafness—he accepts it and is comfortable with it. His mother is very aware of using sign language whenever Raphael is in the room, even if she is speaking to someone else. "If Raphael is watching, then I will sign. He deserves it."

Raphael does very well integrating with his hearing peers at recess. There are a group of guys—little boys—10 or 11 years old who are always coming around, "Can Raphael come out? Can Raphael do this? . . . Just ask him if he'll play with me." A lot of them are picking up the basic signs. So there's a lot of interaction going on.

"He's one of the most popular kids in the neighborhood, and he can play with anybody. He knows how to get his point of view across to the others, and the others— they make up their own little signs that are not really sign language or anything, but they know what they're talking about. When we first moved to this neighborhood, the responses we got from our neighbors, that we have a deaf kid is, 'Wow. That's neat,' and then they'd kind of go, 'Alright, now let's hold back.' But when he goes out there, they see that he can play basketball with any kid in his neighborhood, that he can play street hockey, he can rollerblade, he can ride bikes, and he's not a problem to anybody. In fact, he's the most popular kid in the neighborhood.

"I see Raphael's future as . . . I'm really not sure yet. He's really getting involved in his computers at school. And I'd like to see him continue that way. His working with computers has made a whole new person out of him."

Denise

"Denise is a 9-year-old African American girl in the fourth grade. Her elementary school is in a midsize city in the southeastern United States. Denise lives with her parents and two older brothers in an apartment complex in a working-class African American neighborhood. Because of recent redistricting, Denise is being bused from an all-black school in her neighborhood to a predominantly middle-class white elementary school across town. This is her first year in the school, and Denise is one of only five African American girls in the fourth grade.

"Denise has always been a good student with no social problems. This had been the case when she started the year at her new school. Recently, however, Denise has gotten into fights with several of her classmates. She has also been failing to complete her classwork and has been talking back to her teacher."[1]

Daniel

"Daniel is an 8-year-old second-grader. He and his family arrived in the United States from Mexico two years ago. Daniel has a 14-year-old brother, Julian, who is in middle school. Julian fills a role that is common for children in recently immigrated families, serving as the family's link to the English-speaking world through his ability to translate. Three additional siblings born between Daniel and his brother are still in Mexico. The family's support system includes the father's brothers and their wives, all recent immigrants from Mexico. Daniel's father is a construction worker, and his mother is a housewife.

"Daniel's academic performance has been average. He has consistently submitted required assignments, he has perfect attendance, and his interactions with teachers and peers have been good. Recently, Daniel's academic performance has declined, and he has become withdrawn. His teacher, Mrs. Strickland, noted that Daniel has failed several tests, that he has not had his parents sign the required school folder (which includes the tests he failed), and that he has not had his parents sign permission slips needed for planned field trips. As a result, Daniel has lost recess privileges, he has had to eat by himself at lunch time, and has not been allowed to participate in two field trips. (Although he had earned the right to participate in the field trips, the fact that he did not have written parental permission prevented him from doing so.)

"Mrs. Strickland wrote the parents a note on Daniel's folder, explaining that they needed to sign his folder and that Daniel needed to study for his tests. She also telephoned Daniel's home and talked to 'someone' there about the situation who said, 'OK.' Mrs. Strickland had become extremely frustrated because there had been no change. Every morning, she reprimanded Daniel for not bringing the required signed folder and demanded an explanation. Daniel did not respond."[2]

[1] *Source:* Excerpted from "Counseling Interventions with African American Youth," by D. C. Locke. In *Counseling for Diversity,* edited by C. C. Lee, 1995, pp. 26–27. Boston: Allyn & Bacon, Inc. Reprinted by permission.

[2] *Source:* Excerpted from "Counseling Hispanic Children and Youth," by J. T. Zapata. In *Counseling for Diversity,* edited by C. C. Lee, 1995, pp. 103–104. Boston: Allyn & Bacon. Reprinted by permission.

ENISE'S SITUATION PRESENTS a significant challenge for the education system, which raises a number of questions. Should someone in the school system be fighting to keep Denise from being labeled? Or should she be classified as having disabilities so she can receive specialized help? Should she receive special education services? Should she be considered as having disabilities because of her behavioral and academic difficulties? Do her problems reflect stress related to the change in school or cultural stressors? In this chapter, we will examine many of the complicated issues related to cultural and ethnic diversity and their impact on public education.

Our complex culture reflects an enormous array of needs because a wide variety of individuals take part in our society. Meeting those needs seriously tests the capacities of many service organizations and agencies. This is certainly true of the education system as well as the many other human services provided by both private and governmental agencies. Advocacy groups have emerged to champion certain causes. In some of these cases a particular group's educational needs have not been adequately met by school systems that are structured to serve the majority. Discontent surfaces when a segment of students is left out, discriminated against, or treated unfairly, or if the individual potential of such students is not being appropriately developed.

When the mainstream activities of a system do not satisfactorily accommodate diversity, the system must be viewed as inadequate, and modifications become necessary. This reasoning played a significant role in the emergence of both multicultural education and special education. **Multicultural education** arose from a belief that the needs of certain children—those with cultural backgrounds that differ from those of the majority—were not being appropriately met. Broad societal unrest related to racial discrimination fueled and augmented this belief. Similarly, **special education** evolved from the failure of general education to meet the needs of youngsters who were not learning as rapidly or in the same way as their age-mates. Reformers believed that two particular groups of students were being mistreated—in one case, because of their cultural or racial background, and in the other, because of their disabilities.

To explore multiculturalism and diversity, we will first discuss the basic purpose of general education and the conventional approaches used to achieve this purpose. We will also compare the underlying purposes and approaches of special education and multicultural education and discuss the connections between the two. After building this background, we will examine multicultural and diversity issues in the context of this book's focus: human exceptionality in society, school, and family.

Purposes of and Approaches to Education

he fundamental purpose of education in the United States is to produce literate citizens. According to this perspective, education is presumably intended for everyone; all children should have access to public education through the level of high school. In general terms, this goal is implemented by grouping and teaching students according to chronological age and evaluating their performance based on what society expects children of each age to achieve. Society uses an average of what youngsters of each age typically can learn as its yardstick for

■ MULTICULTURAL EDUCATION. Education that promotes learning about multiple cultures and their values.

■ SPECIAL EDUCATION. As defined in IDEA, the term means specially designed instruction provided to students with disabilities in all settings, including the workplace and training centers.

focus **1**

Identify three ways in which the purposes of and approaches to general education in the United States sometimes differ from those of special education and multicultural education.

assessing their progress. Thus, American education is aimed at the masses, and performance is judged according to an average. Through this system, schools attempt to bring most students to a similar, or at least a minimal, level of knowledge.

■ CULTURAL PLURALISM AND THE ROLE OF EDUCATION

Understanding diverse cultures has become a goal of many educators in the United States. Multicultural education values and promotes **cultural pluralism.** It teaches *all* students about cultural diversity and how to function in a multicultural society and is not aimed only at students of cultural or racial minorities (Banks, 1999; Hollins & Oliver, 1999; Tiedt & Tiedt, 1999). Gollnick and Chinn (1998) asserted that multicultural education is a concept that addresses cultural diversity and cited six beliefs and assumptions on which it is based:

1. *Cultural differences have strength and value.*
2. *Schools should be models for the expression of human rights and respect for cultural differences.*
3. *Social justice and equality for all people should be of paramount importance in the design and delivery of curricula.*
4. *Attitudes and values necessary for the continuation of a democratic society can be promoted in schools.*
5. *Schooling can provide the knowledge, dispositions, and skills for the redistribution of power and income among cultural groups.*
6. *Educators working with families and communities can create an environment that is supportive of multiculturalism. (p. 28)*

Rather than seeking to homogenize the population, current multicultural education promotes the notion that schools should encourage students to gain information about and competence in understanding multiple cultures, both those present in our society and throughout the world (Banks, 1999; Chavez & O'Donnell, 1998; Grant & Gomez, 2001). This perspective opposes the once-prevalent view that schools should minimize cultural differences.

A goal of many educators is to promote an understanding of the world's diverse cultures.

Multicultural education is intended to teach all students about different cultures (Seeberg, Swadener, Vanden-Wyngaard, & Rickel, 1998). Yet despite some progress, we still largely lack an awareness of how members of different cultural groups have contributed to major developments in our country's history. To illustrate, the 1990s PBS series on the Civil War, produced by Kenneth Burns, highlighted significant roles played by African Americans that many of us did not learn about in school. Also, during World War II, Native Americans, known as "Code Talkers," served in critical communications roles by transmitting messages in their native tongue, which could not be decoded by Axis forces. And despite the degrading abuse that they received from many sources, Japanese Americans volunteered for critical assignments and served the United States with distinction during World War II. Such stories need to be told.

Young people develop many of their enduring attitudes and a significant knowledge base at school. Their thoughts and feelings about diverse cultures are at least partially shaped by what they learn in the classroom. Incomplete information or stereotypical presentations about different cultures detract from gaining an understanding of the variety of people that characterizes our world (e.g., Arboleda, 1999). Careless treatment of this important topic perpetuates two problems: a lack of factual information about numerous cultures and a lack of skill in relating to those of different backgrounds. A complete education must include recognition of the roles of many peoples in shaping our country and our world, while fostering attitudes of respect and appreciation.

General education, special education, and multicultural education have some very important differences in their fundamental purposes. From the outset, the primary purpose of general education runs counter to those of the other two. Aimed at serving the masses, general education attempts to create a leveling effect by bringing everyone to more or less the same level, teaching similar topics in groups, and evaluating achievement based on a norm, or average. Special education, in contrast, tends to focus on the individual. Special education professionals would agree that the basic purpose of special education is to provide an opportunity for each child with a disability to learn and develop to his or her individual potential. Current special education efforts focus on individual needs, strengths, and preferences. This individualized approach is important because many students in special education seem unable to learn well through instruction that is broadly directed at large groups. Thus, special education tends to emphasize individuals and specific skill levels. Evaluation, at least in part, is based on individual growth to a specified mastery level and only partly on **norm-based averages** (average performance scores of age-mates).

Contemporary multicultural education promotes recognition and respect for differences and diversity (Hollins & Oliver, 1999; Seeberg et al., 1998). At a certain level, this is somewhat at odds with the goal of general education to achieve consistency (to bring the population to a comparable level of performance in similar areas of knowledge). Further, general education largely reflects a societal self-portrait of the United States as a "melting pot" for peoples of all backgrounds, emphasizing similarities and downplaying differences. Contemporary multicultural education, on the other hand, sees the school as a powerful tool for appreciating and promoting diversity.

The differences in goals and approaches of general, special, and multicultural education can create considerable difficulty within school systems and among educators. As one faction (multicultural education) attempts to make inroads into the broader domain of another (general education), an adversarial or competitive situation may result. Yet such misunderstandings may be diminished through thoughtful discussion and examination of the issues.

■ MULTICULTURAL AND DIVERSITY LINKAGES TO SPECIAL EDUCATION

Linkages between multicultural education and special education have not always been comfortable. They have often involved issues of racial discrimination and inappropriate educational programming. One linkage between multicultural and special education surfaces in special education's role of serving children who are failing in the general education system. Unfortunately, a disproportionately large number of students placed in special education are from minority backgrounds (Kea & Utley, 1998; Valles, 1998). This issue continues to surface (Sheets & Hollins, 1999), suggesting that special education has been used as a tool of discrimination, a means of separating racial and ethnic minorities from the majority.

Connections between special education and multicultural education are numerous. Some of the environmental influences noted earlier that appear to have an

■ CULTURAL PLURALISM. Arrangement in which multiple cultural subgroups live together in a manner that maintains group differences, thereby continuing each group's cultural or ethnic traditions.

■ NORM-BASED AVERAGES. Comparison of a person's performance with the average performance scores of age-mates.

impact in special education also seem operative in multicultural education. These influences can cause behavioral or academic difficulties in school. Additionally, certain instructional approaches common to both special and multicultural education can meet a student's academic needs.

Our discussion of special and multicultural education will focus on four major elements of the Individuals with Disabilities Education Act (IDEA, presented in Chapter 1): nondiscriminatory and multidisciplinary assessment, parental involvement in developing each child's educational program, education in the least restrictive environment, and a free and appropriate public education delivered through an individualized education plan (IEP).

■ PREVALENCE AND OVERREPRESENTATION OF CULTURALLY DIVERSE STUDENTS IN SPECIAL EDUCATION

focus 2

Describe the population status of and trends among culturally diverse groups in the United States. How do they have an impact on the educational system?

The term *prevalence* generally refers to the number of people in a given population who exhibit a condition, problem, or particular status (e.g., who have a hearing loss or who have red hair). In general terms, a phenomenon's prevalence is determined by counting how often it occurs. In this section, we will examine prevalence in a somewhat different sense, discussing certain factors relevant to the relationship between human exceptionality and multicultural issues.

We identified several factors associated with students at risk for academic failure. They included diverse cultural backgrounds, limited background in speaking English, and poverty. It is important to emphasize that these factors only indicate risk for difficulties in school; they do not necessarily destine a student for a special education placement. Yet a disproportionate number of special education students are from culturally divergent backgrounds (Artiles, 1998; Kea & Utley, 1998; Valles, 1998). The overrepresentation of students of color in groups labeled as having disabilities is cause for concern. African American children, for instance, appear more frequently than would be expected in classes for those with serious emotional disturbance and mental retardation, and Hispanic Americans also represent a large and rapidly growing group in special education (Drew & Hardman, 2000). At the other end of the spectrum, programs for the gifted and talented seem to have fewer than expected students who are African American, Hispanic American, or Native American (Daniels, 1998; Gollnick & Chinn, 1998).

Some culturally diverse students may be inappropriately placed into special education classes resulting in overrepresentation.

These are issues concerning school placement and result from assessments that are heavily influenced by the academic situation. Some contend that in these circumstances, social factors play a significant role in shaping definitions, diagnoses, and resulting intervention or treatment (Horwitz & Scheid, 1999). However, research results are mixed, even under these definitional situations. Some results indicate that people of color and those of Asian descent exhibit a lower prevalence than their Caucasian counterparts in a number of mental disorder categories (Zhang & Snowden, 1999), which should bode well for their placement and performance in school.

However, cultural minority students do not complete school as frequently as their peers from the cultural majority. Banks (1999) cited school dropout figures for African American youngsters 18 to 24 years of age at 16.3%, and at 33.9% for Hispanic Americans. This compares with 12.2% for whites in the same age range. Dropout rates also correlate closely with family income and vary across income groups. Ten percent of students from families having annual incomes below $20,000 dropped out of high school whereas only 2.1% of those above $40,000 quit school (Bruno, 1998).

Several culturally or ethnically diverse populations are growing rapidly because of increasing birthrates and immigration levels. For example, African Americans represented approximately 12.3% of the total population in the United States in 1990, but their number is increasing at a more rapid rate than the Caucasian population (Spencer & Hollmann, 1998). Figure 2.1 graphically portrays the U.S. population by ethnic background in 1990 with growth projections through 2050. The increase of culturally and ethnically diverse groups will affect education, presenting diverse needs that will require a spectrum of educational services.

Language differences often contribute to academic difficulties for students from diverse backgrounds who are educated in a system designed by the cultural majority (Upsure & Turner, 1999). Baca and de Valenzuela (1998) noted that approximately 10 million children of school age spoke languages other than English in 1990, a growth of nearly 2 million students over 1980 figures. These authors also estimated that nearly 1.2 million of these youngsters were both disabled and linguistically different. Census data indicate that, although the overall enrollment of 8- to 15-year-olds decreased from 1979 to 1995, the number of students in this age range speaking a language other than English at home increased (Lamison-White, 1997).

People from Southeast Asia constitute a rapidly growing sector of the U.S. population. This influx has had a significant impact on the school systems; the number of youngsters speaking Asian languages in the schools has significantly increased recently (Bennett & Debarros, 1998; U.S. Bureau of the Census, 1998). Such growth places a heavy demand on U.S. school systems to provide linguistically appropriate instruction and to exercise vigilance and caution in assessment. And this trend continues—it is anticipated that the number of students with limited English proficiency (LEP students) will continue to grow more rapidly than other groups of students (De Valenzuela & Cervantes, 1998; Lamison-White, 1997).

Such figures only broadly reflect students who are either bilingual or linguistically diverse. Certainly, many come from backgrounds that permit them to achieve academically in a school system based primarily on the English language. Not all

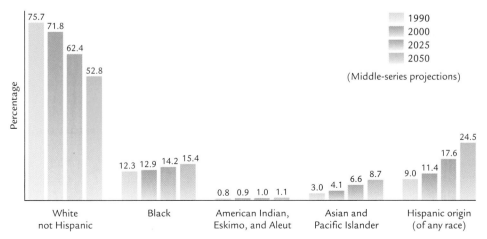

FIGURE 2.1

Percentage of population by race and Hispanic origin: 1990 to 2050

[*Source:* From "National Population Projections," by G. Spencer and F. W. Hollmann. In *Population Profile of the United States: 1997*, 1998, pp. 8–9. U.S. Bureau of the Census, Current Population Reports, Series P23-194. Washington, DC: U.S. Government Printing Office.]

■ NONDISCRIMINATORY AND MULTIDISCIPLINARY ASSESSMENT. One of the provisions of IDEA, requiring that testing be done in a child's native or primary language. It also stipulates procedures to prevent cultural or racial discrimination, validated assessment tools, and assessment conducted by a multidisciplinary team using several pieces of information to formulate a placement decision.

■ MEASUREMENT BIAS. Unfairness or inaccuracy of test results related to cultural background, sex, or race.

students accounted for here will need special supports or programs. Also, estimates and actual census data are always subject to a certain level of error. However, analyses thus far suggest that such error is relatively small and that, if anything, these data are likely to be somewhat conservative (De Valenzuela & Cervantes, 1998). The need for linguistically appropriate instruction is magnified considerably when we consider other multicultural factors such as a careful examination of educational goals and the methods of achieving them.

Nondiscriminatory and Multidisciplinary Assessment

Perhaps nowhere is the link between special and multicultural education more obvious than in issues of **nondiscriminatory assessment.** As mentioned earlier, disproportionate numbers of minority students are found in special education classes (Kea & Utley, 1998; Valles, 1998). Decisions regarding referral and placement in these classes are based on psychological assessment, which typically is based on standardized evaluations of intellectual and social functioning. Such assessments often discriminate or are biased against children from ethnically and culturally diverse backgrounds (Linn & Gronlund, 2000; Venn, 2000).

In several early cases, courts determined that such evaluations were indeed discriminatory to Hispanic American students (*Diana v. State Board of Education,* 1970, 1973) and African American students (*Larry P. v. Riles,* 1972, 1979). Additionally, assessment and instruction for Asian American children were addressed in the case of *Lau v. Nichols* (1974). These California cases had a national impact and greatly influenced the drafting of IDEA. Two prominent precedents in IDEA, for example, were established in the case of *Diana v. State Board of Education:* (1) children tested for potential placement in special education must be assessed in their native or primary language, and (2) children cannot be placed in special classes on the basis of culturally biased tests.

To prevent discriminatory evaluation practices, students must be tested in their native or primary language whenever possible. Additionally, the evaluation procedures must be selected and administered in a way that prevents cultural or racial discrimination, and assessment tools must be validated (shown to measure what they purport to measure). Finally, IDEA also mandates that evaluation should involve a multidisciplinary team using several sources of information to make a placement decision. To place these safeguards in context, it is necessary to examine the assessment process and how cultural bias can occur.

■ CULTURAL BIAS AND ASSESSMENT ERROR

Assessment is a powerful tool. Results of tests that assess academic and behavioral differences often determine placement in particular instructional programs—to the student's benefit or detriment. Assessment error constitutes a major controversy in both special education and multicultural education. Many have found that bias exists in the measurement instruments employed in assessment. **Measurement bias** produces error during testing, leading to unfair or inaccurate test results that do not reflect the student's actual mental abilities or skills (Lyman, 1998). In many cases cultural bias is involved in both the construction and development of assessment instruments and in their use (Rogler, 1999). Standardized, norm-referenced instruments, in which minority children's performances are often compared with norms

focus 3

Identify two ways in which assessment may contribute to the overrepresentation of culturally diverse students in special education programs.

developed from other populations, have been particularly criticized. Under these testing conditions, minority children often appear disadvantaged by cultural differences (Allen, 1998; Dana, 1998a; Hopkins, 1998; Lindsey, 1998).

Bias in psychological assessment has been recognized as a problem for many years (Burt, 1921) and continues to concern professionals (Jencks, 1998; Linn & Gronlund, 2000; Russo & Lewis, 1999). Some assessment procedures simply fail to document the same level of performance by individuals with diverse cultural backgrounds, even if they have similar abilities. This phenomenon is referred to as **test bias.**

Considerable effort has been expended to develop tests that are culture-free or culture-fair. This effort was rooted in the belief that the test itself was the major element contributing to bias or unfairness. This simplistic perspective was flawed because it focused solely on the test instrument itself and did not adequately attend to bias in the *use* of an instrument or data interpretation. Over the years, however, this effort did lead to some improvements in areas where cultural bias *was* involved in instrument or protocol design or construction. Revision minimized the most glaring problems by reducing both the amount of culture-specific content in test items and the culture-specific language proficiency required to perform test tasks.

Educators must avoid test bias in assessing children for potential special education placement.

However, test instrument refinements have limited effectiveness when the use of the test and interpretation of results are not appropriate and conceptually sound. Although administration and interpretation concern is not new, recent attention has presented a more balanced focus on procedures as well as the test instrument itself (Allen, 1998; Dana, 1998b, 2000). One of the best ways to ensure fair testing is to more adequately prepare those who give tests and interpret the results so that they understand cultural issues in assessment. Professionals need explicit and focused training to help them see how easily bias can creep in (Lyman, 1998; Merrell, 1999; Sue, Bingham, Porche'-Burke, & Vasquez, 1999). Lasting personal impressions can be formed based on very little evidence that can, in turn, trigger bias and incorrect categorization of a student—even in the face of evidence to the contrary.

■ LANGUAGE DIVERSITY

A significant challenge in assessing culturally diverse students has always been language differences. Assessment of non-English-speaking children has often been biased, providing an inaccurate reflection of abilities (Sandoval & Duran, 1998; Upshur & Turner, 1999). If language diversity is not considered as a factor during assessment and educational planning, a child may receive an inappropriate special education placement (McMillan, 1997). Test results may suggest limited academic performance or a significant difference in performance capacity partially because the youngster does not have the necessary language skills to do well on the assessment. This may make his or her evaluation performance appear like that of a student that needs specialized instructional assistance such as special education when, in fact, the level of performance is due to a language difference.

A particularly difficult situation exists for non-English-speaking students with a language disorder, such as delayed language development (Puckett, 2001; Sandoval &

focus 4

Identify three ways in which language diversity may contribute to assessment difficulties with students who are from a variety of cultures.

■ TEST BIAS. An unfairness of a testing procedure or test instrument, which gives one group a particular advantage or another a disadvantage due to factors unrelated to ability, such as culture, sex, or race.

Duran, 1998; Trawick-Smith, 2000). Determining the degree to which each factor contributes to academic deficiency is difficult. In fact, it may not be important to apportion a certain amount of performance deficit to language differences versus intellectual or academic ability. What may be vitally important, however, is identifying students with language differences and finding appropriate educational services to help them *other than special education.* Such services may mean intensive language assistance or other tutorial help, but not placement in special education classes or the special education part of the system. It may be difficult to decide whether such a child should be placed in special education. Special education placement will surely raise questions regarding whether such placement is occurring because the child is linguistically *diverse* due to culture or linguistically *deficient* for developmental reasons. Though these questions are not easily answered, the field is enormously strengthened because these questions are now being asked and addressed (e.g., Dana, 2000; Hernandez, 2001; Jencks, 1998).

As indicated earlier, census data show a substantially increasing number of children in the American educational system who speak languages other than English (Bennett & Debarros, 1998; Lamison-White, 1997). Therefore all teachers, related education personnel, social workers, psychologists, and administrators must become aware of the challenges and possible solutions to making appropriate educational assessments of student with language diversity (Hernandez, 2001; Hollins & Oliver, 1999; Sheets & Hollins, 1999). In many cases this means that specific, focused training must be included in professional preparation programs.

One of the seemingly positive safeguards in IDEA, requiring assessment of a child in his or her native language, also raises new questions. Although this law represents a positive step toward fair treatment of linguistically diverse students, some difficulties have emerged in its implementation. Specifically, the legislation defines *native language* as that used in the home, yet a regulation implementing IDEA defined it as that which is normally used by the youngster in school. This latter definition may present problems for a bilingual student who has achieved a conversational fluency in English, yet whose proficiency may not be adequate to sustain academic work. For this child, testing in English is likely to be biased, even though it is considered a proper procedure according to regulations.

■ ASSESSMENT AND THE PREPARATION OF PROFESSIONALS

Proper training of assessment professionals working with ethnic minority children is particularly important to obtain accurate data and minimize interpretations that may lead to bias (Merrell, 1999). Additionally, professionals must be constantly alert to potential bias due to language differences as well as other factors that may mask students' true abilities. In many cases, information about the child's home life and other environmental matters can provide valuable insight to aid evaluators in both administering assessment and interpreting results. That information includes languages spoken in the household and by whom, who the child's caregivers are (parents and others), the amount of time the child spends with caregivers, and the child's out-of-school activities. Uninformed assumptions about family and circumstances can lead to inaccurate assessment, so the evaluator must obtain all information possible about the child and his or her life. It is vitally important to understand the child in the context of his or her family (Kalyanpur, 1998). These training challenges are often addressed unsuccessfully in courses in psychology, teacher education, and a number of related areas (e.g., Bynoe, 1998; Sue et al., 1999; Valles, 1998).

Assessment is a very important tool in education, particularly in special and multicultural education. Effective, unbiased assessment requires that instruments be correctly constructed and used. To that end, the purposes of assessment, and education itself, must be considered from the outset: Are we attempting to bring the bulk of citizenry to a similar point in education or knowledge? Are we creating a leveling effect, attempting to make all people alike to some degree? Or are we promoting individual growth and development and encouraging cultural diversity and individual differences?

Parents from Different Cultures and Their Involvement in Special Education

arental involvement in the education of students with disabilities is required by IDEA. Parent rights, however, are based on certain assumptions. One fundamental assumption is that parents are consistently proactive and will challenge the school if their child is not being treated properly. Although true of some parents of children in special education, the assumption is not true for all. Many parents are reluctant or afraid to interact with the educational system.

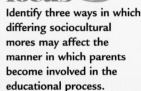

focus 5

Identify three ways in which differing sociocultural mores may affect the manner in which parents become involved in the educational process.

The acceptance of a child's disability is not easy for any parent, and a family's attitude toward exceptionality can influence how a child's intervention proceeds. People of diverse cultural backgrounds have perspectives and beliefs regarding illness, disability, and specialized services that may differ from those of the majority culture (Bailey, Skinner, Rodriguez, & Correa, 1999; Bussing et al., 1998). For example, some cultures have great difficulty accepting disabilities because of religious beliefs and values. Views about the family also can affect treatment of children with disabilities. The extended family structures common in African American and Hispanic American cultures can cause hesitation about accepting care from outside the family and anxieties about special education. Parents of children with disabilities who are poor, have a minority background, and speak a primary language other than English face enormous disadvantages in interacting with the special education system.

Sensitivity in interpersonal communication is very important when professionals deliver service to children of families who are culturally diverse (McNamara, 1998). The meaning and interpretation of certain facial expressions, expression of emotions, manners, and behaviors denoting respect and interpersonal matters vary greatly among cultures (e.g., Choi, Nisbett, & Norenzayan, 1999). Such connotations affect the interactions between minority family members, between these individuals and those of the cultural majority, and certainly with educational professionals. Some minority families may be reluctant to receive assistance from outside the family for a variety of reasons. For example, some parents may feel shame regarding the fact that their child has been identified as having disabilities, which will likely influence their acceptance of the situation (Hatton, Azmi, Caine, & Emerson, 1998). Moreover, professionals should keep in mind that the immigration status of some families may affect the manner in which they react to attempts to provide services for their children. Although this constitutes a pragmatic consideration rather than a cultural difference, a family residing in the United States illegally or feeling somewhat unsure about its residency status will likely avoid interacting with an educational system.

U.S. public education predominantly reflects the philosophy of the cultural majority. This is not surprising, since social institutions—in this instance, formal schooling—are typically founded on such mainstream views. In general, when multiple cultures live together, as in the United States, minorities tend to influence public matters less than the cultural majority. Yet the social mores of the minority subcultures may continue to flourish in private and often emerge in individual interactions and behaviors. Activities or beliefs that are of the utmost importance to

Families can support multicultural education by working with children on school projects that are focused on their cultural heritage.

one cultural group may be less crucial to another or even viewed with disdain (Gauvain, 1998; Lillard, 1998; Wellman, 1998). Such differences surface in discussion of disabilities. For example, although mental retardation is universally recognized by all cultures, its conceptualization, social interpretation, and treatment are culturally specific (Drew & Hardman, 2000). The condition may be considered as negative, such as a punishment on the family, or may be viewed favorably, such as the blessing of knowing an unusual, rare person, depending upon the cultural context. Similarly, certain behaviors that a professional of the majority culture might view as a learning problem may in fact be a product of the acculturation process or considered normal within a child's cultural background. Some level of cultural bias and insensitivity is present in all aspects of professional work, including the research we read. This is important to understand as we attempt to understand cultural differences and provide services in a society characterized by cultural pluralism (e.g., Rogler, 1999; Sue, 1999).

Parental involvement in the educational process is generally thought to be beneficial. This is one reason that legislators included such participation as a major element in IDEA. However, such a perspective overlooks the fact that all parents do not view the educational system in the same way and may not interact or participate actively with the schools because of their diverse cultural views (Griffith, 1998). A child's educational planning may not be viewed similarly by members of all cultures, and these differences may affect work in all service areas.

Education for Culturally Diverse Students

■ INDIVIDUALIZED EDUCATION

focus 6

Identify two areas that require particular attention when developing an individualized education plan (IEP) for a student who is culturally diverse.

Developing an individualized education plan (IEP) for each student with a disability is required by IDEA. Most school districts have considerable experience in this process but face further requirements when addressing the needs of a child with cultural and/or linguistic differences (Hendrick, 2001; Morrison, 2001). Depending on background and capabilities, such a student may need remediation for a specific disability, catch-up work in academic subjects, and instruction in English as a second language. The IEP must consider cultural factors, such as language differences, as well as learning and behavior disabilities and perhaps provide for specialized instruction from different professionals for each facet of education. Rarely will a single person have the training and background in culture, language, and the specialized skills needed to remediate disabilities. Yates and Ortiz noted that "education professionals are generally unprepared to serve language minority students, an issue which is exacerbated when these students have disabilities" (1998, p. 190). Effective educational programming for culturally diverse students requires a team effort (Craig, Hull, Haggart, & Perez-Selles, 2000).

An IEP for a student who is culturally diverse and has a disability may address many facets of his or her life. For example, children from different economic levels may have different instructional needs and substantial developmental differences. The IEP should address these matters if it is to be maximally effective for each particular child. Additionally, it may be important to employ facets of the child's cultural background as a strategy in instruction—taking advantage of it as an instructional resource.

Stereotypical assumptions about ethnic and cultural background should be discarded. These may involve well-intentioned but misguided efforts to integrate into instruction culturally relevant foods, activities, or holidays. The utmost care should be taken to make sure that such content is specifically correct (not just an uninformed generalization about a religious celebration or folk dance) and actually related to the student's experience—some foods typical to an ethnic group may not be eaten in a particular child's family or neighborhood. Insensitive use of such material may do more to perpetuate an unfortunate stereotype than to enrich a child's understanding of his or her heritage (Yates & Ortiz, 1998). Selection of culturally appropriate instructional materials requires a knowledge base that is beyond that held by many educational professionals and requires a thorough analysis (Santos, Fowler, Corso, & Bruns, 2000; Taylor, 2000). IEPs written for children who are culturally diverse must truly be developed in an individualized fashion, perhaps even more so than for children with disabilities who come from the cultural majority.

■ THE LEAST RESTRICTIVE ENVIRONMENT

Education in the least restrictive environment (LRE) involves a wide variety of placement options (see Chapter 1). The guiding principle is that instruction for students with disabilities should take place in an environment as similar to that of the educational mainstream as possible and in settings with nondisabled peers to the maximum extent appropriate. For the child who is culturally diverse and receiving appropriate special education services, the same is true, although some unique circumstances require additional attention.

Exceptional children who have language differences may also receive assistance from bilingual education staff. In some cases, the language instruction may be incorporated into other teaching that focuses on remediation of a learning problem. In situations in which the disability is more severe or the language difference is extreme (perhaps little or no English

Culturally diverse children receiving special education services must be taught in settings with nondisabled peers to the maximum extent appropriate.

FIGURE 2.2

Bilingual–bicultural inclusion models: Teacher competencies for mainstreaming bilingual exceptional children

[*Source:* From "Including Bilingual Exceptional Children in the General Education Classroom," by C. Collier. In *The Bilingual Special Education Interface* (3rd ed.), edited by L. M. Baca and H. T. Cervantes, 1998, p. 297. Columbus, OH: Merrill/Macmillan.]

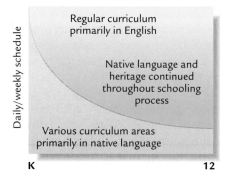

I. Transition Model

Daily/weekly schedule

English language

Regular curriculum in both languages, increasing in English over time

Native language

K — 12

II. Pull-Out Model

Daily/weekly schedule

Instruction in English as 2nd language

K — 12

III. Restoration/Maintenance Model

Daily/weekly schedule

Regular curriculum in English

Instruction in native language and ethnic heritage

K — 12

IV. Restoration/Maintenance Model

Daily/weekly schedule

Regular curriculum primarily in English

Native language and heritage continued throughout schooling process

Various curriculum areas primarily in native language

K — 12

focus 7

Identify two considerations that represent particular difficulties in serving children who are culturally diverse in the least restrictive environment.

■ PULL-OUT PROGRAMS. Programs that move the student with a disability from the general education classroom to a separate class for at least part of the school day.

proficiency), the student may be placed in a separate setting for a portion of instructional time.

Cultural and language instruction may vary as the child grows older, according to the model used in a given school district. Figure 2.2 illustrates how various approaches might be structured into a daily or weekly educational schedule as a student moves from kindergarten to the 12th grade. Each approach differs somewhat in the degree of integration it recommends. Part I, the transition model, moves the student into the instructional mainstream as rapidly as possible while addressing issues of linguistic performance and disability remediation. Parts III and IV involve instruction that takes place while the student remains in an integrated setting as much as possible. Part II represents what has long been known as a **pull-out program** and does not reflect integrated instruction. Although some students may require placement in such a setting, pull-out programs have not been viewed favorably in recent years. Collier noted that "there is still considerable debate concerning how and where the bilingual exceptional child should be served" (1998, p. 295).

Other Diversity Considerations

Many influences come into play as we consider multicultural and diversity issues in education. In some cases, societal problems contribute to the development of a child's learning difficulties. In other cases, the complications involved in educating people from a variety of cultures who also have differing abilities produce a host of challenges in assessment and instruction. It is important to note that the study of culture and associated variables, such as poverty and migrancy, is complicated by attempts to identify simplistic causal relationships (e.g., a finding of a higher frequency of depression in people of certain ethnic backgrounds may be due to poverty, not culture). Research on race and culture involves complex and interacting variables that defy simple conclusions (Frisby, 1998).

■ CHILDREN LIVING IN POVERTY

One important example of how social and cultural factors interrelate is found in the conditions pertaining to poverty. A child from an impoverished environment may be destined for special education even before birth. Gelfand, Jenson, and Drew (1997) cited statistical data about prenatal development, a defining factor in the child's latter development: "Only 5 percent of white upper-class infants have some complications at birth, compared with 15 percent of low SES [socioeconomic status] whites and *51 percent of all nonwhites who have very low incomes as a group*" (p. 92, emphasis in the original). Children who begin their lives facing such challenges are more likely to have difficulty later than those who do not. Children who live in poverty may be more frail, be sick more often, and exhibit more neurological problems that later contribute to academic difficulties (Drew & Hardman, 2000; Dunbar & Reed, 1999; Trawick-Smith, 2000).

As children develop during the important early years, an impoverished environment places them at risk of malnutrition, toxic agents (e.g., lead), and insufficient parental care (Masten & Coatsworth, 1998). As with the statistics already cited, these conditions are more prevalent in the lives of cultural and ethnic minorities (Horton & Allen, 1998; Wachtel, 1999). Additionally, poverty is associated with ethnic minority status. Census data indicate that 29.3% of all African Americans and 30.3% of Hispanic Americans lived below the poverty level, compared to 11.2% of the White population (Proctor, 1998). Other census data present an even more disturbing picture for children: 20.8% of all children were considered to be living below the poverty level (U.S. Bureau of the Census, 1998). Figure 2.3 summarizes 1995 poverty rates across several characteristics.

The conditions of poverty often contribute to poor academic performance, place children in at-risk situations, and generate special education referrals (National Research Council, 1997). For example, inadequate access to health care, particularly prenatal care, among cultural minorities can present at-risk circumstances (e.g., Drew & Hardman, 2000). The effects of impoverished environments continue to assert health risk influences into the adolescent years and are associated with premature "morbidity and mortality" in some ethnic groups (Pack, Wallander, & Browne, 1998, p. 409). Conditions of poverty are found more often in populations having multicultural education needs and are associated with homelessness and academic risk (Gelfand et al., 1997), contributing to the link between special and multicultural education.

■ CHILDREN IN MIGRANT FAMILIES

Although migrancy is often associated with minority status and poverty, this is not always the case. Frequent mobility sometimes characterizes families of considerable affluence, such as those who move from a summer home to a winter home or take extended trips when it suits parents, rather than school schedules. Similarly, children of military personnel may change schools frequently on a schedule that does not coincide with the academic year.

focus 8
Identify two ways in which poverty may contribute to the academic difficulties of children from culturally diverse backgrounds, often resulting in their referral to special education.

focus 9
Identify two ways in which migrancy among culturally diverse populations may contribute to academic difficulties.

FIGURE 2.3

Poverty rates for people and families with selected characteristics: 1995

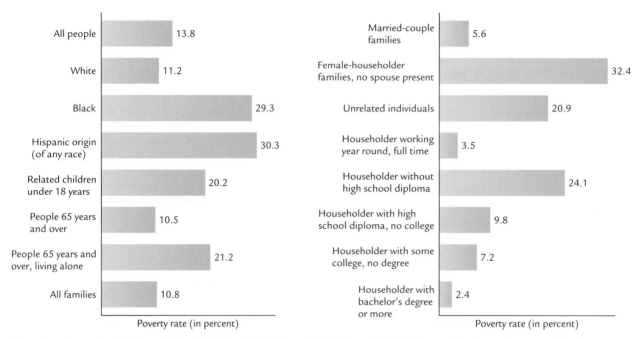

[*Source:* From "Poverty," by B. D. Proctor. In *Population Profile of the United States:* 1997, 1998, pp. 40–41. U.S. Bureau of the Census, Current Population Reports, Series P23-194. Washington, DC: U.S. Government Printing Office.]

Forces that interrupt the continuity of schooling have an impact on learning, teacher and peer relationships, and general academic progress. Often this is a detrimental influence. The mobility of wealthy people and others subject to frequent reassignment also has an impact, but it is often offset by other circumstances that contribute to a child's general education (e.g., opportunity for travel, help of tutors). These children are not subject to the same risks as children from families who migrate as a way of life without the financial resources to offset negative impacts. Unlike military personnel, for example, migrant workers are not assured of employment, housing, or a welcoming sponsor.

In many cases, the circumstances of migrancy are associated with ethnic or cultural diversity as well as economic disadvantage, language differences, and social and physical isolation from much of the larger community. Often the proportion of migrant workers from minority backgrounds is extremely high, and it varies geographically. For example, evidence indicates that over 80% of the farm laborers employed in California and other western states are recent immigrants from Mexico. Although reliable data are not available for other regions, it is known that migrancy is rather widespread and involves seasonal or migrant workers throughout the nation (Drew & Hardman, 2000).

The issues created by poverty and language diversity are even more difficult to address when a child moves three or four times each year. Migrant children experience limited continuity and considerable inconsistency in educational programming. They often have limited access to services because of short-term enrollment or a school's limited service capabilities. While it is difficult to single out the exact effects of mobility on children's academic progress, the problem is significant.

▪ OTHER FACTORS

A number of other factors link special and multicultural education. Some elicit serious concern regarding the placement of minority children in special education, and others pertain to how such placements might best occur.

Special education focuses on differences. If a young girl has academic difficulty, perhaps failing in reading and math, she is singled out as different. She is different in that her math and reading performances are far below those of her peers, and so she may receive special help in these subjects. Several questions emerge as we consider this example: How do we determine that the student is doing poorly in reading and math? Is the student a candidate for special education? What is the primary reason that the student might be a candidate for special education?

What if the student comes from a culturally different background, as does Denise in the opening snapshot? Is Denise considered disabled because of her academic performance or her culturally different background? This question may not have a clear answer, for contributing factors may be so intertwined that they cannot be separated and weighed in a meaningful manner. Denise may be appropriately considered for special education as long as her performance is not preeminently a cultural matter (merely because she is from a background other than that of the majority). Some might argue that the reason for Denise's receiving special help is irrelevant as long as she gets extra instructional assistance and help with behavioral problems. This perspective may have intuitive appeal, but it is not a satisfactory position for professionals involved in multicultural education. If Denise is receiving special education because of her cultural background and not primarily because she is disabled, she is being labeled and placed inappropriately.

Special education often carries an unfavorable stigma. Many people infer that children in special education are somehow inferior to those who do not require such instruction. Unfortunately, this view persists despite efforts by professionals to change it. Peers may ridicule children who are in special education. Some parents are more comfortable with having their child placed in the general education classes—even if the child might do better in special education. Even parents of children who are gifted and talented are often quick to point out that their children are in an accelerated class so that no one assumes that they are attending a special education class.

This negative perspective on special education is especially harmful to children like Denise if their placement stems from mislabeling or flawed assessment. Multicultural advocates may correctly claim that placing students in special education because of cultural differences is nothing more than means of discrimination and perhaps oppression by the cultural majority. This view explains why multicultural education advocates become concerned, even angry, when culturally diverse children appear to be overrepresented in special education.

An additional problem may occur if a child's special education placement is not multiculturally sensitive and appropriate. The wrong special education intervention can do more harm than good. Even the best instruction will be ineffective if it is provided in English and the student does not comprehend or speak it fluently. As noted earlier, designing appropriate instructional programs for children from culturally different backgrounds is complex and will likely involve a number of different specialists operating in a team (Craig et al., 2000; Morrison, 2001). Such instruction may also require some structural or organizational adaptations in order to progress satisfactorily through the academic material (Boudah et al., 2000).

focus 10

Identify three conceptual factors that have contributed to heightened attention and concern regarding the placement of children from ethnic and cultural groups in special education.

This checklist provides professionals with points to consider in the process of educating children from culturally diverse backgrounds. These matters should be considered during each of the following: referral and testing or diagnostic assessment; classification, labeling, or class assignment change; teacher conferences or home communication.

Process	Issues	Question to Be Asked
Referral, testing, or diagnostic assessment	Language issues	Is the native language different than the language in which the child is being taught, and should this be considered in the assessment process? What is the home language? What is the normal conversational language? In what language can the student be successfully taught or assessed—academic language?
	Cultural issues	What are the views toward schooling of the culture from which the child comes? Do differences exist in expectations between the school and family for the child's schooling goals? What are the cultural views toward illness or disability?
	Home issues	What is the family constellation, and who are the family members? What is the family's economic status?
Classification, labeling, or class assignment change	Language issues	Does the proposed placement change account for any language differences that are relevant, particularly academic language?
	Cultural issues	Does the proposed placement change consider any unique cultural views regarding schooling?
	Home issues	Does the proposed change consider pertinent family matters?
Teacher conferences or home communication	Language issues	Is the communication to parents or other family members in a language they understand?
	Cultural issues	Do cultural views influence communication between family members and the schools as a formal governmental organization? Is there a cultural reluctance of family members to come to the school? Are home visits a desirable alternative? Is communication from teachers viewed positively?
	Home issues	Is the family constellation such that communication with the schools is possible and positive? Are family members positioned economically and otherwise to respond to communication from the schools in a productive manner? If the family is low SES, is transportation a problem for conferences?

Denise's placement in special education may impede her academic progress to the extent that her failure becomes a self-fulfilling prophecy (see Chapter 1). In short, Denise may become what she has been labeled. Her poor academic and social performance may be due to cultural differences, not a disability. If the initial assessment inaccurately construes her cultural differences as showing a low level of ability, Denise may be made into a poor student by the system. The concept of the self-fulfilling prophecy has been discussed for many years. First mentioned directly by Merton (1948), the concept was catapulted to the center of attention by the work of Rosenthal and Jacobson (e.g., 1968a, 1968b), which stimulated controversy that still continues (Bushman, Baumeister, & Stack, 1999; Woods et al., 1998; Zebrowitz et al., 1998). A great deal remains unknown about the effects of expectations. This factor warrants particular attention as we study multicultural issues and specialized instruction.

Multicultural Issues and Specialized Instruction

Specialized instruction for students with disabilities from culturally diverse backgrounds must be based on individual need. The IEP must include specific cultural considerations that are relevant for a particular child, addressing language dominance and language proficiency both in terms of conversational and academic skills. The IEP may need to address the type of language intervention needed, which might include enrichment (either in a native tongue or in English) or language development intervention, which may also be in either a native tongue or in English. Instruction may target language enhancement through a strategy integrated with existing curriculum material, such as children's literature.

These are only examples of the considerations that may need attention, and they primarily relate to language diversity. Environmental conditions, such as extreme poverty and developmental deprivation, may dictate that services and supports focus on cognitive stimulation that was lacking in the child's early learning (Guralnick, 1998; Hendrick, 2001). The possible individual strategies are as varied as the factors that make up a child's background. Effective services must be based on the principles of individualized educational planning.

It is also important to note that most children from culturally diverse backgrounds do not require special education. Although the factors discussed here may place such students at risk for such referral, available instruction may meet their needs without special education services. When this is possible, it would be a mistake to label such students as disabled. Table 2.1 outlines points to consider as educators address various elements of the referral process with children from diverse backgrounds.

Case Study

A CASE OF OVERREPRESENTATION, FINANCES, AND SCHOOL REFORM

An associate dean of education, who happens to be African American, was labeled as having mental retardation and placed in special education for a significant portion of his school life. This is just one example of egregious misdiagnoses and possible discrimination in special education placement. Although IDEA is aimed at integrating youngsters with disabilities into the educational mainstream and guarding against ethnic discrimination, overrepresentation still occurs at the beginning of the 21st century. In fact, a 1993 report by *U.S. News & World Report* suggests that placement of disproportionately high numbers of minorities in special education programs continues at a level far beyond what would be expected based on population demographics. This report indicates that nearly 80% of the states have an overrepresentation of African American students in special education. This information is based on Department of Education survey data provided by the states themselves.

Overrepresentation of students of color in special education has been a continuing concern as indicated throughout this chapter. Concerns regarding misdiagnosis (which occurred in the case of the associate dean) and discriminatory practices have always surfaced in examinations of this problem; sociocultural issues are raised as well as the personal implications for individual children and their families. Other matters also seem notable and relate to serious and broadbased school reform.

Cost factors, for example, cannot be overlooked. The national price tag for special education services has risen *thirtyfold,* to over $30 billion since 1977. And there is considerable inducement for school districts to expand special education (even in separate rather than integrated programs). First, districts often receive additional funding for special education students over those not receiving such labels. Texas, for example, pays local districts 10 times the normal per-student rate for teaching a youngster in a special education class (the national average is 3 times the normal per-student rate). Second, many states exclude special education scores in the statistical analysis of statewide competency exams. Consequently, their average scores are higher and these districts receive more favorable publicity and have more supportive boards of education. Such circumstances may translate into a better budget once again, to say nothing of enhancing the reputation of the administrator.

So this is a multihorned dilemma. An administrator can increase his or her budget and enhance the prestige of a district by channeling low-achieving students into special education. Such pragmatism, however, runs counter to the fundamental concepts of IDEA and contributes to overrepresentation of minorities in special education. In addition to these serious moral issues, there are also some risks that may capture one's attention. Litigation has been an alternative of continually increasing significance for remedying educational problems, and lawsuits can be very disruptive to the operation of a school district as well as an administrator's personal life. Of five district administrators at a meeting in August 1994 (unrelated to any administrative problems), the one with the *least* crises had *"only one half-million-dollar lawsuit pending."*

■ **APPLICATION**
1. How can we balance the various facets of cultural diversity, integrated special services to students with disabilities, and a large public educational system within the context of our general society?

2. How should school finances and other incentives be coordinated with public policy and federal and state legislation?

Some vocal critics claim that the educational system should be discarded and a new approach developed from ground zero. However, there is no clear evidence that there would be a financial savings, nor that reforming our existing system would not be an equally effective alternative.

3. What would you do as an administrator?

4. What would you suggest as the parent of a minority child?

Debate Forum

ENGLISH-ONLY OR BILINGUAL EDUCATION?

Declaring English as the official language has had a certain level of support by lawmakers at several levels during the past few years, as recently as 2000. Initiatives to promote such legislation have been evident in nearly 75% of the states as recently as 1987. Yet English is not the primary language for many Americans. Students from culturally diverse backgrounds represent a very large portion of the school enrollment across the country. Critics claim that bilingual education places an unacceptable burden on the educational system, compromising its ability to provide specialized educational services to meet students' needs.

■ **POINT**
Children from different cultures must have certain skills to survive in the world of the cultural majority. They should be taught in English and taught the knowledge base of the cultural majority for their own good. This knowledge will prepare them for success and more efficiently utilize the limited funds available, since specialized culturally sensitive services will not be required.

■ **COUNTERPOINT**
Children from cultures different from that of the majority must have an equal advantage to learn in the most effective manner possible. This may mean teaching them in their native language, at least for some of the time. To do otherwise is a waste of talent, which can ultimately affect the overall progress of our country. To force students who are culturally diverse to use English is also a means of discrimination by the cultural majority.

Review

focus 1

Identify three ways in which the purposes of and approaches to general education in the United States sometimes differ from those of special education and multicultural education.

■ A major purpose of general education is to provide education for everyone and to bring all students to a similar level of performance.

■ Special education focuses on individual differences and often evaluates performance on an individually set or prescribed performance level.

■ Multicultural education promotes cultural pluralism and therefore differences.

focus 2

Describe the population status of and trends among culturally diverse groups in the United States. How do they have an impact on the educational system?

- Ethnically and culturally diverse groups, such as Hispanic Americans, African Americans, and others, represent substantial portions of the U.S. population.
- Population growth in ethnically and culturally diverse groups is increasing at a phenomenal rate, in some cases at twice that of Caucasians. Both immigration and birthrates contribute to this growth.
- Increased demands for services will be placed on the educational system as culturally diverse populations gradually acquire appropriate services and as significant growth rates continue.

 focus 3

Identify two ways in which assessment may contribute to the overrepresentation of culturally diverse students in special education programs.

- Through assessment instruments that are designed and constructed with specific language and content favoring the cultural majority.
- Through assessment procedures (and perhaps due to personnel) that are negatively biased, either implicitly or explicitly, toward people who are culturally different.

focus 4

Identify three ways in which language diversity may contribute to assessment difficulties with students who are from a variety of cultures.

- Non-English-speaking students may be thought to have speech or language disorders and be referred and tested for special education placement.
- A child's native language may appear to be English because of conversational fluency at school, but he or she may not be proficient enough to engage in academic work or assessment in English.
- A child's academic or psychological assessment may inaccurately portray ability because of his or her language differences.

 focus 5

Identify three ways in which differing sociocultural mores may affect the manner in which parents become involved in the educational process.

- Parents from some cultural backgrounds may have a different view of special assistance than the educational institutions do.
- Parents from certain cultural backgrounds may be reluctant to take an active role in interacting with the educational system.
- Certain behaviors that may suggest a disabling condition needing special education assistance are viewed as normal in some cultures, and parents may not see them as problematic.

focus 6

Identify two areas that require particular attention when developing an individualized education plan (IEP) for a student who is culturally diverse.

- Coordination of different services and professional personnel becomes crucial.
- Cultural stereotypes should not be perpetuated by assumptions that are inappropriate for an IEP.

 focus 7

Identify two considerations that represent particular difficulties in serving children who are culturally diverse in the least restrictive environment.

- Cultural or language instruction may be superimposed on other teaching that focuses on remediation of a learning problem, making integration into the educational mainstream more difficult.
- Training limitations of school staff, rather than the child's needs, may influence placement decisions.

 focus 8

Identify two ways in which poverty may contribute to the academic difficulties of children from culturally diverse backgrounds, often resulting in their referral to special education.

- Circumstances resulting in disadvantaged prenatal development and birth complications occur much more frequently among those of low socio-economic status and non-white populations.
- Environmental circumstances, such as malnutrition and the presence of toxic agents, that place children at risk are found most frequently in impoverished households, and poverty is most frequently evident among ethnic minority populations.

 focus 9

Identify two ways in which migrancy among culturally diverse populations may contribute to academic difficulties.

- In many cases, migrant families are characterized by economic disadvantages and language differences.
- Children in migrant households may move and change educational placements several times a year, contributing to limited continuity and inconsistent educational programming.

 focus 10

Identify three conceptual factors that have contributed to heightened attention and concern regarding the placement of children from ethnic and cultural groups in special education.

- A stigma is attached to special education.
- Special education placement for children from culturally and ethnically diverse groups may not be educationally effective in meeting their academic problems.
- A self-fulfilling prophecy may be operative, resulting in youngsters' becoming what they are labeled.

3

Exceptionality and the Family

To begin with . . .

It was 4:30 A.M. Three hours later, Hillary was born. Ten hours later, we learned that Hillary had Down syndrome. Twelve hours later, I was drunk. Twenty-four hours later, Michelle [my wife] was dealing with two infants, Hillary and me. (Shaw, 1994, p. 44)

For a person with a disability, the family will typically be the most important life influence from day-to-day, and the only constant over time. (Berry & Hardman, 1998, p. XX)

I have a special child, John, who is 9 years old and autistic. He has come along so well in the past year. He has been smiling and laughing and seems to be wanting more affection. He actually came and hugged and kissed me and said, "I love you, Mommy." That was the greatest feeling! I was so happy, I hugged him and I did not want to let him go. John wants to learn. He is starting to write letters off the chalkboard and put them on his own paper. He really likes to do homework now. He comes home from school and tells us he has homework that has to be done. John has been learning, through occupational and speech therapy, to hold a conversation, play, and use his hands appropriately. He is starting to want to talk and hold a conversation. I am seeing a great difference in my son and I wanted to share it with the world.
—B.G., Cleveland, OH (Resource Foundation for Children with Challenges, 2000, p. 1)

When Justin was born, I was as excited as a sister could possibly be. I had waited seven long years to have a younger sibling . . . and now I finally had one. Justin acted just like a normal baby, laughing and crying and being adorable. But he wasn't a normal baby. He had a terrible disease and nobody knew it. In fact, we didn't find out that he had cystic fibrosis until four years after he was born. During the first few weeks of his diagnosis, things were really scary for me. My whole life changed eight hours after my brother was given a sweat test. (This is a test that pretty much diagnoses cystic fibrosis.) Justin was whisked off to the hospital the day after Christmas for two weeks. Let me tell you, it's pretty hard to have only half your family around for two weeks. It was also hard to spend my whole weekend at the hospital, seeing my tiny brother with a needle stuck in his arm (actually it was an IV and it probably didn't bother him nearly as much as it did me). The few weeks after Justin got

home, my life changed drastically. We could no longer just run out to the store, because Justin had to get his treatment done or take his medicine. Justin was always getting things because everyone felt bad for him. I began to envy him, and I even wished that I had the disease so people would pay attention to me. Jessica (Parent Project for Muscular Dystrophy Research, Inc., 2000a, p. 1)

Carlyn

Carlyn is 3 years old. Her brother, Parker, and sister, Rachel, love to laugh and play with Carlyn. They take her sledding; her brother enjoys wrestling with her. They just love being together. In fact, Parker tells his mother that Carlyn is his favorite person in the whole world.

When Carlyn was first born, she wasn't breathing. When the doctors got her breathing, they found other physical difficulties and diagnosed her as having mental retardation. Her mother, Janna, explains, "It was heartbreaking. I can't explain how you feel inside when you know there's something wrong with your baby."

Carlyn's father is very involved with Carlyn. "Janna and I have had a lot of conversations about Carlyn. One of the things that we have noticed is sometimes people tend to treat Carlyn a little differently when they interact with her. You know, they feel good about it, which is okay and right, but we want Carlyn to have the same things that our other children have. We want people to know that it's normal to talk and interact with children with disabilities, that it should just be an everyday occurrence. I have a lot of faith and hope that Carlyn will have a bright future to look forward to. And I'm very grateful—I think all of us are—that we have Carlyn. That really sustains us at times, because some times are stressful, and they're very difficult, but nevertheless we're very grateful for Carlyn. That gives us a lot of joy."

When Carlyn first went to the elementary school, she was in preschool. The school seemed quite large and was probably frightening for her. At first she just observed; she didn't interact with the children. But now she loves to play cars with the boys and dolls with the girls. She's learning and enjoys being with the others. She uses all the children around her to learn; she has good role models.

At school, Carlyn works on her feeding and drinking. Academically, she practices fine motor skills. Her teacher sends notes home when Carlyn passes a milestone—when she walked 10 feet, when she took 5 swallows of a liquid, when she put a puzzle together. Carlyn's teacher hopes that when Carlyn turns 5 she will go to an integrated kindergarten class that will provide any of the services she may need.

According to Carlyn's teacher, "Carlyn's growing leaps and bounds. She's benefiting from us as much as we are from her."

OWHERE IS THE IMPACT of an individual who is exceptional felt so strongly as in the family (Fine & Simpson, 2000; Turnbull & Turnbull, 1997). The birth of an infant with disabilities may alter the family as a social unit in a variety of ways (Fuller & Olsen, 1998). Parents and siblings may react with shock, disappointment, anger, depression, guilt, and confusion. Over time, many parents and siblings develop coping skills that enhance their sense of well-being and their capacity to deal with the stressful demands of caring for a child, youth, or adult with a disability (McNab & Blackman, 1998). Additionally, relationships between family members often change.

A child with physical, intellectual, or behavioral disabilities presents unique and diverse challenges to the family unit (Cuskelly, Chant, & Hayes, 1998; Simpson, 1996). In one instance, the child may hurl the family into crisis, resulting in major conflicts among its members. Family relationships may be weakened by the added and unexpected physical, emotional, and financial stress (Chedd, 1996; Falik, 1995; Shelton, Jeppson, & Johnson, 1987). In another instance, this child may be a source of unity that bonds family members together and strengthens their relationships (Beach Center, 1998g). Many factors influence the reactions of the family, including the emotional stability of each individual, religious values and beliefs, socioeconomic status, and the severity and type of the child's disability (Fuller & Olsen, 1998; Lian & Aloia, 1994).

focus 1

Identify five factors that influence the ways in which families respond to infants with birth defects or disabilities.

This chapter discusses how raising children with disabilities affects parents and other children in the family, as well as grandparents. We will examine an array of family and parental issues directly related to families with children who are disabled. Additionally, this chapter examines the family as a social/ecological system defined by a set of purposes, cultural beliefs, parent and child roles, expectations, and family socioeconomic conditions (Cook, Cook, & Tran, 1997; Danseco, 1997; Fine & Simpson, 2000; Howie, 1999; Sontag, 1996; Turbiville, 1997). A **social/ecological system** approach looks at how each family member fulfills roles consistent with expectations established by discussion, traditions, beliefs, or other means. In the process, each member functions in an interdependent manner with other members to pursue family goals and to achieve various expectations (Danseco, 1997; Howie, 1999). This approach also examines the cultural and socioeconomic factors that impinge on the children with disabilities and their families. Using a social/ecological framework, one can easily see how changes in one family member can affect every other member and consequently the entire family system and how cultural and socioeconomic factors influence families and their functioning (Powell-Smith & Stollar, 1997).

Understanding Families

▪ REACTING TO CRISIS

The birth of an infant with significant disabilities has a profound impact on the family. The expected or fantasized child whom the parents and other family members have anticipated does not arrive, and the parents are thrown into a state of emotional shock.

Some conditions, such as **spina bifida** or **Down syndrome,** are readily apparent at birth, whereas others, such as hearing impairments and learning disabilities, are not detectable until later. Even if attending physicians suspect the presence of a disabling condition, they may be unable to give a confirmed diagnosis without the passage of some time and further testing. When the parents also suspect that something may be wrong, waiting for a diagnosis can be agonizing.

The most immediate and predictable reaction to the birth of a child with a disability is shock, characterized by feelings of disappointment, sadness or depression, loneliness, fear, anger, frustration, shock, devastation, numbness, unsureness, and feeling trapped. Both mothers and fathers report having these or similar feelings reoccur intermittently during the lifespan of their child (Blaska, 1998; Fuller & Olsen, 1998). Another reaction is depression, often exhibited in the form of grief or mourning. Some

▪ SOCIAL/ECOLOGICAL SYSTEM; also called SOCIAL SYSTEM. An organization that provides structure for human interactions, for defining individual and group roles, for establishing expectations concerning behavior, and for specifying individual and group responsibilities in a social environment. The system is ecological; changes in one individual or element in the environment often create changes for other individuals within the system.

▪ SPINA BIFIDA. A developmental defect of the spinal column.

▪ DOWN SYNDROME. A condition resulting from a chromosomal abnormality that results in unique physical characteristics and varying degrees of mental retardation. The condition was earlier described as "mongolism," a term no longer acceptable.

Professionals must be able to communicate meaningful information to parents about their child's potential disability.

parents describe such emotions as very much like those suffered after the death of a loved one. Many mothers whose babies with abnormalities survive suffer more acute feelings of grief than mothers whose infants with defects die. Additionally, recurrent sorrow and frequent feelings of inadequacy are persistent emotions that many parents experience as they gradually adjust to having an infant with a disability (Turbiville, 1997). Ongoing feelings of grief may be triggered by health or behavior challenges presented by the child, unusual child care demands, lack of achievement of developmental milestones in the child, and insensitivity of extended family and community members (Blaska, 1998; Powell-Smith & Stollar, 1997).

Parents of children with disabilities experience common feelings and reactions during certain time intervals. However, the nature of the feelings, their intensity and relationship to specific stages, and the eventual adjustments made individually and collectively by family members vary from one person to another (Blacher, 1984; Kroth & Edge, 1997; Simpson, 1996; Turnbull & Turnbull, 1997). Stages associated with various kinds of emotions may overlap one another (see Figure 3.1) and resur-

focus 2

What three statements can be made about the stages that parents may experience in responding to infants or young children with disabilities?

FIGURE 3.1

Potential parent reactions and possible interventions

[*Source: Adapting Early Childhood Curricula for Children*, 4/E. by Cook et al., © 1996. Reprinted by permission of Prentice-Hall, Inc., Upper Saddle River, NJ.]

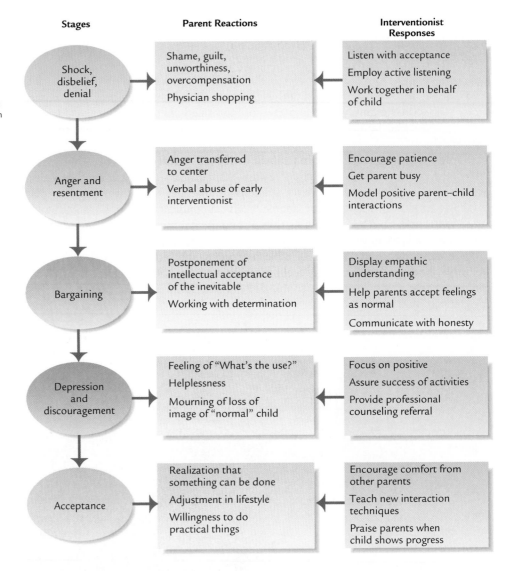

Stages	Parent Reactions	Interventionist Responses
Shock, disbelief, denial	Shame, guilt, unworthiness, overcompensation · Physician shopping	Listen with acceptance · Employ active listening · Work together in behalf of child
Anger and resentment	Anger transferred to center · Verbal abuse of early interventionist	Encourage patience · Get parent busy · Model positive parent–child interactions
Bargaining	Postponement of intellectual acceptance of the inevitable · Working with determination	Display empathic understanding · Help parents accept feelings as normal · Communicate with honesty
Depression and discouragement	Feeling of "What's the use?" · Helplessness · Mourning of loss of image of "normal" child	Focus on positive · Assure success of activities · Provide professional counseling referral
Acceptance	Realization that something can be done · Adjustment in lifestyle · Willingness to do practical things	Encourage comfort from other parents · Teach new interaction techniques · Praise parents when child shows progress

face during another period. Some parents may go through distinct periods of adjustment, whereas others may adjust without passing through any sequence of stages. The process of adjustment for parents is continuous and distinctively individual (Fine & Nissenbaum, 2000; Powell-Smith & Stollar, 1997):

When our son was born, my husband and I were told that the parents of a child [with a disability] move through certain stages of reaction: shock, guilt, reaction, and anger, all terminating in the final, blissful stage of adjustment. I do not believe in this pattern. I now know too many parents of children [with disabilities] to be a believer in any set pattern.

I feel we do move through these emotions, and just because we have come to adjustment (which I prefer to call "acceptance" because we spend our whole lives adjusting, although we may at one point accept the situation), that does not mean we never return to other emotions. We may continue to feel any of these emotions at any time, in any order. (West, 1981, p. S10)

Some parents, siblings, and even relatives of children with disabilities employ a kind of cognitive coping that allows them to think about the child, sibling, or grandchild with disabilities in ways that enhance their sense of well-being and capacity for responding positively (Beach Center, 1998c; Turnbull & Turnbull, 1993). For example, read the following account of one mother and her response to the birth of a child with a disability:

Something like this could tear a marriage apart . . . but instead it has brought us closer.

Right after she was born, I remember this revelation. She was teaching us something . . . how to keep things in perspective . . . to realize what's important. I've learned that everything is tentative and that you never know what life will bring.

I've learned that I'm a much stronger person than I had thought. I look back, see how far I've come, and feel very pleased.

The good that's come from this is that I marvel at what a miracle she is . . . it is a miracle that she's alive and that we are going to take her home. (Affleck & Tennen, 1993, p. 136)

This mother was able to interpret the birth and subsequent events in a positive manner. Her thinking or cognitive coping helped her to reduce or successfully manage feelings of shock, distress, and depression. Additionally, her positive interpretation of this event aided her adjustment and contributed to her capacity to respond effectively to her child's needs.

In sum, having children with disabilities affects mothers, fathers, and families in diverse ways. The range and sequence of emotions can be highly variable, with some parents moving through distinct stages and phases and others not following any specific pattern. The following descriptions illustrate the vast array of feelings parents may experience.

■ SHOCK   The initial response to the birth of an infant with a disability is generally shock, distinguished variously by feelings of anxiety, guilt, numbness, confusion, helplessness, anger, disbelief, denial, and despair. Parents sometimes also have feelings of grief, detachment, bewilderment, or bereavement. At this time, when many parents are most in need of assistance, the least amount of help may be available. How long parents deal with these feelings or move through this period depends on their psychological makeup, the types of assistance rendered, and the nature and severity of the disabling condition (Fuller & Olsen, 1998; Lian & Aloia, 1994; Turnbull & Turnbull, 1997). Over time, many parents move from being victims to survivors of trauma (Affleck & Tennen, 1993).

During the initial period of shock, parents may be unable to process or comprehend information provided by medical and other health-related personnel. For this reason, information may need to be communicated to parents repeatedly until they have fully grasped the important concepts. Parents may experience the greatest assaults on their self-worth and value systems during this time. They may blame themselves for their child's disabilities and may seriously question their positive self-perceptions. Likewise, they may be forced to reassess the meaning of life and the reasons for their present challenges. Blacher (1984) has referred to this stage as the *period of emotional disorganization*.

■ REALIZATION   The stage of realization is characterized by several types of parental behavior. Parents may be anxious or fearful about their ability to cope with the demands of caring for a child with unique needs. They may be easily irritated or upset and spend considerable time in self-accusation, self-pity, or self-hate. They may continue to reject or deny information provided by health care professionals (Powell-Smith & Stollar, 1997). During this stage, however, parents do come to understand the actual demands and constraints that will come with raising a child with a disability:

When Jessica was diagnosed with cerebral palsy at age 1, I knew something really bad, really terrible, had happened. I was very confused, upset, and scared. I personally did not have to make up the interpretation about the badness or wrongness of the situation. It was something everyone knew, a given: To be disabled or to have a child with a disability is a tragedy. Of course, by the time she was a year old, I was hopelessly in love with her. And, from early in Jessica's infancy, I was committed to having a life of joy with her. (Vohs, 1993, p. 52)

■ DEFENSIVE RETREAT   During the stage of defensive retreat, parents attempt to avoid dealing with the anxiety-producing realities of their child's condition. Some try to solve their dilemma by seeking placement for the child in a clinic, institution, or residential setting. Other parents disappear for a while or retreat to a safer and less demanding environment. One mother, on returning home from the hospital with her infant with Down syndrome, quickly packed her suitcase and left with the infant in the family car, not knowing what her destination would be. She simply did not want to face her immediate family or relatives. After driving around for several hours, she decided to return home. Within several months, she adapted very well to her daughter's needs and began to provide the stimulation necessary for gradual, persistent growth. Her daughter is now married and works full time in a day-care center for young children.

■ ACKNOWLEDGMENT   Acknowledgment is the stage in which parents mobilize their strengths to confront the conditions created by having a child with a disability. At this time, parents begin to involve themselves in the intervention and treatment process. They are also better able to comprehend information or directions provided by a specialist concerning their child's condition and treatment. Some parents become interested in joining an advocacy organization that is suited to their child's condition and the needs of the family (Fuller & Olsen, 1998). Parents begin to accept the child with the disability. It is during this stage that parents can direct their energies to challenges external to themselves. (See nearby Reflect on This feature.)

Reflect on This

SESAME STREET: MODELING A WORLD THAT RESPECTS EVERY CHILD

In 1970, *Sesame Street* was a very young television program, only in its second season. And I was the show's newest, youngest writer . . .

I became pregnant. In June 1974, my son, Jason, was born—with Down syndrome. Overnight, my academic interest in disability issues became intensely personal. Suddenly, I was struck by the absolute and total *absence* of children like mine in the media. Everyone on television looked so "perfect," so very—the word still catches in my throat— "normal." I looked at television programming, advertising, catalogs, illustrations in magazines; the media was not depicting *my* experience at all!

It was as if my child and I had instantaneously fallen off the face of the earth. We had, in fact, just joined America's largest minority group, but as far as the media was concerned, we were insignificant to the point of invisibility. It was a terrible feeling—a feeling of isolation, of alienation, of hurt and pain at society's total disregard for the integrity and value of my precious son.

Suddenly, the inclusion of children with disabilities—children like *my* child—on *Sesame Street* was an issue of profound personal importance. Fortunately, all the people at *Sesame Street* were being sensitized at the same time.

I am extremely proud to have written many of the "disability segments" for *Sesame Street* during the past 26 years. But it is the real and sincere commitment to those principles shared by all the other writers and, in fact, every member of the show's staff and crew that makes me so grateful and proud to have been associated with *Sesame Street* and Children's Television Workshop for all these years. I am confident that as long as *Sesame Street* exists, it will continue to model a world in which *all* children are understood, accepted, cherished, and respected.[1]

As a young boy, Jason Kingsley, who has Down syndrome, made several appearances on *Sesame Street, All My Children,* and other television programs. In 1994, Jason and his friend, Mitchell Levitz, published their book *Count Us In: Growing Up with Down Syndrome.* The book, published by Harcourt Brace & Company, is currently in its fourth printing.

Jason lived in Chappaqua, New York, where he graduated from high school with a full academic diploma in June 1994. He attended the Maplebrook School in Armenia, New York, a postsecondary program for students with learning disabilities. He was the school's first student with Down syndrome and was voted dorm representative.

Kingsley, now 24, enjoys some of the benefits of adulthood—like a nice cold beer in the shade. Jason's dreams for the future include getting a job, living in his own place, getting married, and maybe even being a father.

Living independently, Jason proudly opens the door of his new apartment.

Currently, Jason is working full time as assistant cultural arts program coordinator for Westchester Arc. He is living independently in his own apartment like Mitchell. Jason explains, "He is a good inspiration for me."[2]

[1] *Source:* From "Sesame Street: Modeling a World That Respects Every Child," by E. P. Kingsley, 1996, *Exceptional Parent, 26*(6), pp. 74–76.

[2] *Source:* From "25 Role Models for the Next 25 Years," 1996, *Exceptional Parent, 26*(6), p. 54.

Jason Kingsley, who was born with Down syndrome, as he appeared at age 3 on *Sesame Street* demonstrating his letter identification skills.

My daughter, Emily, is 14. Like many teenagers, she is a young woman in some respects, a child in others. We began preparing her for the journey through puberty four years ago, when her body first began to change. The onset of puberty reawakened in us the same fears and uncertainties we felt the day Emily was born, the day we first learned she had Down syndrome. We experience intense feelings when our children enter puberty. It is not an easy time. In fact, it may be very uncomfortable. A father may have to help his daughter with her bra or sanitary napkin. A mother may have to bathe her adolescent son. The child may have questions about his or her sexuality and disability: "Will I be able to marry, to have sex, to have children?" These questions may be difficult to answer. But our feelings of fear, anger, and uncertainty can be worthwhile if they motivate us to prepare our children for this new phase of life.

■ A TYPICAL REACTION

When her older sister's body began to change, Emily was very interested—much to Stephanie's embarrassment. She wondered when she, too, would get pubic hair and when her breasts would grow. We began to talk about these developments and about menstruation, answering her questions as she examined tampons and sanitary napkins. I realized I would have to lose some of my modesty and desire for privacy in order to help Emily learn what a period looks like, and how we change and dispose of the supplies.

When Emily got her first period, she reacted like many teenage girls "I don't like it. I don't want it anymore." But Emily's teachers helped her see this developmental milestone in a more positive light. They privately congratulated Emily and told her how excited they were that she was growing up.

■ "SEX AND STUFF"

For two years, we had read books and talked with Emily about how babies are made, using the appropriate terminology to describe sexual intercourse. Then, one day, she came home from school and said, "I know what sex is." When I invited her to explain, she said, "It's when people get married and stuff."

I asked, "Do you mean when the man puts his penis in the woman's vagina?" And suddenly, I saw her face light up with understanding! Discussions with friends at school must have contributed partially to her understanding, but she didn't quite get it until I repeated it again.

A few weeks later, we saw a public service announcement in which a 15-year-old girl talks about how hard it is to be a teenage mother and how she should have said "no" to her boyfriend. When I asked Emily if she knew what the girl was talking about, Emily replied, "Sex and stuff."

Emily has the same expectations for love, marriage, and children as most other teenage girls. We spend a lot of time talking about the responsibilities and realities of all those life choices. I believe it is important to present the facts, to share my values, to talk about the responsibilities of sexual behavior, and to help Emily feel good about herself, so she has the confidence to make good, independent decisions.

Puberty forces us to think about our children's future, which often looks scary. But I've found that sharing these feelings with other parents has been immensely helpful, both for practical tips and reassurance. We may never really be ready for our children to start growing up, but, alas, puberty comes anyway.

Source: From "Puberty Comes Anyway," by J. Noll, 1996, *Exceptional Parent, 26*(12), pp. 61–63.

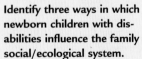

focus 3

Identify three ways in which newborn children with disabilities influence the family social/ecological system.

■ FAMILY CHARACTERISTICS AND INTERACTIONS

The birth and continued presence of a child with disabilities strongly influence how family members respond to one another, particularly if the child is severely disabled or has multiple disabilities. In many families, it is often the mother who experiences the greatest amount of trauma and strain. In caring for such a child, she may no longer be able to handle many of the tasks she once performed, and her attention to other family members may be greatly reduced because of time spent caring for the child's unique needs.

When the mother is drawn away from the tasks she used to perform, other family members often must assume more responsibility. Adjusting to the new roles and routines may be difficult, and family members may need to alter their personal routines in order to assist the mother. Responses of family and extended family members may vary according to their cultural backgrounds and related beliefs about children with disabilities. In this regard, we are just beginning to understand the influences of various cultures on the ways in which children with disabilities are viewed and treated within these cultures (Beach Center, 1998d; Linan-Thompson & Jean, 1997; Skinner, Bailey, Correa, & Rodriguez, 1999). For families that are already experiencing serious emotional, financial, or other problems, the addition of a child with a disability may serve as the catalyst for dissolution (Beach Center, 1998h). (See nearby Reflect on This feature.)

As the child with disabilities grows older, the mother frequently faces a unique dilemma: how to strike a balance between the nurturing activities she associates with her role as caregiver and the activities associated with fostering independence. Seeing her child struggle with new tasks and suffer some of the natural consequences of trying new behaviors can be difficult. For many mothers, overprotectiveness is extremely difficult to conquer, but it can be accomplished with help from those who have already experienced and mastered this problem (Beach, 1998g). If the mother or other care providers continue to be overprotective, the results can be problematic, particularly when the child reaches late adolescence and is unprepared for entry into adulthood or semi-independent living.

Each family exhibits a characteristic pattern of conveying information to family members. The pattern and type of communication vary according to the size of the family, its cultural background, and its members' ages (Alper, Schloss, & Schloss, 1994; Misra, 1994; Turnbull & Turnbull, 1997). Generally, the father conveys such information, particularly if the exceptionality is diagnosed at birth, then the older children provide additional clarification to younger ones.

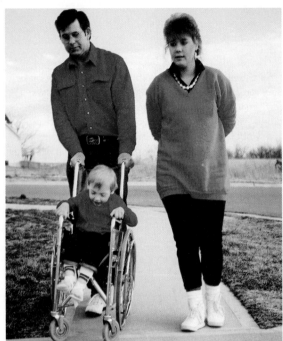

Mothers often develop strong dyadic relationships with their children with a disability (Fuller & Olsen, 1998). **Dyadic relationships** are evidenced by very close ties between these children and their mothers. Rather than communicate with all members of the family, a child may use his or her mother as the exclusive conduit for communicating needs and making requests.

Other dyadic relationships may also develop between other members of the family. Certain siblings may turn to each other for support and nurturing. Older siblings may take on the role of parent substitutes as a result of their new caregiving responsibilities, and their younger siblings, who come to depend on older siblings for care, then tend to develop strong relationships with them.

Every family has a unique power structure. In some families the father holds most of the power or control, and in others the governance of the family lies with the mother or the family at large. *Power,* in the context of this discussion, is defined as the amount of control or influence one or more family members exert in managing family decisions, assigning family tasks, and implementing family activities. Just as families vary greatly in their membership and their organization, the power structure within each family varies according to the characteristics of each member. That power structure is often altered substantially by the arrival of an infant with disabilities, with siblings assuming greater power as they assume more responsibility.

Parents must work together to make mutually satisfactory adaptations to the responsibilities and life-style changes that come with caring for a child with a disability.

■ HUSBAND–WIFE RELATIONSHIPS   The following statements illustrate the interactions and outcomes a couple experiences in living with a child with a disability:

When I think about having another child, I panic. In fact, I have consumed hours of psychological time thinking about my little boy and our response to him. Actually, my husband and I really haven't dealt successfully with our feelings.

Two years ago, I gave birth to a little boy who is severely disabled. I was about 26 years old and my husband was 27.

We didn't know much about children, let alone children with disabilities, nor did we ever think that we would have a child who would be seriously disabled. When the pediatrician suggested institutionalization for the child, we just nodded our heads. Believe it or not, I had merely looked at him through the observation windows once or twice.

Recently, my husband gave me an ultimatum: "Either you decide to have some children, or I'm going to find someone who will." (There are, of course, other things that are bothering him.) Since the birth of this child, I have been absolutely terrified of becoming pregnant again. As a result, my responses to my husband's needs for physical affection have been practically absent—or should I say, nonexistent. I guess you could say we really need some help.

According to the National Council on Disability (1998),

families of children with special needs are often torn apart because of the high stress levels and lack of emotional assistance provided in coping with the challenges of a child with a chronic health condition, as well as the enormous financial pressures. Lacking healthy coping mechanisms, husbands and wives can tear at each other and, without emotional assistance and support, may find it difficult to support each other and maintain the marriage or the family unit. Single parents face tremendous challenges because of a lack of support. A

Identify three factors in raising a child with a disability that contribute to marital stress.

■ DYADIC RELATIONSHIP. Two individuals who develop and maintain a significant affiliation.

child's chronic health condition affects the entire family. The family must be supported to enable it to do what must be done for the child. (p. 43)

An infant with a chronic health condition or disability may require more immediate and prolonged attention from the mother for feeding, treatment, and general care, and her attention may become riveted on the life of the child. The balance that once existed between being a mother and a wife is now absent. The mother may become so involved with caring for the child that other relationships may lose their quality and intensity. The following statements express the feelings that may surface as a result:

Angela spends so much time with Juan that she has little energy left for me. It is as if she has become consumed with his care.

You ask me to pay attention to Juan, but you rarely spend any time with me. When am I going to be a part of your life again?

I am developing a resentment toward you and Juan. Who wants to come home when all your time is spent waiting on him?

Though these feelings are typical of some husbands, others have the opposite reaction. Some may become excessively involved with their disabled children's lives, causing their wives to feel neglected. Wives deeply involved in caregiving may feel overworked, overwhelmed, and in need of a break or reprieve. They may wonder why their husbands are not more helpful and understanding. (See nearby Reflect on This feature.)

Marital partners may also have other types of feelings. Fear, anger, guilt, resentment, and other related feelings often interfere with a couple's capacity to communicate and seek realistic solutions. Fatigue also profoundly affects how couples function and communicate. As a result, some parents join together to create **respite care** programs, which give them a chance to get away from the demands of childrearing and to relax and renew their relationship (Beach Center, 1998e; Benson, 1992).

Other factors may also contribute to marital stress: unusually heavy financial burdens for medical treatment or therapy; frequent visits to treatment facilities; forgone time in couple-related activities; lost sleep, particularly in the early years of the child's life; and social isolation from relatives and friends (Beckman-Bell, 1981; Blackard & Barsh, 1982; Fredericks, 1985; Gallagher, Beckman-Bell, & Cross, 1983).

Research related to marital stress and instability is limited and contradictory (Powell-Smith & Stollar, 1997; Seligman & Darling, 1989; Turbiville, 1997; Turnbull & Turnbull, 1997). Some families appear to experience extreme marital turmoil (Gabel, McDowell, & Cerreto, 1983; McHugh, 1999; Schell, 1981), yet others "report no more frequent problems than comparison families" (Seligman & Darling, 1989, p. 93). Still other families report an improvement in the marital relationship following diagnosis of a child with a disability (Turnbull & Turnbull, 1997). Research suggests that husbands who assist regularly with the care and nurture of their children with disabilities contribute support that is genuinely valued by their wives. Additionally, this support is predictive of marital satisfaction for these couples (Willoughby & Glidden, 1995).

Identify four general phases that parents may experience in rearing a child with a disability.

■ PARENT–CHILD RELATIONSHIPS   The relationships between parents and children with disabilities are a function of many factors. Some of the most crucial factors include the child's age and gender; the family's socioeconomic status, coping strength, and composition (one-parent family, two-parent family, or blended family); and the nature and seriousness of the disability.

Families go through a developmental cycle in responding to the needs and nuances of caring for children with disabilities:

1. The time at which parents learn about or suspect a disability in their child
2. The period in which the parents make plans regarding the child's education
3. The point at which the individual with a disability has completed his or her education
4. The period when the parents are older and may be unable to care for their adult offspring (Turner, 2000)

The nature and severity of the disability and the willingness of the parents to adapt and to educate themselves regarding their role in helping the child have an appreciable influence on the parent–child relationship that eventually emerges.

Many mothers of children with severe disabilities or serious illnesses face the dilemma of finding a baby-sitter. The challenge is far greater than one might imagine, as typified by the following comments:

Marcia's a very mature girl for her age, but she becomes almost terrified when she thinks that she might have to hold our new son, Jeremy. He has multiple disabilities.

I don't dare leave him with our other two children, Amy and Mary Ann. They're much too young to handle Jeremy. But I need to get away from the demands that seem to be ever present in caring for Jeremy. If I could just find one person who could help us, even just once a month, things would be a lot better for me and my family.

Locating a youth or adult who is willing and capable of providing quality care for an evening or weekend is extremely difficult. In some areas of the country, however, enterprising teenagers have developed baby-sitting businesses that specialize in tending children with disabilities. Frequently, local disability associations and parent-to-parent programs can help families find qualified baby-sitters or other respite care providers (Beach Center, 1998h).

Time away from the child with a disability or serious illness provides parents and siblings with a chance to meet some of their own needs. Parents can recharge themselves for their demanding regimens, and siblings can use the exclusive attention of their parents to reaffirm their importance in the family and their value as individuals (Beach Center, 1998e; Powell-Smith & Stollar, 1997).

■ MOTHER–CHILD RELATIONSHIPS   If a child's impairment is congenital and readily apparent at birth, it is often the mother who becomes primarily responsible for relating to the child and his or her needs. If the infant is born prematurely or needs extensive, early medical assistance, the relationship that emerges may be slow in coming, for many reasons. The mother may be prevented from engaging in the feeding and caregiving activities common to other mothers, as the child may need to spend many weeks in an isolette supported by sophisticated medical equipment. Some mothers even come to question whether they really had a baby because of the remoteness they experience in interacting with their infants in a personally satisfying manner. As a result, the process of mother–child attachment may be impeded (Powell-Smith & Stollar, 1997).

In other cases, a mother may be virtually forced into a close physical and emotional relationship with her child with a disability or injury. The bond that develops between mother and child is one that is strong and often impenetrable (Leigh, 1987). She assumes primary responsibility for fostering the child's emotional adjustment and becomes the child's personal representative or interpreter. In this role, the mother becomes responsible for communicating the child's needs and desires to other family members.

Because of the sheer weight of these responsibilities, other relationships often wane or even disappear. The mother who assumes this role and develops a very close relationship with her offspring with a disability often walks a variety of tightropes. In her desire to protect her child, she may become overprotective and thus prevent the child from having optimal opportunities to practice the skills and participate in the activities that ultimately lead to independence. The mother may also underestimate her child's capacities and so may be reluctant to allow her child to engage in challenging or risky ventures. Such mothers might be described as overprotective. In contrast, other mothers may neglect their children with disabilities and not provide the stimulation so critical to their optimal development.

focus **6**

Identify four factors that influence the relationship that develops between infants with disabilities and their mothers.

It is important for the mother of a child with a disability to develop a relationship with her child that does not prevent him or her from ultimately achieving independence.

■ FATHER–CHILD RELATIONSHIPS   Information about fathers and children with disabilities is primarily anecdotal in nature or appears in case studies, web sites, magazine articles, and books (Beach Center, 1998l; Meyer, 1995). Some research suggests that the child-care involvement of fathers with children with disabilities is not significantly different from that of fathers of other children (Turbiville, 1997; Young & Roopnarine, 1994). As indicated earlier, the father is often

focus

Identify three ways in which fathers may respond to their children with disabilities.

responsible for conveying the news that the mother has given birth to a child with a disability, and for a time, the father may be responsible for keeping the family aware of the mother's status and the child's condition (Fuller & Olsen, 1998). The father's reactions to the birth of a child with a disability strongly affect the ways in which other members of the family adjust to the child with a disability (Brotherson & Dollahite, 1997). Moreover, fathers are generally more reserved and guarded in expression of their feelings than other family members (Lamb & Meyer, 1991). Fathers are more likely to internalize their feelings and may respond with coping mechanisms such as withdrawal, sublimation, and intellectualization. Fathers of children with mental retardation are typically more concerned than mothers are about their children's capacity to develop socially adequate behavior and eventual social and educational status, particularly their sons' social behavior (Turbiville, 1997). Likewise, they are more affected by the visibility and severity of their children's condition than are mothers (Lamb & Meyer, 1991; Turbiville, 1997). Often fathers of children with severe disabilities spend less time interacting with them, playing with them, and engaging in school-related tasks. Also, fathers are more likely to be involved with their children with disabilities if the children are able to speak or interact with words and phrases.

The relationships that emerge between fathers and children with disabilities are a function of the same factors concerning mother–child relationships. One important factor may be the gender of the child (Turbiville, 1997). If the child is male and the father had idealized the role he would eventually assume in interacting with a son, the adjustment for the father can be very difficult. The father may have had hopes of playing football with the child, having him eventually become a business partner, or participating with his son in a variety of recreational activities. Many of these hopes will not be realized with a son with a severe disability. When fathers withdraw or remain uninvolved with the child, other family members, particularly mothers, shoulder the caregiving responsibilities (Lamb & Meyer, 1991; Turbiville, 1997). This withdrawal often creates significant stress for mothers and other family members.

Fathers of children with disabilities prefer events and learning activities that are directed at the whole family, not just themselves. They want to learn with other family members and other families how to encourage learning, language development, and so on (Beach Center, 1998l). Often service providers neglect fathers, not realizing the important contributions they are capable of making (Beach Center, 1998a, 1998k). Children whose fathers are involved in their education perform better in school, evidence better social skills, are more highly motivated to succeed in school, and are less likely to exhibit violent or delinquent behavior (Beach Center, 1998k; 1998l; Turbiville, 1997).

focus

Identify four ways in which siblings respond to a brother or sister with a disability.

■ SIBLING RELATIONSHIPS   The responses of siblings to a sister or brother with a disability vary (Masson, Kruse, Farabaugh, Gershberg, & Kohler, 2000; McLoughlin & Senn, 1994; Meyers, 1997; Powell & Gallagher, 1993; Stoneman & Berman, 1993). Upon learning that a brother or sister has a disability, siblings are frequently encumbered with different kinds of concerns. A number of questions are commonly asked: "Why did this happen?" "Is my brother contagious? Can I catch what he has?" "What am I going to say to my friends?" "I can't baby-sit him!" "Am I going to have to take care of him all of my life?" "Will I have children who are disabled too?" "How will I later meet my responsibilities to my brother with a disability and also meet the needs of my future wife and children?"

Like their parents, siblings want to know and understand as much as they can about the condition of their sibling. They want to know how they should respond

Siblings often play a major role in the social and intellectual development of a brother or a sister with a disability.

and how their lives might be different as a result of this event. If these concerns can be adequately addressed, the prognosis for positive sibling involvement with the brother or sister with a disability is much better (Cramer, Erzkus, Mayweather, Pope, Roeder, & Tone, 1997; Masson et al., 2000; Seligman, 1991b).

Parents' attitudes and behaviors significantly impact those of their children toward siblings with disabilities, since children tend to mirror the attitudes and values of their parents (Fuller & Olsen, 1998). If parents are optimistic and realistic in their views toward the child with a disability, then siblings are likely to share these attitudes (Brotherson & Dollahite, 1997). Generally, siblings have positive feelings about having a sister or brother with a disability and believe that their experiences with these siblings with disabilities made them better individuals (Beach Center, 1998d; Fuller & Olsen, 1998; McHugh, 1999; Powell-Smith & Stollar, 1997). Siblings who are kindly disposed toward assisting the child with a disability can be a real source of support (McHale, Sloan, & Simeonsson, 1986). In fact, many siblings play a crucial role in fostering the intellectual, social, and affective development of a brother or sister with a disability.

Negative feelings do exist among siblings of children with disabilities (Cuskelly et al., 1998; Fine & Nissenbaum, 2000; Lobato, 1990; Masson et al., 2000; Powell & Gallagher, 1993). Loneliness, anxiety, guilt, and envy are common. Feelings of loneliness may surface in children who wanted a brother or sister with whom they could play. Anxiety may be present in a youth who wonders who will care for the sibling with a disability when the parents are no longer capable or alive. Guilt may come for many reasons. Siblings, believing they are obligated to care for the sibling with a disability, believe that failure to provide such care would make them bad or immoral. Similarly, they may feel guilty about the real thoughts and feelings they have about their sibling, including anger, frustration, resentment, and even hate. Realizing that many parents would not respond positively to the expression of such feelings, some siblings carry them inside for a long time. One sibling put it this way:

The more I learn about sibling relationships, the more impressed I am with what ambivalent *relationships they are—even when there is no disability. It seems that when disabilities are present, the ambivalence only gets stronger—the highs are higher. (For example, "Donny has brought me unending joy and laughter, and probably increased my sensitivity a hundredfold." Would many of us make such a comment about a sibling who wasn't disabled?) And the lows are lower (e.g., "On the other hand, sometimes I can't help but feel frustrated and cheated"). The challenge, I suppose, is to celebrate the insights and sensitivity one gains as a result of the relationship, learn sometimes painful lessons from the frustrations, and then—somehow—move on. (Parent Project for Muscular Dystrophy Research, Inc., 2000b, p.1)*

With increased inclusion of students with disabilities in neighborhood schools and other general education settings (Berry & Hardman, 1998), siblings are often "called into action." They may be asked to explain their brother or sister's behavior, to give ongoing support, and respond to questions teachers and others might ask. Furthermore, they may be subject to teasing and other related behaviors. Because of these and other factors, some siblings experience a greater risk for behavior problems (Lobato, Faust, & Spirito, 1988).

Many siblings resent the time and attention parents devote to their sister or brother (Therrien, 1993). This resentment may also take the form of jealousy (Forbes, 1987; McHale et al., 1986; Simeonsson & Bailey, 1986). Some siblings feel emotionally neglected, that their parents are not responsive to their needs for attention and emotional support (McHugh, 1999). For some siblings, the predominant feeling is one of bitter resentment or even rage (Seligman, 1991b). For others, the predominant attitude toward the family experience of growing up with a brother or sister with a disability is a feeling of deprivation, that their social, educational, and recreational pursuits have been seriously limited.

The following statements are examples of such feelings: "We never went on a family vacation because of my brother, Steven." "How could I invite a friend over? I never knew how my autistic brother would behave." "How do you explain to a date that you have a sister who is retarded?" "Many of my friends stopped coming to my house because they didn't know how to handle my brother, Mike, who is deaf. They simply could not understand him." "I was always shackled with the responsibilities of tending my little sister. I didn't have time to have fun with my friends." "I want a real brother, not a retarded one."

Siblings of children with disabilities may also believe they must compensate for their parents' disappointment about having a child with a disability (McHugh, 1999). They may feel an undue amount of pressure to excel or to be successful in a particular academic or artistic pursuit. Such perceived pressure can have a profound effect on siblings' physical and mental health, as can the expressed expectations of parents: "Why do I always feel as if I have to be the perfect child or the one who always does things right? I'm getting tired of constantly having to win my parents' admiration. Why can't I just be average for once?"

Support groups for siblings of children with disabilities are emerging and can be particularly helpful to adolescents. These groups introduce children and youth to the important aspects of having such a sibling in the family (Atkins, 1987). They establish appropriate expectations and discuss questions that children may be hesitant to ask in a family context. These groups also provide a therapeutic means by which these individuals analyze family needs and identify practical solutions (McHugh, 1999).

The best way to help siblings of children with disabilities is to support their parents and families (Berry & Hardman, 1998; Powell-Smith & Stollar, 1997). Sibling participation in programs that allow them to share information, to express feelings, and to learn how to be meaningfully involved with their sister or brother with a disability contribute much to their well-being.

■ EXTENDED FAMILY RELATIONSHIPS   The term **extended family** is frequently used to describe a household in which an immediate (nuclear) family lives with relatives. For the purposes of this section, the term refers to close relatives with which the immediate family has regular and frequent contact even though they do not necessarily live in the same household. These individuals may include grandparents, uncles, aunts, cousins, close neighbors, or friends.

When a grandchild is born with a disability, the joy of the occasion may dissipate. Like parents, grandparents are hurled into a crisis that necessitates reevaluation and reorientation (Scherman, Gardner, & Brown, 1995; Seligman & Darling, 1989). They must decide not only how they will respond to their child, who is now a parent, but also how they will relate to the new grandchild. Many grandparents, growing up in a time when deviation from the norm was barely tolerated, much less understood, enter the crisis process without much understanding. In their day such a birth may have signified the presence of "bad blood" within a family, and so the mother or father of the newborn child may be selected as the scapegoat. Blaming provides only a temporary form of relief. It does little to promote the optimal family functioning that becomes so necessary in the weeks and months to come.

Often, the initial response of grandparents to the newly born child with a disability may be to provide evidence that they are "pure and not responsible for the present suffering" (McPhee, 1982, p. 14). This is, of course, very counterproductive to the well-being of the mother and father of the newborn child. Research indicates that grandparents, particularly during the diagnostic phase, play an influential role in how their children, the new parents, respond to the child with a disability. If the grandparents are understanding and emotionally supportive and provide good role models of effective coping, they may have a positive impact on their own children, the mother and father. If the grandparents are critical or not accepting, they may add to the present burden and complicate it even further (Beach Center, 1998b; Seligman & Darling, 1989).

Grandparents and other family members may contribute a great deal to the primary family unit (Hastings, 1997; Lian & Aloia, 1994; Powell-Smith & Stollar, 1997). The correlation between grandparent support and positive paternal adjustment is significant (Sandler, Warren, & Raver, 1995). If grandparents live near the family, they may become an integral part of the resource network and as such may be able to provide support before the energies of their children are so severely depleted that they require additional, costly help. To be of assistance, grandparents must be prepared and informed, which can be achieved in a variety of ways. They must have an opportunity to voice their questions, feelings, and concerns about the disability and its complications, and they must have means by which they can become informed. Parents can aid in this process by sharing, with their own parents and siblings, the pamphlets, materials, and books suggested by health and educational personnel. They may also encourage their families to become involved in parent and grandparent support groups (Bell & Smith, 1996; Kroth & Edge, 1997; Fuller & Olsen, 1998).

Grandparents may be helpful in several ways (Seligman & Darling, 1989), providing much needed respite care and sometimes financial assistance in the form of a special needs trust for long-term support of the grandchild (Harmon, 1999). Furthermore, they may be able to give parents a weekend reprieve from the pressures of maintaining the household and assist with transportation or baby-sitting. Grandparents may often serve as third-party evaluators, providing solutions to seemingly unresolvable

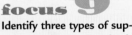

focus 9

Identify three types of support grandparents and other extended family members may render to families with children with disabilities.

■ EXTENDED FAMILY. Close relatives who visit or interact with a family on a regular basis.

problems. The child with a disability profits from the unique attention that only grandparents can provide. This attention can be a natural part of special occasions such as birthdays, vacations, fishing trips, or other traditional family activities.

■NONNUCLEAR FAMILIES   Although discussion has focused on a traditional, nuclear family of a mother, father, and children, there are many types of families (Fish, 2000). Very few children, fewer than 40%, will live with both biological parents through age 18. Thirty percent of children begin life with married parents who will later divorce. The remaining 30% will be born out of wedlock (Berger, 1994). Some families consist of the father and children or have the grandparents as primary caregivers for the children, without the mother or father. Other types of families include foster children living with foster parents and gay couples with adopted children. A number of organizations provide support to these families, including the Single Parent Resource Center, Single Parents (an Internet relay chat channel), SafeTPlace, the Single Parents Association Online, Parents without Partners, and the Single Parent Network.

The nature of families can vary, but one important common factor is the presence of a child with a disability. This child deserves the attention and professionalism of school personnel and other professionals—no matter what type of family unit this child is part of. The persons who serve as primary caregivers or legal guardians of the child should be invited to participate fully in any programs and support services (Fish, 2000). (See nearby Reflect on This feature.)

Family Support

Patterns of family support vary as a function of the life cycle of the family, in parallel with the changing needs of parents, children with disabilities, and their siblings (Berry & Hardman, 1998; Lustig & Akey, 1999; Whitehead, Jesien, & Ulanski, 1998). During the early childhood years, parents are responsible for a variety of important functions, including seeking out appropriate early intervention programs for the child with disability, contributing to their children's self-esteem, teaching daily living skills, and advancing overall development. Early intervention programs are directed at the achievement of goals as specified in an individualized family service plan (IFSP). (See Chapter 4 for an in-depth discussion of the IFSP.) The IFSP addresses child and family needs, details specific services to be provided by multidisciplinary team members, and identifies dates for achieving various goals. Achievements accomplished during this phase of the family cycle lay the foundation for subsequent growth and learning for children with disabilities. Moreover, services and supports provided during this time often prevent the development of other secondary, disabling conditions (U.S. Department of Education, 1999).

Family support during this period focuses on assisting family members to develop an understanding of the child's disability, provide appropriate home-based services, become knowledgeable about their legal rights, learn how to deal with the stress in their lives, and learn how to communicate effectively with professionals (Whitehead et al., 1998). Many home-based services and supports are directed at motor development, speech and language stimulation, and cognitive development. Other assistance may include helping parents deal with specific physical or health conditions that may require specific diets, medications, or therapy regimens. Training programs can sensitize parents to the importance of helping their young child with a disability develop appropriate independence, given the tendency of some parents to be overly protective.

During the elementary school years, parents become increasingly concerned about their children's academic achievement and social relationships (Berry & Hardman, 1998). With the movement in many school systems to more inclusionary programs, parents may be particularly anxious about their children's social acceptance by nondisabled peers (Bennett, Lee, & Lueke, 1998; Lian & Aloia, 1994; Staub, 1998) and the intensity and appropriateness of instructional programs delivered in general education settings. Overall, parents are pleased with the possibilities associated with inclusion, particularly its social aspects (Yasutake & Lerner, 1997). Intervention efforts during this period are based on the individualized education program (IEP). Consistent collaboration between parents and various multidisciplinary team members is crucial to the actual achievement of IEP goals and objectives (Hobbs & Westling, 1998).

The secondary school years frequently pose significant challenges for adolescents with disabilities, their parents, and their families. Like their peers, adolescents with disabilities experience significant physical and psychological issues, including learning how to deal with their emergent sexuality, developing satisfactory relationships with individuals outside of the home environment, and becoming appropriately independent. Other issues must also be addressed during these years, including pursuing employment preparation, learning how to access adult services, and developing community living skills.

During their children's adolescence, parents often experience less compliance to their requests and greater resistance to their authority (Lian & Aloia, 1994). Parents who are attuned to the unique challenges and opportunities of this developmental phase work closely with education and other personnel to develop IEPs that address these issues and prepare the adolescent with disabilities for entry into adulthood. Parents may also benefit from training that is directly related to dealing with teenage behavior and the challenges it presents (Kroth & Edge, 1997; Simpson, 1996).

During adolescence, parents are taught how to "let go," how to access adult services, and how to further their son or daughter's independence. Parents need information about the steps necessary to develop trusts and other legal documents for the welfare of all of their children (Powell-Smith & Stollar, 1997).

The movement from high school to community and adult life can be achieved successfully by adolescents with disabilities if parents and other support personnel have consistently planned for this transition (Levinson, McKee, & DeMatteo, 2000). Transition planning is mandated by IDEA and is achieved primarily through the IEP planning process. IEP goals during this period are directed at providing instruction that is specifically related to succeeding in the community and functioning as adults. The challenge for parents and care providers is to help adolescents with disabilities realize as much independence as possible, given their strengths and challenges (Powell-Smith & Stollar, 1997).

focus 10

Identify three types of professional understanding that are essential to establishing positive relationships with parents and families of children with disabilities.

■ COLLABORATING WITH PROFESSIONALS

The interaction between professionals and parents is too often marked by confusion, dissatisfaction, disappointment, and anger (Powell & Graham, 1996; Powell-Smith & Stollar, 1997; Scherzer, 1999). However, available research and other new developments have led many observers to believe that relationships between parents and professionals can be significantly improved (Fine & Nissenbaum, 2000; Jacobs, 1999; Kay & Fitzgerald, 1997; Kroth & Edge, 1997). Indeed, progress has been made in helping professionals communicate and relate more effectively to parents and others responsible for children and youth with disabilities (Simpson & Zurkowski, 2000). This is particularly true in the preparation of special educators and other care providers who serve as direct and indirect service providers in family, school, and community-based programs. There is now great interest in preparing professionals to be effective collaborators and consultants (U.S. Department of Education, 1999).

Many people with disabilities can successfully make the transition from school to adult life with the support of parents and professionals.

Seligman and Seligman (1980) identified three types of professional understanding essential to establishing positive working relationships with families. First, professionals need to understand their impact on parents. Second, they need to understand the impact the individual with a disability has on the family over time. Finally, they need to understand the impact the child and family have on them, the professionals. Developing these kinds of understanding requires open communication, a willingness to learn about others and their cultures, and time for relationship building (Misra, 1994; Wisniewski, 1994).

Quality family support programs provide "whatever it takes" to help families function like families without children with disabilities (Covert, 1995). Essential components of family-centered support include the following:

- Focusing upon the family as the unit of attention
- Organizing assistance collaboratively (e.g., ensuring equal, mutual respect and teamwork between teamworkers and clients)
- Organizing assistance in accordance with each individual family's wishes so that the family ultimately directs decision making
- Considering family strengths (versus dwelling on family deficiencies)

- Addressing family needs holistically (rather than focusing on the [family] member with a "presenting problem")
- Individualizing services for each family
- Giving families complete information in a supportive manner
- Normalizing perspectives (i.e., recognizing that much of what those receiving services are experiencing is normal)
- Structuring service delivery to ensure accessibility and minimal disruption of family integrity and routine (Beach Center, 1998h)

Superb family support programs work at keeping families together, enhancing their capacity to meet the needs of the individual with a disability, reducing the need for out-of-home placement, and giving families access to typical social and recreational activities.

■ STRENGTHENING FAMILY SUPPORTS

The primacy of the family in contributing to the well-being of children is obvious. This is also true for children with disabilities (U.S. Department of Education, 1999). Research indicates that family members provide one another with the most lasting and often most meaningful support (Turnbull & Turnbull, 1997). Much of what has been done to assist children with disabilities, however, has supplanted rather than supported families in their efforts to care and provide for these children (Bradley, Knoll, & Agosta, 1992). Monies and resources have been directed historically at services and supports outside of the family environment or even beyond the neighborhood or community in which the family resides.

focus 11
What are the five goals of family support systems?

Increasingly, policy makers and program providers are realizing the importance of the family and its crucial role in the development and ongoing care of a child or youth with a disability. Services are now being directed at the family as a whole rather than just the child with the disability (U.S. Department of Education, 1999). This support is particularly evident in the individualized family service plan (IFSP) as discussed earlier in this chapter and in Chapter 4 of this text. Such an orientation honors the distinctive and essential role of parents, siblings, and other extended family members as primary caregivers, nurturers, and teachers. Additionally, these services provide parents and siblings with opportunities to engage in other activities that are important to their physical, emotional, and social well-being.

Family supports are directed at several goals. These include enhancing the caregiving capacity of the family; giving parents and other family members respites from the often tedious and sometimes unrelenting demands of caring for a child with a serious disability; assisting the family with persistent financial demands related to the disability; providing valuable training to families, extended family members, concerned neighbors, and caring friends; and improving the quality of life for all family members.

Research suggests that family support services, particularly *parent-to-parent* programs, have reduced family stress, increased the capacity of family members to maintain arduous care routines, improved the actual care delivered by family members, and reduced out-of-home placements (Agosta, 1992; Beach Center, 1998j; Knoll, 1992). Parent-to-parent programs carefully match a parent in a one-to-one relationship with a trained and experienced supporting parent. The support parent is a volunteer parent who has attended a training program and is open to listening, sharing, and being available when a parent needs support (Herbert, Klemm, & Schimanski, 1999, p. 58).

Because of these family support services and parent-to-parent programs, many children and youth enjoy the relationships and activities that are a natural part of living in

Reflect on This

ALONE NO MORE: PARENT-TO-PARENT MATCHES BRING BENEFITS TO THE WHOLE FAMILY

Suzy Quirogo, a parent living in Columbia, South Carolina, was finding life in her new home very isolated. Daniel, her son, has obsessive compulsive disorder and will not leave their house. "When I would talk to other parents or my family about Daniel's situation, they just couldn't understand. It has to be difficult for them to understand how my physically robust son couldn't use the phone or touch the door knob because he thought it was contaminated," Suzy shares. "It was hard for them to believe how threatened Daniel felt around other people—so threatened that he couldn't even leave the house to go to school." Then she found the Family Connection of South Carolina.

Suzy recalls how the Family Connection took time to get to know her and to understand what she was dealing with. They listened to her explain what she was looking for in a match. Like most parents who request a match, Suzy was hoping to be matched with a parent who had a child with a similar disability. Family Connection searched their database, with her preferences in mind, and found a match for her—Jenny, one of their trained Support Parents. Jenny has a son, David, who also has obsessive compulsive disorder. Knowing there was another family out there in the same situation brought so much excitement and hope to Suzy. "Jenny and I met and shared a lot of information during our short but emotional meeting. I knew exactly where she was coming from and I'm sure she felt the same."

Jenny's son, David, and Daniel also became friends. At the first visit, Daniel had a panic attack and ran to his room. But Jenny let Suzy know that I was okay and that they would come over as many times as needed until Daniel felt at ease. David went home that first day and e-mailed Daniel, telling him it was "okay" and that he felt the same way at times. Over time, through e-mail—which was not threatening for Daniel—and through short visits, the boys' friendship grew.

Source: From "The Match: Everyone Benefits When Parents Find a Connection through Parent to Parent," by D. Klemm and B. Santelli, 1999, *Exceptional Parent,* 29(11), pp. 80–81.

---

their own homes, neighborhoods, and communities (Beach Center, 1998f, 1998h). Additionally, these services allow children or youth with disabilities to truly be a part of their families, neighborhoods, and communities. (See nearby Reflect on This feature.)

■ TRAINING FOR PARENTS, PROFESSIONALS, AND FAMILY MEMBERS

■ **TRAINING FOR PARENTS** Parent training is an essential part of most early intervention programs for young children as well as older children with disabilities (U.S. Department of Education, 1999). As part of the IDEA amendments, the thrust of parent training is now helping parents acquire the essential skills that will help them implement their child's IEP or IFSP (National Information Center for Children and Youth with Disabilities, 1998). No longer is the child viewed as the primary recipient of services; instead, services and training are directed at the complex and varied needs of each family and its members. The thrust of much of this training is directed at family empowerment; that is, the training is designed to help families effectively meet their needs and those of their child as they see them (Beach Center, 1998h). Much of the training is conducted by experienced and skilled parents of children with disabilities who volunteer their time as part of their affiliation with an advocacy or support group. These support groups play an invaluable role in helping parents, other family members, neighbors, and friends effectively respond to the child or youth with a disability.

Training may be focused on feeding techniques, language development activities, toilet training programs, behavior management approaches, motor development activities, or other related issues important to parents (Kroth & Edge, 1997; Simpson,

focus 12

What are five goals of parent training?

1996). For parents of youth or adults with disabilities, the training may be directed at understanding adult services, accessing recreational programs, finding postsecondary vocational programs, or locating appropriate housing. In some instances, the training centers on giving parents meaningful information about their legal rights, preparing them to participate effectively in IEP meetings, helping them understand the nature of their child's disability, making them aware of recreational programs in their communities, or alerting them to specific funding opportunities (Amlund & Kardash, 1994). Through these training programs, parents learn how to engage effectively in problem solving and conflict resolution and thus are empowered and prepared to advocate for their children and themselves. Parent involvement with the schooling of their children with disabilities significantly benefits the children's learning and overall school performance (U.S. Department of Education, 1999).

■ TRAINING FOR PROFESSIONALS   Training for professionals—educators, social workers, psychologists, medical professionals—focuses primarily on relationship building, communication, collaboration skills, and cross-cultural understanding (Correa & Jones, 2000; Powell-Smith & Stollar, 1997). Additionally, the training is aimed at helping professionals understand the complex nature of family cultures, structures, functions, and interactions as well as taking a close look at their own attitudes, values, and perceptions about families with children, youth, and adults with disabilities (Correa & Jones, 2000; Garland, Gallagher, & Huntington, 1997; Lynch & Hansen, 1998; Misra, 1994; Turnbull & Turnbull, 1997). Unfortunately, professionals often see parents as part of the child's or youth's problem rather than as partners on a team (Powell-Smith & Stollar, 1997; Seligman, 1991a). Moreover, they are frequently insensitive to the daily demands inherent in living with a child, youth, or adult who presents persistent challenges. As such, they may use vocabulary that is unfamiliar to parents, may speak a language that is foreign to parents, may not give parents adequate time to express their feelings and perceptions, and may be insensitive to cultural variations in relating and communicating (Simpson, 1996). Communication and collaboration skills that are stressed include effective communication, problem-solving strategies, negotiation, and conflict resolution.

■ TRAINING FAMILY MEMBERS   The training of family members is directed at siblings, grandparents, and other relatives. The training may even involve close neighbors or caring friends who wish to contribute to the well-being of the family. Often these are individuals who are tied to the family through religious affiliations or long-standing friendships (Kroth & Edge, 1997). Some families use a process referred to as GAP (group action planning) (Beach Center, 1998b). On a regular basis, family members meet with service providers (case workers, speech clinicians, and other professionals) to learn together, to plan, and to make adjustments in the interventions currently in place.

Siblings of children with disabilities need information about the nature and possible course of disabilities affecting their brother or sister. Furthermore, they need social and emotional support directed at their needs for nurturing, attention, and affirmation (Powell-Smith & Stollar, 1997). Some research suggests that many siblings know very little about their brother's or sister's disability, its manifestations, and its consequences (Seligman, 1991b). Additionally, siblings need to understand that they are not responsible for a particular condition or disability. Other questions also need addressing. These questions deal with the inheritability of the disability, the siblings' future role in providing care, the ways in which siblings might explain the disability to their friends, and how the presence of the brother or sister with a disability will affect their family and themselves.

In most instances, the training of siblings occurs through support groups that are specifically designed for a particular age group. In these groups, siblings can express feelings, vent frustrations, and learn from others. Additionally, they may learn how to deal with predictable situations, that is, what to say or how to respond. They may learn sign language, how to complete certain simple medical procedures, how to manage misbehavior, or how to use certain incentive systems. In some cases, they may be prepared for the eventual death of a brother or sister who has a life-threatening condition.

Training of grandparents, other relatives, neighbors, and friends is crucial. They, like the siblings of children with disabilities, must be informed, have opportunities to express feelings, be able to ask pertinent questions, and receive training that is tailored to their needs. If informed and well trained, they often provide the only consistent respite care that is available to families. Also, they may contribute invaluable help to families in the way of transportation, recreational activities, baby-sitting, critical emotional support, and short-term and long-term financial assistance (Harmon, 1999).

Case Study

FAMILY VOICES ARE HEARD

Garret Frey, a Cedar Rapids, Iowa, high school student was paralyzed in a childhood accident. Currently, he uses a power wheelchair, has a tracheotomy, needs a ventilator, and is catheterized daily. His equipment and health status require monitoring 24 hours a day.

When he started school, Garret had a specially trained attendant. Later, the Cedar Rapids school district insisted that he have the assistance of a licensed practical nurse (LPN), paid for through his family's insurance. Once his family's insurance cap was reached, Garret was ineligible for private insurance. The school district claimed that because they believed that Garret's condition required "medical treatment" by a registered nurse during school hours, it was not obliged to pay for the care. It suggested the Frey family

1. pay for a nurse at school, or
2. have Garret tutored at home one hour per day.

The Freys believed that IDEA (Individuals with Disabilities Education Act) obligates school districts to pay for related school health services. Earlier federal court decisions agreed. Unable to reach a compromise with the school district, the Frey family sought a legal solution.

Garret's case won at several court levels, finally reaching the United States Supreme Court. In August 1998, Family Voices, the American Academy of Pediatrics, and the National Association of School Nurses filed an amicus brief on Garret's behalf.

On March 3, 1999, in a 7-to-2 ruling, the U.S. Supreme Court said that IDEA requires schools to provide health supports for students who need them. This support should be provided as long as it is not medical in nature and performed by doctors, "to help guarantee that students like Garret are integrated into the public school." This means that all students, whatever their health condition, have a right to safely attend school, with necessary services paid by the school district. In most cases a well-trained attendant, backed up by a regular school nurse, is sufficient.

Cedar Rapids says Garret's nurse will cost $30,000 to $40,000 annually, and his attendant will cost an additional $12,000. Garret's lawyer says the two positions can be combined for $18,000. The National School Board Association argues that with $17,000 students like Garret, federal dollars are inadequate for school districts' obligations. How many students need such support or what those services cost is really unknown. Institutional care can run $80,000 per year. And the ultimate price Garret and society will pay if he does not attend school is impossible to calculate. (*Exceptional Parent*, 1999a, p. 31).

■ APPLICATION

1. What are the key issues in this dispute?
2. What steps need to be taken to resolve the financial issues associated with Garret's placement in an integrated school setting?
3. What should a school district do to address funding issues such as this one?
4. What should state boards of education do to provide assistance for students like these?
5. On what basis would you seek funding for Garret from a philanthropical agency?

MANAGED CARE AND CHILDREN WITH CHRONIC ILLNESSES OR DISABILITIES

■ REAL LIVES—REAL CONCERNS

Joanne Kocourek is one of these warriors. A registered nurse who manages clinical research for a large hospital in Chicago, Illinois, she is exhausted, frustrated, "financially drained," at wit's end—but persevering. The family's former health plan denied vital services and constantly threatened to reduce others for Kristen, the Kocoureks' 9-year-old daughter, who is adopted. Kristen has congenital central hypoventilation syndrome, which causes breathing problems, and mitochondrial cytopathy, an inherited metabolic disorder in which the body cannot generate enough cellular energy. Her sister, Annalies, 13, also has mitochondrial cytopathy.

Of the two, Kristen requires more care. A private nurse spends week nights at the family's home so Joanne and her husband, Tom, can sleep. On weekends, Joanne provides most of the care for Kristen, including intermittent ventilation. The fourth-grader also needs megadose vitamin supplements.

About four years ago, their former health plan pressured the Kocoureks to reduce in-home nursing care to just three nights a week—an effort they successfully fought with the help of their doctors. Their current health plan has pushed for institutional care, which the family maintains would be just as expensive, if not more so, than in-home care: $7,000 to $9,000 per month. The Kocoureks also believe that institutional care would not be the best arrangement in terms of Kristen's quality of life.

Moreover, says Joanne Kocourek, the health plan won't pay for the costly vitamin supplements because lower dose—and less expensive—supplements are available over the counter. It also will not pay for the physical or occupational therapy that clinicians believe would help develop both Kristen's and Annalies's delayed motor skills, arguing that the children's parents are responsible for such therapy.

There are other snags that the family has run into. One is the insurer's refusal to commit itself in writing when denying or granting coverage. The other is the family's financial status—it is "too well off" to qualify for public aid, but they do not have enough money to pay many medical bills out of pocket. "It has been a battle all the way," Joanne Kocourek says with a sigh.

■ PUTTING CHILDREN'S NEEDS FIRST

Recent media reports have focused on the misdeeds of health maintenance organizations (HMOs) among the general population. They tend to overlook how managed care has affected treatment for kids with a chronic illness or disability.

About 20% of all children have a chronic physical or mental condition requiring services that typically extend well beyond the services most healthy children receive, according to national data. These difficult and expensive-to-treat conditions run the gamut—from asthma and attention deficit disorder to sickle cell disease, cerebral palsy, cystic fibrosis, spina bifida, craniofacial abnormalities, and adolescent depression.

Around 5% of all children with special needs account for about 90% of all pediatric health care spending. Particularly pricey are treatments by specialists, physical and speech therapy, medical supplies and equipment, and long-term care.

And there is the rub in this age of cost-conscious managed care. To keep a lid on spending, managed care organizations—HMOs, preferred-provider organizations, or medical groups with managed care contracts—have strong incentives for enrollees to obtain health care from a selected pool of physicians, therapists, and hospitals.

They also impose preauthorization and other techniques to limit hospitalizations, prescription-drug and medical-gear purchases, and access to specialty care, diagnostic tests, and the like. Managed care physicians receive a per-person, or capitated, fee. They do not bill for the actual cost of their services, so there is a financial incentive for them not to provide what they deem to be unnecessary care.

As of late 1998, about 85% of all workers were covered by some type of managed care plan, up 50% since 1994. Some of these health plans simply don't have the capacity to care for children with special health needs. Their panels of physicians and ancillary providers may not include all of the pediatric specialists, therapists, and others who are best qualified to treat these young patients.

Furthermore, the needs of children with chronic illnesses or disabilities—even those with the same condition—can vary tremendously, a situation that health plans may overlook. As Peter D. Rappo, MD, a pediatrician, wrote in 1997 in *Medical Economics* magazine: "Even within one diagnosis code, there's a range of severity. Some of my spina bifida patients can kick a soccer ball, while others are confined to a wheelchair."

My own research indicates that some health plans may not have the necessary experience or knowledge to adequately oversee the care of children with chronic illnesses or disabilities, and sometimes they don't reimburse for critical aspects of preventive care. For example, one of the leading causes of death among kids with spina bifida is renal failure. Yet some plans routinely don't cover urological tests with the frequency that could lead to early detection and treatment of urological complications of the disease.

■ **POINT**

Families with children with disabilities should have access to health insurance that covers reasonable health care for all family members. Insurance companies currently base their coverage on "experience ratings" rather than "community ratings." Using experience ratings, they identify groups of individuals with whom they can make significant profits given their past health care requirements. They should use community ratings that consider the health needs of all individuals in a given area or location and base their pricing and potential profit structures on these community ratings. As a society, we should be willing to share the expense of providing basic medical care to all families and their members. Present insurance policies are patently discriminatory.

■ **COUNTERPOINT**

Insurance companies are private entities and for-profit businesses. As such, they must operate in ways that allow them to make profits as well as fund the expenses incurred in paying for health care delivered to families and individuals. If insurance companies were to alter their current underwriting standards, their expenses would exceed their incomes and they would not be able to provide health insurance for anyone.

Source: From "Managed Care and Children with Chronic Illnesses or Disabilities," by E. J. Jameson, 1999, *Exceptional Parent, 29*(9), pp. 104–105.

Review

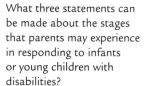

focus 1

Identify five factors that influence the ways in which families respond to infants with birth defects or disabilities.

- The emotional stability of each family member
- Religious values and beliefs
- Socioeconomic status
- The severity of the disability
- The type of disability

focus 2

What three statements can be made about the stages that parents may experience in responding to infants or young children with disabilities?

- The stage approach needs further refinement and validation before it can be used accurately to understand, predict, or help parents deal with young infants and children with disabilities.

- Parental responses are highly variable.
- The adjustment process, for most parents, is continuous and distinctively individual.

focus 3

Identify three ways in which a newborn child with disabilities influences the family social/ecological system.

- The communication patterns within the family may change.
- The power structure within the family may be altered.
- The roles and responsibilities assumed by various family members may be modified.

focus 4

Identify three factors in raising a child with a disability that contribute to marital stress.

- A decrease in the amount of time available for the couple's activities
- Heavy financial burdens
- Fatigue

focus 5

Identify four general phases that parents may experience in rearing a child with a disability.

- The diagnostic period: Does the child truly have a disability?
- The school period (elementary and secondary, with their inherent challenges: dealing with teasing and other peer-related behaviors, as well as learning academic, social, and vocational skills): Included in this period are the challenges of adolescence.
- The postschool period: The child makes the transition from school to other educational or vocational activities.
- The period when the parents are no longer able to provide direct care and guidance for their son or daughter.

focus 6

Identify four factors that influence the relationship that develops between infants with disabilities and their mothers.

- The mother may be unable to engage in typical feeding and caregiving activities because of the intensive medical care being provided.
- Some mothers may have difficulty bonding to children with whom they have little physical and social interaction.
- Some mothers are given little direction as to how they might become involved with their children. Without minimal involvement, some mothers become estranged from their children and find it difficult to begin the caring and bonding process.
- The expectations that mothers have about their children and their functions in nurturing them play a significant role in the relationship that develops.

focus 7

Identify three ways in which fathers may respond to their children with disabilities.

- Fathers are more likely to internalize their feelings than are mothers.
- Fathers often respond to sons with disabilities differently from how they respond to daughters.
- Fathers may resent the time their wives spend in caring for their children with disabilities.

 focus 8

Identify four ways in which siblings respond to a brother or sister with a disability.

- Siblings tend to mirror the attitudes and behaviors of their parents toward a child with disabilities.
- Siblings may play a crucial role in fostering the intellectual, social, and affective development of the child with a disability.
- Some siblings respond by eventually becoming members of helping professions that serve populations with disabilities.
- Some siblings respond with feelings of resentment or deprivation.

 focus 9

Identify three types of support grandparents may render to families with children with disabilities.

- They may provide their own children with weekend reprieves from the pressures of the home environment.
- They may assist occasionally with baby-sitting or transportation.
- They may help their children in times of crisis by listening and helping them deal with seemingly unresolvable problems and by providing short-term and long-term financial assistance.

 focus 10

Identify three types of professional understanding that are essential to establishing positive relationships with parents and families of children with disabilities.

- Professionals need to understand the impact that they have on the family over time.
- Professionals need to understand the impact that the child with disabilities has on the family over time.
- Professionals need to understand the impact that the child with disabilities and his or her family have on them.

focus 11

What are the five goals of family support systems?

- Enhancing the caregiving capacity of the family
- Giving parents and other family members respites from the demands of caring for a child with a disability
- Assisting the family with persistent financial demands related to the child's disability
- Providing valuable training to families, extended family members, concerned neighbors, and caring friends
- Improving the quality of life for all family members

 focus 12

What are five goals of parent training?

- To help them with specific needs such as feeding their children, teaching them language skills, helping them become toilet trained; accessing adult services; finding appropriate housing; locating appropriate postsecondary vocational training
- To help them understand their legal rights
- To contribute to their understanding of the nature of the disability or disabilities
- To make them aware of services in the community
- To alert them to financial assistance that is available

The Early Childhood and Elementary School Years: Special Education, Inclusion, and Collaboration

To begin with . . .

In 1970, before the enactment of the federal protections in IDEA, schools in America educated only one in five students with disabilities. More than one million students were excluded from public schools and another 3.5 million did not receive appropriate services. Many states had laws excluding certain students, including those who were blind, deaf, or labeled "emotionally disturbed" or "mentally retarded." Almost 200,000 school-age children with mental retardation and emotional disabilities were institutionalized. The likelihood of exclusion was greater for children with disabilities living in low-income, ethnic and racial minority, or rural communities. (National Council on Disability, 2000, p. 6)

Special education works! John, 23, has a severe reading disability. Despite his disability, he graduated from high school and received training as an electrician. After working for a national company for two years, he now runs his own company. . . . Alfie, 25, has Down syndrome. Though the "medical experts" said there was "no hope" and that he would never even speak, Alfie is bilingual, reads at a 6th grade level, and is in a job training program. Lindsay, 11, has severe cerebral palsy. Though she is unable to use her hands, she maintains an A/B average and also keeps up with her classmates in written work—she types with her feet. The stories of John, Becky, Alfie, and Lindsay are not atypical. Every special educator can look at the students he or she has taught and mark their progress—and the often remarkable success—students with disabilities achieve with the support of special education. (Council for Exceptional Children, 1999)

The most recent descriptor for the effort to create greater integration of children with disabilities into school programs is the term *inclusion*. For many educators, the term is viewed as a more positive description of efforts to include children with disabilities in genuine and comprehensive ways in the total life of schools. . . . The most effective and needed services that special education can provide must be preserved. At the same time, the education of children with disabilities must be viewed by all educators as a shared responsibility and privilege. Most important, every child must have a place and be made welcome in a regular classroom. (Smith, 1998, pp. 17, 18)

As long as there are people with disabilities, there will be a need for special services that goes beyond anything a regular [general] classroom teacher can provide. . . . Regular classroom teachers attempt to meet physical–motor, cognitive–intellectual, and social–emotional needs just as special educators do. Yet, their focus tends to be different. Regular class teachers are given an agenda called the curriculum. They are provided with it prior to seeing any student. They are told that this is what they have to teach, and sometimes what book to use and even how to use it. This more standardized approach to education for the masses generally succeeds. . . . It misses some individual children by a mile, children who may be normal and a little bit different, or who may have a disability and be a lot different. The greater the difference, the greater the chance that the student will fall through the cracks of any standard educational setting. (Lieberman, 1996, p. 24)

99

Matt

One day, 4-year-old Matt was playing across the street from his house. As he crossed the street to return home, he was hit by a car. Matt suffered a severe trauma as a result of the accident and was in a coma for more than 2 months. Now he's in school and doing well.

Matt wears a helmet to protect his head, and he uses a walker in his general education kindergarten class in the morning and special education class in the afternoon. The general education kindergarten children sing songs together and work on handwriting, before they work at centers in the classroom. Matt's favorite center is the block area. He

spends most of his time there. Recently, however, he has become interested in the computer and math centers.

He is working on his fine motor skills and speech skills so he can learn to write and use a pencil again. The focus of his academic learning is mastering the alphabet, learning how to count, and recognizing numbers. He also receives regular speech therapy. He speaks in sentences, but it is very difficult for others to understand what he is saying.

Matt is well liked by his classmates. His teacher enjoys seeing his progress. "Well, it's our hope that he'll be integrated with the other kids eventually, and through the activities we do in the classroom here (in special education) and in the kindergarten, we hope the kids will get to know him and interact with him and that this will help pull up his skills to the level where he can eventually go back to the general education classroom."

Yvonne

■ THE EARLY CHILD-HOOD YEARS

Anita was elated. She had just learned during an ultrascan that she was going to have twin girls. As the delivery date neared, she thought about how much fun it would be to take them on long summer walks in the new double stroller. Two weeks after her estimated delivery date, she was in the hospital, giving birth to the first of her two twins. The first little girl arrived without a problem. Unfortunately, this was not the case for the second.

There was something different about her; it became obvious almost immediately after the birth. Yvonne just didn't seem to have the same body tone as her sister. Within a couple of days, Yvonne was diagnosed as having cerebral palsy. Her head and the left side of her body seemed to be affected most seriously. The pediatrician calmly told the family that Yvonne would

undoubtedly have learning and physical problems throughout her life. She referred the parents to a division of the state health agency responsible for assisting families with children who have disabilities. Further testing was done, and Yvonne was placed in an early intervention program for infants with developmental disabilities. When she reached the age of 3, Yvonne's parents enrolled her in a preschool program where she would have the opportunity to learn communication and social skills while interacting with children of her own age with and without disabilities. As neither of the parents had any previous direct experience with a child with disabilities, they were uncertain how to help Yvonne. Would this program really help her that much, or should they work with her at home only? It was hard for them to see this little girl go to school so very early in her life.

tHIS CHAPTER EXPLORES THE world of infants, toddlers, preschoolers, and elementary school children with disabilities. For infants, toddlers, and preschool-age children, the world is defined primarily through family and a small, same-age peer group. As the child progresses in age and development, the world expands to include the neighborhood, the school, and eventually, a larger heterogeneous group called the community. For educators, the question is this: How can schools and families work together to individualize a child's instructional program to effectively foster full participation in the home, the school, and eventually the community setting?

The Early Childhood Years

Over the past decade, there has been a growing recognition of the educational, social, and health needs of young children with disabilities. The early experiences of infants and children at risk provide a foundation for future learning, growth, and development (Burchinal, Campbell, Bryant, Wasik, & Ramey, 1997; Noonan & McCormick, 1993; Ramey & Ramey, 1999; Young, 1996). These first years of life are critical to the overall development of children, including those defined as at risk. Moreover, classic studies in the behavioral sciences from the 1960s and 1970s indicated that early stimulation is critical to the later development of language, intelligence, personality, and a sense of self-worth (Bloom, 1964; Hunt, 1961; Piaget, 1970; White, 1975).

Advocates of **early intervention** services for children at risk believe that intervention should begin as early as possible in an environment free of traditional disability labels (such as *mentally retarded* or *emotionally disturbed*). Carefully selected services and supports can lessen the long-term impact of the disability and counteract any negative effects of waiting to intervene. The postponement of services may, in fact, undermine a child's overall development as well as his or her acquisition of specific skills (Guralnick, 1998).

focus 1

Why is it so important to provide early intervention services as soon as possible to young children at risk?

■ BRINGING ABOUT CHANGE FOR YOUNG CHILDREN WITH DISABILITIES

For the better part of the 20th century, comprehensive educational and social services for young children with disabilities were nonexistent or were provided sporadically at best. For families of children with more severe disabilities, often the only option was institutionalization. Harbin (1993) reported that as recently as 1950, many parents were advised to institutionalize a child immediately after birth if he or she had a recognizable physical condition associated with a disability (such as Down syndrome). By doing so, the family would not become attached to the child in the hospital or after returning home.

The efforts of parents and professionals to gain national support to develop and implement community services for young children at risk began in 1968 with the passage of Public Law (PL) 90-538, the Handicapped Children's Early Education Program (HCEEP). A primary purpose of HCEEP was to fund model demonstration programs focused on experimental practices for young children with disabilities. Many of the best practice approaches coming out of these experimental projects were transferred to other early intervention programs through outreach efforts funded through HCEEP. The documented success of HCEEP eventually culminated in the passage of PL 99-457, in the form of amendments to the Education of the Handicapped Act, passed in 1986 (see Chapter 1). The most important piece of legislation ever enacted on behalf of infants and preschool-age children with disabilities, the act opened up a new era of services for young children with disabilities. It required that all states ensure a free and appropriate public education to every eligible child with a disability between 3 and 5 years of age. For infants and toddlers (birth to 2 years of age), a new program, Part H (changed to Part C in the 1997 Amendments to IDEA), was established to help states develop and implement programs for early intervention services. Every state now provides services for infants and toddlers with disabilities under Part C. IDEA 97 described the critical need for Part C early intervention services, namely, to do the following:

■ EARLY INTERVENTION. Comprehensive services for infants and toddlers who are disabled, or at risk of acquiring a disability. Services may include education, health care, and/or social or psychological assistance.

1. Enhance the development of infants and toddlers with disabilities and to minimize their potential for developmental delay.
2. Reduce the educational costs to our society, including our nation's schools, by minimizing the need for special education and related services after infants and toddlers with disabilities reach school age.
3. Minimize the likelihood of institutionalization of individuals with disabilities and maximize the potential for their living independently in society.
4. Enhance the capacity of families to meet the special needs of their infants and toddlers with disabilities.
5. Enhance the capacity of state and local agencies and service providers to identify, evaluate, and meet the needs of historically underrepresented populations, particularly minority, low-income, inner-city, and rural populations. (Public Law 105-17, Part C, Section 631)

In the next two sections, we will discuss the comprehensive services necessary to meet the needs of infants, toddlers, and preschool-age children with disabilities.

focus 2

Identify the components that must be included in the individualized family service plan.

■ EARLY INTERVENTION SERVICES FOR INFANTS AND TODDLERS

Early intervention is defined in myriad ways. McConnell (1994) emphasized its preventive aspects. "Early intervention must provide early identification and provision of services to reduce or eliminate the effects of disabilities or to prevent the development of other problems, so that the need for subsequent special services is reduced" (p. 78). Early intervention for infants and toddlers is comprehensive when it provides services and supports in education, health care, and social services. IDEA 97 defines eligible infants and toddlers as those under 3 years of age who need early intervention services for one of two reasons: (1) there is a developmental delay in one or more of the areas of cognitive development, physical development, communication development, social or emotional development, and adaptive development; or (2) there is a diagnosis of a physical or mental condition that has a high probability of resulting in a developmental delay (Sec. 632[1]).

Effective early intervention services are not only directed to the young child with a disability but to family members as well (Sontag & Schacht, 1994). Berry and Hardman (1998) suggested that all early intervention services must be designed and delivered within the framework of informing and empowering family members.

Advancements in health care have increased the number of at-risk infants who survive birth. **Intensive care specialists,** working with sophisticated medical technologies in newborn intensive care units and providing **developmentally supportive care,** are able to save the lives of infants who years ago would have died in the first days or weeks of life. Developmentally supportive care views the infant as "an active collaborator" in determining what services are necessary to enhance survival. Using this approach, infant behavior is carefully observed to determine what strategies (such as responding to light, noise, or touch) the infant is using to try to survive. Specially trained developmental specialists then focus on understanding the infant's "developmental agenda," in order to provide appropriate supports and services to assist the infant's further growth and development (Als & Gilkerson, 1995).

Timing is critical in the delivery of early intervention services. The maxim "the earlier, the better" is very true. Moreover, early intervention may be less costly and more effective than providing services later in the individual's life (Garber et al.,

■ INTENSIVE CARE SPECIALISTS. Health care professionals (such as physicians and nurses) trained specifically to provide medical care to newborns who are seriously ill, disabled, or at risk of serious medical problems; also referred to as *neonatal specialists.*

■ DEVELOPMENTALLY SUPPORTIVE CARE. Approach to care that views the infant as "an active collaborator" in determining what services are necessary to enhance survival.

1991; Guralnick, 1998; Liaw, F., & Brooks-Gunn, J., 1994; Noonan & McCormick, 1993; Young, 1996).

Comprehensive intervention services are broad in scope. The Infant and Toddlers Program under IDEA, Part C, specified that programs include the following services:

- Special instruction
- Speech and language instruction
- Occupational and physical therapy
- Psychological testing and counseling
- Service coordination
- Diagnostic and evaluative medical services
- Social work services
- **Assistive technology** devices and services
- Family training, counseling, and home visits
- Early identification, screening, and assessment
- Health services necessary to enable the infant or toddler to benefit from the other early intervention services
- Transportation and related costs as necessary to ensure the infant and toddler and the family receive appropriate services.

These services are provided to infants and toddlers according to their needs as determined in the individualized family service plan (IFSP) (see the Reflect on This feature on page 104). The IFSP is structured much like the individualized education program (IEP), but it broadens the focus to include not only the individual, but also all members of the family. The IFSP must contain the following components:

1. The infant's or toddler's present levels of physical development, cognitive development, communication development, social or emotional development, and adaptive development, based on objective criteria
2. The family's resources, priorities, and concerns relating to enhancing the development of the family's infant or toddler with a disability
3. The major outcomes expected to be achieved for the infant or toddler and the family, and the criteria, procedures, and timelines used to determine the degree to which progress toward achieving the outcomes is being made and whether modifications or revisions of the outcomes or services are necessary
4. Specific early intervention services necessary to meet the unique needs of the infant or toddler and the family, including the frequency, intensity, and method of delivering services
5. The natural environments in which early intervention services shall appropriately be provided, including a justification of the extent, if any, to which the services will not be provided in a natural environment
6. The projected dates for initiation of services and the anticipated duration of the services
7. The identification of the service coordinator from the profession most immediately relevant to the infant's or toddler's or family's needs (or who is otherwise qualified to carry out all applicable responsibilities under this part) who will be responsible for the implementation of the plan and coordination with other agencies and persons
8. The steps to be taken to support the transition of the toddler with a disability to preschool or other appropriate services (IDEA 97, Sec. 636[d])

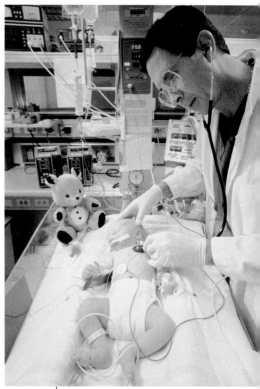

Today, infant care specialists working with sophisticated medical technology save the lives of many seriously ill newborns who only a few years ago would have died in the first days or weeks of life.

▪ ASSISTIVE TECHNOLOGY. Technology devices that help an individual with disabilities adapt to the natural settings of home, school, and family. The technology may include computers, hearing aids, wheelchairs, and so on.

IT TAKES A WHOLE VILLAGE TO DEVELOP AN IFSP

The African proverb, "It takes a whole village to raise a child," best illustrates the individual family service plan (IFSP). No one person can accurately decide what is the best treatment or care necessary for a child with special needs. That's why Part C of IDEA stipulates that infants and toddlers with disabilities must have an IFSP. The IFSP is an ongoing written service plan for children from birth to age 3 until they transition into preschool. Anything of concern to a family is outlined and highlighted in the IFSP:

- *Medical history/developmental information:* Includes diagnosis, medications, strengths, concerns such as a breakdown of the child's fine and gross motor skills, communication, social–emotional issues, and self-help as well as play and cognitive skills

- *Family interest and concerns:* Everything from housing, transportation, health and financial issues, to employment, social service programs, legal services, early intervention programs, and therapy
- *Timeline:* A breakdown in months detailing when the family would like to see events occur in a child's development; includes a plan of action, a provider, cost, and outcome
- *Preschool transition plan:* Includes what school district the child resides in, the district contact person, and a plan of action for how and when the transition to preschool services will take place.

An assigned person, known as a service coordinator, generally initiates an IFSP and works with the family to complete it as the child grows to preschool age. The service

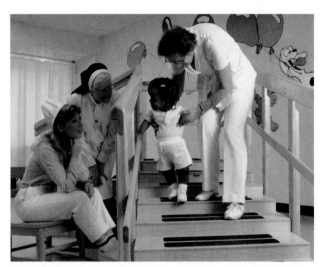

The IFSP is a team effort involving families and professionals.

coordinator works with a variety of people and agencies to ensure that the child's and family's needs are met. A family's priorities can easily change, and for that reason, the IFSP is a working, flexible document. Its focus is to help provide families with support and encourage them to seek community resources.

Source: The Individualized Family Service Plan, by Resources for Young Children and Families, 2000, Colorado Springs, CO: Author. Available: *http://www.rycf.org/ifsp.html*

■ EARLY INTERVENTION SERVICE DELIVERY

In addition to the intensive services provided in hospital newborn intensive care units, three types of basic programs are available for early intervention services: center-based, home-based, or a combination of the two (McDonnell, Hardman, McDonnell, & Kiefer-O'Donnell, 1995; Noonan & McCormick, 1993). The center-based model requires that families take their child from the home to a setting where comprehensive services are provided. These sites may be hospitals, churches, schools, or other community facilities. The centers use various instructional approaches, including both developmental and therapeutic models, to meet the needs of infants and toddlers. Noonan and McCormick have suggested that because many center-based programs are heavily furnished with "therapeutic equipment," they tend to look more like "hospital therapy rooms than an early childhood program" (1993, p. 15).

In contrast to the center-based model, a home-based program provides services to the child and family in their natural living environment. Using the resources of the home, professionals address the needs of the child in terms of individual family values and lifestyles. As suggested by Craig and Haggart (1994), home-based programs are consistent with the goals of the Americans with Disabilities Act to develop functional independence for people with disabilities in natural settings.

Finally, early intervention may be provided through a combination of services at both a center and the home. Infants or toddlers may spend some time in a center-based program, receiving instruction and therapy in individual or group settings, and also receive in-home services to promote learning and generalization in their natural environment.

Whether the intervention is delivered at a center or in the home, programs for infants and young children who are at risk or have disabilities should be based on the individual needs of the child, as well as being intensive over time, and comprehensive. Intensity refers to the frequency and amount of time an infant or child is engaged in intervention activities. An intensive approach requires that the child participate in intervention activities that involve two to three hours of contact each day, at least four or five times a week. Until the 1980s, this child-centered model of service delivery placed parents in the role of trainers, who provided direct instruction to the child and helped him or her transfer the learning activities from the therapeutic setting to the home environment. The model of parents as trainers eventually was questioned by many professionals and family members. Families were dropping out of programs, and many parents did not use the intervention techniques effectively with their children or simply preferred to be parents, not trainers (Bailey & Wolery, 1992; McDonnell et al., 1995). With the passage of PL 99-457 in 1986 (now IDEA), early intervention evolved into a more family-centered approach in which individual family needs and strengths became the basis for determining program goals, supports needed, and services to be provided.

Providing the breadth of services necessary to meet the individual needs of an infant or toddler within the family constellation requires a multidisciplinary intervention team. It should include professionals with varied experiential backgrounds—such as speech and language therapy, physical therapy, nursing, and education—and also at least one of the child's parents or his or her guardian. The team should review the IFSP at least annually and issue progress updates to the parents every six months. Coordination of early intervention services across disciplines and with the family is crucial if the goals of the program are to be realized.

The traditional academic-year programming (lasting approximately nine months) common to many public school programs is not in the best interests of infants and toddlers who are at risk or have disabilities. Continuity is essential. Services and support must be provided throughout the early years without lengthy interruptions.

■ EARLY CHILDHOOD SERVICES FOR PRESCHOOL-AGE CHILDREN WITH DISABILITIES

Services for preschool-age children begin with a referral to a local education agency in order to formally assess the type and extent of a child's perceived delays or differences from nondisabled peers of the same age. Once a child's needs have been identified and the educational team determines eligibility for special education services, appropriate developmental and age-appropriate instructional practices are implemented in a home or school-based classroom.

■ **REFERRAL AND ASSESSMENT** Programs for preschool-age children with disabilities have several important components. First, a **child-find** system is set up in each state to locate preschool-age (ages 3 to 5) children at risk and make referrals to

■ CHILD FIND. A system within a state or local area that attempts to identify all children who are disabled or at risk in order to refer them for appropriate support services.

the local education agency. Such referrals may come from parents, the family physician, health or social service agencies, or the child's day-care or preschool teacher. Referrals for preschool services may be based on a child's perceived delays in physical development (such as not walking by age 2), speech and language delays (such as nonverbal by age 3), excessive inappropriate behavior (such as frequent temper tantrums, violent behavior, extreme shyness, or excessive crying), or sensory difficulties (unresponsive to sounds or unable to visually track objects in the environment).

Following a referral, a child-study team initiates an assessment to determine whether the child is eligible for preschool special education services under IDEA. A preschool-age child with disabilities is eligible if he or she meets both of the following requirements. First, developmental delays are evident as measured by appropriate diagnostic instruments and procedures, in one or more of the following areas: physical development, cognitive development, communication development, social or emotional development, or adaptive development. Second, as a result of these delays, the child needs special education and related services (IDEA, Sec. 602, 3B).

If the child is eligible, an individualized education program (IEP) is developed. Specialists from several disciplines—including physical therapy, occupational therapy, speech and language therapy, pediatrics, social work, and special education—participate in the development and implementation of IEPs for preschool-age children.

The purpose of preschool programs for young children with disabilities is to assist them in living in and adapting to a variety of environmental settings, including home, neighborhood, and school. Depending on individual needs, preschool programs may focus on developing skills in communication, social and emotional learning, physical well-being, self-care, and coping (Davis, Kilgo, & Gamel-McCormick, 1998; Wolery, 1994). The decision regarding which skill areas are to be the focus of instruction should be based on a **functional assessment**[1] of the child and the setting where he or she spends time. Functional assessments determine the child's skills, the characteristics of the setting, and the family's needs, resources, expectations, and aspirations (Bailey & Wolery, 1992; Wolery, 1994). Through a functional assessment, professionals and parents come together to plan a program that supports the preschool-age child in meeting the demands of the home, school, or community setting. (See Table 4.1.)

■ INSTRUCTIONAL APPROACHES TO PRESCHOOL EDUCATION

Developmentally Appropriate Practice. Early child educators share the common philosophy that programs for young children should be based upon **developmentally appropriate practice (DAP).** DAP is grounded in the belief that traditionally there has been too much emphasis in preparing preschool-age children for academic learning and not enough on activities that are child initiated, such as play, exploration, social interaction, and inquiry. Child-initiated activities are based on the assumption that "young children are intrinsically motivated to learn by their desire to understand their environment" (Udell, Peters, & Templeman, 1998, p. 44). DAP is viewed as culturally sensitive because it emphasizes interaction between children and adults. Adults become "guides" for student learning rather than controlling what, where, and how students acquire knowledge.

DAP is based on helping the child achieve "normal developmental milestones." As described by McDonnell et al. (1995), regardless of a child's chronological age, if he or she acts like a 2-year-old, the learning environment should be structured in ways that are congruent to those that would facilitate learning for a 2-year-old. In other words, learning environments and teaching practices for a specific child must be based on

■ FUNCTIONAL ASSESSMENT. An approach emphasizing the relationship between individual functioning and the environment in which the individual lives, learns, and works.

■ DEVELOPMENTALLY APPROPRIATE PRACTICES (DAP). Instructional approaches that use curriculum and learning environments consistent with the child's developmental level. These approaches provide young children with opportunities to explore, discover, choose, and acquire skills that are sensitive and responsive for their ages and abilities.

---

[1]Also referred to as an ecological assessment

TABLE 4.1	Information needed to plan programs for young children with disabilities
Goals for the Child	■ What is the child's current level of developmental functioning in communication, social, physical, cognitive, and self-care areas? ■ What does the child need to be independent in the classroom, home, and community? ■ What are the effects of adaptations and assistance on the child's performance? ■ What usual patterns of responding and what relationships with environmental variables appear to influence the child's performance? ■ What are the child's most important behaviors, skills, abilities, and patterns of responding?
Child's Environments	■ In what environments (home, classroom, etc.) does the child spend time? ■ How much time is spent in each environment? ■ Who cares for and interacts with the child in those environments?
Physical Dimensions and Organization of Environment	■ What materials and toys are in each environment? ■ How are those toys and materials organized and placed about the room? ■ Can the child access all areas and materials and, if so, how? ■ How much space is available, and how many children and adults are in it? ■ What adaptations of equipment and materials are needed?
Temporal Dimensions and Organization of Routines	■ What is the child's typical daily schedule (from awakening to bedtime)? ■ How are activities within the classroom sequenced? ■ How long do activities last? ■ What routines (e.g., meals, toileting) happen every day?
Adults' Usual Roles in Activities	■ For each part of the day, what do adults do in relation to the child? ■ When do adults observe children, interact with them, and take care of organizational tasks (prepare materials)? ■ When, if ever, do adults lead activities? ■ How do adults interact with children (e.g., direct a child, respond to a child)? ■ What types of verbal interactions (e.g., questions, commands, comments) do adults use, and when?
Activity Structures	■ How is each activity in the classroom organized? ■ How does the child get into and out of each activity? ■ How does the child know what is expected in each activity? ■ What is the child expected to do in each activity? ■ How are expectations communicated to the child?

Source: From "Implementing Instruction for Young Children with Special Needs in Early Childhood Classrooms," by M. Wolery. *Including Children with Special Needs in Early Childhood Programs,* edited by M. Wolery and J. S. Wilbers, 1994, pp. 151–166. Washington, DC: National Association for the Education of Young Children.

what is expected of other young children of comparable developmental levels. DAP is strongly advocated by the National Association for the Education of Young Children (NAEYC), the nation's largest national organization for professionals in early childhood education. NAEYC has developed several guiding principles for DAP:

■ *Create a caring community of learners.* Developmentally appropriate practices occur within a context that supports the development of relationships between adults and children, among children, among teachers, and between teachers and families.

■ *Teach to enhance development and learning.* Adults are responsible for ensuring children's healthy development and learning. From birth, relationships with adults are critical determinants of children's healthy social and emotional development and serve as well as mediators of language and intellectual development.

- *Construct appropriate curriculum.* The content of the early childhood curriculum is determined by many factors, including the subject matter of the disciplines, social or cultural values, and parental input. In developmentally appropriate programs, decisions about curriculum content also take into consideration the age and experience of the learners.

- *Assess children's learning and development.* Assessment of individual children's development and learning is essential for planning and implementing appropriate curriculum. In developmentally appropriate programs, assessment and curriculum are integrated, with teachers continually engaging in observational assessment for the purpose of improving teaching and learning.

- *Establish reciprocal relationships with families.* Developmentally appropriate practices derive from deep knowledge of individual children and the context within which they develop and learn. The younger the child, the more necessary it is for professionals to acquire this knowledge through relationships with the child's family. (National Association for the Education of Young Children Position Statement, 1997)

Age-Appropriate Placements and Functional Skill Learning. While DAP is widely accepted throughout the larger early childhood community, many special educators see DAP as a base or foundation to build on in order to meet the individual needs of young children with disabilities. Early childhood programs for students with disabilities must also take into account age-appropriate placements and functional skill learning.

Age-appropriate placements emphasize the child's chronological age over developmental level. As such, a 2-year-old with developmental delays is first and foremost a 2-year-old, regardless of whether or not he or she has disabilities. A young child with disabilities should be exposed to the same instructional settings as a nondisabled peer of the same chronological age. Age-appropriate learning prepares the child to live and learn in inclusive environments with same-age peers. Arguing that DAP and age-appropriate practice are compatible, McDonnell et al. suggested that there are many ways to create learning experiences for young children that are both developmentally appropriate and age appropriate. The following shows one example:

Mark is a 4-year-old with limited gross and fine motor movement and control. His cognitive development is similar to a typically developing 11-month-old. Mark is learning to use adaptive switches to activate toys and a radio or [CD] player. Mark enjoys listening to music and toys that make noise and move simultaneously. Mark would also enjoy the lullabies and battery-operated lamb and giraffe toys that might usually be purchased for an 11-month-old. However, he also enjoys Raffi songs and songs from Disney movies, as well as automated race tracks and battery-operated dinosaurs and robots. The latter selection of music and toys would also interest other children of his age, and could provide some familiar and pleasurable experiences for Mark to enjoy in classroom and play settings with typical peers. (p. 153)

Teaching Functional Skills. Consistent with the individualized needs of the child and the expectations of the family, teaching functional skills facilitates the young child's learning in the natural setting (such as home and family). Functional skill development helps the child adapt to the demands of a given environment—that is, it creates an adaptive fit between the child and the setting in which he or she must learn to function. (See the later section in this chapter on Basic Skills, Adaptive Instruction, and Functional Life Skills.) Udell et al. (1998) indicated that in early childhood settings, functional skills are important because the child learns to be more independent and to interact positively with others in his or her immediate environment. "For example, it is probably more functional for a child to be able to carry out his or her own toileting functions independently than to be able to name 10 farm animals" (p. 46).

■ PRESCHOOL PROGRAM MODELS   Programs for preschool-age students with disabilities have been organized using home-based, school-based, or combined home- and school-based models. *Home-based programs* remain an important option for families who want their preschool-age children to spend most of their time at home. These programs concentrate on ways to teach members of the family to work directly with the child in the natural environment of the home and within the context of daily family routines (Berry & Hardman, 1998).

Beginning at age 3, the use of *school-based programs* expands considerably to meet the needs of young children with disabilities. These preschool programs may be full- or part-day self-contained special classes or inclusive classes within a general preschool or day-care program. The self-contained preschool special education classroom may be located in a special school housing other educational programs for school-age students with disabilities or in a general education school building. The students spend most, if not all, of their day alongside other preschool-age students with disabilities with similar needs, as designated in the IEP. Support personnel, such as speech and language therapists and occupational therapists, work directly with the child in the special classroom setting.

■ INCLUSIVE PRESCHOOL CLASSROOMS   In the inclusive classroom, preschool-age students with disabilities receive their educational program side by side with nondisabled peers in a regular preschool or day-care program. Effective programs are staffed by both child care providers and paraprofessionals with a special education preschool teacher in a co-teaching or consultant role. The following are nine indicators of quality for an inclusive early childhood program:

1. *A holistic view of child development.* Teachers must enter the classroom with a thorough understanding of child development to support the inclusion of diverse learners.
2. *Class as community.* Educators provide students with opportunities to enhance feelings of self-worth, social responsibility, and belonging.
3. *Collaboration.* Critical to the success of collaboration is that colleagues view each other as equals. They must share a common body of knowledge and repertoire of skills.
4. *Authentic assessment.* **Authentic assessment** procedures consist of a variety of performance-based assessments that require children to demonstrate a response in a real-life context.
5. *Heterogeneous grouping.* All children should have opportunities throughout the day to work and play in diverse and heterogeneous groups that are responsive to individual strengths and needs.
6. *Range of individualized supports and services.* Successful inclusion is dependent upon the belief that all children can learn, participate in, and benefit from all areas of the curriculum.
7. *Engagement and active learning.* "Actively engage" is a concept from classic child development theories that emphasize the importance of learning by doing in meaningful contexts.
8. *Reflective teaching.* Teachers must become good observers of their own behavior, as well as the behavior of their children. This type of thoughtful inquiry allows teachers to study individual child behavior within the context of the learning environment.

■ AUTHENTIC ASSESSMENT. An alternative to traditional use of standardized tests to measure student progress. Assessment is based on student progress in meaningful learning activities.

Inclusive preschool classrooms staffed by professionals and a special education teacher allow students with disabilities to be educated with their nondisabled peers.

9. *Multiple ways of teaching and learning.* Teachers who support diverse learners are more likely to use a variety of teaching and learning strategies that challenge the strengths and support the needs of their students. Children in these classrooms are encouraged to use multiple methods to solve problems. (Schwartz & Meyer, 1997, p. 9–10)

In a recent study (Devore & Hanley-Maxwell, 2000), child care providers identified five critical factors that contributed to successfully serving young children with disabilities in inclusive, community-based child care settings: (1) a willingness on the part of the child care provider to make inclusion work; (2) a realistic balance between the resources available in the program and the needs of the student; (3) continual problem-solving with parents; (4) access to emotional support and technical assistance from special educators and early intervention therapists; and (5) access to other supports, such as other child care providers, respite care providers, and houses of worship.

There are many reasons for the increasing number of inclusive classrooms for preschool students with disabilities. Inclusive classrooms create opportunities for social interaction and the development of friendships among children with disabilities and same-age nondisabled peers. The social development skills learned in inclusive settings are applied at home and community as well as in future educational and social settings. Nondisabled preschool-age children learn to value and accept diversity (Drew & Hardman, 2000; Schwartz, Billingsley, & McBride, 1998; Strain, 1990).

■ HEAD START **Head Start,** the nation's largest federally funded early childhood program, was enacted as law in 1965 and has served 17.7 million children over the past 35 years (U.S. Department of Health and Human Services, 1999a). The program was developed around a strong research base, suggesting that early enrichment experiences for economically disadvantaged children would better prepare them for elementary school (Davis et al., 1998). Although the original legislation did not include children with disabilities, the law was eventually expanded in 1992 to require that at least 10% of Head Start enrollment be reserved for these children. The U.S. Department of Health and Human Services (1999a) reported that of the 822,316 children in Head Start programs in 1998, children with disabilities accounted for 13% of this population. Head Start has been hailed through the years as a major breakthrough in federal support for early childhood education.

In January 1993, federal regulations for children with disabilities under Head Start were expanded to ensure that a disabilities service plan be developed to meet the needs of children with disabilities and their families, that the programs designate a coordinator of services for children with disabilities, and that the necessary special education and related services be provided for children who are designated as disabled under IDEA.

■ HEAD START. A federally funded preschool program for disadvantaged students to give them "a head start" prior to elementary school.

■ TRANSITION FROM PRESCHOOL TO ELEMENTARY SCHOOL

Transitions, although a natural and ongoing part of everyone's life, are often difficult even under the best of circumstances. For preschool-age children with disabilities and their families, the transition from early childhood programs to kindergarten can be very stressful. Early childhood programs for preschool-age children with disabilities commonly employ many adults (both professional and paraprofessional). In contrast, kindergarten programs are often not able to offer the same level of staff support, particularly in more inclusive educational settings. Additionally, children in kindergarten programs are expected to "work more independently, follow group directions, and attend to their own needs" (Rous & Hallam, 1998, p. 17). As such, it is important for preschool professionals responsible for transition planning to attend not only to the needs and skills of the individual student, but also to how he or she can match the performance demands of the elementary school and classroom setting. Conn-Powers, Ross-Allen, and Holburn (1990, p. 94) summarized the goals that professionals should focus on as they plan for the preschooler's transition to school:

- Promote the speedy adjustment of the child and family to the new educational setting.
- Enhance the child's independent and successful participation in the new educational setting.
- Ensure the uninterrupted provision of appropriate services in the least restrictive school setting.
- Support and empower the family as an equal partner in the transition process.
- Promote collaboration among all constituents in the transition process.
- Increase the satisfaction of all constituents with (1) the outcomes of the transition process, and (2) the transition process itself, including their participation.
- Increase the likelihood that the child is placed and maintained in the regular kindergarten and elementary school mainstream.

In order to identify the skills needed in the elementary school environment, the preschool transition plan should begin at least one to two years prior to the child's actual move. This move is facilitated when the early intervention specialist, the child's future kindergarten teacher, and the parents engage in a careful planning process that recognizes the significant changes that the child and the family will go through as they engage a new and unknown situation (Udell et al., 1998).

In summary, early childhood programs for children with disabilities focus on teaching skills that will improve a child's opportunities for living a rich life and on preparing the child to function successfully in family, school, and neighborhood environments. Young children with disabilities are prepared as early as possible to share meaningful experiences with same-age peers. Additionally, early childhood programs lessen the impact of conditions that may deteriorate or become more severe without timely and adequate intervention and that may prevent children from developing other secondary disabling conditions. The intended outcomes of these programs will not, however, be accomplished without consistent family participation and professional collaboration.

The Elementary School Years

The move from preschool into the elementary school years shifts the emphasis to whether the child with a disability can adapt (academically, behaviorally, and physically) to the demands of the general education environment. The degree to which the child is able to cope with these demands depends on the type and severity of the disability as well as how effectively the school will accommodate his or her needs. A student with a mild disability may be viewed

Yvonne

■ THE ELEMENTARY
SCHOOL YEARS

Yvonne left her preschool
program at age 5 to attend
her neighborhood elementary
school. From kindergarten

through sixth grade, she
divided her day between a
general education classroom
with her nondisabled friends
and a special education class.
Her educational program
during the elementary years
focused on developing basic
academic skills, learning to

manage her own personal
affairs, and participating in
social activities with her
friends. Yvonne's rate of academic learning was significantly slower than that of
other children of her age, and
she required extensive specialized instruction in reading

and arithmetic. She also
needed assistance in developing age-appropriate personal
care skills, managing her
time, socially interacting with
her peers, and participating
in recreation and leisure
activities.

---

as a discipline problem, a slow learner, or a poorly motivated child. From the school's
perspective, the differences are more pronounced for students with moderate and
severe disabilities requiring more extensive educational support. The need for ongoing special education services and supports for these individuals is evident in several
environmental settings.

■ CHARACTERISTICS OF SPECIAL EDUCATION

focus 4

Identify three characteristics
of special education that enhance learning opportunities
for students with disabilities.

Ensuring an appropriate educational experience for students with disabilities
depends upon the provision of effective special education services. Characteristics
of special education that enhance learning opportunities for students of all ages and
across multiple settings include the following:

- *Individualization*—a student-centered approach to instructional decision making
- *Intensive instruction*—frequent instructional experiences of significant duration
- *The explicit teaching of basic, adaptive, and/or functional life skills* (McLaughlin,
  Fuchs, & Hardman, 1999; National Research Council, 1997)

■ INDIVIDUALIZATION   The hallmark of special education is **individualization**—developing and implementing an appropriate educational experience based
on the individual needs of each student. Research indicates that fundamental differences characterize the ways in which special educators approach instruction, distinguishing them from their general education colleagues. Hocutt (1996) suggested
that instruction in general education is most often oriented to the masses and centered on the curriculum:

*Undifferentiated large-group instruction appears to be the norm in general education. Indi-
vidual assignments, small group work, and student pairing occur, but much less frequently
than whole-class instruction. Teachers typically follow the sequence of lessons outlined in
teachers' manuals and focus on content coverage. . . . When surveyed, teachers do not perceive themselves as having the skills for adapting instruction in ways that facilitate individual or small-group instruction. (p. 81)*

Special education, on the other hand, is designed to meet the unique needs of every
student, regardless of educational need or ability. Using an individually referenced
approach to decision making, special education teachers must continually plan and
adjust curriculum and instruction in response to the student. Teachers must have at
their disposal multiple ways to adapt curriculum, modify their instructional
approaches, and motivate their students to learn (Downing, 1996; National Research
Council, 1997; Nevin, 1998). Hardman, McDonnell, and Welch (1998) suggested that

■ INDIVIDUALIZATION. A student-
centered approach to instructional decision making.

the vast majority of teachers, whether in general or special education, do not have expertise in both the subject matter being taught and in adapting curriculum and instruction. Thus, general and special educators need (1) to acquire a core of knowledge and skills that facilitates their ability to teach *all* students, and (2) to work collaboratively in meeting the instructional needs of students with disabilities.

■ INTENSIVE INSTRUCTION **Intensive instruction** involves (1) actively engaging students in their learning by requiring high rates of appropriate response to the material presented, (2) carefully matching instruction to student ability and skill level, (3) providing instructional cues and prompts to support learning and then fading them when appropriate, and (4) providing detailed feedback that is directly focused on the task the student is expected to complete (McLaughlin et al., 1999). Intensive instruction may involve both group and one-to-one learning.

Research suggests that intensive instruction can significantly improve academic achievement and functional skill levels of students with disabilities (Alexander et al., 1991; Billingsley, Liberty, & White, 1994; Torgesen, 1996; Wasik & Slavin, 1993). In the area of learning disabilities, Lyon (1996) reported that "intensive instruction of appropriate duration provided by trained teachers can remediate the deficient reading skills of many children" (p. 70). This is exemplified in a 1991 study of severely dyslexic children, in which Alexander et al. found that an intensive program of 65 hours of individual instruction in addition to group instruction resulted in significant gains in reading skill. In the area of severe disabilities, Billingsley et al. (1994) found that one-to-one intensive instruction resulted in significant gains in functional skills (such as dressing, money management, sexual behavior, etc.).

■ BASIC SKILLS, ADAPTIVE INSTRUCTION, AND FUNCTIONAL LIFE SKILLS APPROACHES In addition to needing individualized and intensive instruction, students with disabilities require more structured and teacher-directed approaches to learning than do students who are not disabled (Harris & Graham, 1995; Tarver, 1996). Learning is a continual process of adaptation for students with disabilities as they attempt to meet the demands of school. These students do not learn as quickly or as efficiently as their classmates and are constantly fighting a battle against time and failure. They must somehow learn to deal with a system that is often rigid and allows little room for learning or behavior differences. Students with mild disabilities must also adapt to a teaching process that may be oriented toward the majority of students within a general classroom and not based on individualized assessment of needs or personalized instruction. Despite these obstacles, however, students with disabilities can learn social and academic skills that will orient them toward striving for success rather than fighting against failure. Success can be achieved only when educators remain flexible, constantly adjusting to meet the needs of these students.

Three general types of instruction may be used when teaching students with disabilities: basic skills, **adaptive instruction,** and **functional life skills.** The basic skills approach stresses that the student must learn a specified set of sequenced skills, each a prerequisite to the next. This process, sometimes referred to as the *developmental approach,* can be illustrated by briefly analyzing the teaching of reading. When learning to read, the student must acquire many individual skills and then be able to link them together as a whole. The student then has the ability to decode abstract information and turn it into meaningful content. When one of the separate skills required for reading is not learned, the entire process may break down. The basic skills approach, whether in reading or any other content area, lays the groundwork for further development and higher levels of functioning.

■ INTENSIVE INSTRUCTION. An instructional approach that involves (1) actively engaging students in their learning by requiring high rates of appropriate response; (2) carefully matching instruction to student ability and skill level; (3) providing instructional cues and prompts to support learning and then fading them when appropriate; and (4) providing detailed feedback directly focused on the task the student is expected to complete.

■ ADAPTIVE INSTRUCTION. Instruction that modifies the learning environment to accommodate unique learner characteristics.

■ FUNCTIONAL LIFE SKILLS. Practical skills that facilitate a person's participation and involvement in family, school, and community life.

focus 5

What is meant by adaptive fit and adaptive instruction for students with disabilities?

However, not all children learn basic skills within the time frame dictated by schools. The degree to which a student is able to cope with the requirements of a school setting and the extent to which the school recognizes and accommodates individual diversity are known as **adaptive fit.** This fit is dynamic and constantly changes in the negotiations between the individual and the environment.

For the student with a disability, adaptive fit may involve learning and applying various strategies that will facilitate the ability to meet the expectations of a learning environment. Such a student may find that the requirements for success within a general education classroom are beyond his or her adaptive capabilities and that the system is unwilling to accommodate academic, behavioral, physical, sensory, or communicative differences. As a result, the student develops negative attitudes toward school. Imagine yourself in a setting that constantly disapproves of how you act and what you do, a place in which activities are difficult and overwhelming, a setting in which your least desirable qualities are emphasized. What would you think about spending more than 1,000 hours a year in such a place?

Over the years, educators have responded in several ways to mismatches between the needs of the student and the demands of the learning environment. The more traditional approach was to leave the student in the negative situation and do nothing until inevitable failure occurs. This changed with the advent of special education and the continuum of placements whereby the student is pulled out of a setting and moved to a classroom or school more conducive to individual needs. In this approach, no attempt is made to modify the student's current environment. A third alternative has been to seek ways of creating a better adaptive fit between the student and the learning environment through a process known as *adaptive instruction.* Adaptive instruction seeks to enhance student performance in a given subject by modifying the *way* in which instruction is delivered and by changing the environment *where* the learning takes place. This approach uses a variety of instructional procedures, materials, and alternative learning sequences in the classroom setting to help students master content consistent with their needs, abilities and interests (Bradley & King-Sears, 1997; Friend & Bursuck, 1998; Wood, 1997a). For example, a student who is unable to memorize multiplication tables may be taught to use a calculator to complete the task. Learning to use the calculator would likely not take place in a large group setting but in a one-to-one or small group situation. The task's degree of difficulty is modified to fit with the conceptual ability of the student, and the alteration within the learning environment allows the student to be taught an *explicit* skill through *intensive* instruction.

For some time, the general classroom teacher has had to work with students who have disabilities without the assistance of any effective support systems. This is no longer the case in many of today's schools. The emergence of inclusive education programs in elementary schools throughout the United States has strengthened collaborative efforts between the general education classroom teacher and the network of supports available in the schools. When student need and ability make it appropriate, instruction in *functional life skills* can be implemented. Students are taught only those skills that will help them succeed in practical matters related to the natural setting, whether it be the classroom, family, or neighborhood. Functional life skills may include daily living (such as self-help, personal finances, and community travel), personal–social development (such as learning **self-determination** and socially responsible behaviors), communication skills, recreational and leisure activities, and employment skills.

The functional life skills approach is based on the premise that, if these practical skills are not taught through formal instruction, they will not be learned. Most students do not need to be taught functional skills because they have already learned them

▪ ADAPTIVE FIT. Compatibility between demands of a task or setting and a person's needs and abilities.

▪ SELF-DETERMINATION. The ability of a person to consider options and make appropriate choices regarding residential life, work, and leisure time.

through everyday experience. This does not mean that students being taught through a functional approach are not also learning basic academic skills. Instruction may occur in academic content areas, but not in the same sequence as in the basic skills approach. For example, a functional life skills reading approach would initially teach frequently used words that are necessary for survival within the environment (e.g., danger, exit, and rest room signs) and then pair them directly with an environmental cue.

■ THE SPECIAL EDUCATION REFERRAL, PLANNING, AND PLACEMENT PROCESS

The special education referral, planning, and placement process, as mandated in the Individuals with Disabilities Education Act (IDEA), is intended to ensure that all eligible students with disabilities have the opportunity to receive a free and appropriate public education. The process involves four sequential phases: (1) initiating the referral, (2) assessing student eligibility and educational need, (3) developing the individualized education program (IEP), and (4) determining the least restrictive environment. (See nearby Table 4.2)

focus 6

Identify the four phases of the special education referral, planning, and placement process.

■ **PHASE 1: INITIATING THE REFERRAL**   Referral for special education can occur at different times for different students, depending on the type and severity of the need. Students with more severe disabilities are likely to be referred prior to elementary school and have probably received early intervention and preschool services. For children with mild disabilities, referral could be initiated at any time during elementary school as they appear to have difficulty in academic learning, in exhibiting appropriate behavior, or in overall development. For these children, the general education teacher is the most likely referral source.

The referral begins with a request to the school's **child-study team** (sometimes referred to as a *special services committee*) for an assessment to determine the student's qualification for special education services. At a minimum, the child-study team consists of the school principal, the school psychologist, and a special education teacher. It may also include a general education teacher, a speech and language specialist, a school nurse, an occupational therapist, or other support personnel as determined by the child's needs. Once the team receives the referral, it may choose one of two paths: (1) attempt to modify or adapt current instruction in the general education class, or (2) conduct a formal evaluation to determine the student's eligibility for special education services.

The first alternative (sometimes referred to as a *prereferral intervention*) is intended to provide additional support services to children who may be at risk for educational failure without inappropriately placing the student in a special education program. Prior to implementing any instructional and/or environmental adaptations in the general education classroom, parents are notified that the child is having difficulty and are asked to meet with the school's child-study team. The team and the parents discuss the student's needs and recommend possible changes. Adaptations vary according to student need but most often involve modifying curriculum, changing a seating arrangement, changing the length and difficulty of homework or classroom assignments, using peer tutors or volunteer parents to assist with instructional programs, or implementing a behavior management program. It is the responsibility of the general education teacher to implement the modified instruction and to assess the student's progress over a predetermined period of time. If the modifications are successful, there will be no further need to make a referral for special education. However, if the team determines that the student's educational progress is not satisfactory, the referral process for special education services continues.

■ CHILD-STUDY TEAM. A term synonymous with *multidisciplinary team* or *special services team*. Required by IDEA, this team develops an individualized education program for the child with a disability.

Phase 1 Initiating the Referral	Phase 2 Assessing Student Eligibility and Educational Need	Phase 3 Developing the Individualized Education Program (IEP)	Phase 4 Determining the Least Restrictive Environment (LRE)
■ School personnel or parents indicate concern about student's learning, behavior, or overall development. ■ If referral is made by school personnel, parents are notified of concerns. ■ Child-study team decides to provide additional support services and adapt student's instructional program prior to initiating formal assessment for eligibility. (This step may be bypassed and team may choose to immediately seek parental permission to evaluate the student's eligibility for special education.) ■ School seeks and receives parents' permission to evaluate student's eligibility for special education services. (This will occur if the additional support services and adaptive instruction are unsuccessful OR if the team has chosen to move directly to a formal evaluation to determine student eligibility.)	■ Multidisciplinary and nondiscriminatory assessment tools and strategies are used to evaluate student's eligibility for special education services. ■ Child study team reviews assessment information to determine (1) whether student meets eligibility requirements for special education services under 1 of 12 disability classifications or meets the definition of developmentally delayed (for students between ages 3 and 9), and (2) whether student requires special education services. ■ If team agrees that the student is eligible for and needs special education services, then the process moves to phase 3: developing the IEP.	■ Appropriate professionals to serve on an IEP team are identified. A team coordinator is appointed. ■ Parents (and student when appropriate) participate as equal members of the team and are provided with written copies of all assessment information. ■ Team meets and agrees upon the essential elements of the student's individualized education program plan: – Measurable annual goals and objectives/benchmarks – Skill areas needing special education and related services – Persons responsible for providing services and supports to meet student's identified needs – Criteria/evaluation procedures to assess progress – Student's access to the general education curriculum – Student's participation in statewide or school district assessments – Beginning and end dates for special education services – A process for reporting to parents on student's progress toward annual goals – Positive behavioral intervention plan if needed	■ Identify potential educational placements based on student's annual goals and special education services to be provided. ■ Adhering to the principle that students with disabilities are to be educated with their nondisabled peers to the maximum extent appropriate, justify any removal of the child from the general education classroom. ■ With parents involved in the decision making process, determine student's appropriate educational placement. ■ Document on the student's IEP justification for any removal from the general education classroom. ■ Team members agree in writing to the essential elements of the IEP and to the educational placement where special education and related services are to be provided. ■ As members of the IEP team, parents must consent in writing to the agreed-upon educational placement for their child.

If a formal referral for special education services is determined to be the appropriate path, the child-study team reviews the information documented by the classroom teacher and other education professionals, describing the child's needs. Documentation may include results from achievement tests, classroom performance tests, samples of student work, behavioral observations, or anecdotal notes (such as teacher journal entries). The team decides whether additional assessment information is needed in order to determine eligibility for special education. At this time a written notice must be provided to parents regarding their child's educational performance indicating that the school proposes to initiate or change the identification, evaluation, or educational placement of the child (U.S. Department of Education, 1999). The content of the notice must include all of the following:

- A full explanation of the procedural safeguards available to the parents
- A description of the action proposed or refused by the school, why the school proposes or refuses to take the action, and a description of any options the school considered and the reasons why those options were rejected
- A description of each evaluation procedure, test, record, or report the school used as a basis for the proposal or refusal
- A description of any other factors relevant to the school's proposal or refusal to take action

Following a written notice the school must seek consent in writing from the parents in order to move ahead with the evaluation process. Informed consent means that parents

- have been fully informed of all information relevant to the activity for which consent is sought, in their native language or other mode of communication.
- understand and agree in writing to the carrying out of the activity for which his or her consent is sought, and the consent describes that activity and lists the record (if any) that will be released and to whom.
- understand that the granting of consent is voluntary on the part of the parent and may be revoked at any time.

■ PHASE 2: ASSESSING EDUCATIONAL NEED AND ELIGIBILITY
Once written consent to evaluate has been obtained from parents, the child-study team moves ahead to assess the student's educational need. The purpose of this assessment is to evaluate whether the student meets eligibility criteria under IDEA and to determine the need for special education services. The assessment should include the student's performance in both school and home environments. When the assessment process is complete, a decision is made regarding the student's eligibility for special education and his or her disability classification.

Presently, the most common way to classify students for special education services is to categorize them into 1 of 12 disability areas (such as specific learning disabilities, autism, etc.) or their counterparts as mandated in state law. IDEA 97 also allows states or LEAs (local education agencies) the option of classifying students with disabilities between the ages of 3 through 9 as developmentally delayed. Developmental delays may be in one or more of the following areas: physical development, cognitive development, communication development, social or emotional development, or adaptive development.

Proponents for maintaining the categorical approach argue that each of the 12 categories represents unique characteristics and needs. For example, students with behavior disorders have different traits and instructional needs than those with learning disabilities or mental retardation. According to the categorical approach,

Snapshot

Ricardo

Ricardo, a third-grader at Bloomington Hill Elementary School, has recently been referred by his teacher, Ms. Thompson, to the school's special services committee for an evaluation. During the first four months of school, Ricardo has continued to fall further behind in reading and language. He entered third grade with some skills in letter and sound recognition, but had difficulty reading and comprehending material beyond a first-grade level. It was also clear to Ms. Thompson that Ricardo's language development was delayed as well. He had a very limited expressive vocabulary and had some difficulty following directions if more than one or two steps were involved.

Ricardo's mother, Maria Galleghos (a single parent), was contacted by Ms. Thompson to inform her that she would like to refer Ricardo for an in-depth evaluation of his reading and language skills. A representative from the school would be calling her to explain what the evaluation meant and to get her approval for the necessary testing. The school psychologist, Jean Andreas, made the call to Ms. Galleghos. During the phone conversation Ms. Galleghos reminded the school psychologist that the primary language spoken in the home was Spanish even though Ricardo, his parents, and siblings spoke English as well. Ms. Andreas indicated that the assessment would be conducted in both Spanish and English in order to determine if Ricardo's problems were related to a disability in reading or problems with English as a second language.

Following written approval from Ricardo's mother, the school special services team conducted an evaluation of Ricardo's academic performance. The formal evaluation included achievement tests, classroom performance tests, samples of Ricardo's work, behavioral observations, and anecdotal notes from Ms. Thompson. An interview with Mrs. Galleghos was conducted as part of the process to gain her perceptions of Ricardo's strengths and problem areas and to give her the opportunity to relate pertinent family history.

The evaluation confirmed his teacher's concerns. Ricardo was more than two years below what was expected for a child his age in both reading and language development. Ricardo's difficulties in these areas did not seem to be primarily related to the fact that he was bilingual, but the issue of English as a second language would need to be carefully taken into consideration in developing an appropriate learning experience.

The team determined that Ricardo qualified for special education services as a student with a specific learning disability. Once again, Ms. Andreas contacted Mrs. Galleghos with the results, indicating that Ricardo qualified for special education services in reading and language. Ms. Andreas pointed out that as a parent of a student with an identified disability, she had some specific legal rights, which would be further explained to her both in writing and orally.

One of those rights is to participate as a partner in the development of Ricardo's individualized education program (IEP). Ms. Andreas further explained that a meeting would be set up at a mutually convenient time to develop a plan to assist Ricardo over the next year. Prior to that formal meeting, however, Ms. Andreas asked Ms. Galleghos to meet with her and the special education teacher, Mr. Lomas, to talk about how IEP teams work and what everyone needed to do in order to be prepared and work together to help Ricardo. Ms. Galleghos was asked to think about the long-range goals she has for Ricardo. What did she see as important for Ricardo to learn in school? What were her experiences at home that would help the team better understand Ricardo's needs and interests, particularly in the areas of reading and language development?

Source: From *Lifespan Perspectives on the Family and Disability* (p. 184), by J. Berry and M. Hardman, 1998, Boston: Allyn & Bacon.

---

using a single label to identify all these students will not result in meeting their educational needs. (Bryan, Bay, Lopez-Reyna, & Donahue, 1991; Lyon, 1996; Walker & Bullis, 1991)

Other professionals argue that such classification prohibits clearly defining or adequately differentiating the needs of these students in a classroom setting (Gottlieb, Alter, & Gottlieb, 1991; Kliewer & Biklen, 1996; Lilly, 1992; Reynolds, 1991). Kliewer and Biklen (1996) stated, "Labels block the essential agenda of good teaching, namely, inquiry through dialogue and interaction, teacher with student" (p. 93). Finally, Reynolds (1991) indicated that the traditional approach to categorization results in unnecessary separation of students and "represents a large and expensive error" (p. 31). Regardless of the approach to disability classification, once a student's eligibility for special education services is established, the next phase is developing the IEP.

■ PHASE 3: DEVELOPING THE IEP   The cornerstone of a free and appropriate public education as defined in IDEA is the IEP (National Information Center for Children and Youth with Disabilities, 1999; Schrag, 1996). Once it has been determined that the student is eligible for special education services under IDEA 97, the next step is to establish an IEP team as determined by the evaluation of the student's educational needs. At a minimum this team consists of the student's parents, the student (when appropriate), a special education teacher, a general education teacher (if the student is participating in the general education environment), and a representative of the local education agency (LEA). As stated in IDEA 97, the LEA representative must be qualified to "provide, or supervise the provision of, specially designed instruction to meet the unique needs of children with disabilities" (20 U.S.C. 1414[d]). This person must also be knowledgeable regarding the general education curriculum and the availability of resources within the district or agency. IDEA 97 requires that someone must be available (either a current team member or someone from outside of the team such as a school psychologist) to interpret the results of the student evaluations. At the discretion of the parents or district/agency, other individuals with knowledge or special expertise, including related services specialists, may also be invited to participate on the IEP team.

Each IEP team should have a coordinator (such as the special education teacher, school psychologist, or school principal) who serves as liaison between the school and the family. The coordinator has the responsibility to (1) inform parents and respond to any concerns they may have regarding the IEP process, (2) assist parents in developing specific goals they would like to see their child achieve, (3) schedule IEP meetings that are mutually convenient for both team members and parents, and (4) lead the IEP meetings. Prior to the initial IEP meeting, parents should be provided with written copies of all assessment information on their child. Individual conferences with members of the IEP team or a full team meeting may be necessary prior to developing the IEP. This will further assist parents in understanding and interpreting evaluation information. Analysis of the assessment information should include a summary of the child's strengths as well as areas in which the child may require special education or related services beyond his or her current program.

Once there is mutual agreement between educators and parents on the interpretation of the assessment results, the team coordinator organizes and leads the IEP meeting(s). Such meeting(s) are meant to achieve the following purposes:

- Document each student's present levels of performance.
- Agree upon measurable annual goals and objectives/ benchmarks.
- Identify skill areas needing special education (including physical education) and related services, the persons responsible for delivering these services, and the criteria/evaluation procedures to assess progress.
- Document student access to the general education curriculum.
- Document student participation in state and districtwide assessment programs with individual modifications or adaptations made, as necessary, in how the tests are administered. For children who cannot participate in regular assessments, the team must document use of state-developed **alternate assessments.**
- Establish beginning and end dates for special education services.
- Determine a process for reporting to parents on student progress toward annual goals.

See Figure 4.1, a sample individualized education program plan.

■ ALTERNATE ASSESSMENTS. Assessments mandated in IDEA 1997 for students who are unable to participate in required state- or districtwide assessments. They ensure that all students, regardless of the severity of their disabilities, are included in the state's accountability system.

FIGURE 4.1   A sample individualized education plan (IEP)

Student's Primary Classification	Serious Emotional Disturbance
Secondary Classification	None

Student Name   _Diane_

Date of Birth   _5-3-90_

Primary Language:
   HOME   _English_   Student   _English_

Date of IEP Meeting   _April 27, 2001_

Entry Date to Program   _April 27, 2001_

Projected Duration of Services   _One school year_

Services Required   _Specify amount of time in educational and/or related services per day or week_

General Education Class   _4–5 hours p/day_

Resource Room   _1–2 hours p/day_

Special Ed Consultation in General Ed Classroom   _Co-teaching and consultation with general education teacher in the areas of academic and adaptive skills as indicated in annual goals and short-term objectives._

Self-Contained   _none_

Related Services   _Group counseling sessions twice weekly with guidance counselor. Counseling to focus on adaptive skill development as described in annual goals and short-term objectives_

P.E. Program   _45 min. daily in general ed PE class with support from adapted PE teacher as necessary_

Assessment

Intellectual   _WISC-R_

Educational   _Key Math Woodcock Reading_

Behavioral/Adaptive   _Burks_

Speech/Language   _____

Other

Vision   _Within normal limits_

Hearing   _Within normal limits_

Classroom Observation Done
   Dates   _1/15–2/25/2001_
Personnel Conducting Observation   _School Psychologist, Special Education Teacher, General Education Teacher_

Present Level of Performance Strengths
   1) Polite to teachers and peers
   2) Helpful and cooperative in the classroom
   3) Good grooming skills
   4) Good in sports activities

Access to General Education Curriculum

Diane will participate in all content areas within the general education curriculum. Special education supports and services will be provided in the areas of math and reading.

Effect of Disability on Access to General Education Curriculum

Emotional disabilities make it difficult for Diane to achieve at expected grade level performance in general education curriculum in the areas of reading and math. It is expected that this will further impact her access to the general education curriculum in other content areas (such as history, biology, English) as she enters junior high school.

Participation in Statewide or District Assessments

Diane will participate in all state and districtwide assessments of achievement.   No adaptations or modifications required for participation.

Justification for Removal from General Education Classroom

Diane's objectives require that she be placed in a general education classroom with support from a special education teacher for the majority of the school day.   Based on adaptive behavior assessment and observations, Diane will receive instruction in a resource room for approximately one to two hours per day in the areas of social skill development.

Reports to Parents on Progress toward Annual Goals

Parents will be informed of Diane's progress through weekly reports of progress on short-term goals, monthly phone calls from general ed teachers, special education teachers, and school psychologist, and regularly scheduled report cards at the end of each term.

FIGURE 4.1 *(continued)*

Areas Needing Specialized Instruction and Support

Team Signatures _____ IEP Review Date _____

LEA Rep. _____

Parent _____

1. Adaptive Skills

Sp Ed Teacher _____

- Limited interaction skills with peers and adults

Gen Ed Teacher _____

- Excessive facial tics and grimaces

School Psych _____

- Difficulty staying on task in content subjects, especially reading and math

Student (as appropriate) _____

- Difficulty expressing feelings, needs, and interests

Related Services Personnel (as appropriate) _____

2. Academic Skills

Objective Criteria and Evaluation Procedures _____

- Significantly below grade level in math—3.9

- Significantly below grade level in reading—4.3

Annual Review: _____   Date: _____

Comments/Recommendations

IEP—Annual Goals and Short-Term Objectives	Persons Responsible	Objective Criteria and Evaluation Procedures
#1 ANNUAL GOAL: *Diane will improve her interaction skills with peers and adults.*	*General education teacher and special ed teacher (resource room)*	*Classroom observations and documented data on target behavior*
S.T. OBJ. *Diane will initiate conversation with peers during an unstructured setting twice daily.*	*School psychologist consultation*	
S.T. OBJ. *When in need of assistance, Diane will raise her hand and verbalize her needs to teachers or peers without prompting 80% of the time.*		

FIGURE 4.1 (continued)

IEP—Annual Goals and Short-Term Objectives	Persons Responsible	Objective Criteria and Evaluation Procedures
#2 ANNUAL GOAL: Diane will increase her ability to control hand and facial movements.	General education teacher and special ed teacher (resource room)	Classroom observations and documented data on target behavior
S.T. OBJ. During academic work, Diane will keep her hands in an appropriate place and use writing materials correctly 80% of the time.	School psychologist consultation	
S.T. OBJ. Diane will maintain a relaxed facial expression with teacher prompt 80% of the time. Teacher prompt will be faded over time.		
#3 ANNUAL GOAL: Diane will improve her ability to remain on task during academic work.	General education teacher and special ed teacher (resource room)	Classroom observations and documented data on target behavior
S.T. OBJ. Diane will work independently on an assigned task with teacher prompt 80% of the time.	School psychologist consultation	
S.T. OBJ. Diane will complete academic work as assigned 90% of the time.		
#4 ANNUAL GOAL: Diane will improve her ability to express her feelings.	General education teacher and special ed teacher (resource room)	Classroom observations and documented data on target behavior
S.T. OBJ. When asked how she feels, Diane will give an adequate verbal description of her feelings or moods with teacher prompting at least 80% of the time.	School psychologist consultation	
S.T. OBJ. Given a conflict or problem situation, Diane will state her feelings to teachers and peers 80% of the time.		
#5 ANNUAL GOAL: Diane will improve math skills by one grade level.	Collaboration of general education teacher and special education teacher through co-teaching and consultation	Precision teaching Addison Wesley Math Program Scope and Sequence Districtwide Assessment of Academic Achievement
S.T. OBJ. Diane will improve rate and accuracy in oral 1- and 2-digit division facts to 50 problems per minute without errors.		
S.T. OBJ. Diane will improve her ability to solve word problems involving $t - x - v$.		
#6 ANNUAL GOAL: Diane will improve reading skills by one grade level.	Collaboration of general education teacher and special education teacher through co-teaching and consultation	Precision teaching Barnell & Loft Scope and Sequence Districtwide Assessment of Academic Achievement
S.T. OBJ. Diane will answer progressively more difficult comprehension questions in designated reading skills program.		
S.T. OBJ. Diane will increase her rate and accuracy of vocabulary words to 80 wpm without errors.		

PHASE 4: DETERMINING THE LEAST RESTRICTIVE ENVIRONMENT
A student's educational placement is determined only after educators and parents have agreed upon annual goals and short-term objectives. The decision regarding placement rests upon the answers to two questions: First, what is the appropriate placement for the student, given his or her annual goals? Second, which of the placement alternatives under consideration is consistent with the least restrictive environment? As stated in IDEA, the student is to be educated with nondisabled peers to the maximum extent appropriate. To ensure that this principle is applied in making placement decisions, IDEA begins with the premise that the general education classroom is where *all* children belong. As such, any movement away from the general education class must be justified and documented on the student's IEP.

Finally, decisions regarding the appropriate placement for a student are most successful when parents are viewed as valued and equal participants in the process. Parents must be fully involved in and eventually consent to the educational placement for their child. Parents should be encouraged not only to share their expectations for the child, but also to express approval for or concerns about the goals, objectives, resources, or timelines that are being proposed by educators. The IEP must be the result of a collaborative process that reflects the views of both the school and the family.

Inclusive Elementary Classrooms and Schools

Since the publication of *A Nation at Risk* (National Commission on Excellence in Education, 1983), a great deal of effort has been expended to identify characteristics that taken together would constitute an effective school for *all* students. There seems to be considerable agreement about the key factors that contribute to a student's success in both school and postschool adjustment. Schools are most successful when they have

- high expectations for success that are linked with a clear and focused mission.
- strong instructional leadership with frequent monitoring of student progress.
- positive relationships with families.
- opportunities for *all students* to learn.

Effective schools are also inclusive schools. Several factors appear to contribute directly to a school's ability to meet the needs of all students, including those with disabilities.

CHARACTERISTICS OF EFFECTIVE INCLUSIVE SCHOOLS

Inclusive schools are characterized by a schoolwide support system that uses both general and special education resources in combination to benefit all students in the school (Ainscow, 1999; Bradley & King-Sears, 1997; Montgomery, 1994; Shulman & Doughty, 1995; Wade & Zone, 2000). The leadership of the school principal is vital. The principal should openly support the inclusion of all students in the activities of the school, advocate for the necessary resources to meet student needs, and strongly encourage cooperative learning and peer support programs (Gee, 1996; Giangreco, Cloninger, & Iverson, 1994; Stainback, Stainback, & Ayres, 1996; Villa & Thousand, 1992). Inclusive classrooms are characterized by a philosophy that celebrates diversity, rewards **collaboration** among professionals, and teaches students how to help and support one another.

Inclusive schools provide services and support to students with disabilities in age-appropriate classrooms within a neighborhood school—the **home school.**

COLLABORATION. As applied in educational settings, the process in which one or more people work together to attain a common goal. Such collaboration is sometimes referred to as *professional partnerships.*

HOME SCHOOL. The school the child would attend if not identified as having a disability.

focus 7
Describe the characteristics of effective inclusive schools and classrooms.

Reflect on This

■ **SCHOOLWIDE APPROACHES**
Inclusion is not a single "pilot" or special inclusion class. The philosophy and practice of inclusive education are accepted by all stakeholders. As a consequence, the school brings together the full range of students, educational personnel, and fiscal and other resources.

■ **ALL CHILDREN CAN LEARN**
Inclusive schools have a belief that all children can learn and that all benefit when that learning is done together.

■ **A SENSE OF COMMUNITY**
The belief is that all children belong and that diversity among students is a positive characteristic for the school (and for society). A child does not have to "prove" his or her way in order to be included.

■ **SERVICES BASED ON NEED RATHER THAN LOCATION**
Each student is recognized as an individual, with strengths and needs, not as a label or as a member of a category. Further, the response to those needs is seen as the provision of services.

■ **NATURAL PROPORTIONS**
Students attend their home school, thus ensuring that each school (and class) has a natural proportion of students with and without disabilities.

■ **SUPPORTS ARE PROVIDED IN GENERAL EDUCATION**
Schools recognize that all students have special needs. In doing so, they do not equate this with the need for separate programs. Rather than addressing those needs in separate locations or programs, in the language of the federal law, supplemental aids and support services are pro-

vided in the general education environment.

■ **TEACHER COLLABORATION**
Various models enable educators to work collaboratively, for example, as co-teachers, in team teaching, through consultation, and in "push-in" programs for special services. Programs of professional development, as well as time for teachers to work collaboratively, are integral in inclusive schools.

■ **CURRICULUM ADAPTATION**
Drawing from the school's general curriculum, inclusion provides adaptations to enable all students to benefit from the common curriculum.

■ **ENHANCED INSTRUCTIONAL STRATEGIES**
Inclusive education requires a wide range of instructional strategies, which enable all students to learn in recognition of students' differences in

intelligence, learning style, strengths, and limitations. These include cooperative learning, peer instruction, hands-on activities, learning outside of the classroom, and the use of instructional technology.

■ **STANDARDS AND OUTCOMES**
The learning outcome for students with disabilities is drawn from that expected of students in general. Their performance, with necessary adaptations and modifications in the measurement instruments and procedures, is incorporated in the school's overall performance. In other words, everybody counts.

Source: From "Inclusive Education: A Requirement of a Democratic Society," by D. K. Lipsky and A. Gartner. *Inclusive Education: World Yearbook of Education,* edited by H. Daniels and P. Garner, 1999, pp. 7–18. London: Kogan Page.

(Giangreco et al., 1994; Hardman et al., 1998; Lipsky & Gartner, 1999; McLaughlin & Warren, 1992; National Association of State Boards of Education, 1992). McDonnell (1993) further suggested that an effective inclusive school is one in which (1) educational programming for all students is individualized, (2) necessary support is provided to all students to ensure their success across learning environments, (3) educational practices have been validated, and (4) the school uses a transdisciplinary model to deliver services. A transdisciplinary model uses a collaborative or team approach to instruction. Team members (such as general educators, special educators, school psychologists, or speech and language therapists) cooperate in developing and implementing a student's instructional program. (See the nearby Reflect on This feature.)

■ COLLABORATION THROUGH SCHOOLWIDE ASSISTANCE AND SUPPORT

In the inclusive classroom, there is something for everyone. Teachers and students work together in a problem-solving approach to meet a common goal and ensure that the needs of all students are met (Ainscow, 1999; Bradley & Switlick, 1997; Hobbs & Westling, 1998; Hunt, Staub, Alwell, & Goetz, 1994; Jorgensen, 1992; Shulman & Doughty, 1995; Welch, 2000). Teachers may take on a variety of roles, depending on the need and situation; for example, a teacher may move into the role of "expert" because he or she has more knowledge or skill in a content area. Through such reciprocity, educators share their expertise with one another in order to achieve a common goal. Teachers will move in and out of the role of expert as a part of the collaboration process. Collaboration should always be viewed as a cooperative, not a competitive, endeavor.

Collaboration may be defined "as *a dynamic framework* for educational efforts which endorses collegial, interdependent and co-equal styles of interaction between at least two partners working jointly together to achieve common goals in a decision-making process that is influenced by cultural and systemic factors" (Welch & Sheridan, 1995, p. 11). Several models for partnerships among general educators, special educators, and other support professionals in the public schools have been conceptualized and practiced in an effort to enhance each student's educational experience. In the next three sections, we will discuss three of these models: the **consulting teacher,** the resource room teacher, and teacher, or **teacher assistance teams.** Although we discuss each of the models independently, they often interact in providing schoolwide assistance and support to meet the needs of all students in a classroom setting. Services provided through each collaborative model are intended to support a student in meeting the demands of the curriculum in a general education environment.

■ THE CONSULTING TEACHER   The general education classroom teacher at the elementary level is often expected to teach nearly every school-related subject area. This teacher is responsible for teaching the basic subjects—reading, writing, and arithmetic—as well as developing students' appreciation for the arts, good citizenship, and physical health. This teacher is trained as a generalist, acquiring basic knowledge of every subject area. However, when the general education classroom teacher is confronted with instructional needs beyond his or her experience and training, the result is often frustration for the teacher and failure for the student. Given the present structure of public education (large class sizes and limited assistance to the classroom teacher), it is unrealistic and unnecessary for classroom teachers to become specialists in every school subject.

Many school districts offer support to general education classroom teachers through the services of specialists with extensive background in certain areas, such as reading, arithmetic, language, motor development, and behavior and classroom management techniques. Professionals in these areas are usually referred to as consulting teachers, although the terms *support teachers, curriculum specialists, master teachers,* and *itinerant teachers* may also be used.

Consulting teachers are professionals with training beyond a basic teacher certification program and have advanced knowledge of instructional strategies across one or more subject content areas (such as reading). They build mutually trusting relationships through positive interactions with other professionals, are responsive to others, and have a good understanding of the dynamics of social interaction. They view consultation as a learning experience for themselves as well as for the professionals and students they serve. Consulting teachers can make both concrete, specific suggestions to improve students' educational experiences and can look at issues from broad theoretical perspectives. Finally, they are good researchers who know how to locate and use resources effectively (Lipsky & Gartner, 1996).

focus

Define *collaboration,* and distinguish between the consulting teacher, resource room teacher, and teacher assistance teams.

■ CONSULTING TEACHER. A teacher who provides support to general education classroom teachers. Consulting teachers train and assist others in modifying curricula and the environment to accommodate students with diverse needs.

■ TEACHER ASSISTANCE TEAMS. Groups of professionals, students, and parents working together toward a common goal of solving problems, providing instructional support, and supporting classroom teachers.

The consulting teacher model offers training and support for general classroom teachers and emphasizes modifying the general education environment to accommodate students with differences, rather than moving them to separate settings. It is not unusual for consulting teachers to *co-teach* with a general education teacher, providing instruction to students with and without disabilities. In a class of 25 to 30 children, 2 or more students are likely to have learning or behavioral needs that require the services of a consulting teacher.

■ **THE RESOURCE ROOM TEACHER** In the resource room model, the student with a disability receives specialized instruction in a classroom that is separate from the general education setting but within the same school building. The student still receives the majority of instruction in the general education classroom but goes to the resource room for short periods to supplement learning. The resource room is not intended to be a study hall, where students do their homework or spend time catching up on other class work; it is directed by a qualified special education teacher. The role of the resource room teacher is to provide individualized instruction to facilitate the student's success in the general education curriculum. Working with the general education teacher and other members of the instructional team, the resource room teacher identifies each student's educational needs. The team then develops and implements the appropriate academic, social–behavioral, or functional skills program.

The resource room model has some important features that differ from the traditional self-contained special education classroom. The resource room allows students to remain with same-age nondisabled peers for the majority of the school day, eliminating a great deal of the stigma associated with segregated special education classrooms. The resource room also provides support to the general education classroom teacher, who, despite realizing that these students have potential for success in the general education classroom, may find it extremely difficult to provide appropriate individualized instruction without some assistance. Approximately 1 or 2 students in a general education classroom of 25 to 30 will need the additional instructional services offered by a resource room program.

■ **TEACHER ASSISTANCE TEAMS** The movement toward a stronger collaborative relationship among general educators, special educators, and other school support personnel has also emphasized developing schoolwide support or assistance to professionals and students. This essentially means sharing a school's human and material resources to meet the needs of students who are at risk or have disabilities. Typically, resources within a school are distributed based on standard staffing patterns: general educators work with "their kids," and special educators work with "their kids." Although this procedure may ensure equitable distribution of resources to students who are at risk or have disabilities, it is not sensitive to their varying needs. Flexibility is a necessary component of accommodating individual diversity.

To meet the challenges posed by student diversity, schools have developed support networks that facilitate collaboration among professionals. Teacher assistance teams (TATs), sometimes referred to as schoolwide assistance teams (SWATs), involve groups of professionals, students, and/or parents working together to solve problems, develop instructional strategies, and support classroom teachers (Vaughn, Bos, & Schumm, 1999). TATs use strategies designed to assist teachers in making appropriate referrals of students who may need special education services as well as those at risk in the general classroom who may not qualify for such services but still need additional support. (See the nearby Reflect on This feature.)

Reflect on This

A team is a group of professionals, parents, and/or students who join together to plan and implement an appropriate educational program for a student at risk or with a disability. Team members may be trained in different areas of study, including education, health services, speech and language, school administration, and so on. In the team approach, these individual people sit down together and coordinate their efforts to help the student, regardless of where or how they were trained. For this approach to work, each team member must clearly understand his or her role and responsibilities as a member of the team. Let's visit with some team members and have them share their perceived role in relationship to working with a student.

■ CONSULTING OR RESOURCE ROOM TEACHER

It's my responsibility to coordinate the student's individualized educational program. I work with each member of the team to assist in selecting, administering, and interpreting appropriate assessment information. I maintain ongoing communication with each team member to ensure that we are all working together to help the student. It's my responsibility to compile, organize, and maintain good, accurate records on each student. I propose instructional alternatives for the student and work with others in the implementation of the recommended instruction. To carry this out, I locate or develop the necessary materials to meet each student's specific needs. I work directly with the student's parents to ensure that they are familiar with what is being taught at school and can reinforce school learning experiences at home.

■ PARENTS

We work with each team member to ensure that our child is involved in an appropriate educational program. We give information to the team about our child's life outside school and suggest experiences that might be relevant to the home and the community. We also work with our child at home to reinforce what is learned in school. As members of the team, we give our written consent for any evaluations of our child and any changes in our child's educational placement.

■ SCHOOL PSYCHOLOGIST

I select, administer, and interpret appropriate psychological, educational, and behavioral assessment instruments. I consult directly with team members regarding the student's overall educational development. It is also my responsibility to directly observe the student's performance in the classroom and assist in the design of appropriate behavioral management programs in the school and at home.

■ SCHOOL ADMINISTRATOR

As the school district's representative, I work with the team to ensure that the resources of my school and district are used appropriately in providing services to the student. I am ultimately responsible for ensuring that the team's decisions are implemented properly.

■ GENERAL EDUCATION CLASSROOM TEACHER

I work with the team to develop and implement appropriate educational experiences for the student during the time that he or she spends in my classroom. I ensure that the student's experiences outside my classroom are consistent with the instruction he or she receives from me. In carrying out my responsibilities, I keep an accurate and continuous record of the student's progress. I am also responsible for referring any other students in my classroom who are at risk and may need specialized services to the school district for an evaluation of their needs.

■ ADAPTED PHYSICAL EDUCATION TEACHER

I am an adapted physical education specialist who works with the team to determine whether the student needs adapted physical education services as a component of his or her individualized education program.

■ RELATED SERVICES SPECIALIST

I may be a speech and language specialist, social worker, school counselor, school nurse, occupational or physical therapist, juvenile court authority, physician, or school media coordinator. I provide any additional services necessary to ensure that the student receives an appropriate educational experience.

■ THE ROLE OF THE GENERAL EDUCATION TEACHER

Today's classroom teachers are faced with growing diversity, including increasing numbers of students with disabilities, students from ethnically diverse backgrounds, and students at risk for educational failure due to a number of complex factors in their lives. General education teachers must meet the challenges of achieving increased academic excellence as mandated in the standards-based reform movement as well as responding to students with many different needs coming together

focus 9
Describe the role of the general education teacher in meeting the needs of students with disabilities.

in a common environment. The inclusion of students with disabilities in general education schools and classrooms need not be met with teachers' frustration, anger, or refusal. These reactions are merely symptomatic of the confusion surrounding inclusive education. Huefner (2000) suggested that the changes in IDEA 97 requiring general education teachers to be members of the IEP team provide these individuals with "new leverage to obtain the supports they need to be effective with special education students" (p. 203). As members of the IEP team, general educators will be in a better position to share their knowledge and insight on individual students and provide important information on how the student will fare in the general education curriculum and classroom setting.

Inclusive education, in the worst cases, can be synonymous with dumping a student with disabilities in a general education classroom without any supports to the teacher or to the student and at the expense of others in the class. In a recent survey, general education teachers attempting to meet the needs of students with disabilities in their classroom identified four major problem areas:

1. Disruptive students who lacked the necessary social and behavioral skills to succeed in a general education setting
2. Lack of specialized assistance from a special education teacher or other school personnel
3. Lack of information regarding the appropriate instructional adaptations necessary to meet the needs of any given student with a disability
4. Concerns regarding the social acceptance of students with disabilities—peers sometimes isolated, rejected, teased, or bullied these students (Hobbs, 1997)

To address these concerns, participate as an informed IEP team member, and meet the needs of students with disabilities within their classroom, general education teachers must receive expanded training during their initial university preparation and as a component of their ongoing professional development. However, as suggested by Hardman et al. (1998), university and college teacher education programs in many parts of the United States provide little, if any training, to general

General education teachers face the challenges of working with a diversity of students that may include students from different ethnic backgrounds and students with disabilities.

Reflect on This

WHAT IS NEEDED TO SUCCESSFULLY IMPLEMENT AN INCLUSIVE EDUCATION PROGRAM?: PERSPECTIVES FROM THE GENERAL EDUCATION TEACHER

- *Time.* Teachers need 1 hour or more per day to plan for students with disabilities.
- *Training.* Teachers need systematic, intensive training, either as part of their certification programs (i.e., as intensive and well-planned in-services) or as an ongoing process with consultants.
- *Personal resources.* Teachers report a need for additional personnel assistance to carry out inclusion

objectives. This could include a part-time aide and daily contact with special education teachers.
- *Material resources.* Teachers need adequate curriculum materials and other classroom equipment appropriate to the needs of students with disabilities.
- *Class size.* Teachers agree that their class size should be reduced to fewer than 20 students if students

with disabilities are included in their general classrooms.
- *Consideration of severity of disability.* Teachers are more willing to include students with mild disabilities than students with more severe disabilities, apparently because of teachers' perceived ability to carry on their teaching mission for the entire classroom. By implication, the more

severe the disabilities represented in the inclusive setting, the more the previously mentioned sources of support would be needed.

Source: From "Teacher Perceptions of Mainstreaming/Inclusion, 1958–1995: A Research Synthesis," by T. E. Scruggs and M. A. Mastropieri, 1996, *Exceptional Children,* 63(1), p. 17.

---

education teacher candidates on instructional strategies for working with at-risk or disabled students. General and special education teachers are often prepared in separate academic programs. Consequently, many newly prepared general education teachers lack the necessary skills to meet the diverse needs of students in their classrooms and to work effectively with their special education colleagues.

In a study of six states' implementation of the least restrictive environment clause of IDEA, Hasazi, Johnston, Liggett, and Schattman (1994) found that university teacher education programs were not taking any leadership in statewide education reform agendas. On the contrary, they were viewed as barriers to change by state offices of education, school districts, and parents. These authors noted further that many universities are in a strategic position to promote teacher education reform in both general and special education because they are receiving considerable funding through state and federal grants to develop in-service training initiatives in model development and innovative practices. Yet, in spite of these initiatives at the doorstep of research institutions, they are not being translated into curricula for teacher candidates. (See the nearby Reflect on This feature.)

The role of the general education classroom teacher extends not only to working with students with mild disabilities, but also to involvement with those with more severe disabilities. Success in the general education environment for students with severe disabilities weighs heavily upon the cooperative relationship among the general education classroom teacher, special education teacher, and school support team. The general education classroom teacher works with the team to create opportunities for inclusion of students with more severe disabilities in natural settings. Inclusion may be achieved by having the general education class serve as a homeroom for the student; by developing opportunities for students with severe disabilities to be with their nondisabled peers as often as possible both within the general education classroom and in school activities such as recess, lunch, and assemblies; or by developing a peer support program and by using **multilevel instruction** and **universal design** in the classroom setting (Eichinger & Downing, 1996; Giangreco & Doyle, 2000; Orkwis & McLane, 1998; Sailor, Gerry, & Wilson,

■ MULTILEVEL INSTRUCTION. Use of different instructional approaches within the same curriculum to address students' individual needs and levels of performance.

■ UNIVERSAL DESIGN. Instructional programs and environments that work for all students, to the greatest extent possible, without the need for adaptation or specialized design. Such curriculum must be accessible and applicable to students, teachers, and parents with different backgrounds, learning styles, abilities, and disabilities in widely varied learning contexts.

■ PEER-MEDIATED INSTRUCTION.
Structured interactions between
two or more students that are
designed by school personnel to
achieve instructional goals.

■ PEER AND CROSS-AGE
TUTORING. A cooperative learning situation wherein one or more
peers, or students of different
ages, provide instruction to other
students to achieve instructional
goals.

■ COOPERATIVE LEARNING.
Learning situation in which students work together to achieve
group goals or group rewards.

focus 10

Distinguish between *peer and
cross-age tutoring* and *cooperative learning.*

1990). In multilevel instruction, teachers use different instructional approaches within the same curriculum *adapted* to individual need and functioning level. The process uses alternative presentation methods to teach key concepts. The teacher must be willing to accept varying types of student activities, evaluation procedures, and multiple outcomes (National Center on Educational Restructuring and Inclusion, 1994). Universal design goes one step beyond multilevel instruction, creating instructional programs and environments that work for all students, to the greatest extent possible, *without the need for adaptation or specialized design.* The basic premise of universal design is that the curriculum must be

accessible and applicable to students, teachers, and parents with different backgrounds, learning styles, abilities, and disabilities in widely varied learning contexts. The "universal" in universal design does not imply one optimal solution for everyone, but rather it underscores the need for inherently flexible, customizable content, assignments, and activities. (Center for Applied Special Technology, 1999, p. 1)

(See the nearby Today's Technology feature.)

■ COOPERATIVE LEARNING AND PEER SUPPORT

Peers serve as a powerful support system within the classroom in both academic and social areas. They often have more influence on their classmates' behavior than the teacher does. Peer support programs may range from simply creating opportunities in the class for students with disabilities to socially interact with their nondisabled peers to highly structured programs of peer-mediated instruction. **Peer-mediated instruction** involves a structured interaction between two or more students under the direct supervision of a classroom teacher. The instruction may use **peer and cross-age tutoring** and/or **cooperative learning.** Cross-age and peer tutoring emphasizes individual student learning, while cooperative learning emphasizes the simultaneous learning of students as they seek to achieve group goals.

Peers are a reliable and
effective resource for students
with disabilities in general
education classrooms.

Today's Technology

TECHNOLOGY AND INCLUSION AT WORK: HERE'S WHAT A FULLY INCLUDED CLASSROOM MIGHT LOOK LIKE

Melissa Graham's fifth-grade urban class has 24 children, ranging in ability level from kindergarten to seventh grade, not an atypical situation for many teachers. What's different about Graham's class is that two special education children are fully included. Stephen is severely learning disabled with impaired visual–motor skills. Maria, a bilingual student, is a high-functioning Down syndrome youngster.

Graham believes that technology helps the fully-included students capitalize on their capabilities and helps her create child-centered learning opportunities. Graham teaches with thematic units and she stresses cooperative learning, both of which reinforce the inclusive nature of her classroom.

Stephen works at a Macintosh LC 520 and a laptop that the special education consultant has outfitted with IntelliKeys, a brightly colored alternative keyboard that allows Stephen to use a large arrow in lieu of a mouse. He also has a scanner for all written work, including homework assignments.

Also essential to Stephen's written communication is *Co-Writer*, a word prediction program that reduces the number of key strokes he has to type to create words and sentences. Stephen functions successfully close to grade level by using this technology.

Graham also uses regular technology programs with all her students during their current thematic unit on exploration. For instance, Maria avidly watches the video series *Building a Book with Sparkle* to help her create a dictionary that she uses in a cooperative group project on Christopher Columbus. The children in her group videotape Maria showing a page from her dictionary about Columbus, which they incorporate into a larger multimedia presentation.

Technology in Melissa Graham's class broadens the possibilities for the class as a whole. *Science in Motion: Planets in Motion,* for example, is a package whose videodisc presentation works well with the whole class and whose activity cards lend themselves to small-group activities in which Stephen and Maria can fully participate. There is a second audio track on the videodisc that has a simplified narration that Maria can review with other students.

In a classroom like Graham's, technology, in combination with innovative curriculum practices, enables all students to benefit academically and socially and prepares them to take their place in our diverse society.

*Barbara Hertz is a special education teacher with the Greenwich, Connecticut, Public School System. . . . She was asked here to describe—both idealistically and realistically—how technology in an inclusive classroom might work. The children and teacher Ms. Hertz portrays are a compilation of the many special education students and teachers she has worked with over the years.

Source: "Here's What a Fully Included Classroom Might Look Like," by B. Hertz. From *Electronic Learning,* March 1994 issue. Copyright © 1994 by Scholastic Inc. Reprinted by permission of Scholastic Inc.

Although often an underrated and underused resource in a general education setting, peers are very reliable and effective in implementing both academic and social programs with their classmates who have disabilities (Graves & Bradley, 1997; Hunt et al., 1994; Jakupcak, 1998; Putnam,1998b; Vaughn et al., 1999). The effectiveness of peers, however, is dependent on carefully managing the program so that students both with and without disabilities benefit. It is important for teachers to carefully select, train, and monitor the performance of students working as peer tutors (McDonnell et al., 1995; Vaughn et al., 1999). In a summary of the available research, Slavin (1991) reported that cooperative learning is

- most effective when it includes goals for the group as a whole as well as individual members
- beneficial for all students from high achievers to those at risk of school failure
- beneficial to student self-esteem, social relationships among group members, overall acceptance of students with disabilities, and attitudes toward school.

Special Education Classrooms and Schools

focus 11

Describe special education classrooms and schools for students with disabilities.

Some professionals and parents believe that inclusive education using a collaborative approach with general education may not be beneficial for some students with disabilities. They support a *continuum of placements* that includes self-contained special education classrooms and special schools. In the judgment of these professionals and parents, some students require more intensive and specialized educational services provided in either a self-contained special education classroom or a special school for students with disabilities.

■ THE SELF-CONTAINED SPECIAL EDUCATION CLASSROOM

The self-contained special education classroom in a general education school is characterized by a qualified special education teacher working during most, if not all, of the school day with students who are disabled. This teacher may still create opportunities for these students to interact with nondisabled peers whenever appropriate, for instance, through academically and nonacademically oriented classes, lunch and playground breaks, school events, peer-tutoring programs, and so forth. However, it is also possible that, in some cases, students with disabilities in self-contained classrooms may never be included in the classrooms or activities of a general education school.

■ THE SPECIAL SCHOOL

Students with disabilities may also be placed in special schools that are completely separate from general education buildings. Proponents of this arrangement have argued that the large numbers of students in special schools provide greater homogeneity in grouping and programming and therefore allow special education teachers to specialize in a subject area and more effectively meet the needs of their students. For example, one teacher would instruct an art class, another physical education, and a third math. In inclusive programs, with only one or two special education teachers

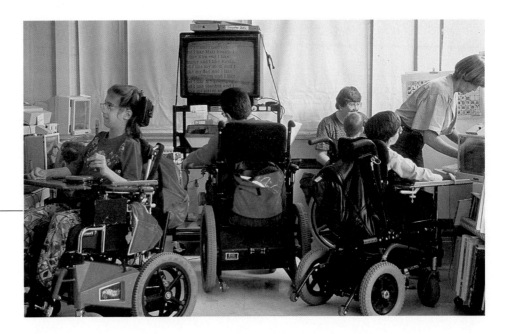

Students in a self-contained special classroom spend most, if not all, of their day working with the special education teacher.

in a general education school, an individual teacher would have to provide instruction for everything from art and home economics to academic subjects. Proponents have also argued that special schools remove students with disabilities from being subjected to the ridicule of their nondisabled peers as well as centralizing supplies, specialized equipment, special facilities, and related services personnel.

Opponents of special schools have argued that research on the efficacy of these facilities does not support the proponents' rationale. Several authors have contended that, regardless of the severity of their disabling condition, students with disabilities benefit from placement in a general education school and classrooms, where opportunities for inclusion with nondisabled peers are systematically planned and implemented (Ferguson et al., 1992; Gee, 1996; Lipsky & Gartner, 1999; Putnam, 1998a; Sailor, Gee, & Karasoff, 2000; Snell, 1991).

Full Inclusion Versus the Continuum of Placements

A number of general and special educators have argued that, in spite of certain accomplishments, pull-out programs (removing the student with a disability from the general education classroom for only part of the day) have caused negative effects or obstacles to the appropriate education of students with disabilities (Laski, 1991; Lipsky & Gartner, 1999; Paul, 1998; Putnam, 1998a; Sailor et al., 2000; Stainback et al., 1996; Vaughn, Moody, & Schumm, 1998). On the other side, proponents of pull-out programs have argued that the available research doesn't support the premise that full-time placement in a general education classroom is superior to special education classes for all students with disabilities (Baker & Zigmond, 1995; Dupre, 1997; Fox & Ysseldyke, 1997; Fuchs & Fuchs, 1991, 1994; Hocutt, 1996; Kauffman & Hallahan, 1997; Lieberman, 1996; Mills, Cole, Jenkins, & Day 1998). In this section, we examine the arguments on both sides of the full inclusion issue.

focus 12

Identify the arguments for and against the full inclusion of students with disabilities in general education classrooms.

■ THE CASE FOR FULL INCLUSION

Advocates of full inclusion have argued that the current continuum of placements that go beyond full-time placement in a general education classroom (such as resource rooms, self-contained classrooms, or special schools) are stigmatizing and fail to serve the individual needs of each student. Such programs result in a fragmented approach to instruction, with little cooperation between general and special educators.

The proponents of full inclusion have contended that general education classrooms that incorporate a partnership between general and special educators result in a diverse and rich learning environment, rather than just a series of discrete programming slots and funding pots. Such a partnership personalizes each student's instructional program and implements it in the least restrictive environment, rather than removing the child to a separate program. Additionally, special educators are more effective in a partnership because they can bring their knowledge and resources to assist general educators in developing intervention strategies that are directly oriented to student needs in the natural setting of the general education classroom. In a study of full-inclusion programs in school districts across four states, Morra (1994) found perceived gains in "the areas of social interaction, language development, appropriate behavior, and self-esteem. Academic progress was also noted. For the nondisabled students, parents and teachers perceived them becoming generally more compassionate, more helpful, and more friendly in relating to . . . students [with disabilities]"

(p. 1). Staub and Peck (1995) reinforced this finding and identified potential benefits of full-inclusion programs for students who are not disabled:

- Greater awareness of and comfort with human differences
- Improved self-esteem and more positive feelings about themselves through a better understanding and insight into the needs of others
- Reduced prejudice toward those who are different and a stronger commitment to moral and ethical principles
- Meaningful and lasting friendship with people who are disabled.

In a summary of the rationale for full-inclusion programs, Putnam (1998a) indicated that efficacy studies comparing special education pull-out programs with full-time placement in a general education classroom continually find superior results for students placed in the full-inclusion programs. Baker, Wang, and Walberg (1995) also reported that students with disabilities achieve better academic and social outcomes in general education classrooms when compared to comparable students in special education pull-out programs.

■ THE CASE AGAINST FULL INCLUSION

Opponents of full inclusion suggest that general education teachers have little expertise in assisting students with learning and behavioral difficulties and are already overburdened with large class size and inadequate support services. On the other hand, special educators have been specifically trained to individualize instruction, develop instructional strategies, and use proven techniques that facilitate learning for students with disabilities. This results in more specialized academic and social instruction in a pull-out setting, where students can more effectively prepare to return to the general education classroom. Specialized pull-out settings also allow for centralization of both human and material resources.

Opponents of full inclusion also contend that if practitioners and consumers don't believe special education is broken, why fix it? In general, both parents and professionals are quite satisfied with the special education continuum of placements (Guterman, 1995). In the study of inclusive education programs in four states noted in the previous section, Morra (1994) found that inclusion programs were viewed by the schools as not being for everyone. School districts indicated that they were struggling with the difficult challenges of "(1) severely emotionally disturbed students who disrupt classrooms and (2) students with learning disabilities who may need a more highly focused, less distracting learning environment than that presented by the general education classroom" (p. 1).

As we conclude this chapter on the elementary years, it is clear that educators are confronted with some difficult decisions about how, what, and where to teach students with disabilities. These decisions must take into account factors such as the student's age, prior learning history, performance demands in the natural setting, and available resources. In addition, educators must consider constraints in making efficient use of limited instructional time. As students with disabilities approach adolescence and eventually the adult years, their life space increases to include a much larger and more heterogeneous environment called "community." In the next chapter, we look at services and supports for adolescents with disabilities during middle school and high school. The chapter concludes with an exploration of the transition out of school and into adult life.

Case Study

Jerald is finishing up his last two months in a second-grade classroom at Robert F. Kennedy Elementary School. Kennedy is a large urban school with a number of students from low economic and culturally diverse backgrounds. Many of its students are described as "disadvantaged" and at significant risk of school failure.

Next year, Jerald will move to third grade, and his parents and teachers have expressed some concerns. "Jerry is an outgoing kid who loves to talk about anything to anyone at anytime," says his mother. His current second-grade teacher, Miss Robins, complains that he is "hyperactive, inattentive, and a behavior problem." His mom, his dad, and his teacher agree that Jerald has a great deal of difficulty with controlling his emotions.

Mother: *I just wish he wasn't so easily frustrated at home when things aren't going his way.*

Miss Robins: *He's always in a state of fight or flight. When he is in a fighting mode, he hits, teases, and screams at me or the other students. When in a state of "flight," he withdraws and refuses to comply with any requests. He may even put his head on his desk and openly cry to vent his frustrations.*

During second grade, his "fight" behavior has increased considerably. Miss Robins, reported that "he has made very little progress and is uncontrollable—a very disruptive influence on the other children in the class." With permission from Jerald's parents, she initiated a referral to the school's child-study team to assess his eligibility for special education services. His overall assessment indicated that he was falling further behind in reading (word decoding skills at grade level 1.5; reading comprehension at grade level 1.0) and math (grade level 1.9). Behaviorally, he has difficulty expressing his feelings in an appropriate manner. He is impulsive, easily distracted, and not well liked by his peers. After determining his eligibility for special education services, the school IEP team developed Jerald's third-grade annual goals and objectives. The focus will be on

1. improving Jerald's reading and math achievement by ensuring access to general curriculum with specialized academic instruction and support—Jerald is to be included in the district and state testing program.
2. teaching Jerald the skills to (a) manage his own behavior when faced with difficult or frustrating situations and (b) improve daily interactions with teachers and peers—the activities for these goals and objectives will be included on the IEP as components of Jerald's *behavioral intervention plan.*

Once the team had agreed upon annual goals, objectives, and activities for Jerald, they discussed various classroom and school settings that would be appropriate to his needs as described in the IEP. Miss Robins and the school principal are concerned that his disruptive behavior will be too difficult to control in a general education classroom. They would like to see him placed in a special self-contained class for students who are emotionally disturbed. They are concerned not only for Jerald's education but also the negative effect he has on his classroom peers. Miss Robins reported that she had to spend a disproportionate amount of her time dealing with Jerald's inappropriate behavior.

In considering the views of Jerald's teachers and the school principal, the team is considering placement in a special education class for students with serious behavior problems. Such a class is not available at his home school, so Jerald would have to be transported to a special education program in another location. Ms. Beckman, the special education consulting teacher, has an alternative point of view. She proposes that Jerald stay at Kennedy Elementary and that his behavioral intervention plan and specialized academic instruction be implemented in next year's third-grade classroom. Working in collaboration with Jerald's general education teacher and other members of the school's assistance team, Ms. Beckman suggests using cooperative learning techniques, co-teaching among the general and resource room teachers, and ongoing support from the school psychologist.

Jerald's parents, while recognizing that his disruptive behavior is increasing and that he is falling further behind academically, are reluctant to have him transferred to another school. They feel it would remove him from his family and neighborhood supports. His brother, who will be in the fifth grade, also goes to Kennedy Elementary.

■ APPLICATION

1. What do you see as the important issues for the team to consider in deciding what educational setting would be most appropriate to meet Jerald's needs?
2. In addition to the recommendations made by Ms. Beckman, the special education resource room teacher, what suggestions would you have to adapt Jerald's academic and behavioral program if he were to remain in his third-grade class at Kennedy Elementary?
3. Should he remain in his third-grade class at Kennedy Elementary?

Debate Forum

PERSPECTIVES ON FULL INCLUSION

Full inclusion: Students are placed in a general education classroom for the entire school day. The necessary support services to ensure an appropriate education come to the student in the general education class setting; the student is *not* "pulled out" into a special education classroom for instruction.

■ POINT

We must rethink our current approach to the educational placement of students with disabilities. Pulling these students out of general education classrooms and into separate, segregated settings does not make sense from a standpoint of both values and "what works." As a moral imperative, inclusion is the right thing to do (Paul, 1998; Putnam, 1998a). Putnam suggested the following:

The most compelling rationale for inclusive education is based on cultural and human rights. The civil rights movement used the legislative mandate of the Brown v. Board of Education *(1954) decision in the fight to eliminate the negative effects of political, social, and educational segregation. [Today], advocates are fighting against another insidious form of segregation—the denial of equal opportunities to students who have disabilities . . . . According to the 14th Amendment to the U.S. Constitution, people are equal under the law and, thus, deserve equal opportunities in U.S. public schools. (pp. 7–8)*

■ COUNTERPOINT

No one is questioning the value of children belonging, of being a part of society. However, it is not necessarily true that placing a child with a disability in a general education classroom is a denial of human rights. Is it a denial of human rights if a student with a disability receives inadequate academic support to meet his or her instructional needs? Is it a denial of human rights to have a child socially isolated in a classroom? How do you translate the moral imperative into action when the social and academic needs of these students are beyond the expertise of a general education teacher? We must separate the vision from the reality. General education does not have the inclination or the expertise to meet the diverse needs of all students with disabilities. General education is already overburdened with the increasing number of at-risk students, large class sizes, and an inadequate support system.

■ POINT

Let's do separate reality from vision. The reality is traditional special education has failed; it does not work (Lipsky & Gartner, 1996, 1999). Setting the values inherent in the inclusion of all students aside, let's look at the reality (Wagner & Blackorby, 1996):

- Only 56% of students in special education graduate with a diploma.
- Thirty-eight percent drop out of school.
- Thirty-one percent receive failing grades in school.
- Only 55% of special education graduates and 40% of the dropouts are employed following their exit from school.
- Only 21% of special education graduates and 5% of the dropouts pursue any type of postsecondary training.

Wagner and Blackorby also pointed out that having positive experiences in school, including interactions with nondisabled peers, puts students with disabilities on a better trajectory toward successful transition into adult life. Several other authors (Baker, Wang, & Walberg, 1995; Lipsky & Gartner, 1999; Stainback et al., 1996; Vaughn, Moody, & Schumm, 1998) have noted that there is no evidence that pulling them out of general education classrooms benefits students with disabilities.

■ COUNTERPOINT

There is always a flip side to the research coin. What about the following research findings?

- Research doesn't support the premise that full-time placement in a general education classroom is superior to special education pull-out programs for all students with disabilities (Baker & Zigmond, 1995; Fox & Ysseldyke, 1997; Mills et al., 1998).
- General education teachers have little expertise in assisting students with learning and behavioral difficulties and are already overburdened with large class size and inadequate support services (Lieberman, 1996; Scruggs & Mastropieri, 1996).
- Special educators have been specifically trained to individualize instruction, develop instructional strategies, and use proven techniques that facilitate learning for students with disabilities (National Research Council, 1997).
- In general, both parents and professionals are quite satisfied with the special education continuum of placements (Guterman, 1995).

Additionally, on what basis do you attach blame to special education for low graduation and high dropout rates or for the lack of access to postsecondary education? Given that 96% of all students with disabilities are spending at least a portion of their day in general classes, shouldn't we be looking at the system as a whole, not just special education, in trying to deal with student failure? Concerning the high unemployment rate for people with disabilities, shouldn't we look at the failure of adult services to expand opportunities for individuals to receive the necessary training and support to find and succeed in community employment settings?

The conclusions from researchers that special education has failed can be countered by other investigators who reached a very different interpretation (Dupre, 1997; Fuchs & Fuchs, 1991, 1994; Hocutt, 1996; Kauffman & Hallahan, 1997). These researchers, while calling for improvements in special education, don't support its abolition.

■ **POINT**

We could forever argue the point about what the research supports or doesn't support, and still not reach any agreement. Let's come back to the issue of values and reality. The goal behind full inclusion is to educate students with disabilities with their nondisabled peers in a general education class setting, as a means to increase their access to, and participation in, all natural settings. The general education classroom is a microcosm of the larger society. For the preschool-age child, the world is defined primarily through family and a small same-age peer group. As the child gets older, the world

expands to the neighborhood, to the school, and eventually to the larger heterogeneous community. As educators, we must ask how we can educate the child with a disability to foster full participation as the life space of the individual is expanded. What are the barriers to full participation, and how do we work to break them down? A partnership between general and special education is a good beginning to breaking down barriers. Each professional brings his or her knowledge and resources into a single setting in the development of an instructional program that is directly oriented to student need. This unified approach to instruction will provide teachers with the opportunity to work across disciplines and gain a

broader understanding of the diversity in all children. Pull-out programs result in a fragmented approach to instruction with little cooperation between general and special education.

Finally, students in pull-out programs are much more likely to be stigmatized. Separate education on the basis of a child's learning or behavioral characteristics is inherently unequal.

■ **COUNTERPOINT**

The value of full inclusion is a laudable goal, but one nevertheless that is misguided as an achievable or even desirable outcome for all students with disabilities. The reality is that specialized academic and social instruction can best be provided, at least for some students, in a pull-

out setting. These more restricted settings are the least restrictive environment for some students. Pull-out programs will more effectively prepare the student to return to less restricted settings, such as the general education class. A move to full inclusion will result in the loss of special education personnel who have been trained to work with students who have diverse needs. In spite of the rhetoric about collaboration between general and special education, the responsibilities for the student's education in a full-inclusion classroom will move to the general education class teacher with little or no support. The result will be dumping these students into an environment that will not meet their needs.

Review

 **1**

Why is it so important to provide early intervention services as soon as possible to young children at risk?

■ The first years of life are critical to the overall development of all children—normal, at risk, and disabled.
■ Early stimulation is crucial to the later development of language, intelligence, personality, and self-worth.

■ Early intervention can prevent and lessen the overall impact of disabilities as well as counteract the negative effects of delayed intervention.
■ Early intervention may in the long run be less costly and more effective than providing services later in the individual's life.

 2

Identify the components that must be included in the individualized family service plan.

■ The infant's or toddler's present levels of physical development, cognitive development, communication development, social or emotional development, and adaptive development
■ The family's resources, priorities, and concerns relating to enhancing the development of the young child with a disability
■ The major outcomes to be achieved for the infant or toddler and the family, and the criteria, procedures, and timelines used to determine progress toward achieving the outcomes

■ Specific early intervention services to meet the unique needs of the infant or toddler and the family
■ The natural environments in which early intervention services are to be provided, including a justification of the extent, if any, to which the services will not be provided in a natural environment
■ The projected dates for initiation of services and the anticipated duration of the services
■ The identification of the service coordinator
■ The steps to be taken to support the transition of

the toddler with a disability to preschool or other appropriate services

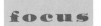 **focus 3**

Identify critical services and programs for preschool-age children.

- A child-find system in each state to locate young children at risk and refer them to appropriate agencies for preschool services
- An individualized education program plan that involves specialists across several disciplines
- Instructional approaches that reflect developmentally appropriate practice, age-appropriate practice, and the teaching of functional skills
- Home-based and school-based (including inclusive preschool classrooms) programs

focus 4

Identify three characteristics of special education that enhance learning opportunities for students with disabilities.

- Individualization
- Intensive instruction
- The explicit teaching of basic, adaptive, and/or functional life skills

 focus 5

What is meant by adaptive fit and adaptive instruction for students with disabilities?

- The degree to which an individual is able to cope with the requirements of

the school setting is described as adaptive fit.
- The purpose of adaptive instruction is to modify the learning environment to accommodate the unique learning characteristics and needs of individual students.
- Adaptive instruction focuses on assessing each student's individual characteristics and capabilities.

 focus 6

Identify the four phases of the special education referral, planning, and placement process.

- Initiating the referral
- Assessing the student's educational need and eligibility for special education
- Developing the individual education program (IEP)
- Determining the least restrictive environment

 focus 7

Describe the characteristics of effective inclusive schools and classrooms.

- Schoolwide support systems that use both general and special education resources to benefit all students
- Strong leadership from the school principal
- A philosophy that celebrates diversity and rewards collaboration among professionals and students
- Service and supports delivered in age-appropriate classrooms within the student's home school

- Educational programming that is individualized
- Support provided to all students regardless of their instructional needs
- Effective educational practices that have been validated
- A transdisciplinary model used to deliver instruction.

 focus 8

Define *collaboration,* and distinguish between the consulting teacher, resource room teacher, and teacher assistance teams.

- *Collaboration* refers to a dynamic framework for educational efforts that endorses collegial, interdependent, and co-equal styles of interaction between at least two partners working together to achieve common goals in a decision-making process that is influenced by cultural and systemic factors.
- Consulting teachers work directly with general education classroom teachers on the use of appropriate assessment techniques and intervention strategies. Students who work with consulting teachers are not removed from the general education classroom program but remain with their nondisabled peers while receiving additional instructional assistance.
- Resource room teachers provide specialized instruction to students with disabilities in a classroom that is separate from the general education room. Under the resource room program, the student still receives the majority of

instruction in the general education classroom, but is removed from the general education class for short periods to supplement his or her educational experience.
- Teacher assistance teams involve professionals, students, and parents working together to solve problems, develop instructional strategies, and support classroom teachers.

 focus 9

Describe the role of the general education teacher in meeting the needs of students with disabilities.

- Implement an appropriate instructional program focused on ensuring student success in the general education curriculum.
- Develop peer support programs, and use multilevel instruction in the classroom.
- Understand how a student's learning, behavior, communication, and physical differences affect his or her ability to acquire academic skills and cope socially in the educational environment.
- Identify students who may be in need of additional educational support.
- Make referrals to the team for testing and evaluation of students perceived as being at risk.
- Work with team members to develop and implement individualized instruction in the general education classroom.
- Initiate and maintain ongoing communication with parents.

focus 10

Distinguish between *peer and cross-age tutoring* and *cooperative learning.*

- Peer and cross-age tutoring emphasizes individual student learning.
- Cooperative learning emphasizes the simultaneous learning of students as they seek to achieve group goals.

focus 11

Describe special education classrooms and schools for students with disabilities.

- The self-contained special education classroom employs the expertise of a qualified special education teacher to work for most, if not all, of the school day with students who have disabilities.
- A teacher in the self-contained classroom may still create opportunities for students with disabilities to interact with nondisabled peers whenever appropriate.
- Special schools provide services and supports for large numbers of students with disabilities in a setting separate from a general education school and classroom.

focus 12

Identify the arguments for and against the full inclusion of students with disabilities in general education classrooms.

- Arguments for the full inclusion of students in the general education classroom. (1) The continuum of placements beyond the general education classroom is stigmatizing, creates a fragmented approach to instruction, and fails to meet the individual needs of each student. (2) Partnerships between general and special education teachers result in a diverse and rich learning environment. Within this partnership, special educators can effectively bring their knowledge and resources to assist general educators in developing intervention strategies that meet student needs in a natural setting. (3) Students with disabilities gain in academic learning, social interaction, language development, appropriate behavior, and self-esteem. (4) Students who are not disabled report improved self-esteem, greater awareness and comfort with human differences, reduced prejudice, and lasting friendships with students who are disabled.
- Arguments against full inclusion. (1) General education teachers have little expertise to assist students with learning difficulties and are already overburdened with large class sizes and inadequate support services. (2) Special educators have been specifically trained to develop instructional strategies and use teaching techniques that are not part of the training of general education teachers. (3) More specialized academic and social instruction can be provided in pull-out settings, and such settings can more effectively prepare students to return to the general education classroom. (4) Specialized pull-out settings allow for centralization of both human and material resources.

Transition from School and the Adult Years

To begin with . . .

A successful schooling experience will provide the student with the tools and skills necessary to make the transition effectively to the next stage of life. For some, this means going on to college or another educational experience. For others, it means entering the workforce. . . . For students with severe disabilities . . . long-term outcomes (e.g., degree of independence, employment) are designated through the IEP process; instruction then focuses on building skills that will lead to these outcomes in age-appropriate natural settings. . . . For students with mild disabilities, a combination of academic, vocational, and functional outcomes is often selected with the specific mix of components dependent on individual student goals and needs. (National Research Council, 1997, pp. 119–120)

As more educators and parents experience the benefits of inclusion in elementary schools, methods to promote inclusion at a secondary level have increased. . . . In secondary settings, however, educators face challenges in collaborating with diverse general educators, handling the logistics of scheduling, and providing staff and peer support. . . . Educators at the secondary level encounter challenging tasks related to inclusion: selecting general education classes; infusing student goals across subject areas; and establishing teaching partnerships and curricular adaptations. (Siegel-Causey, McMorris, McGowen, & Sands-Buss, 1998, p. 66)

Today, there are more students with documented disabilities in higher education than ever before—over 95% of all freshmen as compared with only 2.6% in 1978. Although the process has been slow, colleges and universities have made their programs more and more accessible, sometimes in good faith, sometimes due to coercion made by federal agencies and courts. Only modest progress was made between 1973 and 1990; however, once the ADA [Americans with Disabilities Act] was passed . . . [universities and colleges] that had made little or no progress in making their building and programs accessible increased their efforts. . . . Of particular significance in recent years has been the growth in the number of students with learning disabilities. Over 35% of the freshmen in 1996 who reported having a disability were purported to have a learning disability. . . . The growth in the number of students with learning disabilities has created a new challenge to professors and colleges. . . . Many professors prefer that all students meet the same set of requirements, within the same time period . . . and in the same way, and are ill-prepared to adapt their instruction to address the individual needs of students or to identify appropriate, fair, and reasonable accommodations. (Thomas, 2000, p. 248)

Lee

Lee is a high school student with a part-time job stocking shelves at a local store. Lee walks from his high school to catch the bus to work. On his way to the bus, everyone says hello to Lee. He's a great friend to everybody. Everyone makes it a point to stop and ask how he's doing.

At work, his employer gives him a checklist indicating how many cases of each item Lee needs to bring from the backroom to stock on the shelves. Lee can't read, but he can associate the item with the cases in the backroom. Most of Lee's education occurs in the community with the assistance of peer tutors who help him learn to purchase foods, bank, use the bus, and perform various work functions.

In his high school classes, Lee also has access to peer tutors who work with him. They may provide one-on-one tutoring or participate with him in a weight-lifting class. They are invaluable to him and his teachers.

Lee has become much more independent because of the skills he has learned in school and practiced in the community. Eventually, he plans to live independently.

Albert

From the time he was 16 years old, Albert's high school program had placed a strong emphasis on planning for his transition from school to adult life. During the first two years of high school, Albert spent part of his day in traditional core subjects such as math and science, working with a general education and special education team on academic and adaptive skill development. The remainder of his day was spent outside the classroom in experiences focusing on employment training, recreation, and management of his personal life. As graduation grew nearer, Albert spent more and more of his school day in an on-the-job employment training program. During his high school years, employment training had included sampling various jobs in the local community to match his interests and abilities with the demands of various employment opportunities. Albert was provided on-the-job training and support from teachers and other school staff, vocational education personnel, and vocational rehabilitation counselors. In his final year of high school, Albert was hired to work in housekeeping and laundry at a local hotel, where he continued to receive training and support from school personnel. The transition program also focused on helping Albert learn how to access various community activities, such as parks, theaters, and restaurants. His training also included hygiene, use of a personal schedule, and a time management system.

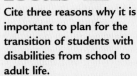

Cite three reasons why it is important to plan for the transition of students with disabilities from school to adult life.

OR MANY YEARS, THE development of appropriate services for people who are exceptional, particularly those with disabilities, has focused primarily on school-age children. With the advent of the 21st century, a crucial issue faces students, parents, and professionals: what is the relationship between school instruction and individual needs and preferences during adulthood? There are some substantial reasons why this issue is receiving a great deal of attention.

Research has suggested that many people with disabilities are not able to access the services necessary for success in postsecondary education or in the community, either during high school or following graduation (Gartin et al., 1996; Hasazi, Furney, & Destafano, 1999; N.O.D./Harris, 2000; Valdes, Williamson, & Wagner, 1990; Wagner & Blackorby, 1996). The U.S. Department of Education's National Longitudinal Transition Study (Wagner & Blackorby, 1996) reported that paid employment during high school had become more common, with 42% of students with disabilities being placed in community vocational or employment programs. However, one out of four of these students worked fewer than 10 hours per week and was paid below minimum wage. Additionally, most students were in service and manual labor positions. Five years out of high school, 57% of these students were in competitive employment and 43% were working full-time. The employment rate of individuals with disabilities lagged far beyond that of nondisabled adults.

The increasing emphasis on the transition from school to adult life has altered many previously held perceptions about people with disabilities. Without question, the potential of adults with disabilities has been significantly underestimated. In recent years, professionals and parents have begun to address some of the crucial issues facing adolescents with disabilities as they prepare to leave school and face life as adults in their local communities. Nearly half a million students with disabilities exit school each year. Since the passage of IDEA, schools have made significant strides in preparing youth with disabilities for adult life, but much remains to be done. Of the students age 17 and older exiting school, only 61% leave with a high school diploma as compared to 90% of their nondisabled peers (U.S. Department of Education, 2000a). Many of the current graduates from special education programs are not adequately prepared for employment and are unable to access further education. They are unable to locate the critical programs and services necessary for success as adults in their local communities (Chadsey-Rusch & Heal, 1998; McDonnell, Mathot-Buckner, & Ferguson, 1996; N.O.D./Harris, 2000; Wehman, 1996). For people with more severe disabilities, long waiting lists for employment and housing services prove frustrating (Prouty & Lakin, 1996). In 1997, Davis reported that over 200,000 adults with disabilities were on waiting lists for residential, day treatment, or family support services. Individuals with disabilities who enroll in postsecondary education will often find that the supports and services necessary for them to find success in college are not available (Gartin et al., 1996; Thomas, 2000).

> ■ TRANSITION SERVICES. A coordinated set of activities for students with disabilities that are designed to facilitate the move from school to employment, further education, vocational training, independent living, and community participation.

Transition Planning and Services

The transition from school to adult life is a complex and dynamic process that should begin as early as possible. Transition planning should culminate with the transfer of support from the school to an adult service agency, access to postsecondary education, or life as an independent adult. The planning process involves a series of choices about which experiences would best prepare students with disabilities in their remaining school years for what lies ahead in the adult world. A successful transition from school to the adult years requires both formal (government-funded) and natural family supports (Ferguson & Ferguson, 2000; Repetto & Correa, 1996; Szymanski, 1994; Turnbull & Turnbull, 1996; Wehman & Revell, 1997). Historically, providing formal supports, such as health care, employment preparation, and supported living, has been emphasized. Only recently has society begun to understand the importance of the family and other natural support networks in preparing the adolescent with disabilities for adult life. Research suggests that the family unit may be the single most powerful force in preparing the adolescent with disabilities for the adult years (Berry & Hardman, 1998).

Legal Requirements for Transition Services

The requirement that every student with a disability receive transition services was enacted as law through the 1990 amendments to the Individuals with Disabilities Education Act (IDEA) and modified by Congress in IDEA 97. Under current law, **transition services** for a student with a disability refers to a coordinated set of activities with the following attributes:

focus 2

How does IDEA define transition services?

- Designed within an outcome-oriented process, which promotes movement from school to postschool activities, including postsecondary education, vocational training, integrated employment (including supported employment), continuing and adult education, adult services, independent living, or community participation
- Based upon the individual student's needs, taking into account the student's preferences and interests
- Includes instruction, related services, community experiences, the development of employment and other postschool adult living objectives, and, when appropriate, acquisition of daily living skills and functional vocational evaluation (Sec. 602[30])

focus 3

What information should be included in each student's IEP statement for transition services? Who should be involved in the planning process?

IDEA requires that beginning at age 14, and updated annually, a student's IEP must include a statement of the transition services that relate to various courses of study (such as participation in advanced placement courses or a vocational education program). Beginning at age 16 (or younger, if determined appropriate by the IEP team), an IEP should include a statement of needed transition services, including, when appropriate, a statement of the responsibilities of other agencies (such as vocational rehabilitation) or any other needed linkages.

Four other pieces of federal legislation are also important in the transition planning process: the Vocational Rehabilitation Act (as amended in 1998), the Carl Perkins Vocational and Applied Technology Education Act of 1990 (PL 98-524), the Americans with Disabilities Act of 1990 (ADA), the School-to-Work Opportunities Act of 1993, and the Work Incentives Act of 1999. The Vocational Rehabilitation Act provides services through rehabilitation counselors in several areas (such as guidance and counseling, vocational evaluation, vocational training and job placement, transportation, family services, interpreter services, and telecommunication aids and devices). Recent amendments to the act encourage stronger collaboration and outreach between the schools and the rehabilitation counselors in transition planning.

Greater linkages between education and vocational rehabilitation are expected to benefit the student with a disability in moving on to postsecondary education or in obtaining employment. The Carl Perkins Act provides students with disabilities greater access to vocational education services. ADA focuses on equal access to public accommodations, employment, transportation, and telecommunication services following the school transition years. Such services are often directly targeted as a part of the student's transition plan.

The School-to-Work Act provides *all* students in the public schools with education and training to prepare them for first jobs in high-skill, high-wage careers and for further education following high school. Students with disabilities are specifically identified as a target population of the act. The Work Incentives Act of 1999 provides greater opportunities for the employment of people with disabilities by allowing them to work and still keep critical health care coverage. Prior to the passage of this act, many people with disabilities were not able to work because federal Social Security laws put them at risk of losing Medicaid and Medicare coverage if they accrued any significant earnings. As such, there was little incentive for people with disabilities to work because they could not access health insurance. The Work Incentives Act made health insurance available and affordable when a person with a disability goes to work or develops a significant disability while working.

The principal components of a transition system include the following:

- Effective middle and high school programs that link instruction to further education (such as college or trade schools) and valued postschool outcomes (such as employment, independent living, recreation/leisure activities)

- A cooperative system of transition planning that involves public education, adult services, and an array of natural supports (family and friends) in order to ensure access to valued postschool outcomes
- The availability of formal government-funded programs following school that are capable of meeting the unique educational, employment, residential, and leisure needs of people with disabilities in a community setting

The Individualized Transition Plan (ITP)

Transition involves much more than the mere transfer of administrative responsibility from the school to an adult service agency. An **individualized transition plan (ITP),** based on an evaluation of student needs and preferences, must be developed and implemented. The ITP should include access to the general education curriculum and/or a focus on the adaptive and functional skills that will facilitate life in the community following school (Alberto, Taber, Brozovic, & Elliot, 1997).

The ITP is a statement within each student's IEP describing needed transition services (see Figure 5.1). The purpose of the transition statement is to (1) identify the type and range of transitional services and supports, and (2) establish timelines and personnel responsible for completing the plan. Wehman (1996) identified seven basic steps in the formulation of a student's ITP: (1) organize ITP teams for all transition-age students; (2) organize a circle of support; (3) identify key activities; (4) hold initial ITP meetings as part of annual IEP meetings; (5) implement the ITP through secondary school and adult services provision; (6) update the ITP annually during the IEP meetings and implement quarterly follow-up procedure; and (7) hold an exit meeting (see Table 5.1).

■ INVOLVING STUDENTS AND PARENTS

In the transition from school to the adult world, many students and parents receive a considerable shock. The services they were entitled to during the school years are no longer mandated by law. The student may receive no further assistance from government programs or, at the least, may be placed on long waiting lists for employment training, housing, or education assistance. As such, the person with a disability may experience a significant loss in services at a crucial time. Many students and their parents know little, if anything, about what life may bring during the adult years.

To fully prepare for the transition from high school to adult life, students and parents must be educated about critical components of adult service systems, including the characteristics of service agencies and what constitutes a good program, as well as current and potential opportunities for employment, independent living, or further education (deFur, 1999; Whitney-Thomas & Hanley-Maxwell, 1996). McDonnell et al. (1996) suggested three strategies that schools could use to facilitate family involvement in the transition process:

- *Adopt a person-centered approach to transition planning.* The student should be at the center of the planning process, and his or her specific needs, preferences, and values should come first.
- *Assist parents in identifying their son's or daughter's preferences.* Families have the most comprehensive understanding of the student with a disability. Schools must work with the family to help the student to understand and verbalize, as much as possible, his or her values, wants, and needs prior to entering adult life.

■ INDIVIDUALIZED TRANSITION PLAN. A statement about transition services within each student's IEP. It identifies the range of services needed, high school activities to facilitate the individual's access to adult programs if necessary, timelines, and responsibilities for completion of these activities.

BACKGROUND INFORMATION	PARTICIPANTS

Student Name: *Lisa O'Neil*	Parents: *Sarah and Gene O'Neil*
Meeting Date: *3/25/2001*	School Principal: *Sally Monroe*
Place of Meeting: *Eastridge High School*	Special Education Teacher: *Dennis Cochran*
Proposed Graduation Date: *6/2003*	School Psychologist: *George Rivera*

PLANNING AREA: *Work Experience in Outdoor Recreation*

Transition Goal: *Lisa will initiate a work experience program for a minimum of 10 hours per week through the local parks and recreation program, state fish and game department, and/or national forest service.*

SUPPORT ACTIVITIES	RESPONSIBLE PERSON	TIMELINES
Complete application to the appropriate agency for work experience program	Lisa O'Neil w/support from Dennis Cochran	4/15/2001
Determine most appropriate work experience site along public transportation route	Team members	5/15/2001
Contact vocational rehabilitation and local job service agency to identify personnel to be involved in transition plan	Dennis Cochran	5/15/2001
Schedule work experience program into school schedule	Dennis Cochran George Rivera	6/1/2001
Meet with director of selected agency to set up logistics for work experience program	Lisa O'Neil Mr. and Mrs. O'Neil Dennis Cochran	9/15/2001
Handle logistics for public transportation to and from work experience site (e.g., insurance, backup, etc.); approve off-campus community-based program	Sally Monroe	9/15/2001
Obtain public transit bus pass	Mr. and Mrs. O'Neil	9/15/2001
Teach bus route to and from work experience site	Dennis Cochran	10/1/2001
Develop objectives for Lisa based on work experience requirements on site	Team members and identified agency supervisor	10/1/2001
Begin work experience program	School: Dennis Cochran Training site: Identified agency supervisor	10/15/2001
Evaluate progress toward identified work experience objectives	Team members	ongoing

[*Source:* Adapted from *Lifespan Perspectives on the Family and Disability* (p. 221), by J. Berry and M. L. Hardman, 1998, Boston: Allyn and Bacon.]

TABLE 5.1	Basic steps in the formulation of an ITP
Step 1: Organize ITP teams for all transition-age students.	■ Identify all students who are at transition age. ■ Identify appropriate school service personnel. ■ Identify adult service agencies.
Step 2: Organize a circle of support.	■ Meet with transition-age student and small circle of friends, family members, coworkers, neighbors, church members, and staff to establish individual's needs and preferences for adult life.
Step 3: Identify key activities.	■ Identify those items that are most important to the individual in the transition from school to adult years.
Step 4: Hold initial ITP meetings as part of annual IEP meetings.	■ Schedule the ITP meeting. ■ Conduct the ITP meeting. ■ Develop the ITP.
Step 5: Implement the ITP.	■ Operate according to guidelines defined in local interagency agreements. ■ Use a transdisciplinary and cross-agency approach.
Step 6: Update the ITP annually during the IEP meetings, and implement follow-up procedures.	■ Phase out involvement of school personnel while increasing involvement of adult services personnel. ■ Contact persons responsible for completion of ITP goals to monitor progress.
Step 7: Hold an exit meeting.	■ Ensure most appropriate employment outcome. ■ Ensure most appropriate recreation outcome. ■ Ensure most appropriate community living outcome. ■ Ensure referrals to all appropriate adult agencies and support services.

Source: Adapted from "Individualized Transition Planning," by P. Wehman. In *Life Beyond the Classroom: Transition Strategies for Young People with Disabilities* (2nd ed.), edited by P. Wehman, 1996, pp. 78–98. Baltimore: Paul H. Brookes. Used with permission.

■ *Help parents explore and identify "their" expectations.* Parents will differ in their individual expectations. Some will have difficulty letting go and giving their son or daughter more responsibility and freedom as adults. Others view greater independence from the family as an important part of their son or daughter's transition into adult life.

■ WORKING WITH ADULT SERVICES

In addition to the student, parents, and school personnel, the team developing the ITP may also involve professionals from **adult service agencies** (such as vocational rehabilitation counselors, representatives from university or college centers for students with disabilities, the state developmental disability agency, etc.). Adult service agencies focus on providing services to assist individuals with disabilities in accessing postsecondary education, employment, supported living, or leisure activities. Agencies may provide support in vocational rehabilitation, social services, and mental health. Examples of supports include *career, education, or mental health counseling, job training and support (such as a job coach), further education (college or trade school), attendant services, and interpreter services.*

▮ ADULT SERVICE AGENCIES. Agencies whose major focus is to provide services necessary to assist individuals with disabilities to become more independent as adults. Adult agencies include rehabilitation services, social services, mental health services, and so on.

Adult service agencies should become involved early in transition planning to begin targeting the services necessary once the student leaves school. This involvement includes direct participation in the development of the student's transition plan. Adult service professionals should collaborate with the student, parents, and the school in establishing transition goals and identifying appropriate activities for the student during the final school years. Additionally, adult service professionals must be involved in developing information systems that can effectively track students as they leave school, and monitor the availability and appropriateness of services to be provided during adulthood (Wehman, 1996).

The importance of developing and implementing effective transition services for students with disabilities cannot be overstated. Despite significant federal and state investment in educational programs for these students, many remain unemployed, are socially isolated, and depend on the family and community service programs during adulthood. That model transition programs and services have been developed in most areas in the United States demonstrates that students with disabilities can achieve postschool outcomes that will enhance their access and opportunities in nearly every aspect of community life (Chadsey-Rusch & Heal, 1998; Hasazi et al., 1999).

Implementing Transition Services in Secondary Schools

Successful transition begins with a solid foundation, and that foundation is the school. Secondary school programs (middle and high school) must provide activities that will facilitate success for the individual during the adult years. For Lee and Albert, in the opening snapshot, these activities included learning to shop in a neighborhood grocery store and training for a job in the community. For another student with a disability who has different preferences, needs, and abilities, the activities may be more academically based and focus on instruction in the general education curriculum with preparation for postsecondary education.

focus 4

Identify three outcomes expected for adolescents with disabilities as they enter adulthood.

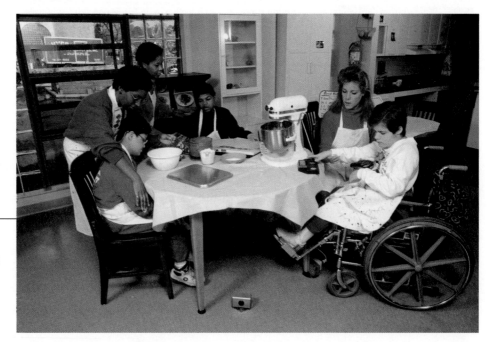

Schools must provide many different activities to facilitate each student's successful transition from school to adult life.

In this chapter, the term *secondary schools* will encompass both middle school (junior high) and high school. This is not to ignore the important distinctions between middle and high school programs. The purpose of middle school education is to be "responsive to the special needs of the young adolescent" (Clark & Clark, 1994, p. 5), and that of high school education is to help the older adolescent "move with confidence from school to work and further education" (Boyer, 1983, p. 305). Middle school grade-level configurations vary; some schools encompass sixth through eighth grades and others seventh through ninth grades.

IDEA provides that transition services begin for students with disabilities as early as age 14. As such, middle schools play an important role in the planning process for many of these students. The cornerstone of this planning will be an "exploratory curriculum" that provides a direct link between the concepts and skills learned during the elementary years and the knowledge to be acquired during high school that will facilitate transition to adult life. A middle school exploratory curriculum exposes the student to as many programs and activities as possible prior to a more narrow focus during the high school years.

Several outcomes are expected for students with disabilities as they enter adulthood. First, as adults they should be able to function as independently as possible in their daily lives; their reliance on others to meet their needs should be minimized. As students with disabilities leave school, they should be able to make choices about where they will live, how they will spend their free time, and whether they will immediately begin working in the community or go on to postsecondary education.

A job in the community is of value to the person with a disability, both for the monetary benefits and for the opportunities for social interaction, personal identity, and contribution to others. All adults should be able to participate in social and leisure activities that are an integral part of community life. These activities might include going to the movies, participating in sports (such as skiing, bowling, swimming, etc.), eating out at a restaurant, or just relaxing in a local park.

There are also increasing opportunities for students with disabilities to further their education as they transition from high school to adult life. The two primary pathways are (1) vocational and community-based instruction leading to eventual employment (Falvey, Gage, & Eshilian, 1995), and (2) academic programs leading to further education at the postsecondary level (Zigmond, 1990). For students considering further education at the postsecondary level, Table 5.2 shows a model for a student's transition from high school to college.

Secondary schools are in the unique position of being able to coordinate activities that enhance student participation in the community and link students such as Lee and Albert with needed programs and services. Schools have many roles in the transition process: assessing individual needs, helping each student develop a transition plan, coordinating transition planning with adult service agencies, and participating with parents in the planning process.

The preferences and needs of adults with disabilities vary according to functioning levels and requirements of each community and family setting. Involvement with community activities may require significant and long-term support for people with severe disabilities. Adults with mild disabilities, in contrast, may need only short-term assistance or no support system whatsoever during their adult years.

■ TEACHING SELF-DETERMINATION

A factor that appears to play a critical role in the transition from school to adult life is the teaching of self-determination (personal choice) (Field & Hoffman, 1999; Morgan, Ellerd, Gerity, & Blair, 2000; Wehmeyer, 1998; Wehymer & Sands, 1998).

TABLE 5.2	Higher education transition model

Essential Curricular Elements	Instructional Objectives
Psychosocial adjustment	1. Self-advocacy skill development
	2. Handling frustration
	3. Social problem-solving
	4. College-level social skills
	5. Mentor relationships
Academic development	1. College entrance exam preparation
	2. Test-taking strategies/accommodations
	3. Career awareness
	4. Goal setting
	5. Academic remediation
	6. Career preparation
	7. Learning strategies/study skills
	8. College services
	9. Transition to college
College/community orientation	1. College-level linkage
	2. Buddy systems
	3. College choices
	4. College resources/activities
	5. College orientation program
	6. Campus support groups
	7. Community services assessment

Source: From "The Higher Education Transition Model: Guidelines for Facilitating College Transition Among College-Bound Students with Disabilities," by B. C. Gartin, P. Rumrill, and R. Serebreni, 1996, *Teaching Exceptional Children, 29*(1), p. 31. Copyright 1996 by the Council for Exceptional Children. Reprinted with permission.

focus 5

Why is it important for students with disabilities to receive instruction in self-determination, academics, adaptive and functional life skills, and employment preparation during the secondary school years?

Self-determination is "the ability of a person to consider options and make appropriate choices regarding residential life, work, and leisure time" (Schloss, Alper, & Jayne, 1993, p. 215). That secondary schools need to focus on self-determination is evident from research revealing the reasons why individuals with disabilities fail in employment situations. In a summary of the research in this area, Schloss et al. stated that individuals with disabilities do not fail because they can't do the required tasks of the job. Instead, "failure has been linked to a lack of appropriate *decision-making* skills related to the job and in ability to adjust to work situations" (p. 216, emphasis added).

Teaching self-determination skills to students with disabilities helps them become more efficient in acquiring knowledge and solving problems (Browder & Bambara, 2000). Students will be better able to achieve goals that will facilitate their transition out of school and become aware of the specific challenges they will face in the adult years. Ultimately, the student leaves school with a more well developed sense of personal worth, social responsibility, and problem-solving skills (Agran & Wehmeyer, 1999). Benjamin (1996) recommended a four-step problem-solving process in which schools and parents can support the development of self-determination for students with disabilities:

1. Through role playing and simulated activities, teach students to observe and analyze a situation by identifying a problem in the situation and giving it a name.
2. Ask students to think about possible options that might solve the problem. If they are unable to do so, teach them how to access resources, such as libraries and knowledgeable people, that will help them generate possible solutions.
3. Once a student has identified possible solutions and selected one, encourage him or her to see if any problem still exists. If yes, ask the student what he or she might do to change the plan and solve the problem.
4. Ask students to think about how to use strategies to solve similar problems in other situations.

Creating opportunities for individual choice and decision making is an important element in the school-to-adult life transition of people with disabilities. Each individual must be able to consider options and make appropriate choices. This means less problem solving and decision making on the part of service providers and family members and a greater focus on teaching and promoting choice. The planning process associated with the development of a student's IEP is an excellent opportunity to promote self-determination. Unfortunately, very few adolescents with disabilities attend their IEP meetings, and fewer yet *actively* participate (Wehman, 1996).

Although we have discussed self-determination in the context of the secondary school years, it is important to remember that instruction in self-determination must begin early in a child's life. As suggested by Abery (1994), "striving to attain self-determination doesn't begin (or end) during adolescence or early adulthood. Rather it is initiated shortly after birth and continues until we have breathed our last breath" (p. 2).

■ TEACHING ACADEMIC SKILLS

As the emphasis on access to the general education curriculum increases (see Chapter 1) for students with disabilities, the IEP team is faced with some difficult curriculum decisions. Should instruction emphasize academic learning in the core content areas such as English, math, or science, or should the focus be on preparation for life (adaptive and functional skills, employment preparation)?

Evidence indicates that students with disabilities are not faring well in the academic content of high school programs or in further postsecondary education (Bursuck & Rose, 1992; Hocutt, 1996; Zigmond & Miller, 1992). These students have high dropout rates and low academic achievement. However, evidence also shows that students with mild disabilities, particularly those with learning disabilities, can achieve in academic content areas beyond their current performance (Gajar, Goodman, & McAfee, 1993; National Research Council, 1997). Zigmond (1990) suggested that high school programs should include more "intensive instruction in reading and mathematics" (p. 20) as well as a strong emphasis on successful completion of content courses (such as history or biology) required for graduation. She suggested two service delivery models for students with learning disabilities, one focusing on continued postsecondary education or training and one emphasizing preparation for work. The model promoting postsecondary educational opportunities has five basic components:

1. Students are assigned to general education classes for content subjects required for graduation and for elective courses.
2. One special education teacher is assigned as a support or consulting teacher to work with general education teachers in whose classes students with learning disabilities are placed.
3. Additional special education teachers are responsible for yearly English and reading courses, one survival skills class, and a supervised study hall that students are scheduled to take each year of high school.
4. From the start of grade 9 (about age 14), students interact regularly with a counselor for transition planning.
5. Courses required for graduation are spaced evenly throughout the four years to reduce academic pressures, particularly in grade 9.

For students with more severe disabilities, the purpose of academic learning may be more functional and compensatory—skills that have immediate and frequent use in the student's environment (Browder & Snell, 2000). Instruction concentrates on skills that occur as part of the student's daily living routine. For example, safety skills may include reading street signs, railroad crossings, entrance/exit signs, or product labels. Information skills may include reading job application forms, classified ads, maps, telephone directories, or catalogs.

▪ TEACHING ADAPTIVE AND FUNCTIONAL LIFE SKILLS

Adaptive and functional life skills training may include accessing socialization activities in and out of school and learning to manage one's personal affairs. A fundamental need of students with disabilities in the secondary school years is access to social activities. It may be important to provide basic instruction on how to develop positive interpersonal relationships and the behaviors that are conducive to successfully participating in community settings (Agran & Wehmeyer, 1999; Wehmeyer, 1998; Wehmeyer & Bolding, 1999). Instruction could include the use of nondisabled peer tutors to both model for, and teach, students with disabilities appropriate social skills in community settings such as restaurants, theaters, or shopping malls.

Adolescence brings on a growing awareness of the requirements of adult life relative to sex-role expectations, personal appearance, and hygiene. Sexual interests are developing, as is conformity to peer opinions, activities, and appearances (Drew & Hardman, 2000). Dramatic physical and psychological changes with the onset of puberty can affect the individual's self-esteem. Secondary school programs face the difficult challenge of identifying their role in providing instruction in these areas. However, if these skills are not taught in the home and the school chooses not to include them in an educational program, students with disabilities may be placed at a significant disadvantage as they move from school to life as an adult in the community.

▪ EMPLOYMENT PREPARATION

People with disabilities are often characterized as consumers of society's resources rather than as contributors, but employment goes a long way toward dispelling this idea. Paid employment means earning wages through which individuals can obtain material goods and enhance their quality of life; it also contributes to personal identity and status (Drew & Hardman, 2000). Today, many adults with disabilities are unemployed or underemployed despite advances in research and development of effective employment practices (N.O.D./Harris & Associates, 2000; Valdes et al., 1990; Wagner & Blackorby, 1996).

In the past, high schools have been somewhat passive in their approach to employment training, focusing primarily on teaching vocational readiness through simulations in a classroom setting. More recently, high schools have begun to emphasize employment preparation for students with disabilities through work experience, career education, and community-referenced instruction. In a *work experience program,* the student spends a portion of the school day in classroom settings (which may emphasize academic and/or vocational skills) and the remainder at an off-campus site receiving on-the-job training. The responsibility for the training may be shared among the high school special education teacher, vocational rehabilitation counselor, and vocational education teacher.

Career education includes training in social skills development as well as general occupational skills. Career education programs usually concentrate on developing an awareness of various career choices, exploring occupational opportunities, and developing appropriate attitudes, social skills, and work habits.

Whereas career education is oriented to developing an awareness of various occupations, *community-referenced instruction* involves direct training and ongoing support as necessary in a community employment site. The demands of the work setting and the functioning level, interests, and wishes of each individual determine the goals and objectives of the training. The most notable difference between community-referenced instruction and work experience programs is that the former focuses on the activities to be accomplished at the work site rather than on the development of isolated skills in the classroom. An employment training program based on a community-referenced approach includes the following elements:

- Primary focus on student and family needs and preferences
- A balance between time spent in inclusive general education classrooms and placement and employment preparation at least until age 18
- A curriculum that reflects the job opportunities available in the local community
- An employment training program that takes place at actual job sites
- Training designed to sample the student's performance across a variety of economically viable alternatives
- Ongoing opportunities for students to interact with nondisabled peers in a work setting
- Training that culminates in employment placement
- Job placement linked to comprehensive transition planning, which focuses on establishing interagency agreements that support the student's full participation in the community (Drew & Hardman, 2000; Moon & Inge, 2000)

The Adult Years

Most of the attention given to exceptionality in the past has focused on children and youth. Only recently have professionals begun to address the challenges encountered by adults, altering our overall perspective of exceptionality and broadening the views of many professionals. Would Adolphe's life (see the nearby Snapshot) have been better if intervention had occurred when he was younger? What can be done now to ensure that Adolphe has the supports he needs to actively participate in the life of his community?

For most people, reaching adulthood is a time when one leaves home, gets a job, and becomes more self-reliant, no longer dependent on parents or caregivers. For adults with disabilities, living conditions and lifestyles vary greatly. Many people

Snapshot

Adolphe

Adolphe was 31 when he came to what may have been the most startling realization of his life: he was learning disabled! Adolphe was uncertain what this label meant, but at least he now had a term for what had mostly been a difficult life. The label came from a clinical psychologist who had administered a number of tests after Adolphe had been referred by his counselor, whom he had been seeing since his divorce a year ago. The past year had been particularly rough, although most of Adolphe's life had been troublesome.

As a young child, Adolphe was often left out of group activities. He was not very adept at sports, was uncoordinated, and could not catch or hit a baseball no matter how hard he tried. School was worse. Adolphe had a difficult time completing assignments and often forgot instructions. Paying attention in class was difficult, and it often seemed as though there were more interesting activities than the assignments.

Adolphe finally gave up on school when he was a junior and took a job in a local service station. That employment did not last long, for he was terminated because of frequent billing errors. The owners said they could not afford to lose so much money because of "stupid mistakes on credit card invoices."

The loss of that job did not bother Adolphe much. An enterprising young man, he had already found employment in the post office, which paid much more and seemed to have greater respectability.

Sorting letters presented a problem, however, and loss of that job did trouble Adolphe. He began to doubt his mental ability further and sought comfort in his girlfriend, whom he had met recently at a YMCA dance. They married quickly when she became pregnant, but things did not become easier. After 12 years of marriage, two children, a divorce, and five jobs, Adolphe is finally gaining some understanding of why he has been so challenged throughout his life.

---

with disabilities lead a somewhat typical existence, living and working in their community, perhaps marrying, and for the most part supporting themselves financially. These adults still need support, however, as do people who are not disabled. That support is most often "time-limited" (such as vocational rehabilitation services) or informal (attention from family members and friends). Those with more severe disabilities reach adulthood still in need of an ongoing formal support system that facilitates their opportunities for paid employment, housing in the community, and access to recreation and leisure experiences.

Next, we look at some of the decisions facing the individual with disabilities and his or her family during the adult years. From there, we move on to discuss what it takes to build a support network for adults with disabilities, concluding with a discussion on issues concerned with aging adults.

■ MAKING CHOICES

Adult status for people with disabilities and their families is often paradoxical. On the one hand, many parents struggle with their child's "right to grow up." On the other hand, they must face the realities of their adult offspring's continuing need for support, further complicated by the issues surrounding what legally or practically constitutes adult status. Just as there is a great deal of variability in the needs and functioning level of people with disabilities, there is also considerable variability in lifestyle during the adult years. Adults with mild disabilities may lead a life similar to those of nondisabled peers, primarily because their challenges while growing up were mostly related to academic performance in school. Some adults with mild disabilities go on to postsecondary education and become self-supporting, eventually working and living independent of their immediate family. As is true for nondisabled people, however, some of these adults may still need assistance, whether it be government-funded or from family, friends, and neighbors. For adults with more severe disabilities, ongoing government-funded and natural supports are critical in order to ensure access and participation in employment, supported residential living, and recreation in their local community. Parents and family members of people with severe disabilities often face the stark reality that their caregiving role may not diminish during the adult years and could well extend through a lifetime. About 60% of adults with more severe disabilities of all ages live at home with their parents and/or siblings (Heller, 2000). One in four of the family caregivers are over the age of 60 years (Braddock, 1999).

Quality of life during the adult years is most often characterized by (1) employment, useful work, and valued activity; (2) access to further education when desired and appropriate; (3) personal autonomy and independence; (4) social interaction and community participation; and (5) participation within the life of the family. As one reaches the adult years, decisions have to be made relative to each of these areas. What kind of career or job do I desire? Should I go on to further education to increase my career choices? Where shall I live, and whom shall I live with? How shall I spend my money? Whom do I choose to spend time with? Who will be my friends? Whereas most people face these choices as a natural part of the transition into adult life, the questions facing a person with disabilities and his or her family may be quite different. Issues concerning the competence of the person with a disability to make decisions in his or her best interest, as well as the role of formal and informal support networks to assist in such decision making, may also arise. (See Table 5.3.)

TABLE 5.3	Adults with disabilities and self-determination	
A Traditional Adult Services Model	**Self-Determination**	**The Principles of Self-Determination**[1]
■ Professionals make all the decisions. ■ People with disabilities are seen as requiring supervision and direction. ■ Services to the person are determined by what's available in any given program.	■ The person with a disability takes charge of and responsibility for his or her life. ■ The person, not the service system, decides where he or she will live, and with whom; what type of services he or she requires, and who will provide them; how he or she will spend time and relate to the community, which may include joining in community events, taking part in civic groups, and developing and maintaining relationships with others in the community. ■ Self-determination is not a program with a predetermined menu of available services and a set way of delivering them. Self-determination is a process that differs from person to person according to what each individual determines is necessary and desirable to create a satisfying and personally meaningful life. They are free to "order off the menu," including those services they desire to be provided in ways that meet their needs.	■ *Freedom*—the ability for an individual, together with freely chosen family and friends, to plan a life with necessary support rather than purchase a program ■ *Authority*—the ability for a person with a disability (with a social support network or circle if needed) to control a certain sum of dollars in order to purchase services ■ *Autonomy*—the arranging of resources and personnel, both formal and informal, that will assist an individual with a disability to live a life in the community rich in community affiliations ■ *Responsibility*—the acceptance of a valued role in a person's community through competitive employment, organizational affiliations, spiritual development, and general caring of others in the community, as well as accountability for spending public dollars in ways that are life-enhancing for persons with disabilities

[1]*Source:* From "Self-Determination for People with Developmental Disabilities," by T. Nerney, 1998, *AAMR News and Notes, 11*(6), pp. 10–11, 12.

■ BUILDING A SUPPORT NETWORK FOR ADULTS WITH DISABILITIES

During the adult years, people with disabilities and their families must not only come to terms with making choices relative to planning for the future, but also they must deal with the maze of options of government-funded programs. Over the past 30 years, adult services have gone through major reform. The system has evolved from a sole focus on protecting, managing, and caring for persons with disabilities in segregated settings to one of providing what is necessary in order for the person to participate in family and community life. As we move into the 21st century, adult services are attempting to be more flexible to the changing needs and preferences of the person with a disability and his or her network of family and friends. However, as suggested by a recent survey of Americans with disabilities (N.O.D./Harris, 2000), there is still a long way to go. (See the nearby Reflect on This feature.)

In this section, we explore the concept of "supports" for people with disabilities in the context of (1) government-funded programs in the areas of income support, health care, supported residential living, and employment, and (2) natural support networks of family and friends.

■ GOVERNMENT-FUNDED PROGRAMS   Two types of adult service programs for people with disabilities are supported by the government: entitlements and eligibility. Under an **entitlement program,** everyone who meets the eligibility criteria must receive the service. **Income support** (such as Supplemental Social Security Income) and medical assistance programs (such as Medicaid and Medicare) are government-supported entitlement programs for adults with disabilities. The Individuals with Disabilities Education Act is an example of an entitlement program for school-age students with disabilities. Entitlement programs require that services be provided to eligible individuals with disabilities without respect to the availability of funds.

Under an eligibility program, in contrast, the person with a disability may meet the eligibility criteria but not receive the service because there are *not* enough funds to serve everyone. When funds are insufficient, some people with disabilities may spend months or even years on waiting lists. Residential services (housing) and many employment programs (such as **supported employment**) are examples of eligibility programs.

Income Support.   Government income support programs, enacted through Social Security legislation (Supplemental Security Income [SSI] and Social Security Disability Insurance [SSDI]), provide direct cash payments to people with disabilities and other eligible individuals, thus providing basic economic assistance. Income support programs have been both praised and condemned. They have been praised because money is provided to people in need who otherwise would have no means to support themselves. They have been condemned because such support programs can make it economically advantageous for people with disabilities to remain unemployed and dependent on society. For many years, an individual who went to work at even 50% of minimum wage would potentially lose income support and medical benefits that far exceeded the amount they would earn on a job. This disincentive to work has been significantly reduced with the passage of the Work Incentives Act of 1999. People with disabilities can now go to work and not worry about losing critical health care coverage.

Health Care.   Government-sponsored health care for people with disabilities comes under two programs: Medicaid and Medicare. **Medicaid,** established in 1965, pays for health care services for individuals receiving SSI cash payments, as

focus 6

What are the purposes of government-funded programs for people with disabilities in the areas of income support, health care, residential living, and employment?

■ ENTITLEMENT PROGRAM. A government-funded program in which everyone who meets the eligibility requirements must receive the designated service. The Individuals with Disabilities Education Act is an entitlement program.

■ INCOME SUPPORT. A government-sponsored program whereby the individual receives cash payments to support living needs.

■ SUPPORTED EMPLOYMENT. Paid work in integrated community settings for individuals with more severe disabilities who are expected to need continuous support services, and for whom competitive employment has traditionally not been possible.

■ MEDICAID. A government-sponsored health care program for people with disabilities and others that pays for certain medical service, such as early screening, diagnosis, treatment and immunizations.

Reflect on This

A DECADE AFTER THE PASSAGE OF ADA, ADULTS WITH DISABILITIES STILL FACE SHARP GAPS IN EMPLOYMENT, EDUCATION, AND DAILY LIVING

A 2000 poll by the National Organization on Disability/Harris found that Americans with disabilities ages 18 to 64 were still lagging far behind nondisabled adults in overall satisfaction with life, employment and income levels, education, health care, civic participation, and access to transportation and recreation.

■ SATISFACTION WITH LIFE
- Only about one in three (33%) adults with disabilities is very satisfied with life in general, compared to fully seven out of ten (67%) nondisabled adults.

■ EMPLOYMENT
- Only 32% of adults with disabilities work full- or part-time, compared to 81% of those who are not disabled, a gap of nearly 50 percentage points.
- Of those with disabilities of working age who are not working, 67% say that they would prefer to work.
- The proportion of working-age adults with disabilities who are employed has remained constant since 1986.
- Forty-three percent of adults say that their disability has prevented or made it more difficult for them to get the kind of job they would like to have.

■ INCOME
- One out of three (29%) adults with disabilities lives in a household with an annual income of less than $15,000, compared to only 12% of those without disabilities.

■ EDUCATION
- One out of five (22%) adults with disabilities has not graduated from high school, compared to only one out of ten (9%) of nondisabled adults.
- Approximately one out of ten people with disabilities graduates from college, compared to slightly more than two out of ten nondisabled people.

■ HEALTH CARE
- One out of five (19%) adults with a disability did not get the medical care that he or she needed on at least one occasion during the past year, compared to only 6% of people of nondisabled adults.
- One in four (28%) adults with disabilities postponed getting health care they thought they needed in the past year because they couldn't afford it.
- Although nine out of ten (90%) adults with disabilities are covered by health insurance, they are more likely than nondisabled adults (28% versus 7%) to

not have their special needs covered.

■ VOTING
- People with disabilities are less likely to be registered to vote than people without disabilities (62% versus 78% respectively).

■ ACCESS TO TRANSPORTATION
- Inadequate transportation is considered a problem by 30% of adults with disabilities but by only 10% of nondisabled adults.

■ FREQUENCY OF SOCIALIZING
- Seven out of ten (70%) adults with disabilities socialize with close friends, relatives, or neighbors at least once a week, compared to more than eight out of ten (85%) of the nondisabled adults.

■ ENTERTAINMENT/GOING OUT
- One in four (40%) of adults with disabilities go to a restaurant at least once a week, compared to six out of ten (59%) of those without disabilities.

■ OTHER KEY FINDINGS
- Over the past 14 years, education has shown signs of improvement for all people with disabilities, and employment has shown signs of improvement for

people who say they are able to work.
- Among people with disabilities who say they are able to work despite their disability or health problem, 56% are working today, compared to only 46% in 1986. These improvements most likely stem from multiple causes, including the Americans with Disabilities Act and the Individuals with Disabilities Education Act.
- Over 70% of people with disabilities agree that access to public facilities such as restaurants, theaters, stores, and museums has gotten better over the past four years.
- In an era of economic expansion, it appears that people with disabilities have been less likely to benefit. They are more likely to have lower incomes than people without disabilities, and lower-income individuals are less likely to benefit from increases in the stock market or an overall economic surge.

Source: From *National Organization on Disability/Harris Survey of Americans with Disabilities (Executive Summary),* by N.O.D./L. Harris and Associates, 2000, pp. 14–20. New York: Author.

well as families receiving welfare payments. Medicaid is an example of a federal–state partnership program that requires participating states to provide matching funds to available federal dollars. The state match can be as low as 22% and as high as 50%, depending on state per capita income.

The Medicaid program can pay for inpatient and outpatient hospital services, laboratory services, and early screening, diagnosis, treatment, and immunization for children. Working within federal regulations, states design their own plans for the delivery of Medicaid services. Thus a service provided in one state may not be provided in another.

Medicare.   Title XVIII of the Social Security Act, Medicare is a national insurance program for individuals over the age of 65 and for eligible people with disabilities. Medicare has two parts: hospital insurance and supplementary medical insurance. The Hospital Insurance Program pays for short-term hospitalization, related care in skilled nursing facilities, and some home care. The Supplementary Medical Insurance Program covers physician services, outpatient services, ambulance services, some medical supplies, and medical equipment.

Supported Residential Living.   For most of the 20th century, federal government support for residential living was directed to large congregate care settings (institutions and nursing homes). As we enter the 21st century, however, people with disabilities, their families, and professionals are advocating for smaller community-based residences within local neighborhoods and communities. In the past 20 years, spending for smaller community residences increased sevenfold (Braddock & Hemp, 1997). People with disabilities and their families are also advocating for choice, individualization, and a focus on the abilities of people rather than on their disabilities in making decisions regarding community living.

Three of the most widely used models for residential living are group homes, semi-independent homes and apartments, and foster family care. Group homes may be large (as many as 15 or more people) or small (4 or fewer people). In the **group home** model, professionals provide ongoing training and support to people with disabilities, aiming to make daily living experiences as similar as possible to those of people who are not disabled. The **semi-independent apartment or home** provides housing for people with disabilities who require less supervision and support. This model for residential living may include apartment clusters (several apartments located close together), a single co-residence home or apartment in which a staff member shares the dwelling, or a single home or apartment occupied by a person with a disability who may or may not receive assistance from a professional.

Foster family care provides a surrogate family for persons with a disability. The goal of foster care is to integrate individuals with disabilities into a family setting where they will learn adaptive skills and work in the community. Foster family care settings may accommodate up to six adults with disabilities.

Employment.   Sustained competitive employment for people with disabilities is important for many reasons, as cited earlier (monetary rewards, adult identity, social contacts, and inclusion in a community setting). Yet the reality is that adults with disabilities are significantly underemployed and unemployed when compared to their nondisabled peers (N.O.D./Harris, 2000).

In spite of the bleak data on the unemployment rates of people with disabilities, there is good reason to be optimistic about their future employment opportunities. There is a greater emphasis on employment opportunities for these people than ever before (Blanck & Braddock, 1998; Reiff, Ginsberg, & Gerber, 1997; Ryan, 2000).

■ GROUP HOME. A supported living arrangement for people with disabilities, in which professionals provide ongoing training and support in a community home setting.

■ SEMI-INDEPENDENT APARTMENT OR HOME. A model for providing housing for persons with disabilities who require less supervision and support.

■ FOSTER FAMILY CARE. A supported living arrangement for persons with disabilities, whereby an individual(s) lives in a family setting, learns adaptive skills, and works in a community job.

Competitive employment can now be described in terms of three alternatives: employment with no support services, employment with time-limited support services, and employment with ongoing support services.

An adult with a disability may be able to locate and maintain employment without support from government-funded programs. Many find jobs through contacts with family and friends, the local job service, want ads, and the like. For people with mild disabilities, the potential for locating and maintaining a job is enhanced greatly if the individual has received employment training and experience during the school years (Gajar et al., 1993).

An adult with a disability may also have access to several employment services on a time-limited, short-term basis, including vocational rehabilitation, vocational education, and on-the-job training. Time-limited employment services provide intensive, short-term support to people with disabilities who have the potential to make it on their own after receiving government assistance. The most widely known time-limited support service is **vocational rehabilitation.**

Vocational rehabilitation provides services to enable people with disabilities, including those with the most severe disabilities, to pursue meaningful careers by securing gainful employment commensurate with their preferences and abilities. Through the vocational rehabilitation program, federal funds pass to the states to provide services in counseling, training, and job placement. The program, funded under the Vocational Rehabilitation Act, requires that the individual have an employment-related disability. In 1986, vocational rehabilitation services expanded to include funding for ongoing job training and support for those who need it: the supported employment model. The 1992 Amendments to the Rehabilitation Act authorized a program to provide grants for special projects and demonstrations to improve the provision of supported employment services to individuals with the most severe disabilities.

Supported employment is work in an integrated setting provided for people with disabilities who need some type of continuing support and for whom competitive employment has traditionally not been possible. The criteria for a supported

▌VOCATIONAL REHABILITATION. A government-sponsored program to assist people with disabilities to find employment consistent with their needs and abilities.

Vocational rehabilitation services include intensive short-term training and support for people with disabilities who are seeking gainful employment.

employment placement requires that (1) the job must provide between 20 and 40 hours of work weekly and be consistent with the individual's stamina, (2) the individual must earn a wage at or above minimum wage or at a wage commensurate with production level and based upon the prevailing wage rate for the job, (3) fringe benefits should be similar to those provided for nondisabled workers or with the public as a regular part of working, and (4) work should take place in settings where no more than eight persons with disabilities work together (1992 Amendments to the Vocational Rehabilitation Act).

Over the past two decades, supported employment has become a viable employment program for people with disabilities in need of long-term support (Mank, Cioffi, & Yovanoff, 1997; McDonnell et al., 1996; Wehman, West, & Kregel, 1999). Whereas there were fewer than 10,000 people with disabilities receiving supported employment in 1984, the number had grown to more than 140,000 in 1995 (Mank et al., 1997). The efficacy of supported employment has been documented through a variety of research studies (Braddock, Hemp, Bachelder, & Fujiura, 1995; McGaughey, Kiernan, McNally, & Gilmore, 1995; Murphy & Rogan, 1995; Revell et al., 1994; Rusch, Chadsey-Rusch, & Johnson, 1991; Tines et al., 1990).

Supported employment consists of four main features: wages, social integration with nondisabled peers, ongoing support provided as necessary by a job coach or through natural supports (coworkers), and application of a zero-exclusion principle. A zero-exclusion principle veers from the more traditional approach of "getting individuals with disabilities ready for work" to a principle of placing the individual on a job and providing the necessary supports to ensure success. The essential element of a successful supported employment program is establishing a match between the needs, preferences, and abilities of the individual with the demands of a particular job.

■ NATURAL SUPPORTS   The importance of natural supports for adults with disabilities, including family, friends, neighbors, and coworkers, cannot be overstated. As is true for all of us, adults with disabilities need a support network that extends beyond government-funded programs. Some adults with disabilities may never move away from their primary family. Parents, and in some cases siblings, assume the major responsibilities of ongoing support for a lifetime (Freedman, Krauss, & Seltzer, 1997). In a study of 43 adults with disabilities, Heller and Factor (1993) found that 63% of the persons interviewed indicated that they wanted to remain in the family home. Respondents suggested two reasons for not wanting to leave the primary family: fear of the alternatives and a desire to be near parents and siblings. It is estimated that about 85% of adults with more severe disabilities live with their parents for most of their lives (Braddock, Hemp, Parish, & Rizzolo, 2000; Seltzer & Krauss, 1994). Smith, Majeski, and McClenny (1996) characterized this situation as "perpetual parenthood" (p. 172). Perpetual parenthood results from an offspring's continuing dependence through the adult years, either because of a lack of formal resources for the family or because the family simply chooses to keep the individual at home.

Many siblings appear to have attitudes similar to those of their parents. A study by Griffiths and Unger (1994) suggested that most siblings believe that families should be responsible for the care of their adult disabled members. Most indicated that they were "willing to assume future caregiving responsibilities for their brothers/sisters" (p. 225). In a longitudinal study of 140 families who had adults with mental retardation still living at home, Krauss, Seltzer, Gordon, and Friedman (1996) found that many siblings remained very actively involved with their brothers or sisters well into the adult years. These siblings had frequent contact with their brother or sister and were knowledgeable about their lives. In addition, they played a major role in their parents' support network. Interestingly, about one in three of these siblings indicated that they planned to reside with their brother or sister at some point during adult life.

Whether the adult with disabilities continues to live with parents or siblings, in a semi-independent living situation, or independently, extended family members (grandparents, aunts, uncles, etc.) often remain important sources of support. Extended family members may help with transportation, meals, housecleaning, or just "being there" for the individual. Similar support may also come from friends, neighbors, and coworkers. The nature and type of support provided by individuals outside of the family will be unique to the individuals involved and will depend on a mutual level of comfort in both seeking and providing assistance. Clear communication regarding what friends or neighbors are willing to do, and how that matches with the needs and preferences of each individual, is essential.

Issues for Aging Adults with Disabilities

Life expectancy for all adults, including those with disabilities, continues to improve. According to present projections, by the year 2025, nearly 20% of U.S. citizens will be over the age of 65. The fastest-growing age group in the United States is people between the ages of 75 and 85 (U.S. Census Bureau, 2000). Due to significant advances in health care and treatment, many more older persons with disabilities are living longer and have expected lifespans similar to those of people who are not disabled (Lavin & Doka, 2000). This includes people with more severe disabilities. Heller (2000) estimated that there are about half a million adults with developmental disabilities age 60 and older in the United States. As life expectancy increases for people with disabilities, concerns have arisen among family members, service providers, and the individuals themselves related to life satisfaction, health care, and living arrangements as they age (Hawkins, 1993). Although the available information on age-related change in adults has increased as a whole, little is known about aging persons with disabilities (Eklund & Martz, 1993).

Although people with disabilities are living longer, they are not necessarily living better. In society's dramatic shift from institutionalization to community services for people with disabilities, new and significant challenges have arisen in areas such as home care and supported living. Today there is a significant gap in the availability of appropriate in-home and supported living services for aging people with

focus 7
Identify two challenges faced by aging people with disabilities.

Snapshot

Roberta

Roberta celebrated her 74th birthday with her dearest friends, Spencer and Josephine. They made a cake in their kitchen and placed a single candle on top.

Roberta's friends seemed like family although none of her actual family were present— they had not visited Roberta for several years. Roberta had lived in a nursing home for people with mental retardation just outside of Bend for

the past 10 years, but she was now living in a small group home with Spencer and Josephine. The three friends enjoy their time together, usually chatting, watching movies, or walking through the neighborhood. The support staff

present during the day assist them in handling the daily chores of the house, cooking, and doing the laundry. While all three are no longer employed, they spend a day a week volunteering at a local day-care center.

Many elderly people with disabilities are not receiving the assistance they need to live as independently as possible in small community settings.

disabilities. Lavin and Doka (2000) suggested that this gap is parallel to the evolution of special education services. "First [education] facilities were separate, then classes were separate, then classes were integrated. The same controversy regarding inclusion and participation extends throughout the life cycle. Individuals with disabilities are considered to be different from us, and there is a tendency to distance ourselves from them and avoid interaction" (p. 25).

In the area of health care, more and more professionals are attempting to expand our knowledge about the functional competence and health status of older people with disabilities. As suggested by Ireys, Wehr, and Cooke (1999), the failure to obtain critical health services may "curtail the ability of these persons to communicate . . . and actively participate in community life" (p. 1).

Similar research is being conducted in the area of community living. Research findings on community living options for older people with disabilities parallel those concerning adults with disabilities in general—a trend toward using smaller community living options. A survey by Martinson and Stone (1993) suggested that although large congregate care facilities (such as nursing homes) remain a major service provider for older people with disabilities, there is a clear trend toward smaller establishments. These authors note that "older adults with developmental disabilities should have the opportunity to participate in the communities in which they live, instead of being neglected into invisibility" (p. 197).

From the high school transition years through adult life, the issues surrounding delivery of quality services and supports to people with disabilities are varied and complex. With the information in this chapter as background, we now move on to focus on each area of exceptionality. The discussion will continue to highlight multicultural, family, and lifespan issues as well as the nature of educational, medical, and social services. Definitions for each of the areas of exceptionality are presented, along with overviews of prevalence, characteristics, causation, services, instructional approaches, and supports.

Case Study

YVONNE

Yvonne is 19 years old and leaving high school to begin her adult life. For most of her high school years, she was in special education classes for reading and math, because she was about three grade levels behind her nondisabled peers. During the last term of high school, she attended a class on exploring possible careers and finding and keeping a job. The class was required for graduation, but it didn't make much sense to Yvonne because she had never had any experience with this area before. It just didn't seem to be related to her other schoolwork.

Although Yvonne wants to get a job in a retail store (such as stocking clothing or shoes), she isn't having much success. She doesn't have a driver's license, and her parents don't have time to run her around to apply for various jobs. The businesses she approached are close by her home and know her well, but they keep telling her she isn't *qualified* for the jobs available. She has never had any on-the-job training in the community. Yvonne's parents are not very enthusiastic about her finding employment because they are afraid she might lose some of her government-funded medical benefits.

■ APPLICATION
1. In retrospect, what transition planning services would you have recommended for Yvonne during her last years of high school?
2. How would you help Yvonne now? Do you see the Americans with Disabilities Act playing a role in Yvonne's story?
3. Whose responsibility is it to work with potential employers to explore "the reasonable accommodations" that would facilitate the opportunity for Yvonne to succeed in a community job?

Debate Forum

STUDENTS WITH DISABILITIES AND THE MEANING OF A HIGH SCHOOL DIPLOMA

Students with disabilities often do not receive the same high school diploma that their nondisabled peers do. Many states and local school districts have adopted graduation requirements that specify successful completion of a number of credits in order to receive a diploma. In these areas, students with disabilities must meet the same requirements as their nondisabled peers in order to receive a "regular" high school diploma. If a student with a disability fails to meet graduation requirements, he or she may be awarded a certificate indicating completion (or attendance) of high school. Certificates of completion communicate that a student was unable to meet the requirements to obtain a standard diploma.

Other states, however, award students with disabilities the standard high school diploma based upon modified criteria that are individually referenced, reflecting the successful completion of IEP goals and objectives as determined by a multidisciplinary team of professionals and a student's parents (National Research Council, 1997).

In 1996–1997, about 25% of students with disabilities exiting school received a standard high school diploma. Students most likely to be awarded a diploma were those with sensory disabilities (vision and hearing loss), visual impairments, and traumatic brain injury. Students least likely to receive a diploma were those with severe multiple disabilities and autism (U.S. Department of Education, 2000a).

■ POINT

The purpose of a high school diploma is to communicate to employers, colleges, and society in general that an individual has acquired a specified set of knowledge and skills that prepares him or her to leave school and enter postsecondary education or the world of work. Every student must be held to the same standards, or the diploma has no meaning as a "signal" of competence. The diploma simply becomes a piece of paper that will make no impression on employers or colleges. It will be ignored, as it often is now, as a means to discriminate between who is competent and who is not. For those students with disabilities who cannot meet graduation requirements, there is certainly the need to signal what an individual has achieved during high school even though it is not to the same performance level as those who are awarded the diploma. This can be accomplished through a certificate of completion with modified criteria for graduation. What is most important is not to engage in the devaluing of the high school diploma by lowering requirements so that everyone gets the credential. Otherwise, employers and colleges will continue to lose faith in public education as a credible system for preparing students for the future.

■ COUNTERPOINT

Although the move to hold all students to specific requirements (or standards) is to be applauded, it is discriminatory to expect every student to meet the "same" standards in order to receive a high school diploma. The purpose of a high school diploma is to communicate that the individual has demonstrated a "personal best" while in school, thus acquiring knowledge and a set of skills consistent with individual ability. I would also support the viewpoint that students with disabilities can achieve at much higher levels than they do now, and expectations should be raised. However, some will never be able to achieve the graduation requirements now in place in many states and school districts. Students with disabilities who cannot perform at the level mandated in graduation requirements should still be awarded a standard diploma based upon requirements consistent with their individual needs and abilities. This is the basis of a free and appropriate public education for students with disabilities. If a standard diploma is not awarded, a student with a disability will be immediately singled out as incompetent and be placed at a major disadvantage with employers, regardless of the skills he or she possesses.

Review

focus 1

Cite three reasons why it is important to plan for the transition of students with disabilities from school to adult life.

- Students with disabilities who leave the public schools are not adequately prepared for postsecondary education or employment.
- Adult service systems do not have the resources to meet the needs of students with disabilities following the school years.
- The capabilities of adults with disabilities have been underestimated.

focus 2

How does IDEA define transition services?

- Transition services are a coordinated set of activities for a student, designed within an outcome-oriented process that promotes movement from school to postschool activities, including postsecondary education, vocational training, integrated employment (including supported employment), continuing and adult education, adult services, independent living, or community participation.
- Activities shall be based upon individual student needs, taking into account preferences and interests.

- Activities shall include instruction, community experiences, development of employment, and other postschool adult-living objectives.

focus 3

What information should be included in each student's IEP statement for transition services? Who should be involved in the planning process?

- The IEP should incorporate a description of inter-agency responsibilities or linkages prior to the student's departure from school.
- The IEP should identify the range of services needed by the individual in order to participate in the community.
- The IEP should identify activities that must occur during high school to facilitate the individual's access to adult service programs if necessary.
- The IEP should establish timelines and responsibilities for completion of these activities.
- In addition to education personnel, transition planning must include the student with disabilities and his or her parents. Students and parents should be educated about adult service systems, including the characteristics of agencies, criteria for evaluating programs, and potential as well as current service alternatives. Professionals from adult service agencies may also be involved to facili-

tate the student's access to employment, postsecondary education, supported living, and leisure activities.

focus 4

Identify three outcomes expected for adolescents with disabilities as they enter adulthood.

- Adults with disabilities should be able to function as independently as possible in their daily lives.
- Adults with disabilities should also begin working in the community or go on to postsecondary education.
- Adults with disabilities should be able to participate in social and leisure activities that are an integral part of community life.

focus 5

Why is it important for students with disabilities to receive instruction in self-determination, academics, adaptive and functional life skills, and employment preparation during the secondary school years?

- Self-determination skills help students solve problems, consider options, and make appropriate choices as they make the transition into adult life.
- Academic skills training is important in meeting school graduation requirements and preparing students with disabilities for further postsecondary education. A functional aca-

demic program helps students learn applied skills in daily living, leisure activities, and employment preparation.
- Adaptive and functional life skills help students learn how to socialize with others, maintain personal appearance, and make choices about how to spend free time.
- Employment preparation during high school increases the probability of success on the job during the adult years and places the individual with a disability in the role of a contributor to society.

focus 6

What are the purposes of government-funded programs for people with disabilities in the areas of income support, health care, residential living, and employment?

- Income support programs are direct cash payments to people with disabilities, providing basic economic assistance.
- Medicaid and Medicare are government-supported health care programs. The Medicaid program can pay for inpatient and outpatient hospital services, laboratory services, and early screening, diagnosis, treatment, and immunization for children. Medicare is a national insurance program with two parts: hospital insurance and supplementary medical insurance. The Hospital Insurance Program pays for short-term hospitalization,

related care in skilled nursing facilities, and some home care. The insurance program covers physician services, outpatient services, ambulance services, some medical supplies, and medical equipment.

■ Residential services show a trend toward smaller, community-based residences located within local neighborhoods and communities. These residences may include group homes, semi-independent homes and apartments, or foster family care. The purpose of residential services is to provide persons with disabilities a variety of options for living in the community.

■ There are essentially three alternative approaches to competitive employment for people with disabilities: employment with no support services, employment with time-limited support services, and employment with ongoing support services. The purpose of all three approaches is to assist people with disabilities obtain a job and maintain it over time.

Identify two challenges faced by aging people with disabilities.

■ Little research information is available on people with disabilities and the effects of aging. We do know that although people with disabilities are living longer, they are not necessarily living better.

■ Many aging people with disabilities are not able to access adequate health care or receive the ongoing services they need at home or in a support living situation.

Olive Octopus

6
People with Learning Disabilities

To begin with . . .

The number of children with learning disabilities has grown at a faster pace than many with other disability categories. In 1998–1999, over 2.8 million children with specific learning disabilities were served under IDEA. (U.S. Department of Education, 2000)

Conventional wisdom has suggested that boys identified with learning disabilities substantially outnumber girls, although some recent research suggests they may be more equal in number. (Lerner, 1997)

The fastest-growing category of disability is "learning disability," especially the variants of attention-deficit disorder. The number of students requesting accommodations on SAT tests—the great majority involving claims for a learning disability—has doubled in five years. Even so, last year they amounted to less than 2% of all test takers. (Begley, 1998, p. 56)

A review of direct instruction by the Division of Learning Disabilities of the Council for Exceptional Children leads to the conclusion that "it is an effective and reliably implementable instructional approach for students with LD in those skill and content domains studied to date." (Division of Learning Disabilities, 1999, p. 3)

Jamaal

Jamaal's difficulties initially became evident in kindergarten, which is somewhat unusual since learning disabilities are more typically identified later in the school years. His parents were frustrated and, like so many parents of children with disabilities, felt that they were not doing something correctly. Jamaal was also aware of some difficulties, mentioning to the teacher that he had trouble concentrating in some cases.

Jamaal expresses himself well verbally and comes up with great ideas; however, he has particular problems with reading and writing. It appears that he falls below his classmates in sight word vocabulary, which influences both academic areas. His fourth-grade teachers are now working very hard to integrate into his instruction the important skills that he will need in order to succeed as he moves on in school. Although he exhibits some disruptive behaviors, they are relatively minor in the overall context of Jamaal's world. He fundamentally has a positive outlook and already has plans for attending college—rather long-range planning for a fourth-grader.

Mathew

Note: The following is a statement prepared by an upper-division psychology undergraduate student who has learning disabilities. Mathew tells his story in his own words, recounting some of his school experiences, his diagnosis, and how his learning disabilities affect his academic efforts.

Imagine having the inability to memorize times tables, not being able to "tell time" until the ninth grade, and taking several days to read a simple chapter from a school textbook.

In elementary and high school, I was terrified of math classes for several reasons. First, it did not matter how many times I practiced my times tables or other numerical combinations relating to division, subtraction, and addition. I could not remember them. Second, I dreaded the class time itself for inevitably the teacher would call on me for an answer to a "simple" problem. Multiplication was the worst! Since I had to count on my fingers to do multiplication, it would take a lot of time and effort. Do you know how long it takes to calculate 9 x 7 or 9 x 9 on your fingers? Suffice it to say too long, especially if the teacher and the rest of the class are waiting.

When I was a sophomore at a junior college, I discovered important information about myself. After two days of clinical cognitive testing, I learned that my brain is wired differently than most individuals. That is, I think, perceive, and process information differently. They discovered several "wiring jobs" which are called learning disabilities. First, I have a problem with processing speed. The ability to bring information from long-term memory to consciousness (into short-term memory) takes me a long time. Second, I have a deficit with my short-term memory. This means that I cannot hold information there very long. When new information is learned, it must be put into long-term memory. This is an arduous process requiring the information to be rehearsed several times. Third, I have a significant problem with fluid reasoning. Fluid reasoning is the ability to go from A to G without having to go through B, C, D, E, and F. It also includes drawing inferences, coming up with creative solutions to problems, solving unique problems, and the ability to transfer information and generalize. Hence, my math and numerical difficulties.

Perhaps the most unique piece of information I learned was that I have scotopic sensitivity to light. This means that the eyes are overly sensitive to light and glare, which tire them rapidly.

With all of this knowledge, I was able to use specific strategies that will help me in compensating for these neurological wiring patterns. Now I tape all lectures rather than trying to keep up taking notes. I take tests in a room by myself and they are not timed. Anytime I need to do mathematical calculations I use a calculator. To compensate for scotopic sensitivity, I use transparent blue–green plastic sheets when I read textbooks and I use green paper when I write assignments, etc.

Source: From *Understanding Child Behavior Disorders* (3rd ed., p. 215), by D. M. Gelfand, W. R. Jenson, and C. J. Drew, 1997, Fort Worth, TX: Harcourt Brace & Co. Used with permission.

THE FIELD OF LEARNING DISABILITIES was virtually unrecognized prior to the 1960s. These disabilities are often considered mild because people with learning disabilities usually have average or near-average intelligence, although learning disabilities can occur at all intelligence levels. People with learning disabilities achieve at unexpectedly low levels, particularly in reading and mathematics. Recent thinking suggests that the term *learning disabilities* functions as a generic label representing a very heterogeneous group of conditions, which range from mild to severe in intensity (Beers, 1998). In many cases, people with learning disabilities have been described as having "poor neurological wiring." Individuals with learning disabilities manifest a highly variable and complex set of characteristics and needs. As such they present a substantial challenge to family members and professionals.

Definitions and Classifications

Confusion, controversy, and polarization have been associated with **learning disabilities** as long as they have been recognized as a family of disabilities. In the past, many children now identified as having specific learning disabilities would have been labeled as remedial readers, remedial learners, or emotionally disturbed or even mentally retarded children, if they received any special attention or additional instructional support at all. Academic performance represents a major element in most current definitions of learning disabilities (Kauffman, Hallahan, & Lloyd, 1998; Wong, 1999). Today, services related to learning disabilities represent the largest single program for exceptional children in the United States. Although relatively new, its growth rate has been unparalleled by any other area in special education (U.S. Department of Education, 2000a).

focus 1
Identify four reasons why definitions of learning disabilities have varied.

■ DEFINITIONS

The definitions of learning disabilities include a considerable amount of variation. This inconsistency may be due to the field's unique evolution, rapid growth, and strong interdisciplinary nature. The involvement of multiple disciplines (such as medicine, psychology, speech and language, and education) has also contributed to confusing terminology. For example, education coined the phrase "specific learning disabilities"; psychology uses terms such as *perceptual disorders* and *hyperkinetic behavior;* speech and language employ the terms *aphasia* and *dyslexia;* and medicine uses the labels *brain damage, minimal brain dysfunction, brain injury,* and *impairment.* Brain injury, minimal brain dysfunction, and learning disabilities are the most commonly used terms, although all appear in various segments of professional terminology.

A child with a brain injury is described as having an organic impairment resulting in perceptual problems, thinking disorders, and emotional instability. A child with minimal brain dysfunction manifests similar problems but often shows evidence of language, memory, motor, and impulse-control difficulties. Individuals with minimal brain dysfunction are often characterized as average or above average in intelligence, distinguishing the disorder from mental retardation.

■ LEARNING DISABILITY. A condition in which one or more of the basic psychological processes in understanding or using language are deficient.

■ EARLY HISTORY   Samuel Kirk first introduced the term *specific learning disabilities* in 1963. His original concept remains largely intact today. The concept is defined by delays, deviations, and performance discrepancies in basic academic subjects (e.g., arithmetic, reading, spelling, and writing) and speech and language problems that cannot be attributed to mental retardation, sensory deficits, or emotional disturbance. The common practice in education is to describe individuals with learning disabilities on the basis of what they are *not*. For example, although they may have a number of problems, they do *not* have mental retardation, emotional disturbance, or hearing loss. Learning disabilities is an umbrella label that includes a variety of conditions and behavioral and performance deficits (Gelfand, Jenson, & Drew, 1997).

■ IDEA AND JOINT COMMITTEE DEFINITIONS   The Individuals with Disabilities Education Act (IDEA) describes learning disabilities as follows in the *Federal Register* (1999) as part of the rules and regulations:

Specific learning disability is defined as follows:

General. *The term means a disorder in one or more of the basic psychological processes involved in understanding or in using language, spoken or written, which may manifest itself in an imperfect ability to listen, think, speak, read, write, spell, or to do mathematical calculations, including conditions such as perceptual disabilities, brain injury, minimal brain dysfunction, dyslexia, and developmental aphasia.*

Disorders not included. *The term does not include problems that are primarily the result of visual, hearing, or motor disabilities, of mental retardation, of emotional disturbance, or of environmental, cultural, or economic disadvantage. (1999, p. 51)*

This definition actually includes many of the concepts that originated in Kirk's description. It also provided a legal focus for the provision of services in the public schools.

The IDEA definition was exclusionary in some ways. It continued to define conditions that are *not* learning disabilities but did not offer a substantive explanation of what does constitute a learning disability. This use of exclusionary criteria remains an issue today (e.g., MacMillan & Speece, 1999). The definition was also somewhat ambiguous because it lacked a clear way to measure a learning disability. Another definition statement presented by the National Joint Committee for Learning Disabilities (1998) had certain important elements not stated in IDEA:

Learning disabilities *is a general term that refers to a heterogeneous group of disorders manifested by significant difficulties in the acquisition and use of listening, speaking, reading, writing, reasoning, or mathematical abilities. These disorders are intrinsic to the individual, presumed to be due to central nervous system dysfunction, and may occur across the lifespan. Problems in self-regulatory behaviors, social perception, and social interaction may exist with learning disabilities but do not by themselves constitute a learning disability. Although learning disabilities may occur concomitantly with other handicapping conditions (e.g., sensory impairment, mental retardation, serious emotional disturbance), or with extrinsic influences (such as cultural differences, insufficient or inappropriate instruction), they are not the result of those conditions or influences. (p. 187)*

This definition is important to our discussion for several reasons. First, it describes *learning disabilities* as a generic term that refers to a heterogeneous group of disorders. Second, a person with learning disabilities must manifest significant difficulties. Use of the word *significant* is an effort to remove the connotation that a learning disability constitutes a mild problem. Finally, this definition highlights learning disabilities as lifelong problems and places them in a context of other disabilities and cultural differences. These are important refinements of earlier definitions.

■ OTHER ISSUES IN DEFINING LEARNING DISABILITIES Varying definitions and terminology related to learning disabilities emerged partly because of different theoretical views of the condition. For example, perceptual-motor theories emphasize an interaction between various channels of perception and motor activity. Perceptual-motor theories of learning disabilities focus on contrasts between normal sequential development of motor patterns and the motor development of children with learning disabilities. Children with learning disabilities are seen as having unreliable and unstable perceptual-motor abilities, which present problems when such children encounter activities that require an understanding of time and space.

Language disability theories, on the other hand, concentrate on a child's reception or production of language. Because language is so important in learning, these theories emphasize the relationship between learning disabilities and language deficiencies. It is clear from examining only these two theories that very different viewpoints exist regarding these disabilities. This field encompasses many theoretical perspectives regarding the nature of learning problems as well as their causation and treatment.

Still another view of learning disabilities has emerged in the past several years. Some researchers have suggested that many different, specific disorders have been grouped under one term. They see *learning disabilities* as a general umbrella term that includes both academic and behavioral problems and have developed terminology to describe particular conditions falling within the broad category of learning disabilities. Some of these terms refer to particular areas of functional academic difficulty (e.g., math, spelling, reading), whereas others reflect difficulties that are behavioral in nature. This perspective has been adopted by the American Psychiatric Association in the *Diagnostic and Statistical Manual of Mental Disorders,* fourth edition (American Psychiatric Association, 2000). This manual uses the term *learning disorders* to refer specifically to disorders in areas such as reading, mathematics, or written expression.

In one sense, this strategy is not surprising. It has long been acknowledged that people with learning disabilities form a very heterogeneous group, yet professionals have continued to describe them as though they were homogeneous. Such characterizations typically reflect the theoretical or disciplinary perspective of the professional, rather than an objective behavioral description of the individual being evaluated. This has resulted in a tendency to focus on defining a particular disorder and then categorizing people according to such definitions, rather than objectively evaluating the *individual* with problems. This approach often leads to error when evaluating members of a population that represents a wide variety of disorders.

Research on learning disabilities also reflects the problems of definition. The wide range of characteristics associated with children having learning disabilities and various methodological problems (such as poor research design and measurement error) have caused multiple difficulties in conducting research on learning disabilities (Carnine, 2000; Gay & Airasian, 2000; Salkind, 2000). Generalizing research results is questionable, and replication of studies is very difficult. Efforts to standardize and clarify definitions continue, and they are important both for research and intervention purposes (Kauffman et al., 1998).

The notion of severity has largely been ignored in earlier definitions and concepts related to learning disabilities. To some degree this has changed, although this issue still receives only limited attention (see Bocian, Beebe, MacMillan, & Gresham, 1999). Learning disabilities have probably been defined in more ways by more disciplines and professional groups than any other type of disability (Mastropieri & Scruggs, 2000). We describe behavioral characteristics of learning disabilities from different theoretical viewpoints because the diversity in approaches makes it impossible to select a single perspective. It is important to know how a person might be classified as having a learning disability according to different perspectives.

■ LEARNING DISABILITIES AND ATTENTION-DEFICIT/HYPERACTIVITY DISORDER

One condition often associated with learning disabilities but not defined in IDEA is **attention-deficit/hyperactivity disorder (ADHD).** Several features of ADHD have long been recognized in many children with learning disabilities. Although ADHD is often associated with learning disabilities, there is not a complete correspondence in characteristics between the two conditions (e.g., Aro et al., 1999; Hazell et al., 1999). Our discussion of the attributes of learning disabilities in this chapter will show that attention problems, impulsiveness, and hyperactivity have emerged periodically in depictions of learning disabilities. Additionally, perception difficulties and discrimination problems, among others, are often associated with learning disabilities. The distinctions between learning disabilities and ADHD as categories are often not clear, in part because the definitions have historically overlapped and been applied to very heterogeneous groups of people (Conte, 1998). Chapter 7 examines ADHD in detail.

■ CLASSIFICATION

Learning disabilities is a term applied to a complex constellation of behaviors and symptoms. Many of these symptoms or characteristics have been used for classification purposes at one time or another. One element that has not emerged as a classification scheme is severity—learning disabilities have generally been seen as mild disorders. Reference to severity appears in the literature on learning disabilities fairly often even though it is not accounted for in most definitions (see Bocian et al., 1999).

IDEA rules and regulations do address the issue of severity to some extent. They mandate that any criterion for classifying a child as having learning disabilities must be based on preexisting severe discrepancy between capacity and achievement. The determination for placement was related to the following criteria:

1. Whether a child achieves commensurate with his or her age and ability when provided with appropriate educational experiences
2. Whether the child has a severe discrepancy between achievement and intellectual ability in one or more of seven areas relating to communication skills and mathematical abilities

The child's learning disability must be determined on an individual basis, and the severe discrepancy between achievement and intellectual ability must be in one or more of the following areas: oral expression, listening comprehension, written expression, basic reading skill, reading comprehension, mathematical calculation, or mathematical reasoning.

The meaning of the term *severe discrepancy* is debated among professionals (Fletcher et al., 1998). Although it is often stipulated as a classification parameter,

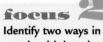
focus 2
Identify two ways in which people with learning disabilities can be classified.

■ ATTENTION-DEFICIT/HYPERAC-TIVITY DISORDER (ADHD). A disorder in youngsters, characterized by difficulties in maintaining attention because of a limited ability to concentrate. Children with ADHD exhibit impulsive actions and hyperactive behavior.

there is no broadly accepted way to measure it. What is an acceptable discrepancy between a child's achievement and what is expected at his or her grade level—25%? 35%? 50%? The idea of severe discrepancy has appeared in the literature for many years, but general agreement regarding its exact definition has never been reached.

A review of the literature on definitions and classifications of learning disabilities, either historical or current, presents a confusing and conflicting array of ideas. Classification schemes have ranged from very general concepts to specific categories based on subgroups such as people with dyslexia (e.g., Padget, 1998). However, lack of agreement about concepts basic to the field has caused difficulties in both research and treatment. The people who display characteristics of learning disabilities, however, present some of the most interesting challenges in behavioral science today.

Prevalence

focus **3**
Identify two current estimated ranges for the prevalence of learning disabilities.

Problems in determining accurate figures related to people with learning disabilities are amplified by differing definitions, theoretical views, and assessment procedures. Prevalence estimates are highly variable, ranging from 2.7% to 30% of the school-age population (Lerner, 1997; Prasad & Srivastava, 1998). Within the total school-age population, the most reasonable estimates range around 5% to 10%, as portrayed in Figure 6.1.

Since learning disabilities emerged as a category, their prevalence has been high compared to that of other exceptionalities, a fact that has been controversial for many years. Learning disabilities are among the most common of all reported causes of disability (Halfon & Newacheck, 1999). However, it is difficult to find one prevalence figure that is agreed on by all involved in the field. In 1998–1999, nearly 5.5 million children with disabilities (ages 6–21) were being served under IDEA in the United States (including Washington, D.C., and Puerto Rico). Of that number, over 2.8 million were classified as having learning disabilities, which represents 51% of the population with disabilities being served (U.S. Department of Education, 2000a).

Professionals and parents involved with other disability groups often question the high prevalence of learning disabilities. In some cases, they simply feel a sense

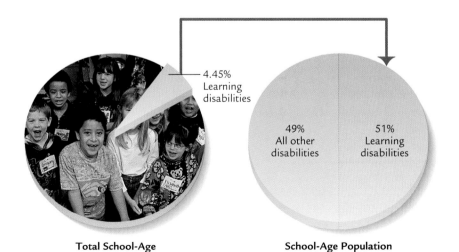

4.45% Learning disabilities

49% All other disabilities

51% Learning disabilities

Total School-Age Population

School-Age Population with Disabilities

FIGURE 6.1

The prevalence of learning disabilities for students 6–21 years of age [U.S. Department of Education, 2000a]

PREVALENCE DISTRIBUTION BY DISABILITY

Despite the difficulties involved with defining and classifying learning disabilities, this term describes one of the largest groups served in special education. Use of the *learning disabilities* label for service still continues to grow, as illustrated in Table 6.1. The percentage of change indicated in the table, although substantial, is not as remarkable as the increased *number* of individuals served under the learning disabilities label. The contin-

ued growth and high level of service for students with learning disabilities have come under some criticism. Reflect on these questions:

- With definitional problems, does it make much sense to have this group of exceptional individuals rep-

resent such a high proportion of those served?

- Do people with learning disabilities really represent such a high proportion of individuals in general?
- Or has this classification become a catchall for those in special education?

of competition for the limited funds distributed among groups of people with different disabilities. Others, however, are concerned that the learning disabilities category is being overused to avoid the stigma associated with other labels or because of misdiagnosis, which may result in inappropriate treatment (see the nearby Reflect on This feature and Table 6.1).

Although discrepancies in prevalence occur in all fields of exceptionality, the area of learning disabilities seems more variable than most. Partly this can be attributed to the different descriptions of disabilities and procedures used by the agencies, states, and researchers who do the counting and estimating (e.g., Halfon & Newacheck, 1999; Kaplan et al., 1998). Another source of discrepancy may be differing or vague definitions of learning disabilities. Prevalence figures gathered

| **TABLE 6.1** | Net change between 1987–1988 and 1998–1999 in number of individuals ages 6–21 served under IDEA by disability condition |

| | School Year | | |
Disability	1987–1988	1998–1999	Net Difference
Learning disability	1,937,827	2,814,278	876,451
Speech or language difficulty	951,512	1,074,044	122,532
Mental retardation	596,928	610,445	13,517
Emotional disturbance	372,048	463,172	91,124
Multiple disabilities	78,588	107,591	29,003
Hearing impairments	56,742	70,813	14,071
Orthopedic impairments	46,837	69,467	22,630
Other health impairments	46,013	220,743	174,730
Visual impairments	22,769	26,100	3,331
Deafness-blindness	1,426	1,602	176
Autism	*	53,576	NA
Traumatic brain injury	*	12,927	NA
All disabilities	4,110,690	5,536,600	1,425,910

* Data not available under IDEA service for this disability in 1987–1988

Source: 1998–1999 data from *The 22nd Annual Report to Congress on the Implementation of the Individuals with Disabilities Act,* by the U.S. Department of Education, 2000, Washington, DC: U.S. Government Printing Office: Author.

Albert Einstein failed math in elementary school and demonstrated little ability or interest in school work. His intellectual genius and capability in science and mathematics was not evident until his early teens. Einstein represents the discrepancy that can exist in an individual student.

through various studies are unlikely to match when different definitions determine what is counted. This situation is common in the field of learning disabilities.

Characteristics

focus 4

Identify seven characteristics attributed to those with learning disabilities, and explain why it is difficult to characterize this group.

Although specific learning disabilities are often characterized as representing mild disorders, few attempts have been made to validate this premise empirically. Identification of subgroups, subtypes, or severity levels in this heterogeneous population has been largely ignored in the past. However, some attempts have been made in the past few years to attend to these issues (Bocian et al., 1999; D'Amato, Dean, & Rhodes, 1998). Subtype and comorbidity research are appearing in the current literature at increasing rates. Subtype research investigates the characteristics of youngsters to search for distinctive groups within

Snapshot

Alice

Alice found herself very frustrated with school. She was in the fourth grade, and her grades were very bad. She had worked very hard, but many of the things that were required just didn't seem to make sense.

History was a perfect example. Alice had looked forward to learning more about history; it seemed so fun and interesting when her grandfather told his stories. Alice thought it would have been fun to live back then, when all the kids got to ride horses. But history in school

was not fun, and it didn't make any sense at all. Alice had been reading last night, supposedly about a girl who was her age and was moving West with a wagon train. As she looked at the book, Alice read strange things. One passage said, "Mary pelieveb that things would get detter.

What they hab left Missouri they hab enough foob dut now there was darely enough for one meal a bay. Surely the wagon-master woulb finb a wet to solve the brodlem." Alice knew that she would fail the test, and she cried quietly in her room as she dressed for school.

the broad umbrella of learning disabilities. Comorbidity research studies the degree to which youngsters exhibit evidence of multiple disabilities or conditions (e.g., ADHD and learning disabilities). In some ways these approaches are exploring similar questions but from differing perspectives. Certainly the learning disabilities category has multiple subgroups because the definitions have been so broad and the group so heterogeneous. Likewise, many students who have learning disabilities also exhibit characteristics of other disorders, such as emotional difficulties. Researchers have investigated a broad array of subgroups ranging from people with reading problems to those with hyperactivity difficulties (e.g., Johnson, Altmaier, & Richman, 1999; Naglieri, 1999; Tirosh & Cohen, 1998). Subtype and comorbidity research may lead to more effective intervention, geared precisely to the specific needs of distinctive groups within the large, heterogeneous population with learning disabilities (Bender, 1998).

Perceptions of teachers and other professionals have also been investigated relative to learning disabilities (Harmon, 1998). Although exhibiting a typical amount of error and variation, such ratings are stable enough to make possible some reliable distinctions regarding both subgroups and severity levels among students with learning disabilities. Some research suggests that teacher judgments resemble those made by school psychologists regarding the nature of a disability and its severity in a particular child (Harmon, 1998). The perceptions and knowledge of teachers have long been cited as a badly overlooked source of assessment information; their input is vital in designing instructional adaptation for students with learning problems. Also, teachers working with students with learning disabilities quite often encounter youngsters who they firmly believe should *not* be considered learning disabled. Such reports support the belief that many students currently being served as having learning disabilities may have been inappropriately referred. Over 20 years ago Larsen (1978) commented on this phenomenon:

It is . . . likely that the large number of students who are referred for mild to moderate underachievement are simply unmotivated, poorly taught, come from home environments

Many students with learning disabilities have difficulties with word recognition, word knowledge, and the use of context in learning to read.

where scholastic success is not highly valued, or are dull–normal in intelligence. For all intents and purposes, these students should not automatically be considered as learning disabled, since there is little evidence that placement in special education will improve their academic functioning. (p. 7)

■ ACADEMIC ACHIEVEMENT

Problems and inconsistencies in academic achievement largely prompted the recognition of learning disabilities as an area of exceptionality. Individuals with learning disabilities, while generally of normal or above-average intelligence, seem to have many academic problems. These problems generally persist from the primary grades through the end of formal schooling, including college (Ward & Bernstein, 1998).

■ READING   Reading problems are observed among students with learning disabilities more often than problems in any other area of academic performance. Historically, as the learning disabilities category began to take shape, it was applied to youngsters who were earlier identified as *remedial reading students*. Estimates have suggested that as many as 80% to 90% of students with learning disabilities have reading difficulties, and even the low estimates range around 60% (Bender, 1998). Supporting this contention, the National Research Council noted that reading disability accounts for 80% of those children identified as having learning disabilities (Snow, Burns, & Griffin, 1998). Clearly, problems with the reading process are very prevalent among these students. This does not mean that they have similar specific difficulties with reading. The specific problems in reading vary as much as the many components of the reading process.

Both word knowledge and word recognition are vitally important parts of reading skill, and they both cause problems for people with learning disabilities. When most of us encounter a word that we know, we recall its meaning from our "mental dictionary." However, for unfamiliar words we must "sound out" the letters and pronounce the words based on our knowledge of typical spelling patterns and pronunciation rules—an important process since we cannot memorize all words.

Students must also be able to generalize letter patterns and draw analogies with considerable flexibility. This task is usually accomplished rather easily, fairly quickly, and almost automatically after a little practice, by good readers (Snow et al., 1998). Students with reading disabilities, however, experience substantial difficulty with this process, and when they can do it, they seem to manage it only slowly and laboriously. Such students need specific training and practice in strategies that will help them succeed at recognizing words (Torgesen, 1999).

Another important component of reading involves the use of context to determine meaning. Here again, good readers tend to be rather adept, but poor readers have difficulty. Though poor readers encounter substantial problems in using context information to recognize words or infer their meaning, specific instruction improves performance. Additionally, students with learning disabilities do not effectively use background information. Good and poor readers differ in the degree to which they have and use background knowledge specifically for reading (Chard & Osborn, 1999; Smith, 1998). Similarly, some students with learning disabilities focus on minor details within a text, without distinguishing the important ideas from those of less significance. A specific focus on learning strategies can help these students. Teaching them skills such as organizing and summarizing, using mnemonics, problem solving, and relational thinking can offset these difficulties and enhance academic performance (Gersten & Baker, 1998).

Reflect on This

DYSLEXIA: SEARCHING FOR CAUSES

For decades there has been a search for *the* cause of learning disabilities, particularly the most severe forms, such as dyslexia. Dyslexia is a condition characterized by a severe impairment of the ability to read. Public interest has continually been high because the conditions seem strange and result in an inability to perform seemingly simple tasks, such as reading the newspaper. The constant search for the single or most prominent cause is jokingly called looking for the "bullet theory" by professionals in the field (who mostly believe that matters are more complicated than singular causation). However, "bullet theory" reports continue to make news in the popular press, perhaps because they are simple enough to report in short accounts (or in sound bites on television) and attribution is simple—the *cause* is _____ (fill in the blank).

Time magazine followed this reporting trend on August 29, 1994, with "Brain Bane," an article reporting that researchers may have found a cause for dyslexia. Beginning with background information on dyslexia, its prevalence and characteristics, this article then moves to the final paragraph, where barely one-third of the article is devoted to the main object for reporting. Here it is noted that Dr. Albert Galaburda of Harvard and Beth Israel Hospital in Boston has been conducting research on the brains of people with dyslexia who have died. Essentially, the research team sampled brain tissue from people with dyslexia (postmortem) and compared it with brain tissue collected from people who did not have dyslexia. Interestingly enough, these researchers found a difference in the size of nerve cells between the left and right hemispheres in tissue from people with dyslexia, but they found no such difference in the tissue from individuals without dyslexia. The researchers were careful to note that the size differential is only between 10 and 15 percent, but it is enough to capture the attention of *Time*. The public thirst for bullet theories is alive and well.

Source: From "Brain Bane: Researchers May Have Found a Cause for Dyslexia" by C. P. Alexander, 1994, *Time, 144*(9), p. 61.

Reading involves many skills (such as the ability to focus on important, rather than irrelevant, aspects of a task, and the ability to remember) that also affect performance in other subject areas. Some difficulties experienced by people with learning disabilities emerge in more than one area, making the exact deficit difficult to pinpoint and explain. For example, does a child with reading disabilities have attention difficulties or working memory problems? The problem could be caused by either disability or a combination of the two. Though specific instruction may improve performance, if the focus of the training is too limited, the student may not generalize it to other relevant areas. Instruction that combines different methods (e.g., using both phonological awareness and specific skill instruction) may serve students with reading disabilities better than single-focused methods (Snow et al., 1998). In cases of more severe disability (such as dyslexia), it may be best to teach the person to compensate for the problem by accessing information through other means (see the nearby Reflect on This feature).

■ WRITING AND SPELLING   Children with learning disabilities often exhibit quite different writing performance than do their peers without disabilities. This problem affects their academic achievement and frequently persists into adulthood. Difficulties may occur in handwriting (slow writing, spacing problems, poor formation of letters), spelling skills, and composition (Berninger, 1999; Graham, 1999). Several such problems are illustrated in Figure 6.2.

Some children are poor at handwriting because they have not mastered the basic developmental skills required for the process, such as grasping a pen or pencil and moving it in a fashion that results in legible writing. In some cases, fine motor development seems delayed in children with learning disabilities, contributing to physi-

As I seT hare Thinking abouT This
simiTe I wundr How someone Like Me Cood
posblee make iT thou This cors. BuT some Howl
I muse over come my fers and Wrese So I muse
Be Calfodn in my sef and be NoT aferad To Trie

3 Reasens I Came To College

Reasen#1   To fofel a Drem that my Parens,
Teichers and I hadd — Adrem that I codd
some day by come ArchuTeck.

Reasen#2   To pouv rong those who sed I
codd NoT make iT.

Reasen#3   Becos I am a bulheded.

The text of these samples reads as follows:

As I sit here thinking about this semester, I wonder how someone like me could possibly make it through this course. But somehow I must overcome my fears and worries. So I must be confident in myself and be not afraid to try.

Three Reasons I Came To College

Reason #1. To fulfill a dream that my parents, teachers, and I had—a dream that I could some day become architect.
Reason #2. To prove wrong those who said I could not make it.
Reason #3. Because I am bullheaded.

FIGURE 6.2

Writing samples of a college freshman with a learning disability

cal difficulty in using writing materials. Handwriting also involves an understanding of spatial concepts, such as *up, down, top,* and *bottom*. These abilities frequently are less well developed in youngsters with learning disabilities than in their age-mates without disabilities (Bender, 1998). The physical actions involved in using pencil or pen, as well as problems in discerning spatial relationships, can make it difficult to form letters and use spacing between letters, words, and lines. Some children with rather mild handwriting problems may be exhibiting slowness in development, which will improve as they grow older, receive instruction, and practice. However, in more severe cases (e.g., the young adult whose writing sample appeared in Figure 6.2), age and practice may not bring about skill mastery.

Some researchers view the handwriting, writing, and composition skills of students with learning disabilities as closely related to their reading ability. For example, research does not clearly indicate that children with learning disabilities write more poorly than their normally achieving peers who are reading at a similar level. Basic transcription processes seem to contribute significantly to writing problems among students with learning disabilities (Berninger, 1999; MacArthur, 1999). Letter reversals and, in severe cases, **mirror writing** have often been used as illustrations of poor handwriting. However, it is also questionable whether children with learning disabilities commit these types of errors more often than their peers without disabilities at the same reading level.

▪ MIRROR WRITING. Writing backwards from right to left, making letters that look like ordinary writing seen in a mirror.

The logic connecting writing and reading abilities has certain intuitive appeal. Most children write to some degree on their own, prior to receiving instruction in school. In general, children who write spontaneously also seem to read spontaneously and tend to have considerable practice at both before they enter school. Their homes (thereby hinting at the influence of parents) tend to have writing materials readily available for experimentation and practice. Likewise, they may often observe their parents writing, and the parents and child may write together. Further research concerning the relationship between reading and handwriting is definitely in order. Instruction in writing for children with learning disabilities has historically been somewhat isolated from the act of reading, focusing instead primarily on the technical skills (Amano, 1999).

Poor spelling is often a problem among students with learning disabilities (also evident in Figure 6.2). These children frequently omit letters or add incorrect ones. Their spelling may also show evidence of letter-order confusion and developmentally immature pronunciation (Smith, 1998). Interestingly, relatively little research has been conducted on these spelling difficulties, and teaching methods have been based primarily on individual opinion rather than proven approaches (Berninger, 1999; Graham, 1999). Recent literature suggests that spelling skills of students with learning disabilities seem to follow developmental patterns similar to those of their peers without disabilities, but are delayed (Bender, 1998; Lerner, 1997). Characteristics such as visual and auditory processing and memory problems, deficiencies in auditory discrimination, and phonic generalizations have also been implicated in the spelling difficulties with learning disabilities. Data are mixed on these characteristics, and further research on spelling is needed to understand this area more clearly (Schulte-Koerne, Deimel, Bartling, & Remshmidt, 1998).

■ MATHEMATICS   Arithmetic is another academic area that causes individuals with learning disabilities considerable difficulty. They often have difficulty with counting, writing numbers, and mastering other simple math concepts (Cawley, Parmar, Yan, & Miller, 1998). Counting objects is perhaps the most fundamental mathematics skill and provides a foundation for the development of the more advanced, yet still basic, skills of addition and subtraction. Some youngsters omit numbers when counting sequences aloud (e.g., 1, 2, 3, 5, 7, 9), and others can count correctly but do not understand the relative value of numbers. Students with arithmetic learning disabilities have additional difficulties when asked to count beyond 9, which requires the use of more than one digit. This skill is somewhat more advanced than single-digit counting and involves knowledge about place value.

Place value is a more complex concept than the counting of objects and is fundamental to understanding addition and subtraction, since it is essential to the processes of carrying and borrowing. Many students with learning disabilities in math have problems understanding place value, particularly the idea that the same digit (e.g., 6) represents different magnitudes when placed in various positions (e.g., 16, 61, 632). Such complexities require strategic problem solving, which presents particular difficulties for students with learning disabilities (Gersten & Chard, 1999; Niu & Zhang, 1998).

Some of these basic mathematics difficulties are often major obstacles in the academic paths of students with learning disabilities, frequently continuing to cause problems throughout high school (Maccini, McNaughton, & Ruhl, 1999). Mastery of fundamental quantitative concepts is vital to learning more abstract and complex mathematics, a requirement for youth with learning disabilities seeking to complete high school and attend colleges or universities. These young adults are increasing in number, and it is essential for them to master algebra and geometry during secondary education. These topics have traditionally received minimal or no attention in curriculum designed for students with learning disabilities. Such coursework has tended to emphasize computational skills, though change is occurring as more attention is given to the need for more advanced instruction in mathematics (Maccini et al., 1999). Further research on mathematics difficulties and effective instruction for students encountering such problems grows more important as such young people seek to achieve more challenging educational goals.

■ ACHIEVEMENT DISCREPANCY   Students with learning disabilities perform below expectations based on their measured potential, in addition to scoring below their age-mates in overall achievement. This discrepancy between academic achievement and the student's assessed ability and age has prompted considerable research and theorizing. Attempts to quantify the discrepancy between academic achievement and academic potential for students with learning disabilities have appeared in the literature for some time, but the field still lacks a broadly accepted explanation of the phenomenon (Bender, 1998; Fisher, Fox, & Wood, 1999). Early in the school years, youngsters with learning disabilities may find themselves two to four or more years behind their peers in level of academic achievement, and many fall even further behind as they continue in the educational system. This discouraging pattern often results in students' dropping out of high school (U.S. Department of Education, 2000) or graduating without proficiency in basic reading, writing, or math skills.

■ INTELLIGENCE

Certain assumptions about intelligence are being reconsidered in research on learning disabilities. Typically, populations with behavior disorders and learning disabilities are thought to include people generally considered above average, or near average in intelligence (MacMillan & Speece, 1999; Niu & Luo, 1999). Differences between students with behavior disorders and those with specific learning disabilities have been defined based on social skill levels and learner characteristics. However, individuals

This teacher is providing several cues to help her students grasp the meaning of the word cytoplasm. She has linked a shaded illustration, the whole word cytoplasm, cytoplasm broken syllable-by-syllable, and the actual writing and visualizing of the word and what it represents. A combination of cues is often important for students with learning disabilities.

with learning disabilities may also exhibit secondary behavioral disorders, and students with behavior disorders may also have learning difficulties. To further complicate the matter, student classroom performance also suggests that behavior problems are not associated with a particular level of intellectual functioning. It is well known that individuals with intellectual deficits and those with learning disabilities may both exhibit a considerable amount of maladaptive social and interpersonal behavior (Frederickson & Furnham, 1998; Prior, Smart, Sanson, & Oberklaid, 1999). Problems in social adjustment must be viewed as a shared characteristic.

These insights have affected traditional ideas about the distinctions between learning disabilities and mental retardation. High variability between measured intelligence and academic performance has long been viewed as a defining characteristic of people with learning disabilities (MacMillan & Speece, 1999; Niu & Luo, 1999). Also, descriptions of learning disabilities have often emphasized great intraindividual differences between skill areas. For example, a youngster may exhibit very low performance in reading but not in arithmetic. Frequently, this variability in aptitude has been used to distinguish populations with learning disabilities from those with mental retardation. A typical view holds that individuals thought to have mental retardation exhibit a consistent profile of abilities (generally, low performance in all areas), in contrast to the pronounced intraindividual variability associated with learning disabilities. However, intraindividual variability is not limited to students with learning disabilities; it is sometimes evident in students with mental retardation and those with behavior disorders. Further, the widely touted intraindividual variability in students with learning disabilities does not always appear; here again the research evidence is mixed (Greenway & Milne, 1999; Mayes, Calhoun, & Crowell, 1998).

■ COGNITION AND INFORMATION PROCESSING

People with learning disabilities have certain characteristics related to **cognition,** or **information processing.** Long used in psychology as a model for studying the processes of the mind, theories about cognition focus on the way a person acquires, retains, and manipulates information (Campbell, Campbell, & Dickinson, 1999; Johnson & Johnson, 1999). These processes often emerge as problematic for individuals with learning disabilities. For example, teachers have long complained that such children have poor memory. In many cases, these students seem to learn material one day but cannot recall it the next. Research on the memory skills of these children has been relatively scanty, although it is central to understanding how information is acquired, stored, selected, and recalled. Certain evidence has suggested that children with learning disabilities do not perform as well as normal children on some memory tasks, whereas on other tasks results have shown no differences (Johnson et al., 1999). Additional research is needed to confirm, refute, or clarify clinical impressions gathered so far.

Research also suggests that children with learning disabilities have differing, rather than uniformly deficient, cognitive abilities (Johnson et al., 1999). This finding has led to the development of specific, highly focused instruction for individuals with learning disabilities to replace generic curricula that assume their cognitive skills are generally poor.

Attention problems have also been associated with learning disabilities. Such problems have often been clinically characterized as **short attention span.** Parents and teachers often note that their children with learning disabilities cannot sustain attention for more than a very short time—in some cases exhibiting considerable daydreaming and high distractibility. Some researchers have observed short atten-

■ COGNITION. The act of thinking, knowing, or processing information.

■ INFORMATION PROCESSING. A model used to study the way people acquire, remember, and manipulate information.

■ SHORT ATTENTION SPAN. An inability to focus attention on a task for a sustained period, even more than a few seconds or minutes.

tion spans in these children, but others have indicated that they have difficulty in certain *types* of attention problems and, in some cases, attend selectively (Bender, 1998; Johnson et al., 1999). **Selective attention** problems make it difficult to focus on centrally important tasks or information rather than peripheral or less relevant stimuli. Such problems might emerge when children with learning disabilities are asked to compute simple math problems that are on the chalkboard (which also means they must copy from the board). They may attend to the copying task rather than the math problems. In this situation, the teacher can easily modify the task (e.g., by using worksheets rather than copying from the board) to facilitate completion of an important lesson. Attention problems remain in the spotlight as the information-processing problems of children with learning disabilities is investigated (e.g., Johnson et al., 1999).

■ LEARNING CHARACTERISTICS

The study of perceptual problems played a significant role early in the history of learning disabilities although interest in this topic has declined. However, some researchers continue to view perception difficulties as important.

Perception difficulties in people with learning disabilities represent a constellation of behavior anomalies, rather than a single characteristic. Descriptions of these problems have referred to the visual, auditory, and **haptic** sensory systems. Visual perception difficulty has been closely associated with learning disabilities. It is important to remember that the definitions of learning disabilities exclude impaired vision in the traditional sense—visual perception problems in persons with learning disabilities refer to something distinctly different. This type of abnormality can cause a child to see a visual stimulus as unrelated parts rather than as an integrated pattern; for example, a child may not be able to identify a letter in the alphabet because he or she perceives only unrelated lines, rather than the letter as a meaningful whole. Clearly, such perception causes severe performance problems in school, particularly during the early years (Smith, 1998).

Visual perception problems may emerge in **figure–ground discrimination,** which is the process of distinguishing an object from its background. Whereas most of us have little difficulty with figure–ground discrimination, certain children labeled as having learning disabilities may have difficulty focusing on a word or sentence on the page of a textbook because they cannot distinguish it from the rest of the page. This, of course, results in difficulties with schoolwork. This deficit illustrates one of the problems in research on learning disabilities: this difficulty could represent a figure–ground discrimination disorder, but it could also reveal an attention deficit or a memory problem. Thus the same abnormal behavior can be accounted for differently by several theories (Bender, 1998).

Other discrimination problems have also surfaced in descriptions of people with learning disabilities. Individuals with difficulties in **visual discrimination** may be unable to distinguish one visual stimulus from another (e.g., the difference between words such as *sit* and *sat* or letters such as *V* and *W*); they commonly reverse letters such as *b* and *d*. This type of error is common among young children, causing great concern for parents. Yet most youngsters overcome this problem in the course of normal development and show few reversal or rotation errors with visual images by about 7 or 8 years of age. Children who make frequent errors beyond that age might be viewed as potential problem learners and may need additional instruction specifically aimed at improving such skills.

Auditory perception problems have historically been associated with learning disabilities. Some children have been characterized as unable to distinguish

■ SELECTIVE ATTENTION. Attending that often does not focus on centrally important tasks or information.

■ HAPTIC. Related to touch sensation and information transmitted through body movement or position.

■ FIGURE-GROUND DISCRIMINATION. The process of distinguishing an object from its background.

■ VISUAL DISCRIMINATION. The act of distinguishing one visual stimulus from another.

between the sounds of different words or syllables or even to identify certain environmental sounds (e.g., a ringing telephone) and differentiate them from others. Such problems have been termed **auditory discrimination** deficits. People with learning disabilities have also been described as having difficulties in auditory blending, auditory memory, and auditory association. Those with **auditory blending** problems may not be able to blend word parts into an integrated whole as they pronounce the word. **Auditory memory** difficulties may result in an inability to recall information presented orally. **Auditory association** deficiencies may result in an inability to process such information. Difficulties in these areas can obviously create school performance problems for a child. However, some questions have emerged regarding the utility of auditory deficit theories in understanding learning disabilities (see Bender, 1998).

Another area of perceptual difficulty long associated with learning disabilities involves *haptic perception* (touch, body movement, and position sensation). Such difficulties are thought to be relatively uncommon but may be important in some areas of school performance. For example, handwriting requires haptic perception because tactile information about the grasp of a pen or pencil must be transmitted to the brain. In addition, **kinesthetic** information is transmitted regarding hand and arm movements as one writes. Children with learning disabilities have often been described by teachers as having poor handwriting and difficulties in spacing letters and staying on the lines of the paper. Such problems could also be due to visual perception abnormalities, however, so precisely attributing some behaviors to a single factor is difficult. Figure 6.2 on page 179 presents an example of writing by a college freshman with learning disabilities. The two samples in this figure were written on consecutive days, each in a 40-minute period. The note translates what was written.

Not all individuals labeled as having learning disabilities exhibit behaviors that suggest perceptual problems. Patterns of deficiencies vary widely. Also, empirical evidence of perceptual problems in those labeled as having learning disabilities is generally lacking. Overall, the notion of perceptual dysfunction is founded on clinical impressions rather than rigorous research. However, this viewpoint is widespread enough to warrant this brief discussion.

■ HYPERACTIVITY

Hyperactivity has commonly been linked to children labeled as having learning disabilities although current literature more often associates it with attention-deficit hyperactivity disorder (ADHD) (Barkley, 1998; Fleck, 1998; Speltz et al., 1999). Also termed **hyperkinetic behavior, hyperactivity** is typically defined as a general excess of activity. Professionals working in the area of learning disabilities, particularly teachers, often mention this behavior first in describing their students, depicting them as fidgeting a great deal and unable to sit still for even a short time (e.g., Aro et al., 1999). Most descriptions portray an overly active child.

Certain points need to be clarified as we discuss hyperactivity in children with learning disabilities. First, not all children with learning disabilities are hyperactive, and vice versa. As many as half the children with learning disabilities may not be hyperactive—certainly it is not a universal characteristic. Currently mixed research results and confusion mark our understanding of how learning disabilities relate to hyperactivity (Aro et al., 1999; Johnson et al., 1999; Kovner et al., 1999).

A second point involves the view that hyperkinesis is characterized as a general pattern of excessive activity. This idea may reveal more about stereotypical expectations than about accurate observations. Some research has suggested that it may

■ AUDITORY DISCRIMINATION. Ability to distinguish between the sounds of different words, syllables, or environmental noises.

■ AUDITORY BLENDING. The act of blending the parts of a word into an integrated whole when speaking.

■ AUDITORY MEMORY. The ability to recall verbally presented material.

■ AUDITORY ASSOCIATION. The ability to associate verbally presented ideas or information.

■ KINESTHETIC. Related to the sensation of body position, presence, or movement, resulting chiefly from stimulation of sensory nerve endings in the muscles, tendons, and joints.

■ HYPERKINETIC BEHAVIOR. An excess of behavior in inappropriate circumstances.

■ HYPERACTIVITY. Perhaps the most frequently mentioned behavioral characteristic in the literature on ADHD. In some cases the term *hyperactivity* refers to too much activity. In others, the term refers to inappropriate activity for a given situation or context.

be more helpful to consider the appropriateness of a child's activity in particular settings rather than make overly broad generalizations about a child's behavior (Bender, 1998). Evidence does indicate that hyperactive children have a higher level of activity than their normal peers in structured settings (such as certain classroom circumstances); however, in relatively unstructured settings (such as play periods), no such differences exist (Smith, 1998).

■ SOCIAL AND EMOTIONAL CHARACTERISTICS

Thus far we have discussed academically related characteristics and behavior of students with learning disabilities. Definitions and labels used for these students tend to focus on the academic perspective. Yet children and adolescents with learning disabilities often encounter emotional and interpersonal difficulties that are quite serious and highly resistant to treatment (Persinger & Tiller, 1999; Prior et al., 1999). Because of their learning problems, they frequently experience low self-esteem and negative emotional consequences that present significant problems (Bender, 1998; Cordell, 1999). They may not be able to interact effectively with others because they misunderstand social cues or cannot discriminate among or interpret the subtleties of typical interpersonal associations.

In some cases the social dimensions of life present greater problems to students with learning disabilities than their specific academic deficits, and yet this dynamic is essentially ignored in the definitions and labels related to learning disabilities. Some view the broad category of learning disabilities as less functional than specific terminology that more precisely describes particular problems. Many people would not support broadening the definition of learning disabilities to incorporate social and emotional dimensions, although it is clear that they are substantial (Hagborg, 1999).

Causation

Researchers have theorized about a number of possible causes for learning disabilities. However, despite substantial work related to this field, determining precise causation has been difficult, and the effort to do so still continues. There are likely many different causes of learning disabilities, and in some cases, a specific type of learning disability may have multiple causes (Silver, 1999). Also, a single cause may underlie multiple disorders in the same child, such as learning disabilities and ADHD (Kaplan et al., 1998). But because it is imperative to assist affected students even before we understand the cause of learning disabilities, frequently the practical issues of assessment and intervention have taken priority in research so that specialized instruction can be offered to such students (Reschly, 1999).

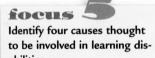

focus 5

Identify four causes thought to be involved in learning disabilities.

■ NEUROLOGICAL FACTORS

For many years, some have viewed the cause of learning disabilities as structural neurological damage, abnormal neurological development, or some type of neurological function abnormality. A substantial portion of the literature in the field has reflected the interest in this proposition (e.g., Kaplan et al., 1998; Samar, Parasnis, & Berent, 1998; Smith, 1998). Neurological factors have been the focus of some research and have been specified as an identification criterion in some literature (Silver, 1999).

Neurological damage associated with learning disabilities can occur in many ways. Damage may be inflicted on the neurological system at birth by conditions such as abnormal fetal positioning during delivery or anoxia (a lack of oxygen).

Infections may also cause neurological damage and learning disabilities, as can certain types of physical injury. As a practical matter, however, neurological damage as a cause of learning disability must be largely inferred, since direct evidence is usually not available (Bender, 1998; Drew & Hardman, 2000) (see also Chapter 9 on the effects of neurological damage as related to mental retardation).

■ MATURATIONAL DELAY

Some theories have suggested that a maturational delay of the neurological system results in the difficulties experienced by some individuals with learning disabilities (Samango-Sprouse, 1999). In many ways, the behavior and performance of children with learning disabilities resemble those of much younger individuals (Lerner, 1997). They often exhibit delays in skills maturation, such as slower development of language skills, and problems in the visual–motor area and several academic areas, as already noted. Although maturational delay is most likely not a causative factor in all types of learning disabilities, it has received considerable support as one of many.

■ GENETIC FACTORS

Genetic causation has also been implicated in learning disabilities. Genetic abnormalities, which are inherited, are thought to cause or contribute to one or more of the problems categorized as learning disabilities (Culbertson, 1998; Silver, 1999). This is always a concern for parents, whatever the learning or behavior disorder. Over the years, some research, including studies of **identical twins** and **fraternal twins,** has suggested that such disorders may be inherited (Alarcon-Cazares, 1998). These findings must be viewed cautiously because of the well-known problems in separating the influences of heredity and environment, but evidence lends a certain degree of support to the idea that some learning disabilities may be inherited.

■ ENVIRONMENTAL FACTORS

Searches for the causes of learning disabilities have also implicated certain environmental influences. Factors such as dietary inadequacies, food additives, radiation stress, fluorescent lighting, unshielded television tubes, smoking, drinking, drug consumption, and inappropriate school instruction have all been investigated at one time or another (Codina, Yin, Katims, & Zapata, 1998; Zapata, Katims, & Yin, 1998). Some environmental factors, such as irradiation, lead ingestion, illicit drugs, and family stress, are known to have negative effects on development (Lefrancois, 1999). In some cases, these influences appear to be primarily prenatal concerns, and in others, the problems seem limited to the postnatal environment or are attributable to both. Research on environmental causation relating specifically to learning disabilities remains inconclusive, but it is the focus of continuing study.

■ IDENTICAL TWINS. Twins that develop from a single fertilized egg in a single placental sac. Such twins will be of the same sex and usually resemble one another closely.

■ FRATERNAL TWINS. Twins that develop from two fertilized eggs and develop in two placentas. Often such twins do not resemble each other closely.

Assessment

Psychoeducational assessment or evaluation of individuals with learning disabilities has multiple purposes. The ultimate goal is to provide an appropriate intervention, if warranted, for the child or adult being evaluated. Assessment and intervention will involve a series of related actions, which includes screening, identification, placement, and delivery of specialized assistance. This may mean additional help with academic work, social skills, or support related to any aspect of life and involving professionals from a number of human service dis-

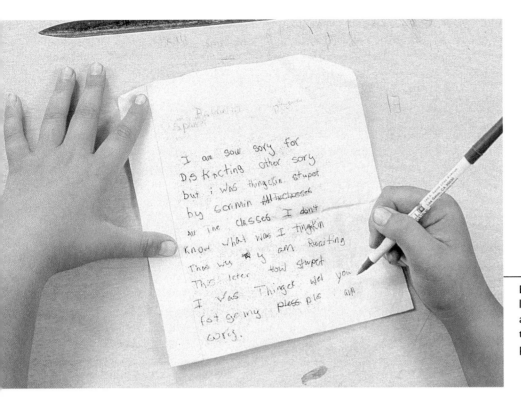

By comparing a student's skill level with a criterion-based assessment, a teacher is able to make a specific instruction plan for the student.

ciplines. Deciding how to meet a student's individual needs requires a spectrum of information obtained through a variety of assessment procedures (Merrell, 1999; National Joint Committee on Learning Disabilities, 1998; Taylor, 2000). This section will examine purposes and domains of assessment for learning disabilities in terms and will focus on intelligence, adaptive behavior, and academic achievement.

■ FORMAL AND INFORMAL ASSESSMENT

An individual's status in performance, skills, and ability can be evaluated in a number of ways, either formally or informally. Formal versus informal assessment has grown to mean standardized tests versus teacher-made tests or techniques. Standardized instruments, such as intelligence tests and achievement tests, are published and distributed on a commercial basis. Teacher-made (or those devised by any professional) techniques or instruments are not commercially available. These may be constructed for specific assessment purposes and are often quite formal, in the sense that great care is taken in the evaluation process (Gronlund, 1998; Nitko, 2001). Both formal and informal assessment techniques are effective ways of evaluating students with learning disabilities, and other students as well (Linn & Gronlund, 2000; Oosterhof, 2001; Watson, 1999). Both are used for evaluation purposes in a number of performance or behavior areas.

Other distinguishing characteristics can be used to describe assessment instruments. **Norm-referenced assessment** compares an individual's skills or performance with that of others, such as age-mates, usually on the basis of national average scores. Thus, a student's counting performance might be compared with that of his or her classmates, others in the school district of the same age, or state or national average scores. In contrast, **criterion-referenced assessment** compares an individual's skills not with a norm, but with a desired level (criterion) of performance or

■ NORM-REFERENCED ASSESS-MENT. Assessment wherein a person's performance is compared with the average of a larger group.

■ CRITERION-REFERENCED ASSESSMENT. Type of assessment that compares a person's performance to a specific established level (the criterion). This performance is not compared with that of other people.

goal. For example, the goal may involve counting to 100 with no errors by the end of the school year. One application of criterion-referenced assessment, **curriculum-based assessment,** has received increasing attention recently. It uses the objectives in a student's curriculum as the criteria against which progress is evaluated (Bishop, Bullock, Martin, & Thompson, 1999; Hasbrouck, Woldbeck, Ihnot, & Parker, 1999; Taylor, 2000).

Both norm- and criterion-referenced assessment are useful for working with students with learning disabilities, although the two approaches tend to be used for different purposes. Norm-referenced assessment is often used for administrative purposes, such as compiling census data on how many students are achieving at the state or national average. Criterion-referenced assessment is helpful for specific instructional purposes and planning.

These two types of assessment do not correspond to two entirely separate types of assessment instruments or procedures. Depending on how a technique, instrument, or procedure is employed, it may be used in a norm-referenced or criterion-referenced manner. Some areas, such as intelligence, are more typically evaluated using norm-referenced procedures. However, even a standardized intelligence test can be scored and used in a criterion-referenced fashion (the test would then function as a source of test items, and a student's performance could not be evaluated exactly as the test developer intended). Assessment should always be undertaken with careful attention to the purpose and future use of the evaluation (Drew & Hardman, 2000; Merrell, 1999).

■ SCREENING

Screening of students who seem to have learning disabilities has always been an important facet of assessment. Such assessment occurs *prior* to labeling or treatment of the student, although clinicians or others (often parents) in contact with the child often suspect a problem exists. Some individuals are screened at a rather young age, and their assessment compares them to children of a similar age. But assessment for potential learning disabilities most often takes place during the school years simply because the performance areas that these children find most problematic place them under stress at this time. However, screening and further assessment steps may be undertaken earlier if a child's difficulties attract attention before school. Such assessment may result in intervention at a very early age, a beneficial step ahead for these children.

The role of screening is to "raise a red flag," or suggest that investigation is needed. Four questions are pertinent at this point of the assessment process:

1. Is there a reason to investigate the abilities of the child more fully?
2. Is there a reason to suspect that the child in any way has disabilities?
3. If the child appears to have disabilities, what are the relevant characteristics, and what sort of intervention is appropriate?
4. How should we plan for the future of the individual?

Answers to these questions might point to a variety of needs: further classification of the disability, planning of intervention services such as psychological treatment or individualized instruction, or ongoing evaluation of progress. For students with learning disabilities, assessment is not a simple, isolated event that results in a single diagnosis, but a complex process involving many different steps (Taylor, 2000). After diagnosis, continuing assessment undergirds all decision making while an individual receives services related to learning disabilities. Approaches to assessment, for our purposes, focus on intelligence, adaptive skills, and academic achievement.

focus 6

Identify four questions that are addressed by screening assessment in learning disabilities.

■ CURRICULUM-BASED ASSESS-MENT. A type of assessment in which the objectives of a student's curriculum are used as the criteria against which progress is evaluated.

■ SCREENING. A preliminary assessment process that may suggest that further evaluation of a child's needs and functioning level is necessary. The role of screening is to "raise a red flag" if a problem is indicated.

■ INTELLIGENCE

For the most part, individuals with learning disabilities are described as having above average, or near-average intelligence, although they experience problems in school typical of students having lower intelligence levels. In many cases, measures of intelligence may be inaccurate due to specific visual, auditory, or other limitations that may affect the student's performance. However, intelligence assessment remains an important matter for individuals with learning disabilities and is often evaluated with a standardized instrument such as an intelligence test.

Issues of where measured intelligence fits into the definition of learning disabilities is somewhat controversial. Some researchers argue that intelligence is irrelevant to the definition of learning disabilities, whereas others see it as important. Still others believe that the traditional way of measuring intelligence is problematic, but not the concept of intelligence per se (MacMillan & Speece, 1999; Naglieri, 1999; Persinger & Tiller, 1999). Such difference of opinion is not unusual in the field of learning disabilities.

■ ADAPTIVE SKILLS

People with learning disabilities are frequently described as exhibiting poor adaptive skills—lacking a sense of what constitutes appropriate behavior within a particular environment. Such descriptions have primarily appeared in clinical reports and have not historically been a routine part of assessment of learning disabilities to the degree they have in other areas of exceptionality, such as mental retardation. However, some work has been undertaken to address adaptive and social skills assessment for individuals with learning disabilities (e.g., Cate et al., 1998; Vallance, Cummings, & Humphries, 1998). Such efforts are based on the assumption that a discrepancy between ability and academic achievement alone is insufficient to fully assess and describe learning disabilities. The study of adaptive skills has contributed to greater understanding of subtypes and severity levels in learning disabilities and is beginning to receive greater attention in the field as researchers focus more on the emotional well-being of students with learning disabilities (see Hagborg, 1999; Hallahan, Kauffman, & Hoyd, 1999).

■ ACADEMIC ACHIEVEMENT

Academic achievement has always been a major problem for students with learning disabilities. Assessment of academic achievement determines whether there is an overall discrepancy between a student's ability and his or her academic achievement. Such assessment also helps evaluate the student's level of functioning in one or more specific academic areas. Instruments have been developed and used to diagnose specific academic problems. For example, a number of reading tests, including the Woodcock Reading Mastery Tests, the Diagnostic Reading Scales, and the Stanford Diagnostic Reading Test, are used to determine the nature of reading problems. Likewise, mathematics assessment employs instruments such as the Key Math Diagnostic Arithmetic Test and the Stanford Diagnostic Mathematics Test (Gronlund, 1998).

Academic assessment for students with learning disabilities is very important. For the most part, assessment techniques resemble those used in other areas of exceptionality, because deficits in academic achievement are a common problem among students with a variety of disabilities. Specific skill-deficit diagnosis, however, has a more prominent history in learning disabilities and has prompted the development of focused, skill-oriented academic achievement assessment in other disability areas, as well. As with other exceptionalities, issues of inclusion and collaboration are prominent considerations in choosing the types of assessments employed with regard to instructional placement and implementation in the educational program (Dettmer, Dyck, & Thurston, 1999; Vallecorsa, deBettencourt, & Zigmond, 2000; Welch, Brownell, & Sheridan, 1999). Assessment with maximum relevance to the setting of application, often termed authentic or alternative assessment, also has attracted growing interest. These methods assess progress or skill using settings and procedures in a context like that in which the student must function, in contrast to the sterile, formal style of test administration used in the past.

The Elementary School Years

focus 7

Identify three types of intervention or treatment employed with people diagnosed as having learning disabilities.

Services and supports for children with learning disabilities have changed over time as professionals have come to view learning disabilities as a constellation of specific individualized needs, rather than a single generic category. Specific disabilities, such as cognitive learning problems, attention deficit and hyperactivity, social and emotional difficulties, and problems with spoken language, reading, writing, and mathematics are receiving research attention. This approach has resulted in services and supports focused on individual need, rather than general treatment of learning disabilities. Greater attention is also being paid to social skills instruction for children with learning disabilities and the effective use of peers as tutors (McConaughy & Ritter, 1999; Petti, 1999). Increasing recognition that these children learn, develop, and live in a broad social context has shifted the focus of services. Rather than intervening in an isolated problem area and ignoring others, a broad spectrum of issues is addressed. Some services and supports focus on strategic instruction (e.g., teaching the children how to learn), counseling and/or peer and family support (e.g., parent training), and medical treatment, all in the context of a structured educational environment (Bender, 1998). Early intervention with the most effective instruction possible is viewed as a crucial factor in the child's overall academic success (Slavin, 1996).

Services and supports for adolescents or adults with learning disabilities may differ from those for children. Some changes in approach are due to shifting goals as individuals grow older (e.g., the acquisition of basic counting skills versus math instruction in preparation for college). Educational support requires a broad range of specialized instruction tailored to individual need. Individuals from varied professions must function as a team and also as unique contributors to create a well-balanced program for the student with learning disabilities (Welch et al., 1999).

■ ACADEMIC INSTRUCTION AND SUPPORT

A wide variety of instructional approaches has been used over the years for children with learning disabilities. These include strategies to develop cognition, attention, spoken language, and skill in reading, writing, and mathematics (Meltzer, Roditi, Houser, & Perlman, 1998). Even within each area, a whole array of instructional procedures has been used to address specific problems. For example, as part of cognitive training, instruction in problem solving, problem-attack strategies, and social competence has been incorporated (Bryan, Sullivan-Burstein, & Mathur, 1998; Welch et al., 1999).

Various approaches to cognitive instruction are needed to teach the heterogeneous population of children with learning disabilities. Such strategies or tactics are often customized or reconfigured to individualize the program and specifically target a student's needs. For example, if a youngster exhibits adaptive skills deficits that interfere with inclusion in general education, such skills may form an instructional focus. Flexible and multiple services or supports may make inclusion possible, providing a well-defined instructional environment, teaching the child important skills, and addressing interpersonal or social–emotional needs (Mastropieri & Scruggs, 2000). Orchestrating such an instructional package is not a simple task. It requires determining the intensity and duration of instruction appropriate for the child, choosing supports that will meet the child's needs, and doing all of this early. Slavin (1996) argued for "neverstreaming," a plan for early intervention and excellent instruction aimed at avoiding both special education and mainstreaming as well as academic failure for children diagnosed as having learning disabilities. The design of the program is complex and labor-intensive, but essential to integrating children with learning disabilities into the educational mainstream (McConaughy & Ritter, 1999). Such a program for elementary-level children can build and improve their deficient skills, giving them a more promising prognosis for success in later school programs.

■ MATHEMATICS   Mathematics instruction for students with learning disabilities exemplifies how building a foundation of basic skills can enhance later learning. Earlier, we noted that children with arithmetic learning difficulties may have problems with basic counting and understanding of place value. For these students, counting may be most effectively taught with manipulative objects. Repetitive experience with counting buttons, marbles, or any such objects provides practice in counting as well as exposure to the concepts of magnitude associated with numbers. Counting and grouping sets of 10 objects can help children begin to grasp rudimentary place-value concepts. These activities must often be quite structured for students with learning disabilities.

Commercial programs of instruction in basic math concepts are also available. Cuisenaire Rods, sets of 291 color-coded rods used for manipulative learning experiences, are an example. These rods, whose differing lengths and colors are associated with numbers, can be used to teach basic arithmetic processes to individual students or groups.

Computer technology has also found its way into math skills instruction for students with learning disabilities (Maccini et al., 1999; Royer & Tronsky, 1998). Microcomputers are particularly appealing for teaching math because content can be presented in the sequence that is most helpful. Computers can also provide drill and practice exercises for those who need it, an instructional goal that is often difficult for teaching staff to accomplish in a classroom with several children. Concern exists, however, regarding the use of computer technology primarily for drill and practice. Although reinforcement of learning is clearly a strength of many math programs, some focus excessively on drill and practice. Some researchers strongly contend that a broad range of instructional applications is needed, extending beyond elementary skill development to serve a broader range of students (see Bitter & Pierson, 1999). Computer technology has yet to meet the high expectations many have had for instruction. It can provide some effective instruction for some students with learning disabilities, but students who find the manipulation of objects helpful in understanding math concepts may find microcomputers less useful. Long-term research is needed to study the effectiveness of computer instruction and to determine its most useful application for these children. (See the Today's Technology feature on page 194.)

■ READING   Students with learning disabilities have long been recognized as having great difficulty with reading. Because of this, reading instruction has received considerable attention, and many different strategies have been developed to address the problem (Snow et al., 1998). Each procedure has succeeded with certain children but not with all. This result lends credence to the current belief that many different disabilities may affect students who experience problems in the same area.

■ EARLY CHILDHOOD YEARS*

TIPS FOR THE FAMILY

■ Play verbal direction games, such as finding certain words or sounds, interspersing those that are difficult with those that are easy for the child with learning disabilities.

■ Give the child practice in identifying different sounds (e.g., the doorbell and phone).

■ Reinforce the child for paying attention.

■ Promote family learning about learning disabilities, their child's specific strengths and limitations, and their respect for their child as a person.

TIPS FOR THE PRESCHOOL TEACHER

■ Limit verbal instructions to simple sentences, presented briefly, one at a time.

■ Determine appropriate content carefully, paying attention to the developmental level of the material.

■ Provide multiple examples to clarify points and reinforce meaning.

■ Provide more practice than usual, particularly on new material or skills.

TIPS FOR PRESCHOOL PERSONNEL

■ Promote a school environment and attitude that encourage respect for children of all abilities.

■ Promote the development of instructional programs focusing on preacademic skills, which may be unnecessary for all children but very important for young students with learning disabilities.

■ Be alert for students that seem to be of average or higher intelligence but, for reasons that may not be evident, are not performing up to ability.

TIPS FOR NEIGHBORS AND FRIENDS

■ Community activities should be arranged to include a broad range of maturational levels so that children with learning disabilities are not shut out or do not experience unnecessary failure at this early age.

■ ELEMENTARY YEARS

TIPS FOR THE FAMILY

■ Become involved in the school through parent–teacher organizations and conferences.

■ Volunteer as a tutor.

■ Learn more about learning disabilities as you begin to understand how they affect your child, perhaps through reading material or enrolling in a short course.

TIPS FOR THE GENERAL EDUCATION CLASSROOM TEACHER

■ Keep verbal instructions simple and brief.

■ Have the student with learning disabilities repeat directions back to you, to ensure understanding.

■ Use mnemonics in instruction to aid memory.

■ Intensify instruction by repeating the main points several times to aid memory.

■ Provide additional time to learn material, including repetition or reteaching.

TIPS FOR SCHOOL PERSONNEL

■ Encourage individual athletic activities (e.g., swimming) rather than competitive team sports.

■ Involve the child in appropriate school activities (e.g., chorus or music) where interests are apparent.

■ Develop peer-tutoring programs, in which older students assist children who are having difficulty.

TIPS FOR NEIGHBORS AND FRIENDS

■ Learn about advocacy or other groups that can help you learn about and interact with the child with learning disabilities.

■ Maintain a relationship with the child's parents, talking with them about the child if and when they feel comfortable doing so.

■ As a friend, encourage parents to seek special assistance from agencies that might provide services such as "talking books."

■ If you are interested, offer assistance to the child's parents in whatever form they may need, or even volunteer to work with the child as a tutor.

■ SECONDARY AND TRANSITION YEARS

TIPS FOR THE FAMILY

■ Provide extra support for your youngster in the family setting, encouraging good school performance despite academic problems that may be occurring.

■ Encourage your adolescent to talk about and think about future plans as he or she progresses into and through the transition from school to young adult life.

- Try to understand the academic and social difficulties the student may encounter. Encourage impulse control if impulsiveness may be causing some of the problems.
- Do not shy away from the difficult task of encouraging the student to associate with peers who are success oriented rather than those who may be involved in inappropriate behavior.
- Encourage your adolescent to consider and plan for the years after high school, whether those involve college or an employment situation.

TIPS FOR THE GENERAL EDUCATION CLASSROOM TEACHER

- Specifically teach self-recording strategies, such as asking, Was I paying attention?
- Relate new material to knowledge the student with learning disabilities already has, making specific connections with familiar information.
- Teach the use of external memory enhancers (e.g., lists and note taking).
- Encourage the use of other devices to improve class performance (e.g., tape recorders).

TIPS FOR SCHOOL PERSONNEL

- Promote involvement in social activities and clubs that will enhance interpersonal interaction.
- Where students with learning disabilities have such interests and abilities, encourage participation in athletics or other extracurricular activities.
- Where interests and abilities are present, involve students in support roles to extracurricular activities (e.g., as team equipment manager).
- Promote the development of functional academic programs that are combined with transitional planning and programs.
- Provide information on college for students with learning disabilities, and encourage them to seek counseling regarding educational options, where appropriate.

TIPS FOR NEIGHBORS AND FRIENDS

- Encourage students to seek assistance from agencies that may provide services (e.g., special newspapers, talking books, and special radio stations).
- Promote involvement in community activities (e.g., scouting, Rotary Club, Chamber of Commerce, or other service organizations for adults).

- Encourage a positive understanding of learning disabilities among neighbors, friends, and community agencies (e.g., law enforcement officials) who may encounter adolescents or adults with disabilities.

ADULT YEARS

TIPS FOR THE FAMILY

- Interact with your adult family member with learning disabilities on a level that is consistent with his or her adult status. Despite all the difficulties experienced in school and while maturing, remember that this person is now an adult.
- While recognizing the person's adult status, also remember that your adult family member with learning disabilities will likely continue to experience specific difficulties related to his or her disability. Help the person to devise ways of compensating.

TIPS FOR THERAPISTS OR OTHER PROFESSIONALS

- In adulthood, it is unlikely that basic academic instruction will be the focus of professional intervention. It may be worthwhile to focus on compensatory skills for particularly difficult problem areas.

- Be alert for signs of emotional stress that may require intervention. This person may have a very deep sense of frustration accrued from a lifelong history of difficulties and failure.

TIPS FOR NEIGHBORS AND FRIENDS

- It may be necessary to be more flexible or understanding with adult friends or neighbors with learning disabilities. There may be good explanations for deviations from what is considered normal behavior. However, if certain behaviors are persistent and particularly aggravating to you, you owe it to your friend to discuss the matter rather than let it interfere with a friendship. You may have numerous friends, but the adult with learning disabilities may have precious few; thus your understanding and honesty are particularly valuable.

*Very young children who may have learning disabilities typically have not been formally diagnosed with the disability, although they may exhibit what appears to be maturational slowness.

Today's Technology

SOFTWARE FOR WRITING

Writing has long been recognized as an academic area that presents considerable difficulty for children with learning disabilities. Advances in educational applications of technology, especially the development of new computer software, have potential for assisting children with writing problems (MacArthur, 1999). An example of such software is Write: OutLoud, a talking word processor. Write: OutLoud cues the user with a beep or a flash on the screen in response to an incorrectly spelled word. This program can also speak! It will read back a sentence or a word so the user can check his or her work for accuracy.

Another software package with a speaking component is the Co: Writer, a word prediction program. It lets users write almost as quickly as they can think by predicting words through a program using artificial intelligence. For example, typing in the first letter or two of a word the user is unsure how to spell will produce a list of possible words from which to choose. It helps those with spelling difficulties and low motor ability; it also helps address grammar and spelling problems.

Research on particular types of skill instruction, such as prereading activities, guided practice with feedback, and the direct teaching of skills in summarizing, has produced significant improvements for students with learning disabilities (see Gardill & Jitendra, 1999). Information gained from such research is being incorporated into instructional programs more than ever before. Combined with the realization that one single approach does not fit all students, this trend promises improved instruction and positive outcomes for students with learning disabilities.

Reading programs that base and sequence instruction within a developmental framework often help students with learning disabilities (Smith, 1998). Such programs typically methodically introduce sight vocabulary based on developmental status, with an analytic phonics emphasis. The most widely used developmental approaches involve basal readers such as the Holt Basic Reading; Ginn 720 Series; Scott, Foresman Reading; and Macmillan Series E. Such basal readers are most useful for group instruction (often designed for three levels), are well sequenced on a developmental basis, and typically provide sufficient detail to be used effectively by somewhat inexperienced teachers. The orientation toward group instruction, however, is likely to present some limitations for those students with learning disabilities who need heavy doses of individual attention. Houghton Mifflin's *Soar to Success* program presents an appealing small-group intervention package that focuses on students performing at a two- to three-grade reading deficit. While this program has previously focused on grades 3–6, grades 7 and 8 were added during the spring of 2000.

Many teachers successfully use whole-language strategies to teach reading to students with learning disabilities. This approach tends to deemphasize isolated exercises and drills. Some are concerned, however, that this population needs a balance between a whole-language approach and focused, intensive, direct instruction related to problem areas (see Hallahan et al., 1999; Lerner, 1997). To make significant progress, a student with a serious reading disability often needs individualized reading instruction. A wide variety of materials (e.g., trade books) may be selected to match the student's reading level and cover topics of high interest to the student. The teacher responsible for developing and providing individualized instruction needs to have considerable knowledge of reading skills and the procedures that will enhance learning them. Effective individualized instruction also requires evaluation of progress, ongoing monitoring, and detailed record keeping. Increasing the student's

THE GET IT STRATEGY: TEACHING THE MTV GENERATION TO TAKE RESPONSIBILITY FOR LEARNING

The GET IT program is a video-mediated instructional strategy aimed directly at appealing to the student. Emulating television game shows, the program also combines real-life situations of students from their perspectives—their lives as they see it, not as adults conceive them. This program is intended to teach basic learning strategies and responsibility to the student as a learner. The strategy title is a mnemonic provided to help students remember the elements and their tasks:

G: Gather the Objectives (or Get objectives).
E: Execute the search for objectives.
T: Take notes.
I: Inspect inventory of objectives.
T: Test your comprehension.

The GET IT strategy has been used effectively with a number of student populations in both general and special education settings. The program emphasizes interactive participation of students and does not permit passive viewing. Larsen-Miller (1994) field-tested the program with mainstreamed sixth-grade students identified as having learning disabilities. She found that significant gains were made in comprehension, attitude toward reading, and knowledge of the parts of a textbook. This strategy emphasizes students' taking responsibility for an increased role in the teaching–learning equation.

Sources: From *Educational Partnerships: An Ecological Approach to Serving Students at Risk,* by M. Welch and S. M. Sheridan, 1995, San Francisco, CA: Harcourt Brace Jovanovich. And from *An Investigation to Determine the Effects of a Video-Mediated Metacognitive Reading Comprehension Strategy in a Complimentary Environment,* by L. Larsen-Miller, 1994, Unpublished Master's Thesis, University of Utah.

responsibility for his or her own learning, including self-monitoring skills, appears to enhance instructional effectiveness for students with learning disabilities (Bender, 1998). This self-directed involvement in learning makes students proactive partners in the instruction–learning process. This idea has led to the development of learning strategies packages that teach students effective skills for being better students. One such program is the GET IT strategy, described by its developers as a cognitive learning strategy for reading comprehension (Welch & Sheridan, 1995). (A brief description of the GET IT strategy is presented in the nearby Reflect on This feature.)

Several commercially available reading programs also provide specific skill-oriented reading instruction that function in a diagnostic–prescriptive manner. Examples include the Fountain Valley Reading Support System, available from Zweig and Associates, and the Ransom Program from Addison-Wesley. Computer-assisted instruction is employed in some diagnostic–prescriptive reading programs, such as the Harcourt Brace CAI Remedial Reading Program and the Stanford University CAI Project. Individualized instruction is a hallmark of diagnostic–prescriptive reading programs. Such materials let students work at their own pace. However, these materials are limited by the fact that they can focus on teaching only the skills that lend themselves to the particular program's format. Notwithstanding this limitation, these programs have considerable strengths. For example, they do not require that the teacher possess a high degree of knowledge and skill, which, as described earlier, is essential for totally individualized, *teacher-generated* reading instruction. Additionally, diagnostic–prescriptive programs generally provide ongoing assessment and feedback, and developmental skills are usually well sequenced. Yet such remedial reading programs are somewhat controversial, both in terms of methodology and conceptual arguments about their function and appropriateness (e.g., Dudley-Marling & Murphy, 1997; Johnston, 1998).

A variety of other programs and approaches to reading instruction are available, each strategy with its own strengths and limitations for students with learning disabilities. Other developmentally based approaches include synthetic phonics basals, linguistic phonemic programs, and language experience approaches. Some procedures use multisensory techniques in order to maximize the student's learning. Selection of method and application of instructional technique should be based on a student's particular disability profile and other relevant needs.

Computer software for use in assessment and instruction in reading can assist students with learning disabilities and will become increasingly common in the future. Computer-presented reading instruction offers some particular advantages. It provides individual instruction, as well as never-ending drill and practice, as mentioned earlier. Programs can also combine feedback with corrective instruction. As computer programs advance, reading instruction software will improve (right now, word-recognition programs seem to be of higher quality than comprehension software) and become more widely available. However, there is continuing concern regarding the appropriate use of software, including enormous needs for long-range planning, faculty training, and other staff development related to technology applications in instruction (see Bitter & Pierson, 1999). There continues to be a gap between technology developments and their effective broad implementation in education, and many matters require debate and resolution before information technology can achieve its full potential in education (Donovan & Macklin, 1999; Katz, 1999).

As children progress into the upper-elementary grades, they may need instruction in compensatory skills or methods to circumvent deficit areas not yet remedied. This instruction may involve tutoring by an outside agency or an individual specializing in the problem or placement in a resource room or even a self-contained class for students with learning disabilities. The chosen approach will reflect the severity of the difficulty, the particular area of deficiency, and, sometimes (for better or for worse), the resources and attitudes of the decision makers (e.g., families and school districts).

■ BEHAVIORAL INTERVENTIONS

Distinctions between behavioral and academic interventions are not always sharp and definitive. Both involve students in learning skills and changing behavior. Behavioral interventions, however, generally use practical applications of learning principles such as reinforcement. Behavioral interventions such as the structured presentation of stimuli (e.g., letters or words), reinforcement for correct responses (e.g., specific praise), and self-monitoring of behavior and performance are used in many instructional approaches (Jitendra, Cole, Hoppes, & Wilson, 1998; Wong, 1999). In this section, we briefly discuss some behavioral interventions that are used outside of traditional academic areas.

With certain children, instruction may focus on social skills training. Some students with learning disabilities who experience repeated academic failure, despite their great effort, become frustrated and depressed. They may not understand why their classmates without disabilities seem to do little more than they do, yet achieve more success. These students may withdraw or express frustration and anxiety by acting out or becoming aggressive. When this type of behavior emerges, it may be difficult to distinguish individuals with learning difficulties from those with behavior disorders as a primary disability, and therefore both diagnosis of the problem and treatment may be quite difficult (e.g., Persinger & Tiller, 1999). In fact, these student groups often manifest many similar behaviors. Social and behavioral difficulties of students with learning disabilities are receiving increasing attention in the literature (Bender, 1998; Prior et al., 1999).

Behavioral contracts represent one type of intervention often used to change undesirable behavior. Using this approach, a teacher, behavior therapist, or parent

■ BEHAVIORAL CONTRACT. Agreement, written or oral, between people, stating that if one party behaves in a certain manner (for example, the student completes homework), the other (for example, teacher or parent) will provide a specific reward.

establishes a contract with the child that provides him or her with reinforcement for appropriate behavior. Such contracts are either written or spoken, usually focus on a specific behavior (e.g., remaining in his or her seat for a given period of time), and reward the child with something that he or she really likes and considers worth striving for (e.g., going to the library or using the class computer). It is important that the pupil understand clearly what is expected and that the event or consequence be appealing to that child, so that it really does reinforce the appropriate behavior. Behavioral contracts have considerable appeal because they give students some responsibility for their own behavior (Gelfand et al., 1997). They can also be used effectively by parents at home. Contracts in various forms can be applied for students at widely different ages.

Token reinforcement systems represent another behavioral intervention often used with youngsters experiencing learning difficulties. **Token reinforcement systems** allow students to earn tokens for appropriate behavior and evenually exchange them for a reward of value to them (Gelfand et al., 1997). Token systems resemble the work-for-pay lives of most adults, and therefore can be generalized to later life experiences. Although token systems require considerable time and effort to plan and implement, they can be truly effective.

Behavioral interventions are based on fundamental principles of learning largely developed from early experimental psychology research. These principles have been widely applied in many settings for students with learning disabilities as well as other exceptionalities. One of their main strengths is that, once the basic theory is understood, behavioral interventions can be modified to suit a wide variety of needs and circumstances.

The Adolescent Years

Services and supports for adolescents and young adults with learning disabilities differ somewhat from those used for children. Age is an important factor to consider when planning services. Even the services and supports used during childhood vary according to age—appropriate assistance for a child of age 6 will not typically work for one who is 12. New issues crop up during the teen-age years. Adolescents and young adults with learning disabilities may, like their nondisabled peers, become involved in alcohol or drug use and sexual activity (Moss, 1998; Watson, Franklin, Ingram, & Eilenberg, 1998). Certainly they are vulnerable to peer pressure and the possibility of engaging in misconduct. However, adolescents are also influenced by their parents' expectations, which may be an important positive factor in academic achievement. Age-appropriate modifications are essential to effective instruction and services for adolescents with learning disabilities, and most often they must be individually designed.

focus 8

How are the services and supports for adolescents and adults with learning disabilities different from those used with children?

■ ACADEMIC INSTRUCTION AND SUPPORT

Academic instruction for adolescents with learning disabilities differs from such programs for younger children. Research suggests that the educational system often fails adolescents with learning disabilities. These students have lower school completion rates than their nondisabled peers do, as well as higher unemployment rates (U.S. Department of Education, 2000). The goal of secondary education is to prepare individuals for postschool lives and careers. These findings suggest a serious doubt that youth with learning disabilities are being adequately supported in meeting this goal. Often these adolescents find that they still need to develop basic academic survival

The goals of adolescents with learning disabilities will vary among individuals. Some students may look forward to employment after high school while others might plan some type of continuing education.

skills (and for some, preparation for college), and they also often lack social skills and comfortable interpersonal relationships (Persinger & Tiller, 1999). Adolescents with learning disabilities are attending college in greater numbers than ever, but they tend to drop out at higher rates than do their nondisabled peers (U.S. Department of Education, 2000). Clearly, a comprehensive model, with a variety of components, needs to be developed to address a broad spectrum of needs for adolescents and young adults with learning disabilities.

Relatively speaking, adolescents with learning disabilities have received considerably less attention than their younger counterparts. Academic deficits that first appeared during the younger years tend to grow more marked as students face progressively more challenging work, and by the time many reach secondary school or adolescence, they may be further behind academically than they were in the earlier grades (Bender, 1998). Although academic performance figures prominently in the federal definition of learning disabilities, there still has been relatively little research on factors that influence academic development in adolescents with learning disabilities. Problems in motivation, self-reliance, learning strategies, social competence, and skill generalization all emerge repeatedly in the literature on adolescents and young adults with learning disabilities (see Gersten & Baker, 1998; Jenkins, 1999). More often than not, however, these findings appear within individual studies on single components of learning disabilities. Comprehensive instruction is difficult to implement and to investigate.

Time constraints represent one difficulty facing teachers of adolescents with learning disabilities. A limited amount of time is available for instruction, student progress can be slow, and determining what to focus on is difficult. These adolescents and their teachers face a difficult task. In some areas, high school students may not have progressed beyond fifth-grade level academically, and they may have only a rudimentary grasp of some academic topics (Bender, 1998). Yet they are reaching an age at which life grows more complex. A broad array of issues must be addressed, including possible college plans (an increasingly frequent goal for students with learning disabilities),

Reflect on This

WRITE, P.L.E.A.S.E.: A LEARNING STRATEGY TO USE IN THE GENERAL CLASSROOM

Using a bologna sandwich to teach writing skills may seem a bit strange, but it serves a definite purpose. It camouflages the academic overtones of a video-assisted learning-strategies program and has been successfully employed with typical students, low-efficiency learners who do not qualify for special education, and students with learning disabilities. This strategy is another in the series developed by Welch and his colleagues that targets the inclusion of students with learning problems (and low-efficiency students) into the instructional mainstream.

Write, P.L.E.A.S.E. provides students with an easily remembered strategy for planning and executing their written compositions, using the mnemonic cues of the title:

Pick: Students pick the topic, audience, and appropriate textual format in view of the topic and audience.

List: Students list information about the topic to be used in generating sentences.

Evaluate: Students evaluate their list and other elements of their writing as they proceed.

Activate: Students activate their paragraph with a topic sentence.

Supply: Students supply supporting sentences, moving from their topic sentence and drawing on their list of ideas.

End: Students end with a concluding sentence and evaluate.

Combining mnemonics and the sandwich visual metaphor has given students a means of remembering important elements of writing paragraphs. This uniquely presented learning strategy is effective in the general education classroom as well as in more specialized instructional circumstances.

Source: From *"Write, P.L.E.A.S.E.: A Video-Assisted Strategic Intervention to Improve Written Expression of Inefficient Learners,"* by M. W. Welch and J. Jensen, 1991, *Journal of Remedial and Special Education, 12,* pp. 37–47.

---

employment goals, and preparation for social and interpersonal life during the adult years. In many areas, instead of building and expanding on a firm foundation of knowledge, many adolescents with learning disabilities are operating on a beginning to intermediate level. They may appear less than fully prepared for the challenges ahead of them, but a well-planned program of supports can do much to smooth the transition to adulthood.

Students' academic learning difficulties intersect with limited instructional time to create some particularly challenging circumstances in teaching adolescents with learning disabilities. This has led researchers to seek alternatives to and supplements for traditional teaching of academic content to students with learning disabilities. Teaching students learning strategies represents one widely used approach that focuses on the learning process. Using this approach, students are taught *how to learn* in addition to the content of a given lesson (e.g., Gersten & Baker, 1998). Thus the learning-strategies approach promotes self-instruction and frequently emphasizes "thinking about" the act being performed. This process is known as metacognition and may focus on rather complex academic content such as writing (Wong, 1999). Learning-strategies programs may be employed in the general education classroom, as illustrated in the nearby Reflect on This feature.

Secondary school instruction for adolescents with learning disabilities may also involve teaching compensatory skills to make up for those not acquired earlier. Compensatory skills often address specific areas of need, such as writing, listening, and social skills. For example, tape recorders may be used in class to offset difficulties in taking notes during lectures and thus compensate for a listening (auditory input) problem. For some individuals, personal problems related to disabilities require counseling or other mental health assistance. And to further complicate matters during adolescence, hormonal changes with strong effects on interpersonal behavior come into play; the literature is barely beginning to emerge on such issues related to adolescents with learning disabilities (see Boucher, 1999; Hollins, Perez, Abdelnoor, & Webb, 1999). These students tend to have low social status among nearly all the people around them, including peers, teachers, and even parents. Some may become involved in criminal activities, as mentioned periodically in the literature, although the research evidence linking learning disabilities and juvenile delinquency is mixed (Lindsay, 1999; O'Callaghan, 1998; Smith, 1998). Generally, evidence does not suggest that arrests and jail terms for individuals with learning disabilities occur at substantially higher rates than for peers without disabilities.

■ TRANSITION FROM SCHOOL TO ADULT LIFE

Some adolescents and adults with learning disabilities have successfully adapted by themselves to a variety of challenges. However, many of the difficulties that adolescents with learning disabilities experience do not disappear as they grow older, and specialized services are often needed throughout adolescence, perhaps into adulthood (Silver, 1999). We currently do not understand the factors that contribute to success or lack of it in young adults with learning disabilities. Some ingredients that would seem to contribute to success as a young adult have not proved to be accurate predictors (e.g., verbal intelligence, length of school enrollment). Such findings may suggest that we still don't know what predicts success in young adults such as these with learning disabilities. Or the findings may reflect difficulties and inaccuracies in measurement as well as challenges in prediction in research on adults (Persinger & Tiller, 1999). Accumulating research on the transition years of adolescents with learning disabilities may begin to illuminate some of these methodology problems. We may find that this period of life is characterized by some unique challenges, as it is for young people with other disabilities (Pangos & Dubois, 1999; Ryan, Nolan, Keim, & Madsen, 1999).

Transition services remain rather sparse for adolescents with learning disabilities. However, this area is beginning to receive increased attention in the literature. We are beginning to learn more about how emotional, interpersonal, and social competence issues affect adults with learning disabilities, and such research will have an impact on transition planning. Research is emerging on factors such as substance abuse; results suggest a possible association between alcohol abuse and learning disabilities (Greenway & Milne, 1999; Zeitlin, 1999). Services and supports that address this problem are beginning to be reported (Rowland, 1999; Wenar & Kerig, 2000). Although the picture remains unclear at this point, the literature is also beginning to focus on adults with learning disabilities and matters such as violence and violent crime, with some suggesting an at-risk situation for these individuals (Willoughy-Booth & Pearce, 1998). Research on interpersonal relationships is also underway, and preliminary findings point to a need for transition services for young adults with learning disabilities in areas of emotional well-being, interpersonal intimacy, and sexuality development (see Moss, 1998). Results suggest that the competence of young adults with learning disabilities in these areas is not notably positive.

Those planning transition programs for adolescents with learning disabilities must consider that their life goals may approximate those of adolescents without disabilities. Some students look forward to employment that will not require education beyond high school. Some plan to continue their schooling in vocational and trade schools (Lerner, 1997). As with other areas of exceptionality, schooling should play a significant role in preparing young adults with learning disabilities for the transition from school to work (National Joint Committee on Learning Disabilities, 1998). Employment preparation activities such as occupational awareness programs, work experience, career and vocational assessment, development of job-related academic and interpersonal skills, and information about specific employment should be part of transition plans and should benefit these students. In addition, professionals may need to negotiate with employers to secure some accommodations at work for young adults with learning disabilities. Limited data are available concerning the employment success of young adults with learning disabilities; most reports combine information on people with a number of disabilities. Most authorities agree, however, that the employment years for these individuals usually are not any easier than their school years, and a definite need exists for transitional programs from school to work (Bender, 1998).

Growing numbers of young people with learning disabilities plan to attend a college or university (see Arries, 1999; Jenkins, 1999; U.S. Department of Education, 2000a). There is little question that they will encounter difficulties and that careful transition planning is essential for success. Their dropout rates are higher and their academic performance indicators are lower than those of their counterparts without learning disabilities (Sinclair, Christenson, Elevo, & Hurley, 1998). It is also clear that, with some additional academic assistance, they not only will survive, but also can be competitive college students (Jenkins, 1999). These students need substantial college preparatory counseling before they leave secondary school. There is a considerable difference in the relatively controlled setting of high school and the more unstructured environment of college. To make this significant transition, students profit from focused assistance, transition planning, and goal setting, perhaps in conjunction with their high school counselors (Raskind, Goldberg, Higgins, & Herman, 1999).

College-bound students with learning disabilities may find that many of their specific needs are related to basic survival skills in higher education. At the college level, it is assumed that students already have adequate ability in taking notes, digesting lecture information auditorily, writing skills, reading, and study habits. Transition programs must strengthen these abilities as much as possible and show the students how to compensate for deficits, using a range of perspectives and strategies to plan the student's pursuit of postsecondary education (National Joint Committee on Learning Disabilities, 1998). Taped lectures can be replayed many times to help the student understand the information. Students with reading disabilities can obtain the help of readers who tape-record the context of textbooks so that they can listen to the material, rather than make slow progress if reading is difficult and time consuming. College students with learning disabilities must also seek out educational support services and social support networks to offset emotional immaturity and personality traits that may impede college achievement (Persinger & Tiller, 1999).

Perhaps the most helpful survival technique that can be taught to an adolescent with learning disabilities is actually more than a specific skill—it is a way of thinking about survival, an overall attitude of resourcefulness and a confident approach to solving problems. Recall Mathew, the psychology student in this chapter's beginning snapshot. Mathew has an amazing array of techniques that he uses to acquire knowledge while compensating for his specific deficit areas. Students need both proven techniques to deal with problem areas and the ability to generate new ways to tackle challenges that inevitably arise in college. This positive attitude also includes knowing how to seek help and how to advocate for oneself. Transition programs that can instill such a mind-set in students preparing for college have truly served an important purpose.

Another important transition element involves establishing a support network. Students with learning disabilities should be taught how to establish an interpersonal network of helpers and advocates. A faculty member advocate can often be more successful than the student in requesting special testing arrangements or other accommodations (at least to begin with). A word of caution is in order, however.

Faculty in higher education are bombarded with student complaints and requests, many of which are not based on extreme needs. Consequently many faculty are wary of granting special considerations such as extra time. However, a request from a faculty colleague may carry more weight. It should also be noted that many faculty are uninformed about learning disabilities, and overtures from a colleague can enhance the credibility of the student's request.

Concern about the accommodations requested by students who claim to have learning disabilities is genuine and is growing. Because these disabilities are invisible, they are hard to understand and there is great room for abuse in requests for accommodations. Such requests have increased dramatically, and many faculty are skeptical about the legitimacy of many of them. Research suggests that some cynicism is understandable; some claims indeed lack a sound justification, and diagnostic documentation provided for many college students claiming to be learning disabled is seriously flawed (see Ward & Bernstein, 1998). Although the Americans with Disabilities Act clearly mandates accommodation, college students with learning disabilities should be aware that many higher education faculty are skeptical about the merits of this mandate. Some incidents pertaining to this issue have become publicized and politicized, and they may have a detrimental influence on the general higher education environment for those with learning disabilities (McGuire, 1998). Providing clear diagnostic evidence of a learning disability will enhance the credibility of a request for accommodation. Even faculty in special education have encountered those who have diagnosed themselves and claimed to have a learning disability; this unprofessional approach is counterproductive to improving the experiences of students with learning disabilities in higher education.

Students with learning disabilities can lead productive, even distinguished, adult lives. But some literature suggests that, even after they complete a college education, adults with learning disabilities have limited career choices (Bender, 1998). A more complete research base is needed in this area. However, we do know that notable individuals have been identified as learning disabled, including scientist and inventor Thomas Edison, president of the United States Woodrow Wilson, scientist Albert Einstein, and governor of New York and vice president of the United States Nelson Rockefeller. We also know that Mathew graduated from college and entered graduate school, and that the young man whose writing we saw in Figure 6.2 did become a successful architect. Such achievements are not accomplished without considerable effort, but they show that the outlook for people with learning disabilities can be very promising.

Inclusive Education

Definitions and descriptions of various approaches to inclusive education were introduced in Chapters 1 and 4. Much of the impetus for the inclusive education movement emerged from efforts of parents and advocacy organizations; the concept has been known by various terms such as *mainstreaming, the regular education initiative,* and *integration service models.* A very large portion of students with learning disabilities receives educational services in settings that are either fully or partially inclusive. In 1997–1998, only 16% of students with learning disabilities from 6 to 21 years of age were served outside the regular classroom more than 60% of the time (U.S. Department of Education, 2000a).

Inclusive education is an important part of the academic landscape for students with learning disabilities, and a variety of specific instructional strategies is employed to enhance success (Rodgers, 1999). Inclusive approaches have received increasing attention in the learning disability literature, including debate regarding appropriate formats and the strengths and limitations of placing students with learning disabilities in fully inclusive educational environments (Silliman, Ford, Beasman, & Evans, 1999).

Instructing students with learning disabilities in inclusive settings requires significant advance planning. Increasingly, the education of these students is guided by complex, comprehensive plans incorporating instructional services and supports and multiple approaches. Each student's instructional plan targets specific areas that need more intense or specialized attention. The academic focus may be on a reading problem or difficulties in some other content area. Social and behavioral issues may emerge in the inclusive environment, and related interventions may form part of the spectrum of services and supports. To be effective, instructional supports must be directly keyed to the student's needs in the context of a general education classroom.

Several factors affect the success of inclusive education for students with learning disabilities. For example, teacher attitudes are very influential. Some evidence suggests that general education teachers feel unprepared to teach students with disabilities, to collaborate with special educators, and to make academic adaptations. Adequate teacher preparation is a very important factor in effective inclusive education. Such preparation requires a significant collaborative partnership between general education and special education teacher education programs, which has largely been lacking to date and is potentially threatened by some market-driven developments in higher education (see Rosenberg & Sindelar, 1998). In addition to curriculum and instructional skills, personal attitudes toward inclusive education are vitally important. General education teachers often have less positive attitudes toward and perceptions of inclusive education than special education teachers do, although such attitudes can be changed (Welch & Tulbert, 1998).

Successful inclusion requires much more than merely placing students with learning disabilities in the same classroom with their nondisabled peers. Because these students need supports and adaptations, some have noted that successful inclusion might better be described as supported inclusion rather than inclusion alone. Inclusive education must be undertaken only after careful planning of the instructional approach, services, and supports. Such a program can effectively promote academic support, student motivation, and social–emotional skill development for students with learning disabilities.

Medical Services

Medical professionals are sometimes involved in the diagnosis of learning disabilities and in prescribing medications used in treating conditions that may coexist with learning disabilities. The involvement of physicians varies somewhat according to the age of the person with disabilities.

■ CHILDHOOD

Physicians often diagnose a child's abnormal or delayed development in the areas of language, behavior, and motor functions. It is not uncommon for pediatricians to participate in diagnosing physical disabilities that may significantly affect learning and behavior and then interpret medical findings to the family and other professionals. Physicians may have early involvement with a child with learning disabilities because of the nature of the problem, such as serious developmental delay or hyperactivity. However, more often a medical professional sees the young child first because he or she has not entered school yet, and the family physician is a primary adviser for parents (Drew & Hardman, 2000). When other professional expertise is needed, the physician may refer the family to other specialists and then function as a team member in meeting a child's needs.

One example of medical service appropriate for some children with disabilities involves controlling hyperactivity and other challenging behaviors (Heimann, 1999; Silver, 1999). On the surface, hyperactive behavior may lead one to believe that the child is suffering from greater than normal physiological arousal. Such notions led many researchers to recommend placing such children in environments with few distracting stimuli, known as low-stimulus or stimulus-free settings. However, one treatment often employed with hyperactive children has called into question the overarousal theory. The medication Ritalin (generic name, methylphenidate), which is most often used to control hyperactivity, is from the amphetamine family, which stimulates, rather than suppresses, physiological arousal (see Elia, Ambrosini, & Rapoport, 1999).

Many professionals have tried to make sense of the seemingly paradoxical reactions to amphetamines shown by some individuals with learning disabilities and ADHD (see Chapter 7). It is popularly believed that although amphetamines increase activity in most people, they decrease activity in children who are hyperactive. Some have suggested that hyperactive individuals may be plagued by abnormally low physiological arousal; they are not functioning at an optimal arousal level and are not, contrary to previous assumptions, generally overly aroused (Lerner, 1997). Although of academic interest, such theories have provided little specific guidance regarding the use of medication to control hyperactivity. On a practical level, psychostimulants appear to result in general improvement for a large portion of children with ADHD (Elia et al., 1999).

Some researchers have expressed concern or caution about such treatment, focusing particularly on matters of effectiveness, overprescription, and side effects (e.g., Jensen et al., 1999; Silver, 1999). Concerns have been consistently expressed regarding the soundness of research methods used to investigate effects of medication (see Gelfand et al., 1997). Clearly, too little is known about the effects of medication on hyperactivity, even as evidence continues to accumulate regarding this avenue of treatment. For example, there are a number of situations where exactly which drug will be effective is not known until after treatment has begun. Uncertainty regarding dosage level and the fact that high doses may have toxic effects are adding to the disconcerting confusion. Some professionals have seriously questioned the use of medication in light of the evidence on its effectiveness. Concern exists about side effects of the medication as well as possible abuse (e.g., Silver, 1999). The physical side effects of using stimulant medication include insomnia, irritability, decreased appetite, and headaches. However, these side effects seem to be relatively minor and mostly temporary, although they vary greatly among individuals. Current thinking suggests that, although there are clear benefits to the use of medication, it may be overprescribed, and expectations that it will produce generalized improvement simply are not supported by research evidence (Jensen et al., 1999).

■ ADOLESCENCE

Like other treatment areas, medical services for adolescents and young adults with learning disabilities differ somewhat from those for children. The literature directly addressing medical services during adolescence is unfortunately scarce, although some have explored specific needs that may require medical attention. For example, stress and serious emotional difficulty, including depression, during the adolescent years are receiving attention (see Boucher, 1999; Hagborg, 1999). In some cases, psychiatry may be involved in treatment, either through interactive therapy or the prescribing of antidepressant medication. A larger body of literature related to medical treatment of serious emotional difficulty will probably emerge, since the need seems to be surfacing. Some efforts are underway to improve assessment of medical, developmental, functional, and growth variables for individuals with learning difficulties, in a variety of settings (e.g., Martin, Scahill, Klin, & Volkmar, 1999). These efforts too are expanding and hopefully will systematically address individuals with learning disabilities at various age levels.

Some adolescents receiving medication to control hyperactivity may have been taking it for a number of years, since many such physician assessments and prescriptions are made during childhood. On the other hand, some treatments are of a rather short duration, and many terminate within two years (Jensen et al., 1999). This finding raises serious questions regarding which type of treatment is most suitable. Other ongoing questions regard problems with side effects and determining which medications are effective in dealing with particular symptoms (Silver, 1999). A number of adolescent youth and adults with learning disabilities have struggled through their earlier years and have not received medication until after childhood. In many cases, the medication to assist with behavior and attention problems is again an amphetamine and appears to have the same beneficial results noted earlier (Elia et al., 1999).

The field of learning disabilities and the individuals served within it represent a most interesting array of challenges, perhaps the most perplexing among the high-incidence disabilities. In the overall picture of disabilities, these challenges are not trivial, both because they are complex and because they involve such a very large portion of the population that we consider to have disabilities. Progress is evident on many fronts although it is also clear that intense and systematic research efforts are essential if improvement in service is to continue.

Case Study

ALICE REVISITED

Recall Alice, whom we met in the last snapshot. Alice was in the fourth grade when we last saw her and was extremely frustrated with school. Unfortunately, she failed the history test for which she was preparing. She could not obtain enough information from the narrative and consequently could not answer the questions on the test. The exam was a paper-and-pencil test, which, to Alice, looked like the book that she was supposed to read about the family who was moving West with the wagon train. When she received her graded test, Alice broke into tears. This was not the first time she had wept about her schoolwork, but it was the first time that her teacher had observed it.

Alice's teacher, Mr. Dunlap, was worried about her. She was not a troublesome child in class and she seemed attentive. But she could not do the work. On this occasion, Mr. Dunlap consoled Alice and asked her to stay after school briefly to visit with him about the test. Since it was early in the year, he had no clue what was wrong, except he knew that this charming girl could not answer his test questions. He was astonished when they sat together and he determined that Alice could not even read the questions. If she could not read the questions, he thought, then she undoubtedly can't read the book. But he was fairly certain that she was not lacking in basic intelligence—her conversations simply didn't indicate such a problem.

After further consoling Alice regarding her test, Mr. Dunlap sent her home and then contacted her parents. He knew a little about exceptional children and the referral process. He set the process in motion, meeting with the parents, the school psychologist, and the principal, who also sat in on all the team meetings at this school. After a diagnostic evaluation, the team met again to examine the psychologist's report. Miss Burns, the psychologist, had tested Alice and found that her scores fell in the average range in intelligence (with a full-scale WISC-III score of 114). She had also assessed Alice's abilities with a comprehensive structural analysis of reading skills. This led her to believe that Alice had a rather severe form of dyslexia, which interfered substantially with her ability to read.

Alice's parents expressed a strong desire for her to remain in Mr. Dunlap's class if possible. This was viewed as a desirable choice by each member of the team, and the next challenge was to determine how an intervention could be undertaken to work with Alice while she remained in her regular class as much as possible. All team members, the parents included, understood that they had a challenge before them to most effectively meet Alice's educational and social needs. However, they all agreed that they were working toward the same objectives, which is a very positive first step.

■ APPLICATION

Placing yourself in the role of Mr. Dunlap and, given the information that you now have regarding Alice, respond to the following questions.

1. How can you facilitate Alice's social needs, particularly focusing on her relationships with her classmates?
2. Should the information regarding Alice's reading difficulties be shared with classmates, or would this be detrimental to their interactions with her?
3. Who should be a part of this broad educational planning?
4. Should you visit with Alice about it?

Debate Forum

REASONABLE ACCOMMODATION VERSUS UNREASONABLE COSTS FOR ACCOMMODATION

No concept could be more acceptable or embraceable by most people than that of having a "fair and level playing field" for all. Yet the accompanying notion of *reasonable accommodation* continues to be controversial and is often challenged in the context of providing services for students with disabilities. In some cases the most vocal participants in the discussion may be those with budget responsibilities for education (in some cases accommodations have significant budgetary ramifications), whereas in others the dissenting viewpoints are voiced by educators and those who are not requesting accommodation—the student's classmates.

■ POINT

Accessing services for students with learning disabilities often involves requests for reasonable accommodations in order to take into account the student's needs resulting from a disability. For students with learning disabilities, such requests may involve extensions of time during exams, oral exams instead of written performances, or modification of homework assignments. In some cases providing accommodations is easily accomplished; in others it is more difficult and creates significant challenges for the teacher, and even the educational institution. It is the law, however, and such requests must be honored.

■ COUNTERPOINT

Interestingly enough, many educators do not know or have a good grasp of what is involved in reasonable accommodation. Their sources of information may be rumor and speculation in the teachers' lounge or at faculty gatherings such as department meetings in colleges or universities. Sometimes identifying sources of good advice is not that easy. In fact, it is probably prudent to consider all requests, but the notion that all requests must be honored is simply not true. For example, students in college often request such accommodations from their professors, inferring a learning disability but not providing evidence beyond the verbal claim. There needs to be solid evidence, such as a diagnostic review by a campus center for assistance to those with disabilities. Written documentation is required in the protocol negotiated by the institution's legal department. Self-diagnosis is not grounds for accommodations that would, in fact, create a playing field that was far from level.

Review

 focus 1

Identify four reasons why definitions of learning disabilities have varied.

- *Learning disabilities* is a broad, generic term that encompasses many different specific problems.
- The study of learning disabilities has been undertaken by a variety of different disciplines.
- The field of learning disabilities per se has existed for only a relatively short period of time and is therefore relatively immature with respect to conceptual development and terminology.
- The field of learning disabilities has grown at a very rapid pace.

 focus 2

Identify two ways in which people with learning disabilities can be classified.

- Whether a child achieves commensurate with his or her age and ability when provided with appropriate educational experiences
- Historically, classified as having a mild disorder, but with increasing attention to varying severity

 focus 3

Identify two current estimated ranges for the prevalence of learning disabilities.

- From 2.7% to 30% of the school-age population, depending on the source
- From 5% to 10% is a reasonable current estimate

 focus 4

Identify seven characteristics attributed to those with learning disabilities, and explain why it is difficult to characterize this group.

- Typically, average or near-average intelligence
- Uneven skill levels in various areas
- Hyperactivity
- Perceptual problems
- Visual and auditory discrimination problems
- Cognition deficits, such as memory
- Attention problems
- The group of individuals included under the umbrella term *learning disabilities* is so varied that it defies simple characterization denoted by a single concept or term.

 focus 5

Identify four causes thought to be involved in learning disabilities.

- Neurological damage or malfunction
- Maturational delay of the neurological system
- Genetic abnormality
- Environmental factors

 focus 6

Identify four questions that are addressed by screening assessment in learning disabilities.

- Is there a reason to investigate the abilities of the child more fully?
- Is there a reason to suspect that the child in any way has disabilities?
- If the child appears to have disabilities, what are the characteristics, and what sort of intervention is appropriate?
- How should we plan for the future of the individual?

focus 7

Identify three types of intervention or treatment employed with people diagnosed as having learning disabilities.

- Medical treatment, in some circumstances involving medication to control hyperactivity
- Academic instruction and support in a wide variety of areas that are specifically aimed at building particular skill areas
- Behavioral interventions aimed at improving social skills or remediating problems in this area (behavioral procedures may also be a part of academic instruction)

 focus 8

How are the services and supports for adolescents and adults with learning disabilities different from those used with children?

- Services and supports for children focus primarily on building the most basic skills.
- Instruction during adolescence may include skill building but also may involve assistance in compensatory skills to circumvent deficit areas.
- Services during adolescence should include instruction and assistance in transition skills that will prepare students for adulthood, employment, and further education, based on their own goals.
- Information for the adult with learning disabilities should include an awareness of how invisible their disability is to others and how requests for accommodation might be viewed with skepticism.

People with Attention-Deficit/Hyperactivity Disorder (ADHD)

To begin with . . .

[With regard to ADHD] there are polarities in true believers in behavior therapy and true believers in medication treatment. (Peter Jensen, quoted in Thomas, 1999)

 I believe our discipline will see increasing emphasis on psychopharmacology research and training, as well as improved integration of pharmacological and psychological therapies. (Kilbey, 1999, discussing prescription privileges for psychologists)

 Ritalin, which is commonly used to treat attention-deficit/hyperactivity disorder (ADHD), carries a warning against its use in children under six. . . . [However,] . . . recent studies show a doubling to tripling of the number of children under age 4 taking Ritalin. (Livni, 2000)

Additional national public school expenditures on behalf of students with ADHD may exceed $3 billion in 1995. (National Institutes of Health, 1998)

Snapshot

James

James has been driving his mother crazy since he was an infant. When he was a baby, he was irritable, colicky, and difficult to predict or manage. His mother recalls that he could run before he could walk, and that he was constantly getting into things. In fact, he was such an active and exploring preschooler, he poisoned himself and was well known in the emergency room for a series of accidents.

However, trouble really started to occur for James when he entered school. He had difficulty listening to the teacher and staying on task.

He had particular problems with acting before thinking. For example, he would raise his hand even before the teacher finished a question and would invariably not know the answer. He would blurt out comments in the classroom, and he seemed incapable of keeping his hands to himself. He always seemed to be on the move, particularly in structured classrooms. In addition to his classroom and academic problems, James also had social problems. His peers did not like him. They commented that he seemed bossy and uncooperative: "He always had to do things his way."

At first, the teacher thought he was immature, and he was retained for a year. This only made things worse. He did not grow out of his problems, and his peers made fun of him for being stupid. James hated school. He became defiant with the teacher and started fights with the other children on the playground.

Things have improved for James since last year. His doctor has him on a stimulant medication, and he spends part of the school day in a resource room classroom. This classroom is particularly good for James because the teacher has a good program

that rewards him for being on task and completing work. The teacher also runs a social skills training group, and James is starting to learn how to cooperate with other children. In addition, James's mother and father have taken a parenting class on how to manage children with ADHD, and things have started to improve at home.

Source: From *Understanding Child Behavior Disorders* (3rd ed., p. 117), by D. M. Gelfand, W. R. Jenson, and C. J. Drew, 1997, Fort Worth: Harcourt Brace & Company.

---

focus 1

Identify three behavioral symptoms commonly associated with ADHD.

■ ATTENTION-DEFICIT/HYPERACTIVITY DISORDER (ADHD). A disorder in youngsters, characterized by difficulties in maintaining attention because of a limited ability to concentrate. Children with ADHD exhibit impulsive actions and hyperactive behavior.

■ HYPERACTIVITY. Perhaps the most frequently mentioned behavioral characteristic in the literature on ADHD. In some cases the term *hyperactivity* refers to too much activity. In others, the term refers to inappropriate activity for a given situation or context.

focus 2

Identify two ways in which the behavior of children with ADHD detrimentally affects instructional settings.

 S A SEPARATE DISABILITY condition, during the 1990s **attention-deficit/hyperactivity disorder (ADHD)** took center stage. The puzzling characteristics associated with ADHD, descriptions of affected individuals, and collections of symptoms have appeared in historic writings as early as 100 years ago (Barkley, 1998). In the past few decades, however, ADHD has been viewed as a set of symptoms accompanying other conditions, such as learning disabilities and emotional–behavior disorders. In more recent years, ADHD has become increasingly treated as a separate and distinct disability although it is still not viewed as such in IDEA (U.S. Department of Education, 2000a).

People with ADHD may exhibit a variety of characteristics including unusually impulsive behavior, fidgeting or **hyperactivity,** an inability to focus attention, or some combination of these behaviors. In many cases, we define ADHD by what we see—hyperactivity, disruptiveness, and perhaps aggressive behavior. In fact, ADHD is actually a variety of physical processes (such as neurological or chemical malfunctions) interacting with social, psychological, or environmental factors (e.g., frustration, social isolation, poor teaching). In grappling with such behaviors, researchers in ADHD have begun to look beyond these characteristics and conceptualize the disability as an intense disorder of self-regulation, impulse control, attention span, and activity level. Increasingly the literature on ADHD reflects attention to impulse control and thinking about the consequences of one's actions, with studies on concepts such as **executive function,** which is the ability to monitor and regulate one's own behavior (Barkley, 1998; Fleck, 1998; Speltz et al., 1999).

People with ADHD often have symptoms intense enough to interfere with performance and life activities in a number of ways. Children with ADHD often have significant difficulties in school and frequently present a substantial challenge to teachers in terms of both instruction and classroom management. Such children may be in and out of their seats, pestering others, or even exhibiting some aggressive behaviors like hitting or pulling hair. They may be unable to focus on the teacher's instructions and impulsively start an assignment before the directions are complete. In many cases an assignment may not be completed, either because the child did not hear the work objective or because he or she darted to another activity that captured his or her roving attention.

Although much of the attention on ADHD has focused on children and adolescents, it may also present major difficulties for adults. Some researchers estimate that ADHD is a lifetime disability for about half of those affected during childhood (Austin, 1999; Mancini, Van Ameringen, Oakman, & Figueiredo, 1999; Silver, 1999). ADHD during adulthood may make it difficult to focus on specific work responsibilities long enough to see them to completion. Such a worker may flit from task to task, making a little headway on each but seeing none of them to completion. Such individuals may have difficulty focusing during discussions with their supervisors. Though such workers may exhibit well-rehearsed social survival skills such as nodding and looking at the boss, their thoughts may be far away, passing over a jumble of unfinished tasks.

Behaviors of children with ADHD often challenge teachers in both instruction and classroom management.

ADHD and Other Disabilities

ADHD has long been associated with learning disabilities. As research evidence has accumulated on both learning disabilities and ADHD, it has become increasingly clear that there is a certain level of overlap, or **comorbidity** (conditions occurring together). Some writers estimate that as much as a 25% overlap exists between learning disabilities and ADHD although certainly not a complete correspondence between the two conditions (Aro et al., 1999; Hazell et al., 1999).

A number of other conditions appear to have a notable level of comorbidity with ADHD (National Institutes of Health, 1998). One, for example, is **Tourette's syndrome,** a condition characterized by motor or verbal tics that cause the person to make repetitive movements, emit strange involuntary sounds, or say words or phrases that are inappropriate for the context. Tourette's syndrome has received some attention in the popular media in the past few years, presenting images of individuals emitting sounds and phrases (sometimes intense swearing) while appearing to exhibit reflexive motor movements. Tourette's does not appear with great frequency among those with ADHD, although about half of the individuals with Tourette's exhibit some ADHD symptoms. There is some evidence that causal culprits in Tourette's may include some of the chemical malfunctions thought to be related to ADHD, although further research is needed in this area (Pauls, Alsobrook, Gelernter, & Leckman, 1999; Sheppard, Bradshaw, Purcell, & Pantelis, 1999; Zohar et al., 1999).

Another area of disability that overlaps with ADHD concerns behavior, conduct, and emotional disorders. Since this covers a very large area, some level of comorbidity is quite understandable. Some of the behaviors exhibited by individuals with ADHD are quite disruptive. In some cases, the level of aggression can easily be seen as a conduct or behavior disorder. The literature suggests that such behavior disorders do occur in as many as half of those with ADHD (Stahl & Clarizio, 1999;

focus 3

Identify four other areas of disability that are often found to be comorbid with ADHD.

■ EXECUTIVE FUNCTION. The ability to monitor and regulate one's own behavior. Executive function reflects an individual's ability to exercise impulse control and to think about and anticipate the consequences of actions.

■ COMORBIDITY. A situation in which multiple conditions occur together.

■ TOURETTE'S SYNDROME. A condition characterized by motor or verbal tics that cause the person to make repetitive movements, emit strange involuntary sounds, or say words or phrases that are inappropriate for the context.

Weller, Rowan, Elia, & Weller, 1999; Weller, Rowan, Weller, & Elia, 1999). There are also interesting overlaps between ADHD and other conditions that might be considered emotional disorders such as anxiety, depression, obsessive-compulsive disorder, and some levels of neurotic behavior (Austin, 1999; Mancini et al., 1999; Sheppard et al., 1999; White, 1999).

As we examine ADHD, it is important to realize it has many faces. ADHD is not a simple condition that can be defined and categorized easily. The distinctions between ADHD and other conditions are often not at all clear, in part because certain definitions have historically overlapped and because groups of people who have been diagnosed with one condition or another represent very heterogeneous populations (Conte, 1998). Some evidence suggests that more than 70% of those with ADHD demonstrate comorbidity with some other identifiable condition (Austin, 1999).

Definitions

ADHD characteristics have often been described in the context of other prominent disabilities where there is substantial comorbidity, most frequently learning disabilities and emotional or behavior disorders. The most often used definition of ADHD is that provided by the American Psychiatric Association (APA) in the fourth edition its *Diagnostic and Statistical Manual of Mental Disorders (DSM-IV)* (APA, 2000). The APA definition is presented in Table 7.1.

The American Psychiatric Association includes three subcategories of ADHD in its description of diagnostic criteria: (1) ADHD, combined type; (2) ADHD, predominantly inattentive type; and (3) ADHD, predominantly hyperactive–impulsive type (APA, 2000). The diagnostic criteria for these as outlined in the *DSM-IV* are summarized in Table 7.2. Although many people exhibit symptoms that combine

focus 4

Identify the three major types of ADHD according to the *DSM-IV*.

TABLE 7.1   APA Definition of ADHD

Criterion	Description
Criterion A	The essential feature of attention-deficit/hyperactivity disorder is a persistent pattern of inattention and/or hyperactivity–impulsivity that is more frequent and severe than is typically observed in individuals at a comparable level of development.
Criterion B	Some hyperactive–impulsive or inattentive symptoms that cause impairment must have been present before age 7 years, although many individuals are diagnosed after the symptoms have been present for a number of years.
Criterion C	Some impairment from the symptoms must be present in at least two settings (e.g., at home and at school or work).
Criterion D	There must be clear evidence of interference with developmentally appropriate social, academic, or occupational functioning.
Criterion E	The disturbance does not occur exclusively during the course of a pervasive developmental disorder, schizophrenia, or other psychotic disorder and is not better accounted for by another mental disorder (e.g., mood disorder, anxiety disorder, dissociative disorder, or personality disorder).

Source: From Diagnostic and Statistical Manual of Mental Disorders (4th ed. Text Revision, p. 85), by the American Psychiatric Association, 2000, Washington, DC: Author.

A. Either (1) or (2):

   1. Six (or more) of the following symptoms of *inattention* have persisted for at least 6 months to a degree that is maladaptive and inconsistent with developmental level:

   Inattention

     a. Often fails to give close attention to details or makes careless mistakes in schoolwork, work, or other activities.

     b. Often has difficulty sustaining attention in tasks or play activities.

     c. Often does not seem to listen when spoken to directly.

     d. Often does not follow through on instructions and fails to finish schoolwork, chores, or duties in the workplace (not due to oppositional behavior or failure to understand instructions).

     e. Often has difficulty organizing tasks and activities.

     f. Often avoids, dislikes, or is reluctant to engage in tasks that require sustained mental effort (such as schoolwork or homework).

     g. Often loses things necessary for tasks or activities (e.g., toys, school assignments, pencils, books, or tools).

     h. Is often easily distracted by extraneous stimuli.

     i. Is often forgetful in daily activities.

   2. Six (or more) of the following symptoms of *hyperactivity–impulsivity* have persisted for at least 6 months to a degree that is maladaptive and inconsistent with developmental level:

   Hyperactivity

     a. Often fidgets with hands or feet or squirms in seat.

     b. Often leaves seat in classroom or in other situations in which remaining seated is expected.

     c. Often runs about or climbs excessively in situations in which it is inappropriate (in adolescents or adults, may be limited to subjective feelings of restlessness).

     d. Often has difficulty playing or engaging in leisure activities quietly.

     e. Is often "on the go" or often acts as if "driven by a motor."

     f. Often talks excessively.

   Impulsivity

     g. Often blurts out answers before questions have been completed.

     h. Often has difficulty awaiting turn.

     i. Often interrupts or intrudes on others (e.g., butts into conversations or games).

B. Some hyperactive-impulsive or inattentive symptoms that caused impairment were presented before age 7 years.

C. Some impairment from the symptoms is present in two or more settings (e.g., at school [or work] and at home).

D. There must be clear evidence of clinically significant impairment in social, academic, or occupational functioning.

E. The symptoms do not occur exclusively during the course of a pervasive developmental disorder, schizophrenia, or other psychotic disorder and are not better accounted for by another mental disorder (e.g., mood disorder, anxiety disorder, dissociative disorder, or a personality disorder).

   Code based on type:

   Attention-Deficit/Hyperactivity Disorder, Combined Type: if both Criteria A1 and A2 are met for the past 6 months.

   Attention-Deficit/Hyperactivity Disorder, Predominantly Inattentive Type: if Criterion A1 is met but Criterion A2 is not met for the past 6 months.

   Attention-Deficit/Hyperactivity Disorder, Predominantly Hyperactive–Impulsive Type: if Criterion A2 is met but Criterion A1 is not met for the past 6 months.

   Coding note: For individuals (especially adolescents and adults) who currently have symptoms that no longer meet full criteria, "In Partial Remission" should be specified.

inattention, impulsivity, and hyperactivity, others have a predominant feature that corresponds to one of the three subtypes.

The American Academy of Pediatrics has issued a set of clinical practice guidelines that build on *DSM-IV* criteria. These guidelines are aimed at primary care clinicians, providing further suggestions to those faced with diagnostic decisions for these children. They include the points summarized in Table 7.3.

TABLE 7.3	American Academy of Pediatrics clinical practice guidelines

1. In a child 6 to 12 years old who presents with inattention, hyperactivity, impulsivity, academic underachievement, or behavior problems, primary care clinicians should initiate an evaluation for ADHD.

2. The diagnosis of ADHD requires that a child meet *Diagnostic and Statistical Manual of Mental Disorders, Fourth Edition* criteria.

3. The assessment of ADHD requires evidence directly obtained from parents or caregivers regarding the core symptoms of ADHD in various settings, the age of onset, duration of symptoms, and degree of functional impairment.

4. The assessment of ADHD requires evidence directly obtained from the classroom teacher (or other school professional) regarding the core symptoms of ADHD, duration of symptoms, degree of functional impairment, and associated conditions.

5. Evaluation of the child with ADHD should include assessment for associated (coexisting) conditions.

6. Other diagnostic tests are not routinely indicated to establish the diagnosis of ADHD but may be used for the assessment of other coexisting conditions (e.g., learning disabilities and mental retardation).

This clinical practice guideline is not intended as a sole source of guidance in the evaluation of children with ADHD. Rather, it is designed to assist primary care clinicians by providing a framework for diagnostic decision making. It is not intended to replace clinical judgment or to establish a protocol for all children with this condition and may not provide the only appropriate approach to this problem.

Source: From "Diagnosis and Evaluation of the Child with Attention-Deficit/Hyperactivity Disorder (AC0002), by the American Academy of Pediatrics, 2000, *Pediatrics, 105*, 1158–1170.

Prevalence

Prevalence estimates for ADHD suggest that from 3% to 5% of all school-aged children may have the disorder. The literature generally indicates that more males are identified with ADHD than females (National Institutes of Health, 1998; Rhee, Waldman, Hay, & Levy, 1999). Male-to-female ratios range from 2:1 to 10:1, depending on the population sampled. For example, young children show higher male/female proportions, whereas older groups show lower proportions. The average male/female ratio across the lifespan appears to be about 3.5:1 (APA, 2000; Barkley, 1998; Bender, 1998). There has been substantial growth in services to ADHD students during the past decade, particularly since the U.S. Department of Education stipulated that such students are eligible for services under the IDEA category of Other Health Impairments. While such eligibility is certainly not the only factor affecting the growing number of people in this category, it is thought to be substantial, with several states showing increases of 20% in this category between 1997–1998 and 1998–1999 (U.S. Department of Education, 2000a).

Males and females with ADHD seem to exhibit different symptoms and may have different intervention needs, which could account for differences in identification and incidence. Young males may exhibit more disruptive or aggressive behaviors, which may more readily bring them to the attention of their teachers. Some questions have been raised about the possibility of gender bias in identification and diagnosis. This

focus 5

Identify two prevalence estimates for ADHD that characterize the difference in occurrence by gender.

assertion suggests that boys may be overidentified and girls underidentified partially because of the differing predominant behaviors (that is, differences in aggressive and disruptive behaviors). The literature remains mixed on this issue, suggesting that while some gender bias may be present, the substantial gender differences also likely reflect some actual difference in the prevalence of ADHD in males and females (Barkley, 1998). There is also some suggestion that different types of ADHD have differing prevalence levels, with over half of those with ADHD manifesting the combined type, 27% the inattentive type, and 18% the hyperactive–impulsive category (McBurnett, 1995). There also appears to be some variation between subgroups by age and gender although considerably more evidence needs to be accumulated on this topic (Turnbull, Turnbull, Shank, & Leal, 1999).

Assessment and Diagnosis

The process of assessing and diagnosing ADHD is a joint venture among multiple disciplines, often including professionals from medicine, psychology, and education (Shaver, 1999). Assessment and diagnostic information for ADHD falls into two broad categories, data that are medical in nature, and data that provide information about educational, behavioral, and contextual circumstances.

Medical data are collected through examinations by pediatricians or other health care professionals. In many cases these health care professionals are family doctors or other referred physicians who are sought out by the parents outside the school system. Clinical interviews and other psychological assessments are undertaken by psychologists who may be on staff in the schools or in private practice. This process will likely include compilation of both psychological and environmental data, including information pertaining to family and school matters. Additionally, direct information from parents and teachers is sought and quantified through completion of rating scales and other such instruments (Barkley, 1998; Venn, 2000).

One instrument used to assess ADHD is the Child Behavior Checklist (CBCL) developed by Achenbach (1991, 1992). CBCL is considered a very useful assessment

focus 6

Identify the two broad categories of assessment information useful in diagnosing ADHD.

Reflect on This

INSURANCE AS A FACTOR IN ASSESSMENT

On the surface, insurance coverage would not seem to play a significant role in assessment and diagnosis of ADHD. However, in many cases it may play more of a role than one might expect. The National Institutes of Health Consensus reported that "The lack of insurance coverage for psychiatric or psychological evaluations, behavior modifi- cation programs, school consultation, parent management training, and other specialized programs presents a major barrier to accurate classification, diagnosis, and management of ADHD. Substantial cost barriers exist in that diagnosis results in out-of-pocket costs to families for services not covered by managed care or other health insurance" (1998, p. 10).

Consider the situation of a parent of a child who has just completed a series of tests, which have in turn led to a long conversation with the family pediatrician. The pediatrician has outlined what she believes are the next steps in information gathering, suggested that ADHD may be involved, and discussed how some treatment recommendations may not be covered by insurance. The costs may be significant, several hundred dollars per month for a while and then unknown after that. This predicament is not unknown to parents of children with ADHD.

Source: From "Diagnosis and Treatment of Attention Deficit Hyperactivity Disorder," by the National Institutes of Health, 1998, *NIH Consensus Statement Online, 16*(2), Nov. 16–18, pp. 1–37.

Snapshot

Doug

Doug is an 11-year-old, fifth-grade male who was referred because of parental and teacher concerns about his school performance. He is suspected of having significant attention problems.

Doug also has significant trouble in peer and other relationships. He often fights and argues with peers, resulting in his often playing by himself.

Doug has a history of significant medical difficulties. He is the product of an at-risk pregnancy. Although he achieved most developmental milestones within normal time frames, he has a history of motor delays. In second grade he was diagnosed with muscular dystrophy. He also suffers from inflammatory bowel disease, resulting in ongoing treatment for ulcers. He does not tolerate many foods well and consequently his appetite is poor.

In first grade Doug was also diagnosed as learning disabled, with problems in reading. He is in a resource special education program. He is described by his teacher as "socially inept." He is often disrespectful of teachers and peers. His grades deteriorated significantly toward the end of the last academic year. His teachers consider him to be a capable underachiever with behavior problems such as inattention, excessive talking, fighting, arguing, and poor work completion.

[Doug was evaluated on the CBCL Scales listed below, which indicated a broad range of difficulties for this youngster.] . . .

- Internalizing
- Withdrawn
- Somatic complaints
- Anxious/depressed
- Externalizing
- Social problems
- Thought problems
- Attention problems
- Delinquent behavior
- Aggressive behavior

His mother's report, however, was also more severe than the majority of the three teacher ratings. His mother's responses to the Parenting Stress Index were also highly significant, revealing stress beyond the 99th percentile on the majority of the PSI scales.

All raters and observations were needed in order to clarify the CBCL results. Aggressive behavior, attention problems, somatic complaints, and depression symptoms were identified by the majority of indices. Enough information was gleaned to make the diagnosis of attention-deficit/hyperactivity disorder and oppositional defiant disorder. Recommendations or intervention also included treatment for significant sadness, although the criteria for a depressive disorder were not met at the time of the evaluation.

Indications of thought problems were not corroborated by other findings. The clinicians thought that the thought problems scale was elevated for some raters due to interpretation of the items by raters as indicators of hyperactivity or inattention.

CBCL social problems scores were corroborated by low scores on social skills measures. The social skills measures were used to develop behavioral objectives for Doug's intervention.

This CBCL profile highlights the need, more pressing in a case like this, to complement the CBCL with other measures. In this case, teacher ratings, observations, self-reports, measures of parent stress, history taking, and observations were all needed to clarify diagnostic impressions and identify treatment objectives.

Source: From *Clinical Assessment of Child and Adolescent Personality and Behavior* (p. 131), by R. W. Kamphaus and P. J. Frick, 1996, Needham Heights, MA: Allyn and Bacon. Reprinted by permission.

---

procedure in child psychopathology (Kamphaus & Frick, 1996; Merrell, 1999). The CBCL provides parent data, teacher ratings, and classroom observation protocols to assess academic competence and social problems beginning at age 4 and to evaluate adolescents through age 18. The snapshot on Doug lists a portion of the CBCL reporting protocol used by parents. The snapshot also touches on the need to use more than one assessment procedure. Other evaluation protocols include the Behavior Assessment System for Children–Teacher Rating Scales (BASC–TRS) (Reynolds & Kamphaus, 1992) and the School Situations Questionnaire (SSQ) (Barkley & Edelbrock, 1987). The SSQ employs a different assessment protocol than many rating scales in that it presents specific situations in which the child being evaluated may encounter problems.

The referral process typically begins with the educational and psychological data-gathering process outlined above, and information may come from educational professionals or the parents. The initial referral is very important because it sets in motion a course of action that will significantly impact the child's life, hopefully for the better, in the form of effective treatment (Shaver, 1999). As with most referrals, a child with ADHD will enter the process because of some aspect of performance or behavior that sets him or her apart and causes concern for the person or professional who initiates the referral process (such as a classroom teacher).

Children with ADHD frequently show aggressive or disruptive behavior that draws attention and invites further evaluation or scrutiny on the part of teachers or parents (Venn, 2000; Weller, Roan, Weller, & Elia, 1999). For many children with ADHD, such behaviors are the most discernible manifestation of their disability, creating significant disruptions in class and contributing to some level of social dysfunction (Henker & Whalen, 1999). These children tend not to exhibit specific difficulties in memory, although their academic performance may well suffer from their inattentiveness, impulsivity, and lack of planning (Tramo, 1999; Tripp, Luk, Schaughency, & Singh, 1999). Parents may also be concerned about the aggressive and disruptive behavior exhibited by many children with ADHD. Evidence suggests that raising children with such disabilities is likely to contribute to significant parental life stress, which may trigger the referral process (Cleveland, 1999; Vitanza & Guarnaccia, 1999).

An important part of the diagnostic evaluation for ADHD is information collected by health care professionals.

An initial referral is a precursor to a more complete evaluation and diagnostic analysis, including a comprehensive clinical interview conducted by a psychologist. At the clinical interview stage more information is collected regarding the nature of the child's behavior and the environment in which it occurs (both school and family settings). Behavior checklists or other protocols that quantify observations in a structured fashion may also be used. One such protocol is the Diagnostic Interview Schedule for Children (DISC-2.3) (Shaffer et al., 1993). The DISC is a structured interview designed for use by trained psychologists or lay interviewers.

The final source of diagnostic evaluation comes from the medical examination. This assessment will likely use all previously gathered information, attempting to eliminate other physical conditions that may contribute to the behavior observed. The medical examination may also produce the first step in intervention if medication is prescribed.

Much of the referral and diagnostic assessment outlined above involves some professional judgment that might be considered subjective. This is no different from the evaluation process for other disabilities—trained professional judgment is extremely critical. However, for ADHD, some questions continue regarding the amount of bias involved and the accuracy of the assessment process (Kamphaus & Frick, 1996). Such questions also raise concerns about how well professionals are prepared to conduct assessments. For example, a teacher may play a very important part in the identification of ADHD. Some evidence suggests that a teacher's choice to refer a student for assessment or identification for ADHD may be influenced considerably by his or her general attitude, style, and beliefs about teaching practices (Shaver, 1999). As illustrated earlier, observations and ratings of children through standardized ADHD protocols form an important part of the evaluation process. Despite the standardized nature of these tools, their accuracy and usefulness depends in large part on the knowledge and care of those who complete them. Some research suggests that considerable error may occur because the raters' own

Snapshot

Jordan

Jordan is a 7-year, 3-month-old boy who was referred for a comprehensive psychological evaluation by his parents upon the recommendation of his teachers. His teachers had reported to Jordan's parents that he was having difficulty paying attention and day-dreaming, interrupting others, and making careless mistakes in his work. His parents requested a comprehensive evaluation to determine the severity and possible cause for these difficulties and to make recommendations for possible interventions to aid in his school adjustments.

Jordan's background, developmental, and medical history were unremarkable. During the testing Jordan had great difficulty concentrating and was easily distracted. He was also very fidgety and restless. Intellectually, Jordan had much better verbal comprehensive ability, especially in the area of verbal reasoning, than nonverbal perceptual–organizational abilities. Consistent with his verbal abilities, Jordan scored in the above-average range on measures of reading and math achievement.

Jordan's emotional and behavioral functioning was assessed through the use of structured interviews conducted with Jordan's parents and teachers and through rating scales completed by his parents, teacher, and Jordan himself. The structured interviews were the parent version of the DISC-2.3 and the experimental teacher version used in the DSM-IV field trials (Frick, Silverthorn, & Evans, 1994). The child version was not given to Jordan because he was below the age of 9, and the DISC has not proven to be reliable in this young age group. The following is an excerpt from the report on Jordan's evaluation that illustrates how information from the DISC-2.3 was integrated with other assessment information:

The only problematic area that emerged from this assessment of Jordan's emotional and behavioral functioning were significant problems of inattention, disorganization, impulsivity, and overactivity that seem to be causing Jordan significant problems in the classroom. Jordan's teachers describe him as being very restless and fidgety, being easily distractible, having very disorganized and messy work habits, having a hard time completing things, and making a lot of careless mistakes. Results from teacher rating scales suggested that these behaviors are more severe than would be typical for children Jordan's age. These behaviors are consistent with a diagnosis of Attention-Deficit Hyperactivity Disorder (ADHD). Also consistent with this diagnosis, his parents reported that many of these behaviors, especially the restless and fidgety behaviors have been present from very early in life, at least since age 4. These behaviors associated with ADHD seem to be causing significant problems for Jordan in school, affecting the amount and accuracy of schoolwork. A sociometric exercise also suggests that these behaviors may be starting to affect his peer relationships.

Source: From *Clinical Assessment of Child and Adolescent Personality and Behavior* (pp. 239–240), by R. W. Kamphaus and P. J. Frick, 1996, Needham Heights, MA: Allyn and Bacon. Reprinted by permission.

---

characteristics influence how they rate a child's behavior problems (Mandal, Olmi, & Wilcznski, 1999). The snapshot on Jordan presents another example of a comprehensive evaluation process completed on a young boy with ADHD.

If teachers make significantly inaccurate evaluations of children with ADHD, then programs that prepare these professionals need to respond. Jerome, Washington, Laine, and Segal (1999) have raised concerns about the way teachers are prepared to work with children who have ADHD. These researchers found that recent graduates from teacher preparation programs were not better prepared than teachers graduating five years earlier. In fact, the more recent sample was less well informed about some aspects of ADHD than the earlier group. Such findings suggest that the teacher education curriculum at least warrants examination and may need to be significantly enhanced with more information and strategies related to ADHD.

Characteristics

The opening snapshot presented James, a child with characteristics associated with ADHD that appeared from a very early age. James's story also illustrates how one type of behavior problem can lead or contribute to another as a child grows older. Discussion of the characteristics of ADHD can clearly become mired in "chicken or egg" issues—which came first, impulsivity and

focus 7
Identify three areas of difficulty that present challenges for individuals with ADHD.

Individuals with ADHD have difficulty paying attention. Here a young woman is lost in a daydream during a teacher's lecture.

problems with self-regulation, or inattention, hyperactivity, and aggression? This is an important debate to the extent that it helps to identify effective interventions.

James's behavior before he received medication included hyperactivity with disruptive and aggressive tendencies. James seemed to not think ahead about the outcomes or consequences of his actions. He appeared to be impulsive, and an observer could easily infer that he had difficulty regulating his own behavior.

■ SELF-REGULATION, IMPULSIVITY, AND HYPERACTIVITY

Difficulty in self-regulation and behavioral inhibition are receiving more attention as theoretical explanations and research models for ADHD (Lazar & Frank, 1998; Raggio, 1999a; Speltz et al., 1999). Some researchers have suggested that this is a very important key to understanding ADHD (e.g., Barkley, 1998; Fleck, 1998). Discussions include terms such as "behavioral inhibition" and "executive function," as well as impulse control, self-regulation, and self-management. Problems encountered by the individual under all of these rubrics are quite similar—substantial difficulty in thinking through one's actions to see what the effects of certain behaviors might be (Dale & Baumeister, 1999; Sakelaris, 1999; Young, 1999). People with ADHD are not able to consider the following question: "If I behave in a certain manner, what is the likely outcome, and how will it affect those around me?" This was true with James when he raised his hand before the question was asked and without having the answer in mind.

Hyperactivity is a primary characteristic of ADHD as suggested in the diagnostic criteria summarized in Table 7.2 on page 213. In accordance with these criteria, the hyperactive behavior must persist for at least six months and must be intense enough to create maladaptive problems for the individual. Many parents, teachers, and others describe such youngsters as those who fidget and squirm constantly; are continually running, jumping, and climbing around; and are generally on the move all the time (Barkley, 1998; Goldstein, 1999). As most parents will confirm, all children can be characterized in these terms from time to time, but the hyperactive child with ADHD far exceeds the norm. The behaviors are seemingly continuous and occur in inappropriate settings and times.

Hyperactivity may be the most frequently mentioned characteristic in the literature addressing various facets of ADHD. Being overly active seems to affect about half of the children diagnosed with ADHD. Although the high-activity characteristic appears to diminish as some children get older, for others this is not true. In some cases the hyperactive behavior begins to surface in adolescence and may be evident through the adult years (Moore & Fombonne, 1999; Stein, Fischer, Szumowski, 1999; Wood, 1997).

■ SOCIAL RELATIONSHIPS

Youngsters with ADHD often encounter difficulties in their social relationships with peers (Henker & Whalen, 1999; Landau, Milich, & Diener, 1998; Lochman & Szczepanski, 1999). Some children encounter difficulty getting along because they exhibit aggressive behavior toward their classmates, which does not promote positive social interactions (Stahl & Clarizio, 1999; Weller, Rowan, Elia, & Weller, 1999; Weller, Rowan, Weller, & Elia, 1999). Other children with ADHD exhibit seriously antisocial or pathological social behavior, such as cruelty to animals, that may suggest other mental health problems (Luk, Staiger, Wong, & Mathai, 1999). These behaviors can contribute to low social status among peers, which may persist for years. This pattern may evolve in a variety of ways over time, such as increased risk for criminal activity (Babinski, Hatsough, & Lambert, 1999; French & Amen, 1999). Such behavioral patterns present enormous challenges for schools as these children proceed through the system.

Individuals with ADHD often feel isolated from others. Social relationships can be a difficult challenge.

The level of severity of ADHD is significant in both males' and females' social relationships, and the outcomes are varied and often serious (Biederman et al., 1999a). Some youngsters with ADHD grow increasingly frantic as they try to gain friends, which can easily aggravate their already poor self-regulating behavior. They may thereby seem even more of a nuisance to the peers whom they wish to befriend. Accumulated frustration due to low social status and having few friends may prompt even stranger behaviors aimed at gaining attention from classmates. Some research also suggests that substance abuse may be more likely among those with ADHD (Biederman et al., 1998; Castaneda, Sussman, Levy, & Trujillo, 1999; Lambert & Hartsough, 1998). Though some researchers have claimed that this may be due to the use of psychostimulants as treatment, not enough research evidence exists to support such an assertion (DuPaul, Barkley, & Conner, 1998). Some researchers have found that it is more likely that other comorbid disabilities may be more predictive of substance abuse than ADHD, such as social impairment, conduct disorders, and aggressive behavior (Disney, Elkins, McGue, & Iacono, 1999; Weissman, Warner, Wickramaratne, & Kandel, 1999). Thus, research results do not pinpoint whether substance abuse is more closely related to ADHD or to other coexisting conditions, but the combination appears to increase risk substantially.

■ ACADEMIC CHARACTERISTICS

Students with ADHD experience significant challenges in an academic setting. Estimates suggest that from 40% to 80% of these children and adolescents face substantial learning problems in school (Wood, 1997b). Such problems increase as they progress through the educational system; demands increase on the skill areas with which they have the greatest difficulty—self-management and thinking ahead (Sakelaris, 1999). Failure and poor academic performance also affect other areas, such as self-esteem, creating a repeating cycle of circumstances and symptoms that some researchers believe accumulate dynamically, increasing the likelihood of further problems (Austin, 1999; Campbell, 1999; Henker & Whalen, 1999).

Children and adolescents with ADHD are characterized by a lack of academic success compared to their nondisabled peers and often do not graduate from high school (Biederman et al., 1999a; Marks, Himelstein, Newcorn, & Halperin, 1999; Zimmermann, 1999). Poor academic achievement by students with ADHD is likely associated with their disruptive and nonproductive social behaviors as well as their poor capacity to self-manage (Henker & Whalen, 1999; Zimmermann, 1999). In academic environments that adapt instruction to individual student needs and abilities, students with ADHD can learn, achieve academically, and improve their self-management skills (Aro et al., 1999; Sakelaris, 1999; Zimmermann, 1999).

Causation and Interventions

■CAUSATION

focus 8
Identify three possible causes of ADHD.

There is considerable difference of opinion regarding the causes of ADHD, and both biological and environmental influences have been identified (e.g., Kaplan, Wilson, Dewey, & Crawford, 1998; Silver, 1999). Speculation has included genetic inheritance, neurological injury during birth complications, and negative impacts of a variety of environmental factors, to name only a few. As we begin to more fully understand ADHD, we will likely find that multiple causes are associated with this condition.

Neurological causes of ADHD have been suspected for many years, although viewpoints regarding the nature of such neurological dysfunction have varied considerably. Early investigation on behaviors exhibited by World War I soldiers who had received head injuries focused on a trauma-based or physical cause for brain malfunction. Current theories still include injury-induced brain malfunction, although more current thinking also views chemical imbalances in serotonin and dopamine as possible causal agents (Ernst et al., 1998; Faraone et al., 1999; Gainetdinov et al., 1999; Sagvolden, 1999).

Documentation of neurological causes for ADHD has progressed enormously through new and developing technology, particularly neuroimaging procedures. Where previously the profession speculated about neurological dysfunction based on behavior, we are now able to examine the brain directly. For example, neuroimaging shows that people with ADHD seem to exhibit brain abnormalities in three areas, the **frontal lobes,** selected areas of the **basal ganglia,** and the **cerebellum** (Berquin et al., 1998; Filipek et al., 1997). Figure 7.1 indicates the general areas in the brain that have been identified as having abnormalities associated with ADHD. (See Today's Technology box.)

In some cases the actual brain structures appear different for individuals with ADHD, whereas in other cases the chemical functioning in the brain may differ (Castellanos, 1997; Ernst et al., 1998; Gainetdinov et al., 1999). Such differences in structure and chemical function may be caused by a variety of factors including physical injury to the brain and developmental factors. It is widely known that environmental influences during prenatal or neonatal periods can have serious detrimental effects. For example, lead exposure, pregnant mothers' alcohol abuse, and exposure to tobacco smoke place developing embryos and infants at high risk for serious learning and developmental delays. Likewise, low birthweight and delivery complications are also high-risk circumstances that may relate to ADHD (Johnson-Cramer, 1999; Levy, Barr, & Sunahara, 1998; Milberger, Biederman, Faraone, & Jones, 1998). Emotional and general health status for both the pregnant mother and

■FRONTAL LOBES. The front parts of the brain, which are nearest the forehead.

■BASAL GANGLIA. Sections of the brain that are near the stem, close to where the spinal cord meets the bottom of the brain matter.

■CEREBELLUM. The part of the brain that coordinates muscular movement. It is located right below the large main sections of the brain.

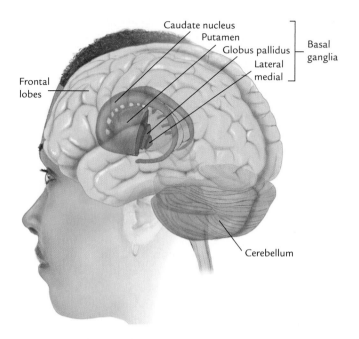

FIGURE 7.1

Brain malfunctions in some areas of the brain—frontal lobes, basal ganglia, and cerebellum—seem to be associated with ADHD.

Caudate nucleus
Putamen
Globus pallidus
Lateral
medial
Basal ganglia

Frontal lobes

Cerebellum

developing fetus appear to be important predictive factors in ADHD causation (Eshleman, 1999). Serious problems during this critical prenatal period of development can result in a wide variety of undesirable outcomes for the baby that may be manifested in what appear to be developmental delays or deficiencies in both intellectual and behavioral functioning (Drew & Hardman, 2000; Trawick-Smith, 2000).

Heredity has long been associated with ADHD, suggesting that there may be a genetic transmission of circumstances that result in the condition. Youngsters appear to have a higher risk of being diagnosed with ADHD if parents or siblings have the condition (Barkley, 1998; Rutter, Silberg, O'Connor, & Siminoff, 1999). Additionally, research on twins suggests a hereditary link, with identical twins (same egg) having a higher coincidence of the condition than fraternal twins (different eggs) (Faraone et al., 1999; Sherman, Iacono, & McGue, 1997; Thapar, Holmes, Poulton, & Harrington, 1999). Evidence also supports the concept that multiple genes may be involved and that they may present a tendency or predisposition in

Today's Technology

A CAUSE OF HYPERACTIVITY?—STUDY SUGGESTS HYPERACTIVE BRAINS GET LESS BLOOD

A new magnetic resonance imaging (MRI) technique has been used by researchers to investigate certain brain malfunctions in young boys with ADHD. In this case, the team led by Dr. Martin Teicher discovered additional evidence

for a biological cause of the disability. The researchers found that the MRI indicated a reduced blood flow to a part of the brain known as the putamen. This part of the brain is associated with motor movement and attention, areas often identified as challenging for youngsters with

ADHD. The MRI technology also indicated an increase in the blood flow for these young boys when they were given Ritalin. Other young boys with some, but not all, ADHD characteristics showed a decreased blood flow when given Ritalin as evidenced on the magnetic resonance imaging.

Source: From "A Cause of Hyperactivity? Study Suggests Hyper Brains Get Less Blood," ABC News, March 28, 2000. Available: http://abcnews.go.com/ sections/living/DailyNews/ hyperativebrains000328. html

an affected individual that may be triggered by various environmental circumstances (Rhee et al., 1999). Research on the genetic bases of ADHD is ongoing, and results continue to emerge.

■ INTERVENTIONS

ADHD requires multiple interventions that fall into two broad categories: behavioral and medical. As is true in many disability areas, effective treatment involves a multidisciplinary team approach and includes combinations of techniques as determined by individual need (Everett & Everett, 1999; Sloan, Jensen, & Kettle, 1999; Taylor, 1999).

focus 9

Identify two approaches to intervention that appear to show positive results with individuals having ADHD.

The Elementary School Years

On a practical level, psychostimulants (e.g., methylphenidate, the generic name for Ritalin) appear to result in behavioral improvement for about 80% of children with ADHD (Cunningham, 1999; Elia, Ambrosini, & Rapoport, 1999; National Institutes of Health, 1998). However, administration of such medication has long presented some perplexing ironies to physicians. While a medication may work well for a child with ADHD, the same medication would *make* most of us hyperactive. Self-regulation theories tend to approach the problem primarily as a functional deficit in self-regulation or impulse control. Administration of methylphenidate arouses the frontal lobes of the brain, which exert a regulatory influence. This regulatory function impacts subcortical and cortical regions that monitor motor activity and distractibility (Barkley, 1998; Teeter & Semrud-Clikeman, 1997).

Controlling hyperactive and impulsive behavior appears to be most effectively accomplished with medication (most often methylphenidate) (Chabot et al., 1999; Murrell, 1999; Pelham, 1999). Evidence is emerging that pharmacological control of behavioral challenges is more effective than nonmedical interventions, such as behavioral treatment (Jensen, 1999; MTA Cooperative Group, 1999a, 1999b). While research supporting the effectiveness of medication is accumulating, such medical intervention shows no effect, or very limited influence, on academic performance (Benedetto-Nasho & Tannock, 1999). Current thinking suggests that although there are clear benefits to the use of medication, it may be overprescribed, and expectations that it will produce generalized improvement, including in academic performance, simply are not supported by available research evidence (Jensen et al., 1999).

Some researchers have expressed caution regarding the use of psychostimulants for both theoretical and practical reasons (e.g., Jensen et al., 1999). First, there are concerns regarding medication side effects, as one would expect with any pharmacological treatment that has such widespread use. In some cases, it is difficult to untangle some psychological characteristics that may appear as potential side effects, such as increased anxiety, from the symptoms of ADHD. Investigators examining these questions are constantly trying to determine whether an increase in anxiety, for example, is due to the use of medication over time or occurs because a child becomes increasingly anxious due to negative personality or interpersonal effects of ADHD (Cherland & Fitzpatrick, 1999; Vance et al., 1999). Additionally, some researchers express ongoing uneasiness about other matters pertaining to appropriate dosage, overprescription, abuse potential, and issues regarding management planning and implementation for children being treated with medication (Beck, Silverstone, Glor, & Dunn, 1999; Biederman et al., 1999b; Miller, 1999). Children at this young age may receive medication over a very long period, and it is unclear what the cumulative effects may be on physical or intellectual development (Buckingham, 1999; National Institutes of Health, 1998). For preschoolers, there is some evidence that susceptibility to side effects might be greater (Handen, Feldman, Lurier, & Murray, 1999). Further investigation in both of these areas is most certainly warranted. Finally, for about 20% of children with ADHD, medications do not improve their behavior (DuPaul & Eckert, 1997). Such concerns about medication interventions have appeared in the popular press and make the news periodically as the field grapples with the challenges presented by these children (e.g., Bank, 2000).

The hyperactive and impulsive behaviors of many children with ADHD clearly present a significant challenge to parents, teachers, and other school personnel during the elementary school years. Elementary teachers describe the characteristics of these children as fidgety, impulsive, and constantly disruptive. These behaviors are often accompanied by deficits in academic performance (Aro et al., 1999; Barkley, 1998; Raggio, 1999b). From a teacher's viewpoint, it is difficult for the child to focus on learning if he or she is in constant motion.

Nonmedical, school-based interventions can also be effective in improving classroom behaviors of elementary-age school children with ADHD, and some are more potent than others. In general, targeted behavior modification strategies appear to be more effective for controlling behavioral problems than those involving cognitive–behavioral or cognitive interventions. Cognitive–behavioral therapies are based on behavioral techniques that are combined with efforts to effectively change the way a person thinks about his or her behaviors—attempting to enhance the cognitive control that a person has over his or her actions. Research evidence does not suggest beneficial results from cognitive–behavioral interventions for children with ADHD (DuPaul & Eckert, 1997; National Institutes of Health, 1998). Using behavior modification interventions aimed at controlling a child's behavioral activity and giving structure to the classroom environment both seem to be academically productive. Descriptions of effective instructional settings for children with ADHD consistently include a good deal of structure.

Educators should arrange the classroom setting to enhance the child's ability to respond, attend, and behave in a manner that is conducive to learning. Teachers may have to constantly monitor the directions they give students with ADHD, often cuing them to the fact that a direction or message is about to be delivered. This

Reflect on This

EXPLORING OTHER OPTIONS

From time to time, the popular press raises concerns about use of methylphenidate with children. Because of concern regarding side effects, overprescription, and other matters, parents are often encouraged to explore other options such as behavioral therapy. Long-term effects of drugs on young developing brains also raise concerns, particularly in view of the frequency of drug treatment for ADHD in children.

Consider the difficult circumstances of a parent with a young child who has ADHD. Research evidence to date shows that the most consistently effective treatment for hyperactivity and other symptoms involves administration of psychostimulant medication. The issues noted above loom large, but you have just "lived through" the week from hell as your young child has been expelled from school for aggressive and disruptive behavior that appears to endanger the health and well-being of other students. You have been told before by your pediatrician that prescription medication is often helpful and she recommended its use. What are you going to do?

Source: From "Misdiagnosing Misbehavior?: First Lady Calls for a Closer Look at Psychotropics for Kids," by E. Livini, ABC News, March 20, 2000.

might be done with prompts such as "Listen, John" or some other signal that is comfortable for the teacher and well-understood by the student as meaning a directive is to follow. The signal may be accompanied with other signals or procedures that add structure and direct the student's attention to the learning task at hand. Such cues or signals must be designed in a developmentally appropriate manner (Folstrom-Bergeron, 1998; Wood, 1997b).

Academic instructions must directly target the specific content area where the child is experiencing problems. Strategies involving considerable structure will enhance learning (DuPaul & Eckert, 1998). For example, reading lessons may be more effective if reinforcement is combined with modeling and increased practice, all of which provides considerable structure aimed at the learning task (Noell et al., 1998). Literature also suggests that children with ADHD need to be taught learning strategies in order to benefit from instruction (Folstrom-Bergeron, 1998). These children need to experience an explicit demonstration of the strategy not just a description of it. Demonstrating a specific tactic is more likely to succeed than simply telling such students to do it. These children often require individualized instruction from a teacher or aide, focused on the specific content area needing attention, such as reading, math, or spelling. Such individual work is clearly a labor-intensive undertaking, and some research suggests that individualized sessions are rarely part of the instructional strategies for children with ADHD (Callwood-Brathwaid, 1998). Further research on the practical implementation and effectiveness of such approaches is clearly required.

Multiple treatment approaches—often termed *multimodal treatments* (such as drug and behavior therapies)—are more effective for children with ADHD (e.g., Goldstein, 1999). But this approach creates a risk factor that may not emerge with a single treatment. The National Institutes of Health consensus report (1998) noted that communication or coordination among educational (school-based) and health-related (medical) assessments and services is often poor. Diagnosticians and interventionists from both disciplines may have difficulty communicating outside of their field, a problem with considerable ramifications, such as worsening the child's condition or promoting additional problems such as antisocial behaviors. Communication and coordination among multiple disciplines have been a challenge in providing services to all people with disabilities (Drew & Hardman, 2000). The circumstances appear exacerbated in the case of children with ADHD because such a high proportion are receiving both medical treatment and school-based instruction. This situation can be improved through explicit attention to facilitating communication among attending physicians and others providing treatment. However, this is unlikely to occur unless it is intentionally included in a child's intervention plans (Barbaresi & Olsen, 1998).

Adolescence and Adulthood

Once viewed as a childhood condition, ADHD now is known to have a significant presence beyond those early years and is accompanied by an array of other behaviors and conditions in adulthood (e.g., Curran & Fitzgerald, 1999; Tucker, 1999). Estimates suggest that 30% to 80% of those who are diagnosed as having ADHD during childhood continue to be challenged by some symptoms and require treatment during adulthood (Campbell, 1999; Turnbull, Turnbull, Shank, & Leal, 1999; Weiss, Hechtman, & Weiss, 1999). Interventions appropriate for adolescents and adults with ADHD must be reassessed and, where appropriate, modified in an age-appropriate manner (Barkley, 1998; Lubell, 1999).

■ EARLY CHILDHOOD YEARS

TIPS FOR THE FAMILY

- Learn about simple applications of behavior modification in a home environment, perhaps by enrolling in a parent training class.
- Try to structure the home environment, family activities, and tasks for the child, perhaps using a similar structure for all family members. This may mean setting a somewhat fixed daily routine or even a fixed routine for portions of the day. Group activities so that each is somewhat separate.
- Describe ADHD to other family members, taking a practical, positive approach. Avoid commenting on the affected child in a manner that has negative implications for him or her (e.g., focusing on the disability or how difficult it is). Instead, find ways to meet the child's needs in a routine approach to family life.
- Maintain communication with the child's physician regarding medical treatment. If questions arise about interventions, do not hesitate to seek additional opinions.
- Give directions while looking the child in the eye, to gain attention and build eye contact as a control mechanism.

TIPS FOR THE PRESCHOOL TEACHER

- Initiate and maintain communication with the child's parents to enhance the information flow and, if possible, to build consistency across environments in rules and reward structures.
- Structure the environment and activities, such as dividing activities into short sessions, each focusing on a single sub-activity.
- Signal or alert the student when a verbal directive is to be given in order to focus attention. You might say, "Jim, listen. I want you to . . ."
- Use a kitchen timer to facilitate time management, and gradually increase periods for activities in which the student is gaining in focus and attentiveness.
- Monitor stress in the child; exceeding his or her stress thresholds may trigger disruptive behavior or inattention.
- Communicate with other school personnel in order to promote a consistent environment throughout the school regarding appropriate behavior and interactions (e.g., praise, structuring).

TIPS FOR PRESCHOOL PERSONNEL

- Communicate with other preschool staff who are primarily involved in the child's instruction—primarily the classroom teacher.
- Try to communicate with the child in a manner consistent with the teacher's program. The setting may be different (e.g., hallways, playground, or bus), but the contingencies for appropriate behavior should be reasonably consistent.

TIPS FOR NEIGHBORS AND FRIENDS

- These children may be noisier and more active than others in the neighborhood. Try to ignore minor transgressions.
- Communicate with the child's parents to learn about the techniques they use for control. Encourage appropriate behavior in a manner that is consistent with the parents' plan.

■ ELEMENTARY YEARS

TIPS FOR THE FAMILY

- Think about modifying the structured family environment to be appropriate for the developmental level of the child.
- While continuing the overall structure begun during the younger years, gradually lengthen the activity periods.
- Consider varying somewhat the distinctive breaks between activities, and modify rewards for older children.
- Be proactive in communicating with the child's

teacher, and facilitate communication between medical and educational professionals.

TIPS FOR THE GENERAL EDUCATION CLASSROOM TEACHER

- Maintain distinctive signals and alerting messages as cues for attention, but make sure they are age-appropriate. Minimize drawing the attention of other students to the child's challenges.
- Divide assignments into smaller or shorter segments as necessary.
- Shorten work sessions as needed. Make clear breaks between activities or subjects.
- Give positive rewards for good academic work and appropriate behavior. Such reinforcement is very important for these children.

TIPS FOR SCHOOL PERSONNEL

- Participate in ongoing communication with other school staff who are involved with the child, including his or her teacher or teachers, the bus driver, counselors, and any extracurricular staff.
- Try to use communication and rules consistent with those employed by the other school team members, which will often be led by the teacher or teachers.

- Recognize that during the elementary years, these children may appear more active or noisy than their playmates in the neighborhood.
- Communicate and collaborate with the child's parents in order to provide a reasonably consistent neighborhood environment. For example, if behavior modification is being used in the home to shape elements of the youngster's behavior, learn the simple components of reinforcement and contingency setting.

SECONDARY AND TRANSITION YEARS

TIPS FOR THE FAMILY

- Set age-appropriate modifications of the family environment. They are vital at this level.
- Maintain structuring, but add more adultlike modeling, and demonstrate how to focus attention.
- Continue communication with school personnel, especially the teacher, in order to maintain consistent ways of supporting and challenging the person with ADHD.

TIPS FOR THE GENERAL EDUCATION CLASSROOM TEACHER

- Help the youngster to modify annoying behavior and characteristics to achieve more appropriate

and acceptable ways of behaving. Handle this delicately, since the youngster is on the brink of adulthood in some ways, yet very immature in others.
- Initiate communication with other school personnel who are involved in the academic and nonacademic life of the youngster, as well as the parents. Collaborate on a plan to provide a relatively consistent environmental structure for the individual.
- Help the youngster to learn strategies for organizing both academic and nonacademic activities. This may involve open acknowledgment of limitations such as a short attention span.

TIPS FOR SCHOOL PERSONNEL

- Collaborate and help open lines of communication with all school personnel who are involved with the youngster.
- Depending on your particular role within the school, don't hesitate to visit with the youngster's parents and others in the broader community (e.g., employers, police organizations).
- Help shape a positive growth environment for the youngster within your realm of responsibility (e.g., coach, etc.). Facilitate this young adult's skill development while acknowledging that his or her daily life may differ in some ways from the lives of others.

TIPS FOR NEIGHBORS AND FRIENDS

- Communicate with the youngster's parents about how this period of development is proceeding for the youngster and how you, as a nonfamily adult, can participate with the youngster, if that is comfortable.
- Recognize that this young person, who is beginning to look like an adult, still may encounter great difficulty with impulse control and task focus. If you are working with him or her, perhaps as an employer, structure the environment in order to take advantage of strengths and minimize the effect of limitations.

ADULT YEARS

TIPS FOR THE FAMILY

- Communicate directly with this family member about his or her personal strengths and limitations. Such communication will facilitate adapting the structure of the family environment for this new stage in the individual's life.
- Work with the affected person and other family members to help structure or organize the family environment. The adult with ADHD may not be hyperactive but still may have some challenges with impulse control and task focus.
- Communicate openly with physicians or other health care professionals who are treating the family mem-

ber with ADHD. This should not be done without the knowledge of the affected individual and will be more productive if all team members work together.

TIPS FOR THERAPISTS OR OTHER PROFESSIONALS

- Open communication with other adult family members in order to promote a consistent and productive environment for the client.
- Help your client organize his or her life in order to emphasize personal strengths and lessen the demands in areas where challenges are most evident.

TIPS FOR NEIGHBORS, FRIENDS, AND EMPLOYERS

- This adult is likely to test your patience. He or she may appear to be a busybody, flitting from task to task without finishing any. If you are an employer, you may find yourself presented with partially completed assignments. Try to be patient.
- Speak directly with the person about his or her strengths, and help the person maintain focus on staying organized.
- Structure the environment in order to take advantage of strengths and minimize the effects of limitations. Limit the areas of responsibility in order to help focus.

However, certain elements of intervention described for children with ADHD seem to frequently carry forward to adolescents and adults as well. For example, a structured environment is beneficial for both school-based instruction and other interventions later in life such as psychological therapy and self-management (Weiss, Hechtman, & Weiss, 1999; Young, 1999). Also reminiscent of treatment at younger ages, academic instruction for adolescents with ADHD is more effective when the students can employ learning strategies (e.g., mnemonics, conceptual organizers) (Dolyniuk, 1999; Schultz, 1999). Further, stimulant medication (such as methylphenidate) remains an effective treatment for impulsivity, difficulty in focusing on tasks, and other related behaviors that continue into the adolescent and adult years for many people with ADHD. However, some research is exploring alternative medications in order to lessen potential for abuse or side effects (Levin, Evans, & Kleber, 1999; Riordan et al., 1999; Weiss et al., 1999). As is the case with other treatments, adaptations and modifications are often required in order to effectively maintain or achieve the most effective intervention during these years (e.g., Low, 1999).

Adolescents and adults with ADHD may not exhibit hyperactivity but may still have considerable difficulty in focusing on tasks and controlling impulses. Though medication may help, it is likely that these individuals will also require a significantly structured environment. Counseling that emphasizes behavior modification may be enormously helpful. At this point in life, it is probably most helpful to openly communicate with the person with ADHD about his or her areas of strength and areas that present challenges. This type of communication works best when both adult family members, such as spouses, and professional therapists use it. Such conversations may be difficult but become easier with practice, particularly when they aim to enhance the lives of all involved.

People with ADHD face significant challenges at every age. While behaviors of adults with ADHD may look somewhat different than those of children with ADHD, similarities exist and significant difficulties remain. Many mysteries remain to be solved concerning this condition, but real progress in treatment is already occurring.

Case Study

COEXISTING CONDITIONS

Jim was a 10-year-old boy enrolled in a mental health day program that treated severely behaviorally disordered children. In this program he was treated for a major fire-setting problem. Jim's developmental history was characterized by deprivation, inadequate parenting, chaotic home life, and a series of foster home placements. He was diagnosed as both conduct disordered and having attention-deficit disorder. His list of referral problems included stealing, hyperactivity, tantrumming, learning disabilities, agression, non-compliance, zoophilia, and fire setting. The fire setting had been a problem since Jim was 3, when he burned down the family home. Since his foster placements, Jim had averaged approximately one fire setting every two weeks.

It was assumed that Jim set fires partly because he enjoyed seeing the fires and partly as a reaction to stress. The stress was related to a series of skill deficits in the social and academic areas. In addition, it was assumed that Jim did not fully realize the dangerous consequences of his behavior. His therapy involved a multiple treatment approach. . . .

After treatment, Jim's fire setting dropped from an average of one every two weeks to virtually zero fires at a one-year follow-up. Jim improved his basic social skills and appeared better prepared to handle stressful situations, although some of his inappropriate behaviors such as stealing and family problems have continued.

■ APPLICATION

1. List the different professionals that may have contact with Jim and his parents as a result of the different types of problems he presents.
2. How important is communication among the various professionals you listed for question 1? What difficulties may crop up if they do not communicate in a coordinated manner?
3. In order to coordinate communication and treatment, who is the best candidate to be the main organizer of Jim's case? Should it be his parents or one of the professionals involved in treatment?

Source: From *Understanding Child Behavior Disorders* (3rd ed., p. 127), by D. M. Gelfand, W. R. Jenson, and C. J. Drew, 1997, Fort Worth: Harcourt Brace & Company.

Debate Forum

IS MEDICATION AN APPROPRIATE TREATMENT FOR CHILDREN WITH ADHD?

Concern continues regarding the use of medication, particularly psychostimulants, to treat students with ADHD. The debate becomes increasingly difficult with mounting evidence that medication is the most effective intervention. Some professionals, however, have seriously questioned the administration of medication as currently practiced.

■ POINT

Several points must be raised regarding the administration of medication to children with ADHD. The use of medication for treating ADHD is very widespread and may be overprescribed. Some estimates place the number of children receiving psychostimulant treatment near 1 million. In the context of such wide usage, a basic concern emerges about how little we actually know regarding long-term influences and side effects. It is unsettling that we know so little about a treatment that is so widely employed.

■ COUNTERPOINT

For some children with ADHD, medication is the only approach that will bring their hyperactivity under control and thereby allow effective instruction to occur. Without such treatment, these students will be unable to attend to their academic work and will be so disruptive in classroom situations that other students will not be effectively taught. Side effects such as insomnia, irritability, and decreased appetite, among others, are relatively minor and temporary for the most part. Research suggests that teachers have reported that a substantial proportion of those children receiving medication do show an improvement in behavior.

Review

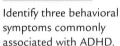

focus 1

Identify three behavioral symptoms commonly associated with ADHD.

- Impulsive behavior
- Fidgeting or hyperactivity
- Inability to focus attention

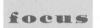

focus 2

Identify two ways in which the behavior of children with ADHD detrimentally affects instructional settings.

- Children with ADHD challenge teachers' skills in classroom management as they are in and out of their seats, pestering their classmates, and perhaps exhibiting aggressive behavior toward other students.
- Children with ADHD challenge teachers' skills in instruction in that they may be unable to focus on instructions, they may impulsively start an assignment before directions are complete, and they may submit incomplete assignments because they did not listen to all the instructions.

focus 3

Identify four other areas of disability that are often found to be comorbid with ADHD.

- Learning disabilities
- Tourette's syndrome
- Conduct disorders
- Emotional disorders

focus 4

Identify the three major types of ADHD according to the *DSM-IV*.

- Attention-deficit/hyperactivity disorder, combined type
- Attention-deficit/hyperactivity disorder, predominantly inattentive type
- Attention-deficit/hyperactivity disorder, predominantly hyperactive-impulsive type

focus 5

Identify two prevalence estimates for ADHD that characterize the difference in occurrence by gender.

- Some estimates of gender differences range from 2:1 to 10:1, with males outnumbering females.
- On the average, the male/female ratio appears to be about 3.5:1.

focus 6

Identify the two broad categories of assessment information useful in diagnosing ADHD.

- Information about medical status
- Information about educational, behavioral, and contextual circumstances

focus 7

Identify three areas of difficulty that present challenges for individuals with ADHD.

- Difficulties in self-regulation, impulsivity, and hyperactivity
- Difficulties in social relationships
- Significant challenges in academic performance

focus 8

Identify three possible causes of ADHD.

- Neurological dysfunction that is trauma-based
- Neurological dysfunction due to brain structure differences
- Hereditary transmission

focus 9

Identify two approaches to intervention that appear to show positive results with individuals having ADHD.

- Medication
- Behavior modification

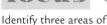

Hunter – Accept
James — Follow Rules
Harry — Follow Directions
David – Problem Solving
Sport Pizza

People with Emotional or Behavior Disorders

To begin with . . .

[I] Am very worried. *60 Minutes* just profiled a GFG [Gift from God] . . . who has ADD (but I'm sure a conduct disorder as well) who has been pulling the usual defiant stuff in school, on the public bus, he has an aide everywhere he goes, typical conduct disorder behavior, you know what I'm talking about, and a political a_____e has arranged to have him kicked out of all of the public schools . . .

He feels that this kid could turn a school into another Columbine—and he is now proposing to the Association of School Boards to overturn IDEA and have special ed. disabled children DISCIPLINED the same as other "normal" kids who mess up in school.

Morley Safer said, "Do you realize what you're doing? Do you realize that you're fighting a federal law, and that if you manage to have these kids disciplined like all the others, they'll be kicked out of school and will run the streets instead of getting an education?" And this man said yes he did, but as far as he was concerned his highest priority was getting "kids like him" out of the public school system because they are dangerous to other children.

I am burning. Steam is coming from my ears. Forgive me if I got a few of the details wrong if you saw the segment, but I am very alarmed. If the school boards across the country are sending representatives to listen to this proposal, we're in deep trouble. Bertie (Kendall, 2000, p. 1)

Schools, too, are no longer safe havens.

One of the most obvious indicators of violence in schools is the fact that approximately 135,000 students bring guns to school each day. . . . Less obvious is the fact that many schools function as setting events for aggressive, antisocial behavior due to overcrowding; harsh, punitive, and inconsistent disciplinary practices; inexperienced teachers; weak staff support; and few allowances (in teaching strategies, curriculum, and discipline) for individual differences. . . . Such situations may have little negative effect on the behavior of students with well-developed self-control and social skills and students who are sufficiently motivated and skillful to overcome such antecedents. . . . Students with, or at risk of, [emotional and behavioral difficulties] do not have these skills. [They] are the ones who react inappropriately to negative setting events, and who then may be severely punished. (Webber & Scheuermann, 1997, pp. 168–169)

Over 100,000 students bring weapons to school each day, and 40 are killed or wounded with these weapons.

■ Large numbers of students fear victimization on the way to and from school.

■ In our nation's schools, 22% of students are afraid to use school bathrooms because these relatively unsupervised areas are often sites for assaults and other forms of victimization.

■ More than 6,000 teachers are threatened annually, and well over 200 are physically injured by students on school grounds.

■ Increasingly, students are intimidated and threatened by mean-spirited teasing, bullying, and sexual harassment occurring at school.

■ Finally, schools are major sites for recruitment and related activities by organized gangs. (Walker, Horner et al., 1996, p. 195)

231

Eric

Eric is a preschooler. In his mother's words, "He's busy. He's hyper . . . , but he is very intelligent, very perceptive." Eric spends about 4 hours a day at Children's Center, a day treatment center for young children with serious emotional and behavior problems. Professionals at this center are helping Eric develop a variety of behaviors, one of which is learning how to express himself verbally, rather than physically striking out at others.

Eric was referred to Children's Center because of his persistent fighting, biting, hitting, and screaming. Additionally, he had great difficulty in responding to directions and giving sustained attention to various age-appropriate tasks. The center's psychologist described him as being the "most extremely hyperactive child that I have tested." Prior to coming to the center, Eric had been ejected from several day-care centers because of his aggressive and noncompliant behaviors.

Eric's mother also experienced great difficulties in managing him. "I feel kind of guilty saying it, but I have to say the truth, I didn't like my son. I couldn't stand him. I couldn't stand being around him for long, I mean I could take about ten minutes. He would, every day, . . . ruin something in the house."

At Children's Center, Eric has the opportunity to interact with some very talented and caring professionals. He spends most of each day with two child therapists who skillfully respond to his negative as well as his positive behaviors. Moreover, each week Eric has a chance to meet one-on-one with Jim, a child therapist, for individual play therapy. At least once a week, his mother meets with Dorothy, a talented social worker who helps Eric's mother with personal concerns and provides suggestions for dealing with Eric at home.

Eric has made significant progress in the past several months. His attention span has increased so significantly that he now can listen to stories and even wait his turn, something that was virtually impossible for him before he came to Children's Center.

Nick

Nick is a very likable, bright kid. He enjoys athletics and is well above average in his reading performance and other academic skills. During the later part of his fifth-grade year, however, he created significant problems for his teacher, whom he saw as being very rude and always picking on him.

The teacher assistance team in the elementary school attempted a variety of prereferral interventions to bring his behavior under control. However, he continued to be noncompliant, problematic during recesses, and generally difficult to manage.

In sixth grade he was placed in a self-contained classroom for students with behavior disorders. He did quite well during this entire year, relating well to his special class teacher, Mrs. Backman, and becoming more self-controlled in his responses to peers and most teachers. The next year he moved on to Northwest, an intermediate school in his neighborhood. Again, he was placed in a self-contained, special education setting with some opportunities for involvement in other classes such as physical education and art.

He made significant progress during his first year at Northwest, partly because of his teacher's social skills program and her expertise in dealing with him. He was now more responsive to verbal redirection and much less reactive to criticism. Because of this progress and other changes in his behavior, he was prepared to spend most of his time outside of the special education classroom. In fact, he now participates for several periods a day in a program for students who are gifted.

His mother sums up his future in this fashion, "I think Nick has a very bright future, but he has to want it." His teachers concur.

Amy

Amy is a very attractive and talented young woman. About midway through the seventh grade, she began to complain about persistent stomachaches, and at the same time, her mother began receiving continual complaints from school personnel about her behavior. In fact, in one year's time, her life went from "beautiful to dismal," as described by her mother. She was not able to eat, was often hostile and suicidal, and did not sleep well. Her behavior at school was "out of control." At this same time, she was prescribed Prozac by one of the physicians with whom her mother was working. Over time, however, her mother took her off this drug, believing that it was not helping her but contributing to her problems in school and at home.

Eventually, Amy was placed in a self-contained classroom at a high school different from the one that she would have attended normally. Her placement in this classroom was based on a number of persistent problems, including a lack of anger control, consistent clashes with authority figures, episodes of inattention, and incomplete school work.

At age 15, after seeing a number of specialists, it was discovered that she had a severe case of endometriosis. She underwent surgery for this condition and gradually things seemed to improve for her.

Amy now spends each morning at a technical training center, where she is learning to become a dental assistant. During the midday hours, she attends several special classes as well as one regular class of biology at her high school. During the afternoon, she works with a dentist who is contributing to her training as a dental assistant.

Amy's mother describes her as follows: "Right now Amy's a capable, fairly happy, well-adjusted 17-year-old kid. Two years ago she was withdrawn, hostile . . . she was suicidal—I never knew what was going to come out of her next. She couldn't eat, she couldn't sleep, but she's progressed really, really well . . . I'm so proud of her."

W E WILL NOW EXPLORE in depth emotional and behavior disorders in children and youth, examining the ways in which we perceive the behavior of others and reviewing factors that give rise to aberrant behaviors. Additionally, you will have opportunities to explore classification systems, learn about the causes of behavior and emotional problems, review assessment techniques, and investigate interventions.

Understanding Emotional or Behavior Disorders

Individuals with **emotional disorders** or **behavior disorders**—such as Eric, Nick, and Amy in the opening snapshots—experience great difficulties in relating appropriately to peers, siblings, parents, and teachers. Students with emotional or behavior disorders are more likely to be economically disadvantaged, male, and African American (Patton, 1998; U.S. Department of Education, 1998). Students with emotional or behavior disorders also have difficulty responding to academic and social tasks that are essential parts of their schooling. Sometimes, they may exhibit too much behavior, or they may be deficient in important academic and social behaviors. For example, Eric's placement in the Children's Center was a function of his excessive aggressive or noncompliant behaviors. In other cases, individuals with emotional or behavior disorders may not have learned the essential skills necessary for successful participation in school settings, as demonstrated by Nick. He, for a variety of reasons, had not learned how to relate well with peers and to accept correction delivered by teachers and others. Amy, as described by her mother, gradually lost her appetite, became suicidal, and dealt with teachers and others in unacceptable ways. However, she is now making great progress with the assistance of her teachers, vocational trainers, and the dentist with whom she works.

■ IDENTIFYING "NORMAL" BEHAVIOR

Many factors influence the ways in which we perceive the behaviors of others (Gelfand, Jenson, & Drew, 1997; Mash & Terdal, 1997). Our perceptions of others and their behaviors are significantly influenced by our personal beliefs, standards, and values about what constitutes normal behavior (Elkind, 1998). Our range of tolerance varies greatly, depending on the behavior and situation. Eric's aggressive and oppositional behaviors were not tolerated at the various preschools where he was enrolled for very short periods of time. Moreover, what may be viewed as normal by some may be viewed by others as abnormal. For example, parents may have little foundation for determining what is normal behavior, since their perceptions are often limited by their lack of experience with children in general. They may see their child's behavior as somewhat challenging, but not abnormal.

The context in which behaviors occur dramatically influences our views of their appropriateness. For example, teachers and parents expect children to behave

■ EMOTIONAL DISORDERS. Behavior problems that are frequently internal in nature. Persons with these problems may have difficulties in expressing or dealing with emotions produced in normal family-, school-, or work-related experiences.

■ BEHAVIOR DISORDERS. Conditions in which the emotional or behavioral responses of individuals in various environments significantly differ from those of their peer, ethnic, and cultural groups. These responses seriously affect social relationships, personal adjustment, schooling, and employment.

focus **1**

Identify five factors that influence the ways in which others' behaviors are perceived.

reasonably well in settings where they have interesting things to do or where children are doing things they seem to enjoy. Often it is in these settings that children with emotional or behavior disorders misbehave. At times, they seem to be oblivious to the environments in which they find themselves. Some have the social skills to act appropriately but choose not to use them. Sometimes the intensity or sheer frequency of some behavior forces parents and others to ask the question, "Is this behavior really normal?" Eric's mother became perplexed not only with the intensity of his behaviors but also with their frequency. Every day something seemed to be broken or damaged by Eric in their home.

■ FACTORS INFLUENCING EMOTIONAL OR BEHAVIOR DISORDERS

Many factors influence the types of behaviors that individuals with emotional or behavior disorders exhibit or suppress: the parents' and teachers' management styles; the school or home environment; the social and cultural values of the family; the social and economic climate of the community; the responses of peers and siblings; and the biological, academic, intellectual, and social-emotional characteristics of the individuals with the disorders (Kauffman, 1997).

■ EXTERNALIZING AND INTERNALIZING DISORDERS

focus **2**

What differentiates externalizing disorders from internalizing disorders?

A number of terms have been used by professionals to describe individuals with emotional, social, and behavior difficulties. These terms include behavior disordered, socially maladjusted, emotionally disturbed, and conduct disordered, among others. Childhood, adolescent, and adult behavior problems can frequently be grouped into two broad but overlapping categories: externalizing and internalizing problems. The latter category refers to behaviors that seem to be directed more at the self than at others. Withdrawal, depression, shyness, and phobias are examples of internalized behaviors (Lambros, Ward, Bocian, MacMillan, & Gresham, 1998); some clinicians would describe individuals with these conditions as emotionally disturbed.

Children or youth who exhibit externalizing disorders may be described as engaging in behaviors that are directed more at others than at themselves. These

Graffiti might be the work of an adolescent who is socially maladjusted and engages in behavior such as defacing property, which directs his feelings and emotions at others.

behaviors could be characterized as aggressive, noncompliant, resistive, disruptive, and dangerous (Lambros et al., 1998). These behaviors significantly impact parents, siblings, classmates, and teachers. The juvenile offender who chronically engages in crimes involving property damage or injury to others might be identified as socially maladjusted. The distinction between these two categories is not clear-cut. For example, adolescents who are severely depressed certainly have an impact on their families and others, although the primary locus of their distress is internal or emotional.

Throughout this chapter, the term *behavior disorders* is used to describe persons with both external and internal (emotional) problems. In reality, most children and youth with behavior disorders experience both external and internal problems associated with their behavioral conditions and related challenges (Boucher, 1999).

Definitions and Classifications

■IDEA DEFINITION

variety of definitions have served to describe people with behavior disorders (Forness & Kavale, 1997). The current definition, used in conjunction with the rules and regulations governing the implementation of the Individuals with Disabilities Education Act Amendments of 1997, is as follows:

Emotional disturbance is defined as . . . :
> *(I) a condition exhibiting one or more of the following characteristics over a long period of time and to a marked degree, which adversely affects educational performance:*
>> *(A) An inability to learn which cannot be explained by intellectual, sensory, or health factors;*
>> *(B) An inability to build or maintain satisfactory relationships with peers and teachers;*
>> *(C) Inappropriate types of behavior or feelings under normal circumstances;*
>> *(D) A general pervasive mood of unhappiness or depression; or*
>> *(E) A tendency to develop physical symptoms or fears associated with personal or school problems.*
> *(ii) The term includes children who are schizophrenic or autistic.[1] The term does not include children who are socially maladjusted, unless it is determined that they are seriously emotionally disturbed. (45 Code of Federal Regulations 1212.5 [b] [8] [1978])*

This description of severe emotional disturbance or behavior disorders was adapted from an earlier definition created by Bower (1959). The IDEA definition for behavior disorders has been criticized for its lack of clarity, incompleteness, and exclusion of individuals described as socially maladjusted (Council for Children with Behavior Disorders, 1987, 1989, 1990; Forness, 1996; Forness & Knitzer, 1990; Webber & Sheuermann, 1997). Additionally, this definition mandates that assessment personnel demonstrate that the disorder is adversely affecting students' school performance. In many cases, students with serious behavior disorders—such as eating disorders, depression, suicidal tendencies, and social withdrawal—do not receive appropriate care and treatment, merely because their academic achievement in school

---

[1]In 1990, the U.S. Department of Education removed autism as a term under the category of serious emotional disturbance. Autism is now a separate category under IDEA.

appears to be normal or above average. In some cases, these students are gifted (see Chapter 17).

■ THE COUNCIL FOR EXCEPTIONAL CHILDREN DEFINITION

The Council for Exceptional Children has proposed a definition for emotional disturbance that goes beyond the language of IDEA (Council for Exceptional Children, 1991; Forness, 1996; Forness & Knitzer, 1990):

Emotional or Behavior Disorders (EBD) refers to a condition in which behavioral or emotional responses of an individual in school are so different from his/her generally accepted, age-appropriate, ethnic, or cultural norms that they adversely affect educational performance in such areas as self-care, social relationships, personal adjustment, academic progress, classroom behavior, or work adjustment.

EBD is more than a transient, expected response to stressors in the child's or youth's environment and would persist even with individualized interventions, such as feedback to the individual, consultation with parents or families, and/or modification of the educational environment. The eligibility decision must be based on multiple sources of data about the individual's behavioral or emotional functioning. EBD must be exhibited in at least two different settings, at least one of which must be school related.

EBD can coexist with other handicapping conditions as defined elsewhere in this law [IDEA].

This category may include children or youth with schizophrenia, affective disorders, or with other sustained disturbances of conduct, attention, or adjustment. (Council for Exceptional Children, 1991, p. 10)

Features of this definition represent significant advantages over the present IDEA definition, including (1) the inclusion of impairments of adaptive behavior as evidenced in emotional, social, or behavioral differences; (2) the use of normative standards of assessment from multiple sources, including consideration of cultural and/or ethnic factors; (3) the examination of prereferral interventions and other efforts to assist children prior to formally classifying them as disabled; and (4) the potential inclusion of individuals previously labeled as socially maladjusted.

The pressure to include children considered to be socially maladjusted in the federal definition of emotional disturbance continues to be a sharply debated issue (Bullock & Gable, 1998; Forness & Kavale, 1997; McIntyre & Forness, 1996; Murray & Myers, 1998; Webber & Scheuerman, 1997). Proponents for the inclusion of the socially maladjusted have argued that professional practice as well as current research run counter to the exclusionary clause found in the present IDEA definition (Center, 1989a, 1989b; Duncan, Forness, & Hartsough, 1995; Kauffman, 1989; Nelson, Rutherford, Center, & Walker, 1991; Rosenblatt et al., 1998; Terrasi, Sennett, & Macklin, 1999; Webber & Scheuerman, 1997). Moreover, the clause in the IDEA definition excluding these children and youth prevents them from receiving "attendant protections with regard to discipline and service delivery" (Webber & Scheuerman, 1997, p. 169). We will discuss these protections later in this chapter.

Many professionals believe that greater numbers of young children with behavior disorders would receive preventive treatment if the more inclusive definition were adopted, thereby decreasing the need for more intensive and expensive services later in students' lives. Additionally, many clinicians believe that adoption of this definition will lead to greater numbers of children and youth receiving needed special education services directly related to their strengths as well as their challenging behaviors.

■ CLASSIFICATION

Classification systems serve several purposes for human services professionals. First, they provide a means for describing various types of behavior problems in children. Second, they provide a common set of terms for communicating with others. For example, children who are identified as having Down syndrome, a type of mental retardation, share some rather distinct characteristics (see Chapter 9). Third, physicians and other health care specialists use these characteristics and other information as a basis for diagnosing and treating these children.

Unfortunately, there is no consistent use of a standardized set of criteria for determining the nature and severity of behavior disorders (Forness, 1988, 1996; Kavale, Forness, & Alper, 1986). If valid eligibility and classification systems did exist, they would provide educational, psychological, and psychiatric clinicians with extremely valuable information about the nature of various conditions, effective treatment outcomes, and associated complications.

The field of behavior disorders is broad and includes many different types of problems, so it is not surprising that many approaches have been used to classify these individuals. Some classification systems describe individuals according to statistically derived categories, whereby patterns of strongly related behaviors are identified through sophisticated statistical techniques. Other classification systems are clinically oriented; they are derived from the experiences of physicians and other social scientists who work directly with children, youth, and adults with behavior disorders. Still other classification systems help us understand behavior disorders in terms of their relative severity.

■ STATISTICALLY DERIVED CLASSIFICATION SYSTEMS For a number of years, researchers have collected information about children with behavior disorders. Data collected from parent and teacher questionnaires, interviews, and behavior rating scales have been analyzed using advanced statistical techniques. Certain clusters or patterns of related behaviors have emerged from these studies. For example, Peterson (1987) found that the behavior disorders exhibited by elementary school children could be accounted for by two dimensions: withdrawal and aggression. Similarly, several researchers have intensively studied child psychiatric patients to develop a valid classification system (Achenbach, 1966, 1991a & 1991b). Statistical analysis of data generated from these studies revealed two broad clusters of behaviors: externalizing symptoms and internalizing symptoms (discussed earlier). Externalizing behaviors included stealing, lying, disobedience, and fighting. Internalizing behaviors included physical complaints (e.g., stomachaches), phobias, fearfulness, social withdrawal, and worrying.

Other researchers (Quay, 1975, 1979; Von Isser, Quay, & Love, 1980), using similar methodologies, have reliably identified four distinct categories of behavior disorders in children:

1. Conduct disorders involve such characteristics as overt aggression, both verbal and physical; disruptiveness; negativism; irresponsibility; and defiance of authority—all of which are at variance with the behavioral expectations of the school and other social institutions.
2. Anxiety–withdrawal stands in considerable contrast to conduct disorders, involving, as it does, overanxiety, social withdrawal, seclusiveness, shyness, sensitivity, and other behaviors implying a retreat from the environment rather than a hostile response to it.

focus 4

Identify three reasons why classification systems are important to professionals who identify, treat, and educate individuals with behavior disorders.

3. Immaturity characteristically involves preoccupation, short attention span, passivity, daydreaming, sluggishness, and other behavior not in accord with developmental expectations.

4. Socialized aggression typically involves gang activities, cooperative stealing, truancy, and other manifestations of participation in a delinquent subculture. (Von Isser et al., 1980, pp. 272–273)

This category, **socialized aggression,** is related to social maladjustment. Presently, children and youth identified as socially maladjusted are not eligible for services through IDEA. Socialized aggression is also related to another term mentioned very briefly, *conduct disordered.* We will review conduct disorders in greater depth later in this section.

In thinking about these categories, recall the descriptions of Eric, Nick, and Amy in the opening snapshots. How would they be classified according to these categories? Did Eric have attention-deficit disorder? Was Nick's behavior serious enough to identify him as conduct disordered, and what about Amy's behavior? Does she qualify for placement in any of these categories?

■ CLINICALLY DERIVED CLASSIFICATION SYSTEMS   Although several clinically derived classification systems have been developed, the system predominantly used by medical and psychological personnel is the American Psychiatric Association's *Diagnostic and Statistical Manual of Mental Disorders* (1994, 4th ed.) *(DSM-IV).* It was developed and tested by groups and committees of psychiatric, psychological, and health care professionals. Participants in each of these groups included persons who served or worked closely with children, adolescents, and adults with behavior disorders. The categories and subcategories of the *DSM-IV* (American Psychiatric Association, 1994) were developed after years of investigation and field testing. Unfortunately, these psychiatric categories do not serve educational clinicians well, as they are not generally considered in identifying children or adolescents for special education services (Duncan et al., 1995).

The current manual, *DSM-IV* (American Psychiatric Association, 1994), identifies ten major groups of disorders that may be exhibited by infants, children, or adolescents. Several of these disorders overlap with other conditions such as mental retardation, autism, and attention-deficit disorders:

■ *Pervasive developmental disorders.* Children with **pervasive developmental disorders** exhibit pervasive and severe deficits in several areas of development. These deficits may include significant problems in relating to parents, siblings, and others; very poor communication skills; and unusual behaviors evidenced in gestures, postures, and facial expressions. Generally these disorders are accompanied by chromosomal abnormalities, structural abnormalities in the nervous system, and congenital infections. Also, these disorders are generally evident at birth or present themselves very early in a child's life. One of these disorders, autism, will be addressed in Chapter 12.

■ *Attention deficit and disruptive behavior disorders.* Children with these disorders manifest a variety of symptoms (see Tables 8.1 and 8.2). For example, children with attention deficits have difficulty responding well to typical academic and social tasks as well as controlling their level of physical activity. Often their activity appears to be very random or purposeless in nature. See Chapter 7 for information on attention-deficit disorders. Children with disruptive behavior disorders frequently cause physical harm to other individuals or animals, often engage in behaviors destructive to others' property, repeatedly participate in

■ SOCIALIZED AGGRESSION. Participation in a delinquent subculture that involves activities such as gang behavior, cooperative stealing, and truancy.

■ PERVASIVE DEVELOPMENTAL DISORDER. A term used by the American Psychiatric Association in *DSM-III-R,* referring to a psychological disorder characterized by impaired development of social interaction abilities and communication skills.

theft and deceitful activities, and regularly violate rules and other social conventions. In some instances, children with these disorders are highly oppositional. They exhibit a pattern of recurrent negativism, opposition to authority figures, and loss of temper. Other typical behaviors include disobeying, arguing, blaming others for problems and mistakes, and being spiteful. Most of the students with behavior disorders who are served in special education through IDEA are conduct disordered or oppositionally defiant (see Tables 8.1 and 8.2 for diagnostic criteria for conduct disorder and oppositional defiant disorder). Think about Nick, identified in the opening snapshots. How would you classify him?

■ *Anxiety disorders.* The category of anxiety disorders of childhood or adolescence is very similar to the anxiety–withdrawal category of the statistically derived classification system. Children with anxiety disorders have difficulty dealing with anxiety-provoking situations and with separating themselves from parents or other attachment figures (e.g., close friends, teachers, coaches). Unrealistic

---

TABLE 8.1   Representative diagnostic criteria for conduct disorder

A. A repetitive and persistent pattern of behavior in which the basic rights of others or major age-appropriate societal norms or rules are violated, as manifested by the presence of three (or more) of the following criteria in the past 12 months, with at least one criterion present in the past 6 months:

Aggression to people and animals

1. Often bullies, threatens, or intimidates others.
2. Often initiates physical fights.
3. Has used a weapon that can cause serious physical harm to others (e.g., a bat, brick, broken bottle, knife, gun).
4. Has been physically cruel to people.
5. Has been physically cruel to animals.
6. Has stolen while confronting a victim (e.g., mugging, purse snatching, extortion, armed robbery).
7. Has forced someone into sexual activity.

Destruction of property

8. Has deliberately engaged in fire setting with the intention of causing serious damage.
9. Has deliberately destroyed others' property (other than by fire setting).

Deceitfulness or theft

10. Has broken into someone else's house, building, or car.
11. Often lies to obtain goods or favors or to avoid obligations (i.e., "cons" others).
12. Has stolen items of nontrivial value without confronting a victim (e.g., shoplifting, but without breaking and entering; forgery).

Serious violations of rules

13. Often stays out at night despite parental prohibitions, beginning before age 13 years.
14. Has run away from home overnight at least twice while living in parental or parental surrogate home (or once without returning for a lengthy period).
15. Is often truant from school, beginning before age 13 years.

B. The disturbance in behavior causes clinically significant impairment in social, academic, or occupational functioning.

Source: Reprinted with permission from the *Diagnostic and Statistical Manual of Mental Disorders,* Fourth Edition (pp. 90–91). Copyright 1994 American Psychiatric Association.

A. A pattern of negativistic, hostile, and defiant behavior lasting at least 6 months, during which four (or more) of the following are present:
1. Often loses temper.
2. Often argues with adults.
3. Often actively defies or refuses to comply with adults' requests or rules.
4. Often deliberately annoys people.
5. Often blames others for his or her mistakes or misbehavior.
6. Is often touchy or easily annoyed by others.
7. Is often angry and resentful.
8. Is often spiteful or vindictive.

Note: Consider a criterion met only if the behavior occurs more frequently than is typically observed in individuals of comparable age and developmental level.

B. The disturbance in behavior causes clinically significant impairment in social, academic, or occupational functioning.
C. The behaviors do not occur exclusively during the course of a psychotic or mood disorder.
D. Criteria are not met for conduct disorder, and, if the individual is age 18 years or older, criteria are not met for antisocial personality disorder.

Source: Reprinted with permission from the *Diagnostic and Statistical Manual of Mental Disorders,* Fourth Edition (pp. 93–94). Copyright 1994 American Psychiatric Association.

worries about future events, over concern about achievement, an excessive need for reassurance, and somatic complaints are characteristic of young people who have anxiety disorders.

■ *Feeding and eating disorders.* The first of these disorders is pica, or the persistent eating of nonnutritive materials for at least one month. Materials consumed may be cloth, string, hair, plaster, or even paint. Often children with pervasive developmental disorders manifest pica. Anorexia and bulimia are common eating disorders evidenced by gross disturbances in eating behavior. In the case of anorexia nervosa, the most distinguishing feature is bodyweight that is 15 percent below the norm. These individuals are intensely afraid of weight gain and exhibit grossly distorted perceptions of the shapes and sizes of their bodies. Bulimia is characterized by repeated episodes of binging, followed by self-induced vomiting or other extreme measures to prevent weight gain. Both of these conditions may result in depressed mood, social withdrawal, irritability, and other more serious medical conditions.

■ *Tic disorders.* Tic disorders involve stereotyped movements or vocalizations that are involuntary, rapid, and recurrent over time. Tics may take the form of eye blinking, facial gestures, sniffing, snorting, repeating certain words or phrases, and grunting. Stress often exacerbates the nature and frequency of tics.

■ *Elimination disorders.* **Elimination disorders** deal with soiling and wetting behaviors in older children. Children who continue to have consistent problems with bowel and bladder control past their fourth or fifth birthday may be diagnosed as having an elimination disorder, particularly if the condition is not a function of any physical disorder.

■ *Other disorders of infancy, childhood, or adolescence.* The remaining categories in the *DSM-IV* refer to other disorders that do not easily fit other categories. Separation anxiety disorder is characterized by inordinate fear about leaving home

■ ELIMINATION DISORDER. A disorder in children who continue to have consistent problems with bowel and/or bladder control past the fourth or fifth birthday; the condition is not caused by a physical disorder.

TABLE 8.3   Characteristics of individuals with behavior disorders

General Factors	Mild Behavior Disorders	Severe Behavior Disorders
Intelligence	Below average intelligence to gifted; generally below average	Generally in the retarded range
Academic achievement	Academic skills and knowledge well below average; dropout rates exceed that of individuals with other disabilities	Severe deficits in academic skills; may exhibit rudimentary reading and mathematics abilities
Social relationships	Major problems in developing and maintaining relationships	Few, if any, stable relationships with others; often avoids relationships with other individuals, even peers
Adaptive skills	Generally skilled in daily living skills and caring for self	Major problems in everyday living skills and caring for self
Behavior problems	Frequently aggressive (verbally and physically), oppositional, noncompliant, and generally obnoxious	Often and consistently violent, assaultive, destructive, or self-injurious
Speech and language problems	Generally normal	Bizarre language, speech problems; sometimes completely lacks functional communication skills
Contact with reality	Contact with reality good; generally aware of environment and other individuals	Out of contact with environment and the persons in it; develops own realities (hallucinates, fantasizes, etc.)
Presence of other disorders	Few, if any, disorders other than learning problems	Other disorders and disabilities may be present (eating disorders, depression, elimination disorders, etc.)
Employment	Sporadically employed or underemployed, according to abilities	Generally unemployed; not self-sustaining; dependent on others

or being separated from persons to whom the child or adolescent is attached. Behaviors indicative of this disorder include persistent refusal to go to school, excessive worry about personal harm or injury to self or other family members, reluctance to go to sleep, and repeated complaints about headaches, stomachaches, and nausea.

The other condition, elective mutism, is a persistent refusal to talk in typical social, school, and work environments. This disorder is really quite rare, occurring less than 1% of the time in psychiatric referrals. This disorder may significantly impact the child's social and educational functioning.

■ CLASSIFICATION ACCORDING TO SEVERITY OF BEHAVIORS
Various researchers have attempted to differentiate mild to moderate from severe behavior disorders. As one might expect, the behavioral characteristics of individuals with severe behavior disorders are identified more easily than those associated with mild disorders. As illustrated in Table 8.3, individuals with severe disorders differ significantly from those with mild disorders in a variety of intellectual, social, academic, and behavioral domains.

Persons who exhibit severe behavior disorders are often described as psychotic. **Psychosis** is a general term. The *DSM-IV* uses such terms as *pervasive developmental*

■ PSYCHOSIS. A general term referring to a serious behavior disorder resulting in a loss of contact with reality and characterized by delusions, hallucinations, or illusions.

People with anorexia nervosa are intensely afraid of weight gain and have seriously distorted perceptions of the shape and size of their bodies.

disorders and *schizophrenia,* among others, to refer to infants, children, adolescents, and adults who are psychotic, or very seriously disturbed.

Prevalence

Estimates of the prevalence of behavior disorders vary greatly from one source to the next, ranging from 0.05% to 15.0%. The U.S. Office of Education estimated that 1.2% to 2% of students in the country have behavior disorders. Estimates provided by the Office of Technology Assessment and the National Institute of Medicine suggest that more than 3% of children and adolescents have severe behavior disorders. Other current research indicates that between 3% and 8% of all school-age children may have emotional or behavior disorders sufficiently severe to warrant treatment (Brandenburg, Friedman, & Silver, 1990; Forness, Kavale, & Lopez, 1993; Rosenblatt et al., 1998; Ruehl, 1998).

Other researchers have suggested that 3% to 6% of the school-age population need specialized services because of behavior disorders (Kauffman, 1997; Ruehl, 1998). Other specialists have suggested that as many as 33% of school-age children experience behavior problems during any given year (Cullinan & Epstein, 1986). Of this number, about one third need the assistance provided by personnel outside the typical classroom. Another third of this number need special education and related services. During the 1998–1999 school year in the United States, fewer than 1% of children 6 to 21 years of age were identified and served as behavior disordered (U.S. Department of Education, 2000a).

Unfortunately, significant numbers of students with behavior disorders remain unidentified and do not receive special education (Kauffman, 1997; Knitzer, Steinberg, & Fleisch, 1990; Ruehl, 1998). Some researchers have suggested that the number of students who receive special education is less than one third of those who actually need this assistance (Brandenburg et al., 1990). The low number of students served is in part due to the lack of standardized criteria, diverse definitions, and meager research about the processes related to labeling students as behavior disordered and related placement decisions (Denny, Gunther, Shores, & Campbell, 1995; Kavale et al., 1986; Knitzer, 1982; Lewitt & Baker, 1996; Ruehl, 1998; Stephens & Lakin, 1995). Another factor that contributes to the problems of identification, classification, and service provision is the fact that many children and youth with behavior disorders manifest other disabling conditions (MacMillan, 1998; Ruehl, 1998).

Characteristics

■ INTELLIGENCE

Researchers from a variety of disciplines have studied the intellectual capacity of individuals with behavior disorders. In an early national study of children with behavior disorders enrolled in public school programs, the majority of these students exhibited above-average intelligence (Morse, Cutler, & Fink, 1964). However, recent research has revealed a different picture.

focus 5
Identify five general characteristics (intellectual, adaptive, social, and achievement) of children and youth with behavior disorders.

The preponderance of evidence leads to the conclusion that children with behavior disorders tend to have average to below-average IQs compared to their normal peers (Greenbaum et al., 1998; Quinn & Epstein, 1998). Additionally, children with severe behavior disorders such as schizophrenia and autism tend to have IQs that fall within the retarded range of functioning.

What impact does intelligence have on the educational and social–adaptive performance of children with behavior disorders? Is the intellectual capacity of a child who is disturbed a good predictor of other types of achievement and social behavior? The answer is yes. Kauffman (1997) asserted that "the IQs of disturbed children appear to be the best single predictor of academic and future social achievement" (p. 245). The below-average IQs of many of these children contribute significantly to the challenges they experience in mastering academic and social tasks in school and other environments.

■ ADAPTIVE AND SOCIAL BEHAVIOR

Individuals with behavior disorders exhibit a variety of problems in adapting to their home, school, and community environments. Furthermore, they have difficulties in relating socially and responsibly to persons such as peers, parents, teachers, and other authority figures. In short, students with behavior disorders are difficult to teach and to parent (Gresham & MacMillan, 1997; Turnbull & Ruef, 1997). In contrast to their peers who generally follow rules, listen to their teachers and parents, finish class work and home chores, and comply promptly with adult requests, children and youth with behavior disorders often defy their teachers, disturb others, do not complete tasks, and behave in ways that produce teacher, parent, and peer rejection (Gresham, Lane, & MacMillan, & Bocian, 1999). These behaviors lead to referral for special education and related services (Gresham & MacMillan, 1997; see Table 8.4).

TABLE 8.4 Behavioral correlates and outcomes associated with teacher and peer-related adjustment

| | Teacher-related adjustment | | Peer-related adjustment | |
	Adaptive	Maladaptive	Adaptive	Maladaptive
Behaviors	Complies promptly	Steals	Cooperates with peers	Disrupts group
	Follows rules	Defies teacher	Supports peers	Acts snobbish
	Works independently	Has tantrums	Defends self in arguments	Uses indirect aggression
	Follows directions	Disturbs others	Remains calm	Starts fights
	Listens to teacher	Cheats	Leads peers	Has a short temper
	Finishes class work	Swears	Compliments peers	Brags
		Is aggressive	Affiliates with peers	Gets in trouble with teacher
		Ignores teacher		Seeks help constantly
Outcomes	Teacher acceptance	Teacher rejection	Peer acceptance	Social rejection
	School achievement and success	Referral to special education	Positive peer relations	Loneliness
		School failure and dropout	Friendships	Weak social involvement
		Low performance expectations		

Source: Adapted from "Social Competence and Affective Characteristics of Student with Mild Disabilities," by F. M. Gresham and D. L. MacMillan, 1997, *Review of Educational Research, 67*(4), pp. 377–415.

Socially, children and youth with behavior disorders may have difficulty sharing, playing typical age-appropriate games, and apologizing for actions that hurt others. They may be unable to deal appropriately with situations that produce strong feelings, such as anger and frustration. Problem solving, accepting consequences for misbehavior, negotiating, expressing affection, and reacting appropriately to failure are behaviors that do not come naturally or easily to these children and youth. In many cases, they have not been taught these behaviors or they chose not to use these behaviors in their interactions with others. Because these children have deficits in these adaptive–social behaviors, they frequently experience difficulties in meeting the demands of the classroom and other environments in which they must participate.

Earlier in the classification section, the statistically derived categories of behaviors that were common to children and adolescents with behavior disorders were reviewed. These categories included conduct disorder, anxiety withdrawal, immaturity, and socialized aggression. Children and adolescents with conduct disorders engage in verbal and physical aggression. They may threaten other children, may extort money from them, or may physically hurt them often without any provocation. In classrooms, these students often defy authority, refuse to follow teacher directions, and frequently engage in power struggles with teachers and administrative personnel (Hester & Kaiser, 1998; Skiba, 1997; Wicks-Nelson & Israel, 2000). Students with behavior disorders are "13.3 times more likely than other students with disabilities to be arrested while in school" (U.S. Department of Education, 1999, p. II-4). Also, 42% of the youth with disabilities in correctional facilities are youngsters with identified behavior disorders (U.S. Department of Education, 1999).

Children and adolescents who are anxious and withdrawn frequently exhibit behaviors such as seclusiveness and shyness. They may find it extremely difficult to interact with others in normal social events. They tend to avoid contact with others and may be often found daydreaming. In the extreme, some of these youth begin to avoid school or refuse to attend school. Their school avoidance or refusal is marked by persistent fear of social situations that might arise in school or related settings. These youth fear being humiliated or embarrassed. Their anxiety may be expressed by tantrums, crying, freezing, and other bodily complaints (stomachaches, sickness, etc.) (Paige, 1997). Children and youth with behavior disorders who manifest low personal and social skills are more likely than other youth with disabilities to be victimized during their school years (U.S. Department of Education, 1999).

Other children and youth with behavior disorders may struggle with depression. Left untreated, these individuals are at risk for suicide, poor school performance, and relationship problems with peers, siblings, parents, and teachers. Manifestations of depression in children and youth include sleep disturbance, fatigue or loss of energy, excessive feelings of guilt or worthlessness, inability to concentrate, and suicidal ideation (Whelan, 1998).

Youth gang activities, drug abuse, truancy, violence toward others, and other delinquent acts characterize children and adolescents who are identified as "undersocialized aggressive" (Kauffman, 1997). These adolescents are often seen as impulsive, hyperactive, irritable, and tenaciously stubborn (U.S. Department of Justice, 1999a). Furthermore, they frequently do not get along well with others, engage in behaviors that draw attention to themselves, are cruel to others, and are sometimes involved in drug distribution and other illegal activities (Thurlow, Christenson, Sinclair, & Evelo, 1997). Youth gang activities in the United States account for an estimated 3,340 homicides each year, 33% of crack cocaine sales, 32% of marijuana sales, 12% of methamphetamine sales, and 9% of heroin sales. Moreover, gang members account for 17% of all violent crimes and 35% of all property crimes (U.S. Department of Justice, 1998, 1999a, 1999b, 1999c).

It is easy to see how the behaviors associated with these categories are maladaptive and interfere with school, family, community, and eventual employment success. Moreover, it is easy to see how youth gang activities would antagonize and agitate community members.

■ ACADEMIC ACHIEVEMENT

Students with behavior disorders experience significant difficulties in academic subject areas (Bauer & Shea, 1999; Greenbaum et al., 1998; Gresham et al., 1999; Kerr & Nelson, 1998; U.S. Department of Education 1998). In contrast to other students with disabilities, students with behavior disorders are absent more often, fail more classes, are retained more frequently, and are less successful in passing minimum competency examinations (Thurlow et al., 1997, U.S. Department of Education, 1998). On the high school level, students with behavior disorders have average grade points of 1.7, compared with 2.0 for all high school students with disabilities (Osher, Osher, & Smith, 1994; Wagner et al., 1991). Moreover, the majority of students with behavior disorders receive their services and instruction in settings outside of general education classrooms (U.S. Department of Education, 2000a).

More so than other groups with disabilities, children and youth with behavior disorders are absent more frequently from school (Bauer & Shea, 1999). Furthermore, the dropout and graduation rates for students with behavior disorders are staggering (Coutinho & Oswald, 1998; Osher, Osher, & Smith, 1994; U.S. Department of Education, 1998). About 50% of these students drop out of school, most before they finish the tenth grade (U.S. Department of Education, 1999). Forty-two percent actually graduate from high school (Osher & Hanley, 1996). About 17% of students with behavior disorders go on to college.

Studies dealing with post–high school employment rates of students are quite revealing. Only 41% of students with behavior disorders who have exited high school are employed two years later, compared with 59% of typical adolescents who have exited high school. Three to five years later, the contrasts are even stronger: 69% of students without disabilities are employed, compared with 47% of students with behavior disorders (D'Amico & Blackorby, 1992).

Some studies have suggested that many programs designed to assist students with behavior disorders overemphasize control and management of behavior rather than the teaching of academic skills or valuable prevocational or vocational competencies (Cheney, Barringer, Upham, & Manning, 1996; Knitzer et al., 1990; Nichols, 1996; Scheuermann & Webber, 1996).

Causation

Throughout history, philosophers, physicians, theologians, and others have attempted to explain why people behave as they do (Elkind, 1998). Historically, people who were mentally disturbed were described as possessed by evil spirits, for which the treatment of choice was religious in nature. Later, Sigmund Freud (1856–1939) and others promoted the notion that behavior could be explained in terms of subconscious phenomena or early traumatic experiences. More recently, some theorists have attributed disordered behaviors to inappropriate learning and complex interactions that take place between individuals and their environments. From a biological perspective, others have suggested that aberrant behaviors are caused by certain biochemical substances, brain abnormalities or injuries, and chromosomal irregularities.

focus 6

What can be accurately said about the causes of behavior disorders?

With such a wealth of etiological explanations, it is easy to see why practitioners might choose different approaches in identifying, treating, and preventing various disorders (Elkind, 1998). However, the variety of theoretical frameworks and perspectives provides clinicians with a number of choices for explaining the presence of certain behaviors.

1. *The biological approach.* The biological framework explains behavior disorders as a function of inherited or abnormal biological conditions within the body or injury to the central nervous system. Behavior problems presumably surface as a result of some physiological, biochemical, or genetic abnormality or disease (Bauer & Shea, 1999; Erickson, 1998; Wicks-Nelson & Israel, 2000).

2. *The psychoanalytical approach.* Subconscious processes, predispositions or instincts, and early traumatic experiences explain the presence of behavior disorders from a psychoanalytic perspective. The internal processes are unobservable events that occur in the mind among the well-known psychic constructs of the id (the drives component), ego (the reality component), and superego (the conscience component). As individuals gain insight into their psychic conflicts by means of psychotherapy, they may be able to eliminate or solve their behavior problems. The return to normalcy may also be aided by a caring ther-

apist or teacher. For children, this process theoretically occurs through play therapy, in which inner conflicts are revealed and subsequently resolved through family therapy and therapeutic play experiences with understanding adults (Bauer & Shea, 1999; Erickson, 1998; Wicks-Nelson & Israel, 2000).

3. *The behavioral approach.* The behavioral approach focuses on aspects of the environment that produce, reward, diminish, or punish certain behaviors. Through treatment, adults and children are given opportunities to learn new adaptive behaviors by identifying realistic goals and receiving reinforcement for attaining these goals. Gradually, aberrant behaviors are eliminated or replaced by more appropriate ones (Bauer & Shea, 1999; Erickson, 1998; Wicks-Nelson & Israel, 2000).

4. *The phenomenological approach.* From a phenomenological point of view, abnormal behaviors arise from feelings, thoughts, and past events tied to a person's self-perception or self-concept. Faulty perceptions or feelings are thought to cause individuals to behave in ways that are counterproductive to self-fulfillment. Therapy using this approach is centered on helping people develop satisfactory perceptions and behaviors that are in agreement with self-selected values.

5. *The sociological–ecological approach.* The sociological–ecological model is by far the most encompassing explanation of behavior disorders. Aberrant behaviors are presumed to be caused by a variety of interactions and transactions with other people. For some, the deviant behaviors are taught as part of one's culture. For others, the behaviors are a function of labeling. Individuals labeled as juvenile delinquents, according to this perspective, gradually adopt the patterns of behavior that are associated with the assigned label. In addition, others who are aware of the label begin to treat the labeled individuals as if they were truly delinquent. Such treatment theoretically promotes the delinquent behavior (Bauer & Shea, 1999; Erickson, 1998; Wicks-Nelson & Israel, 2000).

   This model also specifies another source of aberrant behavior—*differential association.* This is closely related to the cultural-transmission explanation of deviance: people exhibit behavior problems in an attempt to conform to the wishes and expectations of a group with which they wish to join or maintain affiliation. Finally, the sociological–ecological perspective views the presence of aberrant behavior as a function of a variety of interactions and transactions that are derived from a broad array of environmental settings.

Each model contributes different explanations for the causes of behavior disorders. Unfortunately, clinicians are rarely able to isolate the exact cause of a child's behavior disorder, but they do understand many factors that contribute to the condition. Many professionals concur with Kauffman (1997), who wrote, "Both the disorder of behavior and their causes are usually multidimensional; life seldom refines disorders or their causes into pure unambiguous forms. Children seldom show teachers or researchers a single disorder uncontaminated by elements of other problems, and the cause of a disorder is virtually never found to be a single factor" (p. 159).

Family and home environments play a critical role in the emergence of behavior disorders. Poverty, drug and alcohol involvement of primary caregivers, child abuse and neglect, malnutrition, dysfunctional family environments, family discord, divorce, and incompetent parenting have a profound impact on the behaviors observed in children and adolescents (Kaiser & Hester, 1997; Walker et al., 1996; Wicks-Nelson & Israel, 2000).

Children reared in low-income families bear increased risks for wide-ranging challenges including lower intellectual development, deficient school achievement, and high rates of behavior problems (Kaiser & Hester, 1997; Quinn, Bell, & Ward, 1997; Wicks-Nelson & Israel, 2000). Antisocial behaviors often emerge in children whose family poverty is accompanied by other stressors such as homelessness, the death of a parent, placement in foster care, or persistent child abuse (Kaiser & Hester, 1997). Family discord and divorce also play a role in the development of behavior disorders in some children. The impact of divorce on children is influenced by a variety of factors (e.g., age of the child, financial status of the family, gender of the child, amount of acrimony between the partners), so it is difficult to predict with great precision who will be severely affected by divorce. Extended marital conflict and distress are associated with several serious child outcomes, including aggressive behavior, difficulty with schoolwork, depression, health problems, and inferior social competence (Walker et al., 1996; Wicks-Nelson & Israel, 2000).

Child-management and discipline procedures also play important roles in the development of behavior disorders. However, the way in which child management may trigger behavior disorders is highly complex. Parents who are extremely permissive, overly restrictive, and/or aggressive often produce children who are conduct disordered. Home environments that are devoid of consistent rules and consequences for child behavior, that lack parental supervision, that reinforce aggressive behavior, and that have parents who model aggression and use aggressive child-management practices produce children who are very much at risk for developing disruptive behavior disorders or conduct disorders (Rutter, 1995; Wicks-Nelson & Israel, 2000).

Child abuse plays a major role in the development of aggression and other problematic behaviors in children and adolescents. Effects of child abuse on young children include withdrawal, noncompliance, aggression, enuresis (bed-wetting), and somatic and physical complaints. Physically abused children exhibit high rates of adjustment problems of all kinds (Erickson, 1998; Wicks-Nelson & Israel, 2000). Neglected children have difficulty in academic subjects and receive below-average grades. Children who have been sexually abused manifest an array of problems, including inappropriate, premature sexual behavior; poor peer relationships; and often serious, life-long mental health problems. Similar difficulties are evident in adolescents who have been abused. These include low-self-esteem, depression, poor peer relationships, and school problems, and self-injurious and suicidal behaviors.

Assessment

■ SCREENING AND REFERRAL

The first step in the assessment process is screening, to identify infants, children, and adolescents most in need of treatment. Screening is based on the belief that early identification leads to early treatment, which may lessen the overall impact of the behavior disorders on the individual and family (see Table 8.5). However, very few school systems or social agencies screen for behavior disorders on a wide scale, for two reasons. First, such a task is generally very expensive and time consuming, beyond the financial and human resources of most school systems and state social service agencies. Most districts and treatment agencies rely on teachers and parents to refer students for screening (Bauer & Shea, 1999). Second, many more children might be identified than could be adequately handled by a school system or social agency.

In most school environments, children are considered for screening only after concerned or perplexed teachers have initiated referrals for them. For example, an

TABLE 8.5 Eligibility decisions

Question	Action
I. Screening	
A. Is student "at risk"?	A. Administer screening procedure, activate teacher assistance team
B. Can student be helped through regular program?	B. Modify or adapt regular program
II. Identification	
A. Has student benefited from adaptations made in regular program?	A. Evaluate effects of regular education interventions
B. Is additional support or service needed?	B. Implement consultative intervention
C. Should the student be identified as behaviorally disordered?	C. Conduct assessment; hold staffing
III. Certification	
A. Should the student be referred for EBD services?	A. Conduct child study team meeting
B. What services are needed?	B. Develop individualized education plan (IEP)
C. Where should services be provided?	C. Identify least restrictive settings for pupil
D. What expectations must the pupil meet to return to the regular classroom?	D. Specify criteria for decertification
IV. Program Evaluation	
A. Is the program working?	A. Implement formative and summative evaluation procedures
V. Decertification	
A. Is special education no longer needed?	A. Evaluate progress against exit criteria, conduct exit child study team meeting

Source: From *Strategies for Managing Behavior Problems in the Classroom* (p. 25), by M. M. Kerr and C. M. Nelson, 1998, Upper Saddle River, NJ: Merrill.

experienced kindergarten teacher became very concerned about one of the boys in her class, John. He was continually involved in behaviors atypical for his age—taking off his clothes, crying for prolonged periods, and physically attacking children—all for no obvious reason. These behaviors and others prompted his teacher to take some action, not only with his parents but also with the principal.

Often prereferral interventions are employed prior to making an official referral for special education testing and services. These interventions are designed to address the students' identified problems and to lessen the likelihood of further, more restrictive actions. Often these interventions are developed, planned, and implemented under the direction of the intervention assistance team. Many states now require prereferral interventions before referrals may be received and processed by school personnel (Bauer & Shea, 1999; Kerr & Nelson, 1998; Yell, 1998).

The actual submission of a referral for a student is generally preceded by several parent–teacher conferences. The conferences help the teacher and parents determine what action ought to be taken. For example, the student's difficulties may be symptomatic of family problems such as a parent's extended illness, marital difficulties, or severe financial challenges. If the parents and teacher continue to be perplexed by a child's behavior, a referral may be initiated. Referrals are generally processed by principals, who review them, consult with parents, and then forward them to a psychologist or assessment team leader. (See nearby Reflect on This feature.)

Once a referral has been appropriately processed and parental or guardian permission for testing and evaluation has been obtained, assessment team members proceed with the tasks of carefully observing and assessing a child's present levels of performance, intellectually, socially, academically, medically, physically, and emotionally

PREREFERRAL INTERVENTION FOR LOUISE

Louise was doing well in Mr. Raphael's fourth-grade classroom until December, when her behavior changed. Louise no longer completed her homework, did not participate in games during recess, and on two occasions, had pinched children who were swinging in "her" swing on the playground. After receiving no responses to notes to Louise's mother regarding concerns about these behaviors, Mr. Raphael telephoned Louise's home. Louise's 19-year-old aunt, who was "helping out with the kids," reported that Louise's mother had entered a hospice program for terminally ill cancer patients. Louise's father was spending a great deal of time at the hospice, but "just couldn't bring himself to take the kids to visit."

Mr. Raphael approached Ms. Turner, the principal, to discuss Louise's behavior. They agreed that an intervention assistance team should be formed. Mr. Raphael recommended that Ms. Holt, the art teacher, with whom Louise had particular rapport, be included in the team. Ms. Turner suggested that Ms. Michael, the school counselor, and Ms. Wang, who had recently worked her classroom through the death of a student's mother in an automobile accident, also be included.

The intervention assistance team met and discussed Louise's behavior. The plan that was formulated included the following:

- Hold weekly meetings for Louise with the school counselor.
- Increase efforts to encourage Louise to participate appropriately during recess, while recognizing her feelings. Louise was to receive a cue such as the following: "I know it's hard to have fun when you're worried about someone. Would you like to talk about how you're feeling before you go join the game?" or "I know you're feeling worried right now, but the rule is to keep your hands to yourself on the playground. How could you ask (child's name) to move to another swing? Could you swing on another one?

- Review materials Ms. Wang had received from the local children's hospital regarding dealing with death, separation, and loss in the classroom.
- Continue communication attempts with the home, recognizing that the family was in crisis and all contacts should be supportive rather than report negative behavior.
- Hold a meeting again in four weeks to evaluate the plan and Louise's behavior.

Source: From *Learner with Emotional and Behavioral Disorders: An Introduction* (p. 192), by A. M. Bauer and T. M. Shea, 1999, Upper Saddle River, NJ: Prentice Hall.

(Bauer & Shea, 1999; Kerr & Nelson, 1998). Their task is to determine whether the child has a behavior disorder and whether he or she qualifies for special education services. Furthermore, the team is responsible for identifying treatment strategies that may be helpful to the parents and teacher.

■ ASSESSMENT FACTORS

focus 7

What three important outcomes are achieved through a functional behavioral assessment?

The severity of behaviors such as those exhibited by the kindergartner John may be examined from several perspectives. First, it is necessary to determine whether any discrepancy exists between his chronological age and the behaviors he consistently displays, so that John's status in relationship to various norms can be scaled. In addition to determining whether John's behaviors are age-appropriate, assessment team members must analyze the frequency and severity of problem behaviors (Mash & Terdal, 1997). New IDEA regulations require assessment team members to conduct a functional behavioral assessment. Its purpose is to identify the functions of a student's behavior in relationship to various school or home settings (Repp & Horner, 1999; Scott & Nelson, 1999; U.S. Department of Education, 1998). Assessment team members conduct observations over a period of days. Through these observations, they hope to find reliable relationships between and among specific problem behaviors, the settings or events that give rise to these behaviors, and the consequences of these behaviors. Several important outcomes are achieved through functional assessment. These include (1) development of a concrete definition of the problem behavior(s); (2) one or more predictions regarding when, and under what

Reflect on This

AMY AND JAY: PROBLEMATIC BEHAVIORS

Amy is a third-grade student who does well academically but who has some serious social deficits. Specifically, her teacher describes her as "impulsive and aggressive." She has been referred to the principal on several occasions for fighting or otherwise being involved in physical altercations with others. Amy has been suspended 4 days during the current school year, continues to have difficulty with peers, and is frequently restrained by adults as a consequence.

Jay is a seventh-grade student who rarely completes his work and whose teacher describes him as being "bizarre and scattered." Jay exhibits an array of disruptive behaviors in the classroom, including loud and (apparently) purposeful flatulence, sticking pencils up his nose, and licking his desk. He has been sent to the counselor several times during the current year but continues to engage in disruptive behaviors.

See Table 8.6 that shows the results of a behavioral assessment for Amy and Jay.

Source: From "Using Functional Behavioral Analysis to Develop Effective Intervention Plans," by T. M. Scott and C. M. Nelson, 1999, *Journal of Positive Behavioral Interventions,* *1*(4), p. 244.

conditions, the problem behavior occurs; and (3) the identification of the function that a behavior serves in meeting the needs of the individual (O'Neill et al.,1997; Scott & Nelson, 1999, p. 244). (See nearby Reflect on This feature.)

Additionally, assessment steps include an evaluation of the influence of John's behaviors on classmates, teachers, and the family. Team members also assess the teacher's contribution to the present problems. John's interactions with individuals in his school setting and his responses to his home environment may significantly

TABLE 8.6   Results of a functional behavioral assessment for Amy and Jay

Event	Problem Pathway	Replacement Pathway	Possible Interventions
Amy			
Setting event	Peer altercation	Peer altercation	Teach problem-solving skills
Antecedent	Verbal insult	Verbal insult	Use prompts and cues
Behavior	Physical aggression	Move away or tell teacher	Teach anger management skills
Consequence	Escape altercation	Escape altercation and access teacher reinforcement	Provide reinforcement for appropriate behavior and response cost for inappropriate behavior
Jay			
Setting event	Classroom setting	Classroom setting	Use group contingency
Antecedent	Peer holds class attention	Peer holds class attention	Use prompts and cues
Behavior	Disruptive sounds and actions	Raise hand and make appropriate comment	Teach student to access peer attention in positive manner
Consequence	Peer attention	Peer attention	Provide praise along with student attention and have peers ignore inappropriate behavior under group contingency

Source: From "Using Functional Behavioral Analysis to Develop Effective Intervention Plans," by T. M. Scott and C. M. Nelson, 1999, *Journal of Positive Behavior Interventions,* *1*(4), p. 249.

influence the recommendations of team members regarding his classification, placement, and eventual treatment.

■ ASSESSMENT TECHNIQUES

A variety of techniques are used to identify children with behavior disorders, all closely paralleling the theoretical framework or philosophical perspective of their evaluators. Usually, an actual diagnosis of the behavioral problems is preceded by a set of screening procedures using functional assessment procedures, teacher and parent interviews, diagnostic academic instruments, behavior checklists, and a variety of sociometric devices (e.g., peer ratings) and teacher rating scales (Mash & Terdal, 1997; Overton, 2000; Venn, 2000). (See nearby Today's Technology feature.)

Typically parents and teachers are asked to respond to a variety of rating-scale items that describe behaviors related to various classifications of behavior disorders. The number of items marked as well as the rating given to each item contribute to the behavior profiles generated from the ratings. (See Table 8.7.) In making their assessments, parents and professionals are asked to consider the child's behavior during the past six months.

A recent development in assessing children and youth with suspected behavior disorders is **strength-based assessment** (Epstein, 1997; Lyons, 1997). In contrast to deficit-oriented instruments, this approach focuses on the individual's strengths. One such instrument is the *Behavior and Emotional Rating Scale* (BERS) (Epstein & Sharma, 1997). Using this instrument, parents, teachers, and other caregivers rate the child or youth's strengths in several important areas, including interpersonal strength, involvement with family, intrapersonal strength, school functioning, and affective or emotional strength. Skilled clinicians use the BERS and other similar approaches to develop strength-centered, rather than deficit-centered, IEPs for children and youth with behavior disorders (see Table 8.8).

Once the screening process has been concluded, specialists and/or consultants—including psychologists, special educators, social workers, and psychiatrists—complete in-depth assessments of the child's academic and social–emotional strengths and weaknesses in various settings, such as the classroom, home, and playground. The assessment team may analyze classroom and playground interactions with peers

Today's Technology

EXPERT SYSTEMS AND ARTIFICIAL INTELLIGENCE FOR ASSESSMENT

Researchers are testing the effectiveness of computers in aiding assessment teams to classify students as having behavior disorders, learning disabilities, or mental retardation. Multidisciplinary team members enter assessment data that they have collected and respond to questions that experts have programmed the computer to ask. The so-called artificial intelligence (AI) that the experts have created examines and processes the data and then makes a reasoned judgment. Additionally, AI systems are also programmed to provide information about interventions that should be applied and the likelihood of their success in treating various learning and behavior problems (Hofmeister & Ferrara, 1986).

Are these expert systems superior to human judgment? This is a difficult question to answer. AI systems represent the best judgment of skilled assessment and intervention specialists. They are much like the expert systems used in medicine that assist physicians in making careful diagnoses and identifying potential treatments.

Imagine having an expert system in your own home for identifying potentially serious behavior problems in your children as well as for ways of dealing with them! You would enter the problem, its duration in time, its average frequency per day, and other salient information, and the computer would provide you with some effective strategies for addressing the problems.

TABLE 8.7		Representative items from the child behavior checklist for ages 4–18		

0	=	Not True (as far as you know)	
1	=	Somewhat or Sometimes True	
2	=	Very True or Often True	

0	1	2	1.	Acts too young for his/her age
0	1	2	5.	Behaves like opposite sex
0	1	2	10.	Can't sit still, restless, or hyperactive
0	1	2	15.	Cruel to animals
0	1	2	20.	Destroys his/her own things
0	1	2	25.	Doesn't get along with other kids
0	1	2	30.	Fears going to school
0	1	2	35.	Feels worthless or inferior
0	1	2	40.	Hears sounds or voices that aren't there (describe):

_____

_____

0	1	2	45.	Nervous, high strung, or tense
0	1	2	50.	Too fearful or anxious

Source: From _Manual for the Child Behavior Checklist/4–18 and 1991 Profile_, by T. M. Achenbach. Burlington: Department of Psychiatry, University of Vermont. Copyright by T. M. Achenbach. Reproduced by permission.

and teachers, using ecological and behavioral analysis techniques (observations with frequency counts of various types of behaviors or interactions); may administer various tests to evaluate personality, achievement, and intellectual factors; and may interview the parents and the child. Additionally, they may observe the child at home and apply an array of other assessment procedures (Mash & Terdal, 1997).

One of the pressing problems for clinicians is the assessment of children and youth who have limited English proficiency and/or are culturally diverse (Council for

TABLE 8.8		Representative items from the Behavioral and Emotional Rating Scale (BERS)		

0	=	Not at all like the child	2	=	Like the child
1	=	Not much like the child	3	=	Very much like the child

0	1	2	3	1.	Demonstrates a sense of belonging to family
0	1	2	3	3.	Accepts a hug
0	1	2	3	6.	Acknowledges painful feelings
0	1	2	3	10.	Uses anger management skills
0	1	2	3	15.	Interacts positively with parents
0	1	2	3	30.	Loses a game gracefully
0	1	2	3	34.	Expresses affection for others
0	1	2	3	39.	Pays attention in class

Source: From the BERS (Behavioral and Emotional Rating Scale), by M. H. Epstein and J. Sharma, 1998, Austin, TX: Pro-Ed, Inc.

TABLE 8.9	Comparison of traditional behavior management and positive behavioral support

Traditional Behavior Management	**Positive Behavioral Support**
Views individual as "the problem"	Views systems, settings, and skill deficiencies as "the problem"
Attempts to "fix" individual	Attempts to "fix" systems, settings, and skills
Extinguishes behavior	Creates new contacts, experiences, relationships, and skills
Sanctions aversives	Sanctions positive approaches
Takes days or weeks to "fix" a single behavior	Takes years to create responsive systems, personalized settings, and appropriate/empowering skills
Implemented by a behavioral specialist often in atypical settings	Implemented by a dynamic and collaborative team using person-centered planning in typical settings
Often resorted to when systems are inflexible	Flourishes when systems are flexible

Source: From "Positive Behavioral Support: Strategies for Teachers," by M. B. Ruef, C. Higgins, B. J. C. Glaeser, and M. Patnode, 1998, *Intervention in School and Clinic, 34*(3), p. 22.

Children with Behavior Disorders, 1989; Overton, 2000; Venn, 2000). Unfortunately, many of these children and youth are disproportionately represented in special education settings for students with behavior disorders. Some progress is being made, particularly as practitioners make use of functional behavioral assessment and related procedures, prereferral interventions, and positive behavioral support. Both prereferral interventions and positive behavioral support (PBS) hold great promise for helping diverse students remain and succeed in less restrictive settings and general education classrooms. Positive behavioral support is a comprehensive research-based approach to producing changes not only for students with behavior disorders, but for all students who present challenging behaviors. Instead of treating the symptom(s) and ignoring the disease, the thrust of PBS is to address all the features and factors that may be related to child or youth's challenging behaviors (see Table 8.9).

FIGURE 8.1

The System of Care Framework

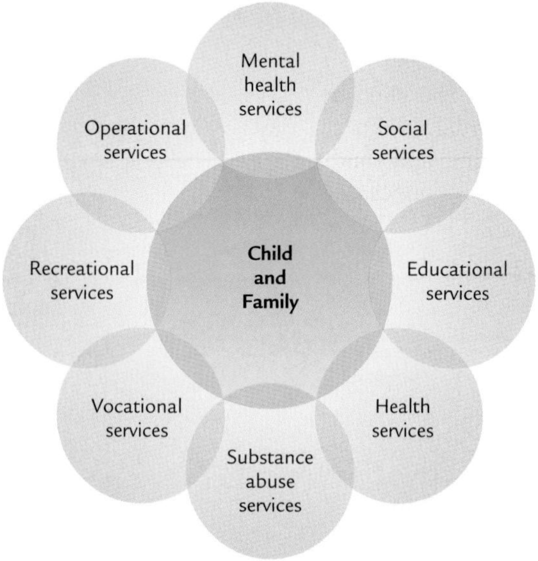

[*Source:* Adapted from *A System of Care for Children and Adolescents with Severe Emotional Disturbances* (p. xxvi), by B. Stroul and R. M. Friedman, 1986 (Rev. ed.), Washington, DC: Georgetown University Child Development Center, National Technical Assistance enter for Children's mental Health. Copyright 1986 by B. Stroul and R. M. Friedman. Adapted by permission.]

Interventions

Historically, most children and youth with behavior disorders received treatments and interventions in isolation from their families, homes, neighborhoods, and communities. This approach was based on the assumption that such students' problems were exclusively of their own making and internal to them. Furthermore, services, if they were delivered, were disconnected. The coordination and orchestration of services were rare or totally absent. Conditions in service delivery systems are changing, however. These changes have been brought about by courageous and vocal advocates who detailed the deplorable plight of these children and youth (Duchnowski & Friedman, 1990; Knitzer, 1982; Peacock Hill Working Group, 1990; Stroul & Friedman, 1986).

Community-based service delivery systems for children and youth with behavior disorders and their families are emerging (Epstein, Kutash, & Duchnowski, 1998;

TABLE 8.10	Core values and guiding principles of systems of care

Core Values	1.	The system of care should be child-centered and family focused, with the needs of the child and family dictating the types and mix of services provided.
	2.	The system of care should be community based, with the locus of services as well as management and decision-making responsibility resting at the community level.
	3.	The system of care should be culturally competent, with agencies, programs, and services that are responsive to the cultural, racial, and ethnic differences of the population they serve.
Guiding Principles	1.	Children with emotional disturbances should have access to a comprehensive array of services that address physical, emotional, social, and educational needs.
	2.	Children with emotional disturbances should receive individualized services in accordance with the unique needs and potentials of each child and guided by an individualized service plan.
	3.	Children with emotional disturbances should receive services within the least restrictive, most normative environment that is clinically appropriate.
	4.	The families and surrogate families of children with emotional disturbances should be full participants in all aspects of the planning and delivery of services.
	5.	Children with emotional disturbances should receive services that are integrated, with linkages between child-serving agencies and programs and mechanisms for planning, developing, and coordinating services.
	6.	Children with emotional disturbances should be provided with case management or similar mechanisms to ensure that multiple services are delivered in a coordinated and therapeutic manner and that they can move through the system of services in accordance with their changing needs.
	7.	Early identification and intervention for children with emotional disturbances should be promoted by the system of care in order to enhance the likelihood of positive outcomes.
	8.	Children with emotional disturbances should be ensured smooth transitions to the adult service system as they reach maturity.
	9.	The rights of children with emotional disturbances should be protected, and effective advocacy efforts for children and youth with emotional disturbances should be promoted.
	10.	Children with emotional disturbances should receive services without regard to race, religion, national origin, sex, physical disability, or other characteristics, and services should be sensitive and responsive to cultural differences and special needs.

[*Source:* From *A System of Care for Children and Adolescents with Severe Emotional Disturbances* (p. xxiv), by B. Stroul and R. M. Friedman, 1986 (Rev. ed.), Washington, DC: Georgetown University Child Development Center, National Technical Assistance Center for Children's Mental Health. Copyright 1986 by B. Stroul and R. M. Friedman. Reprinted by permission.]

Ollendick & Prinz, 1998; U.S. Department of Education, 1999). Educational, medical, and community care providers are beginning to pay greater attention to families and parents of children and youth with behavior disorders and the communities in which they live. This new approach is referred to as community-based systems of care (Lourie, Stroul, & Friedman, 1998) (see Figure 8.1). This approach is based on several core values and guiding principles (see Table 8.10). One of the basic features of the system-of-care concept is that it does not represent a prescribed structure for assembling a network of services and agencies. Rather, it presents a philosophy about the way in which services should be delivered to children and their families (Lourie et al., 1998, p. 6). The child and family become the focus of the delivery system, with vital services surrounding them. These services might include home-based services,

focus 8
What five guiding principles are associated with systems of care?

Reflect on This

PETER: PART ONE

■ INTRODUCTION

Peter was referred for individualized care by the local elementary school basic staffing team. His first-grade teacher reported that he was often aggressive, unable to sit still, and uncompliant. In addition, she complained that his hygiene was very poor and that he often came to school tired. At the time of referral, his parents refused to participate on the school planning team and were openly hostile toward school staff. Despite Peter's above-average intellectual abilities, he was failing in his academic subjects, was disliked by his peers, and spent approximately 70% of his school day in "time-out" situations. Peter's teacher felt that his needs could no longer

be met within a mainstream setting. The initial assessments in school indicated that Peter was a child with significant undercontrolled behaviors occurring approximately every five minutes. Some of his more disruptive and dangerous behaviors included running around the classroom, jumping on the desks, hitting, spitting at the other children and the teacher, bolting out of the school, running into the street, and refusing to work and comply with instructions.

Peter's parents were unable to cope with equally problematic behaviors at home. If they placed any limits on his behavior he would destroy things. They reported that he constantly fought

with his younger brother, wet the bed every night, hit and kicked his parents, and required constant supervision because he was like a revved-up engine and would get into everything. Their approach to child management was quite punitive and involved yelling, spanking, and locking Peter in his room. An assessment of the home environment revealed a highly punitive and restrictive home situation. Peter's mother and father felt inadequate as parents and rarely interacted with their children. They lacked an understanding of developmental norms and expectations for children, expressed only hostile feelings toward their children, and demanded 100% compliance at all

times. Their marital relationship was explosive; during one episode the children were physically hurt and had to be placed in foster care for a short period of time. The child protection agency and school personnel felt that there was considerable potential for further abuse.

Source: Excerpted from J. D. Burchard and R. T. Clarke, "The Role of Individualized Care in a Service Delivery System for Children and Adolescents with Severely Maladjusted Behavior," *Journal of Mental Health Administration, 17*(1), pp. 48–60. Copyright 1990 by *Journal of Mental Health Administration.* Reprinted by permission of Sage Publications, Inc.

---

special class placement, therapeutic foster care, financial assistance, primary health care, outpatient treatment, career education, after-school programs, and family support. An integral part of the systems of care is schoolwide primary prevention. Interventions associated with this kind of prevention include teaching conflict resolution, emotional literacy, and anger management to all students in the school—not just those identified with behavior disorders. This kind of prevention program can avert 75% to 85% of the student adjustment problems (U.S. Department of Education, 1999).

Take a moment now to read about Peter and his family (see Reflect on This, Peter: Part One and Peter: Part Two). This is a solid example of a community-based system of care in which professionals from a variety of social service agencies help not only Peter but also his parents and family.

The Early Childhood Years

The early childhood years are important for all children, particularly those at risk for developing behavior disorders. Recent research suggests that behavior disorders can be prevented (Bryant & Maxwell, 1997; Kauffman, 1999; Landrum & Tankersley, 1999; Walker et al., 1996; Walker et al., 1998; Walker, Stiller, & Golly, 1998). However, as a society, we seem to favor the immense financial, social, and emotional costs of hospitalization, residential placement, incarceration, and other related youth and adult services. Again, the research

Reflect on This

PETER: PART TWO

■ INTERAGENCY CARE AND INTENSIVE FAMILY-BASED SERVICES

Following initial contacts with Peter's family, a multidisciplinary team was formed consisting of the parents and appropriate representatives from mental health, social services, and education. The interdisciplinary team met as needed for three reasons: (1) to plan and coordinate the various services that were provided to the family and child; (2) to provide multiagency ownership with respect to funding services as well as to discuss the utilization of private third-party payments; and (3) to ensure that all efforts were made to provide the least restrictive care prior to any placement of the child into more costly and/or restrictive educational or residential programs.

Peter's parents participated in the interagency team to aid in the identification of services.

Due to the necessity to intervene immediately to prevent the child from being placed in a more restrictive environment, the comprehensive ecological assessment was performed as intervention was being applied. As the evaluation process was progressing, services and plans were revised to meet the individual needs of the family, child, and school. For example, an immediate family concern was the parents' lack of appropriate discipline and child management strategies. A family intervention specialist entered the home within seven hours of the referral and initiated interventions designed to assist the parents in developing alternative approaches. As the parents

progressed through the training, the ongoing individualized assessment revealed that the parents did not know how to play with their children and felt insecure about interacting with them. Interventions were then applied to educate them about child play situations. At all stages of the assessment process, emphasis was placed on the parents' realistically identifying needs and assisting in the development of services to meet those needs. Although the needs identified by the parents did not always coincide with the priorities of the clinician, involving the parents in this manner ensured more commitment from them to participate and empowered them to be effective advocates for themselves and their children. During a two-year period, the family experienced intensive home-

based services, significant respite care, a variety of interventions designed to meet the individual needs of the child such as dry-bed training and conflict resolution training, individual counseling to address alcohol and physical abuse issues, and two summer education programs to assist the children in skill building around safety, social skills, and cooperative play.

Source: Excerpted from J. D. Burchard and R. T. Clarke, "The Role of Individualized Care in a Service Delivery System for Children and Adolescents with Severely Maladjusted Behavior," *Journal of Mental Health Administration, 17*(1), pp. 48–60. Copyright 1990 by *Journal of Mental Health Administration.* Reprinted by permission of Sage Publications, Inc.

---

evidence is clear. Many children would not develop serious behavior disorders if they and their families received early, intensive, community-based and family-centered services. Moreover, the cost of delivering these prevention services would be far less than providing services to these same individuals as teens, young adults, or adults. We are simply unwilling to make investments now that would produce remarkable financial, social, and emotional dividends for us, our children, and our communities (Umansky & Hooper, 1998). Key elements of the prevention process include early identification, family-driven needs assessment, home-based and community-based interventions, and collaborative teaming with an array of educational and community agencies (Kauffman, 1999; McKinney, Montague, & Hocutt, 1998; Umansky & Hooper, 1998).

Interventions for young children with behavior disorders are child-, family-, and home-centered. Often they are directed at lessening the impact of the behavior disorders or even preventing them, as indicated earlier in this section. They are directed at the needs of the children with behavior disorders and their families. Thus, the goals associated with the individualized family service plans (IFSPs) go well beyond the typical educational goals found in IEPs for older children. Interventions for young children with behavior disorders and their families may include respite care, specific parent training, home-centered interventions provided by a family specialist, marital and family therapy, drug therapy, and specialized day care or day treatment. The nature, intensity, and duration of the services or interventions are determined by the

■ EARLY CHILDHOOD YEARS

TIPS FOR THE FAMILY

- Become involved with parent training and other community mental health services.
- Work closely with family support personnel (e.g., social workers, nurses, and parent group volunteers) in developing effective child-management strategies.
- Use the same intervention strategies at home that are used effectively in the preschool setting.
- Establish family routines, schedules, and incentive systems that reward positive behaviors.
- Join advocacy or parent support groups.

TIPS FOR THE PRESCHOOL TEACHER

- Work closely with the support personnel in your preschool (e.g., director, psychologist, social worker, parent trainers, special educators, etc.) to identify effective and realistic strategies.
- Establish clear schedules, class routines, rules, and positive consequences for all children in your classroom.
- Create a learning and social environment that is nurturing and supportive for everyone.
- Teach specific social behaviors (e.g., following directions, greeting other children, sharing toys, using words to express anger, etc.) to all children.
- Do not be reluctant to ask for help from support per-

sonnel. Remember, collaboration is the key.

TIPS FOR PRESCHOOL PERSONNEL

- Use older, socially competent children to assist with readiness skills and social skills training.
- Help others (e.g., teaching assistants, aides, volunteers, etc.) know what to do in managing children with behavior disorders.
- Make every effort to involve the children in all schoolwide activities and special performances.
- Orient and teach the other preschool children about disabling conditions and how they should respond and relate to their peers with behavior problems.
- Collaborate with parents in using the same management systems in your preschool classroom that are used in the home and other specialized settings.

TIPS FOR NEIGHBORS AND FRIENDS

- Become familiar with the things you should do as a neighbor or friend in responding to the positive and negative behaviors of a child with behavior disorders.
- Be patient with parents who are attempting to deal with their child's temper tantrum or other equally challenging behaviors at the grocery store or other like environments.
- Offer parents some time away from their preschooler by watching him or her for a couple of hours.
- Involve the child in your family activities.

- Help parents become aware of advocacy or parent support groups.
- Encourage parents to involve their child in neighborhood and community events (e.g., parades, holiday celebrations, and birthday parties).

■ ELEMENTARY YEARS

TIPS FOR THE FAMILY

- Use the effective management techniques that are being used in your child's classroom in your home environment.
- Help your other children (who are not disturbed) to develop an understanding of behavior disorders.
- Establish rules, routines, and consequences that fit your child's developmental age and interests.
- Take advantage of parent training and support groups that are available in your community.
- Obtain counseling when appropriate for yourself, your other children, and your spouse from a community mental health agency or other public or private source.
- Help your other children and their friends understand the things they can do to assist you in rearing your child with behavior disorders.

TIPS FOR GENERAL EDUCATION CLASSROOM TEACHER

- Provide a structured classroom environment (e.g., clearly stated rules, helpful positive and negative consequences, well-conceived

classroom schedules, and carefully taught classroom routines).
- Teach social skills (e.g., dealing with teasing, accepting criticism, etc.) to all of the children with the aid of members of the teacher assistance team.
- Teach self-management skills (e.g., goal selection, self-monitoring, self-reinforcement, etc.) to all children with the aid of members of the teacher assistance team.
- Use cooperative learning strategies to promote the learning of all children and to develop positive relationships among students.
- Do not be reluctant to ask for help from members of your teacher assistance team or the child's parents.

TIPS FOR SCHOOL PERSONNEL

- Use same-age or cross-age peers to provide tutoring, coaching, and other kinds of assistance in developing the academic and social skills of children with behavior disorders.
- Develop a schoolwide management program that reinforces individual and group accomplishments.
- Work closely with the teacher assistance team to create a school environment that is positive and caring.
- Use collaborative problem-solving techniques in dealing with difficult or persistent behavior problems.
- Help all children in the school develop an understanding of how they

should respond to students with behavior problems.

TIPS FOR NEIGHBORS AND FRIENDS

- Involve the child with behavior problems in appropriate after-school activities (e.g., clubs, specialized tutoring, recreational events, etc.).
- Invite the child to spend time with your family in appropriate recreational events (e.g., swimming, hiking, etc.).
- Teach other children (without behavior problems) how to ignore or support certain behaviors that may occur.
- Catch the child being good rather than looking for "bad" behaviors.
- As a youth leader, coach, or recreational specialist, get to know each child with behavior disorders well so that you can respond with confidence in directing his or her activities.

■ SECONDARY AND TRANSITION YEARS

TIPS FOR THE FAMILY

- Continue your efforts to focus on the positive behaviors of your child with behavior disorders.
- Assist your child in selecting appropriate postsecondary training, education, and/or employment.
- Give yourself a regular break from the tedium of being a parent, and enjoy a recreational activity that is totally enjoyable for you.
- Ask for help from community mental health services, clergy, or a close friend when you are feeling overwhelmed or stressed.

- Consult regularly with treatment personnel to monitor progress and to obtain ideas for maintaining the behavioral gains made by your child.
- Continue your involvement in advocacy and parent support groups.

TIPS FOR GENERAL EDUCATION CLASSROOM TEACHER

- Create positive relationships within your classroom with cooperative learning teams and group-oriented assignments.
- Use all students in creating standards for conduct as well as consequences for positive and negative behaviors.
- Focus your efforts on developing a positive relationship with the student with behavior disorders by greeting him or her regularly to your class, informally talking with him or her at appropriate times, attending to improvements in his or her performance, and becoming aware of his or her interests.
- Work closely with the members of the teacher assistance team to be aware of teacher behaviors that may adversely or positively affect the student's performance.
- Realize that changes in behavior often occur very gradually, with periods of regression and sometimes tumult.

TIPS FOR SCHOOL PERSONNEL

- Create a school climate that is positive and supportive.
- Provide students with an understanding of their roles and responsibilities

in responding to peers who are disabled.
- Use peers in providing social skills training, job coaching, and academic tutoring, and the like.
- Use members of the teacher assistance team to help you deal with crisis situations and to provide other supportive therapies and interventions.
- Be sure schoolwide procedures are in place for dealing quickly and efficiently with particularly difficult behaviors.

TIPS FOR NEIGHBORS, FRIENDS, AND POTENTIAL EMPLOYERS

- If you have some expertise in a content area (e.g., math, English, history, etc.), offer to provide regular assistance with homework or other related school assignments for students with behavior disorders.
- Provide opportunities for students with behavior disorders to be employed in your business.
- Give parents an occasional reprieve by inviting the youth to join your family for a cook-out, video night, or other family-oriented activities.
- Encourage other children (who are not disordered) to volunteer as peer partners, job coaches, and social skills trainers.
- Do not allow others in your presence to tease, harass, or ridicule a youth with behavior disorders.

■ ADULT YEARS

TIPS FOR THE FAMILY

- Continue to build on efforts to develop appro-

priate independence and interdependence.
- Maintain contact with appropriate medical personnel, particularly if the individual is on some form of medication for his or her condition.
- Make use of appropriate adult service agencies that are required by law to assist with your child's employment, housing, and recreation.
- Prepare your other children or other caregivers as appropriate to assume the responsibilities that you may be unable to assume over time.

TIPS FOR NEIGHBORS, FRIENDS, AND EMPLOYERS

- Be willing to make sensible and reasonable adjustments in the work environments.
- Be aware of adjustments that may need to take place with new medications or treatment regimens.
- Get to know the individual as a person—his or her likes, heroes or heroines, and leisure activities.
- Be willing to involve the individual in appropriate holiday and special occasion, events such as birthdays, athletic activities, and other social gatherings.
- Be aware of what might be irritating or uncomfortable to the individual.
- Make yourself available to communicate with others who may be responsible for the individual's well-being—a job coach, an independent living specialist, and others.

needs of the families and the speed with which they develop new skills and coping strategies (Stoneman & Manders, 1998; Umansky, 1998; Umansky & Hooper, 1998). The interventions are delivered in multiple contexts—the places where children, family members, and others play, work, learn, and grow (Hester & Kaiser, 1998; Quinn & Rutherford, 1998).

Often the interventions for young children with behavior disorders are directed at beginning communication skills; appropriate social interaction with siblings, parents, and peers; beginning social skills; and responding effectively to developmentally appropriate tasks (Umansky, 1998). Also, with the press for inclusive or integrated settings, family intervention and transition specialists will need to pay greater attention to preparing young children for successful participation in less restrictive environments (Hester & Kaiser, 1998; Umansky & Hooper, 1998).

The Elementary School Years

Elementary children with behavior disorders often present overlapping behavioral problems. Think about Eric, Nick, and Amy, who were highlighted at the beginning of this chapter. Each presented behavioral problems related to accepting consequences, interacting successfully with others, controlling themselves in various school and family situations, and expressing strong feelings. These behaviors become the focus of intervention efforts. With the assistance of parents, IEP team members strive to construct a complete picture of each child, determining his or her present levels of intellectual, social, emotional, and academic performance and the contexts that give rise to these behaviors. Also, these identified levels of performance become the basis for identifying important goals and objectives for the child's IEP.

A new instrument, the *Behavioral Objective Sequence (BOS)* (Braaten, 1998), provides teachers and clinicians with a means for determining developmentally appropriate long-term goals and objectives for children and youth with behavior disorders. The BOS helps intervention personnel assess students' behavioral competencies in six areas: adaptive, self-management, communication, interpersonal, task, and personal behaviors (see Table 8.11). This kind of instrument is also very helpful to teachers, parents, and others who are responsible for developing high-quality IEPs.

Typically, programs for children with behavior disorders focus on developing appropriate academic skills, increasing self-awareness, building self-esteem, and acquiring age-appropriate self-control. Children need these skills and behaviors to succeed in their classrooms, homes, and communities. In the past, many programs for children with behavior disorders were restrictive, controlling, and punitive in nature (Knitzer et al., 1990). More than teaching new behaviors, these programs focused on controlling the behaviors of children and youth. These programs employed the **curriculum of control** (Knitzer et al., 1990) or the *curriculum of noninstruction* (Shores & Wehby, 1999, p. 196). Rather than developing replacement behaviors or new behaviors, children and youth in many of these programs languished or regressed (Knitzer, 1982; Knitzer et al., 1990). (See Reflect on This, Peter: Part Three.)

New systems of care for children and youth with behavior disorders have emerged (Center for Effective Collaboration and Practice, 1999). These systems deliver wraparound services to children and youth with behavior disorders and their families. As is implied by the word *wraparound,* children, youth, and their families receive the support that they need to solve the problems and to address the conditions in the family, home, and school that give rise to the behavior disorders. Ser-

■CURRICULUM OF CONTROL. Classroom routine, structures, and instructional strategies focused on controlling children and youth rather than teaching them new, success-related social and academic behaviors.

TABLE 8.11 Representative long-term goals and behavioral objectives from the Behavioral Objective Sequence (BOS)

BOS Subscale Areas	Potential Long-Term Goal	Representative Objectives
Adaptive behaviors	The student will attend school regularly. The student will participate in routine school activities.	The student will remember routine daily schedule without reminders. The student will comply with written bus-riding rules. The student will remain in school for its duration daily.
Self-management behaviors	The student will attempt structured new experiences and seek success. The student will differentiate between intentional and unintentional acts and accept responsibility for own behaviors. The student will accept and utilize adult help and directions.	The student will respond when angry without abuse of or damage to property. The student will respond when angry without verbal threats of intent to harm someone, peer or adult
Communication behaviors	The student will use verbal language to get adults to respond to personal needs and wishes. The student will use words and behaviors to affect others in positive and appropriate ways.	The student will respond appropriately with words to greetings and farewells. The student will verbally recall group rules and/or give reasons for rules, when requested by an adult.
Interpersonal behaviors	The student will participate in selected adult-structured activities with other students. The student will demonstrate knowledge of and compliance with basic social rules for constructive interactions.	The student will respond appropriately, when requested, to come to an adult in non-crisis situations. The student will play simple competitive games according to rules.
Task behaviors	The student will attempt assigned individualized tasks. The student will accept and seek adult assistance. The student will minimally participate in group tasks.	The student will refrain from inappropriate behavior when asked by an adult to correct errors on academic tasks. The student will work independently for 10 to 20 minutes on assigned tasks.
Personal behaviors	The student will attend to and accept input/feedback from an adult. The student will demonstrate a developing trust with selected adults by responding appropriately to help that is offered. The student will accurately label personal feelings to an adult.	The student will accept feedback from an adult about his/her feelings. The student will remain seated in appropriate place during counseling sessions.

Source: Reprinted with permission from the *Behavioral Objective Sequence (BOS)* by S. Braaten (1998), Champaign, IL: Research Press.

Reflect on This

PETER: PART THREE

■ INTENSIVE SCHOOL-BASED SERVICES

Due to pervasive, cross-setting difficulties, a school-based planning team was established consisting of the classroom teacher, a case worker from social services, a special educator, the parents, a school-based integration specialist, and the school nurse. This team met for one hour each week to coordinate a variety of school programs aimed at helping Peter adjust and improve academic skills and to track his progress in school. Again, all services used were child-centered and designed to meet Peter's needs in the various school environments.

The integration specialist assigned to Peter's planning team provided a variety of services including teacher training in behavior management; behavioral analysis of Peter's behaviors in school; technical assistance to the planning team in designing, implementing, and monitoring treatment services within the school; and direct counseling to Peter. The direct counseling Peter received revolved around structured programs to help him gain control of his impulses and manage his own behavior. These programs were supplemented by the school counselor and the classroom teacher through training in social skills and cooperative play behaviors carried out with the entire class. In-school counseling service was provided an average of four times a week.

In addition to individual and group counseling, Peter engaged in a behavior token program with the whole class focusing on improving time on task and work achievement. More structured restitution and time-out procedures were implemented for aggressive behaviors. Over time it was felt that Peter would benefit from more structured positive interactions with other children and the teacher. For this reason, the classroom teacher engaged in scheduled reinforcement of Peter. He was instructed to use a soft voice, work on his assigned task cooperatively, and wait his turn. This reinforcement occurred every five minutes and was decreased by the end of the year to once every half hour.

■ SUMMARY

To date, Peter and his family have received a host of intensive home and school-based treatment services. They have participated in 2½ years of service planning and have been, at one point or another, involved in the mental health, social service, educational, and recreational systems of care. The approach of all these services emphasized individual care and incorporated program tracking of services and adjustment. While Peter and his family continue to access services, their needs are less intensive than they were two years ago. His parents are better able to manage his behavior and spend more time interacting with him in positive activities. In addition, both parents are full participants on the school planning team. At present, Peter requires little one-on-one attention, although an intervention is still being provided to foster additional social skills. A major component of Peter's plan at this point in time involves tracking progress and assessing long-term changes. Peter's parents understand that additional services will be provided if they are necessary.

Source: Excerpted from J. D. Burchard and R. T. Clarke, "The Role of Individualized Care in a Service Delivery System for Children and Adolescents with Severely Maladjusted Behavior," *Journal of Mental Health Administration,* 17(1), pp. 48–60. Copyright 1990 by *Journal of Mental Health Administration.* Reprinted by permission of Sage Publications, Inc.

---

vices may include in-home, child-management training; employment assistance; and family therapy—whatever is needed to help families become successful. The essential features of these systems and related programs are as follows:

- *The use of clinicians or other student support providers in the schools.* These professionals work with students, their families, and all members of the school community, including teachers and administrators.
- *The use of school-based and school-focused wraparound services to support learning and transition.*
- *The use of school-based case management.* Case managers help determine needs; they help identify goals, resources, and activities; they link children and families to other services; they monitor services to ensure that they are delivered appropriately; and they advocate for change when necessary.
- *The provision of schoolwide prevention and early intervention programs.* Prevention helps those students with or at risk of developing emotional and behavior

problems to learn the skills and behaviors that help in following school rules and enjoying positive academic and social outcomes. Early intervention allows schools to provide students with the support and training they need to be more successful in managing their behavior.

- *The creation of "centers" within the school.* These centers provide support to children and youth with emotional and behavior needs and their families. Students in the centers interact with caring staff members who can help students and their families connect with the entire system of care to help in meeting their needs.

- *The use of family liaisons or advocates.* These people strengthen the role and empowerment of family members in their children's education and care. All three sites studied have harnessed the power that involving family members as equal partners brings to their comprehensive programs. (Center for Effective Collaboration and Practice, 1999, pp. 6–7)

At the heart of many new programs is positive behavioral support (PBS). Instead of trying to eliminate or control behaviors, teachers, parents, and clinicians seek to understand the purposes behind children's behaviors. As highlighted in the assessment section of this chapter, professionals use functional behavioral assessment to determine the patterns and functions of certain behaviors. Once these patterns and functions are well understood, teachers and others help children develop positive approaches to achieving their goals. They are also taught how to deal with their thoughts and feelings in positive ways (Kaplan, 2000). The development of self-control, academic competence, and social skills takes time and great effort.

Children who exhibit moderate to severe behavior disorders may be served in special classes, located in various kinds of facilities. In some school systems, special classes are found in elementary schools. They may be grouped in small clusters of two to three classes in selected buildings. Other special classes may be found within hospital units, special schools, residential programs, and specialized treatment facilities.

Special classes for children with moderate to severe disorders have certain basic characteristics. The first is a high degree of structure; in other words, rules are clear and consistently enforced. The second feature is teacher monitoring of student performance; students receive frequent feedback and reinforcement based on their academic and social behaviors. Often point systems or token economies are used, although some concerns have been raised about them. These systems provide students with a specific number of points or tokens when they maintain certain behaviors or achieve certain goals. The points can be exchanged for various rewards (Schmid & Evans, 1998), such as things to eat; school supplies such as pencils, notebooks, or erasers; or activities that students enjoy. Further-

Over 50% of adolescents with behavior disorders drop out of high school.

FIGURE 8.2   Point card for IEP goals

Name: _Mike_   **Date:** _26 November_

1. My IEP goal today is: *Raising my hand to get teacher help, to answer questions, or to participate in class discussions.*

Goal "Positives"	Goal "Negative"
7H/L ///	//

Percent "Positives"
8/10 = 80%

Points Earned on IEP Goal Today __8__

2. Returned Daily Home Note: Yes __✓__   No _____   Points Earned on Daily Home Note __10__

3. Bus Report: Poor __✓__   Good _____   Excellent _____   Points Earned on Bus Report __3__

POSITIVE CLASSROOM BEHAVIORS	APPROPRIATE LOCATION	ON TASK, LISTENED, WORKED CONSISTENTLY, ETC.	APPROPRIATE LANGUAGE	RESPECTFUL OF OTHERS AND THEIR THINGS	APPROPRIATE SOCIAL SKILLS
Time					
8:30 to 9:00	2	0	2	2	0
9:00 to 10:00	2	2	2	2	2
11:00 to 12:00	2	0	2	2	0
12:00 to 1:00	2	2	2	2	0
1:00 to 2:00	2	0	2	2	0
2:00 to 3:00	2	2	2	2	0
3:00 to 3:30	2	2	2	2	0
Points Earned	14	8	14	14	2

Total Positive Classroom Points Earned Today	52
Total Points Earned Today	73
Total Points Spent Today	−10
Total Points Banked Today	63

more, all special class members are well informed about behavioral expectations (see Figure 8.2).

In addition to behaviorally oriented interventions, students may also receive individual counseling or group and family therapy (Erickson, 1998; Nelson-Wicks & Israel, 2000). Many children with behavior disorders may take some form of medication (Brown & Sawyer, 1998; Wicks-Nelson & Israel, 2000).

The Adolescent Years

Individually and collectively, adolescents with behavior problems pose significant challenges for parents, teachers, and other care providers. These problems include violent exchanges with parents and others, bullying, fighting, withdrawal, substance abuse, and other difficult behaviors. In the past, interventions and programs for adolescents with behavior disorders, like those created for elementary children, were often punitive, controlling, and negative (Wehby, Symons, & Canale, 1998). As indicated in the previous section, the *curriculum of control* or the *curriculum of noninstruction* predominated (Knitzer et al., 1990; Shores & Wehby, 1999).

Fortunately, perspectives are changing. Professionals in education, medicine, social work, and mental health are developing systems of care (see Figure 8.1 on page 254) (Hodges, Nesman, & Hernandez. 1999). These systems of care are characterized by *family–provider* collaboration (Osher et al., 1999; Simpson, Koroloff, Friesen, & Gac, 1999). Ideally, the care is comprehensive, family-centered, and diversity-sensitive. In these systems, the knowledge and views of parents and family members are taken seriously. They assist with the designing, shaping, and assessment of intervention programs. If a family needs parent training, family therapy, and employment assistance, the agencies and school work together to provide these needed services (Woodruff et al., 1999). If the youth needs services beyond those typically delivered in a school, they are delivered.

Another approach that is beginning to pick up momentum is **individualized care (IC)** (Burchard & Clarke, 1990). IC is integrally linked to the **wraparound approach (WRAP)** (Burns & Goldman, 1999; Eber, 1996; U.S. Department of Education, 1999). WRAP centers on improving the outcomes for children and adolescents with behavior disorders through coordinated, flexible approaches to integrated, family-centered care. Rather than providing services to students only in school settings or at a mental health agency, services are delivered to children and adolescents, their

■ INDIVIDUALIZED CARE (IC). Improving the outcomes for children and adolescents with behavior disorders through coordinated, flexible approaches to integrated, family-centered care. Services are delivered to children and adolescents, their parents, and families where needed, frequently in their homes.

■ WRAPAROUND APPROACH (WRAP). Care that provides comprehensive services to youth and their families, addressing individual and family needs through flexible approaches coordinated and orchestrated through a team of caring professionals and paraprofessionals.

These young people are working together on a program to prevent gang violence. Programs like Gang Peace are having success in developing social skills training, anger control instruction, and conflict resolution to replace aggression and violence among adolescence.

TABLE 8.12	Risk factors for youth gang membership

Domain	Risk Factors	
Community	■ Social disorganization, including poverty and residential mobility ■ Underclass communities ■ Presence of gangs in the neighborhood ■ Availability of drugs in the neighborhood ■ Availability of firearms	■ Barriers to and lack of social and economic opportunities ■ Lack of social capital ■ Cultural norms supporting gang behavior ■ Feeling unsafe in neighborhood; high crime ■ Conflict with social control institutions
Family	■ Family disorganization, including broken homes and parental drug/alcohol abuse ■ Troubled families, including incest, family violence, and drug addiction ■ Family members in a gang ■ Lack of adult male role models	■ Lack of parental role models ■ Low socioeconomic status ■ Extreme economic deprivation, family management problems, parents with violent attitudes, sibling antisocial behavior
School	■ Academic failure ■ Low educational aspirations, especially among females ■ Negative labeling by teachers ■ Trouble at school ■ Few teacher role models	■ Educational frustration ■ Low commitment to school, low school attachment, high levels of antisocial behavior in school, low achievement test scores, and identification as being learning disabled
Peer Group	■ High commitment to delinquent peers ■ Low commitment to positive peers ■ Street socialization ■ Gang members in class	■ Friends who use drugs or who are gang members ■ Friends who are drug distributors ■ Interaction with delinquent peers
Individual	■ Prior delinquency ■ Deviant attitudes ■ Street smartness; toughness ■ Defiant and individualistic character ■ Fatalistic view of the world ■ Aggression ■ Proclivity for excitement and trouble ■ *Locura* (acting in a daring, courageous, and especially crazy fashion in the face of adversity) ■ Higher levels of normlessness in the context of family, peer group, and school ■ Social disabilities	■ Illegal gun ownership ■ Early or precocious sexual activity, especially among females ■ Alcohol and drug use ■ Drug trafficking ■ Desire for group rewards such as status, identity, self-esteem, companionship, and protection ■ Problem behaviors, hyperactivity, externalizing behaviors, drinking, lack of refusal skills, and early sexual activity ■ Victimization

Source: Adapted from "Youth Gangs: An Overview," by J. C. Howell, 1998, *Juvenile Justice Bulletin,* August, pp. 1–19.

parents, and families where they are needed, frequently in their homes. The case study of Peter provides powerful examples of IC and WRAP in action.

Adolescents who are chronically delinquent or are found guilty of felony offenses (e.g., physical assault, armed robbery) present considerable challenges for school and clinical personnel. Additionally, the proliferation of gangs in many communities poses serious problems for schools, teachers, community members, and gang members themselves (U.S. Department of Justice, 1999b). As natural gathering places for gang members, schools provide many opportunities for income through extortion, drug sales, and other illegal activities. With a lack of role models and the decline of family structure and support, young people seek power, friendship, fame, and reputation among their peers through gang membership (Evans & Taylor, 1995; Huff, 1998; Mathews, 1996). Gangs provide these young people with a sense of family, personal identity, and affiliation. All too often, violence and death become everyday realities for gang members, their families, and other innocent bystanders (Howell, 1998; U.S. Department of Justice, 1999b) (See Table 8.12).

Programs directed at preventing and treating gang violence are emerging. Generally, these programs center on group support systems, specific competence training, and the development of healthy relationships with caring adults and other authority figures. Young people are specifically taught how to deal with substance abuse, challenging interpersonal relationships, depression, and situations that may produce uncontrolled anger and violence. Also, these young people are taught how to assess provocations that lead to aggression, how to analyze and change their self-statements (what they actually say to themselves) in response to these provocations, and how to deal with provocations in healthy and appropriate ways (Glick & Goldstein, 1999).

One exemplary program for adolescents who are severely aggressive and otherwise very difficult to manage is the *aggression replacement training (ART) program* (Goldstein & Glick, 1999). This program emphasizes social skills training, anger control, self-management, and moral education. Adolescents involved in this multi-element program learn how to respond to anger appropriately, avoid fights, deal with group pressure, and express affection, as well as other pertinent social skills. Additionally, they learn to think about their behavior and to engage in self-talk, a self-instructional strategy to control verbally or physically aggressive behaviors. In this brief example of self-talk, the individual talks himself through a situation that, in the past, may have caused him to behave very aggressively: "I am beginning to get very angry. I feel like punchin' this guy, but I need to calm down. If I lose it now, I will get myself in big, _____ trouble. I need to move away from this _____ situation—now!"

The third component of the ART program, moral development, gives adolescents experiences that are directed at improving their reasoning and problem-solving skills as well as other related behaviors. Groups are formed and directed by trained leaders who carefully expose adolescents to moral dilemmas and conflicts. Through these discussions and related activities, adolescents develop new ways of thinking and reasoning about moral conflicts and learn how it feels to be someone who has been injured, abused, stolen from, or otherwise hurt. Moreover, adolescents learn how to behave in new, socially appropriate ways when confronted with moral dilemmas.

FULL INCLUSION. The delivery of appropriate, specialized services to children or adolescents with behavior disorders or other disabilities in general education settings. These services are usually directed at improving students' social skills, developing satisfactory relationships with peers and teachers, building targeted academic skills, and improving the attitudes of nondisabled peers.

Inclusive Education

Few issues in recent years have received as much attention in the professional literature as inclusion, particularly the full inclusion of students with behavior disorders (Braaten et al., 1988; Bullock & Gable, 1994; Fuchs & Fuchs, 1994; Kauffman & Lloyd, 1995; Lewis, Chard, & Scott, 1994; MacMillan, Gresham, & Forness, 1996). The term **full inclusion** is generally defined as the delivery of appropriate, specialized services to children or adolescents with behavior disorders or other disabilities in general education settings. These services are usually directed at

focus

What five factors should be considered in placing a child or youth with behavior disorders in general education settings and related classes?

Snapshot

Jane

■ STUDENTS AS SOLUTIONS

Jane, a 12-year-old student, started doing strange things at school. The principal, teacher, and resource teacher agreed to call in the "behavior specialists" to design a "compliance training" program.

For a short while Jane stopped being a nuisance and life went on, until she suddenly attacked a schoolmate in the schoolyard, knocking the girl to the ground and touching her breasts and genital area. She had to be physically pulled away. The "attack" frightened the other child involved but did not seriously injure her.

The principal immediately phoned both sets of parents and to his surprise, the mother of the student who was "attacked" did not become hysterical; she realized her daughter was not hurt. Jane's entire family was called in for a serious talk with the principal.

Two months later these responses were gathered from her classroom peers:

Our SWAT (Students Who Are Together) team has a weekly meeting with Mrs. Gill (the resource teacher). Jane comes to every meeting. At the first meeting we told Jane we wanted to help and be her friends. We told her that no matter what she did, we'd be there for her. We apologized for not being around enough before. Sarah invited her to a party and Sue went to visit her at home. Danny, Rose, and Linda call her a lot. Jane's happy now because she's got the SWAT team and because she has friends. We're making new friends, too. Jane's whole attitude has changed and she hasn't hit or attacked anyone since we talked to her. (p. 191)

Jane has changed since her first meeting with the SWAT team. These past couple of weeks she's really opened up. She now feels that she belongs, and she knows we are her friends. She hasn't been acting up or annoying us like she used to. Instead she has been cheery and always talks to us.

She was just recently invited to her first party with boys. She really enjoyed it. I think that Jane has really changed. She used to be so quiet and always kept to herself. Now she is more outgoing and talkative. Like any teenager, Jane needs friends and a social life. (p. 192)

Before SWAT I found Jane moody, babyish, she swore, she spat, and once in a while she would pee in her pants. When SWAT started helping, Jane was overjoyed. Jane would always say that she didn't care about anyone or school. About four days after saying how she didn't care about school she got suspended because she touched a kid in a private spot.

Because of SWAT she is really changing now. I called her at home and she talked to me for 10 minutes on the phone. Jane is trying to act like us. She's becoming like us! (p. 192)

Krystyne Banakiewiczm

A POEM ABOUT JANE
Jane came three years ago
No one did she really know
We tried to teach her wrong
    from right
Tried to make her days sunny
    and bright
Still she walked around so sad
And we knew that we had
To make her feel like one of us
And over her we'd all fuss
Now Jane has many good
    friends
And I hope "our" friendship
    never ends.

Tammi Washnuk

Source: From "Supports for Addressing Severe Maladaptive Behavior" by M. Forest and J. Pearpoint, 1990, *Support Networks for Inclusive Schooling: Interdependent Integrated Education,* W. Stainback and S. Stainback (Eds.), Baltimore: Paul H. Brookes Publishing Company. Copyright 1990 by Paul H. Brookes Publishing Company. Reprinted with permission.

Jack Pearpoint and Marsha Forest are the Directors and Founders of the Centre for Integrated Education and Community and Inclusion Press. For information, write 24 Thome Crescent, Toronto, Ontario, Canada M6H 255, 416-658-5363.

improving students' social skills, developing satisfactory relationships with peers and teachers, building targeted academic skills, and improving attitudes of nondisabled peers (Cheney & Barringer, 1999; Snell, 1990; Stainback & Stainback, 1990).

Another aspect of the full inclusion movement is the recommendation by some professionals that the present delivery systems or variety of placement options be eliminated (Stainback & Stainback, 1992). They would be replaced by a model in which all students, regardless of disabling condition, would be educated in their neighborhood schools. These schools would serve all students with disabilities, including those with behavior disorders; thus special schools, special classes, and other placements associated with the typical continuum of placements would no longer be available. Because of this movement and other factors, many services that were once available for students with behavior disorders have been diminished or eliminated (Webber & Scheuermann, 1997).

Critics of this movement have expressed strong concerns about its short- and long-term impact on children and adolescents with behavior disorders and their families. They argue that little research supports the elimination of the current placement and service delivery continuum (MacMillan et al., 1996). They believe that the current continuum provides a range of options and specialized services in keeping with the unique needs of many students with behavior disorders and their families. Additionally, they feel that many general education teachers and related personnel are not adequately prepared to respond to the needs of children and adolescents with behavior disorders (Braaten et al., 1988; Fuchs & Fuchs, 1994; Kauffman, 1993; Kauffman & Lloyd, 1995; MacMillan et al., 1996; Walker & Bullis, 1990).

Recent court decisions and the 1997 Amendments to the Individuals with Disabilities Act (IDEA) are informative (Yell, 1998). "The courts have indicated that there are two primary grounds for removing a student from the general education classroom: if the child does not benefit educationally (considering both academic and nonacademic benefits), and if the student disrupts the learning environment or adversely affects the education of other students" (Yell, 1995, p. 188). If a student under consideration poses no significant management problems for the teacher, does not interfere with the safety or learning of other classmates, and can benefit from a parallel or similar curriculum given to other students in general classroom settings, he or she will be placed in these environments (Yell, 1998). (See the nearby Reflect onThis feature.)

The 1997 Amendments to IDEA authorize school personnel to order a change in placement to an appropriate interim alternative educational setting, another setting, or suspension, for not more than 10 school days, if the student carries a weapon to school or knowingly possesses or uses illegal drugs or sells or solicits the sale of a controlled substance while at school. During the 10 days the school must conduct functional behavior assessment, if it has not already done so, and implement a behavioral intervention plan through the IEP process. Any alternative setting for a student must be determined by the IEP team. Additionally, a hearing officer may order a change in placement to an appropriate interim alternative educational setting for not more than 45 days, if the hearing officer determines that the current placement is substantially likely to result in injury to the child or others. In making the decision, the hearing officer must consider whether the school has made reasonable efforts to minimize risks of harm in the current placement and that the interim placement meets the student's needs as described in the IEP.

Interestingly, most students with behavior disorders are served in settings separated from general education classrooms (Knitzer et al., 1990; Stephens & Lakin, 1995; U.S. Department of Education, 2000a). In fact, students with behavior disorders are far more likely to be served in special schools and separate facilities than any other group of students with disabilities. Additionally, a fifth of all students served in special day schools and half of all students served in residential facilities are children and youth with behavior disorders (Koyangi & Gaines, 1993; Stephens & Lakin, 1995).

Inclusion of students with behavior disorders in general education settings should be determined ultimately by what the child or adolescent with behavior dis-

Reflect on This

WHAT IS A FUNCTIONAL BEHAVIORAL ASSESSMENT?

Maurice, a 10-year-old who finds multiplication of fractions difficult, becomes frustrated and throws tantrums when asked to complete worksheets requiring him to multiply fractions.

Kerry, a 12-year-old who has problems paying attention, is so overstimulated by what she sees out of the window and hears in the nearby reading, she slams her text shut and loudly declares that she cannot work.

Functional behavioral assessment is an approach that incorporates a variety of techniques and strategies to diagnose the causes and to identify likely interventions intended to address the problem behaviors [identified in Maurice and Kerry]. In other words, functional behavioral assessment looks beyond the overt topography of the behavior, and focuses instead upon identifying biological, social, affective, and environmental factors that initiate, sustain, or end the behavior in question. This approach is important because it leads the observer beyond the "symptom" (the behavior) to the student's underlying motivation to escape, "avoid," or "get" something (which is, to the functional analyst, the root of all behavior). Research and experience have demonstrated that behavior intervention plans stemming from the knowledge of why a student misbehaves (i.e., based on a functional behavioral assessment) are extremely useful in addressing a wide range of problems.

The functions of behavior are not usually considered inappropriate. Rather, it is the behavior itself that is judged appropriate or inappropriate. For example, getting high grades and acting out may serve the same function (i.e., getting attention from adults), yet the behaviors that lead to good grades are judged to be more appropriate than those that make up acting-out behavior. For example, if the IEP team determines through a functional behavioral assessment that a student is seeking attention by acting out, they can develop a plan to teach the student more appropriate ways to gain attention, thereby filling the student's need for attention with an alternative behavior that serves the same function as the inappropriate behavior.

By incorporating functional behavioral assessment into the IEP process, team members can develop a plan that teaches and supports replacement behaviors, which serve the same function as the problem behavior itself (e.g., teaching Maurice to calmly tell the teacher when he feels frustrated, and to ask for assistance when he finds a task too difficult to accomplish). At the same time, strategies may be developed to decrease or even eliminate opportunities for the student to engage in behavior that hinders positive academic outcomes (e.g., making sure that Maurice's assignments are at his instructional level).

Source: From *Addressing Student Problem Behavior: An IEP Team's Introduction to Functional Behavioral Assessment and Behavior Intervention Plans, Why a Functional Assessment of Behavior is Necessary,* by the Center for Effective Collaboration and Practice, 1998, Washington, DC: Center for Effective for Collaboration and Practice, American Institutes for Research.

orders genuinely needs (Kauffman & Smucker, 1995; Keenan, 1997). These needs are established through the thoughtful deliberations of parents, professionals, and, as appropriate, the child or adolescent, through the IEP process. This process and resultant outcomes create the basis for determining the services and supports required to address the child or adolescent's needs, both present and anticipated. If the identified services and supports can be delivered with appropriate intensity and skill in the general education environment without adversely affecting the learning and safety of other students, placement in this environment should occur. However, if the needs of the student cannot be successfully met in the general education setting, other placement alternatives should be explored and selected. Recent studies suggest that the inclusion of students with behavior disorders is greatly enhanced when general education school personnel receive excellent training; timely, intensive consultation; and appropriate in-class supports (Gibb et al., 1997; Gibb et al., 1999; Shapiro et al., 1999).

Promising Practices

In summary, the National Information Center for Children and Youth with Disabilities (NICHCY) has developed a list of promising practices for chronic behavior problems in children and youth. As you review this list, think about Eric, Nick, and Amy, whom you met at the beginning of this chapter, as well as your own experiences with children and youth with behavior disorders. Would these practices benefit our schools and communities?

focus 10

What are 13 promising practices for dealing with challenging behavior in children and youth?

1. Assessment of the student's behavior must be linked with interventions that follow the student through whatever placements the student has.
2. Multiple interventions are necessary for improving the behavior of most students. Any positive effect of a single strategy, especially when the intervention is short-term, is likely to be temporary. Just as behavior problems and risk factors come in packages, so too should interventions.
3. To produce lasting effects, interventions must address not only the behavior that led to disciplinary action but a constellation of related behaviors and contributing factors.
4. Interventions must be sustained and include specific plans for promoting maintenance over time and generalization across settings. Focusing on the student's behavior while placed in any short-term setting, such as an interim alternative educational setting, is not sufficient. Interventions need to follow the student to his or her next placement (and elsewhere).
5. A combination of proactive, corrective, and instructive classroom management strategies is needed. Interventions must target specific prosocial and antisocial behaviors and the "thinking skills" that mediate such behaviors. Such a combination provides an atmosphere of warmth, care, support, and necessary structure.
6. Interventions must be developmentally appropriate and address strengths and weaknesses of the individual student and his or her environment.
7. Parent education and family therapy are critical components of effective programs for antisocial children and youth.
8. Interventions are most effective when provided early in life. Devoting resources to prevention reduces the later need for more expensive treatment.
9. Interventions should be guided by schoolwide and districtwide policies that emphasize positive interventions over punitive ones.
10. Interventions should be fair, consistent, culturally and racially nondiscriminatory, and sensitive to cultural diversity.
11. Interventions should be evaluated as to their short-term and long-term effectiveness in improving student behavior. Both the process and outcome of each intervention should be evaluated.
12. Teachers and support staff need to be well trained with respect to assessment and intervention. Staff working with students who have behavior problems will require ongoing staff development and support services.
13. Effective behavioral interventions require collaborative efforts from the school, home, and community agencies. Helping children and youth must be a shared responsibility. (NICHY, 1999, p. 5)

When these practices are consistently and effectively applied, children and youth with behavior disorders have greater chances of realizing their full potential, living and succeeding with their families, and making meaningful contributions to their neighborhoods and communities.

Case Study

SHOULD KARL STAY AT HOME OR BE HELPED ELSEWHERE?

Karl is a 7-year-old boy who was referred to the study by a staff member at the mental health clinic where he was receiving weekly outpatient therapy. Though his mother, Ms. S., found their current therapist to be helpful, she felt her family needed more comprehensive assistance. As Karl grew older, his aggressive behaviors were increasingly difficult to manage and residential placement had been discussed. Ms. S. was adamant that "even with all of his problems, he belongs at home." On referral to the study, Karl was randomly assigned to FCICM (Family-Centered Intensive Case Management).

Karl likes to bowl, fish, and play soccer. His mother described him as a very loving and generous child who could be helpful when he wanted to be. Karl liked school but had low-average school achievement and received additional help in reading and math. Karl's teacher reported that he had some behavioral problems in school and difficulty with peer relationships.

At home, Karl behaved aggressively toward his younger sister and mother. Ms. S. reported that he had violent temper tantrums. He was found once putting a pillow over his sister's face, and he had harmed her in other ways. Ms. S. did not feel that she could leave the two children alone for even a few minutes. Karl had purposely injured a pet hamster and animals he found, and he had also set several small fires. His mother was concerned about his increasing withdrawal and "not telling me how he was feeling." He had tried to hang himself with a belt, dashed into busy roads, and engaged in other risk-taking behaviors. He experienced sleep problems, was diagnosed with depression, and was assessed as functionally impaired in social relationships and self-direction.

Karl's needs contributed to the tension between his mother and stepfather, and the relationship between Karl and his stepfather was difficult. Karl was confused and distressed by the lack of contact with his birth father and imagined his father to be coming for a visit or being able to live with him when there was virtually no contact between them. Karl and his mother had made allegations of psychological abuse and neglect (Evans et al., pp. 563–564).

■ APPLICATION

1. With appropriate human and material resources, what would need to be put in place so Karl could remain at home rather than be placed in a residential setting?
2. What family-centered services would help his mother and other family members?
3. What advocacy assistance might the mother profit from in working with Karl's school?
4. On what basis should Karl be removed from his home for other more intensive treatments or services?

Debate Forum

60 MINUTES: THE COLUMBINE EFFECT: WHAT SHOULD THEY (WE) DO WITH LANCE?

■ PROGRAM EXCERPT ONE

Morley Safer: Sixteen-year-old Lance Landers looks like a typical American kid, but everyone who knows him, including his mother, says he's a very troubled American kid. At school in Gulf Shores, Alabama, he picked fights with students, he spit in their food, he threatened to kill his teacher and his classmates, he addressed the principal in the most offensive language. When Columbine happened and

Baldwin County's district attorney, David Whetstone, heard about Lance, he decided to act.

Mr. David Whetstone: I looked at Columbine and I was shocked, like the rest of the country, and then I found something in my school I thought could be the same thing. And we had to take a stand. I think in Columbine, if you could have removed those kids before the acts took place, that would have been a preferable act to do.

Safer: What you're saying, in effect, is that—that Lance will probably kill somebody if left in the school system.

Whetstone: I think there's a chance that he will act violently, because that has been his situation throughout his life.

Safer: The final straw came on a school bus full of children. When Lance erupted and threatened to cause a crash, a teacher's aide had to restrain him. Lance hit and kicked the aide. The district attorney went to

court and asked a judge to throw Lance not just out of the school, but out of the entire state school system.

Whetstone: I wanted to ask the question, "Do the other children and the teachers have the right to go to school in safety and not being disturbed? And can a court of law protect that in the state of Alabama?" The answer to that was yes.

Ms. Ann Vinson: There was no call for him to have been pulled out of all the schools in Alabama.

PROGRAM EXCERPT TWO

Safer: If any other student had done the things Lance did, the principal could have expelled him. But Lance was special, considered disabled, and the school had to find a way to continue to educate him. It consulted his mother, and together they agreed to send Lance to a treatment program that offered psychiatric help. He wouldn't cooperate, so doctors sent him back to public school, which felt it had no choice but to take him. The behavior continued. The school assigned Lance his own private teacher. That didn't work out. His mother tried home schooling him, but he was violent there, too. She called the police a number of times.

He assaulted her.

PROGRAM EXCERPT THREE

Safer: The school finally recommended that Lance go to a special public school for at-risk children. The closest one was an hour and a half away. His mother refused, said her son could not handle the daily commute, so he was put back into his regular classroom.

Whetstone: Because of his status—of his special protected status, he was allowed to continue and continue to do the acts and get worse and worse and worse.

Safer: Is Lance himself aware that he's got this, what you would call, I guess, a free pass?

Whetstone: Yeah. Lance has said, "You can't touch me. I'm d—I'm special." Well, I wanted to touch him. I wanted to let him know that somebody could touch him, and we did.

Safer: What District Attorney Whetstone did was to take Lance to state court, which flew in the face of federal law and banned the boy from public school. Just describe how this federal law works.

Whetstone: If you fall under a certain type of disabilities set by Congress, then you cannot be disciplined as other children. For example, if you threaten to hurt someone at school, you are—you are protected more so than all the other children.

Safer: That's because the lawmakers felt that disabled children needed more protection. Until the mid-1970s, . . . , schools were allowed to exclude children they considered too difficult to educate. That changed in 1975 when Congress passed a law forcing public schools to accept the disabled and to protect them. Lance had the same rights as any student in a wheelchair. There are mechanisms in the law for schools to keep potentially dangerous students out of class, but they can involve long, drawn-out legal proceedings, and many schools fear the consequences.

Whetstone: We have schools so afraid they're going to be personally sued because they have not given someone all the rights under this disability act, that they're afraid to do anything.

PROGRAM EXCERPT FOUR

Vinson: Let me ask you a question. Which is more dangerous: a child who is in a classroom learning, or someone who's out on the streets not learning, becoming angry?

Safer: For Lance, it's neither the street nor his classroom. As punishment for the bus incident, a state agency sent him to Glenwood, a tough, private institution for troubled kids. He's getting an education and treatment, and his mother says he's making progress.

Vinson: We have not given up on Lance, and we won't give up on Lance. He's part of our family; he's part of us. And I think that he deserves a public, appropriate education. And I truly believe that when he finishes this program, he'll be able to attend a school—a regular public school, and do well.

Safer: That's if he wins the right to. When he's released, probably this summer, he'll still be banned from all schools in the state, if David Whetstone has his way.

Whetstone: I—I hope he gets a good education, and I hope he becomes a good person. But as long as he's going to act the way he is, he's not welcome in the public schools of Alabama.[1]

POINT

Students with behavior disorders, particularly those served in general education settings, should be treated like other students in schools. If they come with weapons, distribute drugs, or engage in behaviors dangerous to others, they should be treated like other students guilty of similar offenses. They should experience the same disciplinary consequences as students without disabilities. When students with behavior disorders violate school rules, state, and national laws, they should forfeit their rights as other students do.

COUNTERPOINT

On the basis of legal and ethical grounds, students with behavior disorders should not be suspended or expelled from schools as nondisabled students are. Removing students with behavior disorders from the school setting without giving them appropriate services as determined in their IEPs merely exacerbates their problems. They need the interventions and services that are targeted to their particular problems and needs. Without these services, they are likely to create even more serious problems for their neighborhoods and communities. Suspending or expelling students with behavior disorders without providing appropriate, ongoing education services, roughly speaking, is equivalent to refusing a child with a serious illness appropriate medical care precisely because the child is sick.

[1]*Source:* Adapted from *60 Minutes: The Columbine Effect,* produced C. Olian of MM CBS, 2000, New York, New York: CBS News.

Review

focus 1

Identify five factors that influence the ways in which others' behaviors are perceived.

- Our personal beliefs, standards, and values
- Our tolerance for certain behaviors and our emotional fitness at the time the behaviors are exhibited
- Our perceptions of normality, which are often based on personal perspective rather than on an objective standard of normality as established by consensus or research
- The context in which a behavior takes place
- The frequency with which the behavior occurs or its intensity

focus 2

What differentiates externalizing disorders from internalizing disorders?

- Externalizing disorders involve behaviors that are directed at others (e.g., fighting, assaulting, stealing, vandalizing).
- Internalizing disorders involve behaviors that are directed inwardly or at oneself more than at others (e.g., fears, phobias, depression).

focus 3

Identify six essential parts of the definitions describing emotional or behavior disorders.

- The behaviors in question must be exhibited to a marked extent.
- Learning problems that are not attributable to intellectual, sensory, or health deficits are common.
- Satisfactory relationships with parents, teachers, siblings, and others are few.
- Behaviors occur in many settings and under normal circumstances are considered inappropriate.
- A pervasive mood of unhappiness or depression is frequently displayed by children with behavior disorders.
- Physical symptoms or fears associated with the demands of school are common in some children.

focus 4

Identify three reasons why classification systems are important to professionals who identify, treat, and educate individuals with behavior disorders.

- They provide a means of describing and identifying various behavior disorders.
- They provide a common language for communicating about various types and subtypes of behavior disorders.
- They sometimes provide a basis for treating a disorder

and making predictions about treatment outcomes.

focus 5

Identify five general characteristics (intellectual, adaptive, social, and achievement) of children and youth with behavior disorders.

- Children and youth with behavior disorders tend to have average to lower-than-average IQs compared to their normal peers.
- Children and youth with severe behavior disorders tend to have IQs that fall within the retarded range of functioning.
- Children and youth who are disturbed have great difficulty relating socially and responsibly to peers, parents, teachers, and other authority figures.
- Children and youth who are disturbed perform worse than their ability would predict, as measured by intellectual instruments.
- Children and youth who are seriously disturbed, particularly those with IQs in the retardation range, are substantially substandard in their academic achievement.

focus 6

What can be accurately said about the causes of behavior disorders?

- Behavior disorders are caused by sets of continu-

ously interacting biological, genetic, cognitive, social, emotional, and cultural variables.

focus 7

What three important outcomes are achieved through a functional behavioral assessment?

- Development of a concrete definition of the problem behavior(s)
- One or more predictions regarding when and under what conditions the problem behavior occurs
- Identification of the function that a behavior serves in meeting the needs of the individual

focus 8

What five guiding principles are associated with systems of care?

- Children with emotional disturbances should have access to services that address physical, emotional, social, and educational needs.
- Children should receive individualized services based on unique needs and potentials and guided by an individualized service plan.
- Children should receive services within the least restrictive environment that is appropriate.
- Families should be full participants in all aspects of

the planning and delivery of services.

- Children should receive integrated services with linkages between child-serving agencies and programs and mechanisms for planning, developing, and coordinating services.

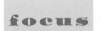

focus 9

What five factors should be considered in placing a child or youth with behavior disorders in general education settings and related classes?

- Will the child or youth be able to achieve his or her IEP goals and objectives in the general education environment?
- Will the child or youth pose significant management problems for teachers

and others in the general education setting?

- Will the behavior(s) of the child or youth pose significant safety problems for other students?
- Will the behavior(s) of the child or youth interfere significantly with the learning of other classmates?
- Will the child or youth benefit from the curriculum delivered in the general education setting?

focus 10

What are 13 promising practices for dealing with challenging behavior in children and youth?

- Behavioral assessment must be linked with interventions that follow the student through all placements.
- Multiple interventions are necessary for most stu-

dents. Any positive effect of a single strategy is likely to be temporary.

- Interventions must address not only the behavior that led to disciplinary action but a constellation of related behaviors and contributing factors.
- Interventions must promote maintenance over time and generalization across settings.
- Combined proactive, corrective, and instructive classroom management strategies must target specific prosocial and antisocial behaviors and the "thinking skills" that mediate such behaviors.
- Interventions must be developmentally appropriate and address strengths and weaknesses of the individual student and his or her environment.
- Parent education and family therapy are critical com-

ponents of effective programs for antisocial children and youth.

- Interventions are most effective when provided early in life.
- Interventions should be guided by schoolwide and districtwide policies that emphasize positive interventions over punitive ones.
- Interventions should be fair, consistent, culturally and racially nondiscriminatory, and sensitive to cultural diversity.
- Interventions should be evaluated as to their short-term and long-term effectiveness.
- Teachers and support staff need to be well trained with respect to assessment and intervention.
- The school, home, and community agencies must collaborate to help children and youth.

People with Mental Retardation

To begin with . . .

At 2:30 A.M. in Boulevard Hospital, Woodside, New York, the obstetric doctor showed me Michael, an hour old in his small crib in the nursery and said, "Your son will be mentally retarded. Notice his features and his hands. I'm sorry." With that, our family would be changed forever. The year was 1960 and at that time our culture favored institutionalization of children like Mike. Today, there are a number of options for support for parents [of children with mental retardation] that we didn't have. (John Murphy, parent, 1999, p. 10).

By the time Scott was 10 years old, he had been in five different schools. Because he has Down syndrome, he began his schooling at 18 months, attending the only public special education in the county once a week. At that time, all children [with mental retardation] were bused to this central location. Scott stayed at the special education school until he was 3½ years old. He could have stayed there until he was 21, but we wanted something different for him. . . . The transition to Coleridge Elementary School wasn't easy. . . . Scott . . . was included in the regular classroom for only short periods . . . . At first, he didn't like going into the regular classroom, but before long it was the reverse: he didn't want to leave. . . . Scott is now fully included. Lately we've noticed that he is more verbal. . . . He is less dependent on an assistant at school and has started to develop independent work skills. (Heather and Bill Bonn, parents, 2000a, p. 174; 2000b, pp. 210–211)

The rates of sexual abuse of children with mental retardation are the highest among all disability areas, and are *four times* the national sexual assault rate. Children with mental retardation are at greater risk because "standards of care" across the nation are inadequate for them, and they are less protected from incest than children of normal intelligence. Children with mental retardation are also at a significantly increased risk for neglect and maltreatment in comparison to children who are not retarded. The highest risk area for these children is physical abuse. (Sullivan, 2000)

Some 526,000 people with mental retardation and other developmental disabilities [in the United States] are now 60 years old or older. Experts project that those numbers could double by the year 2030. And as the bulge of baby boomers hits senior status, the lifespan of individuals [with mental retardation] also continues to lengthen. People with mental retardation who were not even surviving their teenage years in the 1930s, or reaching their sixtieth year in the 1970s, are now 66.2 years old at their mean age of death. Those without severe [mental retardation] may soon be expected to have life expectancies equal to that of the general population. (Herr, 1998, p. 2)

277

Lilly

Lilly is an 8-year-old with mental retardation. When she was adopted at the age of 2, her new parents were told she would never talk and might not walk. Through the untiring efforts of her family during the early childhood years, Lilly is able to say some words and use short sentences that are understood by her family and friends. She can now walk without support. Lilly's greatest challenge, according to her mother, is to stay focused. If directed step by step, Lilly is capable of participating in family activities and helping out around the house. Her brother Josh is always there for Lilly, helping her with homework, reading to her, and helping her get dressed in the morning.

At school, Lilly spends part of her day in a classroom with other students who also have mental retardation and part of the day in a general education class with second-grade nondisabled students. While in the special education classroom, Lilly works with peer tutors from the sixth-grade general education class to help her with schoolwork. Her two peer tutors, Nita and Amy, work with Lilly on using the computer to better develop her communication skills. A computer is a wonderful tool for Lilly because all she has to do is learn to hit the right buttons on the Touch Talker program to communicate with family, friends, and teachers. Lilly's second-grade teacher, Mrs. Roberts, describes Lilly as one of the most popular students in her class. The second-grade students love her "neat talking machine." When in the second-grade class, Lilly participates in learning centers where she is paired up with nondisabled students working on a variety of activities.

Lilly's mother and teachers are optimistic about her future. The special education teacher hopes that Lilly will be able to go to her neighborhood school next year and spend even more time with nondisabled students of her own age. "And from there, with her great social skills and her persistence, I see her as being independent in the future, working in a job setting."

Roger

Roger is 19 years old and lives at home with his parents. During the day, he attends high school and works in a local toy company in a small work crew with five other individuals who also have disabilities. Roger and his working colleagues are supervised by a job coach. Roger assembles small toys and is learning how to operate power tools for wood- and metal-cutting tasks. His wages are not enough to allow Roger to be financially independent, so most likely he will always need some financial support from his family or society.

Roger is capable of caring for his own physical needs. He has learned to dress and feed himself and understands the importance of personal care. He can communicate many of his needs and desires verbally but is limited in his ability to participate in social conversations, such as discussing the weather or what's new at the movies. Roger has never learned to read, and his leisure hours are spent watching television, listening to the radio, and visiting with friends.

Becky

Becky is a 6-year-old who has significant delays in intellectual, language, and motor development. These developmental differences have been evident from very early in her life. Her mother experienced a long, unusually difficult labor, and Becky endured severe heart-rate dips; at times, her heart rate was undetectable. During delivery, Becky suffered from birth asphyxiation and epileptic seizures. The attending physician described her as flaccid (soft and limp), with abnormal muscle reflexes. Becky has not yet learned to walk, is not toilet trained, and has no means of communication with others in her environment. She lives at home and attends a local elementary school during the day.

Her education program includes work with therapists to develop her gross motor abilities in order to improve her mobility. Speech and language specialists are examining the possibility of teaching her several alternative forms of communication (e.g., a language board or manual communication system) because Becky has not developed any verbal skills. The special education staff is focusing on decreasing Becky's dependence on others by teaching some basic self-care skills such as eating, toileting, and grooming. The professional staff does not know what the ultimate long-term impact of their intervention will be, but they do know that, although Becky is a child with severe mental retardation, *she is learning.*

THIS CHAPTER IS ABOUT PEOPLE whose intellectual and social capabilities may differ significantly from the average. Their growth and development depend on the educational, social, and medical supports made available throughout life. Lilly (see nearby snapshot) is a child with mental retardation who has a wonderful support network of family, friends, and teachers. As she grows older, she may achieve at least partial independence economically and socially within her community. Most likely, Lilly will continue to need some assistance from family, friends, and government-sponsored programs to help her adjust to adult life.

Roger has completed school and is just beginning life as an adult in his community. Roger is a person with moderate mental retardation. Although he will probably require lifetime support on his job, he is earning wages that contribute to his success and independence as an adult. Within a few years, Roger will most likely move away from his family and into a supported living arrangement, such as house or apartment of his own.

Becky has severe mental retardation. Although the long-term prognosis is unknown, she has many opportunities for learning and development that were not available until recently. Through a positive home environment and a school program that supports her learning and applying skills in natural settings, Becky can reach a level of development that was once considered impossible.

Lilly, Roger, and Becky are people with mental retardation, but they are not necessarily representative of the wide range of people who are characterized as having mental retardation. A 6-year-old described as mildly retarded may be no more than one or two years behind in the development of academic and social skills. Many children with mild mental retardation are not identified until they enter elementary school at age 5 or 6, because they may not exhibit physical or learning delays that are readily identifiable during the early childhood years. As these children enter school, developmental delays become more apparent. During early primary grades, it is not uncommon for the intellectual and social differences of children with mild mental retardation to be attributed to immaturity. However, within a few years, educators generally recognize the need for specialized services to support the child's development in the natural settings of school, neighborhood, and home.

People with moderate to severe mental retardation have challenges that transcend the classroom. Many are delayed in nearly every facet of life. Some have significant multiple disabling conditions, including sensory, physical, and emotional problems. People with moderate retardation are capable of learning adaptive skills that allow a degree of independence, with ongoing support. These skills include the abilities to dress and feed themselves, to care for their personal care and health needs, and to develop safety skills that allow them to move without fear wherever they go. These individuals have some means of communication. Most can develop spoken language skills, but some may be able to learn only manual communication (signing). Their social interaction skills are limited, however, making it difficult for them to relate spontaneously to others.

Contrast the preceding characteristics with those of people who have severe to profound retardation, and the diverse nature of people with mental retardation becomes clear. Individuals with profound retardation often depend on others to maintain even their most basic life functions, including eating, toileting, and dressing. They may not be capable of self-care and often do not develop functional communication skills. Their disabilities will require a lifetime of support, whether it be in a special-care setting or at home. In terms of treatment or interventions, the only realistic conclusion that can be drawn about this group is that the long-term prognosis for development is unknown.

This does not mean that education and treatment beyond routine care and maintenance are not beneficial. The extreme nature of these disabilities is the primary reason such individuals were excluded from the public schools for so long. Exclusion was often justified on the basis that schools did not have the resources, facilities, or trained personnel to deal with the needs of lower-functioning students (Drew & Hardman, 2000). Given society's present emphasis on research and alternative approaches to support people with mental retardation, the future may hold some answers and bring about a more positive outlook.

Definitions and Classification

People with mental retardation have been studied for centuries, by a variety of professional disciplines. They are often stereotyped as a homogeneous group of individuals—"the retarded"—with similar physical characteristics and learning capabilities. Nothing could be further from the truth. In fact, mental retardation encompasses a broad range of functioning levels and learning capabilities.

focus 1

Identify the three components of the AAMR definition of mental retardation.

■ DEFINITION

The most widely accepted definition of mental retardation is that of the **American Association on Mental Retardation (AAMR),** an organization of professionals of varied backgrounds such as medicine, law, and education. As defined by AAMR,

mental retardation [also known as intellectual disabilities] refers to substantial limitations in present functioning. It is characterized by significantly subaverage intellectual functioning, existing concurrently with related limitations in two or more of the following applicable adaptive skill areas: communication, self-care, home living, social skills, community use, self-direction, health and safety, functional academics, leisure, and work. Mental retardation manifests itself before age 18. (AAMR Ad Hoc Committee on Terminology and Classification, 1992, p. 5)

This definition has evolved through years of effort to more clearly reflect the ever-changing perceptions of mental retardation. Historically, definitions of mental retardation were based solely on the measurement of intellect, emphasizing routine care and maintenance rather than treatment and education. In recent years, the concept of adaptive skills has played an increasingly important role in defining and classifying people with mental retardation. The importance of adaptive skills is evident in the 1992 AAMR definition that includes ten primary adaptive skill areas that must be addressed in considering the overall functioning level of a person with mental retardation. Additionally, legislation (such as the Americans with Disabilities Act and the Individuals with Disabilities Education Act, IDEA) has opened new doors for people with mental retardation and put pressure on professionals to develop and use definitions aimed at assisting individuals in receiving the appropriate supports necessary to improve the quality of their lives.

In the next section, we address the three major components of the AAMR definition: significantly subaverage general intellectual functioning, impairments in adaptive behavior (skills), and age of onset.

■ AMERICAN ASSOCIATION ON MENTAL RETARDATION (AAMR). An organization of professionals from many disciplines involved in the study and treatment of mental retardation.

■ INTELLIGENCE   Significantly subaverage general intellectual functioning is assessed by a standardized intelligence test. On an intelligence test, a person's score is compared to the average of other people who have taken the same test (referred to as a normative sample). The statistical average for an intelligence test is generally set at 100. We state this by saying that the person has an intelligence quotient (IQ) of 100. Psychologists use a mathematical procedure called a **standard deviation** to determine the extent to which any given individual's score deviates from this average of 100. An individual who scores more than two standard deviations below 100 on an intelligence test meets AAMR's definition of subaverage general intellectual functioning. This means that people with IQs of approximately 70 to 75 and lower would be considered as having mental retardation.

■ STANDARD DEVIATION. A statistical measure of the amount that an individual score deviates from the average.

■ ADAPTIVE SKILLS   AAMR describes ten adaptive skill areas that are important in life: communication, self-care, home living, social skills, community use, self-direction, health and safety, functional academics, leisure, and work (see Table 9.1). If a person has limitations in these adaptive skills, he or she may need some additional assistance or *supports* in order to participate more fully in both family and community life. Consider Becky from the chapter opening snapshot. She has significant limitations in her adaptive skills. She is unable to walk and take care of her basic needs (self-care skills). At 6 years old, she still has no means of communicating with others.

TABLE 9.1   1992 AAMR adaptive skill areas

Skill Area	Portrayal
Communication	The ability to understand and communicate information by speaking or writing, through symbols, sign language, or nonsymbolic behaviors such as facial expressions, touch, or gestures
Self-care	Skills in such areas as toileting, eating, dressing, hygiene, and grooming
Home living	Functioning in the home, including clothing care, housekeeping, property maintenance, cooking, shopping, home safety, and daily scheduling
Social	Social interchange with others, including initiating and terminating interactions, responding to social cues, recognizing feelings, regulating own behavior, assisting others, and fostering friendships
Community use	Appropriate use of community resources, including traveling in the community, shopping at stores, obtaining services such as at gas stations, receiving medical and dental services, and using public transportation and facilities
Self-direction	Making choices, following a schedule, initiating contextually appropriate activities, completing required tasks, seeking assistance, resolving problems, and demonstrating appropriate self-advocacy
Health and safety	Maintaining own health, including eating; identifying, treating, and preventing illness; basic first aid; sexuality; physical fitness; and basic safety
Functional academics	Abilities and skills related to learning in school that also have direct application in life
Leisure	Developing a variety of leisure and recreational interests that are age- and culturally appropriate
Work	Abilities that pertain to maintaining part- or full-time employment in the community, including appropriate social and related work skills

Source: Adapted from *Mental Retardation: Definition, Classification, and Systems of Supports* (9th ed., pp. 40–41), Washington, DC: American Association on Mental Retardation. Copyright 1992 by the American Association on Mental Retardation, by permission.

Learning and applying adaptive skills in community work settings contribute to the independence of a person with mental retardation during the adult years.

As is true with intelligence, adaptive skills also may be measured by standardized tests. These tests, most often referred to as *adaptive behavior scales,* generally use structured interviews or direct observations to obtain information. Adaptive behavior scales measure the individual's ability to take care of personal needs (such as hygiene) and to relate appropriately to others in social situations. Adaptive skills may also be assessed through informal appraisal, such as observations by family members or professionals who are familiar with the individual or through anecdotal records.

■ AGE OF ONSET The AAMR defines the age of onset for mental retardation as prior to 18 years. The reason for choosing 18 as a cutoff point is that mental retardation is part of a family of conditions referred to as **developmental disabilities.** By definition, developmental disabilities are mental and/or physical impairments that are diagnosed at birth or during the childhood and adolescent years. A developmental disability results in substantial functional limitations in at least three areas of major life activity (i.e., self-care, language, learning, mobility, self-direction, capacity for independent living, or economic self-sufficiency. Although it is likely that developmental disabilities will continue throughout life, adults over 18 with no history of mental retardation are prevented from ever receiving the label.

■ PUTTING THE DEFINITION INTO PRACTICE The AAMR (1992) developed four criteria viewed as essential for professionals to follow as they put the definition into practice.

1. Assessments used to determine whether an individual meets the definition of mental retardation must take into account a person's cultural and linguistic background as well as communication or behavior problems that could affect performance on any given test.
2. A person's limitations in adaptive skills must occur in age-appropriate community environments and are indexed to each individual's need for support.
3. When assessing adaptive skills or personal capabilities, it is important to identify both limitations and strengths.
4. With appropriate supports over a sustained period, the life functioning skills of the person with mental retardation will generally improve.

■ CLASSIFICATION

To more clearly understand the diversity of people labeled as having mental retardation, several classification systems have been developed. We discuss four methods of classifying individuals with mental retardation: the severity of the condition, educability expectations, medical descriptors, and type and extent of needed support. Each classification method reflects an attempt by a particular discipline (such as medicine or education) to better understand and respond to the needs of individuals with mental retardation.

■ SEVERITY OF THE CONDITION The extent to which a person's intellectual capabilities and adaptive skills differ from what is considered "normal" can be described by using terms such as *mild, moderate, severe,* or *profound.* Mild describes the highest level of performance; profound describes the lowest level.

■ DEVELOPMENTAL DISABILITIES. Mental and/or physical impairments that are diagnosed at birth or during the childhood and adolescent years. Result in substantial functional limitations in at least three areas of major life activity (i.e., self-care; language, learning, mobility, self-direction, capacity for independent living, or economic self-sufficiency.

Distinctions between severity levels associated with mental retardation are determined by scores on intelligence tests and limitations in adaptive skills. Historically, four levels of intellectual functioning have been used to group people with mental retardation according to the severity approach: (1) mild, IQ 55 to 70; (2) moderate, IQ 40 to 55; (3) severe, IQ 25 to 40; and (4) profound, IQ 25 or lower (IQ scores based on standard deviations of the Wechsler Intelligence Scales).

A person's adaptive skills, or the ability to cope with environmental demands, can also be categorized by severity. Adaptive skill limitations can be described in terms of the degree to which an individual's performance differs from what is expected for his or her chronological age. For example, in the area of independent functioning, average 3-year-olds are expected to feed themselves unassisted with the proper eating utensils, take care of their own personal hygiene, and be fully toilet trained. A child with mild adaptive skill limitations may be able to use eating utensils, but with considerable spilling. This child can dress and take care of personal needs, but only with assistance. The child may be partially toilet trained; toileting accidents are common. The level of independence decreases for people with moderate, severe, and profound adaptive skill limitations. A 3-year-old with profound adaptive skill limitations often must be fed by another individual, drinks from a cup with help, cannot take care of personal needs, and has no effective speech.

To better understand adaptive skills, let's look at Lilly, Roger, and Becky from our opening snapshot. As an 8-year-old, Lilly has learned some of the required self-care skills for a child of her age, and although her socialization and communication skills are below what is expected, she is able to successfully interact with others through the use of **assistive technology.** Roger, at age 19, has developed many skills that allow him to successfully live in his own community with some supervision and support. It took longer for Roger to learn to dress and feed himself than it did for Lilly, but he has learned these skills. Although his verbal communication skills are somewhat rudimentary, he is capable of communicating basic needs and desires. Becky is a child with severe to profound mental retardation. At age 6, her development is significantly delayed in nearly every area. However, it is clear that with appropriate intervention, she is learning.

■ EDUCABILITY EXPECTATIONS   To distinguish among the diverse needs of students with mental retardation, the field of education developed its own classification system. As the word *expectations* implies, students with mental retardation have been classified according to how well they are expected to achieve in a classroom situation. The specific descriptors used vary greatly from state to state, but most often specify an approximate IQ range, and a statement of predicted achievement:

- *Educable (IQ 55 to about 70).* Second- to fifth-grade achievement in school academic areas. Social adjustment skills will result in independence with intermittent or limited support in the community. Partial or total self-support in a paid community job is a strong possibility.
- *Trainable (IQ 40 to 55).* Learning primarily in the area of self-care skills; some achievement in functional academics. A range of more extensive support will be needed to assist the student to adapt to community environments. Opportunities for paid work include supported employment in a community job.

Historically, the schools have also used the term *custodial* to describe individuals with IQs below 40, who may be unable to care for even their most basic needs. The custodial category described children who could be maintained or cared for only in a specialized setting. Inherent within this category was the assumption that learning experiences in a

focus 2

Identify four approaches to classifying people with mental retardation.

■ ASSISTIVE TECHNOLOGY. Technology devices that help an individual with disabilities adapt to the natural settings of home, school, and family. The technology may include computers, hearing aids, wheelchairs, and so on.

Today's schools are moving away from pejorative classifications (such as trainable and custodial) to a system that describes the type and extent of support a student needs to function in a natural setting.

public school would be fruitless. We have learned that such an assumption is entirely false, for many of the children labeled custodial only a few years ago are now receiving educational experiences that are increasing their adaptive skills and creating opportunities for successful living in family and community settings. *Custodial* is seldom used in today's public schools, having been replaced in most states with the symptom-severity descriptors *severely retarded* and *profoundly retarded*.

The classification criterion for educability expectation was originally developed to determine who would be able to benefit from school and who would not. The term *educable* implied that the child could cope with at least some of the academic demands of the classroom, meaning that the child could learn basic reading, writing, and arithmetic skills. The term *trainable* indicated that the student was noneducable and only capable of being trained in settings outside of the public school. In fact, until the passage of PL 94-142 in 1975 (now IDEA), many children who were labeled trainable could not get a free public education. In some school systems, the terms *educable* and *trainable* have now been replaced by symptom-severity classifications (mild through severe mental retardation).

■ MEDICAL DESCRIPTORS   Mental retardation may be classified on the basis of the biological origin of the condition. A classification system that uses the cause of the condition to differentiate people with mental retardation is often referred to as a medical classification system because it emerged primarily from the field of medicine. Common medical descriptors include **fetal alcohol syndrome, chromosomal abnormalities** (e.g., Down syndrome), **metabolic disorders** (e.g., phenylketonuria, thyroid dysfunction), and infections (e.g., syphilis, rubella). These medical conditions will be discussed more thoroughly in the section on causation.

■ CLASSIFICATION BASED ON NEEDED SUPPORT   When the AAMR revised its definition of mental retardation in 1992, it also recommended a different way to classify these individuals. Instead of the more traditional classification approaches based on intelligence quotient, educability expectations, or medical origin, the AAMR recommended classifying persons with mental retardation on the basis of *the type and extent of the support* they would need to function in the natural settings of their home and community. The AAMR recommended four levels of support:

■ *Intermittent.* Supports are provided on an "as-needed basis." These supports may be (1) episodic—that is, the person does not always need assistance; or

■ FETAL ALCOHOL SYNDROME (FAS). Damage caused to the fetus by the mother's consumption of alcohol.

■ CHROMOSOMAL ABNORMALITIES. Defects or damage in the chromosomes of an individual. Chromosomes are threadlike material that carries the genes and therefore plays a central role in inherited characteristics.

■ METABOLIC DISORDERS. Problems in the body's ability to process (metabolize) substances that can become poisonous and damage the central nervous system.

(2) short-term, occurring during lifespan transitions (e.g., job loss or acute medical crisis). Intermittent supports may be of high or low intensity.

- *Limited.* Supports are characterized by consistency; time required may be limited but not intermittent. Fewer staff may be required, and costs may be lower than those associated with more intensive levels of support (e.g., time-limited employment training or supports during transition from school to adulthood.

- *Extensive.* Supports are characterized by regular involvement (e.g., daily) in at least some environments, such as work or home; supports are not time limited (e.g., long-term job and home-living support will be necessary).

- *Pervasive.* Supports must be constant and of high intensity. They have to be provided across multiple environments and may be life-sustaining in nature. Pervasive supports typically involve more staff and are more intrusive than extensive or time-limited supports.

The AAMR's emphasis on classifying people with mental retardation on the basis of needed support is an important departure from the more restrictive perspectives of the traditional classification approaches. Supports may be described not only in terms of the level of assistance needed, but also by type: formal and natural support systems. Formal supports may be funded through government programs, such as income maintenance, health care, education, housing, or employment. Another type of formal support is the advocacy organization (e.g., **Arc, A National Organization on Mental Retardation**) that lobbies on behalf of people with mental retardation for improved and expanded services as well as provides family members a place to interact and support one another. **Natural supports** differ from formal supports in that they are not provided by agencies or organizations, but by the nuclear and extended family members, friends, or neighbors. Natural supports are often more effective than formal supports in helping people with mental retardation access and participate in a community setting. Research has suggested that adults with mental retardation who are successfully employed following school find more jobs through their natural support network of friends and family than through formal support systems (Berry & Hardman, 1998).

Prevalence

The U.S. Department of Education (2000a) reported that 611,076 students between the ages of 6 and 21 were labeled as having mental retardation and receiving service under IDEA during 1998–1999. Approximately 11% of all students with disabilities between the ages of 6 and 21 have mental retardation. Overall, students with mental retardation constitute about 0.97% of the total school population (see Figure 9.1).

The National Health Survey–Disability Supplement (Research and Training Center on Community Living, 1999) found that noninstitutionalized people with mental retardation constitute 0.78% of the total population, or about 1.9 million people in the United States. If you add in people with mental retardation living in nursing homes and institutional settings of four or more residents, the prevalence figure increases to 0.83% of the total population, or 2 million people. Adults constitute the lowest overall percentage of the total population (0.42%). People with mild mental retardation constitute about 90% of all people labeled as mentally retarded, or about 0.75% of the total population. Those with more severe mental retardation constitute a much smaller percentage of the general population (0.25%).

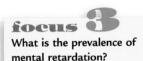
focus 3
What is the prevalence of mental retardation?

FIGURE 9.1

Prevalence of mental
retardation

[*Source:* From "To Assure the Free
Appropriate Public Education of All
Children with Disabilities," by the U.S.
Department of Education. In *Twenty-
second Annual Report to Congress on the
Implementation of the Individuals with
Disabilities Education Act,* 2000,
Washington, DC: U.S. Government
Printing Office.]

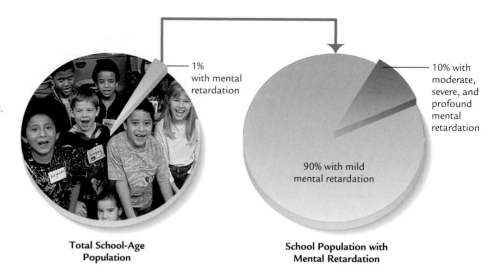

1%
with mental
retardation

10% with
moderate,
severe, and
profound
mental
retardation

90% with mild
mental retardation

**Total School-Age
Population**

**School Population with
Mental Retardation**

The prevalence figures reported from the National Health Survey are considerably lower than prior estimates of mental retardation. Based on an intelligence test
score of 70 or lower, it is estimated people with mental retardation would constitute about 3% of the total population, or about 6.6 million people in the United
States (U.S. Census Bureau, 2000). The President's Committee on Mental Retardation (2000) also estimates that between 6.2 and 7.5 million Americans of all ages, or
3% of the general population, experience mental retardation. The above figures are
considerably higher than the 2 million people reported in the National Health Survey. It is important to note that we are only able to *estimate* the prevalence of mental retardation since no one has actually counted the number of people with mental
retardation. The closest we can come to actual numbers is through the data from
the National Health Survey, which used a random sample of 108,000 people across
the United States to make their estimates.

Characteristics

In this section, we examine the many characteristics of people with mental
retardation that can affect their academic learning, as well as their ability to
adapt to home, school, and community environments.

**Identify four intellectual and
adaptive skills characteristic
of individuals with mental
retardation.**

■ LEARNING AND MEMORY

Intelligence is the ability to acquire, remember, and use knowledge. The primary
characteristic of mental retardation is an intellectual deficit that translates to a difference in the rate at and efficiency with which the person acquires, remembers, and
uses new knowledge in comparison to the general population (Benson et al., 1993).

The learning and memory capabilities of people with mental retardation are significantly below average in comparison to their nondisabled peers. Children with
mental retardation, as a group, are less able to grasp abstract, as opposed to concrete, concepts. As such, they benefit from instruction that is meaningful and useful, and they learn more from contact with real objects than they do from representations or symbols.

Intelligence is also associated with learning how to learn and with the ability to apply what is learned to new experiences. This process is known as establishing learning sets and generalizing them to new situations. As described by Cipani and Spooner (1994), **generalization** occurs "when a learned response is seen to occur in the presence of 'untaught' stimuli" (p. 157). Children and adults with mental retardation develop learning sets at a slower rate than nonretarded peers, and they are deficient in relating information to new situations (Beirne-Smith, Ittenbach, & Patton, 1998; Hughes, 1992; Turner, Dofny, & Dutka, 1994). The greater the severity of intellectual deficit, the greater the difficulties with memory. Memory problems in children with mental retardation have been attributed to several factors. People with mental retardation have difficulty in focusing on relevant stimuli in learning and real-life situations, sometimes attending to the wrong things (Benson et al., 1993; Henry & Gudjonsson, 1999; Westling & Fox, 2000).

■ SELF-REGULATION

People with mental retardation do not appear to develop efficient learning strategies, such as the ability to rehearse a task (to practice a new concept, either out loud or to themselves, over and over). The ability to rehearse a task is related to a broad concept known as **self-regulation,** or the ability to mediate or regulate one's own behavior (Jay, Grote, & Baer, 1999). Whereas most people will rehearse to try to remember, it does not appear that individuals with retardation are able to apply this skill.

Some researchers have begun to focus on information-processing theories to better understand learning differences in people with mental retardation. Information-processing theorists study how a person processes information from sensory stimuli to motoric output. In information-processing theory, the learning differences in people with mental retardation are seen as the underdevelopment of metacognitive processes. Metacognitive processes help the person plan how to solve a problem. First, the person decides on which strategy he or she thinks will solve a problem. Then the strategy is implemented. During implementation, the person monitors whether the strategy is working and makes any adaptions necessary. Finally, the results of the strategy are evaluated in terms of whether the problem has been solved and how the strategy could be used in other situations (Sternberg, 1997a). Even though children with mental retardation may be unable to use the best strategy when confronted with new learning situations, researchers have suggested that they can be taught ways to do so (Agran & Hughes, 1997; Mithaug et al.,1998; Wehmeyer & Kelchner, 1995).

■ ADAPTIVE SKILLS

The abilities to adapt to the demands of the environment, relate to others, and take care of personal needs are all important aspects of an independent lifestyle. In the school setting, adaptive behavior is defined as the ability to apply skills learned in a classroom to daily activities in natural settings.

For people with mental retardation, adaptive skills are often not comparable to those of their nondisabled peers. A child with mental retardation may have difficulty in both learning and applying skills for a number of reasons, including a higher level of distractibility, inattentiveness, failure to read social cues, and impulsive behavior (Agran & Wehmeyer, 1999; Benavidez & Matson, 1993; Bergen & Mosley, 1994; McAlpine, Kendall, & Singh, 1991; Merrill & Peacock, 1994). As such, these children will need to be taught appropriate reasoning, judgment, and social skills that lead to more positive social relationships and personal competence. Adaptive skill differences for people with mental retardation may also be associated with a lower self-

■ GENERALIZATION. The process of applying previously learned information to new settings or situations.

■ SELF-REGULATION. The ability to regulate one's own behavior.

Reflect on This

MAKING A DIFFERENCE IN THE LIVES OF PEOPLE WITH MENTAL RETARDATION: A LASTING KENNEDY FAMILY LEGACY

Most people will remember John Kennedy Jr. as the son of a president of the United States and member of the famous Kennedy family. Many people mourned his death on July 19, 1999, as a tragic loss of a potential national leader and statesman for the 21st century. Others, albeit fewer in number, will remember John Kennedy Jr. for his dedication to improving the lives of people with mental retardation. His commitment began in the 1980s as he struggled to understand why direct care workers in community programs, such as supported employment and support living, were always the lowest paid, had the least chance for career advancement, and received little or no training for their jobs. Yet these were the very people who were closest to those being served, working day after day and side by side to help make the lives of people with mental retardation a little better.

In 1989, John Kennedy Jr. founded Reaching Up, an organization devoted to improving educational and career opportunities for direct care staff in community settings. He provided college scholarships to community direct care staff so they could be better trained and receive higher pay in their jobs. In the past decade, more than 400 Kennedy Fellows have completed degrees that prepared them for occupations in fields such as psychology, social work, rehabilitation, recreation therapists, agency administrators, and special education.

The initial funds for John's Reaching Up program came from a close personal source—his family. In the early 1950s, the patriarchs of the Kennedy family, Joseph and Rose, established the Joseph P. Kennedy Jr. Foundation in remembrance of their son Joe Jr. who was killed in action during World War II while flying a dangerous, volunteer mission in Europe. As was true when it began 50 years ago, the Kennedy Foundation remains today as the only family foundation in the world devoted to people with mental retardation. Under the leadership of Eunice Kennedy Shriver, Senator Edward Kennedy, Ambassador Jean Kennedy Smith, and Patricia Lawford, the foundation has played a major role in bettering the lives of people who are mentally retarded.

In early 1962, Eunice Kennedy Shriver talked with her brother, then president of the United States, John F. Kennedy, about revealing a close-kept family secret. She wanted to write an article for the *Saturday Evening Post* and tell the world about their mentally retarded sister, Rosemary. The president was supportive, and the article, read by millions, changed forever the view that people with mental retardation should be kept in closets, hidden from view, and treated as objects of scorn. Spurred on by the positive public and scientific reception to the article, Mrs. Shriver and the Kennedy family moved forward in their quest to bring people with mental retardation out of the darkness and into the lives of their families, schools, and communities.

- In 1961, President John F. Kennedy created the President's Panel on Mental Retardation (later established in law as the President's Committee on Mental Retardation) and called upon America to address the significant needs of people with mental retardation and their desire to be part of everyday life in America. The PCMR acts in an advisory capacity to the president of the United States and the secretary of health and human services on matters relating to programs and services for persons with mental retardation. The committee organizes national planning, stimulates policies and programs, and advances community participation in the field of mental retardation.

- The Kennedy Foundation was instrumental in establishing (1) the first research and training program focused on people with mental retardation in a major research center, Massachusetts General Hospital and Harvard University—which led to the development of Mental Retardation Research Centers around the country; (2) the National Institute of Child Health and Human Development in the National Institutes of Health; (3) University Affiliated Programs—cross-disciplinary training for professionals working in the field of mental retardation; and (4) the Kennedy Public Policy Fellows Program, which provides opportunities to professionals and parents to serve as fellows in the Congress or executive branch of the U.S. government.

- In 1968, Eunice Kennedy Shriver founded the Special Olympics sports training and competition for people with mental retardation. Special Olympics provides year-round training and athletic competition for more than 1 million athletes in nearly 150 countries and all 50 states in the United States. Over the years, millions of children and adults with mental retardation have participated in Special Olympics. Today, Special Olympics continues to be a Shriver family passion. Sargent Shriver is chairman of the board of directors, and son Timothy Shriver is the organization's chief executive officer.

- Ambassador Jean Kennedy Smith founded Very Special Arts (now VSA Arts) in 1974 as an affiliate of the John F. Kennedy Center for the Performing Arts. VSA Arts is an international organization that creates learning opportunities through the arts for people with disabilities. VSA Arts operates in 41 states and the District of Columbia and in 83 countries, serving 4.3 million Americans and 1.3 million people with disabilities in other parts of the world.

- Senator Edward M. Kennedy has been a leading advocate in Congress on behalf of people with mental retardation for nearly 40 years. Most recently, he co-sponsored the Work Incentives Act, landmark legislation that would remove the barriers that prevent so many people with mental retardation from working and living independent and productive lives.
- Patricia Kennedy Lawford has been instrumental in the success of the Kennedy Child Study Center in New York. The center provides early intervention and special education services to young children with mental retardation.

In addition to John Kennedy Jr., many of the third-generation Kennedy family members continue the legacy passed down from their grandparents and parents. Here are but a few examples. In 1989 Anthony Shriver founded Best Buddies, a national service program that provides one-on-one friendship opportunities for people with mental retardation and people who are not disabled. Best Buddies has grown to an international organization involving 13,000 participants annually on more than 400 high school and college campuses in the United States, Canada, and Greece. More than 80,000 individuals have volunteered in its ten years of existence. Kathleen Kennedy Townsend (lieutenant governor of Maryland) established one of the first community service programs in the country to directly involve high-school-age students with mental retardation in volunteer community service projects. Dr. William Kennedy Smith developed a physician and nurse training program in the area of fetal alcohol syndrome. Filmmaker Rory Kennedy has produced documentaries on the challenges that parents with mental retardation face in raising their families and on the plight of welfare families who have mentally retarded children. Ted Kennedy Jr. established a safe home at the Yale Medical Center to serve as a treatment site for lead-poisoned children and their families. Robin Lawford helped build a garden at the Kennedy Child Study Center in New York as a place of respite for young children with mental retardation and their parents.

---

image and a greater expectancy for failure in both academic and social situations. In a study of 764 children in regular education classrooms, Siperstein and Leffert (1997) identified the characteristics of 20 socially accepted and 20 socially rejected students with mental retardation. Characteristics of socially accepted children included a higher level of social skills. These children were not perceived by their nondisabled peers as aggressive in their behavior. The authors suggested that there is value in recognizing and teaching the skills that distinguish between those children who are accepted and those who are not (see nearby Reflect on This feature).

ACADEMIC ACHIEVEMENT

Research on the academic achievement of children with mild to moderate mental retardation has suggested that they will experience significant delays in the areas of literacy and mathematics. Reading comprehension is generally considered the weakest area of learning. In general, students with mild retardation are better at decoding words than comprehending their meaning (Drew & Hardman, 2000) and read below their own mental-age level (Katims, 2000).

focus 5

Identify the academic, motivational, speech and language, and physical characteristics of children with mental retardation.

Children with mental retardation also perform poorly with mathematical computations, although their performance may be closer to what is typical for their mental age. These children may be able to learn basic computations but be unable to apply concepts appropriately in a problem-solving situation (Beirne-Smith et al., 1998).

A growing body of research has indicated that children with moderate and severe mental retardation can be taught functional academics. In a functional reading program, the students are able to develop a useful vocabulary that will facilitate their inclusion in school and community settings (Browder & Snell, 2000). The goal of functional reading is for "students to have enough of a sight word vocabulary to be able to scan printed materials and glean the key information needed in a given activity" (Browder & Snell, p. 526). These children may be able to recognize their names and those of significant others in their lives, as well as common survival words, including *help, hurt, danger,* and *stop.* In a functional math program, students learn such skills as how to tell time, add and subtract small sums to manage finances (such as balancing a checkbook), and appropriately exchange money for products in community settings (e.g., grocery stores, movie theaters, vending machines, etc.).

■ MOTIVATION

People with mental retardation are often described as lacking motivation, or *outer-directed behavior.* They may seem unwilling or unable to complete tasks, take responsibility, and be self-directed. Although people with mental retardation may appear to be less motivated than their nondisabled peers, such behavior may be more attributable to the way they have learned to avoid certain situations because of a fear of failure. A child with mental retardation may have a history of failure, particularly in school, and may be afraid to take risks or participate in new situations. The result of failure is often **learned helplessness**—"No matter what I do or how hard I try, I will not succeed." To overcome such children's feelings of learned helplessness, it is important for professionals and family members to focus on providing experiences that have high probabilities for success. The opportunity to strive for success, rather than to avoid failure, is a very important learning experience for these children. Dever and Knapczyk (1997, p. 280) suggested several considerations in motivating students with mental retardation:

- Reward the learner for doing what he or she is supposed to do.
- Develop a different activity that is more inherently motivating for the learner, to teach the same objective.
- Change the objective.
- Forget about teaching until other considerations are addressed, such as health problems, abuse, and development of rapport.

■ SPEECH AND LANGUAGE CHARACTERISTICS

One of the most serious and obvious characteristics of individuals with mental retardation is delayed speech and language development (Warren & Yoder, 1997). The most common speech difficulties involve **articulation problems, voice problems, and stuttering.** Language problems are generally associated with delays in language development rather than a bizarre use of language (Beirne-Smith et al., 1998; Warren & Yoder, 1997). Kaiser (2000) emphasized that "the overriding goal of language intervention is to increase the functional communication of students" (p. 457).

There is considerable variation in the language skills of people with mental retardation. In general, the severity of the speech and language problems is positively correlated with the cause and severity of the mental retardation: the milder the mental retardation, the less pervasive the language difficulty (Tager-Flusberg & Sullivan, 1998). Speech and language difficulties may range from minor speech defects, such as articulation problems, to the complete absence of expressive language. Speech and language pathologists are able to correct minor speech differences for most students with mental retardation.

Mental retardation may cause speech problems, but some speech difficulties (such as **echolalia**) may also directly contribute to the severity of the mental retardation. Table 9.2 describes the range of speech and language skills for people with moderate to profound mental retardation.

■ PHYSICAL CHARACTERISTICS

The physical appearance of most children with mental retardation does not differ from that of same-age children who are not disabled. However, there is a rela-

■ LEARNED HELPLESSNESS. Refusal or unwillingness to take on new tasks or challenges, resulting from repeated failures or control by others.

■ ARTICULATION PROBLEMS. Speech problems such as omissions, substitutions, additions, and distortions of words.

■ VOICE PROBLEMS. Abnormal acoustical qualities in a person's speech.

■ STUTTERING. A speech problem involving abnormal repetitions, prolongations, and hesitations as one speaks.

■ ECHOLALIA. A meaningless repetition or imitation of words that have been spoken.

TABLE 9.2   Speech and language skills for individuals with moderate to profound mental retardation

Severity of Mental Retardation		
Moderate	Severe	Profound
Most individuals have delays or deviations in speech and language skills, but many develop language abilities that allow them some level of communication with others.	Individuals exhibit significant speech and language delays and deviations (such as lack of expressive and receptive language, articulation difficulties, and little, if any, spontaneous interaction).	Individuals do not exhibit spontaneous communication patterns. Echolalic speech, speech out of context, and purposeless speech may be evident.

tionship between the severity of the mental retardation and the extent of physical differences for the individual (Beirne-Smith et al., 1998; Drew & Hardman, 2000; Horvat, 2000). For the person with severe mental retardation, there is a significant probability of related physical problems; genetic factors are likely behind both disabilities. The individual with mild retardation, in contrast, may exhibit no physical differences because the retardation may be associated with environmental, not genetic, factors. Table 9.3 describes the range of physical characteristics associated with individuals who have moderate to profound mental retardation.

The majority of children with severe and profound retardation have multiple disabilities that affect nearly every aspect of intellectual and physical development (Westling & Fox, 2000). Increasing health problems for children with mental retardation may be associated with genetic or environmental factors. For example, people with Down syndrome have a higher incidence of congenital heart defects and respiratory problems directly linked to their genetic condition (Marino & Pueschel, 1996). On the other hand, some children with mental retardation experience health problems because of their living conditions. A significantly higher percentage of children with mental retardation come from low socioeconomic backgrounds in comparison to nondisabled peers. Children who do not receive proper nutrition and are exposed to inadequate sanitation have a greater susceptibility to infections (Drew & Hardman, 2000). Health services for families in these situations may be minimal or nonexistent, depending on whether they are able to access government medical support. As such, children with mental retardation may become ill more often than those who are not retarded. Consequently, children with retardation may miss more school.

TABLE 9.3   Physical characteristics of individuals with moderate to profound mental retardation

Severity of Mental Retardation		
Moderate	Severe	Profound
Gross and fine motor coordination is usually delayed. However, the individual is often ambulatory and capable of independent mobility. Perceptual-motor skills exist (e.g., body awareness, sense of touch, eye–hand coordination) but are often delayed in comparison to the norm.	As many as 80% have significant motor difficulties (i.e., poor or nonambulatory skills). Gross or fine motor skills may be present, but the individual may lack control, resulting in awkward or uncontrolled motor movement.	Some gross motor development is evident, but fine motor skills are delayed. The individual is usually nonambulatory and not capable of independent mobility within the environment. The individual may lack perceptual–motor skills.

The more severe the mental retardation, the more likely the person's physical appearance will differ from those who are not disabled.

Causation

focus 6

Identify the causes of mental retardation.

Mental retardation is the result of multiple causes, some known, many unknown. For about 30% of all people with mental retardation, the cause of the condition is unknown. This percentage is much higher for people with *mild* mental retardation wherein the specific cause cannot be determined in 75% of the cases (The ARC, 2000). Possible known causes of mental retardation include sociocultural influences, biomedical factors, behavioral factors, and unknown prenatal influences.

▪ SOCIOCULTURAL INFLUENCES

For individuals with mild retardation, the cause of the problem is not generally apparent. A significant number of these individuals come from families of low socioeconomic status and diverse cultural backgrounds; their home situations often offer few opportunities for learning, which only further contributes to their challenges at school. Additionally, because these high-risk children live in such adverse economic conditions, they generally do not receive proper nutritional care. In addition to poor nutrition, high-risk groups are in greater jeopardy of receiving poor medical care and living in unstable families (Children's Defense Fund, 1998a; Manning & Baruth, 1995).

An important question to be addressed concerning people who have grown up in adverse sociocultural situations is this: how much of the person's ability is related to sociocultural influences, and how much to genetic factors? This issue is referred to as the **nature-versus-nurture** controversy. Numerous studies over the years have focused on the degree to which heredity and environment contribute to intelligence. These studies show that, although we are reaching a better understanding of the interactive effects of both heredity and environment, the exact contribution of each to intellectual growth remains unknown.

The term used to describe retardation that may be attributable to both sociocultural and genetic factors is **cultural–familial retardation.** People with this condition are often described as (1) being mildly retarded, (2) having no known biological cause for the condition, (3) having at least one parent or sibling who is also mildly retarded, and (4) growing up in a low socioeconomic home environment.

▪ NATURE-VERSUS-NURTURE. Controversy concerning how much of a person's ability is related to sociocultural influences (nurture) as opposed to genetic factors (nature).

▪ CULTURAL–FAMILIAL RETARDATION. Mental retardation that may be attributable to both sociocultural and genetic factors.

▪ BIOMEDICAL FACTORS. Biologic processes, such as genetic disorders or nutrition, that can cause mental retardation or other disabilities.

For the majority of people with moderate, severe, and profound mental retardation, problems are evident at birth. To differentiate among the diversity of causes associated with moderate through profound levels of mental retardation, we will briefly review the biomedical and behavioral factors associated with this condition. As defined by the AAMR, **biomedical factors** "relate to biologic processes, such as genetic disorders or nutrition," and **behavioral factors** relate to "potentially causal behaviors, such as dangerous (injurious) activities or maternal substance abuse" (AAMR Ad Hoc Committee, 1992, p. 71).

■ BIOMEDICAL FACTORS

Many biomedical factors are associated with mental retardation. In this section, we will discuss three major influences: chromosomal abnormalities, metabolism and nutrition, and postnatal brain disease.

■ CHROMOSOMAL ABNORMALITIES

Chromosomes are threadlike bodies that carry the genes that play the critical role in determining inherited characteristics. Defects resulting from chromosomal abnormalities are typically severe and accompanied by visually evident abnormalities. Fortunately, genetically caused defects are relatively rare. The vast majority of humans have normal cell structures (46 chromosomes arranged in 23 pairs) and develop without accident. Aberrations in chromosomal arrangement, either before fertilization or during early cell division, can result in a variety of abnormal characteristics.

One of the most widely recognized types of mental retardation, Down syndrome, results from chromosomal abnormality. About 5% to 6% of people with mental retardation have Down syndrome (Beirne-Smith et al., 1998) A person with Down syndrome is characterized by slanting eyes with folds of skin at the inner corners (epicanthal folds); excessive ability to extend the joints; short, broad hands with a single crease across the palm on one or both hands; broad feet with short toes; a flat bridge of the nose; short, low-set ears; a short neck; a small head; a small oral cavity; and/or short, high-pitched cries in infancy.

Down syndrome has received widespread attention in the literature and has been a favored topic in both medical and special education textbooks for many years. Part of this attention is due to the ability to identify a cause with some degree of certainty. The cause of such genetic errors has become increasingly associated with the ages of both the mother and the father. The National Information Center for Children and Youth with Disabilities (NICHCY) (2000) estimated that about 4,000 infants with Down syndrome are born each year in the United States, or about 1 in every 1,000 live births. Approximately 350,000 people in the United States have Down syndrome. Although parents of any age may have a child with Down syndrome, the incidence is higher for women over 35. The probabilities increase significantly (1 in 20) for mothers older than 45 years of age. The most common type of Down syndrome is **trisomy 21.** In about 25% of the cases associated with trisomy 21, the age of the father (particularly when over 55 years old) is also a factor (see nearby Reflect on This feature).

Other chromosomal abnormalities associated with mental retardation include **Williams syndrome** and **fragile X syndrome.** Williams syndrome is a rare genetic disease that

The most common cause of Down syndrome is a chromosomal abnormality known as trisomy 21, in which the twenty-first chromosomal pair carries an extra chromosome.

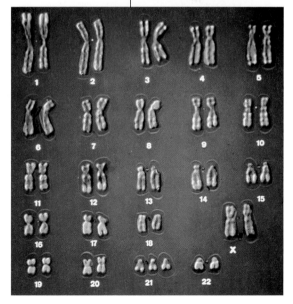

Reflect on This

MYTHS AND TRUTHS ABOUT DOWN SYNDROME

■ *Myth:* Down syndrome is a rare genetic disorder.

■ *Truth:* Down syndrome is the most commonly occurring genetic condition. One in every 800 to 1,000 live births is a child with Down syndrome, representing approximately 5,000 births per year in the United States alone. Today, Down syndrome affects more than 350,000 people in the United States.

■ *Myth:* Most children with Down syndrome are born to older parents.

■ *Truth:* Eighty percent of children born with Down syndrome are born to women younger than 35 years old. However, the incidence of births of children with Down syndrome increases with the age of the mother.

■ *Myth:* People with Down syndrome are severely retarded.

■ *Truth:* Most people with Down syndrome have IQs that fall in the mild to moderate range of retardation. Children with Down syndrome are definitely educable, and educators and researchers are still discovering the full educational potential of people with Down syndrome.

■ *Myth:* Most people with Down syndrome are institutionalized.

■ *Truth:* Today people with Down syndrome live at home with their families and are active participants in the educational, vocational, social, and recreational activities of the community. They are integrated into the regular education system and take part in sports, camping, music, art programs, and all the other activities of their communities. In addition, they are socializing with people with and without disabilities, and as adults are obtaining employment and living in group homes and other independent housing arrangements.

■ *Myth:* Parents will not find community support in bringing up their child with Down syndrome.

■ *Truth:* In almost every community of the United States, parent support groups and other community organizations are directly involved in providing services to families of individuals with Down syndrome.

■ *Myth:* Children with Down syndrome must be placed in segregated special education programs.

■ *Truth:* Children with Down syndrome have been included in regular academic classrooms in schools across the country.

In some instances they are integrated into specific courses, while in other situations students are fully included in the regular classroom for all subjects. The degree of mainstreaming is based in the abilities of the individual; but the trend is for full inclusion in the social and educational life of the community.

■ *Myth:* Adults with Down syndrome are unemployable.

■ *Truth:* Businesses are seeking young adults with Down syndrome for a variety of positions. They are being employed in small and medium-sized offices: by banks, corporations, nursing homes, hotels, and restaurants. They work in the music and entertainment industry, in clerical positions, and in the computer industry. People with Down syndrome bring to their jobs enthusiasm, reliability, and dedication.

■ *Myth:* People with Down syndrome are always happy.

■ *Truth:* People with Down syndrome have feelings just like everyone else in the population. They respond to positive expressions of friendship, and they are hurt and upset by inconsiderate behavior.

■ *Myth:* Adults with Down syndrome are unable to form close interpersonal relationships leading to marriage.

■ *Truth:* People with Down syndrome date, socialize, and form ongoing relationships. Some are beginning to marry. Women with Down syndrome can and do have children, but there is a 50% chance that their child will have Down syndrome. Men with Down syndrome are believed to be sterile; there is only one documented instance of a male with Down syndrome having fathered a child.

■ *Myth:* Down syndrome can never be cured.

■ *Truth:* Research on Down syndrome is making great strides in identifying the genes on chromosome 21 that cause the characteristics of Down syndrome. Scientists now feel strongly that it will be possible to improve, correct, or prevent many of the problems associated with Down syndrome in the future.

Source: From *Down Syndrome: Myths and Truths,* by the National Down Syndrome Society, 2000, New York: Author. *[on-line].* Available: *http://www.ndss.org/aboutds/aboutds.html#Down*

occurs in about 1 in every 20,000 births and is characterized by an absence of genetic materials on the seventh pair of chromosomes. Most people with Williams syndrome have some degree of mental retardation and associated medical problems (e.g., heart and blood vessel abnormalities, low weight gain, dental abnormalities, kidney abnormalities, hypersensitive hearing, musculoskeletal problems, and elevated blood calcium levels). While exhibiting deficits in academic learning and spatial ability typical of people with mental retardation, they are often described as highly personable and verbal, exhibiting unique abilities in spoken language.

Fragile X syndrome is a common hereditary cause of mental retardation associated with genetic anomalies in the 23rd pair of chromosomes. Males are usually more severely affected than females because they have an X and a Y chromosome. Females have more protection because they have two X chromosomes; one X contains the normal functioning version of the gene and the other is nonfunctioning. The normal gene partially compensates for the nonfunctioning gene. The term *fragile X* refers to the fact that this gene is pinched off in some blood cells. For those affected with fragile X, intellectual differences can range from mild learning disabilities and a normal IQ to severe mental retardation and autism. Physical features may include a large head and flat ears; a long, narrow face with a broad nose; a large forehead; a squared-off chin; prominent testicles; and large hands. People with fragile X are also characterized by speech and language delays or deficiencies, and behavioral problems. While some people with fragile X are socially engaging and friendly, others have autistic-like characteristics (e.g., poor eye contact, hand flapping, hand biting, and fascination with spinning objects) and may be aggressive. Males may also exhibit hyperactivity.

■ METABOLISM AND NUTRITION   Metabolic problems are characterized by the body's inability to process (metabolize) certain substances that can then become poisonous and damage tissue in the central nervous system. With **phenylketonuria (PKU),** one such inherited metabolic disorder, the baby is not able to process phenylalanine, a substance found in many foods, including the milk ingested by infants. The inability to process phenylalanine results in an accumulation of poisonous substances in the body. If untreated or not treated promptly (mostly through dietary restrictions), PKU causes varying degrees of mental retardation, ranging from moderate to severe deficits. If treatment is promptly instituted, however, damage may be largely prevented or at least reduced. For this reason, most states now require mandatory screening for all infants in order to treat the condition as early as possible and prevent lifelong problems.

Milk also presents a problem for infants affected by another metabolic disorder. With **galactosemia,** the child is unable to properly process lactose, which is the primary sugar in milk and is also found in other foods. If galactosemia remains untreated, serious damage results, such as cataracts, heightened susceptibility to infection, and reduced intellectual functioning. Dietary controls must be undertaken, eliminating milk and other foods containing lactose.

■ POSTNATAL BRAIN DISEASE   Some disorders are associated with gross postnatal brain disease. **Neurofibromatosis** is an inherited disorder that results in multiple tumors in the skin, peripheral nerve tissue, and other areas such as the brain. Mental retardation does not occur in all cases, although it may be evident in a small percentage of patients. The severity of mental retardation and other problems resulting from neurofibromatosis seems to relate to the location of the tumors (e.g., in the cerebral tissue) and their size and pattern of growth. Severe disorders due to postnatal brain disease occur with a variety of other conditions, including

■ PHENYLKETONURIA (PKU). A metabolic disorder that may cause mental retardation if left untreated.

■ GALACTOSEMIA. A metabolic disorder causing an infant to have difficulty in processing lactose. The disorder may cause mental retardation and other problems.

■ NEUROFIBROMATOSIS. An inherited disorder resulting in tumors of the skin and other tissue (such as the brain).

tuberous sclerosis, which also involves tumors in the central nervous system tissue and degeneration of cerebral white matter.

■ BEHAVIORAL FACTORS

Mental retardation may result from behavioral factors that are not genetically based. Behavioral causes of mental retardation include infection and intoxication (such as HIV and fetal alcohol syndrome), as well as traumas and physical accidents.

■ INFECTION AND INTOXICATION   Several types of **maternal infections** may result in difficulties for the unborn child. In some cases, the outcome is spontaneous abortion of the fetus; in others, it may be a severe birth defect. The probability of damage is particularly high if the infection occurs during the first three months of pregnancy. **Congenital rubella** (German measles) causes a variety of conditions, including mental retardation, deafness, blindness, cerebral palsy, cardiac problems, seizures, and a variety of other neurological problems. The widespread administration of a rubella vaccine is one major reason that mental retardation as an outcome of rubella has declined significantly in recent years.

Another infection associated with mental retardation is the **human immunodeficiency virus (HIV).** When transmitted from the mother to the unborn child, HIV can result in significant intellectual deficits. The virus actually crosses the placenta and infects the fetus, damaging the infant's immune system. HIV is a major cause of preventable infectious mental retardation (Cohen, 1991).

Several prenatal infections can result in other severe disorders. **Toxoplasmosis,** an infection carried by raw meat and fecal material, can result in mental retardation and other problems such as blindness and convulsions. Toxoplasmosis is primarily a threat if the mother is exposed during pregnancy, whereas infection prior to conception seems to cause minimal danger to the unborn child. Intoxication refers to cerebral damage that occurs due to an excessive level of some toxic agent in the mother–fetus system. Excessive maternal use of alcohol or drugs or exposure to certain environmental hazards such as x-rays or insecticides can cause damage to the child. Damage to the fetus from maternal alcohol consumption is characterized by facial abnormalities, heart problems, low birthweight, small brain size, and mental retardation. Fetal alcohol syndrome (FAS) and fetal alcohol effects (FAE) (a lesser number of the same symptoms associated with FAS) refer to a group of physical and mental birth defects resulting from a woman's drinking alcohol during pregnancy. FAS is recognized as a leading preventable cause of mental retardation. The National Organization on Fetal Alcohol Syndrome (2000) estimated that more than 50,000 babies with alcohol-related problems are born in the United States each year. Similarly, pregnant women who smoke are at greater risk of having a premature baby with complicating developmental problems such as mental retardation (Carta et al., 1994; Shiono & Behrman, 1995). The use of drugs during pregnancy has varying effects on the infant, depending on frequency, usage, and drug type. Drugs known to produce serious fetal damage include LSD, heroin, morphine, and cocaine. Prescription drugs such as **anticonvulsants** and antibiotics have also been associated with infant malformations.

Maternal substance abuse is also associated with gestation disorders involving prematurity and low birthweight. **Prematurity** refers to infants delivered before 35 weeks from the first day of the last menstrual period. **Low birthweight** characterizes babies that weigh 2,500 grams (5.5 pounds) or less at birth. Prematurity and low birthweight significantly increase the risk of serious problems at birth, including mental retardation.

■ TUBEROUS SCLEROSIS. A birth defect that does not appear until late childhood, is related to mental retardation in about 66% of the cases, and is characterized by tumors on many organs.

■ MATERNAL INFECTION. Infection in a mother during pregnancy, sometimes having the potential to injure the unborn child.

■ CONGENITAL RUBELLA. German measles contracted by a mother during pregnancy, which can cause a variety of conditions including mental retardation, deafness, blindness, and other neurological problems.

■ HUMAN IMMUNODEFICIENCY VIRUS (HIV). A virus that reduces immune system function and has been linked to AIDS.

■ TOXOPLASMOSIS. An infection caused by protozoa carried in raw meat and fecal material.

■ ANTICONVULSANTS. Medication prescribed to control seizures (convulsions).

■ PREMATURITY. Status of infants delivered before 37 weeks from the first day of the last menstrual period.

■ LOW BIRTHWEIGHT. A weight of 5½ pounds (2,500 grams) or less at birth.

Another factor that can seriously affect the unborn baby is an incompatible blood type between the mother and the fetus. The most widely known form of this problem occurs when the mother's blood is Rh-negative, whereas the fetus has Rh-positive blood. In this situation, the mother's system may become sensitized to the incompatible blood type and produce defensive antibodies that damage the fetus. Medical technology can now prevent this condition through the use of a drug known as Rhogam.

Mental retardation can also occur as a result of postnatal infections and toxic excess. For example, **encephalitis** may damage the central nervous system following certain types of childhood infections (e.g., measles or mumps). Reactions to certain toxic substances—such as lead, carbon monoxide, and drugs—can also cause central nervous system damage.

■ TRAUMAS OR PHYSICAL ACCIDENTS   Traumas or physical accidents can occur either prior to birth (e.g., exposure to excessive radiation), during delivery, or after the baby is born. Consider Becky from the chapter opening snapshot: the cause of her mental retardation was trauma during delivery. She suffered from birth asphyxiation as well as epileptic seizures. The continuing supply of oxygen and nutrients to the baby is a critical factor during delivery. One threat to these processes involves the position of the fetus. Normal fetal position places the baby with the head toward the cervix and the face toward the mother's back. Certain other positions may result in damage to the fetus as delivery proceeds. One of these, breech presentation, occurs when the buttocks of the fetus, rather than the head, are positioned toward the cervix. The head exits last, rather than first, and can be subjected to several types of stress that would not occur in a normal delivery. The head passes through the birth canal under stress, and the pressure of the contractions has a direct impact on the fetal skull rather than on the buttocks, as in a normal position. In a breech presentation, the umbilical cord may not be long enough to remain attached while the head is expelled, or it may become pinched between the baby's body and the pelvic girdle. In either case, the baby's oxygen supply may be reduced for a period of time until the head is expelled and the lungs begin to function. The baby's lack of oxygen may result in damage to the brain. Such a condition is known as **anoxia** (oxygen deprivation).

Other abnormal positions can also result in delivery problems and damage to the fetus. The fetus may be situated across the birth canal in what is known as a *transverse position,* which either prevents the baby from exiting through the birth canal or causes such stress during exit that severe damage may occur. In other cases, labor and delivery proceed so rapidly that the fetal skull does not have time to mold properly or in a sufficiently gentle fashion. Rapid births (generally less than two hours) are known as **precipitous births** and may result in mental retardation as well as other problems.

■ UNKNOWN PRENATAL INFLUENCES

Several conditions associated with unknown prenatal influences can result in severe disorders. One such condition involves malformations of cerebral tissue. The most dramatic of these malformations is known as **anencephaly,** a condition in which the individual has a partial or even complete absence of cerebral tissue. In some cases, portions of the brain appear to develop and then degenerate. In **hydrocephalus,** also resulting from unknown origins, an excess of cerebrospinal fluid accumulates in the skull and results in potentially damaging pressure on cerebral tissue. Hydrocephalus may involve an enlarged head and result in decreased intellec-

■ ENCEPHALITIS. An inflammation of brain tissue that may damage the central nervous system.

■ ANOXIA. A lack of oxygen that may result in permanent damage to the brain.

■ PRECIPITOUS BIRTH. A delivery wherein the time between the onset of labor and birth is unusually short (generally less than two hours).

■ ANENCEPHALY. A condition in which the person has a partial or complete absence of cerebral tissue.

■ HYDROCEPHALUS. An excess of cerebrospinal fluid, often resulting in enlargement of the head and pressure on the brain, which may cause mental retardation.

tual functioning. If surgical intervention occurs early, the damage may be slight because the pressure will not have been serious or prolonged.

Although we have presented a number of possible causal factors associated with mental retardation, cause is often unknown and undeterminable in many cases. Additionally, many conditions associated with mental retardation are due to the interaction of both hereditary and environmental factors. Although we are unable to always identify the causes of mental retardation, measures can be taken to prevent its occurrence.

Prevention

Preventing mental retardation is a laudable goal and has been the focus of health care professionals for many years. Historically, prevention has taken many forms, including the sterilization of people with mental retardation. More recently, preventive measures have focused on immunization against disease, improvement of maternal nutritional habits during pregnancy, addressing maternal substance abuse, appropriate prenatal care, and screening for genetic disorders prior to and at birth.

Immunization can protect family members from contracting serious illness and guard against the mother's becoming ill during pregnancy. Diseases such as rubella, which may result in severe mental retardation, heart disease, or blindness, can be controlled through routine immunization programs.

Poor nutritional habits and substance abuse during pregnancy may also contribute to fetal problems and are part of a much larger social problem: the lack of appropriate prenatal care. Delays in prenatal care can have significant consequences for the health of the baby and the mother. Many conditions that are amenable to timely medical treatment can have serious complications if neglected.

A medical history can alert the attending physician to potential dangers for the mother or the unborn infant that may result from family genetics, prior trauma, or illness. The physician will be able to monitor the health of the fetus, including heart rate, physical size, and position in the uterus. At the time of birth, several factors relevant to the infant's health can be assessed. A procedure known as **Apgar scoring** evaluates the infant's heart rate, respiratory condition, muscle tone, reflex irritability, and color. This screening procedure alerts the medical staff to infants who may warrant closer monitoring and more in-depth assessments. Other screening procedures conducted in the medical laboratory within the first few days of life can detect anomalies that, if not treated, will eventually lead to mental retardation, psychological disorders, physical disabilities, or even death.

Other methods of prevention involve issues of morality and ethics. These include genetic screening and counseling and therapeutic abortion. Genetic screening is a search for certain genes that are predisposed to disease, are already diseased, or can lead to disease in future generations of the same family. Genetic screening may be conducted at various times in the family-planning process or during pregnancy. Screening prior to conception seeks parental predisposition to genetic anomalies that could be inherited by their offspring. Screening after conception seeks any genetic abnormalities in the fetus and can be accomplished through one of several medical procedures, including **amniocentesis, fetoscopy,** and **ultrasound.**

Once genetic screening has been completed, it is the responsibility of a counselor to inform parents of the test results, potential outcomes, and options. The genetic counselor does not make decisions for the parents regarding family planning, but he

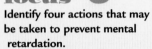

Identify four actions that may be taken to prevent mental retardation.

▪ APGAR SCORING. An evaluation of a newborn, which assesses heart rate, respiratory condition, muscle tone, reflexes, and color.

▪ AMNIOCENTESIS. A prenatal assessment of a fetus, which involves analysis of amniotic fluid to screen for possible abnormalities.

▪ FETOSCOPY. A procedure for examining the unborn baby, using a needle-like camera that is inserted into the womb to videoscan the fetus for visible abnormalities.

▪ ULTRASOUND. A prenatal evaluation procedure that employs high-frequency sound waves that are bounced through the mother's abdomen to record tissue densities. Ultrasound may be used as a prenatal assessment to locate fetal abnormalities.

or she does prepare the parents to exercise their rights. The primary outcome of genetic counseling can be viewed in terms of informing parents about decisions they have to make concerning (1) whether to have children, based on the probability of the occurrence of a genetic anomaly, or (2) whether to abort a pregnancy if prenatal assessment indicates that the developing fetus has a genetic anomaly.

Abortion involves a moral controversy that society has been debating for years. For example, if it is detected that a fetus has Down syndrome, what intervention options are available? Certainly, one option involves continuing the pregnancy and making mental, physical, and financial preparations for the additional care that may be required for the child. The other option is to terminate the pregnancy through a **therapeutic abortion.** This is abortion, nonetheless, and presents ethical dilemmas for many people.

The time immediately following birth, known as the *neonatal period,* may present some of the most difficult ethical dilemmas for parents and professionals. During the neonatal period, the issue is usually whether to withhold medical treatment from a defective newborn. This raises a number of ethical and moral questions: Who makes these decisions? Under what circumstances are such decisions made? What criteria are used to determine whether treatment is to be withheld?

Educational Assessment

Just as a physician assesses a person with mental retardation to determine the extent of needed health care services, professionals from several disciplines assess a student's need for special education. Once the needs have been identified, this multidisciplinary team joins with the student and his/her parents to plan and implement the appropriate educational services and supports. Depending on the student's identified needs, many professionals may be involved (such as classroom teachers, a school psychologist, a school administrator, a social worker, a speech or language specialist, an occupational or physical therapist, an adaptive physical education teacher, a school counselor, and a school nurse).

The multidisciplinary team has two important functions in the assessment of a student: to determine whether the student meets the criteria of mental retardation before placing him or her in a special education program, and to assess the educational needs of the student so that an appropriate educational program can be developed and implemented.

An intelligence test and a measure of adaptive skills must be completed to determine whether the child meets criteria. The most commonly used scales for measuring intelligence in school-age children are the Wechsler Intelligence Scales and the Stanford-Binet Intelligence Scale. Adaptive skills may be measured by both formal and informal appraisals. Informal appraisals include functional or ecological assessments (either through direct observations of the child in the environment or asking people in regular contact with the child, such as parents and classroom teachers, about his or her ability to cope with the demands of the environment). Formal appraisals include the use of standardized adaptive behavior scales such as the Vineland Social Maturity Scale, the Scales of Independent Behavior, and the AAMR Adaptive Behavior Scale.

Once it has been determined that the student meets the criteria for mental retardation, the team sets in place specific procedures to assess the nature of an appropriate educational experience. The team members' areas of expertise build a broad base for determining the student's needs. The psychologist and the classroom

■ THERAPEUTIC ABORTION. Termination of a pregnancy when a defect is found in the fetus during prenatal evaluation.

teacher select, administer, and interpret appropriate psychological, educational, and behavioral assessment instruments. In addition, they observe the student's performance in an educational setting and consult with parents and other team members regarding overall development. Parents provide the team with information regarding their son or daughter's performance outside of the school setting. Physical therapists, occupational therapists, and adaptive physical education specialists assess the motor development of the student. The speech or language specialist assesses the child's communication abilities. The social worker may collect pertinent information from the home setting as well as other background data relevant to the child's needs. The school nurse assists in the interpretation of information regarding the child's health (e.g., screening of hearing and vision, conferring with physicians, and monitoring medications).

Although each team member has specific responsibilities in assessing the educational needs of the child, it is important that the members work together as a unit. Each member of the team has the responsibility to maintain ongoing communication with other members, to actively participate in problem-solving situations, and to follow through with assigned tasks.

The Early Childhood Years

The provision of appropriate services and supports for people with mental retardation is a lifelong process. For people who have severe retardation, interventions should begin at birth and continue through the adult years. The importance of early intervention cannot be overstated.

Significant advances have been made in the area of early intervention, including improved assessment, curricular, and instructional technologies; increasing numbers of children receiving services; and appreciation of the need to individualize services for families as well as children (Guralnick, 1998; McDermott & Altrekruse, 1994; Noonan & McCormick, 1993; Young, 1996). Early intervention techniques, such as **infant stimulation** programs, focus on the acquisition of sensorimotor skills and intellectual development. Infant stimulation involves learning simple reflex activity and equilibrium reactions. Subsequent intervention then expands into all areas of human growth and development.

Intervention based on normal patterns of growth is referred to as the *developmental milestones approach* (Bailey & Wolery, 1992) because it seeks to develop, remedy, or adapt learner skills based on the child's variation from what is considered normal. This progression of skills continues as the child ages chronologically; rate of progress depends on the severity of the condition. Some children who are profoundly retarded may never exceed a developmental age of 6 months. Those with moderate retardation may develop to a level that will enable them to have fulfilled lives as adults, with varying levels of support.

The child with mild retardation may exhibit subtle developmental delays in comparison to age-mates, but parents may not view these discrepancies as significant enough to seek intervention during the preschool years. Even if parents are concerned and seek help for their child prior to elementary school, they are often confronted with professionals who are apathetic toward early childhood education. Some professionals believe that early childhood services may actually create, rather than remedy, problems, since the child may not be mature enough to cope with the pressures of structured learning in an educational environment. Simply stated, the maturation philosophy means that prior to entering school, a child should reach a

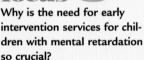

focus 8

Why is the need for early intervention services for children with mental retardation so crucial?

■ INFANT STIMULATION. Early intervention procedures that provide an infant with an array of visual, auditory, and physical stimuli to promote development.

level of growth at which he or she is ready to learn certain skills. Unfortunately, this philosophy has kept many children out of the public schools for years.

The antithesis of the maturation philosophy is the prevention of further learning and behavior problems through intervention. **Head Start,** initially funded as a federal preschool program for disadvantaged students, is a prevention program that attempts to identify and instruct high-risk children prior to their entering public school. Although Head Start did not generate the results that were initially anticipated (the virtual elimination of school-adjustment problems for the disadvantaged student), it has represented a significant move forward and continues to receive widespread support from parents and professionals alike. The rationale for early education is widely accepted in the field of special education and is an important part of the IDEA mandate (see Chapters 1 and 4).

■HEAD START. A federally funded preschool program for disadvantaged students to give them "a head start" prior to elementary school.

The Elementary School Years

Public education is a relatively new concept as it relates to students with mental retardation, particularly those with more severe characteristics. Historically, many of these students were defined as noneducable by the public schools because they did not fit the programs offered by general education. Because such programs were built on a foundation of academic learning that emphasized reading, writing, and arithmetic, students with mental retardation could not meet the academic standards set by the schools, and as such were excluded. Public schools were not expected to adapt to the needs of students with retardation; rather, the students were expected to adapt to the schools.

focus 9
Identify five skill areas that should be addressed in programs for elementary-age children with mental retardation.

Through both state and federal mandates (such as IDEA), the schools that excluded these children for so long are facing the challenge of providing an appropriate education for all children with mental retardation. Based on a new set of values, education has been redefined. Instruction and support for elementary school-age children with mental retardation focus on decreasing dependence on others while concurrently teaching adaptation to the environment. Therefore, instruction must concentrate on those skills that facilitate the child's interaction with others and emphasize independence in the community. Instruction for children with mental retardation generally include development of motor skills, self-help skills, social skills, communication skills, and academic skills.

■ MOTOR SKILLS

The acquisition of motor skills is a fundamental component of the developmental process and a prerequisite to successful learning in other content areas, including self-help and social skills. Gross motor development involves general mobility, including the interaction of the body with the environment. Gross motor skills are developed in a sequence, ranging from movements that make balance possible to higher-order locomotor patterns. Locomotor patterns are intended to move the person freely through the environment. Gross motor movements include controlling the head and neck, rolling, body righting, sitting, creeping, crawling, standing, walking, running, jumping, and skipping.

Fine motor development requires more precision and steadiness than the skills developed in the gross motor area. The development of fine motor skills, including reaching, grasping, and manipulating objects, is initially dependent on the ability of the child to visually fix on an object and visually track a moving target. Coordination of the eye and hand is an integral factor in many skill areas as well as in fine

The development of fine motor skills and eye-hand coordination is important in fostering independence for the young child with mental retardation.

motor development. Eye–hand coordination is the basis of social and leisure activities and is essential to the development of the object-control skills required in employment.

■ SELF-HELP SKILLS

The development of self-help skills is critical to a child's progression toward independence from caregivers. Self-help skills include eating, dressing, and maintaining personal hygiene. Eating skills range from finger feeding, drinking from a cup, and using proper table behaviors, such as employing utensils and napkins, serving food, and following etiquette. Dressing skills include buttoning, zipping, buckling, lacing, and tying. Personal hygiene skills are developed in an age-appropriate context. Basic hygiene skills include toileting, face and hand washing, bathing, tooth brushing, hair combing, and shampooing. Skills associated with adolescent and adult years include skin care, shaving, hair setting, use of deodorants and cosmetics, and menstrual hygiene.

■ SOCIAL SKILLS

Social skills training emphasizes the importance of learning problem-solving and decision-making skills and using appropriate communication in a social context. Agran and Wehmeyer (1999) indicated that poor problem-solving and decision-making skills have been barriers to the success of people with mental retardation in community and school settings. These authors further suggested that students with mental retardation will not learn these skills through observation but must be specifically taught how to solve problems. Benjamin (1996) proposed a four-step process:

1. Students learn to observe and analyze a problem situation through role playing and simulation, identify the problem(s) within the situation, and name the problem.
2. Students learn to come up with possible options that could solve the problem. If they are unable to produce options, they learn how to access resources (e.g., talking to other people) that will help generate possible solutions.
3. Once possible options have been identified, students select the most viable option to solve the problem. Once the option is implemented, the student checks to see if the problem has been solved. If the problem remains, students decide what can be done to change the plan.
4. Students learn how to use strategies from one problem to solve similar problems in other situations.

In the use of appropriate communication in a social context, Westling and Fox (2000) suggested several learning outcomes for students. They must be able to initiate and maintain a conversation (whether it be verbal, signed, or pictorial) while using appropriate social conventions and courtesies (e.g., staying on topic, not interrupting the speaker, appropriate body posture). These authors suggested a list of social skills that are important instructional targets for students with mental retardation. (See Table 9.4.)

TABLE 9.4	Instructional targets in social skills training

Establish eye contact.	Ask questions.
Establish appropriate proximity.	Make requests.
Maintain appropriate body posture during conversation.	Respond to request.
	Ask for information.
Speak with appropriate volume, rate, and expression.	Provide information.
	Ask for clarification.
Maintain attention during exchange.	Respond to requests for clarification.
Initiate greetings.	Extend social invitation.
Respond to greetings.	Deliver refusal.
Initiate partings.	Respond to refusals.
Respond to partings.	Use social courtesies (please, thank you, apology).
Discriminate appropriate times to greet or part.	
	Maintain topic.
Answer questions.	Initiate a new topic.

Source: From *Teaching Students with Severe Disabilities* (p. 242), by D. Westling and L. Fox, 2000, Upper Saddle River, NJ: Merrill.

■ COMMUNICATION SKILLS

The ability to communicate with others is an essential component of growth and development. Without communication, there can be no interaction. Communication systems for children with mental retardation take three general forms: verbal language, augmentative communication (including sign language and language boards), and a combination of the verbal and augmentative approaches. The approach used depends on the child's capability. A child who can develop the requisite skills for spoken language will have greatly enhanced everyday interactive skills. For a child unable to develop verbal skills as an effective means of communication, manual communication must be considered. What is important is that the child develop some form of communication that will facilitate interaction within natural settings. (See nearby feature, Interacting in Natural Settings.)

Some students with mental retardation will benefit from the use of augmentative communication. Augmentative communication refers to

the variety of communication approaches that are used to assist persons who are limited in their ability to communicate messages through natural modes of communication. These approaches may be unaided (e.g., manual sign and adapted gestures) or aided (utilization of communication boards or electronic devices). Regardless of the communication mode employed, the goals of augmented communicators are similar to those of natural speakers, that is, to express wants and needs, to share information, to engage in social closeness, and to manage social etiquette. (Franklin & Beukelman, 1991, p. 321)

■ ACADEMIC SKILLS

Students with mental retardation can benefit from instruction in basic or functional academic programs. In the area of literacy, students with mild mental retardation will require a systematic instructional program that accounts for differences in the rate of learning, but they will learn to read when given "rich, intensive, and extensive literary experiences" (Katims, 2000). In fact, these students may achieve as high as a fourth- or fifth-grade level in reading. In a 1996 study, Katims found that students with mental retardation made significant progress in literacy programs that

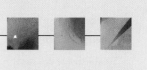

PEOPLE WITH MENTAL RETARDATION

▪ EARLY CHILDHOOD YEARS

TIPS FOR THE FAMILY

- Promote family learning about the diversity of all people in the context of understanding the child with intellectual differences.
- Create opportunities for friendships to develop between your child and children without disabilities, both in family and neighborhood settings.
- Help facilitate your child's opportunities and access to neighborhood preschools by actively participating in the education planning process. Become familiar with the individualized family service plan (IFSP) and how it can serve as a planning tool to support the inclusion of your child in preschool programs that involve students without disabilities.

TIPS FOR THE GENERAL EDUCATION PRESCHOOL TEACHER

- Focus on the child's individual abilities first. Whatever labels have been placed on the child (e.g., "mentally retarded") will have little to do with instructional needs.
- When teaching the child, focus on presenting each component of a task clearly, while reducing outside stimuli that may distract learning.
- Begin with simple tasks, and move to more complex ones as the child masters skills.
- Verbally label stimuli, such as objects or people, as often as possible to pro-

vide the child with both auditory and visual input.
- Provide a lot of practice in initial learning phases, using short but frequent sessions to ensure that the child has mastered the skill before moving on to more complex tasks.
- Create success experiences by rewarding correct responses to tasks as well as appropriate behavior with peers who are not disabled.
- It is important for the young child with mental retardation to be able to transfer learning from school to the home and neighborhood. Facilitate such transfer by providing information that is meaningful to the child and noting how the initial and transfer tasks are similar.

TIPS FOR PRESCHOOL PERSONNEL

- Support the inclusion of young children with mental retardation in classrooms and programs.
- Support teachers, staff, and volunteers as they attempt to create success experiences for the child in the preschool setting.
- Integrate families into the preschool programs as well as children. Offer parents as many opportunities as possible to be part of the program (e.g., advisory boards, volunteer experiences).

TIPS FOR NEIGHBORS AND FRIENDS

- Look for opportunities for young neighborhood children who are not disabled to interact during play times with the child who is mentally retarded.

- Provide a supportive community environment for the family of a young child who is mentally retarded. Encourage the family, including the child, to participate in neighborhood activities (e.g., outings, barbecues, outdoor yard and street cleanups, crime watches).
- Try to understand how the young child with mental retardation is similar to other children in the neighborhood rather than different. Focus on those similarities in your interactions with other neighbors and children in your community.

▪ ELEMENTARY YEARS

TIPS FOR THE FAMILY

- Actively participate in the development of your son or daughter's individualized education program (IEP). Through active participation, fight for the goals that you would like to see on the IEP that will focus on your child's developing social interaction and communication skills in natural settings (e.g., the general education classroom).
- To help facilitate your son or daughter's inclusion in the neighborhood elementary school, help educators and administrators understand the importance of inclusion with peers who are not disabled (e.g., riding on the same school bus, going to recess and lunch at the same time, participating in schoolwide assemblies).
- Participate in as many school functions for parents (e.g., PTA, parent advisory

groups, volunteering) as is reasonable, to connect your family to the mainstream of the general education school.
- Create opportunities for your child to make friends with same-age children without disabilities, both within the family and neighborhood.

TIPS FOR THE GENERAL EDUCATION CLASSROOM TEACHER

- View children with mental retardation as children, first and foremost. Focus on their similarities with other children rather than their differences.
- Recognize children with mental retardation for their own accomplishments within the classroom rather than comparing them to those of peers without disabilities.
- Employ cooperative learning strategies wherever possible to promote effective learning by all students. Try to use peers without disabilities as support for students with mental retardation. This may include establishing peer-buddy programs or peer and cross-age tutoring.
- Consider all members of the classroom when you organize the physical environment. Find ways to meet the individual needs of each child (e.g., establishing aisles that will accommodate a wheelchair, and organizing desks to facilitate tutoring on assigned tasks).

TIPS FOR SCHOOL PERSONNEL

- Integrate school resources as well as children.

- Wherever possible, help general classroom teachers access the human and material resources necessary to meet the needs of students with mental retardation. Instructional materials and programs should be made available to whoever needs them, not just those identified as being in special education.
- Assist general and special education teachers to develop nondisabled peer-partner and support networks for students with mental retardation.
- Promote the heterogeneous grouping of students. Try to avoid clustering large numbers of students with mental retardation in a single general education classroom. Integrate no more than one or two in each elementary education classroom.
- Maintain the same schedules for students with mental retardation as for all other students in the building. Recess, lunch, school assemblies, and bus arrival and departure schedules should be identical for all students, with and without disabilities.
- Create opportunities for all school personnel to collaborate in the development and implementation of instructional programs for individual children.

TIPS FOR NEIGHBORS AND FRIENDS
- Support families who are seeking to have their child with mental retardation educated in their local school with children who are not disabled. This will help children with mental retardation have more opportunities for interacting with children who are not disabled, both in school and in the local community.

■ SECONDARY AND TRANSITION YEARS

TIPS FOR THE FAMILY
- Create opportunities for your son or daughter to participate in activities that are of interest to him or her beyond the school day with their same-age peers who are not disabled, including high school clubs, sports, or just hanging out in the local mall.
- Promote opportunities for students from your son's or daughter's high school to visit your home. Help arrange get-togethers or parties involving students from the neighborhood and/or school.
- Become actively involved in the development of the individualized education and transition program. Explore with the high school their views on what should be done to assist your son or daughter in the transition from school to adult life.

TIPS FOR THE GENERAL EDUCATION CLASSROOM TEACHER
- Collaborate with special education teachers and other specialists to adapt subject matter in your classroom (e.g., science, math, or physical education) to the individual needs of students with mental retardation.
- Let students without disabilities know that the student with mental retardation belongs in their classroom. The goals and activities of this student may be different from those of other students, but with support, the student with mental retardation will benefit from working with you and the other students in the class.
- Support the student with mental retardation in becoming involved in extracurricular high school activities. If you are the faculty sponsor of a club or organization, explore whether this student is interested and how he or she could get involved.

TIPS FOR SCHOOL PERSONNEL
- Advocate for parents of high-school-age students with mental retardation to participate in the activities of the school (e.g., committees and PTA).
- Help facilitate parental involvement in the IEP process during the high school years by valuing parental input that focuses on a desire for including their child in the mainstream of the school. Parents will be more active when school personnel have general and positive contact with the family.
- Provide human and material support to high school special education or vocational teachers seeking to develop community-based instruction programs that focus on students learning and applying skills in actual community settings (e.g., grocery stores, malls, theaters, parks, work sites).

TIPS FOR NEIGHBORS, FRIENDS, AND POTENTIAL EMPLOYERS
- Work with the family and school personnel to create opportunities for students with mental retardation to participate in community activities (such as going to the movies, "hanging out" with nondisabled peers in the neighborhood mall, going to high school sports events) as often as possible.
- As a potential employer, work with the high school to locate and establish community-based employment training sites for students with mental retardation.

■ ADULT YEARS

TIPS FOR THE FAMILY
- Become aware of what life will be like for your son or daughter in the local community during the adult years. What are the formal (government-funded, advocacy organizations) and informal supports available in your community? What are the characteristics of adult service programs? Explore adult support systems in the local community in the areas of supported living, employment, and recreation and leisure.

TIPS FOR NEIGHBORS, FRIENDS, AND POTENTIAL EMPLOYERS
- Seek ways to become part of the community support network for the individual with mental retardation. Be alert to ways that this individual can become and remain actively involved in community employment, neighborhood recreational activities, and functions at a local house of worship.
- As potential employers in the community, seek information on employment of people with mental retardation. Find out about programs (e.g., supported employment) that focus on establishing work for people with mental retardation while meeting your needs as an employer.

emphasized **direct instruction** (the direct teaching of letters, words, and syntactic, phonetic, and semantic analysis) in conjunction with written literature that was meaningful to the student, or from the student's own writings.

A significant relationship exists between measured IQ and reading achievement: Students with mental retardation read well below nondisabled students of the same age. This relationship seems to suggest that reading instruction should be limited to higher-functioning students with mental retardation. A growing body of research, however, indicates that students with more severe mental retardation can learn "useful" academic skills in a functional reading program. Browder and Snell (2000) described functional academics as "simply the most useful parts of the three R's— reading, writing, and arithmetic. . . . *Useful* must be defined individually by studying each student's current daily routines, predicting future needs, and establishing a set of priorities in basic math and reading" (p. 497). A functional reading program uses materials that are a part of a person's normal routines in work, everyday living, and leisure activities. For example, functional reading involves words that are frequently encountered in the environment, such as those used on labels or signs in public places; words that warn of possible risks; and symbols such as the skull and crossbones to denote poisonous substances.

Students with mental retardation are also deficient in arithmetic skills, but the majority of those with mild retardation can learn basic addition and subtraction. However, these children will have significant difficulty in the areas of mathematical reasoning and problem-solving tasks (Beirne-Smith et al., 1998). Arithmetic skills are taught most efficiently through the use of money concepts. For example, functional math involves activities such as learning to use a checkbook, shop in a grocery store, or operate a vending machine. The immediate practical application motivates the student. Regardless of the approach used, arithmetic instruction must be concrete and practical to compensate for the child's deficiencies in reasoning ability.

The Adolescent Years

focus 10

Identify four educational goals for adolescents with mental retardation.

The goals of an educational program for adolescents with mental retardation are to increase personal independence, enhance opportunities for participation in the local community, prepare for employment, and facilitate a successful transition to the adult years.

■ PERSONAL INDEPENDENCE AND PARTICIPATION IN THE COMMUNITY

Independence refers to the development and application of skills that lead to greater self-sufficiency in daily personal life, including personal care, self-help, and appropriate leisure activities. Participation in the community includes access to programs, facilities, and services that those without disabilities often take for granted: grocery stores, shopping malls, restaurants, theaters, and parks. Adolescents with mental retardation should have opportunities for interaction with nondisabled peers other than caregivers, access to community events, sustained social relationships, and involvement in choices that affect their lives. Work is a crucial measure of any person's success during adulthood, providing the primary opportunity for social interaction, a basis for personal identity and status, and a chance to contribute to the community. These needs are basic to adults who have mental retardation, just as they are to their nondisabled peers.

For adolescents with severe mental retardation, employment preparation during high school is shifting from segregated sheltered workshops to the skills needed for supported employment in an integrated setting.

■ EMPLOYMENT PREPARATION

Employment preparation for adolescents with mental retardation was historically fraught with problems because professionals and the general public held a pessimistic attitude about its effectiveness. Today, that negative philosophy has largely been replaced by a commitment to the development of relevant employment-training programs, particularly in competitive employment settings (Blanck & Braddock, 1998; McDonnell, Mathot-Buckner, & Ferguson, 1996; Ryan, 2000; Wehman, 1996).

Employment training during the high school years is shifting from the isolation and "getting ready" orientation of a **sheltered workshop** to activities accomplished in community employment. Goals and objectives are developed according to the demands of the community work setting and the functioning level of the individual. The focus is on assisting each person to learn and apply skills in a job setting while receiving the support necessary to succeed. Providing ongoing assistance to the individual on the job is the basis of an approach known as **supported employment.** Supported employment is defined as work in an integrated setting for individuals with severe disabilities (including those with mental retardation) who are expected to need continuous support services and for whom competitive employment has traditionally not been possible (see Chapter 5).

Research indicates that individuals with mental retardation, including those with moderate and severe differences, can work in community employment if provided adequate training and support (Reiff, Ginsberg, & Gerber, 1997; Tines, Rusch, McCaughrin, & Conley, 1990; Wehman, 1996). Effectively preparing these adolescents for community work settings requires a comprehensive employment-training program during the high school years. Adherence to the following guidelines will help enable the student to access and succeed in a community job following school:

1. The student should have the opportunity to make informed choices about what jobs he or she wants to do and where he or she wants to work.
2. The student should receive employment training in community settings prior to graduation from high school.
3. Employment training should focus on work opportunities present in the local area where the individual currently lives.

■ SHELTERED WORKSHOP. A segregated vocational training and employment setting for people with disabilities.

■ SUPPORTED EMPLOYMENT. Paid work in integrated community settings for individuals with more severe disabilities who are expected to need continuous support services, and for whom competitive employment has traditionally not been possible.

Today's Technology

HOW TECHNOLOGY HELPS ADOLESCENTS WITH MENTAL RETARDATION IN TRANSITION FROM SCHOOL TO WORK

■ What opportunities do high school youth with mental retardation have when it comes to job placement?

■ Why do special educators and others in secondary transition programs place most of these youth in fast-food jobs, custodial positions, and other service occupations? Is it because they prefer these jobs, or do they have insufficient information about other opportunities?

■ To what extent are the scope and breadth of information about jobs and careers limited by what educators provide these young people?

■ Are the career choices of these youth "self-determined" only in a narrow sense, bounded by the information at hand?

■ How can we provide youth with realistic, efficient information about career paths and ensure that their choices guide transition planning?

The above questions are central to some of the dilemmas encountered by adolescents with mental retardation and the educators who support their transition. One way to provide more information to youth and to represent the complexity of employment environments is to use motion video on CD-ROM. The video medium realistically portrays the complex stimuli in employment envi-

ronments, presents information efficiently, and offers a permanent resource for future use. The YES Project, funded by a grant from the U.S. Department of Education and based at Utah State University, is developing a job preference program using motion video on CD-ROM. A student with mental retardation or other disabilities works with a facilitator, such as a special education teacher or a transition specialist, at a computer. The student makes computer selections by using a mouse or by pointing to a touch screen. The outcome is a short list of 5–10 preferred jobs selected by the student. The transition team can then use this list as the focus of transition activities. This program is appropriate for adolescents and adults with disabilities, such as mental retardation and autism, who are unable to take advantage of reading-based programs.

The CD-ROM program distinguishes six job domains based on various characteristics (e.g., work location, required physical stamina, level of social activity). Working individually with a facilitator, the youth will initially identify general work conditions. This screening process allows the youth to identify preferences in employment conditions (e.g., inside vs. outside work, heavy vs. light physical involvement, working mostly alone vs. mostly with people).

■ RYAN'S STORY: FROM JOB PLACEMENT CHALLENGE TO EMPLOYEE OF THE MONTH

Ryan is a 22-year-old young man with mental retardation. I first met Ryan when he was referred after a series of unsuccessful community-based job placements. The background information I received from his previous service provider described him as unmotivated and sloppy in both appearance and job performance. The professionals who had worked with Ryan in the past recommended that he return to a sheltered day program for "work skills training."

During the intake process, I asked Ryan to name his three most desired jobs. The jobs he identified as most preferred were the same ones from which he had been fired due to extensive absence or poor performance. Documentation indicated that although Ryan was able to perform the tasks associated with each job, he would lose interest after a short time.

To further assist Ryan in identifying and obtaining employment, staff from a local university project, the Yes Program provided him the opportunity to view a number of jobs on a video. After watching the video, Ryan identified motel housekeeping as a desired job. He seemed really excited about this particular job. So together, he and I began our job search. After a few weeks

of job development, we found a rather reluctant employer who was willing to give Ryan a job on a 30-day trial basis. I explained the agreement to Ryan, and again he assured me that this was the job he wanted.

Within 3 weeks, Ryan had become the fastest and most dependable housekeeper on the motel's staff. His employer was so impressed with his work that she asked me if I had other people with disabilities looking for employment. Within 6 weeks of his start date, Ryan was awarded Employee of the Month and was given a cash bonus. Less than 2 months after starting the job, he was promoted to "second floor supervisor" and received a raise. In my last contact with him, Ryan was supervising a crew of employees — adults without disabilities — on an entire motel wing. The once hesitant and skeptical employer now brags about Ryan's performance to anyone who will listed.

—Becky Blair,
Employment Specialist

Source: Adapted from "'That's the Job I Want': How Technology Helps Young People in Transition," by R. L. Morgan, D. A. Ellerd, B. P. Gerity, and R. J. Blair, 2000, *Teaching Exceptional Children, 32*(4), pp. 44–49.

4. The focus of the employment training should be on specific job training as the student approaches graduation.
5. Collaboration between the school and adult service agencies must be part of the employment-training program. (Drew & Hardman, 2000; Morgan, Ellerd, Gerity, & Blair, 2000) (See nearby Today's Technology feature.)

Inclusive Education

The educational placement of students with mental retardation has been a critical issue for school personnel and parents for many years. Prior to the late 1960s, special education for students with mental retardation meant segregated education. Since then, much of the focus on educational placement has been concerned with including these students with their nondisabled age-mates. Inclusive education may be defined as the placement of students with mental retardation in general education classrooms with nondisabled peers, consistent with an established individualized education program for each student. Some students with mental retardation may be only partially included for a small part of the school day and attend only those general education classes that their individualized education program (IEP) teams consider consistent with their needs and functioning levels (such as physical education, industrial arts, home economics). Other students with mental retardation may attend general education classes for all or the majority of the school day. For these students, special education consists primarily of services and supports intended to facilitate their opportunities and success in the general education classroom. Placement information from the U.S. Department of Education (2000a) indicated that in 1998–1999 approximately 94% of students with mental retardation between the ages of 6 and 21 were placed in general education schools for the entire day. Of these students, about 10% were served in a general education class for at least 80% of their time, and 50% spent more than half of their time outside the general education class.

Another placement option for students with disabilities is the special school. Special schools are defined as facilities exclusively for students with mental retardation or other disabilities. Approximately 4.6% of students with mental retardation attended public special schools in 1998–1999, and another 1.2% attended private special schools. (See Debate Forum at the end of this chapter.)

focus 11

Why is the inclusion of students with mental retardation with their nondisabled peers important to an appropriate educational experience?

Medical and Social Services

The diverse needs of people with mental retardation require the intervention of several professionals. Because most individuals with moderate to profound mental retardation exhibit problems evident at birth, a physician is usually the first professional to come in contact with these children.

The physician's primary roles are as diagnostician, counselor, and caregiver. As a diagnostician, the physician analyzes the nature and cause of the child's condition and then, based on the medical information available, counsels the family concerning the medical prognosis. The physician's role as a family counselor has been challenged by some professionals in the behavioral sciences and by parents because such counseling often exceeds the medical domain. This concern reflects the opinion that medical personnel should counsel families only on medical matters and recommend

focus 12

Identify the roles of medicine and social services in meeting the diverse needs of people with mental retardation.

FIGURE 9.2

Categories of social services

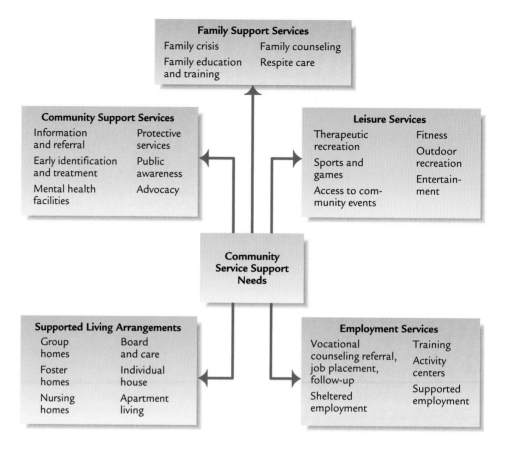

other resources—educators, psychologists, social workers, clergy, or parent groups—when dealing with issues other than the child's medical needs.

The appropriate social services for a person with mental retardation extend into many realms of life: the primary family, the extended family, the neighborhood, the educational environment, and the community at large. Thus appropriate social services may be classified in five general categories: family support services, community support services, supported living arrangements, leisure services, and employment services. Figure 9.2 illustrates some of the supports included within each of these general categories.

Social services provide individuals with mental retardation a greater opportunity to achieve what is commonly referred to as normalization. The principle of **normalization** emphasizes the need to make available to the individual "the patterns and conditions of everyday life which are as close to the norms and patterns of mainstream society" as possible (Nirje, 1970, p. 181). Normalization goes far beyond the mere physical inclusion of the individual into a community. In addition, it promotes the availability of needed supports, such as training and supervision, without which the individual with mental retardation may not be prepared to cope with the demands of community life.

▪ NORMALIZATION. Making the patterns and conditions of everyday life, and of mainstream society available to persons with disabilities.

Case Study

LARA

Lara Clark has two jobs, which is quite an achievement for someone who, according to the records, couldn't walk or talk until age 12. Today, at age 51, Lara works at a medical center and at the local sheltered workshop. She also volunteers at the public library. Her days are full, which as she says, "Is better than doin' nothin'. Nothing is what I used to do." It is hard to imagine how this situation came about until you begin to examine her history.

In a world full of records and files, details about Lara's past are hard to find. From her records, it appears that she lived at home until she was 22 years old, at which time her mother died and Lara was placed in an institution. In 1966, at age 30, Lara went to live in a community care home, where she remained for 11 years even though rumors of physical abuse surrounded the home. After moving to yet another group home, she moved to a rural community where Lara now lives with Carrie and Bob Hanson, their 2-year-old daughter, and two other women with disabilities.

Lara talks about the things she did when she lived with her mother and about her new job and her new friends. She doesn't mention the time that has elapsed between living with her mother and her current life.

Her life of "doin' nothin'" has changed to one bustling from place to place. On Mondays and Tuesdays she goes to the sheltered workshop. On Wednesdays and Fridays she works at the medical center where she places stickers on EKG equipment. On Thursdays she volunteers at the public library where she cleans and stacks books:

I like what I do at the library and the hospital. It's more serious than the workshop. I also like being home most afternoons by 1:30 p.m. I take a nap or work on my afghan.

Although it is hard work, she likes working at the medical center. Her only complaint concerns the times when she worked half-days "because I got home too early." She's happy that she has made friends outside the workshop. However, as suggested by Lara, "The best part of my job at the hospital is that I get paid."

Lara's social activities have also increased since she began work at the medical center. She now goes out to eat with her boyfriend and other friends. She is able to buy her own yarn for her afghans. "Shopping for clothes" is one of the most important benefits of the money, she says.

If the staff at the workshop and the medical center have anything to say about it, Lara's time and pocketbook may fill up even more. Plans are being made for Lara to work five days a week at the medical center instead of splitting her time between the two employment sites.

Working has provided Lara with activities that keep her life busy. However, it would appear that the most important byproduct of her experiences is a change of attitude. Carrie Hanson thinks that the job has provided Lara an independence that she didn't have before:

Lara feels rewarded by what she does at the hospital. She feels she is doing something worthwhile, and getting paid for it. As a result she pays more attention to having money and works harder to get it.

Whether it was the new job, the increased income, or her friends, it is evident to those that meet her that Lara Clark is proud of the work she does, the friends she has, and the life she leads. She no longer thinks she's "doin' nothin'."

■ APPLICATION

In the past few years, Lara has been moving from a sheltered workshop to more paid work in a community setting. Brainstorm and list some of the ongoing support that Lara will need as she makes the transition to full-time integrated employment.

Beyond monetary rewards, what are some other benefits that will exist for Lara as a result of her job at the medical center?

Lara is 51 years old. How might life have been different for her had she been born 30 years later?

Source: Adapted from *Stories of Work,* by B. Guy, J. Scott, S. Hasazi, and A. Patten, (n.d.), (unpublished manuscript), Burlington: University of Vermont.

Debate Forum

CAN SPECIAL SCHOOLS FOR STUDENTS WITH MENTAL RETARDATION BE JUSTIFIED?

■ POINT

There will always be a need for a special school. Although inclusion may be appropriate for many students with mental retardation, special schools are the least restrictive environment for a small number of children who require intensive instruction and support that cannot be provided in a general education school or classroom. Special schools provide for greater homogeneity in grouping and programming. Teachers can specialize in particular areas such as art, language, physical education, and music. Teaching materials can be centralized and, thus, used more effectively with larger numbers of students. A special school more efficiently uses available resources. In addition, some parents of students with severe mental retardation believe that their children will be happier in a special school that "protects" them.

■ COUNTERPOINT

Research on the efficacy of special schools does not support the contention that such a placement is ever the least restrictive environment (Downing & Eichinger, 1996; Gee, 1996; Sailor, Gee, & Karasoff, 2000). On the contrary, investigations over the past 20 years have strongly indicated that students with mental retardation, regardless of the severity of their condition, benefit from placement in general education environments where opportunities for interaction with students who are not disabled are systematically planned and implemented (Hunt, Staub, Alwell, & Goetz, 1994a; Meyer, Peck, & Brown, 1991; Sailor et al., 2000). Inclusion for students with mental retardation embodies a variety of opportunities, both within the general education classroom and throughout the school. Besides interaction in a classroom setting, ongoing inclusion may be found in the halls, on the playground, in the cafeteria, and at school assemblies.

Stainback, Stainback, and Ayres (1996) also reported that general education teachers who have the opportunity for interaction with children with mental retardation are not fearful of or intimidated by their presence in the school building. Special schools generally offer little, if any, opportunity for interaction with normal peers and deprive the child of valuable learning and socialization experiences. Special schools cannot be financially or ideologically justified. Public school administrators must now plan to include children with retardation in existing general education schools and classes.

Review

focus 1

Identify the three components of the AAMR definition of mental retardation.

- Significantly subaverage intellectual functioning is defined as two standard deviations below the mean on an individual test of intelligence.
- Adaptive skill limitations may occur in communication, self-care, home living, social skills, community use, self-direction, health and safety, functional academics, leisure, or work.
- The condition is manifested before 18 years of age.

focus 2

Identify four approaches to classifying people with mental retardation.

- Severity of the condition may be described in terms of mild, moderate, severe, and profound mental retardation.
- Educability expectations are designated for groups of children who are educable, trainable, and custodial.
- Medical descriptors classify mental retardation on the basis of the origin of the condition (e.g., infection, intoxication, trauma, chromosomal abnormality).
- Classification based on the type and extent of support needed categorize people with mental retardation according to intermittent, limited, extensive, or pervasive needs for support in order to function in natural settings.

focus 3

What is the prevalence of mental retardation?

- There are over 600,000 students between the ages of 6 and 21 labeled as having mental retardation and receiving service under IDEA. Approximately 11% of all students with disabilities between the ages of 6 and 21 have mental retardation.

- The National Health Survey–Disability Supplement found that people with mental retardation constitute 0.83% of the total population, or 2 million people.
- The President's Committee on Mental Retardation (2000) estimated that between 6.2 and 7.5 million Americans of all ages, or 3% of the general population, experience mental retardation. These figures are considerably higher than the 2 million people reported in the National Health Survey.

 focus 4

Identify four intellectual and adaptive skills characteristic of individuals with mental retardation.

- Intellectual characteristics may include learning and memory deficiencies, difficulties in establishing learning sets, and inefficient rehearsal strategies.
- Adaptive skills characteristics may include difficulties in coping with the demands of environment, developing interpersonal relationships, developing language skills, and taking care of personal needs.

 focus 5

Identify the academic, motivational, speech and language, and physical characteristics of children with mental retardation.

- Students with mental retardation exhibit significant deficits in the areas of reading and mathematics.

- Students with mild mental retardation have poor reading mechanics and comprehension, compared to their same-age peers.
- Students with mental retardation may be able to learn basic computations but be unable to apply concepts appropriately in a problem-solving situation.
- Motivational difficulties may reflect learned helplessness—"No matter what I do or how hard I try, I will not succeed."
- The most common speech difficulties involve articulation problems, voice problems, and stuttering.
- Language differences are generally associated with delays in language development rather than the bizarre use of language.
- Physical differences generally are not evident for individuals with mild mental retardation because the retardation is usually not associated with genetic factors.
- The more severe the mental retardation, the greater the probability of genetic causation and compounding physiological problems.

 focus 6

Identify the causes of mental retardation.

- Mental retardation is the result of multiple causes, some known, many unknown. The cause of mental retardation is generally not known for the individual who is mildly retarded.
- Causes associated with moderate to profound mental retardation include sociocultural influences,

biomedical factors, behavioral factors, and unknown prenatal influences.

 focus 7

Identify four actions that may be taken to prevent mental retardation.

- Immunizations against disease
- Appropriate nutrition for the mother during pregnancy
- Appropriate prenatal care
- Screening for genetic disorders at birth

 focus 8

Why is the need for early intervention services for children with mental retardation so crucial?

- Early intervention services are needed to provide a stimulating environment for the child to enhance growth and development.
- Early intervention programs focus on the development of communication skills, social interaction, and readiness for formal instruction.

 focus 9

Identify five skill areas that should be addressed in programs for elementary-age children with mental retardation.

- Motor development skills
- Self-help skills
- Social skills
- Communication skills
- Academic skills

 focus 10

Identify four educational goals for adolescents with mental retardation.

- To increase the individual's personal independence
- To enhance opportunities for participation in the local community
- To prepare for employment
- To facilitate a successful transition to the adult years

 focus 11

Why is the inclusion of students with mental retardation with their nondisabled peers important to an appropriate educational experience?

- Regardless of the severity of their condition, students with mental retardation benefit from placement in general education environments where opportunities for inclusion with nondisabled peers are systematically planned and implemented.

 focus 12

Identify the roles of medicine and social services in meeting the diverse needs of people with mental retardation.

- The physician's roles include diagnostician, counselor, and caregiver.
- Appropriate social services include community support services, family support services, alternative living arrangements, employment services, and leisure services.

People with Communication Disorders

10

To begin with . . .

Nineteen percent of the children (6–21 years old) with disabilities who were served under federal law during 1997–1998 had speech or language difficulties. (U.S. Department of Education, 2000)

"It's her self-expression, her ability to express her feelings and goals. Just being understood makes her feel valued, . . . That's the purpose of technology—to not hold people back." (Norma Velez, speaking about her daughter's voice machine, as quoted by Horiuchi, 1999)

Maternal input, social interaction, play, and cognitive development all play a dynamic role in early language development. Although children come to the language acquisition process biologically equipped to learn language, the role they play is an active one. (Bernstein, 1997b, p. 98)

Snapshot

Meghan

Meghan is 12 years old. She is a respected member of her sixth-grade class in a school that has become a powerful inclusive community for her. People are drawn to Meghan because of her courage, humor, and her belief in living for her dreams.

Meghan has a strong circle of friends who pay attention to who she is as a person and know how to be with her and share in many different mutual experiences. Meghan enjoys skiing, playing tennis, swimming, music, and movies. Meghan's friends call her on the phone and talk to her—even if she chooses only to listen. If they could just see her smile over the telephone! She goes to birthday parties and has slumber parties. Her friends have given her the opportunity to be a typical sixth grader.

When Meghan was born, we knew she had cerebral palsy. We saw that she had a projected motor delay and cognitive delay, but how much was uncertain. As parents, we wanted a language-based environment, not a life skills environment for Meghan. We wanted her to have a childhood where her strengths were recognized, and her hopes for learning encouraged. Meghan may never tell us on demand the 26 letters of the alphabet, a readiness requirement in the developmental center program, but she was able to return to an inclusive fourth-grade community, where she learned the history of California. She knew the people who built the railroad and could tell us this through an adapted curriculum and picture cues, and she was accurate.

Meghan is apraxic. It is hard for her to come up with words—it is hard for her to retrieve them and it is hard for her to summon the motor skills to utter them. But she is driven to talk and to get her messages out. We use many forms of communication with her: verbal modeling, singing because it builds vocabulary (music uses another part of the brain), sign language for a visual way to focus, and a Dynavox. The Dynavox is touch-activated and creates verbal speech. We can program information on its screen to increase practical language skills as well as link up with the curriculum she is being taught in school. Meghan just completed an oral presentation on the Alaskan oil spill. We created a page on the Dynavox with picture cues that had verbal messages sequencing the key topics of her report.

One of Meghan's friends helped her program "I'm having a bad hair day" into her Dynavox diary. She uses sassy sixth-grade language now, and we think of it as an increase in language skills. We can be the great Mom, Dad, teachers in her life, but it is her peers who are the most valuable resources, for they see Meghan as a person first and her disability second. They will make the difference in her tomorrows, for they pay attention to what they have in common and not what makes them different.

focus **1**

Identify four ways in which speech, language, and communication are interrelated.

OMMUNICATION IS A DAILY EVENT; we engage in this activity many times each day. We order food in a restaurant, thank a friend for doing a favor, ask a question in class, call for help in an emergency, follow instructions regarding the assembly of a gift received by mail, or give directions to someone who is lost. Our lives revolve around communication in many central ways. Despite its importance and constant presence in our lives, we seldom think much about communication unless there is a problem with it. Communication is also one of the most complicated processes people undertake. Speech and language are two highly interrelated components of communication. Problems in either can significantly affect a person's daily life. Because of their complexity, determining the cause of a problem in these areas is often perplexing.

Communication is the exchange of ideas, opinions, or facts between senders and receivers. It requires that a sender (an individual or group) compose and transmit a message and that a receiver decode and understand the message (Bernstein, 1997b). The sender and receiver are therefore partners in the communication process. Com-

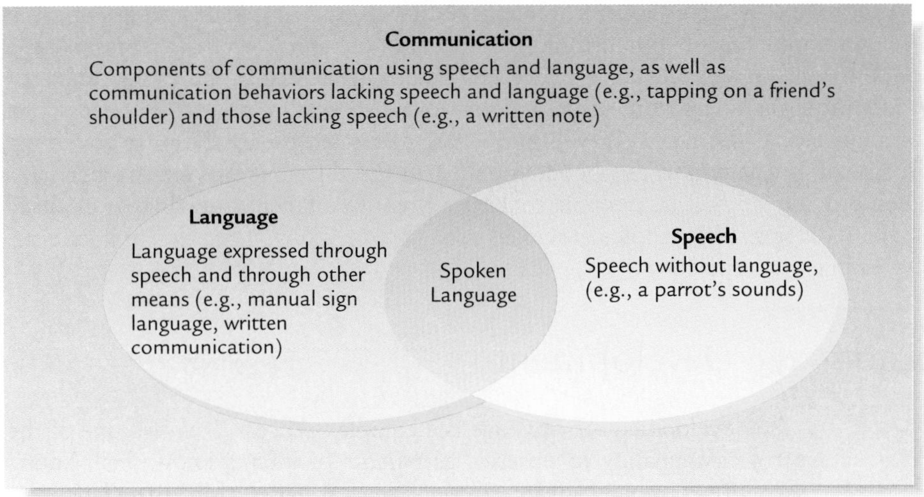

FIGURE 10.1

A conceptual model of communication, language, and speech

Communication
Components of communication using speech and language, as well as communication behaviors lacking speech and language (e.g., tapping on a friend's shoulder) and those lacking speech (e.g., a written note)

Language
Language expressed through speech and through other means (e.g., manual sign language, written communication)

Spoken Language

Speech
Speech without language, (e.g., a parrot's sounds)

munication is perhaps our most important tool in interacting with our environment. Part of this tool involves the use of speech and language.

Although related, speech and language are not synonymous. Speech is the audible representation of language. It is one means of expressing language but not the only means. Language represents the message contained in speech. It is possible to have language without speech, such as sign language used by people who are deaf, and speech without languages, such as the speech of birds that are trained to talk. Communication is the broader concept. Language is a part of communication. Speech is often thought of as a part of language, although language may exist without speech. Figure 10.1 illustrates the interrelationship of speech, language, and communication.

The Structure of Language

Language consists of several major components, including phonology, syntax, morphology, semantics, and pragmatics. Phonology refers to the system of speech sounds that an individual utters, that is, rules regarding how sounds can be used and combined (Post, 1999; Stahl & Murray, 1998). For example, the word cat has three phonemes, C–A–T. Syntax involves the rules governing sentence structure, the way sequences of words are combined into phrases and sentences. For example, the sentence *Will you help Janice?* changes in meaning when the order of words is changed to *You will help Janice.* Morphology is concerned with the form and internal structure of words, that is, the transformations of words in terms of areas such as tense and number—present to past tense, singular to plural, and so on. When we add an *s* to *cat,* we have produced the plural form, *cats,* with two morphemes, or units of meaning—the concept of cat and the concept of plural. Such transformations involve prefixes, suffixes, and inflections (Grinstead, 2000; Szagun, 2000). Grammar is constituted from a combination of syntax and morphology. Semantics represents the understanding of language, the component most concerned with meaning. Semantics addresses whether the speaker's intended message is conveyed by the words and their combinations in an age-appropriate manner. It involves the meaning of a word to an individual, which may be unique in each of our personal mental dictionaries (e.g., the meaning of the adjective *nice* in the phrase *nice house*).

Pragmatics is a component of language that is receiving increased attention in recent literature (e.g., Nippold, 2000; Toppelberg & Shapiro, 2000). It represents the "rules that govern the reason(s) for communicating (called communicative functions or intentions) as well as the rules that govern the choice of codes to be used when communicating" (Bernstein, 1997b, p. 9). Pragmatics represents the rules governing the use of language and can be exemplified in the different ways a teacher talks when providing direct instruction, making a point in a faculty meeting, or chatting at a party. Pragmatics includes processes such as turn taking, initiating, maintaining, and ending a conversation.

Language Development

The development of language is a complex process. It is also one of the most fascinating to observe, as parents of infants know well. Young children normally advance through several stages in acquiring language, from a preverbal stage to the use of words in sentences. An infant's initial verbal output is primarily limited to crying, usually associated with discomfort (e.g., from hunger, pain, or being soiled or wet). Before long (around 2 months), babies begin to coo as well as cry, verbally expressing reactions to pleasure as well as discomfort. They begin to babble at about 3 to 6 months of age, which involves making some consonant and vowel sounds. At this point, babies often make sounds repeatedly when they are alone, seemingly experimenting with their sound-making and not necessarily trying to communicate with anyone (Puckett, 2001). They may also babble when their parents or others are with them, playing or otherwise handling them.

A baby's first word is a momentous, long-anticipated event. In fact, eager parents often attach words to sounds that stretch the imagination of more objective observers and likely have no meaning to the child. What usually happens is that the baby begins to string together sounds that occasionally resemble words. To the parents' delight, these sounds frequently include utterances such as "Da-Da" and "Ma-Ma," which, of course, are echoed, repeated, and reinforced greatly by Father and Mother. As the baby actually begins to listen to the speech of adults, exchanges or "conversations" seem to occur, where the youngster responds by saying "Da-Da" when a parent says that sound. Although this type of interchange sounds like a conversation, the child's vocal productions may be understood only by those close to him or her (e.g., parents or siblings); people other than immediate family members may not be able to interpret meaning at all. The baby also begins to use different tones and vocal intensity, which makes the vocalization vaguely resemble adult speech. The interactions between babies and their parents can do much to enhance babies' developing language at this time. Parents often provide a great deal of reinforcement for word approximations, like praise in excited tones, or hugs. They also provide stimulus sounds and words for the baby to mimic, giving the youngster considerable directed practice.

Within a broad range of 4 to 8 years of age, children with normal language development can correctly articulate most speech sounds in context.

The timing of a baby's actual first word is open to interpretation although it usually happens between 9 and 14 months. These words often involve echoing (repeating what has been heard) or mimicking responses based on verbalizations by those around him or her. At first the words may have little or no meaning, although they soon become attached to people or objects in the child's immediate environment, such as Daddy, Mommy, or milk. Before long these words begin to have more perceptible intent, as the child uses them for requests and an apparent means of pleasing parents. Strings of two and three words that resemble sentences typically begin between 18 and 24 months. At this stage, there is little question about meaning because the child can clearly indicate that he or she wants something. The child uses fairly accurate syntax, usually with word order consisting of subject-verb-object.

Most children with normally developing language are able to use all the basic syntactical structures by 3 to 4 years of age. By 5 years, they have progressed to using six-word sentences, on the average. A child who is developing language normally articulates nearly all speech sounds correctly and in context somewhere between 4 and 8 years of age. These illustrations are couched in terms of when children produce language, that is, expressive language development. However, some observations suggest that a child's receptive skills precede his or her ability to express language (Keith, 1999). Thus, children are able to understand a great deal more than they can express. Most children show some understanding of language as early as 6 to 9 months, often responding first to commands such as "no-no" and their names (Puckett, 2001).

In outlining normal language development, we used variable age ranges for each milestone, some with rather broad approximations. Several factors contribute to this variability. For one thing, children exhibit substantial differences in their rates of development, even those that are considered normal. Some variations are due to general health and vitality, others are due to inheritance, and still others relate to environmental influences, such as the amount and type of interaction with parents and siblings (Rice, Spitz, & O'Brien, 1999; Twachtman-Cullen, 1998). Note also that age ranges become more variable in more advanced stages of development (e.g., 3 to 6 months for babbling; 18 to 24 months for two- and three-word strings), partially because there is more variation regarding when advanced developmental events occur than is the case for earlier stages. It is also true, however, that these advanced developments are more complex, some involving subtleties that are not as singularly obvious as, say, the first "Da-Da." Therefore, observation of when they first occur is perhaps less accurate. Table 10.1 summarizes general milestones of normal language and prelanguage development.

We will also see considerable variability as we discuss abnormal language and speaking ability. In some cases, the same factors contributing to variability in normal language are also considered to be disorders if they result in extreme performance deviations. In others, we will find that definitions differ in the literature and that characteristics vary between people—variability we have encountered with other disorders.

Language Disorders

History has witnessed language in many different forms. Some early Native Americans communicated using systems of clucking or clicking sounds made with the tongue and teeth. Such sounds were also used in combination with hand signs and spoken language that often differed greatly

Age	Behavior
Birth	Crying and making other physiological sounds
1 to 2 months	Cooing as well as crying
3 to 6 months	Babbling as well as cooing
9 to 14 months	Speaking first words as well as babbling
18 to 24 months	Speaking first sentences as well as words
3 to 4 years	Using all basic syntactical structures
4 to 8 years	Articulating correctly all speech sounds in context

TABLE 10.1 Normal language and prelanguage development

Source: Reprinted with permission of Merrill, an imprint of Macmillan Publishing Company, from *Mental Retardation: A Life Cycle Approach,* Seventh Edition by Clifford J. Drew and Michael L. Hardman. Copyright 2000 by Macmillan Publishing Company.

between tribes. Such differing language systems have been described extensively in a variety of historical documents and continue to be of interest (e.g., Bartens, 2000).

Current definitions of language reflect the breadth necessary to encompass diverse communication systems. For the most part, these definitions make reference to the systems of rules and symbols people use to communicate, including matters of phonology, syntax, morphology, and semantics (Den-Dikken, 2000; Fodor & Inoue, 2000). Considerable attention is given to meaning and understanding in definitions of language. For example, Bernstein (1997b) defined language as encompassing the "complex rules that govern sounds, words, sentences, meaning, and use. These rules underlie an individual's ability to understand language (language comprehension) and his or her ability to formulate language (language production)" (p. 6).

Speech disorders include problems related to verbal production, that is, vocal expression. Language disorders represent serious difficulties in the ability to understand or express ideas in the communication system being used. The distinction between speech and language disorders is like the difference between the sound of a word and the meaning of a word. As we examine language disorders, we will discuss difficulties in meaning, both expressing it and receiving it. Table 10.2 lists behaviors that might emerge if a child has a language disorder.

■ DEFINITION

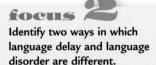

focus 2

Identify two ways in which language delay and language disorder are different.

A serious disruption of the language acquisition process may result in language disorders. Such irregular developments may involve comprehension (understanding) or expression in written or spoken language (Bernstein, 1997b; Denes & Pizzamiglio, 1999). Such malfunctions may occur in one or more of the components of language. Because language is one of the most complex sets of behaviors exhibited by humans, language disorders are complex and present perplexing assessment problems. Language involves memory, learning, message reception and processing, and expressive skills. An individual with a language disorder may have deficits in any of these areas, and it may be difficult to identify the nature of the problem (Johnson & Slomka, 2000). In addition, language problems may arise in the form of language delays or language disorders.

Language delay occurs when the normal rate of developmental progress is interrupted but the systematic sequence of development remains essentially intact. For

The following behaviors may indicate that a child in your classroom has a language impairment that is in need of clinical intervention. Please check the appropriate items.

_____ Child mispronounces sounds and words.

_____ Child omits word endings, such as plural -s and past tense -ed.

_____ Child omits small unemphasized words, such as auxiliary verbs or prepositions.

_____ Child uses an immature vocabulary, overuses empty words, such as *one* and *thing,* or seems to have difficulty recalling or finding the right word.

_____ Child has difficulty comprehending new words and concepts.

_____ Child's sentence structure seems immature or overreliant on forms, such as subject-verb-object. It's unoriginal, dull.

_____ Child's question and/or negative sentence style is immature.

_____ Child has difficulty with one of the following:

_____ Verb tensing	_____ Articles	_____ Auxiliary verbs
_____ Pronouns	_____ Irreg. verbs	_____ Prepositions
_____ Word order	_____ Irreg. plurals	_____ Conjunctions

_____ Child has difficulty relating sequential events.

_____ Child has difficulty following directions.

_____ Child's questions often inaccurate or vague.

_____ Child's questions often poorly formed.

_____ Child has difficulty answering questions.

_____ Child's comments often off topic or inappropriate for the conversation.

_____ There are long pauses between a remark and the child's reply or between successive remarks by the child. It's as if the child is searching for a response or is confused.

_____ Child appears to be attending to communication but remembers little of what is said.

_____ Child has difficulty using language socially for the following purposes:

_____ Request needs	_____ Pretend/imagine	_____ Protest
_____ Greet	_____ Request information	_____ Gain attention
_____ Respond/reply	_____ Share ideas, feelings	_____ Clarify
_____ Relate events	_____ Entertain	_____ Reason

_____ Child has difficulty interpreting the following:

_____ Figurative language	_____ Humor	_____ Gestures
	_____ Emotions	_____ Body language

_____ Child does not alter production for different audiences and locations.

_____ Child does not seem to consider the effect of language on the listener.

_____ Child often has verbal misunderstandings with others.

_____ Child has difficulty with reading and writing.

_____ Child's language skills seem to be much lower than other areas, such as mechanical, artistic, or social skills.

Source: From R. E. Owens, *Language Disorders: A Functional Approach to Assessment and Intervention* (2nd ed., p. 392). Copyright 1995. All rights reserved. Reprinted by permission of Allyn and Bacon.

youngsters with a language delay, the development follows a normal pattern or course of growth but is substantially slower than in most children of the same age; in other words, affected children use the language rules typical of a younger child. The term *language disorder* differs in that it refers to circumstances when language acquisition is not systematic and/or sequential; a child with language disorders is not progressing in a sequential acquisition of the rule-governed linguistic behavior.

We will use the term *language disorder* in a general sense to discuss several types of behaviors. Where evidence suggests that delay may be a major contributor, we discuss it as such.

■ CLASSIFICATION

Terminology varies widely regarding the processes involved in language as well as disorders in those processes. In many cases, language disorders are classified according to their causes, which may be known or only suspected (Boucher, 1998; Segalowitz, 2000). In other cases, specific labels, such as aphasia, tend to be employed. There is some uncertainty in the literature regarding classification of language disorders, although one approach is to view them in terms of receptive and expressive problems (Toppelberg & Shapiro, 2000). We examine both of these categories as well as aphasia, a problem that may occur in both children and adults.

■ RECEPTIVE LANGUAGE DISORDERS People with **receptive language disorders** have difficulty in comprehending what others say. In many cases, receptive language problems in children are noticed when they do not follow an adult's instructions. These children may seem inattentive, as though they do not listen to directions, or they may be very slow to respond. Individuals with receptive language disorders have great difficulty understanding other people's messages and may process only part (or none) of what is being said to them (Keith, 1999). They have a problem in language processing, which is basically half of language (the other part being language production). Language processing is essentially listening to and interpreting spoken language.

Some of this behavior is reminiscent of the discussion in Chapter 6 on learning disabilities. It is not uncommon for receptive language problems to appear in students with learning disabilities (Johnson & Slomka, 2000; Ward-Lonergan, Liles, & Anderson, 1998). Such language deficits contribute significantly to academic performance problems and difficulties in social interactions for these students. Receptive language disorders appear as high-risk indicators of other disabilities and may frequently remain undiagnosed because they are not as evident as problems in language production (Toppelberg & Shapiro, 2000).

■ EXPRESSIVE LANGUAGE DISORDERS Individuals with **expressive language disorders** have difficulty in language production, or formulating and using spoken or written language. Those with expressive language disorders may have limited vocabularies and use the same array of words regardless of the situation. Expressive language disorders may appear as immature speech, often resulting in interaction difficulties (Vicari et al., 2000). People with expressive disorders also use hand signals and facial expressions to communicate.

■ APHASIA Definitions of aphasia have varied over time, but they still employ strikingly consistent themes. **Aphasia** involves a loss of the ability to speak or comprehend because of an injury or developmental abnormality in the brain. Aphasia most often involves those who have acquired a language disorder because of a specific acquired brain lesion resulting in impairment of language comprehension, formulation, and use. Thus, definitions of aphasia commonly link the disorder to brain injury, either through mechanical accidents or other damage, such as that caused by a stroke. Over the years, many types of aphasia and/or conditions associated with aphasia have been identified and labeled, such as paraphasia and dysprosody (Coppens, Lebrun, & Basso, 1998; Tsvetkova, 1998). Aphasic language disturbances have also been classified in terms of receptive and expressive problems.

■ RECEPTIVE LANGUAGE DISORDERS. Difficulties in comprehending what others say.

■ EXPRESSIVE LANGUAGE DISORDERS. Difficulties in language production.

■ APHASIA. An acquired language disorder caused by brain damage that is characterized by complete or partial impairment of language comprehension, formulation, and use.

Aphasia may be found both during childhood and the adult years. The term *developmental aphasia* has been widely used with affected children, despite the long-standing association of such problems with neurological damage. Children with aphasia often begin to use words at age 2 or later and phrases at age 4. The link between aphasia and neurological abnormalities in children has been of continuing interest to researchers, and some evidence has suggested a connection. Despite theories and assumptions, in many cases of aphasia in children, objective evidence identifying neurological dysfunction has been difficult to acquire.

Adult aphasia typically can be linked to accidents or injuries likely to occur during this part of the lifespan, such as gunshot wounds, motorcycle or auto accidents, and strokes. For this group, it is clear why terms such as *acquired language disorder* emerge, since these disorders are typically acquired through specific injury. Current research suggests that varying symptoms result from damage to different parts of the brain (e.g., Fadda et al., 1998; Kertesz, Davidson, & McCabe, 1998). Those with injury to the front part of the brain often can comprehend better than they can speak; they also have considerable difficulty finding words, have poor articulation with labored and slow speech, omit small words such as *of* and *the,* and generally have reduced verbal production. Individuals with aphasia resulting from injury to the posterior (back part) of the brain seem to have more fluent speech, but it lacks content. Speech may also be characterized by use of an unnecessarily large number of words to express an idea or use of unusual or meaningless terms. The speech of these individuals appears to reflect impaired comprehension. In some such cases, research has shown adult aphasia occurring in a selective fashion where progressive illness effects a broad range of comprehension deficits though superficial conversational speech may remain (Kertesz et al., 1998).

■ CAUSATION

Determining the causes of different language disorders with a high level of accuracy can be difficult. We do not have precise answers regarding what contributes to normal language acquisition, exactly how those contributions occur, and how malfunctions influence language disorders. We do know that certain sensory and other physiological systems must be intact and developing normally for language processes to develop normally. For example, if vision or hearing is seriously impaired, a language deficit may result (House & Davidson, 2000; Shriberg, Tomblin, & McSweeny, 1999). Likewise, serious brain damage might deter normal language functioning. Learning must also progress in a systematic, sequential fashion for language to develop appropriately. For example, children must attend to communication before they can mimic it or attach meaning to it. Language learning is like other learning: it must be stimulated and reinforced to be acquired and mastered (Bernstein, 1997a).

In discussing other communication disorders, we have encountered many of the physiological problems that may also cause language difficulties. Neurological damage that may affect language functioning can occur prenatally, during birth, or anytime throughout life (Indefrey et al., 2000; Molfese & Molfese, 2000). For example, language problems can clearly result from oxygen deprivation before or during birth, which are times of high vulnerability (e.g., Drew & Hardman, 2000). Likewise, a serious accident later in life can disrupt a person's language skills. Beyond specific incidents that contribute to problems, serious emotional disorders may be accompanied by language disturbances if an individual's perception of the world is substantially distorted (Prizant, Wetherby, & Roberts, 2000).

focus 3

Identify three factors thought to cause language disorders.

Language disorders may also occur if learning opportunities are seriously deficient or otherwise disrupted. As with speech, children may not learn language if the environment is not conducive to such learning (Chapman, 2000). Modeling in the home may be so infrequent that a child cannot learn language in a normal fashion. This might be the case in a family where no speaking occurs because the parents are deaf, even when the children have normal hearing. Such circumstances are rare, but when they do occur, a language delay is likely. The parents cannot model language for their children, nor can they respond to and reinforce such behavior.

It is important to remember that learning outcomes are highly variable. In situations that seem normal, we may find a child with serious language difficulty. In circumstances that seem dismal, we may find a child whose language facility is normal. The next snapshot presents an example involving four brothers with normal hearing who were born to and raised by parents who were both deaf and had no spoken language facility. The boys seemed to develop language quite normally, although they could not explain that development. They have distinguished themselves in various manners, from earning Ph.D.'s and M.D.'s (one holds both degrees) to becoming a millionaire through patented inventions.

This illustration represents a rare set of circumstances, but it is a good illustration of how variable and poorly understood language learning is. The assumption has long been that language-deprived environments place children at risk for exhibiting language delays or disorders. For example, it has been thought that language acquisition may be delayed when parents use baby talk in communicating with their young children. Such a view is based on the fundamental principles of learning theory that children learn what is modeled and taught. There is little question that this perspective is sound concerning most skill acquisition. Many clinical reports of language problems uphold such a notion, and research has also supported certain relationships between parental verbalizations and child language development (D'Odorico, Salerni, Cassibba, & Jacob, 1999; Laakso, Poikkeus, & Lyytinen, 1999). Although some questions have been raised regarding the presumed effects of baby talk, the general influence of parent modeling on child language development is positive.

Snapshot

Cy

■ LANGUAGE DIFFERENCES: WE DIDN'T KNOW THEY WERE DIFFERENT

My name is Cy, and I am one of the four brothers mentioned. Both of my parents were deaf from a very early age; they never learned to speak. When you ask me how we learned speech, I can't really answer, knowing what I now know about how those very early years are so impor-

tant in this area. When we were really young, we didn't even know they were deaf or different (except for Dad's active sense of humor). Naturally, we didn't talk; we just signed. We lived way out in the country and didn't have other playmates. Grandma and Grandpa lived close by, and I spent a lot of time with them. That is when I began to know something was different. We probably began learning to talk there.

When we were about ready to start school, we moved

into town. My first memory related to school is sitting in a sandbox, I guess on the playground. We had some troubles in school, but they were fairly minor as I recall. I couldn't talk or pronounce words very well. I was tested on an IQ test in the third grade and had an IQ of 67. Both Mom and Dad worked, and so we were all sort of out on our own with friends, which probably helped language, but now I wonder why those kids didn't stay away from us because we were a

bit different. Probably the saving grace is that all four of us seem to have pretty well developed social intelligence or skills. We did get in some fights with kids, and people sometimes called us the "dummy's kids." I would guess that all four of us pretty much caught up with our peers by the eighth grade. One thing is for certain: I would not trade those parents for any other in the world. Whatever they did, they certainly did right.

Cy, Ph.D.

Distinctions between speech problems and language problems are blurred because they overlap as much as the two functions of speech and language overlap. Thus, receptive and expressive language disorders are as intertwined as speech and language. When an individual does not express language well, does he or she have a receptive problem or an expressive problem? These disorders cannot be clearly separated, nor can causation be clearly divided into categories.

This student uses a computer that prints in large type that he can easily read. An individual using a computer to communicate probably has a severe physical or cognitive disability that affects communication.

■ INTERVENTION

Any treatment for a language disorder must take into account the nature of the problem and the manner in which an individual is affected. It is also important to give full consideration to cultural and linguistic background as an intervention is being planned (Toppelberg & Shapiro, 2000). Intervention is an individualized undertaking, just as it is with other types of disorders (Bowen & Cupples, 1999; Fey, 1999). Some causes are rather easily identified and may or may not be remedied by mechanical or medical intervention. Other types of treatment basically involve instruction or language training.

■ INDIVIDUALIZED LANGUAGE PLANS

A number of integrated steps are involved in effective language training, including identification, assessment, development of instructional objectives, development of a language intervention program, implementation of the intervention program, reassessment of the child, and reteaching, if necessary. These steps are similar to the general stages of specialized educational interventions for other disorders. The customary approach to language disorder intervention follows the basic steps for treatment as outlined in IDEA. Specific programs of intervention may also involve other activities aimed at individualized intervention (see, for example, Bowen & Cupples, 1999; Fey, 1999).

Programs of language training are tailored to an individual's strengths and limitations. In fact, current terminology labels them individualized language plans (ILPs), similar in concept to the individualized education plans (IEPs) mandated by IDEA. These intervention plans include long-range goals (annual), more short-range and specific behavioral objectives, a statement of the resources to be used in achieving the objectives, a description of evaluation methods, program beginning and ending dates, and an evaluation of the individual's generalization of skills. For young children, interventions often focus on beginning language stimulation. Treatment is intended to mirror the conditions under which children normally learn language, but the conditions may be intensified and taught more systematically. In many cases, parents or other family members are involved in the intervention (e.g., Grela & Illerbrun, 1998; Iacono, Chan, & Waring, 1998; Scheidler, 1998).

Many different approaches have been used to remediate aphasia although consistent and verifiable results have been slow to emerge. Intervention typically involves the development of an individual's profile of strengths, limitations, age, and developmental level, mono/bilingual background, literacy, as well as considerations regarding temperament issues that may affect therapy (Coppens et al., 1998; Varney, 1998). From such a profile, an individualized treatment plan can be designed. Several questions or points immediately surface, including what to teach or remediate first and whether teaching should focus on an individual's strong or weak areas. These questions have been raised from time to time with respect to many disorders.

focus 4

Describe two ways in which treatment approaches for language disorders generally differ for children and for adults.

Today's Technology

COMPUTERS: A LANGUAGE TUTORIAL PROGRAM

Computer technology has made inroads in many areas of human disability in the past few years and will become increasingly important in the future. Language disability intervention is one area where technology is being used with increasing frequency. Advances in both hardware and software have impacted language training and have substantial potential for future development.

First Words is a language tutorial program that may have a number of applications for teaching those who are developing or reacquiring language functions. This program uses graphic presentations combined with synthesized speech to teach and test a student's acquisition of high-frequency nouns. The student is presented with two pictures of an object and asked to decide which one represents the word being taught. Students can select an answer using a computer keyboard or a special selection switch or by touching the object on the screen. First Words is a relatively inexpensive program, costing about $200. The voice synthesizer and the touch screen options must be added to the basic package but may be essential elements to effective intervention, depending on the student's capability.

Nearly all clinicians have their own opinions or some personal formula for balancing the extremes. Teaching exclusively to a child's weak areas may result in more failure experiences than are either necessary or helpful to his or her overall progress—the child receives so little success and reinforcement that he or she may become discouraged about the whole process. Good clinical judgment needs to be exercised in balancing remediation attention to the aphasic child's strengths and weaknesses. Intervention programs include the collaborative participation of parents and other family members as well as any other professionals who may be involved with the overall treatment of the youngster (Grela & Illerbrun, 1998; Iacono et al., 1998; Scheidler, 1998).

The perspective for remediation of adults with aphasia begins from a point different from that for children, in that it involves relearning or reacquiring language function. Views regarding treatment have varied over the years. Early approaches included the expectation that adults with aphasia would exhibit spontaneous recovery. This approach has largely been replaced by the view that patients are more likely to progress if direct therapeutic instruction is implemented.

The nature of therapy for adults with aphasia has some predictable similarities to treatment for children. Areas of strength and limitation must receive attention when an individualized remediation program is being planned. However, development of a profile of strengths and deficits may involve some areas different from those of children because of age differences. For example, social, linguistic, and vocational readjustments represent three broad areas that need attention for most adults with aphasia. Although children need attention beyond just language therapy, some aspects of adult treatment are not necessarily relevant (e.g., vocational readjustment), and the notion of readjustment differs substantially from initial skill acquisition. Language learning treatment (relearning) is often employed in a way that focuses on the individual's needs and is practical in terms of service delivery (Ferguson, 1999; LeDorze, Croteau, Brassard, & Michallet, 1999; Wambaugh, Martinez, McNeil, & Rogers, 1999). In some cases individuals with aphasia are effectively treated in group settings, and for others individual therapy works well (e.g., Byng, Swinburn, & Pound, 1999). Advances in technology are continually being integrated into diagnosis and treatment (Denes & Pizzamiglio, 1999; Fox, 1999; Weitzel, 2000), such as those illustrated in the nearby Today's Technology features.

An individualized treatment plan for adults with aphasia also involves evaluation, profile development, and teaching/therapy in specific areas within each of the

Today's Technology

ASSISTIVE DEVICES HELP TO LEVEL THE PLAYING FIELD

Using a pink cap rigged with a long gold stick and pencil eraser, 11-year-old Marisa Velez punches a few buttons on a computerized box.

"Hello, my name is Marisa Velez," the box says in a computerized voice, customized to sound like a girl. "This device lets me speak like anyone else."

For Marisa, who was born with quadriplegia cerebral palsy, the Liberator and other devices in her home and school are the key to a productive life.

Such assistive technology usually is associated with devices that help people with disability, but it also includes commonplace items such as glasses, hearing aids, or canes.

Assistive technology has allowed Marisa to attend regular classes at Westvale Elementary School like any other student. She uses a motorized wheelchair to get around the building and a computer touch-screen to write papers. She also can use the Liberator voice machine, which has a built-in printer, to complete assignments and quizzes.

"It's her self-expression, her ability to express her feelings and goals. Just being understood makes her feel valued," said Marisa's mother, Norma Velez. "That's the purpose of technology—to not hold people back." . . .

Norma Velez had to scream and shout to get her insurance to pay for Marisa's Liberator.

"Marisa was the first individual our [insurance] company provided a speech device for," she said. "At first, they said it was not a medical necessity. But the object is to not give up. If she is ill and cannot communicate what is wrong, of course that is a medical necessity."

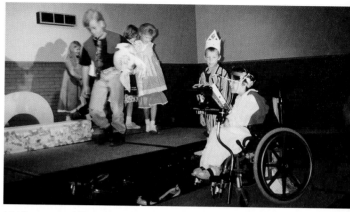

Marisa uses a Liberator voice machine to talk, a computer touch-screen to write, and a motorized wheelchair. All these devices enable her to participate in a school play.

Source: Excerpted from: "Assistive Devices Help to Level Playing Field: Machines Can Be Key to Productive Life and Individual Self-Esteem," by V. Horiuchi, 1999, *The Salt Lake Tribune,* April 10, p. D8.

broad domains (Byng et al., 1999). Such training should begin as soon as possible, depending on the patient's condition. Some spontaneous recovery may occur during the first 6 months after an incident resulting in aphasia, but waiting beyond 2 months to begin treatment may not only be unnecessary but also seriously delay recovery to whatever degree may be possible.

■ AUGMENTATIVE COMMUNICATION   Some individuals require intervention using means of communication other than oral language. In some cases, the person may be incapable of speaking because of a severe physical or cognitive disability and so will require that a nonspeech means of communication be designed and implemented. Known variably as assistive, alternative, or **augmentative communication,** these strategies may involve a variety of approaches, some employing new technological developments. Augmentative communication strategies have received increasing attention in the past few years, some because of the rapid development of technology and others due to interest from the popular press. Applications include a range of circumstances and disability conditions including mental retardation, autism, and multiple disabilities that are often in the severe functioning range (Antona, Stephanidis, & Kouroupetroglou, 1999; Fox, 1999; Petersen, Reichle, & Johnston, 2000). These strategies must also be individualized to meet the specific needs of those being treated as well as taking into account their strengths and limitations in operating the technology. Augmentative communication strategies are providing therapists with

■ AUGMENTATIVE COMMUNICATION. Forms of communication that employ nonspeech alternatives.

important new alternatives for intervention with individuals having language disorders. Research is increasingly addressing this area and indicating considerable effectiveness when techniques and devices are carefully chosen to meet an individual's capacities and preferences as well as the environmental context (e.g., Antona et al., 1999; Beck, Fritz, Keller, & Dennis, 2000).

Speech Disorders

Speech disorder definitions vary greatly; some are very detailed in terms of characteristics whereas others are more general. However, one common theme among definitions is that speech disorders involve deviations of sufficient magnitude to interfere with communication. Such speaking patterns are so divergent from what is normal and accepted that they draw attention to the speaking act, thereby distracting from the meaning of the message being sent. The detrimental effect of such a deviant speaking behavior can impact the listener, the speaker, or both.

Speech is extremely important in contemporary society. Speaking ability can influence a person's success or failure in both the personal–social and professional arenas. Most people are about average in terms of their speaking ability, and they may envy those who are unusually articulate and pity those who have a difficult time with speech. What is it like to have a serious deficit in speaking ability? Certainly, it is different for each individual, depending on the circumstances in which he or she operates and the severity of the deficit.

For many individuals with speech disorders, speaking difficulties seriously affect their lives. They often carry strong emotional reactions to their speech that may significantly alter their behavior. It is not difficult to imagine the impact that stuttering, for example, may have in classroom settings or in social encounters. Speech is so central to functioning in society that such disorders often have a significant impact on affected individuals. Children may be ridiculed by peers, begin to feel inadequate, and suffer emotional stress.

There are many different speech disorders and considerable diversity in terms of theoretical perspectives regarding causes and treatment. Volumes much longer than this book have focused solely on the topic. In this section, we will discuss several speech disorders that represent major communication disorders, including fluency disorders, delayed speech, articulation disorders, and voice disorders.

Fluency Disorders

In normal speech we are accustomed to a reasonably smooth flow of words and sentences. For the most part, it has a rhythm and timing that is steady, regular, and rapid. Most of us also have times when we pause to think about what we are saying, either because we have made a mistake or want to mentally edit what we are about to say. However, these interruptions are not frequent and do not constitute a disturbance in the ongoing flow of our speaking. In general, our speech is considered fluent with respect to speed and continuity.

Fluency of speech is a significant problem for people with a fluency disorder. Their speech is characterized by repeated interruptions, hesitations, or repetitions that seriously interfere with the flow of communication. Some people have a fluency disorder known as cluttered speech, or **cluttering,** which is characterized by

CLUTTERING. A speech disorder characterized by excessively rapid, disorganized speaking, often including words or phrases unrelated to the topic.

328

speech that is overly rapid, disorganized, and occasionally filled with unnecessary words. Stuttering is by far the most well known type of fluency disorder and has fascinated researchers for years.

DEFINITION OF STUTTERING

Stuttering occurs when the flow of speech is abnormally interrupted by repetitions, blocking, or prolongations of sounds, syllables, words, or phrases (Perino, Famularo, & Tarroni, 2000). Although familiar to most, stuttering occurs rather infrequently, between 1% and 5% of the general population, and has one of the lower prevalence rates among all speech disorders (e.g., Mansson, 2000; Van Borsel, Verniers, & Bouvry, 1999). For example, articulation disorders (e.g., omitting, adding, or distorting certain sounds) occur in the United States much more often than do stuttering problems.

Laypeople's high awareness of stuttering partly comes from the nature of behavior involved. Stuttering is a disturbance in the rhythm and fluency of speech. It may only involve certain sounds, syllables, words, or phrases, and the problem elements may differ among individuals. Such interruptions in speech flow are very evident to both speaker and listener and are perhaps more disruptive to communication than any other type of speech disorder. Furthermore, listeners often become uncomfortable and may try to assist the stuttering speaker, providing missing or incomplete words (Dorsey & Guenther, 2000; Whaley & Golden, 2000). The speaker's discomfort may be magnified by physical movements, gestures, or facial distortions that often accompany stuttering. All of this may make the experience very vivid and easily remembered.

Parents often become concerned about stuttering as their children learn to talk. Apprehension is usually unnecessary, however, since most children exhibit some normal nonfluencies that diminish and cease with maturation. However, these normal nonfluencies have historically played a role in some theories regarding the causes of stuttering.

The way in which parents speak greatly affects their child's speech patterns.

CAUSATION OF STUTTERING

Behavioral scientists have looked in many directions, searching for a cause of stuttering. One difficulty has been the search for a single cause. Current thinking suggests that stuttering may have a variety of causes (e.g., Gottwald, 1999; Ludlow, 1999), and the search for a single cause has been discarded by many. Theories regarding causes follow three basic perspectives: as a symptom of some emotional disturbance, as a result of one's biological makeup or some neurological problem, and as a learned behavior.

Many professionals have become less interested in both the emotional and biological causation theories of stuttering. Investigation of this perspective is scarce, and the topic is difficult to study due to research methodology problems. Some investigations of emotional problems have explored psychosocial factors emerging from the parent–child interaction, although this work is somewhat fragmentary. The emotional component has been included in many descriptions of contributors to stuttering, including speculation that stuttering may be caused by an individual's capacity being exceeded by demands. Such theories, however, often consider a person's cognitive, linguistic, and motor capacities as other contributors, placing the emotional role as one of several possible culprits. Research and theoretical literature relating stuttering to emotion continues but at a relatively sporadic level (Guitar, 1998; Ratner & Healy, 1999).

Research continues to explore biological-causation in a number of different areas, producing different theories. Limited evidence indicates that the brains or neurological structures of some who stutter may be organized or function differently from those of their fluent counterparts, although the nature of such differences remains unclear and a matter for speculation (Ludlow, 1999; Salmelin et. al., 1998; Webster, 1998). There is also some suggestion that individuals who stutter use different sections of the brain to process material than do their counterparts with fluent speech. A few authors suggest that people who stutter may have differences in brain-hemisphere function than those who are fluent. For example, the hemispheres of the brain may compete with each other in information processing (e.g., Dmitrieva & Zaitseva, 1998). Some researchers also suggest that nervous system damage, such as from an injury, can result in stuttering (Van Borsel et al, 1998). Other theories imply that a variety of problems may disrupt the person's precise timing ability, which is an important element in speech production. There is also speculation that control mechanisms for speech production may be unsynchronized in people who stutter or may produce an elevated activity of the muscles involved in speech production. Thus research continues on several fronts related to biological causation.

Learned behavior has long persisted as a theory concerning the cause of stuttering. According to this perspective, learned stuttering emerges from the normal nonfluency evident in early speech development. Stuttering often begins between 3 to 5 years of age, the years when children are still developing language (e.g., Mansson, 2000). From a learning causation point of view, a typical child may become a stuttering child if considerable attention is focused on normal disfluencies at that stage of development. The disfluency of early stuttering may be further magnified by negative feelings about the self as well as anxiety (e.g., Murphy, 1999; Whaley & Golden, 2000). Interest in this theory persists, although like others, it also has its critics (e.g., Max & Caruso, 1998; Ratner, 2000).

Theories about causes of stuttering have also included consideration of heredity (Ludlow, 1999). Some evidence suggests that stuttering may be gender related since males who stutter outnumber females about four to one, although this hypothesis remains speculative. Heredity has also been of interest because of the high incidence of stuttering and other speech disorders within certain families as well as with twins (Guitar, 1998; Stagg & Burns, 1999). However, there is great difficulty in separating hereditary and environmental influences, a problem long evident in human development and behavior disorders research (Drew & Hardman, 2000; Yairi, 1999).

When reviewing the research on stuttering, it becomes clear that causation has been an elusive and perplexing matter for workers in speech pathology. Some recent literature has raised questions regarding definitions, assessment, and some of the theoretical logic about stuttering (e.g., Conture, 1999; Prins, 1999; Yairi, 1999). Researchers and clinicians continue their search for a cause, with the hope of identifying more effective treatment and prevention measures. Some researchers are combining elements of previous theoretical models and multiple disciplines where evidence is suggestive and logical. For example, Murphy (1999) suggested that a careful examination of the literature in psychology helps to understand the emotional status of children and others who stutter. While some cling to the notion of a single cause for this condition, an emerging trend favors examining any and all relevant components, irrespective of their theoretical domain.

■ INTERVENTION

Many approaches have been used to treat stuttering over the years, with mixed results. Interventions such as play therapy, creative dramatics, self-monitoring, specialized auditory feedback, parental counseling and training, and involvement of parents, teachers, and classmates have been all studied and shown to be somewhat useful for children who stutter (e.g., Howell, Sacking, & Williams, 1999; Kalinowski, Stuart, Wamsley, & Ratstatter, 1999; Onslow & Packman, 1999). Some research on medication treatment has shown improvements although pharmacological intervention has not been widely employed (Anderson et al., 1999; Lavid, Franklin, & Maguire, 1999; Maguire et al., 1999). Hypnosis has been used to treat some cases of stuttering, but its success has been limited. Speech rhythm has been the focus of some therapy, in some cases using a metronome to establish a speaking pattern. Relaxation therapy and biofeedback have also been used, since tenseness is often observed in people who stutter (Gilman & Yaruss, 2000). In all the techniques noted, outcomes are mixed, and it is common for those who stutter to repeat treatments using several approaches. The inability of any one treatment or cluster of treatments to consistently help people who stutter demonstrates the ongoing need for research in this area. There is also need for research investigating the most effective timing of intervention. Some have favored postponing intervention whereas others have argued that early intervention is essential (e.g., Onslow & Packman, 1999). Early intervention, although it carries a certain risk of labeling, has long been popular in many areas of exceptionality.

Research to date does not provide a complete understanding of stuttering. However, for several years treatment models have increasingly focused on direct behavioral therapy, attempting to teach children who stutter to use fluent speech patterns (e.g., Bray & Kehle, 1998; Miltenberger & Woods, 1998; Onslow & Packman, 1999). In some cases, children are taught to monitor and manage their stuttering, for example, by speaking more slowly or rhythmically. Using this model, they are also taught to reward themselves for increasing periods of fluency. Some behavioral therapies include information regarding physical factors (e.g., regulating breathing) and direct instruction about correct speaking behaviors. Such research combines several dimensions to create the overall therapy, such as an interview regarding the inconvenience of stuttering, behavior modification training, and follow-up. Because stuttering is a complex problem, effective interventions are likely to be complicated.

Spoken communication is seriously disturbed by fluency disorders because they interrupt the flow of ideas. For people who stutter, the stream of communication is broken by severe rhythm irregularities. For people with cluttered speech, the flow of ideas is interrupted by extraneous words and disorganization. However, other people with speech disorders are not dysfluent; rather, they are delayed in their speaking ability.

Delayed Speech

▪ DEFINITION

Delayed speech is a deficit in communication ability in which the individual speaks like a much younger person. From a developmental point of view, this problem involves a delayed beginning of speech and language development. Young children can typically communicate before they learn verbal behaviors, at least to some degree. They use gestures, gazing or eye contact, facial expressions, other physical movements, and nonspeech vocalizations, such as grunts or squeals. This early development illustrates the relationships among communication, language, and speech.

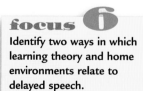

focus 6
Identify two ways in which learning theory and home environments relate to delayed speech.

Preschool teachers should use all occasions possible to increase the vocabulary of a child with delayed speech. This child may be more comfortable using a puppet to interact with his teacher or other children.

Delayed speech, a failure of speech to develop at the expected age, is often associated with other maturational delays. It may be associated with a hearing impairment, mental retardation, emotional disturbance, or brain injury (e.g., Drew & Hardman, 2000). Delayed speech may occur for many reasons and take various forms, and treatment differs accordingly (Gruber, 1999).

Children with delayed speech often have few or no verbalizations that can be interpreted as conventional speech. Some communicate solely through physical gestures. Others may use a combination of gestures and vocal sounds that are not even close approximations of words. Still others may speak but in a very limited manner, perhaps using single words (typically nouns without auxiliary words, like *ball* instead of *my ball*) or primitive sentences that are short or incomplete (e.g., *get ball* rather than *would you get the ball*) (Cheng, 2000). Such communication is normal for infants and very young children, but not for children who are well beyond the age of speaking in at least a partially fluent fashion.

Differences between stuttering and delayed speech are obvious, but the distinctions between delayed speech and articulation disorders are not as clear. In fact, children with delayed speech usually make many articulation errors in their speaking patterns. However, their major problems lie in grammatical and vocabulary deficits, which are more matters of developmental delay. The current prevalence of delayed speech is not clear, and government estimates do not even provide data regarding provision of services for delayed speech on a continuing basis (U.S. Department of Education, 2000). Such data problems, plus definitional differences among studies, have led many to place little confidence in existing prevalence figures.

■ **CAUSATION**

Because delayed speech can take a variety of forms, it is not surprising that the causes of these problems also vary greatly. Several types of environmental deprivation contribute to delayed speech. For example, partial or complete hearing loss may seriously limit an individual's sensory experience and contribute to or cause serious delays in speech development (e.g., Schriberg et al., 1999). A child's broader environment may also be a contributing factor in delayed speech for those with normal hearing (Tartter, 1998). For example, some children's homes provide little opportunity to learn speech, such as in families where there is minimal conversation or chance for the child to speak. Other problems may contribute to delayed speech, such as cerebral palsy and emotional disturbances.

Negativism involves a conflict between parents' expectations and a child's ability to perform, often occurring as children develop speech. Considerable pressure is placed on children during the period when they normally develop their speaking skills: to go to bed when told, to control urination and defecation properly, and to learn appropriate eating skills, among other things. The demands are great, and they may exceed a child's performance ability. Children react in many ways when more is demanded than they are able to produce. They may refuse. They may simply not talk, seeming to withdraw from family interactions, remaining silent. In normal development, children occasionally refuse to follow the directions of adults. One very effective refusal is silence, to which the parents' reprisal options are few and

■ DELAYED SPEECH. A deficit in speaking proficiency whereby the individual performs like someone much younger.

may be ineffective. As a parent, it is relatively simple to punish refusal misbehaviors when they involve acts such as refusing to go to bed or to clean one's room, but it is a different matter when parents encounter the refusal to talk. It is not easy to force a child to talk through conventional punishment techniques. Viewing negativism from another angle, children may be punished for talking in other situations. Parents may be irritated by a child's attempt to communicate. A child may speak too loudly or at inappropriate times, such as when adults are reading, watching television, resting, or talking with other adults (even more rules to learn at such a tender age). Delayed speech may occur in extreme cases of prolonged negativism related to talking (Chapman, 2000).

In the previous paragraph we can see that some children might experience delayed speech as a result of environmentally controlled learning due to refusal or rebellion. In some instances, not speaking may be rewarded, whereas in others, it may be a way of expressing refusal that is unlikely to result in punishment. Thus, in some cases, children may not learn to speak, and in others, they may learn not to speak. Imagine the effect on a baby who is yelled at for practicing his or her babbling (perhaps loudly) while a parent is on the telephone. Frightened, the child begins to cry, which further angers the parent, who screams, "Shut up!" Of course, the baby does not understand, and this episode escalates and becomes even more frightening to the child. Such situations may alternate with more calm periods when the parent hugs the baby and talks in soothing tones. A baby in this type of environment is likely to become very confused about the reaction to vocal output; sometimes it is punished, and at other times it is rewarded. If such circumstances exist at the time a child normally develops speech and persist for a substantial length of time, seriously delayed speech may result.

Thus delayed speech may emerge from experience deprivation in at least two ways. In one, the environment limits the opportunity to learn, and in the second, an opportunity to learn speech is hindered. Basic principles of learning suggest that, when one is first learning a skill, the stimulus and reward circumstances are important. A skill that is just beginning to develop is fragile. Stimuli and reinforcement must be reasonably consistent, appropriate, and properly timed. If such conditions do not exist, the skill development may be retarded or even negated. A child left alone for many hours each day, perhaps with only a single light bulb and four walls as stimuli, will not be rewarded for cooing, babbling, or approximating the first word. Over an extended period, this baby will fall behind his or her peers who are being hugged for each sound they make and who hear adults talk, modeling speech. This does not mean that the home environment must be an orchestrated language development program. Most households involve adequate circumstances to promote speech learning.

Although very complex, learning to speak is little different from learning other skills. In some homes, conversation may be unusually infrequent; parents may rarely speak either to each other or to the children. A child in this type of environment may experience infrequent speech modeling and little reinforcement for speaking, so delayed speech may result. Also, if verbal interchanges between parents reflect a strained relationship or emotional problems, the environment may be unpleasant, involving threats, arguments, and shouting. Children learning to speak in such a setting may learn that speech is associated with unpleasant feelings or even punishment. Seriously delayed speech can result from these environmental circumstances as well. When such contingencies are combined with infrequent interchanges, the learning—whether not to speak or not learning to speak—may be particularly potent.

Such an unpleasant environment may raise concerns about the amount of love and caring in such a situation and the role that emotional health plays in learning to

■ EARLY CHILDHOOD YEARS

TIPS FOR THE FAMILY

- Model speech and language to your infant by talking to him or her in normal tones from a very early age, even though he or she may not yet be intentionally communicating directly with you.
- Respond to babbling and other noises the young child makes with conversation, reinforcing early verbal output.
- Do not overreact if your child is not developing speech at the same rate as someone else's infant; great variation is found between children.
- If you are concerned about your child's speech development, have his or her hearing tested to determine whether that source of stimulation is normal.
- Observe other areas of development to assure yourself that your child is progressing within the broad boundaries of normal variation.
- If you are seeking day-care or a preschool program, search carefully for one that will provide a rich, systematic communication environment.

TIPS FOR THE PRESCHOOL TEACHER

- Encourage parental involvement in all dimensions of the program, including systematic speech and language stimulation at home.
- Consider all situations and events as opportunities to teach speech and language, perhaps focusing initially on concrete objects and later moving to the more abstract, depending on the individual child's functioning level.
- Ask "wh" questions, such as *what, who, when,* and so on, giving the child many opportunities to practice speaking as well as thinking.

- Practice with the child the use of prepositions *in, on, out,* and so on.
- Use all occasions possible to increase the child's vocabulary.

TIPS FOR PRESCHOOL PERSONNEL

- Communicate with the young child. Consider involvement in either direct or indirect communication instruction.

TIPS FOR NEIGHBORS AND FRIENDS

- Interact with young children with communication disorders as you would with any others, speaking to them and directly modeling appropriate communication.
- Intervene if you encounter other children ridiculing the speech and language of these youngsters; encourage sensitivity to individual differences among your own and other neighborhood children.

■ ELEMENTARY YEARS

TIPS FOR THE FAMILY

- Stay involved in your child's educational program through active participation with the school.
- Work in collaboration with the child's teacher on speaking practice, blending it naturally into family and individual activities.
- Communicate naturally with the child; avoid "talking down" and thereby modeling the use of "simpler language."

TIPS FOR THE GENERAL EDUCATION CLASSROOM TEACHER

- Continue promoting parental involvement in their child's intervention program in whatever manner they can participate.
- Encourage the child with communication disorders to talk about events and things in his or her environment, describing experiences in as much detail as possible.

speak. But delayed speech can also occur in families that exhibit great love and caring. In some environments, a child may have little need to learn speech. Most parents are concerned about satisfying their child's needs or desires. However, carrying this ambition to the extreme, a "superparent" may anticipate the child's wants (e.g., toys, water, or food) and provide them even before the child makes a verbal request. Such children may only gesture and their parents immediately respond, thereby rewarding gestures and not promoting the development of speech skills. Learning to speak is much more complex and demanding than making simple movements or facial grimaces. If gesturing is rewarded, speaking is less likely to be learned properly.

Delayed speech is a complex phenomenon and its causation is equally complicated—as complicated as the speech development process itself. If you are a new parent or anticipating parenthood, you should know that the vast majority of children learn to speak normally. Certainly, parents should not become so self-conscious that they see a problem before one exists.

- Use all situations possible to provide practice for the child's development of speech and language skills.
- Promote the enhancement of vocabulary for the child in a broad array of topic areas.

TIPS FOR SCHOOL PERSONNEL
- Promote an environment where all who are available and in contact with the child are involved in communication instruction, if not directly then indirectly through interaction and modeling.
- Begin encouraging student involvement in a wide array of activities that can also be used to promote speech and language development.

TIPS FOR NEIGHBORS AND FRIENDS
- Interact with children with communication disorders normally; do not focus on the speaking difficulties that may be evident.
- As a neighbor or friend, provide support for the child's parents, who may be struggling with difficult

feelings about their child's communication skills.

■ SECONDARY/ TRANSITION YEARS

TIPS FOR THE FAMILY
- Children who still exhibit communication problems at this level are likely to perform on a lower level, suggesting that communication may focus on functional matters such as grooming, feeding, and so on.
- For some children, communication may involve limited verbalization; consider other means of interacting.
- Interact with your child as much and as normally as possible.

TIPS FOR THE GENERAL EDUCATION CLASSROOM TEACHER
- Embed communication instruction in the context of functional areas (e.g., social interactions, request for assistance, choice making).
- Consider adding augmented communication devices or procedures to the student's curriculum.

TIPS FOR SCHOOL PERSONNEL
- Develop school activities that will encourage use of a broad variety of skill levels in speaking (i.e., not just the debate club).
- Promote school activities that permit participation through communication modes other than speaking (although with caution, keeping consistent with therapy goals).

TIPS FOR NEIGHBORS AND FRIENDS
- To the degree that you are comfortable, interact with children using alternative communication approaches (e.g., signs, gesturing, pantomiming).

■ ADULT YEARS

TIPS FOR THE FAMILY
- Interact with the adult having communication disorders on a level that is functionally appropriate for his or her developmental level. For some adults with communication disorders, the developmental level may vary depending on the topic (e.g., individuals also

having mental retardation). For others, the communication disorder is an inconvenience rather than another disability.

TIPS FOR THERAPISTS OR OTHER PROFESSIONALS
- Recognize the maturity level of the person with whom you are working. Do not assume you know the interests or inclinations of a younger client simply because the individual has a communication difficulty.
- Be aware of the lifestyle context of the adult when suggesting augmentative devices. Some techniques may not serve a person well who is employed or otherwise engaged in adult activities.

TIPS FOR NEIGHBORS AND FRIENDS
- Communicate in as normal a fashion as possible, given the severity and type of disorder. If the person uses alternative communication methods, consider learning about them to the degree that you feel comfortable.

■ INTERVENTION

Delayed speech treatment approaches are as varied as its causes. Whatever the cause, an effective treatment should teach the child appropriate speaking proficiency for his or her age level. In some cases, matters other than just defective learning, such as hearing impairments, must be considered in the treatment procedures (Radziewicz & Antonellis, 1997). Such cases may involve surgery and prosthetic appliances like hearing aids, as well as specially designed instructional techniques aimed at teaching speech.

Treatment is likely to focus on the basic principles of learned behavior if defective learning is the primary cause of delayed speech. In this situation, stimulus and reinforcement patterns contributing to delayed speech must be changed so that appropriate speaking behaviors can be learned. Although the process sounds simple, identification and control of such contingencies may be complicated (Johnson & Slomka, 2000; Mogford-Bevan, 2000). Some success has been achieved through direct instruction as well as other procedures aimed at increasing spontaneous speech. Such instruction emphasizes positive reinforcement of speaking to modify the child's behavior in favor of more normal speech. Other interventions involve collaborative efforts between speech clinicians, teachers, and parents (Grela & Illerbrun, 1998; Iacono, Chan, & Waring, 1998; Scheidler, 1998), focusing on modifying not only the child's speech but also the family environment that contributed to the problem. Because different elements cause the delay in each case, therapies must be individually tailored.

Articulation Disorders

■ DEFINITION

Articulation disorders represent the largest category of all speech problems, also known as phonological disorders in the *DSM-IV* (American Psychiatric Association, 2000). For most people with this type of difficulty, the label **functional articulation disorders** is used. This term refers to articulation problems that are not due to structural physiological defects, such as cleft palate or neurological problems, but are likely a result of environmental or psychological influences.

Articulation disorders refer to abnormal speech-sound production, characterized by inaccurate or otherwise inappropriate execution of speaking. This category of problems often includes omissions, substitutions, additions, and distortions of certain sounds (Shuster, 1998). Omissions most frequently involve dropping consonants from the ends of words (e.g., *los* for *lost*), although omissions may occur in any position in a word. Substitutions frequently include saying *w* for *r* (e.g., *wight* for *right*), *w* for *l* (e.g., *fowo* for *follow*), and *th* for *s* (e.g., *thtop* for *stop, thoup* for *soup*). Articulation errors may also involve transitional lisps, where a *th* sound precedes or follows an *s* (e.g., *sthoup* or *yeths* for *soup* or *yes*). Articulation difficulties come in many forms.

Articulation disorders are a rather prevalent type of speech problem (American Psychiatric Association, 2000). Research suggests that most problems encountered by speech clinicians involve articulation disorders, with the vast majority being functional (e.g., Cicci, 1998). Some estimates suggest that articulation problems represent about 80% of the speech disorders diagnosed by such professionals (Gelfand, Jenson, & Drew, 1997). Although most of these difficulties are functional disorders, some articulation problems do not fit into the functional type and may be attributed to physiological abnormalities.

The treatment of articulation disorders has been somewhat controversial, due in part to the large number that are functional in nature. A predictable developmental progression occurs in a substantial number of functional articulation disorders. In such cases, articulation problems diminish and may even cease to exist as the child matures. For instance, the *r, s,* or *th* problems disappear for many children after the age of 5. This phenomenon makes many school administrators reluctant to treat functional articulation disorders in younger students, basically because of limited school resources. In other words, if a significant proportion of articulation disorders is likely to be corrected as the child continues to develop, why expend precious resources to treat them early on? The logic has a certain appeal, particularly in times where there is a shortage of educational resources and their use is constantly questioned. However, this argument must be applied with considerable caution. In general, improvement of articulation performance continues until a child is about 9 or

focus 7

Identify two reasons why some professionals are reluctant to treat functional articulation disorders in young schoolchildren.

■ FUNCTIONAL ARTICULATION DISORDERS. Articulation problems that are not due to structural defects or neurological problems but more likely result from environmental or psychological influences.

Timothy

■ I THINK I TALK OKAY, DON' YOU?

My name is Timothy. I am almost 7½ years old. Mondays after school, I go to the university where I meet "wif a lady who help me talk betto. It was my teacha's idea 'cause she said I don' say "l" and "r" good an some othos too. I kinda like it [coming here] but I think I talk okay, don' you? I can say "l" good now all the time and "r" when I reeeally think about it. I have lots of friends, fow, no—five. I don' talk to them about comin' hea, guess I'm jus not in the mood. Hey, you witing this down, is that good? You know the caw got hit by a semi this mowning and the doow hanle came off. I'm a little dizzy 'cause we wecked."

Timothy, age 7½

10 years of age. If articulation problems persist beyond this age, they are unlikely to improve unless intense intervention occurs. Furthermore, the longer such difficulties are allowed to continue, the more difficult treatment will become and the less likely it will be successful. Although some suggest that the impact of articulation difficulties is ultimately minimal, some hold that affected individuals may still have residual indications of the disorder many years later (e.g., Johnson & Slomka, 2000; Molfese & Molfese, 2000).

Decisions whether to treat articulation problems in young children are not easily made, and interventions can be quite complex. One option is to combine articulation training with other instruction for all very young children. This approach may serve as an interim measure for those who have continuing problems, facilitate the growth of articulation for others, and not overly tax school resources. It does, however, require some training for teachers of young children.

■ CAUSATION

Articulation disorders develop for many reasons. Some are caused by physical malformations, such as abnormal mouth, jaw, or teeth structures, and others result from nerve injury or brain damage (Lohmander-Agerskov, Soederpalm, Friede, & Lilja, 1998). Functional articulation disorders are often seen as caused by defective learning of the speaking act in one form or another. However, such categories of causation are not as distinct in practice, and a definite blurring is seen between even such broad types as functional and structural. Function and structure, although often related, are not perfectly correlated, as illustrated by the fact that some people with physical malformations that should result in articulation problems do not have problems, and vice versa.

Despite this qualifying note, we will examine causation of articulation performance deficits in two general categories: those due to physical oral malformations and those that are clearly functional because there is no physical deformity. These distinctions remain useful for instructional purposes, since it is the unusual individual who overcomes a physical abnormality and articulates satisfactorily.

In addition to oral cavity physical abnormalities, other types of physical defects can also affect articulation performances, such as an abnormal or absent larynx. Many different physical structures influence speech formulation, and all must be synchronized with learned muscle and tissue movements, auditory feedback, and a multitude of other factors. Although these coordinated functions are almost never perfect, they occur for most people in a remarkably successful manner. Oral structure malformations alter the manner in which coordinated movements must take place and sometimes make normal or accurate production of sounds extremely difficult, if not impossible.

FIGURE 10.2

Normal and cleft palate configurations:
(a) normal palate configuration;
(b) unilateral cleft palate;
(c) bilateral cleft palate;
(d) repaired cleft palate

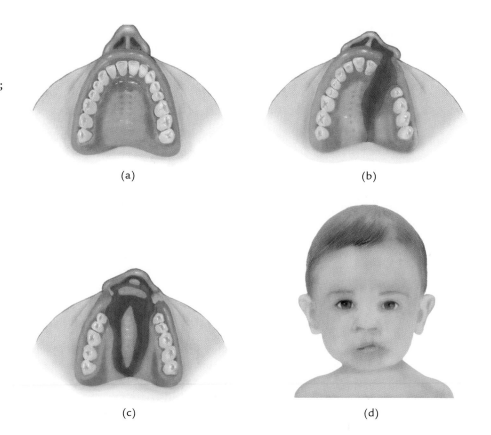

(a)

(b)

(c)

(d)

One faulty oral formation recognized by most people is the **cleft palate,** often referred to by speech pathologists as clefts of the lip or palate or both. The cleft palate is a gap in the soft palate and roof of the mouth, sometimes extending through the upper lip. The roof of the mouth serves an important function in accurate sound production. A cleft palate reduces the division of the nasal and mouth cavities, influencing the movement of air so important to articulation performance (Lohmander-Agerskov et al., 1998). Clefts are congenital defects that occur in about 1 of every 700 births and may take any of several forms (e.g., Benson, Gross, & Kellum, 1999; Cochrane & Slade, 1999). Figure 10.2 shows a normal palate in part (a) and unilateral and bilateral cleft palates in parts (b) and (c), respectively; it is easy to see how articulation would be impaired. These problems are caused by developmental difficulties in utero and are often corrected by surgery.

Articulation performance is also significantly influenced by a person's dental structure. Because the tongue and lips work together with the teeth in an intricate manner to form many sounds, dental abnormalities may result in serious articulation disorders. Some dental malformations are side effects of cleft palates, as portrayed in parts (b) and (c) of Figure 10.2, but other dental deformities not associated with clefts also cause articulation difficulties.

The natural meshing of the teeth in the upper and lower jaws is important to speech production. The general term used for the closure and fitting together of dental structures is **occlusion,** or dental occlusion. When the fit is abnormal, the condition is known as **malocclusion.** Occlusion involves several factors, including the biting height of the teeth when the jaws are closed, the alignment of teeth in the upper and lower jaws, the nature of curves in upper and lower jaws, and teeth positioning. A normal adult occlusion is portrayed in part (a) of Figure 10.3. The upper

▪CLEFT PALATE. A gap in the soft palate and roof of the mouth, sometimes extending through the upper lip.

▪OCCLUSION. The closing and fitting together of dental structures.

▪MALOCCLUSION. An abnormal fit between the upper and lower dental structures.

FIGURE 10.3   Normal and abnormal dental occlusions: (a) normal dental occlusion; (b) overbite malocclusion; (c) underbite malocclusion

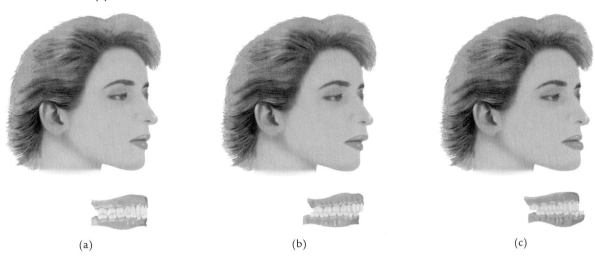

(a)   (b)   (c)

teeth normally extend slightly beyond those of the lower jaw, and the bite overlap of those on the bottom is about one third for the front teeth (incisors) when closed.

Occlusion abnormalities take many forms, although we will discuss only two here. When the overbite of the top teeth is unusually large, the normal difference between the lower and upper dental structure is exaggerated. Such conditions may be due to the positioning of the upper and lower jaws, as illustrated in part (b) of Figure 10.3. In other cases, nearly the opposite situation occurs, as illustrated in part (c) of Figure 10.3, forming another kind of jaw misalignment. Both exaggerated overbites and underbites may also be the result of abnormal teeth positioning or angles as well as jaw misalignment. All can result in articulation difficulties.

Many functional articulation disorders are thought to be due to faulty language learning. The sources of defective speech learning are frequently unknown or difficult to precisely identify (Cicci, 1998; Gibbon, 1999; Stimley & Hambrecht, 1999). Like other articulation problems, those of a functional nature have many specific causes. For example, interactions between children and their mothers tend to make considerable contribution to language acquisition (D'Odorico et al., 1999; Laakso et al., 1999). In some cases, the existing stimulus and reinforcement patterns may not support accurate articulation. For example, parents may be inconsistent in encouraging and prompting accurate articulation. Parents are busy in their daily routines. Routinely encouraging their children to speak properly may not be high on their priority list. However, such encouragement is important, particularly if misarticulation begins to emerge as a problem.

Also, adults may unthinkingly view some normal inaccuracies of speech in young children as cute or amusing. "Baby talk," for example, may be reinforced in a powerful manner by parents asking the young child to say a particular word in the presence of grandparents or other guests and rewarding him or her with laughter and hugs and kisses. Such potent rewards can result in misarticulations that linger long beyond the time when normal maturation would diminish or eliminate them. Related defective learning may come from modeling. Parents (or other adults) may model and thus reinforce articulation disorders when they imitate the baby talk of young children. If parents, grandparents, or friends realized the potential results of such behavior, they would probably alter the nature of verbal interchanges with young children. Modeling is a potent tool in shaping learned behavior. Although the influence of baby talk between parents and children has been questioned, modeling and imitation are used in interventions and are thought to influence natural verbal development (Chapman, 2000; Rice et al., 1999; Shuster, 1998).

■ INTERVENTION

There are many types of treatment for articulation disorders. Clearly, the treatment for disorders due to physical abnormalities differs from that for disorders that are functional. In many cases, however, treatment may include a combination of procedures.

Considerable progress has been made over the years in various types of surgical repair for cleft palates. Such techniques may be complex because of the dramatic nature of the structural defect. Some procedures include Teflon implants in the hard portion of the palate, as well as stretching and stitching together the fleshy tissue. As suggested by Figure 10.2, surgery is often necessary for the upper lip and nose structures, and corrective dental work may be undertaken as well. It may also be necessary to train or retrain the individual in articulation and assess his or her emotional status related to appearance or speech skills, depending on age at the time of surgery (Cochran & Slade, 1999). A child's continued development may introduce new problems later; for example, the physical growth of the jaw or mouth may create difficulties for someone who underwent surgery at a very young age. Although early correction has resulted in successful healing and speech for a very high percentage of treated cases, the permanence of such results is questionable in light of later growth spurts.

Treatment of cleft palate may also involve the use of prosthetic appliances. For example, a prosthesis that basically serves as the upper palate or at least covers the fissures may be employed. Such an appliance may be attached to the teeth to hold it in position and resembles the palate portion of artificial dentures.

Dental malformations other than those associated with clefts can also be corrected. Surgery can alter jaw structure and alignment. In some cases, orthodontic treatment may involve the repositioning of teeth through extractions and the use of braces. Prosthetic appliances, such as full or partial artificial dentures, may also be used. As in other types of problems, the articulation patient who has orthodontic treatment often requires speech therapy to learn proper speech performance.

Treatment of functional articulation disorders often focuses on relearning the speaking act; in some cases, muscle control and usage are the focus (Skelton, 1999). Specific causes of defective learning are difficult to identify precisely, but the basic assumption in such cases is that an inappropriate stimulus and reinforcement situation was present in the environment during speech development (e.g., inappropriate modeling by parents). Following this assumption, treatment attempts to correct that set of circumstances so that accurate articulation can be learned. Several behavior modification procedures have been employed successfully in treating functional articulation disorders. In all cases, treatment techniques are difficult to implement because interventions must teach proper articulation plus the generalization of that learning to a variety of word configurations and diverse environments beyond the treatment setting (Dehaney, 2000; Skelton, 1999). Further research on the treatment of articulation disorders is seriously needed, particularly in view of its prevalence. Additionally, some advocate improving the quality of measurement and research methods employed in this and other areas of communication disorders (Johnson & Slomka, 2000; Skelton, 1999).

It should also be noted that differences in language and dialect can create some interesting issues regarding treatment. When a child's first language is other than

English or involves a significant specific ethnic dialectic component, that youngster may demonstrate an articulation distinctiveness that makes his or her speech different and perhaps difficult to understand (Holm, Dodd, Stow, & Pert, 1999; Wilcox & Anderson, 1998). Does this circumstance require an intervention similar to that for articulation disorders? Such a question involves cultural, social, and political implications far beyond those typically considered by professionals working with speech disorders.

▪ VOICE DISORDER. A condition in which an individual habitually speaks with a voice that differs in pitch, loudness, or quality from the voices of others of the same sex and age in a particular cultural group.

Voice Disorders

▪ DEFINITION

oice disorders involve unusual or abnormal acoustical qualities in the sounds made when a person speaks. All voices differ significantly in pitch, loudness, and other qualities from others of the same gender, cultural group, and age. All people have varying acoustical qualities in their voices. However, voice disorders involve characteristics that are habitually and sufficiently different such that they are noticeable and may divert a listener's attention from the content of a message.

Relatively little attention has been paid to voice disorders in the research literature, for several reasons. First, the determination of voice normalcy involves a great deal of subjective judgment. Moreover, what is normal varies considerably according to the circumstances (e.g., football games, barroom conversation, or seminar discussion) and geographical location (e.g., the West, a rural area, New England, the Deep South), as well as family environments, personality, and physical structure of the speech mechanism. Another factor contributing to the lack of attention to voice disorders is related to the acceptable ranges of normal voice. Most individuals' voices fall within acceptable tolerance ranges. Because of limited attention, children with voice disorders are often not referred for help, and their problems are persistent when not treated (Cicci, 1998).

Children with voice disorders often speak with an unusual nasality, hoarseness, or breathiness. Nasality involves either too little resonance from the nasal passages (hyponasality or denasality), which sounds as if the child has a continual cold or stuffy nose, or too much sound coming through the nose (hypernasality), which causes a twang in the speech. People with voice disorders of hoarseness have a constant husky sound to their speech, as though they had strained their voices by yelling. Breathiness is a voice disorder with very low volume, like a whisper; it sounds as though not enough air is flowing through the vocal cords. Other voice disorders include overly loud or soft speaking and pitch abnormalities (e.g., monotone speech).

Like so many speech problems, the nature of voice disorders varies greatly. Our description provides considerable latitude, but it also outlines the general parameters of voice disorders often dismissed in the literature: pitch, loudness, and quality. An individual with a voice disorder may

Factors in voice disorders that interfere with communication are pitch, loudness, and quality. A voice disorder exists when these factors, singly or in combination, cause the listener to focus on the sounds being made rather than the message to be communicated.

exhibit problems with one or more of these factors, significantly interfering with communication (i.e., the listener will focus on the sound rather than the message).

■ CAUSATION

An appropriate voice pitch is efficient and suited to the situation and the speech content as well as the speaker's laryngeal structure. Correct voice pitch permits inflection without voice breaks or excessive strain. Appropriate pitch varies as emotion and meaning change and should not distract attention from the message. Acoustic characteristics of voice quality include factors such as degree of nasality, breathy speech, and hoarse-sounding speech. Like the other parameters of voice, determination of appropriate loudness is subjective. The normal voice is not habitually characterized by excessive loudness or unusual softness. A normal level of loudness depends greatly on circumstances.

Pitch disorders take several forms. The person's voice may have an abnormally high or low pitch, may be characterized by pitch breaks or a restricted pitch range, or may be monotonal or monopitched. Many individuals experience pitch breaks as they progress through adolescence. Although more commonly associated with young males, pitch breaks also occur in females. Such pitch breaks are a normal part of development, but if they persist much beyond adolescence, they may signal laryngeal difficulties. Abnormally high- or low-pitched voices may signal a variety of problems. They may be learned through imitation, as when a young boy attempts to sound like his older brother or father. They may also be learned from certain circumstances, such as when an individual placed in a position of authority believes a lower voice pitch is necessary to suggest the image of power. Organic conditions, such as a hormone imbalance, may also result in abnormally high- or low-pitched voices.

Voice disorders involving volume may also have varied causes. Voices that are excessively loud or soft may be learned through imitation, perceptions and characteristics of the environment, and even aging (Goozee, Murdoch, Theodoros, & Thompson, 1998; Vilkman, 2000). An example is mimicking the soft speaking of a female movie star. Other cases of abnormal vocal intensity occur because an individual has not learned to monitor loudness. Beyond learning difficulties, however, some intensity voice disorders occur because of organic problems. For example, abnormally low vocal intensity may result from problems such as paralysis of vocal cords, laryngeal trauma (e.g., larynx surgery for cancer, damage through accident or disease), and pulmonary diseases such as asthma or emphysema (e.g., Weitzel, 2000). Excessively loud speech may occur as a result of organic problems such as hearing impairments and brain damage.

Voice disorders relating to the quality of speech include production deviances such as those of abnormal nasality as well as the hoarse and breathy speech noted earlier. Abnormal nasality may take the form of a voice that sounds overly nasal (hypernasality) or a voice with reduced acoustic sound (denasality or **hyponasality**) that dulls the resonance of consonants. **Hypernasality** occurs essentially because the soft palate does not move upward and back to close off the airstream through the nose properly. Such conditions can be due to improper tissue movement in the speech mechanism, or they may result from organic defects such as an imperfectly repaired cleft palate (Lohmander-Agerskov et al., 1998). Excessive hypernasality may also be learned, as in the case of country music or certain rural dialects. **Denasality** is the type of voice quality experienced during a severe head cold or hay fever. The sounds are congested and/or dulled, with reduced acoustic resonance. In some cases, however, denasality is the result of learning or abnormal physical structures rather than these more common problems.

■ HYPONASALITY. A voice disorder involving resonance whereby too little air passes through the nasal cavity (denasality).

■ HYPERNASALITY. A voice resonance disorder that occurs when excessive air passes through the nasal cavity, often resulting in an unpleasant twanging sound.

■ DENASALITY. A voice resonance problem that occurs when too little air passes through the nasal cavity.

■ INTERVENTION

The approach to voice disorder treatment depends on causation. In cases when abnormal tissue development and/or dental structures result in unusual voice production, surgical intervention may be necessary. Surgery may also be part of the intervention plan in cases where the larynx requires removal. Such an intervention will also involve relearning communication through alternative mechanisms, including prostheses, and learning communication techniques to replace laryngeal verbalizations (Weitzel, 2000). In some situations, treatment may involve direct instruction to help the affected individual's learning or relearning of acceptable voice production. Such interventions often include counseling regarding the effects of unusual voice sounds on others and behavior modification procedures aimed at retraining the person's speaking. These efforts are more difficult if the behavior has been long-standing and is well ingrained. We have already discussed interventions such as these in the discussions of other speech disorders.

Voice disorders are seldom the focus of referral and treatment in the United States. However, some researchers have argued that voice disorders should be treated more aggressively, even to the point of imposing legislative guidelines for workplace conditions affecting vocal stress (Vilkman, 2000). One important element in planning interventions with voice disorders is clear and open communication with the person seeking treatment. It is important to avoid setting unrealistic expectations about outcomes since those being treated are the ultimate evaluators of success.

Prevalence

We have already noted the difficulties involved in estimating the prevalence of other disorders, due to differences in definitions and data-collection procedures. The field of speech disorders is also vulnerable to these problems, and so prevalence estimates vary considerably.

The most typical prevalence figures cited for speech disorders indicate that between 7% and 10% of the population is affected. Approximately 19% of all children (ages 6 to 21) served in programs for those with disabilities were categorized as having speech or language impairments in 1998–1999 (U.S. Department of Education, 2000a). These figures do not deviate greatly from other estimates over the years, although some data have suggested substantial differences between geographic locales (e.g., significantly higher percentages in some areas of California than in parts of the Midwest). To some degree, these figures present difficulties when we consider the overall 12% ceiling for services to all students with disabilities, as specified in the Individuals with Disabilities Education Act (IDEA). Obviously, individuals with speech disorders of a mild nature cannot be eligible for federally funded services. However, the *22nd Annual Report to Congress on the Implementation of IDEA* cited speech or language impairments as the second most frequently occurring disability (next to learning disabilities) receiving special services during the 1998–1999 school year (U.S. Department of Education, 2000a).

The frequency with which speech problems occur diminishes in the population as age increases. Speech disorders are identified in about 12% to 15% of children in kindergarten through grade 4. For children in grades 5 through 8, the figure declines to about 4% to 5%. The 5% rate remains somewhat constant after grade 8 unless treatment intervenes. Thus, age and development diminish speech disorders considerably, more so with certain types of problems (e.g., articulation difficulties) than others.

Case Study

RICKY

The following is a statement by Ricky Creech, a person with a serious communication disorder due to cerebral palsy. Ricky communicates by using a computer-controlled electronic augmentative communication device. He provides some insights regarding assumptions people make about individuals who cannot communicate. This is a portion of a presentation made at the National Institutes of Health.

"There is a great need for educating the public on how to treat physically limited people. People are still under the misconception that somehow the ability to speak, hear, see, feel, smell, and reason are tied together. That is, if a person loses one, he has lost the others.

"The number one question people ask my parents is, 'Can he hear?' When I reply that I can, they bend down where their lips are not two feet away from my eyes and say very loudly, 'How—are—you? Do—you—like—that—talking—machine?' Now, I don't mind when that person is a pretty, young girl. But when it is an older or married woman, it is a little embarrassing. When the person is a man, I'm tempted to say something not very nice. . . .

"I would make a great spy. When I am around, people just keep talking—because I can't speak, they think I can't hear or understand what is being said. I have listened to more private conversations than there are on the Watergate tapes. It is a good thing that I am not a blackmailer. If people knew that I hear and understand everything they say, some would die of embarrassment.

"There is another conclusion which people make when first seeing me, which I don't kid about; I don't find it a bit humorous. That is, that I am mentally retarded.

"The idea that if a person can't speak, something must be wrong with his mind is the prevalent belief in every class, among the educated as well as the not-so-educated. I have a very good friend who is a nuclear scientist, the most intelligent person I have ever known, but he admitted that when he first saw me, his first conclusion was that I was mentally retarded. This was in spite of my parents' assertions that I was not.

"However, this man had a special quality—when he was wrong he could admit it with his mind and his heart—most people can't do both. There are people who know me who know with their minds that I am not mentally retarded, but they treat me as a child because in their hearts they have not really accepted that I have the mentality of an adult. I am an adult and I want to be treated as an adult. I have a tremendous amount of respect for anyone who does."

■ **APPLICATION**

1. Have you ever made the same error that the nuclear scientist made in the case study? Explain what you felt and how you acted.
2. Having read Ricky Creech's description, how would you react now?
3. As a professional, how would you explain to people Ricky's communication disorder so they would understand his abilities?

Source: From "Consumers Speak Out on the Life of the Nonspeaker," by R. Creech and J. Viggiano, 1981, *ASHA, 23,* pp. 550–552. Reprinted by permission of the American Speech-Language-Hearing Association.

Debate Forum

TO TREAT OR NOT TO TREAT?

Articulation problems represent about 80% of all speech disorders encountered by speech clinicians, making this type of difficulty the most prevalent of all communication disorders. It is also well known that young children normally make a number of articulation errors during the process of maturation as they are learning to talk. A substantial portion do not conquer all the rules of language and produce all the speech sounds correctly until they are 8 or 9 years old, yet they eventually develop normal speech and articulate properly. In lay terminology, they seem to "grow out of" early articulation problems. Because of this maturation outcome and the prevalence of articulation problems, serious questions are asked regarding treatment in the early years.

■ **POINT**

Some school administrators are reluctant to treat young children who display articulation errors because the resources of school districts are in very short supply and budgets are extremely tight. If a substantial proportion of young children's articulation problems will correct themselves through maturation, then shouldn't the precious resources of school districts be directed to other more pressing problems? Articulation problems should not be treated unless they persist beyond the age of 10 or 11.

Although articulation does improve with maturation, delaying intervention is a mistake. The longer such problems persist, the more difficult treatment will be. Even the issue of financial savings is a false one. If all articulation difficulties are allowed to continue, those children who do not outgrow such problems will be more difficult to treat later, requiring more intense and expensive intervention than if treated early. Early intervention for articulation problems is vitally important.

Review

focus 1

Identify four ways in which speech, language, and communication are interrelated.

- Both speech and language form part, but not all, of communication.
- Some components of communication involve language but not speech.
- Some speech does not involve language.
- The development of communication, language, and speech overlap to some degree.

focus 2

Identify two ways in which language delay and language disorder are different.

- In language delay, the sequence of development is intact, but the rate is interrupted.
- In language disorder, the sequence of development is interrupted.

focus 3

Identify three factors thought to cause language disorders.

- Defective or deficient sensory systems
- Neurological damage occurring through physical trauma or accident
- Deficient or disrupted learning opportunities during language development

focus 4

Describe two ways in which treatment approaches for language disorders generally differ for children and for adults.

- Treatment for children generally addresses initial acquisition or learning of language.
- Treatment for adults involves relearning or reacquiring language function.

focus 5

Identify three factors thought to cause stuttering.

- Learned behavior, emotional problems, and neurological problems can contribute to stuttering.
- Some research has suggested that people who stutter have a brain organization differing from those who do not.
- People who stutter may learn their speech patterns as an outgrowth of the normal nonfluency evident when speech development first occurs.

focus 6

Identify two ways in which learning theory and home environments relate to delayed speech.

- The home environment may provide little opportunity to learn speech.
- The home environment may interfere with speech development when speaking is punished.

focus 7

Identify two reasons why some professionals are reluctant to treat functional articulation disorders in young schoolchildren.

- Many articulation problems evident in young children are developmental in nature, and so speech may improve with age.
- Articulation problems are quite frequent among young children, and treatment resources are limited.

People with Severe and Multiple Disabilities

To begin with . . .

"Yvonne belongs with us!" we firmly told the psychiatrist when he insisted that we place our 2-year-old daughter in an institution. To us, Yvonne's sudden regression meant that she needed us more than ever—we could not abandon her, we could not reject her. At first we struggled on our own; there were no community supports. Then, together with other parents, we advocated for appropriate supports in the community for children who were labeled "severely mentally handicapped." We believed that Yvonne, and children like her, had a right to live at home, had a right to go to school, and had a right to participate in the life of the community. Our vision was shared and supported by some service providers, but other professionals opposed our view and worked against us. (Penner, 1999)

For as long as she can remember, Mrs. Brown has been told that she and other general education teachers were not appropriately trained or qualified to teach students with a wide range of disabilities. She was told, "That's why we have special education classes and schools where students with special educational needs can get the specialized instruction they need." . . . Recently, people started talking about educating students with more significant disabilities in the general education classroom; they referred to it as "inclusive education." Mrs. Brown felt that she had never excluded children before because of their disabilities, but rather, was trying to help them by sending them to a place that would better meet their needs. Now, she was about to have a student with more significant disabilities in her class. She wondered how this would work and what she should do to make sure it worked for her whole class. (Giangreco & Doyle, 2000, pp. 51–52)

Remarkable progress has been made during the past 10 years in using technology to meet the needs of students with disabilities. In particular, researchers have customized technology to meet the needs of students with severe cognitive and physical disabilities. . . . Students with severe impairments [disabilities] have increased independence levels through "low tech" solutions such as specially designed pencils, scissors, and silverware and "high tech" advances such as voice recognition systems, word prediction systems, and virtual reality. (U.S. Department of Education, 1997, p. xii)

At 37, Kathleen McAuliffe found herself pregnant but in a terrible predicament. An amniocentesis performed at 16 weeks had brought bad news: a large section of chromosome 2 in the fetus's DNA had done a flipflop. The genetic counselor said that if either parent had the same alteration, there was a 10% chance, at most, of a serious birth defect. But chromosome tests on the parents were not reassuring. Neither had the defect. . . . She and her husband debated the risks. He favored continuing the pregnancy, but she had serious doubts and decided to abort. She has since had two healthy babies, a boy and a girl. Though McAuliffe never asked for the results of the autopsy on her aborted fetus, they were sent to her anyway: the baby would have had "crushing" deformities. "If there is a moral to my story," she lamented in the *New York Times,* "it is that there is no moral." (When Genetic Testing Says No, 1999)

Sarina

Sarina never had the opportunity to go to preschool and didn't begin her formal education in the public schools until the age of 6. She is now 15 years old and goes to Eastmont Junior High—her neighborhood school. Sarina does not verbally speak, walk, hear, or see. Professionals have used several labels to describe her, including *severely disabled, severely multiply handicapped, deaf–blind,* and *profoundly mentally retarded.* Her teenage classmates at Eastmont call her Sarina. Throughout the day, Sarina has a support team of administrators, teachers, paraprofessionals, and peers that work together to meet her instructional, physical, and medical needs. And she has many, many needs. Sarina requires some level of support in everything she does, ranging from eating and taking care of personal hygiene to communicating with others. In the last few years, she has learned to express herself through the use of assistive technology. Sarina has a personal communication board with picture symbols that keeps her in constant contact with teachers, friends, and family. Through the use of an electronic wheelchair and her ability to use various switches, Sarina is able to maneuver her way through just about any obstacle in her environment. She is also learning to feed herself independently.

Sarina lives at home with her family, including three older brothers. Her parents, siblings, and grandparents are very supportive, always looking for ways to help facilitate Sarina's participation in school, family, and community activities. What she loves to do most is go shopping with her mom at the local mall, eat with friends at a fast-food restaurant, relax on the lawn in the neighborhood park, and play miniature golf at Mulligan's Pitch and Putt.

SARINA, IN THE OPENING SNAPSHOT, is a person with **severe and multiple disabilities.** In one way or another, she will require services and support in nearly every facet of her life. Some people with severe disabilities have significant intellectual, learning, and behavioral differences; others are physically disabled with vision and hearing loss. Most have significant, multiple disabilities. Sarina certainly has multiple needs, one of which is communication. Yet, although she is unable to communicate verbally, she is able to express herself through the use of a communication board. Thus, in many circumstances, a disability may be described as severe, but through today's technology and our understanding of how to adapt the environment, the impact on the person may be diminished.

Definitions

The needs of people with severe and multiple disabilities cannot be met by one profession. The nature of their disabilities extends equally into the fields of education, medicine, psychology, and social services. Since these individuals present such diverse characteristics and require the attention of several professionals, it is not surprising that numerous definitions have been used to describe them.

■ HISTORICAL DESCRIPTIONS OF SEVERE DISABILITIES

Throughout history, terminology associated with severe disabilities has communicated a sense of hopelessness and despair. The condition was described as "extremely debilitating," "inflexibly incapacitating," or "uncompromisingly crippling." Abt Associates (1974) described individuals with severe handicaps as unable "to attend to even the most pronounced social stimuli, including failure to respond

■ SEVERE AND MULTIPLE DISABILITIES. A cross-classification of disabilities that involve significant physical, sensory, intellectual, and/or social–interpersonal performance deficits. The need for extensive services and supports is evident in all environmental settings. Individuals with severe and multiple disabilities may need significantly altered environments for care, treatment, and accommodation.

to invitations from peers or adults, or loss of contact with reality" (p. v). The definition went on to use terms such as *self-mutilation* (e.g., head banging, body scratching, and hair pulling), *ritualistic behaviors* (e.g., rocking and pacing), and *self-stimulation* (e.g., masturbation, stroking, and patting). The Abt definition focused almost exclusively on the individual's deficits and negative behavioral characteristics.

In 1976, Justen proposed a definition that moved away from negative terminology to descriptions of the individual's developmental characteristics. "The 'severely handicapped' refers to those individuals . . . who are functioning at a general development level of half or less than the level which would be expected on the basis of chronological age and who manifest learning and/or behavior problems of such magnitude and significance that they require extensive structure in learning situations" (p. 5).

Whereas Justen emphasized a discrepancy between normal and atypical development, Sailor and Haring (1977) proposed a definition that was oriented to the educational needs of each individual:

A child should be assigned to a program for the severely/multiply handicapped according to whether the primary service needs of the child are basic or academic. . . . If the diagnosis and assessment process determines that a child with multiple handicaps needs academic instruction, the child should not be referred to the severely handicapped program. If the child's service need is basic skill development, the referral to the severely/multiply handicapped program is appropriate. (p. 68)

In 1991, Snell further elaborated on the importance of defining severe disabilities on the basis of educational need, suggesting that the emphasis be on supporting the individual in inclusive classroom settings. The Association for Severe Handicaps (Meyer, Peck, & Brown, 1991b), while agreeing in principle with Snell, proposed a definition that focused on inclusion in all natural settings: family, community, and school.

■ THE TASH DEFINITION OF SEVERE DISABILITIES

The Association for Persons with Severe Handicaps (TASH) proposed the following definition of severe disabilities:

These people include individuals of all ages who require extensive ongoing support in more than one major life activity in order to participate in integrated community settings and to enjoy a quality of life that is available to citizens with fewer or no disabilities. Support may be required for life activities such as mobility, communication, self-care, and learning as necessary for independent living, employment, and self-sufficiency. (Meyer et al., 1991b, p. 19)

The TASH definition focused on the relationship of the individual with the environment (adaptive fit), the need to include people of all ages, and "extensive ongoing support" in life activities. The adaptive fit between the person and the environment is a two-way street. First, it is important to determine the capability of the individual to cope with the requirements of family, school, and community environments. Second, how do these various environments recognize and accommodate the need of the person with severe disabilities? The adaptive fit of the individual with the environment is a dynamic process requiring continuous adjustment that fosters a mutually supportive coexistence. The TASH definition of severe disabilities suggests that an adaptive fit can be created only when there is extensive ongoing support (formal and/or natural) for each person as he or she moves through various life activities, including social interactions, taking care of personal needs, and making choices about lifestyle, working, and moving from place to place.

focus 1

What are the three components of the TASH definition of severe disabilities?

focus 2

Define the terms *multiple disabilities and deaf–blindness* as described in IDEA.

THE IDEA DEFINITIONS OF SEVERE AND MULTIPLE DISABILITIES

The Individuals with Disabilities Education Act (IDEA) does not include the term *severe disabilities* as one of the categorical definitions of disability identified in federal regulation. Individuals with severe disabilities may be subsumed under any one of IDEA's categories, such as mental retardation, autism, serious emotional disturbance, speech and language impairments, and so on. (These disability conditions are discussed in other chapters in this text.) IDEA does include multiple disabilities and deaf–blindness as specific disability categories.

MULTIPLE DISABILITIES

Multiple disabilities as defined in IDEA federal regulations means

concomitant impairments (such as mental retardation–blindness mental retardation–orthopedic impairment, etc.), the combination of which causes such severe educational needs that they cannot be accommodated in special education programs solely for one of the impairments. The term does not include deaf–blindness [34 C.F.R. 300.7(c) (7) (1999)].

This definition includes multiple conditions that can occur in any of several combinations. One such combination is described by the term **dual diagnosis.** Dual diagnosis involves persons who have serious emotional disturbance or present challenging behaviors in conjunction with severe mental retardation. Estimates of people with mental retardation also having serious challenging behaviors vary, ranging from 5% to 15% of those living in the community to a much higher percentage for people living in institutions (Beirne-Smith, Ittenbach, & Patton, 1998; Griffiths, Nugent, & Gardner, 1998). So, why do people with mental retardation and other developmental disabilities often have higher rates of challenging behaviors? Griffiths et al. (1998) indicated that "it is important to understand that the challenging behaviors are not a fundamental characteristic of developmental disabilities" (p. 3). These authors further suggested that the increase is related to various risk factors. People with developmental disabilities have

- an increased prevalence of neurological , sensory, and physical abnormalities.
- lifestyles that frequently are characterized by restrictiveness, prejudice, limited personal independence, restricted personal control, paucity of mentally healthy experiences, and victimization.
- skill deficits in critical functional areas. These skill deficits make it more difficult to appropriately deal with stresses in life.
- atypical learning histories. Often, positive behaviors have not been acknowledged and negative and disruptive behaviors have attracted excessive attention. (Griffiths et al., pp. 3–4)

The term *dual diagnosis* has raised apprehension among some professional groups, particularly TASH. TASH suggests that the term may be misapplied as a rationale for the use of aversive behavioral procedures, psychotropic medications, and punishment through the judicial system. To deal with the confusion surrounding the use of this label more effectively, TASH recommended the following:

- Programs for people described as having a dual diagnosis must include individualized, personalized services and nonaversive methods.
- Additional research must be undertaken to determine the influence of environmental factors affecting the increase in behaviors associated with mental illness.
- Support and assistance must be based on individual need rather than labels. (Meyer et al., 1991b) (See nearby Reflect on This feature.)

DUAL DIAGNOSIS. Identification of both serious emotional problems and mental retardation in the same individual.

Reflect on This

MAT'S STORY: JOINING THE COMMUNITY

Mat is a 23-year-old man with autism and mental retardation. He lives in a home with one roommate and holds two jobs. One job involves cleaning at a local bar and restaurant for an hour each morning. The second job is delivering a weekly advertiser to 170 homes in his neighborhood. In addition to working in the community, Mat goes shopping, takes walks around a nearby lake, goes to the movies, attends concerts and special events, and eats at a fast-food restaurant where he uses a wallet-sized communication picture board to order his meal, independently.

Mat hasn't always been so integrated into his local community. In the past he engaged in a number of challenging behaviors including removing pictures from the wall, taking down drapes and ripping them, dismantling his bed, ripping his clothing, breaking windows, smearing his bowel movements on objects, urinating on his clothing, hurting others, stripping naked, and other similar behaviors. For almost one entire year Mat refused to wear clothing and spent most of his time wrapped in a blanket. He would often cover his head with the blanket and lie on the couch for hours. He frequently stripped in community settings, on those few occasions when staff were able to coax him to go out.

After this had continued for months, the assistance of a behavioral analyst was sought. An analysis of the function that the behaviors served revealed that Mat's stripping and subsequent refusal to wear clothing were the result of his attempt to exert control over his environment, primarily to escape or avoid undesirable events. For this reason, the behavior analyst suggested not focusing directly on the issue of wearing clothing, but rather addressing the development of a communication system for Mat. Mat was reported to know over 200 signs; however, he was rarely observed to use the signs spontaneously. When he did sign, others in his environment were unable to interpret his signing. Consequently, the behavior analyst and a consultant in augmentative and alternative communication suggested that a communication system using picture or symbols be implemented to supplement his existing system.

The support program that was developed for Mat had two main components. The first was to enhance his communication and choice-making skills and the second was to provide opportunities for him to participate in activities that were motivating and required him to wear clothing. To address communication and choice-making skills, several photographs were taken of people Mat knew and had worked with, activities he liked or was required to engage in (e.g., watching MTV, go to McDonald's, shaving, taking a shower, etc.), and a variety of objects (e.g., lotion, pop, cookies, etc.). Then a minimum of four times each hour, Mat was presented with a choice. Mat would then pick one of the pictures, and staff would help him complete whatever activity he had chosen. Soon he had over 130 photographs in his communication system. The photographs were mounted on hooks in the hallway of the house where he lived, ensuring he had easy access to them. Over time, staff reported that Mat began spontaneously using some of the pictures to request items. He would, for example, bring staff the photo for a Diet Pepsi to request a Diet Pepsi. So the communication enhanced his ability to make his wants and needs known as well as helped him understand choices presented to him.

While Mat's communication system was being developed, staff were also trying to indirectly address his refusal to wear clothes by capitalizing on the fact that he seemed to genuinely like to go out into the community. Staff would periodically encourage Mat to dress. On those occasions when he would dress, he was then able to participate in a community activity that was reinforcing for him. The length of these outings was gradually increased.

As time went on, staff tried to increase the amount of time Mat was dressed at home by requiring him to wait for short periods of time once he was dressed to go out in the community. For example, if he indicated that he wanted to go to the store, he was encouraged to get dressed before he could go. Once he was dressed, staff would say, "Mat, I have to do these dishes quickly before we go. Why don't you just watch MTV, and we'll be ready to go in just a few minutes. Staff employed similar "stalling" techniques once Mat returned from a community outing. For example, after returning home from the store, he was encouraged to help carry in the bags of groceries and to put them away. Staff continued to implement these stalling and delaying techniques over an 11-month period, gradually increasing the amount of time he would remain clothed. Mat now wears clothes an average of 17 hours a day, and during the past year he has not attempted to undress while in the community. This is not to say his challenging behaviors have disappeared. He still experiences periods when many of these behaviors escalate. But now, these periods generally last only days, not months. And staff now feel more confident in their ability to implement strategies that have been successful in the past. Perhaps most important, Mat's challenging behavior no longer stands in the way of his full participation in the local community.

Sources: From *A Little Help from My Friends* (pp. 14–15), by A. Hewitt and S. O'Nell, 1998, Washington, DC: President's Committee on Mental Retardation [on-line] Available: http://www.acf.dhhs.gov/programs/pcmr/help4.pdf Adapted from "Joining the Community," by L. Piche, P. Krape, and C. Wiczek, 1991, *IMPACT, 4*(1), pp. 3, 18.

■ DEAF–BLINDNESS   For some multiple disabilities, mental retardation may not be a primary symptom. One such condition is deaf–blindness, a **dual sensory impairment.** The concomitant vision and hearing difficulties exhibited by people with **deaf–blindness** result in severe communication deficits as well as developmental and educational difficulties that require extensive support across several professional disciplines. IDEA defines deaf–blindness as:

concomitant hearing and visual impairments, the combination of which causes such severe communication and other developmental and educational needs that they cannot be accommodated in special education programs solely for children with deafness or children with blindness. [34 C.F.R. 300.7(c) (2) (1999)].

The impact of both vision and hearing loss on the educational needs of the student is a matter of debate among professionals. One view of deaf–blindness is the individuals are so severely mentally retarded that both vision and hearing are also affected. Another view is that they are average in intelligence and lost their hearing and sight after having acquired language. Intellectual functioning for persons with deaf–blindness may range from normal or gifted to severe mental retardation. All people with deaf–blindness experience challenges in learning to communicate, access information, and comfortably move through their environment. These individuals may also have physical and behavioral disabilities. However, the specific needs of each person will vary enormously according to age, onset, and type of deaf–blindness (Deafblind International, 2000).

A child with severe disabilities will need extensive ongoing support in many areas, including learning functional academics in a school setting.

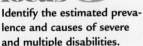

focus 3

Identify the estimated prevalence and causes of severe and multiple disabilities.

■ DUAL SENSORY IMPAIRMENTS. A condition characterized by both vision and hearing sensory impairments (deaf-blindness). The condition can result in severe communication problems as well as developmental and educational difficulties that require extensive support across several professional disciplines.

■ DEAF-BLINDNESS. A disorder involving simultaneous vision and hearing impairments.

Prevalence

People with severe and multiple disabilities constitute a very small percentage of the general population. Even if we consider the multitude of conditions, prevalence is no more than 0.1% to 1.0%. Approximately 4 out of every 1,000 persons are severely disabled where the primary symptom is mental retardation. The U.S. Department of Education (2000a) estimated that about 107,763 students between the ages of 6 and 21 were served in the public schools under the label *multiple disabilities* during the 1998-1999 school year. These students account for 2% of the over 5.5 million students considered eligible for services under IDEA. The Department of Education also reported that there were 1,609 students between the ages of 6 and 21 labeled as deaf–blind. These students account for 0.0002% of students with disabilities served under IDEA. Overall, about 14,000 individuals in the United States are identified as deaf–blind.

Causation

Multiple disabilities result from multiple causes. For the vast majority of people with severe and multiple disabilities, the differences are evident at birth. Severe disabilities may be the result of genetic or metabolic disorders, including chromosomal abnormalities, phenylketonuria, or Rh incompatibility. Most identifiable causes of severe mental retardation and related developmental disabilities are genetic in origin (The Arc, 2000). Other causes include prenatal conditions: poor maternal health during pregnancy, drug abuse, infectious diseases (e.g., HIV), radiation exposure, venereal disease, and advanced maternal age. Severe and multiple disabilities can also result from incidents or conditions that occur later in life, such as poisoning, accidents, malnutrition, physical and emotional neglect, and disease. (See Chapter 9 for a more in-depth discussion of genetic and behavioral factors associated with severe disabilities in which a primary symptom is mental retardation.)

Characteristics

The multitude of characteristics exhibited by people with severe and multiple disabilities is mirrored by the numerous definitions associated with these conditions. A close analysis of these definitions reveals a consistent focus on people whose life needs cannot be met without substantial support from others, including family, friends, and society. With this support, however, people with severe and multiple disabilities have a much greater probability of escaping the stereotype that depicts them as totally dependent consumers of societal resources. People with severe disabilities can become contributing members of families and communities.

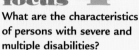

focus 4
What are the characteristics of persons with severe and multiple disabilities?

School-age students with severe and multiple disabilities may be characterized according to their instructional needs. Sailor, Gee, and Karasoff (2000) suggested that professionals concentrate more on "the way in which special education services are defined and implemented in inclusive educational settings" (p. 11) and less on general, often stereotyped population characteristics. For Sarina (see the opening snapshot), this would mean concentrating on educational outcomes that will decrease her dependence on others in her environment and create opportunities to enhance her participation at home, at school, and in the community. Instruction would be developed with these outcomes in mind, rather than on the basis of a set of general characteristics associated with the label *severely disabled*. Snell and Brown (2000a, pp. 115–116), described three desirable outcomes that are achieved for students with severe disabilities when they attend inclusive school settings:

- *Skills.* Inclusive classrooms appear to offer the opportunity to learn more useful and age-appropriate functional academic, social, motor, and communication skills and to generalize them to a variety of settings.
- *Membership.* Inclusive schools present more and varied occasions to join peer groups and experience affiliation with classmates during and after school hours than do noninclusive schools.
- *Relationships.* Inclusive schools provide the context for one or more ongoing, familiar, social interactions with other individuals (disabled and nondisabled) that may take on various patterns, including play and companionship, helper, helpee, reciprocal peer, and adversarial.

■ INTELLIGENCE AND ACADEMIC ACHIEVEMENT

Most people with severe and multiple disabilities have mental retardation as a primary condition. As such, their learning and memory capabilities are diminished. The greater the mental retardation, the more difficulty the individual will have in learning, retaining, and applying information. People with severe and multiple disabilities will require specialized and intensive instruction in order to acquire and use new skills across a number of settings.

Given the diminished intellectual capability of many people with severe and multiple disabilities, academic learning is often a low instructional priority. The vast majority of students with severe disabilities are unable to learn from basic academic programs in reading, writing, and mathematics. Instruction in functional skills is the most effective approach to academic learning. Basic academic subjects are taught in the context of daily living. A functional program in reading focuses on those words that facilitate a child's access to the environment (*rest room, danger, exit,* etc.). Functional math skill development relates more to developing strategies for telling time or the consumer's use of money. As suggested by Drew and Hardman (2000), a functional approach teaches academic skills in the context of environmental cues. The learning of new skills is always paired directly with environmental stimuli. Snell and Brown (2000a) stressed that the teacher must use instructional materials that are realistic. Traditional materials, such as workbooks, basal readers, flash cards, and so on, do not work for students with severe disabilities because they are unable to relate the materials to the natural setting of home or community.

■ ADAPTIVE SKILLS

The learning of **adaptive skills** is critical to success in natural settings. These skills involve both personal independence and social interaction. Personal independence skills range from the ability to take care of one's basic needs, such as eating, dressing, and hygiene, to living on one's own in the community (including getting and keeping a job, managing money, or finding ways to get around in the environment). Social interaction skills involve being able to communicate one's needs and preferences, as well as listening and appropriately responding to others. People with severe and multiple disabilities often do not have age-appropriate adaptive skills and need ongoing services and supports to facilitate learning and application in this area. We do know that when given the opportunity to learn adaptive skills through participation in inclusive settings with nondisabled peers, individuals with severe disabilities have a higher probability of maintaining and meaningfully applying this learning over time (Sailor et al., 2000; Snell & Brown, 2000a; Westling & Fox, 2000).

■ SPEECH AND LANGUAGE SKILLS

People with severe and multiple disabilities generally have significant deficits and delays in speech and language skills, ranging from articulation and fluency disorders to an absence of any expressive oral language (Westling & Fox, 2000) Speech and language deficits and delays are positively correlated with the severity of mental retardation (McLean, Brady, & McLean, 1996). As is true for adaptive skill learning, people with severe and multiple disabilities will acquire and use appropriate speech and language if these skills are taught and applied in natural settings. It is also important that functional communication systems (such as signing, picture cards, communication boards, gesturing) form an integral part of instruction. Regardless of the communication system(s) used to teach speech and language skills, they must be applied across multiple settings. For example, if picture cards are used in the classroom, they must also be a part of the communication system used at home and in other environments.

■ PHYSICAL AND HEALTH CHARACTERISTICS

People with severe and multiple disabilities have significant physical and health care needs. For instance, these individuals have a higher incidence of congenital heart disease, **epilepsy,** respiratory problems, diabetes, and metabolic disorders. They also exhibit poor muscle tone and often have conditions such as **spasticity,**

■ ADAPTIVE SKILLS. Skills that facilitate an individual's ability to function in community, family, and school settings. Adaptive skills may include communication, self-care, home living, social skills, community use, self-direction, health and safety awareness, functional academics, leisure activities, and work.

■ EPILEPSY. A condition that from time to time produces brief disturbances in the normal electrical functions of the brain, affecting a person's consciousness, bodily movements, or sensations for a short time. Intensity and length of these effects depend on the severity of the seizure.

■ SPASTICITY. A condition that involves involuntary contractions of various muscle groups.

■ ATHETOSIS. A condition characterized by constant, contorted twisting motions in the wrists and fingers.

athetosis, and **hypotonia.** Such conditions require that professionals in the schools and other service agencies know how to administer medications, **catheterization, gastronomy tube feeding,** and **respiratory ventilation** (Ault, Rues, Graff, & Holvoet, 2000; Sobsey & Cox, 1991).

■ VISION AND HEARING CHARACTERISTICS

Although the prevalence of vision and hearing loss is not well documented among people with severe disabilities, Sobsey and Wolf-Schein (1996) suggest that sensory impairments do occur more frequently in people with severe disabilities in comparison to the general population. Some individuals, particularly those described as deaf–blind, have significant vision *and* hearing disorders that require services and supports beyond those for a person who is blind *or* deaf.

Educational Supports and Services

The axiom "the earlier, the better" is certainly applicable to educational services and supports for children with severe and multiple disabilities. There is no question of whether or when services should begin—they must begin at birth and continue throughout the lifespan. We begin this section with a discussion of various types of educational assessments for students with severe and multiple disabilities. We then examine the characteristics of effective programs during the early childhood, elementary, and adolescent years.

■ ASSESSMENT

■ IDENTIFYING THE DISABILITY   Traditionally, there has been a heavy reliance on standardized measurements, particularly the IQ test, in identifying people with severe and multiple disabilities, particularly when the primary condition is mental retardation. For example, the American Association on Mental Retardation (AAMR) defined mental retardation as "significantly subaverage general intellectual functioning" as determined by the results of an intelligence (IQ) test (AAMR Ad Hoc Committee, 1992). Some professionals (Evans, 1991; Silberman & Brown, 1998) have suggested that standardized tests, particularly the IQ test, do not provide useful information in either diagnosing the disability or providing instruction to individuals with severe disabilities. Others (Wehman & Parent, 1997) believe that IQ tests may be appropriate for diagnosis but provide no "meaningful information for making curriculum decisions such as what to teach and how to teach it" (p. 158).

■ ASSESSING FOR INSTRUCTION   Assessments that focus on valued skills to promote independence and quality of life in natural settings are referred to as functional, ecological, or **authentic assessment** (Knowlton, 1998; Siegel-Causey & Allinder, 1998). A functional assessment has the following characteristics:

- It focuses on practical *independent living skills* that enable the person to survive and succeed in the real world.
- It has an *ecological* emphasis that looks at the individual functioning in his or her surrounding environment.
- It examines the *process* of learning and performance.
- It suggests *intervention* techniques that may be successful.
- It specifies ongoing *monitoring procedures* that can evaluate treatment progress. (Gaylord-Ross & Browder, 1991, p. 45)

■ HYPOTONIA. Poor muscle tone.

■ CATHETERIZATION. The process of introducing a hollow tube (catheter) into body cavities to drain fluid, such as introducing a tube into an individual's bladder to drain urine.

■ GASTRONOMY TUBE FEEDING. The process of feeding the individual through a rubber tube that is inserted into the stomach.

■ RESPIRATORY VENTILATION. Use of a mechanical aid (ventilator) to supply oxygen to an individual with respiratory problems.

■ AUTHENTIC ASSESSMENT. An alternative to traditional use of standardized tests to measure student progress. Assessment is based on student progress in meaningful learning activities.

focus 5
Identify three types of educational assessments for students with severe and multiple disabilities.

■ **WHAT IS AN ALTERNATE ASSESSMENT?**

An alternate assessment is different from the assessment given to most students. An assessment generally is viewed as a process for collecting information about what a student knows and can do and consists of taking a test. Most statewide assessments involve test-taking, although some states also use a portfolio approach that allows for collecting samples of student work. The majority of students are assessed by tests, some by using accommodations. However, some students are unable to take a test even with accommodations or modifications. For these students there must be an alternate way of determining their learning progress.

■ **WHAT ARE ALTERNATE COLLECTION STRATEGIES?**
■ Observing the child in the course of the school day over a specified period of time
■ Interviewing parents or family members about what the child does outside of school
■ Asking the child to perform a specific activity or task and noting the level of performance
■ Administering a commercially developed assessment instrument (e.g., Brigance) and comparing the results with a set of state-established standards
■ Reviewing records that have been developed over a designated period of time

Source: Adapted from *Alternate Assessment: Questions and Answers. IDEA Practices,* by C. Massanari, 2000. *[on-line]* Available: *http://www.idea practices.org/ideaquests/Alternate Assess.htm#whatisalt*

As described in the TASH definition of severe disabilities, functional assessment is concerned with the match between the needs of the individual and the demands of the environment (adaptive fit). The purpose of the assessment is to determine what supports are necessary to achieve the intended outcomes of access and participation in natural settings. Skills are never taught in isolation from actual performance demands. Additionally, the individual does not "get ready" to participate in the community through a sequence of readiness stages as in the developmental model, but learns and uses skills in the setting where the behavior is expected to occur.

■ **SCHOOL ACCOUNTABILITY AND THE ASSESSMENT OF STUDENTS WITH SEVERE DISABILITIES** During the past decade, there has been an increasing emphasis on holding schools more accountable for student learning and progress (see Chapter 1). States are setting educational standards and then assessing how students progress toward the intended goals. A major challenge for education is to demonstrate accountability for *all* students, including those with disabilities. IDEA 97 requires that students with disabilities must participate in statewide or districtwide assessments of achievement or provide a statement of why that assessment is not appropriate for the child. The law also requires that individual modifications in the administration of statewide or districtwide assessments be provided as appropriate in order for the child to participate. Examples of student accommodations include large-print text, testing in a separate setting, or extended time. Ysseldyke, Olsen, and Thurlow (1997) estimate that about 85% of students with disabilities have mild or moderate disabilities and can take state or district assessments, either with or without accommodations. For many students with severe disabilities, these assessments are inappropriate, and such students are excluded from taking them. Schools are still accountable, however, for the progress of these students. IDEA 1997 mandated that by July 2000, states must be conducting **alternate assessments** to ensure that all students are included in the state's accountability system. Ysseldyke and Olsen (1997) indicated four assumptions that are the foundation of alternate assessments:

■ **ALTERNATE ASSESSMENT.** Assessments mandated in IDEA 1997 for students who are unable to participate in required state- or districtwide assessments. It ensures that all students, regardless of the severity of their disabilities, are included in the state's accountability system.

- Alternate assessments focus on authentic skills and on assessing experiences in community and other real-life environments.
- Alternate assessments should measure integrated skills across domains.
- If at all possible, alternate assessment systems should use continuous documentation methods.
- Alternate assessment systems should include as critical criteria the extent to which the system provides the needed supports and adaptations, and trains the student to use them.

Alternate assessments may involve either normative or absolute performance standards (Ysseldyke & Olsen, 1997). If a normative assessment is used, then a student's performance is compared to that of peers (other students of comparable age or ability participating in the alternate assessment). If an absolute standard is used, then a student's performance is compared against a set criterion. For example, the student is able to cross the street when the "walk" sign is flashing 100% of the time without assistance. (See nearby Reflect on This feature.)

The Early Childhood Years

Effective early intervention services that start when the child is born are critical to the prevention and amelioration of social, medical, and educational problems that can occur throughout the life of the individual (Burchinal et al., 1997; Guralnick, 1998; Ramey & Landesman-Ramey, 1992; Ramey & Ramey, 1999).

During the early childhood years, services and supports are concentrated on two age groups: infants and toddlers, and preschool-age children.

■ SERVICES AND SUPPORTS FOR INFANTS AND TODDLERS

Effective programs for infants and toddlers with severe and multiple disabilities are both child- and family-centered. A child-centered approach is focused on identifying and meeting individual needs. Services begin with infant stimulation programs intended to elicit sensory, cognitive, and physical responses in newborns that will connect them with their environment. As the child develops, health care, physical therapy, occupational therapy, and speech and language services may become integral components of a child-centered program.

Family-centered programs are characterized by a holistic approach that involves the child as a member of the family unit. The needs, structure, and preferences of the family drive the delivery of services and supports (Bailey & Wolery, 1992; Eiserman, Weber, & McCoun, 1995; Ramey & Ramey, 1999). The overall purpose of family-centered intervention is to enable family members to initially cope with the birth of a child with a severe disability and eventually become empowered to grow together and support one another. Berry and Hardman (1998) suggested that family-centered approaches build on and increase family strengths, address the needs of every family member, and support mutually enjoyable family relationships. Supports for families may include parent-training programs, counseling, and **respite care.**

■ SERVICES AND SUPPORTS FOR PRESCHOOL-AGE CHILDREN

Preschool programs for young children with severe and multiple disabilities continue the emphasis on family involvement while extending the life space of the

focus 6
Identify the features of effective services and supports for children with severe and multiple disabilities during the early childhood years.

■RESPITE CARE. Assistance provided by individuals outside of the immediate family allowing parents and other children within the family for time away from the child with a disability for a recreational event, a vacation, and so on. Some states provide funding to families to secure this kind of care.

In this music class, students with severe disabilities are learning social interaction and classroom participation skills.

child to a school setting. McDonnell, Hardman, McDonnell, & Kiefer-O'Donnell (1995) suggested four goals for preschool programs serving children with severe disabilities:

1. Maximize the child's development in a variety of important developmental areas. These include social communication, motor skills, cognitive skills, preacademic skills, self-care, play, and personal management.
2. Develop the child's social interaction and classroom participation skills. Focus on developing peer relationships and teaching the child to follow adult directions, respond to classroom routines, and become self-directed (complete classroom activities without constant adult supervision).
3. Increase community participation through support to family members and other caregivers. Work to identify alternative caregivers so that the family has a broader base of support and more flexibility to pursue other interests. Help the family to identify activities within the neighborhood that their preschooler would enjoy to provide the child with opportunities to interact with same-age peers. Activities may involve swimming or dancing lessons, joining a soccer team, attending a house of worship, and so on.
4. Prepare the child for inclusive school placements, and provide support for the transition to elementary school. The transition out of preschool will be facilitated if educators from the receiving elementary school work collaboratively with family and preschool personnel.

To meet these goals, Grenot-Scheyer, Schwartz, and Meyer (1997) proposed that preschool programs for children with severe disabilities blend the principles and elements of developmentally appropriate practices (DAP), multicultural education, and special education. DAP was developed by the National Association for the Education of Young Children as an alternative to an academic curriculum for preschoolers. It emphasizes age-appropriate child exploration and play activities that are consistent with individual need (see Chapter 4). Multicultural education emphasizes acceptance of people from different cultural and ethnic backgrounds within and across the preschool curriculum. Successful culturally inclusive programs blend principles and practices that guide special education, inclusive education, and multicultural education (Grenot-Scheyer et al., 1997). Special education focuses on assessing individual needs, providing intensive instruction, and teaching explicit skills within the context of an individualized education program (IEP).

The combination of DAP, multicultural education, and special education work together to provide a quality experience for preschool-age children with severe disabilities. The following factors characterize an effective and inclusive preschool program using the three practices in combination:

- The program has a holistic view of child development. Teachers have a thorough understanding of child development and support the inclusion of diverse learners in the classroom.
- The classroom is viewed as a community of learners. Students have opportunities to enhance feelings of self-worth, social responsibility, and belonging.
- The program is based on a collaborative ethic. Colleagues view each other as equals, sharing their knowledge and skills.
- Educators use authentic assessment. Authentic assessment consists of a variety of performance-based assessments that require children to demonstrate a response in a real-life context.
- The classroom is heterogeneous. Children must have the opportunity to work and play in diverse and heterogeneous groups that attend to individual strengths and needs.
- A range of individualized supports and services are available. Teachers and therapists provide support in the natural setting of the classroom in the context of ongoing activities.
- The program engages children and uses an active learning model. Learning by doing is emphasized in meaningful contexts.
- The program emphasizes reflective teaching. Teachers are good observers of their own behavior as well as the behavior of the children.
- The program emphasizes multiple ways of teaching and learning. Children are encouraged to use multiple methods to solve problems. Teaching approaches are selected for a "goodness of fit" between the teacher and the learner. (Grenot-Scheyer et al., 1997)

The Elementary School Years

Historically, services and supports for students with severe and multiple disabilities have been oriented to protection and care. The objective was to protect the individual from society, and society from the individual. This philosophy resulted in programs that isolated the individual and provided physical care rather than preparation for life in a heterogeneous world. Today, educators working in tandem with parents are concentrating their efforts on preparing students with severe and multiple disabilities to participate actively in the life of the family, school, and community (see the nearby Reflect on This feature).

Given the emphasis on lifelong learning and living in natural settings, educators have identified several features that characterize quality programs for elementary-age students with severe and multiple disabilities:

- Self-determination—student preferences and needs are taken into account in developing educational objectives.
- The school values and supports parental involvement.
- Instruction focuses on frequently used functional skills related to everyday life activities.
- Assistive technology and augmentative communication are available to maintain or increase the functional capabilities of the student with severe and multiple disabilities.

focus 7

Identify the features of effective services and supports for children with severe and multiple disabilities during the elementary school years.

Reflect on This

Kipps Elementary School is one of 13 elementary schools in the Montgomery County Public School Division in the southwestern part of Virginia. Kipps is a new school, which opened in the fall of 1994. At Kipps, like other schools in the system, students with disabilities attend general education classes in their neighborhood schools with their peers who do not have disability labels. Principals and staff in each school are involved in shared decision-making teams whereby decisions about the school's resources are made cooperatively with staff and with the input of parents; these decisions are consistent with the schools' and district's philosophy of providing special education services in the least restrictive environment within the neighborhood school. The special education services and supports needed for each student are planned collaboratively by the student's educational team to address the individual student's strengths and needs; supports are implemented, evaluated, and revised by the team on an individual basis, not prescribed by a disability category. Collaboration between the special education teachers, classroom teachers, parents, and other team members (e.g., related services personnel) provides the essential mechanism for planning and problem-solving.

At Kipps, Benjamin is one of 10 students with severe disabilities, each of whom is enrolled full-time in a general education classroom. These students range from 5 to 11 years old and are placed in kindergarten through grade 5. These students have special education labels such as "multi-handicapped," "developmental delay," "autism," and "mental retardation" and have one or more of the following conditions or characteristics: cerebral palsy, visual impairment, Down syndrome, challenging behavior, and nonsymbolic communication.

Benjamin's first year of inclusive education was in preschool within Head Start. He is now 7 years old and in Tricia William's second-grade classroom with others of his age. Benjamin has cerebral palsy, moves about with a walker, and has a special education label of multiple handicaps. He has developmental delays, visual impairments, and speech and language impairments, and hydrocephalus. He communicates primarily by words and phrases, gestures, and facial expressions. Benjamin, who is well known for being highly social, is described by some of his classmates as being "a very popular kid."

Benjamin's classroom has the same number of students as other classrooms in the school but is assigned one teaching assistant in the morning, who alternates with another in the afternoon. Both assistants attend to special needs presented by Benjamin, assist with general classroom activities, and also support educational needs of other stu-

■ SELF-DETERMINATION

People with severe and multiple disabilities, like everyone else, must be in a position to make their own life choices as much as possible. School programs that promote self-determination enhance each student's opportunity to become more independent in the life of the family and in the larger community setting. Providing students with severe disabilities the opportunity to communicate their needs and preferences enhances autonomy, problem-solving skills, adaptability, and self-efficacy expectations (Agran & Wehmeyer, 1999; Whitney-Thomas, Shaw, Honey, & Butterworth, 1998).

■ PARENTAL INVOLVEMENT

Schools are more successful in meeting the needs of students when they establish positive relationships with the family (Fuller & Olsen, 1998). The important role that parents play during the early childhood years must continue and be supported during elementary school. Parents who actively participate in their child's educational program exert more influence on the development and implementation of instruction that is consistent with individual needs and preferences. Parental involvement can be a powerful predictor of postschool adjustment for students with severe and multiple disabilities. A strong home–school partnership requires that parents and educators

- acknowledge and respect each other's differences in values and culture.
- listen openly and attentively to each other's concerns.

dents who do not have disability labels. By dividing their time across two different classrooms, these assistants develop more versatile skills, and capacity is created within the school that minimizes the disruption caused by the inevitable absence of the teachers or assistants. Benjamin's special education teacher, Kenna Colley, distributes her time among the classrooms at Kipps where the 10 students with severe disabilities on her "caseload" are placed by working with the classroom teachers, teaching assistants, related services personnel, and peers. Through this collaboration, Benjamin participates in the same educational activities as his classmates although at times he may be pursuing different learning outcomes than they are, and/or he may need individualized adaptations to ensure that his involvement is meaningful (e.g., enlarged print materials, specialized seating, peer assistance).

Benjamin's educational program is oriented toward his participation in school routines with an emphasis on skills needed for communication, peer relationships, mobility, and self-care. Though these represent the focus of his individualized curriculum, he is exposed to a broad array of curricular content in general education areas such as physical education, music, art, science, social studies, and language arts. The related services providers work with classroom staff to provide educationally relevant input that is required to support Benjamin's program in general class and school activities.

Mr. Van Dyke established twice-monthly "inclusion meetings" devoted to collaborative problem-solving. Teachers share their successes and concerns in a round-robin fashion, and the group makes decisions about solutions, determines who is responsible, and sets timelines. When complex problems arise, Mr. Van Dyke meets with a smaller group of teachers and facilitates solution finding. "Whole school" strategies also result from collaborative problem solving at Kipps. For Benjamin, who is very social and is learning to move more quickly through the school, a whole school strategy was put in place this year by requesting that everyone reduce their socialization with him in the hall, and instead, wait for times when he is not moving through the schools on a schedule. Teachers in turn advised their classes with sensitive explanations of the reasons.

Peer support is central to the inclusive school program in Montgomery County and takes several forms. For example, peers' questions are answered in respectful ways; teachers model appropriate interactions and help to students with disabilities as needed; teachers work with peers to problem-solve and discuss issues of concern (e.g., "How can we help Benjamin participate?"); and cooperative groups and activity-based instruction are frequently used within classroom activities. All staff members at Kipps Elementary School share responsibility for welcoming, including, and educating *all* the students in the school including those with severe disabilities.

Source: From "Severe and Multiple Disabilities," by M. F. Giangreco & M. E. Snell. In *Improving the Implementation of the Individuals with Disabilities Education Act: Making Schools Work for All of America's Children (Supplement)*, 1996, pp. 97–132. Washington, DC: National Council on Disability. Reprinted with permission.

- value varying opinions and ideas.
- discuss issues openly and in an atmosphere of trust.
- share in the responsibility and consequences of making a decision. (Berry & Hardman, 1998)

■ TEACHING FUNCTIONAL SKILLS

Effective educational programs focus on the functional skills necessary for students with severe and multiple disabilities to live successfully in the natural settings of family, school, and community. A functional skill is one that will have frequent and meaningful use across multiple environments. If the student with severe disabilities is to learn how to cross a street safely, shop in a grocery store, play a video game, or eat in a local restaurant, the necessary skills should be taught in the actual setting where the behavior is to be performed. It should not be assumed that a skill learned in a classroom will transfer to a setting outside of the school. Instruction in a more natural environment can ensure that the skill will be useful and maintained over time. This instruction should involve the following elements:

- Many different people
- A variety of settings within the community
- Varied materials that will interest the learner and match performance demands

When teaching functional skills, teachers should use a variety of materials that will interest the learner and have meaning within the school and community setting.

■ ASSISTIVE TECHNOLOGY AND AUGMENTATIVE COMMUNICATION

Assistive technology, as defined in federal law, means any item, piece of equipment, or product system that can be used to increase, maintain, or improve the functional capabilities of students with disabilities (The Technology-Related Assistance for Individuals with Disabilities Act, PL 100-407, [20 U.S.C. Sec. 140(25)]). An assistive technology service "directly assists an individual with a disability in the selection, acquisition, or use of an assistive technology device [20 U.S.C. Sec 140(26)]. Wehman (1997) identified several categories of assistive technology:

- Mobility (wheelchairs, lifts, adaptive driving controls, scooters, laser canes)
- Seating and positioning (assistance in choosing and using a wheelchair)
- Computers (environmental control units, word processors, software, keyboards)
- Toys and games (software, switch-operated toys)
- Activities of daily living (feeders, lifts, watch alarms, memory books)
- Communication (touch talkers, reading systems, talking keyboards (p. 475)

Students with severe and multiple disabilities will benefit from any one or more of these assistive devices or activities. For students with severe disabilities who are unable to use speech and need an additional communication mode, **augmentative communication** will nearly always be an integral component of their individualized education program. Augmentative communication systems involve adapting existing vocal or gestural abilities into meaningful communication; teaching manual signing (such as American Sign Language), static symbols, or icons (such as **Blissymbols**); and using manual or electronic communication devices (such as electric communication boards, picture cues, or synthetic speech) (Mirenda, Iacono, & Williams, 1990; Westling & Fox, 2000). (See Today's Technology feature on page 364.)

The Adolescent Years

Describe four outcomes that are important in planning for the transition from school to adult life for adolescents with severe and multiple disabilities.

Societal perceptions about the capabilities of people with severe and multiple disabilities have been significantly altered over the past several years. There is little question that until very recently, the potential of these individuals to learn, live, and work in community settings was significantly underestimated. Giangreco and Snell (1996) indicated that there is now strong evidence that people with severe and multiple disabilities can become active participants in the lives of their community and family. This realization has prompted professionals and parents to seek significant changes in the ways that schools prepare students for the transition into adult life.

In a review of the research on successful community living for people with severe disabilities, McDonnell, Mathot-Buckner, and Ferguson (1996) have pointed out four outcomes that are important in planning for the transition to adult life: (1) establishing a network of friends and acquaintances, (2) developing the ability to use community resources on a regular basis, (3) securing a paid job that supports the use of community resources and interaction with peers, and (4) establishing independence and autonomy in making lifestyle choices (p. 9).

Inclusive Education

Many professionals argue that the provision of services and supports in an inclusive educational setting is a critical factor in delivering a quality program for students with severe and multiple disabilities (Gee, 1996; Giangreco & Doyle, 2000; Putnam, 1998; Sailor et al., 2000; Sax, Fisher, & Pumpian, 1999; Thousand, Villa, & Nevin, 1994). Effective educational programs include continual opportunities for interaction between students with severe disabilities and their nondisabled peers. Frequent and age-appropriate interactions between students with disabilities and their nondisabled peers can enhance opportunities for successful participation in the community during the adult years. Social interaction can be enhanced by creating opportunities for these students to associate both during and after the school day. Successful inclusion efforts are characterized by the following features:

- Physical placement of students with severe and multiple disabilities in the general education schools and classes they would attend were they not disabled
- Systematic organization of opportunities for interaction between students with severe and multiple disabilities and students without disabilities
- Specific instruction in valued postschool outcomes that will increase the competence of students with severe and multiple disabilities in the natural settings of family, school, and community
- Access to the appropriate services and support necessary to ensure participation in natural settings. This includes highly trained teachers competent in the necessary instructional and assistive technology that facilitates learning that is functional across multiple environments

One of the most important characteristics of the postschool environments in which students ultimately must function is the need for frequent interaction with people who are not disabled. Consequently, it is logical to plan educational programs that duplicate this feature of the environment and actively build skills required for successful interaction.

As students with severe and multiple disabilities are included in general education schools and classrooms, it is important to find ways to encourage social interactions between these students and students who are not disabled. Planned opportunities for interaction may include the use of in-class peer supports (tutors, circles of friends) as well as access to everyday school activities such as assemblies, recess, lunch, or field trips. (See the Interacting in Natural Settings feature on pages 366 and 367.)

Severe Disabilities and Biomedical Dilemmas

Rapid advances in medical technology have resulted in the survival of an increasing number of infants with severe and multiple disabilities. Today, many such infants who would have died at birth only five to ten years ago now often live well into their adult years. However, this decrease in infant mortality and increase in lifespan have raised a number of serious ethical issues regarding decisions about prevention, care, and selective nontreatment of

ASSISTIVE TECHNOLOGY. Technology devices that help an individual with disabilities adapt to the natural settings of home, school, and family. The technology may include computers, hearing aids, wheelchairs, and so on.

AUGMENTATIVE COMMUNICATION. Communication systems that involve adapting existing vocal or gestural abilities into meaningful communication; teaching manual signing, static symbols, or icons; and using manual or electronic communication devices.

BLISSYMBOLS. A rebus system developed by C. K. Bliss that ties a specific symbol to a word. There are four types of Blissymbols: pictographic, ideographic, relational, and abstract.

focus

Describe four features that characterize successful inclusive education for students with severe and multiple disabilities.

Today's Technology

MEET JOEY

Identified as having cerebral palsy and also being "deaf-blind with cognitive disabilities," Joey spent the first four years of his school career in a special day class, where he spent a great deal of time lying in a beanbag chair. He had no consistent method of communication other than screaming and crying, which he used when staff attempted to engage him in an activity. Even the peer helpers from general education classes avoided contact with Joey. The majority of interactions that students or staff had with Joey were to provide personal care services, such as feeding and changing his diaper. About the time that Joey turned 8, his life changed significantly as assistive technology was introduced into his range of supports and services.

Four years ago, when he was 8 years old and still attending a special day class, Joey began to learn about cause and effect through the use of a set of adapted switches connected to a Bart Simpson toy. The standard remote control switch for the toy featured one button to move Bart forward and a second to move him backward. The remote control was rewired so that Joey could hit either a large plate for forward motion or a large pillow switch to reverse the movement. Due to Joey's limited vision, the toy was placed on a table so that, at the very least, he could feel the vibration of the toy moving across the table's surface. As soon as Joey became engaged in the activity, exciting things happened. First, he clearly began to follow the movement of Bart's yellow head as it moved across his field of vision. Second, peers in the room saw this activity as a way to interact with Joey. Finally, as his peers helped him to press the switches, Joey began to associate the operation of the switch with the movement of the toy. As a result, his peers began to consider many more activities in which Joey could participate. The classroom teacher set up a variety of appliances that could be switch controlled so that Joey could practice throughout the day. It became obvious that Joey could perform these same activities in general education classes.

Over the next couple of years, Joey began spending more time in general education classes where he participated in activities instead of simply observing them. He became more proficient at switch use and was able to operate a number of individualized devices. One device was used for climate control. Because the school operated on a year-round schedule, the children had to acclimate to warm classrooms. Some teachers permitted students to take turns "misting" the classroom. Joey participated by using a switch-operated spray bottle which was modified from a sports bottle. While a classmate pointed the sprayer in different directions, Joey operated the water flow. Other adaptations included a Plexiglas display board that was used for communication, and a variety of appliances that he controlled with his switches.

By the time Joey entered fifth grade, he made the transition from being a "visitor from Room #5" to being a full-time member of the class. New situations required new adaptations. Joey's classmates had been responsible for raising Joey's hand to summon the teacher, but they felt that Joey needed his own method. A "low-tech" light switch was mounted on Joey's laptray so that he could attract the teacher's attention. His ability to use a switch increased so that he could use several of them, coded with Picture Communication Symbols to operate a Speakeasy communication device with messages recorded by a student whom he chose. He used another switch to turn on a tape recorder to play the same book on tape that the other students were reading during "silent reading" time. Consistent use of switches helped to increase his motivation and dexterity for accessing the computer through the Ke:nx program. These abilities would be essential for participating at his neighborhood middle school.

Joey's seating and positioning needs were adjusted, including time scheduled to be out of his wheelchair and sitting at a desk. His therapy needs were met during the regular physical education periods, as coordinated by his teacher, with consultative support from the school district's physical therapist and adaptive physical education specialist. The special education teacher worked closely with the fifth-grade teacher to adapt the curriculum and make accommodations as necessary. Joey's classmates were an invaluable source of creativity who thought of innovative strategies to increase Joey's participation. As they became more familiar with Joey and the way in which he responded, they were key players in identifying new goals based on their keen insights and perceptions of Joey's needs and desires. The entire range of services and supports that were listed on his IEP were designed and implemented through effective collaboration of all of the professionals involved. People learned to perform their roles in new settings and under different circumstances. By the end of the school year, everyone agreed that Joey had surpassed all earlier expectations. Eventually it was determined that Joey no longer required services from the vision and hearing specialists, as he was obviously using both of these sensory modes adequately in all of his daily activities. His transition plan for moving to the middle school included a discussion of scheduling him into classes where he would remain with a number of his fifth-grade classmates. The possibilities for Joey are endless, and as luck would have it, his new school is a technology magnet, a perfect place for him to continue to build his skills in using all kinds of technology.

Source: Adapted from Sax, C., Pumpian, I., & Fisher, D. (1997, March). *Assistive Technology and Inclusion.* Issue Brief. Pittsburgh, PA: Consortium on Inclusive Schooling Practices, Allegheny University of the Health Sciences, pp. 1–5. Reprinted with permission.

infants with severe disabilities. In recent years, there has been an increasing awareness and interest in **bioethics,** particularly as it relates to serious illness and severe disabilities. Bioethical issues include concerns about the purpose and use of genetic engineering, screening for genetic diseases, abortion, and the withholding of life-sustaining medical treatment. A number of questions have been raised by both professionals and parents. When do individual rights begin? Who should live, and who should die? What is personhood? Who defines quality of life? What are the rights of the person with severe disabilities in relationship to the obligations of a society? Who shall make the difficult decisions?

focus 10

Describe four bioethical dilemmas that can have an impact on people with severe disabilities and their families.

■ GENETIC ENGINEERING

The purpose of genetic engineering is to conquer disease. Through the identification of a faulty gene that causes a disease, such as cystic fibrosis, scientists are able to prevent future occurrence and treat those who have the condition. In 1990, the United States and the United Kingdom joined together with more than 3,000 research scientists in the **Human Genome Project.** The purpose of the project was to

- identify the 80,000 genes in human DNA.
- determine the sequences of the 3 billion chemical base pairs that make up human DNA.
- store this information in databases.
- develop tools for data analysis.
- address the ethical, legal, and social issues that may arise from the project. (U.S. Department of Energy, 2000)

In June 2000, scientists from the Human Genome Project and scientists from a private company, Celera Genomics of Rockville, Maryland, announced they had successfully completed the first phase of the research. They had sequenced 99% of the human genome and had assembled more than 1 billion letters of genetic code. The next step, which may be the most challenging and controversial, is the interpretation of what all the codes mean.

The work of scientists to map the secrets of the genetic code has attracted the attention of professionals and parents concerned with the rights of people with severe and multiple disabilities. Although genetic engineering may be seen as holding considerable promise for reducing human suffering in the future, it can also be viewed as a means to enhance or perfect human beings. Since the vast majority of people with

■ BIOETHICS. The study of ethics in medicine.

■ HUMAN GENOME PROJECT. Project developed by the United States and the United Kingdom to identify the 80,000 genes in human DNA; determine the sequences of the 3 billion chemical base pairs that make up human DNA; store this information in databases; develop tools for data analysis; and address the ethical, legal, and social issues that may arise from the project.

Genes are studied and compared by a geneticist who, by identifying a faulty gene, can provide valuable information to a doctor indicating the potential for disease.

■ EARLY CHILDHOOD YEARS

TIPS FOR THE FAMILY

■ During the infant and toddler years, seek out family-oriented programs that focus on communication and the building of positive relationships among all individual members.

■ Seek supports and services for your preschool-age child that promote communication and play activities with same-age nondisabled peers.

■ Seek opportunities for friendships to develop between your child and children without disabilities in family and neighborhood settings.

■ Use the individualized family service plan (IFSP) and the individualized education plan (IEP) as a means to establish goals that develop your child's social interaction and classroom participation skills.

TIPS FOR THE GENERAL EDUCATION PRESCHOOL TEACHER

■ Establish a classroom environment that promotes and supports diversity.

■ Use a child-centered approach to instruction that acknowledges and values every child's strengths, preferences, and individual needs.

■ Ignore whatever labels have been used to describe the child with severe and multiple disabilities. There is no relationship between the label and the instruc-

tion needed by the child to succeed in natural settings.

■ Create opportunities for ongoing communication and play activities among children with severe disabilities and their same-age nondisabled peers. Nurture interactive peer relationships across a variety of instructional areas and settings.

TIPS FOR PRESCHOOL PERSONNEL

■ Support the inclusion of young children with severe and multiple disabilities in all preschool classrooms and programs.

■ Always refer to children by name, not by label. If you must label, use child-first language—"children with severe disabilities."

■ Communicate genuine respect and support for all teachers, staff, and volunteers who look for ways to include children with severe disabilities in preschool classrooms and schoolwide activities.

■ Welcome families into the preschool programs. Listen to what parents have to say about the importance of, or concerns about, including their child in school programs and activities. Create opportunities for parents to become involved in their child's program through volunteering, school governance, and so on.

TIPS FOR NEIGHBORS AND FRIENDS

■ First and foremost, see the child with severe disabilities as an individual who

has needs, preferences, strengths, and weaknesses. Avoid the pitfalls of stereotyping and "self-fulfilling prophecies."

■ Support opportunities for your children and those of friends and neighbors to interact and play with a child with severe and multiple disabilities.

■ Help children without disabilities build friendships rather than caregiving roles with children who have severe and multiple disabilities.

■ Provide a supportive community environment for the family of a young child with severe and multiple disabilities. Encourage the family, including the child, to participate in neighborhood activities.

■ ELEMENTARY YEARS

TIPS FOR THE FAMILY

■ Actively participate in the development of your son's or daughter's IEP. Write down the priorities and educational goals that you see as important to allow your child to participate in the natural settings of home, school, and community.

■ Follow up at home on activities that the school suggests are important to help your child generalize skills learned at school to other natural settings.

■ Actively participate as a volunteer in the school whether it be in your child's classroom or in another situation. Show your appreciation and sup-

port for administrators, teachers, and staff who openly value and support the inclusion of your child in the school and classroom.

■ Continually communicate with administrators and teachers how important it is to include children with severe disabilities in classroom and schoolwide activities (such as riding on the same school bus, going to recess and lunch at the same time, participating in schoolwide assemblies).

TIPS FOR THE GENERAL EDUCATION CLASSROOM TEACHER

■ See children with severe and multiple disabilities as individuals, not labels. Focus on their similarities with other children rather than their differences.

■ Openly value and support diversity in your classroom. Set individualized goals and objectives for all children.

■ Develop a classroom environment and instructional program that recognize multiple needs and abilities.

■ Become part of a team that works together to meet the needs of all children in your classroom. View the special education teacher as a resource that can assist you in developing an effective instructional program for the child with severe and multiple disabilities.

TIPS FOR SCHOOL PERSONNEL

■ Communicate that diversity is a strength in your

school. Openly value diversity by providing the resources necessary for teachers to work with students who have a range of needs and come from heterogeneous backgrounds.

- Integrate school resources as well as children. Develop schoolwide teacher-assistance or teacher-support teams that use a collaborative ethic to meet the needs of every student.
- Support general and special education teachers in the development of peer-partner and support networks for students with severe and multiple disabilities.
- Include all students in the programs and activities of the school.

TIPS FOR NEIGHBORS AND FRIENDS

- Openly communicate to school personnel, friends, and neighbors your support of families who are seeking to have their child with severe and multiple disabilities be a part of an inclusive school setting.
- Communicate to your children and those of friends and neighbors the value of inclusion. Demonstrate this value by creating opportunities for children with severe disabilities and their families to play an active role in the life of the community.

SECONDARY AND TRANSITION YEARS

TIPS FOR THE FAMILY

- Seek opportunities for students from your son's or daughter's high school

to visit your home. Help arrange get-togethers or parties involving students from the neighborhood or school.

- Communicate to the school what you see as priorities for your son or daughter in the transition from school to adult life. Suggest goals and objectives that promote and support social interaction and community-based activities with nondisabled peers. Work with the school to translate your goals into an individualized transition plan (ITP).

TIPS FOR THE GENERAL EDUCATION CLASSROOM TEACHER

- Become part of a school-wide team that works together to meet the needs of all students in high school. Value the role of the special educator as teacher, collaborator, and consultant who can serve as a valuable resource in planning for the instructional needs of students with severe disabilities. Collaborate with special education teachers and other specialists to adapt subject matter in your classroom (e.g., science, math, or physical education) to the individual needs of students with severe and multiple disabilities.
- Communicate the importance of students with severe disabilities being included in school programs and activities. Although the goals and activities of this student may differ from those of other students, with support they will benefit from

working with you and other students in the class.

- Support the student with severe disabilities becoming involved in extracurricular high school activities. If you are the faculty sponsor of a club or organization, explore whether this student is interested and how he or she could get involved.

TIPS FOR SCHOOL PERSONNEL

- Advocate for parents of high-school-age students with severe and multiple disabilities to participate in the activities and governance of the school.
- Support parental involvement in the transition-planning process during the high school years by listening to parents.
- Support high school special education or vocational teachers seeking to develop community-based instruction programs that focus on students learning and applying skills in actual community settings (e.g., grocery stores, malls, theaters, parks, work sites).

TIPS FOR NEIGHBORS, FRIENDS, AND POTENTIAL EMPLOYERS

- Work with the family and school personnel to create opportunities for students with severe and multiple disabilities to participate in community activities (such as going to the movies, "hanging out" with nondisabled peers in the neighborhood mall, going to high school sporting events) as often as possible.
- As a potential employer, work with the high school

to locate and establish community-based employment training sites for students with severe and multiple disabilities.

ADULT YEARS

TIPS FOR THE FAMILY

- Develop an understanding of life after school for your son or daughter during the adult years. What are the formal (government-funded, parent organizations) and informal supports (family and friends) available in your community? What are the characteristics of adult service programs? Explore adult support systems in the local community in the areas of supported living, employment, and recreation and leisure.

TIPS FOR NEIGHBORS, FRIENDS, AND POTENTIAL EMPLOYERS

- Become part of the community support network for the individual with severe and multiple disabilities. Be alert to ways that this individual can become and remain actively involved in community employment, neighborhood recreational activities, and functions at a local house of worship.
- As potential employers in the community, seek information on employment of people with severe and multiple disabilities. Find out about programs (such as supported employment) that focus on establishing work for people with severe disabilities while meeting your needs as an employer.

severe and multiple disabilities have genetic disorders (e.g., fragile X and Down syndrome), they are greatly affected by this debate. The Arc of the United States (a national organization of and for people with mental retardation and related developmental disabilities and their families) is concerned that people with severe disabilities have been subjected to a long history of discrimination. As such, it is important that the complex ethical issues surrounding the work of the Human Genome Project receive widespread public attention. The Arc (2000, pp. 1–2) suggested numerous questions in the area of genetic engineering that have yet to be answered:

Should therapies for genetic conditions causing mental retardation [severe disabilities] even be considered? Is there positive value in [human] diversity? How can we avoid stigmatizing those living with a genetic condition while trying to eliminate the condition in others? Are some conditions so destructive to the individual that if a therapy is possible it should be undertaken? Should parents include their newborn child in experimental gene therapy research?

■ GENETIC SCREENING AND COUNSELING

Genetic screening is a search for genes in the human body that are predisposed to disease, are already diseased, or may lead to disease in future generations of the same family. Genetic screening has become widespread throughout the world but is not without controversy and potential for abuse. The Human Genome Project has raised several ethical questions regarding genetic screening. As the availability of genetic information increases, how will society make sure that insurers, employers, courts, schools, adoption agencies, law enforcement, and the military use it in a fair and equitable manner and not discriminate against certain groups of people? What might be the potential psychological impact and stigmatization related to an individual's genetic differences? How does the information affect society's perceptions of that individual (New Goals for the U.S. Human Genome Project, 1998)?

The next step following genetic screening is counseling for family members to understand the results and implications of the screening. The concerns surrounding genetic counseling focus on the neutrality of the counselor. The role of the genetic counselor is one of giving information and not becoming a "moral adviser" or psychotherapist for the family. Drew and Hardman (2000) noted that it is difficult for genetic counselors to maintain neutrality when they have personal beliefs and strong feelings about what should be done. However, it is critical for counselors to remain neutral and not become directive to family members in their attempts to help them make the "right" decision in regard to future pregnancies or ongoing treatment of a condition.

■ SELECTIVE ABORTION AND WITHHOLDING MEDICAL TREATMENT

No other issue polarizes society like the unborn child's right to life versus a woman's right to choose. Rapidly advancing medical technology makes the issue of abortion even more complex. A number of chromosomal and metabolic disorders that may result in severe and multiple disabilities can now be identified in utero. Thus, parents and physicians are placed in the untenable position of deciding whether or not to abort a fetus diagnosed with severe anomalies. On one side are those who argue that the quality of life for the child born with severe disabilities may be so diminished that, if given the choice, they would choose not to live under such circumstances. Additionally, the family may not be able to cope with a child who is severely disabled. On the other side are those who point out that no one has the right to decide for someone else whether a life is "worth living." For people with severe disabilities, major strides in education, medical care, technology, and social inclusion have enhanced their quality of life.

Controversy also surrounds the issue of denying medical treatment to a person with a disability (Drew & Hardman, 2000). The application of one standard for a person who is not disabled and another for a person with a severe disability has resulted in some difficult issues in the medical field (see Debate Forum: Disabilities May Keep Brian Cortez from Heart Transplant). Several national organizations (The Association for Persons with Severe Handicaps, the Arc—A National Organization on Mental Retardation, the American Association on Mental Retardation) have strongly opposed the withholding of medical treatment when the decision is based on the individual's being disabled. These organizations hold that everyone is entitled to the right to life, and it is the obligation of society to protect people from the ignorance and prejudices that may be associated with disability.

Case Study

THE BEGINNING OF A NEW CIRCLE OF FRIENDS

Joanne and Jennifer are new students in the fifth-grade homeroom. It's midafternoon of their first day at the new school, and time for recess. The special education aide has a break now, so Tom and Maria, two students in the homeroom, volunteer to help Jennifer outside to the playground. Halfway down the hall, Jennifer begins to wheel her chair—slowly, but by herself. Tom lights up.

"Hey, I didn't know that you could do that. Why didn't you tell me before?"

Jennifer first smiles and then lets out a full laugh. The two other fifth-graders join in. They continue slowly outside, where Tom leaves to play softball. Joanne, the other new student, has been invited to join an impromptu soccer game, serving, because of her height, as goalie. Maria, not wanting to leave Jennifer simply to sit by herself during recess, asks, "Do you want to play jump rope?"

Again, Jennifer smiles, and looks toward the group of girls next to the building who have already begun to play jump rope. Maria understands and helps Jennifer over a curb, as the two girls move on to the game.

Once there, Maria asks, "Do you know how to twirl?"

Jennifer shakes her head no, so Maria places the end of the rope in her hand, and holding it together, says, "Okay, hold it like this, and go round this way," guiding her movements with her hand.

Soon, Jennifer gets the hang of it, and Maria is able to let go. It's her turn to jump, so she leaves Jennifer's side, and begins her routine. She is able to jump longer than any of the other girls. As she spins around to complete a maneuver, she faces Jennifer as she jumps. Seeing her twirl, Maria sticks out her tongue and both girls laugh. Unfortunately, the twirling stops, ending Maria's turn. It doesn't really matter, because a new game will start again tomor-

row and Maria usually wins anyway.

In a moment Ms. Nelson calls to the students to return to class, and Maria and Jennifer come in together. As they enter the room, Ms. Nelson asks the classmates to take out their library books and use the remaining time to read silently. Marsha, who had been playing soccer with Joanne, asks her teacher if she could loan her one of her books to read. Ms. Nelson approves, and the girls go to the reading corner of the room to choose among Marsha's three books.

The special education aide, in seeing Jennifer enter the class, takes her chair and moves her to the side of the room to work on her communication board. Maria asks her teacher, "Ms. Nelson, is it okay if I give Jennifer one of my books to look at?"

The special education aide hearing the request interrupts, saying, "Honey, Jennifer really can't read your books. But thanks anyway."

"Well, what if we read together?"

Both her teacher and the aide think for a second, and simultaneously give their approval. Together, Maria and Jennifer spend the remainder of class reading her two books, one on raising tropical fish and the other about a girl on a ranch and her pet horse. Class ends, and the special education aide helps Jennifer place her papers in her backpack and go out to the special education bus.

From a young child's perspective, establishing friends is one of the more important activities of school. Taking advantage of natural opportunities that occur at school is crucial for all students, including those with severe disabilities. Learning to communicate, including new ways to listen, is all part of the process of building bonds. With positive experiences come new opportunities. Often, the best action on the part of team members is to not act and to let the natural events and efforts of peers begin to evolve.

■ **APPLICATION**

1. Could this experience have as easily occurred in a special school or if Jennifer had to be served solely in a self-contained classroom?
2. How can this relationship be continued outside of school?
3. Under what conditions is it appropriate to change scheduled instruction (such as working on a communication board) for more spontaneous opportunities?
4. Why is being a "member" of the homeroom so important to establishing friendships for children with severe disabilities?

Source: Adapted from *Introduction to Persons with Severe Disabilities* (p. 194), by J. M. McDonnell, M. L. Hardman, A. P. McDonnell, R. Kiefer-O'Donnell, 1995, Boston: Allyn and Bacon. Reprinted with permission.

Debate Forum

DISABILITIES MAY KEEP BRIAN CORTEZ FROM HEART TRANSPLANT

Moving a step to his right, Brian Cortez dribbles the basketball and arcs a 15-foot shot that sails through the curbside hoop. He flashes a smile, and his fingers move quickly to sign his pleasure to his friends.

It is a happy moment in the troubled times of Cortez, 20. In a life filled with challenges, he is facing perhaps his most difficult.

Cortez is developmentally disabled, almost deaf, and has lived in poverty since birth. Four years ago he was diagnosed with mild mental illness. Now his heart is sick and eventually will fail without a transplant.

Yet his limited mental abilities may disqualify him from the procedure. University of Washington physicians have said in an initial evaluation that they don't think Cortez, who lives in an adult home, can follow a strict medication regimen or articulate any problems after a transplant. A scarcity of donor hearts nationwide makes patients like Cortez less able to compete for a spot on the waiting list.

Advocates for Cortez—his teacher, his mother, adult-home caregivers, and caseworkers disagree. They say University of Washington physicians and a social worker did not speak in depth with key people in the young man's support network. If they had, they would have learned Cortez takes medications when asked, is aware of his physical condition, and can tell caregivers how he feels.

"They didn't have a true picture of his ability to deal with things," said Ted Karanson, deaf-education teacher at North Thurston High School, where Cortez was a student until his heart problems became worse this winter. "Brian deserves a chance at a transplant like anyone else."

Karanson and Cortez's mother, Gabriele Cortez, have contacted the American Civil Liberties Union and the state Human Rights Commission about the young man's case. David Merchant, an Olympia, Washington, attorney, is studying possible legal action under the Americans with Disabilities Act.

University of Washington physicians will not comment on specifics of the case. Dan Fishbein, medical director of the University of Washington heart-transplant program, will say only that Cortez will be further evaluated.

Cortez's situation frames the consequences of a national shortage of vital organs for transplantation. About 800 people a year die while waiting for heart transplants. More than 5,000 patients nationwide die while waiting for other organs.

The government-contracted agency that allocates organs nationally—the United Network for Organ Sharing—has an elaborate system to channel organs to patients who have the best chance of benefiting.

And the law of supply and demand applies: scarce organs go to those with the best chance of surviving an operation and caring for themselves afterward.

Fishbein is adamant that heart-transplant candidates are selected solely on medical need and chances of survival.

Laurence O'Connell, president of the Park Ridge Center, a Chicago bioethics institute, said the University of Washington is using a widely accepted standard, and the decision couldn't be more difficult:

"To offer the organ to this young man will almost certainly mean another patient will die," O'Connell said.

Brian Cortez's life began with a difficult birth, when his brain was briefly deprived of oxygen. Months later, he was diagnosed with severe hearing loss, impaired mental development, poor fine-motor control, and a faulty heart valve. At age 16, he began occasionally hearing voices. He banged his head against his locker and mumbled threats at other students at North Thurston High School. He was diagnosed with a "thought disorder" and was prescribed medication that silences the voices most of the time. Through it all, Cortez has been undiscouraged and struggled to learn, Karanson said. He has friends from school, reads the newspaper to keep up with the Sonics and Mariners, and has firm opinions about current affairs. He expresses himself through signing, speaking, and writing. Last year he worked two days a week for a landscape nursery as part of his school's job-training program.

With a successful transplant, "He could work a job, part time if not full time," said Lisa Flatt, a sign-language interpreter for the North Thurston School District. "He could do something repetitious—landscaping, assembly-line work, working in a mail room. . . . He would be really good at it." Cortez's medical record shows he was given test after

test during his two-week stay at the University of Washington hospital. Communication was poor, his mother said, because he did not understand the hospital's sign-language interpreter. The tests and treatment frightened and angered him.

At one point he was restrained in bed because he was spitting at and biting nurses. He wet his bed and hoarded food. He was given heavy doses of anti-psychotic medications to calm him. In the end, doctors wrote in his record: "It was thought during his admission that, due to his developmental delay and inability to understand and comply with instructions, the patient was not a candidate for heart transplant. . . . Due to his mental and psychiatric condition, he is not a candidate for heart transplant and should be medically managed with medications as best as possible." David Smith, an Olympia physician who has seen Cortez in recent months, said he doesn't think doctors at the University of Washington or elsewhere exclude patients from scarce resources because they are disabled. Rather, they consider whether the patient's quality of life would improve with surgery, and whether the patient can do his part to make it successful. Arthur Caplan, director of the University of Penn-

sylvania Center for Bioethics, said that the University of Washington's selection standard is appropriate. But he said it is essential that a patient's support system be considered when evaluating the chances of success.

The Cortez case likely would be watched closely if advocates make a claim under the Americans with Disabilities Act, which requires "reasonable accommodation" be provided to the disabled to ensure they have equal opportunities.

"There has never been an ADA case involving transplantation," said Caplan, who has written and lectured widely on organ transplantation, "and this could be one."

■ POINT

Brian Cortez is clearly a qualified candidate for a heart transplant and should immediately be placed on the waiting list. His support network of family and caregivers have made a strong case that Brian is able to follow a strict medication regimen and communicate any problems he is having following the transplant. His disabilities should not in anyway be a factor in the decision. Brian clearly qualifies on the basis of medical need. With reasonable accommodations and his strong family and caregivers support network, there is no

reason to believe that Brian's chances for survival from the transplant would be less than anyone else.

■ COUNTERPOINT

The primary issue here is a scarcity of organs that requires that difficult life and death decisions be made on the basis of who has the best chance of benefitting from the operation. To give to one person, means that another person must die. As suggested by Brian's behavior during his hospital stay, he has poor communication even with an interpreter; is easily upset by tests and medical treatment; and requires heavy doses of medication to calm him down. Clearly, his developmental disabilities make it difficult for him to understand the critical instructions necessary for him to meet the required medical regimen following the heart transplant. Brian's condition is better managed by medications and not a risky operation and difficult recovery that are beyond his abilities to cope with over the long run.

Source: From "Disabilities May Keep Man from Transplant," by W. King, 2000, *Salt Lake Tribune*, May 2, pp. A1, A7.

Review

 focus 1

What are the three components of the TASH definition of severe disabilities?

- The relationship of the individual with the environment (adaptive fit)
- The inclusion of people of all ages
- The necessity of extensive ongoing support in life activities

focus 2

Define the terms *multiple disabilities* and *deaf–blindness* as described in IDEA.

- *Multiple disabilities* refers to concomitant impairments (such as mental retardation–orthopedic impairments, etc.). The combination causes educational problems so severe that they cannot be accommodated in special education programs solely for one impairment. One such combination is "dual diagnosis," a condition characterized by serious emotional disturbance (challenging behaviors) in conjunction with severe mental retardation.
- Deaf–blindness involves concomitant hearing and visual impairments. The combination causes communication and other developmental and educational problems so severe that they cannot be accommodated in special education programs solely for children who are deaf or blind.

 focus 3

Identify the estimated prevalence and causes of severe and multiple disabilities.

- Prevalence estimates generally range from 0.1% to 1% of the general population.
- Students with multiple disabilities accounted for about 2% of the 5.5 million students with disabilities served in the public schools. Approximately 0.0002% of students with disabilities were labeled deaf–blind.
- There are many possible causes of severe and multiple disabilities. Most severe and multiple disabilities are evident at birth. Birth defects may be the result of genetic or metabolic problems. Most identifiable causes of severe mental retardation and related developmental disabilities are genetic in origin. Factors associated with poisoning, accidents, malnutrition, physical and emotional neglect, and disease are also known causes.

focus 4

What are the characteristics of persons with severe and multiple disabilities?

- Mental retardation is often a primary condition.

- Most children will not benefit from basic academics instruction in literacy and mathematics. Instruction in functional academics is the most effective approach to learning academic skills.
- People with severe and multiple disabilities often do not have age-appropriate adaptive skills and need ongoing services and supports to facilitate learning in this area.
- Significant speech and language deficits and delays are a primary characteristic.
- Physical and health needs are common, involving conditions such as congenital heart disease, epilepsy, respiratory problems, spasticity, athetosis, and hypotonia. Vision and hearing loss are also common.

 focus 5

Identify three types of educational assessments for students with severe and multiple disabilities.

- Traditionally, there has been a heavy reliance on standardized measurements, particularly the IQ test, in identifying people with severe and multiple disabilities.
- Assessments that focus on valued skills to promote independence and quality of life in natural settings are referred to as functional, ecological, or authentic assessment.
- Students with disabilities must participate in statewide or districtwide

assessments of achievement or provide a statement of why that assessment is not appropriate for the child. For many students with severe disabilities, these assessments are inappropriate and they are excluded from taking them. Alternate assessments are conducted instead.

focus 6

Identify the features of effective services and supports for children with severe and multiple disabilities during the early childhood years.

- Services and supports must begin at birth.
- Programs for infants and toddlers are both child- and family-centered.
- The goals for preschool programs are to maximize development across several developmental areas, to develop social interaction and classroom participation skills, to increase community participation through support to family and caregivers, and to prepare the child for inclusive school placement.
- Effective and inclusive preschool programs have a holistic view of the child, see the classroom as community of learners, base the program on a collaborative ethic, use authentic assessment, create a heterogeneous environment, make available a range of individualized supports and services, engage educators

in reflective teaching, and emphasize multiple ways of teaching and learning.

 focus 7

Identify the features of effective services and supports for children with severe and multiple disabilities during the elementary school years.

- Self-determination—student preferences and needs are taken into account in developing educational objectives.
- The school values and supports parental involvement.
- Instruction focuses on frequently used functional skills related to everyday life activities.
- Assistive technology and augmentive communication are available to maintain or increase the functional capabilities of the student with severe and multiple disabilities.

 focus 8

Describe four outcomes that are important in planning for the transition from school to adult life for adolescents with severe and multiple disabilities.

- Establishing a network of friends and acquaintances
- Developing the ability to use community resources on a regular basis
- Securing a paid job that supports the use of community resources and interaction with peers
- Establishing independence and autonomy in making lifestyle choices

 focus 9

Describe four features that characterize successful inclusive education for students with severe and multiple disabilities.

- Physical placement of students with severe and multiple disabilities in the general education schools and classes they would attend were they not disabled.
- Systematic organization of opportunities for interaction between students with severe and multiple disabilities and students without disabilities.
- Specific instruction to increase the competence of students with severe and multiple disabilities in interacting with students who are not disabled.
- Highly trained teachers competent in the necessary instructional and assistive technology to facilitate social interaction between students with and without disabilities.

 focus 10

Describe four bioethical dilemmas that can have an impact on people with severe disabilities and their families.

- Genetic engineering may be used to conquer disease or as a means to enhance or perfect human beings.
- Genetic screening may be effective in preventing disease but can also be used by insurance companies, employers, courts, schools, adoption agencies, law enforcement, and the military to discriminate against people with severe disabilities.
- Genetic counselors can provide important information to families but may also lose neutrality and give their own personal beliefs about what the family should do.
- Selective abortion and options for the withholding of medical treatment may allow parents to make the very personal decision about whether the quality of life for their unborn child may be so diminished that life would not be worth living. However, it can also be argued that no one has the right to decide for someone else whether a life is worth living.

People with Autism

12

To begin with . . .

Some parents and others believe increasing prevalence of autism in the past 10 years is partially due to multiple vaccines, like those for measles, mumps, and rubella all given in one. In certain cases it may be that such vaccinations serve as a mechanism that triggers the onset of autistic behaviors. (Fox, 2000)

"Knowing Chris; he does not speak. He throws his food. When unrestrained, he often bangs his knee against his forehead. When he leaves, not only will I miss him; a small part of my personality will be gone too. . . . Next week, after two years here, Chris will be moved to another institution, one with better access to medical crisis intervention." (Whitaker, 2000, p. Z12)

If you're looking for a camp to accommodate a child with special needs, the search is getting easier. There is a growing number of camps that work with special needs children. Programs like those at *Bradford Woods* in Indiana work with children who are physically and mentally challenged. These camps provide kids living with conditions like . . . autism . . . the opportunity to meet and bond with others who share similar experiences. (ABCNEWS.com, 2000, pp. 1–2)

375

Josh

Josh is in a general education class at his elementary school. His friend Marshall, who has learning disabilities, is a close friend to Josh. Marshall says, "Josh likes to dribble the basketball. Other people help Josh, but I help him a lot, too."

When Josh was born, his parents thought he was deaf, but tests showed he could hear. At age 30 months, Josh was diagnosed with autism. His parents couldn't afford a specialized clinic or treatment facility and felt at a loss for what to do. They visited a school with a separate unit for children with autism, mental retardation, and other disabilities. During the visit, Josh mingled with other children and mimicked their behavior—shouts, some violent movements. Josh's parents decided not to place Josh in that school.

Josh entered a general education class. The special education teacher at the school was concerned at first because Josh would bite his nails, scratch his legs. He wasn't interacting with the other students. Gradually, he started to talk and interact with the other students. His special education teacher says, "I think this wouldn't have happened if he were only interacting with other autistic children."

Josh's dad feels strongly about including students with disabilities in the general education classroom: "When wheelchairs come in (to school) in the morning and the Down syndrome (students) come in in the morning, and Josh comes in in the morning, they are the students. They are not the special education students. It's a long process and it's just becoming comfortable."

Billy

Billy is a blue-eyed, blond little boy of striking beauty; he is almost too perfect physically. His parents first became aware that Billy was different and had special problems when he was 5 years old but had not yet begun to talk. Some of his other behaviors also bothered Billy's parents a great deal. Billy didn't seem to play like other children. He would rock for long periods of time in his crib, and he had little interest in toys. At best, Billy would just spin the wheels of his trucks and stare as they turned. Most disturbing to Billy's parents was the fact that he showed little affection. Billy was not a warm baby. When his mother picked him up to cuddle, Billy would start to cry and arch his back until he was put back in his crib. Billy treated other children and adults as objects of no consequence in his life. He didn't care about people; he would rather be left alone.

Since Billy's behavior was recognized as different from normal, other changes have occurred. Billy developed language very slowly and in a strange way. His language is what specialists call "echolalic" in nature. When asked a question, Billy simply responds by echoing the question. Billy also has a great deal of trouble using pronouns and prepositions correctly when trying to talk. He will commonly reverse pronouns and refer to himself as "you" or refer to another person as "I." The correct use of prepositions also causes Billy a great deal of difficulty. Up or down, on or under, or a yes-or-no answer to a question are very confusing concepts for Billy. He simply answers yes or no at random. When viewed as a whole, Billy's language is not just delayed; it is also disturbed in some fundamental way. He simply does not learn. Over and over he makes the same language mistakes.

Aside from Billy's atypical language development, he now spends a great deal of time in repetitive, non-goal-oriented behavior, called *self-stimulatory* or *stereotypic* behavior. He has progressed from simple rocking and spinning the wheels on his toys to flapping his hands and twirling in circles until he falls from dizziness. If made to stop this behavior, Billy will throw ferocious temper tantrums that include screaming, biting, and often head banging. This self-destructive behavior is very disconcerting because, in his tantrums, Billy not only breaks things but hurts himself as well.

Billy also has a tremendous need to protect himself against any sort of change, including changes in his daily routine or his physical environment. Billy's mother recently rearranged the furniture in the living room while he was napping. When Billy awoke and entered the rearranged room, he immediately started to cry and whine; then he had a tantrum until the furniture was returned to its original position. Changes in his daily schedule also produce near-panic reactions that end up in tantrums. It seems as though Billy has memorized his environment and daily schedule, and any change produces the unknown for Billy. Adjustment and relearning are very difficult for him. Billy's behavior cripples his family as well as himself. The furniture arrangement episode is only one of many incidents in which Billy requires his parents' constant attention. If left alone for even short periods of time, Billy can hurt himself or break something. After claiming all the attention his parents and older brother can give, Billy returns little. He is not affectionate and will not even look his brother in the eye, nor does he seek his mother's affection. Billy suffers from a rare childhood developmental disorder known as infantile autism.

Source: Adapted from *Understanding Child Behavior Disorders* (2nd ed., p. 288), by D. M. Gelfand, W. R. Jenson, and C. J. Drew, 1988, New York: Holt, Rinehart and Winston.

EDERAL LAW FIRST RECOGNIZED autism as a disability category in the Individuals with Disabilities Education Act of 1990 (IDEA). Although only recently acknowledged in federal law, autism began to appear in the research literature in the first half of the 20th century and is thought to have been described as early as the early 1800s (Ward & Meyer, 1999). **Autism** is taken from the Greek "autos," meaning "self," to indicate the extreme sense of isolation and detachment from the world around them that characterizes individuals with autism.

focus 1

Identify four areas of functional challenge often found in children with autism.

Autism symptoms tend to emerge very early in a child's life. Most cases become evident before the age of 2½, and few are diagnosed after the age of 5. Autism is one of the most seriously disruptive of all childhood disabilities. It is characterized by combinations of varying degrees of deficiencies in language, interpersonal skills, emotional or affective behavior, and intellectual functioning (Eisenmajer et al., 1998; Folstein et al., 1999; Shriver, Allen, & Mathews, 1999). It is a disability that impairs the normal development of many areas of functioning.

Autism has received significant attention in the past several years by both researchers and the public media. Examples of public visibility are found in the words of Rick Whitaker, mentioned in the chapter opening, which portray Chris both through the challenging behaviors he exhibits and also through the personal fingerprint he leaves on at least one person who knows him. Although some of the more public portrayals of autism are perhaps not typical of the condition, they educate and capture the interest of a considerable segment of the lay public.

Definition

he federal regulations for IDEA employ the following definition of autism:

Autism means a developmental disability significantly affecting verbal and nonverbal communication and social interaction, generally evident before age 3, that adversely affects educational performance. Characteristics of autism include—irregularities and impairments in communication, engagement in repetitive activities and stereotyped movements, resistance to environmental change or change in daily routines, and unusual responses to sensory experiences. (U.S. Department of Education, 1991, p. 41,271)

This definition refers to the appearance of deviations from normal development before 3 years of age, since the symptoms of autism tend to emerge during the early years. The definition does not intend, however, to preclude a diagnosis of autism if a child develops symptoms after age 3. Federal regulations also note that a diagnosis of autism should not be used in cases where children show characteristics of serious emotional disturbance, since they are addressed elsewhere in the law. Such attention to autism is relatively recent. The 1991–1992 school year was the first during which data were collected regarding the number of children identified as having autism and served in the public schools (U.S. Department of Education, 2000a).

Definitional statements provide a partial picture of autism although most professionals are reluctant to make broad generalizations regarding people with autism. People with autism are certainly not all alike, and it is more accurate to speak of characteristics than to characterize. The diagnostic criteria outlined for autism by the American Psychiatric Association add to our description of these individuals and are found in Table 12.1 (APA, 2000).

■ AUTISM. A childhood disorder with onset prior to 36 months of age. It is characterized by extreme withdrawal, self-stimulation, intellectual deficits, and language disorders.

TABLE 12.1	Diagnostic criteria for autism

A. A total of six (or more) items from (1), (2), and (3), with at least two from (1), and one each from (2) and (3):

1. Qualitative impairment in social interaction, as manifested by at least two of the following:

   a. Marked impairment in the use of multiple nonverbal behaviors such as eye-to-eye gaze, facial expression, body postures, and gestures to regulate social interaction.

   b. Failure to develop peer relationships appropriate to developmental level.

   c. A lack of spontaneous seeking to share enjoyment, interests, or achievements with other people (e.g., by a lack of showing, bringing, or pointing out objects of interest).

   d. Lack of social or emotional reciprocity.

2. Qualitative impairments in communication as manifested by at least one of the following:

   a. Delay in, or total lack of, the development of spoken language (not accompanied by an attempt to compensate through alternative modes of communication such as gestures or mime).

   b. In individuals with adequate speech, marked impairment in the ability to initiate or sustain a conversation with others.

   c. Stereotyped and repetitive use of language or idiosyncratic language.

   d. Lack of varied, spontaneous make-believe play or social imitative play appropriate to developmental level.

3. Restricted repetitive and stereotyped patterns of behavior, interests, and activities, as manifested by at least one of the following:

   a. Encompassing preoccupation with one or more stereotypic and restricted patterns of interest that is abnormal either in intensity or focus.

   b. Apparently inflexible adherence to specific, nonfunctional routines or rituals.

   c. Stereotypic and repetitive motor mannerisms (e.g., hand or finger flapping or twisting, or complex whole-body movements).

   d. Persistent preoccupation with parts of objects.

B. Delays or abnormal functioning in at least one of the following areas, with onset prior to age 3 years: (1) social interaction, (2) language as used in social communication, or (3) symbolic or imaginative play.

C. The disturbance is not better accounted for by Rett's Disorder or Childhood Disintegrative Disorder.

Source: From *Diagnostic and Statistical Manual of Mental Disorders (DSM-IV-TR)* (4th ed.—text revision, p. 92), by the American Psychiatric Association, 2000, Washington, DC: Author.

Prevalence

Compared to other conditions, the occurrence of autism is relatively rare. The American Psychiatric Association has estimated that the prevalence is about 5 cases per 10,000 (APA, 2000). Although this is the commonly accepted prevalence range (Rosenberg, Wilson, Maheady, & Sindelar, 1997), some research has shown both lower and higher figures (Bryson & Smith, 1998; Creswell & Skuse, 1999; Kadesjoe et al., 1999). The wide variation in prevalence is

focus 2

What is the general range of prevalence estimated for autism?

likely due to differences in definition and diagnostic criteria employed but may diminish over time as greater consensus about what constitutes autism is achieved. Gender differences are evident in autism, with males outnumbering females substantially. Estimates of these prevalence differences range from 2.1 to 1, to 4 to 1 (Creswell & Skuse, 1999; Fombonne, 1999).

Characteristics

Unusual behaviors often appear very early in the lives of children with autism. They may, for example, exhibit significant impairment in interpersonal interaction as babies. Parents often report that these babies may be particularly unresponsive to physical contact or affection (Hobson, 1999; Okyere, 1998; Ratey et al., 2000). It is not unusual for parents to note that their infants become rigid when picked up and are "not cuddly," that they avoid eye contact, averting their gaze rather than looking directly at another person. Such behavior may continue in older children. In some cases, children with autism rely heavily on using peripheral vision rather than direct, face-to-face visual contact.

focus 3
Identify six characteristics of children with autism.

Children with autism are frequently described in terms of social impairments, social unresponsiveness, extreme difficulty relating others, and difficulty understanding or expressing emotion (Floriana, 1998; Heaton, Hermelin, & Pring, 1999; Serra, Minderaa, vanGeert, & Jackson, 1999). Often, these children seem to prefer interacting with inanimate objects, forming attachments to objects rather than people. They appear to be insensitive to the feelings of others and in many cases treat other people as objects, even physically pushing or pulling others around to suit their needs. Clearly, children with autism interact with their environment in ways that are not typical, as though they have difficulty making sense of the world around them.

A person with autism often has difficulty forming attachments with other people.

■ IMPAIRED OR DELAYED LANGUAGE

Children with autism often exhibit impaired or delayed language development (Eisenmajer, et al., 1998; Folstein et al., 1999). Approximately half do not develop speech, and those who do often engage in strange language and speaking behavior, such as **echolalia** (repeating back only what has been said to them) (Malvy et al., 1999; Rhode, 1999). In many cases, children with autism who speak reproduce parts of conversations that they have heard but do so in a very mechanical fashion, with no sign that they attach meaning to what was said. This echolalic behavior is sometimes misinterpreted as an indicator of high intellectual abilities. Children with autism who develop language often have a limited speaking repertoire, exhibit an uneven level of development between language skill areas, and fail to use pronouns in speech directed at other people (Parisse, 1999; Wilkinson, 1998). These children differ from their peers in grammatical complexity and make little use of semantics in sentence structure (Botting & Conti-Ramsden, 1999). Additionally, the tonal quality

■ ECHOLALIA. A meaningless repetition or imitation of words that have been spoken.

of their speech is often unusual or flat, and in some cases, their speech appears to serve the purpose of self-stimulation rather than communication. Further investigation is needed on language development in children with autism as well as using stronger and novel research methodologies; research techniques have limited research evidence in the past (Leonard, 2000; Tager-Flusberg, 2000).

■ SELF-STIMULATION

Behavior of a self-stimulative nature is often associated with autism, although self-stimulation is not always present. Children with autism often engage in physical forms of **self-stimulation,** such as flicking their hands in front of their faces repeatedly (Dawson et al., 1998). They also tend to manipulate objects in a repetitive fashion, suggesting self-stimulation. Behavior such as spinning objects, rocking, or hand flapping may continue for hours (Berkson, 1998). Some behaviors that seem to start as self-stimulation may worsen or take different forms and create potential injury to the child, such as face slapping, biting, and head banging. Behavior that becomes self-injurious is more often found in low-functioning children and can understandably cause concern and stress for parents and others around them.

■ RESISTANCE TO CHANGE IN ROUTINE

Intense resistance to change, or rigidity, is often mentioned in discussions of children with autism. Familiar routines—for example, during meals or at bedtime—are obsessively important to them, and any deviation from the set pattern may upset them greatly. Youngsters who are affected in this manner may insist on a particular furniture arrangement or one type of food for a given meal (for example, specific cereal for breakfast); they may even wash themselves in a particular pattern, somewhat approximating obsessive–compulsive or stereotypic-like behaviors (Aman, Arnold, & Armstrong, 1999; Nilsson, Gillberg, Gillberg, & Rastam, 1999). Often, items must be arranged in a symmetrical fashion to seem proper to the child with autism. There have also been reports relating the rigidity or perseveration of those with autism to obsessive behaviors including self-mutilation (Aman et al., 1999; Verri et al., 2000).

Such obsessive, ritualistic behaviors create numerous problems, as one might expect, particularly if an effort is made to integrate the child into daily life activities. For example, most people pay little attention to the exact route they take when driving to the grocery store or to the precise pattern of moving through the store once they arrive. For parents attempting to take their child with autism along, however, minor deviations may cause serious crisis situations. Transitions from one activity to another may present challenges for these children both in school and home activities. Research is beginning to address questions on such matters, with structured verbal and visual cues facilitating smoother transitions from one activity to another (Schmidt, Alper, Raschke, & Ryndak, 2000; Trillingsgaard, 1999).

■ INTELLIGENCE

Most children with autism exhibit a lower intellectual functioning; about 75% having measured IQs below 70 (Kauffman, 2001; Mastropieri & Scruggs, 2000; O'Neill, 1997). The verbal and reasoning skills required in intelligence testing pose particular difficulty for these children. It has long been thought that they have a tendency to imitate what they hear, as evidenced by their echolalic speech. However, more recent thinking suggests that this is more appropriately seen as one or more specific information processing or cognition deficits (Parisse, 1999). Intellectual ability varies among children having autism, with high-functioning individuals testing

■ SELF-STIMULATION. Repetitive behavior that has no apparent purpose other than providing the person with some type of stimulation.

Snapshot

Steven

■ REFLECTIONS OF A PARENT

Steven was 2½ years old when our daughter, Katherine, was born. This was the time when I seriously began to search for help. I knew something was wrong shortly after Steve's birth, but when I tried to describe the problem, no one seemed to understand what I was saying. In spite of chronic ear infections, Steve looked very healthy. He was slow in developing language, but that could easily be attributed to his ear trouble. Since he was our first baby, I thought that maybe we just weren't very good parents.

When he was 2½, we enrolled Steven in a diagnostic nursery school. He did not seem to understand us when we spoke. I wondered whether he was retarded or had some other developmental problem. The nursery school gave us their opinion when he was 4. They said Steve seemed to have normal intelligence, but he perseverated, was behind socially, and did not seem to process verbs. The school said he had some signs of autism and some signs of a learning disability.

When Steve was 4½, he did some amazing things. He began to talk, read, write, and play the piano. I was taking beginning adult piano lessons at the time, and Steve could play everything I did. In fact, he could play any song he heard and even added chords with his left hand. Relatives and friends began to tell us that he was a genius and that this accounted for his odd behavior. I really wanted to believe this genius theory.

I enrolled Steven in a public kindergarten at age 5. This teacher had another theory about Steve's strange behavior. She believed that we were not firm enough with him. She also sent the social worker to our home to see what we were doing with him.

I often wondered if we were just very poor parents. I certainly had enough people tell us so! Whenever I went to anyone for help, I was likely to begin crying. Then the doctor or whoever would start to watch my behavior closely. I could just see each of them forming a theory in his or her mind: The child is okay, but the mother is a mess. I wondered if I was a very cold mother. Maybe I was subtly rejecting my son. Then again, maybe it was his father. My mother always said he didn't spend enough time with Steve.

I didn't understand when the psychiatrist told me Steve had a *pervasive developmental disorder*. I began to get the picture when the other terms were used. I had heard of autism before. Something was terribly wrong, but it had a physical basis. It was not my fault at all. This was a relief but also a tremendous blow. It has really helped to have a name for the problem. We used to wonder whether Steve was lying awake nights, dreaming up new ways to get our attention. We lived from crisis to crisis. We would finally handle one problem, only to have a new one develop in its place. Steve still does unusual things, but it doesn't send us into a panic anymore.

—*Sheri*, Steve's Mother

---

at a normal or near-normal level. High-functioning individuals may have rather substantial vocabularies, but they do not always know the appropriate use of terms that they can spell and define (Sigman & Kim, 1999; Volkmar & Marans, 1999). In some cases, very high functioning people with autism appear to use language quite well, although there may still be clues that something is different. Such is the case with the description of Mike FitzPatrick in the Reflect on This feature on page 382, about how Mike was wrongly accused of robbery.

Approximately 10% to 15% of those with autism exhibit what are known as splinter skills, areas of ability in which performance levels are unexpectedly high compared to those of other domains of functioning. For instance, a student with autism may perform unusually well at memory tasks or drawing but have serious deficiencies in language skills and abstract reasoning. For parents of such students, these splinter skills create enormous confusion. Although most parents realize early on that their child with autism is exceptional, they also hope that he or she is healthy. These hopes may be fueled by the child's demonstration of unusual skills. In some cases, the parents may believe that whatever is wrong is their fault, as portrayed in the second snapshot. A great deal remains unknown about autism. For example, are the savant characteristics portrayed in the movie *Rain Man* simply extremes of splinter skills? Can splinter skills be effectively exploited in a functional way to facilitate school or work activity—some preliminary evidence suggests it is

Reflect on This

A SIMPLE MAN: AUTISTIC MAN WRONGLY ACCUSED OF ROBBERY

Mike Fitz-Patrick has autism . . . but he has managed to meet the challenges of life. He holds down a job as a night janitor in this hometown of Syracuse, New York. He drives a car and does his own shopping.

But, incredibly, this gentle, simple man was charged with the brazen daylight robbery of a bank.

Police looking into the April 15, 1999, robbery of the Ontario National Bank in Clifton Springs, New York,

zeroed in on FitzPatrick, 48, as the chief suspect. . . . He had visited the town on vacation in late April. Authorities thought his behavior suspicious and came to believe he was casing yet another bank to rob.

Police interrogated Fitz-Patrick after picking him up at his job one night. He told the police he had robbed the bank. "Mike tries to please people," explains Anne Fitz-Patrick, Mike's mother. "He thought in his mind if he told them what they wanted to hear, they'd let him go. He

didn't know that would complicate things."

FitzPatrick's confession did complicate things. He was charged with bank robbery and faced 25 years in prison if convicted.

But the real bank robber came forward and told authorities he had robbed the Ontario National Bank on April 15. David Harrington was already in jail, awaiting trial for other bank robberies. He was outraged that an autistic man should be charged for a crime he did not commit. Harrington, 30,

confessed to the robbery, giving authorities details only the robber could have known.

Charges against FitzPatrick were finally dropped. . . . He's back at his job as a night janitor. He says he's grateful to Harrington, the man who admitted robbing the bank, for clearing his name. Harrington is still awaiting trial.

Source: From "A Simple Man: Autistic Man Wrongly Accused of Robbery," by J. Siceloff, December 13, 1999. Available: *ABCNEWS.com.*

---

possible, and research continues in this fascinating area (e.g., Cox & Eames, 1999; Happe, 1999; Heaton, Hermelin, & Pring, 1999a).

The challenging behavior patterns found in children with autism often cause a variety of difficulties. Restricted behavioral repertoires, communication limitations, stereotypic self-stimulation, resistance to changes in routine, and unusual responses to their environment pose problems and may limit integration options for some individuals with autism (Westling & Fox, 2000). Many may have the ability to perform and the skills necessary to participate in community jobs or living arrangements, yet the presence of a challenging behavior may lead to placement in a more restricted setting. Continued research on behavior management, social interactions, and program development is essential if these individuals are to achieve maximum integration into the community (Okyere, 1998).

▪ LEARNING CHARACTERISTICS

Learning characteristics of children with autism are frequently different from those of their normally developing peers and may present significant educational challenges. Some characteristics described earlier are prominent in this respect. For example, students who resist change may perseverate on a specific item to be learned and encounter cognitive shifting difficulties in changing attention to the next topic or problem in an instructional sequence (Durand, 1999; Olley, 1999). Because of problems understanding social cues and relating to people, students with autism may experience difficulty interacting with teachers and other students in a school setting (Heaton, Hermelin, & Pring, 1999b; Serra et al., 1999).

The abilities of children with autism frequently develop unevenly, both within and among skill areas. These children may or may not generalize already-learned skills to other settings or topics (Watanabe, Yamaguchi, Uematsu, & Kobayashi, 1999). They are often impulsive and inconsistent in their responses, which is a matter that teachers may have to address. Children with autism frequently have diffi-

One of the many mysteries surrounding the phenomenon of autism is the extraordinary talents and abilities demonstrated by some individuals. . . . In the past, such individuals were referred to as *idiot savants*. *Idiot is* an antiquated term for someone with mental retardation, and *savant* means "knower" in French. Some professionals now prefer the term *savant syndrome* to describe a condition in which persons with serious mental limitations demonstrate spectacular "islands of brilliance in a sea of mental disability."

Given the scope of talents in the human repertoire, these "islands" are confined to a narrow range of abilities: a flair for music or visual arts, mathematical aptitude, mechanical wizardry, or mnemonic skills such as calendar calculation (being able to report instantly on what day of the week a particular date will fall in a given year, past or future). The trait that binds these unique abilities is superior memory skills that are idiosyncratic, emotionless, and enigmatic. Indeed, savants often seem to accomplish feats of brilliance

as if by rote. No emotion shades their performance.

How are savants able to do what they do? While no conclusive findings exist, theories abound. For example, one theory has suggested that the sensory deprivation and social isolation experienced by many individuals with autism causes them to be bored and thus they adopt trivial preoccupations. Another theory has suggested that autism is associated with deficits in the left hemisphere of the brain, which governs the use of language and other logical, conceptual, and abstract skills. Savants' skills are usually

associated with right-brain functions—spatial perception, visualization, mechanical dexterity, and movement—suggesting that the right hemisphere is dominant.

Clearly, much remains unknown about both autism and the savant syndrome. Certainly, little is understood about how they exist in the same person. Increased understanding will hopefully benefit those who struggle with autism.

Source: Reprinted by permission of Omni, copyright 1989, Omni Publications International, Ltd.

culty with information processing and abstract ideas and may focus on one or more select stimuli while failing to understand the general concept (Weldy, 1998).

Some children with autism possess certain qualities that can be viewed as educational strengths or at least be focused on for instructional purposes. For example, although generalizations about these youngsters are difficult to make, individuals with autism are sometimes noted as enjoying routine, which is consistent with their desire to maintain sameness. If a child shows this tendency, teachers can employ it when practice or drill is warranted to learn a skill. In certain cases, splinter skills may be capitalized on for positive, productive purposes (Happe, 1999). Additionally, some individuals with autism seem to have relatively strong, specific, long-term memory skills, particularly for factual information like names, numbers, and dates (Heavey, Pring, & Hermelin, 1999). For these students, once they have learned a piece of information, they may not forget it. Their long-term memory skills may equal those of their normally developing peers.

Generalizations regarding children with autism are difficult to make. Despite the many stereotypes about these individuals, they are highly variable. Learning characteristics, both limitations and strengths, must be individually assessed and considered in educational programming (Olley, 1999).

Causation

Historically, two broad theories about the causes of autism have been most prominent: biological and psychodynamic. The **psychodynamic perspective** has implicated family interactions as causal factors in autism. Theorists subscribing to this view have speculated that the child withdraws from rejection and erects defenses against psychological pain. In so doing,

■ PSYCHODYNAMIC PERSPECTIVE. An approach to psychological disorders that views unconscious conflicts and anxieties as the cause of such disorders.

The teacher who works with a child with autism should be prepared to use different teaching strategies that compensate for the uneven skills development of the child.

focus 4

Identify the two broad theoretical views regarding the causes of autism.

he or she retreats to an inner world and essentially does not interact with the outside environment that involves people. Psychodynamic theories have largely fallen out of favor as research has failed to support this position. However, some literature continues to explore this area with topics such as fears, the newborn's anxieties, and searching for the meaning of the child's autistic symptoms (Edwards & Lanyado, 1999; Reid, 1999). Other authors discuss psychodynamic theories as part of a balanced theoretical description (Wenar & Kerig, 2000).

Biological causation in a variety of forms predominates the current research on autism, particularly genetics (Berney, 2000). For instance, damage to the chromosome structure in a condition known as **fragile X syndrome** emerged in the late 1960s as a potential cause of autism. Researchers found that this condition appeared in a certain percentage of males with autism (e.g., York, vonFraunhofer, Turk, & Sedgwick, 1999). Work continues on this genetic linkage although it appears that fragile X is not a major cause of autism (Robertson & Murphy, 1999).

Research has established genetic causation in autism, but it has not provided a complete and clear explanation of how causation occurs (Berney, 2000; Minshew, 2000; Mueller & Courchesne, 2000). One problem in developing a body of genetic information arises from the relative infrequency with which autism appears in the population at large. Although some research on twins has suggested a genetic link (Cook, 1998; Piven, 1999), additional evidence is clearly needed.

Abnormal development and damage to the central nervous system have received attention recently as a cause of autism along with other investigations of neurological problems, such as brain cell differences, absence of specialization in the brain hemispheres, arrested neurological development, and neurological chemical imbalances (Rapin, 2000; Saugstad, 1999). Major developments in technology have enabled research once possible only through autopsy, if at all. For example, some people with autism appear to have an abnormality in a portion of the brain. One abnormal area, known as the **vermis** and located in the cerebellum, may be related to the cognitive malfunctions found in autism (Levitt et al., 1999; Simon, 2000). Further research is needed to confirm this finding as well as the damage theories in general.

Neurological damage, such as that noted earlier, may be caused by a number of problems during prenatal development as well as early infancy. Maternal infections, alcohol abuse, and other problems during pregnancy have great potential of dam-

▪ FRAGILE X SYNDROME. A condition involving damage to the chromosome structure, which appears as a breaking or splitting at the end of the X chromosome. The condition is found in some males with autism.

▪ VERMIS. A portion of the brain in the cerebellum that appears to be underdeveloped in children with autism.

aging the developing fetus and have been associated with autism and other disabilities involving the central nervous system (Drew & Hardman, 2000; Howard, Williams, Port, & Lepper, 2001). In particular, viral infections such as rubella have been implicated, although a great deal of research is still needed to explore this area. Problems during the birth process—such as unusual hemorrhaging, difficult deliveries, and anoxia—are also known causes of neurological injuries in babies (Barak et al., 1999; Wenar & Kerig, 2000). Children with autism seem to have more frequent histories of delivery problems than do children without disabilities. Despite the multitude of potential neurological causes, no single type of trauma has been consistently identified (Berney, 2000).

Causes of autism remain as unsolved puzzles in the face of ongoing research and interest in the condition. Accumulated evidence has strongly implicated biological factors, although some biological malfunctions may be related to environmental influences (Courchesne, Yeung-Courchesne, & Pierce, 1999; Saugstad, 1999; Whiteley, Rodgers, & Shattock, 1998). Many current researchers have viewed autism as a behavioral syndrome with multiple biological causes (Berney, 2000; Mueller & Courchesne, 2000). To date, researchers have not identified any single specific factor that causes autism. Rather, it appears to be an assortment of symptoms rather than a specific disease, which is why it is often called a syndrome. As with many areas of disability, an understanding of causation is important as we attempt to improve treatment. Research continues to unravel the sources of this perplexing disability, and improved research methodology is vital for further progress in autism investigation (e.g, Menn & Bernstein-Ratner, 2000; Tager-Flusberg, 2000).

Interventions

Identifying causation in autism is a companion activity of the continual attention to discovering effective treatments. Different approaches have been used as interventions with autism. Some have been based on theories of causation, others have focused on specific observable behaviors, and some appear to be rather trendy and controversial (e.g., Ivey & Ivey, 1999). Significant progress has been made in successful interventions for those with autism, although researchers continually emphasize the importance of further systematic investigation on the effectiveness of various treatment strategies (e.g., Koegel, Koegel, Shoshan, & McNerney, 1999).

focus 5

Identify four major approaches to the treatment of autism.

■ EDUCATIONAL INTERVENTIONS

The configuration of autism features and the severity of specific problem areas vary significantly from individual to individual. Consequently, a wide variety of instructional options are required for effective education of these children. These alternatives range from specialized individual programs to integrated placement with support services. The unusual maladaptive behaviors mentioned earlier have led to the emergence of stereotypes about youngsters with autism and to undue segregation. However, the current literature has emphasized integration for educational purposes to the maximum degree possible, with educational placement and instructional programming dependent on the student's age and functioning level (Durand, 1999; Kasari, Freeman, Bauminger, & Alkin, 1999; Wolfberg et al., 1999). In most cases the ultimate goal is to prepare individuals with autism to live in their home community and in the least restrictive setting. The research literature also supports early interventions as an important element in promoting growth for children with

The IEP of a child with autism should focus on developing functional communication skills and social skills.

autism (Anderson & Romanczyk, 1999; McGee, Morrier, & Daly, 1999; Parisy, 1999). Under IDEA, students with autism are entitled to a free appropriate education in the least restrictive environment.

Children with autism require an individualized educational plan (IEP), including statements of short- and long-term goals (Olley, 1999). For most students with autism, it is vital that the IEP have a central component of functional communication and social skills and focus on individual strengths and skills required for maximum independence. Functional skills and knowledge will vary among individuals. For some, functional instruction will mean heavy use of language training, augmentative communication, and social, self-help, and self-protection skills (Drash, High, & Tudor, 1999; Hedrick, Katims, & Carr, 1999). For others, functional instruction will focus on what may be traditional academic subjects as well as some not always included in general education curricula, such as sexual awareness, sexual behavior, and sex education; others may be topics of concern to the children's parents (Lunsky & Konstantareas, 1998; U.S. Department of Education, 2000a). Educational interventions for children with autism and other disabilities are beginning to include increased use of technology enhancements in the teaching process (Bernard-Opitz, Sriram, & Sapuan, 1999; Roblyer & Edwards, 2000; Yamamoto & Miya, 1999). Additional research on the effectiveness of such applications is essential, particularly since research on technology applications is still maturing.

Creative, innovative, and positive teachers are particularly important in providing effective education for students with autism (Koegel, Kern-Koegel, & Carter, 1999). As noted earlier, these children present some unique and challenging qualities for instruction. Some seemingly insignificant actions by teachers can create great difficulties for students who have autism, difficulties that can easily be avoided if teachers are informed. For example, many high-functioning individuals with autism who have language skills interpret speech literally, so it is important to avoid using slang, idiom, and sarcasm. Such phrases might be translated literally by the individual with autism and teach something other than what is desired.

Parental participation in preparing children with autism for school and other segments of life can be of great assistance (Dunlap, 1999; Olley, 1999; U.S. Department of Education, 2000a). Such preparation can include objectives like instilling a positive attitude in the child, helping him or her with scheduling, and teaching him or her how to find the way around in school (for example, perhaps drawing a map of where to go based on the daily schedule). Also helpful is identifying a "safe" place and a "safe" person, should the child become confused or encounter a particularly upsetting event. The case study at the end of this chapter illustrates parental involvement as we revisit Billy, the youngster we met in the chapter opening snapshot.

■ PSYCHOLOGICAL AND MEDICAL INTERVENTIONS

Interventions based on the psychodynamic theory of causation historically focused on repairing emotional damage and resolving inner conflict. This approach is aimed at remedying the presumably faulty relationship between the child with autism and his or her parents, which often involved parental rejection or absence and resulted in withdrawal by the child (Frost, 1999; Heinemann, 1999). This treatment model has been criticized because of a relative absence of solid empirical evidence supporting its effectiveness. The internal psychological nature of problems, as seen by this approach, makes it very difficult to evaluate its effectiveness.

Various medical treatments have also been used for children with autism. Some early medical therapies (for example, electroconvulsive shock and psychosurgery) have been discarded for children with autism because these treatments appeared to have questionable results and harmful side effects. Likewise, certain medications used in the past had doubtful therapeutic value and were very controversial (like D-lysergic acid, more commonly known as LSD). Other medications used for people with autism have often included antipsychotic drugs, anticonvulsants, serotonergic drugs, and dopamine medication (Aman & Madrid, 1999; Hellings, 1999; Martin, Scahill, Klin, & Volkmar, 1999). Specific symptoms tend to be addressed with specific medication, such as obsessive–compulsive behaviors with clomipramine (Aman, et al., 1999); other antipsychotic drugs seem to help reduce some of the unusual speech patterns and self-injurious behaviors, particularly with older patients. Decreasing self-injury and social withdrawal has also been evident in some research on responses to other drugs (Aman & Madrid, 1999). However, other research on drug therapy has shown mixed or no improvement in the condition (Martin, Koenig, Scahill, & Bregman, 1999).

Generally, medication has shown some promising but mixed results in the treatment of autism. There appears to be potential for improvement, but such treatment should be used thoughtfully in conjunction with a multicomponent, comprehensive treatment plan (Tsai, 1999; Zager, 1999). Most authorities agree that autism represents such a heterogeneous set of symptoms that no single medication will effectively treat all children with the condition (Zimmerman, Jinnah, & Lockhart, 1998).

■ BEHAVIORAL INTERVENTIONS

Interventions using behavioral treatment for children with autism are undertaken without concern for an underlying causation of the disability. This approach focuses on enhancing appropriate behaviors and decreasing inappropriate or unadaptive behaviors (Kauffman, 2001). Behavior management for individuals with autism requires a statement of precise operational definition, observation, and recording of data on behaviors viewed as appropriate and inappropriate. Accurate and reliable data collection is a cornerstone of behavioral intervention, a process greatly enhanced by new technology. (See the Today's Technology box on page 390.)

Behavioral interventions may focus on conduct such as self-stimulation, tantrum episodes, or self-inflicted injury. Behavioral therapy has substantially reduced or eliminated these problem behaviors in many cases (Snell & Brown, 2000b; Westling & Fox, 2000). Behavioral treatment has also been effective in remediating deficiencies in fundamental social skills and language development as well as facilitating community integration for children with autism (Okyere, 1998; Smith & Philippen, 1999). Parental involvement in behavioral treatment has shown promising results. Research has also demonstrated that certain students with autism can be effectively taught to employ self-directed behavior management, which further enhances efficiency (Erba, 2000; U.S. Department of Education, 2000a).

It is important to emphasize that behavioral therapy does not make claims of curing autism. The procedures involved are very specific in focusing on limited behavioral areas that need attention. This approach seems effective for many children with autism, prompting decreases in problem behaviors and potential improvement of survival skills (e.g., Gerdtz, 2000). Such gains constitute a significant step toward normalization for both the children and their families.

In the early 1990s autism literature gave some attention to a treatment being used in Australia that specifically focuses on communication problems for people with autism. Known as *facilitative communication,* this procedure emphasizes the use of

■ EARLY CHILDHOOD YEARS

TIPS FOR THE FAMILY

■ Seek out and read information regarding autism, and become knowledgeable about the disability in all areas possible. Be an active partner in the treatment of your child; take parent training classes (e.g., behavior management workshops).

■ When working with the child with autism, concentrate on one behavior at a time as the target for change; emphasize work on the positive, increasing appropriate behavior rather than focusing solely on inappropriate behavior.

■ Involve all family members in learning about your child's disability and working with him or her when appropriate.

■ Protect your own health by obtaining respite care when needed to get rest or to get a break. You may need to devise a family schedule that allows adequate time for ongoing sleep and respite. Plan ahead for respite; otherwise, when you need it most, you will be too exhausted to find it.

■ Help prepare your child for school by instilling a positive attitude about it, helping him or her with the idea of a school schedule and how to find a "safe" place and "safe" person at school.

TIPS FOR THE PRESCHOOL TEACHER

■ Depending on the child's level of functioning, you may have to use physical cues or clear visual modeling to persuade him or her to do something; children

with autism may not respond to social cues.

■ Pair physical cues with verbal cues to begin teaching verbal compliance.

■ Limit instruction to one thing at a time; focus on what is concrete rather than abstract.

■ Avoid verbal overload by using short, directive sentences.

TIPS FOR PRESCHOOL PERSONNEL

■ Encourage the development of programs where older children model good behavior and interact intensely with children with autism.

■ Promote ongoing relationships between the preschool and medical personnel who can provide advice and assistance for children with autism.

■ Promote the initiation of parent–school relationships to assist both parents and preschool personnel in working together to meet the child's needs and offer mutual support.

■ Promote the appropriate involvement of nonteaching staff through workshops that provide information and awareness. Consistent interaction and expectations are important.

TIPS FOR NEIGHBORS AND FRIENDS

■ Be supportive of the parents and siblings of a child with autism. They may be under a high level of stress and need moral support.

■ Be positive with the parents. They may receive information that places blame on them, which should not be magnified by their friends.

■ Offer parents a respite to the degree that you're

comfortable; you may only give them a short time away to go to the store, but the break will be very helpful to them.

■ ELEMENTARY YEARS

TIPS FOR THE FAMILY

■ Be active in community efforts for children with autism; join local or national parent groups.

■ Use your knowledge and resources to identify a good program for your child; participate in this program in whatever arrangement might be available to parents.

■ Consistently follow through with the basic principles of your child's treatment program at home. This may mean taking more workshops or training on various topics.

■ Siblings of children with autism may find it difficult to understand the level of attention afforded to the sibling with autism. Siblings and parents need support and information.

■ Continue family involvement; be sensitive to the feelings of siblings who may be feeling left out or embarrassed by the child with autism.

■ It may be necessary to take safety precautions in the home (e.g., installing locks on all doors).

TIPS FOR THE GENERAL EDUCATION CLASSROOM TEACHER

■ Help with organizational strategies, assisting the student with autism with matters that are difficult for him or her (e.g., remembering how to use an eraser). Keep instruc-

tion as unrestrictive as possible, perhaps using a prompting note or picture somewhere.

■ Avoid abstract ideas unless they are necessary in instruction. Be as concrete as possible.

■ Communicate with specific directions or questions, not vague or open-ended statements.

■ If the child becomes upset, he or she may need to change activities or go to a place in the room that is "safe" for a period of time.

■ Use rules and schedules that are written with accompanying pictures so students clearly understand what is expected of them.

■ If the child is not learning a particular task, it may need to be broken down into smaller steps or presented through more than one medium (e.g., visual and verbal).

■ Begin preparing the child with autism for a more variable environment by programming and teaching adaption to changes in routine. Involve the child in planning for the changes, mapping out what they might be.

TIPS FOR SCHOOL PERSONNEL

■ Promote an all-school environment where children model appropriate behavior and receive reinforcement for it.

■ Develop peer-assistance programs, where older students can help tutor and model appropriate behavior for children with autism.

■ Encourage the development of strong, ongoing, school–parent relationships and support groups working together to meet the child's needs. Consistent expectations are important.

- Do not depend on the child with autism to take messages home to parents for any reason, except trying out this skill for him or her to learn; communication is a major problem, and even a note may be lost.

TIPS FOR NEIGHBORS AND FRIENDS

- If you interact with the child with autism, be positive and praise him or her for appropriate behavior.
- To the degree possible, ignore trivial disruptions or misbehaviors; focus on positive behaviors.
- Don't take misbehaviors personally; the child is not trying to make your life difficult or manipulate you.
- Avoid using nicknames or cute names such as "buddy" or "pal."
- Avoid sarcasm and idiomatic expressions, such as "beating around the bush." These children may not understand and may interpret what you say literally.

■ SECONDARY AND TRANSITION YEARS

TIPS FOR THE FAMILY

- Be alert to developmental and behavioral changes as the child grows older, watching for changing effects of a medication.
- Continue as an active partner in your child's educational and treatment program, planning for the transition to adulthood.
- Begin acquainting yourself with the adult services that will be available when your child leaves school. If he or she functions at a high level, consider or plan for adult living out of the family home.

TIPS FOR THE GENERAL EDUCATION CLASSROOM TEACHER

- Gradually increase the level of abstraction in teaching, remaining aware of the individual limitations the child with autism has.
- Continue preparing the student for an increasingly variable environment through instruction and example.
- Focus increasingly on matters of vital importance to the student as he or she matures (e.g., social awareness and interpersonal issues between the sexes).
- Teach the student with an eye toward postschool community participation, including matters such as navigating the community physically, activities, and employment. Teach the student about interacting with police in the community, since they require responses different from those appropriate for other strangers.*

TIPS FOR SCHOOL PERSONNEL

- To the degree possible for children with autism, promote involvement in social activities and clubs that enhance interpersonal interaction.
- Encourage the development of functional academic programs for students with autism that are combined with transition planning and programs.
- Promote a continuing working relationship with school staff and other agency personnel that might be involved in the student's overall treatment program (e.g., health care providers, social service agencies, and others).
- Work with other agencies that may encounter the child in the community

(e.g., law enforcement). Provide workshops, if possible, to inform officers regarding behavioral characteristics of people with autism that might be misinterpreted.

TIPS FOR NEIGHBORS AND FRIENDS

- Encourage a positive understanding of people with autism among other neighbors and friends who may be in contact with the child; help them to provide environmentally appropriate interaction.
- Promote the positive understanding of people with autism by community agencies that may encounter these individuals at this stage of life (e.g., law enforcement officials, fire department personnel).
- Support the parents as they consider the issues of adulthood for their child. Topics such as guardianship and community living may be difficult for parents to discuss.

■ ADULT YEARS

TIPS FOR THE FAMILY

- Continue to be alert for behavioral or developmental changes that may occur as the individual matures. Continued biological maturation may require medication adjustments.
- Continue to seek out adult services that are available to individuals with disabilities.
- Seek legal advice regarding plans for the future when you are no longer able to care for the family member with autism. Plan for financial arrangements and other needs that are appropriate, such as naming an advocate. Backup plans should be made; do not always count on the youngster's siblings. Con-

sider guardianship by other persons or agencies.

TIPS FOR THERAPISTS OR OTHER PROFESSIONALS

- Remain cognizant of the maturity level of the individual with whom you are working. Despite the presence of autism, some individuals have mature interests and inclinations. Do not treat the person as a child.
- Promote collaboration between appropriate adult service agencies to provide the most comprehensive services possible.

TIPS FOR NEIGHBORS AND FRIENDS

- Encourage a positive understanding of people with autism by other neighbors and friends who may be in contact with the adult having autism.
- Promote the positive understanding of people with autism by community agencies that may encounter these individuals at this stage of life (e.g., law enforcement officials, fire department personnel).
- Support the family members as they consider the issues of adulthood for the individual. Topics such as guardianship and community living may be difficult for parents and siblings to discuss.

*The authors appreciate Cathy Pratt's review of and contribution to this material (1994).

Source: A portion of this material is adapted from *High-Functioning Individuals with Autism: Advice and Information for Parents and Others Who Care*, by S. J. Moreno and A. M. Donellan, 1991, Crown Point, IN: Maap Services.

Today's Technology

COLLECTING DATA: THE VIDEX TIMEWAND

Most of us are familiar with the bar-code scanners used at checkout stands in many stores. The clerk passes the code symbol over a scanner, the price is instantly entered into the cash register, and a record of the sale is made for inventory control. This same technology is now being applied to coding and recording data on behavioral observations.

Known as the *Videx Time-Wand,* this device simplifies reliable data collection for behavioral interventions with a variety of conditions, such as autism. Appropriate and inappropriate behaviors are defined very specifically, and then each is given a code, which is translated into a bar-code symbol much like we see at the market. These bar codes are then placed on an observation sheet to be used by the observer. The observer also carries a small, portable bar-code reader with a wand that is passed over the relevant code symbol when that particular behavior is observed. Data on behavioral occurrences are recorded as well as clock-time stamped to indicate when the behavior occurred. These data are stored electronically (the unit will hold up to 16,000 characters of information) and transferred to a portable computer at the end of an observation session, for analysis and graphing.

Use of the TimeWand reduces the strain on therapists who were previously required to physically write down behavioral codes while attempting to continue observation. Use of this technology thereby improves the accuracy of data collection and also expedites data processing and translation into treatment action. Information regarding this automated data-collection method is available from Walter Nelson and Gordon Defalco at the Fircrest School in Seattle, Washington, or Richard Saunders at the Parson Research Center, University of Kansas.

---

typing as a means of communicating. A therapist–facilitator provides physical support by touching and putting light pressure on the student's arm or shoulder and interpersonal support through positive attitudes and interactions. Facilitative communication as a treatment for autism has been sufficiently controversial to prompt a number of special programs on national television news shows, featuring both proponents and critics. Although advocates of this treatment are emphatic in their support, other researchers are unable to obtain results supporting its effectiveness, raising serious questions regarding its soundness (Gresham, Beebe-Frankenberger, & MacMillan, 1999; Huebner & Emery, 1998; Witte-Bakken, 1998). Because of the facilitator's participation through touching the arm of the person, some question whether it is the facilitator communicating or the person with autism. While some interest continues, further objective research is clearly needed to clarify the role of

In a general education elementary school classroom, a young boy with autism receives help in language through verbalizing to a teacher's aide what he has drawn.

facilitated communication with individuals having autism (Cormier & Cormier, 1998; Ivey & Ivey, 1999).

Impact on the Family

The impact of a child with autism on his or her family members is enormous (Dewey, 1999; Randall & Parker, 1999). Living with such a child is exhausting and presents many challenges, including strained relationships, vastly and permanently increased financial burdens, social isolation, grief, and considerable physical and emotional fatigue (Lainhart, 1999; Rivers, 1999). The youngster with autism may sleep only a few hours each night and spend many waking hours engaged in self-abusive or disruptive behavior. It is easy to see how parents may feel as if they are in a marathon, 24 hours a day, seven days per week, with no respite. Not only is the family routine interrupted, but the constant demands are physically and emotionally draining, resulting in a number of problems for family members such as high stress levels, depression, and some affective disorders among mothers (Hecimovic, Powell, & Christensen, 1999; Randall & Parker, 1999; Rivers, 1999). The picture may be rather confusing for family members if the child with autism also has savant-like skills in some areas.

Siblings of children with autism may experience a number of problems, particularly during the early years. They may have difficulty understanding their parents' distress regarding their brother or sister and the level of attention afforded this child, and they may manifest stress or some depression (El Ghoroury & Romanczyk, 1999; Lainhart, 1999). Siblings may also have difficulty accepting the emotional detachment of the youngster, who might seem not to care for them at all. Like the siblings of children with other disabilities, brothers and sisters of a child with autism may be embarrassed and reluctant to bring friends home. However, if they can become informed and move beyond the social embarrassment, siblings can be a significant resource in assisting parents.

The arrival or diagnosis of a child with autism will present a significant challenge to parents and other family members (Mickelson, Wroble, & Helgeson, 1999; Midence & O'Neill, 1999; Rivers, 1999). Parents usually have to turn to multiple sources for assistance and information, and relations between professionals and parents are not simple or easy (Freedman & Boyer, 2000; Randall & Parker, 1999). Groups such as the Autism Society of America can provide a great deal of help and support from a perspective not available elsewhere. Parents may find that they have to become aggressive and vocal in their search for services from various agencies (Choutka, 1999). They must also be conscious of their own health and vitality, since their ability to cope will be significantly affected if they allow personal well-being to diminish. This requires respite time and care from a number of sources, from the family as a whole and outside agencies. Perhaps the most difficult issue is the realization that there are no clear-cut answers to many of the questions they have. Intervention to help different families and family members will need to be tailored for the specific needs of the circumstances and affected individuals (Freedman & Boyer, 2000; Hecimovic, et al., 1999; O'Neill, 1997).

Temple Grandin, an assistant professor of animal science at Colorado State University, is a high-functioning person with autism. In addition to writing several hundred papers on autism, she has revolutionized the treatment of animals and barn design for animals that are being raised for consumption.

Case Study

BILLY

What happens to a boy like Billy, who was discussed in the chapter opening snapshot? His parents are exhausted from years of caring for their son, who seems oblivious to their efforts. Placing him in the state hospital would be an easy answer, but Billy's parents sense that this would be disastrous for his development and later adjustment. If admitted to the state hospital, he could spend the rest of his life there.

This family was lucky. When Billy was ready to start school, the school district and the local mental health center arranged to place him in a special classroom within a regular public school. The classroom was well staffed, so that he had individual instruction and treatment from a teacher who was trained to manage children with behavior disorders. Billy's disruptive self-stimulation and tantrums were decreased through the use of time-out procedures (seclusion for short periods of time). Intense language training was implemented, and slowly he has learned more appropriate language. His echolalia has begun to disappear. When his appropriate behavior becomes stabilized in the classroom, he will begin an academic program and learn reading and writing.

There have also been changes for Billy's family. The mental health center offered a series of child management classes that taught the family, including Billy's brother, how to handle his disruptive behavior. The classes also gave Billy's family a chance to see that they were not alone and that other families had similar problems with their children who had disturbances. When the course was officially finished, the parents decided to continue meeting and planning for their children. The group members supported one another in times of need and worked actively to keep their children out of large institutions.

Although Billy is now making progress both behaviorally and academically, he will probably always have autism and be in need of special help. But great things are beginning to happen. The other day, just before the bus came to get Billy, he hugged his mother and kissed her good-bye for the first time, just like a normal boy.

■ APPLICATION

1. What impact do you think Billy's parents had on his ultimate prognosis as a child with autism?
2. How might the outcome been different if they had placed him in the state hospital?
3. Is it realistic for his mother to expect him to "grow out" of his autistic behaviors?

Source: Adapted from *Understanding Child Behavior Disorders* (2nd ed., p. 312) by D. M. Gelfand, W. R. Jenson, and C. J. Drew, 1988, New York: Holt, Rinehart and Winston.

Debate Forum

SELF-STIMULATION AS A REINFORCER?

Reinforcers as behavioral treatments are sometimes difficult to find for some children having autism. Teachers must often take what the client gives them to work with and remain flexible in designing an intervention program. Many individuals with autism do not respond to the same types of rewards that others do, and social rewards may not provide reinforcement or have any effect at all on these youngsters, at least in the initial stages of a treatment program. Research has also shown that, in some cases, tangible reinforcers may produce desired results, but they often seem to lose their power for individuals with autism. Given these circumstances, some researchers have suggested that self-stimulation, which appears to be a powerful and durable reinforcer, should be used to assist in teaching appropriate behavior. Self-stimulation is very different for each child and may involve manipulation of items such as coins, keys, and twigs.

■ POINT

Because reinforcers are often difficult to identify for children with autism, it is important to use whatever is available and practical in teaching these youngsters. Self-stimulation has been recognized as providing strong reinforcement for those who engage in it. Although typically viewed as an inappropriate behavior, self-stimulation may be very useful in teaching the beginning phases of more adaptive behavior and other skill acquisition. For some children with autism, it may be the most efficient reinforcer available, so why not use it, at least initially?

■ **COUNTERPOINT**

Using inappropriate behavior as a reinforcer carries with it certain serious problems and in fact may be unethical. The use of self-stimulation as a reinforcer may cause an increase in this behavior, making it an even more pronounced part of the child's inappropriate demeanor. Should this occur, it may make self-stimulation more difficult to eliminate later.

Review

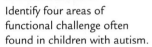 **focus 1**

Identify four areas of functional challenge often found in children with autism.

■ Language
■ Interpersonal skills
■ Emotional or affective behaviors
■ Intellectual functioning

 focus 2

What is the general range of prevalence estimated for autism?

■ Approximately 2 to 5 cases per 10,000

 focus 3

Identify six characteristics of children with autism.

■ As infants, they are often unresponsive to physical contact or affection from their parents and later have extreme difficulty relating to other people.
■ Most have impaired or delayed language skills, with about half not developing speech at all.
■ Those who have speech often engage in echolalia and other inappropriate behavior.
■ They frequently engage in self-stimulatory behavior.

■ Changes in their routine are met with intense resistance.
■ Most have a reduced level of intellectual functioning.

 focus 4

Identify the two broad theoretical views regarding the causes of autism.

■ The psychoanalytic view places a great deal of emphasis on the interaction between the family and the child.
■ The biological view has included neurological damage and genetics.

 focus 5

Identify four major approaches to the treatment of autism.

■ Psychoanalytic-based therapy focuses on repairing the emotional damage presumed to have resulted from faulty family relationships.
■ Medically based treatment often involves the use of medication.
■ Behavioral interventions focus on enhancing specific appropriate behaviors or on reducing inappropriate behaviors.
■ Educational interventions employ the full range of educational placements.

People with Traumatic and Acquired Brain Injury

To begin with . . .

ATLANTA (CNN)— An estimated 5.3 million Americans, a little more than 2% of the U.S. population, currently live with disabilities from traumatic brain injuries, according to a new report by the Centers for Disease Control and Prevention (CDC).

Each year, approximately 80,000 Americans experience the onset of disabilities resulting from brain injuries, the report says. The data released in the CDC study is considered the most complete picture of the impact of traumatic brain injuries (TBIs) in the United States. The National Center for Injury Prevention and Control, a division of the CDC and the Brain Injury Association, plans to use the data to assess the availability of proper medical, social, and support services across the country.

Other TBI statistics reported by the CDC indicated that each year, 1 million people are treated and released in hospital emergency rooms, and 50,000 people die.

The three leading causes of TBI are motor vehicle crashes, violence—mostly from firearms—and falls, particularly among the elderly. The risk of TBI in men is twice the risk in women. The risk is higher in adolescents, young adults, and people older than 75 years. Additionally:

- Each year, 230,000 persons are hospitalized with TBI and survive.
- Twenty-two percent of persons with TBI die.
- Two thirds of firearm-related TBIs are classified as suicidal in intent.
- Falls are the leading cause of TBI for persons age 65 and older; transportation-related injuries lead among the 5–64 population.
- Ninety-one percent of firearm-related TBIs result in death.
- Eleven percent of fall-related TBIs proved fatal. (Brain Injury Association, Inc., 1999a, p.1)

395

Ashley

Ashley was a very normal child, inquisitive and active. One of her great pleasures was having her picture taken at the local mall. Additionally, she loved to run and to blow bubbles. Her favorite activity was visiting the local pet and fish store. There she would move from aquarium to aquarium, pointing with great delight at her favorite fish. Her vocalizations were exuberant and elaborate even though they were not well understood. Nevertheless, it was clear that she delighted in seeing the fish and being with her mom in the store.

When Ashley was about 18 months old, her life changed in a matter of seconds. She and her mother had just attended a family party. On the way home, Ashley's mom decided to visit a friend and just say hi. After leaving the friend's home, they approached an intersection with the usual stoplight. The light was red and they stopped. Their car's left signal lights indicated their intention to turn, and they waited for traffic opposite them to clear. Ashley was comfortably placed in her car seat. As soon as the oncoming traffic cleared, they appropriately began the left turn.

Her mother relates the remainder of the story as follows: "As I looked out the left side, I saw this van coming toward us. I don't remember him hitting us. We know he did. Then the next thing I remember is being in the emergency room and thinking that everything was okay. If I'm fine, I knew Ashley was on the other side of the car in her car seat, in the back, strapped in, and I figured if I was okay, she was."

Several days passed before Ashley's mom was able to see her. "I went down and saw her a couple of days later. I was released from the hospital and that was the first time I was able to see her. And it was kind of hard to go down there and see your child hooked up to all these machines and just not move, just lie there."

Ashley spent the next 24 days in the intensive care unit (ICU) at Primary Children's Medical Center. She was then moved to a rehabilitation unit where she spent the next 4 months.

"During the time in rehab she went in and out of surgery. She had two internal shunts and two external shunt surgeries to relieve the pressure that had built up inside her head from the accident. When we brought her home she couldn't see. She was diagnosed cortically blind. She couldn't talk. It was just as if she was a newborn child. She had just barely learned to hold her head up before we left Primary, so it was like having this 30-pound newborn. One thing we missed the most was her smile. It's so nice to see it back."

C HILDREN, YOUTH, OR ADULTS who have experienced traumatic brain injuries are affected in many ways. Memory loss, concentration problems, slowed information processing, seizures, vision problems, severe headaches—any and all of these problems may be present in individuals who have suffered severe head trauma. Think what it might be like to lose your sense of taste; to be able to think of things to say, but not be able to actually speak them; and to know what it is like to throw a ball, but not be able to release the ball from your hand. The challenges associated with traumatic brain injury (TBI) can be fromidable.

Definition

■ TRAUMATIC BRAIN INJURY (TBI). Direct injuries to the brain, such as tearing of nerve fibers, bruising of the brain tissue against the skull, brain stem trauma, and swelling.

T raumatic brain injury (TBI) "may occur when there is a blow to the head or when the head slams against a stationary object. Such injuries happen, for example, in car accidents when the head hits the windshield, or in bicycle accidents when the head hits the ground. The brain may also be injured by [the] penetration of foreign objects, such as bullets or lawn darts" (Tyler & Mira, 1999, p. 1). The trauma caused by the rapid acceleration or deceleration of the brain may cause the tearing of important nerve fibers in the brain, the bruising of brain itself as it impacts the skull, brain stem injuries, and brain swelling (see nearby Reflect on This feature). Injuries that do not involve the penetration of the skull are referred to as closed-head or generalized head injuries. Head injuries in children are usually of this type. Focal or open-head injuries, such as gunshot wounds, are not common among children.

Two types of brain damage, primary and secondary, have been described by medical professionals. *Primary damage* is a direct outcome of the initial impact to the brain. *Secondary damage* develops over time as the brain responds to the initial trauma (Hill, 1999). For instance, an adolescent who is hit accidentally with a baseball bat may develop a hematoma, an area of internal bleeding within the brain. This may be the primary damage. However, with the passage of time, the brain's response to the initial injury may be pervasive swelling, which may cause additional insult to the brain. This is referred to as secondary damage.

focus 1
Identify three key elements of traumatic brain injury.

The Individuals with Disabilities Act (IDEA) defines traumatic brain injury as

an acquired injury to the brain caused by an external force, resulting in total or partial functional disability or psychosocial impairment, or both, that adversely affects a student's educational performance. The term applies to open and closed head injuries resulting in impairments in one or more areas, such as cognition, language, memory, attention, reasoning, abstract thinking, judgment, problem-solving, sensory, perceptual, and motor abilities; psychosocial behavior, physical functions, information processing, and speech. The term does not apply to brain injuries that are congenital or degenerative or brain injuries induced by birth trauma. (Federal Register, Vol. 57, No. 189, p. 44,802).

A student must have an injury that significantly influences educational performance in order to receive special education services.

Another term, **acquired brain injury (ABI),** "refers to both traumatic brain injuries, such as open or closed head injuries, and nontraumatic brain injuries, such as strokes and other vascular accidents, infectious disease (e.g., encephalitis, meningitis), anoxic injuries (e.g., hanging, near-drowning, choking, anesthetic accidents, severe blood loss), metabolic disorders (e.g., insulin shock, liver and kidney disease), and toxic products taken into the body through inhalation or ingestion. The term does not refer to brain injuries that are congenital or brain injuries induced by birth trauma" (Savage & Wolcott, 1994a, pp. 3–4). These traumatic and acquired brain injuries result in disabilities that may adversely affect individuals' information processing, social behaviors, memory capacities, reasoning and thinking, speech and language skills, and sensory and motor abilities (Tyler & Mira, 1999). (See the nearby Reflect on This feature.)

Prevalence

According to the most recent data from the Centers for Disease Control and Injury Prevention, "it is now estimated that there are 5.3 million children and adults living with the consequences of sustaining a traumatic brain injury in the United States. This number represents nearly 2% of the population" (Brain Injury Association, Inc., 1999b, p. 3). About 1 in 5 children of school age is hospitalized each year because of head injuries. In fact, 1 out of every 30 students will experience some form of significant head injury before they are 16 years of age

■ ACQUIRED BRAIN INJURY (ABI). A more global term than *traumatic brain injury (TBI)*. It refers to injuries that may result from strokes and other vascular accidents, infectious diseases, anoxic injuries (hanging, near-drowning), anesthetic accidents, severe blood loss, metabolic disorders, and ingestion of toxic products.

Reflect on This

(Hill, 1999). Of all the head injuries that occur, 40% involve children. The statistics associated with traumatic brain injury are sobering (see Table 13.1). About 2% to 5% of the children and youth who experience TBI develop severe neurologic complications (Jaffe et al., 1992; Rudolph & Kamei, 1994). Most of these injuries could be prevented with proper use of seat belts, child restraints, helmets, and other preventive measures.

The incidence of TBI peaks during three specific age periods. Children below five years of age, individuals between 15 and 24 years of age, and individuals over 70 years of age are more likely to experience head injuries (Novack, 1999). The peaking of injuries in the 15–24 years age bracket is attributable to several factors, including increased participation in contact sports, greater access to and use of automo-

TABLE 13.1 TBI in the United States

- 1 million to 5 million head injuries occur every year in children alone.
- 4 people sustain a TBI every minute.
- 40% of all head injuries occur in children.
- 75,000 to 100,000 Americans die per year as a result of TBI; 1 person dies every 12 minutes.
- TBI is the leading cause of death related to trauma; since 1980, the death rate from TBI has exceeded total deaths from all wars during the past 200 years.
- 10 of every 100,000 children between infancy and age 14 die each year from head trauma; this rate is 5 times greater than death from leukemia, the second leading cause of mortality in children.
- 75% of people sustaining TBI are under the age of 34; TBI occurs most often in persons aged 15 to 24.
- 25,000 children are killed or permanently injured as a result of TBI annually.
- 166,000 children are hospitalized annually as a result of TBI; 16,000 to 20,000 children display moderate to severe symptoms of injury.
- 70,000 to 90,000 Americans suffer lifelong physical, intellectual, and psychological disabilities annually as a result of TBI.
- There are 5,000 new cases of epilepsy and 2,000 cases of persistent vegetative state per year resulting from TBI.
- Each severe head injury survivor requires between $4.1 and $9.0 million for a lifetime of care.
- In 1974, the total lifetime costs for survivors of acute TBI were estimated at $2.43 billion; by 1985, the costs had risen tenfold to $24 billion.

Source: Adapted from Table 13.3, p. 256, in *Meeting the Needs of Students with Special Needs,* by J. L. Hill, 1999, Upper Saddle River, NJ: Merrill.

DON'T FEEL SORRY FOR ME. I'M A FIGHTER!

When Skyline High School named Emily Jensen junior prom queen, she struggled to the stage, clinging to the arm of the student body president. She is, after all, learning how to walk again.

Ten months ago, a 15-passenger van smashed into Jensen's car, putting her into the most severe coma possible for three months. Upon awakening, a tear in her brain prevented her from performing even basic functions like swallowing.

But when her name was announced in the auditorium Friday, Jensen claimed her crown and sash, wearing a red satin dress, black jacket, and rhinestone necklace, and row after row of her classmates rose and cheered as she passed.

"It was such a touching moment, an amazing victory," Emily's mother, Terri Jensen, recalled Monday. "For a kid who has had so many hard and painful moments, it was a very sweet one."

In a contest usually won by cheerleaders and athletes, the student body reached a "higher level" by picking Jensen, said principal Kathy Clark.

Terri Jensen said her youngest daughter probably always will have some difficulties. Though doctors have not given the Jensen family any prognosis, they have their own ideas. Mom, who spends nearly every hour with her youngest daughter of three, expects to return to work as a fourth-grade teacher next year.

In a poem she dictated to her mother, that was later printed in a Skyline newsletter, Emily explained her determination.

"The pain of having my life taken away from me is more tangible than anything I know," she wrote. "But don't feel sorry for me. I'm a fighter."

Source: From "Prom Queen Raises the Bar at Skyline," by Heather May, *Salt Lake Tribune* (1999, February 15), pp. B1, B10.

■ POSTSCRIPT FROM EMILY'S NEUROLOGIST, DR. VERA FRANCES TAIT

As a pediatric neurologist and a bureau director of children with special health care needs, I had the opportunity of caring for Emily during her 6-month hospitalization and subsequent rehabilitation. Because of the traumatic brain injury that she sustained, she has had to relearn everything, almost as if from birth—chewing, swallowing, eating orally, talking, crawling, sitting, standing, and walking. In 20 years of working as a neurologist, I have never seen anyone more determined than Emily (nor have I seen anyone work harder than Emily). When I describe the situation to others, I compare her work to doing a cognitive and physical marathon—every day. Throughout this terrible ordeal, she has never lost her hope, her discipline, her love of learning, or her sense of humor. She has even insisted on additional exercise at home after school and after her daily regimen of physical, occupational, and speech therapy. I have seen very few young adults or adults, for that matter, with the courage that Emily displays daily.

Source: From a personal communication by Dr. Vera Frances Tait, 20 March 2001.

---

biles, more frequent use of racing and mountain bikes, and injuries sustained from firearms. The number of head injuries in males exceeds that in females. As a rule, males are two to three times more likely to sustain serious head injuries, particularly during the adolescent years (Hill, 1999). (See the nearby Reflect on This feature.)

The rate of mortality for TBI is 30 per 100,000. Fifty percent of those who die as a result of their injuries do so within the first two hours following the accident or insult to the brain. Obviously, medical care at the scene of the accident is crucial. Emergency treatment in the field and in the hospital can make a big difference in survival rates of injured individuals. Nevertheless, many die as a result of severe head injuries (Novack, 1999).

Characteristics

Individuals with traumatic or acquired brain injury present a variety of challenges to families and professionals. The injuries may affect every aspect of an individual's life (Bigler, Clark, & Farmer, 1997; Bowe, 2000; Hill, 1999; Raymond et al., 1999; Tyler & Mira, 1999). Additionally, the resulting disabilities have a profound effect on the individual's family (Conoley & Sheridan, 1997; Tyler & Mira,

Most of the head injuries five million children experience annually could be prevented with the proper use of such preventative aids as helmets, seat belts, and child restraints.

focus 2

Identify four general characteristics of individuals with traumatic or acquired brain injuries.

1999; Wade et al., 1997). Often the injuries radically change the individuals' capacity for learning (Hill, 1999; Lord-Maes & Obrzut, 1997).

Generally, the individual will need services and supports in four areas: cognition, speech and language, social and behavioral skills, and physical functioning. Cognitive problems have an impact on thinking and perception. For example, individuals with a brain injury may be unable to remember or retrieve newly learned information. They may be unable to attend or concentrate for appropriate periods of time. Another serious problem is the person's inability to adjust or respond flexibly to changes in home or school environments (D'Amato & Rothlisberg, 1997; Lord-Maes & Obrzut, 1997).

A person with TBI may also struggle with speech, producing unintelligible sounds or indistinguishable words. Speech may be slurred and labored. The individual may know what he or she wants to say, but be unable to express it. Professionals use the term **aphasia** to describe this condition. **Expressive aphasia** refers to an inability to express one's own thoughts and desires. Language problems may also be evident. For example, a school-age student may be unable to retrieve a desired word or expression, particularly during a "high demand" instructional setting or during an anxiety-producing social situation. Given their difficulties with word retrieval, individuals with TBI may reduce their overall speech output or use repetitive expressions or word substitutions. Interestingly, many children with brain injuries express great frustration in knowing an answer to a question, but being unable to retrieve it when called on by teachers. (See Chapter 10 for additional information on expressive aphasia.)

Social and behavior problems may present the most challenging aspects of TBI and ABI. For many individuals, the injury produces significant changes in their personalities, their temperaments, their dispositions for certain activities, and their behaviors. In fact, the social and behavior problems may worsen over time, depending on the nature of the injury, the pre-injury adjustment of the individual and family, and other factors such as the age at time of the injury and the treatment provided immediately following the injury. Behavior effects include increased irritability and emotionality, compromised motivation and judgment, an inability to restrict socially inappropriate behaviors, insensitivity to others, and low thresholds for frustration and inconvenience (D'Amato & Rothlisberg, 1997; Kehle, Clark, & Jenson, 1997).

▪ APHASIA. An acquired language disorder caused by brain damage that is characterized by complete or partial impairment of language comprehension, formulation, and use.

▪ EXPRESSIVE APHASIA. An inability to express verbally one's own thoughts and desires.

Neuromotor and physical disabilities are also characteristic of individuals with brain injuries. Neuromotor problems may be exhibited through poor eye–hand coordination. For example, an adolescent may be able to pick up a ball, but be unable to produce the motions and efforts to throw it to someone else. In addition, there may be impaired balance, an inability to walk unassisted, significantly reduced stamina, or paralysis. Impaired vision and hearing may also be present. The array and depth of the challenges faced by individuals with brain injuries and their families can be overwhelming and disheartening. However, with appropriate support and coordinated, interdisciplinary treatment, the individual and family can move forward with their lives and develop effective coping skills (Farmer, 1997; Silver & Oakland, 1997).

Causation

The causes of brain injury vary according to the age and developmental status of the affected individual (Hill, 1999). The highest incidence of injury in all age groups is automobile-related accidents. For small children, the most common cause is a "fall from a short distance" (Haslam, 1996, p. 325). Such children may fall from a tree, playground equipment, their parent's arms, or furniture. Another major cause of injury in young children is physical abuse. These injuries generally come from shaking or striking infants. The actions may cause sheering of brain matter or severe bleeding (Hill, 1999; Tyler & Mira, 1999). Other common causes of head injuries in older children include falls from playground swings or climbers, bicycles, or trees; blows to the head from baseball bats, balls, or other sports equipment; and pedestrian accidents.

The first signs of brain injury often manifest themselves in a coma. The severity and nature of complications and the eventual outcomes of the trauma are a function of the location and degree of injury to the brain (see Table 13.2). Jennett and Teasdale (1974) developed a scale to assess the potential impact of head injuries in children and predict their eventual functioning (see Table 13.3). Scores of 3 to 5 generally indicate poor outcomes in children over time (Haslam, 1996).

The number of children and others who experience serious head trauma would be significantly reduced if seat belts and other child-restraint devices were consistently used. Further reductions in such injuries would be achieved by significantly

focus 3

Identify the most common causes of brain injury in children, youth, and adults.

TABLE 13.2	Descriptors of TBI severity
Minor	No loss of consciousness; head injury not seen by a physician; a minor bump.
Mild	Mild or transient loss of consciousness, if any; child may be lethargic and not be able to recall the injury; child may vomit (if more than three times, should be seen by emergency room staff).
Moderate	Loss of consciousness is typically less than 5 minutes; on recovery, the child may be able to move spontaneously and purposefully; opens eyes in response to pain. Older children or youth may be combative, telling others to "leave me alone."
Severe	Loss of consciousness ranges from 5 to 30 minutes. Surgery may be needed if skull is fractured significantly; neurologic consequences are common.
Serious	Loss of consciousness more that 30 minutes, notable neurologic consequences are typical.

Source: Adapted from *Head Injuries* (p. 255), by J. L. Hill, 1999, Upper Saddle River, NJ: Merrill.

TABLE 13.3 Glasgow Coma Scale

Activity	Score	Description
Best Motor Response		
Obeys commands	6	Follows simple verbal directions
Localized pain	5	Moves arms and legs to escape painful stimuli
Withdrawal from pain	4	Normal reflex responses
Abnormal flexion	3	"Decorticate"—abnormal adduction of shoulder
Extensor posturing	2	"Decerebrate"—internal rotation of shoulder and pronation of forearm
No response	1	Limp, without evidence of spinal transection
Best Verbal Response		
Oriented	5	Aware of self, environment, time, and situation
Confused	4	Attention is adequate and patient is responsive, but responses suggest disorientation and confusion
Inappropriate	3	Understandable articulation, but speech is used in a nonconversational (exclamatory or swearing manner); conversation is not sustained
Incomprehensible	2	Verbal response (moaning) but without recognizable words
No response	1	
Eye Opening		
Spontaneous	4	Eyes are open; scored without reference to awareness
To speech	3	Eyes are open to speech or shout without implying a response to a direct command
To pain	2	Eyes are open with painful stimulus to limbs or chest
None	1	No eye opening, not attributable to swelling

Source: Adapted from "Assessment of Coma and Impaired Consciousness," by B. Jennett & G. Teasdale, 1974, *Lancet,* 2, pp. 81–84.

decreasing accidents due to driving under the influence of alcohol and other mind-altering substances (Bowe, 2000).

Programs directed at reducing the number of individuals who drive while under the influence of alcohol or other substances should be vigorously supported. Likewise, steps should be taken to use other accident-prevention procedures, including wearing appropriate protective devices such as helmets and obeying safety rules that reduce the probability of serious accidents. (See nearby Reflect on This feature.)

Educational Supports and Services

Educational supports focus on environmental changes and critical transition issues in returning the child or youth to appropriate school settings. Specific teaching techniques and practices should be informed by current research about learning, the brain, and acquired brain injuries (Jensen, 1999). It is

YOU REALLY WANT TO RIDE A BICYCLE?

Riding a bicycle can be a lot of fun. Bicycles can be a means of transportation, physical fitness, or racing. However, bicycle riding poses many risks and should always be done correctly. Children should never abuse the right to ride a bicycle.

CRASH STATISTICS

- A child is four times more likely to be seriously injured in a bicycle crash than kidnapped by a stranger.

- More kids, ages 5 to 14, go to hospital emergency rooms with injuries related to biking than with any other sport.
- Each year, about 567,000 people go to hospital emergency departments with bicycle-related injuries; about 350,000 of those injured are children under 15. Of those children, about 130,000 sustain brain injuries.
- Each year, bicycle crashes kill about 900 people; about 200 of those killed are children under age 15.

- Statistics show that between 70% and 80% of all fatal bicycle crashes involve brain injuries.
- Ninety percent of bicycle-related deaths involve collisions with motor vehicles.

WHO, WHAT, WHEN, AND WHY

- The number of people who ride bicycles rose from 66.9 million in 1991 to 80.6 million in 1998.
- Distribution of bicycle deaths in 1996: 49% of all deaths occurred between 3 P.M. and 9 P.M.

BICYCLE HELMETS

- Ninety-six percent of bicyclists killed in 1996 were reportedly not wearing helmets.
- Medical research shows that 88% of cyclists' brain injuries can be prevented by a bicycle helmet.
- Universal use of helmets could prevent one death every day and one brain injury every four minutes.

Source: From *Bicycle Safety,* developed by the Brain Injury Association, Inc., 2000a, Alexandria, Virginia.

---

essential that educators and health providers work together in effectively blending clinical, educational, and family interventions (Tyler & Mira, 1999). Unfortunately, many children with brain injuries leave hospitals or rehabilitation settings without adequate preparation for the new environments in which they find themselves (Clark, 1997). They are not ready to return to school. Many teachers who receive these students are not adequately prepared to respond to their cognitive, academic, and behavioral needs (Clark, 1997; Savage & Mishkin, 1994).

Before the child or youth exits the hospital or rehabilitation facility, several issues and questions need to be addressed by medical, psychological, and educational personnel (see Figure 13.1). Pertinent questions include the following:

- *How severe was the injury? What is the prognosis for continued recovery?*
- *What are the major health-related needs of the child? Is an individual health plan needed to establish a protocol for treatment at school?*
- *Are seizures or other neurological problems likely? What changes in behavior indicate that a physician should be contacted?*
- *Are activity restrictions needed to ensure safety and well-being?*
- *What medications are prescribed? Do they have side effects? Do they need to be administered at school?*
- *What is the impact of the brain injury on the child's ability to learn new information in verbal and visual–spatial modalities? Are problems with new learning due primarily to deficits in attention, comprehension, memory, response insufficiency, speed of processing, or reasoning?*
- *In what areas (e.g., language arts, mathematics, science) is the child most likely to experience success?*
- *What content area may prove difficult or overwhelming for the learner? What modifications, if any, would facilitate the child's performance in those areas (reading partners,*

FIGURE 13.1   Suggested School Reintegration Checklist

Student: _____   School/Grade: _____

Date of Injury: _____   Parent Name: _____   Phone #: _____

1. IMMEDIATELY FOLLOWING INJURY

A school representative will be assigned to the case by administrator. The school representative will:

Contact parent(s) to:

- inquire about their child's condition
- obtain release for hospital contact (get release to and from school)

Contact the child's case manager at the hospital to:

- inform them of the school's concern

Meet with the child's classroom teacher(s) to:

- inform them of the child's condition
- obtain/review current educational records

2. AFTER STUDENT'S CONDITION HAS STABILIZED

The school representative will:

Arrange a meeting with the hospital care manager to:

- obtain information regarding the child's condition
- determine if/when to send schoolwork

3. PRIOR TO DISCHARGE

The school representative will:

Visit with student and rehabilitation staff

Obtain copies of hospital evaluations (psychological, educational, physical therapy/occupational therapy, speech)

Conduct in-service in school to:

- provide specific information about the school's condition
- provide more general information about TBI
- discuss potential modifications (ramp, wheelchair, lighting)

4. IMMEDIATELY AFTER HOSPITAL DISCHARGE

The school representative will:

Contact parent(s) to:

- determine if the child will be getting post-acute rehabilitation care
- set a tentative date for return to school if no further rehabilitation is being provided

Follow up with a hospital case manager to:

- get update on discharge condition/special needs (i.e., tracheotomy, ambulation)

Establish a TBI team and designate a case manager (if different from representative) to:

- develop a tentative plan for school reentry (consider need for environmental modifications, special education, 504, and related services)

5. ARRIVAL AT SCHOOL

The team will:

- assign further personnel to conduct initial evaluation and give feedback to teachers and parents
- further modify classroom environment to meet student's needs

6. AFTER FIRST WEEKS AT SCHOOL

The team will:

- reassess the student's needs and modify educational plan accordingly
- maintain contact with parents and teachers

Source: From *Children and Adolescents with Traumatic Brain Injury: Reintegration Challenges in Educational Settings* (p. 202), by E. Clark, 1997, Austin, TX: Pro-Ed, Inc. Reprinted with permission.

cooperative learning activities, peer tutoring, . . . calculators)? (Farmer et al., 1997, pp. 40–41, 43, & 49)

These questions provide valuable information for school personnel and others who must plan for and implement the youngster's reentry into school (Farmer et al., 1997). Generally, a liaison or case manager works with other medical and health personnel to make certain that the child or youth is safe and sufficiently healthy to leave the health care facility. Additionally, the transition liaison ensures that parents and teachers are adequately prepared to receive and care for the child (Clark, 1997; Stuart & Goodsitt, 1996).

Students with traumatic or acquired brain injuries may return to one of several school placements, depending on their needs. Appropriate teaching activities include establishing high expectations, reducing antecedents that elicit challenging behaviors, using appropriate reductive techniques for stopping or significantly reducing aggressive or noncompliant behaviors, eliminating rewards for negative or problematic behaviors, providing precise feedback, giving students strategies for organizing information, and providing many opportunities for practice (Blosser & DePompei, 1994; Gillis, 1996; Kehle et al., 1997).

focus 4

Describe the focus of educational interventions for students with traumatic or acquired brain injuries.

Educational services must be tailored to a student's specific needs. Effort should be directed at improving students' general behaviors, such as problem solving, planning, and developing insight. Teaching may also focus on appropriate social behaviors (performing in stressful situations, improving initiative taking, working with others, etc.), expressive and receptive language skills (word retrieval, event description, understanding instructions, reading nonverbal cues, etc.), and writing skills (sentence development, legibility, etc.) (see Table 13.4).

The initial individualized education programs (IEPs) for students with brain injuries should be written for short periods of time, perhaps six to eight weeks (D'Amato & Rothlisberg, 1997). Moreover, these IEPs should be reviewed often to make adjustments based on the progress and growth of students. Often, students improve dramatically in the first year following their injuries. Children and youth with TBI generally experience the most gains in the first year following the injury, with little progress made thereafter (Tyler & Mira, 1999). Flexibility and responsiveness on the part of teachers and other support staff are essential to the well-being of students with traumatic and acquired brain injuries (D'Amato & Rothlisberg, 1997).

For students who want to move on to postsecondary education, interdisciplinary team members may contribute significantly to the transition process. Critical factors include the physical accessibility of the campus, living arrangements, support for academic achievement, social and personal support systems, and career/vocational training and placement (Bergland & Hoffbauer, 1996; Tyler & Mira, 1999).

For students who might find it difficult to continue their schooling after high school, transition planning for employment is essential. Prior to leaving high school, these students with TBI should have skills associated with filling out job applications, interviewing for jobs, and participating in supervised work experiences. State vocational agencies also play key roles in assisting young people with TBI following high school. They provide services related to aptitude assessment, post–high school training opportunities, and trial job placements (Tyler & Mira, 1999).

Collaboration and cooperation are the key factors in achieving success with individuals with traumatic and acquired brain injuries. A great deal can be accomplished when families, students, and care providers come together, engage in appropriate planning, and work collaboratively (Farmer, 1997; Hill, 1999).

Impairment	Classroom Behaviors	Skills and Teaching Strategies
General Behaviors		
Decreased judgment	Is impulsive	Establish a system of verbal or nonverbal signals to cue the student to alter behavior (e.g., call the student's name, touch the student, use a written sign or hand signal).
Poor problem-solving skills	Does not carefully think through solutions to situations	To help develop problem-solving skills, ask questions designed to help the student identify the problem. Plan and organize implementation of a solution together.
Social Behaviors		
Subtle noncompliance with classroom rules and activities	Is withdrawn and unwilling to participate in group activities (e.g., work on a science project, small group discussion) Refuses to recite in class even when called upon	Help the student strengthen his or her self-concept. Begin to elicit responses from the student during individual activities and seat work when you can be assured that the student can answer correctly; gradually request occasional responses in front of the student's friends, then in small groups; repeat until the student feels comfortable participating in a large group.
Rudeness, silliness, immaturity	Makes nasty or inappropriate comments to fellow students and teachers Laughs aloud during serious discussions or quiet seat work	Help the student develop better judgment by presenting "what if" situations and choices. Discuss the student's responses together. Give the student opportunities to verbally express judgment and decision making regarding appropriate behavior as well as opportunities to role-play such behaviors.
Expressive Language		
Tangential (rambling) communication	Tends to ramble without acknowledging the listener's interest or attention May discuss the appropriate topic, but not focus on the key concept (e.g., when asked to name the major food groups, the student might begin a discussion about growing crops)	When the student begins to digress from the topic, either provide a nonverbal cue or stop the student from continuing in front of classmates. Teach the student to recognize nonverbal behaviors indicating lack of interest or desire to make a comment. (Work with this skill during private conversations with the student.) Teach about the beginning, middle, and ending of stories. Stop the student's response and restate the original question, focusing the student's attention on the key issues.

TABLE 13.4 *(continued)*

Impairment	Classroom Behaviors	Skills and Teaching Strategies
Expressive Language		
Word retrieval errors	Answers using many vague terms ("this," "that," "those things," "whatchamacallits")	To improve word recall, teach the student to use association skills and to give definitions of words he or she cannot recall.
	Has difficulty providing answers in fill-in-the-blank tests	Teach memory strategies (rehearsal, association, visualization, etc.).
Receptive Language		
Inability to determine salient features of questions asked, information presented, or assignments read	Completes the wrong assignment (e.g., teacher requested that the class complete problems 9–12; this student completed problems 1–12)	Encourage the student to write assignments in a daily log.
Inability to read nonverbal cues	Is unaware that the teacher or other classmates do not want to be bothered while they are working	To raise social awareness, use preestablished nonverbal cues to alert the student that the behavior is inappropriate. Explain what was wrong with the behavior and what would have been appropriate.
Written Language		
Simplistic sentence structure and syntactic disorganization	Uses sentences and chooses topics that are simplistic compared with expectations for age and grade; writes themes that are short and dry	Provide the student with worksheets that focus on vocabulary, grammar, and proofreading skills.
Decreased speed and accuracy; poor legibility	Is slower on timed tests than classmates	Accept that the student will take longer to complete assignments; reduce and alter the requirements.

Source: From "Creating an Effective Classroom Environment," by J. L. Blosser and R. DePomei. In *Educational Dimensions of Acquired Brain Injury,* edited by R. C. Savage and G. F. Wolcott, 1994, pp. 413–451. Austin, TX: Pro-Ed, Inc. Reprinted by permission.

Medical and Psychological Services

New medical technologies have revolutionized diagnostic and treatment procedures for traumatic and acquired brain injuries (Bigler et al., 1997). In previous decades, the vast majority of these individuals died within a short time of their accidents. With the development of **computed tomography (CT)** scans, intracranial pressure monitors, **magnetic resonance imaging (MRI),** and the capacity to control bleeding and brain swelling, many individuals with truamatic brain injury survive (Savage & Wolcott, 1994a). Also, CT scans of individuals without brain injuries now provide physicians and other health care providers with essential, normative information about the extent of the injury to the brain in comparison to the uninjured brains of other individuals of the same age and gender (Bigler, 1997).

Head injuries may be described according to the nature of the injury. Injuries include concussions, contusions, skull fractures, and epidural and subdural hemorrhages.

focus 5

Identify four common types of head injuries.

▪ COMPUTED TOMOGRAPHY (CT). A technique of x-ray imaging by which computers create cross-sectional images of specific body areas or organs.

▪ MAGNETIC RESONANCE IMAGING (MRI). An imaging technique by which computers create cross-sectional images of specific body areas or organs.

■ EARLY CHILDHOOD YEARS

TIPS FOR THE FAMILY

- Become fully informed about your child's condition.
- Become familiar with special services available in your school and with health care systems.
- Develop positive relationships with care providers.
- Seek out appropriate assistance through advocacy and support groups.
- Pursue family or individual counseling for persistent relationship-centered problems.
- Develop sensible routines and schedules for the child.
- Communicate with siblings, friends, and relatives; help them become informed about the injury and their role in the treatment process.

TIPS FOR THE PRESCHOOL TEACHER

- Communicate with parents, special education personnel, and health care providers to develop appropriate expectations, management, and instruction.
- Interact frequently with parents, special education

personnel, and health care providers.
- Watch for abrupt changes in the child's behavior. If they occur, notify parents and other professionals immediately.
- Involve socially sophisticated peers and other older children in working with the preschooler with TBI.
- Become familiar with events that "set the child off."
- Use management procedures that promote appropriate independence and foster learning.

TIPS FOR PRESCHOOL PERSONNEL

- Participate in orientation and team meetings with the preschool teacher.
- Develop an understanding of the child and the condition.
- Communicate frequently with the preschool teacher and parents about concerns and promising developments.
- Employ the same management strategies used by the parents and preschool teacher.
- Be patient with the rate of progress behaviorally, socially, and academically.

- Help other children understand the child.

TIPS FOR NEIGHBORS AND FRIENDS

- Offer to become educated about the condition and its impact on the child.
- Become familiar with recommended management procedures for directing the child.
- Inform your own children about the dynamics of the condition; help them understand how to react and respond to variations in behavior.
- Involve the child in appropriate family activities.

■ ELEMENTARY YEARS

TIPS FOR THE FAMILY

- Remember that the transition back to the school and family environment requires explicit planning and preparation.
- Prepare siblings, peers, and neighbors for the child's return to the home and community.
- Learn about and use management procedures that promote the child's well-being.
- Carefully plan with school personnel the child's re-entry into school.

TIPS FOR THE GENERAL EDUCATION CLASSROOM TEACHER

- Become fully familiar with the child's condition.
- Communicate with medical and other personnel about expectations, management strategies, and approaches for dealing with persisting problems.
- Use appropriate routines and schedules to foster learning and good behavior.
- Help other children understand how they can contribute to the child's growth and healing within the classroom setting.
- Let peers and older youngsters work with the student on academic and social tasks.
- Do not be reluctant to communicate with other professionals and parents when problems occur.
- Remember that teamwork among caring professionals and parents is essential to the child's success.

TIPS FOR SCHOOL PERSONNEL

- Become informed; seek to understand the unique characteristics of TBI.
- Behave as if the child were your own.

- Seek to understand and use instructional and management approaches that are well suited to the child.
- Use the expertise that is present in the school and school system; collaborate with other specialists.

TIPS FOR NEIGHBORS AND FRIENDS

- Adopt an inclusive attitude about family and neighborhood events; invite the child or youth to join in family-centered activities, picnics, appropriate recreational and sports activities, and holiday events.
- Learn how to respond effectively and confidently to the common problems that the child or youth may present.
- Communicate concerns and problems immediately in a compassionate fashion.

SECONDARY AND TRANSITION YEARS

TIPS FOR THE FAMILY

- Prepare and plan for the secondary, transitional, and adult years.
- Work closely with school and adult services personnel in developing a transition plan.
- Develop a thoughtful and comprehensive transition plan that includes educa-tion, employment, housing, and use of leisure time.
- Become aware of all the services and resources that are available through state and national funding.
- Begin to develop plans for the individual's care and support over the lifespan.

TIPS FOR THE GENERAL EDUCATION CLASSROOM TEACHER

- Be sure that appropriate steps have been taken to prepare the youth to return to school and related activities.
- Realize that there will be significant changes in the youth's functioning—academically, socially, and behaviorally.
- Work closely with members of the multidisciplinary team in developing appropriate schooling and employment experiences.
- Report any changes in behavior immediately to parents and other specialists within the school.

TIPS FOR SCHOOL PERSONNEL

- Determine what environmental changes need to be made.
- Employ teaching procedures that best fit the youth's current cognitive status and academic functioning.
- Consider having the youth gradually phased into a complete school day.
- Be prepared for emotions of anger, depression, and rebellion.
- Focus on the youth's current strengths.
- Help the youth develop appropriate compensatory skills.

TIPS FOR NEIGHBORS, FRIENDS, AND POTENTIAL EMPLOYERS

- Remember that the injury will significantly alter the youth's personality and functioning in many areas.
- Involve the youth in appropriate family, neighborhood, and community activities, particularly youth activities and parties.
- Use successful management procedures employed in the home and school settings.
- Become informed about the youth's capacities and interests.
- Work with vocational and special education personnel in providing employment explorations and part-time employment.

ADULT YEARS

TIPS FOR THE FAMILY

- Begin developing appropriate independence skills throughout the school years.
- Determine early what steps can be taken to prepare the youth for meaningful part-time or full-time employment.
- Become thoroughly familiar with postsecondary education opportunities and adult services for individuals with disabilities.
- Explore various living and housing options early in the youth's secondary school years.
- Provide opportunities for the young adult to experience different kinds of living arrangements.

TIPS FOR NEIGHBORS, FRIENDS, AND EMPLOYERS

- Keep up a spirit of neighborliness.
- Create opportunities for the adult to be involved in age-relevant activities, including movies, sports events, going out to dinner, and so on.
- Work closely with educational and adult support services personnel in creating employment opportunities, monitoring performance on the job, and making appropriate adjustments.

Services for the person with brain injury do not stop as he or she becomes an adult. Family and care providers should be aware of the services available. They can also create opportunities for the adult with disabilities to be involved in leisure and recreational events.

■ *Concussions.* The most common effects of closed-head injuries, **concussions** occur most frequently in children and adolescents through contact sports such as football, hockey, and martial arts. Children who display weakness on one side of the body or a dilated pupil may have a concussion and should be examined immediately by a physician.

■ *Contusions.* This kind of injury is characterized by extensive damage to the brain, including laceration of the brain, bleeding, swelling, and bruising. The resulting effect of a **contusion** is intense stupor or coma. Individuals with contusions should be hospitalized immediately.

■ *Skull fractures.* The consequences of **skull fractures** depend on the location, nature, and seriousness of the fracture. Unfortunately, some fractures are not easily detectable through radiological examination. Injuries to the lower back part of the head are particularly troublesome and difficult to detect. These basilar skull fractures may set the stage for serious infections of the central nervous system. Immediate medical care is essential for skull fractures to determine the extent of the damage and to develop appropriate interventions.

■ *Epidural and subdural hemorrhages.* Hemorrhaging or bleeding is the central feature of epidural and subdural hematomas. Hematomas are collections of blood, usually clotted. An **epidural hematoma** is caused by damage to an artery (a thick-walled blood vessel carrying blood from the heart) between the brain and the skull (see Figure 13.2). If this injury is not treated promptly and appropriately, the affected individual will die. A **subdural hematoma** is caused by damage to tiny veins that draw blood from the outer layer of the brain (cerebral cortex) to the heart. The aggregation of blood between the brain and its outer covering (dura) produces pressure that adversely affects the brain and its functioning (see Figure 13.3). If the subdural bleeding is left untreated, the result can be death (Haslam, 1996).

■ CONCUSSION. A condition of impaired brain functioning derived from brutal shaking, violent blows, or other serious impacts to the head.

■ CONTUSION. A condition in which the brain is bruised as a result of a severe hit or blow.

■ SKULL FRACTURE. A break, crack, or split of the skull resulting from a violent blow or other serious impact to the head.

■ EPIDURAL HEMATOMA. A collection of blood between the skull and the covering of the brain, which puts pressure on vital brain structures.

■ SUBDURAL HEMATOMA. A collection of blood between the covering of the brain and the brain itself, resulting in pressure on vital brain structures.

FIGURE 13.2

An epidural hematoma. (a) A forceful injury occurs in the temporal area of the brain. (b) The injury may result in a fractured skull, causing bleeding in the middle meningeal artery. Blood collects between the skull and the dura—a tough membrane covering the brain. (c) As the blood collects, pressure builds on vital structures within the brain.

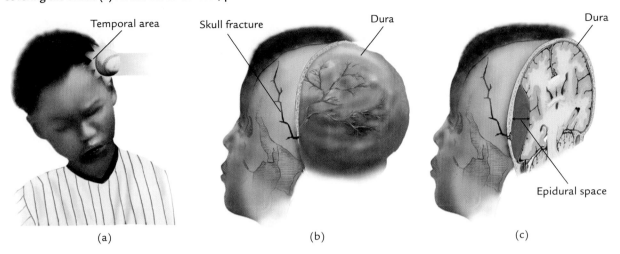

(a)   (b)   (c)

[*Source:* Adapted from Common Neurological Disorders in Children by Robert H. A. Haslam (p. 330) in R. H. A. Haslam & P. J. Valletutti (eds.) *Medical Problems in the Classroom,* Copyright 1996, Austin, TX: Pro-Ed, Inc. Reprinted by permission.]

Medical treatment of traumatic and acquired brain injury proceeds in stages. At the onset of the injury, medical personnel focus on maintaining the child's life, treating the swelling and bleeding, minimizing complications, reducing the level of coma, and completing the initial neurologic examination. This stage of treatment is often characterized by strained interactions between physicians and parents. Many

FIGURE 13.3

A subdural hematoma. (a) Violent shaking or hitting a child may cause damage to the cerebral cortex. (b) Trauma to the brain results in the rupturing of small veins. (c) Blood gathers between the dura and the brain, resulting in pressure on vital brain structures.

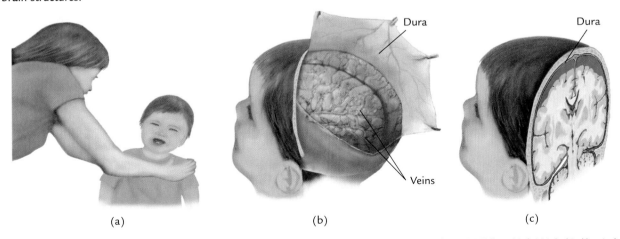

(a)   (b)   (c)

[*Source:* Adapted from Common Neurological Disorders in Children by Robert H. A. Haslam (p. 332) in R. H. A. Haslam & P. J. Valletutti (eds.) *Medical Problems in the Classroom,* Copyright 1996, Austin, TX: Pro-Ed, Inc. Reprinted by permission.]

The medical and psychological services available to Russian skater Elena Berezhnaya enabled her to successfully return to skating after receiving a traumatic head injury in practice. After months of care and rehabilitation, she and her partner were bronze medal winners in the XVIII Winter Olympics.

physicians are unable to respond satisfactorily to the overwhelming psychological needs of parents and family members because of the complex medical demands presented by the injured child. Other trained personnel—including social workers, psychologists, and clergy—should address the parents' and family's needs.

If the child remains in a coma, physical or occupational therapists may use special stimulation techniques to reduce the depth of the coma. If the child becomes agitated by stimuli in the hospital unit, such as visitors' conversations, noises produced by housecleaning staff, obtrusive light, or touching, steps may be taken to control or reduce the problem. As the injured individual comes out of the coma, orienting him or her to the environment becomes a priority. This may include explaining where the patient is located, introducing care providers, indicating where loved ones are, sharing what has transpired since the injury, and responding to the individual's other questions. Many persons who have been injured do not remember the accident or medical interventions.

The next stage of treatment helps the person relearn and perform preinjury skills and behaviors. This treatment may take time and considerable effort. Gradually, children are prepared for return to their homes and appropriate school environments. Their families prepare as well, receiving ongoing support and counseling (Conoley & Sheridan, 1997). Additionally, arrangements are made for appropriate speech/language, physical, and occupational therapies and specialized teaching as necessary (Gillis, 1996).

Many individuals return to their homes, schools, or employment settings as vastly different people. These differences often take the shape of unpredictable or extreme expression of emotion. Furthermore, these individuals may have difficulties recognizing and accepting their postinjury challenges and deficits (Bowe, 2000; Hill, 1999). The last stages of intervention focus on providing counseling and therapy to help the individual cope with the injury and residual effects; assisting the family in maintaining gains achieved; terminating specific head injury services; and referring the person to community agencies, educational programs, and vocational rehabilitation for additional services as needed.

Case Study

F.T.

F.T. is a 15-year-old . . . boy with a history of a TBI 5 years ago. He was referred for a neuropsychological assessment by his school district because educators were unsure of how to manage F.T.'s academic and behavior problems. F.T. had recently entered their school district as a ninth grader, and he was failing all of his classes except for a D- in science and a B+ in physical education. He had particular problems with written expression, following oral and written directions, and identifying the main idea in materials presented to him. Teachers were also concerned about his short attention span, staring spells, and poor work completion. F.T. had received special education services under a diagnosis of learning disabilities in his previous school district. This consisted of 1 hour per day of resource room assistance to help him organize his assignments and complete his homework. Since beginning in the new school, F.T.'s attendance has been adequate, and teachers perceived him as a friendly, outgoing young man. However, they were considering a secondary educational diag-

nosis of behavior disorder because of the disruption caused by his impulsive and off-task behaviors.

F.T. sustained a severe TBI in an amusement park accident at the age of 10 years. He experienced full cardiopulmonary arrest at the scene of the accident and remained in a coma for 3 days. His initial Glasgow Coma Scale score was 6. A computerized tomography (CT scan) of the brain showed a large left temporaparietal contusion, but he had no other significant injuries. Upon transfer to acute rehabilitation 15 days post-injury, F.T. displayed a dense right-side hemiparesis and could not talk, but he could follow simple one-step commands. During rehabilitation, he showed a rapid recovery of physical mobility, self-care skills, and basic language functioning. His attention span was extremely short, his short-term memory was poor, and he was impulsive and noncompliant in therapies.

Behaviorally, F.T. was perceived somewhat differently by his teachers and parents. The teachers and his father reported clinically significant problems with attention/concentration, work production, and noncompliance. In addi-

tion to these problems, F.T.'s mother also indicated significant concerns about social withdrawal; aggressive behaviors (arguing, fighting, mood swings, temper tantrums); and delinquent behaviors (associating with bad companions, stealing, swearing, and truancy). On a behavioral self-report measure, F.T. identified mild, but not clinically significant problems with daydreaming and arguing, suggesting a lack of insight and self-awareness.

F.T. certainly had multiple risk factors that could lead to a poor long-term outcome. He experienced a severe head injury with persistent cognitive and behavioral sequelae that interfered with his ability to keep up with same-age peers, as indicated by neuropsychological testing and by the decline in his IQ scores over time. He had experienced academic problems prior to his TBI that were likely associated with his history of physical and sexual abuse. His home environment was chaotic, and litigation over the TBI fueled family conflict and divisions. His single mother had multiple stressors, including the injury of two of her children and severe financial problems,

and she did not exhibit strong behavioral management or limit-setting skills. F.T.'s recovery from TBI was affected by frequent family moves and inconsistent (and sometimes inadequate) educational services due to educators' inexperience and limited educational resources.

Source: From "Epilogue: An Ecological Systems Approach to Childhood Traumatic Injury," by J. E. Farmer. In *Childhood Traumatic Brain Injury: Diagnosis, Assessment, and Intervention,* edited by E. E. Bigler, E. Clark, & J. E. Farmer, 1997, pp. 177–190. Austin, TX: Pro-Ed, Inc.

■ APPLICATION

1. What steps should be taken by medical and educational personnel in responding to F.T. and his particular needs?
2. What ongoing information should be delivered by the mother that would be helpful to F.T.'s teachers?
3. What ongoing information should be delivered by his teachers that would be helpful to F.T.'s mother?
4. How should other agencies and care providers in the community be involved with F.T. and his family?

Debate Forum

Hundreds of brain injuries could be avoided if parents limited children's access to firearms.

■ SCOPE OF THE PROBLEM

- In 1992, firearms surpassed motor vehicles as the number one cause of brain injury fatalities in the United States.
- It is estimated that every two hours in the United States, someone's child is killed with a loaded gun.
- Firearm violence is a uniquely American problem, with a rate 90 times greater than that of any other similar country.
- It is estimated that half of all American households have firearms.
- Every day, 14 American children under the age of 20 are killed and many more are wounded by guns.
- It costs more than $14,000 to treat each child wounded by gunfire—enough to pay for a full year at a private college.

■ FIREARM USAGE

- Although firearms are often kept in the home for protection, they are rarely used for this purpose. Of 198 cases of home invasion crimes, only three victims (1.5%) used a gun for self-defense.
- The risk of suicide is five times greater if there is a gun in the home, and the risk of domestic homicide is three times greater.
- Most children kill themselves or other children unintentionally while they are playing with a gun they found in their home or the home of a family member or friend.
- News reports state that nearly 90% of accidental shootings involving children are linked to easy-to-find, loaded handguns in the home.
- Over half of all handgun owners keep their guns loaded at least some of the time, and over half do not keep their guns locked up.

An estimated 30% of all unintentional shootings could be prevented by the presence of safety features such as trigger locks and loading indicators, but American-made guns are not subject to federal safety standards like other consumer products such as automobiles, aspirin bottles, and children's toys.

■ POINT

Gun control of any kind is repugnant to many individuals, particularly those who have strong feelings about the "right to bear arms." These individuals argue that controlling firearms is a violation of their civil rights. Any restriction of access to firearms or control of their use is seen by these individuals as undue government intervention and control.

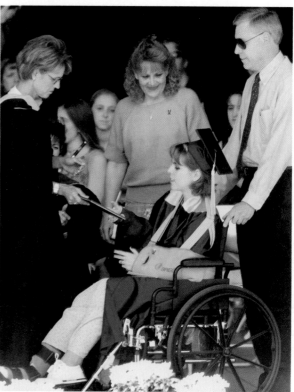

Lisa Kreutz, one of the Columbine High School seniors wounded in the shooting attack at the school, receives her diploma at commencement ceremonies with her mother and father. Two students of the class of 1999 were killed in the shootings and three injured.

■ COUNTERPOINT

As a society, we can no longer ignore the deaths and injuries to children and youth that are caused by firearms. We ought to treat firearms as we treat cars. Cars must have certain safety devices, or they are not available for purchase or use. Likewise, only those licensed to drive may legally get behind the wheel of a car. These governmental measures are directed at providing safety to citizens. The same measures should apply to firearms. The essential goal is prevention, not control.

Source: From *Firearm Safety,* developed by the Brain Injury Association, Inc., 2000b, Alexandria, Virginia.

Review

focus 1

Identify three key elements of traumatic brain injury.

- The brain is damaged by external forces that cause tearing, bruising, or swelling.
- The injuries, open and/or closed head, dramatically influence the individual's functioning in several areas, including psychosocial behavior, speech and language, cognitive performance, vision and hearing, and motor abilities.
- The brain injury often results in permanent disabilities.

focus 2

Identify four general characteristics of individuals with traumatic or acquired brain injuries.

- Individuals with traumatic or acquired brain injuries often exhibit cognitive deficits, including problems with memory, concentration, attention, and problem solving.
- Speech and language problems are frequently evident, including word retrieval problems, slurred or unintelligible speech, and aphasia.

- These individuals may also present social and behavioral problems, including increased irritability, inability to suppress or manage socially inappropriate behaviors, low thresholds for frustration, and insensitivity to others.
- Neuromotor and physical problems may also be present, including eye-hand coordination impairments, vision and hearing deficits, and paralysis.

focus 3

Identify the most common causes of brain injury in children, youth, and adults.

- The most common causes of brain injury in young children are falls, neglect, and physical abuse.
- For children in the elementary grades, the most common causes are falls; pedestrian or bicycle accidents involving a motor vehicle, and sports.
- For high school students and adults, the most common causes are motor vehicle accidents and sports-related injuries.

focus 4

Describe the focus of educational interventions for individuals with traumatic or acquired brain injuries.

- Educational interventions are directed at improving the general behaviors of the individual, including problem solving, planning, and developing insight; building appropriate social behaviors such as working with others, suppressing inappropriate behaviors, and using appropriate etiquette; developing expressive and receptive language skills, including word retrieval, event description, and understanding instructions; and writing skills.
- Other academic skills are also taught that are relevant to the students' needs and developmental level of functioning.
- Transition planning for postsecondary education and training is also essential to the well-being of the individual with traumatic or acquired brain injury.

focus 5

Identify four common types of head injuries.

- Common head injuries include concussions, contusions, skull fractures, and epidural and subdural hemorrhages.

focus 6

Describe five important elements of medical treatment for individuals with traumatic or acquired brain injuries.

- The first stage of treatment is directed at preserving the individual's life, addressing swelling and bleeding, and minimizing complications.
- Once the individual regains consciousness or can benefit from more active therapies, the learning and relearning of pre-injury skills begin.
- The last stage focuses on preparing the individual to return to home, school, or work settings; and readying the individual to work with other health care and training providers.
- The last stage is also characterized by the provision of psychological services directed at helping individuals and their families cope with the injuries and their effects.
- Throughout all the stages of treatment, interdisciplinary collaboration and cooperation are essential to the individual's success.

People with Hearing Loss

To begin with . . .

 Quick Facts: There are nearly 11 million people in the United States (6% of the population) who have a significant irreversible hearing loss. Of those with a hearing loss, about 1 million are deaf. American Sign Language is the third most used language in the United States after English and Spanish. The first and oldest American school for the deaf was founded in 1817 in Hartford, Connecticut. Today, there are nearly 71,000 special education students between the ages of 6 and 21 with hearing impairments in America's schools. Gallaudet University in Washington, D.C., the world's only university in which all programs and services are specifically designed to accommodate deaf and hard of hearing students, has nearly 2,000 enrolled students. Gallaudet was founded in 1864 by an act of Congress, and its charter was signed by President Abraham Lincoln. (Deaf World Web, 2000; U.S. Department of Education, 2000a)

A couple facing their first pregnancy is going through a frightening and vulnerable time, particularly when the pregnancy is high risk. For a couple in Oregon, the situation became even more difficult when their doctor refused to provide a qualified sign language interpreter. . . . Approximately seven months into the mother's first pregnancy, the last thing the hearing mother-to-be and the deaf father-to-be were thinking about was discrimination based on disability. In July of 1998, tests on their unborn child revealed a congenital heart condition. The couple's obstetrician sent them to a Oregon doctor . . . who specializes in high-risk pregnancies. When the couple contacted [the doctor's] office to make an appointment, they requested that an interpreter be provided so that the father-to-be could communicate. . . . The doctor refused. On behalf of the young couple . . . an Oregon attorney filed suit, alleging discrimination in violation of the Ameri-

cans with Disabilities Act. . . . In November, all of the parties entered into a consent judgment ending the lawsuit. . . . [The doctor and his associates] agreed to pay the young couple $25,000 and to adopt a policy for effective communication. This policy provides that deaf patients and their companions will be offered auxiliary aids and services at no charge. The defendants also agreed to provide a mandatory, in-service training to all of its staff members to make sure that they are aware of and complying with the new policy. (Vargas, 1999)

No one has ever accused guitar showman and outdoor enthusiast Ted Nugent of being the strong silent type. The Motor City Madman is famous for his loud mouth and even louder concerts. But you might be surprised to learn that while the 51-year-old Nugent has no trouble being heard, he does have trouble hearing. "My left ear is only there for aesthetic purposes. It just balances my head so I don't fall over," jokes Nugent. "I've played over 5,000 concerts and have subjected myself via my cravings to massive sonic punishment. My left ear is beat to hell." . . . While Nugent's rock 'n' roll profession has certainly contributed to the decline of his aural capacity, a new study by the University of Wisconsin in Madison reveals that his passion for firearms may have been equally injurious. [The study found that people who engage in target shooting had a 57% higher risk for high-frequency hearing loss than those who did not shoot guns.] (Morgan & Shoop, 2000)

Shelley

Shelley is the third oldest in a family of six children. At the age of 18 months, she was diagnosed with a severe hear-ing loss and immediately fitted with hearing aids for both ears. Although her parents have no hearing problems, Shelley has an older brother and a younger sister who are profoundly deaf and a younger brother with a severe hearing loss. She and her non-hearing siblings were all born deaf or hard-of-hearing. While growing up, Shelley's parents worked diligently to ensure that she had every chance possible to develop and use speech. Through the support of her family, the use of hearing aids, and the combination of speech and signing skills, Shelley grew up in a hearing world where she successfully completed public school and went on to receive a graduate degree with an emphasis in teaching children who are deaf or hard-of-hearing. She is now a specialist in early childhood education and the mother of two children, Matthew and Molly. Matthew and Molly, ages 10 and 8 years old, are both hearing children. Shelley describes herself as the kind of person who clearly wants to be perceived as an individual first. She likes to say, "I've got a desire or a drive in me that I just wanted to be the same as everyone else. So basically, I just have broken ears."

aLTHOUGH SHELLEY IS UNABLE to hear most sounds, her life is one of independence and fulfillment (see the opening snapshot). In Shelley's case, as well as those of many people who are deaf or hard of hearing, the obstacles presented by the loss of hearing are not insurmountable.

In a world often controlled by sound and spoken language, the ability to hear and speak can be an important link in the development of human communication. Children who can hear learn to talk by listening to those around them. Everyday communication systems depend on sound. So, what would it be like to live in a world that is silent? People talk, but you hear nothing. The television and movie screens are lit up with moving pictures, but you can't hear and understand what is going on. Your friends talk about their favorite music and hum tunes that have no meaning to you. A fire engine's siren wails as it moves through traffic, but you are oblivious to its warning. To people with hearing, the thought of such a world can be very frightening. To those without hearing, it is quite simply their world—a place that one day can be very lonely, frustrating, and downright discriminatory, and in the next bring joy, fulfillment, and a life of endless possibilities that is no different from those experienced by "hearing people." The National Academy on an Aging Society (1999) indicated that in comparison to those with "normal" hearing, people with a hearing loss are less likely to participate in social activities; are less satisfied with their life; express greater dissatisfaction with their friendships, family life, health, and financial situation; are less healthy; and are underemployed.

People with a hearing loss are able to learn about the world around them in any number of ways, such as lipreading, gestures, pictures, and writing. Some people are able to use their residual hearing with the assistance of a hearing aid. For others, a hearing aid doesn't help because it only makes distorted sounds louder. To express themselves, some people prefer to use their voices; others prefer to use a visual sign language. Most people with a hearing loss use a combination of speech and signing.

People with a hearing loss, such as Shelley from our opening snapshot, may seek and find success in the hearing world. Others seek to be part of a Deaf community or Deaf culture to share a common language (American Sign Language) and customs. In a Deaf culture, there are heritages and traditions shared by those within the community. People often marry others who are deaf from within the community. They also have a shared literature, and participate in the Deaf community's political, business, arts, and sports programs. People in the Deaf community do not see the loss of hearing as a disability. From their perspective, being deaf is not an impairment and should not be looked upon as a pathology or disease that requires treatment.

The Hearing Process

udition is the act or sense of hearing. The auditory process involves the transmission of sound through the vibration of an object to a receiver. The process originates with a vibrator—such as a string, reed, membrane, or column of air—that causes displacement of air particles. To become sound, a vibration must have a medium to carry it. Air is the most common carrier, but vibrations can also be carried by metal, water, and other substances. The displacement of air particles by the vibrator produces a pattern of circular waves that move away from the source.

focus 1
Describe how sound is transmitted through the human ear.

This movement, referred to as a sound wave, can be illustrated by imagining the ripples resulting from a pebble dropped in a pool of water. Sound waves are patterns of pressure that alternately push together and pull apart in a spherical expansion. Sound waves are carried through a medium (e.g., air) to a receiver. The human ear is one of the most sensitive receivers there is, capable of being activated by incredibly small amounts of pressure and able to distinguish more than half a million different sounds.

The ear is the mechanism through which sound is collected, processed, and transmitted to a specific area in the brain that decodes the sensations into meaningful language. The anatomy of the hearing mechanism is discussed in terms of the external, middle, and inner ears. These structures are illustrated in Figure 14.1.

■ THE EXTERNAL EAR

The external ear consists of a cartilage structure on the side of the head called the auricle, or pinna, and an external ear canal referred to as the meatus. The only outwardly visible part of the ear, the auricle, is attached to the skull by three ligaments. Its purpose is to collect sound waves and funnel them into the meatus. The meatus secretes a wax called cerumen, which protects the inner structures of the ear by trapping foreign materials and lubricating the canal and eardrum. The eardrum, or tympanic membrane, is located at the inner end of the canal between the external and middle ear. The concave membrane is positioned in such a manner that, when struck by sound waves, it can vibrate freely.

■ THE MIDDLE EAR

The inner surface of the eardrum is located in the air-filled cavity of the middle ear. This surface consists of three small bones that form the **ossicular chain**: the malleus, incus, and stapes, often referred to as the hammer, anvil, and stirrup because

■ AUDITION. The act or sense of hearing.

■ OSSICULAR CHAIN. The three small bones (malleus, incus, and stapes, or hammer, anvil, and stirrup) that transmit vibrations through the middle-ear cavity to the inner ear.

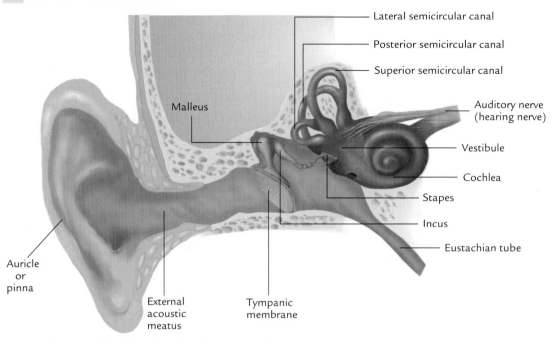

FIGURE 14.1   Structure of the ear

Lateral semicircular canal

Posterior semicircular canal

Superior semicircular canal

Malleus

Auditory nerve
(hearing nerve)

Vestibule

Cochlea

Stapes

Incus

Eustachian tube

Auricle
or
pinna

External
acoustic
meatus

Tympanic
membrane

of similarities in shape to these common objects. The three bones transmit the vibrations from the external ear through the cavity of the middle ear to the inner ear.

The **eustachian tube,** extending from the throat to the middle-ear cavity, equalizes the air pressure on the eardrum with that of the outside by controlling the flow of air into the middle-ear cavity. Although air conduction is the primary avenue through which sound reaches the inner ear, conduction can also occur through the bones of the skull. Bone conduction appears comparable to air conduction in that the patterns of displacement produced in the inner ear are similar.

■ THE INNER EAR

The inner ear consists of a multitude of intricate passageways. The cochlea lies horizontally in front of the vestibule (a central cavity where sound enters directly from the middle ear), where it can be activated by movement in the ossicular chain. The cochlea is filled with fluid similar in composition to cerebral spinal fluid. Within the cochlea is **Corti's organ,** a structure of highly specialized cells that translate vibrations into nerve impulses that are sent directly to the brain.

The other major structure within the inner ear is the **vestibular mechanism,** containing the semicircular canals that control balance. The semicircular canals have enlarged portions at one end and are filled with fluid that responds to head movement. The vestibular mechanism integrates sensory input passing to the brain and assists the body in maintaining equilibrium. Motion and gravity are detected through this mechanism, allowing the individual to differentiate between sensory input associated with body movement and input coming from the external environment. Whenever the basic functions of the vestibular mechanism or any of the structures in the external, middle, and inner ear are interrupted, hearing loss may occur.

■ EUSTACHIAN TUBE. A structure that extends from the throat to the middle-ear cavity and controls air flow into the cavity.

■ CORTI'S ORGAN. A structure in the cochlea made of highly specialized cells that translate vibration into nerve impulses that are sent directly to the brain.

■ VESTIBULAR MECHANISM. A structure in the inner ear containing three semicircular canals filled with fluid. It is sensitive to movement and assists the body in maintaining equilibrium.

Definitions and Classification

Two terms, *deaf and hard-of-hearing* (or *partial hearing*), are commonly used to distinguish the severity of a person's hearing loss. *Deaf* is often overused and misunderstood, commonly applied to describe a wide variety of hearing loss. However, as discussed in this section, the term should be used in a more precise fashion.

■ DEFINITIONS

Deafness and hearing loss may be defined according to the degree of hearing impairment, which is determined by assessing a person's sensitivity to loudness (sound intensity) and pitch (sound frequency). The unit used to measure sound intensity is the decibel (db); the range of human hearing is approximately 0 to 130 db. Sounds louder than 130 db (such as those made by jet aircraft at 140 db) are extremely painful to the ear. Conversational speech registers at 40 to 60 db, loud thunder at about 120 db, and a rock concert at about 110 db.

The frequency of sound is determined by measuring the number of cycles that vibrating molecules complete per second. The unit used to measure cycles per second is the **hertz (Hz).** The higher the frequency, the higher the hertz. The human ear can hear sounds ranging from 20 to approximately 15,000 Hz. The pitch of speech sounds ranges from 300 to 4,000 Hz, whereas the pitches made by a piano keyboard range from 27.5 to 4,186 Hz. Although the human ear can hear sounds at the 15,000-Hz level, the vast majority of sounds in our environment range from 300 to 4,000 Hz.

■ DEAF AND HARD-OF-HEARING

Deafness describes people whose hearing loss is in the extreme—90 db or greater. Even with the use of hearing aids or other forms of amplification, for people who are **deaf** the primary means for developing language and communication is through the visual channel. *Deafness,* as defined by the Individuals with Disabilities Education Act (IDEA), means "a hearing impairment which is so severe that the child is impaired in processing linguistic information through hearing, with or without amplification, which adversely affects educational performance" (IDEA 97, 34 C.F.R. 300.7).

A person who is deaf is most often described as someone who cannot hear sound. As such, the individual is unable to understand human speech. However, many people who are deaf have enough residual hearing to recognize sound at certain frequencies, but still may be unable to determine the meaning of the sound pressure waves.

For persons defined as **hard-of-hearing,** audition is deficient but remains somewhat functional. Individuals who are hard-of-hearing have enough residual hearing that, with the use of a hearing aid, they are able to process human speech auditorily.

The distinction between deaf and hard-of-hearing, based on the functional use of residual hearing, is not as clear as many traditional definitions imply. New breakthroughs in the development of hearing aids as well as improved diagnostic procedures have enabled many children labeled as deaf to use their hearing functionally under limited circumstances.

In addition to measuring a person's sensitivity to loudness and pitch, two other factors are involved in defining deafness and hard-of-hearing: the age of onset and the anatomical site of the loss.

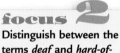

focus 2

Distinguish between the terms *deaf* and *hard-of-hearing.*

■ HERTZ (HZ). A unit used to measure the frequency of sound in terms of the number of cycles that vibrating molecules complete per second.

■ DEAF. A term used to describe individuals who have a hearing loss greater than 90 dB, have vision as their primary input, and cannot understand speech through the ear.

■ HARD-OF-HEARING. A term used to describe individuals with a sense of hearing that is deficient but somewhat functional.

TABLE 14.1	Classification of hearing loss	
Hearing Loss in Decibels (db)	Classification	Effect on Ability to Understand Speech
0–15	Normal hearing	None
15–25	Slight hearing loss	Minimal difficulty with soft speech
25–40	Mild hearing loss	Difficulty with soft speech
40–55	Moderate hearing loss	Frequent difficulty with normal speech
56–70	Moderate–severe hearing loss	Occassional difficulty with loud speech
71–90	Severe hearing loss	Frequent difficulty with loud speech
>91	Profound hearing loss	Near total or total loss of hearing

focus 3

Why is it important to consider age of onset and anatomical site when defining a hearing loss?

■ PRELINGUAL LOSS. Pertaining to hearing impairments occurring prior to the age of two, or the time of speech development.

■ POSTLINGUAL LOSS. Pertaining to hearing impairments occurring at any age following speech development.

■ CONDUCTIVE HEARING LOSS. A hearing loss resulting from poor conduction of sound along the passages leading to the sense organ.

■ SENSORINEURAL HEARING LOSS. A hearing loss resulting from an abnormal sense organ (inner ear) and a damaged auditory nerve.

■ AGE OF ONSET   Hearing loss may be present at birth (congenital) or acquired at any time during life. **Prelingual loss** occurs prior to the age of 2, or before speech development. **Postlingual loss** occurs at any age following speech acquisition. About 90% of deafness in children occurs at birth or prior to the child's learning to speak (Dolnick, 1993). The distinction between a congenital and an acquired hearing loss is important. The age of onset will be a critical variable in determining the type and extent of interventions necessary to minimize the effect of the individual's disability. This is particularly true in relation to speech and language development. A person who is born with hearing loss has significantly more challenges, particularly in the areas of communication and social adaptation (Chouard, 1997; Magnuson, 2000; Talbott & Wehman, 1996).

■ ANATOMICAL SITE OF THE LOSS   The two primary types of hearing loss based on anatomical location are peripheral problems and central auditory problems. There are three types of peripheral hearing loss: conductive, sensorineural, and mixed. A **conductive hearing loss** results from poor conduction of sound along the passages leading to the sense organ (inner ear). The loss may result from a blockage in the external canal, as well as from an obstruction interfering with the movement of the eardrum or ossicle. The overall effect is a reduction or loss of loudness. A conductive loss can be offset by amplification (hearing aids) and medical intervention. Surgery has proved to be effective in reducing or even restoring a conductive loss.

Sensorineural hearing losses are a result of an abnormal sense organ and a damaged auditory nerve. A sensorineural loss may distort sound, affecting the clarity of human speech, and cannot presently be treated adequately through medical intervention. A sensorineural loss is generally more severe than a conductive loss and is permanent. Losses of greater than 70 db are usually sensorineural and involve severe damage to the inner ear. One common way to determine whether a loss is conductive or sensorineural is to administer an air and bone conduction test. An individual with a conductive loss would be unable to hear a vibrating tuning fork held close to the ear, because of blocked air passages to the inner ear, but may be able to hear the same fork applied to the skull as well as someone with normal hearing would. An individual with a sensorineural loss would not be able to hear the vibrating fork, regardless of its placement. This test is not always accurate, however, and must therefore be used with caution in distinguishing between conductive and sensorineural losses. **Mixed hearing loss,** a combination of conductive and sensorineural problems, can also be assessed through the use of an air and bone conduction test. In the case of a mixed loss, abnormalities are evident in both tests.

Although most hearing losses are peripheral, such as conductive and sensorineural problems, some occur where there is no measurable peripheral loss. This type of loss, referred to as a central auditory disorder, occurs when there is a dysfunction in the cerebral cortex. The cerebral cortex, the outer layer of gray matter of the brain, governs thought, reasoning, memory, sensation, and voluntary movement. Consequently, a central auditory problem is not a loss in the ability to hear sound but a disorder of symbolic processes, including auditory perception, discrimination, comprehension of sound, and language development (expressive and receptive).

■ CLASSIFICATION

Hearing loss, like other disabilities, may be classified according to the severity of the condition. Table 14.1 illustrates a symptom severity classification system and presents information relative to a child's ability to understand speech patterns at the various severity levels.

Classification systems based solely on a person's degree of hearing loss should be used with a great deal of caution when determining appropriate services and supports. These systems do not reflect the person's capabilities, background, or experience; they merely suggest parameters for measuring a physical defect in auditory function. As a young child, for example, Shelley from our opening snapshot was diagnosed as having a severe hearing loss in both ears, yet throughout her life she successfully adjusted to both school and community experiences. She went on to college and now has a successful career as a specialist in early childhood education. Consequently, many factors beyond the severity of the hearing loss must be assessed when determining the potential of an individual. In addition to severity of loss, factors such as general intelligence, emotional stability, scope and quality of early education and training, the family environment, and the occurrence of other disabilities must also be considered.

Prevalence

Hearing loss gets worse over time and increases dramatically with age. Estimates of hearing loss in the United States go as high as 28 million people. Of the 28 million, approximately 11 million people have significant irreversible hearing loss, and 1 million are deaf. Only 5% of people with hearing loss are under the age of 17, while nearly 43% are over the age of 65. Contrast this to the fact that only 12% of the general population is over the age of 65 years (Deaf World Web, 2000; National Academy on an Aging Society, 1999). Men are more likely

■ MIXED HEARING LOSS. A hearing loss resulting from a combination of conductive and sensorineural problems.

to have a hearing loss than women; Caucasians are proportionately overrepresented among people with a hearing loss; and prevalence of hearing loss decreases as family income and education increase (National Academy on an Aging Society, 1999).

The U.S. Department of Education (2000a) indicated that 70,883 students defined as having a hearing impairment between the ages of 6 and 21 were receiving special education services in U.S. schools in 1998–1999. These students account for approximately 1.5% of school-age students identified as having a disability. It is important to note that these figures represent only those students who receive special services; a number of students with hearing loss who could benefit from additional services do not receive them. Of the students with a hearing loss receiving special education, 26,697 (38%) were being served in general education classrooms for at least 80% of the school day. This is nearly double the number of students in these classrooms a decade ago. Another 30,547 spent at least a part of their day in a general education classroom; 5,056 in separate public or private day schools for students with a hearing loss; and 6,331 in public or private residential living facilities (U.S. Department of Education, 2000a).

Causation

A number of congenital (existing at birth) or acquired factors may result in a hearing loss. Approximately one in a thousand children is born deaf because of factors associated with heredity, maternal rubella or German measles, or drugs taken during pregnancy. Substance abuse, disease, and constantly being subjected to loud noises are all causes of hearing loss. Loss of hearing is also a normal part of the aging process, beginning as early as the teen years when we lose some of the high frequency hearing we had in childhood.

■ CONGENITAL FACTORS

■ HEREDITY   Although more than 200 types of deafness have been related to hereditary factors, the cause of 50% of all hearing loss remains unknown (Schildroth, 1994). One of the most common diseases affecting the sense of hearing is **otosclerosis.** The cause of this disease is unknown, but it is generally believed to be hereditary and is manifested most often in early adulthood. About 10% of adults have otosclerosis, and it can be passed from one generation to the next but not manifest itself for several generations.

■ OTOSCLEROSIS. A disease of the ear characterized by destruction of the capsular bone in the middle ear and the growth of a web-like bone that attaches to the stapes. The stapes is restricted and unable to function properly.

For a student who is deaf, the visual channel is the primary means for developing language. Here a student in a general education classroom is assisted by an interpreter using sign language to explain the class homework assignment.

The disease is characterized by destruction of the capsular bone in the middle ear and the growth of weblike bone that attaches to the stapes. As a result, the stapes is restricted and unable to function properly. Hearing loss results in about 15% of all cases of otosclerosis and at twice the rate for females as for males. Victims of otosclerosis suffer from high-pitched throbbing or ringing sounds known as **tinnitus,** a condition associated with disease of the inner ear. There is no specific treatment or any medication that will improve the hearing in people with otosclerosis. Surgery (stapedectomy) may be recommended when the stapes (stirrup) bone is involved.

■ PRENATAL DISEASE   Several conditions, although not inherited, can result in sensorineural loss. The major cause of congenital deafness is infection, of which rubella, cytomegalovirus (CMV), and toxoplasmosis are the most common. The rubella epidemic of 1963–1965 dramatically increased the incidence of deafness in the United States. During the 1960s, approximately 10% of all congenital deafness was associated with women contracting rubella during pregnancy. For about 40% of the individuals who are deaf, the cause is rubella. About 50% of all children with rubella acquire a severe hearing loss. Most hearing losses caused by rubella are sensorineural, although a small percentage may be mixed. In addition to hearing loss, children who have had rubella sometimes acquire heart disease (50%), cataracts or glaucoma (40%), and mental retardation (40%). Since the advent of the rubella vaccine, the elimination of this disease has become a nationwide campaign and the incidence of rubella has dramatically decreased.

Congenital cytomegalovirus (CMV) is a viral infection that spreads by close contact with another person who is shedding the virus in body secretions. It is also spread by blood transfusions and from a mother to her newborn infant. CMV is the most frequently occurring virus among newborns, with about 40,000 newborns contracting the disease each year. CMV disease is characterized by jaundice, microcephaly, hemolytic anemia, mental retardation, hepatosplenomegaly (enlargement of liver and spleen), and hearing loss. Although no vaccine is currently available to treat CMV, some preventive measures can be taken, such as ensuring safe blood transfusions and good hygiene and avoiding contact with persons who have the virus (*Pediatric Bulletin,* 2000). CMV is detectable in utero through amniocentesis. However, there is considerable debate regarding the accuracy of amniocentesis in identifying the condition (Moaven, Gilbert, Cunningham, & Rawlinson, 1995).

Congenital toxoplasmosis infection is characterized by jaundice and anemia, but frequently the disease also results in central nervous system disorders (e.g., seizures, hydrocephalus, microcephaly). Approximately 15% of infants born with this disease are deaf.

Other factors associated with congenital sensorineural hearing loss include maternal Rh-factor incompatibility and the use of ototoxic drugs. Maternal Rh-factor incompatibility does not generally affect a firstborn child, but as antibodies are produced during subsequent pregnancies, multiple problems can result, including deafness. Fortunately, deafness as a result of Rh-factor problems is no longer common. With the advent of an anti-Rh gamma globulin (RhoGAM) in 1968, the incidence of Rh-factor incompatibility has significantly decreased. If injected into the mother within the first 72 hours after the birth of the first child, she does not produce antibodies that harm future unborn infants.

Ototoxic drugs are so labeled because of their harmful effects on the sense of hearing. If taken during pregnancy, these drugs can result in a serious hearing loss in the infant. Congenital sensorineural loss can also be caused by congenital syphilis, maternal chicken pox, anoxia, and birth trauma.

■ TINNITUS. High-pitched throbbing or ringing sounds in the ear, associated with disease of the inner ear.

A condition known as **atresia** is a major cause of congenital conductive loss. Congenital aural atresia results when the external auditory canal is either malformed or completely absent at birth. A congenital malformation may lead to a blockage of the ear canal through an accumulation of cerumen, which is a wax that hardens and blocks incoming sound waves from being transmitted to the middle ear.

■ ACQUIRED FACTORS

■ POSTNATAL DISEASE   One of the most common causes of hearing loss in the postnatal period is infection. Postnatal infections—such as measles, mumps, influenza, typhoid fever, and scarlet fever—are all associated with hearing loss. Meningitis is an inflammation of the membranes that cover the brain and spinal cord and is a cause of severe hearing loss in school-age children. Sight loss, paralysis, and brain damage are further complications of this disease. The incidence of meningitis has declined, however, because of the development of antibiotics and chemotherapy.

Another common problem that may result from postnatal infection is known as **otitis media,** an inflammation of the middle ear. This condition, resulting from severe colds that spread from the eustachian tube to the middle ear, is the most common cause of conductive hearing loss in younger children. Otitis media ranks second to the common cold as the most common health problem in preschool children. Three out of every four children have had at least one episode by the time they reach three years of age. The disease is difficult to diagnose, especially in infancy, at which time symptoms are often absent. Otitis media has been found to be highly correlated with hearing problems (Giebink, 1990; National Institute on Deafness and Other Communication Disorders, 2000a).

■ ENVIRONMENTAL FACTORS   Environmental factors—including extreme changes in air pressure caused by explosions, physical abuse of the cranial area, impact from foreign objects during an accident, and loud music—also contribute to acquired hearing loss. Loud noise is rapidly becoming one of the major causes of hearing problems, with about 30 million people subjected to dangerous levels of noise in everyday life (National Institute on Deafness and Other Communication Disorders, 2000a). All of us are subjected to hazardous noise, such as noise from jet engines and loud music, more often than ever before. With the increasing use of headphones, such as those on portable compact disc or DVD players, many people (particularly adolescents) are subjected to damaging noise levels. Occupational noise (e.g., from jackhammers, tractors, and sirens) is now the leading cause of sensorineural hearing loss. Other factors associated with acquired hearing loss include degenerative processes in the ear that may come with aging, cerebral hemorrhages, allergies, and intercranial tumors.

Characteristics

The effects of hearing loss on the learning or social adjustment of individuals are extremely varied, ranging from far reaching, as in the case of prelingual sensorineural deafness, or quite minimal, as in the case of a mild postlingual conductive loss. Fortunately, prevention, early detection, and intervention have recently been emphasized, resulting in a much improved prognosis for individuals who are deaf and hard-of-hearing.

■ ATRESIA. The absence of a normal opening or cavity.

■ OTITIS MEDIA. An inflammation of the middle ear.

■ INTELLIGENCE

Research on the intellectual characteristics of children with hearing loss has suggested that the distribution of IQ scores for these individuals is similar to that of hearing children (Braden, 1992; Paul & Quigley, 1990; Prinz et al., 1996; Schirmer, 2000). Findings suggested that intellectual development for people with hearing loss is more a function of language development than cognitive ability. Any difficulties in performance appear to be closely associated with speaking, reading, and writing the English language, but are not related to level of intelligence. For example, Wood (1991) suggested that children using sign language have to divide their attention between the signs and the instructional materials. Although the child may seem slower in learning, the reality may be that the child is carrying an additional cognitive load and simply needs more time to process the information. Rodda, Cumming, and Fewer (1993) suggested that a hearing loss does make it difficult for the individual to process auditory information. However, these authors emphasize that, when people with a hearing loss have compensated for this barrier, they appear to use cognitive strategies similar to those employed by hearing people.

focus 5

Describe the basic intelligence, speech and language skills, educational achievement, and social development associated with people who are deaf or hard-of-hearing.

■ SPEECH AND ENGLISH LANGUAGE SKILLS

Speech and English language skills are the areas of development most severely affected for those with a hearing loss, particularly for children who are born deaf. These children have a very difficult time learning to speak (Cole, 1992). The effects of a hearing loss on English language development vary considerably. For children with mild and moderate hearing losses, the effect may be minimal. Even for individuals born with moderate losses, effective communication skills are possible because the voiced sounds of conversational speech remain audible. Although individuals with moderate losses cannot hear unvoiced sounds and distant speech, English language delays can be prevented if the hearing loss is diagnosed and treated early (Luetke-Stahlman & Luckner, 1991; Schirmer, 2000). The majority of people with hearing loss are able to use speech as the primary mode for English language acquisition.

For the person who is congenitally deaf, most loud speech is inaudible, even with the use of the most sophisticated hearing aids. These people are unable to receive information through speech unless they have learned to lip-read. Sounds produced by the person who is deaf may be extremely difficult to understand. Children who are deaf exhibit significant articulation, voice quality, and tone discrimination problems. Even as early as 8 months of age, babies who are deaf appear to babble less than their hearing peers. One approach to assist these babies in developing language is to provide early and extensive training in English language production and comprehension. Another approach is to teach them sign language long before they learn to speak. (See the nearby Reflect on This feature.)

■ EDUCATIONAL ACHIEVEMENT

The educational achievement of students with a hearing loss may be significantly delayed in comparison to that of their hearing peers. Students who are deaf or have a partial hearing loss have considerable difficulty succeeding in an educational system that depends primarily on the spoken word and written language to transmit knowledge. Low achievement is characteristic of students who are deaf (Gustason, 1990; Paul & Quigley, 1990; Schirmer, 2000); they average 3 to 4 years below their age-appropriate grade levels. Reading is the academic area most negatively affected for students with a hearing loss. Any hearing loss, whether mild or profound, appears to have detrimental effects on reading performance (Gallaudet Research Institute, 1994, 2000; Leybaert, 1993). Students who are deaf obtain their

Reflect on This

A NEW LANGUAGE FOR BABY

Languishing in front of the tube, watching a gripping episode of *Teletubbies*, a baby of 10 months waves down Mom and signals for a bottle of the good stuff. No crying, no fuss. He just moves his hands in a pantomime of milking a cow—the international sign for *milk*. Mom smiles, signs back her agreement, and fetches Junior's bottle. No, this is not science fiction, but a portrayal of what's now possible at a U.S. university research facility where babies as young as 9 months old are taught sign language, long before they can speak. In a pilot program at Ohio State University, infants and their teachers learned to use a number of specific signs from American Sign Language to communicate with each other. Researcher Kimberlee

Whaley says parents, when they think about it, won't be surprised to hear that children can communicate physically, before they can verbally. "Think of an infant raising his or her hands up in the air," says Ms. Whaley. "What does the baby want? To be picked up, and we all recognize that."

What we didn't recognize is that kids also have the cognitive ability, and the motor skills, to sign for simple words, such as *eat, more, stop,* and *share.*

It's almost spooky to think that babies who aren't even walking yet are capable of basic understanding and communication. That's not the half of it, says Ms. Whaley. She says it's not unusual for babies to teach the signs to adults who have forgotten them. It happened to Ms. Whaley when one baby girl

indignantly reminded the researcher of the sign for *juice.* "I felt about two inches tall," said Ms. Whaley, an associate professor of human development and family science.

The sign language, she says, has allowed for much more effective communication between teachers and infants. "It is so much easier for our teachers to work with 12-month-olds who can sign that they want their bottle, rather than just cry and have us try to figure out what they want. This is a great way for infants to express their needs before they can verbalize them."

It's interesting, too, that some babies will grunt to be noticed, then use sign language to get more specific about what they want to say, she says.

The researchers are embarking on a larger, two-

year study and hope to answer questions raised by the early study: How early can babies learn sign language? And is there a gender difference? Girls appear to learn or use sign language more easily. Ms. Whaley thinks children of 6 or 7 months, who are able to sit up on their own, will learn basic signs.

But what about at night? What happens to a hungry or wet baby when Mom and Dad are asleep? "They revert back to crying," Ms. Whaley says.

Source: From "A New Language for Baby," by S. McKeen, *The Ottawa Citizen,* February 26, 1999. *[on-line]* Available: *http://www.deafworldweb.org/ pub/b/baby.news99.html*

---

highest achievement scores in reading during the first three years of school, but by third grade, reading performance is surpassed by both arithmetic and spelling performance. By the time students who are deaf reach adolescence (age 13), their reading performance is equivalent to that of about a third-grade child with normal hearing (Gallaudet Research Institute, 1994).

To counteract the difficulty with conventional reading materials, specialized instructional programs have been developed for students with a hearing loss (McAnally, Rose, & Quigley, 1999; Quigley & King, 1984). One such program is the Reading Milestones series, which uses content that focuses on the interests and experiences of children with a hearing loss while incorporating linguistic controls: the careful pacing of new vocabulary, the clear identification of syntactic structures, and the movement from simple to complex in introducing new concepts (e.g., idioms, inferences). Reading Milestones has become the most widely used reading program for students who are deaf.

■ SOCIAL DEVELOPMENT

A hearing loss modifies a person's capacity to receive and process auditory stimuli. People who are deaf or have a partial hearing loss receive a reduced amount of auditory information. That information is also distorted, compared to the input received by those with normal hearing. Consequently, the perceptions of auditory information by people with a hearing loss, particularly those who are deaf, will differ from the norm. "Deaf children will experience a somewhat different world than hearing children and these differences undoubtedly will have implications for their psychological development" (Marschark, 1993, p. 9).

■ ADJUSTMENT TO THE HEARING WORLD Reviews of the literature on social and psychological development in children who are deaf have suggested that there are differences in development when compared to hearing peers (Charlson, Strong, & Gold, 1992; Marschark, 1993). Different or delayed language acquisition may lead to more limited opportunities for social interaction. Children who are deaf may have more adjustment challenges when attempting to communicate with their hearing peers but appear to be more secure when conversing with nonhearing peers (Stinson & Whitmire, 1992; Vernon & Andrews, 1990).

■ THE DEAF CULTURE For some people who are deaf, social isolation from the hearing world is not considered an adjustment problem. On the contrary, it is a natural state of being where people are bonded together by a common language, customs, and heritage. People in a deaf culture seek each other out for social interaction and emotional support. The language of the culture is sign language where communication is through hand signs, body language, and facial expressions. Sign language is not one universal language. American Sign Language (ASL) is different from Russian Sign Language (RSL), which is different from French Sign Language (FSL), and so on. ASL is not a form of English or any other language. It has its own grammatical structure, which must be mastered in the same way as the grammar of any other language. (For more in-depth information on American Sign Language, see pages 435–437 of this chapter.)

In addition to a common language, the Deaf culture also has it own unique set of interactive customs. For example, people value physical contact with one another even more so than in a hearing community. It is common to see visual and animated expressions of affection, such as hugs and handshakes both in greetings and departures. Regardless of the topic, discussions are frank, and there is no hesitation in getting to the point (Lane, Hoffmeister, & Bahan, 1996; Lane, 1992). Gatherings within the Deaf culture may last longer because people like to linger. This may be particularly true at a dinner where it is perfectly okay to sign (talk) with your mouth full. It will obviously take longer to eat since it is difficult to sign and hold a knife and fork at the same time.

Within the Deaf community, the social identity of being a deaf person is highly valued, and there is a fierce internal loyalty. Everyone is expected to support activities within the Deaf culture, whether it be sports, arts and literature, or political networks. The internal cohesion among the community's members includes a strong expectation that people will marry within the group. In fact, 9 out 10 people in the Deaf culture marry others within the same community. This loyalty is so strong that deaf parents may hope for a deaf child in order to pass on the heritage and tradition of the Deaf culture to their offspring. While hearing people may be welcomed

When 20-year-old Terence Parkin arrived at the Sydney 2000 Olympic Games, his goal was to make his mark for South Africa and show the world what people who are deaf can accomplish. Terence, who was born with a severe hearing disability and uses sign language to communicate with his coach, achieved his goal by swimming to a silver medal in the 200-meter breaststroke. "I think it will confirm that deaf people can do things," he said afterwards. . . . "Other people will hopefully think now that we're just like other people. The only thing deaf people can't do is hear."

DEFIANTLY DEAF

How to reconcile this Deaf experience with the rest of the world? Should it be reconciled at all? M. J. Bienvenu has been one of the most vocal and articulate opponents of the language of disability. "I am Deaf," she says to me in Knoxville, drawing out the sign for "Deaf," the index finger moving from chin to ear, as though she is tracing a broad smile. "To see myself as Deaf is as much of a choice as it is for me to be a lesbian. I have identified with my culture, taken a public stand, made myself a figure within this community." Considerably gentler now than in her extremist heyday in the early 1980s, she acknowledges that "for some deaf people, being deaf is a disability. Those who learn forced English while being denied sign emerge semilingual rather than bilingual, and they are disabled people. But for the rest of us, it is no more a disability than being Japanese would be."

This is tricky territory. If being deaf is not a disability, then people who are deaf should not be protected under the Americans with Disabilities Act. It should not be legally required (as it is) that interpreters be provided in hospitals and other public service venues, that a relay operator be available on all telephone exchanges, that all televisions include the chip for caption access. It should not be necessary for the state to provide for separate schools. Deaf people should not be eligible for Social Security Disability Insurance (which they often claim). Those who say that being deaf is not a disability open themselves up to a lot of trouble. . . . It is tempting, in the end, to say there is no such thing as a disability. Equally, one might admit that almost everything is a disability. There are as many arguments for correcting everything as there are for correcting nothing.

Perhaps it would be most accurate to say that "disability" and "culture" are really matters of degree. Being deaf is a disability and a culture in modern America; so is being gay; so is being African American; so is being female; so even, increasingly, is being a straight white male; so is being paraplegic, or having Down syndrome. What is at issue is which things are so "cultural" that you wouldn't think of "curing" them, and which things are so "disabling" that you must "cure" them—and the reality is that for some people each of these experiences is primarily a disability experience while for others it is primarily a cultural one. Some African Americans are handicapped by blackness; some who are gay are handicapped by gayness; some paraplegics thrive on the care they receive and would be lost if their mobility were returned. Some people who are deaf are better off deaf and some would be better off hearing. Some could perhaps be both.

Source: Adapted from "Defiantly Deaf," by A. Solomon, August 28, 1994, *The New York Times Magazine*, Section 6, pp. 1–7, xx.

within the Deaf community, they are seldom accepted as full members. (See the nearby Reflect on This.)

Educational Services and Supports

In the United States, educational programs for children who are deaf or hard-of-hearing emerged in the early 19th century. The residential school for the deaf was the primary model for educational service delivery; it was a live-in facility where students were segregated from the family environment. In the latter half of the 19th century, day schools were established in which students lived with their families while receiving an education in a special school exclusively for deaf students. As the century drew to a close, some public schools established special classes for children with a hearing loss within general education schools.

The residential school continued to be a model for educational services well into the 20th century. However, with the introduction of electrical amplification, advances in medical treatment, and improved educational technology, more options became available within the public schools. Today, educational programs for students who are deaf or hard of hearing range from the residential school to inclusive education in a general education classroom with support services.

Since 1986, with the advent of early childhood amendments in Public Law 99-457, an expanding emphasis has been placed on early intervention. Luetke-Stahlman and Luckner (1991) suggested that children with a hearing loss must receive early intervention as soon as possible if they are to learn the language skills necessary for reading and other academic subjects. There is little disagreement that the education of the child with a hearing loss must begin at the time of the diagnosis. Educational goals for students with a hearing loss are comparable to those for their hearing peers. The student with a hearing loss brings many of the same strengths and weaknesses to the classroom as the hearing student. Adjustment to learning experiences is often comparable for both groups, as well. Students with a hearing loss, however, face the formidable problems associated with being unable to communicate effectively with hearing teachers and peers. (See nearby Interacting in Natural Settings.)

■ TEACHING COMMUNICATION SKILLS

Four approaches are commonly used in teaching communication skills to students with a hearing loss: auditory, oral, manual, and total communication. There is a long history of controversy regarding which approach is the most appropriate. However, no single method or collection of methods can meet the individual needs of all children with a hearing loss. It is not our purpose to enter into the controversy regarding these approaches but to present a brief description of each approach.

focus 6

Identify four approaches to teaching communication skills to persons with a hearing loss.

■ **THE AUDITORY APPROACH**   The auditory approach emphasizes the use of amplified sound and residual hearing to develop oral communication skills. The auditory channel is considered the primary avenue for language development, regardless of the severity or type of hearing loss. The basic principles of the auditory approach are as follows:

- Detecting hearing impairment as early as possible through screening programs, ideally in the newborn nursery and throughout childhood
- Pursuing prompt and vigorous medical and audiologic management, including selection, modification, and maintenance of appropriate hearing aids, cochlear implants, or other sensory aids
- Guiding, counseling, and supporting parents and caregivers as the primary models for spoken language through listening and to help them understand the impact of deafness and impaired hearing on the entire family
- Helping children integrate listening into their development of communication and social skills
- Supporting children's auditory–verbal development through one-to-one teaching
- Helping children monitor their own voices and the voices of others in order to enhance the intelligibility of their spoken language
- Using developmental patterns of listening, language, speech, and cognition to stimulate natural communication
- Continually assessing and evaluating children's development in the above areas and, through diagnostic intervention, modifying the program when needed
- Providing support services to facilitate children's educational and social inclusion in regular [general] education classes (Auditory–Verbal International, 2000)

The auditory approach uses a variety of electroacoustic devices to enhance residual hearing, such as binaural hearing aids, acoustically tuned earmolds, and FM units. FM units employs a behind-the-ear hearing aid connected to a high-powered frequency-modulated radio-frequency (FM-RF) system. These units use a one-way

■ EARLY CHILDHOOD YEARS

TIPS FOR THE FAMILY

- Promote family learning about diversity in all people in the context of understanding the child with a hearing loss.
- Keep informed about organizations and civic groups that can provide support to the young child with a hearing loss and also the family.
- Get in touch with your local health, social services, and education agencies about infant, toddler, and preschool programs for children with a hearing loss. Become familiar with the individualized family service plan (IFSP) and how it can serve as a planning tool to support the inclusion of your child in early intervention programs.
- Focus on the development of communication for your child. Work with professionals to determine what mode of communication (oral, manual, and/or total communication) will be most effective in developing early language skills.
- Label stimuli (e.g., objects and people) both visually and verbally as often as possible to provide the child with multiple sources of input.

TIPS FOR THE PRESCHOOL TEACHER

- Language deficits are a fundamental problem for young children with a hearing loss. Focus on developing some form of expressive and receptive communication in the classroom as early as possible. Help young children with a hearing loss to understand words that are abstract, have multiple meanings, and are part of idiomatic expressions (e.g., *run down the street* versus *run for president*).
- Help hearing classmates interact with the child with a hearing loss. Help hearing children be both verbal and visual with the student who is deaf or hard of hearing. If the child with a hearing loss doesn't respond to sound, have the hearing children learn to stand in the line of sight. Teach them to gain the attention of the child with a hearing loss without physical prompting.
- Work closely with parents so that early communication and skill development for the young child with a hearing loss is consistent across school and home environments.
- Become very familiar with acoustical devices (e.g., hearing aids) that may be used by the young child with a hearing loss. Make sure that these devices are worn properly and work in the classroom environment.

TIPS FOR PRESCHOOL PERSONNEL

- Support the inclusion of young children with a hearing loss in your classrooms and programs.
- Support teachers, staff, and volunteers as they attempt to create successful experiences for the young child with a hearing loss in the preschool setting.

- Work very closely with families to keep them informed and active members of the school community.

TIPS FOR NEIGHBORS AND FRIENDS

- Work with the family of a young child with a hearing loss to seek opportunities for interactions with hearing children in neighborhood play settings.
- Focus on the capabilities of the young child with a hearing loss, rather than the disabilities. Understand how the child communicates: orally? manually? or both? If the child uses sign language, take the time to learn fundamental signs that will enhance your communication with him or her.

■ ELEMENTARY YEARS

TIPS FOR THE FAMILY

- Learn about your rights as parents of a child with a hearing loss. Actively participate in the development of your child's individualized education plan (IEP). Through active participation, fight for goals on the IEP that will focus on your child's developing social interaction and communication skills in natural settings.
- Participate in as many school functions for parents as is reasonable (e.g., PTA, parent advisory groups, volunteering) to connect your family to the school.
- Seek information on in-school and extracurricular activities available that will enhance opportunities for

your child to interact with hearing peers.
- Keep the school informed about the medical needs of your child. If he or she needs or uses acoustical devices to enhance hearing capability, help school personnel understand how these devices work.

TIPS FOR THE GENERAL EDUCATION CLASSROOM TEACHER

- Outline schoolwork (e.g., the schedule for the day) on paper or the blackboard so the student with a hearing loss can see it.
- As much as possible, require classroom work to be answered in complete sentences to provide the necessary practice for students with a hearing loss.
- Remember that students with hearing loss don't always know how words fit together to make understandable sentences. Help them develop skills by always writing in complete sentences.
- Have the student with a hearing loss sit where he or she can see the rest of the class as easily as possible. Choose a buddy to sit by and keep him or her aware of what is going on in class.
- When lecturing, have the student with a hearing loss sit as close to you as possible.
- Don't be surprised to see gaps in learning. Demonstrations of disgust or amazement will make the student feel he or she is at fault.

- Be sure to help the student with a hearing loss know what is going on at all times (e.g., pass on announcements made over the intercom).
- Always give short, concise instructions and then make sure the student with a hearing loss understood them by having him or her repeat the information before performing the task.
- Type scripts (or outlines of scripts) for movies and videotapes used in class. Let the student read the script for the movie.
- When working with an interpreter, remember to:
  - Introduce the interpreter to the class at the beginning of the year, and explain his or her role.
  - Always speak directly to the student, not the interpreter.
  - Pause when necessary to allow the interpreter to catch up, since he or she may often be a few words behind.
  - Face the class when speaking. (When using a blackboard, write on the board first, then turn to face the class to speak.)
  - Include students who are deaf in class activities and encourage these students to participate in answering questions.

TIPS FOR SCHOOL PERSONNEL
- Integrate school resources as well as children. Wherever possible, help general education classroom teachers access the human and material resources necessary to meet the needs of students with a hearing loss. For example:
  - The audiologist. Keep in close contact with this

professional, and seek advice on the student's hearing and the acoustical devices being used.
- The special education teacher trained in hearing loss. This professional is necessary as both a teacher of students with a hearing loss and as a consultant to general educators. Activities can range from working on the development of effective communication skills to dealing with behavioral difficulties. The general education teacher may even decide to work with the special education teacher on learning sign language, if appropriate.
- Speech and language specialists. Many students with a hearing loss will need help with speech acquisition and application in the school setting.
- Assist general and special education teachers to develop peer partner and support networks for students with a hearing loss. Peer partners may help by serving as tutors or just by reviewing for tests and class assignments.
- Work to help the student with a hearing loss strive for independence. Assistance from peers is sometimes helpful, but it should never reach the point where other students are doing work for the student with a hearing loss.

TIPS FOR NEIGHBORS AND FRIENDS
- Help families with a child who is deaf or hard-of-hearing to be an integral part of neighborhood and friendship networks. Seek ways to include the family and the

child wherever possible in neighborhood activities (e.g., outings, barbecues, outdoor yard and street cleanups, crime watches).

SECONDARY AND TRANSITION YEARS

TIPS FOR THE FAMILY
- Become familiar with adult services systems (e.g., rehabilitation services, social security, health care) while your son or daughter is still in high school. Understand the type of vocational or employment training that he or she will need prior to graduation. Find out the school's view on what a high school should be doing to assist someone who is deaf or hard-of-hearing make the transition from school to adult life.
- Create opportunities out of school for your son or daughter to participate in activities with same-age hearing peers.

TIPS FOR THE GENERAL EDUCATION CLASSROOM TEACHER
- Collaborate with specialists in hearing loss and other school personnel to help students adapt to subject matter in your classroom (e.g., science, math, physical education).
- Become aware of the needs of and resources available for students with a hearing loss in your classroom. Facilitate student learning by establishing peer-support systems (e.g., note takers) to help students with a hearing loss be successful.
- Use diagrams, graphs, and visual representations

whenever possible when presenting new concepts.
- Help the student with a hearing loss become involved in extracurricular high school activities. If you are the faculty sponsor of a club or organization, explore whether the student is interested and how he or she could get involved.

TIPS FOR SCHOOL PERSONNEL
- Advocate for parents of high-school-age students with a hearing loss to participate in school activities (such as committees, PTA).
- Parents will be more active when school personnel have general and positive contact with the family.

TIPS FOR NEIGHBORS, FRIENDS, AND POTENTIAL EMPLOYERS
- Work with family and school personnel to create opportunities for students with a hearing loss to participate in community activities as much as possible with individuals who are deaf or hard-of-hearing, as well as those who are not.
- As a potential employer for people with a hearing loss, work with the high school and vocational rehabilitation counselors to locate and establish employment training sites.

ADULT YEARS

TIPS FOR THE FAMILY
- Become aware of the supports and services available for your son or daughter in the local community in which they will live as adults. What formal supports are available in

the community through government-funded programs or advocacy organizations for people with a hearing loss? through informal supports (family and friends)? What are the characteristics of quality adult services for people with a hearing loss?

■ Explore adult services in the local community in the areas of postsecondary education, employment, and recreation.

TIPS FOR NEIGHBORS, FRIENDS, AND POTENTIAL EMPLOYERS
■ Seek ways to become part of a community support

network for individuals with a hearing loss. Be alert to ways that these individuals can become and remain actively involved in community employment, neighborhood recreational activities, and local church functions.

■ As potential employers in the community, seek out information on employment of people with a hearing loss. Find out about programs that focus on establishing employment opportunities for people with a hearing loss, while meeting your needs as an employer.

wireless system on radio-frequency bands. The receiver unit (about the size of a deck of cards) is worn by the student, and a wireless microphone-transmitter-antenna unit is worn by the teacher. One advantage of using an FM-RF system is that the teacher can be connected to several students at a time.

■ THE ORAL APPROACH The oral approach to teaching communication skills also emphasizes the use of amplified sound and residual hearing to develop oral language. This approach emphasizes the need for persons with a hearing loss to function in the hearing world. Individuals are encouraged to speak and be spoken to. In addition to electroacoustic amplification, the teacher may employ **speechreading,** reading and writing, and motokinesthetic speech training (feeling an individual's face and reproducing breath and voice patterns). Speechreading is the process of understanding another person's speech by watching lip movement and facial and body gestures. This skill is difficult to master, especially for the person who has been deaf since an early age and thus never acquired speech. Problems with speechreading include that many sounds are not distinguishable on the lips and that the reader must attend carefully to every word spoken, a difficult task for preschool and primary-age children. Additionally, the speechreader must be able to see the speaker's mouth at all times.

Auditory–Verbal International (2000), a major international organization whose principal objective is to promote listening and speaking as a way of life for children who are deaf or hard-of-hearing, indicated that there is compelling evidence for the auditory and oral approach to teaching communication skills:

■ The majority of children with hearing loss have useful residual hearing.
■ When properly aided, children with hearing loss can detect most, if not all, of the speech spectrum.
■ Once residual hearing is accessed through amplification technology, a child will have the opportunity to develop language in a natural way through the auditory modality.
■ In order to benefit from the "critical periods" of neurological and linguistic development, appropriate amplification and medical technology and stimulation of hearing must occur as early as possible.
■ If hearing is not accessed during the critical language-learning years, a child's ability to use acoustic input meaningfully will deteriorate due to physiological (retrograde deterioration of auditory pathways) and psychosocial (attention, practice, learning) factors.
■ Current information about normal language development provides the framework and justification for the structure of auditory–verbal practice. That is,

■ SPEECHREADING. The process of understanding another person's speech by watching lip movement and facial and body gestures.

infants, toddlers, and children learn language most efficiently through consistent and continual meaningful interactions in a supportive environment with significant caretakers.

- As verbal language develops through the auditory input of information, reading skills can also develop.
- Parents in auditory–verbal programs do not have to learn sign language or cued speech. More than 90% of parents of children with hearing loss have normal hearing.
- Studies show that over 90% of parents with normal hearing do not learn sign language beyond a basic preschool level of competence.
- If a severe or profound hearing loss automatically makes an individual neurologically and functionally "different" from people with normal hearing, then the auditory–verbal philosophy would not be tenable. The fact is, however, that outcome studies show that individuals who have, since early childhood, been taught through the active use of amplified residual hearing are indeed independent, speaking, and contributing members of mainstream society.

■ **THE MANUAL APPROACH** The manual approach to teaching communication skills stresses the use of signs in teaching children who are deaf to communicate. The use of signs is based on the premise that many such children are unable to develop oral language and consequently must have some other means of communication. Manual communication systems are divided into two main categories: **sign languages and sign systems.**

Sign languages are a systematic and complex combination of hand movements that communicate whole words and complete thoughts rather than the individual letters of the alphabet. One of the most common sign languages is the **American Sign Language (ASL),** with a vocabulary of more than 6,000 signs. Examples of ASL signs are shown in Figure 14.2. ASL is currently the most widely used sign lan-

Alabama, Hawaii

Arkansas, Florida, Maine, Kentucky, Louisiana, Virginia, North Carolina, South Carolina

California, Illinois, Utah

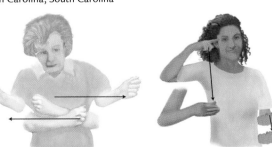
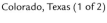
Colorado, Texas (1 of 2)

Massachusetts

Michigan, Ohio

FIGURE 14.2

Examples of one concept (Faint) expressed in American Sign Language

Faint: My mother fainted from the ammonia fumes.

[*Source:* Reprinted by permission of the publisher, from E. Shroyer and S. Shroyer, *Signs Across America,* (1984): 79–80. Washington, DC: Gallaudet University Press. Copyright © 1984 by Gallaudet University.]

guage among many adults who are deaf because it is easy to master and has historically been the preferred mode of communication. It is a language, but it is not English. Its signs represent concepts rather than single words. The use of ASL in a school setting has been strongly recommended by some advocates for people who are deaf, because it is considered their natural language (Lane et al., 1996; Lane, 1992). In fact, two studies by Bonvillian and Folven (1993) suggested that "sign language acquisition provides support for the view that ASL acquisition in young children [who are deaf] closely resembles that of spoken language development. . . . The general order of language emergence in sign was quite similar to that previously reported for spoken language development" (p. 241).

Sign systems differ from sign languages in that they attempt to create visual equivalents of oral language through manual gestures. With finger spelling, a form of manual communication that incorporates all 26 letters of the English alphabet, each letter is signed independently on one hand to form words. Figure 14.3 illustrates the

FIGURE 14.3

The American manual alphabet

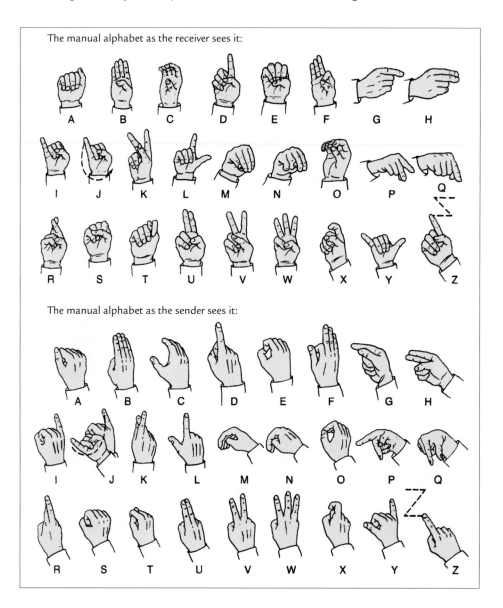

manual alphabet. In recent years, finger spelling has become a supplement to ASL. It is common to see a person who is deaf using finger spelling when there is no ASL sign for a word. The four sign systems used in the United States are Seeing Essential English, Signing Exact English, Linguistics of Visual English, and Signed English.

There is an emerging national debate regarding the use of ASL and signing English systems in providing academic instruction to students who are deaf. Should ASL or English be the primary language for instruction? Those advocating a **bicultural–bilingual approach** believe that ASL should be the primary language and English the second language. As the primary language, ASL would then serve as the foundation for the learning of English. The rationale for ASL as the primary language emerges from the values held dear by the Deaf community: children who are deaf must learn academic content in the language of their culture, their natural language. The primary language for children who are deaf is visual, not verbal. Children who are deaf should be considered bilingual students, and not students with disabilities. As is true in bilingual education programs for students with differing language backgrounds, there is also the debate as to whether ASL should be taught first and then English, or whether both should be taught simultaneously (Drasgow, 1993). One side emphasizes the importance of the child first acquiring the natural language (ASL). The other stresses the need to expose the child to both ASL and English simultaneously and as early as possible. There is little research to support either position. What is available (Prinz et al., 1996; Strong & Prinz, 1997) suggests that exposure to ASL at an early age enhances English skills.

■ TOTAL COMMUNICATION   **Total communication** has roots traceable to the 16th century. Over the past four centuries, many professionals advocated for an instructional system that employed every method possible to teach communication skills: oral, auditory, manual, and written. This approach was known as the combined system or simultaneous method. The methodology of the early combined system was imprecise; essentially, any recognized approach to teaching communication was used as long as it included a manual component. The concept of total communication differs from the older combined system in that it is not used only when the oral method fails or when critical learning periods have long since passed. In fact, total communication is not a system at all, but a philosophy.

The philosophy of total communication holds that the simultaneous presentation of signs and speech will enhance each person's opportunity to understand and use both systems more effectively. Total communication programs use residual hearing, amplification, speechreading, speech training, reading, and writing in combination with manual systems. A method that may be used as an aid to total communication but is not a necessary component of the approach is cued speech. **Cued speech** is intended to facilitate the development of oral communication by combining hand signals with speechreading. Gestures provide additional information concerning sounds not identifiable by speechreading. The result is that an individual has access to all sounds in the English language through either the lips or the hands. (See nearby Reflect on This feature.)

■ TECHNOLOGY

Educational and leisure opportunities for people with a hearing loss have been greatly expanded through technological advances such as **closed-caption television,** computers, and the Internet. In this section, we examine 21st-century technology for persons with a hearing loss.

■ BICULTURAL–BILINGUAL APPROACH. Instructional approach advocating ASL as the primary language and English as the second language for students who are deaf. ASL would thus serve as the foundation for learning English.

■ TOTAL COMMUNICATION. A communication philosophy and approach used by people with hearing impairments. It employs various combinations of elements from manual, oral, and any other techniques available to facilitate understanding.

■ CUED SPEECH. A communication method used by people with hearing impairments. It combines hand signals with speechreading. Gestures provide additional information regarding sounds not identifiable by lipreading.

■ CLOSED-CAPTION TELEVISION. Process by which people with hearing impairments are provided translated dialogue, in the form of subtitles, from television programs. Also called the "line-21" system since the caption is inserted into blank line 21 of the picture.

Reflect on This

COMMUNICATING THROUGH AN INTERPRETER

Interpreters can help facilitate communication during lectures, meetings, or other group situations. Before hiring an interpreter, keep in mind that an interpreter is a trained professional bound by a code of ethics. Knowing sign language does not qualify a person to act as an interpreter. It is best to use a professional interpreter.

Before requesting an interpreter, ask the person who is deaf if he or she has any interpreter preferences. Some may prefer an interpreter skilled in signed English or American Sign Language (ASL); others may rely on speechreading and thus need an oral interpreter. If the person who is deaf will be doing most of the talking, an interpreter who is skilled in voicing what is signed will be needed. Here are some tips to keep in mind when scheduling interpreting services:

■ Inform the interpreting service of the needs of the person who is deaf and in what setting the interpreting will occur.

■ Discuss fees and privileges with the interpreter beforehand.

Speak directly to the person who is deaf, not the interpreter. The interpreter is not part of the conversation and is not permitted to voice personal opinions or enter the conversation.

Remember that the interpreter is a few words behind the speaker. Give the interpreter time to finish before you ask questions so that the person who is deaf can ask questions or join in the discussion.

Treat the interpreter as a professional. It is courteous to introduce the interpreter to the group and explain why he or she is attending. The interpreter should be given the same privileges as the other group members.

If a meeting will last more than 2 hours, it is preferable to have two interpreters. It is difficult to interpret for more than an hour and a half.

Schedule breaks about every hour. Following a manual or oral interpreter for a long time is tiring for a person who is deaf.

Provide good lighting for the interpreter. If the situation requires darkening the room to view slides, for example, auxiliary lighting is necessary so that the person who is deaf can see the interpreter.

Permit only one person to speak at a time during group discussions. It is difficult for an interpreter to follow several people speaking at once. Ask for a brief pause between speakers to permit the interpreter to finish before the next speaker starts.

Speak clearly and in a normal tone when using an interpreter. Do not rush through a speech.

Allow time for people to study handouts, charts, or overheads. A person who is deaf cannot watch the interpreter and study written information at the same time.

When facilitating discussions, call on individual speakers rather than waiting for people to speak up. Because the interpreter needs to be a few words behind, people who are deaf don't always have an opportunity to become involved in discussions. Also, they sometimes don't realize that other people are starting to speak—often their contributions are passed over.

As a final courtesy, thank the interpreter after the service has been performed. If there have been any problems or misunderstandings, let the interpreter or referral service know. Also ask the person who is deaf if the service was satisfactory.

Source: Adapted from Seattle Community College, Regional Education Program for Deaf Students, Seattle, WA.

---

focus 7

Describe the uses of closed-caption television, computers, and the Internet for people with a hearing loss.

■ CLOSED CAPTIONING   The closed-caption TV process translates dialogue from a television program into printed words (captions or subtitles). These captions are then converted to electronic codes that can be inserted into the television picture on sets specially adapted with decoding devices. The process is called the line-21 system because the caption is inserted into blank line 21 of the picture.

Captioning is not a new idea. In fact, it was first used on motion picture film in 1958. Most libraries in the United States distribute captioned films for individuals with a hearing loss. Available only since 1980, closed captioning on television has experienced steady growth over the past 20 years. In its first year of operation, national closed-caption programming was available about 30 hours per week. By 1987, more than 200 hours per week of national programming were captioned in a wide range of topics, from news and information to entertainment and commercials. By 1993, all major broadcast networks were captioning 100% of their prime-time broadcasts, national news, and children's programming. With the passage of the Television Decoder Circuitry Act of 1993, the numbers of viewers watching cap-

This teacher embraces the philosophy of total communication. Students use residual hearing, amplification, and speech reading in combination with sign language.

tion expanded even more dramatically. This act required that all television sets sold in the United States be equipped with a decoder that allows captions to be placed anywhere on the television screen. This prevents captions from interfering with on-screen titles or other information displayed on the TV broadcast. In 1997, the U.S. Congress passed the Telecommunications Act of 1996, which required virtually all new television programming to be captioned by January 2006. While the Congress provided some exemptions to this requirement (e.g., non-English programming, commercials and public service announcements, and late night programs), the clear intent of the law was to continue expanded access to television for millions of people who are deaf.

There is the mistaken belief that the Americans with Disabilities Act (ADA) mandates captioning for television and movies. In fact, the ADA only requires captioning on government-funded television public service announcements. Federal law does not extend beyond television since the Federal Communication Commission has jurisdiction only over the airwaves. As such, there is no law covering the captioning of movies in theaters or videotapes (Robson, 2000).

■ COMPUTERS AND THE INTERNET   Personal computers offer an exciting dimension to information access for persons with a hearing loss. The computer places the person in an interactive setting with the subject matter. It is a powerful motivator. Most people find computers fun and interesting to work with on a variety of tasks. Additionally, computer-assisted instruction can be individualized so that students can gain independence by working at their own pace and level. (See nearby Today's Technology feature.)

Computer programs are now available for instructional support in a variety of academic subject areas, from reading and writing to learning basic sign language. Software is now available that will display a person's speech in visual form on the screen to assist in the development of articulation skills. Another innovative computer system is called C-print, developed by the National Technical Institute for the Deaf. Using a laptop computer equipped with a computer shorthand system and

Today's Technology

FIRST THE WORD, THEN—CLICK!—THE SIGN

Despite her teaching experience, Michele Cournoyer realized she needed new skills to reach the 14-year-old boy who had just enrolled at Willie Ross School for the Deaf.

"When you have a student looking at you who can't read or write but is intelligent and has a full language system, you have to do something," she said.

Cournoyer's new student was fluent in American Sign Language, with its rich vocabulary and its own syntax. He could say whatever he wanted, but only in sign.

The youngster did not have enough command of written English to use an ordinary dictionary or even an ASL dictionary. Cournoyer turned to

Smith College psychology professor Peter de Villiers, who has a special interest in how people with hearing loss acquire language.

They decided to use the youngster's existing knowledge of ASL and a computer.

"He could express concepts," recalled Cournoyer. "He had a fully working vocabulary, but it was not English."

Aided by Becky Haines, his research assistant, and Hampshire College student Nat Sims, they turned to hypercard software. Such software enables a user to flip through a stack of cards on the computer screen. A teacher types as much of a story as he or she wishes on a card, underlining the words that will be unfamiliar to the student.

Using an ASL dictionary and a scanner, the teacher transfers the sign for each underlined word to a separate card.

"They read a story. When they come to an unfamiliar word, they click the mouse and up pops a card with a sign," de Villiers said.

"Getting information about the meaning online as you are reading is much more effective in learning than looking it up in a dictionary or learning a list of words," de Villiers said. "They are better able to learn English words if they see them in sign rather than English."

"I already have data to show these students learn English words better if they get sign feedback than if they see an English definition."

"We are not teaching a new concept, we are giving them a label for a pre-existing concept," Cournoyer said. "It is so motivating, such a tremendous incentive when they see a sign which is their language. They have pride that is really remarkable."

Before using the computer, Cournoyer said, it was a chore for children to read three pages in a book; now, they read three or four whole stories.

"It makes them feel good," she said. "They hit a button and see their language right there for them."

Source: Adapted from "First the Word, Then—Click!—the Sign," by J. Caldwell, October 2, 1994, *Boston Sunday Globe,* pp. B23–B24.

---

commercially available software packages, C-print provides real-time translations of the spoken word. A trained operator is required to listen to speech, then type special codes representing words into the computer. These codes are transcribed into words that are shown almost simultaneously on a screen sitting atop an overhead projector. A printout of the transcription can be obtained as well. C-print provides a major service to students with a hearing loss as they attend college classes or oral lectures; they typically find note taking an extremely difficult activity, even when an oral interpreter is available (Northeast Technical Assistance Center, 2000).

The interactive videodisc is another important innovation in computer-assisted instruction. The videodisc, a record-like platter, is placed in a videodisc player that is connected to a microcomputer and television monitor. The laser-driven disc is interactive, allowing the individual to move through instruction at his or her own pace. Instant repetitions of subject matter are available to the learner at the touch of a button.

Perhaps the most important advance in technology for people with a hearing loss is access to information through the Internet. Whether it be e-mail, interactive chatrooms, or the infinite number of *web sites,* the World Wide Web provides people with a hearing loss access to all kinds of visual information through the quickest and most convenient means possible. *Web sites,* such as Deaf World Web (*http://dww.deafworld web.org/*), Deaf Resources (*http://www.deafresources.com/*), and the American Sign Language Browser (*http://commtechlab.msu.edu/sites/aslweb/*) are just a few examples of

This student can work at her own pace and level using computer-assisted instruction.

sites designed specifically for people who are deaf. In addition, people with a hearing loss can access information from national organizations, such as Alexander Graham Bell Association for the Deaf and Hard of Hearing (*http://www.agbell.org/*) and the National Association of the Deaf (*http://nad.policy.net/*).

■ TELECOMMUNICATION DEVICES   A major advance in communication technology for people with a hearing loss is the telecommunication device (TDD). In 1990, the Americans with Disabilities Act renamed them **text telephones (TTs).** TTs send, receive, and print messages through thousands of stations across the United States. People with a hearing loss can now dial an 800 number to set up conference calls, make appointments, or order merchandise or fast food. Anyone wanting to speak with a person using a TT can do so through the use of a standard telephone.

The teletypewriter and printer (TTY) is another effective use of technology for people who are deaf. It allows them to communicate by phone via a typewriter that converts typed letters into electric signals through a modem. These signals are sent through the phone lines and then translated into typed messages and printed on a typewriter connected to a phone on the other end. Computer software is now available that can turn a personal computer into a TTY.

Medical and Social Services

I n this new century, advances in medicine and social services are opening up opportunities never thought possible for people with a hearing loss. Medical services play a major role in the prevention, early detection, and remediation of a hearing loss. Community services and supports are helping to reduce the social isolation of people who are deaf or have a partial hearing loss. As suggested by Stokoe (1993), "Perspectives on deafness are changing in a radical way. . . . A first generation of deaf people are at last breaking down the prejudicial barriers to professional education. Deaf psychologists, linguists, and anthropologists are beginning to show the world new landscapes of the country they live in" (p. 374).

■ **MEDICAL SERVICES**

Several specialists are integrally involved in medical assessment and intervention, including the geneticist, the pediatrician, the family practitioner, the otologist, the neurosurgeon, and the audiologist.

focus 8
Why is the early detection of hearing loss so important?

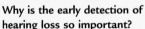

■ TEXT TELEPHONES (TTS). Telephones that send, receive, and print messages through thousands of stations across the United States.

■ **THE GENETICIST**   Prevention of a hearing loss is a primary concern of the genetics specialist. A significant number of hearing losses are inherited or occur during prenatal, perinatal, and postnatal development. Consequently, the genetics specialist plays an important role in preventing disabilities through family counseling and prenatal screening.

■ **THE PEDIATRICIAN AND FAMILY PRACTITIONER**   Early detection of a hearing loss can prevent or at least minimize the impact of the disability on the overall development of an individual. Generally, it is the responsibility of the pediatrician or family practitioner to be aware of a problem and to refer the family to an appropriate hearing specialist. These responsibilities require that the physician be familiar with family history and conduct a thorough physical examination of the child. The physician must be alert to any symptoms (e.g., delayed language development) that indicate potential sensory loss. (See nearby Reflect on This feature.)

focus 9

Distinguish between an otologist and an audiologist.

■ **THE OTOLOGIST**   The **otologist** is the medical specialist who is most concerned with the hearing organ and its diseases. Otology is a component of the larger specialty of diseases of the ear, nose, and throat. The otologist, like the pediatrician, screens for potential hearing problems, but the process is much more specialized and exhaustive. The otologist also conducts an extensive physical examination of the ear to identify syndromes that are associated with conductive or sensorineural loss. This information, in conjunction with family history, provides data regarding appropriate medical treatment.

Treatment may involve medical therapy or surgical intervention. Common therapeutic procedures include monitoring aural hygiene (e.g., keeping the external ear free from wax), blowing out the ear (e.g., a process to remove mucus blocking the eustachian tube), and administering antibiotics to treat infections. Surgical techniques may involve the cosmetic and functional restructuring of congenital malformations such as a deformed external ear or closed external canal (atresia). Fenestration refers to the surgical creation of a new opening in the labyrinth of the ear to restore hearing. A stapedectomy is a surgical process conducted under a microscope whereby a fixed stapes is replaced with a prosthetic device capable of vibrating, thus permitting the transmission of sound waves. A myringoplasty is the surgical reconstruction of a perforated tympanic membrane (eardrum).

Another widely used surgical procedure involves a **cochlear implant.** This electronic device is surgically placed under the skin behind the ear. It consists of four parts: (1) a microphone for picking up sound; (2) a speech processor to select and arranges sounds picked up by the microphone; (3) a transmitter and receiver/stimulator to receive signals from the speech processor and convert them into electric impulses; and (4) electrodes to collect the impulses from the stimulator and send them to the brain. The implant does not restore or amplify hearing. Instead, it provides the person who is deaf or profoundly hard-of-hearing with a useful "sense" of sound in the world around them. The implant overcomes "nerve deafness" (sounds blocked from reaching the auditory nerve) by getting around damage to the tiny hair cells in the inner ear and directly stimulating the auditory nerve. An implant electronically finds useful or meaningful sounds, such as speech, and then sends these sounds to the auditory nerve.

Cochlear implants are becoming more widely used with both adults and children. More than 25,000 people worldwide (50% children and 50% adults) have had the surgery (National Institute on Deafness and Other Communication Disorders, 2000b). Some adults who were deafened in their later years reported useful hearing following the implant, and others still needed speechreading to understand the spo-

■ OTOLOGIST. One who is involved in the study of the ear and its diseases.

■ COCHLEAR IMPLANT. A surgical procedure that implants an electronic device under the skin behind the ear. The implant overcomes "nerve deafness" by getting around damage to the cells in the inner ear and directly stimulating the auditory nerve.

Reflect on This

THE CRIES GROW LOUDER: CHECK NEWBORNS' HEARING

Some deaf babies are lucky enough to be born in a hospital where inexpensive hearing tests are performed on all newborns. Those babies are leaving the hospital on a road toward hearing and developing normal language skills.

But because the tests are so rarely administered, an estimated 30 U.S. newborns a day go home with significant hearing impairment, and it will take an average of 2½ years for their disability to be discovered. By then, the children's brains will have developed largely without the influence of words.

This disparity reflects the sporadic way in which new technologies are being introduced across the United States.

The technologies are simple tests that expose an infant to clicking noises and register the responses in either the child's ear or the brain. Both are used widely and cost less than $50 a child.

Since the National Institutes of Health recommended in 1993 that all babies undergo such testing within the first three months of life,

about 20 states have passed laws encouraging the tests; 12 of those demand that babies be tested. Federal legislation is being considered that would make it a national requirement.

One of every 300 newborns has some hearing loss. Half of those children have moderate to severe hearing loss in both ears.

Through traditional screening methods and limited mandatory testing of all babies, only about 19% of newborns have their hearing checked, but traditional screening methods have had major limitations.

A complex brain scan that showed some hearing loss was expensive and applied only to babies known to be at high risk of hearing loss—some premature babies and those born after problems during pregnancy.

More commonly, doctors could do little but expose babies to a loud noise and try to judge by the reaction whether the child could hear.

But at least half of all babies born with hearing loss are not considered at high risk.

"We knew by following that protocol we would miss 50%

of the babies with hearing loss," says Gilbert Herer, chairman of the hearing and speech department at Children's National Medical Center in Silver Spring, Maryland. "I never thought I would see the day when I had the technology to identify hearing loss during the newborn period."

Sometimes the problem is easy to fix. Some babies are born with "gunk" in the ear that is removed surgically. Other times, the hearing is permanently damaged because the tiny "hairs" deep inside the ear that transmit sound signals to the brain don't work properly.

But today's high-tech hearing aids and cochlear implants allow babies whose hearing loss is identified early to grow up tuned in to the world around them. One hearing aid has a radio that allows parents or teachers to wear a microphone that transmits their voices directly to the ear. The mother washing dishes can chatter as the child plays nearby, teaching the baby language.

"The brain is developing so rapidly during this time," Herer says. "If you don't stimulate the auditory system,

these neural tracks and neural clusters don't develop to support what we as human beings use all the time."

■ EARLY SIGNS OF EAR TROUBLE

If the baby doesn't have the following behavior, a doctor should be consulted.

Birth to 3 months
- Reacts to sounds
- Is soothed by your voice
- Turns head to you when you speak
- Is awakened by loud voices and sounds
- Smiles when spoken to
- Seems to know your voice and quiets down if crying

3 to 6 months
- Looks upward or turns toward a new sound
- Responds to "no" and to changes in tone of voice
- Imitates his/her own voice
- Enjoys rattles and other toys that make sound
- Begins to repeat sounds (such as *ooh, aah* and *ba-ba*)
- Becomes scared by a loud voice

Source: From "The Cries Grow Louder: Check Newborns' Hearing," by R. Davis, *USA Today,* May 24, 1999, 10D.

---

ken word (Tye-Murray, 1993). Most children receive the implants between the ages of 2 and 6. There is a debate about which age is optimal for the surgery but it appears that the earlier, the better. The Cochlear Implants Association (2000) suggests that children from 18 months to 17 years of age are appropriate candidates for an implant if they have profound hearing loss in both ears, little or no useful benefit from hearing aids, no medical contraindications, and high motivation and appropriate expectations (both child and family). The association also recommends that following surgery the child be placed in an educational program that emphasizes development of auditory skills. They suggest similar criteria for adults with the additional caveat that the person must have a strong desire to be part of the hearing world.

The learning of speech and language following a cochlear implant remains difficult for young prelingual deaf children (Geers & Tobey, 1992). Additionally, caution should be exercised because of the risk of possible damage to an ear that has some residual hearing and the risk of infection from the implant.

Some people who are deaf view cochlear implants as a direct attack on the values and heritage of the Deaf culture; others view the implants as a medical miracle.

There are many deaf and hard-of-hearing people who are against the use of implants with children; and there are many who support its use with children. There are people who are opposed to use of implants in anyone at any age; and there are people who don't care if a deaf or hard-of-hearing adult makes a personal decision to be implanted. Cochlear implants have been controversial in our [Deaf] community because some people feel that the implants are being used in an attempt to eradicate our community; but the medical community and the parents seem to see implants as a miraculous way to conquer deafness and keep their implanted children in the mainstream society on a permanent basis. (National Association of the Deaf, 2000)

■ THE AUDIOLOGIST   The degree of hearing loss, measured in decibel and hertz units, is determined by an **audiologist,** using a process known as audiometric evaluation. The listener receives tones that are relatively free of external noise (pure-tone audiometry) or spoken words, in which speech perception is measured (speech audiometry). An **audiometer** detects the person's response to sound stimuli, and a record **(audiogram)** is obtained from the audiometer that graphs the individual's threshold for hearing at various sound frequencies.

Whereas an otologist presents a biological perspective on hearing loss, an audiologist emphasizes the functional impact of losing one's hearing. The audiologist first screens the individual for a hearing loss, then determines both the nature and severity of the condition. Social, educational, and vocational implications of the hearing loss are then discussed and explored. Although audiologists are not specifically trained in the field of medicine, these professionals interact constantly with otologists to provide a comprehensive assessment of hearing.

Working together, audiologists and otologists provide assistance regarding the selection and use of hearing aids. At one time or another, most people with a hearing loss will probably wear hearing aids. Hearing aids amplify sound, but they do not correct hearing. Hearing aids have been used for centuries. Early acoustic aids included cupping one's hand behind the ear as well as the ear trumpet. Modern electroacoustic aids do not depend on the loudness of the human voice to amplify sound but utilize batteries to increase volume. Electroacoustic aids come in three main types: body-worn aids, behind-the-ear aids, and in-the-ear aids. Which hearing aid is best for a particular person depends on the degree of hearing loss, the age of the individual, and the physical condition of the individual.

Body-worn hearing aids are typically worn on the chest, using a harness to secure the unit. The hearing aid is connected by a wire to a transducer, which is worn at ear level and delivers a signal to the ear via an earmold. Body-worn aids are becoming less common because of the disadvantages of being chest-mounted, the location of the microphone, and inadequate high-frequency response. The behind-the-ear aid (also referred to as an ear-level aid) is the most common electroacoustical device for children with a hearing loss (Maxon & Brackett, 1992). All components of the behind-the-ear aid are fitted in one case behind the outer ear. The case then connects to an earmold that delivers the signal directly to the ear. In addition to their portability, behind-the-ear aids have the advantage of producing the greatest amount of electroacoustic flexibility (amount of amplification across all frequen-

■ AUDIOLOGIST. A specialist in the assessment of a person's hearing ability.

■ AUDIOMETER. An electronic device used to detect a person's response to sound stimuli.

■ AUDIOGRAM. A record obtained from an audiometer that graphs an individual's threshold of hearing at various sound frequencies.

cies). The primary disadvantage is problems with acoustic feedback. As discussed earlier in this chapter, the behind-the-ear aid may be used with an FM-RF system. These aids may be fitted monaurally (on one ear) or binaurally (on both ears).

The in-the-ear aid fits within the ear canal. All major components (microphone, amplifier, transducer, and battery) are housed in a single case that has been custom made for the individual user. The advantage of the in-the-ear aid is the close positioning of the microphone to the natural reception of auditory signals in the ear canal. In-the-ear aids are recommended for individuals with mild hearing losses who do not need frequent changes in earmolds. As such, these aids are not usually recommended for young children. Additionally, in-the-ear aids have more problems with feedback because of the close proximity of the microphone to the transducer (Maxon & Brackett, 1992).

Although the quality of commercially available aids has improved dramatically in recent years, they do have distinct limitations. For example, hearing-aid use has been found to be positively related to speech use but appears to have little effect on reading ability (Mertens, 1990). The criteria for effectiveness must be measured against wearability, the individual's communication skills, and educational achievement.

The stimulation of residual hearing through a hearing aid enables most people with a hearing loss to function as hard-of-hearing. However, the use of a hearing aid must be implemented as early as possible, before sensory deprivation takes its toll on the child. It is the audiologist's responsibility to weigh all the factors involved (e.g., convenience, size, weight) in the selection and use of an aid for the individual. The individual should then be directed to a reputable hearing-aid dealer.

focus 10

Identify factors that may affect the social integration of people who are deaf into the hearing world.

■ SOCIAL SERVICES

The social consequences of being deaf or hard of hearing are highly correlated with the severity of the loss. For the individual who is deaf, social integration may be extremely difficult because societal views of deafness have reinforced social isolation. The belief that such a person is incompetent has been predominant from the time of the early Hebrews and Romans, who deprived these people of their civil rights, to 20th-century America, where, in some areas, it is still difficult for adults who are deaf to obtain driver's licenses or adequate insurance coverage or to be gainfully employed. Individuals with the greatest difficulty are those born with congenital deafness. The inability to hear and understand speech has often isolated these people from their hearing peers. For example, people who are deaf tend to marry other people who are deaf. Solomon (1994) reported that when people who are deaf do marry people who can hear, the marriage ends in divorce about 90% of the time.

A segment of individuals who are deaf are actively involved in organizations and communities specifically intended to meet their needs. The National Association for the Deaf (NAD) was organized in 1880. The philosophy of the NAD is that every person who is deaf has the same rights as those in the hearing world—the right to life, liberty, and the pursuit of happiness. NAD emphasizes that the exercise of these rights must be to the satisfaction of those who are deaf and not to their teachers and parents who do not have the condition. NAD serves individuals who are deaf in many capacities. Among its many contributions, NAD publishes books on deafness, sponsors cultural activities, and lobbies throughout the United States for legislation promoting the rights of persons who are deaf.

Another prominent organization is the Alexander Graham Bell Association for the Deaf, which advocates the integration of persons with a hearing loss into the social mainstream. The major thrust of this approach is the improvement of proficiency in

In the past, an inability to hear often isolated these children from their hearing peers. Today, about 8 out of 10 students with a hearing loss are educated in the general education classroom for at least part of the school day.

speech communications. As a clearinghouse for information for people who are deaf and their advocates, the association publishes widely in the areas of parent counseling, teaching methodology, speech reading, and auditory training. In addition, it sponsors national and regional conferences that focus on a variety of issues pertinent to the social adjustment of people who are deaf.

Case Study

MARIO AND SAMANTHA

■ MARIO

It's a Monday in May, near the end of the school year. The classroom door is open, and the hearing students are pouring in, greeting their friends and talking excitedly about their weekend experiences. Mario, who is deaf, slips in silently, sits down alone, and buries his head in a book as he waits for class to begin. He cannot hear the buzz of activity and conversation around him. He was not a part of the weekend activities. No one speaks to him. He looks up as a girl he likes comes up the row to her seat and drops her books down on the desk. He ventures to speak softly to her, not noticing that she is already talking and joking with a guy across the room. Mario finally captures

her glance and asks his question, but the girl doesn't understand what he says. (His speech is slightly impaired, and the room is noisy.) After two more repetitions of "How was your weekend?" he is rewarded with a perfunctory "Oh, fine!" before she turns around and gets wrapped up in a detailed, secret exchange with her best girlfriend, who sits right behind her. They giggle and talk, glancing up once in a while to catch the eye of the boy across the room. Mario rearranges the papers on his desk.

Finally, the teacher begins to lecture, and the lively conversational exchanges become subdued. The hearing students settle into pseudo-attentive postures, reverting to subtle, subversive

communications with those around them. Mario, in his front row, corner seat, turns his eyes on the interpreter. He keeps his focus there, working to grasp visually what the other students are effortlessly half-listening to. The teacher questions a student in the back of the room. Her hearing friends whisper help. Their encouragement boosts her confidence and she boldly answers the teacher. Satisfied, the teacher moves on to question someone else. The first student joins those whispering to the boy who's now on the spot. He picks up the quiet cues and impresses the instructor with his evident mastery of the subject. A peer support system of companionable cooperation helps keep everyone afloat.

However, only those with sensitive hearing and social support can tap into this interwoven network of surreptitious assistance. When a pointed question is directed to Mario, he is on his own. No student schemes bring him into the "we" of class camaraderie. Instead, when he speaks, the students suddenly stop talking and stare. But he is oblivious to the awkward silence in the room. He is verbally stumbling, searching for an answer that will pacify the teacher, and yet not be too specific. He strains to minimize the risk of opening himself up for embarrassment of saying something that misses the mark entirely. While he is still speaking, the bell rings and the other students pack up and start moving out the back door. Mario, his eyes on the teacher, doesn't notice the interpreter's signal that the bell has already sounded. The teacher smiles uncomfortably and cuts him off to give last-minute instructions as the students pour out the door.[1]

SAMANTHA

It is a crisp autumn morning, the kind that some people breathe in deeply as they look forward to the challenges of the day. School has begun an hour ago. Mrs. Jones's algebra class is examining some equations. Puzzled by Mrs. Jones's explanation, Samantha raises her hand and questions her teacher about an equation. While Samantha signs her question, Mrs. Jones watches Samantha (pleased that she understands much of what Samantha is signing) and listens to Samantha's interpreter. Several of Samantha's classmates watch her signing, nodding in agreement that the explanation was not clear.

Later, as the students work some math problems, Samantha and a hearing friend exchange suggestions through signs. As Samantha and her classmates leave for their next class, Mrs. Jones calls out to the class and signs to Samantha, "Have a nice day."

Samantha and two of her hearing friends hurry to their next class. On the way, they animatedly sign to each other about the upcoming school dance. Samantha's planning to go with one of her friends who is deaf from the mainstream program, Jason. As they reach their next class, they meet Mike and Ernestine, two other students in the mainstream program who are deaf. Samantha and her two friends greet Mike and Ernestine and they enter the class together. During the civics class the students and teachers have a lively exchange about the responsibility of citizens when faced with a law they feel is immoral. (Occasionally the teacher reminds the students not to interrupt one another

or talk so fast so that all of the students, deaf and hearing, can catch what is being said.) Samantha, Mike, and Ernestine join in through sign language, and several of the hearing students sign as they speak. An interpreter speaks and signs as needed.

After civics, Samantha and Ernestine head to an English class and Mike to a physical education class. The English class is taught by Mr. Roberts, a deaf education teacher in the mainstream program. Being deaf, Mr. Roberts signs gracefully and eloquently. The class is alive as they discuss poetry by hearing and deaf poets. Tony, Margaret, and Lee, three hearing students, are in the class with Samantha and her deaf classmates. They will attend for two weeks as the class discusses and dramatizes poetry. Mr. Roberts uses his voice to help them understand, though they sign quite well. At the end of the two weeks, the class will dramatize and sign several poems for other deaf and hearing students.[2]

APPLICATION

1. Compare and contrast the social and educational isolation of Mario in a general education setting with the inclusive nature of Samantha's school experiences.

2. Are the two case studies of Mario and Samantha representative of your experiences with students who are deaf in general education classroom settings? Why or why not?

3. How is a school like Samantha's organized? What is needed to support and include students who are deaf in the social and academic life of the school?

[1]*Source:* Adapted from "Alone in the Crowd," by C. Wixtrom, 1988, *The Deaf American, 38*(12), pp. 14–15.

[2]*Source:* Adapted from "The Challenges of Educating Together Deaf and Hearing Youth: Making Mainstreaming Work," by P. C. Higgins, 1990, Springfield, IL: Charles C. Thomas.

Debate Forum

LIVING IN A DEAF CULTURE

*Deaf Culture: a cultural group comprised of persons who share similar and positive attitudes toward deafness. The "core Deaf culture" is comprised of those persons who have a hearing loss, share a common language, values, and experiences and a common way of interacting with each other. The broader Deaf community is comprised of individuals (both deaf and hearing) who have posi-*tive, accepting attitudes toward deafness which can be seen in their linguistic, social, and political behaviors. People in a Deaf culture seek each other out for social interaction and emotional support.*

The inability to hear and understand speech may lead an individual to seek community ties and social relationships primarily with other individuals who are deaf. These individuals may choose to isolate themselves from hearing peers and live, learn, work, and play in a social subculture known as "a Deaf culture or Deaf community."

POINT

The Deaf culture is a necessary and important component of life for many peo-ple who are deaf. The person who is deaf has a great deal of difficulty adjusting to life in a hearing world. Through the deaf culture, he or she can find other individuals with similar problems, common interests, a common language (American Sign Language), as well as a common heritage and culture. Membership in the Deaf culture is an achieved status that must be earned by the individual who is deaf. The individual must demonstrate a strong identification with the deaf world, understand and share experiences that come with being deaf, and be willing to actively participate in the Deaf community's educational, cultural and political activities. The Deaf culture gives such persons a positive identity that can't be found among their hearing peers.

Participation in the Deaf culture only serves to isolate people who are deaf from those who hear. A separate subculture unnecessarily accentuates the differences between people who can and cannot hear. The life of the person who is deaf need not be different from that of anyone else. Children who are deaf can be integrated into general education schools and classrooms. People who are deaf can live side by side with their hearing peers in local communities, sharing common bonds and interests. There is no reason why they can't participate together in the arts, enjoy sports, and share leisure and recreational interests. Membership in the Deaf culture will only further reinforce the idea that people who have disabilities should grow up and live in a culture away from those who do not. The fact is, the majority of people who are deaf do not seek membership in the Deaf culture. These people are concerned that the existence of such a community makes it all the more difficult for them to assimilate into society at large.

Review

 1

Describe how sound is transmitted through the human ear.

- A vibrator—such as a string, reed, or column of air—causes displacement of air particles.
- Vibrations are carried by air, metal, water, or other substances.
- Sound waves are displaced air particles that produce a pattern of auricular waves that move away from the source to a receiver.
- The human ear collects, processes, and transmits sounds to the brain, where they are decoded into meaningful language.

 2

Distinguish between the terms *deaf* and *hard-of-hearing*.

- A person who is deaf typically has profound or total loss of auditory sensitivity and very little, if any, auditory perception.
- For the person who is deaf, the primary means of information input is through vision; speech received through the ears is not understood.
- A person who is hard-of-hearing (partially hearing) generally has residual hearing through the use of a hearing aid, which is sufficient to process language through the ear successfully.

 3

Why is it important to consider age of onset and anatomical site when defining a hearing loss?

- Age of onset is critical in determining the type and extent of intervention necessary to minimize the effect of the hearing loss.
- Three types of peripheral hearing loss are associated with anatomical site: conductive, sensorineural, and mixed.
- Central auditory hearing loss occurs when there is a dysfunction in the cerebral cortex (outer layer of gray matter in the brain).

 4

What are the estimated prevalence and causes of hearing loss?

- It has been extremely difficult to determine the prevalence of hearing loss. Estimates of hearing loss in the United States go as high as 28 million people; approximately 11 million people have significant irreversible hearing loss, and 1 million are deaf.
- Nearly 71,000 students between the ages of 6 and 21 have a hearing impairment and are receiving special education services in U.S. schools. These students account for approximately 1.5% of school-age students identified as having a disability.
- Although more than 200 types of deafness have been related to hereditary factors, the cause of 50% of all hearing loss remains unknown.
- A common hereditary disorder is otosclerosis (bone destruction in the middle ear).
- Nonhereditary hearing problems evident at birth may be associated with maternal health problems: infections (e.g., rubella), anemia, jaundice, central nervous system disorders, the use of drugs, sexually transmitted disease, chicken pox, anoxia, and birth trauma.
- Acquired hearing losses are associated with postnatal infections, such as measles, mumps, influenza, typhoid fever, and scarlet fever.
- Environmental factors associated with hearing loss include extreme changes in air pressure caused by explosions, head trauma, foreign objects in the ear, and loud noise. Loud noise is rapidly becoming one of the major causes of hearing problems.

focus 5

Describe the basic intelligence, speech and language skills, educational achievement, and social development associated with people who are deaf or hard-of-hearing.

- Intellectual development for people with hearing loss is more a function of language development than cognitive ability. Any difficulties in performance appear to be closely associated with speaking, reading, and writing the English language, but are not related to level of intelligence.
- Speech and English language skills are the areas of development most severely affected for those with a hearing loss. The effects of a hearing loss on English language development vary considerably. For children with mild and moderate hearing losses, the effect may be minimal.
- Most people with a hearing loss are able to use speech as the primary mode for language acquisition. People who are congenitally deaf are unable to receive information through the speech process unless they have learned to speechread. Sounds produced by the person who is deaf are extremely low in intelligibility.
- Reading is the academic area most negatively affected for students with a hearing loss. Any hearing loss, whether mild or profound, appears to have detrimental effects on reading performance.
- The social and psychological development in children

is different in comparison to hearing peers. Different or delayed language acquisition may lead to more limited opportunities for social interaction. Children who are deaf may have more adjustment challenges when attempting to communicate with their hearing peers but appear to be more secure when conversing with nonhearing peers.

- For some people who are deaf, social isolation from the hearing world is not considered an adjustment problem. It is a natural state of being where people are bonded together by a common language, customs, and heritage. People in a Deaf culture seek out one another for social interaction and emotional support

 focus 6

Identify four approaches to teaching communication skills to persons with a hearing loss.

- The auditory approach to communication emphasizes the use of amplified sound and residual hearing to develop oral communication skills.
- The oral approach to communication emphasizes the use of amplified sound and residual hearing but may also employ speechreading, reading and writing, and motokinesthetic speech training.
- The manual approach stresses the use of signs in teaching children who are deaf to communicate.
- The total communication approach employs the use of

residual hearing, amplification, speechreading, speech training, reading, and writing in combination with manual systems to teach communication skills to children with a hearing loss.

 focus 7

Describe the uses of closed-caption television, computers, and the Internet for people with a hearing loss.

- Closed-caption television translates dialogue from a television program into captions (subtitles) that are broadcast on the television screen. Closed-caption television provides the person with a hearing loss greater access to information and entertainment.
- Computers place people with a hearing loss in interactive settings with access to vast amounts of information. Computer programs are now available for instructional support in a variety of academic subject areas, from reading and writing to learning basic sign language. Certain software can display a person's speech in visual form on the screen to assist in the development of articulation skills.
- One of the most important advances in technology for people with a hearing loss is access to information through the Internet. E-mail, interactive chatrooms, and the infinite number of web sites provide people with a hearing loss access to all kinds of visual information.
- TT systems provide efficient ways for people who are deaf to communicate over

long distances. TTY devices allow people who are deaf to use a personal computer or typewriter, modem, and printer to communicate over the phone.

 focus 8

Why is the early detection of hearing loss so important?

- Early detection of hearing loss can prevent or minimize the impact of the disability on the overall development of an individual.

focus 9

Distinguish between an otologist and an audiologist.

- An otologist is a medical specialist who is concerned with the hearing organ and its diseases.
- An audiologist is concerned with the measurement of hearing loss and its sociological and educational impact on an individual.
- Both the audiologist and otologist assist in the process of selecting and using a hearing aid.

 focus 10

Identify factors that may affect the social integration of people who are deaf into the hearing world.

- The inability to hear and understand speech has isolated some people who are deaf from their hearing peers.
- Societal views of deafness may reinforce isolation.

People with Vision Loss

To begin with . . .

Jorge Luis Borges (1899–1986) was one of the most original and influential of modern writers. Borges regarded his progressive blindness, the result of an inherited eye disease, not as entirely tragic but as an opportunity. "Blindness has not been for me a total misfortune; it should not be seen in a pathetic way. It should be seen as a way of life; one of the styles of living. . . . The world of the blind is not the night that people imagine." (Borges, cited in Lopate, 1994)

Print-to-speech reading machines for the blind are now very small, inexpensive, palm-sized devices that can read books (those that still exist in paper form) and other printed documents, and other real-world text such as signs and displays. These reading systems are equally adept at reading the trillions of electronic documents that are instantly available from the ubiquitous wireless worldwide network. After decades of ineffective attempts, useful navigation devices have been introduced that can assist blind people in avoiding physical obstacles in their path and finding their way around, using global positioning system (GPS) technology. A blind person can interact with her personal reading-navigation systems through two-way voice communication, kind of like a Seeing Eye dog that reads and talks. (Kurzweil, 2000)

Braille readers can now read their books on the Internet, thanks to a historic technological breakthrough by The Library of Congress called Web-Braille. Readers now have access to [more than 3,000] electronic braille books placed on the Internet for the use of eligible braille readers by the Library's National Library Service for the Blind and Physically Handicapped (NLS). Each year many hundreds of new titles will be added. As a result of new computer technology, braille readers may now access Web-Braille digital braille book files with a computer and a refreshable braille display (electronic device that raises or lowers an array of pins to create a line of braille characters) or a braille embosser. About 40 new titles per month are released in braille and immediately available online to users. The Library of Congress also produces braille versions of many national magazines and is now exploring the feasibility of adding these magazines to Web-Braille for its users. (Library of Congress, 1999)

451

John

Born prematurely and weighing only 1 pound 13 ounces, John is a child with vision loss. Now 9 years old, John lives with his parents and brother Michael, none of whom have any visual problems. John loves technology and has a CB radio, several TVs, a computer, and a tape recorder. He doesn't care for outdoor activities and isn't into sports. He uses braille to read, and has a cane to help him find his way through the world.

John: "I really like to be blind, it's a whole lot of fun. The reason I like to be blind is because I can learn my way around real fast and I have a real fast thinking memory. I can hear things that some people can't hear and smell. Actually, my sense of hearing is the best. . . . I have a CB radio that [I] talk to different people on and sometimes I can talk to people in different places around the world."

John's parents: "John can do anything he wants to do if he puts his mind to it. He's smart enough, he loves all kinds of radio communications. He talks about being on the radio, on TV, and there's no reason why he can't do that as long as he studies hard in school."

Michael: "I didn't want a blind brother."

John: "Sometimes my brother gets along good and sometimes he comes here in my room and under my desk there's a little power switch that controls all my TVs, scanner, CB, and tape recorder. He'll flip that then he'll laugh about it, run and go somewhere and I'll have to turn it back on, lock my door, and go tell Mom. So that's how he handles it and she puts him in time out."

John's third-grade teacher: "John is very well adjusted. He has a wonderful, delightful personality. He's intelligent. We were a little worried about his braille until this year. Probably because of his prematurity, [he has] a little trouble with the tactual. Of course, braille is all tactual. . . . But he's pulling out of that and that was his last problem with education. He's very bright. He could do many things. He loves computers."

John: "I'd like to be a few different things, and I'll tell you a few of them. I'd like to be a newscaster, an astronaut, or something down at NASA and a dispatcher. So, that's three of the things out of a whole million or thousand things I'd like to be."

T HROUGH THE VISUAL PROCESS, we observe the world around us and develop an appreciation for and a greater understanding of the physical environment. Vision is one of our most important sources for the acquisition and assimilation of knowledge, but we often take it for granted. From the moment we wake up in the morning, our dependence on sight is obvious. We rely on our eyes to guide us around our surroundings, inform us through the written word, and give us pleasure and relaxation.

What if this precious sight was lost or impaired? How would our perceptions of the world change? Losing sight is ranked right behind cancer and AIDS as our greatest fear (Jernigan, 1992). This fear is often nurtured by the misconception that persons with vision loss are helpless and unable to lead satisfying or productive lives. It is not uncommon for people with sight to have little understanding of those with vision loss. People who are sighted may believe that most adults who are blind are likely to live a deprived socioeconomic and cultural existence. Children who have sight may believe that their peers who are blind are incapable of learning many basic skills, such as telling time or using a computer, or enjoying leisure and recreational activities such as swimming or watching television. Throughout history some religions have even promoted the belief that blindness is a punishment for sins.

As the chapter opening snapshot about John strongly suggests, these negative perceptions of people with vision loss are often inaccurate. John is an active child who has not allowed his vision loss to keep him from the activities that he values.

▪ VISUAL CORTEX. The visual center of the brain, located in the occipital lobe.

▪ OPTIC NERVE. The nerve that connects the eye to the visual center of the brain.

▪ CORNEA. The external covering of the eye.

▪ PUPIL. The expandable opening in the iris of the eye.

▪ IRIS. The colored portion of the eye.

To understand more clearly the nature of vision loss within the context of normal sight, we begin our discussion with an overview of the visual process. Since vision is basically defined as the act of seeing with the eye, we first review the physical components of the visual system.

The Visual Process

The physical components of the visual system include the eye, the **visual cortex** in the brain, and the **optic nerve,** which connects the eye to the visual cortex. The basic anatomy of the human eye is illustrated in Figure 15.1. The **cornea** is the external covering of the eye, and in the presence of light, it bends or refracts visual stimuli. These light rays pass through the **pupil,** which is an opening in the **iris.** The pupil dilates or constricts to control the amount of light

focus 1

Why is it important to understand the visual process as well as know the physical components of the eye?

FIGURE 15.1

The parts of the human eye   [Source: The Salt Lake Tribune, February 8, 1996, p. C1.]

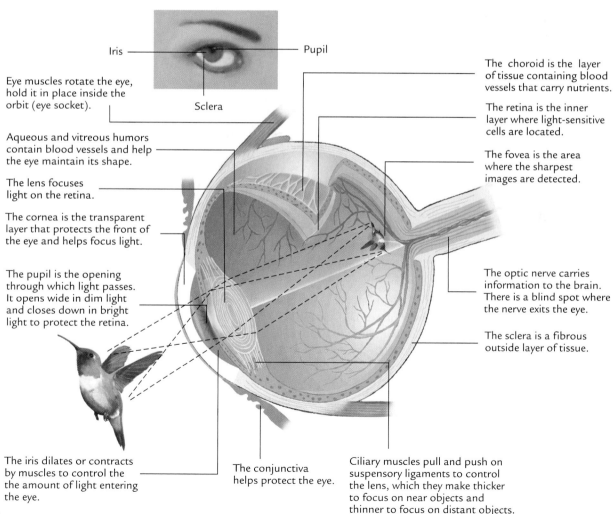

Iris

Pupil

Sclera

Eye muscles rotate the eye, hold it in place inside the orbit (eye socket).

Aqueous and vitreous humors contain blood vessels and help the eye maintain its shape.

The lens focuses light on the retina.

The cornea is the transparent layer that protects the front of the eye and helps focus light.

The pupil is the opening through which light passes. It opens wide in dim light and closes down in bright light to protect the retina.

The iris dilates or contracts by muscles to control the the amount of light entering the eye.

The conjunctiva helps protect the eye.

Ciliary muscles pull and push on suspensory ligaments to control the lens, which they make thicker to focus on near objects and thinner to focus on distant objects.

The choroid is the layer of tissue containing blood vessels that carry nutrients.

The retina is the inner layer where light-sensitive cells are located.

The fovea is the area where the sharpest images are detected.

The optic nerve carries information to the brain. There is a blind spot where the nerve exits the eye.

The sclera is a fibrous outside layer of tissue.

entering the eye. The iris is the colored portion of the eye and consists of membranous tissue and muscles whose function is to adjust the size of the pupil. The lens, like the cornea, bends light rays so they strike the **retina** directly. As in a camera lens, the lens of the eye reverses the images. The retina consists of light-sensitive cells that transmit the image to the brain by means of the optic nerve. Images from the retina remain upside down until they are flipped over in the visual cortex occipital lobe of the brain.

The visual process is a much more complex phenomenon than suggested by a description of the physical components involved. The process is an important link to the physical world, helping us to gain information beyond the range of other senses, while also helping us to integrate the information acquired primarily through hearing, touch, smell, and taste. For example, our sense of touch can tell us that what we are feeling is furry, soft, and warm, but only our eyes can tell that it is a brown rabbit with a white tail and pink eyes. Our nose may perceive something with yeast and spices cooking, but our eyes can confirm that it is a large pepperoni pizza with bubbling mozzarella and green peppers. Our hearing can tell us that a friend sounds angry and upset, but only our vision can perceive the scowl, clenched jaw, and stiff posture. The way we perceive visual stimuli shapes our interactions with and reactions to the environment while providing a foundation for the development of a more complex learning structure.

Definitions and Classification

The term *vision loss* encompasses people with a wide range of conditions, including those who have never experienced sight; those who had normal vision prior to before becoming partially or totally blind; those who experience a gradual or sudden loss of acuity across their field of vision; and those with a restricted field of vision.

■ DEFINITIONS

A variety of terms are used to define vision loss, a practice that has created some confusion among professionals in various fields of study. The rationale for the development of multiple definitions is directly related to their intended use. For example, eligibility for income-tax exemptions or special assistance from the American Printing House for the Blind requires that individuals with vision loss qualify under one of two general subcategories: blind or partially sighted (low vision).

■ **BLINDNESS** The word *blindness* has many meanings. In fact, there are over 150 citations for **blind** in an unabridged dictionary. **Legal blindness,** as defined by the Social Security Administration (2000), refers to vision that cannot be corrected to better than 20/200 in the better eye as measured on the **Snellen test,** or to a visual field of 20 degrees or less, even with corrective lenses. Many people who meet the legal definition of blindness still have some sight and may be able to read large print and get around without support (e.g., a guide dog or cane). As described above, the definition of legal blindness includes both acuity and field of vision (Corn & Koenig, 1996).

Visual acuity is determined by the use of an index that refers to the distance from which an object can be recognized. The person with normal eyesight is defined as having 20/20 vision. However, if an individual is able to read at 20 feet what a person with normal vision can read at 200 feet, then his or her visual acuity would be described as 20/200. Most people consider those who are legally blind to have some light perception; only about 20% are totally without sight.

■ **RETINA.** Light-sensitive cells in the interior of the eye that transmit images to the brain via the optic nerve.

■ **BLINDNESS.** According to the American Medical Association, the condition in which one's central visual acuity does not exceed 20/200 in the better eye with correcting lenses or in which visual acuity, if better than 20/200, is limited in the central field of vision.

■ **LEGAL BLINDNESS.** Visual acuity of 20/200 or worse in the best eye with best correction as measured on the Snellen test, or a visual field of 20% or less.

■ **SNELLEN TEST.** A test of visual acuity.

■ **VISUAL ACUITY.** Sharpness or clearness of vision.

A person is also considered blind if his or her field of vision is limited at its widest angle to 20 degrees or less (see Figure 15.2). A restricted field is also referred to as **tunnel vision,** pinhole vision, or tubular vision. A restricted field of vision severely limits a person's ability to participate in athletics, read, or drive a car.

Blindness can also be characterized as an educational disability. Educational definitions of blindness focus primarily on students' ability to use vision as an avenue for learning. Children who are unable to use their sight and rely on other senses, such as hearing and touch, are described as functionally blind. Functional blindness, in its simplest form, may be defined by whether vision is used as a primary channel of learning. Regardless of the definition used, the purpose of labeling a child as functionally blind is to ensure that he or she receives an appropriate instructional program. This program must assist the student who is blind in utilizing other senses as a means to succeed in a classroom setting and in the future as an independent and productive adult.

■ PARTIAL SIGHT (LOW VISION) People with partial sight or low vision have a visual acuity greater than 20/200 but not greater than 20/70 in the best eye after correction. The field of education also distinguishes between being blind and partially sighted when determining the level and extent of additional support services required by a student. The term **partially sighted** describes students who are able to use vision as a primary source of learning.

A vision specialist often works with students with vision loss to make the best possible use of remaining sight. This includes the elimination of unnecessary glare in the work area, removal of obstacles that could impede mobility, use of large-print books, and use of special lighting to enhance visual opportunities. Although children with low vision often use printed materials and special lighting in learning activities, some use **braille** because they can see only shadows and limited movement. These children require the use of tactile or other sensory channels to gain maximum benefit from learning opportunities (Barraga & Erin, 1992; Bishop, 1996a).

Two very distinct positions have been formed regarding individuals who are partially sighted and their use of residual vision. The first suggests that such individuals should make maximal use of their functional residual vision through the use of magnification, illumination, and specialized teaching aids (e.g., large-print books and posters), as well as any exercises that will increase the efficiency of remaining vision. This position is contrary to the more traditional philosophy of sight conservation or sight saving, which advocates restricted use of the eye. It was once believed that students with vision loss could keep what sight they had much longer

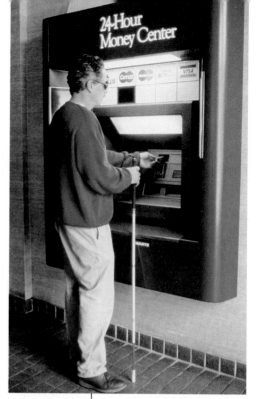

This talking ATM machine allows people with a vision loss to conveniently access their bank account and complete a transaction.

■ TUNNEL VISION. A restricted field of vision that is 20 degrees or less at its widest angle.

■ PARTIALLY SIGHTED. Having visual acuity greater than 20/200 but not greater than 20/70 in the better eye after correction.

■ BRAILLE. A system of writing used by many people who are blind. It involves combinations of six raised dots punched into paper, which can be read with the fingertips.

FIGURE 15.2

The field of vision

(a) Normal field of vision is about 180°.

(b) A person with a field of vision of 20° or less is considered blind.

(a) 180°

(b) 20°

if it was used sparingly. However, extended reliance on residual vision in conjunction with visual stimulation training now appears to actually improve a person's ability to use sight as an avenue for learning.

■ CLASSIFICATION

Vision loss may be classified according to the anatomical site of the problem. Anatomical disorders include impairment of the refractive structures of the eye, muscle anomalies in the visual system, and problems of the receptive structures of the eye.

■ REFRACTIVE EYE PROBLEMS

Refractive problems are the most common type of vision loss and occur when the refractive structures of the eye (cornea or **lens**) fail to focus light rays properly on the retina. The four types of refractive problems are hyperopia, or farsightedness; myopia, or nearsightedness; astigmatism, or blurred vision; and cataracts.

Hyperopia occurs when the eyeball is excessively short from front to back (has a flat corneal structure), forcing light rays to focus behind the retina. The person with hyperopia can clearly visualize objects at a distance but cannot see them at close range. This individual may require convex lenses so that a clear focus will occur on the retina.

Myopia occurs when the eyeball is excessively long (has increased curvature of the corneal surface), forcing light rays to focus in front of the retina. The person with myopia can view objects at close range clearly but cannot see them from a distance (e.g., 100 feet). Eyeglasses may be necessary to assist in focusing on distant objects. Figure 15.3 illustrates the myopic and hyperopic eyeballs and compares them to the normal human eye.

Astigmatism occurs when the curvature or surface of the cornea is uneven, preventing light rays from converging at one point. The rays of light are refracted in different directions, producing unclear, distorted visual images. Astigmatism may occur independently of or in conjunction with myopia or hyperopia.

Cataracts occur when the lens becomes opaque, resulting in severely distorted vision or total blindness. Surgical treatment for cataracts (such as lens implants) has advanced rapidly in recent years, returning to the individual most of the vision that was lost.

■ MUSCLE DISORDERS

Muscular defects of the visual system occur when one or more of the major muscles within the eye are weakened in function, resulting in a loss of control and an inability to maintain tension. People with muscle disorders cannot maintain their focus on a given object for even short periods of time. The

focus 3

What are the distinctive features of refractive eye problems, muscle disorders of the eye, and receptive eye problems?

■ REFRACTIVE PROBLEMS. Visual disorders that occur when the refractive structures of the eye fail to properly focus light rays on the retina.

■ LENS. The clear structure in the eye that focuses light rays on the retina.

■ HYPEROPIA. Farsightedness; a refractive problem wherein the eyeball is excessively short, focusing light rays behind the retina.

■ MYOPIA. Nearsightedness; a refractive problem wherein the eyeball is excessively long, focusing light in front of the retina.

■ ASTIGMATISM. A refractive problem that occurs when the surface of the cornea is uneven or structurally defective, preventing light rays from converging at one point.

■ CATARACT. A clouding of the eye lens, which becomes opaque, resulting in visual problems.

FIGURE 15.3

The normal (a), myopic (b), and hyperopic (c) eyeballs. The image is focused on the retina upside down, but the brain immediately reverses it.

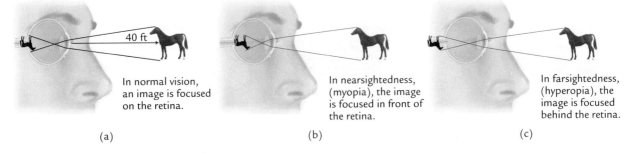

40 ft

In normal vision, an image is focused on the retina.

(a)

In nearsightedness, (myopia), the image is focused in front of the retina.

(b)

In farsightedness, (hyperopia), the image is focused behind the retina.

(c)

three types of muscle disorders are nystagmus (uncontrolled rapid eye movement), strabismus (crossed eyes), and amblyopia (an eye that appears normal but does not function properly). **Nystagmus** is a continuous, involuntary, rapid movement of the eyeballs in either a circular or side-to-side pattern. **Strabismus** occurs when the muscles of the eyes are unable to pull equally, thus preventing the eyes from focusing together on the same object. Internal strabismus **(esotropia)** occurs when the eyes are pulled inward toward the nose; external strabismus **(exotropia)** occurs when the eyes are pulled out toward the ears. The eyes may also shift on a vertical plane (up or down), but this condition is rare. Strabismus can be corrected through surgical intervention. Persons with strabismus often experience a phenomenon known as double vision, since the deviating eye causes two very different pictures coming to the brain. To correct the double vision and reduce visual confusion, the brain attempts to suppress the image in one eye. As a result, the unused eye loses its ability to see. This condition, known as **amblyopia,** can also be corrected by surgery or by forcing the affected eye into focus by covering the unaffected eye with a patch.

■ RECEPTIVE EYE PROBLEMS   Disorders associated with the receptive structures of the eye occur when there is a degeneration of or damage to the retina and the optic nerve. These disorders include optic atrophy, retinitis pigmentosa, retinal detachment, retrolental fibroplasia, and glaucoma. **Optic atrophy** is a degenerative disease that results from the deterioration of nerve fibers connecting the retina to the brain. **Retinitis pigmentosa,** the most common hereditary condition associated with loss of vision, appears initially as night blindness and gradually degenerates the retina. Eventually, it results in total blindness.

Retinal detachment occurs when the retina separates from the choroid and the sclera. This detachment may result from disorders such as glaucoma, retinal degeneration, or extreme myopia. It can also be caused by trauma to the eye, such as a boxer's receiving a hard right hook to the face.

Retinopathy of prematurity (ROP), formerly known as *retrolental fibroplasia,* is one of the most devastating eye disorders in young children. It occurs when too much oxygen is administered to premature infants, resulting in the formation of scar tissue behind the lens of the eye, which prevents light rays from reaching the retina. ROP gained attention in the early 1940s, with the advent of improved incubators for premature infants. These incubators substantially improved the concentration of oxygen available to the infant but resulted in a drastic increase in the number of children with vision loss. The disorder has also been associated with neurological, speech, and behavior problems in children and adolescents. Now that a relationship has been established between increased oxygen levels and blindness, premature infants can be protected by careful control of the amount of oxygen received in the early months of life.

Prevalence

The prevalence of vision loss is often difficult to determine. For example, although about 20% of children and adults have some vision loss, most of these conditions can be corrected to a level where they do not interfere with everyday tasks (e.g., reading, driving a car). It is estimated that about 3% of the population (9 million people) have a significant vision loss that will require some type of specialized services and supports. Approximately 5% of American children (1.2 million) have a serious eye disorder (KidSource, 2000). This figure increases to 20% for elderly people over the age of 65. If cataracts are included, nearly 50% of people over the age of 65 have a significant vision loss (U.S. National Center for Health

■ NYSTAGMUS. Uncontrolled rapid eye movements.

■ STRABISMUS. Crossed eyes (internal) or eyes that look outward (external).

■ ESOTROPIA. A form of strabismus causing the eyes to be pulled inward toward the nose.

■ EXOTROPIA. A form of strabismus in which the eyes are pulled outward toward the ears.

■ AMBLYOPIA. Loss of vision due to an imbalance of eye muscles.

■ OPTIC ATROPHY. A degenerative disease caused by deteriorating nerve fibers connecting the retina to the brain.

■ RETINITIS PIGMENTOSA. A hereditary condition resulting from a break in the choroid.

■ RETINAL DETACHMENT. A condition that occurs when the retina is separated from the choroid and sclera.

■ RETINOPATHY OF PREMATURITY. A term now used in place of *retrolental fibroplasia.*

focus 4
What are the estimated prevalence and causes of vision loss?

Advances in neonatal medicine over the past decade have allowed doctors to save growing numbers of very premature infants. But some of those surviving babies are part of a far less publicized trend: an alarming rise in the numbers of blind children. Doctors say retinopathy of prematurity (ROP)—a condition in which abnormal blood vessels and scar tissue grow over the retina of a very premature and tiny infant—is the primary cause of the increase.

Blindness in infancy and childhood is still a relatively rare disability. According to the American Printing House for the Blind, 53,576 American children under age 18 are legally blind. That figure is growing by about 3% per year, says Tuck Tinsley, president of the printing house, a government-funded institution that supplies virtually all educational materials for the blind.

Previous decades have brought about temporary surges in childhood blindness, Tinsley notes—including a swell of premature babies born in the late 1940s and early 1950s who were overtreated with oxygen in incubators. In the '80s, the crack cocaine epidemic led to another wave of blind children.

But, Tinsley says, "Retinopathy of prematurity is the thing today causing the increase. These are children who wouldn't even have survived a few years ago."

Directors of blind children's centers in Phoenix, San Francisco, Boston, Los Angeles, and other cities report increased enrollments because of ROP and cortical visual impairment, but there is no official tracking or registry of blind children nationwide, so the increase cannot be officially verified.

"The scientific studies that actually prove the increase haven't been done," says Dennak L. Murphy, executive director of San Francisco's Blind Babies Foundation, which has maintained one of the most accurate and long-running registries of blind children in the nation.

"Blindness is a low-incidence disability," he says, "so no one studies it."

Retinopathy of prematurity usually occurs in babies born at 26 weeks gestation—more than three months premature—and weighing less than two pounds. About 40% of infants weighing less than two pounds will develop ROP, compared to 5% of babies born at three pounds, according to the American Academy of Ophthalmology.

ROP often clears up by itself. But in some babies laser surgery or cryosurgery is attempted to reverse the abnormal growth. If that is unsuccessful, ROP can lead to detached retinas. In these cases, surgery can sometimes restore limited vision, but many children are left legally blind.

Experts estimate that 2% of all very low birthweight babies develop ROP-related blindness or severe vision impairment.

"And since [neonatologists] are saving so many more babies at low birthweights, the total number of blind babies is going up," says Kay Ferrell, a professor of special education at the University of Northern Colorado, who is directing one of the largest U.S. studies of blind children.

Source: From "Infant Blindness," by S. Roan, August 17, 1995, *Salt Lake Tribune,* pp. C1, C8. Reprinted by permission.

Statistics, 1994). Based on the U.S. Department of Education's *22nd Annual Report to Congress* (2000a), 26,132 school-age children with vision loss between the ages of 6 and 21 received specialized services in U.S. public schools in 1998–1999.

Thousands of children born blind during the maternal rubella epidemic in 1963 and 1964 constituted a significant percentage of the enrollment in special education and residential schools for the blind in the 1970s and 1980s. Maternal rubella is now essentially under control, since the introduction of a rubella vaccine. Retrolental fibroplasia (now known as retinopathy of prematurity) has been a major cause of blindness in infants since the 1960s and continues to be a factor into the 21st century. (See the nearby Reflect on This feature.)

Causation

GENETIC DISORDERS

■ ALBINISM. Lack of pigmentation in eyes, skin, and hair.

■ PHOTOPHOBIA. An intolerance to light.

A number of genetic conditions can result in vision loss, including **albinism** (resulting in **photophobia** due to lack of pigmentation in eyes, skin, and hair), retinitis pigmentosa (degeneration of the retina), **retinoblastoma** (malignant tumor in the retina), optic atrophy (loss of function of optic nerve fibers), cataracts, severe myopia associated with retinal detachment, lesions of the cornea, abnormalities of the iris (coloboma or aniridia), **microphthalmia** (abnormally small eyeball), hydrocephalus (excess cerebrospinal fluid in the brain) leading to optic atrophy, **anophthalmia** (absence of the eyeball), and **glaucoma** or **buphthalmos** (abnormal distention and enlargement of the eyeball).

Glaucoma occurs in about 1 in every 10,000 births and results from an increased pressure in the eye (Teplin, 1995). This pressure can damage the optic nerve if left untreated. The incidence of glaucoma is highest in persons over the age of 40 who have a family history of the disease. Glaucoma is treatable, either through surgery to drain fluids from the eye or through the use of medicated eye drops to reduce pressure (Isenberg, 1992).

■ ACQUIRED DISORDERS

Acquired disorders can occur prior to, during, or after birth. Several factors present prior to birth, such as radiation or the introduction of drugs into the fetal system, may result in vision loss. A major cause of blindness in the fetus is infection, which may be due to diseases such as rubella and syphilis. Other diseases that can result in blindness include influenza, mumps, and measles.

The leading cause of acquired blindness in children worldwide is vitamin A deficiency **(xeropthalmia)**. Approximately 70% of the 500,000 children who become blind each year do so because of xeropthalmia (Thylefors, Nagrel, Pararajasegaram, & Dadzie, 1995).

Another cause of acquired blindness is retinopathy of prematurity. As noted earlier, ROP results from administering of oxygen over prolonged periods of time to low-birthweight infants. Almost 80% of preschool-age blind children lost their sight as a result of ROP during the peak years of the disease (1940s through 1960s).

Vision loss after birth may be due to several factors. Trauma, infections, inflammations, and tumors are all related to loss of sight. **Cortical visual impairment (CVI)** is a leading cause of acquired blindness. CVI, which involves damage to the occipital lobes and/or the visual pathways to the brain, can result from severe trauma, asphyxia, seizures, infections of the central nervous system, drugs, poisons, or other neurological conditions. Most children with CVI have residual vision (Jan & Wong, 1991).

> ▪ RETINOBLASTOMA. A malignant tumor in the retina.
>
> ▪ MICROPHTHALMIA. An abnormally small eyeball.
>
> ▪ ANOPHTHALMIA. Absence of the eyeball.
>
> ▪ GLAUCOMA. A disorder of the eye, which is characterized by high pressure inside the eyeball.
>
> ▪ BUPHTHALMOS. An abnormal distention and enlargement of the eyeball.
>
> ▪ XEROPTHALMIA. A condition caused by vitamin A deficiency that can lead to blindness. Vitamin A deficiency leads to a lack of production of mucous-producing cells (known as dry eye).
>
> ▪ CORTICAL VISUAL IMPAIRMENT (CVI). A leading cause of acquired blindness, which involves damage to the occipital lobes and/or the visual pathways to the brain. CVI can result from severe trauma, asphyxia, seizures, infections of the central nervous system, drugs, poisons, or various neurological conditions.

Characteristics

A vision loss present at birth will have a more significant effect on individual development than one that occurs later in life. Useful visual imagery may disappear if sight is lost prior to the age of 5. If sight is lost after the age of 5, it is possible for the person to retain "some visual memories which may help in imagining and understanding many concepts" (Best, 1992, p. 3). These visual memories can be maintained over a period of years. Total blindness that occurs prior to age 5 has the greatest negative influence on overall functioning. However, many people who are blind from birth or early childhood are able to function at a level consistent with sighted persons of equal ability.

■ INTELLIGENCE

Children with vision loss sometimes base their perceptions of the world on input from senses other than vision. This is particularly true of the child who is congeni-

focus 5

Describe how a vision loss can affect intelligence, speech and language skills, educational achievement, social development, physical orientation and mobility, and perceptual-motor development.

tally blind, whose learning experiences are significantly restricted by the lack of vision. Consequently, everyday learning opportunities that people with sight take for granted, such as reading the morning newspaper or watching television news coverage, may be substantially altered.

Reviews of the literature on intellectual development suggest that children with vision loss differ from their sighted peers in some areas of intelligence, ranging from understanding spatial concepts to a general knowledge of the world (Hull, 1990; Warren, 1989). However, comparing the performances of individuals with and without sight may not be appropriate if those with sight have an advantage. The only valid way to compare the intellectual capabilities of these children must be based on tasks in which vision loss does not interfere with performance. Hull (1990) suggested that persons who are blind rely much more on their tactile and auditory senses than do their sighted peers. He described the phenomenon as "seeing with one's fingers."

■ SPEECH AND LANGUAGE SKILLS

For children with sight, speech and language development occurs primarily through the integration of visual experiences and the symbols of the spoken word. Depending on the degree of loss, children with vision loss are at a distinct disadvantage in developing speech and language skills because they are unable to visually associate words with objects. Because of this, such children must rely on hearing or touch for input, and their speech may develop at a slower rate. Once these children have learned speech, however, it is typically fluent.

Preschool-age and school-age children with vision loss may develop a phenomenon known as **verbalisms,** or the excessive use of speech (wordiness), in which individuals may use words that have little meaning to them (e.g., "Crusaders are people of a religious sex" or "Lead us not into Penn Station"). Silberman and Sowell (1998) indicated that children with visual impairments have particular difficulties in expressing themselves verbally because of their "incomplete awareness of all the details of an experience" (p. 163). These authors suggested that these children have a restricted oral vocabulary in comparison to that of sighted peers because they lack the visual input necessary for them to piece together all of the information available in a given experience.

■ ACADEMIC ACHIEVEMENT

The academic achievement of students with vision loss may be significantly delayed when compared to that of sighted peers. In fact, the academic achievement of these students often resembles that of children with learning disabilities (Bishop, 1996b). In the area of reading, for example, a study of school-age students in the public schools indicated that 31% of students who are blind could not read; an additional 22% were at a reading readiness level (American Printing House for the Blind, 1992).

Numerous variables influence academic achievement for students with vision loss. In the area of written language, these students have more difficulty organizing thoughts to write a composition because they lack the same opportunities as sighted peers to read newspapers and magazines. Decoding in the area of reading may be delayed because students with a visual impairment often uses braille or large-print books as the media to decode. Decoding is a much slower process when using these two media. Reading comprehension is also affected because it depends so much on the experiences of the reader. Once again, the experience of students with visual impairments may be limited in comparison to that of sighted peers, and therefore these children don't bring as much information to the reading task (Silberman & Sowell, 1998).

■ VERBALISM. Excessive use of speech (wordiness) in which individuals use words that have little meaning to them.

Other possible reasons for delays in academic achievement range from excessive school absences due to the need for eye surgery or treatment as well as years of failure in programs that did not meet each student's specialized needs.

On the average, children with vision loss may lag 2 years behind sighted children in grade level. Thus, any direct comparisons of students with vision loss to those with sight would indicate significantly delayed academic growth. However, this age phenomenon may have resulted from entering school at a later age, absence due to medical problems, or lack of appropriate school resources and facilities.

■ SOCIAL DEVELOPMENT

The ability of children with vision loss to adapt to the social environment depends on a number of factors, both hereditary and experiential. It is true that each of us experiences the world in his or her own way, but common bonds provide a foundation on which to build perceptions of the world around us. One such bond is vision. Without vision, perceptions about ourselves and those around us can be drastically different.

For the person with vision loss, these differences in perception may produce some social–emotional challenges. For example, Crocker and Orr (1996) found that although preschool-age children with significant vision loss were capable of interacting with same-age nondisabled peers, there were some differences between the two groups of children. Children with vision loss were less likely to initiate a social interaction and had fewer opportunities to socialize with other children. These authors pointed out that the success of an inclusive preschool depends on the "presence of specialized programs [supports] to encourage and reinforce interactions between children with visual impairments and their peers with full sight" (p. 461).

Kekelis (1992) found that school-age children with severe vision loss have difficulty in "play" situations, seek attention inappropriately, and ask a lot of irrelevant questions. People with vision loss are unable to imitate the physical mannerisms of others and therefore do not develop one very important component of social communication: body language. Because the subtleties of nonverbal communication can significantly alter the intended meaning of spoken words, a person's inability to learn and use visual cues (e.g., facial expressions, hand gestures) has profound consequences for interpersonal interactions. The person with vision loss can neither see the visual cues that accompany the messages received from others nor sense the messages that he or she may be conveying through body language.

Differences between people with a vision loss and those who are sighted may also result from the exclusion of the person with a vision loss from social activities that are integrally related to the use of sight (e.g., sports, movies). People with vision loss are often excluded from such activities without a second thought, simply because they cannot see. This reinforces the mistaken notion that they do not want to participate and would not enjoy these activities. Social skills can be learned and effectively used by a person with vision loss (MacCuspie, 1992). Excluding them from social experiences more often stems from negative public attitudes than from the individuals' lack of social adjustment skills. (See nearby Reflect on This feature—Losing Sight.)

■ ORIENTATION AND MOBILITY

A unique limitation facing people with vision loss is the basic problem of getting from place to place. Such individuals may be unable to orient themselves to other people or objects in the environment simply because they cannot see them, and therefore they will not understand their own relative position in space. Consequently, they may be unable to move in the right direction and may fear getting

Reflect on This

LOSING SIGHT: REFLECTION ON A FRIEND WHO IS BLIND

Twelve years ago, at the birthday party of a friend, was the first time I met somebody my own age who had a disability. He was tall for his age, thin, and wore eyeglasses, just like I did. It was this commonality that initially attracted me to him, since I didn't know very many kindergartners who wore glasses. I had begun wearing glasses to correct a case of strabismus at age 2 and was able to see perfectly when I put them on. However, I was not aware of the fact that his glasses did very little to sharpen his vision and that he was legally blind.

On the last day of second grade, at the unofficial annual picnic at Westland Hills Park, we became good friends. As we moved from the swings to the jungle gym to the sprinklers, I realized how much we truly had in common. We enjoyed the same things: Legos, swimming, and being Cub Scouts.

Throughout third grade, we spent nearly every weekend together. During this time, though I had been informed of his disability, I never made any differentiation between his abilities or personality and my own. Although I often helped to direct him when he didn't seem to quite have his bearings, I never doubted that his capabilities were similar to my own.

After that year, we were not assigned the same teachers for fourth grade, and unfortunately, we drifted apart. As we finished elementary school and I watched him from a greater distance, his disability somehow became more apparent to me. When other kids asked me if I knew him, I would think of him as the boy who couldn't see well, or the one in the class who had to read large-type books. Why was I doing this? In part, it may have been because I was forced to look at his situation with less subjectivity. Perhaps it was because I began to recognize there were a few things he couldn't do as well as others. Most of all, I believe that my feelings came from the fact that society emphasizes disabilities as a difference between human beings.

While it is necessary to be aware of others' disabilities, they should not be the distinguishing factor between two people. As we continued through middle school, I realized that losing contact often causes one to lose sight of somebody's true personality and the characteristics that make the person who he or she is. However, I would eventually notice his maturity, perseverance, and determination in all areas of his life, qualities which have led him to develop into a young man I truly admire.

During my junior year, we were placed in the same aquatics class. I discovered our interests now differed, but that we had both pursued and achieved a number of personal goals. The last time we spoke, at his parents' New Year's party, I was inspired by the amount of things he had accomplished in the past year. He had become manager of the school store and had won Albany High School's only gold medal in the regional DECA business competition. He got a job at Eastern Mountain Sports. Over the summer, he had participated in a rigorous mountain climbing and hiking trip in the Adirondacks, not for a second letting his disability get in the way of doing something he loved.

I thought back to that first day at the park, when I had worried that his sight might cause him to fall and hurt himself. Now, he had pushed himself to do something considered difficult for anybody. This inspirational individual has never allowed his disability to become his most prominent quality, and consequently, he has encouraged me to view disabilities in the same way. I feel that he has served as an example to society, showing that disabilities do not dictate an individual's personality or quality of life.

—Nathaniel Lewis, Albany High School, New York

Source: From "Losing Sight," by N. Lewis, Summer 1999, *Newsletter of the New York State Commission on Quality of Care,* p. 76. *[on-line]* Available: *http://www.cqc.state.ny.us/76nlewis.htm*

---

injured, and so attempt to restrict their movements in order to protect themselves. In addition, parents and professionals may contribute to such fears by overprotecting the person who has vision loss from the everyday risks of life. Shielding the individual in this way will hinder acquisition of independent mobility skills and create an atmosphere promoting lifelong overdependence on caregivers (see nearby Reflect on This feature—Bleeding Hearts).

Vision loss can affect fine motor coordination and interfere with the ability to manipulate objects. Poor eye–hand coordination interferes with learning how to use tools related to job skills and daily living skills (e.g., using eating utensils, a toothbrush, a screwdriver). Prevention or remediation of fine motor problems may require training in the use of visual aid magnifiers and improvement of basic fine

Reflect on This

I was the only person who was blind attending a birthday party at a friend's house. Though I had been in the company of this friend, along with others, countless times in the past 2 years, I had not been to her house before, and I appreciated being given a tour. My favorite place—the area that attracted all of us—was the deck. This friend has a wonderful, spacious deck upon which we found beautiful, comfortable outdoor furniture. At one end I observed a wooden stairway going down into the yard. As I approached the stairs, this friend panicked, admonishing me to "Watch out!" Before I could utter a word, Barbara, another friend, spoke. She had also seen me approach the stairs, but she has spent much time with me and is very aware of the fearful behavior of those who do not or will not understand that it is all right for me to move around on my own.

Accurately observing the situation from her more enlightened perspective, she said, "Don't worry about it, that's what her cane is for." I assumed that was the end of the incident. During the course of the meal and the frivolity, Barbara and several others remarked on how beautiful the bleeding heart flowers were. She said, "You and I can go down and look at them before we leave." I agreed that this would be a pleasant experience, and I looked forward to it.

I have often been the only person who is blind in a group of sighted people and have desired to marvel as much as they do at our natural surroundings. I have always known I could do so, albeit at times in a different way. However, quite often, due to fear and apparent lack of information, many of those attending such gatherings seem reluctant to allow me the opportunity to "see for myself." Through the years I have come to realize that, if I want to look at something in my own way, I would do well simply to do it, regardless of the possible consternation around me. I am not usually one to upset the apple cart, but when the apples would benefit from a good stirring up, I'm likely to do it. I do this because of my belief that the world is as much mine as anyone else's, and the beauty and grandeur of nature beckon me no less. I am a part of nature, and nature is a part of me. I also believe that, though we learn from other humans, our learning is not limited to this source. Nature teaches us as well. In fact, this broader teaching and bonding of hearts is exactly what occurred during this birthday party in May.

After the party had ended and most of the guests had departed, I remembered the bleeding hearts. Since Barbara was busy inside the house and since she and I both knew I was perfectly capable of looking at the flowers without waiting for her, I approached the stairs and began to descend. The owner of the house and another woman named Ruth were observing me. The owner scolded Ruth: "Watch her; don't let her go down there; it's weird out in the yard." Ruth ignored the admonition, commenting that she'd like to see the flowers too. She quietly followed me down the stairs. I attempted to reassure anyone listening that I was okay. As I finished my descent, what I found at the bottom of the stairs was some uneven terrain, certainly nothing particularly dangerous or weird. Ruth walked over to the flowers, and I met her there. We knelt down to examine them—their dainty little hearts with strands of bloom dangling from them. How delicate and vulnerable they seemed. Yet they showed no sign of worry or fear as I touched their beauty, and their beauty touched me.

At that moment I felt such an awareness of the bleeding hearts—the human one above me on the deck, bleeding worry and fear, and the blossoms bleeding only beauty. I am deeply grateful for the power in me to take steps beyond such worry and fear and to receive nature's beauty. I am also grateful for the two women, Barbara and Ruth, whose loving and respectful responses to the situation enhanced that beauty for us all. I am also grateful for the woman who invited me to the party at which this event occurred—and just think of the opportunity she had to learn something new about people who are blind and to participate also in nature's beauty.

Could it be, after all, that these were not bleeding hearts, but bonding hearts?

Source: Adapted from "Bleeding Hearts," by L. L. Eckery (1994, November), *The Braille Monitor*, pp. 649–650. © National Federation of the Blind.

motor skills. This training must begin early and focus directly on experiences that will enhance opportunities for independent living (Best, 1992).

■ PERCEPTUAL-MOTOR DEVELOPMENT

Perceptual-motor development is essential in the development of locomotion skills, but it is also important in the development of cognition, language, socialization, and personality. Most children with vision loss appear to have perceptual discrimination abilities (e.g., discriminating texture, weight, and sound) comparable to those of sighted peers (Bishop, 1996b). Obviously, children with vision loss do not perform as well on more complex tasks of perception, including form identification, spatial relations, and perceptual-motor integration. In fact, Ochaita and Huertas (1993) suggested that people who are blind are delayed in the development of spatial abilities in comparison with sighted peers and will not reach full development until well into their teen years. An early visual experience prior to the onset of blindness or partial loss of sight may provide a child with some advantage in developing manipulatory and locomotor skills.

A popular misconception regarding the perceptual abilities of persons with vision loss is that, because of their diminished sight, they develop greater capacity in other sensory areas. For example, people who are blind are supposedly able to hear or smell some things that people with normal vision cannot perceive. This notion has never been empirically validated.

Educational Supports and Services

■ ASSESSMENT

focus 6
What is a functional approach to assessment for students with a vision loss?

In addition to assessing the cognitive ability, academic achievement, language skills, motor performance, and social–emotional functioning of a student with a vision loss, an IEP team must also focus on how the student utilizes any remaining vision (visual efficiency) in conjunction with other senses. The Visual Efficient Scale, developed by Barraga and Erin (1992), assesses the overall visual functioning of the individual to determine how he or she uses sight to acquire information. As suggested by Bishop (1996a, p. 92), "When a child still has some useful vision, it should be utilized; it cannot be 'conserved' by not using it, as was once thought; it must be practiced to reach maximum efficiency."

A functional approach to assessment goes beyond determining visual acuity and focuses on capacity, attention, and processing (Blanksby & Langford, 1993). Visual capacity includes both acuity and field of vision, but also encompasses the response of the individual to visual information. The assessment of visual attention involves observing the individual's sensitivity to visual stimuli (alertness), ability to use vision to select information from a variety of sources, attention to a visual stimulus, and ability to process visual information. Visual-processing assessment determines which, if any, of the components of normal visual functioning are impaired.

The nature and severity of the visual problem determine the assessment instruments to be used. Some assessment instruments have been developed specifically for students with vision loss (See Boehm, 1986) and others are intended for sighted students but can be adapted to students with vision loss. Some instruments developed for sighted students are used in their original form with students with vision loss (see Brown, Sherbenou, & Johnsen, 1990; Burns & Roe, 1993; Connolly, 1988). Regardless of the instruments used, educational assessment, in conjunction with medical and psychological data, must provide the diagnostic information that will ensure that students with vision loss receive an appropriate educational experience.

■ MOBILITY TRAINING AND DAILY LIVING SKILLS

The educational needs of students with vision loss are comparable to those of their sighted counterparts. In addition, many instructional methods currently used with students who are sighted are appropriate for students with vision loss. However, educators must be aware that certain content areas usually unnecessary for sighted students are essential to the success of students with vision loss in a classroom situation. These areas include mobility and orientation training as well as acquisition of daily living skills.

focus 7

Identify two content areas that should be included in educational programs for students with vision loss.

The ability to move safely, efficiently, and independently through the environment enhances the individual's opportunities to learn more about the world and thus be less dependent on others for survival. Lack of mobility restricts individuals with vision loss in nearly every aspect of educational life. Such students may be unable to orient themselves to physical structures in the classroom (e.g., desks, chairs, and aisles), hallways, rest rooms, library, or cafeteria. Whereas a person with sight can automatically establish a relative position in space, the individual with vision loss must be taught some means of compensating for a lack of visual input. This may be accomplished in a number of ways. It is important that students with vision loss not only learn the physical structure of their school but also develop specific techniques to orient them to unfamiliar surroundings.

These orientation techniques involve using the other senses. For example, the senses of touch and hearing can help identify cues that designate where the bathroom is in the school. Although it is not true that people who are blind have superior hearing abilities, they may learn to use their hearing more effectively by focusing on subtle auditory cues that often go unnoticed. The efficient use of hearing, in conjunction with the other senses (including any remaining vision), is the key to independent travel for people with vision loss.

Independent travel with a sighted companion but without the use of a cane, guide dog, or electronic device is the most common form of travel for young school-age children. The major challenges for children with low vision in moving independently and safely through their environment include the following:

- Adjusting to glare
- Adapting to lighting changes
- Negotiating drop-offs (stairs and curbs)
- Negotiating street crossings
- Negotiating changes in terrain
- Walking through crowded areas
- Bumping into objects and obstacles
- Walking in inclement weather
- Seeing details (street names and house numbers) during travel (Smith & Geruschat, 1996, pp. 307–308)

With the increasing emphasis on instructing young children in orientation at an earlier age, the introduction of the long cane (Kiddy Cane) for young children has become more common (Pogrund, Fazzi, & Schreier, 1993) . As these children grow older, they may be instructed in the use of a Mowat Sensor. The **Mowat Sensor,** approximately the size of a flashlight, is a hand-held ultrasound travel aid that uses high-frequency sound to detect objects. Vibration frequency increases as objects become closer; the sensor vibrates at different rates to warn of obstacles in front of the individual. The device ignores everything but the closest object within the beam.

Guide dogs or electronic mobility devices may be appropriate for the adolescent or adult, since the need to travel independently significantly increases with age. A variety of electronic mobility devices is currently being used for everything from enhancing hearing efficiency to detecting obstacles.

The **Laser cane** converts infrared light into sound as light beams strike objects in the path of the person who is blind. It uses a range-finding technique with a semi-

▪ MOWAT SENSOR. A hand-held travel aid, approximately the size of a flashlight, used by people who are blind. It serves as an alternative to a cane for finding obstacles in the person's pathway.

▪ LASER CANE. A mobility device for people who are blind. It converts infrared light into sound as light beams strike objects.

Many different devices are available to assist with mobility. Here a student who is blind holds his walking cane while also using a device called the "Talking Sign." This device has an AM receiver that picks up audible signals from a transmitter located at strategic points in the environment. The transmitter orally communicates the location to the student, such as "east cafeteria exit" or "second floor boys' restroom."

■SONICGUIDE. An electronic mobility device for people who are blind, which is worn on the head, emits ultrasound, and converts reflections of objects into audible noise.

conductor laser and a Position Sensitive Device (PSD). Proximity to an obstacle is warned by vibration at different levels of frequency.

The **Sonicguide,** or Sonic Pathfinder, worn on the head, emits ultrasound and converts reflections from objects into audible noise in such a way that the individual can learn about the structure of objects. For example, loudness indicates size: the louder the noise, the larger the object. To effectively use the Sonicguide, the person with low vision should have mobility skills. It is designed for outdoor use in conjunction with a cane, a guide dog, or residual vision.

The acquisition of daily living skills is another content area important to success in the classroom and overall independence. Most people take for granted many routine events of the day, such as eating, dressing, bathing, and toileting. A person with sight learns very early in life the tasks associated with perceptual-motor development, including grasping, lifting, balancing, pouring, and manipulating objects. These daily living tasks become more complex during the school years as a child learns personal hygiene, grooming, and social etiquette. Eventually, people with sight acquire many complex daily living skills that later contribute to their independence as adults. Money management, grocery shopping, doing laundry, cooking, cleaning, household repairs, sewing, mowing the lawn, and gardening are all daily tasks associated with adult life and are learned from experiences that are not usually a part of an individual's formal educational program.

For children with vision loss, however, routine daily living skills are not easily learned through everyday experiences. These children must be encouraged and supported as they develop life skills and not overprotected from everyday challenges and risks by family and friends.

■ INSTRUCTIONAL CONTENT

Mobility training and daily living skills are components of an educational program that must also include an academic curriculum. Corn et al. (1995) suggested that "educational and developmental goals, including instruction, will reflect the assessed needs of each student [with a visual impairment] in all areas of academic and disability-specific core curricula" (p. 5). Koenig and Rex (1996, p. 285) suggested that teachers of students with low vison focus on several disability-specific core areas:

- Ensuring that students develop a solid experiential and conceptual basis for literacy
- Structuring early literacy experiences in the home so as not to rely solely on incidental experiences
- Teaching the efficient use of visual skills in authentic contexts, such as efficient scanning skills to locate words in a dictionary or to interpret a map
- Teaching students to interpret pictures of increasing complexity
- Teaching students to use optical and non-optical low-vision devices
- Providing practice to build automatic skills in the use of low-vision devices
- Providing targeted instruction to increase fluency and stamina in reading

- Teaching functional applications of reading and writing skills, if they have not already been taught in the classroom
- Arranging the physical environment to maximize the visual learning and increase the comfort of young students
- Helping the student assume responsibility for gaining access to print
- Teaching keyboarding and computer word-processing skills if these skills are not part of the early regular curriculum
- Teaching a variety of literacy tools for gaining access to print independently, such as a monocular (magnified eye glass) to take notes from a chalkboard

Particular emphasis must be placed on developing receptive and expressive language skills. Students with vision loss must learn to listen in order to understand the auditory world more clearly. Finely tuned receptive skills contribute to the development of expressive language, which allows these children to orally describe their perceptions of the world. Koenig and Rex (1996) suggested the use of a language experience approach (LEA) as a means to develop language skills and prepare students for reading. The LEA involves several steps, as described in Table 15.1.

Oral expression can be expanded to include handwriting as a means of communication. The acquisition of social and instructional language skills opens the door to many areas, including reading and mathematics. Reading can greatly expand the knowledge base for children with vision loss. For people who are partially sighted, various optical aids are available: video systems that magnify print, hand-held magnifiers, magnifiers attached to eyeglasses, and other telescopic aids. Another means to facilitate reading for partially sighted students is the use of large-print books, generally available through the American Printing House for the Blind and the Library of Congress in several print sizes. Other factors that must be considered in teaching reading to students who are partially sighted include adequate illumination and the reduction of glare. Advance organizers prepare students by previewing the instructional approach and materials to be used in a lesson. These organizers essentially identify the topics or tasks to be learned, give the student an organizational framework, indicate the concepts to be introduced, list new vocabulary, and state the intended outcomes for the student.

Abstract mathematical concepts may be difficult for students who are blind. These students will probably require additional practice in learning to master symbols, number facts, and higher-level calculations. As concepts become more complex, additional aids may be necessary to facilitate learning. Specially designed talking microcomputers, calculators, rulers, compasses, and the Crammer abacus have been developed to assist students in this area.

■ COMMUNICATION MEDIA

For students who are partially sighted, their limited vision remains a means of obtaining information. The use of optical aids in conjunction with auditory and tactile stimuli allows these individuals an integrated sensory approach to learning. However, this approach is not possible for students who are blind. Because they do not have access to visual stimuli, they may have to compensate through the use of tactile and auditory media. Through these media, children who are blind develop an understanding of themselves and the world around them. One facet of this development process is the acquisition of language, and one facet of language acquisition is learning to read.

For the student who is blind, the tactile sense represents entry into the symbolic world of reading. The most widely used tactile medium for teaching reading is the

focus 8

How can communication media facilitate learning for people with vision loss?

■ EARLY CHILDHOOD YEARS

TIPS FOR THE FAMILY

- Assist your child with vision loss in learning how to get around in the home environment. Then give him or her the freedom to move freely about.
- Help your child become oriented to the environment by removing all unnecessary obstacles around the home (e.g., shoes left on the floor, partially opened doors, a vacuum cleaner left out). Keep him or her informed of any changes in room arrangements.
- Instruction in special mobility techniques should begin as early as possible with the young child who has vision loss.
- Keep informed about organizations and civic groups that can provide support to the child and the family.
- Get in touch with your local health, social services, and education agencies about infant, toddler, and preschool programs for children with vision loss. Become familiar with the individualized family service plan (IFSP) and how it can serve as a planning tool to include your child in early intervention programs.

TIPS FOR THE PRESCHOOL TEACHER

- Mobility is a fundamental part of early intervention programs for children with vision loss. Help them learn to explore the environment in the classroom, school, and local neighborhood.
- Work with the child on developing a sense of touch and using hearing to acquire information. The young child may also need assistance in learning to smile and make eye contact.
- Work closely with the family to develop orientation and mobility strategies that can be learned and applied in both home and school settings.
- Help other sighted children in the classroom interact with the young child with vision loss by teaching them to speak directly to him or her in a normal tone of voice so as not to raise the noise level.
- Become very familiar with both tactile (e.g., braille) and auditory aids (e.g., personal readers) that may be used by the young child to acquire information.

TIPS FOR PRESCHOOL PERSONNEL

- Support the inclusion of young children with vision loss in your classrooms and programs.
- Support teachers, staff, and volunteers as they attempt to create successful experiences for the young child with vision loss in the preschool setting.
- Work very closely with families to keep them informed

and active members of the school community.

TIPS FOR NEIGHBORS AND FRIENDS

- Never assume that, because a young child has a vision loss, he or she cannot or should not participate in family and neighborhood activities that are associated with sight (e.g., board games, sports, hide-and-seek).
- Work with the young child's family to seek opportunities for interaction with sighted children in neighborhood play settings.

■ ELEMENTARY YEARS

TIPS FOR THE FAMILY

- Learn about the programs and services available during the school years for your child with vision loss. Learn about your child's right to an appropriate education, and actively participate in the development of your child's individual education plan (IEP).
- Participate in as many school functions for parents as is reasonable to connect your family to the school (e.g., PTA, parent advisory groups, volunteering).
- Seek information on in-school and extracurricular activities that will enhance opportunities for your child to interact with sighted peers.
- Keep the school informed about the medical needs of your child.

- If your child needs or uses specialized mobility devices to enhance access to the environment, help school personnel to understand how these devices work.

TIPS FOR THE GENERAL EDUCATION CLASSROOM TEACHER

- Remove obstacles in the classroom that may interfere with the mobility of students with vision loss, including small things like litter on the floor, to desks that are blocking aisles.
- Place the child's desk as close as necessary to you during group instruction. He or she should also sit as close as possible to visual objects associated with instruction (e.g., blackboard, video monitor, or classroom bulletin board).
- Be consistent in where you place classroom materials so that the child with vision loss can locate them independently.
- When providing instruction, always try to stand with your back to the windows. It is very difficult for a person with vision loss to look directly into a light source.
- Work closely with a vision specialist to determine any specialized mobility or lighting needs for the student with vision loss (e.g., special desk lamp, cassette recorder, large-print books, personal reader).
- Help the student gain confidence in you by letting him or her know

where you are in the classroom. It is especially helpful to let the student know when you are planning to leave the classroom.

TIPS FOR SCHOOL PERSONNEL

- Integrate school resources as well as children. Wherever possible, help general education classroom teachers access the human and material resources necessary to meet the needs of students with vision loss. For example:
  — *A vision specialist.* A professional trained in the education of students with vision loss can serve as an effective consultant to you and the children in several areas (e.g., mobility training, use of special equipment, communication media, instructional strategies).
  — *An ophthalmologist.* Students with a vision loss often have associated medical problems. It is helpful for the teacher to understand any related medical needs that can affect the child's educational experience.
  — *Peer-buddy and support systems.* Peer support can be an effective tool for learning in a classroom setting. Peer-buddy systems can be established in the school to help the child with initial mobility needs and/or any tutoring that would help him or her succeed in the general education classroom.

- Support keeping the school as barrier free as possible; this includes providing adequate lighting in classrooms and hallways.
- It is critical that children with vision loss have access to appropriate reading materials (e.g., braille books, large-print books, cassette recordings of books) in the school library and media center.

TIPS FOR NEIGHBORS AND FRIENDS

- Help the family of a child who is visually impaired be an integral part of the neighborhood and friendship networks. Seek ways to include the family and child wherever possible in neighborhood activities.

■ SECONDARY AND TRANSITION YEARS

TIPS FOR THE FAMILY

- Become familiar with the adult services system (e.g., rehabilitation services, Social Security, health care) while your son or daughter is still in high school. Understand the type of vocational or employment training that he or she will need prior to graduation.
- Find out the school's view on what it should do to assist students with vision loss in making the transition from school to adult life.
- Create opportunities for your son or daughter to participate in out-of-school activities with same-age sighted peers.

TIPS FOR THE GENERAL EDUCATION CLASSROOM TEACHER

- Assist students with vision loss to adapt to subject matter in your classroom while you adapt the classroom to meet their needs (e.g., in terms of seating, oral instruction, mobility, large-print or braille textbooks).
- Access to auditory devices (e.g., cassette recorders for lectures) can facilitate students' learning.
- Support the student with vision loss in becoming involved in extracurricular activities. If you are the faculty sponsor of a club or organization, explore whether the student is interested and how he or she could get involved.

TIPS FOR SCHOOL PERSONNEL

- Assist parents of students with vision loss to actively participate in school activities (e.g., parent/ teacher groups and advisory committees).
- Maintain positive and ongoing contact with the family.

TIPS FOR NEIGHBORS, FRIENDS, AND POTENTIAL EMPLOYERS

- Seek ways of becoming part of a community support network for the individuals with a vision loss. Be alert to ways that individuals can become and remain actively involved in community employment, neighborhood recreational activities, and local church functions.

- As potential employers in the local community, seek information on employment of people with a vision loss.

■ ADULT YEARS

- Become aware of the support and services available for your son and daughter in the local community in which they will live as adults. Identify the government-supported programs available to assist people with vision loss in the areas of postsecondary education opportunities, employment, and recreation/ leisure. Identify informal supports, such as family and friends, to assist your son or daughter.
- Work with the person who has vision loss and the family to become part of a community support network for individuals with vision loss. Help the individual with vision loss to become and remain involved in community employment, neighborhood recreational activities, and local church functions.
- As an employer in the community, seek out information on the employment of people with vision loss. Find out about the programs that focus on establishing employment opportunities for people with a vision loss, while meeting your needs as an employer.

TABLE 15.1	General steps in the language experience approach

1. Arrange an experience for the student, or use a naturally occurring one.

2. Have the student tell a story about the experience. Write down the story as the student tells it and watches.

3. Read the story back to the student immediately, pointing to each word.

4. Continue to reread the story with the student over several days or weeks. The student will systematically read more and more of the story independently.

5. Structure appropriate activities around the story, such as the following:
   - *Word recognition* (for example, place selected words from the story on note cards and review them with the student; have the student find the words in the story)
   - *Phonics* (for instance, identify a recurring consonant or vowel sound from the story, make up other words that start with the identified sound, and read words with the identified sound)
   - *Comprehension* (for example, make up a title for the story that expresses its main idea; suggest titles that may be too broad or too narrow for the story)
   - *Art activities* (for instance, draw pictures or create other works of art that depict the experiences in the story)

Source: From "Instruction of Literacy Skills to Children and Youth with Low Vision," by A. J. Koenig and E. J. Rex. In *Foundations of Low Vision: Clinical and Functional Perspectives,* edited by the American Foundation for the Blind Press, 1996, p. 292, New York: Author.

braille system. (See nearby Reflect on This feature.) This system, which originated with the work of Louis Braille in 1829, is a code that utilizes a six-dot cell to form 63 different alphabetical, numerical, and grammatical characters. To become a proficient braille reader, a person must learn 263 different configurations, including alphabet letters, punctuation marks, short-form words, and contractions.

Braille is not a tactile reproduction of the standard English alphabet but a separate code for reading and writing.

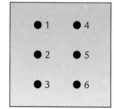
Braille is composed of from one to six raised dots depicted in a cell or space that contains room for two vertical rows of three dots each. On the left the dots are numbered 1, 2, and 3 from top to bottom; on the right the dots are numbered 4, 5, and 6 (see Figure 15.4). This makes it easy to describe braille characters. For example, a is dot 1, p is dots 1, 2, 3, and 4, and h is dots 1, 2, and 5.

. . . In braille any letter becomes a capital by putting dot 6 in front of it. For example, if a is dot 1, A is dot 6 followed by dot 1 and if p is dots 1, 2, 3, and 4, P is dot 6 followed by dots 1, 2, 3, and 4. This sure is easier than print, which requires different configurations for more than half of the capital letters. If h is dots 1, 2, and 5, what is H?

Research has shown that the fastest braille readers use two hands. Using two hands also seems to make it easier for beginning braille readers to stay on the line. Do you think this might have something to do with two points constituting a line as my geometry teacher used to tell us? (Pester, 1998).

Braille is used by about 1 out every 10 students who are blind and is considered by many to be an efficient means for teaching reading and writing. The American Printing House for the Blind produces about 28 million pages in English braille each year (Pester, 1998). Critics of the system argue that most readers who use braille are much slower than those who read from print and that braille materials are bulky and tedious. It can be argued, however, that without braille, people who are blind

Reflect on This

BRAILLE READERS FOUND TO USE VISUAL CORTEX

When blind people "read" Braille with their fingertips, they are somehow able to use the same part of the brain—called the visual cortex—that sighted persons use to interpret things they see. That's the conclusion of new experiments that challenge traditional ideas about how sensory information is processed in the brain.

According to orthodox neuroscience, tactile stimuli are processed in a region of the brain's convoluted outer layer called the somatosensory cortex. Visual information goes by a completely different route to an area at the back of the brain called the visual cortex. Eventually, the twain may meet and be integrated into a single perception—but only after each has been separately processed. There are no known nerve pathways that would permit tactile signals to get to the visual cortex directly.

But in the journal *Nature,* researchers from the National Institute of Neurological Disorders and Stroke report that persons who are blind from an early age seem to have rearranged their neural wiring so that sensory information

from a forefinger running over patterns of raised Braille dots prompts a flurry of action in the brain's visual processing centers. Norihiro Sadato and colleagues at NINDS monitored the cerebral activity of eight adept Braille readers, six other blind subjects, and ten sighted subjects, using a technique called positron emission tomography. PET scans show which areas of the brain are most active (that is, which cells are consuming the most blood-borne nutrients) during a given task.

In this case, the eight blind subjects were scanned while they read raised dot patterns in Braille. The other subjects were monitored while performing various analogous tasks: running their fingers over a uniform grid of Braille dots; feeling the size and angle of grooves in an array of dots; and detecting dot patterns of English letters. When sighted subjects performed those tasks, their scans showed diminished activity in the visual cortex and the expected levels of action in somatosensory areas that normally process tactile information. But when any of the 14 blind subjects read Braille or interpreted dot patterns, they exhibited substantial

increases in the visual cortex. Neither group showed any visual cortex activity during the "non-discriminatory" task of merely sweeping their fingers over the uniform dot grid, which involved purely tactile sensation.

Recent research has shown that when people create imaginary mental images of objects, brain activity increases in the same parts of the visual cortex that are used when actually viewing an object. But none of the NINDS subjects was asked to form mental pictures during any of the tasks, and none reported doing so. Moreover, some of the subjects were blind from birth and presumably had no way to form imagined visual images.

So how did the Braille readers use the visual cortex, and what mechanism might make that possible? "That's the million-dollar question," said NINDS neuropsychologist Jordan Grafman, a co-author of the *Nature* paper. "One hypothesis is that there are certain properties of cells in the visual cortex that resemble properties of cells in the somatosensory cortex"—especially in their ability to discriminate geometrical information about a stimulus. "If

that's true," he said, "then it might be possible under special conditions that cells in either . . . cortex could adapt to sensory input coming from the other area."

It is conceivable, the NINDS team suspects, that information can travel from region to region through some unknown "indirect preexisting pathway." In normal circumstances, in which a sighted person is touching something, that pathway would be shut down to focus attention on tactile stimuli and avoid confusing the brain.

But that pathway might be opened "in an emergency of unusual situation" such as blindness, Grafman said.

Once the phenomenon is better understood, he said, it might be possible to concoct drugs that would encourage this kind of compensatory rerouting, known as neural plasticity.

Source: From "Braille Readers Found to Use Visual Cortex: Results Defy Traditional Ideas of Brain Function," by C. Suplee, April 11, 1996, *Washington Post,* p. A4. © 1996 The Washington Post. Reprinted with permission.

would be much less independent. Some people who are unable to read braille (such as people with diabetes who have decreased tactile sensitivity) are more dependent on sight readers and recordings. Simple tasks—such as labeling cans, boxes, or cartons in a bathroom or kitchen—become nearly impossible to complete.

Braille writing is accomplished through the use of a slate and stylus. Using this procedure, a student writes a mirror image of the reading code, moving from right to left. The writing process may be facilitated by using a braille writer, a hand-operated machine with six keys that correspond to each dot in the braille cell.

Innovations for braille readers that reduce some of the problems associated with the medium include the Mountbatten Brailler and the Braille 'n Speak. The Mountbatten Brailler is electronic, thus making it easier to operate than a manual unit. The Mountbatten Brailler weighs about 15 pounds and can be hooked up to a computer keyboard attachment to input information.

The Braille 'n Speak is a pocket-size battery-powered Braille note-taker with keyboard for data entry with voice output. The device can translate braille into synthesized speech or print. Files may be printed in formatted text to a printer designed to enable users to input information through a braille keyboard. The Braille 'n Speak has accessories for entering or reading text for a host computer, for reading computer disks, and for sending or receiving a fax.

In regard to educational programs for students who are blind, the U.S. Congress responded to concerns that services for these students were not addressing their unique educational and learning needs, particularly their needs for instruction in reading, writing, and composition. In the reauthorization of IDEA 1997, the Congress mandated that schools must make provision for instruction in braille and the use of braille unless the IEP team determines that such instruction and use are not appropriate to the needs of the student (U.S. Department of Education, 2000b, June).

One tactile device that does not use the braille system is the Optacon Scanner. This machine exposes printed material to a camera and then reproduces it on a fingerpad, using a series of vibrating pins that are tactile reproductions of the printed material. Developed by J. C. Bliss and available commercially since 1971, thousands of Optacons are currently in use worldwide. Although the Optacon greatly expands access to the printed word, it has drawbacks as well. It requires tactile sensitivity; as such, reading remains a slow, laborious process. Additionally, the Optacon requires considerable training for the individual to become a skilled user. These drawbacks, along with the development of reading machines, have resulted in the declining use and production of the Optacon Scanner.

Many of the newer communication systems do not make use of the tactile sense because it is not functional for all people who are blind (many do not have tactile sensitivity, including some elderly people). Such individuals must rely solely on the auditory sense to acquire information. Specialized auditory media for people who are blind are becoming increasingly available. One example is the reading machine, hailed as a major breakthrough in technology for persons with a vision loss. Reading machines, manufactured by Kurzweil, IBM, and Arenstone, convert printed matter into synthetic speech at a rate of 1 to 2.5 pages per minute. They can also convert print to braille. The costs associated with reading machines have decreased substantially in the past few years, and most can be purchased with computer accessories for about $1,000. Several advocacy organizations for those with blindness and many banks throughout America cur-

Special computers such as PowerBraille are designed for people who read and write braille. Such electronic aids are faster and easier to use than a braille writer.

rently provide low-interest loans for people with vision loss so they can purchase the device. (See nearby Today's Technology feature.)

Other auditory aids that assist people who are blind include microcomputers with voice output, talking calculators, talking-book machines, compact disc players, and audiotape recorders. For example, the Note Teller is a small, compact machine that can identify denominations of U.S. currency using a voice synthesizer that communicates in either English or Spanish.

Communication media that facilitate participation of people with vision loss in the community include specialized library and newspaper services that offer books in large print, on cassette, and in braille. The *New York Times,* for example, publishes a weekly special edition with type three times the size of its regular type. The sale of large-print books has increased during the past ten years, and many have also become available through the Internet or on computer disk (electronic books).

Responding to a human voice, devices known as **personal digital assistants (PDAs)** can look up a telephone number and dial it. Using a synthesized voice, some PDAs can read a newspaper delivered over telephone lines, balance a checkbook, turn home appliances on and off, and maintain a daily appointment book.

Closed-circuit television (CCTV) systems are another means to enlarge the print from books and other written documents. Initially explored in the 1950s, the design of CCTV systems became more practical in the 1970s, and they are now in wider use than ever before. The components of the CCTV systems include a small television camera with variable zoom lens and focusing capacity, a TV monitor, and a sliding platform table for the printed materials (Zimmerman, 1996). An individual sits in front of the television monitor to view printed material that can be enhanced up to 60 times its original size through the use of the TV camera and zoom lens. Some CCTVs are also available with split-screen capability to allow near and distant objects to be viewed together. These machines can also accept input directly from a computer as well as printed material (Best, 1992; Zimmerman, 1996).

▪ EDUCATIONAL PLACEMENT

Historically, education for students with vision loss—specifically, blindness—was provided through specialized residential facilities. These segregated centers have traditionally been referred to as asylums, institutions, or schools. One of the first such facilities in the United States was the New England Asylum for the Blind, later renamed the Perkins School. This facility opened its doors in 1832 and was one of several eastern U.S. schools that used treatment models borrowed from well-established European institutions. For the most part, the early U.S. institutions operated as closed schools, where a person who was blind would live and learn in an environment that was essentially separate from the outside world. The philosophy was to get the person who was blind "ready for the outside world," even though this approach provided little real exposure to it.

More recently, some residential schools have advocated an open system of intervention. These programs are based on the philosophy that children who are blind should have every opportunity to gain the same experiences that would be available if they were growing up in their own communities.

Both open and closed residential facilities exist today as alternative intervention modes, but they are no longer the primary social or educational systems available to people who are blind. As was true for John in the chapter opening snapshot, the vast majority of individuals who are blind or partially sighted now live at home, attend local public schools, and interact within the community.

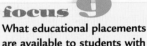

focus 9

What educational placements are available to students with vision loss?

▪PERSONAL DIGITAL ASSISTANT. Hand-held computer device that can be programmed to perform multiple functions such as dialing a telephone, reading a newspaper, or maintaining a daily calendar or address book.

▪CLOSED-CIRCUIT TELEVISION (CCTV). A TV system that includes a small television camera with zoom lens, TV monitor, and sliding platform table, which allows an individual with vision loss to view printed material enlarged up to 60 times its original size.

Today's Technology

THE MAGIC MACHINES OF RAY KURZWEIL[1]

In the late 1960s Ray Kurzweil walked on stage, played a composition on an old upright piano, and then whispered to *I've Got a Secret* host Steve Allen, "I built my own computer." "Well, that's impressive," Steve Allen replied, "but what does that have to do with the piece you just played?" Ray then whispered the rest of his secret: "The computer composed the piece I just played." . . . Ray programmed his computer to analyze the patterns in musical compositions by famous composers and then compose original new melodies in a similar style. For the project, Ray won first prize in the International Science Fair and was one of the 40 Westinghouse Science Talent Search winners that got to meet President Lyndon Johnson in a White House award ceremony.

As a sophomore at MIT, Ray started and ran a business matching up high school kids with colleges using a computer program he had written. In 1974, Ray started his first major enterprise, Kurzweil Computer Products, Inc. (KCP)

to pursue his interest in pattern recognition, attacking the then classical and unsolved problem of teaching a computer to identify printed or typed characters regardless of type style and printing quality. Existing systems could recognize only certain special fonts (e.g., Courier, OCRA). Ray and his colleagues taught the computer how to extract the abstract qualities of letter shapes, defining what essential properties made, for example, all capital A's different from all capital B's. Ray and his team created the first "omni-font" (i.e., any font) Optical Character Recognition (OCR). This new technology became a solution in search of a problem. A chance plane flight during which he sat next to a blind gentleman convinced Ray that the most exciting application of this new technology would be to create a machine that could read printed and typed documents out loud, thereby overcoming the reading handicap of blind and visually impaired individuals. This goal introduced new hurdles as there were no readily available flat bed scanners or speech synthesizers in 1974. So

in addition to the omni-font OCR, Ray and his colleagues developed the first CCD flatbed scanner and the first full text-to-speech synthesizer, and combined these three technologies into the first print-to-speech reading machine for the blind. Ray, along with leaders of the National Federation of the Blind, announced the Kurzweil Reading Machine at a press conference on January 13, 1976, which was covered by all of the networks and leading print publications. Walter Cronkite used it to deliver his signature sign-off "And that's the way it was, January 13, 1976." Stevie Wonder happened to catch Ray demonstrating the Kurzweil Reading Machine on the *Today Show* and dropped by Kurzweil Computer Products to pick up their first production unit. This led to a long-term friendship between the inventor and the musical star, which led to Ray Kurzweil's subsequent innovations in computer-based music.

In 1982, as he was showing Ray a new studio he had built in Los Angeles, Stevie Wonder lamented the state of affairs of musical instruments. On

the one hand there was the world of acoustic instruments (e.g., piano, guitar, violin), which provided rich, complex sounds but were difficult to play, and suffered from a wide range of limitations. On the other hand, the world of computer-based instruments allowed advanced control techniques such as multi-track sequencing and layering, but was capable of creating only thin synthetic sounds. "Wouldn't it be great," Stevie asked Ray, "if we could use the extraordinarily flexible computer-control methods on the beautiful sounds of acoustic instruments." The result of this challenge was Ray's 1982 founding of Kurzweil Music Systems with Stevie Wonder as musical adviser. In 1984, Kurzweil Music introduced the Kurzweil 250, the first computer-based instrument that could realistically recreate the musical response of the grand piano and other orchestral instruments. In A-B tests, musicians were unable to distinguish the Kurzweil 250 from a concert grand piano. With this technology,

---

Educational programs for students with vision loss are based on the principle of flexible placement. As suggested by Corn et al. (1995), schools are responsible for ensuring that every student with a visual impairment has access to a full array of placement options. As such, a wide variety of services must be available to these students in the public schools, ranging from general education class placement, with little or no assistance from specialists, to separate residential schools. Between these two placements, the public schools generally offer several alternative classroom structures, including the use of consulting teachers, resource rooms, part-time special classes, or full-time special classes. Placement of a student in one of these programs depends on the extent to which the loss of vision affects his or her overall educational achievement. Many students with vision loss are able to function suca teenager could play an entire orchestra or rock band in her bedroom.

Ray also started Kurzweil Applied Intelligence in 1982 to develop computer-based speech recognition. The company introduced the first commercially marketed large-vocabulary speech-recognition system in 1987. The company also combined its speech recognition technology with expert systems for the creation of medical reports. Kurzweil Applied Intelligence was sold to Lernout & Hauspie (L&H) in 1997. Shortly after this sale, Microsoft entered into a strategic alliance with the dictation division of L&H (formerly Kurzweil Applied Intelligence) to share technology in the speech field (which included a substantial investment by Microsoft). Ray continues as chief technologist of the dictation division of L&H, which recently introduced the first product to combine continuous large-vocabulary speech recognition with natural language commands. With this product, called Voice Xpress Pro, you can command your personal computer by talking to it in your own words. Ray started his fourth company, Kurzweil Educational Systems,

in 1996. This company quickly became dominant in the print-to-speech reading technology field. In August 1998, Ray and his colleagues received the first SAP/Stevie Wonder "Product of the Year" Vision Award for the Kurzweil 1000 Reading System.

■ THE KURZWEIL 1000 READING SYSTEM CHANGES THE LIVES OF BLIND COUPLE[2]

"It's incredible!" declares Patricia Baxtermoore of Kentucky. "Now we have immediate access to an unlimited amount of reading materials, and this makes our lives a lot simpler. A person can definitely get spoiled with L&H Kurzweil 1000." Patricia is blind and was one of the first to reap the benefits of L&H Kurzweil 1000, an advanced PC-based reading system for people who are blind or visually impaired. "My husband and I started a business, and we needed something that will read clearly and accurately, and give us immediate access to the amount of paperwork we handle," explains Patricia, whose husband, Earl, is also blind. "When we heard that Ray Kurzweil had developed a new reading machine, we decided to give it a try. We had used

everything else available and were not satisfied."

For the Baxtermoores, L&H Kurzweil 1000 has become an integral part of their lives, bringing them greater independence and improved productivity that enhances their lives. Patricia states, "It's an amazing feeling to suddenly be able to read all kinds of printed materials whenever we want, as often as we want—especially after years of not being able to. We no longer have to wait a week for a sighted reader to come and help us."

According to Patricia, L&H Kurzweil 1000 has many unparalleled features. Some of these features include an electronic dictionary, the ability to read complicated texts along with graphical elements, 14 different voices, and highly accurate optical character recognition (OCR).

"L&H Kurzweil 1000 can do so much in so little time," Patricia continues. "And the OCR is just astounding. For instance, when my husband needs to read his law books—which have multiple columns, symbols, footnotes, and different fonts throughout—the Kurzweil easily scans every page without a problem.

That's the way a reading machine ought to work."

As an example of what this powerful reading system can do, the Baxtermoores enthusiastically cite a weekend during which they scanned in 3,000 pages that they wanted to work on immediately. Patricia observes, "Other systems require at least 50 hours for this amount of pages. L&H Kurzweil 1000 finished in less than half that time—just 20 hours." So what do the Baxtermoores do with the 30 hours they saved on that occasion? "L&H Kurzweil 1000 has increased our efficiency by at least 300% and gives us the time to do more," Patricia concludes. "We spend more time reading what we never had time to read before. Now we read for fun, too."

[1]*Source:* From *A Brief Biography of Ray Kurzweil,* by Kurzweil Technologies, 2000, Burlington, MA: Lernout & Hauspie. *[on-line]* Available: http://www.kurzweiltech.com/raybio.htm

[2]From *L&H Kurzweil 1000's Access to Information and Fun,* by A. Pobre, 2000, Burlington, MA: Lernout & Hauspie. *[on-line]* Available: http://www.LHSL.com/pressroom/case studies/motivate.asp

cessfully within general education settings if the learning environment is adapted to meet their needs.

Some organizations advocating for students who are blind strongly support the concept of flexible placements within a continuum ranging from general education classroom to residential school (American Foundation for the Blind, 2000; Joint Organizational Committee, 1993). The report of the Joint Organizational Committee, which represented eight national organizations, opposed the "full inclusion" of students who are blind as the only educational option in the public schools. The American Foundation for the Blind recommended a full continuum of alternative placements, emphasizing that students who are visually impaired are most likely to succeed in educational systems where appropriate instruction and services are provided in a full array of program options by qualified staff to address each student's unique educational needs. Some professionals have also indicated that graduates of inclusive programs in general education classrooms lack the skills needed for independent functioning during the adult years (Sacks, Kekelis, & Gaylord-Ross, 1992).

Whether the student is to be included in the general education classroom or taught in a special class, a vision specialist must be available, either to support the general education classroom teacher or to provide direct instruction to the student. A vision specialist has received concentrated training in the education of students with vision loss. This specialist and the rest of the educational support team have knowledge of appropriate educational assessment techniques, specialized curriculum materials and teaching approaches, and the use of various communication media. Specialized instruction for students who have vision loss may include a major modification in curricula, including teaching concepts that children who are sighted learn incidentally (e.g., walking down the street, getting from one room to the next in the school building, getting meals in the cafeteria, and using public transportation).

Medical and Social Services

Medical services for vision loss include initial screenings based on visual acuity; preventive measures that include genetic screening, appropriate prenatal care, and early developmental assessments; and treatment ranging from optical aids to surgery. Some people with vision loss may have social adjustment difficulties, including lack of self-esteem and general feelings of inferiority. To minimize these problems, social services should be made available as early as possible in the person's life.

■ MEDICAL SERVICES

focus 10
What steps can be taken to prevent and medically treat vision loss?

Initial screenings for vision loss are usually based on the individual's visual acuity. Visual acuity may be measured through the use of the Snellen test, developed in 1862 by Dutch ophthalmologist Herman Snellen. This visual screening test is used primarily to measure central distance vision. The subject stands 20 feet from a letter chart, or E-chart (the standard eye-test chart), and reads each symbol, beginning with the top row. The different sizes of each row or symbol represent what a person with normal vision would see at the various distances indicated on the chart. As indicated earlier in this chapter, a person's visual acuity is then determined by the use of an index that refers to the distance at which an object can be recognized. The person with normal eyesight is defined as having 20/20 vision.

Since the Snellen test measures only visual acuity, it must be used primarily as an initial screening device that is supplemented by more in-depth assessments, such as a thorough ophthalmological examination. Parents, physicians, school nurses, and educators must also carefully observe the child's behavior, and a complete history of possible symptoms of a vision loss should be documented. These observable symptoms fall into three categories: appearance, behavior, and complaints. Table 15.2 describes some warning signs of vision loss. The existence of symptoms does not necessarily mean a person has a significant vision loss, but it does indicate that an appropriate specialist should be consulted for further examination.

■ **PREVENTION** Prevention of vision loss is one of the major goals of the field of medicine. Since some causes of blindness are hereditary, it is important for the family to be aware of genetic services. One purpose of genetic screening is to identify those who are planning for a family and who may possess certain detrimental

TABLE 15.2   Warning signs of visual problems

Physical Symptoms	Observable Behavior	Complaints
Eyes are crossed.	Blinks constantly	Frequent dizziness
Eyes are not functioning in unison.	Trips or stumbles frequently	Frequent headaches
Eyelids are swollen and crusted, with red rims.	Covers one eye when reading	Pain in the eyes
Eyes are overly sensitive to light.	Holds reading material either very close or very far away	Itching or burning of the eyes or eyelids
Sties occur frequently.	Distorts the face or frowns when concentrating on something in the distance	Double vision
Eyes are frequently bloodshot.		
Pupils are of different sizes.	Walks cautiously	
Eyes are constantly in motion.	Fails to see objects that are to one side or the other	

genotypes (such as albinism or retinoblastoma) that can be passed on to their descendants. Screening may also be conducted after conception to determine whether the unborn fetus possesses any genetic abnormalities. Following screening, a genetic counselor informs the parents of the test results so that the family can make an informed decision about conceiving a child or carrying a fetus to term.

Adequate prenatal care is another means of preventing problems. Parents must be made aware of the potential hazards associated with poor nutritional habits, the use of drugs, and exposure to radiation (e.g., x-rays) during pregnancy. One example of preventive care during this period is the use of antibiotics to treat various infections (e.g., influenza, measles, syphilis), thus reducing the risk of infection to the unborn fetus.

Developmental screening is also a widely recognized means of prevention. (It was through early developmental screening that a medical specialist confirmed that John—in the chapter opening snapshot—had a serious vision loss and would require the assistance of a trained vision specialist.) Early screening of developmental problems enables the family physician to analyze several treatment alternatives and, when necessary, to refer the child to an appropriate specialist for a more thorough evaluation of developmental delays.

This screening—which also includes examination of hearing, speech, motor, and psychological development—includes attention to vision as well. Early screening involves a medical examination at birth, examining the physical condition of the newborn, and also obtaining a complete family medical history. The eyes should be carefully examined for any abnormalities, such as infection or trauma.

At 6 weeks of age, visual screening forms part of another general developmental assessment. This examination should include input from the parents concerning how their child is responding (e.g., smiling and looking at objects or faces). The physician should check eye movement and search for infection, crusting on the eyes, or **epiphora** (an overflow of tears resulting from obstruction of the lacrimal ducts).

The next examination should occur at about 6 months of age. A defensive blink should be present at this age, and eye movement should be full and coordinated. If any imbalance in eye movements is noted, a more thorough examination should be

▌EPIPHORA. An overflow of tears from obstruction of the lacrimal ducts of the eye.

conducted. Family history is extremely important, since in many cases there is a familial pattern of vision problems.

Between the ages of 1 and 5, visual evaluation should be conducted at regular intervals. An important period occurs just prior to the child's entering school. Visual problems must not go undetected as children attempt to cope with the new and complex demands of the educational environment.

■ TREATMENT   In addition to medicine's emphasis on prevention of vision loss, significant strides have also been made in the treatment of these problems. The nature of medical interventions depends on the type and severity of the loss. For people who are partially sighted, use of an optical aid can vastly improve access to the visual world. Most of these aids take the form of corrective glasses or contact lenses, which are designed to magnify the image on the retina. Some aids magnify the retinal image within the eye, and others clarify the retinal image. Appropriate use of optical aids, in conjunction with regular medical examinations, not only helps correct existing visual problems but may also prevent further deterioration of existing vision.

Surgery, muscle exercises, and drug therapy have also played important roles in treating persons with vision loss. Treatment may range from complex laser surgical procedures and corneal transplants to the process known as atropinization. **Atropinization** is the treatment for cataracts that involves washing out the eye with the alkaloid drug atropine, which permanently dilates the pupil.

■ SOCIAL SERVICES

Social services can begin with infant stimulation programs and counseling for the family. As the child grows older, group counseling can assist in coping with feelings concerning blindness and provide guidance in the area of human sexuality (limited vision may distort perception of the physical body). Counseling eventually extends into matters focusing on marriage, family, and adult relationships. For the adult with vision loss, special guidance may be necessary in preparation for employment and independent living.

Mobility of the person with vision loss can be enhanced in large cities by the use of auditory pedestrian signals at crosswalks, known as audible traffic signals (ATS). The *walk* and *don't walk* signals are indicated by auditory cues, such as actual verbal messages (e.g., "Please do not cross yet"), different bird chirps for each signal, or a sonalert buzzer (Peck & Uslan, 1990). ATS is somewhat controversial among people who are blind and professionals in the field. Those not supporting the use of ATS have two basic concerns. First, the devices promote negative public attitudes, indicating a presumption that such assistance is necessary for a person who is blind to be mobile. Second, the devices may actually contribute to unsafe conditions because they mask traffic noise for the person who is blind.

Restaurant menus, elevator floor buttons, and signs in buildings (such as rest rooms) can be produced in braille. Additionally, telephone credit cards, personal checks, ATM cards, special mailing tubes, and panels for household appliances are also available in braille. Access to community services is greatly enhanced by devices that use synthesized speech for purchasing subway and rail tickets or obtaining money from automatic teller machines.

Despite advancements in electronic mobility devices, the guide dog continues to be an important source of support for people who are blind. The dog's intelligence and companionship contribute to its popularity.

Case Study

MICHAEL

Clasping a cane in his right hand and book bag in the other, Michael Harris is darting though Kearns High School on his way to his next class. Peer tutor Rebecca Hale is helping this student, who is blind, negotiate the crowd.

"Hi, Mike!" blurt passers-by.

Suddenly, in a rich baritone voice, Michael belts out the first chorus of "I'll Be Home for Christmas."

No one marvels. The voice is familiar and pleasant. Frequently, the 17-year-old stays after school, where he sits cross-legged, propped against a locker, and sings. He even takes requests.

"The most important thing is these kids are just like any other kids," says Deanne Graves, teacher for those with visual impairments in Granite School District. "They have ups and downs. We need to treat them just like everybody else. Just because they have a disability does not mean they cannot aspire to whatever they want."

Michael has been part of the inclusion movement since he was a fifth-grader at Western Hills Elementary. He prefers it to his time at the Utah Schools for the Deaf and the Blind.

"One of the things I like about mainstreaming [is that there are kids from my neighborhood]. When I went to the School for the Blind, there were kids from all over the valley," he says. "So basically there was nobody from my neighborhood."

During his third-period college prep English course, the class is reading *Cyrano de Bergerac* aloud. Since Michael has fallen slightly behind, he sits outside the room with his tutor, Rebecca, listening to *Cyrano* on tape.

Unexpectedly, the fire alarm sounds. It is a routine fire drill. Rebecca, who gets credit for helping Michael, leads him out of the building in the mass student exodus.

About three minutes later, Michael is swarmed by a crowd as they listen to his jokes.

"What do you call twins before they are born?" he asks. "Womb mates." The crowd laughs; Michael loves it.

■ APPLICATION

1. Are Michael's experiences similar to or different from those of other students with vision loss that you have known in high school?

2. Describe any accommodations or supports that Michael is probably receiving that help him function so well in a general education classroom.

Source: Adapted from *Disabled Students Making It in the Mainstream,* by S. A. Autman (October 31, 1994), *Salt Lake Tribune,* pp. B1, B2. Reprinted by permission of S. A. Autman and The Salt Lake Tribune.

Debate Forum

GENERAL EDUCATION SCHOOLS VERSUS SPECIAL SCHOOLS: WHERE SHOULD STUDENTS WHO ARE BLIND BE EDUCATED?

In 1900, the first class for students who were blind opened in the Chicago public schools. Prior to this, such children were educated in state residential schools, where they lived away from their families. Until 1950, the ratio of students attending schools for the blind to those in general education public schools was about 10 to 1. In that year, however, the incidence of children with retrolental fibroplasia (now known as retinopathy of prematurity) increased, resulting in significant numbers of children who were blind attending public schools. By 1960, more children with blindness were being educated with their nondisabled peers in general education public schools than in schools for the blind. Nonetheless, the issue of what is the most appropriate educational environment for children who are blind continues to be debated internationally.

■ POINT

Children who are blind should be educated in public schools and classrooms alongside their seeing peers. Inclusion allows children who are blind to remain at home with their family and live in a local neighborhood, which is just as important for these children as it is for their sighted friends. It also allows children who are blind to have greater opportunities for appropriate modeling of acceptable behaviors.

Schools for children who are blind have endeavored over the years to offer the best education possible, one intended to be equivalent to that offered to children who can see. However, these schools cannot duplicate the experiences of living at home and being part of the local community. Although it can be argued that the special school is geared entirely to the needs of the child who is blind, there is much more to education than a segregated educational environment can provide. During the growing years, the child must be directly involved in the seeing world in order to have the opportunity to adjust and become a part of society.

■ COUNTERPOINT

The special school for children who are blind provides a complete education that is oriented entirely to the unique needs of these individuals. The teachers in these schools have years of experience in working exclusively with children who are blind and are well aware of what educational experiences are needed to help them reach their fullest potential. Additionally, special schools are equipped with a multitude of educational resources developed for children who are blind. General education schools and classrooms cannot offer the intensive, individualized programs in areas such as music, physical education, and arts and crafts that are available through schools for the blind. The strength of the special school is that it is entirely geared to the specialized needs of the child who is blind. Thus, it can more effectively teach him or her the skills necessary to adapt to life experiences.

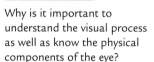

Review

 focus 1

Why is it important to understand the visual process as well as know the physical components of the eye?

- The visual process is an important link to the physical world, helping people to gain information beyond that provided by the other senses and also helping to integrate the information acquired primarily through sound, touch, smell, and taste.
- Our interactions with the environment are shaped by the way we perceive visual stimuli.

focus 2

Distinguish between the terms *blind* and *partially sighted*.

- Legal blindness is visual acuity of 20/200 or worse in the best eye with best correction, or a field of vision of 20% or less.
- Educational definitions of blindness focus primarily on the student's inability to functionally use vision as an avenue for learning.
- A person who is partially sighted has a visual acuity greater than 20/200 but not greater than 20/70 in the best eye after correction.
- A person who is partially sighted can still use vision as a primary means of learning.

 focus 3

What are the distinctive features of refractive eye problems, muscle disorders of the eye, and receptive eye problems?

- Refractive eye problems occur when the refractive structures of the eye (cornea or lens) fail to focus light rays properly on the retina. Refractive problems include hyperopia (farsightedness), myopia (nearsightedness), astigmatism (blurred vision), and cataracts.
- Muscle disorders occur when the major muscles within the eye are inadequately developed or atrophic, resulting in a loss of control and an inability to maintain tension. Muscle disorders include nystagmus (uncontrolled rapid eye movement), strabismus (crossed eyes), and amblyopia (loss of vision due to muscle imbalance).
- Receptive eye problems occur when the receptive structures of the eye (retina and optic nerve) degenerate or become damaged. Receptive eye problems include optic atrophy, retinitis pigmentosa, retinal detachment, retrolental fibroplasia, and glaucoma.

 focus 4

What are the estimated prevalence and causes of vision loss?

- Approximately 20% of all children and adults have some vision loss; 3% (9 million people) have a significant vision loss that will require some type of specialized services and supports.
- Fifty percent of elderly people over the age of 65 experience a significant loss of vision (includes cataracts).
- Over 26,000 students have visual impairments and received specialized services in the U.S. public schools.
- A number of genetic conditions can result in vision loss, including albinism, retinitis pigmentosa, retinoblastoma, optic atrophy, cataracts, severe myopia associated with retinal detachment, lesions of the cornea, abnormalities of the iris, microphthalmia, hydrocephalus, anophthalmia, and glaucoma.
- Acquired disorders that can lead to vision loss prior to birth include radiation, the introduction of drugs into the fetal system, and infections. Vision loss after birth may be due to several factors, including trauma, infections, inflammations, and tumors.
- The leading cause of acquired blindness in children worldwide is vitamin A deficiency (xerophthalmia). Cortical visual impairment (CVI) is also a leading cause of acquired blindness.

 focus 5

Describe how a vision loss can affect intelligence, speech and language skills, educational achievement, social development, physical orientation and mobility, and perceptual-motor development.

- Performance on tests of intelligence may be negatively affected in areas ranging from spatial concepts to general knowledge of the world.
- Children with vision loss are at a distinct disadvantage in developing speech and language skills because they are unable to visually associate words with objects. They cannot learn speech by visual imitation but must rely on hearing or touch for input. Preschool-age and school-age children with vision loss may develop a phenomenon known as ver-

balisms, or the excessive use of speech (wordiness), in which individuals may use words that have little meaning to them.

- In the area of written language, students with vision loss have more difficulty organizing thoughts to write a composition. Decoding for reading may be delayed because such students often use braille or large-print books as the media to decode. Decoding is a much slower process when using these two media. Reading comprehension is also affected because it depends so much on the experiences of the reader.

- Other factors that may influence the academic achievement include (1) late entry to school; (2) failure in inappropriate school programs; (3) loss of time in school due to illness, treatment, or surgery; (4) lack of opportunity; and (5) slow rate of acquiring information.

- People with vision loss are unable to imitate the physical mannerisms of sighted peers and thus do not develop body language, an important form of social communication. A person with sight may misinterpret what is said by a person with a vision loss because his or her visual cues may not be consistent with the spoken word.

- People with vision loss are often excluded from social activities that are integrally related to the use of vision, thus reinforcing the mistaken idea that they do not want to participate.

- Lack of sight may prevent a person from understanding his or her own relative position in space. A vision loss may affect fine motor

coordination and interfere with a person's ability to manipulate objects.

- The perceptual discrimination abilities of people with vision loss in the areas of texture, weight, and sound are comparable to those of sighted peers.

- People who are blind do not perform as well as people with sight on complex tasks of perception, including form identification, spatial relations, and perceptual-motor integration.

 focus 6

What is a functional approach to assessment for students with a vision loss?

- Assessment focuses specifically on how the student utilizes any remaining vision (visual efficiency) in conjunction with other senses to acquire information.

- A functional approach to assessment goes beyond determining visual acuity and focuses on capacity, attention, and processing.

 focus 7

Identify two content areas that should be included in educational programs for students with vision loss.

- *Mobility and orientation training.* The ability to move safely, efficiently, and independently through the environment enhances the individual's opportunities to learn more about the world and thus be less dependent on others for survival. Lack of mobility restricts individuals with vision loss in nearly every aspect of educational life.

- *The acquisition of daily living skills.* For children with a vision loss, routine daily liv-

ing skills are not easily learned through everyday experiences. These children must be encouraged and supported as they develop life skills and not overprotected from everyday challenges and risks by family and friends.

 focus 8

How can communication media facilitate learning for people with vision loss?

- Through communication media, such as optical aids in conjunction with auditory and tactile stimuli, individuals with vision loss can better develop an understanding of themselves and the world around them.

- Tactile media, including the raised-dot braille system and the Optacon Scanner, can greatly enhance the individual's access to information.

- Specialized media—including personal readers, microcomputers with voice output, closed-circuit TV systems, personal digital assistants, talking calculators, talking-book machines, CD players, and audiotape recorders—provide opportunities for people with vision loss that were not thought possible even a few years ago.

 focus 9

What educational placements are available to students with vision loss?

- Residential facilities provide children who are blind with opportunities for the same kinds of experiences that would be available if they were growing up in their own communities.

- The vast majority of people with vision loss live at home, attend public schools, and interact within their own communities.

- Services available within the public schools range from general education class placement, with little or no assistance, to special day schools.

 focus 10

What steps can be taken to prevent and medically treat vision loss?

- Vision loss can be prevented through genetic screening and counseling, appropriate prenatal care, and early developmental assessment.

- The development of optical aids, including corrective glasses and contact lenses, has greatly improved access to the sighted world for people with vision loss.

- Medical treatment may range from complex laser surgical procedures and corneal transplants to drug therapy (e.g., atropinization).

 focus 11

Why is the availability of appropriate social services important for people with vision loss?

- Social services address issues of self-esteem and feelings of inferiority that may stem from having a vision loss.

- Social services include infant stimulation programs, family counseling, and individual counseling relative to preparation for employment and independent living.

People with Physical and Health Disabilities

16

To begin with . . .

Mr. [Christopher] Reeve,

I just wanted to say thank you for all the inspiration that you give to the World in your fight. You are truly someone that many of us look up to. Keep fighting, keep trying, and keep striving. One day very soon they'll find a way to beat spinal cord injury and we'll be able to see a true Super Man walk again. Bill Boxler (Boxler, 1997)

As of the end of 1999, an estimated 33.6 million people worldwide—32.4 million adults and 1.2 million children younger than 15 years—were living with HIV/AIDS. More than 69% of these people (23.3 million) live in Sub-Saharan Africa; another 18% (6.0 million) live in South and Southeast Asia. (National Institute of Allergy and Infectious Diseases, 2000d, p. 1)

There are 15.7 million people or 5.9% of the population in the United States who have diabetes. While an estimated 10.3 million have been diagnosed, unfortunately, 5.4 million people are not aware that they have the disease. Each day approximately 2,200 people are diagnosed with diabetes. About 798,000 people will be diagnosed this year. (American Diabetes Association, 2000b, p. 1).

Now approaching epidemic proportions, suicide is currently the third leading cause of death among teenagers in the United States. It is estimated that 300 to 400 teen suicides occur per year in Los Angeles County; this is equivalent to one teenager lost every day. Evidence indicates that for every suicide, they are 50 to 100 attempts at suicide. Due to the stigma associated with suicide, available statistics may well underestimate the problem. Nevertheless, these figures do underscore the urgent need to seek a solution to the suicide epidemic among our young people. (Youth Suicide Prevention Information, 2000, p. 1).

483

Linda

I just turned 21. I never thought I would actually reach the official age of adulthood, but it has come and gone; and I am, at least according to law, a little more responsible for my behavior. Actually, I've been responsible for a lot of my behavior since I was a young child. For reasons that I don't completely understand, I've always had a personal resilience that helped me deal with the challenges that have been an integral part of my life.

My mother, who is an exquisitely beautiful woman, was very excited about my birth. I was her first child. The expectations she had for me were wonderful. But, within moments of my delivery, it was discovered that I had a serious birth defect known as spina bifida. This discovery altered many of my mom's expectations for me. Although my parents didn't know a great deal about spina bifida at the time, they shortly became specialists.

Their major concern at the time of my birth was not my physical appearance, even though the sac on my spine was quite gross, but the prevention of infection, my intellectual capacity, and the degree of paralysis.

The sac and related nerve tissue were surgically cared for very early in my life through several operations. Fortunately, the infection that was an ever-present threat during the first days and months of my existence was successfully prevented. Because of the location of the sac with neural tissue, I'm paralyzed from the waist down. I walk with the aid of crutches now.

As for my intellectual capacity, I've just completed my second year of college. I'm not an academic superstar, but I do hold my own in my major, which is fashion merchandising.

To be frank with you, my greatest challenge hasn't been my paralysis per se, but my lack of bowel control. I'd love to have the facility that most normal people have, but I don't. I'm working on my attitude about this particular problem. I'm not nearly as sensitive about it as I once was.

■ PHYSICAL DISABILITIES. A category of disability pertaining to physical problems that interfere with the ability to function.

■ OTHER HEALTH IMPAIRED. A category of disability under the Individuals with Disabilities Education Act that includes students with limited strength due to health problems.

■ HEALTH DISABILITIES. Disabling conditions characterized by limited stamina, vitality, or alertness due to chronic or acute health problems.

■ MEDICALLY FRAGILE. Disability category within health disabilities that describes people who are at risk for medical emergencies and often depend on technological support such as a ventilator or nutritional supplements to sustain health or even life.

■ TECHNOLOGICALLY DEPENDENT. Disability category in which the individual requires some technology to breathe, to pass urine, or to meet other essential health needs while participating in home, school, or community activities.

PHYSICAL DISABILITIES CAN AFFECT a person's ability to move about, to use arms and legs effectively, to swallow food, and to breathe independently. They may also affect other capacities such as vision, cognition, speech, language, hearing, and bowel control. The Individuals with Disabilities Education Act (IDEA) uses the term *orthopedically impaired* to describe students with **physical disabilities** and the term **other health impaired** to describe students with health disabilities.

As described in IDEA, **health disabilities** cause individuals to have "limited strength, vitality, or alertness, due to chronic or acute health problems such as a heart condition, tuberculosis, rheumatic fever, nephritis, asthma, sickle cell anemia, hemophilia, epilepsy, lead poisoning, leukemia, or diabetes which adversely affect . . . educational performance" (23 Code of Federal Regulations, Section 300.5 [7]). For example, children and youth with sickle cell anemia often experience periods of persistent pain in their arms, legs, abdomen, or back that often interfere with their school performance and also prevent them from participating in activities that are important to their social and emotional well-being.

In recent years, new subgroups have emerged within the health disabilities area. They are often referred to as **medically fragile** and/or **technologically dependent.** These individuals are at risk for medical emergencies and often require specialized support in the form of ventilators or nutritional supplements. Often children or youth who are medically fragile have progressive diseases such as cancer or AIDS. Other children have episodic conditions that lessen their attentiveness, stamina, or energy. Sickle cell anemia is a good example of a condition that is episodic in nature.

Technology-dependent or technology-assisted individuals use devices such as ventilators for breathing, urinary catheters and colostomy bags for bowel and bladder care, tracheotomy tubes for supplying oxygen-enriched air to congested lungs, or suctioning equipment for the removal of mucus from airways. Some of these devices will be discussed in greater detail later in the chapter.

Physical and health disabilities also impact how individuals with various conditions or diseases view themselves and how they are seen by others—parents, brothers and sisters, peers, teachers, neighbors, and employers. The impact of these disabilities is also felt on a number of social, educational, and psychological fronts. For example, children and youth who must spend significant periods of time away from their homes, neighborhoods, or schools for medical care or support may have limited opportunities to develop friendships with neighborhood and school peers, to attend special social events, and to develop certain social skills. The degree to which individuals with physical and health disabilities become integral participants in their neighborhoods and communities is directly related to the quality and timeliness of treatment received from various professionals, the nurturing provided by parents, siblings, and teachers, and the support and acceptance supplied by neighbors and other community members. In this regard, significant progress has been made in civil rights legislation, particularly with the passage of the Americans with Disabilities Act (ADA) (see Chapter 1). The intent of this act is to give men, women, and children with disabilities full access to public services, transportation, telecommunications, public accommodations, and employment. It attempts to put persons with disabilities on the same team and playing field as those without disabilities; also, it is designed to make environments and services deficit-free for individuals with disabilities.

One of the first provisions of ADA addresses employment. It prohibits employers from discriminating against qualified persons with disabilities in the workplace. Additionally, it requires employers to make reasonable accommodations so that these persons can fully use their skills and truly contribute to the success of the business, industry, or other enterprise of which they are a part. Other provisions in the act ensure that children, youth, and adults with disabilities have access to and the ability to participate in integrated recreational programs. These programs might include "open plunge" swimming, regular participation in community center aerobics classes, membership in a neighborhood bowling league, and involvement in summer camping programs for youth.

ADA also addresses transportation, public accommodations and services, and telecommunication assistance. All new buses and at least one car on every passenger train must be wheelchair accessible, and public and private accommodations and services will be readily accessible to persons with disabilities. For example, hair salons, dentist offices, fitting rooms, fast-food restaurants, locker rooms, video arcades, and playgrounds must be designed with persons with disabilities in mind. No longer should children, youth, or adults with disabilities and their families worry about bathroom facilities or whether they can enter and participate in certain social or recreational environments. The community should truly be open to them for employment, for recreation, and for other commonplace services that many without disabilities take for granted.

Individuals with physical and health disabilities often require highly specialized interventions to realize their maximum potential. Moreover, the range of medical services, educational placements, and therapies is extremely diverse and highly specific to the person and his or her needs. Students with physical and health disabilities may be served in general education, special education, hospital, home, or residential settings.

This chapter concludes with a discussion of several pressing social and health-related problems. Although not typically included in a chapter dealing with physical or health disabilities, these problems are of vital importance to many families, neighborhoods, schools, as well as local and state governments. They include child abuse and neglect, adolescent pregnancy, suicide among youth, and parental drug and alcohol abuse. Each problem will be discussed in some depth, with emphasis on current interventions or prevention strategies.

PHYSICAL DISABILITIES

The discussion of physical disabilities will be limited to a representative sample of physically disabling conditions: cerebral palsy, spina bifida, spinal cord injuries, and muscular dystrophy. We will present pertinent information about definitions, prevalence and causation, and interventions.

Cerebral Palsy

■ DEFINITIONS AND CONCEPTS

group of chronic conditions affecting body movement and muscle coordination is identified by the term **cerebral palsy**. "It is caused by damage to one or more specific areas of the brain, usually occurring during fetal development; before, during, or shortly following birth; or during infancy. *Cerebral* refers to the brain, and *palsy* to muscle weakness and poor control. Cerebral palsy itself is not progressive (i.e., it does not get worse); however, secondary conditions can develop, which may get better over time, get worse, or remain the same. Cerebral palsy is not communicable. It is not a disease and should never be referred to as such. Although cerebral palsy is not 'curable' in the accepted sense, training and therapy can help improve function" (United Cerebral Palsy, 2000, p. 1). There are three major types of CP: "spastic—stiff and difficult movement; athetoid—involuntary and uncontrolled movement; ataxic—disturbed sense of balance and depth perception" (United Cerebral Palsy Resource Center, 1997a, p. 2).

CP is a complicated and perplexing condition. Individuals with CP are likely to have mild to severe problems in nonmotor areas of functioning, including hearing impairments, speech and language disorders, intellectual deficits, visual impairments, and general perceptual problems. Because of the multifaceted nature of this condition, many individuals with CP are considered to be multidisabled. Thus, CP cannot be characterized by any set of homogeneous symptoms; it is a condition in which a variety of problems may be present in differing degrees of severity (Taft, 1999).

■ PREVALENCE AND CAUSATION

In the United States, 500,000 children and adults present one or more of the features of CP (United Cerebral Palsy, 2000). The prevalence of CP is about 4 to 5 per 2,000 live births (Miller & Bachrach, 1995). These figures fluctuate as a function of several variables. For example, some children born with severe forms of CP do not survive, and the birth prevalence rate does not include these children who die. Other children may be diagnosed with CP several months or years after birth.

The causes of CP are varied (see Table 16.1). Any condition that can adversely affect the brain can cause CP. Chronic disease, insufficient oxygen to the brain, premature birth, maternal infection, birth trauma, blood incompatibility, fetal

focus 1

Why are many individuals with cerebral palsy considered multidisabled?

| TABLE 16.1 | Factors influencing the occurrence of cerebral palsy |

Period of Time	Factors
Preconception (parental background)	■ Biological aging (parent or parents over age 35) ■ Biological immaturity (very young parent or parents) ■ Environmental toxins ■ Genetic background and genetic disorders ■ Malnutrition ■ Radiation damage
First trimester of pregnancy (0 to 3 months)	*Early weeks:* ■ Nutrition: malnutrition, vitamin deficiencies, amino acid intolerance ■ Toxins: alcohol, drugs, poisons, toxins from smoking *Late weeks:* ■ Maternal disease: thyrotoxicosis (abrupt oversecretion of thyroid hormone, resulting in elevated heart rate and potential coma), genetic disorders ■ Nutrition: malnutrition, amino acid intolerance
Second trimester of pregnancy (3+ to 6 months)	*Early weeks:* ■ Infection: CM (cytomegalo) virus, rubella, HIV, syphilis, chicken pox, uterine infection *Late weeks:* ■ Placental abnormalities, vascular blockages, fetal malnutrition, chronic hypoxia, growth factor deficiencies
Third trimester of pregnancy (6+ to 9 months)	*Early weeks:* ■ Prematurity and low birthweight ■ Blood factors: Rh incompatibility, jaundice ■ Cytokines: neurological tissue destruction ■ Inflammation and infection of the uterine lining *Late weeks:* ■ Prematurity and low birthweight ■ Hypoxia: insufficient blood flow to the placenta, perinatal hypoxia ■ Infection: listeria, meningitis, streptococcus group B (bacterial infection), septicemia (bacteria growing in the bloodstream), inflammation and infection of the uterine lining
Perinatal period and infancy (first 2 postnatal years)	■ Endocrine: hypoglycemia, hypothyroidism ■ Hypoxia: perinatal hypoxia, respiratory distress syndrome ■ Infection: meningitis, encephalitis ■ Multiple births: death of a twin or triplet ■ Stroke: hemorrhagic or embolic stroke ■ Trauma: abuse, accidents

Source: Adapted from "Cerebral Palsy: Contributing Risk Factors and Causes," Research Fact Sheets; September 1995; by United Cerebral Palsy Research and Education Foundation, Copyright 1995. Reprinted by permission.

Interventions for people with cerebral palsy focus on movement, social and emotional development, learning, speech, and hearing. Here a teacher and student work together on a computer to facilitate the development of speech and motor skills.

infection, and postbirth infection may all be sources of this neurological–motor disorder (United Cerebral Palsy, 2000).

■ INTERVENTIONS

Rather than treating CP, professionals and parents work at managing the condition and its various manifestations (Taft, 1999). It is essential that the management and interventions begin as early as the CP is diagnosed. The interventions center on the child's movement, social and emotional development, learning, speech, and hearing (United Cerebral Palsy, 2000).

Effective interventions for the various forms of CP are based on accurate and continuous assessments. Motor deficits and other related challenges associated with CP are not unchanging, but evolve over time. Continuous assessment allows care providers to adjust treatment programs and select placement options in accordance with the emerging needs of the child or youth.

Treatment of CP is a multifaceted process that involves many medical and human service specialties aggregated in interdisciplinary and transdisciplinary teams (Delagado, 1999; United Cerebral Palsy, 2000). These teams, composed of medical experts, physical and occupational therapists, teachers, social workers, volunteers, and family members join together to help children, youth, and adults with CP realize their full potential.

The thrust of treatment efforts depends on the nature of the problems and strengths presented by the individual child or youth. Generally, treatments are directed at preventing additional physical deformities; developing useful posture and movements; providing appropriate orthopedic surgery when needed to lengthen heel cords, hamstrings, or tendons; dealing with feeding and swallowing problems; securing suitable augmentative communication and other assistive devices; prescribing appropriate medications (muscle relaxants), and developing mobility and independence (Delagado, 1999; Hill, 1999). Because of the multifaceted nature of CP, other specialists may also be involved, including ophthalmologists, audiologists, speech and language clinicians, and vocational and rehabilitation specialists.

Physical and occupational therapists play very significant roles in the lives of children and youth with CP (Bowe, 2000). These individuals provide essentially three types of crucial services: assessments to detect deformities and deficits in movement quality; program planning such as assisting with the writing of IEPs, selection of adaptive equipment and assistive devices, and development of home programs for parents and other family members; and delivery of therapy services (Delagado, 1999). School-centered services may include indirect treatment provided in the form of consultation, in-service training, and informal monitoring of student performance; direct service through regular treatment sessions in out-of-class settings; and in-class or multisite service delivery to students in general education classrooms, on playgrounds, in their homes, or at other community sites.

Recent developments in augmentative communication have had a tremendous impact on children, youth, and adults with CP and other conditions that impair speech and language production. Many augmentative communication devices are electronic in nature or computer-based. Once such device is the Touch Talker with Minispeak. This device provides children with symbols or icons that, when pressed in certain sequences, produce audio output such as "I'd like a quarter-pounder with fries and a large Coke, please." "I need to go to the bathroom." "Do you know what we are having for lunch?" Selecting augmentative communication devices for a child or youth is a team effort. Teachers, parents, speech and language specialists, physical and occupational therapists, and rehabilitation engineers play important roles in providing essential information (Bowe, 2000).

As persons with CP move into adulthood, they may require various kinds of support, including continuing therapy, personal assistance services, independent living services, vocational training, and counseling. These kinds of support help individuals with CP realize their full potential in employment, relationships with others, and participation in their own neighborhoods and communities (Hill, 1999; United Cerebral Palsy Resource Center, 1997a).

Spina Bifida

■ DEFINITIONS AND CONCEPTS

The most frequently occurring permanently disabling birth defect is called **spina bifida** (Spina Bifida Association of America, 1999, p. 1). It is characterized by an abnormal opening in the spinal column. It originates in the first days of pregnancy, often before a mother even knows that she is expecting a child. Through the process of cell division and differentiation, a neural tube forms in the developing fetus. At about 26–27 days, this neural tube fails to completely close, for reasons not completely understood. This failure results in various forms of spina bifida, frequently involving some paralysis of various portions of the body, depending on the location of the opening (Sujansky, Stewart, & Manchester, 1997). It may or may not influence intellectual functioning. Spina bifida is usually classified as either spina bifida occulta or spina bifida cystica.

Spina bifida occulta is a very mild condition in which a small slit is present in one or more of the vertebral structures. Most people with spina bifida occulta are unaware of its presence unless they have had a spinal x-ray for diagnosis of some other condition. Spina bifida occulta has little if any impact on a developing infant.

Spina bifida cystica is a malformation of the spinal column in which a tumorlike sac herniates through an opening or cleft on the infant's back (see Figure 16.1). Spina bifida cystica exists in many forms; however, two prominent forms will receive attention in this discussion: spina bifida meningocele and spina bifida myelomeningocele. In **spina bifida meningocele**, the sac contains spinal fluid but no nerve tissue. In the myelomeningocele type, the sac contains nerve tissue.

■ SPINA BIFIDA. A developmental defect of the spinal column.

■ SPINA BIFIDA OCCULTA. A very mild condition of spina bifida in which an oblique slit is present in one or several of the vertebral structures.

■ SPINA BIFIDA CYSTICA. A malformation of the spinal column in which a tumorlike sac is produced on the infant's back.

■ SPINA BIFIDA MENINGOCELE. A cystic swelling or tumorlike sac that contains spinal fluid but no nerve tissue.

FIGURE 16.1

Side views of a normal spine (a) and spines affected by spina bifida occulta (b) and spina bifida cystica (c)

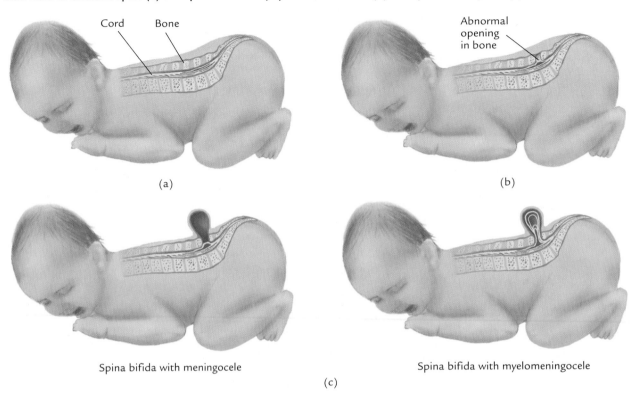

(a)

(b)

Spina bifida with meningocele

Spina bifida with myelomeningocele

(c)

focus 2
What is spina bifida myelomeningocele?

Spina bifida myelomeningocele is the most serious form of spina bifida. It generally results in weakness or paralysis in the legs and lower body, an inability to voluntarily control the bladder or bowel, and the presence of other orthopedic problems (club feet, dislocated hip, etc.). There are two types of myelomeningocele: one in which the tumorlike sac is open, revealing the neural tissue, and one in which the sac is closed or covered with a combination of skin and membrane.

Children with spina bifida occulta exhibit the normal range of intelligence. Most children with myelomeningocele also have normal IQs. For children whose learning capacity is normal or above average, no special educational programming is required.

■ PREVALENCE AND CAUSATION

Prevalence figures for spina bifida, both myelomeningocele and meningocele, vary. Spina bifida affects about 1 out of every 1,000 newborns in the United States (Spina Bifida Association of America, 1999).

The exact cause of spina bifida is unknown, although there is a slight tendency for the condition to run in families (Spina Bifida Association of America, 1999). In fact, myelomeningocele appears to be transmitted genetically, probably as a function of certain prenatal factors interacting with genetic predispositions. It is also possible that certain harmful agents taken by the mother prior to or at the time of conception, or during the first few days of pregnancy, may be responsible for the defect.

■ SPINA BIFIDA MYELOMENINGO-CELE. A cystic swelling or tumor-like sac that contains both spinal fluid and nerve tissue.

Teratogens that may induce malformations in the spine include radiation, maternal hyperthermia (high fever), and excess glucose. Other causative factors include congenital rubella and chromosome abnormalities (Sujansky, Stewart, & Manchester, 1997). (See the nearby Reflect on This feature.)

Folic acid deficiencies have been implicated strongly in the cause of spina bifida (Spina Bifida Association of America, 1999). Pregnant mothers should take particular care to augment their diets with 0.4 mg of folic acid each day. Folic acid is a common water-soluble B vitamin. Intake of this vitamin reduces the probabilities for neural tube defects in developing infants.

■ INTERVENTIONS

Several tests are now available to identify babies with myelomeningocele before they are born. One such test involves the analysis of the mother's blood for the presence of a specific fetal protein (alfa-fetoprotein, AFT). This protein leaks from the developing child's spine into the amniotic fluid of the uterus and subsequently enters the mother's bloodstream. If blood tests prove to be positive for this AFT, ultrasonic scanning of the fetus may be performed to confirm the diagnosis.

Children with spina bifida have normal intelligence. The vast majority of students with spina bifida are in general education classes. This student with a serious form of spina bifida is also able to enjoy the experience of summer camp.

Confirmation of the myelomeningocele creates intense feelings in parents. If the diagnosis is early in the child's interuterine development, parents are faced with the decision of continuing or discontinuing the pregnancy. If parents decide to continue the pregnancy, they have time to process their intense feelings and to prepare for the child's birth and care. If the decision is to discontinue the pregnancy, they must deal with the feelings produced by this action as well. If the condition is discovered at the time of the child's birth, it also produces powerful and penetrating feelings, the first of which is generally shock. All members of the health team (physicians, nurses, social workers, etc.) as well as other persons (religious advisers, siblings, parents, and close friends) assist in coping with the feelings and the decisions that must be made.

Immediate action is often called for when the child with myelomeningocele is born, depending on the nature of the lesion, its position on the spine, and the presence of other related conditions. Decisions regarding medical interventions are extremely difficult to make, for they often entail problems and issues that are not easily or quickly resolved. For example, in 80% of children with myelomeningocele, a portion of the spinal cord is exposed, placing them at great risk for developing bacterial meningitis, which has a mortality rate of over 50%.

The decision to undertake surgery is often made quickly if the tissue sac is located very low on the infant's back. The purpose of the surgery is to close the spinal opening and lessen the potential for infection. Another condition that often accompanies myelomeningocele is hydrocephalus, a condition characterized by excessive accumulation of cerebral fluid within the brain. More than 25% of children with myelomeningocele evidence this condition at birth. Moreover, 80% to 90% of all children with myelomeningocele develop it after they are born. Surgery may also be performed for this condition in the first days of life. The operation includes inserting a small, soft plastic tube between the ventricles of the brain and connecting this tube with an absorption site in the abdomen. The excessive spinal fluid is diverted from the ventricles of the brain to a thin layer of tissue, the peritoneum, which lines the abdominal cavity (see Figure 16.2).

■ TERATOGENS. Substances or conditions that cause malformations.

Reflect on This

GENE THERAPY: IS IT REALLY HERE?

It is estimated that by the end of the year [2001], the entire human genome will have been "cloned." This means that scientists will have identified the 80,000 or so genes that serve as the blueprint for the production and function of a human being. This is but the first step of what we are hopeful will lead to the determination of which specific genes, when defective, cause various developmental disabilities. Once we can assess the linkage between these genetic defects and a developmental disorder, it may allow us to develop more specific and earlier approaches to the treatment of children with special needs. It is estimated that over half of all developmental disabilities in childhood are genetically determined or influenced. Thus, these advances are likely to have a significant impact on the care of our exceptional children.

One such innovative approach is gene therapy. The idea here is to correct a disorder by giving copies of a new gene that will serve in place of the defective gene. This idea is currently being tested in certain inborn errors of metabolism of childhood. In these disorders, the gene "mutation," or error, results in the deficient production of an enzyme that normally breaks down a toxic material produced by the body. A common example of an inborn error is PKU, or phenylketonuria (a metabolic disorder caused by an enzyme deficiency, in which certain amino acids accumulate in body fluids, resulting in mental retardation). In PKU, specific dietary restriction has been found to have enormous benefit by preventing the buildup of toxins, but in many other inborn errors, there remains no effective treatment. Gene therapy studies are now going on, using viruses to act as "taxis" to move copies of the new gene into the body. These studies are being done first in animal models of human disease, to determine if gene therapy is feasible and safe. It is likely that gene therapy trials in children will become common over the next five years, with the goal that some of these will be successful, adding a new approach to our armamentarium for treatment of children with disabilities.

Source: From "Medical Research Update 1999," by M. L. Batshaw, 1999, *Exceptional Parent, 29*(6), p. 92.

Children with spina bifida myelomeningocele may have little if any voluntary bowel or bladder control. This condition is directly attributable to the paralysis caused by malformation of the spinal cord and removal of the herniated sac containing nerve tissues. Very early on, however, children as young as 4 years old can be taught effective procedures to manage bladder problems. As they mature, they can develop effective regimens and procedures for bowel management.

Physical therapists play a critical role in helping children as they learn to cope with the paralysis caused by myelomeningocele. Paralysis obviously limits the children's exploratory activities so critical to later learning and perceptual-motor performance. With this in mind, many such children are fitted with modified skateboards, which allow them to explore their surroundings. Utilizing the strength in their arms and hands, they may become quite adept at exploring their home environments. Gradually, they move to leg braces, crutches, a wheelchair, or a combination of the three. Additionally, some children are ambulatory and do not require the use of a wheelchair. (See the nearby Reflect on This feature.)

Education programs for students with serious forms of spina bifida vary according to the needs of each student. The vast majority of students with myelomeningocele are served in general education settings. School personnel can contribute to the well-being of these students in several ways: making sure that physical layouts permit students to move effectively with their crutches or wheelchairs through

FIGURE 16.2

Ventriculoperitoneal shunt

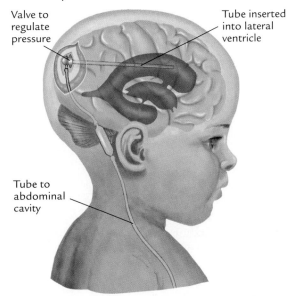

Valve to regulate pressure

Tube inserted into lateral ventricle

Tube to abdominal cavity

When 14-year-old Allie Schneider was born with spina bifida, her mother, Nata Schneider remembers, "Kirk and I felt we had to put some of our dreams for her in a box, and being avid skiers ourselves, one of those dreams was to have Allie learn." That perception changed when the Salt Lake City, Utah, couple heard about an adaptive alpine ski program run by the Ability Center.

Once their daughter was enrolled, the Schneiders soon realized that Allie would be able to experience the excitement of weaving through fresh fallen powder and tackling moguls (mini hills). She was 6 when she had her first lesson on a mono-ski. She remembers vividly: "It scared me a little bit because I thought I wouldn't be able to do it, but the very first time I tried it, I thought I could actually learn to ski, and that maybe I could learn to do other things."

Allie is now involved in horseback riding, water skiing, and tennis through the center. In addition, both Kirk and Nata have noticed a marked increase in their daughter's self-esteem and her willingness to try new things. "Skiing has become a way for Allie to reach other goals," explains Nata. "Math is not an easy subject for Allie, but skiing wasn't easy at first either. However, she did that, and so she uses her experience with learning how to ski to get past the tough spots."

The couple feels that programs like those at the Ability Center, which provide adaptive recreation in an inclusive setting, open up a world of opportunity for individuals who have disabilities. Kirk asserts, "The Ability Center has opened Allie up to socialization, and an awareness about other individuals who have disabilities." Allie's younger sisters, Kacey, 9, and Carli, 7, have also benefited from inclusion in recreational activities with their sister.

"They really don't recognize any barriers, and the Ability Center is the same way," notes Nata. As an example, she points out the center's "ski buddy program," which matches skiers who have a disability with mainstream skiers the same age.

When Nata thinks about how far her family has come with the center's help, her voice takes on a tone of intense emotion. "Kirk, myself, and all three girls were at the top of the mountain at Park City, and it just hit me. Those dreams we thought needed to be stored away, were right in front of us. We were up there as a family and it was just . . . wonderful!"

Source: From "The National Ability Center: Enhancing Mind, Body, and Soul," by J. C. Stolting, 1999, *Exceptional Parent, 29*(3), pp. 32–35.

classrooms and other settings; supporting students' efforts in using various bladder and bowel management procedures and ensuring appropriate privacy in using them; requiring these students to be as responsible as anyone else in the class for customary assignments; involving them fully in field trips, physical education, and other school-related activities; and communicating regularly with parents. Additionally, if the student has a shunt, teachers should be alert to signs of its malfunctioning, including irritability, neck pain, headache, vomiting, reduced alertness, and decline in school performance. As with all physical disabilities, collaboration and cooperation among all caregivers are critical to the well-being of each child or youth.

Spinal Cord Injury

■ DEFINITIONS AND CONCEPTS

When the spinal cord is traumatized or severed, **spinal cord injury (SCI)** occurs. Trauma can result through extreme extension or flexing from a fall, an automobile accident, or a sports injury. The cord can also be severed through the same types of accidents, although such occurrences are extremely rare. Usually in such cases, the cord is bruised or otherwise injured, after which swelling and, within hours, bleeding often occur. Gradually, a self-destructive process ensues, in which the affected area slowly deteriorates and the damage becomes irreversible (Bowe, 2000; Spinal Cord Injury Resource Center, 2000b).

■ SPINAL CORD INJURY (SCI). An injury in which the spinal cord is traumatized or transected.

John Gilpatrick is seen with his guide dog Ice at his Hanover, Mass. home. Gilpatrick, a former hockey player, suffered a spinal injury in 1996 after crashing into a goalpost; he is now able to walk again.

The overall impact of injury on an individual depends on the site and nature of the insult. If the injury occurs in the neck or upper back, the resulting paralysis and effects are usually quite extensive. If the injury occurs in the lower back, paralysis is confined to the lower extremities. Like individuals with spina bifida, loss of voluntary bowel and bladder function may result from the injuries sustained in an SCI. For a brief review of the topographical descriptions of paralytic conditions, see Table 16.2.

Spinal cord injuries rarely occur without individuals sustaining other serious damage to their bodies. Accompanying injuries may include head trauma, fractures of some portion of the trunk, and significant chest injuries (Bowe, 2000).

The physical characteristics of spinal cord injuries are similar to those of spina bifida myelomeningocele except there is no tendency for the development of hydrocephalus. The terms used to describe the impact of spinal cord injuries are as follows: **paraplegia, quadriplegia,** and **hemiplegia.** Note, however, that these terms are global descriptions of functioning and are not precise enough to accurately convey an individual's actual level of motor functioning.

■PREVALENCE AND CAUSATION

About 450,000 people live with SCI in the United States. Every year there are about 10,000 new cases of individuals with SCI (National Spinal Cord Injury Statistical Center, 1997). Spinal cord injuries are primarily a male phenomenon. From 85% to 90% of patients treated for spinal cord injuries are young men between the ages of 16 and 30 (Spinal Cord Injury Resource Center, 2000b). The incidence of spinal cord injuries increases during the summer months. These injuries generally occur in the early hours of the morning. Causes include motor vehicle accidents (36%); violence, primarily gunshot wounds (28.9%); and falls (21.2%) (Spinal Cord Injury Resource Center, 2000b). Twenty-five percent of the injuries are alcohol related (Baskin, 1996). A small 6.9% of the injuries are caused by sporting activities (National Spinal Cord Injury Statistical Center, 1997).

TABLE 16.2	Topographical descriptions of paralytic conditions

Description	Affected Area
Monoplegia	One limb
Paraplegia	Lower body and both legs
Hemiplegia	One side of the body
Triplegia	Three appendages or limbs, usually both legs and one arm
Quadriplegia	All four extremities and usually the trunk
Diplegia	Legs more affected than arms
Double hemiplegia	Both halves of the body, with one side more affected than the other

The immediate care rendered to a person with an SCI is crucial. The impact of the injury can be magnified if proper procedures are not employed soon after the accident or onset of the condition.

The first phase of treatment provided by a hospital is the management of shock. Quickly thereafter, the individual is immobilized to prevent movement and possible further damage. As a rule, surgical procedures are not undertaken immediately. The major goal of medical treatment at this point is to stabilize the spine, manage swelling, and prevent further complications. Pharmacological interventions are critical during this phase of treatment. Recent studies support the use of high and frequent doses of methylprednisolone. This medication often reduces the severity of the injury, improves the functional outcome for the affected individual, and reduces secondary damage (Spinal Cord Injury Resource Center, 2000b).

Catheterization may be employed to control urine flow, and steps may be taken to reduce swelling and bleeding at the injury site. Traction may be used to stabilize certain portions of the spinal column and cord. Medical treatment of spinal cord injuries is lengthy and often tedious.

Once physicians have successfully stabilized the spine and treated other medical conditions, the rehabilitation process promptly proceeds. The individual is taught to use new muscle combinations and take advantage of any and all residual muscle strength. He or she is also taught to use orthopedic equipment, such as handsplints, braces, reachers, headsticks (for typing), and plateguards. Together with an orthopedic specialist, occupational and physical therapists become responsible for the physical reeducation and training process.

Psychiatric and other support personnel are also engaged in rehabilitation activities. Psychological adjustment to a SCI and its impact on the individual's functioning can take a great deal of time. The goal of all treatment is to help the injured individual become as independent as possible.

As the individual masters necessary self-care skills, other educational and career objectives can be pursued with the assistance of the rehabilitation team. The members of this team change constantly with the skills and needs of the individual.

Education for individuals with spinal cord injuries is similar to that for uninjured children or adults. Teachers must be aware, however, that some individuals with spinal cord injuries will be unable to feel pressure and pain in the lower extremities, so pressure sores and skin breakdown may occur in response to prolonged sitting. Opportunities for repositioning and movement will help prevent these problems. Parents and teachers should be aware of signs of depression that may accompany the school reentry process. (See the nearby Reflect on This feature.)

Muscular Dystrophy

■ DEFINITIONS AND CONCEPTS

The term **muscular dystrophy** refers to a group of genetic diseases marked by progressive weakness and degeneration of the skeletal, or voluntary, muscles, which control movement. The muscles of the heart and some other involuntary muscles are also affected in some forms of muscular dystrophy, and a few forms involve other organs as well (Muscular Dystrophy Association, 2000, p. 1). Muscular dystrophy is a progressive disorder that may affect the muscles of the hips, legs, shoulders, and arms, progressively causing these

■ PARAPLEGIA. Paralysis that involves the legs only.

■ QUADRIPLEGIA. A condition characterized by paralysis of all four extremities and usually the trunk.

■ HEMIPLEGIA. Paralysis that involves one side of the body.

■ MUSCULAR DYSTROPHY. A group of inherited, chronic disorders that are characterized by gradual wasting and weakening of the voluntary skeletal muscles.

He once played a man who could fly. Christopher Reeve has since demonstrated a rare ability that exceeds the speed of flight. Christopher has learned to live outside his body in a way that few people have the strength or courage to do.

All of us are, in some ways, prisoners in life—some by limited thinking, others by physical limitation. But rarely has a man demonstrated such a wonderful ability to face limitation, to cry for all that it has robbed him of, and then step beyond it into a life that knows no limitation. Each morning, being human, Christopher sheds a few tears. But then he brushes them away, stops feeling sorry for himself, and goes on to be an example to others. He creates his own freedom to be truly alive. Christopher Reeve has found the Superman within, and we celebrate his courage to be free.

We proudly give to Christopher Reeve the Courage to Be Free Award.

The former Superman admits that he cries every day, dealing with the reality of being in a wheelchair. "In the morning, I need twenty minutes to cry," he says. "To wake up and make that shift, you know, and to just say, 'This really sucks' . . . to really allow yourself the feeling of loss, even two years later . . . still needs to be acknowledged."

But after his long, hard cry each day, he tells himself, "And now, forward!" Christopher Reeve has been an example to us all . . .

Source: Adapted from *The Courage To Be Free Award, Christopher Reeve,* by Role Models on the Web, sponsored by Geddes and Company, 2000, p. 1.

---

focus 4

Describe the physical limitations associated with muscular dystrophy.

individuals to lose their ability to walk and also to use their arms and hands effectively. The loss of ability is attributable to fatty tissue that gradually replaces muscle tissue. Heart muscle may also be affected, resulting in symptoms of heart failure. There are actually nine different types of muscular dystrophy. The seriousness of the various dystrophies is influenced by heredity, age of onset, the physical location and nature of onset, and the rate at which the condition progresses (Muscular Dystrophy Association, 2000a).

Duchenne-type muscular dystrophy (DMD) is the most common form of childhood muscular dystrophy. DMD generally manifests itself between the ages of 2 and 6. Early in the second decade of life, individuals with DMD use wheelchairs to move from place to place. By the second or early in the third decade of life, young adults with DMD die from respiratory insufficiency or cardiac failure (Muscular Dystrophy Association, 2000a).

DMD is first evidenced in the pelvic girdle, although it sometimes begins in the shoulder girdle muscles. With the passage of time, individuals begin to experience a loss of respiratory function and are unable to cough up secretions that may result in pneumonia. Also, severe spinal curvature develops over time with wheelchair use, which may be prevented with spinal fusion. (See the nearby Today's Technology feature.)

■ PREVALENCE AND CAUSATION

"Flaws in muscle protein genes cause muscular dystrophies. Each cell in our bodies contains tens of thousands of genes. Each gene is a string of the chemical DNA and is the "code" for a protein. (Another way to think of a gene is that it is the "instructions" or "recipe" for a protein.) If the recipe for a protein is wrong, the protein is made wrong or in the wrong amount or sometimes not at all" (Muscular Dystrophy Association, 2000a, p. 2).

About 200,000 people are affected by muscular dystrophies and related disorders. About 1 in every 3,000 to 3,500 males is affected by DMD. Mothers who are carriers transmit this condition to 50% of their male offspring. One third of the cases of DMD arise by mutation in families with no history of the disease (Muscular Dystrophy Association, 2000a).

Today's Technology

A REVOLUTIONARY NEW WHEELCHAIR

We have the know-how to fly to the moon, but most people who can't walk still get around with what's essentially 200-year-old technology: the wheelchair. One inventor has decided it's time to get wheelchair riders rolling into the 21st century. He says his machine can take you just about anywhere you want to go. He's been keeping his top-secret invention under wraps until now.

Wheelchairs can get you around, but they don't get close enough to the places disabled people might like to go. You've heard the expression "confined to a wheelchair"? Well, actually, if you think about it, it's the wheelchairs that are confined to the relatively few smooth, easy-rolling places in the world. But what if somebody came up with a device that, as they say, could go where

no wheelchairs have gone before?

It would take someone on a mission. Someone with the money and genius and time to put into the project. It would take someone like Dean Kamen. He's one of this nation's most prestigious inventors. He's a sort of Thomas Edison in the medical world.

Kamen thought about this old problem in a revolutionary new way. What if instead of getting a chair that could go upstairs, you could make a machine that could stand up and balance the way humans do? "Your mother remembers your first steps. It's a big deal that humans walk erect," says Kamen. "It's difficult to do. But once we've learned to do it, we're capable of dealing with curbs and a world with stairs."

Kamen and his engineers came up with a two-wheeled balancing prototype that worked and became a top-secret patented invention crammed full of sophisticated gyroscopes, electric motors, and computers.

■ *What is this extraordinary machine capable of doing?*

It can climb stairs, roll through sand, and can even raise its height to reach the top of shelves. What's exciting about this device is not the technology, it's the choices: you could go from point A to point B anyway you want. And this isn't some

Dean Kamen's revolutionary wheelchair.

exotic experiment on a device that no one is ever going to see. The builders of this machine intend that it's going to be used out in the world, and soon.

Since a wheelchair is a medical device, it has to be tested by the Food and Drug Administration. It's more like a drug than like a bicycle or a lawnmower. With the idea that virtually any failure could be catastrophic, Kamen's engineers have rocked, rolled, bounced, drowned, and pounded their new machine. Can Dean Kamen's new device change the world? Nobody knows until the FDA approves it for use outside of the lab and beyond the inventor's own property. But one thing is certain: the emotional impact can already be felt.

Brace yourself for the price: Dean Kamen's invention will cost about $20,000 when it becomes available to the public. But because it could spare the expense of customizing homes with ramps and wider doorways, and mechanical lifts in cars, the money spent could be offset in money saved.

Source: From "Research and New Updates: A Revolutionary New Wheelchair on the Horizon," by the Spinal Cord Injury Research Center, 2000. *[online]* Available: *http://www .spinalinjury.net/html/wheelchair.html* And from "A Revolutionary New Wheelchair on the Horizon," by MSNBC, 1999 (June). *[online]* Available: *http://www.msnbc.com/ news/285231.asp*

Molecular genetics has contributed greatly to our understanding of neuromuscular diseases and their causes. In some cases, the specific genetic locus of the dystrophy can be identified. Such is the case with DMD, which is tied to a sex-linked recessive gene. Additionally, the biochemical defects associated with various dystrophies can now be recognized.

■ INTERVENTIONS

There is no known cure for muscular dystrophy. The focus of treatment is maintaining or improving the individual's functioning and preserving his or her ambulatory independence for as long as possible. The first phases of maintenance and prevention are handled by a physical therapist, who works to prevent or correct contractures (a permanent shortening and thickening of muscle fibers). As the condition becomes more serious, treatment generally includes prescribing supportive devices, such as walkers, braces, nightsplints, surgical corsets, and hospital beds. Eventually, the person with muscular dystrophy will need to use a wheelchair.

The terminal nature of DMD poses challenging problems to affected individuals, their families, and caregivers. Fortunately, significant progress has been made in helping individuals with terminal illnesses deal with death. Programs developed for families who have a terminally ill child, youth, or adult serve several purposes. They give children with terminal illnesses opportunities to ask questions about death, to express their concerns, and to work through their feelings. Programs for parents are designed to help them understand their children's conceptions about death, to suggest ways in which they might respond to certain questions or concerns, and to relate the steps they might take in successfully preparing for and responding to the child's death and related events. One such program is Compassionate Friends. This organization, composed of parents who have lost children to death, provides sensitive support and resources to other parents who have lost a child due to injury or disease. (See the nearby Reflect on This feature.)

Reflect on This

DEALING WITH THE DEATH OF A CHILD

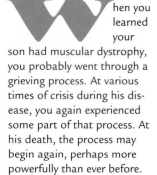

When you learned your son had muscular dystrophy, you probably went through a grieving process. At various times of crisis during his disease, you again experienced some part of that process. At his death, the process may begin again, perhaps more powerfully than ever before.

Most psychologists think that having some warning of a major loss allows you to begin grieving in advance and helps diminish the pain. This is called anticipatory grief. But what's more important to understand is that there's no set way to grieve or time to spend feeling the emotions that come with the death of your son.

Reaching acceptance takes as long as it takes. Even if your son is an adult, even if you thought you were prepared, losing him will be painful. Don't judge your feelings. Sometimes the deepest bereavement, sadness, and depression don't occur until several months after the death. Physical reactions to the death of a child may include loss of appetite or overeating, sleeplessness, and sexual difficulties.

Holidays and the anniversaries of your child's birth and death can be stressful times. Consider the feelings of the entire family in planning how to spend the day. Allow time and space for your own emotional needs.

A child's death often causes a parent to challenge and examine his faith or philosophy of life. Don't be disturbed if you are questioning old beliefs. Talk about it. For many, faith offers help to accept the unacceptable.

Source: From "Facts About Muscular Dystrophy," by the Muscular Dystrophy Association, 2000. *[online]* Available: *http://www.mdausa.org*

HEALTH DISABILITIES

Health disabilities affect children, youth, and adults in a variety of ways. For example, a child with juvenile diabetes who has engaged in a vigorous game of volleyball with classmates may need to drink a little fruit juice or soda pop just before or after the activity to regulate blood sugar levels. An adult with diabetes may need to follow a special diet and regularly receive appropriate doses of insulin. By way of review, IDEA describes persons with health disabilities as individuals with "limited strength, vitality, or alertness, due to chronic or acute health problems such as a heart condition, tuberculosis, rheumatic fever, nephritis, asthma, sickle cell anemia, hemophilia, epilepsy, lead poisoning, leukemia, or diabetes which adversely affect . . . educational performance" (23 Code of Federal Regulations, Section 300.5 [7]).

Of these health conditions, acquired immune deficiency syndrome (AIDS), seizure disorders (epilepsy), diabetes, cystic fibrosis (CF), and sickle cell anemia (SCA) will be reviewed in some depth in this chapter.

Human Immunodeficiency Virus (HIV) and Acquired Immune Deficiency Syndrome (AIDS)

■ DEFINITIONS AND CONCEPTS

IDS in children and youth is defined by the following characteristics: (1) the presence of the **human immunodeficiency virus (HIV),** a virus that attacks certain white blood cells within the body, and/or the presence of antibodies to HIV in the blood or tissues as well as (2) recurrent bacterial diseases (Landau, Mangione, & Pryor, 1997). The first reports regarding some of the features of AIDS, received by the Centers for Disease Control in the spring of 1981, dealt exclusively with young men who had a rare form of pneumonia. Reports were received simultaneously by the Centers for Disease Control regarding an increased incidence of a rare skin tumor, Kaposi's sarcoma. Individuals who had developed these conditions were homosexual men in their 30s and 40s. Many died or were severely debilitated within 12 months of diagnosis.

Prior to the spring of 1981, primary-care physicians in New York, San Francisco, and other large cities had seen many cases of swollen lymph nodes in homosexual men. Many of these individuals exhibited this condition for months or even years after their initial diagnosis without suffering serious side effects. However, those who developed **opportunistic infections** often experienced severe side effects or even death. Eventually, these opportunistic infections were linked to a breakdown in the functioning of the **immune system.** People affected with these infections exhibit pronounced depletions of a particular subset of white blood cells, T lymphocytes. White blood cells fight infections; without sufficient numbers and kinds of them, the body is rendered defenseless. Individuals with this condition become subject to a wide range of opportunistic infections and tumors affecting the gastrointestinal system, central nervous system, and skin.

Individuals with AIDS move through a series of disease stages (Landau, Mangione, & Pryor, 1997). The first stage is the exposure stage, or the period during which the transmission of the HIV occurs. Young people may be infected with HIV but may not

■ HEALTH DISABILITIES. Disabling conditions characterized by limited stamina, vitality, or alertness due to chronic or acute health problems.

■ HUMAN IMMUNODEFICIENCY VIRUS (HIV). A virus that reduces immune system function and has been linked to AIDS.

■ OPPORTUNISTIC INFECTION. An infection caused by germs that are not usually capable of causing infection in healthy people but can do so given certain changes in the immune system (opportunity).

■ IMMUNE SYSTEM. The normally functioning system within a person's body that protects from disease.

If prevention is the most effective means of controlling the spread of AIDS, adolescents must be fully informed about the nature and cause of the disease.

yet exhibit the life-threatening conditions associated with AIDS. The second stage is characterized by the production of antibodies in infected individuals. These antibodies appear about 2 to 12 weeks after the initial transmission of the virus. About 30% of individuals experience flu-like symptoms for a few days to several weeks. During stage three, the immune system declines, and the virus begins to destroy cells of the immune system. However, many individuals with HIV are asymptomatic during this stage. This asymptomatic phase may continue for 3 to 10 years. About half of all individuals with HIV develop AIDS within 10 years. For children, the onset of AIDS ranges from 1 to 3 years. At stage four, individuals begin to manifest symptoms of a damaged immune system, including weight loss, fatigue, skin rashes, and night sweats. In more severe cases, opportunistic diseases begin to evidence themselves in individuals with AIDS. At stage five, recurrent and chronic diseases begin to take their toll on individuals. Gradually the immune system fails and death occurs.

Researchers have identified two patterns of disease development in HIV-infected children. Some 20% develop serious disease complications in the first year of life. Most of these children die before they reach their fourth birthday. The other 80% experience a slower rate of serious symptoms associated with AIDS. Often the most serious symptoms do not evidence themselves until these children enter school or begin their adolescent years.

■ PREVALENCE AND CAUSATION

The Centers for Disease Control and Prevention (CDC) estimate that 650,000 to 900,000 individuals in the United States are HIV-infected, *of whom more than 200,000 are not aware of their infection* (National Institute of Allergy and Infectious Diseases, 2000d, pp. 1–2). In the United States, the average prevalence rate for AIDS cases is 19.9 per 100,000 individuals. About 8,600 children under age 13 in the United States have been diagnosed with AIDS. About 420,000 individuals die of AIDS each year in the United States; of this number about 5,000 are children or youth less than 15 years of age (Centers for Disease Control and Prevention, 1999).

Information regarding the prevalence of AIDS among children and youth is far less accurate and complete than that for adults. About 1% of the recognized cases of AIDS involve children and youth. Adolescents account for much less than 1% of the individuals with AIDS in the United States (Centers for Disease Control and Prevention, 1999). However, about 25% of all individuals with HIV developed the HIV infection when they were teenagers (Kirby, 1997).

The cause of AIDS is the human immunodeficiency virus (HIV). This virus is passed from one person to another through sexual contact that includes the exchange of bodily fluids, usually semen or vaginal secretions; blood exchange through injection drug use (IDU); and transfusions, perinatal contact, and breast milk (Landau, Mangione, & Pryor, 1997).

Sixty percent of adolescents develop AIDS through sexual activity or intravenous drug use. Adolescent males acquire the HIV infection primarily through homosexual activity. Adolescent females generally acquire the infection through heterosexual activity and intravenous drug use (Centers for Disease Control and Prevention, 1999).

Many children with AIDS do not grow normally, do not achieve appropriate weight gains, are slow to achieve important motor milestones (crawling, walking, etc.), and evidence neurological damage. As the HIV turns into AIDS, these children are attacked by life-threatening opportunistic infections. Also, many of the children, as indicated earlier, develop more serious neurological problems associated with mental retardation, cerebral palsy, seizure disorders, and autism (National Institute for Allergy and Infectious Diseases, 2000d).

■ INTERVENTIONS

To date, there is no known cure for AIDS. The best cure for AIDS in children and youth is prevention. Much progress has been made in testing new antiretroviral therapies to combat AIDS and in developing agents to treat opportunistic infections. Nevertheless, there is still much work to be done to find satisfactory drugs and related therapies for HIV infections and AIDS. Despite this progress, 10% to 15% of infected children develop AIDS in the first months of life and die shortly thereafter, and another 15% to 20% develop AIDS following the infancy period. Sixty-five percent to 75% of children who test positive for HIV thrive.

focus 5

What steps should be taken to assist infants and children with AIDS?

Early diagnosis of infants with HIV is crucial. Early antiviral therapy and prophylactic treatment of opportunistic diseases can contribute significantly to the infected child's well-being and prognosis over time. The frequency and nature of treatment depend on the age of onset and the age at which the child develops the first opportunistic infection.

Providing appropriate interventions for infants with AIDS can be challenging. These infants, like others without AIDS, are totally dependent on others for their care. Many mothers who pass the AIDS virus on to their children are not prepared to care effectively for their infants. Typically, these mothers come from impoverished environments with little access to health care and other appropriate support services. Additionally, these mothers are often intravenous drug users and as such are not reliable caregivers (American Academy of Pediatrics, 1995).

The Centers for Disease Control have developed a number of recommendations in responding to children and youth with AIDS in day-care and school settings. With regard to type of education and care settings, the CDC suggests that placement be based on "the behavior, neurologic development, and physical condition of the child and the expected type of interaction" (Hanlon, 1991, p. 695). The only children or youth to be excluded are those "who lack control of body secretions, or who display behavior such as biting, and those children who have uncoverable, oozing lesions" (Hanlon, 1991, p. 695).

Treating adolescents with HIV and AIDS can be very challenging. For example, compliance with medical regimens for all age groups is difficult. However, for those who are HIV-positive and have no obvious symptoms, keeping regular medical appointments and taking antiviral medications are not only highly problematic but also constant reminders of an impending fatal disease. Youth with HIV and AIDS need to learn how to make medical regimens a regular part of their lives to maintain good health and longevity. They also need assistance in dealing with the psychological reactions of anxiety and depression that often accompany the discovery of HIV infection. Finally, they and others benefit significantly from instruction directed at helping them understand AIDS, making wise decisions about their sexual behavior, using assertiveness skills, and effectively communicating with others (National Institute of Allergy and Infectious Disease, 2000a).

At this point, prevention is the single most effective means of controlling the spread of AIDS (McFarland, 1997). At the heart of prevention is informed choice and individual empowerment to make responsible decisions regarding one's own health, as well as that of others.

Seizure Disorders (Epilepsy)

■ DEFINITIONS AND CONCEPTS

neurological condition, "**epilepsy** from time to time produces brief disturbances in the normal electrical functions of the brain. Normal brain function is made possible by millions of tiny electrical charges passing between nerve cells in the brain to all parts of the body. When someone has epilepsy [or a seizure disorder], this normal pattern may be interrupted by intermittent bursts of electrical energy that are much more intense than usual. They may affect a person's consciousness, bodily movements, or sensations for a short time" (Epilepsy Foundation of America, 2000a, p. 1). A **seizure** is a cluster of behaviors that occur in response to abnormal neurochemical activity in the brain. It typically alters the individual's level of consciousness and simultaneously results in certain characteristic motor patterns.

Several classification schemes have been employed to describe the various types of seizure disorders. We will briefly discuss two types of seizures: tonic/clonic and absence.

Generalized **tonic/clonic seizures,** formerly called grand mal seizures, affect the entire brain. The **tonic** phase of these seizures is characterized by a stiffening of the body, the **clonic** phase by repeated muscle contractions and relaxations. Tonic/clonic seizures are often preceded by a warning signal known as an **aura,** in which the individual senses a unique sound, odor, or physical sensation just prior to the onset of the seizure. In some instances, the seizure is also signaled by a cry or other similar sound. The tonic phase of the seizure begins with a loss of consciousness, after which the individual falls to the ground. Initially, the trunk and head of the body become rigid during the tonic phase. The clonic phase follows and consists of involuntary muscle contractions (violent shaking) of the extremities. Irregular breathing, blueness in the lips and face, increased salivation, loss of bladder and bowel control, and perspiration may occur to some degree.

The nature, scope, frequency, and duration of tonic/clonic seizures vary greatly from person to person. Such seizures may last as long as 20 minutes or less than 1 minute. One of the most dangerous aspects of tonic/clonic seizures is potential

■ EPILEPSY. A condition that from time to time produces brief disturbances in the normal electrical functions of the brain, affecting a person's consciousness, bodily movements, or sensations for a short time. Intensity and length of these effcts depend on the severity of the seizure.

■ SEIZURE. A cluster of behaviors (altered consciousness, characteristic motor patterns, etc.) that occurs in response to abnormal neurochemical activity in the brain.

FIGURE 16.3   First aid for seizures

1. Cushion the head.

2. Loosen tight neck tie or collar.

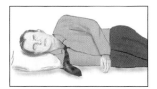
3. Turn on side.

4. Put nothing in the mouth.

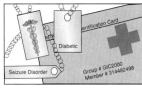
5. Look for identification.

6. Don't hold the person down.

7. Seizure ends.

8. Offer help

[*Source:* Adapted from *Information and Education: First Aid for Seizures* (p. 1), by the Epilepsy Foundation of America, 2000b. *[online]* Available: *http://www. efa.org/education/firstaid/chart/html*

injury from falling and striking objects in the environment. (See Figure 16.3, first aid for seizures.)

A period of sleepiness and confusion usually follows a tonic/clonic seizure. The individual may exhibit drowsiness, nausea, headache, or a combination of these symptoms. Such symptoms should be treated with appropriate rest, medication, or other therapeutic remedies. Seizure characteristics and after effects vary along a number of dimensions and should be treated with this in mind.

Absence seizures, formerly identified as *petit mal seizures,* are characterized by brief periods (moments or seconds) of inattention that may be accompanied by rapid eye blinking and head twitching. During these seizures, the brain ceases to function as it normally would. The individual's consciousness is altered in an almost imperceptible manner. People with this type of seizure disorder may experience these seizures as often as 100 times a day. Such inattentive behavior may be viewed as daydreaming by a teacher or work supervisor, but the episode is really due to a momentary burst of abnormal brain activity that the individual does not consciously control. The lapses in attention caused by this form of epilepsy can greatly hamper the individual's ability to respond properly to or profit from a teacher's presentation or a supervisor's instruction. Treatment and control of absence seizures are generally achieved through prescribed medication.

■ PREVALENCE AND CAUSATION

Prevalence figures for seizure disorders vary, in part because of the social stigma associated with them. About 2,500,000 people in the United States evidence some form of seizure disorders. Of this number, 30% are children. Also, a large number of adults and children have seizure disorders that remain undiscovered and untreated (Epilepsy Foundation of America, 2000a). Seizure disorders or epilepsies occur in about 1% of the population by age 20 (Bailet & Turk, 1997).

The causes of seizure disorders are many, including perinatal factors, tumors of the brain, complications of head trauma, infections of the central nervous system, vascular diseases, alcoholism, infection, maternal injury or infection, and genetic factors. Also, some seizures are caused by ingestion of street drugs, toxic chemicals,

■ TONIC/CLONIC SEIZURES. A seizure in which the entire brain is affected. These seizures are characterized by stiffening of the body, followed by a phase of rapid muscle contractions (extreme shaking).

■ TONIC. The phase of a seizure in which the entire body becomes rigid and stiff.

■ CLONIC. The phase of a seizure in which the muscles of the body contract and relax with rapid repetitions.

■ AURA. A sensation just before a seizure, which the person is able to remember.

■ ABSENCE SEIZURES. Seizures characterized by brief lapses of consciousness, usually lasting no more than ten seconds. Eye blinking and twitching of the mouth may accompany these seizures.

and poisons (Haslam, 1996). Nevertheless, no cause can be found in seven out of ten individuals with seizure disorders.

■ INTERVENTIONS

The treatment of seizure disorders begins with a careful medical investigation in which the physician develops a thorough health history of the individual and completes an in-depth physical examination. Moreover, it is essential that the physician receive a thorough description of the actual seizure itself. These preliminary treatment steps may be followed by other diagnostic procedures, including blood tests, CT scans or MRIs, and spinal fluid taps to determine if the individual has meningitis. EEGs may also be performed to confirm clinical impressions of the physician. However, it should be noted that many seizure disorders are not detectable through electroencephalographic measures (Lancman, 1999).

Many types of seizures can be treated successfully with precise drug management. Significant headway has been made with the discovery of effective drugs, particularly for children with tonic/clonic, complex partial, and absence seizures. Anticonvulsant drugs must be chosen very carefully, however. The potential risk and benefit of each medication must be balanced. Once a drug has been prescribed, families should be educated in its use to be aware of any side effects and the necessity for consistent administration. Maintaining a regular medication regimen can be very challenging for children and their parents. In some instances, medication may be discontinued after several years of seizure-free behavior. This is particularly true for those young children who do not have some form of underlying brain pathology.

Other treatments for seizure disorders include surgery, stress management, and diet modifications. The goal of surgery is to remove the precise part of the brain that is damaged and causing the seizures (Zimmerman & Kingsley, 1997). Surgery is considered for those individuals with uncontrollable seizures, essentially those who have not responded to anticonvulsant medications. Using a variety of sophisticated scanning procedures, physicians attempt to isolate the damaged area of the brain that corresponds with the seizure activity. The outcomes of surgery for children and youth with well-defined foci of seizure activity are excellent (Epilepsy Foundation of America, 2000c). Obviously the surgery must be done with great care. Brain tissue, once removed, is gone forever. Additionally, the function that the tissue performed is eliminated or only marginally restored (Zimmerman & Kingsley, 1997).

Stress management is designed to increase the child or youth's general functioning. Because seizures are often associated with illnesses, inadequate rest, and other stressors, parents and other care providers work at helping children, youth, and adults understand the importance of attending consistently to their medication routines, developing emotional resilience, and maintaining healthy patterns of behavior.

Diet modifications are designed to alter the way the body uses energy from food. Typically our bodies convert the carbohydrates we consume into glucose (sugar). Several types of seizures can be controlled by instituting a ketogenic diet. This diet focuses on having individuals consume fats rather than carbohydrates. Instead of producing glucose, individuals on this diet produce ketones, a special kind of molecule. This change in food consumption causes alterations in the metabolism of the brain that normally uses sugars to "fire" its functions. For reasons that are not completely understood, the brain is less receptive to certain kinds of seizures under this diet. However, the diet is extraordinarily difficult to maintain on a long-term basis (Zimmerman & Kingsley, 1997). (See nearby Today's Technology feature.)

Individuals with seizure disorders need calm and supportive responses from others. Treatment efforts of various professionals and family members must be care-

Today's Technology

THE FIRST NEW, FDA-APPROVED APPROACH TO TREATING EPILEPSY IN 100 YEARS

NeuroCybernetic Prosthesis (NCP)

Vagus Nerve Stimulation (VNS) with the Cyberonics NeuroCybernetic Prosthesis (NCP) system is the first new approach to the treatment of epilepsy in over 100 years. After 15 years of research and clinical studies, VNS was approved on July 16, 1997, as an add-on therapy in reducing the frequency of seizures in adults and adolescents over 12 years of age with partial onset seizures that are refractory to antiepileptic medications. To date, over 8,000 patients of all ages with a variety of seizure types have been treated by physi-

cians at over 350 centers in the United States and Europe.

VNS sends signals from the vagus nerve in the neck to the brain. The device is implanted in the chest and neck. The implant procedure does not involve the brain.

VNS consists of electrical signals that are applied to the vagus nerve in the neck for transmission to the brain. *Vagus* means "wanderer" in Greek. The vagus nerve is appropriately named, considering that it averages 22 inches in length in adults and wanders throughout the upper body. The vagus nerve has proven to be a good way

to communicate with the brain because

- there are few if any pain fibers in the vagus nerve.
- over 80% of the electrical signals applied to the vagus nerve in the neck are sent upwards to the brain.
- the stimulation lead may be attached to the vagus nerve in a surgical procedure that does not involve the brain and is not brain surgery.

Source: From "The First New, FDA-Approved Approach to Treating Epilepsy in 100 Years," by Cyberonics, 2000, pp. 1–2. *[online]* Available: *http://www.cyberonics.com/pat_guide.htm*

---

fully orchestrated to provide these individuals with opportunities to use their abilities and talents. Educators should be aware of the basic fundamentals of seizure disorders and their management. Also, they should be aware of their critical role in observing seizures that may occur at school. The astute observations of a teacher may be invaluable to a health care team in developing appropriate medical interventions for the child or youth.

Diabetes

■ DEFINITIONS AND CONCEPTS

he term **diabetes mellitus** refers to a developmental or hereditary disorder characterized by inadequate secretion or use of **insulin** produced by the pancreas to process carbohydrates. There are two types of diabetes mellitus: insulin-dependent diabetes mellitus (IDDM), commonly known as Type I or juvenile onset; and noninsulin-dependent diabetes mellitus (NIDDM), referred to as Type II or adult onset (American Diabetes Association, 1999; Children with Diabetes, 1997).

Glucose—a sugar, one of the end products of digesting carbohydrates—is used by the body for energy. Some glucose is used quickly, while some is stored in the liver and muscles for later use. However, muscle and liver cells cannot absorb and store the energy produced by glucose without insulin, a hormone produced by the pancreas that converts glucose into energy for use in body cells to perform their various functions. Without insulin, glucose accumulates in the blood, causing a condition known as hyperglycemia. Left untreated, this condition can cause serious,

focus 7

Identify three problems that individuals with diabetes may eventually experience.

■ DIABETES MELLITUS. A disease characterized by inadequate use of insulin, resulting in disordered metabolism of carbohydrates, fats, and proteins.

■ INSULIN. A secretion of the pancreas that assists the body by allowing glucose to enter the body's cells.

Diabetes affects 1 in every 600 children. Here 7-year-old Kaitlyn helps Ivan, age 13, and his mother administer a test to measure blood sugar level. Both Kaitlyn and Ivan have diabetes.

immediate problems for people with IDDM, leading to loss of consciousness or to a diabetic coma (American Diabetes Association, 2000a).

Typical symptoms associated with glucose buildup in the blood are extreme hunger, thirst, and frequent urination. Although progress has been made in regulating insulin levels, the prevention and treatment of the complications that accompany diabetes—including blindness, cardiovascular disease, and kidney disease—still pose tremendous challenges for health care specialists.

IDDM, or juvenile onset diabetes, is particularly troublesome. Compared to the adult form, this disease tends to be more severe and progresses more quickly. Generally, the symptoms are easily recognized. The child develops an unusual thirst for water and other liquids. His or her appetite also increases substantially, but listlessness and fatigue occur despite increased food and liquid intake (Children with Diabetes, 1999).

NIDDM is the most common form of diabetes and is often associated with obesity in individuals over age 40. Individuals with this form of diabetes are at less risk for diabetic comas, and most individuals can manage the disorder through exercise and dietary restrictions. If these actions fail, insulin therapy may be necessary (American Diabetes Association, 2000b).

■ PREVALENCE AND CAUSATION

It is estimated that about 6% of the U.S. population has diabetes. The prevalence rate for children with insulin-dependent (i.e., must administer insulin) diabetes is approximately 1 per 600 children. About 500,000 to 1 million individuals have Type I or juvenile onset diabetes. About 14.9 million individuals have Type II or adult onset. Of this number, about one third do not know that they have the disease (American Diabetes Association, 2000b).

The causes of diabetes remain obscure, although considerable research has been conducted on the biochemical mechanisms responsible for it (Hill, 1999). Diabetes develops gradually in individuals. Individuals with Type I diabetes have a genetic predisposition to the disease (Children with Diabetes, 1997). A youngster's environment and heredity interact in determining the severity and the long-term nature of the condition. However, even in identical twins, when one twin develops Type I diabetes, the other twin is affected only 25% to 50% of the time. There must be an environmental trigger that activates the onset of the disease. Some researchers believe that to be a particular virus, *Coxsackie B.* Progressively, the body's immune system is affected and the destruction of the beta cells occurs (Hill, 1999). These are the cells in the pancreas that produce and regulate insulin production. Without insulin, the child develops the classic symptoms of Type I diabetes: excessive thirst, urination, and hunger; weight loss, fatigue, blurred vision, and high blood sugar levels (Children with Diabetes, 1997).

■ INTERVENTIONS

Medical treatment centers on the regular administration of insulin, which is essential for children and youth with juvenile diabetes. Several exciting advances have been made in recent years to monitor blood sugar levels and deliver insulin to people with diabetes (MiniMed, 2000a). Recent success with pancreas transplants has virtually eliminated the disease for some individuals. Also, significant progress is being made with the development of the bioartificial pancreas (Children with Diabetes, 1997) and gene therapy (Cable News Network, 1997).

Other medical interventions are also being pursued. Solid headway has been made in transplanting insulin-producing islet cells to individuals with Type I diabetes (Warnock, 1999). However, this approach is complicated by shortages in available, whole pancreases and the rejection of these new cells in recipients. Other sources of pancreatic tissue are present in fetal tissue. This controversial approach makes use of tissues derived from aborted fetuses. Also, animal islet cells are currently being investigated, particularly islet cells derived from pigs whose insulin differs by only one molecule from that of humans. However, transplantation of these cells poses similar rejection problems for recipients (see the nearby Today's Technology).

Hybrid technologies are also being pursued. Perhaps the most promising is the production of artificial beta cells that could be used in an artificial pancreas. This approach centers on inserting new genes into naturally occurring cells that would produce insulin and be sensitive to the rise and fall of blood glucose (Children with Diabetes, 2000).

Maintaining normal levels of glucose is now achieved in many instances with an **insulin infusion pump,** which is worn by persons with diabetes and powered by

■ INSULIN INFUSION PUMP. Battery-operated devices that dispense insulin continuously to diabetic patients.

Today's Technology

NO MORE SHOTS!

Canadian researchers . . . have developed a cell transplant technique that eliminates the need for insulin injections in the treatment of diabetes. The development is so striking that the *New England Journal of Medicine* released the University of Alberta study almost two months early and put it up on its *Web site.*

Scientists injected pancreas cells near the liver of eight diabetes patients. The cells took up residence in the liver and began producing the long-lost insulin that controls blood sugar levels.

If the results are confirmed in a larger study and if doctors can find a better source for the cells, which must now be harvested from cadavers, it could mean the end of insulin-dependent diabetes.

The long-term safety and effectiveness of the technique must still be established. In addition, the recipients must now take a combination of three drugs designed to prevent the body from rejecting the transplanted cells. Those drugs increase the risk of cancer and infection.

Source: Adapted from "Diabetes Cure," by CBS News, June 6, 2000, pp. 1–2.

small batteries. The infusion pump operates continuously and delivers the dose of insulin determined by the physician and the patient. This form of treatment is effective only if used in combination with carefully followed diet and exercise programs. These pumps, if carefully monitored and operated, contribute greatly to "controlling" diabetes, thus reducing or slowing the onset and risks for eye disease, nerve damage, and kidney disease (MiniMed, 2000b, p. 1).

Juvenile diabetes is a lifelong condition that can have a pronounced effect on the child in a number of areas. Complications for children with long-standing diabetes include blindness, heart attacks, and kidney problems. Many of these problems can be delayed or prevented by maintaining adequate blood sugar levels with appropriate food intake, exercise, and insulin injections.

Cystic Fibrosis

■ DEFINITIONS AND CONCEPTS

An inherited, systemic, generalized disease that begins at conception is known as **cystic fibrosis (CF)**. Although the lifespan of persons with CF has been lengthened through new treatments, death within the early adult years is often inevitable. CF is a disorder of the secretion glands, which produce abnormal amounts of mucus, sweat, and saliva. Three major organ systems are affected: the lungs, pancreas, and sweat glands. The gluelike mucus in the lungs obstructs their functioning and increases the likelihood of infection, gradually destroying the lungs after repeated infections (Cystic Fibrosis Foundation, 2000b). As lung deterioration occurs, the heart is burdened, and heart failure may result. The pancreas is affected in a similar fashion when excessive amounts of mucus prevent critical digestive enzymes from reaching the small intestine. Without these enzymes, proteins and fats consumed by the individual with CF are lost in frequent, greasy, flatulent stools.

■ PREVALENCE AND CAUSATION

Cystic fibrosis is primarily a Caucasian phenomenon. It affects 30,000 children and adults in the United States (Cystic Fibrosis Foundation, 2000b). CF is virtually absent in the countries of Japan and China. Males and females appear to be influenced in about equal numbers (Hill & Lebenthal, 1995). CF manifests itself in slightly more than 3 infants in every 10,000 live births (Bowe, 2000).

CF is a genetically transmitted disease. A child must inherit a defective copy of the CF gene from each parent to develop the disease. The gene for the CF transfer regulator (CFTR) is very large, and some 2,000 mutations have already been identified with the disease (Rudolph & Kamei, 1994). CFTR, a protein, produces improper transportation of sodium and salt (chloride) within cells that line organs such as the lungs and pancreas (Cystic Fibrosis Foundation, 2000b; Minty, 1996). CFTR prevents chloride from exiting these cells. This blockage affects a broad range of organs and systems in the body, including reproductive organs in men and women, the lungs, sweat glands, and digestive system (Cystic Fibrosis Foundation, 2000b).

■ INTERVENTIONS

The prognosis for an individual with CF depends on a number of factors. The two most critical are early diagnosis of the condition and the quality of care provided after diagnosis. If the diagnosis occurs late, irreversible damage may be present. With early

■ CYSTIC FIBROSIS (CF). A hereditary disease that usually appears during early childhood. This generalized disorder of the exocrine glands is characterized by respiratory problems and excessive loss of salt in perspiration.

diagnosis and appropriate medical care, most individuals with CF can achieve weight and growth gains similar to those of their normal peers. Early diagnosis and improved treatment strategies have lengthened the average lifespan of children with CF; more than half now live beyond their 31st year (Cystic Fibrosis Foundation, 2000a).

The best and most comprehensive treatment is provided through CF centers located throughout the United States. These centers provide experienced medical and support staff (respiratory care personnel, social workers, dieticians, genetic counselors, and psychologists). Moreover, they maintain diagnostic laboratories especially equipped to perform pulmonary function testing and sweat testing. Sweat of children with CF has abnormal concentrations of sodium or chloride; in fact, sweat tests provide the definitive data for a diagnosis of CF in infants and young children.

Interventions for CF are varied and complex, with treatment continuing throughout the person's lifetime. Consistent and appropriate application of medical, social, educational, and psychological components of treatment allow these individuals to live longer and with less discomfort and fewer complications than in years past.

Treatment of CF is designed to accomplish a number of goals. The first is to diagnose the condition before any severe symptoms are exhibited. Other goals include control of chest infection, maintenance of adequate nutrition, education of the child and family regarding the condition, and provision of a suitable education for the child.

Management of respiratory disease caused by CF is critical. If respiratory insufficiency can be prevented or minimized, the individual's life will be greatly enhanced and prolonged. Antibiotic drugs, postural drainage (chest physical therapy), and medicated vapors play important roles in the medical management of CF (Cystic Fibrosis Foundation, 2000b).

Diet management is also essential for the child with CF. Generally, the child with this condition requires more caloric intake than his or her normal peers. The diet should be high in protein and adjusted appropriately if the child fails to grow and/or make appropriate weight gains. Individuals with CF benefit significantly from the use of replacement enzymes that assist with food absorption. Also, the intake of vitamins is very important to individuals with digestive system problems.

The major social and psychological problems of children with CF are directly related to chronic coughing, small stature, offensive stools, gas, delayed onset of puberty and secondary sex characteristics, and unsatisfying social relationships. Also, these children and youth may spend significant amounts of time away from school settings. Thus teachers, counselors, and other support personnel play essential roles in helping these students feel at home in school settings, making up past due work, and forming friendships with others. Moreover, support groups play important roles in helping students with CF understand themselves and their disease and in developing personal resilience and ongoing friendships.

Emerging and exciting interventions for CF are being explored, including gene therapy, lung transplants, mucus-thinning drugs, and the use of high doses of ibuprofen with young children. Gene therapy is particularly promising as it addresses the root cause of CF. (See nearby Today's Technology feature.)

Development of new drugs has improved treatment for many individuals with CF. One such antibiotic is Pulmozyme. It has proved effective in reducing respiratory infections and in improving lung functioning in individuals with CF. On the horizon are new antibiotics such as TOBI™ (tobramycin solution for inhalation) and IB 367. These promising compounds and others yet to be developed should help physicians and individuals with CF more effectively manage chronic lung infections and related conditions (Cystic Fibrosis Foundation, 2000b).

focus 8

Identify present and future interventions for the treatment of children and youth with cystic fibrosis.

Today's Technology

HOW CYSTIC FIBROSIS GENE THERAPY WORKS

CF scientists manufacture normal genes in the laboratory by using state-of-the-art biotechnology. Several teams of researchers are developing innovative gene delivery systems to determine the best way to deposit these healthy genes, such as modified viruses, liposomes (fat cap-sules), and synthetic vectors.

The initial strategy uses a modified adenovirus to act as a delivery van, depositing the normal genes directly to damaged CF airway cells. In these experiments, researchers are delivering the adenovirus as nose drops or drizzling it down a bronchoscope (flexible tube) to reach CF cells lining the airways. They envi-sion that gene therapy for CF eventually will be adminis-tered via an aerosol.

These early trials test the safety and efficiency of the adenovirus delivery system. Patients are monitored to detect whether the normal CF gene has turned on. If so, the gene will produce a normal protein that is vital to the health of cells lining the respi-ratory tract. The treatments are not expected to improve lung function yet, because only a small portion of the airways are being treated.

Source: From *Gene Therapy and Cystic Fibrosis,* by the Cystic Fibrosis Foundation, 2000, p. 2.

Sickle Cell Anemia

■ DEFINITIONS AND CONCEPTS

An inherited disorder that profoundly impacts the function and struc-ture of red blood cells is called **sickle cell anemia (SCA).** The hemo-globin molecule in the red blood cells of individuals with SCA is abnormal, in that it is vulnerable to structural collapse when the blood-oxygen level is significantly diminished. As the blood-oxygen level declines, these blood cells become distorted and form bizarre shapes. This process, known as *sickling,* distorts the normal donutlike shapes of cells into shapes like microscopic sickle blades. Obstructions in vessels of affected individuals can lead to stroke and damage of other organs in the body (American Medical Association, 1999; Sickle Cell Information Center, 1997a).

People affected by sickle cell anemia experience unrelenting **anemia.** In some cases, it is tolerated well; in others, the condition is quite debilitating. Another aspect of SCA involves frequent infections; periodic vascular blockage, which occurs as the sickled cells block microvascular channels, can often cause severe and chronic pain in the extremities, abdomen, or back. In addition, the disease may affect any organ sys-tem of the body. SCA also has a significant negative effect on the physical growth and development of infants and children (Sickle Cell Information Center, 1997b).

■ PREVALENCE AND CAUSATION

Approximately 1 in 400 African American infants has SCA (Sickle Cell Informa-tion Center, 1997b). Moreover, about 7% to 10% of African Americans carry the sickle cell gene (Ezekowitz & First, 1994). Sickle cell disease is most prevalent in areas of the world in which malaria is widespread. Individuals from the Mediter-ranean basin—from Greece, Italy, and Sardinia—may carry the mutant gene for SCA. Also, individuals from India and the Arabian Peninsula may be carriers of the gene (Mayfield, 1999).

Sickle cell anemia is caused by various combinations of genes. A child who receives a mutant S-hemoglobin gene from each parent exhibits SCA to one degree or another. The disease usually presents itself at 6 months of age and continues throughout the individual's lifetime.

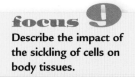

focus 9

Describe the impact of the sickling of cells on body tissues.

■ SICKLE CELL ANEMIA (SCA). An inherited disease that has a pro-found effect on the function and structure of red blood cells.

■ ANEMIA. A condition in which the blood is deficient in red blood cells.

510   CHAPTER 16   PEOPLE WITH PHYSICAL AND HEALTH DISABILITIES

■ INTERVENTIONS

A number of treatments may be employed to deal with the problems caused by sickle cell anemia; however, the first step is early diagnosis. Babies should be screened at birth, particularly infants who are at risk for this disease. Early diagnosis lays the groundwork for the prophylactic use of antibiotics to prevent infections in the first 5 years of life. This treatment, coupled with appropriate immunizations and nutrition, prevents further complications of the disease (Sickle Cell Information Center, 1997a). Moreover, these treatments significantly reduce the death rate associated with SCA.

Children, youth, and adults usually learn to adapt to their anemia and lead relatively normal lives. When their lives are interrupted by crises, a variety of treatment approaches can be used. For children, comprehensive and timely care is crucial. For example, children with SCA who develop fevers should be treated aggressively. In fact, parents of these children may be taught how to palpate the spleen and recognize early signs of potentially serious problems. Hydration is also an important component of treatment. Lastly, pain management may be addressed with narcotic and nonnarcotic drugs.

Several factors predispose individuals to SCA crises: dehydration from fever, reduced liquid intake, and hypoxia (a result of breathing air that is poor in oxygen content). Stress, fatigue, and exposure to cold temperatures should be avoided by those who have a history of SCA crises.

Treatment of crises is generally directed at keeping the individual warm, increasing liquid intake, ensuring good blood oxygenation, and administering medication for infection. Assistance can also be provided during crisis periods by partial-exchange blood transfusions with fresh, normal red cells. Transfusions may also be necessary for individuals with SCA who are preparing for surgery or are pregnant.

SOCIAL AND HEALTH-RELATED PROBLEMS

In this section we review child abuse and neglect, adolescent pregnancy, suicide among youth, and maternal drug and alcohol abuse. Although these conditions are not typically thought of as physical and health disabilities, they do influence significant numbers of families and place children and youth at risk for problems in their schools and communities.

Child Abuse and Neglect

■ DEFINITIONS AND CONCEPTS

Child abuse and neglect have been defined by both state and federal legislation. The Child Abuse Prevention and Treatment Act (CAPTA) (Public Law 104-235, Section 111; 42; U.S.C. 510g) provides the following definitions:

Child is a person who has not attained the lesser of:
- *The age of 18*
- *Except in cases of sexual abuse, the age specified by the child protection law of the state in which the child resides*

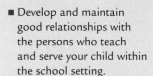

■ EARLY CHILDHOOD YEARS

TIPS FOR THE FAMILY

■ Work closely with medical personnel to lessen the overall impact of the disorder over time. This may include using prophylactic medications, monitoring the impact of certain medications, asking for reading materials, following dietary routines, communicating honest concerns, and asking questions about instructions not well understood.

■ Provide the child with physical or health disabilities opportunities to freely explore his or her environment to the maximum degree possible. This may require some adaptations or specialized equipment (e.g., custom-made wheelchairs, prosthetic devices).

■ Involve the child with other children as time and energy permit. Only children can teach one another certain things. This may include inviting one or several children to your home for informal play activities, celebration of social events, and other age-appropriate activities.

■ Join advocacy and support groups that provide the information and assistance you need.

TIPS FOR THE PRESCHOOL TEACHER

■ Be sure that the physical environment in the classroom lends itself to the needs of children who may have physical or health disorders (e.g., aisles in the classroom are sufficiently large for free movement in a wheelchair). Like any other children, these children benefit from moving around and fully exploring every inch of every environment. Also, it readies them in a gradual way to become appropriately independent.

■ Become aware of specific needs of the child by consulting with parents. For example, the child may need to refrain from highly physical activities.

TIPS FOR PRESCHOOL PERSONNEL

■ Be sure that other key personnel in the school who interact directly with the child are informed of his or her needs.

■ Orient all the children in your classroom to the needs of the child with physical or health disabilities. This could be done by you, the parents or siblings, or other educational personnel in the school. Remember, your behavior toward the child will say more than words will ever convey.

■ Be sure that arrangements have been made for emergency situations. For example, peers may know exactly what to do if a fellow class member begins to have a seizure. Additionally, classmates should know how they may be helpful in directing and assisting the child during a fire drill or other emergency procedure.

TIPS FOR NEIGHBORS AND FRIENDS

■ Involve the child with physical or health disabilities and his or her family in holiday gatherings. Be sensitive to dietary regimens, opportunities for repositioning, and alternative means for communicating.

■ Become aware of the things that you may need to do. For example, you may need to learn what to do if a child with insulin-dependent diabetes shows signs of glucose buildup.

■ ELEMENTARY YEARS

TIPS FOR THE FAMILY

■ Maintain a healthy and ongoing relationship with the care providers that are part of your child's life. Acknowledge their efforts and reinforce behaviors and actions that are particularly helpful to you and your child.

■ Continue to be involved with advocacy and support groups.

■ Stay informed by subscribing to newsletters that are produced and disseminated by advocacy organizations.

■ Develop and maintain good relationships with the persons who teach and serve your child within the school setting.

TIPS FOR THE GENERAL EDUCATION SCHOOL TEACHER

■ Be informed and willing to learn about the unique needs of the child with physical or health disorders in your classroom. For example, schedule a conference with the child's parents before the year begins to talk about medications, prosthetic devices, levels of desired physical activities, and so on.

■ Inform the other children in the class. Help them become aware of their crucial role in contributing to the well-being of the child with physical or health disorders.

■ Use socially competent and mature peers to assist you (e.g., providing tutoring, physical assistance, social support in recess activities).

■ Be sure that plans have been made and practiced for dealing with emergency situations (e.g., some children may need to be carried out of a building or room).

■ If the child's condition is progressive and life threatening, begin to discuss the ramifications of death and loss. Many excellent books about this topic are available for children.

TIPS FOR SCHOOL PERSONNEL

- Be sure that all key personnel in the school setting who interact with the child on a regular basis are informed about treatment regimens, dietary requirements, and signs of potentially problematic conditions such as fevers and irritability.
- Meet periodically as professionals to deal with emergent problems, brainstorm for solutions, and identify suitable actions.
- Children can be involved periodically in brainstorming activities that focus on involving the child with physical or health disorders to the maximum degree possible.
- Institute cross-age tutoring and support. When possible, have the child with a physical or health condition become a tutor.

TIPS FOR NEIGHBORS AND FRIENDS

- Involve the child with physical or health disorders in your family activities.
- Provide parents with some respite care. They will appreciate the time to themselves.
- Be informed! Be aware of the needs of the child by regularly talking to his or her parents. They will sincerely appreciate your concern.

■ SECONDARY AND TRANSITION YEARS

TIPS FOR THE FAMILY

- Remember that, for some individuals with physical

or health disabilities, the secondary or young adult years may be the most trying, particularly if the conditions are progressive in nature.
- Begin planning early in the secondary school years for the youth's transition from the public school to the adult world. Incorporate goals related to independent living in the IEP.
- Be sure that you are well informed about the adult services offered in your community and state.

TIPS FOR THE GENERAL EDUCATION SCHOOL TEACHER

- Continue to be aware of the potential needs for accommodation and adjustment.
- Treat the individual as an adult.
- Realize that the youth's studies may be interrupted from time to time with medical treatments or other important health care services.

TIPS FOR SCHOOL PERSONNEL

- Acknowledge individuals by name, become familiar with their interests and hobbies, joke with them occasionally, and involve them in meaningful activities such as fund raisers, community service projects, and decorating for various school events.
- Provide opportunities for all students to receive recognition and be involved in school-related activities.

- Realize that peer assistance and tutoring may be particularly helpful to certain students. Social involvement outside the school setting should be encouraged (e.g., going to movies, attending concerts).
- Use members of teacher assistance teams to help with unique problems that surface from time to time. For example, you may want to talk with special educators about management ideas that may improve a given child's behavior in your classroom.

TIPS FOR NEIGHBORS, FRIENDS, AND POTENTIAL EMPLOYERS

- Continue to be involved in the individual's life.
- Be aware of assistance that you might provide in the event of a youth's gradual deterioration or death.
- Involve the individual in age-appropriate activities (e.g., cookouts, video nights, or community events).
- Encourage your own teens to volunteer as peer tutors or job coaches.
- If you are an employer, provide opportunities for job sampling, on-the-job training, or actual employment.

■ ADULT YEARS

TIPS FOR THE FAMILY

- Make provisions for independent living away from home. Work with adult service personnel and advocacy organizations in

lining up appropriate housing and related support services.
- Provide support for appropriate employment opportunities.
- Work closely with local and state adult services personnel. Know what your rights are and how you can qualify your son or daughter for educational or other support services.

TIPS FOR NEIGHBORS, FRIENDS, AND EMPLOYERS

- Provide appropriate accommodations for leisure and work activities.
- Adopt an adult for regular recreational and social activities.
- Provide regular opportunities for recognition and informative feedback. When persons with disabilities are hired, be sure that they regularly receive specific information about their work performance. Feedback may include candid comments about their punctuality, rate of work completion, and social interaction with others. Withholding information, not making reasonable adjustments, and not expecting these individuals to be responsible for their behaviors are great disservices to them.

Child abuse and neglect occur among all ethnic groups and at all socioeconomic levels. Educators must be aware of its existence and be willing to address it.

Child abuse and neglect [are], at a minimum:
- *Any recent act or failure to act on the part of the parent or caregiver which results in death, serious physical harm, sexual abuse, or exploitation*
- *An act or failure to act which presents imminent risk of serious harm*

Sexual abuse is:
- *The employment, use, persuasion, inducement, enticement, or coercion to engage in, or assist any other person to engage in, any sexually explicit conduct or stimulation of such conduct for the purpose of producing a visual depiction of such conduct*
- *The rape, and in cases of caretakers or interfamilial relationships, statutory rape, molestation, prostitution, or other form of sexual exploitation of children, or incest with children*

Withholding of medically indicated treatment is: the failure to respond to the infant's life-threatening conditions by providing treatment (including appropriate nutrition, hydration, and medication) that in the treating physician's or physicians' reasonable medical judgment, would most likely to be effective in ameliorating or correcting all such conditions. (National Clearinghouse on Child Abuse and Neglect Information, 2000c, p. 1)

Child abuse and **child neglect** can be regarded as means of maladaptive coping by parents. Abusive parents and caregivers are confronted with personal and family challenges that influence their responses to children. Some parents are able to cope with these challenges with adaptive behaviors that help their children; other parents, unfortunately, respond with maladaptive, harmful behaviors.

Many factors contribute to the neglect of children. Many parents living in poverty cannot provide the necessary shelter, food, clothing, and health care required for the well-being of their children. Often the stress experienced by these parents is overwhelming, and little is available in the way of support systems and services to help them. Many parents who neglect their children simply do not understand their chil-

There are no bruises.
And no broken bones.
She seems the picture of the perfect child. But if you look closely you can see how rejection, fear and constant humiliation have left scars that have tragically affected her childhood.

So now only a shattered spirit remains. And the light of laughter has gone out. Remember that words hit as hard as a fist. So watch what you say.
You don't have to lift a hand to hurt your child.
Take time out. Don't take it out on your kid.

 Write: National Committee for Prevention of Child Abuse, Box 2866E., Chicago, IL 60690

Words hit as hard as a fist.
Next time, stop and listen to what you're saying.
You might not believe your ears.

Take time out. Don't take it out on your kid.
Write: National Committee for Prevention of Child Abuse, Box 2866E., Chicago, IL 60690

dren's behaviors and their important roles in caring for them. Moreover, many parents who neglect their children have very serious problems themselves, including substance abuse and serious psychiatric problems.

Child neglect results when parents abandon their children or fail to care for them in healthy ways. In short, children who are not adequately cared for are considered neglected. These children are often malnourished, infrequently bathed or changed, left without suitable supervision, and rarely held or appropriately stimulated.

Neglect is evidenced in many ways. Some of these children are grossly underweight for their age. They often fail to thrive yet display no medical problems. Some may exhibit persistent and severe diaper rashes because of inconsistent care.

Physical abuse of children generally results in serious physical harm or injury to the affected child and sometimes even death (National Clearinghouse on Child Abuse and Neglect Information, 2000c). Abusive parents often exhibit inconsistent childrearing practices. Furthermore, their child management approaches are often hostile and aggressive in nature. These parents may also experience stress-eliciting problems arising from unemployment, youthful parenthood, limited incomes, and other related factors.

Another form of child mistreatment is **sexual abuse**—incest, assault, or sexual exploitation (Horton & Cruise, 1997). "Sexual abuse involves any sexual activity with a child where consent is not or cannot be given" (Berliner & Elliott, 1996, p. 51). Girls are at greater risk for sexual abuse than are boys. Additionally, children and youth with disabilities are 1.75 times more likely than children without disabilities to be sexually abused (Sullivan, 2000).

Behavioral indicators of sexual abuse include anxiety, depression, age-inappropriate knowledge about sex, running away from home, suicide attempts, substance abuse problems, and fantasies with sexual connotations. However, many children who have been sexually abused show no signs. Manifestations of their maltreatment may not surface until the adult years and are often evidenced in interpersonal relationship problems (Berliner & Elliott, 1996).

Emotional abuse or psychological maltreatment is often the result of behaviors related to rejecting, terrorizing, isolating, and exploiting (Brassard, 1997). Outcomes of this kind of abuse are many and varied. Children who have been severely ignored are often lethargic and apathetic. Often they are developmentally delayed in physical development, language acquisition, and cognitive development.

■ PREVALENCE AND CAUSATION

Establishing accurate and precise prevalence estimates for child abuse is very difficult. In addition to the problem of underreporting, much of the difficulty is attributable to the lack of consistent criteria for child abuse and sundry reporting procedures used in various states. Annually, about 1 million children experience child abuse or neglect. Recent studies suggest that the prevalence for child abuse and neglect is about 13 to 14 cases per 1,000 children. More than half of these children experience neglect, and 22.7% suffer from physical abuse. Almost 12% of the children were sexually abused. Six percent were victims of psychological abuse or medical neglect. Moreover, 25% of the victims experienced several forms of child maltreatment. The age group that experienced the highest rates of abuse was the 0–3 age group (National Clearinghouse on Child Abuse and Neglect Information, 2000a).

Several factors may cause a parent or caregiver to be abusive. These include crises caused by unemployment, poverty, unwanted pregnancy, serious health problems, substance abuse, high levels of mobility, isolation from natural and community support networks, marital problems, death of a significant other, inadequate

focus 10

Identify five factors that may contribute to child abuse and neglect.

■ SEXUAL ABUSE. A form of mistreatment involving sexual misconduct such as incest, assault, or sexual exploitation.

intellectual and moral development, and economic difficulties (Brassard, 1997). Other potential factors include the withdrawal of spousal support, having a child at a very young age, having a particularly challenging infant (one with severe disabilities), or caring for a nonbiologically related child (Dukewich, Borkowski, & Whitman, 1999; Sullivan, 2000). Several personality traits frequently characterize abusive parents, including poor impulse control, deficits in role-taking and empathy, and low self-esteem (Baumrind, 1995).

Interestingly, research suggests that parents who were abused as children are at risk of engaging in child abuse themselves. However, most children who were abused do not grow up to be abusive parents (Buchanan, 1995).

Child abuse and neglect occur among all ethnic groups and at all socioeconomic levels. Thus, all educators of children and youth must be aware of its existence and be willing to address it. State laws designate educators and other professionals who work with children (e.g., health care providers, police officers, social workers, clergy) as mandated reporters, which means they have a legal responsibility to report suspected abuse or neglect to their administrators and/or appropriate law enforcement or child protection agencies. Laws vary from state to state; thus, educators must become familiar with the definition of abuse used in their jurisdiction, as well as what their responsibilities are in reporting.

Clearly, reporting child abuse or neglect is a serious undertaking; however, the responsibility need not be intimidating. Although the reporter should have ample reason to suspect that abuse or neglect has occurred, he or she is not responsible for proving that it has. Moreover, laws often protect individuals who report abuse and neglect by ensuring some level of confidentiality. The reporter's primary consideration should be the welfare of the child.

■ INTERVENTIONS

Treatment of child abuse and neglect is a multifaceted process (Greenwalt, Sklare, & Portes, 1998; Lutzker, 1998). The entire family must be involved. The first goal is to treat the abused or neglected child for any serious injuries and simultaneously prevent further harm or neglect. Hospitalization may be necessary to deal with immediate physical injuries or other complications, during which the child protection and treatment team, in conjunction with the family, develops a comprehensive treatment plan. Once the child's immediate medical needs have been met, a variety of treatment options may be employed: individual play therapy, therapeutic playschool, regular preschool, foster care, residential care, hospitalization, and/or group treatment.

Prevention and treatment programs for parents and families of abused and neglected children are directed at helping parents and other family members function more appropriately in responding to their children's needs as well as their own (National Clearinghouse on Child Abuse and Neglect Information, 2000d). These programs focus on behaviors and skills such as personal impulse control, alternative methods of disciplining, and anger management. Neglectful parents may receive one-on-one assistance with practical child-care tasks such as feeding and diapering an infant, managing a challenging 2-year-old, and effectively dealing with various kinds of crying. Additionally, needed resources may be provided to assist with the provision of adequate and nutritious food, suitable clothing, regular medical and dental care, and appropriate housing. Reviews of treatment programs for abusive and neglecting families suggest that these programs achieve mixed results and are generally ineffective (Brassard, 1997). Some are effective in producing the desired changes, particularly with parents who have been involved in child neglect (Paget,

1997). The most effective approaches seem to be directed at the children themselves (Brassard, 1997; Paget, 1997).

Some programs are directed at reducing economic and emotional stress by providing affordable day care, helping parents become employable and employed, providing opportunities for additional education and training. Also, collaboration among service providers is beginning to emerge. Such collaboration makes it possible for families to receive services that are tailored to their specific needs (Burns & Goldman, 1999; National Clearinghouse on Child Abuse and Neglect Information, 2000d; Paget, 1997).

Adolescent Pregnancy

■ DEFINITIONS AND CONCEPTS

Adolescent pregnancy is the outcome of conception in girls 19 years or younger. The impact of adolescent pregnancy is highly variable, depending on age, class, and race. More than 80% of the pregnancies that occur during the adolescent years are unwanted. Of these, the vast majority of adolescent mothers remain unmarried, leave school, experience severe financial problems, and frequently become reliant on welfare (Kaplan & Mammel, 1997). Moreover, very few negotiate the challenges associated with adolescent pregnancy, complete their schooling, and eventually enter the work force without being dependent on welfare services (Maynard, 1997).

Teens undergo a number of developmental changes during adolescence: the construction of an identity; development of personal relationships and responsibilities; gradual preparation for vocational or professional work through education; independence from their parents; and various adjustments to a complex society. Many if not all of these developmental changes are significantly affected by pregnancy (Budd, Stockman, & Miller, 1998).

The risks and consequences associated with adolescent pregnancy are substantial, particularly if the young mother is 15 years of age or younger. Children born to these mothers experience higher rates of infant mortality, birth defects, mental retardation, central nervous system problems, and intelligence deficits (Kaplan & Mammel, 1997; March of Dimes, 2000). Additionally, fathers of adolescent mothers are not generally adolescents themselves (Maynard, 1997). These dads are often fathers in absentia; few truly assume the role of parent or even partial provider. It is the adolescent mother and her immediate family who shoulder the burdens of caring for and supporting the child (Kaplan & Mammel, 1997; Maynard, 1997).

■ PREVALENCE AND CAUSATION

The United States has the highest rate of teen pregnancies among developed nations (National Women's Health Information Center, 1997). The prevalence of adolescent pregnancy is staggering. About 1 million girls become pregnant each year in the United States. This number represents about 10% of all 15- to 19-year-olds. Of these pregnancies, 13% are deliberate choices (Maynard, 1997; National Center for Health Statistics, 1999).

"About 45% of 15- to 19-year-old females are sexually active, and more than one third of these become pregnant in within 2 years after the onset of sexual activity" (Kaplan & Mammel, 1997, p. 153). Furthermore, most adolescents do not employ

focus **11**
Identify factors that may contribute to the increased prevalence of adolescent pregnancy.

The United States has the highest rate of teen pregnancies among developed nations. About one million teenagers become pregnant each year in the United States. Of these, only one in ten is a deliberate choice.

any contraception measures until after they have been sexually active for about 15 months (Moore et al., 1997).

Adolescent girls become pregnant for a number of varied and complex reasons. Contributing factors include a lack of knowledge about conception and sexuality, lack of access to or misuse of contraceptives, desires to escape family control, need to be more adult, aspirations to have someone to love, means of gaining attention and care, and inability to make sound decisions. Societal factors also play a role in the increased number of adolescents who become pregnant: greater permissiveness and freedom, social pressure from peers, and continual exposure to sexuality through the media (Johnson, 1995; Stoiber, 1997).

■ INTERVENTIONS

The goals of treatment for the pregnant adolescent are varied. The first goal is to help the prospective mother cope with the discovery of being pregnant. What emerges from this discovery is a crisis—for her, for the father, and for the families of both individuals, although responses vary among various ethnic and socioeconomic groups. Some adolescents may respond with denial, disbelief, bitterness, disillusionment, or a variety of other feelings. Parents often react to the announcement with anger, then shame and guilt.

Treatment during this period focuses on reducing interpersonal and intrapersonal strain and tension. A wise counselor involves the family in crisis intervention, which is achieved through careful mediation and problem solving. For many adolescents, this period involves some very intense decision making: Should I keep the baby? Should I have the baby and then put it up for adoption? Should I have an abortion? Should I get married? If the adolescent chooses to have the baby, nutritional support for the developing infant, quality prenatal and perinatal care, training for eventual child care, education, and employment skills become the focus of the intervention efforts.

Many programs for adolescent mothers are community-based (National Institute on Early Childhood Development and Education, 1999). These programs focus on strengthening parenting skills, building parent–child relationships, and enhancing mothers' personal functioning. Additionally, these programs provide for prenatal and well-baby care, psychosocial support, vocational training, and family-planning education. Also, every effort is made to help young mothers stay in school and to continue or conclude their secondary education (Budd, Stockman, & Miller, 1998).

Unfortunately, many services rendered to pregnant adolescents fade after delivery of the child. One the major problems for these mothers is becoming pregnant again (Kaplan & Mammel, 1997). Steps should be taken to help these mothers explore options and approaches that significantly reduce the potential for further dilemmas. Problems do not cease with delivery; the development of functional life skills for independent living is a long-term educational and rehabilitation process.

Suicide in Youth

■ DEFINITIONS AND CONCEPTS

Suicide during youth is generally a premeditated act that culminates in the taking of one's life. Several other terms have been developed to describe **suicide,** including completed suicide, attempted suicide, and suicidal ideation. Completed suicide refers to death caused by a set of acts meant to end life. Attempted suicide is defined by self-harm behaviors that could end in

■ SUICIDE. The taking of one's own life.

518

Reflect on This

SUICIDE NOTE FROM JASON

■ **TO WHOM IT MAY CONCERN:**

Why? Because my life has been nothing but misery and sorrow for 20¾ years! Going backwards: I thought Susan loved me, but I suppose not. "I love you Jason" was only a lie. I base my happiness on relationships with girls—when I'm "going steady," I'm happy. When a girl dumps me (which is always the case) I'm terribly depressed. In fact, over the last three years I've been in love at least four times seriously, but only to have my heart shattered—like so many icicles falling from a roof. But I've tried to go out with at least 30–40 girls in the last few years—none of them ever fell in love with me. My fate was: "To love, but not be loved."

My mother threw me out of the house in March. I guess she must really hate me; she doesn't even write me letters. I think she always hated me.

In high school, and even before that, nobody liked me. They all made fun of me and no girl would ever go to the proms with me.

I haven't anything to live for. Hope? Five years ago I wanted to end my life—I've been hoping for five years! Susan was just the straw that broke the camel's back. I simply cannot take it anymore! I only wanted someone to love; someone who would love me back as much as I loved her.

Yeah, I had pretty good grades, but the way my luck runs, I wouldn't have gotten a job anyway. I got fired over the summer 'cause the boss said, "Jason, you don't have any common sense." Gee, that really made my day.

I walk down the streets of Madison and people call out of dorm windows: "Hey Asshole!" What did I do to them? I don't even know them!

I've been pretty miserable lately . . . , so I think I will change the scenery. What's the big deal! I was gonna die in 40 or 50 years anyway. (Maybe sooner: when George [Bush] decides to push the button in Washington, D.C.!)

Good-bye Susan, Sean, Wendy, Joe, Mr. Montgomery, Dr. Johnston, Jack, and everyone else who made my life a little more bearable while it lasted.

Jason

P.S. You might want to print this in the newspaper. It would make excellent reading!

■ **LAST WILL**

(Only will. I never made one before.)

I probably am wasting my time, because you need a lawyer or a witness for a will to be legal, but here goes:

To Sean—go my records, tapes, cassette player, clock/radio, and my camera (in the doctor's bag in closet).

To Wendy—I leave my car (if you want it, if not, give it to ET), my big black coat and my military school uniform—you said you wanted them.

To Joe and Wendy—all my posters, if you want them.

To Jack—miscellaneous items left over (that's still a lot, so don't complain).

To Susan—I leave memories of nice times we had. Also my airbrush (in doctor bag w/camera), and all my love; I'll miss you forever.

If I've forgotten anyone— I'm sorry.

Jason

Please: No autopsy.

Source: Adapted from *Suicide Across the Lifespan* (pp. 110–111), by J. M. Stillion & E. E. McDowell, 1996, Washington, DC: Taylor and Francis. Copyright, 1996. Reprinted by permission.

---

death. Suicidal ideation refers to the thoughts one has about suicide and the frequency of these thoughts during a set period of time (Brock & Sandoval, 1997).

Suicide is a means of satisfying needs, alleviating pain, dealing with depression, and coping with the challenges and stressors inherent in being a youth in today's society. Suicide is now the third leading cause of death in young people 15 to 24 years of age in the United States (National Institute of Mental Health, 1999b). "Over 50% of suicides occur in young people who are sad, despairing, or depressed; another 20% are described as angry, with the suicidal attempt occurring rather impulsively (see Table 16.3). Substance abuse is implicated in at least 20% of the suicides" (Clark, 1997, p. 197).

■ PREVALENCE AND CAUSATION

The prevalence of suicide among young people ages 15–19 is 9.5 per 100,000 (National Institute of Mental Health, 1999b). The prevalence rate for children 14 years and younger is 1.06 per 100,000 (National Institute of Mental Health, 1999b). Many professionals believe that these figures represent only a small portion of the actual number of youth suicides, particularly if one considers the number of youth whose deaths are described as accidental. Far more young males than females commit suicide; the ratio is 5:1 (National Institute of Mental Health, 1999b). However,

focus 12
Identify the major causes of youth suicide.

TABLE 16.3 Common warning signs of suicidal behavior

Warning Signs	Discussion
Suicide notes	Suicide notes are a very real sign of danger and should always be taken seriously.
Direct and indirect suicide threats	Most individuals give clues they have suicidal thoughts. Clues include direct ("I have a plan to kill myself") and indirect threats ("I might as well be dead").
Making final arrangements	Making funeral arrangements, writing a will, paying debts, saying good-bye, and the like could be signs a youth is suicidal.
Giving away prized possessions	In effect, the youth is executing a will.
Talking about death	This could be a sign the youth is exploring death as a solution to problems.
Reading or writing, and/or creating artwork about death	Sometimes warnings include writing death poems or filling sheets of paper with macabre drawings.
Hopelessness or helplessness	A youth who feels there is no hope that problems will improve and who feels helpless to change things may consider suicide.
Social withdrawal and isolation	These behaviors may be a sign of depression and may be a precursor of suicide.
Loss of involvement in interests and activities	A youth who is considering suicide may see no purpose in continuing previously important interests and activities.
Increased risk taking	Youths who choose high-risk sports, daredevil hobbies, and other unnecessarily dangerous activities may be suicidal.
Heavy use of alcohol and drugs	Substance abusers have a six times greater risk for suicide than the general population.
Abrupt changes in appearance	Youths who no longer care about their appearance may be suicidal.
Sudden weight or appetite change	These changes may be a sign of depression that can increase the risk of suicide.
Sudden changes in personality or attitude	The shy youth who suddenly becomes a thrill seeker or the outgoing person who becomes withdrawn and unfriendly may be giving signals that something is seriously wrong.
Inability to concentrate or think rationally	This inability may be a sign of depression or other mental illness and may increase the risk of suicide.
Sudden unexpected happiness	Sudden happiness, especially following prolonged depression, may indicate the person is profoundly relieved after having made a decision to commit suicide.
Sleeplessness or sleepiness	This behavior may be a sign of depression and may increase the risk of suicide.
Increased irritability or crying easily	Depressed, stressed, and potentially suicidal youths demonstrate wide mood swings and unexpected displays of emotion.
Low self-esteem	Youths with low self-esteem may consider suicide.
Abrupt changes in attendance	Remain alert to excessive absenteeism in a student with a good attendance record, particularly when the change is sudden.
Dwindling academic performance	Question unexpected and sudden decrease in performance.
Failure to complete assignments	Sudden failure is often seen in the depressed and suicidal.

TABLE 16.3 (*continued*)

Warning Signs	Discussion
Lack of interest and withdrawal	One of the first signs of potentially suicidal youth is withdrawal, disengagement, and apathy. A sudden lack of interest in extracurricular activities may be seen.
Changed relationships	Evidence of personal despair may be abrupt changes in social relationships.
Despairing attitude	Students may make comments about being unhappy, feeling like a failure, not caring about the future, or even not caring about living or dying.

Source: Adapted from *California's Helper's Handbook for Suicide Intervention,* by R. F. Ramsay, B. L. Tanney, R. J. Tierney, & W. A. Lang, 1990, Sacramento, CA: State Department of Mental Health.

females are three times more likely to attempt suicide. In contrast to males, females use far less violent and lethal means.

The causes of suicide are multidimensional. Suicide is best viewed as a collection of interacting risk factors (Brock & Sandoval, 1997), including psychopathological (mental or addictive disorders), biological, familial (family history of suicide, parental separation, etc.), and situational factors (available firearms in the home, interpersonal loss or conflict with a boyfriend or girlfriend, etc.) (Brock & Sandoval, 1997). For example, some studies suggest that alterations in brain chemistry place some youth at risk for suicide (Jurich & Collins, 1996). Personal factors associated with suicide include clinical depression and other psychiatric conditions. In fact, many clinicians believe that depression is the most powerful discriminant for suicidal behavior (National Institute of Mental Health, 2000).

Families of suicidal youth may present several problems. These include family violence, rejection, indifference, a lack of warmth or connectedness with their children, extreme rigidity or chaos, severe marital discord, and parental death or suicide (Brock & Sandoval, 1997).

Peers strongly influence the views adolescents have about themselves and how they behave. The youth who feels rejected or isolated is at risk for suicide. This is also true of youth whose romantic relationships are problematic or highly unstable (Brock & Sandoval, 1997). Another factor related to suicide in youth is sexual identity. Youth who struggle with their sexual identity and experience extreme peer rejection are vulnerable to suicide.

Generally, suicide is the culmination of serious, numerous, and long-standing problems. As a child moves into adolescence, these problems often become more serious. Findings from psychological autopsy studies suggest that 93% to 95% of adults who die by suicide met objective criteria for a mental disorder in the weeks preceding their deaths, most commonly major depression, substance abuse, and schizophrenia. Similar studies have been conducted with populations of youth. Findings suggest that drug abuse is the most common problem encountered, followed closely by depression (Brock & Sandoval, 1997; National Institute of Mental Health, 1999a).

■ INTERVENTIONS

Treatment of suicidal youth is directed at protecting them from further harm, decreasing acute suicidal tendencies, decreasing suicide risk factors, and treating mental disorders (Clark, 1997). Interventions are also aimed at enhancing factors that protect against suicidal tendencies and decrease vulnerability to repeated suicidal behavior. These interventions may include "sterilizing" the home of pills, guns, knives, razor blades, and other dangerous items. Also, driving restrictions may be included as one of the interventions. Moreover, school counseling personnel may initiate a *no-suicide* contract in which the youth commits to certain positive actions and coping strategies, particularly as they relate to situations that might evoke suicidal thoughts. These contracts may be tied to one day or several days. Counseling personnel may provide key phone numbers for obtaining assistance or support (Brock & Sandoval, 1997). Such contracts are recommended for students whose risk for suicidal behaviors is low.

Hospitalization may be the first step. Any physical injuries or complications that the youth may have suffered are addressed first. Then, a variety of professionals, together with parents, begin the planning process and implementation of treatment. Therapies directed at decreasing the problems manifested by suicide attempters include individual, peer-group, and family therapy (Clark, 1997).

Multiple levels and kinds of prevention may be implemented for youth who are suicidal. For example, crisis intervention is directed at moving youth away from imminent suicide and making referrals for appropriate treatment. In contrast, prevention programs are designed to provide early intervention, assist children and youth in developing coping skills, teach them how to manage stress, and provide counseling and other therapeutic services for children and adolescents throughout their school years (Obiakor, Mehring, & Schwenn, 1997). Prevention is a community endeavor in many ways, aimed at developing a network of social connections that give adolescents meaningful experiences with peers and other individuals. These connections may avert problems associated with loneliness and alienation.

Schools may be at risk for lawsuits if they have not developed plans for dealing with potentially harmful situations or suicide prevention. Typically, schools develop programs centered on the warning signs of suicide, legal issues, crisis management, causes of suicides, and suicide postvention issues (Brock & Sandoval, 1997).

Maternal Drug and Alcohol Abuse

■ DEFINITIONS AND CONCEPTS

Expectant mothers who use drugs place their children at risk for a variety of problems (American Academy of Pediatrics, 1995, 1998). Substance-exposed infants are affected in several ways (American Academy of Pediatrics, 1995). For example, infants exposed prenatally to cocaine exhibit low birthweights, sleeping and eating disorders, and increased irritability. Other known effects for young infants are presented in Table 16.4.

Drug abuse in parents produces other problems that affect young children. Caring for infants and young children requires a great deal of selflessness and patience. If the children's parents are primarily concerned about obtaining and using drugs, they are not able to provide the essential nurturing, stimulation, and care necessary for normal development and attachment (American Academy of Pediatrics, 1998).

■ PREVALENCE AND CAUSATION

The actual prevalence of babies directly affected by substance abuse is difficult to determine. Many expectant mothers are reluctant to reveal their substance abuse for fear that they will be prosecuted for child abuse.

Each year more than 2.6 million infants have been exposed prenatally to alcohol. Fetal alcohol syndrome (FAS) affects about 1.3 to 2.2 infants per 100 live births in

focus 13
Identify the potential effects of maternal substance abuse on the developing child.

TABLE 16.4 Known effects of prenatal drug and alcohol exposure

	Cocaine	Opiates	Alcohol
At birth	Low birthweight; small head circumference; increased muscle tone; sleeping and eating disorders; resistance to being comforted	Low birthweight; small head circumference; increased muscle tone; sleeping and eating disorders; neonatal abstinence syndrome (decreased attentional and social abilities); social responsiveness; heightened sensitivity to various stimuli; exaggerated reflexes; stuffy/runny nose; rapid respirations; apnea; chest contractions	Low birthweight; small head circumference; craniofacial malformations (small eyes or eye openings; malformed ears; poorly defined philtrum; thin upper lip or nose; flattened midfacial features; crossed eyes); heart murmurs; kidney/liver problems; undescended testicles; hernias; increased muscle tension; sleep problems; hard to comfort; reflex abnormalities; mental retardation
In childhood	*Toddler*: Lower scores on measures of development; less appropriate play; more impulsive; less securely attached *Preschooler*: Most test normally on development, language, and behavior tests; some show expressive language and behavior and organization deficits	*Toddler*: Functions normally on developmental and cognitive tests *Preschooler*: Normal results for most; some show memory, perceptual, and other cognitive deficits	Small for height or weight; alert; talkative; friendly; exhibits fluttering movements; difficulty making transitions; severe tantrums; unable to handle wide range of stimuli; difficulty attending; motor and developmental delays; learning disabilities

Source: From *Working with Children and Families Affected by Substance Abuse,* by Kathleen Pullan Watkins and Lucius Durant, Jr. Copyright 1996. Reprinted with permission of Prentice-Hall/Center for Applied Research in Education.

the United States. Moreover, 11% of all newborns have been exposed to illicit drugs. Every year more than 739,000 expectant mothers use one or more illicit drugs during their pregnancies (National Adoption Information Clearinghouse, 1999).

About 15% of the women of childbearing age are substance abusers. Research conducted by the National Association of Perinatal Addiction Research and Education suggests that about 11% of pregnant women use illicit drugs, most of whom use cocaine during their pregnancies (Bellenir, 1996).

Cocaine is inexpensive, readily available, easily ingested, and highly addictive. In fact, it is the drug of choice for many substance abusers. Because of the low molecular weight of cocaine, it readily crosses the placenta to the developing fetus or child. Also, cocaine easily passes through the blood–brain barrier, thereby altering the chemistry and functioning of the brain. Cocaine may also be passed from the mother to the child through her breast milk. The regular presence of cocaine in the developing fetus or child impacts its development and functioning in a variety of detrimental ways (see Figure 16.4).

■ INTERVENTIONS

Implementing interventions for mothers and their babies who have been exposed to drugs is a challenging and complex process, particularly if the mother is

FIGURE 16.4

The effects of maternal cocaine use on mothers and fetuses/babies

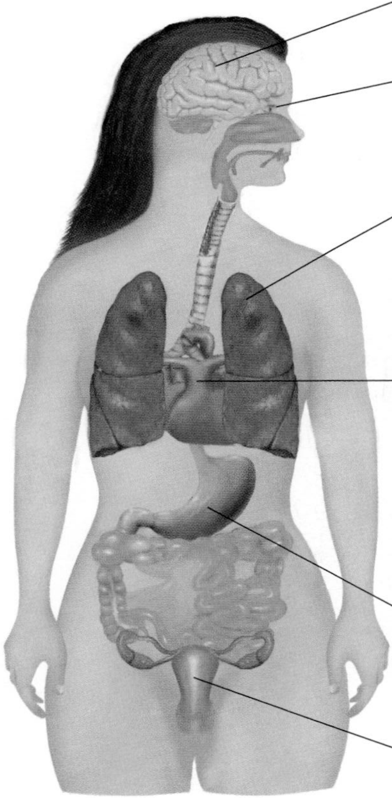

Mother		Fetus/Baby	
Neurological system	Seizures *Neural damage Insomnia	Neurological system	Increased irritability Increased startle response Difficult to console Tremors Jittery
Eyes	Retinal crystals causing flashes of light called snow lights	Eyes	*Eye defects
Respiratory system	Shortness of breath Lung damage, if smoked Nasal membrane burns and lesions Respiratory paralysis in overdose	Respiratory system	Increased respiratory rate Abnormal ventilatory patterns
Cardiovascular system	Acute hypertension Angina Arrhythmias Tachycardia[a] Palpitations Cerebral artery injury/cerebrovascular accident Cardiac failure	Cardiovascular system	*Increased risk for sudden infant death syndrome Intrauterine growth retardation Tachycardia *Cerebral artery injury/infarction[b] *Acute hypertension[b]
Gastrointestinal system	Sore throat Hoarseness Anorexia leading to weight loss and malnutrition	Gastrointestinal system	Diarrhea Poor tolerance for oral feeding *Prune-belly syndrome[c]
Reproductive system	Increased uterine contractility Abruptio placentae Spontaneous abortion Premature labor Stillbirth	Renal system	*Hydronephrosis[d]
		Reproductive system	*Cryptorchidism[e]

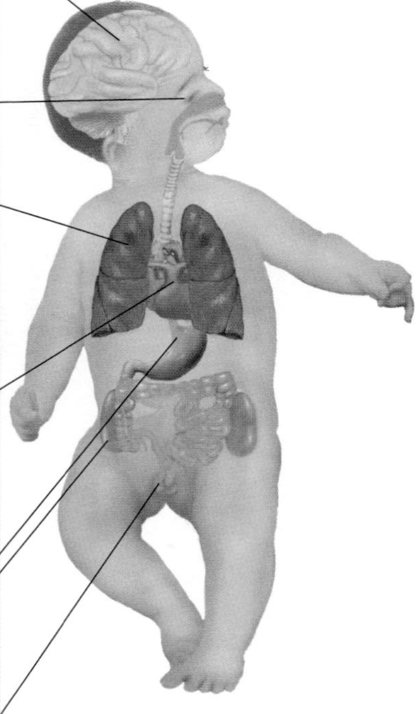

* Suspected but not established
[a] Abnormally high heart rate
[b] An episode of dangerously high blood pressure
[c] Abdominal musculature does not develop, resulting in a stomach that protrudes
[d] Swollen kidney(s)
[e] Testicles remain in the abdominal cavity

[Source: From "The Dangers of Prenatal Cocaine Use," by J. Smith, 1988, American Journal of Maternal Child Nursing 13(3), p. 175. Copyright 1988 by American Journal of Maternal Child Nursing.]

addicted. Mothers with serious drug abuse histories may need as much treatment as their affected infants. In fact, often, mothers may need more assistance. Think for a moment about being a pediatrician, faced with the decision of releasing an infant who is at risk and needs sophisticated care to a mother suspected of drug abuse. What action would you take? Some babies are initially placed with grandparents or other caregivers until their mothers are capable of caring for them.

Educationally oriented treatments for preschoolers affected by substance abuse focus on designing well-structured learning environments, creating small classes (eight children per teacher), and providing developmentally appropriate learning environments that are child-sized, visually interesting, and suitably stimulating. These environments also provide learning activities that are experiential rather than paper-and-pencil tasks. Programs for school-age children are beginning to emerge as practitioners and researchers learn more about the effects of substance abuse on the development and performance of young children.

Comprehensive models of treatment for drug-abusing women and their children are emerging. These models include intake screening and comprehensive health assessment; medical interventions for mothers, their children, and other family members; early intervention services for drug-exposed infants and toddlers; home-based support; counseling for HIV and AIDS; linkages to other service providers for outreach, residential, and outpatient services; substance abuse and psychological counseling; parenting education; health education; life skills education; training and remediation services; child care services; transportation support; housing assistance; and continuing care after intensive forms of therapies and interventions have been applied (Department of Health and Human Services, 1999).

Case Study

LIVING WITH CEREBRAL PALSY

I do not know many scientific facts about CP (cerebral palsy), but I do know how it has affected my life. This is what I want to share with you. I hope it will help you to better understand people with CP.

When I was young, having cerebral palsy was never an issue in our home. I was treated no differently than my brothers or sisters. However, things changed when I started school. The first few years of school were great, to the best of my recollection. I was probably in the 3rd or 4th grade when I became aware that children, in their innocence, can be cruel. I wore a brace on my leg and was faced with much teasing and ridicule. This caused me to become shy and introverted. I did not easily make friends and still don't!

My grandfather liked to take walks on sunny afternoons, so one day I went with him and was having a very pleasant time until we saw someone walking toward us. My grandpa made me change sides so that it would be harder to see that his granddaughter had cerebral palsy. That was a very hurtful thing to learn. I realized that he was ashamed of me.

A person should be judged by their heart and not by their looks. I have learned to judge myself harshly and I strive for perfection in all I attempt to do. Needless to say, I constantly fail miserably! It is easier to not try than fail.

I need to learn to like me even with all my many imperfections. I need to learn that it is okay that not everyone I meet will like me.

■ APPLICATION
1. Given what you have learned about children and youth with disabilities and their families, how would you as a teacher help your students without disabilities treat children with disabilities well? How do we help children look beyond the outward appearance?
2. How would you help your grandparents respond well to a new grandchild with a challenging disability?
3. How would you help a child with a disability deal with the teasing that is often delivered by other children? How do we help children with disabilities become resilient and appropriately optimistic?

Source: Adapted from "Living with cerebral palsy," Author, 2000. Available at *http://www.geocities.com/ Athens/Ithaca/2418/cp.html*

Debate Forum

AIDS AND THE PUBLIC SCHOOLS

Guillermo is a first-grader. Unless you knew him well, you would assume that he was a very normal kid. He likes cold drinks and pizza and watches cartoons every Saturday morning.

In school, he performs reasonably well. He's not an academic superstar, but he is learning to read and write quite well. His teacher likes him and says that he is quite sociable for his age and size. Guillermo is a little on the small side, but he doesn't let that get in the way of his enjoying most things in life.

Since his foster parents have had him, he has been quite happy. The crying and whining that characterized his first weeks in their home have disappeared. He is now pretty much a part of the family.

His older foster brother, John, likes him a lot. John and Guillermo spend a good deal of time together. They are about 16 months apart in age. John is a second-grader and a mighty good one at that. He has always excelled in school, and he loves to help Guillermo when he can.

Guillermo, from day one of his placement, has been ill regularly. He has one infection after another. Of course, his foster parents knew that this would be the case, since Guillermo has AIDS. His biological mother could not care for him, as she was a drug addict and has AIDS herself.

Keeping a secret is sometimes very hard, and such was the case for John. From the very beginning of Guillermo's placement in his home, John knew that there was something special about him. His parents have talked to him about Guillermo and his condition. It was a family decision to have Guillermo live in their home. John is often scared, not for himself but for Guillermo. He wonders how long he will be able to play with his young friend and constant companion. Also, it is often hard to keep the family secret about Guillermo.

Guillermo attends the neighborhood school. Those who are aware of his condition are his classmates, their parents, his teacher, the principal, the school board members, and, of course, John. Just about everyone kept the secret at first, and Guillermo was well received by the overwhelming majority of his classmates. He played with them, enjoyed stories with them, and had a good wrestle now and then with some of the boys in his class.

Over time, other parents and students learned about Guillermo's condition, and a big uproar ensued about his being in school. The PTA was divided. The principal was in favor of Guillermo's continued attendance, but a few vocal parents began a petition to have Guillermo taught by a teacher for the homebound.

■ POINT

Given our current knowledge about the ways in which AIDS is spread in adults and children, there is no reason to remove Guillermo from his neighborhood school. His behavior and physical condition do not place other children at risk for acquiring the HIV virus or developing AIDS.

■ COUNTERPOINT

With the limited knowledge we have about AIDS and its transmission, we should not let children with AIDS or the HIV virus attend neighborhood schools. We should wait until we know a great deal more about the disease. The potential risks for other children are too great and far reaching.

Review

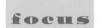 **focus 1**

Why are many individuals with cerebral palsy considered multidisabled?

- Often, individuals with cerebral palsy have several disabilities, including hearing impairments, speech and language disorders, intellectual deficits, visual impairments, and general perceptual problems.

 focus 2

What is spina bifida myelomeningocele?

- Spina bifida myelomeningocele is a defect in the spinal column. This type of spina bifida presents itself in the form of a tumorlike sac on the back of the infant, which contains spinal fluid and nerve tissue.
- Myelomeningocele is also the most serious variety of spina bifida in that it generally includes paralysis or partial paralysis of certain body areas, causing lack of bowel and bladder control.

 focus 3

Identify specific treatments for individuals with spinal cord injuries.

- Immediate pharmacological interventions are needed, with high and frequent doses of methylprednisolone. These doses reduce the severity of the injury and improve the functional outcome over time.
- Stabilization of the spine is critical to the overall outcome of the injury.
- Once the spine has been stabilized, the rehabilitation process begins. Physi-

---

cal therapy helps the affected individual make full use of any and all residual muscle strength.

- The individual is also taught to use orthopedic devices, such as hand-splints, braces, reachers, headsticks, and other augmentative devices.
- Psychological adjustment is aided by psychiatric and psychological personnel.
- Rehabilitation specialists aid the individual in becoming retrained or reeducated; they may also help in securing employment.
- Some individuals will need part-time or full-time attendant care for assistance with daily activities (e.g., bathing, dressing, and shopping).

 **focus 4**

Describe the physical limitations associated with muscular dystrophy.

- Individuals with muscular dystrophy progressively lose their ability to walk and use their arms and hands effectively because fatty tissue begins to replace muscle tissue.

 focus 5

What steps should be taken to assist infants and children with AIDS?

- Infants and children should be provided with the most effective medical care available, particularly care addressed as controlling opportunistic infections with appropriate medications.
- Children with AIDS should attend school unless they

exhibit behaviors that are dangerous to others or are at risk for developing infectious diseases that would exacerbate their condition.

 focus 6

Describe immediate treatment for a person who is experiencing a tonic/clonic seizure.

- Cushion the head.
- Loosen tight neck tie or collar.
- Turn the person onto his or her side.
- Put nothing in the mouth of the individual.
- Look for identification.
- Don't hold the person down.
- As seizure ends, offer help.

 focus 7

Identify three problems that individuals with diabetes may eventually experience.

- Structural abnormalities that occur over time may result in blindness, cardiovascular disease, and kidney disease.

 focus 8

Identify present and future interventions for the treatment of children and youth with cystic fibrosis.

- Drug therapy for prevention and treatment of chest infections
- Diet management, use of replacement enzymes for food absorption, and vitamin intake
- Family education regarding the condition

- Chest physiotherapy and postural drainage
- Inhalation therapy
- Psychological and psychiatric counseling
- Use of mucus-thinning drugs, gene therapy, and lung or lung/heart transplant

 focus 9

Describe the impact of the sickling of cells on body tissues.

- Sickled cells are more rigid than normal cells; as such, they frequently block microvascular channels. The blockage of channels reduces or terminates circulation in these areas, and tissues in need of blood nutrients and oxygen die.

 focus 10

Identify five factors that may contribute to child abuse and neglect.

- Unemployment, poverty, and substance abuse
- Isolation from natural and community support networks
- Marital/relationship problems
- Having a particularly challenging, needy, or demanding infant
- Poor impulse control

 focus 11

Identify factors that may contribute to the increased prevalence of adolescent pregnancy.

- General factors include a lack of knowledge about conception and sexuality, a desire to escape family

control, an attempt to be more adult, a desire to have someone to love, a means of gaining attention and love, and an inability to make sound decisions.

- Societal factors include greater sexual permissiveness and freedom, social pressure from peers, and continual exposure to sexuality through the media.

 focus 12

Identify the major causes of youth suicide.

- The causes of suicide are multidimensional. These causes involve biological, personal, family, peer, and community factors.
- Alterations in brain chemistry put some individuals at risk for suicide.
- Often, clinical depression or other psychiatric conditions precede suicide.
- Other causative factors include extreme peer rejection, problems with sexual identity, and substance abuse.

 focus 13

Identify the potential effects of maternal substance abuse on the developing child.

- The effects include low birth weight, sleeping and eating disorders, heightened sensitivity, and challenging temperaments
- Children exposed to cocaine are at greater risk for neurological problems, eye defects, respiratory problems, cardiovascular complications, and other health problems.

People Who Are Gifted, Creative, and Talented

To begin with . . .

The general objects— are to provide an education adapted to the years, the capacity, and the condition of everyone, and directed to their freedom and happiness—We hope to avail the state of those talented which nature has sown as liberally among the poor as the rich, but which perish without use, if not sought for and cultivated. (Thomas Jefferson, *Notes on Virginia*)

"Dear Adam and Eve,
Did you guys feel yourself being created? What did you eat besides the apple you weren't supposed to eat? Tell me, how did you keep fit and trim? Where is the garden now?" (Interview composed by Samantha W., age 8, in a class for gifted and talented children.)

Renda F. Subotnick: What role can families play in supporting their talented child?
Vladimir Feltsman: Huge. It's impossible to develop a child's musical talent without the parents' support, especially here in the United States. There has to be a certain understanding of what the child is doing and what he or she needs, like time for concentration and privacy. Families must provide instruments, and certain sacrifices have to be made. It's not great fun to listen to someone practice, especially violin. (Vladimir Feltsman, piano virtuoso and educational innovator, cited in Subotnik, 1997, p. 313)

As many as 540,000 children and youth with disabilities may be gifted (Johnson, Karnes, & Carr, 1997)

Gifted and talented students can be found in any community in this country. They come from all kinds of ethnic, cultural, and socioeconomic backgrounds. They are boys and girls. They may have disabilities. Most families rely on the public schools to meet the educational needs of their gifted and talented students. They do not have the resources to do otherwise. Therefore, it is critically important that public schools have access to the research about how these students learn so that all gifted and talented students will have an opportunity to excel because they have access to an appropriate education.

When appropriate gifted and talented programs are not provided in the public schools, only children in wealthy families will have access to the challenging curriculum they need.

When these students do not learn in school because of the lack of programs, learning must take place at home or in private schools. In such cases families must decide either to have one parent stay home or to pay for private school. Either choice requires resources that most families do not have. (Christensen, 1999)

529

Snapshot

Dwight

Dwight spends most of his time in a variety of creative business endeavors. For nearly 18 years he served as a senior executive and board member of a publicly traded communications firm that specialized in the delivery of business information via satellite, FM wireless, cable, and Internet technologies. Dwight has been a pioneer in developing and utilizing these technologies for videoconferencing, data transfer, and advertising in businesses throughout North America.

Dwight is an exceptionally talented musician, composer, and arranger, aided in part by a rare phenomenon known as "perfect pitch." He began his professional career performing with the New Christy Minstrels, based in Los Angeles. He soon became their musical director and continued to arrange music for the group long after he left their performing ranks. Subsequently, Dwight was hired by the Osmond family. During several years of association there, he became responsible for the music coordination and contracting of numerous projects, including the *Donny & Marie Show* for ABC television as well as several other network specials and syndicated programs. Dwight's musical arrangements have been played on programs such as *The Tonight Show, The Bob Hope 80th Anniversary Special, The Suzanne Sommers Special,* and numerous other national programs. His vocal talent has been heard on commercials and television products on a national basis, including work for ABC television and the Disney Channel.

As a youngster, Dwight's siblings and classmates referred to him as "the little professor" or "Doc." Throughout his school years, Dwight easily mastered the content in his classes, from science to math to creative writing. His interests were broad, including four stints as a student body or class officer. He finished high school with scholarship offers from several colleges and universities as well as recognition by the local newspaper as one of the top three scholars statewide in his field.

■ GIFTED, CREATIVE, AND TALENTED. Terms applied to those with extraordinary abilities in one or more areas and capable of superior performance.

■ MENTAL AGE. A concept used in psychological assessment that relates to the general mental ability possessed by a child or youth of a given chronological age.

■ STANFORD-BINET INDIVIDUAL INTELLIGENCE SCALE. A standardized individual intelligence test, originally known as the Binet-Simon Scales, which was revised and standardized by Lewis Terman at Stanford University.

■ INTELLIGENCE QUOTIENT (IQ). A score obtained from an intelligence test that provides a measure of mental ability in relation to age.

THE TERMS GIFTED, CREATIVE, AND TALENTED are associated with people who have extraordinary abilities in one or more areas of performance. In many cases, we admire such individuals and occasionally are a little envious of their talents. The ease with which they are able to master diverse and difficult concepts is impressive. Because of their unusual abilities and skills, educators and policy makers frequently assume that these individuals will reach their full potential without any specialized programs or assistance.

For many years, behavioral scientists described children with exceptionally high intelligence as being **gifted.** Only recently have researchers and practitioners included the adjectives **creative** and **talented** in their descriptions, to suggest domains of performance other than those measured by traditional intelligence tests. Capacities associated with creativity include *elaboration,* the ability to embellish or enrich an idea; *transformation,* the ability to construct new meanings or change an idea into something new and novel; and *visualization,* the capacity to mentally manipulate ideas or images. Individuals who are talented display extraordinary skills in mathematics, sports, music, or other performance areas. Dwight is one of those individuals who is gifted, creative, and talented (see the chapter opening snapshot). Not only did he excel in intellectual (traditional academic) endeavors, but he also exhibited tremendous prowess with regard to producing and performing music. Certainly, the behaviors and traits associated with these terms interact to produce the various constellations of gift-edness. Some individuals soar to exceptional heights in the talent domain, others achieve in intellectual areas, and still others excel in creative endeavors. Furthermore, a select few exhibit remarkable levels of behavior and achievement across several domains or areas.

Historical Background

Definitions describing the unusually able in terms of intelligence quotients and creativity measures are recent phenomena. Not until the beginning of the 20th century was there a suitable method for quantifying or measuring the human attribute of intelligence (Clark, 1997). The breakthrough occurred in Europe when Alfred Binet, a French psychologist, constructed the first developmental assessment scale for children in the early 1900s. This scale was created by observing children at various ages to identify specific tasks that ordinary children were able to perform at each age. These tasks were then sequenced according to age-appropriate levels. Children who could perform tasks well above that which was normal for their chronological age were identified as being developmentally advanced.

Binet and Simon (1905, 1908) developed the notion of **mental age.** The mental age of a child was derived by matching the tasks (memory, vocabulary, mathematical, comprehension, etc.) the child was able to perform according to the age scale (typical performance of children at various stages). Although this scale was initially developed and used to identify children with mental retardation in the Parisian schools, it eventually became an important means for identifying those who had higher than average mental ages, as well.

Lewis M. Terman, an American educator and psychologist, expanded the concepts and procedures developed by Binet. He was convinced that Binet and Simon had developed an approach for measuring intellectual abilities in all children. This belief prompted him to revise the Binet instrument, adding greater breadth to the scale. In 1916, Terman published the **Stanford-Binet Intelligence Scale** in conjunction with Stanford University. During this period, Terman developed the term **intelligence quotient,** or **IQ.** The IQ score was obtained by dividing a child's mental age by his or her chronological age and multiplying that figure by 100 (MA/CA **x** 100 = IQ). For example, a child with a mental age of 12 and a chronological age of 8 would have an IQ of 150 (12/8 **x** 100 = 150).

Gradually, other researchers became interested in studying the nature and assessment of intelligence. They tended to view intelligence as an underlying ability or capacity that expressed itself in a variety of ways. The unitary IQ scores that were derived from the Stanford-Binet tests were representative of and contributed to this notion.

Over time, however, other researchers came to believe that intellect was represented by a variety of distinct capacities and abilities (Cattell, 1971; Guilford, 1959). This line of thinking suggested that each distinct intellectual capacity could be identified and assessed. Several mental abilities were investigated, including memory capacity, divergent thinking, vocabulary usage, and reasoning ability (see Figure 17.1). Gradually, use of the multiple ability approach outgrew that of the unitary intelligence notion. Its proponents were convinced that the universe of intellectual functions was extensive, that the intelligence assessment instruments utilized at that time measured a very small portion of an individual's true intellectual capacities.

focus **1**
Briefly describe several historical developments directly related to the measurement of various types of giftedness.

Lewis Terman

Snapshot

Eduardo

Eduardo and his family are recent immigrants to the United States. At age 10, he has become quite adept at speaking English. His primary language is Spanish. He is the oldest of seven children.

Eduardo's father is a supervisor on a large farm in southern California. With a lot of effort, he developed sufficient English skills to be of great value to farm owners who now employ him full time. They have hired him to work directly with migrant workers who regularly assist with the harvest of various kinds of produce and fruit. He is also skilled mechanically and, in the off-season, repairs equipment and farm machinery.

Eduardo's schooling has been quite irregular until the past two years. Prior to having a stable residence, he traveled with his family up and down the West Coast of the United States, like many migrant families.

Eduardo's schoolmates really enjoy him. He has lots of friends and is invited frequently to birthday parties and social events. He seems to have a real knack for making friends and having adults like him.

Eduardo's parents view him as being especially alert and bright. He seems to be interested in many topics and is rarely bored. At the moment, he is intrigued with tractors. His mother indicates that he always "questioned her to death." Moreover, he seems to be capable of easily entertaining himself. Recently, he spent an entire afternoon looking through a farm magazine and drawing farm equipment that caught his attention.

Since the beginning of this school year, Eduardo has made phenomenal gains in reading, math, and English. In fact, he has become an avid reader of both Spanish and English books that are available at his school. Although it has been difficult to assess his innate ability, he appears to be a child of some promise, intellectually and socially. However, his parents are worried about providing him with the necessary resources to fully utilize his curiosity and ability. They are also concerned about his late start with consistent schooling.

One of the key contributors to the multidimensional theory regarding intelligence was J. P. Guilford (1950, 1959). He saw intelligence as a diverse range of intellectual and creative abilities. Guilford's work led many researchers to consider intelligence more than a broad, unitary ability and to focus their scientific efforts on the emerging field of creativity and its various subcomponents, such as divergent thinking, problem solving, and decision making. Gradually, tests or measures of creativity were developed, using the constructs drawn from models created by Guilford and others.

FIGURE 17.1

Guilford's structure of the intellect model. Each little cube represents a unique combination of one kind of operation, one kind of content, and one kind of product, and hence a distinctly different intellectual ability or function.

[*Source:* From *Way Beyond the IQ: Guide to Improving Intelligence and Creativity* (p. 151), by J. P. Guilford, 1977, Buffalo, NY: Creative Education Foundation. Copyright 1977 by Creative Education Foundation. Reprinted by permission.]

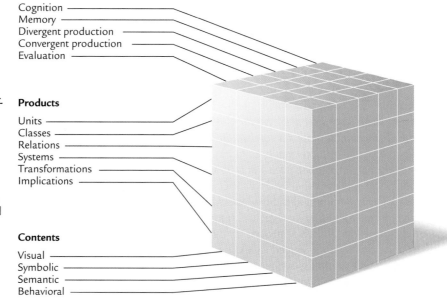

Operations
Cognition
Memory
Divergent production
Convergent production
Evaluation

Products
Units
Classes
Relations
Systems
Transformations
Implications

Contents
Visual
Symbolic
Semantic
Behavioral

In summary, conceptions of giftedness during the early 1920s were closely tied to the score that an individual obtained on an intelligence test. Thus, a single score, an IQ, was the index by which one was identified as being gifted. Commencing with the work of Guilford (1950, 1959) and Torrance (1961, 1965, 1968), notions regarding giftedness were greatly expanded. Giftedness began to refer not only to those with high IQs but also to those who demonstrated high aptitude on creativity measures such as Torrance Tests of Creative Thinking (Torrance, 1966), PRIDE (Preschool and Primary Interest Descriptor, Rimm, 1982), Sternberg Triarchic Abilities Test (Sternberg, 1993), and GIFT (Gift Inventory for Finding Talent, Rimm & Davis, 1983). More recently, the term *talented* has been added to the descriptors associated with giftedness. As a result, individuals who demonstrate remarkable skills in the visual or performing arts or who excel in other areas of performance may be designated as gifted. (See Figure 17.2.)

Currently, there is no federal mandate in the United States requiring educational services for students identified as gifted, as is the case with other exceptional conditions. Some funding is provided through the federal government through the Jacob K. Javits Gifted and Talented Students Act. This act supports a national research center, demonstration programs, and activities for leadership personnel throughout the United States (Feldhusen, 1998a; Gallagher, 1997). The actual funding of services for individuals who are gifted is a state-by-state, local challenge, and as such, there is tremendous variability in the quality and types of programs offered to students (see the nearby Reflect on This feature). "Local-level programming in the 1990s might be characterized as embattled, dealing with reduced staff and funding as well as reduced philosophical support for special programs [for the gifted]" (VanTassal-Baska, 1998e, p. 10). Much of this embattlement has been attributed to the movement away from grouping students for instruction, particularly gifted students (Davis & Rimm, 1998).

In coming years, we will probably see the emergence of the designation *talent development* rather than gifted education. This description suggests a kind of programming that is directed at all students, not just the so-called gifted (Davis & Rimm, 1998; VanTassel-Baska, 1998e).

Definitions and Concepts

Definitions of giftedness have been influenced by a variety of innovative and knowledgeable individuals (Cattell, 1971; Gardner, 1983; Guilford, 1959; Ramos-Ford & Gardner, 1997; Sternberg, 1997b; Torrance, 1966). As you will discover, there is no generally accepted definition of giftedness (Davis & Rimm, 1998). The Javits Gifted and Talented Education Act defines giftedness as follows:

focus 2
Identify six major components of definitions that have been developed to describe giftedness.

Children and youth with outstanding talent perform or show the potential for performing at remarkably high levels of accomplishment when compared with others of their age, experience, or environment.

These children and youth exhibit high performance capability in intellectual, creative, and/or artistic areas, possess an unusual leadership capacity, or excel in specific academic fields. They require services or activities not ordinarily provided by the schools.

Outstanding talents are present in children and youth from all cultural groups, across all economic strata, and in all areas of human endeavor. (U.S. Department of Education, 1993, p. 3)

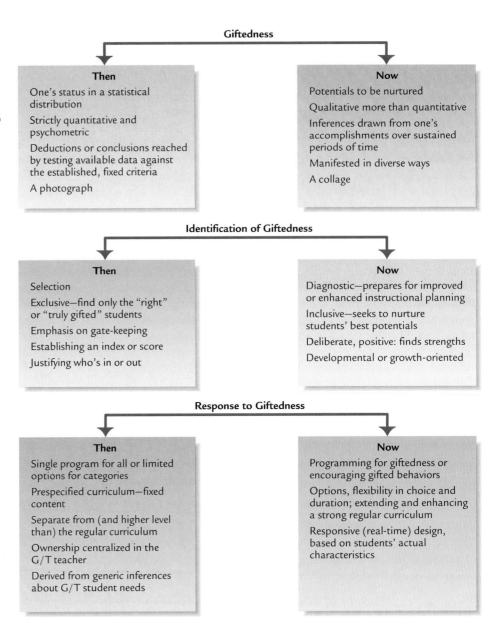

This definition helped schools and school personnel achieve a variety of important objectives. They include identifying a variety of students across disciplines with diverse talents, using many different kinds of assessment measures to identify gifted students, providing students of all backgrounds with equal access to opportunities to develop their potential, identifying capacities not readily apparent in some students, and taking into account students' drives and passions for achievement in various areas.

Tannenbaum (1997), a renowned authority in gifted education, has developed a new definition for giftedness in children:

Keeping in mind that developed talent exists only in adults, I propose a definition of giftedness in children to denote their potential for becoming critically acclaimed performers or exemplary producers of ideas in spheres of activity that enhance moral, physical, emotional, social, intellectual, or aesthetic life of humanity.

John is just a few days away from being 11 years old. On the Washington Pre-College Test (WPC), a test for college-bound high school seniors, he recently scored at the 80th percentile on the verbal portion and at the 10th percentile on the quantitative portion. For the past two years, he has been enrolled at California State University, Los Angeles (CSULA), taking math and other college-level courses. During this time period, he has endeavored to improve his math performance. John has been enrolled in an excellent program for students who are gifted in his junior high; however, he finds his university classes to be more challenging and varied.

John's initial experiences with his university course work were fraught with problems. His elementary school training had not provided him with any skill in taking notes. His parents, however, were and are very supportive. When they discovered that he was having difficulty in taking notes, his mother obtained permission to attend some of his courses with him. They both took notes and then made comparisons each day after class. Within three weeks, John had mastered the skill and was well on his way to becoming a competent note taker.

When he first began his university work, John viewed himself as being a "mathematical moron" because of his low entry scores on the WPC. The change in his self-perception as a mathematician came when he enrolled in a chemistry course at CSULA. It really captured his attention and interest. He soon discovered that an understanding of algebra was central to succeeding in the course. Motivated by this discovery, he soon became proficient in algebra. In his most recent test, he scored at the 70th percentile on the quantitative portion of the WPC.

John's general feelings about himself and his capacity fluctuated a lot after his early entrance to college. Sometimes he felt overconfident and other times discouraged. Now he has a realistic view of his strengths and weaknesses and is pursuing his university course work with a balanced perspective on himself.

This fall, John will enroll full time as a college student. He is now 14 and has a full year of college credit under his belt. By the time he is 15 he will be a junior. Today, he is probably thinking about the graduate school he would like to attend after finishing his bachelor's degree.

In detailing this proposed definition as it pertains to childhood promise, it is useful to answer three basic questions about giftedness in its maturity, most often in adulthood.

1. *Who qualifies to join the pool of possibly gifted individuals?*
2. *What broad realms of achievement among pool members are judged for signs of excellence?*
3. *How do pool members demonstrate their giftedness in these domains of human accomplishment? (Tannenbaum, 1997, p. 27)*

Tannenbaum (1997) believes that there are two types of gifted individuals, performers and producers. (See Table 17.1.) Performers provide "staged artistry" or highly skilled "human services" (p. 27). Producers, on the other hand, generate remarkable "thoughts" and "tangibles" (p. 27). What makes these individuals extraordinary or gifted? Tannenbaum believes that such individuals prove their excellence through "proficiency" and "creativity" (p. 27).

New conceptualizations of giftedness and intelligence have recently emerged from theoretical and research literature (Ramos-Ford & Gardner, 1997; Sternberg, 1997). One of the new approaches to intelligence is Sternberg's triarchic theory of human intelligence (Sternberg, 1997a), according to which intellectual performance is divided into three parts: analytic, synthetic, and practical. Analytic intelligence is exhibited by people who perform well on aptitude and intelligence tests. Individuals with synthetic giftedness are unconventional thinkers who are creative, intuitive, and insightful. People with practical intelligence are extraordinarily adept in dealing with problems of everyday life and those presented in their work environments.

Who	What	How	Who	What	How
Producer	Thoughts	Creativity Proficiency	Performer	Staged artistry	Creativity Proficiency
	Tangibles	Creativity Proficiency		Human services	Creativity Proficiency

Source: From "The Meaning and Making of Giftedness," by A. Tannenbaum. In *Handbook of Gifted Education,* edited by N. Colangelo & G. Davis, 1997, p. 28. Copyright © 1997 by Allyn and Bacon. Reprinted by permission.

Another conceptualization of giftedness or talent development has been proposed by Gagné (1999a). It centers on catalysts that have both positive and negative impacts (see Figure 17.3). These catalysts (intrapersonal and environmental) shape and influence developmental processes that give rise to talents. It is clear from this conceptualization of giftedness that the emergence of talent(s) is dependent on environmental, motivational, and interpersonal factors (Piirto, 1999). Gagné has also recommended the reexamination of IQ thresholds by which giftedness would be defined; the development of subcategories of talents such as musical improvisation, mechanical prowess, and social precocity; and acknowledgment of talents in non-traditional areas of performance including cooking, building, and farming (Piirto, 1999). These recommendations as suggested by Gagné would democratize the field of gifted education, giving many more children and youth opportunities for talent development (Gagné, 1999b).

Another emerging view of giftedness has been developed by Ramos-Ford and Gardner (1997). They have defined intelligence or giftedness as "an ability or set of

Snapshot

Jon

Jon worked with the first- and second-grade class for gifted students for half of his kindergarten time each day. By the end of kindergarten, he was reading at a fourth-grade level and doing math far advanced for his age. The individualized math program in which he participated in first grade enabled him to complete the third-grade book by the end of the year. By fourth grade, he took algebra I at the middle school, and in fifth grade he took advanced geometry at the high school. By the end of eighth grade, he completed advanced placement (AP) calculus and had earned a 5 on the AP test. During high school, he completed three more college-level math courses through a correspondence program.

"I know that without the school's advanced study program, Jon would not have been able to excel at the level he has," his mother said. "The aspect for which I am most grateful is that while he has had the opportunity to work at his own level in most subjects, he has also been with his age-mates in all classes except mathematics."

Alicia

Alicia is a 5-year-old African American who lives in central Harlem. She is one of 11 children under the age of 13. Her mother is addicted to crack, and her absentee father is an alcoholic.

Despite the daily challenges that face Alicia, she is a survivor. Her academic profile is astonishing: she can carry out sophisticated math computations, is teaching herself to read, can weave imaginative stories, and is passionate about playing card games with her teacher in the Project Synergy Summer Program at Teachers College. Her stan-dardized math assessment places her in the 85th percentile, despite her difficult home environment and low-achieving school.

Source: From *National Excellence: A Case for Developing America's Talent,* 1993, the U.S. Department of Education, Office of Education Research and Improvement.

FIGURE 17.3

Catalysts for the development of gifts and talents

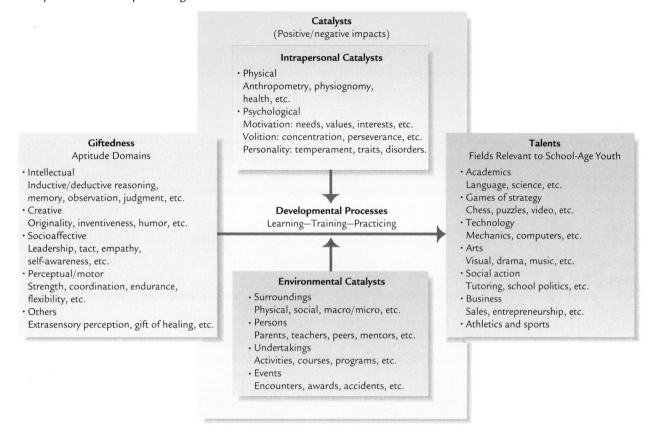

[*Source:* From "Is There Any Light at the End of the Tunnel?" by F. Gagné, 1999, *Journal of the Education of the Gifted, 22*(2), pp. 191-234.]

abilities that permit an individual to solve problems or fashion products that are of consequence in a particular cultural setting" (Ramos-Ford & Gardner, 1991, p. 56). This perspective of giftedness is referred to as the theory of multiple intelligences. Intelligence manifests itself in linguistic, logical–mathematical, spatial, musical, bodily–kinesthetic, interpersonal, and intrapersonal behaviors. Table 17.2 provides a brief definition of each behavior as well as the child and adult roles associated with each type of intelligence.

More recently, Piirto has developed a pyramid of talent development that details various aspects of talent development (see Figure 17.4).

She defines the "'gifted' . . . as those individuals who by way of learning characteristics such as superior memory, observational powers, curiosity, creativity, and the ability to learn school-related subject matters rapidly and accurately with a minimum of drill and repetition, have a right to an education that is differentiated according to their needs. These children become apparent early and should be served through their educational lives, from preschool through college" (p. 28).

The definitions of giftedness have moved from unitary measures of IQ as the major measure of an individual's potential giftedness to multiple measures of cre-

TABLE 17.2   The seven intelligences

Intelligence	Brief Description	Related Child and Adult Roles
Linguistic	The capacity to express oneself in spoken or written language with great facility	Superb storyteller, creative writer, or inventive speaker: Novelist, lyricist, lawyer
Logical–mathematical	The ability to reason inductively and deductively, to complete complex computations	Thorough counter, calculator, notation maker, or symbol user: Mathematician, physicist, computer scientist
Spatial	The capacity to create, manipulate, and represent spatial configurations	Creative builder, sculptor, artist, or skilled assembler of models: Architect, talented chess player, mechanic, navigator
Bodily–kinesthetic	The ability to perform various complex tasks or activities with one's body or part of the body	Skilled playground game player, emerging athlete or dancer: Surgeon, dancer, professional athlete
Musical	The capacity to discriminate musical pitches, hear musical themes, sense rhythm, timbre, and texture	Good singer, creator of original songs or musical pieces: Musician, composer, director
Interpersonal	The ability to understand others' actions, emotions, and intents, and to act effectively in response to verbal and nonverbal behaviors of others	Child organizer or orchestrator, child leader, or a very social child: Teacher, therapist, political social leader
Intrapersonal	The capacity to understand well and respond to one's own thoughts, desires, feelings, and emotions	A sensitive child, a resilient child, or an optimistic child: Social worker, therapist, counselor, hospice worker

ativity, problem solving ability, talent, and intelligence. However, despite the movement away from IQ scores and other changes in definitions of giftedness, critics argue that many, if not most, local, district, and state definitions are elitist in nature and favor the "affluent" and "privileged" (Margolin, 1996; Richert, 1997).

Capturing the essence of any human condition in a definition can be very perplexing. This is certainly the case in defining the human attributes, abilities, and potentialities that constitute giftedness. Definitions do serve a number of important purposes, however. For example, definitions may have a profound influence on the following: the number of students ultimately selected, the types of instruments and selection procedures utilized, the scores an individual must obtain in order to qualify for specialized instruction, the types of education provided, the amount of funding required to provide services, and the types of training individuals need to teach the gifted and talented. The problems of definition and description are not easily resolved, yet such efforts are vital to both research and practice (Gagné, 1999b).

Prevalence

Determining the number of children who are gifted is a challenging matter. The complexity of the task is directly related to problems inherent in determining who is gifted and what constitutes giftedness (Richert, 1997). The numerous definitions of giftedness range from being quite restric-

FIGURE 17.4

The Piirto pyramid of talent development

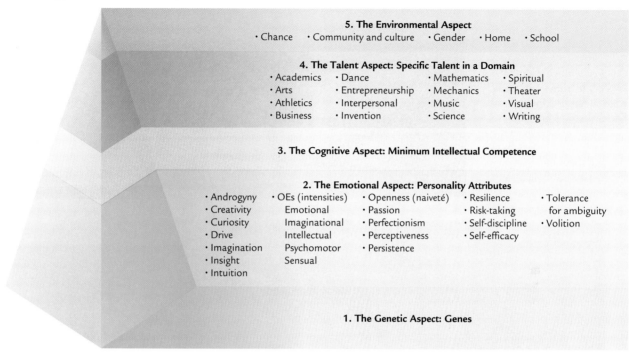

5. The Environmental Aspect
· Chance   · Community and culture   · Gender   · Home   · School

4. The Talent Aspect: Specific Talent in a Domain
· Academics   · Dance   · Mathematics   · Spiritual
· Arts   · Entrepreneurship   · Mechanics   · Theater
· Athletics   · Interpersonal   · Music   · Visual
· Business   · Invention   · Science   · Writing

3. The Cognitive Aspect: Minimum Intellectual Competence

2. The Emotional Aspect: Personality Attributes
· Androgyny   · OEs (intensities)   · Openness (naiveté)   · Resilience   · Tolerance
· Creativity   Emotional   · Passion   · Risk-taking   for ambiguity
· Curiosity   Imaginational   · Perfectionism   · Self-discipline   · Volition
· Drive   Intellectual   · Perceptiveness   · Self-efficacy
· Imagination   Psychomotor   · Persistence
· Insight   Sensual
· Intuition

1. The Genetic Aspect: Genes

[*Source:* From *Talented Children and Adults: Their Development and Education* (p. 30), by J. Piirto, 1999, Upper Saddle River, NJ: Prentice-Hall.]

tive in terms of the number of children to which they apply to very inclusive and broad. Consequently, the prevalence estimates are highly variable.

Prevalence figures prior to the 1950s were primarily limited to the intellectually gifted: those identified for the most part by intelligence tests. At that time, 2% to 3% of the general population was considered gifted. During the 1950s, when professionals in the field advocated an expanded view of giftedness (Conant, 1959; DeHann & Havighurst, 1957), the prevalence figures suggested for program planning were substantially affected. Terms such as *academically talented* were used to refer to the upper 15% to 20% of the general school population.

Thus, prevalence estimates have fluctuated, depending on the views of policy makers, researchers and professionals during past decades. Currently, 3% to 20% of the students in the school population may be identified as gifted, depending on the regulations, which vary from state to state (Davis & Rimm, 1998).

Characteristics

ccurately identifying the characteristics of gifted people is an enormous task (Piirto, 1999). Many characteristics attributed to those who are gifted have been generated by different types of studies (MacKinnon, 1962; Terman, 1925), many of them catalysts for the production of lists of distinctive characteristics. Gradually, what emerged from these studies were stereotypical views of giftedness.

Children with gifts and talents come from every ethnic, cultural, and socioeconomic background. While some individuals achieve in intellectual endeavors, others excel through the arts.

focus 3

Identify four problems inherent in accurately describing the characteristics of individuals who are gifted.

For example, shortly after the publication of the Stanford-Binet Intelligence Scale, Terman (1925) received funding to begin his intriguing studies that would be published in *Genetic Studies of Genius*. His initial group of subjects included more than 1,500 students, drawn from both elementary and secondary classroom settings, who had obtained IQ scores at or above 140 on the Stanford-Binet. In conjunction with other associates, he investigated their physical characteristics, personality attributes, psychological and marital adjustment, educational attainment, and career achievement at the average ages of 20, 35, and so on (see Table 17.3). Terman's work provided the impetus for the systematic study of gifted individuals.

TABLE 17.3	Terman's findings in the study of people who are gifted
Domains	**Differentiating Characteristics**
Physical characteristics	■ Robust and in good health ■ Above average in physical stature
Personality attributes and aesthetic psychological adjustment	■ Above average in willpower, popularity, perseverance, emotional maturity, aesthetic perceptivity, and moral reasoning ■ Keen sense of humor and high levels of self-confidence ■ Equal to peers in marital adjustment ■ Well adjusted as adults; few problems with substance abuse, suicide, and mental health
Educational attainment	■ Generally read before school entrance ■ Frequently promoted ■ Excelled in reading and mathematical reasoning ■ Consistently scored in the top 10% on achievement tests
Career achievement	■ Mates primarily involved in professional and managerial positions ■ Women primarily teachers or homemakers (probably due to cultural expectations at the time) ■ By age 40 had completed 67 books, 1,400 scientific and professional papers, 700 short stories, and a variety of other creative and scholarly works ■ Adult achievers came primarily from encouraging home environments

Unfortunately, much of the initial research related to the characteristics of giftedness was conducted with restricted population samples. Generally, the studies did not include adequate samples of females or individuals from various ethnic and cultural groups; nor did early researchers carefully control for factors directly related to socioeconomic status. Therefore, the characteristics generated from these studies were not representative of gifted individuals as a whole but reflected characteristics of gifted individuals from advantaged environments.

Given the present multifaceted definitions of giftedness and emerging views of intelligence (Gallagher, 1997; Piirto, 1999), we must conclude that gifted people are members of a heterogeneous population. Consequently, research findings of the past must be interpreted with great caution as practitioners assess a particular child's or youth's behavior, attributes, and talents. Frasier et al. (1995) have identified ten core attributes for recognizing giftedness in children from economically disadvantaged environments and minority groups (see Table 17.4).

Clark (1997) synthesized the work of past investigators and developed a comprehensive listing of differential characteristics of gifted individuals, their needs, and their possible problems. Table 17.5 presents a representative listing of some of the characteristics of children who are gifted, according to Clark's five domains: cognitive, affective, physical, intuitive, and societal. Again, remember that individuals who are gifted vary greatly in the extent to which they exhibit any or all of the characteristics identified by researchers. One of the interesting features of Clark's list is the delineation of possible concomitant problems that may surface as a result of the individual's giftedness or characteristics.

Clark (1997) has also developed a listing of characteristics of children, adolescents, and adults described as extraordinarily creative. Table 17.6 lists behaviors associated with different kinds of creativity.

TABLE 17.4	Recognizing gifted potential in minority and economically disadvan

Core Attributes	Description
Motivation: Exhibits evidence of desire to learn.	Forces that initiate, direct, and sustain individual or group behavior in order to satisfy a need or attained goal
Communication skills: Highly expressive and effective use of words, numbers, symbols, etc.	Transmission and reception of signals or meanings through a system of symbols (codes, gestures, language, numbers)
Interest: intense (sometimes unusual) interests	Activities, avocations, objects, etc., that have special worth or significance and are given special attention
Problem-solving ability: Effective (often inventive) strategies for recognizing and solving problems	Process of determining a correct sequence of alternatives leading to a desired goal or to successful completion or performance of a task
Imagination/Creativity: Produces many ideas, highly original	Process of forming mental images of objects, qualities, situations, or relationships that are not immediately apparent to the senses; solves problems by pursuing nontraditional patterns of thinking
Memory: Large storehouse of information on school or non-school topics	Exceptional ability to retain and retrieve information
Inquiry: Questions, experiments, explores	Method or process of seeking knowledge, understanding, or information
Insight: Quickly grasps new concepts and makes connections; senses deeper meanings	Sudden discovery of the correct solution following incorrect attempts based primarily on trial and error
Reasoning: Finds logical approaches to figuring out solutions	Highly conscious, directed, controlled, active, intentional, forward-looking, goal-oriented thought
Humor: Conveys and picks up on humor well	Ability to synthesize key ideas or problems in complex situations in a humorous way; Exceptional sense of timing in words and gestures

Source: Adapted from *Core Attributes of Giftedness,* by Frasier et al., 1995, National Research Center on the Gifted and Talented, Storrs, CT: University of Connecticut.

Origins of Giftedness

cientists have long been interested in identifying the origins of intelligence. Conclusions have varied greatly (Gagné, 1999a). For years, many scientists adhered to a hereditary explanation of intelligence: people inherit their intellectual capacity at conception. Thus, intelligence was viewed as an innate capacity that remained relatively fixed during an individual's lifetime. The prevailing belief then was that little could be done to enhance intellectual ability.

During the 1920s and 1930s, scientists such as John Watson began to explore the new notion of behavioral psychology, or behaviorism. Like other behaviorists who followed him, Watson believed that the environment played an important role in the development of intelligence as well as personality traits. Initially, Watson largely discounted the role of heredity and its importance in intellectual development. Later, however, he moderated his views, moving somewhat toward a theoretical

focus 4

Identify three factors that appear to contribute significantly to the emergence of various forms of giftedness.

TABLE 17.5   Representative characteristics of people who are gifted and potential

Domains	Differentiating Characteristics	Problems
Cognitive (thinking)	Extraordinary quantity of information, unusual retentiveness	Boredom with regular curriculum; impatience with waiting for group
	High level of language development	Perceived as showoff by children of the same age
	Persistent, goal-directed behavior	Perceived as stubborn, willful, uncooperative
	Unusual capacity for processing information	Resent being interrupted; perceived as too serious; dislike for routine and drill
Affective (feeling)	Unusual sensitivity to the expectations and feelings of others	Unusually vulnerable to criticism of others; high level of need for success and recognition
	Keen sense of humor—may be gentle or hostile	Use of humor for critical attack on others, resulting in damage to interpersonal relationships
	Unusual emotional depth and intensity	Unusual vulnerability; problem focusing on realistic goals for life's work
	Advanced levels of moral judgment	Intolerance of and lack of understanding from peer group, leading to rejection and possible isolation
Physical (sensation)	Unusual discrepancy between physical and intellectual development	Results in adults who function with a mind/body dichotomy; children are comfortable expressing themselves only in mental activity, resulting in a limited development both physically and mentally
	Low tolerance for lag between standards and athletic skills	Refusal to take part in any activities where they do not excel, limiting experience with otherwise pleasurable, constructive physical activities
Intuitive	Early involvement and concern for intuitive knowing and metaphysical ideas and phenomena	Ridiculed by peers; not taken seriously by elders; considered weird or strange
	Creativity apparent in all areas of endeavor	Seen as deviant; become bored with mundane tasks; may be viewed as troublemaker
Societal	Strongly motivated by self-actualization needs	Frustration of not feeling challenged; loss of unrealized talents
	Leadership	Lack of opportunity to use social ability constructively may result in its disappearance from child's repertoire or its being turned into a negative characteristic (e.g., gang leadership)
	Solutions to social and environmental problems	Loss to society if these traits are not allowed to develop with guidance and opportunity for meaningful involvement

Source: From *Growing Up Gifted* 5/E by Clark, Barbara, © 1979. Adapted by permission of Prentice-Hall, Inc., Upper Saddle River, NJ.

TABLE 17.6 Characteristics of creative people

Rationally Thinking Creative Individuals
- Self-disciplined, independent, often anti-authoritarian
- Zany sense of humor
- Able to resist group pressure, a strategy developed early
- Greater tolerance for ambiguity and discomfort
- Little tolerance for boredom

Feeling Creative Individuals
- Unfrightened by the unknown, the mysterious, the puzzling; often attracted to it
- More self-accepting; less afraid of what others would say; less need for other people; lack of fear of own emotions, impulses, and thoughts
- Have more of themselves available for use, for enjoyment, for creative purposes; waste less of their time and energy protecting themselves against themselves
- Capacity to be puzzled

- Ability to accept conflict and tension from polarity rather than avoiding them
- Physical/Sensing Creative Individuals
- An ability to toy with elements and concepts
- Perceiving freshly
- Ability to defer closure and judgment
- Ability to accept conflict and tension
- Skilled performance of the traditional arts

Intuitive Creative Individuals
- Are able to withstand being thought of as abnormal or eccentric
- Are more sensitive
- Have a richer fantasy life and greater involvement in daydreaming
- When confronted with novelty of design, music, or ideas, get excited and involved (less creative people get suspicious and hostile)

Source: From *Growing Up Gifted* 5/E by Clark, Barbara,. © 1979. Adapted by permission of Prentice-Hall, Inc., Upper Saddle River, NJ.

perspective in which both heredity and environment contributed to an individual's intellectual ability.

During the 1930s, many investigators sought to determine the proportional influence of heredity and environment on intellectual development. Some genetic proponents asserted that as much as 70% to 80% of an individual's capacity is determined by heredity and the remainder by environmental influences. Environmentalists believed otherwise. The controversy regarding the respective contributions of heredity and environment to intelligence (known as the **nature versus nurture** controversy) is likely to continue for some time, in part because of the complexity and breadth of the issues involved (Plomin, 1997). However, important progress had been made in teasing out the genetic and environmental contributors to high intelligence. For example, the heritability of intelligence increases with age. "This finding is especially interesting because it is counterintuitive. People usually assume that environmental factors increasingly account for variance in intelligence as experiences accumulate during the course of life" (Plomin, 1997, p. 70). From an environmental perspective, recent research suggests that the influence of nurture is far more profound in the preadolescent years than thereafter (Plomin, 1997). Additionally, more research is needed to investigate the role of young children in "selecting, modifying, and creating their own environments" for growth and stimulation (Plomin, 1997, p. 72).

Thus far, we have focused on the origins of intelligence rather than giftedness per se. Many theories regarding the emergence or essence of giftedness have been derived from the study of general intelligence. Few authors have focused directly on the origins of giftedness. Moreover, the ongoing changes in the definitions of giftedness have further complicated the precise investigation of its origins.

Research continues to provide a range of answers about the inheritability of high intellectual capacity, creativity, and other exceptional talents. Of particular interest is the investigative work currently underway in the field of genetics. In coming decades, investigators will be able to identify precise genes responsible for various manifestations of intelligence (Plomin, 1997). We do know, however, that early

■ NATURE VS. NURTURE. Controversy concerning how much of a person's ability is related to sociocultural influences (nurture) as opposed to genetic factors (nature).

Research on the origins of giftedness in high-achieving individuals, such as grand master chess champions, indicates a strong interaction of natural ability and appropriate environmental stimulation.

environmental factors play important roles in the crystallization of intellectual abilities, and far more attention needs to be devoted to improving early learning environments for young children (Gallagher, 1997).

Several researchers have investigated the origins of giftedness and precocity in children (Morelock & Feldman, 1997; Sosniak, 1997). Individuals such as Bobby Fisher (a grand master chess player at 15), Wolfgang Amadeus Mozart, and others were studied. Several researchers have concluded that their giftedness was a fusion of individual, environmental, and historical forces (Morelock & Feldman, 1997).

Thus, the precise origins of the various forms of giftedness and extraordinary talent are yet to be determined. Current thinking favors an interaction of natural endowment and appropriate environmental stimulation (Gagné, 1999a; Gallagher, 1997; Jackson & Klein, 1997; Plomin, 1997; Davis & Rimm, 1998).

Assessment

The focus of assessment procedures for identifying potential giftedness is beginning to change (Frasier, 1997; Richert, 1997). Elitist definitions and exclusive approaches are being replaced with more defensible, inclusive methods of assessment (Davis & Rimm, 1998). Tests for identifying persons with potential for gifted performance are being more carefully selected; that is, tests are being used with the children for which they were designed. Children who were once excluded from programs for the gifted because of formal or standard cut-off scores that favored particular groups of students are now being included as candidates. Multiple, rather than limited, sources of information are now collected and reviewed in determining who is potentially gifted (Davis & Rimm, 1998; Frasier, 1997; Richert, 1991). In ideal cases, the process is now directed at identifying needs and potentials rather than merely labeling individuals as gifted.

Young gifted children are identified using several approaches. Parents and other care providers are to be aware of the behaviors that may signal giftedness in their child or children (Jackson & Klein, 1997). Given the heterogeneous nature of giftedness, this can be a challenging task. Children identified as gifted develop in vastly different ways. Some may read, walk, and talk quite early, whereas others may be slow in these areas. Aspects of giftedness may emerge early in a child's development

focus 5

Describe the range of assessment devices used to identify the various types of giftedness.

or later on as the child matures. Consequently, the identification process should continue throughout a child's developmental years.

Several approaches have been developed to identify more accurately children who are disadvantaged and also gifted. Some theorists and practitioners have argued for the adoption of a *contextual paradigm* or approach. Rather than using information derived solely from typical intelligence tests or other talent assessments, this approach centers on divergent views of giftedness as valued and determined by community members, parents, grandparents, and competent informants (Frasier, 1997). Other like approaches focus on nontraditional measures of giftedness. These approaches use multiple criteria; broader ranges of scores for inclusion in special programs; peer nomination; assessments by persons other than educational personnel; and information provided by adaptive behavior assessments. Furthermore, these approaches seek to understand students' motivations, interests, capacity for communication, reasoning abilities, capacity for imagination, and humor (Davis & Rimm, 1998; Frasier, 1997). For example, if 60% of the students in a given school population come from a certain cultural minority group and only 2% are identified as gifted using traditional measures, the screening committee may want to reexamine and adjust its identification procedures.

Elementary and secondary students who are gifted are identified in a variety of ways. The first step is generally screening. During this phase, teachers, psychologists, and other school personnel attempt to select all students who are potentially gifted. A number of procedures are employed in the screening process. Historically, information obtained from group intelligence tests and teacher nominations has been used to select the initial pool of students. However, many other measures and data-collection techniques have been instituted since the perspective of giftedness changed from a unidimensional to multidimensional approach (Davis & Rimm, 1998; Richert, 1997). They may include developmental inventories, parent and peer nominations, achievement tests, creativity tests, motivation assessments, teacher nominations, and evaluations of student projects (Assouline, 1997; Hunsaker, Finley, & Frank, 1997; Richert, 1997).

Many schools and districts are adopting the Renzulli's talent pool strategy, which is an integral part of the Schoolwide Enrichment Model. This model has several advantages, including liberal percentages of students who may qualify and participate; a focus on continuous identification of students, not one-time assessment; and access for children and youth whose talents may not be readily recognized or assessed.

In summary, Richert (1997) has developed six principles that should be followed carefully in identifying children and youth as gifted (see Table 17.7). Using these principles, students from a variety of backgrounds and cultures have a good opportunity to be identified as gifted.

■ TEACHER NOMINATION

Teacher nomination has been an integral part of many screening approaches. This approach is fraught with problems, however. Teachers often favor children who are well dressed, cooperative, and task oriented. Students who are bright underachievers as well as those who are bright and disruptive may be overlooked. Also, many teachers are unfamiliar with the general traits, behaviors, and dispositions that underlie giftedness (Hunsaker et al., 1997).

Fortunately, some of these problems have been addressed. Several scales, approaches, and guidelines are now available to aid teachers and others responsible for making nominations (Davis & Rimm, 1998). In fact, several researchers have

TABLE 17.7	Principles for identifying gifted children and adolescents

1.	Defensibility	■ Procedures should be based on the best available research and recommendations.
2.	Advocacy	■ Identification should be designed in the best interests of all students. Students should not be harmed by the procedures.
3.	Equity	■ Procedures should guarantee that no one is overlooked. Students from all groups should be considered for representation according to their demographic representation in the district.
		■ The civil rights of students should be protected.
		■ Strategies should be specified for identifying the disadvantaged gifted student.
		■ Cutoff scores should be avoided because they are the most common way that disadvantaged students are discriminated against. (High scores should be used to include students, but if students meet other criteria—through self or parent nominations, for example—then a lower test score should not be used to exclude them.)
4.	Pluralism	■ The broadest defensible definition of giftedness should be used.
5.	Comprehensiveness	■ As many learners with gifted potential as possible should be identified and served.
6.	Pragmatism	■ Whenever possible, procedures should allow for the cost-effective modification and use of available instruments and personnel.

Source: From "Excellence with Equity in Identification and Programming," by S. Richert. In *Handbook of Gifted Education,* 2/E edited by N. Colangelo and G. Davis, 1997, p. 79. Copyright © 1997 by Allyn and Bacon. Reprinted by permission.

developed nomination procedures that are highly correlated with success in gifted programs, particularly in areas such as language skills, creativity, and groups skills (Hunsaker et al., 1997).

■ INTELLIGENCE AND ACHIEVEMENT TESTS

Intelligence testing continues to be a major source of information for screening and identifying general ability or intellectual giftedness in children and adolescents (Assouline, 1997). Past research related to intelligence assessment, however, reveals some interesting findings. Wallach (1976) analyzed a series of studies on the relationship between future professional achievement and scores obtained earlier on academic aptitude tests or intelligence tests. He found that performance scores in the upper ranges, particularly those frequently used to screen and identify students who are gifted, served as poor criteria for predicting future creative and productive achievement.

Other criticisms have been aimed at intelligence tests and their uses, some of which were discussed earlier in this chapter. One major criticism relates to the restrictiveness of such instruments. Many of the higher mental processes that characterize the functioning of individuals who are gifted are not measured adequately, and some are not assessed at all. However, one of the clear advantages of intelligence tests, both individual and group, is the identification of students whose grades and classroom performance may not reflect their true ability or capacity.

Other limitations associated with intelligence tests are their use with individuals who are culturally different. Very few intelligence tests are adequately constructed to assess the abilities of children and adolescents from cultures substantially different from the core culture for which the tests were designed. However, some progress is

■ CEILING EFFECTS. A restricted range of test questions or problems that does not permit academically gifted students to demonstrate their true capacity or achievement.

being made in helping educators identify gifted children who are members of minority groups, underachievers, or at risk (Davis & Rimm, 1998; Richert, 1997).

Similar problems are inherent in achievement tests. For example, achievement tests are not generally designed to measure the true achievement of children who are academically gifted. Such individuals are often prevented from demonstrating their unusual prowess because of the restricted range of the test items. These **ceiling effects,** as they are known, prevent children who are gifted from demonstrating their achievement at higher levels. However, achievement tests do play a very useful role in identifying students with specific academic talents (Davis & Rimm, 1998).

■ CREATIVITY TESTS

Concerns have been raised about the measurement of creativity independent of some talent or performance domain (Davis, 1997; Davis & Rimm, 1998; Gallagher, 1997). Because of the nature of creativity and the many forms in which it can be expressed, developing tests to assess its presence and magnitude is a formidable task (Davis, 1997). In spite of these challenges, a number of creativity tests have been formulated (Rimm, 1982; Rimm & Davis, 1983; Torrance, 1966; Williams, 1980). Two main categories of creativity tests are presently in use: (1) tests designed to assess divergent thinking and (2) inventories that provide information about students' personalities and biographical traits. Several prominent researchers have suggested the use of multiple measures of creativity to substantiate prowess in this area of performance (Davis & Rimm, 1998). A typical question on a divergent thinking test may read as follows: what would happen if your eyes could be adjusted to see things as small as germs?

Once the screening steps have been completed, the actual identification and selection of students is begun. During this phase, each of the previously screened students is carefully evaluated again, using more individualized procedures and assessment tools. Ideally, these techniques should be closely related to the definition of giftedness used by the district or school system and the nature of the program envisioned or offered to students. (See the nearby Reflect on This feature.)

Reflect on This

SUGGESTIONS FOR CREATING A CLIMATE OF CREATIVITY

- Remember that students will be most creative when they enjoy what they are doing.
- Use tangible rewards as little as possible; instead, encourage students to take pride in what they have accomplished.
- Avoid competitive situations within the classroom.
- Downplay your evaluation of students' creative work; instead, help them become more proficient at recognizing their own strengths and weaknesses.
- Whenever possible, give students choices about what they will do and how they will accomplish their goals.
- Make intrinsic motivation a regular focus of class discussions; encourage students to become aware of their own special interests, and help them to distance themselves from extrinsic constraints.
- Encourage students to become active, independent learners, and allow them to take confident control of their own learning process.
- In any ways that you can, show students that you value creativity— that you not only allow it but also actively engage in it.
- Show students that you are an intrinsically motivated individual who enjoys thinking creatively.

Source: From "Creativity, Thinking Skills, and Eminence," by B. A. Hennessey. In *Handbook of Gifted Education,* edited by N. Colangelo and G. A. Davis, 1997, p. 290. Boston: Allyn and Bacon.

Services and Supports

Gifted children and youth benefit from a variety of services and supports that are tailored to their needs. In the following sections, we address instructional approaches and service delivery systems that are designed for each age group—preschool through the young adult years.

Parents can promote early learning and development in the young child by providing a variety of sensory experiences and encouraging creativity.

■ EARLY CHILDHOOD

Parents can promote the early learning and development of their children in a number of ways (Seeley, 1998). During the first 18 months of life, 90% of all social interactions with children take place during activities such as feeding, bathing, changing diapers, and dressing (Clark, 1997). Parents who are interested in advancing their child's mental and social development use these occasions for talking to him or her; providing varied sensory experiences such as bare-skin cuddling, tickling, and smiling; and conveying a sense of trust.

As children progress through infancy, toddler, and preschool periods, the experiences provided become more varied and uniquely suited to the child's emerging interests. Language and cognitive development is encouraged by means of stories that are read and told. Children are also urged to make up their own stories. Spontaneous conversations arise from events that have momentarily captured a child's attention. Requests for help in saying or printing a word are promptly fulfilled. Thus, many children who are gifted learn to read before they enter kindergarten or first grade. (See the nearby Reflect on This feature.)

During the school years, parents continue to advance their children's development by providing opportunities that correspond to their children's strengths and

Reflect on This

TRACEY, SOMEONE SPECIAL

Recently, the mother of a 5-year-old girl called me, looking for advice about finding a good school for her daughter. She had taken her daughter Tracey to the neighborhood public school "kindergarten roundup," where the children were screened prior to regular enrollment. She said Tracey had never been evaluated by a psychologist, but that she suspected she was very bright.

When I asked what Tracey did that made her think that, I heard an incredible list of outstanding abilities. Tracey was talking in complete sentences when she was 18 months old, and she began reading before age 3. Her mother reported that Tracey now had an "adult vocabulary." When I asked what that meant, she reported that Tracey was able to do most newspaper crossword puzzles successfully. She also said that Tracey was

good at playing cards and could fill in easily as a fourth for bridge with her mother's bridge club when one of the members was absent. When I asked what the school said after the kindergarten screening, the mother reported that the teacher was very excited about Tracey's skills, saying that Tracey knew all of her letters and could count to 100. That started the search for a school and ultimately a call to me as part of the search.

Clearly, we all have a lot of work to do to find and nurture the Traceys of the world and to create appropriate educational opportunities.

Source: From "Giftedness in Early Childhood," by Ken Seeley. In *Excellence in Educating Gifted and Talented Learners,* edited by J. VanTassel-Baska, 1998, 3rd edition, p. 67. Denver, CO: Love.

interests. The simple identification games played during the preschool period now become more complex. Discussions frequently take place with peers and other interesting adults in addition to parents. Discussions and questions become more sophisticated. Parents assist their children in moving to higher levels of learning by asking questions that involve analysis (comparing and contrasting ideas), synthesis (integrating and combining ideas into new and novel forms), and evaluation (judging and disputing information in books, newspaper articles, etc.). Other ways parents can help include (1) furnishing books and reading materials on a broad range of topics; (2) providing appropriate equipment as various interests surface (e.g., microscopes, telescopes, chemistry sets); (3) encouraging regular trips to the public library and other learning resource centers; (4) providing opportunities for participation in cultural events, lectures, and exhibits of various kinds; (5) encouraging participation in extracurricular and community activities outside the home; and (6) fostering relationships with potential mentors and other resource people in the community.

■ PRESCHOOL PROGRAMS   A variety of preschool programs have been developed for young children who are gifted. Some children are involved in traditional programs, which focus on activities and curricula devoted primarily to the development of academic skills. Many traditional programs emphasize affective and social development, as well. The entry criteria for these programs are varied, but the primary considerations are usually the child's IQ and social maturity. Moreover, the child must be skilled in following directions, attending to tasks of some duration, and controlling impulsive behavior.

Creativity programs are designed to help children develop their natural endowments in a number of artistic and creative domains. Another purpose of such programs is to help the children discover their own areas of promise. Children in these programs are also prepared for eventual involvement in traditional academic areas of schooling.

A current trend in early childhood education for typical and gifted children is the provision of *developmentally appropriate practice (DAP)*. The thrust of this approach is to provide young children with opportunities to explore, discover, choose, and acquire skills that are developmentally appropriate for their age and abilities. Fusing or blending early childhood education with gifted education can be quite challenging. As a rule, early childhood educators of gifted young children are not well informed about DAP. Often they employ programming or intervention models that have been designed for older gifted children (Seeley, 1998).

A very popular model of early childhood education for gifted young children is the Cognitively Oriented Curriculum (Seeley, 1998). Its essential components are active learning, language development, learning to recognize and represent experiences and objects, developing logical reasoning, and understanding spatial relations and time.

■ CHILDHOOD AND ADOLESCENCE

Giftedness in elementary and secondary students may be nurtured in a variety of ways (Clark, 1997). A number of service delivery systems and approaches are used in responding to the needs of students who are gifted. Frequently, the nurturing process has been referred to as **differentiated education,** that is, an education uniquely and predominately suited to the capacities and interests of individuals who are gifted, not unlike the developmentally appropriate practice (DAP) referred to in the early childhood section (Cline & Schwartz, 1999). Generally, programs for the gifted are targeted at delivering content more rapidly, delivering more content, examining content in greater depth, pursuing highly specialized content, and/or dealing with more complex and higher levels of subject matter (Feldhusen, 1998b, 1998c).

■ DIFFERENTIATED EDUCATION. Instruction and learning activities that are uniquely and predominantly suited to the capacities and interests of gifted students.

■ INSTRUCTIONAL APPROACHES The selection of instructional approaches and occurs as a function of a variety of factors. First, a school system must determine what types of giftedness it is capable of serving. It must also establish identification criteria and measures that allow it to select qualified students fairly. For example, if the system is primarily interested in advancing creativity, measures and indices of creativity should be utilized. If the focus of the program is accelerating math achievement and understanding, instruments measuring mathematical aptitude and achievement should be employed. A variety of formal and informal approaches have been developed that allow practitioners to measure potential giftedness in culturally diverse students (Richert, 1997). Second, the school system must select the organizational structures through which children who are gifted are to receive their differentiated education. Third, school personnel must select the instructional approaches to be utilized within each program setting. Fourth, school personnel must select continuous evaluation procedures and techniques to assess the overall effectiveness of the program. Data generated from program evaluation efforts can serve as a catalyst for making appropriate changes.

■ SERVICE DELIVERY SYSTEMS Once the types of giftedness to be emphasized have been selected and appropriate identification procedures have been established, suitable service delivery systems must be planned. Organizational structures for students who are gifted are similar to those found in other areas of special education. Clark (1997) described several options that have been used to develop services for students who are gifted (see Figure 17.5). Each learning environment in the model has inherent advantages and disadvantages. For example, students who are enrolled in general education classrooms and are given opportunities to spend time in seminars, resource rooms, special classes, and other novel learning circumstances profit from the experiences because they are allowed to work at their own levels of ability (Lando & Schneider, 1997). Furthermore, such pull-out activities provide a means for students to interact with one another and to pursue areas of interest that may not be part of the usual school curriculum. However, the disadvantages of such

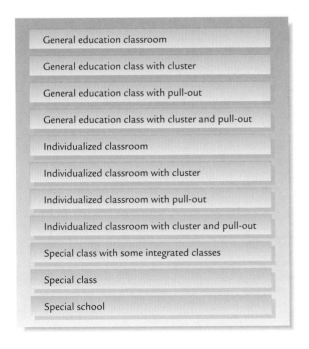

General education classroom

General education class with cluster

General education class with pull-out

General education class with cluster and pull-out

Individualized classroom

Individualized classroom with cluster

Individualized classroom with pull-out

Individualized classroom with cluster and pull-out

Special class with some integrated classes

Special class

Special school

FIGURE 17.5

Clark's continuum model for ability grouping.

[*Source:* From *Growing Up Gifted*, 5/E by Clark, Barbara, Copyright © 1979. Adapted by permission of Prentice-Hall, Inc., Upper Saddle River, NJ.]

a program are numerous. The major part of the instructional week is spent doing things that may not be appropriate for students who are gifted, given their abilities and interests. Also, when they return to general education classes, they are frequently required to make up missed assignments.

Another example from Clark's continuum model for ability grouping is the special class with opportunities for course work integrated with regular classes. This approach has many advantages. Students have the best of both worlds, academically and socially. Directed independent studies, seminars, mentorships, and cooperative studies are made possible through this arrangement. Students who are gifted interact intensively with other able students as well as regular students in their integrated classes. This program also has disadvantages, however. A special class requires a well-trained teacher, and many school systems simply do not have sufficient funds to secure the services of a specially trained teacher. Without a skilled teacher, the special class instruction or other specialized learning activities may just amount to more of the general education curriculum.

VanTassel-Baska (1997) has generated several beliefs that should be considered in developing curricula for gifted students (see Table 17.8). The beliefs provide a basis for development of the Integrated Curriculum Model. This model focuses on advanced content, including sophisticated literature and writing activities, process/product development in the form of scientific research, and issues-oriented themes that tie students' research to specific social, political, or economic problems.

The selection of service delivery systems and curricula for gifted students is a function of several factors: sufficient financial and human resources (e.g., trained personnel, specialists in gifted education, mentors), flexibility in determining student placement and progress, and a climate of excellence characterized by high standards and significant student engagement in learning activities (VanTassel-Baska, 1997). Optimally, delivery systems should facilitate the achievement of curricular goals and should correspond with the types of giftedness being nurtured.

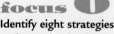

focus 6

Identify eight strategies used to foster the development of children and adolescents who are gifted.

Conditions and strategies associated with successful classrooms and programs for gifted students include teachers who have advanced preparation and knowledge specifically related to gifted education, who relish change, and who enjoy working collaboratively with other professionals. Furthermore, these teachers believe in differentiated instruction, have access to a variety of strategies for delivering this kind of instruction, and have a disposition for leadership and some autonomy in fulfilling their teaching responsibilities (Westberg & Archambault, 1997).

TABLE 17.8	Guiding beliefs for curriculum development for the gifted

1. All learners should be provided curriculum opportunities that allow them to attain optimum levels of learning.
2. Gifted learners have different learning needs compared with typical learners. Therefore, the curriculum must be adapted or designed to accommodate these needs.
3. The needs of gifted learners cut across cognitive, affective, social, and aesthetic areas of curriculum experiences.
4. Gifted learners are best served by a confluent approach that allows for both accelerated and enriched learning.
5. Curriculum experiences for gifted learners need to be carefully planned, written down, implemented, and evaluated in order to maximize potential effect.

Source: From "What Matters in Curriculum for Gifted Learners: Reflections on Theory, Research, and Practice," by J. VanTassel-Baska. In *Handbook of Gifted Education*, 2/E edited by N. Colangelo and G. Davis, 1997, p. 126. Copyright © 1997 by Allyn and Bacon. Reprinted by permission.

■ ACCELERATION Traditionally, programs for students who are gifted have emphasized the practices of acceleration and enrichment (Feldhusen, 1998b, 1998c). Schiever and Maker (1997) define **acceleration** as both a curriculum and program delivery service. Early entrance to kindergarten or college, part-time grade acceleration, and grade skipping are all examples of acceleration. Acceleration allows students to achieve at rates consonant with their capacities. In the past, grade skipping was a common administrative practice in providing for the needs of learners of high abilities. The decline in this practice is attributed to the conviction of some individuals that grade skipping may heighten a student's likelihood of becoming socially maladjusted. Others believe that accelerated students will experience significant gaps in learning because of grade skipping. Acceleration is generally limited to two years in the typical elementary school program. Unfortunately, acceleration does not provide gifted students with opportunities to receive a differentiated curriculum suited to their specific needs (Schiever & Maker, 1997).

Another practice related to grade skipping is telescoped or condensed schooling, which enables students to progress through the content of several grades in a significantly reduced time span. An allied practice is that of allowing students to progress rapidly through a particular course or content offering. Acceleration of this nature provides students with the sequential, basic learning at a pace commensurate with their abilities. School programs without standard grade levels are particularly suitable for telescoping. In such programs, students, regardless of chronological age, may progress through a learning or curriculum sequence that is not constricted by artificial grade boundaries.

Other forms of condensed programming at the high school level include earning credit by examination, enrolling in extra courses for early graduation, reducing or eliminating certain course work, enrolling in intensive summer programs, and taking approved university courses while completing high school requirements. Many of these options enable students to enter college early or begin bachelor's programs with other advanced students. Dwight, the talented musician and broadcasting entrepreneur described in the chapter opening snapshot, was able to profit from honors courses in high school by earning college credit before his actual enrollment in a university. Many students who are gifted are ready for college-level course work at age 14, 15, or 16. Some students of unusually high abilities are prepared for college-level experiences prior to age 14 (Feldhusen, 1998b).

Research on acceleration and its impact suggests that carefully selected students profit greatly from such experiences (Feldhusen, 1998a; Schiever & Maker, 1997). The major benefits of acceleration, as established by research and effective practice, include improved motivation and confidence and early completion of advanced or professional training.

■ ENRICHMENT **Enrichment** like acceleration refers to curricular as well as service delivery systems (Feldhusen, 1998b, 1998c; Schiever & Maker, 1997). Enrichment experiences extend or broaden a person's knowledge. Enrichment refers to courses of study such as music appreciation, foreign languages, and mythology that are added to a student's curriculum and are usually not any more difficult than other classes in which the student is involved. Other examples of enrichment involve

Accelerated programs allow students to achieve at a rate consonant with their capabilities, often by skipping a grade. Enrichment experiences broaden the student's knowledge through the curriculum by providing courses in areas such as music appreciation, foreign language, or mythology.

■ ACCELERATION. A process whereby students are allowed to achieve at a rate that is consonant with their capacity.

■ ENRICHMENT. Educational experiences for gifted students that enhance their thinking skills and extend their knowledge in various areas.

experiences in which the student develops sophisticated thinking skills (i.e., synthesis, analysis, interpretation, and evaluation) or opportunities to develop and master advanced concepts in a particular subject area. Some forms of enrichment are actually types of acceleration. A student whose enrichment involves having an opportunity to fully pursue mathematical concepts that are well beyond his or her present grade level is experiencing a form of acceleration. Obviously, the two approaches are interrelated.

The enrichment approach is the most common administrative provision utilized in serving students who are gifted. It is also the most abused approach in that it is often applied in name only and in a sporadic fashion, without well-delineated objectives or rationale. There are also other problems with the enrichment approach. It is often used by school systems in a superficial fashion, as a token response to the demands of parents of children who are gifted. Enrichment activities are viewed by some professionals as periods devoted to educational trivia or instruction heavy in student assignments but light in content. Quality enrichment programs are characterized by carefully selected activities, modules, or units; challenging but not overwhelming assignments; and evaluations that are rigorous yet fair. Additionally, good enrichment programs focus on thoughtful and careful plans for student learning and learning activities that stress higher-order thinking and application skills (Feldhusen, 1998b, 1998c; Schiever & Maker, 1997).

Enrichment may include activities such as exploring exciting topics not normally pursued in the general curriculum, group-centered activities that focus on cognitive or affective skills and/or processes, or small-group investigations of actual, real-life problems (Renzulli, 1994). The key to these endeavors is high student interest and high-quality teaching and mentoring (Feldhusen, 1998b, 1998c).

There is a paucity of systematic experimental research regarding enrichment programs. Despite many of the limitations of current and past research, evidence supports the effectiveness of enrichment approaches, particularly when it is delivered to specific ability groups (Maker & Nielsen, 1995, 1996). However, little long-term experimental research addressing the effectiveness of enrichment programs has been conducted. Nonexperimental evaluations of enrichment programs have indicated that students, teachers, and parents are generally satisfied with their nature and content.

■ SPECIAL PROGRAMS AND SCHOOLS Programs designed to advance the talents of individuals in nonacademic areas, such as the visual and performing arts, have grown rapidly in recent years (Schiel, 1998). Students involved in these programs frequently spend half their school day working in academic subjects and half in arts studies. Often the arts instruction is provided by an independent institution, but some school systems maintain their own separate schools. Most programs provide training in the visual and performing arts, but a few emphasize instruction in creative writing, motion picture and television production, and photography.

So-called governor's schools (distinctive summer programs generally held at university sites), talent identification programs, and specialized residential or high schools in various states also provide valuable opportunities for students who are talented and academically gifted (Kolloff, 1997). Competitively selected students are provided with curricular experiences that are closely tailored to their individual aptitudes and interests. Faculties for these schools are meticulously selected for competence in various areas and for their ability to stimulate and motivate students. Nevertheless, these schools and special programs are few in number and serve a small number of students who profit from them.

■ CAREER EDUCATION   Career education, career guidance, and counseling are essential components of a comprehensive program for students who are gifted (Perrone, 1997; VanTassel-Baska, 1998a). Ultimately, career education activities and counseling are designed to help students make educational, occupational, and personal decisions. Differentiated learning experiences provide elementary and middle school students with opportunities to investigate and explore. Many of these investigations and explorations are career related and designed to help students understand what it might be like to be a zoologist, neurosurgeon, or filmmaker. Students also become familiar with the training and effort necessary for work in these fields. For gifted students in the elementary grades, these explorations often take place on Saturdays. These explorations help them understand themselves, their talents, and the preparation needed for entry into specific fields of study (Feldhusen, 1998a).

In group meetings, gifted students and talented professionals may discuss the factors that influenced a scientist or group of researchers to pursue a given problem or conduct experiments that led to important discoveries or products. As students grow and mature, both cognitively and physically, the nature and scope of their career education activities become more sophisticated and varied.

■ MENTORING   Some students are provided opportunities to work directly with research scientists, artists, musicians, or other professionals. Students may spend as many as two days a week, 3 or 4 working hours a day, in laboratory facilities, mentored by the scientists and professionals with whom they work (Clasen & Clasen, 1997). Other students rely on intensive workshops or summer programs in which they are exposed to specialized careers through internships and individually tailored instruction (Olszewski-Kubilius, 1997).

The benefits of mentoring gifted students are numerous (VanTassel-Baska, 1998b). Students receive sophisticated learning experiences that are highly motivating and stimulating. They gain invaluable opportunities to explore careers and confirm their interests and commitments to certain areas of study. Mentoring experiences may affirm potential in underachieving or disabled students, potential that was not otherwise demonstrated through conventional means. Mentoring may also promote the development of self-reliance, specific interpersonal skills, and life-long, productive friendships (Clasen & Clasen, 1997).

■ CAREER CHOICES AND CHALLENGES   Career interests, values, and dispositions appear to crystallize early in gifted students. In fact their interests are neither broader nor more restricted than those of their classmates (Achter, Benbow, & Lubinski, 1997). Many gifted students know early on what paths they will follow in postsecondary schooling. These paths often fall within the fields of engineering, health professions, and physical sciences.

Appropriate interest and "above-level ability" assessments (Achter et al., 1997, p. 12), career guidance and exploration (Olszewski-Kubilius, 1997), and other forms of counseling play an important role in helping young people who are gifted utilize their remarkable abilities and talents. These assessments should be made available to these young people in early adolescence. As gifted students come to understand more clearly their individual strengths, talents, interests, and challenges, they will make better choices in appropriate studies and professional careers (Achter et al., 1997; Moon, Kelly, & Feldhusen, 1997).

Every gifted program ought to provide differentiated counseling services to help gifted students and their families deal with personal, social, and educational/career problems (VanTassel-Baska, 1998a, 1998c; Moon et al., 1997). The approaches used by counselors, therapists, and educators will vary according to the nature of the problems

TABLE 17.9   Useful questions for group counseling discussions

1. What does it mean to be gifted?
2. What do your parents think it means to be gifted?
3. What do your teachers think it means to be gifted?
4. What do other kids in school think it means to be gifted?
5. How is being gifted an advantage for you? How is it a disadvantage?
6. Have you ever deliberately hidden your giftedness? If so, how?

Source: From "Counseling Gifted Students: Issues and Practices," by N. Colangelo. In *Handbook of Gifted Education*, 2/E edited by N. Colangelo & G. A. Davis, 1997, p. 356. Copyright © 1997 by Allyn and Bacon. Reprinted by permission.

and the student's needs. One promising approach is the use of group counseling. Colangelo (1997), a long-time advocate for counseling for gifted individuals put it this way, "It is my observation that gifted students are considerably smarter about course work than about themselves. They have the ability to be insightful about themselves, but seldom have the opportunity to articulate and share their insights" (pp. 257–358). Group counseling conducted by a well-trained therapist or counselor would be helpful to many gifted students. Table 17.9 provides some interesting questions that gifted young people might pursue in group therapy sessions.

Problems caused by excessive or inappropriate parental expectations or other related problems may need to be addressed in a family context. Counselors and therapists may help parents develop realistic expectations that fit their child's abilities, aspirations, and true interests (Silverman, 1997). As with other exceptionalities, the provision of counseling services is best achieved through interdisciplinary efforts (Moon et al., 1997).

focus 7
What are some of the social–emotional needs of students who are gifted?

■ PROBLEMS AND CHALLENGES OF GIFTEDNESS   Students who are gifted must cope with a number of problems (Delisle, 1997; Kerr, 1997; Perrone, 1997). One problem is the expectations they have of themselves and those that have been explicitly and implicitly imposed by parents, teachers, and others. Students who are gifted frequently feel an inordinate amount of pressure to achieve high grades or to select particular professions. They often feel obligated or duty-bound to achieve and contribute with excellence in every area, a syndrome called *perfectionism* (Adderholdt-Elliott, 1987). Such pressure often fosters a kind of conformity,

People with gifts and talents often have a variety of interests. Marjorie Scardino is Chief Executive Officer of Pearson plc, one of the world's largest media/education conglomerates. She is also a rodeo barrel racer, prairie populist, attorney, and First Amendment Scholar as well as a former reporter and publisher of the Pulitzer-prize winning *Georgia Weekly*. Ms. Scardino is pictured here with Sir Dennis Stevenson, Chairman of Pearson.

preventing students from selecting avenues of endeavor that truly fit them and their personal interests.

VanTassel-Baska (1989) identified a number of social–emotional needs of students who are gifted that differentiate them from their same-age peers:

- Understanding how they are different from and similar to their peers
- Appreciating and valuing their own uniqueness as well as that of others
- Understanding and developing relationship skills
- Developing and valuing their high-level sensitivity
- Gaining a realistic understanding of their own abilities and talents
- Identifying ways of nurturing and developing their own abilities and talents
- Adequately distinguishing between pursuits of excellence and pursuits of perfection
- Developing the behaviors associated with negotiation and compromise

Students who are gifted need ongoing and continual access to adult role models who have interests and abilities that parallel theirs; the importance of these role models cannot be overestimated (Clasen & Clasen, 1997). Role models are particularly important for gifted students who grow up and receive their schooling in rural and remote areas. Such students often complete their public schooling without the benefit of having a mentor or professional person with whom they can talk or discuss various educational and career-related issues.

Historically Neglected Groups

For years, programs for the gifted and talented were developed and directed primarily at individuals with high IQs and children and youth who were privileged in some fashion. Now more than ever, educators and researchers are examining the emergence and encouragement of giftedness in girls, in persons with disabilities, and in children living in poverty. The sections that follow discuss current practices and issues in nurturing giftedness in these historically neglected groups.

■ FEMALES

Gifted females face several problems, particularly during the middle school years (VanTassel-Baska, 1998d). During this time period, "their confidence fades and [it] is replaced with self-doubt and lowered expectations" (Silverman, 1998, p. 156). These girls begin to discount their intelligence and related abilities, thus enhancing their chances for social acceptance and minimizing their risks for social isolation.

The number of girls identified as gifted appears to decline with age. Olshen (1987) referred to this decline as the disappearance of giftedness in girls. This phenomenon is surprising when we realize that girls tend to walk and talk earlier than their male counterparts; that girls, as a group, read earlier; that girls score higher than boys on IQ tests during the preschool years; and that the grade-point averages of girls during the elementary years are higher than those of boys.

Just exactly what happens to girls? Is the decline in the number of girls identified as gifted related to their socialization? Does some innate physiological or biological mechanism account for this decline? Why do some gifted females fail to realize their potential? To what extent do value conflicts about women's roles contribute to mixed achievement in gifted women? The answers to these and other important questions are gradually emerging.

One explanation given for this decline is the gender-role socialization that girls receive. Behaviors associated with competitiveness, risk taking, and independence are not generally encouraged in girls. Behaviors that are generally fostered in girls include dependence, cooperation, and nurturing. The elimination of independent behaviors in girls is viewed by Silverman (1986) as being the most damaging aspect of their socialization. More recent research suggests that girls who develop social self-esteem, "the belief that one has the ability to act effectively and to make decisions independently," are more likely to realize their potential (Davis & Rimm, 1998; Kerr, 1997). Without independence, the development of high levels of creativity, achievement, and leadership is severely limited. Overcoming the impact of sociocultural influences requires intentional *counterconditioning* and heightened levels of awareness (Davis & Rimm, 1998, p. 320).

focus 8

Identify four important aspects of counterconditioning for gifted girls.

This counterconditioning should begin at home. Often career modeling provided by a talented mother or other close family role model encourages a gifted girl to pursue her dreams and aspirations. Also, fathers play important roles in promoting their daughters' achievement and talent development. Their attitudes and willingness to promote alternative views of what girls ought to be play an important role in the emergence of giftedness in a daughter. Second only to families, schools play an essential role in shaping and encouraging giftedness in girls. Unfortunately, schools often reinforce dependence and docility in girls. With heightened awareness, teachers and school counselors should pay greater attention to girls and their giftedness; should provide girls with access to female role models who have embraced and developed their talents; and should encourage participation in courses and activities that advance their development (Davis & Rimm, 1998).

Females who are gifted and talented experience other unique problems (Davis & Rimm, 1998). They include fear of appearing "unfeminine" or unattractive when competing with males, competition between marital and career aspirations, stress induced by traditional cultural and societal expectations, and self-imposed and/or culturally imposed restrictions related to educational and occupational choices

Itzhak Perlman is one of the most gifted violinists of our time. Performing here with the University of Southern Mississippi Symphony Orchestra, he has been a friend and mentor to countless numbers of young musicians. He was struck with polio at the age of four and has been a tireless advocate for the rights of persons with disabilities throughout his life.

ENCOURAGING GIFTEDNESS IN GIRLS

■ SUGGESTIONS FOR THE FAMILY

- Hold high expectations for daughters.
- Do not purchase gender-role-stereotyped toys.
- Avoid overprotectiveness.
- Encourage high levels of activity.
- Allow girls to get dirty.
- Instill beliefs in their capabilities.
- Support their interests.
- Identify them as gifted during their preschool years.
- Find for them playmates who are gifted to identify with and emulate.
- Foster interests in mathematics outside of school.
- Consider early entrance and other opportunities to accelerate.
- Encourage enrollment in mathematics courses.
- Introduce them to professional women in many occupations.
- Encourage their mothers to acknowledge their own giftedness.
- Encourage their mothers to work at least part time outside the home.
- Encourage fathers to spend time alone with daughters in so-called masculine activities.
- Share household duties equally between the parents.
- Assign chores to siblings on a nonsexist basis.
- Discourage the use of sexist language or teasing in the home.
- Monitor television programs for sexist stereotypes, and discuss these with children of both genders.
- Encourage siblings to treat each other equitably, rather than according to the traditional gender-role stereotypes they may see outside the home.

■ SUGGESTIONS FOR TEACHERS AND COUNSELORS

- Believe in girls' logicomathematical abilities, and provide many opportunities for them to practice mathematical reasoning within other subject areas.
- Accelerate girls through the science and mathematics curriculum whenever possible.
- Have special clubs in mathematics for girls who are high achieving.
- Design coeducational career development classes in which both girls and boys learn about career potentialities for women.
- Expose boys and girls to role models of women in various careers.
- Discuss nontraditional careers for women, including salaries for men and women and schooling requirements.
- Help girls set long-term goals.
- Discuss underachievement among females who are gifted and ask how they can combat it in themselves and others.
- Have girls read biographies of famous women.
- Arrange opportunities for girls to "shadow" a female professional for a few days to see what her work entails.
- Discourage sexist remarks and attitudes in the classroom.
- Boycott sexist classroom materials, and write to the publishers for their immediate correction.
- Discuss sexist messages in the media.
- Advocate special classes and after-school enrichment opportunities for students who are gifted.
- Form support groups for girls with similar interests.

Source: From "What Happens to the Gifted Girl?" by L. K. Silverman. In *Critical Issues in Gifted Education, Vol. 1: Defensible Programs for the Gifted,* edited by C. J. Maker, 1986, pp. 43–89. Austin, TX: Pro-Ed. (Copyright owned by author.) Adapted by permission.

(Delisle, 1997; Kerr, 1997; Silverman, 1997). Although many of these problems are far from being resolved at this point, some progress is being made. Women in greater numbers are choosing to enter professions traditionally pursued by men (Davis & Rimm, 1998; Kerr, 1997). (See the nearby Reflect on This feature.)

Fortunately, multiple role assignments are emerging in many families, wherein the usual tasks of mothers are shared by all members of the family or are completed by someone outside the family. Cultural expectations are changing, and as a result, options for women who are gifted are rapidly expanding (Davis & Rimm, 1998).

■ PERSONS WITH DISABILITIES

For some time, intellectual giftedness has been largely associated with high IQs and high scores on aptitude tests. These tests, by their very nature and structure, measure a limited range of mental abilities. Because of their limitations, they have not been particularly helpful in identifying persons with disabilities who are intellectually

■ EARLY CHILDHOOD YEARS

TIPS FOR THE FAMILY

- Realize that giftedness is evidenced in many ways (e.g., concentration, memory, pleasure in learning, sense of humor, social knowledge, task orientation, ability to follow and lead, capacity and desire to compete, information capacity).
- Provide toys for children who are gifted that may be used for a variety of activities.
- Take trips to museums, exhibits, fairs, and other places of interest.
- Provide an environment that is appropriately challenging.
- Supply proper visual, auditory, verbal, and kinesthetic stimulation.
- Talk to the child in ways that foster a give-and-take conversation.
- Begin to expose the child to picture books and ask him or her to find certain objects or animals or respond to age-appropriate questions.
- Avoid unnecessary restrictions.
- Provide play materials that are developmentally appropriate and may be a little challenging.

TIPS FOR THE PRESCHOOL TEACHER

- Look for ways in which various talents and skills may be expressed (e.g., cognitive, artistic, leadership, socialization, motor ability, memory, special knowledge, imagination).
- Provide opportunities for the child who is gifted to express these talents.
- Capitalize on the child's curiosity. Develop learning activities that relate to his or her passions.
- Allow the child to experiment with all the elements of language—even written language—as he or she is ready.

TIPS FOR PRESCHOOL PERSONNEL

- Remember that conversation is critical to the child's development. Do not be reluctant to spend a great deal of time asking the child various questions as he or she engages in various activities.
- Become a specialist in looking for gifts and talents across a variety of domains (e.g., artistic, social, cognitive).
- Allow for rapid mastery of concepts and then allow the child to move on to other more challenging activities rather than holding him or her back.

TIPS FOR NEIGHBORS AND FRIENDS

- Recognize that people have a variety of gifts and talents that can be encouraged.
- Provide preschool opportunities for all children who are potentially gifted to have the necessary environmental ingredients to fully use their talents or gifts.
- Enjoy and sometimes endure the neighborhood child who has chosen your home as his or her lab for various experiments in cooking, painting, and building.

■ ELEMENTARY YEARS

TIPS FOR THE FAMILY

- Maintain the search for individual gifts and talents; some qualities may not be evident until the child is older.
- Provide out-of-school experiences that foster talent or skill development (e.g., artistic, physical, academic, leadership).
- Enroll the child who is gifted in summer programs that are offered by universities or colleges.
- Monitor the child's school environment to be sure that adequate steps are being taken to respond to his or her unique skills.
- Join an advocacy group for parents in your community or state.
- Subscribe to child publications that are related to your child's current interests.
- Encourage your child's friendships and associations with other people who have like interests and aptitudes.

TIPS FOR THE GENERAL EDUCATION SCHOOL TEACHER

- Provide opportunities for enrichment as well as acceleration.
- Allow students who are gifted to pursue individual projects that require sophisticated forms of thinking or production.
- Become involved in professional organizations that provide assistance to teachers of students who are gifted.
- Take a course that specifically addresses the instructional strategies that might be used with children who are gifted.
- Encourage children to become active participants in various events that emphasize particular skill or knowledge areas (e.g., science fairs, music competitions).

---

or otherwise gifted. However, persons with disabilities such as cerebral palsy, learning disabilities, and other disabling conditions can be gifted (Cline & Schwartz, 1999; Davis & Rimm, 1998). Helen Keller, Vincent van Gogh, and Ludwig von Beethoven are prime examples of individuals with disabilities who were also gifted. Some theorists and practitioners suggest that as many as 2% of individuals with disabilities are gifted (Johnson et al., 1997). Fortunately, we have begun to look for various kinds of

- Develop clubs and programs that allow children who are gifted to pursue their talents.
- Create award programs that encourage talent development across a variety of domains.
- Involve community members in offering enrichment and acceleration activities (e.g., artists, engineers, writers).
- Foster the use of inclusive procedures for identifying students who are potentially gifted from groups that are culturally diverse, disadvantaged, or have disabilities.

TIPS FOR NEIGHBORS AND
FRIENDS

- Contribute to organizations that foster talent development.
- Volunteer to serve as judges for competitive events.
- Be willing to share your talents with young, emergent scholars, musicians, athletes, and artists.
- Become a mentor for someone in your community.

SECONDARY AND TRANSITION YEARS

TIPS FOR THE FAMILY

- Continue to provide sources of support for talent development outside of the home.

- Regularly counsel your child about courses that he or she will take.
- Provide access to tools (e.g., computers, video cameras) and resources (e.g., specialists, coaches, mentors) that contribute to the child's performance.
- Expect variations in performance from time to time.
- Provide opportunities for rest and relaxation from demanding schedules.
- Continue to encourage involvement with peers who have similar interests and aptitudes.

TIPS FOR THE GENERAL
EDUCATION SCHOOL
TEACHER

- Provide a range of activities for students with varying abilities.
- Provide opportunities for students who are gifted to deal with real problems or develop actual products.
- Give opportunities for genuine enrichment activities, not just more work.
- Remember that giftedness manifests itself in many ways. Determine how various types of giftedness may be expressed in your content domain.
- Help eliminate conflicting and confusing signals about career choices and fields of study often given to young women who are gifted.

TIPS FOR SCHOOL
PERSONNEL

- Provide, to the degree possible, a variety of curriculum options, activities, clubs, and the like.
- Acknowledge excellence in a variety of performance areas (e.g., leadership, visual and performing arts, academics).
- Continue to use inclusive procedures in identifying individuals who are potentially gifted and talented.
- Encourage participation in competitive activities in which students are able to use their gifts and talents (e.g., science fairs, debate tournaments, music competitions).

TIPS FOR NEIGHBORS,
FRIENDS, AND POTENTIAL
EMPLOYERS

- Provide opportunities for students to "shadow" talented professionals.
- Volunteer as a professional to work directly with students who are gifted in pursuing a real problem or producing an actual product.
- Become a mentor for a student who is interested in what you do professionally.
- Support the funding of programs for students who are gifted and talented and who come from disadvantaged environments.
- Provide summer internships for students who have a particular interest in your profession.

- Serve as an adviser for a high school club or other organization that gives students additional opportunities to pursue talent areas.

ADULT YEARS

TIPS FOR THE FAMILY

- Continue to nurture appropriate interdependence and independence.
- Assist with the provision of specialized assistance.
- Celebrate the accomplishments and provide support for challenges.
- Let go.

TIPS FOR EDUCATIONAL
PERSONNEL

- Exhibit behaviors associated with effective mentoring.
- Provide meaningful ways to deal with pressure.
- Allow the individuals to be themselves.
- Provide adequate time for discussion and interaction.
- Be aware of other demands in the individuals' lives.

TIPS FOR POTENTIAL
EMPLOYERS

- Establish appropriately high expectations.
- Provide opportunities for diversion and fun.
- Be sensitive to changing interests and needs.
- Allow employees to be involved with young gifted students on a volunteer basis.

giftedness in children with disabilities. They are "individuals with exceptional ability or potential and who are able to achieve high performance despite such disabilities as hearing, speech, orthopedic or emotional impairments, learning disabilities, or health problems, either singly or in combination" (Davis & Rimm, 1998, p. 342). Although many challenges are still associated with identifying individuals with disabilities who are gifted, much progress has been made.

Reflect on This

OLIVIA, I DON'T WANT HER

During the years of beatings by her mother, years of being whipped with an extension cord, smacked in the mouth with a telephone, pounded against a wall, punched in the lip, dragged by the hair through the hallway, tossed in the shower, and scalded with hot water, school was Olivia's salvation. The only kind words she heard, the only love she felt, the only compliments she received, were from her teachers. At home, no matter how she was tormented, no matter how long she cried, when the beatings were over, she always read her assignments and prepared for her tests.

But one afternoon after school, when her mother left for work, Olivia decided to run away instead. She ripped out of the Yellow Pages the shelter listings for abused children and battered women.

She stuffed them in her back pocket and filled a duffle bag with clothes. Then, as an afterthought, she grabbed her mother's black leather jacket.

A few months later a court hearing was held to determine Olivia's fate. She felt as if she were in a fog as the judge and social workers discussed her case. She remembers only the end of the hearing, when the judge told her mother that if she wanted the opportunity to regain custody of her daughter, she would have to undergo psychological testing, individual counseling, and family counseling. Olivia's mother told the judge, "She's the crazy one. Not me." The last words Olivia remembers her mother saying were "I don't want her!"

When Olivia was about to start high school, a compassionate group-home administrator gave her a pamphlet that listed the magnet schools in the Los Angeles school district. These schools were for students who had an interest in a particular field of study, or who had a talent for music or art, or who were classified as gifted because of their high IQ or standardized test scores. Olivia studied the pamphlet and discovered that one of the two high schools in the city for gifted students was located at Crenshaw High School, only a few miles from her South-Central group home.

One afternoon, she took the bus from her junior high school to Crenshaw and talked to several administrators. They told Olivia that her IQ and her standardized test scores—which were in the top 5th percentile of the nation—were well above the minimum requirement. She enrolled in the gifted magnet program in the ninth grade.

The gifted magnet program, however, was a refuge for Olivia, and she immedi-

ately felt comfortable in the program. She met many other students who, like her, had wretched childhoods, yet had managed to stay focused on school and retain a love of learning. Olivia thrived in the program, and at the end of her first year, she was one of only two ninth graders who received all A's in their academic subjects. Her home life remained chaotic, but school, once again, was her escape, her respite from the loneliness of having no family, the rootlessness of having no home. Olivia enjoyed the courses in the gifted program and the challenging class discussions. But most of all she appreciated the interest and concern of her teachers, the camaraderie among her classmates. This, she felt, was the family she never had.

Source: From *And Still We Rise* (pp. 9–13), by M. Corwin, 2000, New York: Morrow.

Unfortunately, the giftedness of these children is often invisible to parents and teachers (Davis & Rimm, 1998). Factors critical to successful identification of giftedness include environments that elicit signs of mental giftedness and information about the individual's performance gathered from many sources. It is important that the child be given opportunities to perform tasks that are not impeded by his or her disabling condition. Also, if and when tests of mental ability are used, they must be appropriately adapted, both in administration and scoring. Additionally, the identification process should occur at regular intervals. Some children with disabilities change dramatically with appropriate instruction and related technologies (Johnson et al., 1997). The developmental delays present in children with disabilities and the disabilities themselves pose the greatest challenges to identification efforts (Davis & Rimm, 1998).

Differential education for children with disabilities who are gifted is still in its infancy. A great deal of progress has been made, particularly in the adaptive uses of computers and related technologies, but much development work remains to be done (Davis & Rimm, 1998). Additionally, a great deal is still unknown about the service delivery systems and materials that are best suited for these individuals. One of the greatest gifts parents and teachers can give to children and youth with disabilities who are gifted is self-confidence and independence. Unfortunately, the necessity for one-to-one instruction provided by parents and teachers gives rise to dependence and diminished self-confidence (Davis & Rimm, 1998). (See the nearby Reflect on This feature.)

■CHILDREN FROM DIFFERENT CULTURAL BACKGROUNDS AND CHILDREN LIVING IN POVERTY

Very rarely are culturally diverse and economically disadvantaged youth identified as gifted (Davis & Rimm, 1998). These youth are dramatically underrepresented in programs for the gifted and talented.

focus 9

Identify eight important elements of programs for gifted children who come from diverse backgrounds and who may live in poverty.

Identification procedures often fail to identify children as being gifted when they come from minority groups or disadvantaged environments. However, many practitioners are now using multiple criteria to reveal potential and giftedness in children who are diverse or poor (Davis & Rimm, 1998; Frasier, 1997). Research conducted by VanTassel-Baska and Chepko-Sade (1986) has suggested that as many as 15% of the gifted population may be children who are disadvantaged.

Instructional programs for children and adolescents who are disadvantaged and gifted have several key components. First and foremost, the teachers in these programs are well trained in "differentiating required subject areas" (Richert, 1997, p. 85). They understand learning styles, how to build and capitalize on students' interests, and how to maximize students' affective, cognitive, and ethical capacities (Richert, 1997). In addition to providing the typical curricular options for enrichment, acceleration, and other talent development approaches, programs for these children and youth include additional elements: (1) maintaining ethnic diversity, (2) providing extracurricular cultural enrichment, (3) addressing learning style differences, (4) providing counseling, (5) fostering parent support groups, and (6) giving these children and youth access to significant models (Davis & Rimm, 1998).

There is a general consensus that programs for these children should begin early and be tailored to the needs and interests of each identified child. These programs should be focused on "individual possibilities rather than norm-defined 'shortcomings'" (Tomlinson, Callahan, & Lelli, 1997, p. 5). Moroever, these programs help parents understand their roles in fostering giftedness and talent development (Tomlinson et al., 1997). Often the emphasis in the early years is on reading instruction, language development, and foundation skills. Other key components include experiential education that provides children with many opportunities for hands-on learning, activities that foster self-expression, plentiful use of mentors and role models who represent the child's cultural or ethnic group, involvement of the community, and counseling throughout the school years that gives serious consideration to the cultural values of the family and the child who is gifted. Lastly, the programs are enhanced by a team approach or "multiavenue approach" in which mentors, parents, teachers, and other community members work together to meet the needs of these children (Tomlinson et al., 1997).

Snapshot

Sadikifu

Sadi's mother, Thelma, who was one week shy of her 41st birthday when her only child was born, considers her son a gift from Allah. He was unexpected and unplanned. Thelma and Sadi's father, who never married, became Muslims in the 1970s, and they gave their son an Islamic name—Sadikifu—which means "truthful and honest."

Because Thelma never had been around children, and Sadi was her only child, she talked to him like a peer. That is one reason, she believes, why he is so bright and articulate. In the third grade he was classified as gifted by the school district when he scored in the 95th percentile on a national achievement test. In the fourth grade he won an oratorical contest, sponsored by a local bank, for a speech on homelessness. Thelma still proudly displays the trophy—next to a picture of Elijah Muhammad—in her small, immaculate two-bedroom apartment (p. 32).

Sadi, unfortunately, went the wrong way. In the ninth grade, he enrolled in Crenshaw's gifted program, but after only two months of high school he was thrown out for instigating a fight between his tagging crew and a rival set. Although his mother was livid, Sadi's expulsion probably saved his life because the next afternoon his best friend was shot to death by a rival tagging crew called "Nothin' But Trouble." Sadi always spent every day after school with his friend, whose street name was Chaos. Sadi knew if he had not been stuck all afternoon enrolling in his new high school, he would have been walking down Vermont Avenue with Chaos. He probably would have been killed, too (pp. 33–34).

On Sadi's first day of school he discovered he was the only black student in his gifted classes. When students passed out worksheets, they skipped him. When he asked for the assignments, the students invariably said, "I thought you were here for detention."

Although he was now attending a surburban high school far from South-Central, at night and on weekends he was immersed in the gang life. He had graduated from his tagging crew to the Front Hood 60s and was known by his street name–Little Cloudy. And even though he had been arrested several times, three of his homies had recently been killed in drive-bys, and about ten were in jail, he kept gangbanging.

One weekday afternoon, when school was canceled because of an earthquake, he and two other 60s were walking down Western Avenue, on their way to buy some Thunderbird at a liquor store near 69th Street. They spotted a teenager across the street whom they did not recognize. Sadi and his two homies threw up the hand sign for the Front Hood 60s. The gangbanger across the street threw up the sign for the Eight-Tray Gangsters, a bitter rival of the 60s. One of Sadi's homies pulled out a semiautomatic .380-caliber pistol and fired at the Eight-Tray. Then everyone sprinted for cover. Two LAPD officers in a patrol car heard the shots, pulled up, and grabbed Sadi and another 60. The shooter and the Eight-Tray, who had not been hit, escaped.

Sadi and his homie were handcuffed, arrested, and taken to the 77th Street Division station. They were questioned by detectives, who then dabbed their hands with a sticky aluminum tab that tests for gunshot residue. When the test came back negative, and a witness told detectives neither of them was the shooter, they were released. But the incident precipitated an epiphany for Sadi.

Seeing the flash of the gun, just inches away, marked a turning point for him. It inalterably changed the course of his life. In an instant, he realized how transitory life was, how transitory *his* life was. How all his decisions were wrong. How he was destined to die in a drive-by, or languish in prison. He realized that maybe his mother had been right about school. Maybe his intelligence was, as his mother told him, a gift from Allah (pp. 34–35).

Source: From *And Still We Rise* (pp. 32–35), by M. Corwin, 2000, New York: Morrow.

Case Study

IS CALVIN GIFTED?

What follows is a series of cartoon strips from *Calvin and Hobbes*. They depict in part the relationship Calvin has with his dad.

■ APPLICATION

1. Is Calvin gifted, creative, and talented? Provide a rationale for your answer.
2. If Calvin's dad asked you how to handle Calvin's "giftedness," what recommendations would you make? Give a rationale for your answers.
3. If Calvin's dad were enrolled in your parenting class and asked for your counsel as the group leader, what would you recommend?

Debate Forum

WHAT WOULD YOU DO WITH JANE?

Many children who are gifted are prevented from accelerating their growth and learning for fear that they will be hurt emotionally and socially. Parents' comments such as these are common: She's so young. Won't she miss a great deal if she doesn't go through the fourth- and fifth-grade experiences? What about her friends? Who will her friends be if she goes to college at such a young age? Will she have the social skills to interact with kids that are much older? If she skips these two grades, won't there be gaps in her learning and social development?

On the other hand, the nature of the questions or comments by parents about acceleration may also be positive: She is young in years only! She will adjust extremely well. Maybe she is emotionally mature enough to handle this type of acceleration. The increased opportunities provided through university training will give her greater chances to develop her talents and capacities. Perhaps the older students with whom she will interact are better suited to her intellectual and social needs.

Consider Jane, a child who is gifted. In third grade, she thrived in school, and just about everything associated with her schooling at that time was positive. Her teacher was responsive and allowed her and others to explore well beyond the usual "read-the-text-then-respond-to-the-ditto-sheet" routine. Much self-pacing was possible, and materials galore were pre-

sented for both independent studies and queries.

In the fourth and fifth grades, however, things began to change radically. Jane's teachers were simply unable to provide enough interesting and challenging work for her. It was during the latter part of the fourth grade that she began to view herself as different. Not only did she know, but her classmates knew, that learning came exceptionally easily to her. At this same time, Jane was beginning to change dramatically in her cognitive capacity. Unfortunately, her teachers persisted in unnecessary drills and other mundane assignments, and Jane gradually became bored and lapsed into a type of passive learning. Rather than attacking assignments with vigor, she performed them carelessly, often making many stupid errors. Gradually, what ensued was a child who was very unhappy in school. School had been the most interesting place for her to be before she entered fourth grade. Then it became a source of pain and boredom.

Jane's parents decided that they needed to know more about her capacities and talents. Although it was expensive and quite time consuming, they visited a nearby university center for psychological services. Jane was tested, and the results were very revealing. For the first time, Jane's parents had some objective information about her capacities. She was in fact an unusually bright and talented young lady. Jane's parents then began to

consider the educational alternatives available to her.

The counselor who provided the interpretation of the results at the university center strongly recommended that Jane be advanced to the seventh grade in a school that provided services to students who were talented and gifted. This meant that Jane would skip one year of elementary school and have an opportunity to move very rapidly through her junior and senior high school studies. Furthermore, she would potentially be able to enter the university well in advance of her peers.

Jane's parents knew that her performance has diminished significantly in the last year. Moreover, her attitude and disposition about school seem to be worsening. What would you do as her parents? What factors would you consider important in making the decision? Or is the decision Jane's and hers alone?

■ POINT

Jane should be allowed to accelerate her educational pace. Moving to the seventh grade will benefit her greatly, intellectually and socially. Most girls develop more rapidly physically and socially than boys do. Skipping one grade will not hinder her social development at all. In fact, she will benefit from the interactions that she will have with other able students, some of whom will also have skipped a grade or two. Additionally, the research regarding the impact of accelerating students is positive, particu-

larly if the students are carefully selected. Jane has been carefully evaluated and deserves to have the opportunity to be excited about learning and achieving again.

■ COUNTERPOINT

There are some inherent risks in having Jane skip her sixth-grade experience and move on to the seventh grade. Jane is neither socially nor emotionally prepared to deal with the junior high environment. She may be very able intellectually and her achievement may be superior, but this is not the time to move her into junior high. Socially, she is still quite awkward for her age. This awkwardness would be intensified in the junior high setting. Acceleration for Jane should be considered later on, when she has matured more socially.

She should be able to receive the acceleration that she needs in her present elementary school. Certainly, other able students in her school would benefit from joining together for various activities and learning experiences. The acceleration should take place in her own school, with other students who are gifted and of her own age. Maybe all Jane needs is some time to attend a class or two elsewhere. Using this approach, she could benefit from involvement with her same-age peers and still receive the stimulation that she so desperately needs. Allowing her to skip a grade now would hurt her emotionally and socially in the long run.

Review

focus 1

Briefly describe several historical developments directly related to the measurement of various types of giftedness.

- Alfred Binet developed the first developmental scale for children during the early 1900s. Gradually, the notion of mental age emerged, that is, a representation of what the child was capable of doing compared with age-specific developmental tasks.
- Lewis M. Terman translated the Binet scale and made modifications suitable for children in the United States.
- Gradually, the intelligence quotient, or IQ, became the gauge for determining giftedness.
- Intelligence was long viewed as a unitary structure or underlying ability. But this view gradually changed, and researchers began to believe that intelligence was represented in a variety of distinct capacities and abilities.
- J. P. Guilford and other social scientists began to develop a multidimensional theory of intelligence, which prompted researchers to develop models and assessment devices for examining creativity.
- Programs were gradually developed to foster and develop creativity in young people.

- More recently, V. Ramos-Ford and H. Gardner have developed the multiple intelligences perspective, which includes linguistic, logical–mathematical, spatial, musical, bodily–kinesthetic, interpersonal, and intrapersonal behaviors.

focus 2

Identify six major components of definitions that have been developed to describe giftedness.

- Children and adolescents who are gifted perform or show potential for performing at remarkably high levels when compared with others of their age, experience, or environment.
- Children who are gifted exhibit high performance capability in intellectual, creative, and/or artistic areas.
- Such children may possess unusual leadership capacity or excel in specific academic fields.
- Gifted children become extraordinarily proficient performers or creative producers, excelling in a wide range of potential activities from cooking to musical improvisation.
- Gifted children have the capacity over time to solve challenging problems and produce products valued and needed by a culture.
- Such children and adolescents need well-designed environments and opportunities to realize their full intellectual and creative potential.

focus 3

Identify four problems inherent in accurately describing the characteristics of individuals who are gifted.

- Individuals who are gifted vary significantly on a variety of characteristics; they are not a homogeneous group.
- Because research regarding the characteristics of people who are gifted has been conducted with different population groups, the characteristics that have surfaced represent the population studied rather than the gifted population as a whole.
- Many early studies of individuals who are gifted led to a stereotypical view of giftedness.
- Historically, studies regarding the characteristics of individuals who are gifted have not included adequate samples of females, minority or ethnic groups, or different socioeconomic groups.

focus 4

Identify three factors that appear to contribute significantly to the emergence of various forms of giftedness.

- Genetic endowment certainly contributes to all varieties of giftedness.
- Environmental stimulation provided by parents, teachers, coaches, tutors, and others contributes significantly to the emergence of giftedness.

- The interaction of innate abilities with environmental influences and encouragement fosters the development and expression of giftedness.

focus 5

Describe the range of assessment devices used to identify the various types of giftedness.

- Developmental checklists and scales
- Parent and teacher inventories
- Intelligence and achievement tests
- Creativity tests
- Other diverse observational information provided by parents, grandparents, and other knowledgeable informants

focus 6

Identify eight strategies used to foster the development of children and adolescents who are gifted.

- Environmental stimulation provided by parents from infancy through adolescence
- Differentiated education and specialized service delivery systems that provide enrichment activities and/or possibilities for acceleration: early entrance to kindergarten or school; grade skipping; early admission to college; honors programs at the high school and college levels; specialized schools in the performing and visual arts,

math, and science; mentor programs with university professors and other talented individuals; and specialized counseling facilities

 focus 7

What are some of the social–emotional needs of students who are gifted?

- Understanding, appreciating and valuing their own uniqueness as well as that of others
- Understanding the importance and the development of relationship skills
- Expanding and valuing their high-level sensitivity
- Gaining a realistic understanding of their own abilities and talents
- Identifying ways of nurturing and developing their own abilities and talents
- Adequately distinguishing between pursuits of excellence and pursuits of perfection
- Developing the behaviors associated with negotiation and compromise

 focus 8

Identify four important aspects of counterconditioning for gifted girls.

- Career modeling by a successful mother or close relative
- Fathers who support alternative views and attitudes about female roles, careers, and professions
- Teachers who attend to girls and young women in ways that support the emergence of talents and capacities
- School and classroom environments that foster independence, provide successful female role models, and provide access and encouragement for courses and experiences that center on talent development

 focus 9

Identify eight important elements of programs for gifted children who come from diverse backgrounds and who may live in poverty.

- The programs are staffed with skilled and competent teachers and other support personnel.
- The staff members work as a team.
- Teachers and others responsible for developing the learning experience understand learning styles, students' interests, and how to build students' affective, cognitive, and ethical capacities.
- The programs maintain and encourage ethnic diversity, provide extracurricular cultural enrichment, provide counseling, foster parent support groups, and provide children and youth access to significant models.
- The programs focus on students' strengths not their deficits.
- The programs help parents understand their key role in developing talents and giftedness.
- The programs provide many opportunities for hands-on learning, activities that foster self-expression, and generous use of mentors and role models from the child's cultural or ethnic group.
- The programs are characterized by a team approach, involving parents, teachers, mentors, and other family members.

References

AAMR Ad Hoc Committee on Terminology and Classification. (1992). *Classification in mental retardation* (9th ed.). Washington, DC: American Association on Mental Retardation.

ABCNEWS.com. (2000, April 9). Summer camps your kids will love. Camping it up: A quick guide for parents on choosing the right camps for your kids 1–2 [On line]. Available: www.ABCNEWS.com

Abery, B. (1994). Self-determination: It's not just for adults. *IMPACT, 6*(4), 2. ERIC Document Reproduction Service No. ED 368 109.

Abramovitch, R., Stanhope, L., Pepler, D. J., & Corter, C. (1987). Patterns of sibling interaction among preschool-age children. In M. E. Lamb & B. Sutton-Smith (Eds.), *Sibling relationships* (pp. 61–68). Hillsdale, NJ: Erlbaum.

Abt Associates. (1974). *Assessments of selected resources for severely handicapped children and youth: Vol. 1. A state-of-the-art paper.* Cambridge, MA: Author. ERIC Document Reproduction Service No. ED 134 614.

Achenbach, T. M. (1966). The classification of children's psychiatric symptoms: A factor analytic study. *Psychological Monographs: General and Applied, 615*, 1–37.

Achenbach, T. M. (1991a). *Manual for the child behavior checklist/4–18 and 1991 profile.* Burlington, VT: University of Vermont, Department of Psychiatry.

Achenbach, T. M. (1991b). *Manual for the teacher's report form and 1991 profile.* Burlington, VT: University of Vermont, Department of Psychiatry.

Achenbach, T. M. (1992). *Manual for the child behavior checklist/2–3 and 1992 profile.* Burlington, VT: University of Vermont, Department of Psychiatry.

Achter, J. A., Benbow, C. P., & Lubinski, D. (1997). Rethinking multipotentiality among the intellectually gifted: A critical review and recommendations. *Gifted Child Quarterly, 41*(1), 5–15.

Adderholdt-Elliott, M. (1987). *Perfectionism: What's bad about feeling too good?* Minneapolis, MN: Free Spirit.

Affleck, G., & Tennen, H. (1993). Cognitive adaptation to adversity: Insights from parents of medically fragile infants. In A. P. Turnbull, J. M. Patterson, S. K. Behr, D. L. Murphy, D. L. Marguis, & M. J. Blue-Banning (Eds.), *Cognitive coping, families, and disability* (pp. 135–150). Baltimore, MD: Brookes.

Agosta, J. (1992). Evaluating family support services: Two quantitative case studies. In V. J. Bradley, J. Knoll, & J. M. Agosta (Eds.), *Emerging issues in family support* (pp. 99–150). Washington, DC: The American Association on Mental Retardation.

Agran, M., & Hughes, C. (1997). Problem solving. In M. Agran (Ed.), *Student-directed learning: Teaching self-determination skills* (pp. 171–198). Pacific Grove, CA: Brooks/Cole.

Agran, M., & Wehmeyer, M. (1999). *Innovations: Teaching problem solving to students with mental retardation.* Washington, DC: American Association on Mental Retardation.

Ainscow, M. (1999). *Understanding the development of inclusive schools.* Studies in inclusive education series. London: Falmer Press.

Alarcon-Cazares, M. (1998). Neuroanatomical correlates of reading disability: A twin study. *Dissertation Abstracts International: Section B: The Sciences and Engineering, 58*(10-B), 5662.

Alberto, P. A., Taber, T., Brozovic, S. A., & Elliot, N. E. (1997). Continuing issues of collaborative transition planning in the secondary schools. *Journal of Vocational Rehabilitation, 8,* 197–204.

Alexander, A., Anderson, H., Heilman, P. C., et al. (1991). Phonological awareness training and remediation of analytic decoding deficits in a group of severe dyslexics. *Annals of Dyslexia, 41,* 193–206.

Allen, J. (1998). Personality assessment with American Indians and Alaska Natives: Instrument considerations and service delivery style. *Journal of Personality Assessment, 70,* 17–42.

Alper, S. K., Schloss, P. J., & Schloss, C. N. (1994). *Families of students with disabilities.* Boston: Allyn and Bacon.

Als, H., & Gilkerson, L. (1995). Developmentally supportive care in the neonatal intensive care unit. *Zero to Three, 15*(6), 1–10.

Aman, M. G., Arnold, L. E., & Armstrong, S. C. (1999). Review of serotonergic agents and perseverative behavior in patients with developmental disabilities. *Mental Retardation and Developmental Disabilities Research Reviews, 5*(4), 279–289.

Aman, M. G., & Madrid, A. (1999). Atypical antipsychotics in persons with developmental disabilities. *Mental Retardation and Developmental Disabilities Research Reviews, 5*(4), 253–263.

Amano, K. (1999). Improvement of schoolchildren's reading and writing ability through the formation of linguistic awareness. In Y. Engestrom and R. Miettinen (Eds.), *Perspectives on activity theory. Learning in doing: Social, cognitive, and computational perspectives* (pp. 183–205). New York: Cambridge University Press.

American Academy of Pediatrics. (1995). Drug-exposed infants. *Pediatrics, 96*(2), 364–367.

American Academy of Pediatrics. (1998). Hospital discharge of high-risk neonate—proposed guideline. *Pediatrics, 102*(2), 411–417.

American Academy of Pediatrics (2000). Diagnosis and evaluation of the child with attention-deficit/hyperactivity disorder (AC 0002). *Pediatrics, 105,* 1158–1170.

American Diabetes Association. (1999). What is insulin dependent diabetes? [Online]. Available: http://www.diabetes.org/ada/Type1.asp

American Diabetes Association. (2000a). Children with diabetes: Information for teachers and child-care providers [Online]. Available: http://www.diabetes.org/ada/teach1.asp

American Diabetes Association. (2000b). Diabetes facts and figures [Online]. Available: http://www.diabetes.org/ada/facts.asp

American Foundation for the Blind. (2000). *Educating students with visual impairments for inclusion in society: A paper on the inclusion of students with visual impairments.* Louisville, KY: Author [Online]. Available: http://www.afb.org/education/jltlipaper.html

American Medical Association. (1999). Facts about sickle cell anemia. *Journal of the American Medical Association, 281*(18), 1768.

American Printing House for the Blind. (1992). *Annual report.* Louisville, KY: Author.

American Psychiatric Association. (1994). *Diagnostic and statistical manual of mental disorders* (4th ed.). Washington, DC: Author.

Amlund, J. T., & Kardash, C. M. (1994). Group approaches to consultation and advocacy. In S. K. Alper, P. J. Schloss, & C. N. Schloss (Eds.), *Families of students with disabilities* (pp. 181–204). Boston: Allyn and Bacon.

Anderson, J. M., Hughes, J. D., Rothi, L. J. G., Crucian, G. P., & Heilman, K. M. (1999). Developmental stuttering and Parkinson's disease: The effects of levodopa treatment. *Journal of Neurology, Neurosurgery, and Psychiatry, 66,* 776–778.

Anderson, S. R., & Romanczyk, R. G. (1999). Early intervention for young children with autism: Continuum-based behavioral models. *Journal of the Association for Persons with Severe Handicaps, 24,* 162–173.

Antona, M., Stephanidis, C., & Kouroupetroglou, G. (1999). Access to lexical knowledge in modular interpersonal aids. *ACC: Augmentative and Alternative Communication, 15,* 269–279.

Arboleda, T. (1999). *In the shadow of race: Growing up as a multiethnic American.* Mahwah, NJ: Erlbaum.

Aro, T., Ahonen, T., Tolvanen, A., Lyytinen, H., & Todd-de-Barra, H. (1999). Contribution of ADHD characteristics to the academic treatment outcome of children with learning difficulties. *Developmental Neuropsychology, 15*(2), 291–305.

Arries, J. F. (1999). Learning disabilities and foreign languages: A curriculum approach to the design of inclusive courses. *Modern Language Journal, 83,* 98–110.

Artiles, A. J. (1998). The dilemma of difference: Enriching the disproportionality discourse with theory and context. *Journal of Special Education, 32*(1), 32–36.

Assouline, S. G. (1997). Assessment of gifted children. In N. Colangelo & A. D. Davis (Eds.), *Handbook of gifted education* (2nd ed., pp. 89–108). Boston: Allyn and Bacon.

Atkins, D. V. (1987). Siblings of the hearing-impaired: Perspectives for parents. *Volta Review, 89*(5), 32–45.

Auditory–Verbal International. (2000). *Principles of auditory-verbal practice* [Online]. Available: http://deafness.miningco.com/health/deafness/gi/dynamic/offsite.htm?site=http://www.auditory%2Dverbal.org/

Ault, M. M., Rues, J. P., Graff, J. C., & Holvoet, J. F. (2000). Special health care procedures. In M. Snell & F. Brown (Eds.), *Instruction of students with severe disabilities* (pp. 245–290). Columbus, OH: Merrill.

Austin, K. M. (1999). Adult attention deficit hyperactivity disorder: Personality characteristics and comorbidity. *Dissertation Abstracts International: Section B: The Sciences and Engineering, 59*(7-B), 3751.

Autman, S. A. (1994, October 31). *Disabled students making it in the mainstream.* Salt Lake Tribune, pp. B1, B2.

Babinski, L. M., Hartsough, C. S., & Lambert, N. M. (1999). Childhood conduct problems, hyperactivity–impulsivity, and inattention as predictors of adult criminal activity. *Journal of Child Psychology and Psychiatry and Allied Disciplines, 40,* 347–355.

Baca, L., & de Valenzuela, J. S. (1998). Background and rationale for bilingual special education. In L. M. Baca & H. T. Cervantes, (Eds.), *The bilingual special education interface* (3rd ed., pp. 2–25). Columbus, OH: Merrill/Macmillan.

Bailet, L. L., & Turk, W. R. (1997). Epilepsy. In G. G. Bear, K. M. Minke, & A. Thomas (Eds.), *Children's needs II: Development, problems, and alternatives* (pp. 801–813). Bethesda, MD: National Association of School Psychologists.

Bailey, D. B., Jr., Skinner, D., Rodriguez, P., & Correa, V. (1999). Awareness, use, and satisfaction with services for Latino parents of young children with disabilities. *Exceptional Children, 65,* 367–381.

Bailey, D. B., Jr., & Wolery, M. (1992). *Teaching infants and preschoolers with disabilities* (2nd ed.). Columbus, OH: Merrill.

Baker, E. T., Wang, W. C., & Walberg, H. J. (1995). The effects of inclusion on learning. *Educational Leadership, 52*(4), 33–35.

Baker, J. M., & Zigmond, N. (1995). The meaning and practice of inclusion for students with learning disabilities: Themes and implications from the five cases. *Journal of Special Education, 29,* 163–180.

Bank, C. (2000, February 1). Coping with attention deficit disorder. *MSNBC report by Philadelphia, PA Channel 10, NBC,* [Online]. Available: www.msnbc.com/local/WCAU/245787.asp

Banks, J. A. (1999). *An introduction to multicultural education* (2nd ed.). Boston: Allyn and Bacon.

Barak, Y., Kimhi, R., Stein, D., Gutman, J., & Weizman, A. (1999). Autistic subjects with comorbid epilepsy: A possible association with viral infections. *Child Psychiatry and Human Development, 29*(3), 245–251.

Barbaresi, W. J., & Olsen, R. D. (1998). An ADHD educational intervention for elementary schoolteachers: A pilot study. *Journal of Developmental and Behavioral Pediatrics, 19*(2), 94–100.

Barkley, R. A. (1998). *Attention-deficit hyperactivity disorder: A handbook for diagnosis and treatment.* New York: Guilford.

Barkley, R. A., & Edelbrock, C. (1987). Assessing situational varia-

tion in children's problem behaviors: The home and school situations questionnaires. In R. J. Prinz (Ed.), *Advances in behavioral assessment of children and families* (Vol. 3, pp. 157–176). New York: JAI.

Baron, R. A., & Byme, D. (1997). *Social psychology: Understanding human interaction* (8th ed.). Boston: Allyn and Bacon.

Barraga, N. C., & Erin, J. N. (1992). *Visual handicaps and learning* (3rd ed.). Austin, TX: Pro-Ed.

Bartens, A. (2000). *Ideophones and sound symbolism in Atlantic creoles.* Helsinki, Finland: Academia Scientiarum Fennica.

Baskin, D. S. (1996). Spinal cord injury. In R. W. Evans (Ed.), *Neurology and trauma* (pp. 276–299). Philadelphia, PA: Saunders.

Bauer, A. M., & Shea, T. M. (1999). *Learner with emotional and behavioral disorders: An introduction.* Upper Saddle River, NJ: Prentice-Hall.

Baumrind, D. (1995). *Child maltreatment and optimal caregiving in social contexts.* New York: Garland.

Beach Center on Families and Disability. (1998a). Dads feel left out [Online]. Available: http://www.lsi.ukans.edu/beach/dis2.htm

Beach Center on Families and Disability. (1998b). Family stories: Gathering for the future [Online]. Available: http://www.lsi.ukans.edu/beach/htmlsfam2.htm

Beach Center on Families and Disability. (1998c). How to: Better cope with a family member's problems [Online]. Available: http://www.lsi.ukans.edu/beach/html/c1.htm

Beach Center on Families and Disability. (1998d). How to: Deal with the news that your baby needs special care [Online]. Available: http://www.lsi.ukans.edu/beach/html/c7.htm

Beach Center on Families and Disability. (1998e). How to: Honor cultural diversity [Online]. Available http://www.lsi.ukans.edu/beach/html/m1.htm

Beach Center on Families and Disability. (1998f). How to: Renew family energy through respite care [Online]. Available: http://www.lsi.ukans.edu/beach/html/fs6.htm

Beach Center on Families and Disabilities. (1998g). Quality indicators for exemplary family empowerment [Online]. Available: http://www.lsi.ukans.edu/beach/html/x5.htm

Beach Center on Families and Disability. (1998h). Quality indicators of exemplary family-centered programs [Online]. Available: http://www.lsi.ukans.edu/beach/html/f19.htm

Beach Center on Families and Disability. (1998i). Research brief: Coping strategies and family well-being [Online]. Available: http://

www.lsi.ukans.edu/beach/html.5c.htm

Beach Center on Families and Disability. (1998j). Research brief: Effectiveness of parent to parent support [Online]. Available: http://www.lsi.ukans.edu/beach/html/12p.htm

Beach Center on Families and Disability. (1998k). Research brief: Father participation in child care programs [Online]. Available: http://www.lsi.ukans.edu/beach/html/28f.htm

Beach Center on Families and Disability. (1998l). What you should know about American Indians and disability [Online]. Available: http://www.lsi.ukans.edu/beach/html/m6.htm

Beck, A. R., Fritz, H., Keller, A., & Dennis, M. (2000). Attitudes to school-aged children toward peers who use augmentative and alternative communication. *AAC: Augmentative and Alternative Communication, 16,* 13–26.

Beck, C., Silverstone, P., Glor, K., & Dunn, J. (1999). Psychostimulant prescriptions by psychiatrists higher than expected: A self-report survey. *Canadian Journal of Psychiatry, 44,* 680–684.

Beckman-Bell, P. (1981). Child-related stress in families of handicapped children. *Topics in Early Childhood Special Education, 1*(3), 45–54.

Beers, S. R. (1998). Rehabilitation assessment and planning for children and adults with learning disabilities. In G. Goldstein and S. R. Beers (Eds.), *Rehabilitation: Human brain function: Assessment and rehabilitation* (pp. 201–228). New York: Plenum.

Begley, S. (1988, January 26). My brain made me do it. *Newsweek,* p. 56.

Beirne-Smith, M., Ittenbach, R. F., & Patton, J. R. (1998). *Mental retardation* (5th ed.). Upper Saddle River, NJ: Merrill.

Belcher, T. L. (1996). Behavioral treatment vs. behavioral control: A case study. *Journal of Developmental and Physical Disabilities, 7,* 235–241.

Bell, M. L., & Smith, B. R. (1996). Grandparents as primary caregivers: Lessons in love. *Teaching Exceptional Children, 28,* 18–19.

Bellenir, K. (1996). *Substance abuse sourcebook.* Detroit, MI: Omnigraphics.

Benavidez, D., & Matson, J. L., (1993). Assessment of depression in mentally retarded adolescents. *Research in Developmental Disabilities, (14),* 179–188.

Bender, W. N. (1998). *Learning disabilities: Characteristics, identification, and teaching strategies* (3rd ed.). Boston: Allyn and Bacon.

Benedetto-Nasho, E., & Tannock, R. (1999). Math computation, error patterns, and stimulant effects in children with attention deficit hyperactivity disorder. *Journal of Attention Disorders, 3*(3), 121–134.

Benjamin, C. (1996). *Problem solving in school.* Upper Saddle River, NJ: Globe Fearon Educational Publisher.

Bennett, C. E., & Debarros, K. A. (1998). The Asian and Pacific Islander population. School enrollment. *Population Profile of the United States: 1997* (pp. 48–49). U.S. Bureau of the Census, Current Population Reports, Series P23-194. Washington, DC: U.S. Government Printing Office.

Bennett, T., Lee, H., & Lueke, B. (1998). Expectations and concerns: What mothers and fathers say about inclusion. *Education & Training in Mental Retardation & Developmental Disabilities, 33*(2), 108–122.

Benson, B. A., Gross, A. M., & Kellum, G. (1999). The siblings of children with craniofacial anomalies. *Children's Health Care, 28,* 51–68.

Benson, G., Aberdanto, L., Short, K., Nuccio, J. B., & Mans, F. (1993). Development of a theory of mind in individuals with mental retardation. *American Journal on Mental Retardation, 98*(6), 427–433.

Benson, H. (1992). *Literature review: Stress, coping, and respite care in families with members with disabilities.* Lawrence, KS: The Beach Center on Families and Disability, the University of Kansas.

Bergen, A. E., & Mosley, J. L. (1994). Attention and attention shift efficiency in individuals with and without mental retardation. *American Journal on Mental Retardation, 98*(6), 732–743.

Berger, K. S. (1994). *The developing person through the lifespan.* New York: Worth.

Bergland, M., & Hoffbauer, D. (1996, Winter). New opportunities for students with traumatic brain injuries: Transition to postsecondary education. *Teaching Exceptional Children, 28*(2), 54–56.

Berkson, G. (1998). Brief report: Control in highly focused top-spinning. *Journal of Autism and Developmental Disorders, 28,* 83–86.

Berliner, L., & Elliott, D. M. (1996). Sexual abuse of children. In J. Briere, L. Berliner, J. A. Bulkley, C. Jenny, & T. Reid (Eds.), *The APSAC handbook on child maltreatment* (pp. 51–71). Thousand Oaks, CA: Sage.

Bernard-Opitz, V., Sriram, N., & Sapuan, S. (1999). Enhancing vocal imitations in children with autism using the IBM SpeechViewer. *Autism, 3*(2), 131–147.

Berney, T. P. (2000). Autism—an evolving concept. *British Journal of Psychiatry, 176,* 20–25.

Berninger, V. W. (1999). Coordinating transcription and text generation in working memory during composing: Automatic and constructive processes. *Learning Disability Quarterly, 22*(2). 99–112.

Bernstein, D. K. (1997a). Language development: The preschool years. In D. K. Bernstein and E. Tiegerman-Farber (Eds.), *Language and communication disorders in children* (4th ed., pp. 97–126). Boston: Allyn and Bacon.

Bernstein, D. K. (1997b). The nature of language and its disorders. In D. K. Bernstein and E. Tiegerman-Farber (Eds.), *Language and communication disorders in children* (4th ed., pp. 1–25). Boston: Allyn and Bacon.

Berquin, P. C., Giedd, J. N., Jacobsen, L. K., Hamburger, S. D., Krain, A. L., Rapoport, J. L., & Castellanos, F. X. (1998). Cerebellum in attention-deficit hyperactivity disorder: A Morphometric MRI study. *Neurology, 50,* 1087–1093.

Berry, J., & Hardman, M. L. (1998). *Lifespan perspectives on the family and disability.* Boston: Allyn and Bacon.

Best, A. B. (1992). *Teaching children with visual impairments.* Philadelphia: Open University Press.

Biederman, J., Faraone, S. V., Mick, E., et al. (1999). Clinical correlates of ADHD in females: Findings from a large group of girls ascertained from pediatric and psychiatric referral sources. *Journal of the American Academy of Child and Adolescent Psychiatry, 38,* 966–975.

Biederman, J., Mick, E., Prince, J., et al. (1999). Systematic chart review of the pharmacologic treatment of comorbid attention deficit hyperactivity disorder in youth with bipolar disorder. *Journal of Child and Adolescent Psychopharmacology, 9*(4), 247–256.

Biederman, J., Willens, T., Mick, E., Faraone, S. V., & Spencer, T. (1998). Does attention-deficit hyperactivity disorder impact the developmental course of drug and alcohol abuse and dependence? *Biological Psychiatry, 44,* 269–273.

Bigler, E. D. (1997). Brain imaging and behavioral outcome in traumatic brain injury. In E. D. Bigler, E. Clark, & J. E. Farmer (Eds.), *Childhood traumatic brain injury: Diagnosis, assessment, and intervention* (pp. 7–29). Austin, TX: Pro-Ed.

Bigler, E. D., Clark, E., & Farmer, J. E. (1997). Traumatic brain injury. In E. D. Bigler, E. Clark, & J. E. Farmer (Eds.), *Childhood traumatic brain injury: Diagnosis, assessment, and intervention* (pp. 3–6). Austin, TX: Pro-Ed.

Billingsley, F. F., Liberty, K. A., & White, O. R. (1994). The chronology of instruction. In E. C. Cipani & F. Spooner (Eds.), *Curricular and instructional approaches for persons with severe disabilities* (pp. 81–116). Boston: Allyn and Bacon.

Binet, A., & Simon, T. (1905). Méthodes nouvelles pour le diagnostique du niveau intellectual des anormaux. *L'Année Psychologique, 11,* 191–244.

Binet, A., & Simon, T. (1908). Le développment de l'intelligence chez les enfants. *L'Année Psychologique, 14,* 1–94.

Bishop, K., Bullock, K., Martin, S., & Thompson, J. (1999). Users' perceptions of the GCSE. *Educational Research, 41*(1), 35–49.

Bishop, V. E. (1996a). Causes and functional implications of visual impairment. In *Foundations of low vision: Clinical and functional perspectives* (pp. 86–114). New York: American Foundation for the Blind Press.

Bishop. V. E. (1996b). *Teaching visually impaired children* (2nd ed.). Springfield, IL: Thomas.

Bitter, G. G., & Pierson, M. E. (1999). *Using technology in the classroom* (4th ed.). Boston: Allyn and Bacon.

Blacher, J. (1984). Sequential stages of parental adjustment to the birth of a child with handicaps: Fact or artifact? *Mental Retardation, 22*(2), 55–68.

Blackard, M. K., & Barsh, E. T. (1982). Parents' and professionals' perceptions of the handicapped child's impact on the family. *Journal of the Association for the Severely Handicapped, 7,* 62–70.

Blanck, D. P. & Braddock, D. L. (1998). *The Americans with Disabilities Act and the emerging workforce: Employment of people with mental retardation.* Washington, DC: American Association on Mental Retardation.

Blanksby, D. C., & Langford, P. E. (1993). VAP-CAP: A procedure to assess the visual functioning of young visually impaired children. *Journal of Visual Impairment & Blindness, 86,* 46–49.

Blaska, J. K. (1998). *Cyclical grieving: Reocurring emotions experienced by parents who have children with disabilities.* Minneapolis: MN: EDRS Price.

Bloom, B. S. (1964). *Stability and change in human characteristics.* New York: Wiley.

Blosser, J. L., & DePompei, R. (1994). Creating an effective classroom environment. In R. C. Savage & G. F. Wolcott (Eds.), *Educational dimensions of acquired brain injury* (pp. 413–451). Austin, TX: Pro-Ed.

Bocian, K. M., Beebe, M. E., MacMillan, D. L., & Gresham, F. M. (1999). Competing paradigms in learning disabilities classification by schools and the variations in the meaning of discrepant achievement. *Learning Disabilities Research and Practice, 14,* 1–14.

Boehm, A. E. (1986). *Boehm test of basic concepts—revised (Boehm-R).* San Antonio, TX: The Psychological Corporation.

Bogdan, W. K. (2000). Celebrating our diversity in the new millennium: An opportunity for success. *Teaching Exceptional Children, 32*(3), 4–5.

Bonn, H., & Bonn, B. (2000a). In the best interests of the child. In S. E. Wade (Ed.), *Inclusive education: A casebook and readings for prospective and practicing teachers* (pp. 173–180). Mahwah, NJ: Erlbaum.

Bonn, H., & Bonn, B. (2000b). Part B of the case: "In the best interests of the child." In S. E. Wade (Ed.), *Preparing teachers for inclusive education* (pp. 209–211). Mahwah, NJ: Erlbaum.

Bonvillian, J. D., & Folven, R. J. (1993). Sign language acquisition: Developmental aspects. In M. Marschark & M. D. Clark (Eds.), *Psychological perspectives on deafness* (pp. 229–265). Hillsdale, NJ: Erlbaum.

Botting, N., & Conti-Ramsden, G. (1999). Pragmatic language impairment without autism: The children in question. *Autism, 3*(4), 371–396.

Boucher, C. R. (1999). *Students in discord: Adolescents with emotional and behavioral disorders.* Westport, CT: Greenwood.

Boucher, J. (1998). Reply: Some issues in the classification of developmental disorders. *International Journal of Language and Communication Disorders, 33,* 95–108.

Boudah, D. J., Lenz, B. K., Bulgren, J. A., Schumaker, J. B., & Deshler, D. D. (2000). Don't water down! Enhance content learning through the unit organizer routine. *Teaching Exceptional Children, 33*(3), 48–56.

Bowe, F. (2000). *Physical, sensory, and health disabilities.* Upper Saddle River, NJ: Merrill.

Bowen, C., & Cupples, L. (1999). Reply: A phonological therapy in depth: A reply to commentaries. *International Journal of Language and Communication Disorders, 34,* 65–83.

Bower, E. M. (1959). The emotionally handicapped child and the school. *Exceptional Children, 26,* 6–11.

Boxler, B. (1997). Available: [Online]. http://www.circleoffriends.org/chris/posstings/0004

Boyer, E. L. (1983). *High school: A report on secondary education in America.* New York: Harper & Row.

Braaten, S., Kauffman, J. M., Braaten, B., Polsgrove, L., & Nelson, C. M. (1988). The regular education initiative: Patent medicine for behavioral disorders. *Exceptional Children, 55*(1), 21–27.

Braddock, D. (1999). Aging and developmental disabilities: Demographic and policy issues affecting American families. *Mental Retardation, 37,* 155–161.

Braddock, D., & Hemp, R. (1997). Medicaid spending reduction and developmental disabilities. *Journal of Disability Policy Studies, 1,* 1–32.

Braddock, D., Hemp, R., Bachelder, L., & Fujiura, G. (1995). *The state of the states in developmental disabilities.* Washington, DC: American Association on Mental Retardation.

Braddock, D., Hemp, R., Parish, S., & Rizzolo, M. (2000). *The state of the state in developmental disabilities: Summary of the 1999 study update.* Chicago: Department of Disability and Human Development, University of Chicago–Illinois.

Braden, J. P. (1992). Intellectual assessment of deaf and hard-of-hearing people: A quantitative and qualitative research synthesis. *School Psychology Review, 21,* 82–94.

Bradley, D. F., & King-Sears, M. E. (1997). The change process: Change for people and schools. In D. F. Bradley, M. E. King-Sears, & D. Tessier-Switlick (Eds.), *Teaching students in inclusive settings: From theory to practice* (pp. 56–82). Boston: Allyn and Bacon.

Bradley, D. F., & Switlick, D. M. (1997). From isolation to cooperation in teaching. In D. F. Bradley, M. E. King-Sears, & D. Tessier-Switlick (Eds.), *Teaching students in inclusive settings: From theory to practice* (pp. 109–128). Boston: Allyn and Bacon.

Bradley, V. J., Knoll, J., & Agosta, J. M. (1992). *Emerging issues in family support.* Washington, DC: American Association on Mental Retardation.

Brain Injury Association, Inc. (1999a). *Special report: CDC report shows prevalence of brain injury.* [Online]. Available: http://www.biausa.org/costsand.htm

Brain Injury Association, Inc. (1999b, September). *Testimony on children's health: Protecting our most precious resource in support of reauthorization of the Traumatic Brain Injury Act of 1996.* U.S. Senate Committee on Health, Education, Labor and Pensions, Subcommittee on Public Health, by Alan I. Bergman [Online]. Available: http://www.biausa.org/childrens_health_testimony.htm

Brain Injury Association, Inc. (1999c). What is a coma? [Online]. Available: http://www.biausa.org/trauma.htm

Brandenburg, N. A., Friedman, R. M., & Silver, S. E. (1990). The epidemiology of childhood psychiatric disorders: Recent prevalence findings and methodologic issues. *Journal of the American Academy of Child and Adolescent Psychiatry, 29,* 76–83.

Brassard, M. R. (1997). Psychological and physical abuse. In G. G. Bear, K. M. Minke, & A. Thomas (Eds.), *Children's needs II: Development, problems, and alternatives* (pp. 707–718). Bethesda, MD: National Association of School Psychologists.

Bray, M., & Kehle, T. J. (1998). Self-modeling as an intervention for stuttering. *School Psychology Review, 27,* 587–598.

Brock, S. E., & Sandoval, J. (1997). Suicidal ideation and behaviors. In G. G. Bear, K. M. Minke, & A. Thomas (Eds.), *Children's needs II: Development, problems, and alternatives* (pp. 361–374). Bethesda, MD: National Association of School Psychologists.

Brotherson, S. E., & Dollahite, D. C. (1997). Generative ingenuity in fatherwork with young children with special needs. In A. J. Hawkins & D. C. Dollahite (Eds.), *Generative fathering: Beyond deficit perspectives* (pp. 89–104). Newbury Park, CA: Sage.

Browder, D., & Bambara, L. M. (2000). Home and community. In M. E. Snell & F. Brown (Eds.), *Instruction of students with severe disabilities* (pp. 543–589). Upper Saddle River, NJ: Merrill.

Browder, D., & Snell, M. E. (2000). Teaching functional academics. In M. E. Snell & F. Brown (Eds.), *Instruction of students with severe disabilities* (pp. 493–542). Upper Saddle River, NJ: Merrill.

Brown, L., Sherbenou, R. J., & Johnsen, S. K. (1990). *Test of nonverbal intelligence (TONI-2): A language-free measure of cognitive ability* (2nd ed.). Austin, TX: Pro-Ed.

Brown, R. T., & Sawyer, M. G. (1998). *Medication for school-age children: Effects on learning and behavior.* New York: Guilford, 1998.

Brown v. Topeka, Kansas, Board of Education, 347 U.S. 483 (1954).

Bruno, R. R. (1998). School enrollment. In *Population profile of the United States: 1997* (pp. 18–19). U.S. Bureau of the Census, Current Population Reports, Series P23-194. Washington, DC: U.S. Government Printing Office.

Bryan, T., Bay, M., Lopez-Reyna, T., & Donahue, M. (1991). Characteristics of students with learning disabilities: The extant database and its implications for educational programs. In J. Lloyd, N. N. Singh, & A. C. Repp (Eds.), *The regular education initiative: Alternative perspectives on concepts, issues, and models* (pp. 113–132). Sycamore, IL: Sycamore.

Bryan, T., Sullivan-Burstein, K., & Mathur, S. (1998). The influence of affect on social-information processing. *Journal of Learning Disabilities, 31,* 418–426.

Bryant, D., & Maxwell, K. (1997). The effectiveness of early intervention for disadvantaged children. In M. J. Guralnick (Ed.), *The effectiveness of early intervention* (pp. 23–46). Baltimore, MD: Brookes.

Bryson, S. E., & Smith, I. M. (1998). Epidemiology of autism: Prevalence, associated characteristics, and implications for research and service delivery. *Mental Retardation and Developmental Disabilities Research Reviews, 4*(2), 97–103.

Buchanan, A. (1996). *Cycles of child maltreatment: Facts, fallacies, and interventions.* Chichester, UK: Wiley.

Buckingham, D. (1999). *Psychopharmacology of children and adolescents.* In J. M. Herrera and W. B. Lawson (Eds.), *Cross-cultural psychiatry* (pp. 373–381). Chichester, UK: Wiley.

Budd, K. S., Stockman, K. D., & Miller, E. N. (1998). Parenting issues and interventions with adolescent mothers. In J. R. Lutzer (Ed.), *Handbook of child abuse, research, and treatment* (pp. 357–376). New York: Plenum Press.

Bullock, L. M., & Gable, R. A. (1994). Monograph on inclusion: Ensuring appropriate services to children and youth with emotional and behavioral disorders. Reston, VA: Council for Exceptional Children.

Bullock, L. M., & Gable, R. A. (1998). *CCBD mini-library series: Successful interventions for the 21st century.* Reston, VA: The Council for Children with Behavior Disorders, a division of the Council for Exceptional Children.

Burchard, J. D., & Clark, R. T. (1990). The role of individualized care in a service delivery system for children and adolescents with severely maladjusted behavior. *Journal of Mental Health Administration, 17*(1), 48–60.

Burchinal, M. R., Campbell, F. A., Bryant, D. M., Wasik, B. H., & Ramey, C. T. (1997). Early intervention and mediating processes in cognitive performance of children of low-income African-American families. *Child Development, 68,* 935–954.

Burns, B. J., & Goldman, S. K. (Eds.). (1999). Promising practices in wraparound for children with serious emotional disturbance and their families. *Systems of care: Promising practices in children's mental health, 1998 series, Vol. 4.* Washington, DC: Center for Effective Collaboration and Practice, American Institutes for Research.

Burns, P. C., & Roe, B. (1993). *Burns Roe informal reading inventory: Preprimer to 12 grade* (4th ed.). Boston: Houghton Mifflin.

Bursuck, W. D., & Rose, E. (1992). Community college options for students with mild disabilities. In F. R. Rusch, L. DeStefano, J. Chadsey-Rusch, L. A. Phelps, & E. Syzmanski, *Transition from school to adult life* (pp. 71–91). Sycamore, IL: Sycamore.

Burt, C. (1921). *Mental and scholastic tests.* London: King.

Bushman, B. J., Baumeister, R. F., & Stack, A. D. (1999). Catharsis, aggression, and persuasive influence: Self-fulfilling or self-defeating prophecies? *Journal of Personality and Social Psychology, 76,* 367–376.

Bussing, R., Schoenberg, N. E., Rogers, K. M., Zima, B. T., & Angus, S. (1998). Explanatory models of ADHD: Do they differ by ethnicity, child gender, or treatment status? *Journal of Emotional and Behavioral Disorders, 6*(4), 233–242.

Byng, S., Swinburn, K., & Pound, C. (1999). *The aphasia therapy file.* Hove, UK: Psychology Press/Taylor and Francis.

Bynoe, P. F. (1998). Rethinking and retooling teacher preparation to prevent perpetual failure by our children. *Journal of Special Education, 32,* 37–40.

Cable News Network. (1997). Experimental gene therapy offers hope to diabetics [Online]. Available: http://cnn.com/HEALTH/9704/30/nfm.diabetes.gene/index.html

Cadray, J. P. (1998). Educating culturally responsive teachers: An introduction to process-oriented or developmental approaches. Paper presented at the annual meeting of the American Association of Colleges for Teacher Education, New Orleans, LA, February 25–28, 1998.

Caldwell, J. (1994, October 2). First the word, then—click!—the sign. *The Boston Sunday Globe,* B23–B24.

Callwood-Brathwaite, D. J. (1998). Co-occurrence of attention deficit/hyperactivity disorder in a school-identified sample of students with emotional and behavioral disorders: Implications for educational programming. *Dissertation Abstracts International Section A: Humanities and Social Sciences, 59*(2-A), 0415.

Campbell, C. E. (1999). MMPI-2 patterns of adults with attention deficit hyperactivity disorder. *Dissertation Abstracts International: Section B: The Sciences and Engineering, 59*(7-B), 36–83.

Campbell, L., Campbell, B., & Dickinson, D. (1999). *Teaching and learning through multiple intelligences* (2nd ed.). Boston: Allyn and Bacon.

Carlson, N. R., & Buskist, W. (1999). *Psychology: The science of behavior* (5th ed.). Boston: Allyn and Bacon.

Carnine, D. (2000). *Why education experts resist effective practices (and what it would take to make education more like medicine).* Washington, DC: Thomas B. Fordham Foundation.

Carta, J. J., Sideridis, G., Rinkel, P., et al. (1994). Behavioral outcomes of young children prenatally exposed to illicit drugs: Review and analysis of experiential literature. *Topics in Early Childhood Special Education, 14*(2), 184–209.

Cassidy, V. M., & Stanton, J. E. (1959). *An investigation of factors involved in the educational placement of mentally retarded children: A study of differences between children in special and regular classes in Ohio.* Columbus: Ohio State University. (U.S. Office of Education Cooperative Research Program, Project No. 043).

Castaneda, R., Sussman, N., Levy, R., & Trujillo, M. (1999). A treatment algorithm for attention deficit hyperactivity disorder in cocaine-dependent adults: A one-year private practice study with long-acting stimulants, fluoxetine, and bupropion. *Substance Abuse, 20*(1), 59–71.

Castellanos, F. X. (1997). Toward a pathophysiology of attention-deficit/hyperactivity disorder. *Clinical Pediatrics, 36,* 381–393.

Cate, I. M. P., Miller, A. C., Rosen, C., Gordon, R. M., Bicchieri, S. M., & Marks, B. C. (1998). Reliability and validity of the Southern California Ordinal Scales of Development for a sample of young children with disabilities. *Journal of Psychoeducational Assessment, 16,* 4–14.

Cattell, R. B. (1971). *Abilities: Their structure, growth, and action.* Boston: Houghton Mifflin.

Cawley, J. F., Parmar, R. S., Yan, W., & Miller, J. H. (1998). Arithmetic computation performance of students with learning disabilities: Implications for curriculum. *Learning Disabilities Research and Practice, 13*(2), 68–74.

Center, D. B. (1989a). *Social maladjustment: An interpretation.* Paper presented at the 67th Annual International Conference of the Council for Exceptional Children, San Francisco, CA.

Center, D. B. (1989b). Social maladjustment: Definition, identification and programming. *Focus on Exceptional Children, 22*(1), 1–12.

Center for Applied Special Technology (1999). Summary of universal design concepts [Online]. Available: http://www.cast.org/concepts/concepts_summary.htm

Centers for Disease Control and Prevention. (1999, Midyear). US HIV and AIDS cases reported through June 1999. *HIV/AIDS Surveillance Report, 11*(1), 1–44.

Center for Effective Collaboration and Practice. (1998, January). *Addressing student problem behavior: An IEP team's introduction to functional behavioral assessment and behavior intervention plans, Why a functional assessment of behavior is necessary.* Washington, DC: Center for Effective Collaboration and Practice, American Institutes for Research.

Center for Effective Collaboration and Practice. (1999). *Executive summary. Volume 3: The role of education in the system of care: Effectively serving children with emotional or behavioral disorders* [Online]. Available: http://cecp.air.org/promisingpractices/documents.htm#3

Chabot, R. J., Orgill, A. A., Crawford, G., Harris, M. J., & Serfontein, G. (1999). Behavioral and electrophysiologic predictors of treatment response to stimulants in children with attention disorders. *Journal of Child Neurology, 14*(6), 343–351.

Chadsey-Rusch, H., & Heal, L. W. (1998). Building consensus from transition experts on social integration outcomes and interventions. *Exceptional Children, 62*(2), 165–187.

Chapman, R. S. (2000). Children's language learning: An interactionist perspective. *Journal of Child Psychology and Psychiatry and Allied Disciplines, 41,* 33–54.

Chard, D. J., & Osborn, J. (1999). Phonics and word recognition instruction in early reading programs: Guidelines for accessibility. *Learning Disabilities Research and Practice, 14*(2), 107–117.

Charlson, E., Strong, M., & Gold, R. (1992). How successful deaf teenagers experience and cope with isolation. *American Annals of the Deaf, 137*(3), 261–270.

Chavez, R. C., & O'Donnell, J. (1998). *Speaking the unpleasant: The politics of (non)engagement in the multicultural education terrain.* Albany, NY: State University of New York Press.

Chedd, N. A. (1996, July). Juggling family and career: Tales from the supernatural. *The Exceptional Parent, 26,* 30+.

Cheney, D., & Barringer, C. (1999). A trandisciplinary model for students' social and emotional development: Creating a context for inclusion. In J. R. Scotti, & L. H.

Meyer (Eds.), *Behavioral intervention: Principles, models, and practices* (pp. 149–174). Baltimore, MD: Brookes.

Cheney, D., Barringer, C., Upham, D., & Manning, B. (1996). Project destiny: A model for developing educational support teams through interagency networks for youth with emotional or behavioral disorders. In R. J. Illback & C. M. Nelson (Eds.), *Emerging school-based approaches for children with emotional and behavioral problems: Research and practice in service integration* (pp. 57–76). Binghamton, NY: Haworth.

Cheng, L. R. L. (2000). Children of yesterday, today and tomorrow: Global implications for child language. *Folia Phoniatrica et Logopaedica, 52*(1–3), 39–47.

Cherland, E., & Fitzpatrick, R. (1999). Psychotic side effects of psychostimulants: A 5-year review. *Canadian Journal of Psychiatry, 44,* 811–813.

Children with Diabetes. (1997). What is Type I diabetes? [Online]. Available: http://www.casleweb.com/diabetes/d_0n_100.htm

Children with Diabetes. (1999). Information for teachers [Online]. Available: http://www.childrenwithdiabetes.com/d_0q_200.htm

Children with Diabetes. (2000). Islet cell transplantation: Working toward a cure [Online]. Available: http://www.childrenwithdiabetes.com/d_0n_701.htm

Children's Defense Fund. (1998a). *Poverty matters: The cost of child poverty in America.* Washington, DC: Author.

Children's Defense Fund. (1998b). *The state of America's children.* Washington, DC: Author.

Children's Defense Fund. (1999). *Moments in America for children.* Washington, DC: Author.

Choi, I., Nisbett, R. E., & Norenzayan, A. (1999). Causal attribution across cultures: Variation and universality. *Psychological Bulletin, 125,* 47–63.

Chouard, C. H. (1997). Cochlear implants in deaf children—medical and social problems today and, perhaps, tomorrow. *Audiologia-Newsletter, 3,* 26–29.

Choutka, C. M. (1999). Experiencing the reality of service delivery: One parent's perspective. *Journal of the Association for Persons with Severe Handicaps, 24,* 213–217.

Christensen, S. M. (1999, June 10). *Testimony submitted for the record.* Hearing before the United States Senate, Health Education, Labor, and Pensions Committee, ESEA Reauthorization—Special Populations (pp. 1–4). Omaha, NE: National Network of Families with Gifted Children.

Cicci, R. (1998). Speech and language evaluation. In H. S. Ghuman and R. M. Sarles (Eds.), *Handbook of child and adolescent outpatient, day treatment, and community psychiatry* (pp. 107–114). Philadelphia: Brunner/Mazel.

Cipani, E., & Spooner, F. (1994). *Curricular and instructional approaches for persons with severe disabilities.* Boston: Allyn and Bacon.

Clark, B. (1997). *Growing up gifted* (5th ed.). Columbus, OH: Merrill.

Clark, E. (1997). Children and adolescents with traumatic brain injury: Reintegration challenges in educational settings. In E. D. Bigler, E. Clark, & J. E. Farmer (Eds.), *Childhood traumatic brain injury: Diagnosis, assessment, and intervention* (pp. 191–211). Austin, TX: Pro-Ed.

Clark, H. B., Prange, M. E., Lee, B., et al. (1998). An individualized wraparound process for children in foster care with emotional and behavioral disturbances: Follow-up findings and implication from a controlled study. In M. H. Epstein, K. Kutash, & A. Duchnowski. (Eds.), *Outcomes for children and youth with emotional and behavioral disorders and their families: Programs and evaluation best practices* (pp. 513–542). Austin, TX: Pro-Ed.

Clark, R. B. (1997). Suicide in children and adolescents. In W. W. Hay, Jr., J. R. Groothuis, A. R. Hayward, & M. J. Levin (Eds.), *Current pediatric diagnosis and treatment* (pp. 197–198). Norwalk, CT: Appleton & Lange.

Clark, S. N., & Clark, D. C. (1994). *Restructuring the middle level school: Implications for school leaders.* New York: State University of New York Press.

Clarke, H. B., & Clarke, R. T. (Eds.). (1996). Research on the wraparound process and individualized services for children with multi-system needs [Special issue]. *Journal of Child and Family Studies, 5*(1).

Clasen, D. R., & Clasen, R. E. (1997). Mentoring: A time-honored option for education of the gifted and talented. In N. Colangelo & A. D. Davis (Eds.), *Handbook of gifted education* (2nd ed., pp. 218–229). Boston: Allyn and Bacon.

Cleveland, J. (1999). Parenting stress in Mexican-American and Caucasian parents of children with ADHD. *Dissertation Abstracts International: Section B: The Sciences and Engineering, 59*(7-B), 3768.

Cline, S., & Schwartz, D. (1999). *Diverse populations of gifted children: Meeting their needs in the regular classroom and beyond.* Upper Saddle River, NJ: Prentice Hall.

Cochlear Implants Association. (2000). What is a cochlear implant?

[Online]. Available: http://www.cici.org/english/englinks.htm

Cochrane, V. M., & Slade, P. (1999). Appraisal and coping in adults with cleft lip: Associations with well-being and social anxiety. *British Journal of Medical Psychology, 72*(4), 485–503.

Codina, G. E., Yin, Z., Katims, D. S., & Zapata, J. T. (1998). Marijuana use and academic achievement among Mexican American school-age students: Underlying psychosocial and behavioral characteristics. *Journal of Child and Adolescent Substance Abuse, 7*(3), 79–96.

Cohen, H. J. (1991, June). The rehabilitation needs of children with HIV infections and associated developmental disabilities. *Physical Medicine and Rehabilitation State-of-the-Art Reviews, 5*(2), 313.

Colangelo, N. (1997). Counseling gifted students: Issues and practices. In N. Colangelo & A. D. Davis (Eds.), *Handbook of gifted education* (2nd ed., pp. 353–365). Boston: Allyn and Bacon.

Cole, E. B. (1992). Promoting emerging speech in birth to 3-year-old hearing-impaired children. *The Volta Review, 94,* 63–77.

Collier, C. (1998). Including bilingual exceptional children in the general education classroom. In L. M. Baca & H. T. Cervantes (Eds.), *The bilingual special education interface* (3rd ed., pp. 290–325). Columbus, OH: Merrill/Macmillan.

Conant, J. B. (1959). *The American high school today.* New York: McGraw-Hill.

Conn-Powers, M. C., Ross-Allen, J., & Holburn, S. (1990, Winter). Transition of young children into the elementary education mainstream. *Topics in Early Childhood Special Education, 9*(4), 91–105.

Connolly, A. (1988). *KeyMath Diagnostic Arithmetic Test.* Circle Pines, MN: American Guidance Services.

Conoley, J. C., & Sheridan, S. M. (1997). Pediatric traumatic brain injury: Challenges and interventions for families. In E. D. Bigler, E. Clark, & J. E. Farmer (eds.), *Childhood traumatic brain injury: Diagnosis, assessment, and intervention* (pp. 177–190). Austin, TX: Pro-Ed.

Conte, D. A. (1998). Differences in parenting stress between parents of children with ADHD, children with internalizing behavior problems, and non-referred children. *Dissertation Abstracts International, 58*(11-B), 6230.

Conture, E. G. (1999). The best day to rethink our research agenda is between yesterday and tomorrow. In N. B. Ratner and C. E. Healey (Eds.), *Stuttering research* and practice: Bridging the gap (pp. 13–26). Mahwah, NJ: Erlbaum.

Cook, E. H., Jr. (1998). Genetics of autism. Mental Retardation and Developmental Disabilities Research Reviews, 4(2), 113–120.

Cook, P., Cook, M., & Tran, L. (1997, June). Children enabling change: A multicultural, participatory, community-based rehabilitation research project involving Chinese children with disabilities and their families. Child and Youth Care Forum, 26, 205–219.

Coppens, P., Lebrun, Y., & Basso, A. (1998). Aphasia in atypical populations. Mahwah, NJ: Erlbaum.

Cordell, A. S. (1999). Self-esteem in children. In J. C. Carlock (Ed.), Enhancing self-esteem (3rd ed., pp. 287–376). Philadelphia: Accelerated Development, Inc.

Cormier, S., & Cormier, B. (1998). Interviewing strategies for helpers: Fundamental skills and cognitive behavioral interventions (4th ed.). Pacific Grove, CA: Brooks/Cole.

Corn, A. L., Hatlen, P., Huebner, K. M., Ryan, F., & Siller, M. A. (1995). The national agenda for the education of children and youth with visual impairments, including those with multiple disabilities. New York: American Foundation for the Blind Press.

Corn, A. L., & Koenig, A. J. (1996). Perspectives on low vision. In Foundations of low vision: Clinical and functional perspectives (pp. 1–21). New York: American Foundation for the Blind Press.

Correa, V. I., & Jones, H. (2000). Multicultural issues related to families of children with disabilities. In M. J. Fine, & R. L. Simpson (Eds.), Collaboration with parents and families of children with exceptionalities (2nd ed., pp. 133–154). Austin, TX: Pro-Ed.

Council for Children with Behavior Disorders. (1987). Position paper on definition and identification of students with behavior disorders. Behavioral Disorders, 13(1), 9–19.

Council for Children with Behavior Disorders. (1989). A new proposed definition and terminology to replace "serious emotional disturbance" in Education of the Handicapped Act. Reston, VA: Author.

Council for Children with Behavior Disorders. (1990). Position paper on the exclusion of children with conduct disorders and behavior disorders. Reston, VA: Author.

Council for Exceptional Children. (1991). Report of the CEC advocacy and governmental relations committee regarding the new proposed U.S. federal definition of serious emotional disturbance. Reston, VA: Author.

Council for Exceptional Children. (1999). Special education works. Today, 6(2), 1, 5.

Courchesne, E., Yeung-Courchesne, R., & Pierce, K. (1999). Biological and behavioral heterogeneity in autism: Roles of pleiotropy and epigenesis. In S. H. Broman & J. M. Fletcher (Eds.), The changing nervous system: Neurobehavioral consequences of early brain disorders (pp. 292–338). New York: Oxford University Press.

Coutinho, M. J., & Oswald, D. P. (1998). Understanding identification, placement, and school completion rates for children with disabilities: The influence of economic, demographic, and educational variables. In T. E. Scruggs & M. A. Mastropieri (Eds.), Advances in learning and behavioral disabilities (pp. 43–78). Greeenwich, CT: JAI Press.

Covert, S. B. (1995). Whatever it takes: Excellence in family support: When families experience a disability. St. Augustine, FL: Training Resource Network.

Cox, M., & Eames, K. (1999). Contrasting styles of drawing in gifted individuals with autism. Autism, 3, 397–409.

Craig, S. E., & Haggart, A. G. (1994). Including all children: The ADA's challenge to early intervention. Infants and Young Children, 7(2), 15–19.

Craig, S. E., Hull, K., Haggart, A. G., & Perez-Selles, M. (2000). Promoting cultural competence through teacher assistance teams. Teaching Exceptional Children, 32(3), 6–12.

Cramer, S., Erzkus, A., Mayweather, K., Pope, K., Roeder, J., & Tone, T. (1997). Connecting with siblings. Teaching Exceptional Children, 30(1), 46–51.

Cresswell, C. S., & Skuse, D. H. (1999). Autism in association with Turner syndrome: Genetic implications for male vulnerability to pervasive developmental disorders. Neurocase: Case Studies in Neuropsychology, Neuropsychiatry, and Behavioural Neurology, 5(6), 511–518.

Crocker, A. D., & Orr, R. R. Social behaviors of children with visual impairments enrolled in preschool programs. Exceptional Children, 62(5), 451–462.

Culbertson, J. L. (1998). Learning disabilities. In T. H. Ollendick & M. Hersen (Eds.), Handbook of child psychopathology (3rd ed., pp. 117–156). New York: Plenum.

Cullinan, D., & Epstein, M. H. (1986). Behavior disorders. In N. Haring (Ed.), Exceptional children and youth (4th ed.). Columbus, OH: Merrill.

Cunningham, C. E. (1999). In the wake of the MTA: Charting a new course for the study and treatment of children with attention-deficit hyperactivity disorder. Canadian Journal of Psychiatry, 44, 999–1006.

Curran, S., & Fitzgerald, M. (1999). Attention deficit hyperactivity disorder in the prison population. American Journal of Psychiatry, 156, 1664–1665.

Cuskelly, M., Chant, D., & Hayes, A. (1998). Behavior problems in the siblings of children with Down syndrome: Associations with family responsibilities and stress. International Journal of Disability, Development, and Education, 45(3), 295–311.

Cystic Fibrosis Foundation. (2000a). Creating a brighter future [Online]. Available: http://www.cff.org/ar1999/section02.htm

Cystic Fibrosis Foundation. (2000b). Facts about cystic fibrosis [Online]. Available: http://www.cff.org/facts.htm

Cystic Fibrosis Foundation. (2000c). Gene therapy and cystic fibrosis [Online]. Available: http://www.cff.org/publications03.htm

Dalaker, J. (1999). Current population reports: Poverty in the United States (P60-207). Washington, DC: U.S. Census Bureau, U.S. Department of Commerce.

Dale, K. L., & Baumeister, R. F. (1999). Self-regulation and psychotherapy. In R. M. Kowalski and M. R. Leary (Eds.), The social psychology of emotional and behavioral problems: Interfaces of social and clinical psychology (pp. 139–166). Washington, DC: American Psychological Association.

D'Amato, R. C., Dean, R. S., & Rhodes, R. L. (1998). Subtyping children's learning disabilities with neuropsychological, intellectual, and achievement measures. International Journal of Neuroscience, 96, 107–125.

D'Amato, R. C., & Rothlisberg, B. A. (1997). How education should respond to students with traumatic brain injury. In E. D. Bigler, E. Clark, & J. E. Farmer (Eds.), Childhood traumatic brain injury: Diagnosis, assessment, and intervention (pp. 213–237). Austin, TX: Pro-Ed.

D'Amico, R., & Blackorby, J. (1992). Trends in employment among out-of-school youth with disabilities. In M. Wagner, L. Newman, C. Marder, R. D'Amico, & J. Blackorby (Eds.), What happens next? Menlo Park, CA: SRI International.

Dana, R. H. (1998a). Cultural identity assessment of culturally diverse groups: 1997. Journal of Personality Assessment, 70(1), 1–16.

Dana, R. H. (1998b). Projective assessment of Latinos in the United States: Current realities, problems, and prospects. Cultural Diversity and Ethnic Minority Psychology, 4(3), 165–184.

Dana, R. H. (2000). Handbook of cross-cultural and multicultural personality assessment. Mahwah, NJ: Erlbaum.

Daniels, V. I. (1998). Minority students in gifted and special education programs: The case for educational equity. Journal of Special Education, 32, 41–43.

Danseco, E. R. (1997, March). Parental beliefs on childhood disability: Insights on culture, child development, and intervention. International Journal of Disability, Development, and Education, 44, 41–52.

Davis, G. A. (1997). Identifying creative students and measuring creativity. In N. Colangelo & A. D. Davis (Eds.), Handbook of gifted education (2nd ed., pp. 269–281). Boston: Allyn and Bacon.

Davis, G. A., & Rimm, S. B. (1998). Education of the gifted and talented. Boston: Allyn and Bacon.

Davis, M. D., Kilgo, J. L., Gamel-McCormick, M. (1998). Young children with special needs. Boston: Allyn and Bacon.

Davis, R. (1999, May 24). The cries grow louder: check newborns' hearing. USA Today, 10D.

Davis, S. (1997). A national status report of waiting lists of people with mental retardation for community services. Arlington, TX: The Arc.

Davis, W. E., & McCaul, E. J. (1991). The emerging crisis: Current and projected status of children in the United States (Monograph). Orono, ME: Institute for the Study of At-Risk Students.

Dawson, G., Meltzoff, A. N., Osterling, J., Rinaldi, J., & Brown, E. (1998). Children with autism fail to orient to naturally occurring social stimuli. Journal of Autism and Developmental Disorders, 28, 479–485.

Deaf World Web. (2000). Deaf America web [Online]. Available: http://deafworldweb.org/int/us/

Deafblind International. (2000). What is deafblindness? [Online]. Available: http://www.deafblindinternational.org/whatisdb/whatisdb.htm

Deaton, A. V., & Waaland, P. (1994). Psychosocial effects of acquired brain injury. In R. C. Savage & G. F. Wolcott (Eds.), Educational dimensions of acquired brain injury (pp. 239–255). Austin, TX: Pro-Ed.

DeFur, S. (1999). Transition planning: A team effort. Washington, DC: The National Information Center for Children and Youth with Disabilities.

Dehaney, R. (2000). Literacy hour and the literal thinker: The inclusion of children with semantic–pragmatic language difficulties in the literacy hour. *Support for Learning, 15,* 36–40.

DeHann, R., & Havighurst, R. J. (1957). *Educating gifted children.* Chicago, IL: University of Chicago Press.

Delagado, M. R. (1999). Management of motor impairment: Approaches for children with cerebral palsy. *Exceptional Parent, 29*(6), 42–45.

Delisle, J. R. (1997). Gifted adolescents: Five steps toward understanding and acceptance. In N. Colangelo & A. D. Davis (Eds.), *Handbook of gifted education* (2nd ed., pp. 475–482). Boston: Allyn and Bacon.

Den-Dikken, M. (2000). The syntax of features. *Journal of Psycholinguistic Research, 29,* 5–23.

Denes, G., & Pizzamiglio, L. (1999). *Handbook of clinical and experimental neuropsychology.* Hove, UK: Psychology Press/Erlbaum (UK) Taylor and Francis.

Denny, R. K., Gunther, P. L., Shores, R. E., & Campbell, C. R. (1995). Educational placements of students with emotional and behavioral disorders: What do they indicate? In J. M. Kauffman, J. W. Lloyd, D. P. Hallahan, & T. A. Astuto (Eds.), *Issues in educational placement: Students with emotional and behavioral disorders* (pp. 119–144). Hillsdale, NJ: Erlbaum.

Department of Health and Human Services. (1999). *Blending perspectives and building common ground. A report to congress and on substance abuse and child protection.* Washington, DC: Department of Health and Human Resources.

DePompei, R., & Williams, J. (1994). Working with families after TBI: A family-centered approach. *Topics in Language Disorders: Collaboration in Assessment and Intervention After TBI, 15*(1), 68–81.

Dettmer, P. A., Dyck, N. J., & Thurston, L. P. (1999). *Consultation, collaboration, and teamwork for students with special needs* (3rd ed.). Boston: Allyn and Bacon.

De Valenzuela, J. S., & Cervantes, H. (1998). Issues and theoretical considerations in the assessment of bilingual children. In L. M. Baca & H. T. Cervantes (Eds.), *The bilingual special education interface* (3rd ed., pp. 144-166). Columbus, OH: Merrill/Macmillan.

Dever, R. B., & Knapczyk, D. R. (1997). *Teaching persons with mental retardation.* Madison, WI: Brown and Benchmark.

Devore, S., & Hanley-Maxwell, C. (2000). "I wanted to see if we could make it work": Perspectives

on inclusive childcare. *Exceptional Children, 66*(2), 241–255.

Dewey, J. T. (1999). Child characteristics affecting stress reactions in parents of children with autism. Dissertation Abstracts International: Section A: Humanities and Social Sciences, 60(2-A), 0388.

Diana v. State Board of Education. (1970, 1973). C–70, 37 RFP (N.D. Cal., 1970, 1973).

Disease [Online]. Available: http://home.coqui.net/myrna/cmv.htm

Disney, E. R., Elkins, I. J., McGue, M., & Iacono, W. G. (1999). Effects of ADHD, conduct disorder, and gender on substance use and abuse in adolescence. *American Journal of Psychiatry, 156,* 1515–1521.

Division of Learning Disabilities. (1999). *Current Practice Alerts* (Issue 2), Council for Exceptional Children.

Dmitrieva, E. S., & Zaitseva, K. A. (1998). Specific sex-linked features of speech function lateralization in stutterers. *Human Physiology, 24,* 171–175.

D'Odorico, L., Salerni, N., Cassibba, R., & Jacob, V. (1999). Stability and change of maternal speech to Italian infants from 7 to 21 months of age: A longitudinal study of its influence on early stages of language acquisition. *First Language, 19*(57, Pt. 3), 313–346.

Dole, R. (1995, April 14). Franklin Delano Roosevelt: A disability hero. *Polio survivor's page* [Online]. Available: http://www.eskimo.com/~dempt/fdr.htm

Dolnick, E. (1993). Deafness as culture. *The Atlantic Monthly, 272*(3), 37–53.

Dolyniuk, C. A. (1999). Using narrative to promote the conceptual development of adolescents with learning disability and attention deficit hyperactivity disorder. *Dissertation Abstracts International Section A: Humanities and Social Sciences, 59*(9-A), 3346.

Donovan, M. C., & Macklin, S. (1999). New learning technologies: One size doesn't fit all. *Planning for Higher Education, 28,* 10–18.

Dorsey, M., & Guenther, R. K. (2000). Attitudes of professors and students toward college students who stutter. *Journal of Fluency Disorders, 25,* 77–83.

Downing, J. (1996) The elementary school child. In J. Downing (Ed.), *Including students with severe and multiple disabilities in typical classrooms* (pp. 83–108). Baltimore, MD: Brookes.

Downing, J., & Eichinger, J. (1996). Educating students with diverse strengths and needs together. In J. Downing (Ed.), *Including students with severe and multiple disabil-*

ities in typical classrooms (pp. 1–14). Baltimore, MD: Brookes.

Drasgow, E. (1993). Bilingual/bicultural deaf education: An overview. *Sign Language Studies, 80,* 243–266.

Drash, P. W., High, R. L., & Tudor, R. M. (1999). Using mind training to establish an echoic repertoire in young children with autism. *Analysis of Verbal Behavior, 16,* 29–44.

Drew, C. J., & Hardman, M. L. (2000). *Mental retardation: A life-cycle approach* (7th ed.). Columbus, OH: Merrill.

Duchnowski, A. J., & Friedman, R. M. (1990). Children's mental health: Challenges for the nineties. *Journal of Mental Health Administration, 17*(1), 3–12.

Dudley-Marling, C., & Murphy, S. (1997). A political critique of remedial reading programs: The example of Reading Recovery. *Reading Teacher, 50*(6), 460–468.

Dukewich, T. L., Borkowski, J. G., & Whitman, T. L. (1999). A longitudinal analysis of maternal abuse potential and developmental delays in children of adolescent mothers. *Child Abuse and Neglect, 23*(5), 405–420.

Dunbar, S. B., & Reed, C. N. (1999). A developmental screening program in primary health care: Meeting the challenges of children in low-income families. *Infant Toddler Intervention, 9*(2), 195–202.

Duncan, B. D., Forness, S. R., & Hartsough, C. (1995). Students identified as seriously emotionally disturbed in school-based day treatment: Cognitive, psychiatric, and special education characteristics. *Behavior Disorders, 20*(4), 238–252.

Dunlap, G. (1999). Consensus, engagement, and family involvement for young children with autism. *Journal of the Association for Persons with Severe Handicaps, 24,* 222–225.

Dunn, L. M. (1968). Special education for the mildly retarded—is much of it justifiable? *Exceptional Children, 35,* 229–237.

DuPaul, G. J., & Eckert, T. L. (1998). Academic interventions for students with attention-deficit/hyperactivity disorder: A review of the literature. *Reading and Writing Quarterly: Overcoming Learning Difficulties, 14,* 59–82.

DuPaul, G. J., & Eckert, T. L. (1997). The effects of school-based interventions for attention deficit hyperactivity disorder: A meta-analysis. *School Psychology Review, 26,* 5–27.

DuPaul, G. J., Barkley, R. A., & Connor, D. F. (1998). Stimulants. In R. A. Barkley (Ed.), *Attention-deficit hyperactivity disorder: A hand-*

book for diagnosis and treatment (pp. 510–551). New York: Guilford.

Dupre, A. P. (1997). Disability and the public schools: The case against "inclusion." *Washington Law Review, 72,* 775–858.

Durand, V. M. (1999). New directions in educational programming for students with autism. In D. B. Zager (Ed.), *Autism: Identification, education and treatment* (2nd ed., pp. 323–343). Mahwah, NJ: Erlbaum.

Eber, L. (1996). Restructuring schools through the wraparound approach: The LADSE experience. In R. J. Illback & C. M. Nelson (Eds.), *Emerging school-based approaches for children with emotional and behavioral problems: Research and practice in service integration* (pp. 135–149). Binghamton, NY: Haworth.

Eckert, T. L., & Shapiro, E. S. (1999). Methodological issues in analog acceptability research: Are teachers' acceptability ratings of assessment methods influenced by experimental design? *School Psychology Review, 28,* 5–16.

Eckery, L. L. (1994, November) Bleeding Hearts. *The Braille Monitor,* pp. 649–650.

Edwards, J., & Lanyado, M. (1999). Autism: Clinical and theoretical issues. In M. Lanyado & A. Horne (Eds.), *The handbook of child and psychotherapy: Psychoanalytic approaches* (pp. 429–444). New York: Routledge.

Eichinger, J., & Downing, J. (1996). Instruction in the general education environment. In J. Downing (Ed.), *Including students with severe and multiple disabilities in typical classrooms* (pp. 83–108). Baltimore, MD: Brookes.

Eisenmajer, R., Prior, M., Leekam, S., Wing, L., Ong, B., Gould, J., & Welham, M. (1998). Delayed language onset as a predictor of clinical symptoms in pervasive developmental disorders. *Journal of Autism and Developmental Disorders, 28,* 527–533.

Eiserman, W. D., Weber, C., & McCoun, M. (1995). Parent and professional roles in early intervention: A longitudinal comparison of the effects of two intervention configurations. *Journal of Special Education, 29*(1), 20–44.

Eklund, S. J., & Martz, W. L. (1993). Maintaining optimal functioning. In E. Sutton, A. R. Factor, B. A. Hawkins, T. Heller, & G. B. Seltzer (Eds.), *Older adults with developmental disabilities* (p. 1). Baltimore, MD: Brookes.

El Ghoroury, N. H., & Romanczyk, R. G. (1999). Play interactions of family members towards children with autism. *Journal of*

Autism and Developmental Disorders, 29, 249–258.

Elia, J., Ambrosini, P. J., & Rapoport, J. L. (1999). Drug therapy: Treatment of attention-deficit-hyperactivity disorder. *New England Journal of Medicine, 340*(10), 780–788.

Elkind, D. (1998). Behavioral disorders: A postmodern perspective. *Behavioral Disorders, 23*(3), 153–159.

Epilepsy Foundation of America. (2000a). Information and education: Frequently asked questions [Online]. Available: http://www.efa.org/education/faq.html#ia

Epilepsy Foundation of America. (2000b). Information and education: First aid for seizures [Online]. Available: http://www.efa.org/education/firstaid/poster.html

Epilepsy Foundation of America. (2000c). *Surgery for epilepsy.* http://www.efa.org/education/surgery/introduction.html.

Epstein, M. H. (1997). Using strength-based assessment in in programs for children with emotional and behavioral disorders. *Beyond Behavior, 9*(2), 25–27.

Epstein, M. H., & Sharma, J. M. (1997). *Behavior and Emotional Rating Scale.* Austin, TX: Pro-Ed.

Epstein, M. H., Kutash, K., & Duchnowski, A. (1998). *Outcomes for children and youth with behavioral and emotional disorders and their families.* Autin, TX: Pro-Ed.

Erba, H. W. (2000). Early intervention programs for children with autism: Conceptual frameworks for implementation. *American Journal of Orthopsychiatry, 70,* 82–94.

Erickson, M. (1998). *Behavior disorders of children and adolescents.* Upper Saddle River, NJ: Prentice Hall.

Erickson, R. N. (1998). *Special education in an era of school reform: Accountability, standards, and assessment.* Washington, DC: The Federal Resource Center.

Erickson, R. N., Thurlow, M. L., & Thor, K. (1995). *1994 state special education outcomes.* Minneapolis, MN: University of Minnesota, National Center on Educational Outcomes.

Ernst, M., Zametkin, A. J., Matochik, J. A., Jons, P. H., & Cohen, R. M. (1998). DOPA decarboxylase activity in attention deficit hyperactivity disorder adults. A [fluorine-18] fluorodopa positron emission tomographic study. *The Journal of Neuroscience, 18,* 5901–5907.

Eshleman, A. S. (1999). Relationship between perinatal complications and attention deficit hyperactivity disorder and other behavioral characteristics. *Dissertation Abstracts International Section A: Humanities and Social Sciences, 59*(10-A), 3836.

Evaluation Guides (SSR 82-53). (2000). Washington, DC: Author [Online]. Available: http://www.ssa.gov/

Evans, I. M. (1991). Testing and diagnosis: A review and evaluation. In L. H. Meyer, C. A. Peck, & L. Brown (Eds.), *Critical issues in the lives of people with severe disabilities* (pp. 25–44). Baltimore, MD: Brookes.

Evans, J. P., & Taylor, J. (1995, February). Understanding violence in contemporary and earlier gangs: An exploratory application of the theory of reasoned action. *Journal of Black Psychology, 21*(1), 71–81.

Evans, M. E., Armstrong, M. I., Kuppinger, A. D., Huz, S., & McNulty, T. L. (1998). Preliminary outcomes of an experimental study comparing treatment foster care and family-centered intensive case management. In M. H. Epstein, K. Kutash, & A. Duchnowski (Eds.), *Outcomes for children and youth with emotional and behavioral disorders and their families: Programs and evaluation best practices* (pp. 543–580). Austin, TX: Pro-Ed.

Everett, C. A., & Everett, S. V. (1999). *Family therapy for ADHD: Treating children, adolescents, and adults.* New York: Guilford .

Exceptional Parent. (1999a). Family voices are heard. *Exceptional Parent, 29*(6), 31.

Exceptional Parent. (1999b). Kids as self-advocates—KASA Project of Family Voices. *Exceptional Parent, 29*(7), 38.

Ezekowitz, R. A., & First, L. R. (1994). Hematology. In M. E. Avery & L. R. First (Eds.), *Pediatric medicine* (2nd ed., pp. 53–606). Baltimore, MD: Williams & Wilkins.

Fadda, L., Turriziani, P., Carlesimo, G. A., Nocentini, U., & Caltagirone, C. (1998). Selective proper name anomia in a patient with asymmetric cortical degeneration. *European Journal of Neurology, 5,* 417–422.

Falik, L. H. (1995). Family patterns of reaction to a child with a learning disability: A meditational approach. *Journal of Learning Disabilities, 28*(6), 335–341.

Falvey, M., Gage, S., & Eshilian, L. (1995). Secondary curriculum and instruction. In M. Falvey (Ed.), *Inclusive and heterogeneous schooling: Assessment, curriculum, and instruction* (pp. 341–362). Baltimore, MD: Brookes.

Faraone, S. V., Biederman, J., Weiffenbach, B., et al. (1999). Dopamine D-sub-4 gene 7-repeat allele and attention deficit hyperactivity disorder. *American Journal of Psychiatry, 156,* 768–770.

Farmer, J. E. (1997). Epilogue: An ecological systems approach to childhood traumatic brain injury. In E. D. Bigler, E. Clark, & J. E. Farmer (Eds.), *Childhood traumatic brain injury: Diagnosis, assessment, and intervention* (pp. 261–276). Austin, TX: Pro-Ed.

Farmer, J. E., Clippard, D. S., Luehr-Wiemann, Y., Wright, E., & Owings, S. Assessing children with traumatic brain injury during rehabilitation: Promoting school and community reentry. In E. D. Bigler, E. Clark, & J. E. Farmer (Eds.), *Childhood traumatic brain injury: Diagnosis, assessment, and intervention* (pp. 33–62). Austin, TX: Pro-Ed.

Federal Register. (1999, March 12). *Rules and Regulations, 64*(48), 51.

Feldhusen, J. F. (1998a). Identification and assessment of talented learners. In J. VanTassel-Baska (Ed.), *Excellence in educating gifted and talented learners* (3rd ed., pp. 193–210). Denver: Love.

Feldhusen, J. F. (1998b). Programs and services at the elementary level. In J. VanTassel-Baska (Ed.), *Excellence in educating gifted and talented learners* (3rd ed., pp. 211–223). Denver: Love.

Feldhusen, J. F. (1998c). Programs and services at the secondary level. In J. VanTassel-Baska (Ed.), *Excellence in educating gifted and talented learners* (3rd ed., pp. 225–240). Denver: Love.

Ferguson, A. (1999). Learning in aphasia therapy: It's not so much what you do, but how you do it! *Aphasiology, 13,* 125–132.

Ferguson, D., Meyer, G., Jeanchild, L., Juniper, L., & Zingo, J. (1992). Figuring out what to do with the grownups: How teachers make inclusion "work" for students with disabilities. *Journal of the Association for Persons with Severe Handicaps, 17*(4), 218–226.

Ferguson, P. M., & Ferguson, D. L. (2000). The promise of adulthood. In M. E. Snell & F. Brown (Eds.), *Instruction of students with severe disabilities* (pp. 629–656). Upper Saddle River, NJ: Merrill.

Fey, M. E. (1999). PACT: Some comments and considerations. *International Journal of Language and Communication Disorders, 34,* 55–59.

Field, S., & Hoffman, A. (1999). The importance of family involvement for promoting self-determination in adolescents with autism and other developmental disabilities. *Focus on Autism and Other Developmental Disabilities, 14*(1), 36–41.

Filipek, P. A., Semrud-Clikemann, M., Steingard, R. J., Renshaw, P. F., Kennedy, D. N., & Biederman, J. (1997). Volumetric MRI analysis comparing subjects hav-

ing attention-deficit hyperactivity disorder with normal controls. *Neurology, 48,* 589–601.

Fine, M. J., & Nissenbaum, M. S. (2000). The child with disabilities and the family: Implications for professionals. In M. J. Fine & R. L. Simpson (Eds.), *Collaboration with parents and families of children with exceptionalities* (2nd ed., pp. 3–26). Austin, TX: Pro-Ed.

Fine, M. J., & Simpson, R. L. (2000). *Collaboration with parents and families of children with exceptionalities* (2nd ed.). Austin, TX: Pro-Ed.

Fish, M. C. (2000). Children with special needs in nontraditional families. In M. J. Fine & R. L. Simpson (Eds.), *Collaboration with parents and families of children with exceptionalities* (2nd ed., pp. 49–68). Austin, TX: Pro-Ed.

Fisher, D., Fox, D., & Wood, K. (1999). The identification of specific reading difficulties: A survey of practice and policy in Scottish local authority psychological services. *Educational and Child Psychology, 16,* 49–53.

Fleck, S. G. (1998). Executive functions in ADHD adults. *Dissertation Abstracts International: Section B: The Sciences and Engineering, 58*(11-B), 6232.

Fletcher, J. M., Francis, D. J., Shaywitz, S. E., et al. (1998). Intelligent testing and the discrepancy model for children with learning disabilities. *Learning Disabilities Research and Practice, 13*(4), 186–203.

Floriana, J. A. (1998). An examination of cerebral processing or auditory nonverbal affective stimuli through event-related desynchronization in autistic and normal adults. *Dissertation Abstracts International: Section B: The Sciences and Engineering, 59*(1-B), 0416.

Fodor, J. D., & Inoue, A. (2000). Syntactic features in reanalysis: Positive and negative symptoms. *Journal of Psycholinguistic Research, 29,* 25–36.

Folstein, S. E., Santangelo, S. L., Gilman, S. E., Piven, J., Landa, R., Lainhart, J., Hein, J., & Wzorek, M. (1999). Predictors of cognitive test patterns in autism families. *Journal of Child Psychology and Psychiatry and Allied Disciplines, 40,* 1117–1128.

Folstrom-Bergeron, B. M. (1998). Metamemory knowledge and application in children with attention deficit hyperactivity disorder: A developmental perspective. *Dissertation Abstracts International: Section B: The Sciences and Engineering, 58*(10-B), 5670.

Fommbonne, E. (1999). The epidemiology of autism: A review. *Psychological Medicine, 29,* 769–786.

Forbes, E. (1987). My brother, Warren. *Exceptional Parent, 17*(5), 50–52.

Forest, M., & Pearpoint, J. (1990). Supports for addressing severe maladaptive behavior. In W. Stainback & S. Stainback (Eds.), *Support networks for inclusive schooling: Interdependent integrated education.* Baltimore, MD: Brookes.

Forness, S. R. (1988). Planning for the needs of children with serious emotional disturbance: The National Special Education and Mental Health Coalition. *Behavioral Disorders, 13*(2), 127–133.

Forness, S. R. (1996). Schoolchildren with emotional or behavioral disorders: Perspectives on definition, diagnosis, and treatment. In B. Brooks & D. Sabatino (Eds.), *Personal perspectives on emotional disturbance/behavioral disorders* (pp. 84–95). Austin, TX: Pro-Ed.

Forness, S. R., & Kavale, K. A. (1997). Defining emotional or behavioral disorders in school and related settings. In J. W. Lloyd, E. J. Kameenui, & D. Chard (Eds.), *Issues in educating students with disabilities* (pp. 45–61). Mahwah, NJ: Erlbaum .

Forness, S. R., Kavale, K. A., & Lopez, M. (1993). Conduct disorders in school: Special education eligibility and comorbidity. *Journal of Emotional and Behavioral Disorders, 1*(2), 101–108.

Forness, S. R., & Knitzer, J. K. (1990). *A new proposed definition and terminology to replace "serious emotional disturbance" in the Education of the Handicapped Act.* Alexandria, VA: National Mental Health Association.

Forts, A. (1998, October). Status and effects of labeling: An interview with Alan Robichaud. *TASH Newsletter,* 13.

Fox, L. E. (1999). Effects of conversational topic self-selection on AAC intervention outcomes for adults with severe broca's aphasia. *Dissertation Abstracts International: Section B: The Sciences and Engineering, 59*(7-B), 3391.

Fox, M. (2000). Vaccine–autism connection? Congressman urges investigation of possible link. Reuters.

Fox, N., & Ysseldyke, J. E. (1997). Implementing inclusion at the middle school level: Lessons from a negative example. *Exceptional Children, 64,* 81–98.

Franklin, K., & Beukelman, D. R. (1991). Augmentative communication: Directions for future research. In J. F. Miller (Ed.), *Research on child language disorders: A decade of progress* (pp. 321–337). Austin, TX: Pro-Ed.

Frasier, M. M. (1997). Gifted minority students: Reframing approaches to their identification and education. In N. Colangelo & A. D. Davis (Eds.), *Handbook of gifted education* (2nd ed., pp. 498–515). Boston: Allyn and Bacon.

Frasier, M. M., Hunsaker, S., Lee, J., et al. (1995). *Core attributes of giftedness: A foundation for recognizing the gifted potential of minority and economically disadvantaged students.* National Research Center on the Gifted and Talented. Storrs, CT: University of Connecticut.

Fredericks, B. (1985). Parents/families of persons with severe mental retardation. In D. Bricker & J. Filler (Eds.), *Severe mental retardation: From theory to practice.* Reston, VA: Council for Exceptional Children.

Frederickson, N. L., & Furnham, A. F. (1998). Sociometric-status-group classification of mainstreamed children who have moderate learning difficulties: An investigation of personal and environmental factors. *Journal of Educational Psychology, 90,* 772–783.

Freedman, R. I., & Boyer, N. C. (2000). The power to choose: Supports for families caring for individuals with developmental disabilities. *Health and Social Work, 25,* 59–68.

Freedman, R. I., Krauss, M. W., & Seltzer, M. (1997). Aging parents' residential plans for adult children with mental retardation. *Mental Retardation, 35*(2), 114–123.

French, A. P., & Amen, D. G. (1999). Criminal recidivism as a neurobehavioral syndrome. *Journal of the American Academy of Child and Adolescent Psychiatry, 38,* 1070–1071.

Frick, P. J., Silverthorn, P., & Evans, C. S. (1994). Assessment of childhood anxiety using structured interviews: Patterns of agreement among informants and association with maternal anxiety. *Psychological Assessment, 6,* 372–379.

Friend, M. P., & Bursuck, W. D. (1998). *Including students with special needs: A practical guide for classroom teachers.* Boston: Allyn and Bacon.

Frisby, C. L. (1998). Poverty and socioeconomic status. In J. H. Sandoval, C. L. Frisby, K. F. Geisinger, J. D. Scheuneman, & J. R. Grenier (Eds.), *Test interpretation and diversity: Achieving equity in assessment* (pp. 241–270). Washington, DC: American Psychological Association.

Frost, E. (1999). Notes on autism research. *Zeitschrift fuer Psychoanalytische Theorie und Praxis, 14,* 416–437.

Fuchs, D., & Fuchs, L. (1991). Framing the REI debate: Abolitionists versus conservationists. In J. W. Lloyd, N. N. Singh, & A. C. Repp (Eds.), *Regular education initiative: Alternative perspectives on concepts, issues, and models* (pp. 241–255). Sycamore, IL: Sycamore.

Fuchs, D., & Fuchs, L. (1994). Inclusive schools movement and the radicalization of special education reform. *Exceptional Children, 60,* 294–309.

Fuller, M. L., & Olsen, G. (1998). *Home–school relations: Working successfully with parents and families.* Boston: Allyn and Bacon.

Gabel, H., McDowell, J., & Cerreto, M. C. (1983). Family adaptation to the handicapped infant. In S. G. Garwood & R. R. Fewell (Eds.), *Educating handicapped infants* (pp. 455–493). Rockville, MD: Aspen.

Gagné, F. (1999a). Is there any light at the end of the tunnel? *Journal for the Education of the Gifted, 22*(2), 191–234.

Gagné, F. (1999b). My convictions about the nature of abilities, gifts, and talents. *Journal for the Education of the Gifted, 22*(2), 109–136.

Gainetdinov, R. R., Wetsel, W. C., Jones, S. R., Levin, E. D., Jaber, M., & Caron, M. G. (1999). Role of serotonin in the paradoxical calming effect of psychostimulants on hyperactivity. *Science, 283,* 397–401.

Gajar, A., Goodman, L., & McAfee, J. (1993). *Secondary schools and beyond.* New York: Merrill.

Gallagher, J. J. (1997). Issues in the education of gifted students. In N. Colangelo & A. D. Davis (Eds.), *Handbook of gifted education* (2nd ed., pp. 27–42). Boston: Allyn and Bacon.

Gallagher, J. R., Beckman-Bell, P., & Cross, A. H. (1983). Families of handicapped children: Sources of stress and its amelioration. *Exceptional Children, 50,* 10–19.

Gallaudet Research Institute. (1994). *Gallaudet Research Institute Working Papers 89-3.* Washington, DC: Author.

Gallaudet Research Institute. (2000). *Literacy and deaf students.* Washington, DC: Author [Online]. Available: http://gri.gallaudet.edu/Assessment/literacy.html

Garber, H. L., Hodge, J. D., Rynders, J., Dever, R., & Velu, R. (1991). The Milwaukee Project: Setting the record straight. *American Journal on Mental Retardation, 95*(5), 493–525.

Gardill, M. C., & Jitendra, A. K. (1999). Advanced story map instruction: Effects on the reading comprehension of students with learning disabilities. *Journal of Special Education, 33,* 2–17.

Gardner, H. (1983). *Frames of mind: The theory of multiple intelligences.* New York: Basic Books.

Garland, C. W., Gallagher, F. G., & Huntington, L. (1997). Caring for infants and toddlers with disabilities: A curriculum for training physicians in early intervention. *Infants & Young Children, 9*(4), 43–57.

Gartin, B. C., Rumrill, P., & Serebreni, R. (1996). The higher education transition model: Guidelines for facilitating college transition among college-bound students with disabilities. *Teaching Exceptional Children, 29*(1), 30–33.

Gauvain, M. (1998). Culture, development, and theory of mind: Comment on Lillard (1998). *Psychological Bulletin, 123,* 37–42.

Gay, L. R., & Airasian, P. (2000). *Educational research: Competencies for analysis and application* (6th ed.). Upper Saddle River, NJ: Prentice-Hall.

Gaylord-Ross, R., & Browder, D. (1991). Functional assessment: Dynamic and domain properties. In L. H. Meyer, C. A. Peck, & L. Brown (Eds.), *Critical issues in the lives of people with severe disabilities* (pp. 45–66). Baltimore, MD: Brookes.

Gee, K. (1996). Least restrictive environment: Elementary and middle school. In The National Council on Disability (Ed.), *Improving the implementation of the Individuals with Disabilities Education Act: Making schools work for all children* (Suppl.) (pp. 395–425). Washington, DC: The National Council on Disability.

Geers, A. E., & Tobey, E. (1992). Effects of cochlear implants and tactile aids on the development of speech production skills in children with profound hearing impairment. *The Volta Review, 94,* 135–163.

Gelb, S. (1995). The best in man: Degenerationism and mental retardation, 1900–1920. *Mental Retardation, 33*(1), 1–9.

Gelfand, D. M., Jenson, W. R., & Drew, C. J. (1997). *Understanding child behavior disorders* (3rd ed.). Fort Worth: Harcourt Brace.

Gerdtz, J. (2000). Evaluating behavioral treatment of disruptive classroom behaviors of an adolescent with autism. *Research on Social Work Practice, 10,* 98–110.

Gersten, R., & Baker, S. (1998). Real world use of scientific concepts: Integrating situated cognition with explicit instruction. *Exceptional Children, 65,* 23–35.

Gersten, R., & Chard, D. (1999). Number sense: Rethinking arithmetic instruction for students with mathematical disabilities. *Journal of Special Education, 33*(1), 18–28.

Giancola, P. R., Mezzich, A. C., & Tarter, R. E. (1998). Executive cognitive functioning, temperament, and antisocial behavior in conduct-disordered adolescent females.

Journal of Abnormal Psychology, 107(4), 629–641.

Giangreco, M. E., & Snell, M. E. (1996). Severe and multiple disabilities. In *Improving the implementation of the Individuals with Disabilities Education Act: Making schools work for all of America's children* (Suppl., pp. 97–132). Washington, DC: National Council on Disability.

Giangreco, M. F., Cloninger, C., & Iverson, V. (1994). *Choosing options and accommodations for children (COACH): A guide to planning inclusive education.* Baltimore, MD: Brookes.

Giangreco, M. F., & Doyle, M. B. (2000). Curricular and instructional considerations for teaching students with disabilities in general education classrooms. In S. E. Wade (Ed.), *Inclusive education: A casebook and readings for prospective and practicing teachers* (pp. 51–70). Mahwah, NJ: Erlbaum.

Gibb, G. S., Young, J. R., Allred, K. W., Dyches, T. T., Egan, M. W., & Ingram, C. F. (1997). A team-based junior high inclusion program: Parent perceptions and feedback. *Remedial and Special Education, 18*(4), 243–249.

Gibb, S. A., Allred, K., Ingram, C., Young, J. R., & Egan, M. W. (1999). Lessons learned from the inclusion of students with emotional and behavioral disorders in one junior high. *Behavioral Disorders, 24*(2), 122–136.

Gibbon, F. E. (1999). Undifferentiated lingual gestures in children with articulation/phonological disorders. *Journal of Speech, Language, and Hearing Research, 42,* 382–397.

Giebink, G. S. (1990). Medical issues in hearing impairment: The otitis media spectrum. In J. Davis (Ed.), *Our forgotten children: Hard-of-hearing pupils in the schools* (pp. 49–55). Bethesda, MD: Self-Help for Hard of Hearing People.

Gillis, R. J. (1996). *Traumatic brain injury rehabilitation for speech–language pathologists.* Boston: Butterworth-Heinemann.

Gilman, M., & Yaruss, J. S. (2000). Stuttering and relaxation: Applications for somatic education in stuttering treatment. *Journal of Fluency Disorders, 25,* 59–76.

Glick, B., & Goldstein, A. (1999). Aggression replacement training: A comprehensive approach for assaultive, violent, and ganging youth. In J. R. Scotti & L. H. Meyer (Eds.), *Behavioral intervention: Principles, models, and practices* (pp. 175–194). Baltimore, MD: Brookes.

Goldstein, A. P., & Glick, B. (1987). *Aggression replacement training: A comprehensive intervention for aggressive youth.* Champaign, IL: Research Press.

Goldstein, S. (1999). Attention-deficit hyperactivity disorder. In S. Goldstein and C. R. Reynolds (Eds.), *Handbook of neurodevelopmental and genetic disorders in children* (pp. 154–184). New York: Guilford.

Gollnick, D. M., & Chinn, P. C. (1998). *Multicultural education in a pluralistic society* (5th ed.). Columbus, OH: Merrill.

Goozee, J. V., Murdoch, B. E., Theodoros, D. G., & Thompson, E. C. (1998). The effects of age and gender on laryngeal aerodynamics. *International Journal of Language and Communication Disorders, 33,* 221–238.

Gottlieb, J., Alter, M., & Gottlieb, B. W. (1991). Mainstreaming academically handicapped children in urban schools. In J. W. Lloyd, N. N. Singh, & A. C. Repp (Eds.), *The regular education initiative: Alternative perspectives on concepts, issues, and models* (pp. 95–112). Sycamore, IL: Sycamore.

Gottwald, S. R. (1999). Family communication patterns and stuttering development: An analysis of the research literature. In N. B. Ratner and C. E. Healey (Eds.), *Stuttering research and practice: Bridging the gap* (pp. 175–191). Mahwah, NJ: Erlbaum.

Graham, S. (1999). Handwriting and spelling instruction for students with learning disabilities: A review. *Learning Disability Quarterly, 22*(2), 78–98.

Grant, C. A., & Gomez, M. L. (2001). *Campus and classroom: Making schooling multicultural* (2nd ed.). Columbus, OH: Merrill/Prentice Hall.

Graves, D. K., & Bradley, D. F. (1997). Establishing the classroom as a community. In D. F. Bradley, M. E. King-Sears, & D. Tessier-Switlick (Eds.), *Teaching students in inclusive settings: From theory to practice* (pp. 365–383). Boston: Allyn and Bacon.

Greenbaum, P. E., Dedrick, R. F., Friedman, R. M., et al. (1998). National adolescent and child treatment study (NACTS): Outcomes for children with serious emotional and behavioral disturbance. In M. H. Epstein, K. Kutash, & A. Duchnowski (Eds.), *Outcomes for children and youth with emotional and behavioral disorders and their families: Programs and evaluation best practices* (pp. 21–54). Austin, TX: Pro-Ed.

Greene, R. W., Biederman, J., Faraone, S. V., Willens, T. E., Mick, E., & Blier, H. K. (1999). Further validation of social impairment as a predictor of substance use disorders: Findings from a sample of siblings of boys with and without ADHD. *Journal of Clinical Child Psychology, 28,* 349–354.

Greenwalt, B. C., Sklare, G., & Portes, P. (1998). The therapeutic treatment provided in cases involving physical abuse. *Child Abuse and Neglect, 22*(1), 71–78.

Greenway, P., & Milne, L. (1999). Relationship between psychopathology, learning disabilities, or both and WISC-III subtest scatter in adolescents. *Psychology in the Schools, 36*(2), 103–108.

Grela, B. G., & Illerbrun, D. (1998). Evaluating rural preschool speech–language services: Consumer satisfaction. *International Journal of Disability, Development, and Education, 45,* 203–216.

Grenot-Scheyer, M., Schwartz, I. S., & Meyer, L. H. (1997, April). Blending best practices for young children: Inclusive early childhood programs. *TASH Newsletter,* 8–11.

Gresham, F., & MacMillan, D. L. (1997). Social competence and affective characteristics of students with mild disabilities. *Review of Educational Research, 67*(4), 377–415.

Gresham, F. M., Beebe-Frankenberger, M. E., & MacMillan, D. L. (1999). A selective review of treatments for children with autism: Description and methodological considerations. *School Psychology Review, 28,* 559–575.

Gresham, F. M., Lane, K. L., MacMillan, D. L., & Bocian, K. M. (1999). Social and academic profiles of externalizing and internalizing groups: Risk factors for emotional and behavioral disorders. *Behavioral Disorders, 24*(3), 231–245.

Griffith, J. (1998). The relation of school structure and social environment to parent involvement in elementary schools. *Elementary School Journal, 99,* 53–80.

Griffiths, D. L., & Unger, D. G. (1994, April). Views about planning for the future among parents and siblings of adults with mental retardation. *Family Relations, 43,* 221–227.

Griffiths, D. M., Nugent, J. A., & Gardner, W. I. (1998). Introduction. In D. M. Griffiths, W. I. Gardner, & J. A. Nugent (Eds.), *Behavioral supports: Individual centered interventions* (pp. 1–5). Kingston, NY: NADD Press.

Grinstead, J. (2000). Case, inflection, and subject licensing in child Catalan and Spanish. *Journal of Child Language, 27,* 119–155.

Gronlund, N. E. (1998). *Assessment of student achievement* (6th ed.). Boston: Allyn and Bacon.

Gronlund, N. E. (2000). *How to write and use instructional objectives* (6th ed.). Columbus, OH: Merrill/Prentice Hall.

Gruber, F. A. (1999). Variability and sequential order of consonant normalization in children with speech delay. *Journal of Speech, Language, and Hearing Research, 42,* 460–472.

Guilford, J. P. (1950). Creativity. *American Psychologist, 5,* 444–454.

Guilford, J. P. (1959). Three faces of intellect. *American Psychologist, 14,* 469–479.

Guitar, B. (1998). *Stuttering: An integrated approach to its nature and treatment* (2nd ed.). Baltimore, MD: Williams & Wilkins.

Guralnick, M. J. (1998). Effectiveness of early intervention for vulnerable children: A developmental perspective. *American Journal of Mental Retardation, 102*(4), 319–345.

Gustaon, G. (1990). Signing exact English. In H. Bornstein (Ed.), *Manual communication: Implications for education.* Washington, DC: Gallaudet University Press.

Gustavsson, A. (1999). Integration in the changing Scandinavian welfare states. In H. Daniels & P. Garner (Eds.), *Inclusive education: World yearbook of education, 1999* (pp. 92–98). London: Kogan Page.

Guterman, B. R. (1995). The validity of categorical learning disabilities services: The consumers' view. *Exceptional Children, 62,* 111–124.

Guy, B., Scott, J. R., Hasazi, S., & Patten, A. (N.D.). *Stories of work.* Unpublished manuscript. Burlington, VT: University of Vermont.

Hagborg, W. J. (1999). Scholastic competence subgroups among high school students with learning disabilities. *Learning Disability Quarterly, 22,* 3–10.

Halfon, N., & Newcheck, P. W. (1999). Prevalence and impact of parent-reported disabling mental health conditions among U.S. children. *Journal of the American Academy of Child and Adolescent Psychiatry, 38,* 600–609.

Hallahan, D. P., Kauffman, J. M., & Lloyd, J. W. (1999). *Introduction to learning disabilities* (2nd ed.). Boston: Allyn & Bacon.

Handen, B. L., Feldman, H. M., Lurier, A., & Murray, P. J. H. (1999). Efficacy of methylphenidate among preschool children with developmental disabilities and ADHD. *Journal of the American Academy of Child and Adolescent Psychiatry, 38,* 805–812.

Hanlon, S. F. (1991). School and day care issues: The legal perspective. In P. A. Pizzo & C. M. Wilfert (Eds.), *Pediatric AIDS: The challenges of HIV infection in infants, children, and adolescents* (pp. 693–703). Baltimore, MD: Williams & Wilkins.

Happe, F. (1999). Understanding assets and deficits in autism: Why success is more interesting than failure. *Psychologist, 12*(11), 540–546.

Harbin, G. L. (1993). Family issues of children with disabilities: How research and theory have modified practice in intervention. In N. J. Anastasiow & S. Harel (Eds.), *At-risk infants: Interventions, families, and research* (pp. 101–114). Baltimore, MD: Brookes.

Hardman, M. L., McDonnell, J., & Welch, M. (1998). *Preparing special education teachers in an era of school reform.* Washington, DC: The Federal Resource Center, Academy for Educational Development.

Harmon, C. G. (1998). An historical and philosophical analysis of the meaning of intelligence and its relationship to the determination of cognitive disabilities. *Dissertation Abstracts International Section: Humanities and Social Sciences, 58*(8-A), 2925.

Harmon, D. (1999). The do's and don'ts planning for your grandchild with special needs. *Exceptional Parent, 29*(12), 74–75.

Harris, K. R., & Graham, S. (1995). Constructivism: Principles, paradigms, and integration. *The Journal of Special Education, 28,* 233–247.

Hartwig, E. P., & Ruesch, G. M. (2000). Disciplining students in special education. *The Journal of Special Education, 33*(4), 240–247.

Hasazi, S. B., Furney, K. S., & Destefano, L. (1999). Implementing the IDEA transition initiatives. *Exceptional Children, 65*(4), 555–566.

Hasazi, S. B., Johnston, A. P., Liggett, A., & Schattman, R. A. (1994). A qualitative policy study of the least restrictive environment provision of the Individuals with Disabilities Education Act. *Exceptional Children, 60*(5), 1–18.

Hasbrouck, J. E., Woldbeck, T., Ihnot, C., & Parker, R. I. (1999). One teacher's use of curriculum-based measurement: A changed opinion. *Learning Disabilities Research and Practice, 14*(2), 118–126.

Haslam, R. H. (1996). Common neurological disorders in children. In R. H. A. Haslam & P. J. Valletutti (Eds.), *Medical problems in the classroom: The teacher's role in diagnosis and management* (3rd ed., pp. 301–332). Austin, TX: Pro-Ed.

Hastings, R. P. (1994). On "good" terms: Labeling people with mental retardation. *Mental Retardation, 32*(5), 363–365.

Hastings, R. P. (1997). Grandparents of children with disabilities: A review. *International Journal of Disability, Development, and Education, 44*(1), 329–340.

Hastings, R. P., & Remington, B. (1993). Connotations of labels for mental handicap and challenging behavior: A review and research evaluation. *Mental Handicap Research, 6,* 237–249.

Hastings, R. P., Songua-Barke, E. J. S., & Remington, B. (1993). An analysis of labels for people with learning disabilities. *British Journal of Clinical Psychology, 32,* 463–465.

Hatton, C., Azmi, S., Caine, A., & Emerson, E. (1998). Informal carers of adolescents and adults with learning difficulties from the South Asian communities: Family circumstances, service support, and carer stress. *British Journal of Social Work, 28,* 821–837.

Hawkins, B. A. (1993). Health and medical issues. In E. Sutton, A. R. Factor, B. A. Hawkins, T. Heller, & G. B. Seltzer (Eds.), *Older adults with developmental disabilities* (p. 1). Baltimore, MD: Brookes.

Hazell, P. L., Carr, V. J., Lewin, T. J., Dewis, S. A. M., Heathcote, D. M., & Brucki, B. M. (1999). Effortful and automatic information processing in boys with ADHD and specific learning disorders. *Journal of Child Psychology and Psychiatry and Allied Disciplines, 40*(2), 275–286.

Heaton, P., Hermelin, B., & Pring, L. (1999a). Can children with autistic spectrum disorders perceive affect in music? An experimental investigation. *Psychological Medicine, 29,* 1405–1410.

Heaton, P., Hermelin, B., Pring, L., (1999b). A pseudo-savant: A case of exceptional musical splinter skills. *Neurocase: Case Studies in Neuropsychology, Neuropsychiatry, and Behavioural Neurology, 5,* 503–509.

Heavey, L., Pring, L., & Hermelin, B. (1999). A date to remember: The nature of memory in savant calendrical calculators. *Psychological Medicine, 29,* 145–160.

Hecimovic, A., Powell, T. H., & Christensen, L. (1999). Supporting families in meeting their needs. In D. B. Zager (Ed.), *Autism: Identification, education, and treatment* (2nd ed., pp. 261–299). Mahwah, NJ: Erlbaum.

Hedrick, W. B., Katims, D. S., & Carr, N. J. (1999). Implementing a multimethod, multilevel literacy program for students with mental retardation. *Focus on Autism and Other Developmental Disabilities, 14*(4), 231–239.

Heimann, S. W. (1999). Pycnogenol for ADHD? *Journal of the American Academy of Child and Adolescent Psychiatry, 38,* 357–358.

Heinemann, E. (1999). Psychoanalytic therapy with an autistic young man: A discussion of Frances Tustin's theories. In J. De Groef & E. Heinemann (Eds.), *Psychoanalysis and mental handicap* (pp. 23–40). London, UK: Free Association Books Ltd.

Heller, T. (2000, Winter). Aging family caregivers: Needs and policy concerns. *Family Support Policy Brief #3, National Center for Family Support,* 1–15.

Heller, T., & Factor, A. R. (1993). Support systems, well-being, and placement decision-making among older parents and their adult children with developmental disabilities. In E. Sutton, A. R. Factor, B. A. Hawkins, T. Heller, & G. B. Seltzer (Eds.), *Older adults with developmental disabilities* (pp. 107–122). Baltimore, MD: Brookes.

Hellings, J. A. (1999). Psychopharmacology of mood disorders in persons with mental retardation and autism. *Mental Retardation and Developmental Disabilities Research Reviews, 5*(4), 270–278.

Hendrick Hudson District Board of Education v. Rowley, 458 U.S. 176 (1982).

Hendrick, J. (2001). *The whole child: Developmental education for the early years* (7th ed.). Columbus, OH: Merrill/Prentice Hall.

Henker, B., & Whalen, C. K. (1999). The child with attention-deficit/hyperactivity disorder in school and peer settings. In H. C. Quay & A. E. Hogan (Eds.), *Handbook of disruptive behavior disorders* (pp. 157–178). New York: Kluwer/Plenum.

Henry, L. A., & Gudjonsson, G. H. (1999). Eyewitness memory and suggestibility in children with mental retardation. *American Journal of Mental Retardation, 104*(6), 491–508.

Herbert, M. J., Klemm, D., & Schimanski, C. (1999). Giving the gift of support: From parent to parent. *Exceptional Parent, 29*(8), 58–62.

Hernandez, M. (2001). *Multicultural education: A teacher's guide to linking context, process, and content* (2nd ed.). Columbus, OH: Merrill/Prentice Hall.

Herr, S. S. (1998, November/December). Life, liberty, and happiness. Part IV: Aging gracefully and rightfully. *AAMR News and Notes, 11*(6), 2.

Hertz, B. (1994, March). Here's what a fully included classroom might look like. *Electronic Learning,* 28.

Hester, P. P., & Kaiser, A. P. Early intervention for the prevention of conduct disorder: Research issues in early identification, implementation, and interpretation of treatment outcome. *Behavioral Disorders, 24*(1), 57–65.

Higgins, P. C. (1990). *The challenges of educating together deaf and hearing youth: Making mainstreaming work.* Springfield, IL: Charles C. Thomas. http://HIVInSite.ucsf.edu/akb/1997/09adol/index.html

Hill, I. D., & Lebenthal, E. (1995). Cystic fibrosis. In W. S. Haubrich, F. Schaffner, & J. E. Berk (Eds.), *Gastroenterology* (5th ed., pp. 3035–3052). Philadelphia: Saunders.

Hill, J. L. (1999). *Meeting the needs of students with special physical and health care needs.* Upper Saddle River, NJ: Merrill.

Hobbs, T. (1997). *Planning for inclusion: A comparison of individual and cooperative procedures.* Unpublished doctoral dissertation, Florida State University, Tallahassee.

Hobbs, T., & Westing, D. L. (1998). Promoting successful inclusion through collaborative problem solving. *Teaching Exceptional Children, 31*(2), 12–19.

Hobson, R. P. (1999). Beyond cognition: A theory of autism. In P. Lloyd & C. Fernyhough (Eds.), *Lev Vygotsky: Critical assessments: Future directions,* Vol. 4 (pp. 253–281). New York: Routledge.

Hocutt, A. M. (1996). Effectiveness of special education: Is placement the critical factor? In The Center for the Future of Children (Ed.), *Special education for students with disabilities* (pp. 77–102). Los Angeles, CA: The Center for the Future of Children.

Hodges, S., Nesman, T., & Hernandez, M. (1999). Promising practices: Building collaboration in systems of care. *Systems of Care: Promising Practices in Children's Mental Health, 1998 Series, Vol. 4.* Washington, DC: Center for Effective Collaboration and Practice, American Institutes for Research.

Hofmeister, A. M., & Ferrara, J. M. (1986). *Artificial intelligence application in special education: How feasible?* [Final report]. Logan, UT: Utah State University.

Hollins, E. R., & Oliver, E. I. (1999). *Pathways to success in school: Culturally responsive teaching.* Mahwah, NJ: Erlbaum.

Hollins, S., Perez, W., Abdelnoor, A., & Webb, B. (1999). *Falling in love.* London, UK: Gaskell/St. George's Hospital Medical School.

Holm, A., Dodd, B., Stow, C., & Pert, S. (1999). Identification and differential diagnosis of phonological disorder in bilingual children. *Language Testing, 16,* 271–292.

Hopkins, K. D. (1998). *Educational and psychological measurement and evaluation* (8th ed.). Boston: Allyn and Bacon.

Horiuchi, V. (1999, April 10). Assistive devices help to level playing field: Machines can be key to productive life and individual self-esteem. *The Salt Lake Tribune*, p. D8.

Horton, C. B., & Cruise, T. K. (1997). Child sexual abuse. In G. G. Bear, K. M. Minke, & A. Thomas (Eds.), *Children's needs II: Development, problems, and alternatives* (pp. 719–727). Bethesda, MD: National Association of School Psychologists.

Horton, H. D., & Allen, B. L. (1998). Race, family structure, and rural poverty: An assessment of population and structural change. *Journal of Comparative Family Studies, 29*(2), 397–406.

Horvat, M. (2000). Physical activity of children with and without mental retardation in inclusive recess settings. *Education and Training in Mental Retardation, 35*(2), 160–167.

Horwitz, A. V., & Scheid, T. L. (1999). *A handbook for the study of mental health: Social contexts, theories, and systems*. New York: Cambridge University Press.

House, S. S., & Davidson, R. C. (2000). Increasing language development through orientation and mobility instruction. *RE:view, 31*(4), 149–153.

Howard, V. F., Williams, B. F., Port, P. D., & Lepper, C. (2001). *Very young children with special needs: A formative approach for the twenty-first century* (2nd ed.). Columbus, OH: Merrill/Prentice Hall.

Howell, J. C. (1998). *Youth gangs: An overview*. [Bulletin.] Washington, DC: U.S. Department of Justice, Office of Justice Programs, Office of Juvenile Justice and Delinquency Prevention.

Howell, P., Sackin, S., & Williams, R. (1999). Differential effects of frequency-shifted feedback between child and adult stutterers. *Journal of Fluency Disorders, 24*(2), 127–136.

Howie, D. (1999). Models and morals: Meanings underpinning the scientific study of special educational needs. *International Journal of Disability, Development, and Education, 46*(1), 9–24.

Huebner, R. A., & Emery, L. J. (1998). Social psychological analysis of facilitated communication: Implications for education. *Mental Retardation, 36,* 259–268.

Huefner, D. S. (2000). The risks and opportunities of the IEP requirements under IDEA 97. *The Journal of Special Education, 33*(4), 195–204.

Huff, C. R. (1998, October). Comparing the criminal behavior of youth gangs and at-risk youths. *Research in Brief*, U.S. Department of Justice, Office of Justice Pro-grams, Office of Juvenile Justice and Delinquency Prevention.

Hughes, C. (1992). Teaching self-instruction utilizing multiple exemplars to produce generalized problem solving among individuals with severe mental retardation. *American Journal on Mental Retardation, 97*(3), 302–314.

Hull, J. M. (1990). *Touching the rock*. New York: Pantheon.

Hunsaker, S. L., Finley, V. S., & Frank, E. L. (1997). An analysis of teacher nominations and student performance in gifted programs. *Gifted Child Quarterly, 4*(2), 19–24.

Hunt, J. M. (1961). *Intelligence and experience*. New York: Ronald Press.

Hunt, P., Staub, D., Alwell, M., & Goetz, L. (1994). Achievement by all students within the context of cooperative learning groups. *Journal of the Association for Persons with Severe Handicaps, 19*(4), 290–301.

Iacono, T. A., Chan, J. B., & Waring, R. E. (1998). Efficacy of a parent-implemented early language intervention based on collaborative consultation. *International Journal of Language and Communication Disorders, 33,* 281–303.

Indefre, P., Levelt, W. J. M., Norris, D., et al. (2000). Language. In M. S. Gazzaniga (Ed.), *The new cognitive neurosciences* (2nd ed., pp. 845–958). Cambridge, MA: The MIT Press.

Insenberg, S. J. (1992). Vision focus: Understanding the medical and functional implications of vision loss in young blind and visually impaired children. In R. L. Pogrun, D. L. Fazzi, & J. S. Lampert (Eds.), *Early focus: Working with young blind and visually impaired children and their families* (pp. 13–35). New York: American Foundation for the Blind Press.

Ireys, H. T., Wehr, E., & Cooke, R. E. (1999). *Defining medical necessity*. Washington, DC: National Center for Education in Maternal and Child Health, U.S. Department of Health and Human Services.

Ivey, A. E., & Ivey, M. B. (1999). *Intentional interviewing and counseling: Facilitating client development in a multicultural society* (4th ed.). Pacific Grove, CA: Brooks/Cole.

Jackson, N. E., & Klein, E. J. (1997). Gifted performance in young children. In N. Colangelo & A. D. Davis (Eds.), *Handbook of gifted education* (2nd ed., pp. 460–474). Boston: Allyn and Bacon.

Jacobs, C. (1999). Communication is a two-way street: In a cooperative program, young people who are non-verbal train medical students in dealing with special populations. *Exceptional Parent, 29*(8), 54–57.

Jaffe, K. M., Fay, G. C., Polissar, N. L., et al. (1992). Severity of pediatric traumatic brain injury and early neurobehavioral outcome: A cohort study. *Archives of Physical Medicine and Rehabilitation, 73*(6), 540–547.

Jakupcak, A. J. (1998). School programs for successful inclusion of all students. In J. Putnam (Ed.), *Cooperative learning and strategies for inclusion* (pp. 203–227). Baltimore, MD: Brookes.

Jan, J., & Wong, P. K. H. (1991). The child with cortical visual impairment. *Seminars in Ophthalmology, 6,* 194–200.

Jay, A. S., Grote, I., & Baer, D. M. (1999). Teaching participants with developmental disabilities to comply with self-instructions. *American Journal on Mental Retardation, 104*(6), 509–522.

Jencks, C. (1998). Racial bias in testing. In C. Jencks and M. Phillips (Eds.), *The Black-White test score gap* (pp. 55–85). Washington, DC: Brookings Institution.

Jenkins, Y. M. (1999). *Diversity in college settings: Directives for helping professionals*. New York: Routledge.

Jennett, B., & Teasdale, G. (1974). Assessment of coma and impaired consciousness. *Lancet, 2,* 81–84.

Jensen, E. (1999). *Teaching with the brain in mind*. Alexandria, VA: Association for Supervision and Curriculum Development.

Jensen, P. S. (1999). Fact versus fancy concerning the multimodal treatment study for attention-deficit hyperactivity disorder. *Canadian Journal of Psychiatry, 44,* 975–980.

Jensen, P. S., Kettle, L., Roper, M. T., et al. (1999). Are stimulants overprescribed? Treatment of ADHD in four U.S. communities. *Journal of the American Academy of Child and Adolescent Psychiatry, 38,* 797–804.

Jernigan, K. (1992, June). Equality, disability, and empowerment. *The Braille Monitor*, 292–298.

Jerome, L., Washington, P., Laine, C. J., & Segal, A. (1999). Graduating teachers' knowledge and attitudes about attention-deficit hyperactivity disorder: A comparison with practicing teachers. *Canadian Journal of Psychiatry, 44*(2), 192.

Jitendra, A. K., Cole, C. L., Hoppes, M. K., & Wilson, B. (1998). Effects of a direct instruction main idea summarization program and self-monitoring on reading comprehension of middle school students with learning disabilities. *Reading and Writing Quarterly: Overcoming Learning Difficulties, 14*(4), 379–396.

Johnson, B. D., Altmaier, E. M., & Richman, L. C. (1999). Attention deficits and reading disabilities: Are immediate memory defects additive? *Developmental Neuropsychology, 15*(2), 213–226.

Johnson, C. R., & Slomka, G. (2000). Learning, motor, and communication disorders. In M. Hersen & R. T. Ammerman (Eds.), *Advanced abnormal child psychology* (2nd ed., pp. 371–385). Mahwah, NJ: Erlbaum.

Johnson, D. W., & Johnson, R. T. (1999). *Learning together and alone: Cooperative, competitive, and individualistic learning* (5th ed.). Boston: Allyn and Bacon.

Johnson, G. (1998). Family members: What you can do in a hospital setting [Online]. Available: http://www.tbiguide.com/familymembers.html

Johnson, G. O. (1961). *A comparative study of the personal and social adjustment of mentally handicapped children placed in special classes with mentally handicapped children who remain in regular classes*. Syracuse, NY: Syracuse University Research Institute, Office of Research in Special Education and Rehabilitation.

Johnson, G. O. (1962). Special education for the mentally handicapped—a paradox. *Exceptional Children, 29,* 62–69.

Johnson, L. J., Karnes, M. B., & Carr, V. W. (1997). Providing services to children with gifts and disabilities: A critical need. In N. Colangelo & A. D. Davis (Eds.), *Handbook of gifted education* (2nd ed., pp. 516–527). Boston: Allyn and Bacon.

Johnson, P. A. (1995). Adolescent sexuality, pregnancy, and parenthood. In I. M. Bobak, D. L. Lowdermilk, & M. D. Jensen (Eds.), *Maternity nursing* (4th ed., pp. 722–747). St. Louis, MO: Mosby.

Johnson-Cramer, N. L. (1999). Assessment of school-aged children with comorbidity of attention deficit hyperactivity disorder and low birth weight classification. *Dissertation Abstracts International Section A: Humanities and Social Sciences, 59*(7-A), 2344.

Johnston, P. (1998). Commentary on a critique. *Reading Teacher, 51*(4), 282–285.

Joint Organizational Committee. (1993). *Full inclusion of students who are blind or visually impaired: A position statement*. Author.

Jordan, A. M., & deCharms, R. (1959). Personal–social traits of mentally handicapped children. In T. G. Thurstone (Ed.), *An evaluation of educating mentally handicapped children in special classes and regular classes*. Chapel Hill: School of Education, University of North Carolina.

Jorgensen, C. M. (1992). Natural supports in inclusive schools: Curricular and teaching strategies. In J. Nisbet (Ed.), *Natural supports in school, at work, and in the community for people with disabilities* (pp. 179–215). Baltimore, MD: Brookes.

Jurich, A. P., & Collins, O. P. (1996). Adolescents, suicide, and death. In C. A. Corr & D. E. Balk (Eds.), *Handbook of adolescent death and bereavement* (pp. 65–84). New York: Springer.

Justen, J. (1976). Who are the severely handicapped? A problem in definition. *AAESPH Review, 1*(5), 1–11.

Kadesjoe, B., Gillberg, C., Hagberg, B., Gillberg, C., & Hagberg, B. (1999). Autism and Asperger syndrome in seven-year-old children: A total population study. *Journal of Autism and Developmental Disorders, 29*(4), 327–33.

Kaiser, A. P. (2000). Teaching functional communication skills. In M. E. Snell & F. Brown (Eds.), *Instruction of persons with severe disabilities* (5th ed., pp.453–492). Columbus, OH: Merrill.

Kaiser, A. P., & Hester, P. P. (1997). Prevention of conduct disorder through early intervention: A social-communicated perspective. *Behavior Disorders, 22*(3), 117–130.

Kalinowski, J., Stuart, A., Wamsley, L., & Rastatter, M. P. (1999). Effects of monitoring condition and frequency-altered feedback on stuttering frequency. *Journal of Speech, Language, and Hearing Research, 42,* 1347–1354.

Kalyanpur, M. (1998). The challenge of cultural blindness: Implications for family-focused service delivery. *Journal of Child and Family Studies, 7*(3), 317–332.

Kammeyer, K. C. W., Ritzer, G., & Yetman, N. T. (1997). *Sociology: Experiencing changing societies* (7th ed). Boston: Allyn and Bacon.

Kamphaus, R. W., & Frick, P. J. (1996). *Clinical assessment of child and adolescent personality and behavior.* Boston: Allyn and Bacon, p. 131.

Kaplan, B. J., Wilson, B. N., Dewey, D., & Crawford, S. G. (1998). DCD may not be a discrete disorder. *Human Movement Science, 17*(4–5), 471–490.

Kaplan, D. W., & Mammel, K. A. (1997). Gynecologic disorders in adolescence. In W. W. Hay, Jr., J. R. Groothuis, A. R. Hayward, & M. J. Levin (Eds.), *Current pediatric diagnosis and treatment* (pp. 153–157). Norwalk, CT: Appleton & Lange.

Kaplan, J. S. (2000). *Beyond functional assessment: A social–cognitive approach to the evaluation of behavior problems in children and youth.* Austin, TX: Pro-Ed.

Kasari, C., Freeman, S. F. N., Bauminger, N., & Alkin, M. C. (1999). Parental perspectives on inclusion: Effects of autism and Down syndrome. *Journal of Autism and Developmental Disorders, 29,* 297–305.

Katims, D. S. (2000). Literacy instruction for people with mental retardation: Historical highlights and contemporary analysis. *Education and Training in Mental Retardation and Developmental Disabilities, 35*(1), 3–15.

Katz, R. N. (1999). Competitive strategies for higher education in the information age. In R. N. Katz (Ed.), *Dancing with the devil: Information technology and the new competition in higher education* (pp. 27–49). San Francisco: Jossey-Bass.

Kauffman, J. M. (1989). *Characteristics of behavior disorders of children and youth* (4th ed.). Columbus, OH: Merrill.

Kauffman, J. M. (1993). How might we achieve the radical reform of special education? *Exceptional Children, 60*(1), 6–16.

Kauffman, J. M. (1997). *Characteristics of emotional and behavioral disorders of children and youth.* Upper Saddle River, NJ: Prentice-Hall.

Kauffman, J. M. (1998). Commentary: Today's special education and its messages for tomorrow. *Journal of Special Education, 32*(3), 127–137.

Kauffman, J. M. (1999). How we prevent the prevention of emotional and behavioral disorders. *Exceptional Children, 65*(4), 448–468.

Kauffman, J. M. (2001). *Characteristics of emotional and behavioral disorders of children and youth* (7th ed.). Columbus, OH: Merrill/Prentice Hall.

Kauffman, J. M., & Hallahan, D. P. (1997). A diversity of restrictive environments: Placement as a problem of social ecology. In J. W. Lloyd, E. J. Kameenui, & D. Chard (Eds.), *Issues in educating students with disabilities* (pp. 325–342). Hillsdale, NJ: Erlbaum.

Kauffman, J. M., Hallahan, D. P., & Lloyd, J. W. (1998). Politics, science, and the future of learning disabilities. *Learning Disability Quarterly, 21,* 276–280.

Kauffman, J. M., & Lloyd, J. W. (1995). A sense of place: The importance of placement issues in contemporary special education. In J. M. Kauffman, J. W. Lloyd, D. P. Hallahan, & T. A. Astuto (Eds.), *Issues in educational placement: Students with emotional and behavioral disorders* (pp. 3–19). Hillsdale, NJ: Erlbaum.

Kauffman, J. M., & Smucker, K. (1995). The legacies of placement: A brief history of placement options and issues with commentary on their evolution. In J. M. Kauffman, J. W. Lloyd, D. P. Hallahan, & T. A. Astuto (Eds.), *Issues in educational placement: Students with emotional and behavioral disorders* (pp. 21–44). Hillsdale, NJ: Erlbaum.

Kavale, K. A., Forness, S. R., & Alper, A. E. (1986). Research in behavioral disorders/emotional disturbance: A survey of subject identification criteria. *Behavioral Disorders, 11*(3), 159–167.

Kay, P. J., & Fitzgerald, M. (1997). Parents + teacher + action research = real involvement. *Teaching Exceptional Children, 30*(1), 8–11.

Kea, C. D., & Utley, C. A. (1998). To teach me is to know me. *Journal of Special Education, 32*(1), 44–47.

Keenan, S. M. (1997). Program elements that support teachers and students with learning and behavior problems. In P. Zionts (Ed.), *Inclusion strategies for students with learning and behavior problems* (pp. 117–138). Austin, TX: Pro-Ed.

Kehle, T. J., Clark, E., & Jenson, W. R. (1997). Interventions for students with traumatic brain injury: Managing behavioral disturbances. In E. D. Bigler, E. Clark, & J. E. Farmer (Eds.), *Childhood traumatic brain injury: Diagnosis, assessment, and intervention* (pp. 135–152). Austin, TX: Pro-Ed.

Keith, R. W. (1999). Clinical issues in central auditory processing disorders. *Language, Speech, and Hearing Services in Schools, 30,* 339–344.

Kekelis, L. S. (1992). Peer interactions in childhood: The impact of visual impairment. In S. Z. Sacks, L. S. Kekelis, & R. J. Gaylord-Ross (Eds.), *The development of social skills by blind and visually impaired students* (pp. 13–35). New York: American Foundation for the Blind Press.

Kendall, R. (2000). *Am very worried* [Online]. Available: http://www. conductdisorders.com/ubb/Forum1/ HTML/010138.html

Kerr, B. (1997). Developing talents in girls and young women. In N. Colangelo & A. D. Davis (Eds.), *Handbook of gifted education* (2nd ed., pp. 483–497). Boston: Allyn and Bacon.

Kerr, M. M., & Nelson, C. M. (1998). *Strategies for managing behavior problems in the classroom.* Upper Saddle River, NJ: Merrill.

Kertesz, A., Davidson, W., & McCabe, P. (1998). Primary progressive semantic aphasia: A case study. *Journal of International Neuropsychological Society, 4*(4), 388–398.

KidSource. (2000). Undetected vision disorders are blinding children; earlier testing needed to preserve good eyesight [Online]. Available: http://www.kidsource.com: 80/kidsource/content/news/Vision. html

Kilbey, M. M. (1999). One academic's viewpoint on prescription privileges. *APA Monitor, 30*(11), 11.

King, W. (2000, May 2). Disabilities may keep man from transplant. *Salt Lake Tribune,* A1, A7.

Kirby, D. (1997). *HIV Prevention Among Adolescents.*

Kirk, S. A. (1963). Behavioral diagnosis and remediation of learning disabilities. *Proceedings: Conference on exploration into the problems of the perceptually handicapped* (Vol. 1). First Annual Meeting, Chicago.

Kliewer, C., & Biklen, D. (1996). Labeling: Who wants to be retarded. In W. Stainback & S. Stainback (Eds.), *Controversial issues confronting special education: Divergent perspectives* (pp. 83–95). Boston: Allyn and Bacon.

Knitzer, J. (1982). *Unclaimed children: The failure of public responsibility to children and adolescents in need of mental health services.* Washington, DC: Children's Defense Fund.

Knitzer, J., Steinberg, Z., & Fleisch, B. (1990). *At the schoolhouse door: An examination of programs and policies for children with behavioral and emotional problems.* New York: Bank Street College of Education.

Knoll, J. (1992). Being a family: The experience of raising a child with a disability or chronic illness. In V. J. Bradley, J. Knoll, & J. M. Agosta (Eds.), *Emerging issues in family support* (pp. 9–56). Washington, DC: American Association on Mental Retardation.

Knowlton, E. (1998). Considerations in the design of personalized curricular supports for students with developmental disabilities. *Education and Training in Mental Retardation, 33*(2), 95–107.

Koegel, L. K., Koegel, R. L., Shoshan, Y., & McNerney, E. (1999). Pivotal response intervention II: Preliminary long-term outcome data. *Journal of the Association for Persons with Severe Handicaps, 24,* 186–198.

Koegel, R. L., Kern-Koegel, L., & Carter, C. M. (1999). Pivotal teaching interactions for children with autism. *School Psychology Review, 28,* 576–594.

Koenig, A. J., & Rex, E. J. (1996). Selection of learning and literacy media for children and youths with low vision. In *Founda-*

tions of low vision: Clinical and functional perspectives (pp. 280–305). New York: American Foundation for the Blind Press.

Kolloff, P. B. (1997). Special residential high schools. In N. Colangelo & A. D. Davis (Eds.), Handbook of gifted education (2nd ed., pp. 198–206). Boston: Allyn and Bacon.

Kovner, R., Budman, C., Frank, Y., Sison, C., Lesser, M., & Halprin, J. (1999). Neuropsychological testing in adult attention deficit hyperactivity disorder: A pilot study. International Journal of Neuroscience, 97, 277.

Koyangi, C., & Gaines, S. (1993). All systems failure: An examination of the results of neglecting the needs of children with serious emotional disturbance. Washington, DC: National Mental Health Association.

Krauss, M. W., Seltzer, M. M., Gordon, R., & Friedman, D. H. (1996, April). Binding ties: The roles of adult siblings of persons with mental retardation. Mental Retardation, 34(2), 83–93.

Kroth, R. L., & Edge, D. (1997). Strategies for communicating with parents and families of exceptional children. Denver, CO: Love.

Kurzweil Technologies. (2000, February). A brief biography of Ray Kurzweil. Burlington, MA: Lernout & Hauspie [Online]. Available: http://www.kurzweiltech.com/raybio.htm

Laakso, M. L., Poikkeus, A. M., & Lyytinen, P. (1999). Shared reading interaction in families with and without genetic risk for dyslexia: Implications for toddler's language development. Infant and Child Development, 8(4), 179–195.

Lainhart, J. E. (1999). Psychiatric problems in individuals with autism, their parents, and siblings. International Review of Psychiatry, 11(4), 278–298.

Lamb, M. E., & Meyer, D. J. (1991). Fathers of children with special needs. In M. Seligman (Ed.), The family with a handicapped child (2nd ed., pp. 151–180). Boston: Allyn and Bacon.

Lambert, N. M., & Hartsough, C. S. (1998). Prospective study of tobacco smoking and substance dependencies among samples of ADHD and non-ADHD participants. Journal of Learning Disabilities, 31, 533–544.

Lambros, K. M., Ward, S. L., Bocian, K. M., MacMillan, D. L., & Gresham, F. M. (1998). Behavioral profiles of children at risk for emotional and behavioral disorders: Implications for assessment and classification. Focus on Exceptional Children, 30(5), 1–16.

Lamison-White, L. (1997). Poverty in the United States: 1996. U.S. Bureau of the Census, Current Population Reports (Ser. P60-198). Washington, DC: U.S. Government Printing Office.

Lancman, M. (1999). Epilepsy: Diagnosis and management. Exceptional Parent, 29(8), 67–69.

Landau, S., Mangione, C., & Pryor, J. B. (1997). HIV & AIDS. In G. G. Bear, K. M. Minke, & A. Thomas (Eds.), Children's needs II: Development, problems, and alternatives (pp. 781–791). Bethesda, MD: National Association of School Psychologists.

Landau, S., Milich, R., & Diener, M. B. (1998). Peer relations of children with attention-deficit hyperactivity disorder. Reading & Writing Quarterly: Overcoming Learning Difficulties, 14, 83–105.

Landers, M. F., & Weaver, M. F. (1997). Inclusive education: A process, not a placement. Swampscott, MA: Watersun Publishing.

Lando, B. Z., & Schneider, B. H. (1997). Intellectual contributions and mutual support among developmentally advanced children in homogeneous and heterogeneous work/discussion groups. Gifted Child Quarterly, 4(2), 44–57.

Landrum, T. J., & Tankersley, M. (1999). Emotional and behavioral disorders in the new millennium. Behavioral Disorders, 24(4), 319–330.

Lane, H. (1992). The mask of benevolence: Disabling the deaf community. New York: Knopf.

Lane, H., Hoffmeister, R., & Bahan, B. (1996). A journey into the deaf world. San Diego, CA: Dawn Sign Press.

Lapadat, J. C. (1998). Implicit theories and stigmatizing labels. Journal of College Reading and Learning, 29(1), 73–81.

Larry P. v. Riles. (1972). C-71-2270 US.C, 343 F. Supp. 1306 (N.D. Cal. 1972).

Larry P. v. Riles. (1979). 343 F. Supp. 1306, 502 F. 2d 963 (N.D. Cal. 1979).

Larsen, S. (1978). Learning disabilities and the professional educator. Learning Disability Quarterly, 1(1), 5–12.

Laski, F. J. (1991). Achieving integration during the second revolution. In L. H. Meyer, C. A. Peck, & L. Brown (Eds.), Critical issues in the lives of people with severe disabilities (pp. 409–421). Baltimore, MD: Brookes.

Lau v. Nichols. (1974, January 21). 414, U.S., 563–572.

Lavelle, N., & Keogh, B. K. (1980). Expectations and attribu-

tions of parents of handicapped children. In J. J. Gallagher (Ed.), New directions for exceptional children, parents, and families of handicapped children. San Francisco: Jossey-Bass.

Lavid, N., Franklin, D. L., & Maguire, G. A. (1999). Management of child and adolescent stuttering with olanzapine: Three case reports. Annals of Clinical Psychiatry, 11(4), 233–236.

Lavin, C., & Doka, K. J. (1999). Older adults with developmental disabilities. Amityville, NY: Baywood.

Lazar, J. W., & Frank, Y. (1998). Frontal systems dysfunction in children with attention-deficit/hyperactivity disorder and learning disabilities. Journal of Neuropsychiatry and Clinical Neurosciences, 10(2), 160–167.

LeDorze, G., Croteau, C., Brassard, C., & Michallet, B. (1999). Research considerations guiding interventions for families affected by aphasia. Aphasiology, 13, 922–927.

Lefrancois, G. R. (1999). The lifespan (6th ed.). Belmont, CA: Wadsworth.

Lehr, E. (1990). Psychological management of traumatic brain injuries in children and adolescents. Rockville, MD: Aspen.

Leigh, J. (1987). Parenting and the hearing-impaired. Volta Review, 89(5), 11–21.

Leonard, L. B. (2000). Understanding grammatical deficits in children with specific language impairment: The evaluation of productivity. In L. Menn & N. Bernstein-Ratner (Eds.), Methods for studying language production (pp. 333–352). Mahwah, NJ: Erlbaum.

Lerner, J. (1997). Learning disabilities: Theories, diagnosis, and teaching strategies (7th ed.). Boston: Houghton Mifflin .

Levin, F. R., Evans, S. M., & Kleber, H. D. (1999). Practical guidelines for the treatment of substance abusers with adult attention-deficit hyperactivity disorder. Psychiatric Services, 50, 1001–1003.

Levinson, E. M., McKee, L., & Dematteo, F. J. (2000). The exceptional child grows up: Transition from school to adult life. In M. J. Fine & R. L. Simpson (Eds.), Collaboration with parents and families of children with exceptionalities (2nd ed., pp. 409–436). Austin, TX: Pro-Ed.

Levitt, J. G., Blanton, R., Capetillo-Cunliffe, L., Guthrie, D., Toga, A., & McCracken, J. T. (1999). Cerebellar vermis lobules VIII-X in autism. Progress in Neuro-Psychopharmacology and Biological Psychiatry, 23, 625–633.

Levy, F., Barr, C., & Sunahara, G. (1998). Directions of aetiologic research on attention deficit hyperactivity disorder. Australian & New Zealand Journal of Psychiatry, 32, 97–103.

Lewis, N. (1999, Summer). Losing sight. Newsletter of the New York State Commission on Quality of Care, 76 [Online]. Available: http://www.cqc.state.ny.us/76nlewis.htm

Lewis, T. J., Chard, D., & Scott, T. M. (1994). Full inclusion and the education of children and youth with behavioral disorders. Behavioral Disorders, 19(4), 277–293.

Lewitt, E. M., & Baker, L. S. (1996). Children in special education. The Future of Children, 6(1), 139–151.

Leybaert, J. (1993). Reading in the deaf: The roles of phonological codes. In M. Marschark & M. D. Clark (Eds.), Psychological perspectives on deafness (pp. 269–309). Hillsdale, NJ: Erlbaum.

Lian, M. J., & Aloia, G. (1994). Parental responses, roles, and responsibilities. In S. K. Alper, P. J. Schloss, & C. N. Schloss (Eds.), Families of students with disabilities (pp. 51–94). Boston: Allyn and Bacon.

Liaw, F., & Brooks-Gunn, J. (1994). Cumulative familial risks and low-birthweight children's cognitive and behavioral development. Journal of Clinical Child Psychology, 23(4), 360–372.

Library of Congress. (1999). Library of Congress launches Web-Braille on the Internet for blind and visually impaired library users [Online]. Available: http://www.loc.gov/nls/nls=wb.html

Lieberman, L. M. (1996). Preserving special education . . . for those who need it. In W. Stainback & S. Stainback (Eds.), Controversial issues confronting special education: Divergent perspectives (2nd ed., pp. 16–27). Boston: Allyn and Bacon.

Lillard, A. (1998). Ethnopsychologies: Cultural variations in theories of mind. Psychological Bulletin, 123, 3–32.

Lilly, M. S. (1992). Labeling: A tired, overworked, yet unresolved issue in special education. In W. Stainback & S. Stainback (Eds.), Controversial issues confronting special education: Divergent perspectives (pp. 85–95). Boston: Allyn and Bacon.

Linan-Thompson, S., & Jean, R. E. (1997, November/December). Completing the parent participation puzzle: accepting diversity. Teaching Exceptional Children, 30, 46–50.

Lindsay, W. R. (1999). Cognitive therapy. Psychologist, 12(5), 238–241.

Lindsey, M. L. (1998). Culturally competent assessment of African

American clients. *Journal of Personality Assessment, 70,* 43–53.

Linn, R. L., & Gronlund, N. E. (2000). *Measurement and assessment in teaching* (8th ed.). Columbus, OH: Merrill/Prentice Hall.

Lipsky, D. K., & Gartner, A. (1996). Inclusive education and school restructuring. In W. Stainback & S. Stainback (Eds.), *Controversial issues confronting special education: Divergent perspectives* (pp. 3–15). Boston: Allyn and Bacon.

Lipsky, D. K., & Gartner, A. (1999). Inclusive education: A requirement of a democratic society. In H. Daniels & P. Garner (Eds.), *Inclusive education: World yearbook of education, 1999* (pp. 12–23). London, UK: Kogan Page.

Livni, E. (2000, March 20). Misdiagnosing misbehavior?: First lady calls for a closer look at psychotropics for kids. *ABC News.*

Lobato, D. J. (1990). *Brothers, sisters, and special needs: Information and activities for helping young siblings of children with chronic illness and developmental disabilities.* Baltimore, MD: Brookes.

Lobato, D. J., Faust, D., & Spirito, A. (1988). Examining the effects of chronic disease and disability on children's sibling relationships. *Journal of Pediatric Psychology, 13,* 389–407.

Lochman, J. E., & Szczepanski, R. G. (1999). Externalizing conditions. In V. L. Schwean & D. H. Saklofske (Eds.), *Handbook of psychosocial characteristics of exceptional children* (pp. 219–246). New York: Kluwer/Plenum.

Locke, D. C. (1995). Counseling interventions with African American youth. In C. C. Lee (Ed.), *Counseling for Diversity* (pp. 21–40). Boston: Allyn & Bacon.

Lohmander-Agerskov, A., Soederpalm, E., Friede, H., & Lilja, J. (1998). A comparison of babbling and speech at pre-speech level, and 5 years of age in children with cleft lip and palate treated with delayed hard palate closure. *Folia Phoniatrica et Logopaedica, 50,* 320–334.

Lopate, P. (Ed.). (1994). *The art of the personal essay: An anthology from the classical era to the present.* New York: Anchor.

Lord-Maes, J., & Obrzut, J. E. (1997). Neurological consequences of traumatic brain injury in children and adolescents. In E. D. Bigler, E. Clark, & J. E. Farmer (Eds.), *Childhood traumatic brain injury: Diagnosis, assessment, and intervention* (pp. 101–114). Austin, TX: Pro-Ed.

Lourie, I. S., Stroul, B. A. & Friedman, R. M. (1998). Community-based systems of care: From advo-cacy to outcomes. In M. H. Epstein, K. Kutash, & A. Duchnowski (Eds.), *Outcomes for children and youth with emotional and behavioral disorders and their families: Programs and evaluation best practices* (pp. 3–19). Austin, TX: Pro-Ed.

Low, C. B. (1999). Attention deficit hyperactivity disorder: Dissociation and adaptation (a theoretical presentation and case study). *American Journal of Clinical Hypnosis, 41*(3), 253–261.

Lubell, E. C. (1999). An examination of the diagnosis of adult attention deficit hyperactivity disorder and incidence of impulsivity, obesity, and alcohol abuse. *Dissertation Abstracts International: Section B: The Sciences and Engineering, 60*(3-B), 1020.

Ludlow, C. L. (1999). A conceptual framework for investigating the neurobiology of stuttering. In N. B. Ratner and C. E. Healey (Eds.), *Stuttering research and practice: Bridging the gap* (pp. 63–84). Mahwah, NJ: Erlbaum.

Luetke-Stahlman, B., & Luckner, J. (1991). *Effectively educating students with hearing impairments.* White Plains, NY: Longman.

Luk, E. S. L., Staiger, P. K., Wong, L., & Mathai, J. (1999). Children who are cruel to animals: A revisit. *Australian and New Zealand Journal of Psychiatry, 33,* 29–36.

Lunsky, Y., & Konstantareas, M. M. (1998). The attitudes of individuals with autism and mental retardation towards sexuality. *Education and Training in Mental Retardation and Developmental Disabilities, 33,* 24–33.

Lustig, D., & Akey, T. (1999). Adaptation in families with adult children with mental retardation: Impact of family strengths and appraisal. *Education & Training in Mental Retardation & Developmental Disabilities, 34*(3), 260–270.

Lutzker, J. R. (1998). *Handbook of child abuse research and treatment.* New York: Plenum.

Lyman, H. B. (1998). *Test scores and what they mean* (6th ed.). Boston: Allyn and Bacon.

Lynch, E. W., & Hanson, M. J. (1998). *Developing cross-cultural competence: A guide for working with children and their families* (2nd ed.). Baltimore, MD: Brookes.

Lyon, G. R. (1996). Learning disabilities. In The Center for the Future of Children (Ed.), *Special education for students with disabilities, 6*(1), pp. 54–76. Los Angeles, CA: The Center for the Future of Children.

Lyons, J. S. (1997). *Child and adolescent strengths assessment.* Chicago, IL: Northwest University, Depart-ment of Psychiatry and Behavioral Sciences.

MacArthur, C. A. (1999). Overcoming barriers to writing: Computer support for basic writing skills. *Reading and Writing Quarterly: Overcoming Learning Difficulties, 15*(2), 169–192.

Maccini, P., McNaughton, D., & Ruhl, K. L. (1999). Algebra instruction for students with learning disabilities: Implications from a research review. *Learning Disability Quarterly, 22*(2), 113–126.

MacCuspie, P. S. (1992). The social acceptance and interaction of visually impaired children in integrated settings. In S. Z. Sacks, L. S. Kekelis, & R. J. Gaylord-Ross (Eds.), *The development of social skills by blind and visually impaired students* (pp. 83–102). New York: American Foundation for the Blind Press.

MacKinnon, D. W. (1962). The nature and nurture of creative talent. *American Psychologist, 17*(7), 484–495.

MacMillan, D. L. (1998). Unpackaging special education categorical variables in the study and teaching of children with conduct disorders. *Education and Treatment of Children, 21*(3), 234–245.

MacMillan, D. L., Gresham, F. M., & Forness, S. R. (1996). Full inclusion: An empirical perspective. *Behavioral Disorders, 21*(2), 145–159.

MacMillan, D. L., & Speece, D. L. (1999). Utility of current diagnostic categories for research and practice. In R. Gallimore, L. P. Bernheimer, D. L. MacMillan, D. L. Speece, & S. Vaughn (Eds.), *Developmental perspectives on children with high-incidence disabilities* (pp. 111–133). Mahwah, NJ: Erlbaum.

Madelaine, A., & Wheldall, K. (1999). Curriculum-based measurement of reading: A critical review. *International Journal of Disability, Development, and Education, 46,* 71–85.

Magnuson, M. (2000) Infants with congenital deafness: On the importance of early sign language acquisition. *American Annals of the Deaf, 145*(1), 6–14.

Maguire, G. A., Gottschalk, L. A., Riley, G. D., Franklin, D. L., Bechtel, R. J., & Ashurst, J. (1999). Stuttering: Neuropsychiatric features measured by content analysis of speech and the effect of risperidone on stuttering severity. *Comprehensive Psychiatry, 40*(4), 308–314.

Maker, C. J., & Nielsen, A. B. (1995). *Teaching models in the education of the gifted.* Austin, TX: Pro-Ed.

Maker, C. J., & Nielson, A. B. (1996). *Curriculum development and teaching strategies for gifted learners.* Austin, TX: Pro-Ed.

Malvy, J., Roux, S., Zakian, A., Debuly, S., Sauvage, D., & Barthelemy, C. (1999). A brief clinical scale for the early evaluation of imitation disorders in autism. *Autism, 3*(4), 357–369.

Mancini, C., Van Ameringen, M., Oakman, J. M., & Figueirdo, D. (1999). Childhood attention deficit/hyperactivity disorder in adults with anxiety disorders. *Psychological Medicine, 29,* 515–525.

Mandal, R. L., Olmi, D. J., & Wilczynski, S. M. (1999). Behavior rating scales: Concordance between multiple informants in the diagnosis of attention-deficit/hyperactivity disorder. *Journal of Attention Disorders, 3*(2), 92–103.

Mank, D., Cioffi, A., & Yovanoff, P. (1997). Analysis of the typicalness of supported employment jobs, natural supports, and wage and integration outcomes. *Mental Retardation, 35,* 185–197.

Manning, M. L., & Baruth, L. G. (1995). *Students at risk.* Boston: Allyn and Bacon.

Mansson, H. (2000). Childhood stuttering: Incidence and development. *Journal of Fluency Disorders, 25,* 47–57.

March of Dimes. (2000). Teenage pregnancy fact sheet [Online]. Available: http://www.modimes.org/HealthLibrary2/factsheets/Teenage_Pregnancy_Fact_Sheet.htm

Margolin, L. (1996). A pedagogy of privilege. *Journal for the Education of the Gifted, 19*(2), 164–180.

Marino, B. R., & Pueschel, S. M. (1996). *Heart disease in persons with Down syndrome.* Baltimore, MD: Brookes.

Marks, D. J., Himelstein, J., Newcorn, J. H., & Halperin, J. M. (1999). Identification of AD/HD subtypes using laboratory-based measures: A cluster analysis. *Journal of Abnormal Child Psychology, 27,* 167–175.

Marschark, M. (1993). Origins and interactions in the social, cognitive, and language development of deaf children. In M. Marschark & M. D. Clark (Eds.), *Psychological perspectives on deafness* (pp. 7–26). Hillsdale, NJ: Erlbaum.

Martin, A., Koenig, K., Scahill, L., & Bregman, J. (1999). Open-label quetiapine in the treatment of children and adolescents with autistic disorder. *Journal of Child and Adolescent Psychopharmacology, 9*(2), 99–107.

Martin, A., Scahill, L., Klin, A., & Volkmar, F. R. (1999). Higher-functioning pervasive developmental disorders: Rates and patterns of psychotropic drug use. *Journal of the*

American Academy of Child and Adolescent Psychiatry, 38, 923–931.

Martinson, M. C., & Stone, J. A. (1993). Small-scale community living options serving three or fewer adults with developmental disabilities. In E. Sutton, A. R. Factor, B. A. Hawkins, T. Heller, & G. B. Seltzer (Eds.), *Older adults with developmental disabilities* (pp. 199–221). Baltimore, MD: Brookes.

Mash, E. J., & Terdal, L. G. (1997). *Assessment of childhood disorders* (3rd ed.). New York: Guilford.

Massanari, C. (2000). Alternate assessment: Questions and answers. IDEA practices [Online]. Available: http://www.ideapractices.org/idea quests/AlternateAssess.htm#whatisalt

Masson, E. J., Kruse, L. A., Farabaugh, A., Gershberg, R., and Kohler, M. S. (2000). Children with exceptionalities: Opportunities for collaboration between family and school. In M. J. Fine & R. L. Simpson (Eds.), *Collaboration with parents and families of children with exceptionalities* (2nd ed., pp. 69–88). Austin, TX: Pro-Ed.

Masten, A. S., & Coatsworth, J. D. (1998). The development of competence in favorable and unfavorable environments. *American Psychologist, 53,* 205–220.

Mastropieri, M. A., & Scruggs, T. E. (2000). The inclusive classroom: Strategies for effective instruction. Upper Saddle River, NJ: Prentice-Hall.

Mathews, F. (1996). Re-framing gang violence: A pro-youth strategy. In N. J. Long, W. C. Morse, & R. G. Newman (Comp.), *Conflict in the classroom: The education of at-risk and troubled students* (5th ed., pp. 217–226). Austin, TX: Pro-Ed.

Max, L., & Caruso, A. J. (1998). Adaptation of stuttering frequency during repeated readings: Associated changes in acoustic parameters of perceptually fluent speech. *Journal of Speech, Language, and Hearing Research, 41,* 1265–1281.

Maxon, A. B., & Brackett, D. (1992). *The hearing impaired child: Infancy through high school years.* Boston: Andover Medical Publishers.

Mayes, S. D., Calhoun, S. L., & Crowell, E. W. (1998). WISC-III profiles for children with and without learning disabilities. *Psychology in the Schools, 35*(4), 309–316.

Mayfield, E. (1999). Sickle cell inheritance [Online]. Available: http://www.fda.gov/fdac/features/496_sick.html

Maynard, R. A. (1997). *Kids having kids.* Lanham, MD: Urban Institute Press.

McAlpine, C., Kendall, K. A., & Singh, N. N. (1991). Recognition of facial expressions of emotion by persons with mental retardation. *American Journal on Mental Retardation, 96,* 29–36.

McAnally, P. L., Rose, S., & Quigley, S. P. (1999). *Reading practices with deaf children.* Austin, TX: Pro-Ed.

McBurnett, K. (1995). The new subtype of ADHD: Predominantly hyperactive–impulsive type. *Attention! 1*(3), 10–15.

McCleary, I. D., Hardman, M. L., & Thomas, D. (1990). International special education. In T. Husen & T. N. Postlewaite (Eds.), *International encyclopedia of education: Research and studies* (pp. 608–615). New York: Pergamon.

McConaughy, S. H., & Ritter, D. R. (1999). Psychological perspectives on exceptionality. In V. L. Schwean & D. H. Saklofske (Eds.), *Handbook of psychosocial characteristics of exceptional children* (pp. 41–68). New York: Kluwer/Plenum.

McConnell, S. R. (1994). Social context, social validity, and program outcome in early intervention. In R. Gardner III, D. M. Sainato, J. O. Cooper, T. E., Heron, W. L. Heward, J. Eshleman, & T. A. Grossi (Eds.), *Behavior analysis in education: Focus on measurably superior instruction* (pp. 75–85). Pacific Grove, CA: Brooks/Cole.

McDermott, S., & Altrekruse, J. (1994). Dynamic model for preventing mental retardation: The importance of poverty and deprivation. *Research on Developmental Disabilities, 15*(1), 49–65.

McDonnell, J. M. (1993). Reflections on supported inclusion programs for students with severe disabilities. *Special Educator, 14*(1), 9–12.

McDonnell, J. M., Hardman, M. L., McDonnell, A. P., & Kiefer-O'Donnell, R. (1995). *Introduction to persons with severe disabilities.* Boston: Allyn and Bacon.

McDonnell, J. M., Mathot-Buckner, C., & Ferguson, B. (1996). *Transition programs for students with moderate/severe disabilities.* Pacific Grove, CA: Brooks/Cole.

McFarland, E. J. (1997). Human immunodeficiency virus (HIV) infections: Acquired immunodeficiency syndrome (AIDS). In W. W. Hay, Jr., J. R. Groothuis, A. R. Hayward, & M. J. Levin (Eds.), *Current pediatric diagnosis and treatment* (pp. 992–1002). Norwalk, CT: Appleton & Lange.

McGaughey, M. J., Kiernan, W. E., McNally, L. C., & Gilmore, D. S. (1995). A peaceful coexis-

tence? MR/DD agency trends in integrated employment and facility-based services. *Mental Retardation, 33,* 170–180.

McGee, G. G., Morrier, M. J., & Daly, T. (1999). An incidental teaching approach to early intervention for toddlers with autism. *Journal of the Association for Persons with Severe Handicaps, 24,* 133–146.

McGuire, J. M. (1998). Educational accommodations: A university administrator's view. In G. Michael & S. Keiser (Eds.), *Accommodations in higher education under the Americans with Disabilities Act (ADA): A no-nonsense guide for clinicians, educators, administrators, and lawyers* (pp. 20–454). New York: Guilford.

McHale, S. M., Sloan, J., & Simeonsson, R. J. (1986). Sibling relationships and adjustment of children with disabled brothers and sisters. *Journal of Children in Contemporary Society, 16,* 131–158.

McHugh, M. (1999). *Special siblings.* New York: Hyperion.

McIntyre, T., & Forness, S. R. (1996). Is there a new definition yet, or are our kids still seriously emotionally disturbed? *Beyond Behavior: A Magazine Exploring Behavior in Our Schools, 7*(3), 4–9.

McKeen, S. (1999, February 26). A new language for baby. *The Ottawa Citizen.* [Online]. Available: http://dww.deafworldweb.org/pub/b/baby.news99.html

McKinney, J. D., Montague, M., & Hocutt, A. M. (1998, April). *A two-year follow-up of children at risk for developing SED: Implications for designing prevention program.* Paper presented at the Annual Convention of the Council for Exceptional Children.

McLaughlin, M. J., Fuchs, L., & Hardman, M. (1999). Individual rights to education and students with disabilities: Some lessons from U.S. policy. In H. Daniels and P. Garner (Eds.), *Inclusive education: World yearbook of education, 1999* (pp. 24–35). London, UK: Kogan Page.

McLaughlin, M. J. & Tilstone, C. (2000). Standards and curriculum: The core of educational reform. In M. Rousa & M. J. McLaughlin (Eds.), *Special education and school reform in the United States and Britain* (pp. 38–65) London, UK: Routledge.

McLaughlin, M. J., & Warren, S. H. (1992). *Issues and options in restructuring schools and special education programs.* College Park: University of Maryland at College Park.

McLaughlin, M. W., Shepard, L. A., & O'Day, J. A. (1995).

Improving education through standards-based reform. *A report by the National Academy of Education Panel on Standards-Based Education Reform.* Stanford, CA: The National Academy of Education.

McLean, L., Brady, N., & McLean, J. (1996). Reported communication abilities of individuals with severe mental retardation. *American Journal of Mental Retardation, 100*(6), 580–591.

McLoughlin, J. A., & Senn, C. (1994). Parental responses, roles, and responsibilities. In S. K. Alper, P. J. Schloss, & C. N. Schloss (Eds.), *Families of students with disabilities* (pp. 51–94). Boston: Allyn and Bacon.

McMillan, J. H. (1997). *Classroom assessment: Principles and practice for effective instruction.* Boston: Allyn and Bacon.

McNab, T. C., & Blackman, J. A. (1998). Medical complications of the critically ill newborn: A review for early intervention professionals. *Topics in Early Childhood Special Education, 18*(4), 197–205.

McNamara, B. E. (1998). *Learning disabilities: Appropriate practices for a diverse population.* Albany, NY: State University of New York Press.

McPhee, N. (1982). A very special magic: A grandparent's delight. *Exceptional Parent, 12*(3), 13–16.

Melich, M. (1996, October 14). Now hear this. *Salt Lake Tribune,* pp. C1, C8.

Meltzer, L., Roditi, B., Houser, R. F., Jr., & Perlman, M. (1998). Perceptions of academic strategies and competence in students with learning disabilities. *Journal of Learning Disabilities, 31,* 437–451.

Menn, L., & Bernstein-Ratner, N. (2000). Methods for studying language production. Mahwah, NJ: Erlbaum.

Merrell, K. W. (1999). *Behavioral, social, and emotional assessment of children and adolescents.* Mahwah, NJ: Erlbaum.

Merrill, E. C., & Peacock, M. (1994). Allocation of attention and task difficulty. *American Journal on Mental Retardation, 98*(5), 588–593.

Mertens, D. M. (1990). A conceptual model for academic achievement: Deaf student outcomes. In D. F. Moores & K. P. Meadow-Orlands (Eds.), *Educational and developmental aspects of deafness* (pp. 25–72). Washington, DC: Gallaudet University Press.

Merton, R. K. (1948). The self-fulfilling prophecy. *Antioch Review, 8,* 193–210.

Metropolitan Life/Louis Harris Associates, Inc. (1996, April). *The*

Metropolitan Life Survey of The American Teacher, 1984–1995. New York: Author.

Meyer, D. J. (1995). *Uncommon fathers: Reflections on raising a child with a disability.* Bethesda, MD: Woodbine.

Meyer, L. H., Peck, C. A., & Brown, L. (Eds.). (1991a). *Critical issues in the lives of people with severe disabilities.* Baltimore, MD: Brookes.

Meyer, L. H., Peck, C. A., & Brown, L. (1991b). Definitions and diagnosis. In L. H. Meyer, C. A. Peck, & L. Brown (Eds.), *Critical issues in the lives of people with disabilities* (p. 17). Baltimore, MD: Brookes.

Meyers, D. (1997). *Views from our shoes: Growing up with a brother or sister with special needs.* Bethesda, MD: Woodbine.

Mian, M. (1996). Child abuse. In R. H. A. Haslam & P. J. Valletutti (Eds.), *Medical problems in the classroom* (pp. 585–600). Austin, TX: Pro-Ed.

Mickelson, K. D., Wroble, M., & Helgeson, V. S. (1999). "Why my child?": Parental attributions for children's special needs. *Journal of Applied Social Psychology, 29,* 1263–1292.

Midence, K., & O'Neill, M. (1999). The experience of parents in the diagnosis of autism: A pilot study. *Autism, 3,* 273–285.

Milberger, S., Biederman, J., Faraone, S. V., & Jones, J. (1998). Further evidence of an association between maternal smoking during pregnancy and attention deficit hyperactivity disorder: Findings from a high-risk sample of siblings. *Journal of Clinical Child Psychology, 27,* 352–358.

Miller, A. (1999). Appropriateness of psychostimulant prescription to children: Theoretical and empirical perspectives. *Canadian Journal of Psychiatry, 44,* 1017–1024.

Miller, F., & Bachrach, S. (1995). *Cerebral palsy: A complete guide for caregiving.* Baltimore, MD: The Johns Hopkins University Press.

Mills, P. E., Cole, K. N., Jenkins, J. R., & Dale, P. S. (1998). Effects of differing levels of inclusion on preschoolers with disabilities. *Exceptional Children, 65,* 79–90.

Mills v. District of Columbia Board of Education, 348 F. Supp. 866 (D.D.C. 1972).

Miltenberger, R. G., & Woods, D. W. (1998). Speech disfluencies. In T. S. Watson and F. M. Gresham (Eds.), *Handbook of child behavior therapy: Issues in clinical child psychology* (pp. 127–142). New York: Plenum.

MiniMed. (2000a). Pump therapy: Why pump therapy? [Online].

Available: http://www.minimed.com/files/whypi.htm

MiniMed. (2000b). Why good control is important [Online]. Available: http://www.minimed.com/files/gd_cntrl.htm

Minow, M. (1991). *Making all the difference: Inclusion, exclusion, and American law.* Ithaca, NY: Cornell Press.

Minshew, N. (2000). Autism's home in the brain: Reply. *Neurology, 54,* 269.

Minty, G. D. (1996, July). What is CF? [Online]. Available: http://www2.cal.ca/distsite/frank/cf-basic.html

Mirenda, P., Iacono, T., & Williams, R. (1990). Communication options for persons with severe and profound disabilities: State of the art and future directions. *Journal of the Association for Persons with Severe Disabilities, 15,* 3–21.

Misra, A. (1994). Partnership with multicultural families. In S. K. Alper, P. J. Schloss, & C. N. Schloss (Eds.), *Families of students with disabilities* (pp. 143–180). Boston: Allyn and Bacon.

Mithaug, D. E., Wehmeyer, M. L., Agran, M., Martin, J. E., & Palmer, S. (1998). The self-determined learning model of instruction: Engaging students to solve their learning problems. In M. L. Wehmeyer & D. J. Sands (Eds.), *Making it happen: Student involvement in education planning, decision making, and instruction* (pp. 299–328). Baltimore, MD: Brookes.

Moaven, L. D., Gilbert, G. L., Cunningham, A. L., & Rawlinson, W. D. (1995). Amniocentesis to diagnose congenital cyomegalovirus infection. *Medical Journal of Australia, 162,* 334–335.

Mogford-Bevan, K. (2000). Developmental language impairments with complex origins: Learning from twins and multiple birth children. *Folia Phoniatrica et Logopaedica, 52,* 74–82.

Molfese, D. L., & Molfese, V. J. (2000). The continuum of language development during infancy and early childhood. In C. Rovee-Collier & L. P. Lipsitt (Eds.), *Progress in infancy research* (Vol. 1, pp. 251–287). Mahwah, NJ: Erlbaum.

Montgomery, A., & Rossi, R. (1994, January). *Educational reforms and students at risk: A review of the current state of the art.* Washington, DC: U.S. Department of Education, Office of Educational Research and Improvement.

Montgomery, J. (1994, July). *Selected strategies for inclusive classrooms.* Paper presented at the

Anglo-American Symposium on Educational Reform and Students with Special Needs. Cambridge, UK: University of Cambridge Institute of Education.

Moon, M. S., & Inge, K. (2000). Vocational preparation and transition. In M. E. Snell & F. Brown (Eds.), *Instruction of students with severe disabilities* (pp. 591–628). Upper Saddle River, NJ: Merrill.

Moon, M. S., Kelly, K. R., & Feldhusen, J. F. (1997). Specialized counseling services for gifted youth and their families: A needs assessment. *Gifted Child Quarterly, 41*(1), 16–25.

Moore, J., & Fombonne, E. (1999). Psychopathology in adopted and nonadopted children: A clinical sample. *American Journal of Orthopsychiatry, 69,* 403–409.

Moore, K. A., Miller, B. C., Sugland, B. W., Morrison, D. R., Glei, D. A., & Blumenthal, C. (1997). *Beginning too soon: Adolescent sexual behavior, pregnancy, and parenthood, a review of research and interventions* [Online]. Available: http://aspe.os.dhhs.gov/hsp/cyp/xsteesex.htm

Morelock, M. J., & Feldman, D. H. (1997). High IQ children, extreme precocity, and savant syndrome. In N. Colangelo & G. A. Davis (Eds.), *Handbook of gifted education* (2nd ed., pp. 430–459). Boston: Allyn and Bacon.

Morgan, J., & Shoop, S. A. (2000, May 19). Rocker sounds off about hearing loss. *USA Today* [Online]. Available: http://www.usatoday.com/life/health/doctor/lhdoc155.htm

Morgan, R. L., Ellerd, D. A., Gerity, B. P., & Blair, R. J. (2000). "That's the job I want": How technology helps young people in transition. *Teaching Exceptional Children, 32*(4), 44–49.

Morra, L. G. (1994, April 28). Districts grapple with inclusion programs. *Testimony before the U.S. House of Representatives on special education reform.* Washington, DC: U.S. General Accounting Office.

Morrison, G. S. (2001). *Early childhood education today* (8th ed.). Columbus, OH: Merrill/Prentice Hall.

Morse, W. C., Cutler, R. L., & Fink, A. H. (1964). *Public school classes for emotionally handicapped: A research analysis.* Washington, DC: Council for Exceptional Children.

Moss, J. (1998). Working with issues of sexual abuse. In E. Emerson & C. Hatton (Eds.), *Clinical psychology and people with intellectual disabilities* (pp. 177–192). Chichester, UK: American Ethnological Press.

MTA Cooperative Group. (1999a). A 14-month randomized clinical trial of treatment strategies for attention-deficit/hyperactivity disorder. *Archives of General Psychiatry, 56,* 1073–1086.

MTA Cooperative Group. (1999b). Moderators and mediators of treatment response for children with attention-deficit/hyperactivity disorder: The multimodal treatment study of children with attention-deficit/hyperactivity disorder. *Archives of General Psychiatry, 56,* 1088–1096.

Mueller, R. A., & Courchesne, E. (2000). Autism's home in the brain: Reply. *Neurology, 54*(1), 270.

Murphy, B. (1999). A preliminary look at shame, guilt, and stuttering. In N. B. Ratner and C. E. Healey (Eds.), *Stuttering research and practice: Bridging the gap* (pp. 131–143). Mahwah, NJ: Erlbaum.

Murphy, J. (1999, Fall). One parent's perspective. *Frontline Initiative, 3*(4), 10.

Murphy, S., & Rogan, P. (1995). *Closing the shop: Conversion from sheltered to integrated employment.* Baltimore, MD: Brookes.

Murray, B. A., & Myers, M. A. (1998). Avoiding the special education trap for conduct disordered students. *NASSP Bulletin, 82*(594), 65–73.

Murrell, J. G. (1999). Behavior profile of children with attention deficit disorder under treatment of Ritalin in elementary schools. *Dissertation Abstracts International: Section B: The Sciences and Engineering, 60*(2-B), 0815.

Muscular Dystrophy Association. (2000a). Facts about muscular dystrophy [Online]. Available: http://www.mdausa.org/publications/fa-md-9.html

Muscular Dystrophy Association. (2000b). *Facts About Muscular Dystrophy: Most frequently asked questions about muscular dystrophy, Part I.* http://www.mdausa.org/publications/fa-md-qa.html

Naglieri, J. A. (1999). How valid is the PASS theory and CAS? *School Psychology Review, 28,* 145–162.

National Academy on an Aging Society. (1999, December). Hearing loss: A growing problem that affects quality of life, 2, 1–6. [Online]. Available: http://www.agingsociety.org/hearing.pdf

National Adoption Information Clearinghouse. (1999). Drug exposed infants [Online]. Available: http://www.calib.com/naic/adptsear/adoption/research/stats/drug.htm

National Advisory Committee on Handicapped Children. (1968). *Special education for handicapped children: First annual report.* Washington, DC: Department of Health, Education, and Welfare.

National Association for the Education of Young Children. (1997). NAEYC position statement [Online]. Available: http://www.naeyc.org/public_affairs/pubaff_index.htm

National Association of State Boards of Education (NASBE). (1992, October). *Winners all: A call for inclusive schools.* Alexandria, VA: Author.

National Association of the Deaf. (2000). I have heard that deaf people are against technology. Is that true? Silver Springs, MD: Author [Online]. Available: http://www.nad.org/infocenter/in fotogo/tech/against.html

National Center for Education Statistics. (1997). *Principal/school disciplinarian survey on school violence.* Washington, DC: U.S. Department of Education.

National Center for Education Statistics. (1998a). *Digest of education statistics.* Washington, DC: U.S. Department of Education.

National Center for Education Statistics. (1998b). *Violence and discipline problems in U.S. public schools: 1996–1997.* Washington, DC: U.S. Department of Education.

National Center for Education Statistics. (1999). *Common core of data, agency universe 1997–1998: State non-fiscal survey and school universe.* Washington, DC: U.S. Department of Education.

National Center for Health Statistics. (1999). FASTATS: Teen births [Online]. Available: http://www.cdc.gov/nchs/fastats/teenbrth.htm

National Center on Educational Restructuring and Inclusion (NCERI). (1994). National survey on inclusive education. *Bulletin of the National Center on Educational Restructuring and Inclusion, 1,* 1–4.

National Clearinghouse on Child Abuse and Neglect Information. (2000a). Child abuse and neglect national statistics [Online]. Available: www.calib.com/nccanch/index.htm

National Clearinghouse on Child Abuse and Neglect Information. (2000b). NCCAN lessons learned [Online]. Available: http://www.calib.com/nccanch/pubs/ot herpubs/lessons/index.htm

National Clearinghouse on Child Abuse and Neglect Information. (2000c). What is child maltreatment? [Online]. Available: http://www.calib.com/nccanch/in dex.htm

National Clearinghouse on Child Abuse and Neglect Information. (2000d). What's new? [Online]. Available: http://www.calib.com/nccanch/whatsnew.htm#cm97

National Commission on Excellence in Education. (1983). *A nation at risk: The imperative for educational reform.* Washington, DC: Author.

National Council on Disability. (1996a). *Achieving independence: The challenge for the 21st century.* Washington, DC: Author.

National Council on Disability. (1996b). Disability demographics. In *Achieving independence: The challenge for the 21st century* (pp. 13–16). Washington, DC: Author.

National Council on Disability. (1998). *Grassroots experiences with government programs and disability policy.* Proceedings from a public hearing in New Orleans, Louisiana, October 1, 1998. Washington, DC: Author.

National Council on Disability. (1999). *National disability policy: A progress report, November 1, 1997–October 31, 1998.* Washington, DC: Author.

National Council on Disability. (2000). *Back to school on civil rights.* Washington, DC: Author.

National Down Syndrome Society. (2000). *Down syndrome: Myths and truths.* New York: Author [Online]. Available: http://www.ndss.org/aboutds/about ds.html#Down

National Information Center for Children and Youth with Disabilities. (1998, June). *Newsdigest: The IDEA amendments of 1997, Volume 26 (Revised Edition).* Washington, DC: Author.

National Information Center for Children and Youth with Disabilities. (1999). *Interventions for chronic behavior problems.* Washington, DC: Author.

National Information Center for Children and Youth with Disabilities. (2000). General information about Down syndrome. Fact Sheet no. 4 (FS4). Washington, DC: Author [Online]. Available: http://www.nichcy.org/pubs/facts he/fs4txt.htm

National Information Center for Children and Youth with Disabilities and the Federal Center. (1999). *Office of Special Education Programs IDEA 97 Training Package.* Washington, DC: Author [Online]. Available: http://www.nichcy.org/Trainpkg/trainpkg.htm

National Institute of Allergy and Infectious Diseases. (2000a). Fact sheet: HIV/AIDS statistics [Online]. Available: http://www.niaid.nih.gov/factsheets/aidsstat.htm

National Institute of Allergy and Infectious Diseases. (2000b).

Fact sheet: HIV infection and adolescents [Online]. Available: http://www.niaid.nih.gov/factsheets/hivadolescent.htm

National Institute of Allergy and Infectious Diseases. (2000c). Fact sheet: How HIV causes AIDS [Online]. Available: http://www.niaid.nih.gov/factsheets/howhiv.htm

National Institute of Allergy and Infectious Diseases. (2000d). Pediatric AIDS [Online]. Available: http://www.niaid.nih.gov/fact-sheets/pedaids.htm

National Institute of Mental Health. (1999a). In harm's way: Suicide in America [Online]. Available: http://www.nimh.nih.gov/publi-cat/harmaway.cfm

National Institute of Mental Health. (1999b). Suicide facts [Online]. Available: http://www.nimh.nih.gov/research/suifact.htm

National Institute of Mental Health. (2000). Depression in children and adolescents [Online]. Available: http://www.nimh.nih.gov/publicat/depchildresfact.cfm

National Institute on Deafness and Other Communication Disorders. (2000a). Cochlear implants. In *Health Information: Hearing and balance* [Online]. Available: http://www.nih.gov/nidcd/health/pubs_hb/coch.htm

National Institute on Deafness and Other Communication Disorders. (2000b). Otitis media. In *Health Information: Hearing and balance* [Online]. Available: http://www.nih.gov/nidcd/health/pubs_hb/otitism.htm#effects

National Institute on Early Childhood Development and Education. (1999). *Compendium of school-based and school-linked programs for pregnant and parenting adolescents.* Washington, DC: Office of Educational Research and Improvement, U.S. Department of Education.

National Institutes of Health. (1998). Diagnosis and treatment of attention-deficit hyperactivity disorder. *NIH Consensus Statement* [Online], *16*(2), Nov. 16–18, 1–37.

National Joint Committee on Learning Disabilities. (1998). Operationalizing the NJCLD definition of learning disabilities for ongoing assessment in schools. *Learning Disability Quarterly, 21,* 186–193.

National Law Center on Homelessness and Poverty. (1999). General information about homelessness: Homelessness and poverty in America [Online]. Available: http://www.nlchp.org/h&pusa.htm

National Organization on Disability (N.O.D.)/Harris, L., & Associates. (1994). *National Organization on Disability/Harris Survey*

of Americans with Disability. New York: Author.

National Organization on Disability/Harris, L., & Associates. (1995). *National Organization on Disability/Harris Survey of Americans with Disability.* New York: Author.

National Organization on Disability/Harris, L., & Associates. (1998). *National Organization on Disability/Harris Survey of Americans with Disability.* New York: Author.

National Organization on Disability/ Harris, L., & Associates. (2000). *National Organization on Disability/Harris Survey of Americans with Disabilities.* New York: Author.

National Organization on Fetal Alcohol Syndrome. (2000). What is fetal alcohol syndrome? [Online]. Available: http://www.nofas.org/stats.htm

National Research Council. (1997). *Educating one and all: Students with disabilities and standards-based reform.* Washington, DC: National Academy Press.

National Spinal Cord Injury Statistical Center (NSCISC). (1997). FAQ data [Online]. Available: http://www.sci.rehabm.uab.edu/s hared/faq.data.html

National Women's Health Information Center. (1997). Teen pregnancy [Online]. Available: http://www.4woman.gov/faq/teenpreg nancy.htm

Natriello, G., McDill, E. L., & Pallas, A. M. (1990). *Schooling disadvantaged children: Racing against catastrophe.* New York: Teachers College Press, Columbia University.

Nelson, C. M., Rutherford, R. B., Center, D. B., & Walker, H. M. (1991). Do public schools have an obligation to serve troubled children and youth? *Exceptional Children, 57*(5), 406–415.

Nevin, A. (1998). Curricular and instructional adaptations for including students with severe disabilities in cooperative groups. In J. Putam (Eds.), *Cooperative learning and strategies for inclusion* (2nd ed.) (pp. 49–65). Baltimore, MD: Paul H. Brookes.

New Goals for the U.S. Human Genome Project: 1998–2003. (1998). *Science, 282,* 682–689.

Nichols, P. (1996). The curriculum of control: Twelve reasons for it, some arguments against it. In N. J. Long, W. C. Morse, & R. G. Newman (Comp.), *Conflict in the classroom: The education of at-risk and troubled students* (5th ed., pp. 82–94). Austin, TX: Pro-Ed.

Nilsson, E. W., Gillberg, C., Gillberg, I. C., & Rastam, M. (1999). Ten-year follow-up of adolescent-onset anorexia nervosa: Personality disorders. *Journal of the American*

Academy of Child and Adolescent Psychiatry, 38, 1389–1395.

Nippold, M. A. (2000). Language development during the adolescent years: Aspects of pragmatics, syntax, and semantics. Topics in Language Disorders, 20(2), 15–28.

Nirje, B. (1970). The normalization principle and its human management implications. Journal of Mental Subnormality, 16, 62–70.

Nisbet, J. (1992). Introduction. In J. Nisbet (Ed.), Natural supports in school, at work, and in the community for people with disabilities (pp. 1–16). Baltimore, MD: Brookes.

Nitko, A. J. (2001). Educational assessment of students (3rd ed.). Columbus, OH: Merrill/Prentice Hall.

Niu, W., & Zhang, M. (1998). A comparative study of the strategies used in mathematical problem solving between learning disabled students and high achieving students. Psychological Science China, 21, 566–567.

Niu, X., & Luo, W. (1999). Patterns of performance of Chinese-American students with learning disabilities: A pilot study. International Journal of Disability, Development, and Education, 46, 117–129.

Noell, G. H., Gansle, K. A., Witt, J. C., et al. (1998). Effects of contingent reward and instruction on oral reading performance at differing levels of passage difficulty. Journal of Applied Behavior Analysis, 31, 659–663.

Noonan, M. J., & L. McCormick. (1993). Early intervention in natural environments: Methods and procedures. Pacific Grove, CA: Brooks/Cole.

Northeast Technical Assistance Center. (2000). C-Print: A computer aided speech to print transition system. Rochester, NY: Author [Online]. Available: http://netac.rit.edu/c-print.html

Novack, T. (1999). Traumatic brain injury resource guide: TBI facts and stats. Center for Neuro Skills [Online]. Available: http://www.neuroskills.com/tbi/facts.shtml

O'Callaghan, D. (1998). Practice issues in working with young abusers who have learning disabilities. Child Abuse Review, 7(6) (Special issue), 435–448.

Obiakor, F. E., Mehring, T. A., & Schwenn, J. O. (1997). Disruption, disaster, and death: Helping students with crises. Reston, VA: The Council for Exceptional Children.

Ochaita, E., & Huertas, J. A. (1993). Spatial representation by persons who are blind: A study of the effects of learning and development. Journal of Visual Impairment and Blindness, 85, 37–41.

O'Day, J. A., & Smith, M. S. (1993). Systemic reform and educational opportunity. In S. H. Fuhrman (Ed.), Designing coherent education policy (pp. 250–313). San Francisco: Jossey-Bass.

Okyere, B. A. (1998). The effect of reinforcement, prompting, and social initiation as intervention strategies on the abnormal social relations of autistic children. IFE Psychologia: An International Journal, 6(2), 29–40.

Ollendick, T. H., & Prinz, R. J. (1998). Advances in child psychology (Vol. 20). New York: Plenum.

Olley, J. G. (1999). Curriculum for students with autism. School Psychology Review, 28, 595–607.

Olshen, S. R. (1987). The disappearance of giftedness in girls: An intervention study. Roeper Review, 18(4), 121–126.

Olszewski-Kubilius, P. (1997). Special summer and Saturday programs for gifted students. In N. Colangelo & A. D. Davis (Eds.), Handbook of gifted education (2nd ed., pp. 180–188). Boston: Allyn and Bacon.

O'Neill, R. (1997). Autism. In J. W. Wood & A. M. Lazzari (Eds.), Exceeding the boundaries: Understanding exceptional lives (pp. 462–502). Fort Worth: Harcourt Brace.

O'Neill, R. E., Horner, R. W., Albin, R. W., Sprague, J. R., Storcy, K., & Newton, J. S. (1997). Functional assessment and program development for problem behavior: A practical handbook (2nd ed.). Pacific Grove, CA: Brooks/Cole.

Onslow, M., & Packman, A. (1999). The Lidcombe Program of early stuttering intervention. In N. B. Ratner and C. E. Healey (Eds.), Stuttering research and practice: Bridging the gap (pp. 193–209). Mahwah, NJ: Erlbaum.

Oosterhof, A. (2001). Classroom application of educational measurement (3rd ed.). Columbus, OH: Merrill/Prentice Hall.

Orkwis, R., & McLane, K. (1998). A curriculum every student can use: Design principles for student access. Reston, VA: ERIC/OSEP Special Project, Council for Exceptional Children.

Osher, D., & Hanley, T. V. (1996). Implications of the national agenda to improve results for children and youth with or at risk of serious emotional disturbance. In R. J. Illback & C. M. Nelson (Eds.), Emerging school-based approaches for children with emotional and behavioral problems: Research and practice in service integration (pp. 7–36). Binghamton, NY: Haworth.

Osher, D., Osher, T., & Smith, C. (1994). Toward a national perspective in emotional and behavioral disorders: A developmental perspective. Beyond Behavior, 6(1), 6–17.

Osher, T., deFur, E., Nava, C., Spencer, S., & Toth-Dennis, D. (1999). New roles for families in systems of care. Systems of care: Promising practices in children's mental health, (1998 Series, Vol. 1). Washington, DC: Center for Effective Collaboration and Practice, American Institutes for Research.

Overton, T. (2000). Assessment in special education (3rd ed.). Upper Saddle River, N.J.: Merrill.

Owens, R. E., Jr. (1995). Language disorders: A functional approach to assessment and intervention (2nd ed.). Needham Heights, MA: Allyn and Bacon.

Pack, R. P., Wallander, J. L., & Browne, D. (1998). Health risk behaviors of African American adolescents with mild mental retardation: Prevalence depends on measurement method. American Journal on Mental Retardation, 102, 409–420.

Padget, S. Y. (1998). Lessons from research on dyslexia: Implications for a classification system for learning disabilities. Learning Disability Quarterly, 21(2), 167–178.

Paget, K. D. (1997). Child neglect. In G. G. Bear, K. M. Minke, & A. Thomas (Eds.), Children's needs II: Development, problems, and alternatives (pp. 729–740). Bethesda, MD: National Association of School Psychologists.

Paige, L. Z. (1997). School phobia, school refusal, and school avoidance. In G. G. Bear, K. M. Minke, & A. Thomas (Eds.), Children's needs II: Development, problems, and alternatives (pp. 339–359). Bethesda, MD: National Association of School Psychologists.

Pangos, R. J., & DuBois, D. L. (1999). Career self-efficacy development and students with learning disabilities. Learning Disabilities Research and Practice, 14, 25–34.

Parent Project for Muscular Dystrophy Research, Inc. (2000). Band-aids and blackboards: Brothers and sisters have something to say, Jessica and Justin [Online]. Available: http://www.parentdmd.org/frame10.htm

Parisse, C. (1999). Cognition and language acquisition in normal and autistic children. Journal of Neurolinguistics, 12(3–4), 247–269.

Parisy, D. (1999). Early intervention: The view from a distance. Journal of the Association for Persons with Severe Handicaps, 24, 226–229.

Patton, J. M. (1998). The disproportionate representation of African-Americans in special education: Looking behind the curtain for understanding and solutions. Journal of Special Education, 32(1), 25–31.

Paul, P. V. (1998, November/December). Radical heart, moderate mind: A perspective on inclusion. TASH Newsletter, 16–18.

Paul, P. V., & Quigley, S. P. (1990). Education and deafness. White Plains, NY: Longman.

Pauls, D. L., Alsobrook, J. P., Gelernter, J., & Leckman, J. F. (1999). Genetic vulnerability. In J. F. Leckman & D. J. Cohen (Eds.), Tourette's syndrome—tics, obsessions, compulsions: Developmental psychopathology and clinical care (pp. 194–212). New York: Wiley.

Peacock Hill Working Group. (1990). Problems and promises in special education and related services for children and youth with emotional and behavioral disorders. Charlottesville, VA: Author.

Peck, A. F., & Uslan, M. (1990, December). The use of audible traffic signals in the United States. Journal of Visual Impairment and Blindness, 547–551.

Pediatric Bulletin. (2000). Congenital cytomegalovirus infection and disease [Online]. Available: http://home.coqui.net/myrna/cmv.htm.

Pelham, W. E., Jr. (1999). The NIMH multimodal treatment study for attention-deficit hyperactivity disorder: Just say yes to drugs alone? Canadian Journal of Psychiatry, 44, 981–990.

Penner, I. (1999). The right to belong: The story of Yvonne [Online]. Available: http://www3.nb.sympatico.ca/ipenner/

Pennsylvania Association for Retarded Citizens v. Commonwealth of Pennsylvania, 334 F. Supp. 1257 (E.D.Pa. 1971).

Perino, M., Famularo, G., & Tarroni, P. (2000). Acquired transient stuttering during a migraine attack. Headache, 40, 170–172.

Perrone, P. A. (1997). Gifted individuals' career development. In N. Colangelo & A. D. Davis (Eds.), Handbook of gifted education (2nd ed., pp. 398–407). Boston: Allyn and Bacon.

Persinger, M. A., & Tiller, S. G. (1999). Personality, not intelligence or educational achievement, differentiate university students who access special needs for "learning disabilities." Social Behavior and Personality, 27, 1–10.

Pester, P. (1998). Braille bits. Louisville, KY: American Printing House for the Blind [Online]. Available: http://www.aph.org/bits898.htm

Petersen, K., Reichle, J., & Johnston, S. S. (2000). Examining preschoolers' performance in linear and row-column scanning techniques. *AAC: Augmentative and Alternative Communication, 16,* 27–36.

Peterson, N. L. (1987). *Early intervention for handicapped and at-risk children: An introduction to early childhood–special education.* Denver, CO: Love.

Petti, V. L. (1999). Emotion perception competence and its relationship to social skills, personality characteristics, and self-concept of children with varied cognitive abilities in a psychiatric sample. *Dissertation Abstracts International: Section B: The Sciences and Engineering, 59*(8-B), 4480.

Piaget, J. (1970). Piaget's theory. In P. H. Mussen (Ed.), *Carmichael's manual of child psychology* (3rd ed., Vol. 1). New York: Wiley.

Piirto, J. (1999). *Talented children and adults: Their development and education.* Upper Saddle River, NJ: Prentice Hall.

Piven, J. (1999). Genetic liability for autism: The behavioural expression in relatives. *International Review of Psychiatry, 11*(4), 299–308.

Plomin, R. (1997). Genetics and intelligence. In N. Colangelo & A. D. Davis (Eds.), *Handbook of gifted education* (2nd ed., pp. 67–74). Boston: Allyn and Bacon.

Pobre, A. (2000). *L&H Kurzweil 1000's Access to Information and Fun.* Burlington, MA: Lernout & Hauspie. [Online] Available: http://www.LHSL.com/pressroom/case studies/motivate.asp

Pogrund, R. L., Fazzi, D. L., & Schreier, E. M. (1993). Development of a preschool "Kiddy Cane." *Journal of Visual Impairment and Blindness, 86,* 52–54.

Post, B. (1999). Restructured phonological phrases in French: Evidence from clash resolution. *Linguistics, 37,* 41–63.

Powell, T. H., & Gallagher, P. H. (1993). *Brothers and sisters: A special part of exceptional families.* Baltimore, MD: Brookes.

Powell, T. H., & Graham, P. L. (1996). Parent–professional participation. In *Improving the implementation of the Individuals with Disabilities Education Act: Making schools work for all of America's children.* (Supplement, pp. 603–628). Washington, DC: National Council on Disability.

Powell-Smith, K. A., & Stollar, S. A. (1997). Families of children with disabilities. In G. G. Bear, K. M. Minke, & A. Thomas (Eds.), *Children's needs II: Development, problems, and alternatives* (pp. 667–680). Bethesda, MD: National Association of School Psychologists.

Prasad, S., & Srivastava, A. N. (1998). Learning disabled children: Diagnosis and remedial measures. *Psycho-Lingua, 28,* 81–87.

President's Committee on Mental Retardation. (2000). Mission [Online]. Available: http://www.acf.dhhs.gov/programs/pcmr/mission.htm

Prins, D. (1999). Describing the consequences of disorders: Comments on Yaruss (1998). *Journal of Speech, Language, and Hearing Research, 42,* 1395–1397.

Prinz, P. M., Strong, M., Kuntze, M., et al. (1996). A path to literacy through ASL and English for deaf children. In C. E. Johnson & J. H. V. Gilbert (Eds.), *Children's language* (Vol. 9, pp. 235–251). Mahwah, NJ: Erlbaum.

Prior, M., Smart, D., Sanson, A., & Oberklaid, F. (1999). Relationships between learning difficulties and psychological problems in preadolescent children from a longitudinal sample. *Journal of the American Academy of Child and Adolescent Psychiatry, 38*(4), 429–236.

Prizant, B. M., Wetherby, A. M., & Roberts, J. E. (2000). Communication problems. In C. H. Zeanah, Jr. (Ed.), *Handbook of infant mental health* (2nd ed., pp. 282–297). New York: Guilford.

Proctor, B. D. (1998). Poverty. In *Population profile of the United States: 1997* (pp. 40–41). U.S. Bureau of the Census, Current Population Reports, Series P23-194. Washington, DC: U.S. Government Printing Office.

Prouty, R. W., & Lakin, K. C. (1996). *Residential services for people with developmental disabilities: Status and trends through 1995.* Minneapolis: University of Minnesota, Research and Training Center on Community Living, Institute on Community Integration.

Puckett, M. (2001). *The young child: Development from prebirth through age 8* (3rd ed.). Columbus: Merrill/Prentice Hall.

Putnam, J. W. (1993). Foreword. In J. W. Putnam (Ed.), *Cooperative learning and strategies for inclusion* (p. xiii). Baltimore, MD: Brookes.

Putnam, J. W. (1998a). The movement toward teaching and learning in inclusive classrooms. In J. W. Putnam (Ed.), *Cooperative learning and strategies for inclusion* (2nd ed., pp. 1–16). Baltimore, MD: Brookes.

Putnam, J. W. (1998b). The process of cooperative learning. In J. W. Putnam (Ed.), *Cooperative learning and strategies for inclusion* (2nd ed., pp. 17–47). Baltimore, MD: Brookes.

Quay, H. C. (1975). Classification in the treatment of delinquency and antisocial behavior. In N. Hobbs (Ed.), *Issues in the classification of children* (Vol. 1, pp. 377–392). San Francisco, CA: Jossey-Bass.

Quay, H. C. (1979). Classification. In H. C. Quay & J. S. Werry (Eds.), *Psychopathological disorders of childhood* (2nd ed., pp. 1–41). New York: Wiley.

Quigley, S. P., & King, C. (Eds.). (1984). *Reading milestones.* Beaverton, OR: Dormac.

Quinn, K. P., & Epstein, M. H. (1998). Characteristics of children, youth, and families served by local interagency systems of care. In M. H. Epstein, K. Kutash, & A. Duchnowski (Eds.), *Outcomes for children and youth with emotional and behavioral disorders and their families: Programs and evaluation best practices* (pp. 81–114). Austin, TX: Pro-Ed.

Quinn, M. M., & Rutherford, R. B. (1998). Alternative program for students with social, emotional, or behavioral problems. In L. M. Bullock & R. A. Gable (Eds.), *Second CCBD mini-library series: Successful interventions for the 21st century* (pp. 1–49). Reston, VA: The Council for Children with Behavior Disorders, a division of the Council for Exceptional Children.

Quinn, W. H., Bell, K., & Ward, J. (1997). The prevention of juvenile delinquency: A review of the research. *The Prevention Researcher, 4*(2), 1–5.

Radziewicz, C., & Antonellis, S. (1997). Considerations and implications for habilitation of hearing impaired children. In D. K. Bernstein and E. Tiegerman-Farber (Eds.), *Language and communication disorders in children* (4th ed., pp. 574–603). Boston: Allyn and Bacon.

Raggio, D. J. (1999a). Use of the School Performance Rating Scale with children treated for attention deficit hyperactivity disorder. *Perceptual and Motor Skills, 88*(3, Pt.1), 957–960.

Raggio, D. J. (1999b). Visuomotor perception in children with attention deficit hyperactivity disorder—combined type. *Perceptual and Motor Skills, 88,* 448–450.

Ramey, C., & Landesman-Ramey, S. (1992). Early educational intervention with disadvantages children—to what effect? *Applied and Preventive Psychology, 1,* 130–140.

Ramey, C. T., & Ramey, S. L. (1999). *Right from birth.* New York: Goddard.

Ramos-Ford, V., & Gardner, H. (1997). Giftedness from a multiple intelligences perspective. In N. Colangelo & A. D. Davis (Eds.), *Handbook of gifted education* (2nd ed., pp. 54–66). Boston: Allyn and Bacon.

Randall, P., & Parker, J. (1999). Supporting the families of children with autism. Chichester, UK: Wiley.

Rapin, I. (2000). Autism's home in the brain: Reply. *Neurology, 54,* 269.

Raskind, M. H., Goldberg, R. J., Higgins, E. L., & Herman, K. L. (1999). Patterns of change and predictors of success in individuals with learning disabilities: Results from a twenty-year longitudinal study. *Learning Disabilities Research and Practice, 14,* 35–49.

Ratey, J. J., Dymek, M. P., Fein, D., Joy, S., Green, L. A., & Waterhouse, L. (2000). Neurodevelopmental disorders. In B. S. Fogel & R. B. Schiffer (Eds.), *Synopsis of neuropsychiatry* (pp. 245–271). Philadelphia: Lippincott-Raven.

Ratner, N. B. (2000). Elicited imitation and other methods for the analysis of trade-offs between speech and language skills in children. In L. Menn and N. B. Ratner (Eds.), *Methods for studying language production* (pp. 291–311). Mahwah, NJ: Erlbaum.

Ratner, N. B., & Healey, C. E. (1999). *Stuttering research and practice: Bridging the gap.* Mahwah, NJ: Erlbaum.

Raymond, M. J., Bennett, T. L., Hartlage, L. C., & Cullum, C. M. (1999). *Mild traumatic brain injury: A clinician's guide.* Austin, TX: Pro-Ed.

Reid, S. (1999). The assessment of the child with autism: A family perspective. *Clinical Child Psychology and Psychiatry, 4,* 63–78.

Reiff, H. B., Ginsberg, R., & Gerber, P. J. (1997). *Exceeding expectations: Successful adults with learning disabilities.* Austin, TX: Pro-Ed.

Renzulli, J. S. (1994). *Schools for talent development.* Mansfield Center, CT: Creative Learning Press.

Repetto, J. B., & Correa, V. I. (1996). Expanding views on transition. *Exceptional Children, 62,* 551–563.

Repp, A. C., & Horner, R. H. (1999). *Functional analysis of problem behavior from effective assessment to effective support.* Belmont, CA: Wadsworth.

Reschly, D. J. (1999). Assessing educational disabilities. In A. K. Hess & I. B. Weiner (Eds.), *The handbook of forensic psychology* (2nd ed., pp. 127–150). New York: Wiley.

Research and Training Center on Community Living. (1999, January). 1994 National Health Interview Survey: Disability Supplement. *MR/DD Data Brief, 1*(1), 1–7.

Resource Foundation for Children with Challenges. (2000). Success stories [Online]. Available: http://www.specialchild.com/success.html

Revell, W. G., Wehman, P., Kregel, J., West, M., & Rayfield, R. (1994). Supported employment for persons with severe disabilities: Positive trends in wages, models, and funding. *Education and Training in Mental Retardation and Developmental Disabilities, 29*(4), 256–264.

Reynolds, C. R., & Kamphaus, R. W. (1992). *Behavior assessment system for children (BASC)*. Circle Pines, MN: American Guidance Services.

Reynolds, M. C. (1991). Classification and labeling. In J. W. Lloyd, N. N. Singh, & A. C. Repp (Eds.), *The regular education initiative: Alternative perspectives on concepts, issues, and models* (pp. 29–41). Sycamore, IL: Sycamore.

Reynolds, M. C. (1994). A brief history of categorical programs: 1945–1993. In K. Wong & M. C. Wang (Eds.), *Rethinking policy for at-risk students* (pp. 3–24). Berkley, CA: McCutchan.

Rhee, S. H., Waldman, I. D., Hay, D. A., & Levy, F. (1999). Sex differences in genetic and environmental influences on DSM-III-R attention-deficit/hyperactivity disorder. *Journal of Abnormal Psychology, 108*, 24–41.

Rhode, M. (1999). Echo or answer? The move toward ordinary speech in three children with autistic spectrum disorder. In A. Alvarez & S. Reid (Eds.), *Autism and personality: Findings from the Tavistock Autism Workshop* (pp. 79–92). New York: Routledge.

Rice, M. L., Spitz, R. V., & O'Brien, M. (1999). Semantic and morphosyntactic language outcomes in biologically at-risk children. *Journal of Neurolinguistics, 12*(3–4), 213–234.

Richert, E. S. (1997). Excellence with Equity™ in identification and programming. In N. Colangelo & A. D. Davis (Eds.), *Handbook of gifted education* (2nd ed., pp. 75–88). Boston: Allyn and Bacon.

Rimm, S. B. (1982). *PRIDE: Preschool and primary interest descriptor*. Watertown, WI: Educational Assessment Service.

Rimm, S. B., & Davis, G. A. (1983, September/October). Identifying creativity, Part II. *G/C/T*, 19–23.

Riordan, H. J., Flashman, L A., Saykin, A. J., Frutiger, S. A., Carroll, K. E., & Huey, L. (1999). Neuropsychological correlates of methylphenidate treatment in adult ADHD with and without depression. *Archives of Clinical Neuropsychology, 14*(2), 217–233.

Rivera, J. B., Jaffe, K. M., Polissar, N. L., et al. (1994). Family functioning and children's academic performance and behavior problems in the year following traumatic brain injury. *Archives of Physical Medicine and Rehabilitation, 75*, 369–379.

Rivers, J. W. (1999). Siblings relationships when a child has autism: Temperament, family stress, and coping. *Dissertation Abstracts International, Section A: Humanities and Social Sciences, 60*(2-A), 0560.

Roan, S. (1995). Infant blindness. *Salt Lake Tribune*, C1, C8.

Robertson, D., & Murphy, D. (1999). Brain imaging and behaviour. In N. Bouras (Ed.), *Psychiatric and behavioural disorders in developmental disabilities and mental retardation* (pp. 49–70). New York: Cambridge University Press.

Roblyer, M. D., & Edwards, J. (2000). *Integrating educational technology into teaching* (2nd ed.). Columbus, OH: Merrill/Prentice Hall.

Robson, G. (2000, January). Captioning and the law. *Journal of Court Reporting* [Online]. Available: http://www.robson.org/gary/writing/jcr-captionlaw.html

Rodda, M., Cumming, C., & Fewer, D. (1993). Memory, learning, and language: Implications for deaf education. In M. Marschark & M. D. Clark (Eds.), *Psychological perspectives on deafness* (pp. 339–352). Hillsdale, NJ: Erlbaum.

Rode, M. (1999). Echo or answer? The move towards ordinary speech in three children with autistic spectrum disorder. In A. Alvarez & S. Reid (Eds.). Autism and personality: Findings from the Tavistock Autism Workshop (pp. 79–92). New York: Routledge.

Rodgers, J. (1999). Trying to get it right: Undertaking research involving people with learning difficulties. *Disability and Society, 14*(4), 421–433.

Rogler, L. H. (1999). Methodological sources of cultural insensitivity in mental health research. *American Psychologist, 54*, 424–433.

Rosenberg, M. S., & Sindelar, P. T. (1999). The impact of market-driven higher education practices on professional teacher development. *Teacher Education and Special Education, 21*, 227–235.

Rosenberg, M. S., Wilson, R., Maheady, L., & Sindelar, P. T. (1997). Educating students with behavior disorders (2nd ed.). Boston: Allyn and Bacon.

Rosenblatt, J., Robertson, L., Bates, M., Wood, M., Furlong, M., & Sosna, T. (1998). Troubled or troubling? Characteristics of youth referred to a system of care without system-level referral constraints. *Journal of Emotional and Behavioral Disorders, 6*(1), 42–54.

Rosenhan, D. I. (1973). On being sane in insane places. *Science, 179*, 250–258.

Rosenthal, R., & Jacobson, L. (1968a). *Pygmalion in the classroom: Teacher expectation and pupils' intellectual development*. New York: Holt, Rinehart & Winston.

Rosenthal, R., & Jacobson, L. (1968b). Self-fulfilling prophecies in the classroom: Teachers' expectations as unintended determinants of pupils' intellectual competence. In M. Deutsch, I. Katz, & A. R. Jensen (Eds.), *Social class, race, and psychological development* (pp. 219–253). New York: Holt, Rinehart & Winston.

Rosman, N. P. (1994). Acute head trauma. In F. A. Oski, C. D. DeAngelis, R. D. Feigin, J. A. McMillan, & J. B. Warshaw (Eds.), *Principles and practice of pediatrics* (2nd ed., pp. 2038–2048). Philadelphia: Lippincott.

Rous, B., & Hallam, M. A. (1998). Easing the transition to kindergarten: Assessment of social, behavioral, and functional skills in young children with disabilities. *Young Exceptional Children, 1*(4), 17–26.

Rowland, G. H. (1999). Polydipsia in adults with learning disabilities: Prevalence, presentation, and aetiology. *British Journal of Developmental Disabilities, 45*(88, Pt. 1), 52–62.

Royer, J. M., & Tronsky, L. N. (1998). Addition practice with math disabled students improves subtraction and multiplication performance. In T. E. Scruggs and M. A. Mastropieri (Eds.), *Advances in learning and behavioral disabilities* (pp. 185–217). Greenwich, CT: JAI Press.

Rudolph, A. M., & Kamei, R. K. (1994). *Rudolph's fundamentals of pediatrics*. Norwalk, CT: Appleton & Lange.

Ruehl, M. E. (1998). Educatiing the child with severe behavioral problems: Entitlement, empiricism, and ethics. *Behavioral Disorders, 23*(3), 184–192.

Rusch, F. R., Chadsey-Rusch, J., & Johnson, J. R. (1991). Supported employment: Emerging opportunities for employment integration. In L. H. Meyer, C. A. Peck, & L. Brown (Eds.), *Critical issues in the lives of people with severe disabilities* (pp. 145–170). Baltimore, MD: Brookes.

Russo, S. A., & Lewis, J. E. (1999). The cross-cultural applications of the KAIT: Case studies with three differentially acculturated women. *Cultural Diversity and Ethnic Minority Psychology, 5*(1), 76–85.

Rutter, M. (1995). Clinical implications of attachment concepts: Retrospect and prospect. *Journal of Child Psychology and Psychiatry, 36*, 549–571.

Rutter, M., Silberg, J., O'Connor, T., & Siminoff, E. (1999). Genetics and child psychiatry: II. Empirical research findings. *Journal of Child Psychology and Psychiatry and Allied Disciplines, 40*(1), 19–55.

Ryan, A. G., Nolan, B. F., Keim, J., & Madsen, W. (1999). Psychosocial adjustment factors of postsecondary students with learning disabilities. *Journal of College Student Psychotherapy, 13*(3), 3–18.

Ryan, D. J. (2000). *Job search handbook for people with disabilities*. Indianapolis, IN: Jist.

Sacks, S. Z., Kekelis, L. S., & Gaylord-Ross, R. J. (1992). *The development of social skills by blind and visually impaired students*. New York: American Foundation for the Blind Press.

Sagor, R. (1993). *At-risk students: Reaching them and teaching them*. Swampscott, MA: Watersun.

Sagvolden, T. (1999). Attention deficit/hyperactivity disorder. *European Psychologist, 4*(2), 109–114.

Sailor, W., Gee, K., & Karasoff, P. (2000). Inclusion and school restructuring. In M. Snell & F. Brown (Eds.), *Instruction of students with severe disabilities* (5th ed., pp. 1–30). Columbus, OH: Merrill.

Sailor, W., Gerry, M., & Wilson, W. C. (1990). Disability and school integration. In T. Husen & T. N. Postlewaite (Eds.), *International encyclopedia of education: Research and studies* (2nd Suppl., pp. 158–163). New York: Pergamon.

Sailor, W., & Haring, N. (1977). Some current directions in the education of the severely/multiply handicapped. *AAESPH Review, 2*, 67–86.

Sakelaris, T. L. (1999). Effects of a self-managed study skills intervention on homework and academic performance of middle school students with attention deficit hyperactivity disorder (ADHD). *Dissertation Abstracts International Section A: Humanities and Social Sciences, 60* (2-A), 0337.

Salkind, N. J. (2000). *Exploring research* (4th ed.). Upper Saddle River, NJ: Prentice-Hall.

Salmelin, R., Schnitzler, A., Schmitz, F., Jaencke, L., Witte, O. W., & Freund, H. J. (1998). Functional organization of the auditory cortex is different in stutterers and fluent speakers. *Neuroreport: An International Journal for the Rapid Communication of Research in Neuroscience, 9,* 2225–2229.

Samango-Sprouse, C. (1999). Frontal lobe development in childhood. In B. L. Miller & J. L. Cummings (Eds.), *The human frontal lobes: Functions and disorders* (pp. 584–603). New York: Guilford.

Samar, V. J., Parasnis, I., & Berent, G. P. (1998). Learning disabilities, attention deficit disorders, and deafness. In M. Marschark & M. D. Clark (Eds.), *Psychological perspectives on deafness* (pp. 199–242). Mahwah, NJ: Erlbaum.

Sandler, A. G. (1998). Grandparents of children with disabilities: A closer look. *Education and Training in Mental Retardation and Developmental Disabilities, 33*(4), 350–356.

Sandler, A. G., Warren, S. H., & Raver, S. A. (1995, August). Grandparents as a source of support for parents of children with disabilities: A brief report. *Mental Retardation, 33,* 248–250.

Sandoval, J., & Duran, R. P. (1998). Language. In J. H. Sandoval, C. L. Frisby, K. F. Geisinger, J. D. Scheuneman, & J. R. Grenier (Eds.), *Test interpretation and diversity: Achieving equity in assessment* (pp. 181–211). Washington, DC: American Psychological Association.

Santos, R. M., Fowler, S. A., Corso, R. M., & Bruns, D. A. (2000). Acceptance, acknowledgment, and adaptability: Selecting culturally and linguistically appropriate early childhood materials. *Teaching Exceptional Children, 33*(3), 14–22.

Saugstad, L. F. (1999). A lack of cerebral lateralization in schizophrenia is within the normal variation in brain maturation but indicates late, slow maturation. *Schizophrenia Research, 39*(3), 183–196.

Savage, R. C., & Mishkin, L. (1994). A neuroeducational model for teaching students with acquired brain injuries. In R. C. Savage & G. F. Wolcott (Eds.), *Educational dimensions of acquired brain injury* (pp. 393–411). Austin, TX: Pro-Ed.

Savage, R. C., & Wolcott, G. F. (Eds.). (1994a). *Educational dimensions of acquired brain injury.* Austin, TX: Pro-Ed.

Savage, R. C., & Wolcott, G. F. (1994b). Overview of acquired brain injury. In R. C. Savage & G. F. Wolcott (Eds.), *Educational dimensions of acquired brain injury* (pp. 3–12). Austin, TX: Pro-Ed.

Sax, C., Fisher, D., & Pumpian, I. (1999). We didn't always learn what we were taught: Inclusion does work. In D. Fisher, C. Sax, & I. Pumpian, *Inclusive high schools* (pp. 5–26). Baltimore, MD: Brookes.

Schaffer, J. (1998). Cocaine use during pregnancy: Its effects on infant development and implications for adoptive parents [Online]. Available: http://www.nysccc.org/cocaine.html

Scheidler, K. B. (1998). Evaluation of a parent education program to address homework completion and accuracy. *Dissertation Abstracts International Section A: Humanities and Social Sciences, 59*(5-A), 1460.

Schell, G. C. (1981). The young handicapped child: A family perspective. *Topics in Early Childhood Special Education, 1*(3), 21–28.

Scherman, A., Gardner, J. E., & Brown, P. (1995, April/May). Grandparents' adjustment to grandchildren with disabilities. *Educational Gerontology, 21,* 261–273.

Scherzer, A. L. (1999). Coming to an understanding: Can parents and professionals learn to be more realistic about a child's disability? *Exceptional Parent, 29*(8), 22–23.

Scheuermann, B., & Webber, J. (1996). Level systems: Problems and solutions. *Beyond Behavior, 7*(2), 18–21.

Schiel, J. (1998). *ACT research report series: Academic benefits in high school of an intensive summer program for academically talented seventh graders.* Iowa City, IA: ACT.

Schiever, S. W., & Maker, C. J. (1997). Enrichment and acceleration: An overview and new directions. In N. Colangelo & A. D. Davis (Eds.), *Handbook of gifted education* (2nd ed., pp. 113–125). Boston: Allyn and Bacon.

Schildroth, A. N. (1994). *Annual survey of hearing-impaired children and youth: 1992-1993 school year.* Center for Assessment and Demographic Studies. Washington, DC: Gallaudet University.

Schirmer, B. R. (2000). *Language and literacy development in children who are deaf* (2nd ed.). Boston: Allyn and Bacon.

Schloss, P. J., Alper, S., & Jayne, D. (1993). Self-determination for persons with disabilities: Choice, risk, and dignity. *Exceptional Children, 60*(3), 215–225.

Schmid, R. E., & Evans, W. (1998). *Curriculum and instruction practices for students with emotional/behavioral disorders.* Reston, VA: The Council for Children with Behavioral Disorders.

Schmidt, J., Alper, S., Raschke, D., & Ryndak, D. (2000). Effects of using a photographic cuing package during routine school transitions with a child who has autism. *Mental Retardation, 38,* 131–137.

Schrag, J. (1996). *The IEP: Benefits, challenges, and future directions.* Alexandria, VA: The National Association of State Directors of Special Education.

Schulte-Koerne, G., Deimel, W., Bartling, J., & Remschmidt, H. (1998). Role of auditory temporal processing for reading and spelling disability. *Perceptual and Motor Skills, 86*(3, Pt. 1), 1043–1047.

Schultz, C. J. (1999). Using narrative to promote the conceptual development of adolescents with attention deficit hyperactivity disorder. *Dissertation Abstracts International Section A: Humanities and Social Sciences, 59*(9-A), 3346.

Schwartz, I. S., Billingsley, F. F., & McBride, B. M. (1998, Winter). Including preschool children with autism in inclusive preschools: Strategies that work. *Young Exceptional Children,* 19–26.

Schwartz, I. S., & Meyer, L. H. (1997, April). Blending best practices for young children: Inclusive early childhood programs. *TASH Newsletter,* 8–10.

Scott, T. M., & Nelson, C. M. (1999). Using functional behavioral analysis to develop effective intervention plans. *Journal of Positive Behavioral Interventions, 1*(4), 242–251.

Scruggs, T. E., & Mastropieri, M. A. (1996). Teacher perceptions of mainstreaming/inclusion, 1958–1995: A research synthesis. *Exceptional Children, 63*(1), 59–74.

Seeberg, V., Swadner, B., Vanden-Wyngaard, M., & Rickel, T. (1998). Multicultural education in the United States. In K. Cushner (Ed.), *International perspectives on intercultural education* (pp. 259–300). Mahwah, NJ: Erlbaum.

Seeley, K. (1998). Giftedness in early childhood. In J. VanTassel-Baska (Ed.), *Excellence in educating gifted and talented learners* (3rd ed., pp. 67–81). Denver: Love.

Segalowitz, S. J. (2000). Predicting child language impairment from too many variables: Overinterpreting stepwise discriminant function analysis. *Brain and Language, 71,* 337–343.

Seifert, K. L., & Hoffnung, R. J. (1997). *Child and adolescent development* (4th ed.). Boston: Houghton Mifflin.

Seligman, M. (1991a). *The family with a handicapped child* (2nd ed.). Boston: Allyn and Bacon.

Seligman, M. (1991b). Siblings of disabled brothers and sisters. In M. Seligman (Ed.), *The family with a handicapped child* (2nd ed., pp. 181–202). Boston: Allyn and Bacon.

Seligman, M., & Darling, R. B. (1989). *Ordinary families, special children.* New York: Guilford.

Seligman, M., & Darling, R. B. (1999). Ordinary families, special children: A systems approach to childhood disability. *Exceptional Parent, 19*(4), 52–54.

Seligman, M., & Seligman, D. A. (1980). The professional's dilemma: Learning to work with parents. *Exceptional Parent, 10*(5), 511–513.

Seltzer, M. M., & Krauss, M. W. (1994). Aging parents with resident adult children: The impact of lifelong caregiving. In M. M. Seltzer, M. W. Krauss, & M. P. Janicki (Eds.), *Life course perspectives on adulthood and old age* (pp. 3–18). Washington, DC: The American Association on Mental Retardation.

Serra, M., Minderaa, R. B., vanGeert, P. L. C., & Jackson, A. E. (1999). Social–cognitive abilities in children with lesser variants of autism: Skill deficits or failure to apply skills? *European Child and Adolescent Psychiatry, 8*(4), 301–311.

Shaffer, D., Schwat-Stone, M., Fisher, P., et al. (1993). The Diagnostic Interview Schedule for Children-Revised Version (DISC-R): I. Preparation, field testing, interrater reliability, and acceptability. *Journal of the American Academy of Child and Adolescent Psychiatry, 32,* 643–650.

Shapiro, E. S., Miller, D. N., Sawka, K., Gardill, M. C., & Handler, M. W. (1999). Facilitating the inclusion of students with EBD into general education classrooms. *Journal of Emotional and Behavioral Disorders, 7*(2), 83–93, 127.

Shapiro, J. P. (1994). *No pity.* New York: Random House, Times Books.

Shaver, S. M. (1999). The relationship among teaching practices, attitudes about ADHD, and medical and special education referral by teachers. *Dissertation Abstracts International Section A: Humanities and Social Sciences, 59*(8-A), 2854.

Shaw, L. (1994). Honor thy son. *Exceptional Parent, 24*(7), 44–45.

Sheets, R. H., & Hollins, E. R. (1999). *Racial and ethnic identity in school practices.* NJ: Erlbaum.

Shelton, T. L., Jeppson, E. S., & Johnson, B. H. (1987). *Family-centered care for children with special health-care needs.* Washington, DC:

Association for the Care of Children's Health.

Sheppard, D. M., Bradshaw, J. L., Purcell, R., & Pantelis, C. (1999). Tourette's and comorbid syndromes: Obsessive compulsive and attention deficit hyperactivity disorder. A common etiology? *Clinical Psychology Review, 19*(5), 531–552.

Sherman, D. K., Iacono, W. G., & McGue, M. K. (1997). Attention-deficit hyperactivity disorder dimensions: A twin study of inattention and impulsivity–hyperactivity. *Journal of the American Academy of Child and Adolescent Psychiatry, 36,* 745–753.

Shiono, P. H., & Behrman, R. E. (1995). Low birth weight: Analysis and recommendations. *The Future of Children, 5*(1) [Online]. Available: http://www.futureofchildren.org/LBW/02LBWANA.htm

Shores, R. E., & Wehby, J. H. (1999). Analyzing the classroom social behavior of students with EBD. *Journal of Emotional and Behavioral Disorders, 7*(4), 194–199.

Shriberg, L. D., Tomblin, J. B., & McSweeny, J. L. (1999). Prevalence of speech delay in 6-year-old children and comorbidity with language impairment. *Journal of Speech, Language, and Hearing Research, 42,* 1461–1481.

Shriver, M. D., Allen, K. D., & Mathews, J. R. (1999). Effective assessment of the shared and unique characteristics of children with autism. *School Psychology Review, 28,* 538–558.

Shulman, M. S., & Doughty, J. F. (1995, December). *The difficult dichotomy: One school district's response. Phi Delta Kappan,* 292–294.

Shuster, L. I. (1998). The perception of correctly and incorrectly produced /r/. *Journal of Speech, Language, and Hearing Research, 41,* 941–950.

Siceloff, J. (1999). A simple man: Autistic man wrongly accused of robbery. December 13, ABCNEWS.com.

Sickle Cell Information Center. (1997a). Sickle cell anemia [Online]. Available: http://www.emory.edu/PEDS/SICKLE/sicklept.htm

Sickle Cell Information Center. (1997b). Sickle cell information—clinician summary [Online]. Available: http://www.emory.edu/PEDS/SICKLE/prod05.htm

Siegel-Causey, E., & Allinder, R. M. (1998). Using alternate assessment for students with severe disabilities: Alignment with best practices. *Education and Training in Mental Retardation and Developmental Disabilities, 33*(2), 168–178.

Siegel-Causey, E., McMorris, C., McGowen, S., & Sands-Buss, S. (1998). In junior high you take earth science. *Teaching Exceptional Students, 31*(1), 66–72.

Sigman, M., & Kim, N. (1999). Continuity and change in the development of children with autism. In S. H. Broman & J. M. Fletcher (Eds.), *The changing nervous system: Neurobehavioral consequences of early brain disorders* (pp. 274–291). New York: Oxford University Press.

Silberman, R. K., & Brown, F. (1998). Alternative approaches to assessing students who have visual impairments with other disabilities in classroom and community environments. In S. Z. Sacks & R. K. Silberman (Eds.), *Educating students who have visual impairments with other disabilities* (pp. 73–98). Baltimore, MD: Brookes.

Silberman, R. K., & Sowell, V. (1998). Educating students who have visual impairments with learning disabilities. In S. Z. Sacks & R. K. Silberman (Eds.), *Educating students who have visual impairments with other disabilities* (pp. 161–185). Baltimore, MD: Brookes.

Silliman, E. R., Ford, C. S., Beasman, J., & Evans, D. (1999). An inclusion model for children with language learning disabilities: Building classroom partnerships. *Topics in Language Disorders, 19*(3), 1–18.

Silver, C. H., & Oakland, T. D. (1997). Helping students with mild traumatic brain injury: Collaborative roles within schools. In E. D. Bigler, E. Clark, & J. E. Farmer (Eds.), *Childhood traumatic brain injury: Diagnosis, assessment, and intervention* (pp. 239–260). Austin, TX: Pro-Ed.

Silver, L. B. (1999). *Attention-deficit/hyperactivity disorders: A clinical guide to diagnosis and treatment for health and mental health professionals* (2nd ed.). Washington, DC: American Psychiatric Press.

Silverman, L. K. (1997). Family counseling for the gifted. In N. Colangelo & A. D. Davis (Eds.), *Handbook of gifted education* (2nd ed., pp. 382–397). Boston: Allyn and Bacon.

Silverman, L. K. (1998). Developmental stages of giftedness: Infancy through adulthood. In J. VanTassel-Baska (Ed.), *Excellence in educating gifted and talented learners* (3rd ed., pp. 145–166). Denver: Love.

Silverstein, R. (1999). *A user's guide to the 1999 IDEA regulations.* Washington, DC: Center for the Study and Advancement of Disability Policy (CSADP) at the George Washington University School of Public Health and Health Services.

Simeonsson, R. J., & Bailey, D. B. (1986). Siblings of the handi-capped child. In J. J. Gallagher & W. Vietze (Eds.), *Families of handicapped persons* (pp. 67–77). Baltimore, MD: Brookes.

Simon, N. (2000). Autism's home in the brain. *Neurology, 24,* 269.

Simpson, J. S., Koroloff, N., Friesen, B. F., & Gac, J. (1999). Promising practices in family provider collaboration. *Systems of Care: Promising Practices in Children's Mental Health, 1998 Series, Vol. II.* Washington, DC: Center for Effective Collaboration and Practice, American Institutes for Research.

Simpson, R. L. (1996). *Parents working with parents and families of exceptional children: Techniques for successful conferencing and collaboration* (3rd ed.). Austin, TX: Pro-Ed.

Simpson, R. L., & Zurkowski, J. K. (2000). Parent and professional collaborative relationships in an era of change. In M. J. Fine, & R. L. Simpson (Eds.), *Collaboration with parents and families of children with exceptionalities* (2nd ed., pp. 89–102). Austin, TX: Pro-Ed.

Sinclair, B., Hamilton, J., Gutmann, B., Daft, J., & Bolcik, D. (1998). *Report on state implementation of the Gun-Free Schools Act—school year 1996–97: Final report.* Washington, DC: U.S. Department of Education.

Sinclair, M. F., Christenson, S. L., Elevo, D. L., & Hurley, C. M. (1998). Dropout prevention for youth with disabilities: Efficacy of a sustained school engagement procedure. *Exceptional Children, 65,* 7–21.

Siperstein, G. N., & Leffert, J. S. (1997). Comparison of socially accepted and rejected children with mental retardation. *Mental Retardation, 101*(4), 339–351.

Skelton, S. L. (1999). A comparison of concurrent and hierarchical task sequencing in single-phoneme phonologic treatment and generalization. *Dissertation Abstracts International: Section B: The Sciences and Engineering, 59*(7-B), 3393.

Skiba, R. J. (1997). Conduct disorders. In G. G. Bear, K. M. Minke, & A. Thomas (Eds.), *Children's needs II: Development, problems, and alternatives* (pp. 119–133). Bethesda, MD: National Association of School Psychologists.

Skinner, D., Bailey, D. B., Correa, V., & Rodriguez, P. (1999). Narrating self and disability: Latino mothers' construction of identities vis-à-vis their child with special needs. *Exceptional Children, 65*(4), 481–495.

Slavin, R. (1991). Synthesis of research on cooperative learning. *Educational Leadership, 48,* 71–82.

Slavin, R. E. (1996). Never-streaming: Preventing learning disabilities. *Educational Leadership, 53*(5), 4–7.

Sloan, M. T., Jensen, P., & Kettle, L. (1999). Assessing the services for children with ADHD: Gaps and opportunities. *Journal of Attention Disorders, 3,* 13–29.

Smith, A. J., & Geruschat, D. R. (1996). Orientation and mobility for children and adults with low vision. In *Foundations of low vision: Clinical and functional perspectives* (pp. 306–321). New York: American Foundation for the Blind Press.

Smith, C. R. (1998). *Learning disabilities: The interaction of learner, task, and setting* (4th ed.). Boston: Allyn and Bacon.

Smith, G. C., Majeski, R. A., & McClenny, B. (1996). Psychoeducational support groups for aging parents: Development and preliminary outcomes. *Mental Retardation, 34*(3), 172–181.

Smith, J. D. (1998). *Inclusion: Schools for all students.* Belmont, CA: Wadsworth.

Smith, M. D., & Philippen, L. R. (1999). Community integration and supported employment. In D. Berkell (Ed.), *Autism: Identification, education, and treatment* (2nd ed., pp. 301–321). Mahwah, NJ: Erlbaum.

Smith, R. W., Osborne, L. T., Crim, D., & Rho, A. H. (1986). Labeling theory as applied to learning disabilities. *Journal of Learning Disabilities, 19*(4), 195–202.

Snell, M. E., & Brown, F. (2000a). Development and implementation of educational programs. In M. E. Snell & F. Brown (Eds.), *Instruction of students with severe disabilities* (pp. 115–172). Upper Saddle River, NJ: Merrill.

Snell, M. E., & Brown, F. (2000b). *Instruction of students with severe disabilities* (5th ed.). Columbus, OH: Merrill/Prentice Hall.

Snow, C. E., Burns, M. S., & Griffin, P. (1998). *Preventing reading difficulties in young children.* Washington, DC: National Academy Press.

Sobsey, D., & Cox, A. W. (1991). Integrating health care and educational programs. In F. P. Orelove & D. Sobsey (Eds.), *Educating children with multiple disabilities: A transdisciplinary approach* (2nd ed., pp. 155–186). Baltimore, MD: Brookes.

Sobsey, D., & Wolf-Schein, E. G. (1996). Children with sensory impairments. In F. P. Orelove & D. Sobsey (Eds.), *Educating children with multiple disabilities: A transdisciplinary approach* (3rd ed., pp. 411–450). Baltimore, MD: Brookes.

Social Security Administration. (2000). Titles II and XVI: Basic Disability. [Online]. Available: www.ssa.gov/disability

Solomon, A. (1994, August 28). Defiantly deaf. *The New York Times Magazine*, Section 6, pp. 1–7, xx.

Sontag, J., & Schacht, R. (1994). An ethnic comparison of parent participation and information needs in early intervention. *Exceptional Children, 16*(5), 422–431.

Sontag, J. C. (1996, Fall). Toward a comprehensive theoretical framework for disability research: Bronfenbrenner revisited. *The Journal of Special Education, 30,* 319–344.

Sosniak, L. (1997). The tortoise, the hare, and the development of talent. In N. Colangelo & G. A. Davis (Eds.), *Handbook of gifted education* (2nd ed., pp. 207–217). Boston: Allyn and Bacon.

Speltz, M. L., DeKlyen, M., Calderon, R., Greenberg, M. T., & Fisher, P. A. (1999). Neuropsychological characteristics and test behaviors of boys with early onset conduct problems. *Journal of Abnormal Psychology, 108,* 315–325.

Spencer, G., & Hollmann, F. W. (1998). National population projections. *Population profile of the United States: 1997* (pp. 8–9). U.S. Bureau of the Census, Current Population Reports, Series P23-194. Washington, DC: U.S. Government Printing Office.

Spina Bifida Association of America. (1996). Spina bifida association of America (SBAA) information about folic acid [Online]. Available: http://www.infohiway.com/spinabifida/folic.html

Spina Bifida Association of America. (1999). Did you know? [Online]. Available: http://www.sbaa.org/html/sbaa_dyk.html

Spinal Cord Injury Resource Center. (2000a). *Research and new updates: A revolutionary new wheelchair on the horizon.* http://www.spinalinjury.net/html/wheelchair.html

Spinal Cord Injury Resource Center. (2000b). *Spinal cord 101: Some basic questions and answers.* http://www.spinalinjury.net/html/_spinal_cord_101.html.

Stagg, V., & Burns, M. S. (1999). Specific developmental disorders. In R. T. Ammerman & M. Hersen (Eds.), *Handbook of prescriptive treatments for children and adolescents* (2nd ed., pp. 48–62). Boston: Allyn and Bacon.

Stahl, N. D., & Clarizio, H. F. (1999). Conduct disorder and comorbidity. *Psychology in the Schools, 36,* 41–50.

Stahl, S. A., & Murray, B. (1998). Issues involved in defining phono-logical awareness and its relation to early reading. In J. L. Metsala & L. C. Ehri (Eds.), *Word recognition in beginning literacy* (pp. 65–87). Mahwah, NJ: Erlbaum.

Stainback, W., & Stainback, S. (1990). *Supportive networks for inclusive schooling.* Baltimore, MD: Brookes.

Stainback, W., & Stainback, S. (1992). *Curriculum considerations in inclusive classrooms: Facilitating learning for all students.* Baltimore, MD: Brookes.

Stainback, S., Stainback, W., & Ayres, B. (1996). Schools as inclusive communities. In W. Stainback & S. Stainback (Eds.), *Controversial issues confronting special education: Divergent perspectives* (pp. 31–43). Boston: Allyn and Bacon.

Staub, D. (1998). *Delicate threads: Friendships between children with and without special needs in inclusive settings.* Bethesda, MD: Woodbine.

Staub, D., & Peck, C. A. (1995). What are the outcomes for nondisabled students? *Educational Leadership, 52*(4), 36–40.

Stein, M. A., Fischer, M., & Szumowski, E. (1999). Evaluation of adults for ADHD. *Journal of the American Academy of Child and Adolescent Psychiatry, 38,* 940–941.

Stephens, S. A., & Lakin, K. C. (1995). Where students with emotional or behavioral disorders go to school. In J. M. Kauffman, J. W. Lloyd, D. P. Hallahan, & T. A. Astuto (Eds.), *Issues in educational placement: Students with emotional and behavioral disorders* (pp. 47–74). Hillsdale, NJ: Erlbaum.

Sternberg, R. J. (1993). Sternberg triarchic abilities test. Unpublished test.

Sternberg, R. J. (1997a). The triarchic theory of intelligence. In D. P. Flanagan, J. Genshaft, & P. L. Harrison (Eds.), *Contemporary intellectual assessment: Theories, tests, and issues* (pp. 92–104). New York: Guilford.

Sternberg, R. J. (1997b). A triarchic view of giftedness: Theory and practice. In N. Colangelo & A. D. Davis (Eds.), *Handbook of gifted education* (2nd ed., pp. 43–53). Boston: Allyn and Bacon.

Stimley, M. A., & Hambrecht, G. (1999). Comparisons of children's single-word articulation proficiency, single-word speech intelligibility, and conversational speech intelligibility. *Journal of Speech Language Pathology and Audiology, 23,* 19–23.

Stinson, M. S., & Whitmire, K. (1992). Students' views of their social relationships. In T. N. Kluwin, D. F. Moores, & M. G. Gaustad (Eds.), *Toward effective public school programs for deaf students: Context, process, and outcomes* (pp. 149–174). New York: Teachers College Press.

Stoiber, K. C. (1997). Adolescent pregnancy and parenting. In G. G. Bear, K. M. Minke, & A. Thomas (Eds.), *Children's needs II: Development, problems, and alternatives* (pp. 653–665). Bethesda, MD: National Association of School Psychologists.

Stokoe, W. C. (1993). The broadening and sharpening of psychological perspectives on deafness. In M. Marschark & M. D. Clark (Eds.), *Psychological perspectives on deafness* (pp. 365–376). Hillsdale, NJ: Erlbaum.

Stoneman, Z., & Berman, P. W. (1993). *The effects of mental retardation, disability, and illness on sibling relationships.* Baltimore, MD: Brookes.

Stoneman, Z., Brody, G. H., Davis, C. H., & Crapps, J. M. (1987). Mentally retarded children and their older same-sex siblings: Naturalistic in-home observations. *American Journal of Mental Retardation, 92,* 290–298.

Stoneman, Z., & Manders, J. E. (1998). Partnerships with families. In W. Umansky & S. R. Hooper (Eds.), *Young children with special needs* (pp. 72–93). Upper Saddle River, NJ: Merrill.

Strain, P. (1990). LRE for preschool children with handicaps: What we know, what we should be doing. *Journal of Early Intervention, 14,* 291–296.

Strong, M., & Prinz, P. M. (1997). A study of the relationship between American Sign Language and English literacy. *Journal of Deaf Studies and Deaf Education, 122,* 37–46.

Stroul, B. A., & Friedman, R. M. (1986). *A system of care for severely emotionally disturbed children and youth.* Washington, DC: Georgetown University.

Stuart, J. L., & Goodsitt, J. L. (1996, Winter). From hospital to school: How a transition liaison can help. *Teaching Exceptional Children, 28*(2), 58–62.

Subotnik, R. (1997). Talent developed: Conversations with masters in the arts and sciences. *Journal for the Education of the Gifted, 20*(3), 306–317.

Sue, D. W., Bingham, R. P., Porche'-Burke, L., & Vasquez, M. (1999). The diversification of psychology: A multicultural revolution. *American Psychologist, 54,* 1061–1069.

Sue, S. (1999). Science, ethnicity, and bias: Where have we gone wrong? *American Psychologist, 54,* 1070–1077.

Sujansky, E., Stewart, J. M., & Manchester, D. K. (1997). Polygenic disease (multifactorial inheritance). In W. W. Hay, Jr., J. R. Groothuis, A. R. Hayward, & M. J. Levin (Eds.), *Current pediatric diagnosis and treatment* (pp. 904–908). Norwalk, CT: Appleton & Lange.

Sullivan, P. M. (2000). *Violence and abuse against children with disabilities.* Omaha, NE: Center for Abused Children with Disabilities, Boys Town National Research Hospital.

Suplee, C. (1996, April 11). *Braille readers found to use visual cortex: Results defy traditional ideas of brain function.* Washington Post, A4.

Szagun, G. (2000). The acquisition of grammatical and lexical structures in children with cochlear implants: A developmental psycholinguistic approach. *Audiology and Neuro-Otology, 5,* 39–47.

Szymanski, E. (1994). Transitions: Life-span and life-space considerations for empowerment. *Exceptional Children, 60,* 402–410.

Taft, L. T. (1999). Accentuating the positive for children with cerebral palsy. *Exceptional Parent, 29*(3), 64–65.

Tager-Flusberg, H. (2000). The challenge of studying language development in children with autism. In L. Menn & N. Bernstein Ratner (Eds.), *Methods for studying language production* (pp. 313–332). Mahwah, NJ: Erlbaum.

Tager-Flusberg, H., & Sullivan, K. (1998). Early language development in children with mental retardation. In J. A. Burack, R. M. Hodapp, & E. Zigler (Eds.), *Handbook of mental retardation and development* (pp. 208–239). New York: Cambridge University Press.

Talbott, R. F., & Wehman, P. (1996). Hearing disorders. In P. Wehman (Ed.), *Exceptional individuals in school, community, and work* (pp. 321–356). Austin, TX: Pro-Ed.

Tannenbaum, A. J. (1997). The meaning and making of giftedness. In N. Colangelo & A. D. Davis (Eds.), *Handbook of gifted education* (2nd ed., pp. 27–42). Boston: Allyn and Bacon.

Tartter, V. C. (1998). *Language processing in atypical populations.* Thousand Oaks, CA: Sage.

Tarver, S. (1996). Direct instruction. In W. Stainback & S. Stainback (Eds.), *Controversial issues confronting special education: Divergent perspectives* (2nd ed., pp. 143–152). Boston: Allyn and Bacon.

Taylor, E. (1999). Development of clinical services for attention-deficit/hyperactivity disorder. *Archives of General Psychiatry, 56,* 1097–1099.

Taylor, R. (2000). *Assessment of exceptional students: Educational and psychological procedures* (5th ed.). Boston: Allyn and Bacon.

Taylor, S. V. (2000). Multicultural is who we are: Literature as a reflection of ourselves. *Teaching Exceptional Children, 33*(3), 24–29.

Teeter, P. A., & Semrud-Clikeman, M. (1997). *Child neuropsychology: Assessment and interventions for neurodevelopmental disorders.* Boston: Allyn and Bacon.

Teplin, S. W. (1995). Visual impairments in infants and young children. *Infants and Young Children, 8,* 18–50.

Terman, L. M. (1925). *Genetic studies of genius: Vol. 1. Mental and physical traits of a thousand gifted children.* Stanford, CA: Stanford University Press.

Terrasi, S., Sennett, K. H., & Macklin, T. O. (1999). Comparing learning styles for students with conduct and emotional problems. *Psychology in the Schools, 36*(2), 159–166.

Thapar, A., Holmes, J., Poulton, K., & Harrington, R. (1999). Genetic basis of attention deficit and hyperactivity. *British Journal of Psychiatry, 174,* 105–111.

The Arc. (2000). *Genetic issues in mental retardation.* Silver Springs, MD: Author [Online]. Available: http://TheArc.org/depts/gbr01.html

The Internet for blind and visually impaired library users [Online]. Available: http://www.loc.gov/nls/nls-wb.html

The Joseph P. Kennedy, Jr. Foundation. (no date). *Opening doors for you.* Washington, DC: Author.

Therrien, V. L. (1993). For the love of Wes. In S. D. Klein and M. J. Schlerfer (Eds.), *It isn't fair!* Westport, CT: Bergin & Garvey.

Thomas, K. (1999, December 15). Study of attention deficit disorder supports medicine over therapy. *USA Today,* p. D14.

Thomas, S. B. (2000). College students and disability law. *The Journal of Special Education, 33*(4), 248–257.

Thousand, J., Villa, R., & Nevin, A. (1994). *Creativity and collaborative learning: A practical guide to empowering students with severe disabilities.* Baltimore, MD: Brookes.

Thurlow, M. L., Christenson, S. L., Sinclair, M. F., & Evelo, D. L. (1997). Wanting the unwanted: Keeping those "out of here" kids in school. *Beyond Behavior, 8*(3), 10–16.

Thurstone, T. G. (1959). *An evaluation of educating mentally handicapped children in special classes and regular classes.* U.S. Office of Education, Cooperative Research Project No. OE-SAE 6452. Chapel Hill, NC: University of North Carolina.

Thylefors, B., Nagrel, A. D., Pararajasegaram, R., & Dadzie,

K. Y. (1995). Global data on blindness. *Bulletin of the World Health Organization, 73*(1), 115–121.

Tiedt, P. L., & Tiedt, I. M. (1999). *Multicultural teaching: A handbook of activities, information, and resources* (5th ed.). Boston: Allyn and Bacon.

Tiegerman-Farber, E. (1997). Autism: Learning to communicate. In D. K. Bernstein and E. Tiegerman-Farber (Eds.), *Language and communication disorders in children* (4th ed.). (pp. 524–573). Boston: Allyn & Bacon.

Tines, J., Rusch, F. R., McCaughrin, W., & Conley, R. W. (1990). Benefit-cost analysis of supported employment in Illinois: A statewide evaluation. *American Journal on Mental Retardation, 95,* 55–67.

Tirosh, E., & Cohen, A. (1998). Language deficit with attention-deficit disorder: A prevalent comorbidity. *Journal of Child Neurology, 13*(10), 493–497.

Titrud, J. (1995). The first sleepover. *Exceptional Parent, 25*(11), 28–29.

Tomlinson, C. A., Callahan, C. M., & Lelli, K. M. (1997). Challenging expectations: Case studies of high-potential, culturally diverse young children. *Gifted Child Quarterly, 4*(2), 5–17.

Toppelberg, C. O., & Shapiro, T. (2000). Language disorders: A 10-year research update review. *Journal of the American Academy of Child and Adolescent Psychiatry, 39*(2), 143–152.

Torgesen, J. K. (1996, January). *The prevention and remediation of reading disabilities.* John F. Kennedy Center Distinguished Lecture Series. Nashville, TN: Vanderbilt University.

Torgesen, J. K. (1999). Reading disabilities. In R. Gallimore, L. P. Bernheimer, D. L. MacMillan, D. L. Speece, & S. Vaughn (Eds.), *Developmental perspectives on children with high-incidence disabilities* (pp. 157–181). Mahwah, NJ: Erlbaum.

Torrance, E. P. (1961). Problems of highly creative children. *Gifted Child Quarterly, 5,* 31–34.

Torrance, E. P. (1965). *Gifted children in the classroom.* New York: Macmillan.

Torrance, E. P. (1966). *Torrance tests of creative thinking.* Bensenville, IL: Scholastic Testing Service.

Torrance, E. P. (1968). Finding hidden talent among disadvantaged children. *Gifted and Talented Quarterly, 12,* 131–137.

Tramo, M. J. (1999). Metamemory knowledge and applications in children with attention deficit hyperactivity disorder: A developmental perspective. *Dissertation Abstracts International: Section B: The*

Sciences and Engineering, 59(10-B), 5670.

Trawick-Smith, J. (2000). *Early childhood development: A multicultural perspective* (2nd ed.). Columbus, OH: Merrill/Prentice Hall.

Trillingsgaard, A. (1999). The script model in relation to autism. *European Child and Adolescent Psychiatry, 8,* 45–49.

Tripp, G., Luk, S. L., Schaughency, E. A., & Singh, R. (1999). DSM-IV and ICD-10: A comparison of the correlates of ADHD and hyperkinetic disorder. *Journal of the American Academy of Child and Adolescent Psychiatry, 38*(2), 156–164.

Tsai, L. Y. (1999). Medical treatment in autism. In D. B. Zager (Ed.), *Autism: Identification, education, and treatment* (2nd ed., pp. 199–257). Mahwah, NJ: Erlbaum.

Tsvetkova, L. S. (1998). New directions in aphasiology. *Journal of Russian and East European Psychology, 36*(3), 5–59.

Tucker, P. (1999). Attention deficit/hyperactivity disorder in the drug and alcohol clinic. *Drug and Alcohol Review, 18*(3), 337–344.

Turbiville, Vicki. (1997). Literature review: Fathers, their children, and disability. Lawrence, KS: The Beach Center on Families and Disability, the University of Kansas.

Turnbull, A. P. & Turnbull, H. P. (1996). *Families, professionals, and exceptionality: A special partnership* (3rd ed.). Upper Saddle River, NJ: Prentice Hall.

Turnbull, A. P., & Turnbull, H. R., III. (1993). Participatory research on cognitive coping: From concepts to research planning. In A. P. Turnbull, J. M. Patterson, S. K. Behr, D. L. Murphy, D. L. Marguis, & M. J. Blue-Banning (Eds.), *Cognitive coping, families, and disability* (pp. 1–14). Baltimore, MD: Brookes.

Turnbull, A. P., Turnbull, R., Shank, M., & Leal, D. (1999). *Exceptional lives: Special education in today's schools* (2nd ed.). Upper Saddle River, NJ: Merrill/Prentice-Hall.

Turnbull, A. P., & Ruef, M. (1997). Family perspectives on inclusive lifestyle issues for people with problem behavior. *Exceptional Children, 63*(2), 211–227.

Turnbull, A. & Turnbull, H. R. III. (1997). *Families, professionals, and exceptionality: A special partnership.* Upper Saddle River, NJ: Merrill/Prentice Hall.

Turner, L., Dofny, E., & Dutka, S. (1994). Effective strategy and attribution training on strategy maintenance and transfer. *American Journal on Mental Retardation, 98*(4), 445–454.

Turner, M. H. (2000). The developmental nature of parent–child relationships: The impact of disabilities. In M. J. Fine & R. L. Simpson (Eds.), *Collaboration with parents and families of children with exceptionalities* (2nd ed., pp. 103–130). Austin, TX: Pro-Ed.

Twatchtman-Cullen, D. (1998). Language and communication in high-functioning autism and Asperger syndrome. In E. Schopler & G. B. Mesibov (Eds.), *Asperger syndrome or high functioning autism? Current issues in autism* (pp. 199–225). New York: Plenum.

Tye-Murray, N. (1993). Vowel and diphthong production by young users of cochlear implants and the relationship between the phonetic level evaluation and spontaneous speech. *Journal of Speech and Hearing Research, 36,* 488–502.

Tyler, J. S., & Mira, M. P. (1999). *Traumatic brain injury in children and adolescents* (2nd ed.). Austin, TX: Pro-Ed.

Udell, T., Peters, J., & Templeman, T.P. (1998, January/February). Inclusive early childhood programs. *Teaching Exceptional Children,* 44–49.

Umansky, W. (1998). Emotional and social development. In W. Umansky & S. R. Hooper (Eds.), *Young children with special needs* (pp. 276–307). Upper Saddle River, NJ: Merrill.

Umansky, W., & Hooper, S. R. (Eds.). (1998). *Young children with special needs* (3rd ed.). Upper Saddle River, NJ: Merrill.

United Cerebral Palsy. (2000). Cerebral palsy: Facts and figures [Online]. Available: http://www.ucp.org/ucp_generaldoc.cfm/1/3/43/43-43/447

United Cerebal Palsy of New York City. (1999). 10 myths and misunderstandings about cerebral palsy. *Exceptional Parent, 29*(3), 66–67.

United Cerebral Palsy Resource Center. (1997a, May). Cerebral palsy—facts and figures [Online]. Available: http://www.ucpa.org/html/esearch/factsfigs.html

United Cerebral Palsy Resource Center. (1997b, May). Fast facts sheet on UCP's 1996 ADA snapshot on America. Available: http://www.ucpa.org/html/resources/1996_fast facts.html

U.S. Bureau of the Census. (1997). *Current population survey.* Washington, DC: Author.

U.S. Bureau of the Census. (1998). *Population Profile of the United States: 1997.* U.S. Bureau of the Census, Current Population Reports, Series P23-194. Washington, DC: U.S. Government Printing Office.

U.S. Census Bureau. (1999). *Census Bureau Population Topics and Household Economic Topics*. Washington, DC: U.S. Census Bureau, Population Division.

U.S. Census Bureau. (2000). *Projections of the total resident population by five-year age groups, and sex with special age categories*. Middle series 2025-2045. Washington, DC: U.S. Census Bureau, Populations Projections Program, Population Division.

U.S. Department of Education. (1991, August 19). Notice of proposed rulemaking. Federal Register, 56(160), 41271.

U.S. Department of Education. (1993). *National excellence: A case for developing America's talent*. Washington, DC: Office of Education Research and Improvement, U.S. Department of Education.

U.S. Department of Education. (1998, October) *Annual report on school safety*. Washington, DC: Author.

U.S. Department of Education. (1998). *To assure the free appropriate public education of all children with disabilities: Twentieth annual report to Congress on the implementation of the Individuals with Disabilities Act*. Washington, DC: U.S. Government Printing Office.

U.S. Department of Education. (1999, March 12). Individuals with Disabilities Education Act Amendments of 1997, Public Law 105-17, *Federal Register*, Sec. 300-503: Prior notice by the public agency, content of notice. Washington, DC: U.S. Government Printing Office.

U.S. Department of Education. (1999). *To assure the free appropriate public education of all children with disabilities: Twenty-first annual report to Congress on the implementation of the Individuals with Disabilities Education Act*. Washington, DC: U.S. Government Printing Office.

U.S. Department of Education. (2000, June). *Educating blind and visually impaired students: Policy guidance*. Washington, DC: Office of Special Education and Rehabilitative Services, 65 FR 36586.

U.S. Department of Education, Office of Special Education Programs. (2000). *Twenty-second annual report to Congress on the Implementation of the Individuals with Disabilities Education Act*. Washington, DC: Author.

U.S. Department of Energy. (2000). Human Genome Project Information [Online]. Available: http://www.ornl.gov/hgmis/

U.S. Department of Health and Human Services. (1996). *National household survey on drug abuse: Population estimates, 1994–1995*. Washington, DC: Substance Abuse and Mental Health Services Administration, U.S. Department of Health and Human Services.

U.S. Department of Health and Human Services. (1999a). *Blending perspectives and building common ground: A report to Congress on substance abuse and child protection*. Washington, DC: U.S. Government Printing Office.

U.S. Department of Health and Human Services. (1999b). 1999 Head Start Fact Sheet. Washington, DC: Administration on Families and Children [Online]. Available: http://www2.acf.dhhs.gov/programs/hsb/research/99_hsfs.htm

U.S. Department of Justice. (1998, August). Youth gangs: An overview. *Juvenile Justice Bulletin*. Washington, DC: U.S. Department of Justice, Office of Justice Programs, Office of Juvenile Justice and Delinquency Prevention.

U.S. Department of Justice. (1999a). *1997 national youth gang survey: OJJDP summary*. Washington, DC: U.S. Department of Justice, Office of Justice Programs, Office of Juvenile Justice and Delinquency Prevention.

U.S. Department of Justice. (1999b). OJJDP research: Making a difference for juveniles. Washington, DC: U.S. Department of Justice, Office of Justice Programs, Office of Juvenile Justice and Delinquency Prevention.

U.S. Department of Justice. (1999c). *Report to Congress: Juvenile violence research*. Washington, DC: U.S. Department of Justice, Office of Justice Programs, Office of Juvenile Justice and Delinquency Prevention.

U.S. National Center for Health Statistics. (1994). Prevalence of selected chronic conditions, by age and sex: 1994. *Vital and Health Statistics*, 10(193). Hyattsville, MD: Center for Disease Control and Prevention, U.S. Department of Health and Human Services.

U.S. News & World Report, "Separate and unequal." December 13, 1993, pp. 46–60.

Upshur, J. A., & Turner, C. E. (1999). Systematic effects in the rating of second-language speaking ability: Test method and learner discourse. *Language Testing, 16*, 82–111.

Valdes, K. A., Williamson, C. L., & Wagner, M. M. (1990). *The national longitudinal transition study of special education students, statistical almanac. Vol. 5: Youth Categorized as Mentally Retarded*. Menlo Park, CA: SRI International.

Vallance, D. D., Cummings, R. L., & Humphries, T. (1998). Mediators of the risk for problem behavior in children with language learning disabilities. *Journal of Learning Disabilities, 31*(2), 160–171.

Vallecorsa, A. L., deBettencourt, L., & Zigmond, N. (2000). *Students with mild disabilities in general education settings: A guide for special educators*. Columbus, OH: Merrill/Prentice Hall.

Valles, E. C. (1998). The disproportionate representation of minority students in special education: Responding to the problem. *Journal of Special Education, 32*(1), 52–54.

Van Borsel, J., Van Lierde, K., Van Cauwenberge, P., Guldemont, I., & Van Orshoven, M. (1998). Severe acquired stuttering following injury of the left supplementary motor region: A case report. *Journal of Fluency Disorders, 23,* 49–58.

Van Borsel, J., Verniers, I., & Bouvry, S. (1999). Public awareness of stuttering. *Folia Phoniatrica et Logopaedica, 51*(3), 124–132.

Vance, A. L. A., Luk, E. S. L., Costin, J., Tonge, B. J., & Pantelis, C. (1999). Attention deficit hyperactivity disorder: Anxiety phenomena in children treated with psychostimulant medication for 6 months or more. *Australian and New Zealand Journal of Psychiatry, 33*(3), 399–406.

VanTassel-Baska, J. (1989). Counseling the gifted. In J. Feldhusen, J. Van Tassel-Baska, & K. Seeley (Eds.), *Excellence in educating the gifted*. Denver, CO: Love.

VanTassel-Baska, J. (1997). What matters in curriculum for gifted learners: Reflections on theory, research, and practice. In N. Colangelo & A. D. Davis (Eds.), *Handbook of gifted education* (2nd ed., pp. 126–135). Boston: Allyn and Bacon.

VanTassel-Baska, J. (1998a). A comprehensive model of program development. In J. VanTassel-Baska (Ed.), *Excellence in educating gifted and talented learners* (3rd ed., pp. 309–333). Denver, CO: Love.

VanTassel-Baska, J. (1998b). Appropriate curriculum for the talented learner. In J. VanTassel-Baska (Ed.), *Excellence in educating gifted and talented learners* (3rd ed., pp. 339–361). Denver, CO: Love.

VanTassel-Baska, J. (1998c). Counseling talented students. In J. VanTassel-Baska (Ed.), *Excellence in educating gifted and talented learners* (3rd ed., pp. 489–509). Denver, CO: Love.

VanTassel-Baska, J. (1998d). Girls of promise. In J. VanTassel-Baska (Ed.), *Excellence in educating gifted and talented learners* (3rd ed., pp. 129–144). Denver, CO: Love.

VanTassel-Baska, J. (1998e). Introduction. In J. VanTassel-Baska (Ed.), *Excellence in educating gifted and talented learners* (3rd ed., pp. 7–18). Denver, CO: Love.

VanTassel-Baska, J., & Chepko-Sade, D. (1986). *An incidence study of disadvantaged gifted students in the Midwest*. Evanston, IL: Center for Talent Development, Northwestern University.

Vargas, M. (1999, November). Doctors agree to provide interpreting services for deaf family members. *The NAD Broadcaster* [Online]. Available: http://nad.policy.net/proactive/newsroom/release.vtml?id=18440

Varney, N. R. (1998). Neuropsychological assessment of aphasia. In G. Goldstein (Ed.), *Neuropsychology: Human brain function—assessment and rehabilitation* (pp. 357–378). New York: Plenum.

Vaughn, S., Bos, C. S., & Schumm, J. S. (1999). *Teaching exceptional, diverse, and at-risk students in the general education classroom* (2nd ed.). Boston: Allyn and Bacon.

Vaughn, S., Moody, S., & Schumm, J. S. (1998). Broken promises: Reading instruction in the resource room. *Exceptional Children, 64*, 211–225.

Venn, J. J. (2000). *Assessing students with special needs*. Upper Saddle River, NJ: Merrill.

Vernon, M., & Andrews, J. F. (1990). *The psychology of deafness: Understanding people who are deaf and hard-of-hearing*. White Plains, NY: Longman.

Verri, A., Uggetti, C., Vallero, E., Ceroni, M. & Federico, A. (2000). Oral self-mutilation in a patient with rhombencephalosynapsys. *Journal of Intellectual Disability Research, 44,* 86–90.

Vicari, S., Albertoni, A., Chilosi, A. M., Cipriani, P., Cioni, G., & Bates, E. (2000). Plasticity and reorganization during language development in children with early brain injury. *Cortex, 36,* 31–46.

Vilkman, E. (2000). Voice problems at work: A challenge for occupational safety and health arrangement. *Folia Phoniatrica et Logopaedica, 52,* 120–125.

Villa, R., & Thousand, J. (1992). *Restructuring for caring and effective education*. Baltimore, MD: Brookes.

Vitanza, S. A., & Guarnaccia, C. A. (1999). A model of psychological distress for mothers of children with attention-deficit hyperactivity disorder. *Journal of Child and Family Studies, 8*(1), 27–45.

Vohs, J. (1993). On belonging: A place to stand, a gift to give. In A. P. Turnbull, J. M. Patterson, S. K. Behr, D. L. Murphy, D. L. Marguis, & M. J. Blue-Banning (Eds.), *Cognitive coping, families, and disability* (pp. 51–66). Baltimore, MD: Brookes.

Volkmar, F. R., & Marans, W. D. (1999). Measures for assessing pervasive developmental and communication disorders. In D. Shaffer & C. P. Lucas (Eds.), *Diagnostic assessment in child and adolescent psychopathology* (pp. 167–205). New York: Guilford.

Von Isser, A., Quay, H. C., & Love, C. T. (1980). Interrelationships among three measures of deviant behavior. *Exceptional Children, 46*(4), 272–276.

Wachtel, P. L. (1999). *Race in the mind of America: Breaking the vicious circle between blacks and whites.* New York: Routledge.

Wade, S. E., & Zone, J. (2000). Creating inclusive classrooms: An overview. In S. E. Wade (Ed.), *Inclusive education: A casebook and readings for prospective and practicing teachers* (pp. 1–27). Mahwah, NJ: Erlbaum.

Wagner, M., & Blackorby, J. (1996). Transition from high school to work or college: How special education students fare. In The Center for the Future of Children (Ed.), *Special education for students with disabilities,* (Vol. 6, pp.103–120). Los Angeles, CA: The Center for the Future of Children.

Wagner, M., Newman, L., D'Amico, R., et al. (1991). *Youth with disabilities: How are they doing? The first comprehensive report from the National Longitudinal Study of special education students.* Menlo Park, CA: SRI International.

Walker, H. M., & Bullis, M. (1991). Behavior disorders and the social context of regular class integration: A conceptual dilemma? In J. W. Lloyd, N. N. Singh, & A. C. Repp (Eds.), *The regular education initiative: Alternative perspectives on concepts, issues, and models* (pp. 75–93). Sycamore, IL: Sycamore.

Walker, H. M., Horner, R. H., Sugai, G., et al. (1996). Integrated approaches to preventing antisocial behavior patterns among school-age children and youth. *Journal of Emotional and Behavioral Disorders, 4*(4), 194–209.

Walker, H. M.; Kavanagh, K., Stiller, B., Golly, A., Severson, H., & Feil, E. G. (1998). First step to success: An early intervention approach for preventing school antisocial behavior. *Journal of Emotional and Behavioral Disorders, 6*(2), 66–80.

Walker, H. M., Stiller, B., & Golly, A. (1998). First step to success: A collaborative home–school intervention for preventing antisocial behavior at the point of school entry. *Young Exceptional Children, 1*(2), 2–6.

Wallach, M. A. (1976). Tests tell us little about talent. *American Scientist, 64,* 57.

Walther-Thomas, C., & Brownell, M. (1999). An interview with Mara Sapon-Shevin: Implications for students and teachers of labeling students as learning disabled gifted. *Intervention in School and Clinic, 34*(4), 244–246, 250.

Wambaugh, J. L., Martinez, A. L., McNeil, M. R., & Rogers, M. A. (1999). Sound production treatment for apraxia of speech: Overgeneralization and maintenance effects. *Aphasiology, 13,* 821–837.

Ward, M. C., & Bernstein, D. J. (1998). Promoting academic performance among students with special needs. *Ethics and Behavior, 8*(3), 276–281.

Ward, M. J., & Meyer, R. N. (1999). Self-determination for people with developmental disabilities and autism: Two self-advocates' perspectives. *Focus on Autism and Other Developmental Disabilities, 14*(3), 133–139.

Ward-Lonergan, J. M., Liles, B. Z., & Anderson, A. M. (1998). Listening comprehension and recall abilities in adolescents with language-learning disabilities. *Journal of Communication Disorders, 31,* 1–32.

Warnock, G. L. (1999). Frontiers in transplantation of insulin-secreting tissue for diabetes mellitus. *Canadian Journal of Surgery, 42*(6), 421–426.

Warren, D. H. (1984). *Blindness and early childhood development.* New York: American Foundation for the Blind Press.

Warren, S. F., & Yoder, P. J. (1997). Communication, language, and mental retardation. In W. E. MacLean (Ed.), *Ellis's handbook of mental deficiency, psychological theory, and research* (pp. 379–403). Mahwah, NJ: Erlbaum.

Wasik, B. A., & Slavin, R. E. (1993). Preventing early reading failure with one-to-one tutoring: A review of five programs. *Reading Research Quarterly, 28,* 179–200.

Watanabe, M., Yamaguchi, T., Uematsu, T., & Kobayashi, S. (1999). Teaching generalized purchasing skills to a youth with autism. *Japanese Journal of Special Education, 36*(4), 59–69.

Watkins, K. P., & Durant, L., Jr. (1996). *Working with children and families affected by substance abuse: A guide for early childhood education and human service staff.* West Nyack, NY: The Center for Applied Research in Education.

Watson, A. (1999). Paradigmatic conflicts in informal mathematics assessment as sources of social inequity. *Educational Review, 51*(2), 105–115.

Watson, A. L., Franklin, M. E., Ingram, M. A., & Eilenberg, L. B. (1998). Alcohol and other drug abuse among persons with disabilities. *Journal of Applied Rehabilitation Counseling, 29*(2), 22–29.

Watson, J. B., & Rayner, R. (1920). Conditioned emotional reactions. *Journal of Experimental Psychology, 3,* 1–14.

Webb-Johnson, G., Artiles, A. J., Trent, S. C., Jackson, C. W., & Velox, A. (1998). The status of research on multicultural education in teacher education and special education: Problems, pitfalls, and promises. *Remedial and Special Education, 19*(1), 7–15.

Webber, J., & Scheuermann, B. (1997). A challenging future. Current barriers and recommended action for our field. *Behavior Disorders, 22*(3), 167–178.

Webster, W. G. (1998). Brain models and the clinical management of stuttering. *Journal of Speech Language Pathology and Audiology, 22,* 220–230.

Wehby, J. H., Symons, F. J., & Canale, J. A. (1998). Teaching practices in classrooms for students with emotional and behavioral disorders: Discrepancies between recommendations and observations. *Behavioral Disorders, 24*(1), 51–56.

Wehman, P. (1996). *Life beyond the classroom: Transition strategies for young people with disabilities* (2nd ed.). Baltimore, MD: Brookes.

Wehman, P. (1997). Traumatic brain injury. In P. Wehman (Ed.), *Exceptional individuals in school, community, and work* (pp. 451–485). Austin, TX: Pro-Ed.

Wehman, P., & Parent, W. (1997). Severe mental retardation. In P. Wehman (Ed.), *Exceptional individuals in school, community, and work* (pp. 145–173). Austin, TX: Pro-Ed.

Wehman, P., & Revell, W. G. (1997). Transition into supported employment for young adults with severe disabilities: Current practices and future directions. *Journal of Vocational Rehabilitation, 8,* 65–74.

Wehman, P., West, M., & Kregel, J. (1999). Supported employment program development and research needs: Looking ahead to the year 2000. *Education and Training in Mental Retardation and Developmental Disabilities, 34*(1), 3–19.

Wehmeyer, M. (1998). Self-determination and individuals with significant disabilities: Examining meanings and misinterpretations. *Journal of the Association for Persons with Severe Handicaps, 23,* 5–16.

Wehmeyer, M., & Bolding, N. (1999). Self-determination across living and working environments: A matched-samples study of adults with mental retardation. *Mental Retardation, 37*(5), 353–363.

Wehmeyer, M., & Kelchner, K. (1995). Interpersonal cognitive problem-solving skills of individuals with mental retardation. *Education and Training in Mental Retardation and Developmental Disabilities, 29,* 265–278.

Wehmeyer, M., & Sands, D. J. (Eds.). (1998). *Making it happen: Student involvement in education planning, decision making, and instruction.* Baltimore, MD: Brookes.

Weiss, M., Hechtman, L. T., & Weiss, G. (1999). *ADHD in adulthood: A guide to current theory, diagnosis, and treatment.* Baltimore, MD: Johns Hopkins University Press.

Weissman, M. M., Warner, V., Wickramaratne, P. J., & Kandel, D. B. (1999). Maternal smoking during pregnancy and psychopathology in offspring followed to adulthood. *Journal of the American Academy of Child and Adolescent Psychiatry, 38,* 892–899.

Weitzel, A. (2000). Overcoming loss of voice. In D. O. Braithwaite & T. L. Thompson (Eds.), *Handbook of communication and people with disabilities: Research and application* (pp. 451–466). Mahwah, NJ: Erlbaum.

Welch, M. (2000). Collaboration as a tool for inclusion. In S. E. Wade (Ed.), *Inclusive education: A casebook and readings for prospective and practicing teachers* (pp. 71–96). Mahwah, NJ: Erlbaum.

Welch, M., Brownell, K., & Sheridan, S. M. (1999). What's the score and game plan on teaming in schools? A review of the literature on team teaching and school-based problem solving teams. *Remedial and Special Education, 20*(1), 36–49.

Welch, M. W., & Jensen, J. (1991). Write, P.L.E.A.S.E.: A video-assisted strategic intervention to improve written expression of inefficient learners. *Journal of Remedial and Special Education, 12,* 37–47.

Welch, M., & Sheridan, S. M. (1995). *Educational partnerships: An ecological approach to serving students at risk.* San Francisco, CA: Harcourt Brace Jovanovich.

Welch, M., & Tulbert, B. (1998). Collaboration in educational settings: Implications for teacher education. Paper presented at the Annual Conference of the American Association of Colleges of Teacher Education, New Orleans.

Weldy, S. R. (1998). Complex memory in high-functioning autistic individuals. *Dissertation Abstracts International: Section B: The Sciences and Engineering, 58*(10–B), 5661.

Weller, E. B., Rowan, A., Elia, J., & Weller, R. A. (1999). Aggressive behavior in patients with attention-deficit/hyperactivity disorder, conduct disorder, and pervasive developmental disorders. *Journal of Clinical Psychiatry, 60* (Suppl. 15), 5–11.

Weller, E., Rowan, A., Weller, R., & Elia, J. (1999). Aggressive behavior associated with attention-deficit/hyperactivity disorder, conduct disorder, and developmental disabilities. *Journal of Clinical Psychiatry Monograph Series, 17*(2), 2–7.

Wellman, H. M. (1998). Culture, variation, and levels of analysis in folk psychologies: Comment on Lillard (1998). *Psychological Bulletin, 123,* 33–36.

Wenar, C., & Kerig, P. (2000). *Developmental psychopathology: From infancy through adolescence* (4th ed.). New York: McGraw-Hill.

West, E. (1981). My child is blind—thoughts on family life. *Exceptional Parent, 1*(1), S9–S12.

West, J. (1991). Implementing the act: Where do we begin? In J. West (Ed.), *The Americans with Disabilities Act: From policy to practice* (pp. xi–xxxi). New York: Millbank Memorial Fund.

Westberg, K. L., & Archambault, F. X., Jr. (1997). A multi-site case study of successful classroom practices for high ability students. *Gifted Child Quarterly, 41*(1), 42–51.

Westling, D. L., & Fox, L. (2000). *Teaching students with severe disabilities* (2nd ed.). Columbus, OH: Merrill/Prentice Hall.

Whaley, B. B., & Golden, M. A. (2000). Communicating with persons who stutter: Perceptions and strategies. In D. O. Braithwaite and T. L. Thompson (Eds.), *Handbook of communication and people with disabilities: Research and application* (pp. 423–438). Mahwah, NJ: Erlbaum.

Whelan, R. J. (1998). *Emotional and behavioral disorders: A 25-year-focus.* Denver, CO: Love.

When genetic testing says no. (1999, January 11). *Time, 153*(1). [Online]. Available: http://www.time.com/time/magazine/articles/0,3266,17683-3,00.html

Whitaker, R. (2000, March 21). Knowing Chris. *Washington Post,* p. Z12.

White, B. L. (1975). *The first three years of life.* Englewood Cliffs, NJ: Prentice Hall.

White, J. D. (1999). Personality, temperament, and ADHD: A review of the literature. *Personality and Individual Differences, 27*(4), 589–598.

Whitehead, A., Jesien, G., & Ulanski, B. K. (1998). Weaving parents into the fabric of early intervention interdisciplinary training: How

to integrate and support family involvement in training. *Infants and Young Children, 10*(3), 44–53.

Whiteley, P., Rodgers, J., & Shattock, P. (1998). Clinical features associated with autism. *Autism, 2,* 415–422.

Whitney-Thomas, J., & Hanley-Maxwell, C. (1996). Packing the parachute: Parents' experiences as their children prepare to leave school. *Exceptional Children, 63,* 75–87.

Whitney-Thomas, J., Shaw, D., Honey, K., & Butterworth, J. (1998). Building a future: a study of student participation in person-centered planning. *Journal of the Association for Persons with Severe Handicaps, 23*(2), 119–133.

Wicks-Nelson, R., & Israel, A. C. (2000). *Behavior disorders of childhood.* Upper Saddle River, NJ: Prentice Hall.

Wilcox, L. D., & Anderson, R. T. (1998). Distinguishing between phonological difference and disorder in children who speak African-American vernacular English: An experimental testing instrument. *Journal of Communication Disorders, 31,* 315–335.

Wilkinson, K. M. (1998). Profiles of language and communication skills in autism. *Mental Retardation and Developmental Disabilities Research Reviews, 4*(2), 73–79.

Williams, D. (1992). *Nobody nowhere: The extraordinary autobiography of an autistic.* New York: Avon Books.

Williams, F. E. (1980). *Creativity assessment packet.* East Aurora, NY: DOK.

Willoughby, J. C., & Glidden, L. M. (1995). Father helping out: Shared child care and marital satisfaction of parents of children with disabilities. *American Journal on Mental Retardation, 99*(4), 399–406.

Willoughy-Booth, S., & Pearce, J. (1998). On the edge: Art therapy for people with learning difficulties and disordered personalities. In M. Rees (Ed.), *Drawing on difference: Art therapy with people who have learning difficulties* (pp. 59–72). New York: Routledge.

Wisniewski, L. (1994). Interpersonal effectiveness in consultation and advocacy. In S. K. Alper, P. J. Schloss, & C. N. Schloss (Eds.), *Families of students with disabilities* (pp. 205–228). Boston: Allyn and Bacon.

Witte-Bakken, J. K. (1998). The effects of feedback on the validity of facilitated communication. *Dissertation Abstracts International: Section B: The Sciences and Engineering, 58*(9-B), 5148.

Wixtrom, C. (1988, Summer). Alone in the crowd. *Deaf American, 38*(12), 14–15.

Wolery, M. (1994). Implementing instruction for young children with special needs in early childhood classrooms. In M. Wolery & J. S. Wilbers (Eds.), *Including children with special needs in early childhood programs* (pp. 151–166). Washington, DC: National Association for the Education of Young Children.

Wolfberg, P. J., Zercher, C., Lieber, J., Capel, K., Matias, S., Hanson, M., & Odom, S. L. (1999). "Can I play with you?" Peer culture in inclusive preschool programs. *Journal of the Association for Persons with Severe Handicaps, 24*(2), 69–84.

Wong, B. Y. L. (1999). Metacognition in writing. In R. Gallimore, L. P. Bernheimer, D. L. MacMillan, D. L. Speece, & S. Vaughn (Eds.), *Developmental perspectives on children with high-incidence disabilities* (pp. 183–198). Mahwah, NJ: Erlbaum.

Wood, D. (1991). Communication and cognition: How the communication styles of hearing adults may hinder—rather than help—deaf learners. *American Annals of the Deaf, 136*(3), 247–251.

Wood, J. W. (1997a). *Adapting instruction to accommodate students in inclusive settings* (3rd ed.). Upper Saddle River, NJ: Prentice Hall.

Wood, J. W. (1997b). Attention deficit disorders. In J. W. Wood and A. M. Lazzari (Eds.), *Exceeding the boundaries: Understanding exceptional lives* (pp. 161–194). Fort Worth: Harcourt Brace.

Woodruff, D. W., Osher, D., Hoffman, C. C., et al. (1999). The role of education in a system of care: Effectively serving children with emotional or behavioral disorders. In *Systems of care: Promising practices in children's mental health, 1998 Series, Vol. 3.* Washington, DC: Center for Effective Collaboration and Practice, American Institutes for Research.

Woods, N. S., Eyler, F. D., Conlon, M., Behnke, M., & Wobie, K. (1998). Pygmalion in the cradle: Observer bias against cocaine-exposed infants. *Journal of Developmental and Behavioral Pediatrics, 19*(4), 283–285.

Yairi, E. (1999). Epidemiologic factors and stuttering research. In N. B. Ratner and C. E. Healey (Eds.), *Stuttering research and practice: Bridging the gap* (pp. 45–53). Mahwah, NJ: Erlbaum.

Yamamoto, J., & Miya, T. (1999). Acquisition and transfer of

sentence construction in autistic students: Analysis of computer-based teaching. *Research in Developmental Disabilities, 20*(5), 355–377.

Yasutake, D., & Lerner, J. (1997). Parents' perceptions of inclusion: A survey of parents of special education and non-special education students. *Learning Disabilities, 8*(2), 117–120.

Yates, J. R., & Ortiz, A. A. (1998). Developing individualized education programs for exceptional language minority students. In L. M. Baca & H. T. Cervantes (Eds.), *The bilingual special education interface* (3rd ed., pp. 188–212). Columbus, OH: Merrill/Macmillan.

Yell, M. L. (1995). *Clyde K. & Sheila K. v. Puyallup School District:* The courts, inclusion, and students with behavior disorders. *Behavior Disorders, 20*(3), 179–189.

Yell, M. L. (1998). *The law and special education.* Upper Saddle River, NJ: Merrill.

York, A., vonFraunhofer, N., Turk, J., & Sedgwick, P. (1999). Fragile-X syndrome and autism: Awareness and knowledge amongst special educators. *Journal of Intellectual Disability Research, 43*(4), 314–324.

Young, D. M., & Roopnarine, J. L. (1994, Winter). Fathers' child-care involvement with children with and without disabilities. *Topics in Early Childhood Special Education, 14,* 488–502.

Young, M. E. (1996). *Early child development: Investing in the future.* Washington, DC: The World Bank.

Young, S. (1999). Psychological therapy for adults with attention deficit hyperactivity disorder. *Counselling Psychology Quarterly, 12*(2), 183–190.

Youth Suicide Prevention Information. (2000). Youth suicide: What a parent needs to know [Online]. Available: http://www.sanpedro.com/spyc/suicide.htm

Ysseldyke, J. E., & Olsen, K. (1997). Putting alternate assessments into practice: What to measure and possible sources of data. NCEO Synthesis Report 28. Minneapolis: The National Center on Educational Outcomes, University of Minnesota [Online]. Available: http://www.coled.umn.edu/NCEO/OnlinePubs/Synthesis28.htm

Ysseldyke, J. E., Olsen, K., & Thurlow, M. (1997). Issues and considerations in alternate assessments. NCEO Synthesis Report 27. Minneapolis: The National Center on Educational Outcomes, University of Minnesota [Online]. Available: http://www.coled.umn.edu/NCEO/OnlinePubs/Synthesis27.htm

Zager, D. B. (1999). *Autism: Identification, education, and treatment* (2nd ed.). Mahwah, NJ: Erlbaum.

Zapata, J. T. (1995). Counseling Hispanic children and youth. In C. C. Lee (Ed.). *Counseling for Diversity* (pp. 85–108). Boston: Allyn & Bacon.

Zapata, J. T., Katims, D. S., & Yin, Z. (1998). A two-year study of patterns and predictors of substance use among Mexican American youth. *Adolescence, 33*(130), 391–403.

Zebrowitz, L. A., Andreoletti, C., Collins, M. A., Lee, S. Y., & Blumenthal, J. (1998). Bright, bad, babyfaced boys: Appearance stereotypes do not always yield self-fulfilling prophecy effects. *Journal of Personality and Social Psychology, 75,* 1300–1320.

Zeitlin, H. (1999). Psychiatric comorbidity with substance misuse in children and teenagers. *Drug and Alcohol Dependence, 55*(3), 225–234.

Zhang, A. Y., & Snowden, L. R. (1999). Ethnic characteristics of mental disorders in five U.S. communities. *Cultural Diversity and Ethnic Minority Psychology, 5*(2), 134–146.

Zigmond, N. (1990). Rethinking secondary school programs for students with learning disabilities. *Focus on Exceptional Children, 23,* 1–22.

Zigmond, N., & Miller, S. (1992). Improving high school programs. In F. R. Rusch, L. DeStefano, J. Chadsey-Rusch, L. A. Phelps, & E. Syzmanski, *Transition from school to adult life* (pp. 17–31). Sycamore, IL: Sycamore.

Zimmerman, A. W., Jinnah, H. A., & Lockhart, P. J. (1998). Behavioral neuropharmacology. *Mental Retardation and Developmental Disabilities Research Reviews, 4*(1), 26–35.

Zimmerman, D. D., & Kingsley, R. E. (1997, June). General information about epilepsy [Online]. Available: http://www.iupui.edu/~epilepsy/general.htm

Zimmerman, G. J. (1996). Optics and low vision devices. In *Foundations of low vision: Clinical and functional perspectives* (pp. 115–142). New York: American Foundation for the Blind Press.

Zimmermann, S. H. (1999). Portrait of success: A situational analysis case study of students challenged by attention-deficit/hyperactivity disorder. *Dissertation Abstracts International Section A: Humanities and Social Sciences, 59*(7-A), 2368.

Zohar, A. H., Apter, A., King, R. A., Pauls, D. L., Leckman, J. F., & Cohen, D. J. (1999). Epidemiological studies. In J. F. Leckman & D. J. Cohen (Eds.), *Tourette's syndrome—tics, obsessions, compulsions: Developmental psychopathology and clinical care* (pp. 177–193). New York: Wiley.

Author Index

Mertens, D. M., 445
Merton, R. K., 66
Metropolitan Life/Louis Harris
        Associates, Inc., 41
Meyer, D. J., 83, 84
Meyer, G., 132
Meyer, L. H., 110, 312, 349, 350, 358,
        359
Meyer, R. N., 377
Meyers, D., 84
Michallet, B., 326
Mick, E., 220, 221, 223
Mickelson, K. D., 391
Midence, K., 391
Milberger, S., 221
Milich, R., 220
Miller, A., 189, 223
Miller, B. C., 518
Miller, D. N., 217
Miller, E. N., 517, 518
Miller, F., 486
Miller, J. H., 180
Miller, S., 151
Mills, P. E., 133, 136
Mills v. District of Columbia Board of
        Education, 22
Milne, L., 182, 200
Miltenberger, R. G., 331
Minderaa, R. B., 379, 382
MiniMed, 507, 508
Minow, M., 4
Minshew, N., 384
Minty, G. D., 508
Mira, M. P., 397, 399, 401, 403, 405
Mirenda, P., 362
Mishkin, L., 403
Misra, A., 79, 90, 93
Mithaug, D. E., 287
Miya, T., 386
Moaven, L. D., 425
Mogford-Bevan, K., 335
Molfese, D. L., 323, 337
Molfese, V. J., 323, 337
Montague, M., 257
Montgomery, A., 41, 43
Montgomery, J., 123
Moody, S., 133, 136
Moon, M. S., 153, 555, 556
Moore, J., 220
Moore, K. A., 518
Morelock, M. J., 545
Moreno, S. J., 389
Morgan, J., 417
Morgan, R. L., 149, 308, 309
Morra, L. G., 133, 134
Morrier, M. J., 386
Morrison, D. R., 518

Morrison, G. S., 60, 65
Morse, W. C., 243
Mosley, J. L., 287
Moss, J., 197, 200
MSNBC, 497
MTA Cooperative Group, 223
Mueller, R. A., 384, 385
Murdoch, B. E., 342
Murphy, D., 384
Murphy, J., 277, 330
Murphy, S., 160, 195
Murray, B., 317
Murray, B. A., 236
Murray, P. J. H., 224
Murrell, J. G., 223
Muscular Dystrophy Association, 495,
        496, 498
Myers, M. A., 236

N

Naglieri, J. A., 176, 189
Nagrel, A. D., 459
National Academy on an Aging Society,
        418, 423, 424
National Adoption Information
        Clearinghouse, 523
National Association of the Deaf, 444
National Association for the Education
        of Young Children, 108
National Association of State Boards of
        Education (NASBE), 40, 124
National Center for Education Statistics,
        31, 32, 41
National Center on Educational
        Restructuring and Inclusion
        (NCERI), 40, 130
National Center for Health Statistics,
        517
National Clearinghouse on Child Abuse
        and Neglect Information, 514,
        515, 516, 517
National Commission on Excellence in
        Education, 34, 123
National Council on Disability, 13, 80,
        99
National Down Syndrome Society, 294
National Information Center for
        Children and Youth with
        Disabilities (NICHCY), 92, 119,
        271, 293
National Institute of Allergy and
        Infectious Diseases, 483, 500,
        501, 502
National Institute on Deafness and
        Other Communication Disorders,
        426, 442

National Institute on Early Childhood
        Development and Education, 518
National Institute of Mental Health,
        519, 521
National Institutes of Health, 209, 211,
        214, 215, 223, 224
National Joint Committee on Learning
        Disabilities, 170, 187, 200, 201
National Law Center on Homelessness
        and Poverty, 42
National Organization on Disability
        (N.O.D.)/Harris, L. & Associates,
        3, 11, 15, 142, 143, 152, 156, 157,
        158
National Organization on Fetal Alcohol
        Syndrome, 296
National Research Council, 35, 63, 112,
        137, 141, 151, 163
National Spinal Cord Injury Statistical
        Center (NSCISC), 494
National Women's Health Information
        Center, 517
Natriello, G., 43
Nava, C., 265
Nelson, C. M., 236, 245, 249, 250, 251,
        260, 267, 269
Nerney, T., 155
Nesman, T., 265
Nevin, A., 112, 364
New Goals for the U.S. Human
        Genome Project, 368
Newacheck, P. W., 173, 174
Newcom, J. H., 221
Newman, L., 245
Newton, J. S., 251
Nichols, P., 246
Nielsen, A. B., 554
Nilsson, E. W., 380
Nippold, M. A., 318
Nirje, B., 310
Nisbet, J., 40
Nisbett, R. E., 59
Nissenbaum, M. S., 75, 85, 90
Nitko, A. J., 187
Niu, W., 180
Niu, X., 181, 182
Nocentini, U., 323
Noell, G. H., 225
Nolan, B. F., 200
Noll, J., 78
Noonan, M. J., 101, 103, 104, 300
Norenzayan, A., 59
Norris, D., 323
Northeast Technical Assistance Center,
        440
Novack, T., 398, 399
Nuccio, J. B., 286, 287

Wambaugh, J. L., 326
Wamsley, L., 331
Wang, W. C., 134, 136
Ward, J., 248
Ward, M. C., 177, 202
Ward, M. J., 377
Ward, S. L., 234, 235
Ward-Lonergan, J. M., 322
Waring, R. E., 325, 326
Warner, V., 220
Warnock, G. L., 507
Warren, D. H., 460
Warren, S. F., 290
Warren, S. H., 87, 124
Washington, P., 218
Washnuk, T., 268
Wasik, B. A., 101, 113
Watanabe, M., 382
Waterhouse, L., 379
Watkins, K. P., 523
Watson, A., 187, 197
Watson, J. B., 18
Watterson, B., 565
Weaver, M. F., 40
Webb, B., 200
Webb-Johnson, G., 49
Webber, J., 231, 235, 236, 246, 269
Weber, C., 357
Webster, W. G., 330
Wehby, J. H., 260, 265
Wehman, P., 143, 147, 148, 151, 160, 307, 355, 362, 422
Wehmeyer, M., 149, 151, 152, 287, 302, 360
Wehr, E., 162
Wehymer, M., 149
Weiffenbach, B., 221, 222
Weiss, G., 225, 228
Weiss, M., 225, 228
Weissman, M. M., 220
Weitzel, A., 326, 342, 343
Weizman, A., 385
Welch, M., 112, 124, 125, 128, 190, 195, 199, 203
Weldy, S. R., 383
Welham, M., 377, 379
Weller, E. B., 212, 217, 220
Weller, R. A., 212, 217, 220
Wellman, H. M., 60
Wenar, C., 200, 384, 385
West, E., 75
West, J., 13
West, M., 160
Westberg, K. L., 552

Westling, D., 89, 125, 287, 291, 302, 303, 354, 362, 382, 387
Wetesel, W. C., 221
Wetherby, A. M., 323
Whalen, C. K., 217, 220, 221
Whaley, B. B., 329, 330
Whelan, R. J., 245
Whitaker, R., 375
White, B. L., 101
White, J. D., 212
White, O. R., 113
Whitehead, A., 88
Whiteley, P., 385
Whitman, T. L., 516
Whitmire, K., 429
Whitney-Thomas, J., 145, 360
Wickramaratne, P. J., 220
Wicks-Nelson, R., 244, 246, 247, 248, 265
Wiczek, C., 351
Wilcox, L. D., 341
Wilcznski, S. M., 218
Wilkinson, K. M., 379
Willens, T., 220
Williams, B. F., 385
Williams, F. E., 548
Williams, R., 331, 362
Williamson, C. L., 142, 152
Willoughby, J. C., 82
Willoughy-Booth, S., 200
Willwerth, J., 12
Wilson, B., 174, 185, 196, 221
Wilson, R., 378
Wilson, W. C., 129
Wing, L., 377, 379
Wisniewski, L., 90
Witt, J. C., 225
Witte, O. W., 330
Witte-Bakken, J. K., 390
Wixtrom, C., 447
Wobie, K., 67
Wolcott, G. F., 397, 407
Woldbeck, T., 188
Wolery, M., 92, 105, 106, 107, 116, 300, 357
Wolf-Schein, E. G., 355
Wolfberg, P. J., 385
Wong, B. Y. L., 169, 196, 199
Wong, L., 220
Wong, P. K. H., 459
Wood, D., 427
Wood, J. W., 114, 220, 225
Wood, K., 181

Wood, M., 242
Woodruff, D. W., 265
Woods, D. W., 331
Woods, N. S., 67
Wright, E., 405
Wroble, M., 391
Wzorek, M., 377, 379

Y

Yairi, E., 330
Yamaguchi, T., 382
Yamamoto, J., 386
Yan, W., 180
Yaruss, J. S., 331
Yasutake, D., 89
Yates, J. R., 61
Yell, M. L., 249, 269
Yetman, N. T., 5, 6, 19, 20
Yeung-Courchesne, R., 385
Yin, Z., 186
Yoder, P. J., 290
York, A., 384
Young, D. M., 83
Young, J. R., 270
Young, M. E., 101, 103, 300
Young, S., 219, 228
Youth Suicide Prevention Information, 483
Yovanoff, P., 160
Ysseldyke, J. E., 133, 136, 356, 357

Z

Zager, D. B., 387
Zaitseva, K. A., 330
Zakian, A., 379
Zametkin, A. J., 221
Zapata, J. T., 50, 186
Zebrowitz, L. A., 67
Zeitlin, H., 200
Zercher, C., 385
Zhang, A. Y., 54
Zhang, M., 180
Zigmond, N., 133, 136, 149, 151, 190
Zimmerman, A. W., 387
Zimmerman, D. D., 504
Zimmerman, G. J., 473
Zimmermann, S. H., 221
Zingo, J., 132
Zohar, A. H., 211
Zone, J., 40, 123
Zurkowski, J. K., 90

Subject Index

Page numbers in **bold** indicate definitions; page numbers followed by *f* or *t* indicate figures or tables, respectively.

Augmentative communication, 303, **327**–329, 344, **363**, 489
Aura, 502, **503**
Authentic assessment, **109, 355**
Autism, **24,** 375–393
  in adults, 389
  behavioral intervention in, 387–391
  biological factors in, 384–385
  causation, 383–385
  challenging behavior in, 382
  characteristics of, 379–383
  definition of, **377**
  diagnostic criteria for, 378*t*
  in early childhood, 388
  and education, 385–386
  in elementary school, 388–389
  facilitative communication in, 387–391
  and family, 388–389, 391
  in IDEA, 235, 235*n,* 377, 386
  impaired or delayed language in, 378*t,* 379–380
  and intelligence, 243, 380–382
  and interacting in natural settings, 388–389
  learning characteristics of, 382–383
  prevalence, 378–379
  psychodynamic theory of, 383–384, 386–387
  psychological and medical services in, 386–387
  resistance to change in routine, 380
  savant syndrome in, 383
  in secondary school, 389
  self-stimulation in, 376, **380,** 392–393
  services and supports in, 385–391
  sex differences in, 379
  social interaction in, 378*t,* 379
Autism Society of America, 391

B

Baby-sitters, 82–83
Barrier-free facility, **15**
Basal ganglia, **221**
Basal readers, 194
BASC-TRS. *See* Behavior Assessment System for Children-Teacher Rating Scale
Basic skills approach, to special education, 113–115
BEH. *See* Bureau of Education for the Handicapped
Behavior
  abnormal, 18–19
  adaptive, 243–245, 244*t*
  challenging, in autism, 382
  normal, identifying, 233–234

social, behavior disorders and, 243–245, 244*t*
Behavior and Emotional Rating Scale, 252, 253*t*
Behavior Assessment System for Children-Teacher Rating Scale, 216
Behavior disorders, **4,** 231–275
  and academic achievement, 245–246
  adaptive and social behavior in, 243–245, 244*t*
  ADHD and, 211–212
  in adolescence, 265–267
  assessment, 248–254
    cultural diversity and, 253–254
    factors, 250–252
    limited English proficiency and, 253–254
    screening and referral, 248–250, 249*t*
    techniques, 252–254, 253*t*
  causation, 246–248
    behavioral approach, 247
    biological approach, 246
    phenomenological approach, 247
    psychoanalytical approach, 246–247
    sociological-ecological approach, 247
  characteristics of, 243–246
  classification, 237–242
    according to severity of behaviors, 241–242
    clinically derived systems, 238–241
    DSM-IV, 238–241
    statistically derived systems, 237–238
  definitions of
    Council for Exceptional Children, 236
    IDEA, 235–236
  in early childhood years, 256–260
  in elementary school, 258–259, 260–265
  and expulsion, 272–273
  externalizing and internalizing disorders, 234–235, 237
  factors influencing, 234
  identifying normal behavior, 233–234
  and inclusive education, 267–270
  and intelligence, 243
  and interacting in natural settings, 258–259
  interventions, 254–256, 255*t*
    behavior therapy, 263–265, 264*f,* 264*t*

community-based, 254–256, 255*t*
  home- and center-based programs, 256–260
  prevalence, 242–243
  traumatic brain injury and, 400
  understanding, **233**–235
Behavior therapy
  for autism, 387–391
  for behavior disorders, 263–265, 264*f,* 264*t*
  data collection in, 390
  for learning disabilities, 196–197
  for stuttering, 331
Behavioral contracts, **196**–197
Behavioral factors, **393**
Behavioral intervention plan, 31, 269
Behavioral Objective Sequence, 260, 261*t*
Behavioral psychology, 542–544
Behaviorism, 542–544
Bernhardt, Sarah, 8
BERS. *See* Behavior and Emotional Rating Scale
Best Buddies, 289
Bicultural-bilingual approach, to American Sign Language, **437**
Bicycle safety, 403
Bilingual and bicultural service delivery, 62, 62*f,* 68
Binet, Alfred, 20, 531
Binet-Simon Scales, 21
Bioartificial pancreas, 507
Bioethics, 364–**365**
Biofeedback, 331
Biological approach, to behavior disorders, 246
Biomedical factors
  in mental retardation, **292,** 293–296
  in severe and multiple disabilities, 364–369
Birth
  precipitous, 297
  trauma during
    and autism, 385
    and language disorders, 323
    and mental retardation, 297
Birth defects, 352
Bladder control and management, 492
Blindness, 451–481, **454**–455. *See also* Vision loss
  with deafness, 352
  educational definitions of, 455
  legal, **454**
Bliss, J. C., 472
Blissymbols, 362, **363**
Blood transfusion, in sickle cell anemia, 511
Blood type, incompatibility in, 297, 425
Bodily-kinesthetic intelligence, 537, 538*t*

Group psychotherapy, in giftedness, 555–556, 556t
Grouping, mathematical, learning disabilities and, 180, 191
Guide dogs, 465
Guilford, J.P., 532
Gun Free Schools Act, 31
Guns, 414

H

Handicap, **3**
Handicapped Children's Early Education Program, 101
Handicapped Children's Protection Act (1986), 25t
Handwriting, learning disabilities and, 178–179, 179f
Haptic perception, learning disabilities and, **183**, 184
Hard of hearing, **421**
Hate crimes, 42
Hawking, Stephen, 8
HCEEP. *See* Handicapped Children's Early Education Program
Head injury, 395–414. *See also* Traumatic brain injury
types of, 407–410, 411f
Head Start, **110, 301**
Health care, 95–96, 157
for aging people with disabilities, 162
government-sponsored, 156–158
Health disabilities, 483, **484**–486, **499**–511. *See also Specific disabilities*
in adolescence, 512–513
in adults, 513
in early childhood, 512
in elementary school, 512–513
and interacting in natural settings, 512–513
Health disorders, **5**
Health insurance, 95–96, 157, 215
Health maintenance organization, 95–96
Hearing aids, 431–434, 444–445
Hearing loss, 417–449
in adolescence, 433
in adults, 433–434
age of onset, 422
anatomical sites of loss, 422–423
causation, 424–426
acquired factors in, 426
congenital factors in, 424–426
environmental factors in, 426
heredity, 424–425
prenatal disease, 425–426
central auditory disorder, 422, 423

characteristics of, 426–430
classification, 422t, 423
conductive, 422
definitions of, 421–423
diagnosis of, in infants, 443
in early childhood, 432
and educational achievement, 427–428
educational services and supports in, 424, 430–441
in elementary school, 432–433
and employment, 434
and intelligence, 427
and interacting in natural settings, 432–434
medical services in, 441–445
mixed, 423
peripheral, 422–423
postlingual disorders, 422
prelingual disorders, 422
prevalence, 423–424
sensorineural, 422–423
in severe and multiple disabilities, 355
and social development, 428–430
social services in, 445–446
speech and language skills in, 323, 332, 427
teaching communication skills in, 431–437
auditory approach, 431–434
manual approach, 435–437
oral approach, 434–435
total communication, 437
technology and, 439–441
closed captioning, 437–439
computer-assisted instruction, 439–441
telecommunication devices, 441
treatment of, 431–434, 442–445
Hearing process, 419–420
Hematoma(s), 410, 411f, 411f
Hemiplegia, 494, 494t, **495**
Hendrick Hudson District Board of Education v. Rowley (1982), 25t, 27
Heredity
and ADHD, 222
and hearing loss, 424–425
in intelligence and giftedness, 542–545
Hertz, **421**
High school. *See also* Secondary school
diplomas, 163
purpose of, 149
Higher education
learning disabilities in, 201–202
transition to, 149, 150t, 201, 405

Hispanic Americans, 54, 55, 55f, 59, 63
HIV. *See* Human immunodeficiency virus
HMO. *See* Health maintenance organization
Hoarseness, 341, 342
Hobsen v. Hansen (1969), 24t
Home(s)
group, 158
semi-independent, 158
Home-based programs
in behavior disorders, 257–260
for infants and toddlers, 104–105
for preschool children, 109, 257–260
Home school, **123**–124
Home school placement, **40, 123**
Homebound programs, 29, 30
Homosexuality, and AIDS, 499
Hospital education programs, 29, 30
Human Genome Project, 364, **365**–368
Human immunodeficiency virus, **296, 499**–502. *See also* Acquired immune deficiency syndrome
Husband-wife relationships, 80–82
Hydration, and sickle cell anemia, 511
Hydrocephalus, **297,** 459, 491
Hyperactivity, **184, 210**
in ADHD, 219–220
learning disabilities and, 184–185
medication for, 204, 205
Hyperglycemia, 505–506
Hyperkinetic behavior, 169, **184**
Hypernasality, 341, **342**
Hyperopia, **456**
Hypnosis, 331
Hyponasality, 341, **342**
Hypotonia, **355**

I

IB 367, 509
IC. *See* Individualized care
IDDM. *See* Insulin-dependent diabetes mellitus
IDEA. *See* Individuals with Disabilities Education Act
IDEA 97. *See* Individuals with Disabilities Education Act amendments
Ideation, suicidal, 519
Identical twins, studies of, **186**
Idiot savant, 383
IEP. *See* Individualized education plan
IFSP. *See* Individualized family service plan
ILP. *See* Individualized language plans
Immaturity, 238, 244
Immune system, **499**

Intelligence *(continued)*
  origins of, 542–545
  practical, 535
  schizophrenia and, 243
  severe and multiple disabilities and, 353–354, 355–357
  spina bifida and, 490
  synthetic, 535
  triarchic theory of, 535
  vision loss and, 459–460
Intelligence quotient, **530**, 531–533. *See also* Intelligence
Intensity, of early intervention, 105
Intensive care specialists, **102**
Intensive instruction, in special education, 112, **113**
Interim alternative educational setting, 33, 269
Intermittent support, 284–285
Internalizing disorders, 234–235, 237
Internet, 439–441
Interpersonal intelligence, 537, 538*t*
Interpreters, 147, 438
Intervention(s). *See also Specific disabilities*
  behavioral, 196–197
  developmental milestones approach to, 300
  early, 101
    center-based model, 104–105
    combination of services, 104–105
    eligibility, 102
    in hearing loss, 431
    home-based model, 104–105
    for infants and toddlers, 102–105
    intensity of, 105
    in mental retardation, 300–301
    service delivery, 104–105
    in severe and multiple disabilities, 357
    for stuttering, 330–331
Intoxication, and mental retardation, 296
Intraindividual variability, in learning disabilities, 182
Intrapersonal intelligence, 537, 538*t*
Intravenous drug use, and AIDS, 501
Introspection, principle of, 18
IQ, 306, **530**, 531–533. *See also* Intelligence
Iris, **452**, 453*f*, 453–454
Islet cells, transplantation of, 507
Isolation, history of, 7–9
Itard, Jean-Marc, 16–17
Itinerant teacher, **30**, 125
ITP. *See* Individualized transition plan

J

Jacob K. Javits Gifted and Talented Students Act, 533
James, William, 18
Job coaches, 147, 160
Jones, James Earl, 8
Juvenile diabetes, 505–506

K

Kamen, Dean, 497
Kaposi's sarcoma, 499
Kennedy, John F., 21
Kennedy family, 288–289
Kennedy Foundation, 288
Ketogenic diet, 504
Kinesthetic information, **184**
Kirk, Samuel, 170
Klippel-Trenauny-Weber syndrome, 45
Kurzweil, Raymond, 474–475

L

L & H Kurzweil 1000, 475
Labeling, 3–7
  approaches to, 5–6, 6*f*
    cultural, **5**–6
    developmental, **5**
    individual, **6**
  effects of, 4, 7
  environmental bias in, 7
  formal *versus* informal, 5
  positive and negative, 4
  reasons for, 4
  separating person and label, 7
Lactose, 295
Language
  in autism, 378*t*, 379–380
  definition of, 317, 320
  development of, 318–319, 320*t*
    giftedness and, 549–550
    vision loss and, 460, 467
  hearing loss and, 323, 332, 427
  interrelationship with speech and communication, 317*f*
  in mental retardation, 290, 291*t*
  in severe and multiple disabilities, 354
  structure of, 317–318
  in traumatic brain injury, 400, 406*t*–407*t*
Language delay, 320–322, 324, 378*t*, 379–380
Language-disability theories, of learning disabilities, 171
Language disorders, **4**, 319–328
  acquired, 323
  aphasia, 322–323, 326–327

behaviors resulting in teacher referral for, 321*t*
  causation, 323–325
  classification, 322–323
  definition of, 320–322
  expressive, 322
  individualized language plans, 325–327
  intervention, 325–328
  receptive, 322
Language diversity
  articulation disorders and, 340–341
  and assessment, 24*t*, 56, 57–58
  and education, 55–56
  and specialized instruction, 67
Language experience approach, 467, 470*t*
Large-print media, 473
Laryngeal structure, 342
Larynx, 337
Laser cane, **465**–466
Lau v. Nichols (1974), 56
LEA. *See* Local education agency
Learned helplessness, **290**
Learning
  in mental retardation, 286–287
  self-directed, 195
Learning difficulties, as label, 7
Learning disabilities, 167–207
  and academic achievement, 151–152, 177–181, 189–190
  academic instruction and support, 190–196, 197–200
  achievement and ability discrepancy, 172–173, 181
  adaptive skills assessment, 189
  in adolescence, 192–193, 197–202, 204–205
  in adults, 193
  assessment, 180–190, 186–190
  and attention-deficit hyperactivity disorder, 172
  behavioral interventions in, 196–197
  causation, 185–186
  characteristics of, 175–177
  classification, 172–173
  and cognition and information processing, 182–183
  compensatory skills in, 199
  computer technology and, 191
  definitions, **169**–172
    early history, 170
    IDEA, 170–171
    National Joint Committee for Learning Disabilities, 170
  in early childhood, 192
  in elementary school, 190–197, 192, 203–204

double hemiplegia, 494*t*
and education, 495
hemiplegia, 494, 494*t*
immediate care in, 495
interventions, 495
monoplegia, 494*t*
paraplegia, 494, 494*t*
pharmacological interventions in, 495
prevalence, 494
quadriplegia, 494, 494*t*
rehabilitation in, 495
topographical descriptions of paralytic conditions, 494*t*
triplegia, 494*t*
Splinter skills, 381–382, 383
SSQ. *See* School Situations Questionnaire
Standard deviation, **281**
Standards-based reform, **34**–35
Stanford-Binet Intelligence Scale, **21, 530,** 531, 540
Stapedectomy, 442
Stereotypic behavior, 376, 378*t*
Stereotyping, 4, 61
Sterilization, **9**
Sternberg Triarchic Abilities Test, 533
Strabismus, **457**
Strength-based assessment, **252**
Stress management, in seizure disorders, 504
Student(s)
with ADHD, 226–227
with AIDS, 501
with autism, 382–383, 385–386, 388–389
with behavior disorders
adolescents, 265–267
elementary school, 258–259, 260–265
with communication disorders, 334–335
culturally diverse, 60–62
giftedness of, 547–548, 563–564
individualized education plans, 60–61
least restrictive environment, 61–62
overrepresentation in special education, 54–56
with disabilities
disciplining, 31–33, 269, 272–273
educational service options for, 29*f*
and goodness of fit, 359
high school diplomas for, 163
inclusion of, 38–41
and school reform, 34–35
special education profile, 31*f*

transition from school, 89–90, 141–165
in transition planning, 145–147
gifted, 545–548, 549–557
with hearing loss, 424, 430–441
with learning disabilities
adolescents, 192–193, 197–202, 204–205
elementary school, 190–197, 203–204
living in poverty, 63
with mental retardation
adolescents, 306–309, 309
elementary school, 301–306
socially accepted *versus* socially accepted, 289
with physical and health disabilities, 485
with severe and multiple disabilities, 353
adolescents, 362–364, 367
elementary school, 359–362, 366–367
with traumatic brain injury, 402–405, 406*t*–407*t*
with vision loss, 458, 460–461, 464–476
Students at risk, **41**–44
Stuttering, **290,** 329–331
biological factors in, 329–330
causation, 329–330
definition of, 329
emotional factors in, 329
heredity and, 329–330
intervention, 330–331
as learned behavior, 330
Subdural hematoma, **410,** 411*f*
Substance use/abuse
ADHD and, 220
intravenous, and AIDS, 501
key substances and effects, 522, 523*t*
learning disabilities and, 200
maternal, 522–525
during pregnancy, 296, 522–525, 523*t,* 524*f*
student discipline for, 31–33, 269
of students at risk, 41–42
and youth suicide, 519
Substitutions, in articulation disorders, 336
Suicidal behavior, 520*t*–521*t*
Suicidal ideation, 519
Suicide, in youth, 43, **518**–522
attempted, 518–519
causation, 521
completed, 519
definitions and concepts, 518–519
interventions, 521–522

prevalence, 519–520
prevention, 522
Supplemental Social Security Income, 156
Support(s)
academic, in learning disabilities, 190–196, 197–200
in autism, 385–391
building network for adults, 156–161
educational, in vision loss, 464–476
employment, **156,** 158–160
family, 88–94, 357
attributes of quality, 90–91
collaboration with professionals, 90–91
strengthening, 91–92
training, 92–94
formal
in inclusive education, **41**
in mental retardation, 284–285
government-funded programs, 156–160
health care, 156–158
in hearing loss, 430–441
in inclusive education, 41
income, 156
in mental retardation, 284–285, 309–310, 310*f*
natural
for adults, 160–161
in inclusive education, **41**
mental retardation, 285
quality, indicators of, 10
residential living, 158–162
in severe and multiple disabilities, 357–359
in transition from school, 143
in traumatic brain injury, 402–405
Support groups
history of, 10, 21
for siblings, 86, 94
Support teachers, 125
Supported employment, **156,** 158–160, **307**
SWATs. *See* Schoolwide assistance teams
Sweat glands, in cystic fibrosis, 508
Sweat testing, 509
Switch control, 363
Syntax, 317
Synthesized speech, 472, 478
Synthetic intelligence, 535
Syphilis, 459

T

T cells, 499
T lymphocytes, 499
Tactile media, in vision loss, 467–472

Talented, 530, 533, 539
Talents, **530.** *See also* Giftedness
  catalyst theory of, 536, 537*f*
  Piirto pyramid of, 537, 538*f*
TASH. *See* The Association for Persons
    with Severe Handicaps
TATs. *See* Teacher assistance teams
TBI. *See* Traumatic brain injury
TDD, 441
Teacher(s)
  consulting, **125,** 127
  general education, 127–130
  of gifted students, 552, 558, 560–561
  and goodness of fit, 359
  itinerant, 30, 125
  master, 125
  perceptions of inclusion, 203
  and reporting child abuse, 516
  resource-room, 125, 126, 127
  special education, 203
  and students with ADHD, 210–211,
      217, 224–225, 226–227
  and students with autism, 382–383,
      386, 388–389
  and students with behavior
      disorders, 258–259
  and students with communication
      disorders, 334–335
  and students with hearing loss,
      432–433
  and students with learning
      disabilities, 176, 192–193,
      198–199
  and students with mental
      retardation, 308–309
  and students with physical and
      health disabilities, 512–513
  and students with severe and
      multiple disabilities, 358–359,
      366–367
  and students with traumatic brain
      injury, 405, 406*t*–407*t*, 408–409
  and students with vision loss, 468–469
  support, 125
Teacher assistance teams, **125,** 126
Teacher nomination, in gifted
    assessment, 546–547
Team(s)
  child-study, **115**
  in educational collaboration, 126
  in IEP process, 27–28, 119
  multidisciplinary, 299, 488
  schoolwide assistance, 125, 126
  teacher assistance, 126
  transdisciplinary, 488
Technologically dependent, **484**–485
Technology
  for assessment, 252

assistive, **103, 283,** 362
  and communication, 303, 326, 327
  and educational inclusion, 131
  in hearing loss, 439–441
  and students with autism, 386
  and students with learning
      disabilities, 191
  and transition services, 308
Technology-Related Assistance for
    Individuals with Disabilities Act,
    362
Teenagers. *See* Adolescent(s)
Telecommunication assistance, 13, 485
Telecommunication devices, in hearing
    loss, 441
Telescoped schooling, 553
Teletypewriter and printer, 441
Television
  closed-caption, 437–439
  closed-circuit, 473
Television Decoder Circuitry Act (1993),
    438–439
Ten-day rule, 32–33
Teratogens, **491**
Terman, Lewis, 21
Terman, Lewis M., 531, 540
Terminal illness, 498
Test bias, **57**
Text telephones, **441**
Therapeutic abortion, 298, **299**
Therapeutic recreation, 15
Tic disorders, 240
Tinnitus, **425**
Tobacco use, 41–42, 296
TOBI, 509
Toddlers
  early intervention for, 102–105, 357
  legal precedents affecting, 22,
      101–102
  prenatal drug and alcohol exposure
      and, 523*t*, 525
  service delivery, 104–105
  severe and multiple disabilities, 357,
      366
Token reinforcement systems, **197,**
    263–265, 264*f*
Tonic/clonic seizures, 502–**503,** 504
Torrance Tests for Creative Thinking,
    533
Total communication, **437**
Touch Talker, 489
Tourette's syndrome, **211**
Toxoplasmosis, **296,** 425
Trainable, 283, 284
Training
  for family members, 93–94
  for general education teachers,
      127–130

for parents, 92–93
  for physicians, 17–18, 93
  for professionals, 93
Training schools, 9
Transdisciplinary teams, 488
Transformation, 530
Transition services, 89–90, **143,**
      143–145
  ADHD and, 227
  adult service agencies and, **147**–148
  autism and, 389
  behavior disorders and, 259
  communication disorders and, 335
  components of, 144–145
  giftedness and, 561
  hearing loss and, 433
  individualized transition plan,
      145–148, 146*f,* 147*t*
  learning disabilities and, 192–193,
      200–202
  legal requirements for, 143–145
  mental retardation and, 306–309,
      309
  parent and student involvement,
      145–147
  physical and health disabilities and,
      513
  in secondary schools, 148–153
  severe and multiple disabilities and,
      362–364, 367
  technology and, 308
  traumatic brain injury and, 403–405,
      404*f,* 409
  vision loss and, 469
Transportation, 13, 157, 485
Transverse position, 297
Trauma
  and aphasia, 323
  during birth, 297, 323, 385
  and spinal cord injury, 493, 494
Traumatic brain injury, **24,** 395–414
  in adolescence, 398–399, 409
  in adults, 409
  causation, 401–402
  characteristics of, 399–401
  and cognition, 400
  definition of, **396**–397
  developing cognitive-communicative
      skills in, 406*t*–407*t*
  in early childhood, 408
  educational supports and services in,
      402–405
  in elementary school, 408–409
  and interacting in natural settings,
      408–409
  medical and psychological services
      in, 407–413
  mortality rate of, 399

Photo Credits